A Bibliography of

AMERICAN CHILDREN'S BOOKS

Printed Prior to 1821

A Bibliography of

AMERICAN

CHILDREN'S BOOKS

Printed Prior to 1821

---

d'ALTÉ A. WELCH

AMERICAN ANTIQUARIAN SOCIETY
and BARRE PUBLISHERS · 1972

TO THE LATE CLARENCE S. BRIGHAM

*A tribute to his remarkable genius
for stimulating younger men to bibliographical endeavor,
and also to having built the superb collection
of early American children's books
of the American Antiquarian Society.*

TABLE OF CONTENTS

Foreword

d'ALTÉ WELCH died tragically on January 4th, 1970. He had been wounded
by a gunman during an attempted robbery near the Cleveland Racquet Club
on December 10th, after which, apparently, he had made good progress toward
recovery. Thus, this most unfortunate event doubly shocked his family and
friends.

James d'Alté Aldridge Welch was born in New York City on April 9, 1907,
to Charles James and Elizabeth (Livingston) Welch. He was educated in private lower and secondary schools in that city and then proceeded to Johns
Hopkins University where, during the academic years of 1927 through 1931,
he earned a master's degree in the biological sciences. After serving as Assistant Malacologist of the Bishop Museum at Honolulu and collecting snails in
the Caribbean Islands, d'Alté was awarded the degree of doctor of philosophy
from Johns Hopkins in 1937. He pursued this interest by means of a long-
standing research project pertaining to the distribution and variation of *Achati-
nella Bulimoides,* a Hawaiian tree snail. Thus, by training and profession he
was a biological scientist. He had followed his trade since 1942 on the faculty
of John Carroll University where he was held with respect and affection.

But, all this is foreign to the humanists and bibliophiles among us who de-
lightedly recall another facet of d'Alté Welch. He was an avid collector of
children's books. His personal collection of English and American examples
is a major one. He numbered over eight hundred of his own books in this
bibliography.

d'Alté's interest in such books began about the year 1922 during a visit
to England with his mother. She was a collector of lace and encouraged d'Alté.
He purchased a few English examples which sparked an enthusiasm which
he never abandoned. His infectious love of his books, his good will, good humor, and knowledge endeared him to fellow collectors, librarians, and booksellers across North America.

The American Antiquarian Society's association with d'Alté began in
the mid-forties. He and Clarence Brigham and Ted Shipton formed an alliance
to which newer staff members were admitted. His admiration of Brigham was
particularly strong and found expression in the dedication of this book. He
took great pleasure in forwarding new data to Avis Clarke, the Society's cata-
loger, for incorporation into our card catalogue.

I vividly remember my first meeting with d'Alté, nearly twenty years ago. He was working with the AAS collection of children's books in his usual, whirlwind manner, catching up everyone with his boundless delight. I was working my way through Vermont imprints. d'Alté insisted that I stay in the same rooming house on Wachusett Street in order that we might spend the evening searching one another's bibliographical notes. After a swim at Bell Pond and supper, we attacked our typescripts, keeping at them until three in the morning. Later visits to Worcester and long, telephoned conversations only strengthened our conviction that he was totally immersed in children's books; yet, we know that he was at the head of a large and lively household, was a sympathetic teacher, and was active in Cleveland affairs.

So it went with us; right through the summer of 1969, when d'Alté came on to inspect the Tighe collection of children's books and to advise us on that most important matter. We all had a grand time together. We shall miss him.

d'Alté bequeathed to the Society his American children's books which were not present in Worcester. His family gave to the library all of his other American books. This truly magnificent bequest and gift have dramatically enriched the Society's already great collections. In addition, his notes, films, and xerographic copies of American children's books are here as an important research tool for the study of children's literature; nevertheless, all poor substitutes for our friend.

d'Alté Welch leaves a family of six—his wife, the former Ann Goddard, whom he married in 1943; two sons, James and Charles; and three daughters, Martha, Elizabeth, and Frances.

The culmination of the life work of d'Alté Welch lies in this volume. It was originally published in six parts in the *Proceedings* of the American Antiquarian Society, as follows: A-C, April 1963; D-G, October 1963; H, October 1964; I-O, October 1965; P-R, April 1967; S-Z, October 1967. It is fortunate that he had finished his notes for the revision before his death. The editing of this version, which incorporates his corrections and additions, has been carefully and completely done by Alice Cecil with the guidance and help of the staff of the Society.

Some editorial decisions were made which require comment. The lengthy lists of prior English editions to many of the titles have been eliminated, with only a note on the first English edition being retained. For the deleted information the reader is referred to the original printing in the *Proceedings* or to Welch's manuscript bibliography of English children's books now located, with his large collection of English juveniles, at the University of California in Los Angeles. With the exception of unique copies in private hands, the location of books held by private collectors has been eliminated because nearly all of those collections have been or will be dispersed.

The book is uniquely d'Alté Welch's. Clifford K. Shipton in his own foreword to the first published part of the bibliography wrote, ". . . Of the importance of this work, there is no need to say anything; it is obviously one of the great bibliographical contributions of our time. Professional bibliographers may complain that the objectives of Dr. Welch's odd descriptive methods could have been attained in a more orthodox system, but our experience proves that it works, and that it is not too hard to grasp. . . . Because of the many years over which this bibliography has been preparing, and because of many revisions and changes in style, it will inevitably show more errors and inconsistencies than are to be expected in a work which could follow some more orthodox plan; but to withhold it longer for further polishing would be to do a wrong to the world of bookmen. Everyone who lives by books, who ever was a child, or had an ancestor, will find in the pages of this bibliography more new information about old friends than he is ever likely to encounter again."

It is a happy event that this book is being published at last. The staff of the Society, for years, has followed it and its late compiler with affection and interest. We thank the generosity of the members of d'Alté Welch's family for encouragement and permission to go on with the book, Mrs. Cecil for her skillful work, and Alden P. Johnson and Barre Publishers for the means to publish it. I am sure that in this sense of gratitude I am joined by all of d'Alté's friends, by collectors of American children's books, and by students of American cultural history.

Marcus A. McCorison

American Antiquarian Society

Introduction & Acknowledgments

THE HIDDEN HISTORY of Mother Goose was my introduction, at the age of sixteen, to the fascinating hobby of collecting early children's books. My father in 1924 returned from a business trip where he heard the story concerning the origin of Little Jack Horner. The story so interested me that I went down to The New York Public Library and did some research on the origin of nursery rhymes and wrote a paper entitled "Old Mother Goose" which was published in the Browning School magazine, *The Browning Buzzer*. Miss Leonore St. John Power, now Mrs. Morris Mendelson of San Francisco, was then head of the Children's Room at The New York Public Library and introduced me to the charm of early children's books. During the summer of the same year I went to London with my mother and visited some bookstores Miss Power had told me about. The Banks sisters in Church Street, Kensington, had a delightful shop, which held forth so many tempting items that I left the store quite penniless after my first visit. My fate as a collector of children's books was sealed.

When I returned in the early fall, I had bought over two hundred early English juveniles. Through Miss Power I met Wilbur Macey Stone, who wrote me a most delightful letter condoning the dreadful disease that I had contracted, namely that of collecting early juveniles, and inviting me to dinner at his home in East Orange, New Jersey. My visit to his library was a rare experience. The walls were lined with especially constructed bookshelves to take miniature children's books. The thumb Bibles were all together on one narrow shelf. Each book was housed in a paper-covered box made by their owner. Ten and twelve centimeter books printed by John Newbery and other publishers were on another shelf. Each book had a cardboard cover with the name of the book on the white cloth back strip. Many were covered with various colored papers, which lent charm to the books. That library was certainly an exciting place in which to browse. Wilbur Macey Stone had a phenomenal knowledge of both English and American juveniles which he generously shared, and my many trips to his home are remembered with great pleasure.

During successive years I collected more American juveniles, because of their availability, than English ones. One of my earliest trips was to Boston. I took the nightboat from New York and visited only two stores in Boston. One was Goodspeed's, the other that of P. K. Foley. One day in Boston was sufficient. I expended all my funds in short order. At P. K. Foley's I obtained a fragment of an edition of *Mother Goose's Melody,* which afterwards proved to be the third Worcester edition printed by Isaiah Thomas in 1799.

Soon after entering the field I keenly felt the need for a guide to collecting children's books: what books were known and what were unique. Therefore, at an early period, I started a card catalogue of juveniles offered in booksellers' catalogues, a card file of miniature bibles in the Stone collection and the holdings of The New York Public Library. In time the Rosenbach catalogue was published, an important milestone in the bibliography of children's books. This catalogue was particularly provocative because it showed me that, although many titles were reprinted by the same publisher year after year, the famous Rosenbach Collection sometimes had only a single imprint. One of the greatest libraries of children's books, therefore, was far from complete and did not even scratch the surface of what had been published prior to 1821.

At the American Antiquarian Society in 1945, I met Clarence S. Brigham who was a constant source of help. Under his stimulus I began to compile the present work in earnest. The following summer and for many succeeding ones I visited libraries, microfilming their holdings. The title page and all pages following the title up to the first arabic numbered page were filmed, as well as the last two numbered pages and any following unnumbered pages. An inch scale and the name of the collector or institution were filmed at the same time. This way I could visit a library and in a few days obtain all the bibliographic knowledge about the collection on film and later transfer it to paper.

A bibliography is not the work of a single person. Unless many people help the compiler, no work of any size can be produced. I have been very fortunate in having friends who have been unstinting in their aid. Foremost among these was Clifford K. Shipton of the American Antiquarian Society who left no stone unturned to do all in his power to help me. He also gave me much good advice. When books were needed they were loaned to me or, when duplicates were available, they were given. This work would never have been brought to completion if it had not been for his interest.

While Clifford K. Shipton was director of the American Antiquarian Society, Marcus McCorison became editor and librarian of the Society and it is to him that I am indebted for generously allowing me to review his card catalogue of Vermont imprints from which I added information to this bibliography. After his bibliography of Vermont imprints was published I quoted the book. I am not only indebted to Marcus McCorison for the editorial work he did but, since he became director of the American Antiquarian Society, for information and gifts of books or duplicates not wanted by the Society. He is carrying on the splendid tradition of the Society of helping and encouraging research. Since 1967 James E. Mooney has been editor of the Society and saw through the press the latter part of this work.

The Very Reverend Hugh E. Dunn, S.J., president of John Carroll University, and the Reverend William H. Millor, S.J., executive dean of John Carroll University, have shown the greatest interest in this project. Without their help in innumerable ways I could not have carried it on. The Reverend Terence Ahearn, S.J., former chairman of the Biology Department of John Carroll University, made the work possible by lending to me the department's graflex microfilm recorder, which enabled me to get the basic data for most of the book. Dr. Philip Vogel, past head of the Biology Department, and Dr. Jean Cummings, present head of the department, have done all in their power to further the undertaking.

I wish to thank the American Council of Learned Societies for a grant in aid of $1,800.00 for the year 1960. By means of the grant I was able to finish the research in checking the holdings of libraries on the Atlantic seaboard, obtain microfilms and photostats of needed material, and defray some of the cost of typing the manuscript. The major cost of typing the manuscript was borne by John Carroll University.

Robert W. G. Vail, former director of the New-York Historical Society, was a lifelong friend who aided me in research and helped me obtain necessary books. He was the first person to allow me to microfilm the holdings of an institutional library. Thompson R. Harlow, director of the Connecticut Historical Society, has been unstinting in his help. Through Frederick R. Goff, Chief of the Rare Book Room of the Library of Congress, photostats of the card catalogue of the children's book collection printed prior to 1821 were obtained, which formed one of the foundations of this bibliography. The entire collection was later studied. The late Frederick G. Melcher lent me books and helped me in any way possible. Jacob Blanck has been kind in showing his interest. Harry B. Weiss has been generous with his papers on children's books. He has the rare ability of selecting the most interesting or important children's books on which to write.

At the American Antiquarian Society, Mary Brown, over the past twenty years, has obtained hundreds of books year after year for me to microfilm and study, and made suggestions of some I might have overlooked. Avis Clarke's wonderful catalogue of the library of the American Antiquarian Society and her catalogue of American printers have been invaluable. She has been most generous in sharing with me her wealth of information on American children's books. Being a perfectionist she has spent hours of time-consuming work going over 18th and early 19th century local newspapers to locate a publisher's advertisement of the first edition of an undated juvenile.

Forrest Bowe, an authority on translations of French books printed in America prior to 1821, has not only allowed me to microfilm books in his collection, but it was he who first gave me the idea of collecting bibliographical data by means of the use of the microfilm recorder. He has spent hours copying data from his manuscript, "French Literature in early American Translation," so that these could be incorporated in my book. These gave me many leads as to where children's books might be found. I have obtained much bibliographical knowledge from him and have followed his advice concerning children's books of French origin, and their entry in this book. Herbert Cahoon of the Pierpont Morgan Library, Howell J. Heaney of the Free Library of Philadelphia, Edwin Wolf II, Director of the Library Company of Philadelphia, and Clifford K. Shipton read the first portion of this bibliography through the letter C. They caught many errors and inconsistencies and gave me valuable advice in the preparation of the manuscript. Miss Ellen Shaffer, sometime head of the Rare Book Room of the Free Library of Philadelphia has also been of invaluable assistance. Mr. John Cooke Wyllie, late Director of the Alderman Library of the University of Virginia, had a wealth of information on early American printing. Thanks to him the first American edition of *The Holy Bible In Verse, 1717* was recognized and identified to be the product of the Boston press of John Allen. He also gave me aid in the dating or identification of other early American children's books. Roger Bristol of the same library showed me methods of correcting manuscript and how to make entry forms consistent. Due to his advice many bibliographical points, of which I was uncertain, were clarified and enabled me to get this book ready for press much sooner.

Mr. George A. Schwegman, Chief of the National Union Card Catalogue at the Library of Congress, has been most helpful. This catalogue has proved to be invaluable in locating books and has a wealth of bibliographical information culled from cataloguers from all over the United States.

Sir Frank Francis, director of the British Museum, was extremely kind and helped me in numerous way, for which I am most grateful.

Listing institutions in alphabetical order and using symbols in parentheses to denote the names, I wish to thank the following people who have been so very helpful and considerate: Ian Williamson, Julian J. Roberts, Albert White (BM); Miss Judith St. John (CaOTP); Wilbur Smith, Leo Linder (CLU); Carey S. Bliss (CSmH); Miss Helma L. Talcott, Mrs. Sylvie Turner (Ct); Miss Ruth Kerr, Miss Jessie M. Kenny (CtHT); Stanley Crane (CtSoP); Miss Alexina P. Burgess (CtSu); Wyman W. Parker (CtW); John H. Ottemiller, Miss Marjorie Gray Wynne (CtY); Harland A. Carpenter (DeWi); Miss Helen R. Belknap (DeWint); Robert Rosenthal, Mrs. Harris B. Rubin (ICU); Miss Isabelle F. Grant (IU); Miss Alexandra Mason (KU); John Eliot Alden, Zoltan Haraszti, Francis O. Mattson, Miss Harriet Swift (MB); Ebenezer Gay (MBAt); Miss Corrine M. Nordquest (MBC); Mrs. Elsie M. Boyle (MBChM); Miss Grace D. Baker (MDeHi); Miss Carolyn Jackman, Mrs. Julie Johnson Sirois (MH); John D. Cushing, Stephen T. Riley (MHi); Mrs. David Wallace (MLuHi); Miss Thelma Paine (MNBedf); Miss Katherine Kuechle (MNe); Lawrence Wilkander (MNF); Miss Rose T. Briggs (MPlyA); Mrs. R. L. Higgin (MSaAt); Walter M. Merrill, David R. Proper (MSaE); Miss Alice Hester Rich, John D. Kilbourne (MdHi); James M. Babcock, Mrs. George E. F. Brewer (MiD); Howard A. Sullivan (MiDW); Mrs. Joyce Bonk, Miss Harriet C. Jameson, Miss Agnes Tysse (MiU); Crawford E. L. Donohugh, Mrs. Joseph E. Ledden, Mason Tolman (N); Mrs. Ruth Stewart, George W. Wakefield (NB); Mrs. Charles S. Mott (NBuG); Miss Dorothy C. Barck (NCooHi); Miss Geraldine Beard, Miss Rachel Minick (NHi); Lewis M. Stark, Mrs. Maud D. Cole, Mrs. Philomena C. Houlihan (NN); Miss Maria Cimino, Miss Helen Mastern (NN-C); Miss Darthula Wilcox (NNC-LS); Roland Baughman, Miss Alice Bonnell, Bernard R. Crystal (NNC-Sp); Mrs. Eva Epstein (NNC-T); A. Hyatt Mayor (NNMM); Miss Dorothy A. Plum (NPV); John R. Russell (NRU); Miss Alice C. Dodge (NUt); Miss Elizabeth Miller (NWebyC); Miss Florence Bakely (NcD); Miss Stella L. Scheckter (Nh); Peter Michael Rainey (NhD); Philip N. Guyol (NhHi); Miss Katherine B. Sherwood (NjN); Miss Julie Hudson, Earle E. Coleman, Howard C. Rice, Paul R. Wagner (NjP); Richard R. Shoemaker, Donald Sinclair (NjR); Mrs. Florence H. Krueger, the Reverend James A. Mackin, S.J., Miss Leah Yabroff (OClJC); Miss Margaret Kaltenbach, Miss Harriet Long (OClW-LS); Miss Alene K. White (OClWHi); Mrs. Catherine deSaint-Rat, L. S. Dutton (OOxM); Charles Ness (P); Miss E. Helen Bongard (PHi); Miss Dorothy J. Smith (PMA); Robert Newkirk (PP); Mrs. Lillian Tonkin (PPL); William H. McCarty (PPRF); Andrew S. Berky

(PPeSchw); Miss Elizabeth Nesbitt (PPi); Mrs. Dellene M. Tweedale (PPiU); Mrs. Neda Westlake (PU); Clarkson A. Collins 3rd. (RHi); Stuart C. Sherman (RP); Mrs. Christine D. Hathaway, David A. Jonah (RPB); Miss Jeannette D. Black, Thomas R. Adams (RPJCB); Mrs. Carol Cable, Mrs. Elese Shoemaker (TxU); Lawrence J. Turgeon (Vt); Miss Clara E. Follette (VtHi).

There are a number of private collectors of children's books who have been of great assistance. Miss Ruth E. Adomeit of Cleveland, Ohio, the leading authority on miniature books, has been of great help on all sections covering miniature books, especially the Bibles. At one time or another she has lent me her entire collection of books for filming or study, and I have often consulted her on various bibliographical matters. Miss Elisabeth Ball, of Muncie, Indiana, opened her magnificent collection of children's books for study and allowed me to microfilm all her early American children's books and her English ones through about 1804. I also wish to thank Gillett G. Griffin of Princeton University; Emerson Greenaway, director of the Free Library of Philadelphia; the late Colonel David M. McKell, of Chillicothe, Ohio, for allowing me to microfilm their collections. Malcolm Stone, son of Wilbur Macey Stone, was very kind to allow me to microfilm the last portion of his father's collection, prior to its sale. Edward Naumburg, Jr., of New York City, granted me the same favor before he disposed of his books. The only record I have of certain unique books in both collections is my microfilms of selected pages. Another collector, whose books I have filmed, is John M. Shaw, formerly of New York City. He has since given his collection to Florida State University, Tallahassee, Florida. Mr. Sinclair Hamilton, who has given his choice collection of illustrated books to Princeton University, has been helpful.

Benjamin and Helen French Tighe assembled a small but important collection of mainly American children's books. Benjamin Tighe is one of the great New England bookmen. He has formed three collections of early American children's books. Two of these he sold to the American Antiquarian Society, and the third to Seven Gables Bookshop in New York City. Rare children's books seem to flow to Benjamin Tighe like iron filings to a magnet. He has also sold many individual books to the American Antiquarian Society. Thanks to these purchases, this greatest of all collections of American children's books is now the proud owner of many choice items. A few years ago he began forming a personal collection jointly owned by himself and Mrs. Tighe. With unbelievable speed he has amassed a fourth collection of around 250 children's books printed prior to 1820 as well as others printed after that date. There are seven editions of Benjamin Sands' *Metamorphosis,* including a copy of the earliest edition [*ca.* 1787] known only by the Sinclair Hamilton copy at NjP, and another entirely new edition [*ca.* 1805–1806]. In this collection there is a copy of the second American edition of Perrault's *Tales of Passed Times. New-York: J. Rivington, 1795,* with all nine plates by Alexander Anderson. The plates are sharp and clean and not daubed with color. Beside these there are about twenty-five new edition or unique editions among which is *The History Of The Holy Jesus* and an unknown fragment of another edition of the same book, *Boston: J. Perkins, 1771.* In addition to this new material there are another twenty-five or more which are either the best known copy of the book or the book is only known by one or two copies. It is without doubt most heartening to have people with such beautiful material who are so helpful. I am most grateful to the Tighes for their assistance. In return for their kindness I have repaired a good number of their books so that they are now in nice strong usable condition. Those books from the fourth Tighe collection which were not located at the American Antiquarian Society or were in better condition than AAS copies have been placed at the Society through the kindness of the Tighes and an anonymous donor.

Other collectors who have helped me by allowing me to see their collections and make cards of their holdings and to whom I am most grateful are: Mrs. William M. Ahstrom, Mentor, Ohio; Mrs. Wallace Baker, Shaker Heights, Ohio; Mrs. Glen E. Bartsche, Cleveland Heights, Ohio; Gordon Block, Jr., Philadelphia, Pennsylvania; Mrs. Joseph Carson, Philadelphia, Pennsylvania; George Creamer, Denver, Colorado; Miss Francis Dunn, Saginaw, Michigan; Julian Edison, St. Louis, Missouri; Wm. M. Fitzhugh, Jr., M.D., Pebble Beach, California; Mrs. A. W. France, Wyncote, Pennsylvania; Frederick R. Gardner, Amityville, New York; Mrs. R. L. Gruen, East Hampton, L.I., New York; W. N. H. Harding, Chicago, Illinois; Haddon Klingberg, New Britain, Connecticut; Roland Knaster, London, England; Mrs. Wilbur Krise, Winchester, Virginia; Robert Massmann, New Britain, Connecticut; Peter and Iona Opie, West Liss, Hampshire, England; the late Dr. Edgar S. Oppenheimer, New York; Ludwig Ries, Forest Hills, New York; Sydney Roscoe, Harrow, England; Mrs. Vera von Rosenberg, London, England; Mr. and Mrs. George Shiers, Santa Barbara, California; Raymond Smith, Meriden, New Hampshire; Bradford F. Swan, Providence, Rhode Island; Miss Virginia Warren, Los Angeles, California; Mrs. Oscar Winterstein, Zollikon, Switzerland; and the late C. Richard Whittemore, Westborough, Massachusetts.

A number of booksellers have made gifts of books or enabled me to procure material used in this bibliography. Foremost among these is Michael Papantonio of Seven Gables Bookshop, New York City. He has been a close friend for years and has suggested many ideas which have been of the greatest value. Ernest Wessen, Mansfield, Ohio, has done me many a favor for which I remember him kindly. The late Aaron Mendoza of New York City, Walter Schatzki, New York, and Michael Walsh of Goodspeed's Bookshop, Boston, have also helped me to obtain fine books.

And last, but not least, I wish to thank my wife Ann Goddard Welch for giving unstintingly of her time to help me. She has been my most helpful critic in preparing parts of this bibliography, which she has read over and corrected for English and punctuation. My daughters Elizabeth and Frances Welch helped me tremendously.

A Chronological History
of American Children's Books

18TH CENTURY

THE EARLIEST CHILDREN'S BOOKS in this bibliography were printed mainly in Boston, where the Puritan ideal was predominate. The majority of the books for children in New England were sermons pointing out the depravity of youth and are not included in this bibliography. Accounts of pious children who died prematurely were popular in the early 18th century. They were usually funeral sermons and except for a few selected ones have been omitted. Many were actually meant for adults rather than children.

There were few narrative books, but the earliest is *A Token For Children. Being An Exact Account of the Conversion, Holy and Exemplary Lives and Joyful Deaths of Several Young Children,* By James Janeway (Boston, 1700). This was published in two parts with an added third part, *A Token for the Children of New England,* an American contribution by Cotton Mather. Janeway's popular compilation of stories of over-pious, preaching children, who died at an early age of some unpleasant disease, first appeared in England in two parts, 1671 and 1672. It was repeatedly issued in America and is represented by twenty-nine editions printed prior to 1816.

The next narrative is Thomas White's gruesome tale, *A Little Book For Little Children* (Boston, 1702), known by a single copy. The book is replete with preachments and includes harrowing accounts of tortures taken from Foxe's *Book of Martyrs.* Such detailed descriptions of martyrdom are disconcerting to a modern reader, but such tortures probably did not faze the Puritan children any more than the death of another cowboy affects the young viewer of today's television.

The Holy Bible In Verse, 1717, is the earliest compilation of the Bible published for children. It was written by Benjamin Harris and probably published in Boston. The first English edition is entitled *The Holy Bible, Containing, The Old and New Testaments, with the Apocryphy. Done into Verse by B. Harris for the Benefit of weak memories.* Only four American editions of this book have survived. From advertisements it appears that more editions were published and the book was probably so popular that copies were loved

xxi

out of existence by their owners. The 1717 edition is particularly interesting, because it contains ten cuts which came from an unknown edition of the *New England Primer*. The earliest *New England Primers* known are the unique Boston editions of 1727 and 1735 and they have these cuts in reverse.

Children's books, like fossils, are found today only because of a combination of factors which were favorable to their survival. Therefore, there are many missing links of children's books between the illustrations of an early book like *The Holy Bible In Verse* and the original book in which the cuts first appeared. Paul Leicester Ford states that Franklin and Hall printed over 3700 copies of the *New England Primer* between 1749 and 1766, but only one copy is known to exist today. He also quotes Isaiah Thomas as saying that Fowle printed, *ca.* 1757, one edition of 10,000 copies. Edwin Wolf, speaking of Dr. Rosenbach's collection of children's books, says, "From Johnson & Warner through M'Carty & Davis and Moses Polock, boxes of unsold books for children descended to the Rosenbach cellar." Sets of these publisher's remainders were sold by Rosenbach. Wolf states, "Of no one of these charming little volumes were there more copies than of *The Death and Burial of Cock Robin*, 1805 [*sic. i.e.* The *Tragic-Comic History Of The Burial of Cock Robin*, 1821] —something like 857 copies when counted in recent years." Tracts published by Flagg and Gould, Andover, Mass., 1815–1819, were printed in editions of 6,000. Judging from these scanty data it is probable that narrative children's books were issued in editions of several thousand copies. Of this number, entire editions are no longer extant, many are known by only one or two copies, and common ones by as few as five copies. Every collector of children's books sooner or later becomes the proud possessor of some unique edition of a child's book. Such chance rarities from the past were possibly the cherished possession of some child who died prematurely. Carefully preserved by a fond parent, the little books were put away in an attic trunk where they lay forgotten for many years.

Not only was the New England child brought up with the fear of the Lord and a knowledge of divine truth by means of the *Bible, The New England Primer,* and the *Catechism,* but attention was given to his deportment in the world. In Connecticut a most interesting little volume was printed setting up rules for behavior which were the standards of children's deportment throughout New England. The earliest American edition extant is *The School Of Good Manners. Containing. I. Sundry Mixt Precepts. II. Rules for Children's Behaviour at the Meeting-house, at Home, at the Table, in Company, in Discourse, at School Abroad; with an Admonition to Children. III. Good advice for the ordering of their Lives* (New-London, T. Green and B. Eliot, 1715). In the preface to the 1754 edition, signed T. Green, the statement is made that it was "compiled (chiefly) by Eleazer Moodey, late a famous School-Master in Boston, etc." This Boston arbiter of manners was an adept pirate lifting bodily the entire section on behaviour from *The School Of Manners. Or Rules for Childrens Behaviour: . . . By the Author of the English Exercises.* [J. Garretson, Schoolmaster] *The Fourth Edition* (London, 1701). Only one copy of any edition of Garretson's work, first published in 1685, has been located. In it and Moodey's pirated book children are admonished, "Pick not thy Teeth at the Table, unless holding up thy Napkin before thy mouth with thine other Hand." The book is known by twenty-eight American editions up to 1818.

Wilbur Macey Stone in 1918 said, "If *The New England Primer* was the 'little Bible' of New England, Dr. Watts' *Divine and Moral Songs* has a worthy place beside it as the 'little Hymnbook', not only of New England but of Old England as well." *Divine Songs Attempted in Easy Language for the Use of Children* was first printed in London in 1715. The earliest American edition extant is the seventh edition which was printed in Boston in 1730 and reprinted, up to 1819, sixty-six times. Watts' *Divine and Moral Songs* did not appear until 1788 and went through another thirty-one editions. If all editions prior to 1821 of Isaac Watts' poems for children are counted, the total comes to 130.

Another hymnal which was popular during this early period was *The New England Psalter* which is known by twenty-eight editions between 1732 and 1784.

In 1736 a small book appeared entitled *Martyrology, or, A Brief Account of the Lives, Sufferings and Deaths of those two holy Martyrs, viz. Mr. John Rodgers, and Mr. John Bradford* (Boston, S. Kneeland and T. Green, 1736). From its size and format it seems to be a child's book. Only two copies of this book, the subject matter of which was reprinted so many times in *The New England Primer*, are known.

While *The Holy Bible In Verse* (1717), had Primer cuts, early extant American children's books were usually not illustrated. It must have been a great pleasure to the children of New England when a crudely illustrated little book was available entitled *The History of The Holy Jesus. Third Edition* (Boston, 1746), which also was in verse. One verse reads:

> The Wise men from the East do come,
> Led by a shining Star,
> And offer to the new-born King
> Frankincense, Gold and Myrrh.

The picture accompanying these verses shows a group of men in Puritan dress, two of them looking through telescopes at a star.

Herod slaying the innocent children is depicted mounted on a spirited horse and holding aloft a sword. On either side stand opposing groups of infantry bearing their respective fluttering flags. One flag looks like the union jack. Recently slain bodies lie on the ground. This battle scene was meant to illustrate the verses:

> The bloody Wretch, enrag'd to think,
> Christ's Death he could not gain,
> Commands that Infants all about
> Bethlehem should be slain.

One of the most delightful cuts depicts Christ's teaching. He stands in a pulpit dressed in minister's robes with three men and three women on either side dressed in their Sunday-best eighteenth century clothes, and holding books. This life of Christ seems to have been the first storybook not patterned after some English work. It had been advertised in 1745, but no copies of the first and second editions are known. It was so popular that in succeeding years, up to about 1817, forty-eight editions had appeared.

Halsey quotes John Locke as saying that reading "be never made a Task" and that learning should be made a play and recreation to children. These advanced ideas of making a school or family book of instruction a storybook came to flower in *The Child's New Play-thing; being a spelling-book intended to make the learning to read a diversion . . . Second edition* (London, M. Cooper, 1743). Mary Cooper, who preceded John Newbery, was a pioneer publisher of children's books in England. Her edition of *Tommy Thumb's Pretty Song Book. Vol. II (ca. 1744)*, is a charming, illustrated, little book containing the first collection of "Mother Goose Nursery Rhymes," printed in the manner which proved so successful to John Newbery, who started printing children's books at about the same time.

The earliest American edition is entitled *The Child's New Plaything; Being A Spelling-Book Intending To make the Learning to Read a Diversion instead of a Task. . . . The Fourth Edition. . . .* (Boston, J. Draper for J. Edwards in Cornhill, 1750). It contains the first printing in America of two famous alphabet rhymes

> A. Apple-Pye
> B. bit it
> C. cut it

A was an Archer, and shot at a frog.

Besides these oft-reprinted rhymes, there are fables, selections from Aesop's Fables, stories from the Bible, proverbs, "An Alphabet of Moral Precepts in Verse," riddles, English romances and fairy stories such as "St. George and the Dragon," "Guy Earl of Warwick," "Fortunatus," and "Reynard the Fox."

Halsey says that the third edition was advertised in the "Boston Evening Post" of January 23, 1744, by Joseph Edwards in Cornhill, so that an English edition had been in Boston six years before the first extant American one. It was reprinted in Philadelphia in 1763.

The first non-biblical storybook not designed for the use of schools is an illustrated book called *A New Gift for Children. Delightful and Entertaining Stories For little Masters and Misses* (Boston, D. Fowle, 1756). Daniel Fowle printed in Boston from 1751 to 1756. It contains ten stories entitled: "The Good Boy," "A Good Girl," "The proud Playfellow," "Good Girl & pretty Girl," "The meanly proud Girl," "The Trifler," "The undutiful Child," "The lost Child," "The Advantages of Truth," and "Story X [Of Master Tommy Fido]." In 1762, Fowle and Draper published an illustrated fourth edition of this book, two parts in one volume. Part one includes five new stories: "The Dutiful Child," "The Thief," "The Generosity of confessing a Fault," "The two good Friends," and "The Rewards of Virtue." The second part has the ten stories first printed by D. Fowle.

Daniel Fowle printed another small typical child's book entitled *A Little Book For Children, Containing A few Rules for the Regulation of their Thots, Words & Actions* (Portsmouth, N. H., 1758). While most of the book is taken up with rules for behaviour and a catechism, the last three pages contain "The Story of Miss Sally Friendly," which certainly is the type of story published for children by John Newbery.

Only a meager number of children's books printed during the period of unrest from 1750 to the American Revolution, are extant today. The children in those years could obtain the first American edition of a miniature Bible written by John Taylor and first published in London in 1614. It was *The Verbum Sempiternum* (New York, Samuel Parker, ca. 1760). *The Children's Bible*, London, 1759, was printed in Philadelphia in 1763.

Tom Thumb's Play Book advertised in Birmingham, England in 1750 is a charming miniature book. In it are reprinted the two famous alphabet rhymes "A Apple pye" and "A was an Archer" first seen in *The Child's New Plaything* (London, 1743). The first American edition, and earliest known one, has the imprint "Boston: Printed for and sold by A. Barclay in Cornhill." This little scrap is historic because Isaiah Thomas, the famous publisher, wrote in the copy he gave to the American Antiquarian Society, "Printed by I. Thomas when A 'prentice in 1764, for A. Barclay." In 1764 Thomas was an apprentice of Zechariah Fowle and at his printing office probably published this extremely fragile little book with the letters of the alphabet enclosed in ornamental borders. It is known by eight American and two Scotch editions published prior to 1801.

Chapbooks were unbound paper pamphlets sold by chapmen or hawkers who roamed the streets or the countryside selling not only chapbooks, but thread, needles, and various other small portable articles. They were referred to as "running stationers", or "traveling stationers." Many editions of Watts' *Divine Songs* are typical chapbooks. One of the most popular chapbooks was *The Prodigal Daughter* which first appeared in Boston about 1758 and went through twenty-six editions before 1820. Another was *The Happy Child* (Boston, 1767). Both books are known only by American editions. But some American chapbooks were reprints of earlier English chapbooks, many of which were published in Aldermary Church Yard, London in the early eighteenth century. These are *The Most Delightful History of The King and the Cobbler* (Boston, *ca.* 1770); *The Famous and Remarkable History Of Sir Richard Whittington* (Boston, *ca.* 1770); and *The Friar and Boy* (Boston, 1767). In this latter book, A. Barclay advertises *Robinson Crusoe, Goose's Tales, Arabian Nights, History Of Mother Bunch, Tom Thumb, Jack the Piper, Jack Horner,* and *Jack and the Giants.* No edition with his imprint of any of these has been located but such advertisements are interesting evidence that American children had books recounting the tales so beloved in England.

The year 1767 is noteworthy in American children's books. In that year Mein and Fleeming of Boston published two little storybooks, *The Story Of The cruel Giant Barbarico,* lifted from Sarah Fielding's *The Governess,* and *The Adventures Of Urad,* pirated from Ridley's *Tales of the Genii.* John Newbery's advertisements and the influx of children's books from England must have stimulated the production of these books because no good businessman could sit idly by and see Boston children catered to so lucratively by a London printer who advertised his wares in American newspapers. The following year they reprinted the first of the Newbery books to be published in America, *The Renowned History Of Giles Gingerbread.* There are no John Newbery editions extant of this book although it was advertised by him in 1766. The earliest copy known is the Newbery and Carnan 1769 edition. In the Boston edition are listed "Books For Children to be had of John Mein at the London Bookstore." Two of them may be English books or they could be American reprints which are no longer extant. One is *The Adventures of Tommy Trip* advertised in 1761 by John Newbery under the title *A Pretty Book of Pictures for little Masters and Misses, Or Tommy Trip's History of Birds and Beasts*. No American edition of this is known before 1796 when Samuel Hall published it under the new title *Pictures of Seventy-Two Beasts and Birds*. The second book listed, *The Famous Tommy Thumb's Little Story Book*, was reprinted in 1771 by J. Boyles in Boston. The original London source book was published by S. Crowder and B. Collins in Salisbury in about 1760. It is one of the important source books of *Mother Goose Rhymes*.

After the American Revolution, especially after 1785, there was a marked increase in the production of children's books. From 1790 to 1800 they were so numerous that it is possible to mention only those that went through seven or more editions. A large proportion of those most often reprinted were originally printed in England by John Newbery and his successors.

Prior to John Newbery, the majority of amusing English storybooks were chapbooks and were printed not only in London, in Aldermary Church Yard, but also in Newcastle-on-Tyne and elsewhere in England. Some of these chapbooks which would appeal to children were coarse, ribald, and even obscene. The strict religious parents of the early 18th century would not go out of their way to place such books in their children's hands. A selected chronological list has been compiled of pleasurable non-biblical books consisting of fairy tales, romances, and poetry, published before 1745 in England. In the list below, and in all following lists, the date of the earliest English edition or advertisement located is given, followed by the title and, if known, the location of the printing of the earliest American edition, its date, and in parenthesis, the number of American editions.

1686 John Bunyan. *A Book For Boys And Girls.* In 1724 the title was changed to *Divine Emblems;* New York, *ca.* 1794, (3).

1692 Aesop. Sir Roger L'Estrange, *tr. A History Of The Life Of Aesop;* Philadelphia, 1788, (2).

1719 D. Defoe. *Robinson Crusoe. Abridged;* New York, 1774, (92).

1722 Aesop. S. Croxall, *tr. Fables Of Aesop And Others;* Philadelphia, 1777, (7).

1724 *The Renowned History Of Valentine And Orson;* Haverhill, Mass., 1794, (11, including variants).

1729 Charles Perrault. *Histories Or Tales of Passed Times;* Haverhill, 1794, (2). Separate stories: Blue Beard, (28); Cinderella (16).

1736 [T. Boreman] *A Description of a Great Variety of Animals and Vegetables.*

[1730] [—] *A Description of three hundred Animals.*

1739 [—] *A Description of some curious and uncommon Creatures, Omitted in the Description of Three Hundred Animals.*

1740–43   [—] "The Gigantick Histories," 10 vols. They describe Guildhall, 2 vols.; The Tower of London, 2 vols.; St. Paul's Cathedral, 2 vols.; Westminster Abbey, 3 vols.; The Giant Cajanus, 1 vol.

1743   *The Child's New Plaything*; Boston, 1750, (2).

[1744?]   Nurse Lovechild. *Tommy Thumb's Pretty Song Book,* vol. II; Worcester, 1788, (1).

Most of these English juveniles were not printed in America until after the American Revolution and frequently as late as fifty years after first publication. The books printed, and probably written, by Thomas Boreman from 1736 to 1743 while never published in America are important. "The Gigantick Histories" are particularly so, because they are only six centimeters high, bound in gilt Dutch paper, and especially aimed at making reading a pleasure rather than a task. There is even a list of subscribers in each volume of the "Gigantick Histories." M. Cooper's edition of *Tommy Thumb's Pretty Song Book* is also a diminutive book, charmingly illustrated, the first compilation of nursery rhymes and a source of some of the rhymes in *Mother Goose's Melody.*

John Newbery has been hailed as the first publisher to cater to a juvenile audience by printing to delight youngsters after the principles laid down by John Locke. It is evident from the above list that John Newbery, when he advertised his first non-instructive child's book, *A Little Pretty Pocket Book* in the *Penny Morning Post,* June 13, 1744, had not invented a new type of recreational book. He merely capitalized on Locke's theories, as other publishers had done and were doing at that time. His genius lay in the number of good children's books he printed and in his methods of successfully marketing them. Newbery left no stone unturned to advertise both his children's books and his patent medicines. Not only did he list them in the back of his books and have them heralded in both English and American newspapers, but he also had them mentioned in the text of his books by some character or hero. It is no wonder, due to his business acumen, that at the time of his death, December 22, 1767, he was a well-to-do man. In twenty-three years, in addition to his numerous diminutive books of instruction, he published twenty which were purely recreational. Of these, twenty-six were published only once in America, by Isaiah Thomas in Worcester. Five were popular and are listed below:

1755 (adv.)   *Nurse Truelove's New Year's Gift.* (Contains *The House That Jack Built*); Worcester, 1786, (6).

1758 (adv.)   *The Holy Bible Abridged;* Boston, 1782?, (23).

1760 (adv.)   *Nurse Truelove's Christmas Box;* Hartford, 1789, (6).

1764 (adv.)   1766—earliest located. *The History of Little Goody Two Shoes;* New York, 1775, (15).

1766 (adv.)   *The Renowned History Of Giles Gingerbread;* Boston, 1768, (21 including variants).

By the terms of John Newbery's will, his son, Francis Newbery, junior, was left the entire patent-medicine business. The general business was left to be carried on for the joint interest of his son Francis Newbery, jun.; daughter, Mary Power; stepson, T. Carnan; and nephew, Francis Newbery, Sr.; with a provision being made for his widow, Mary Newbery, and his daughter-in-law, Mary Smart. However, the interest to rights in books and pamphlets was divided between his wife; F. Newbery, Jun.; Mary Power; and T. Carnan; with the nephew, F. Newbery, Sr., excluded.

Francis Newbery, jun. and Thomas Carnan continued the business under the joint name of Newbery and Carnan at No. 65 St. Paul's Church yard. Charles Welsh says that the partners were not on the best of terms because Carnan believed he had been harshly treated by the terms of the will. Francis Newbery, jun. gradually withdrew from active participation in the firm and devoted himself to his patent-medicine business. Their joint names have been noted as late as 1778 on children's books, but Welsh says that they were together until about 1782. Even before 1778, Carnan's name appears alone on certain books dated from 1771. Carnan continued to manage the firm alone until his death January 15, 1788.

At Carnan's death Francis Newbery, jun. appears to have again taken an active interest in the publishing business with Mary Power's son, Francis Power, doing the managing and using the imprint *F. Power and Co.* (*Successors to the late T. Carnan*), or (*Grandson to the late Mr. J. Newbery*). All the Newbery publications came into the possession of Elizabeth Newbery, the widow of Francis Newbery, Sr. How this came about is unknown, but it may have been through purchase or transfer of title.

The firm of Newbery and Carnan did not add a large number of books which caught the fancy of the American juvenile public. Only the few below are of importance.

1768 (adv.)   D. Defoe. *Robinson Crusoe. Abridged;* New York, 1774, ([version 3] 18).

1768   *Tom Thumb's Folio;* Boston, *ca.* 1780, (12).

1770 (adv.)   *London Cries;* Philadelphia, 1787, (2).

These books have not been located on John Newbery's lists. Those printed in 1768 may have been unpublished ones belonging to John Newbery who had not yet printed them at the time of his death. The earliest English abridgement of *Robinson Crusoe,* with a format surely copied by Hugh Gaine in his first American abridgement of Defoe's work, has an imprint which reads: "Printed for the inhabitants of his Island, and Sold by all the Booksellers in the World." It is a typical, whimsical John Newbery imprint, and is in a similar vein to the one Newbery used in *A Pretty Play-Thing* . . . Alexandria: "Printed for the Booksellers of Egypt and Palmyra, and Sold at the Bible and Sun in St. Paul's Church-Yard, London."

When T. Carnan completely took over the management of the firm, *ca.* 1778, he was not successful in selecting books which became popular in America. An important advertisement of his appeared in the *London Chronicle* for Dec. 30, 1780–January 2, 1781: "This Day was published, Price 3d. Mother Goose's Melody; Or Sonnets for the Cradle . . . Now first published from the papers of that very great writer of little books the late Mr. John Newbery, and sold by T. Carnan in St. Paul's Churchyard." For some reason none of the Newbery successors advertised the book in any of their lists except Francis Power in *The Adventures of a Bee* (1790). A unique copy printed by F. Power in 1791 is in Miss Elisabeth Ball's collection. This had always been an enigma, because it was the earliest known English edition and Isaiah Thomas had advertised an American edition in 1786. A fragmentary copy is in the American Antiquarian Society, lacking a title page and wanting most of the lower part of each page. Evans and others considered it to have been printed in 1785 by Thomas. This fragment, the 1794, and 1799 editions of Isaiah Thomas are very close to the English one of 1791. Now we know T. Carnan advertised that he had published the book in 1780. Therefore, even though John Newbery probably had compiled or hired someone to compile the manuscript, T. Carnan gets the distinction of having published the most famous child's book ever written. The actual book is known by only eight American editions before 1821, including abridged versions. Many of the poems were published in books with other titles.

Francis Newbery, Sr. who had not chosen to remain in business with his relatives, had immediately set up business at 20 Ludgate Street, corner of St. Paul's Church yard. He continued there until the time of his death, January 1780. The firm was continued by his widow, Elizabeth Newbery, until 1801 when she was succeeded by her manager, J. Harris. Francis Newbery, Sr. did much more for juvenile literature than his cousins' firm of Newbery and Carnan. He published John Newbery's books, much to his cousins' displeasure, and added twenty-eight new titles. On the verso of the title of *The Holy Bible Abridged* (1775), is this notation: "The Public are desired to observe that F.

Newbery, at the corner of St. Paul's Church Yard and Ludgate-street has not the least concern in any of the late Mr. John Newbery's Entertaining Books for Children; and to prevent having paltry compilations obtruded on them, instead of Mr. John Newbery's useful publications, they are desired to be particularly careful to apply for them to T. Carnan and F. Newbery, jun. (Successors to the late Mr. John Newbery) at No. 65, near the Bar in St. Paul's church yard."

A chronological list of the most popular F. Newbery, Sr. books printed in America are:

1769 (adv.)   S. Richardson. *Clarissa. Abridged;* Boston, 1795, (2).

1769 — *Pamela Abridged;* Boston, 1794, (14).

1769 (adv.)   — *Sir Charles Grandison. Abridged;* Philadelphia, *ca.* 1790, (8).

1773 (adv.)   *The Brother's Gift;* Worcester, 1786, (17).

1773 (adv.)   *The Sister's Gift;* Worcester, 1786, (14).

1775   *The Cries Of London;* Philadelphia, 1805, (19).

1775 (adv.)   *The Father's Gift;* Worcester, 1786, (8).

1775 (adv.)   *The History of Little King Pippin;* Philadelphia, 1786, (13).

1775 (adv.)   *The Puzzling Cap;* Boston, 1792, (10).

1777 (adv.)   J. Swift. *The Adventures of Captain Gulliver. Abridged;* Philadelphia, 1787, (10).

The abridgements of Richardson's *Clarissa* and *Pamela* were first advertised by Newbery and Carnan in *The History of Little Goody Two-Shoes* (1768). No copies have been located nor have they been found on any of their other lists. They were frequently advertised by F. Newbery, Sr. and a copy of *Pamela* published in 1769, with his imprint, has advertisements of abridged editions of *Clarissa* and *Sir Charles Grandison.* For some reason these books seem to have become the property of F. Newbery, Sr. rather than that of Newbery and Carnan. Since they originally appeared on the lists of both firms they also may have been unpublished John Newbery books inherited by his heirs.

The Cries of London, while not the source book of the first American edition entitled *London Cries,* a Newbery and Carnan book, is the one which was more frequently published in America although later editions varied greatly from it.

When Elizabeth Newbery took over the management of her husband's firm on the decease of F. Newbery, Sr., the business flourished still more. She was assisted by Abraham Badcock until his death in 1797. He was followed by her manager, J. Harris, who succeeded her in 1801 as head of the firm. According to C. Welsh, Harris paid her a yearly allowance of £500 until her death in 1821. During Elizabeth's reign, from 1781–1801, ninety-nine or more new titles were added to the lists of John Newbery, Francis Newbery, Sr., Newbery and Carnan and T. Carnan. *Mother Goose's Melody* and a number of books on Francis Power's lists do not appear to have been published by her. The hack writer Richard Johnson wrote a number of the new books published by E. Newbery. Although his children's books bought by T. Carnan were not outstanding, Johnson's productions bought by Abraham Badcock were among the most popular books reprinted in America. They are as follows:

1787 Berquin, A. [R. Johnson] *comp. The Looking Glass For The Mind;* Providence, 1794, (17).

1787 [—] *The History of Tommy Careless;* New York, *ca.* 1788, (10).

1788 [—] *The Hermit Of The Forest;* Boston, *ca.* 1789, (31).

1789 [—] *The Blossoms Of Morality;* Philadelphia, 1795, (7).

A rival of the Newbery successors was John Marshall, who published in London from *ca.* 1780 to after 1820. He was the publisher for Dorothy Kilner, Mary Ann Kilner, Mrs. Trimmer, Lady Eleanor Fenn and others. His publications listed in *Nancy Cock's Pretty Song Book,* dated, *ca.* 1780, include some exceedingly popular books reprinted in America. They are:

The Life Death and Burial Of Cock Robin; Worcester, 1787, (34).

The History of Master Jackey And Miss Hariot; Worcester, 1787, (10).

The House That Jack Built; Philadelphia, 1786, (25 including variants).

Jacky Dandy's Delight; Worcester, 1787, (10).

In the preceding lists of popular books issued by John Newbery, his successors, and John Marshall, a number of first American editions were printed in Worcester. They came from the press of Isaiah Thomas who was one of the pioneer American publishers of children's books. Contemporary with him were other publishers such as Samuel Hall, J. White, C. Cambridge, J. Folsom, all in Boston; John Trumbull in Norwich, Conn.; N. Patten, Hartford; William Durell, Evert Duyckinck, New York; A. Stoddard, Hudson, New York; Young and McCulloch, J. Crukshank, R. Aikin, in Philadelphia; W. Spotswood in Philadelphia and later Boston; and others.

A number of books published in England by others besides the Newbery clan and John Marshall played an important role in the production of much-read children's books in America. Those most often reprinted in America were:

1593 *The Affecting History of The Children in the Wood.* Hartford, 1796. ([all editions of *The Children* or *Babes in the Wood*] 29).

1761 Aesop. R. Dodsley, *tr. Select Fables of Aesop;* Philadelphia, 1777, (13).

1771 J. Macgowan. *The Life Of Joseph Son Of Israel;* Hartford, 1791, (33).

1772 H. Wynne. *Choice Emblems;* Philadelphia, 1790, (11).

1781 A. L. Barbauld. *Hymns In Prose;* Norwich, 1786, (38).

1782 W. Cowper. *John Gilpin.* Newburyport, 1793, ([all editions] 10).

1783 *Heiroglyphic Bible;* Worcester, 1788, (14).

[1784 adv.?] John Bunyan. *The Christian Pilgrim;* Worcester, 1798, (11).

1783–84 A. Berquin. *The Children's Friend;* Boston, 1790?, (8).

1783–1786 T. Day. *Sandford and Merton.* Philadelphia, 1788, (12).

19TH CENTURY PRIOR TO 1821

The bulk of every collection of children's books is made up of post-1800 imprints. A veritable flood of books were published. Many were reprints of books published earlier in the eighteenth century. A selected list of books first issued in America in the early nineteenth century and represented by more than seven editions are listed chronologically below. The first English edition or the earliest source book of some of them has not been located. A number are American in origin.

1795 *Juvenal (or Juvenile) Poems, or The Alphabet In verse;* Hartford, 1800, (17).

1796 More, H. *The Shepherd Of Salisbury Plain.* [Cheap Repository]; Philadelphia, 1800, (12).

[1800] J. Campbell, *Worlds Displayed;* New York, 1801, (13).

Clara English, *The Children in the Wood;* Philadelphia, 1803, (11, including variants).

The History Of Beasts; Philadelphia, adv., 1805, (11).

J. Horner [pseud.] *The Silver Penny;* New Haven, 1805, (10).

Trip's History of Beasts; Hudson, 1805, (15).

Will Whistle. The History of the Birds in the air; Philadelphia, 1805, (14, including variants).

Aesop's Fables (various selections); New Haven, 1806, (9).

1804–5 Gilbert, Ann (Taylor). *Original Poems;* Philadelphia, 1806, (9).

The Wonderful History of The Enchanted Castle; Albany, 1806, (9).

More, Hannah. *T's All For The Best;* Hartford, 1807, (10).

Corry, John. *Biographical Memoirs of . . . General George Washington;* Philadelphia, 1808, (12).

The Cries Of New York; New York, 1808, (7).

The Book of Riddles; New York, 1808, (10).

The History of Insects; New York, 1808, (8).

xxxiii

1795 Edgeworth, M. *The Parent's Assistant;* Georgetown, 1809, (6).

The Seven Wonders Of The World; New York, 1810, (7).

Old Age; New York, S. Wood, 1810, (7).

The History of Birds; New York, 1810, (10).

1808 Gilbert, Ann (Taylor). *Hymns For Infant Minds,* Boston, *ca.* 1810, (32).

[–] *Little Poems For Little Readers,* New York, 1811, (8).

[–] *Poems For Children;* New York, 1811, (6).

Campbell, John. *Walks of Usefulness;* Boston, 1812, (11).

[Gilbert, Ann (Taylor)]. *Hymns For Little Children;* New York, 1812, (8).

1809 Richmond, Leigh. *The Dairyman's Daughter;* Harrisonburg, Va., 1813, (17).

The Story of Ali Baba; Boston, 1813, (8).

[written 1803] Cameron, Lucy L. (Butt). *The Two Lambs;* Hartford, 1815, (7).

1814 Sherwood, Mary M. (Butt). *The History Of Little Henry And His Bearer;* Andover, 1817, (15).

In the above list Ann Taylor Gilbert's *Hymns For Infant Minds* was by far the leading best seller. If S. Wood's editions of *Poems For Children* and *Little Poems For Little Readers,* which contain mainly selections from *Original Poems,* are included, fourteen more would be added. Three of the six issues of Maria Edgeworth's *Parent's Assistant* were published in 1816, 1818, and 1819 by Wells and Lilly in Boston and broken up into separate booklets with one or more stories in them.

The moral and religious tracts of the *Cheap Repository* were published in profusion in England during the 1790's. Spinney states that in one year over 2,000,000 copies were sold. A selection first appeared in America gathered together in book form under the title *The Entertaining Moral and Religious Repository* (Elizabeth-Town, N.J., 1798). In 1800 the *Cheap Repository* tracts were brought out separately in Philadelphia. One of the most frequently printed was Hannah More's *The Shepherd Of Salisbury Plain,* which from 1806 to 1818 is known by eleven editions. Among the early tract societies were the New York Religious Tract Society, 1812; The New England Tract Society, Andover, Mass., 1814; The Philadelphia Female Tract Society, 1816. They published tracts in great numbers and the most popular tract of all was Leigh Richmond's *The Dairyman's Daughter.*

The publications of Samuel Wood, New-York; Sidney's Press, New-Haven; and E. and E. Hosford, Albany were undoubtedly more numerous than listed in this bibliography. They seem to have published a complete edition of all their advertised publications once and sometimes twice a year. Their publications must each have been represented by at least a dozen or more editions.

The big change in children's books which came during the early nineteenth century was in books not known by a large number of extant editions. In London a number of firms began publishing books with beautiful copperplate engravings, many of which were colored by hand. Not only were the books finely illustrated, but some were written with a sense of humor. William Darton wrote the text and engraved the plates for some delightfully illustrated books such as *The First, Second and Third Chapter of Accidents, A Present For a Little Boy,* and *A Present For A Little Girl.* These appeared between 1797 and 1805. Jacob Johnson reprinted them in Philadelphia, 1802–1807, and later. He seemed to specialize in pirating English copperplate books. John Harris, who succeeded Elizabeth Newbery, brought out *The Comic Adventures Of Old Mother And Her Dog* (1805), with beautiful hand-colored illustrations. The book was so successful that thousands of copies were sold in a short time. *The Butterfly's Ball* (London, J. Harris, January 1, 1807), was another amusing book. It was one of the earliest nonsense rhyming books. It was illustrated with six engravings after Mulready, the designer of the famous Mulready envelope. Roscoe had written the verses for his son Robert. Harris commissioned Mrs. Dorset to write the sequel, *The Peacock At Home,* which also came out in 1807. Forty thousand copies of these two books were sold in 1807 alone. *Dr. Goldsmith's Celebrated Elegy On That Glory of Her Sex. Mrs. Mary Blaize* (London, J. Harris, 1808), was another amusing book. *The Butterfly's Ball* and its sequel had a host of imitators and an entire pattern of juvenile literature was established by those entertaining children's books. William Godwin, under the name of his manager, Thomas Hodgkins, published in 1806 *The Little Woman And The Pedlar.* He previously had published in 1805 *The King And Queen Of Hearts* by Charles Lamb, which was not very successful.

William Charles, an American engraver and publisher, copied all the above books, with the exception of Lamb's book, and many like them. He published in New York City from 1806–1814, and then moved to Philadelphia where he lived until his death on August 29, 1820. Editions of William Charles' books are not numerous, possibly because the majority of them were completely destroyed. Many books advertised by him are as yet unlocated. His wife, Mary Charles, after his decease, and later Morgan and Yeager, reprinted his plates and books. Even these reprints are anything but common and extant copies of many are unknown.

It is strange that Charles Lamb's *King and Queen of Hearts* was not published in America before 1821. Only a single edition was printed in America. It has the imprint, "Baltimore Published by F. Lucas, Jr. No. 138 Market Street. Philadelphia Ash & Mason, No. 139 Chestnut Street," (*ca.* 1825). Lamb's *Tales from Shakespeare, Mrs. Leicester's School,* and *Poetry For Children* were all published in America but did not go through many editions.

A very delightful colorplate child's book undoubtedly of American origin, executed in the format of J. Harris and William Charles, is entitled *Some very gentle touches to Some very gentle-Men By a humble country Cousin of Peter Pindar, Esq. Dedicated to all the little Girls & Boys, of the City of New York* (*ca.* 1806). The book is engraved throughout and the plates colored by hand. The text in verse starts:

> In a City far fam'd
> Which must not be Nam'd
> A City most wise & most fine;
> There is to be seen
> A sight most clean.
> The streets all alive with swine.

The story then proceeds to relate the havoc swine caused in the streets of New York City.

It is interesting to note that of all the books printed in America before 1821 none equaled the popularity of Watts' *Divine Songs* and *Robinson Crusoe,* both of which were first published in the early part of the 18th century.

Much needs to be done in tracing English source books of American children's publications. Only a beginning has been made in this bibliography. The catalogues of the British Museum, Harvey Darton Collection given to the Teacher's College Library of Columbia University by Mr. Carl H. Pforsheimer, Osborne Collection, and Percy Muir's *Children's Books of Yesterday* are invaluable in this search. Added to these are Welch microfilms and notes held by the American Antiquarian Society and the University of California at Los Angeles.

COLLECTIONS

The majority of American children's books printed prior to 1820 are in institutional libraries. Many libraries in the "dark ages" of book-care turned over their fragile volumes to people determined on one thing, namely that the book should henceforth be branded, as a cattleman brands a steer, so that nobody could possibly steal the textual slave delivered into their unfeeling hands. Some of the most priceless juveniles in the world are hopelessly branded with ink stamps, perforated or embossed stamps which seriously impair the value of the book. Owing to the zeal of past generations, hundreds of children's books have been so damaged. Usually a disgraceful library seal or catalogue number has been permanently branded across the title page, the frontispiece, or some important page of the text. Luckily, such practices are now frowned upon by reputable libraries. Books defaced by library seals are today replaced as fast as possible with unstamped ones. Because of the scarcity of juveniles, many collections have had to buy stamped books with the seals of other libraries. This miserable practice of stamping books has put unstamped juveniles at a premium. Collectors should be very sure that the library to which they are leaving their cherished volumes will not mutilate them.

A twentieth century refinement of book mutilation is the improper use of the bookplate in delicate juveniles not having a blank page. Bookplates, usually oversize ones, are often pasted over the frontispiece, title page, or some important page of the text, when a blank leaf is not available. Bookplates properly used are a definite addition. But sad is the day when a library has a blanket rule which insists that every book have a bookplate regardless of whether there is a place for it or not. This results in the bookplate becoming all important and a case of "the tail wagging the dog." Wilbur Macey Stone made delightful colored paper covers for his rare fragile juveniles. He pasted his bookplate onto the cover when no blank leaf was available and was sure he put a bookplate of an appropriate size in the book. This cover protected the book's cover when being handled and was an excellent place on which to write notes.

Many juveniles in institutions are in ragged condition. Unless these books are expertly repaired, they will be doomed to extinction. The amateur should not try to repair books with the run-of-the-mill materials available in a stationery store. Children's books must be carefully repaired by someone used to working with old paper.

In the last thirty-five years a good many private collections have been dispersed. The most notable of these was that of Wilbur Macey Stone, which not only was a very sizable one containing both English and American material, but also had a large bibliographical collection on juveniles. Some time after the sale of the Stone books, the collections of Miss Beatrice Gunn and Edward Naumburgh, Jr. were sold. Many choice items from these now enrich the American Antiquarian Society and others.

Some private collections have been preserved in their entirety. The famous Rosenbach collection went to the Free Library of Philadelphia. A large portion of Miss Elisabeth Ball's collection is now deposited at the Pierpont Morgan

Library. She had an outstanding collection of English children's books. She acquired both the C. T. Owen and Gumuchian collections which were exceptionally fine. Among her American books was a unique copy of *The Renowned History of Giles Gingerbread*, Newport, [R. I.], 1771. The Albert C. Bates collection was left to the Connecticut Historical Society. Mrs. C. Scuyler Davis' collection was given to the University of Rochester, that of John M. Shaw to Florida State University at Tallahassee. The Harold Rugg collection of Vermontiana, replete with juveniles, went to the Vermont Historical Society. The University of California at Los Angeles bought the Olive Percival, Bernard Meeks, and Mrs. Elvah J. Karshner collections. The H. Friedman collection was bought by the Encyclopedia Britannica and given to the University of Chicago. The McKell collection is now housed in the David McCandless McKell Library, Ross County Historical Society, Chillicothe, Ohio. In the years to come, all present day collections in private hands will probably be in some institutional library.

There are still holdings of children's books in private hands. Miss Ruth E. Adomeit has a small but representative series of children's books, and an outstanding collection of miniature books. She has the ability of picking up the most interesting material in out-of-the-way places. Her Dodsley's *Select Fables of Aesop*, Montreal, 1800, and *A History of The Holy Bible*, Cincinnati, 1815, are choice. Gillett G. Griffin has a choice collection of New England imprints, some of which are unique. He owns the entire Wilbur Macey Stone collection of *New England Primers*, and his copy of the 1724 fragment of *The Holy Bible In Verse*. He also has a unique edition of Isaac Watts' *Divine Songs Attempted In Easy Language For The Use Of Children*, Norwich [Conn.], Green & Spooner, 1777, and *The Brother's Gift*, Hartford, N. Patten, 1789.

Mrs. Joseph Carson's collection includes a unique copy of *Robinson Crusoe* printed in Philadelphia by Charles Cist, 1792, as well as other rare and unique juveniles. Miss Virginia Warren has an interesting collection of *Cries* both English and American. Emerson Greenaway owns *The Prodigal Daughter*, Boston [*ca.* 1769] and a unique copy of *The Father's Gift*, Worcester, 1794.

The late Dr. Edgar S. Oppenheimer was an omnivorous collector of all types of children's books in English and foreign languages, and did not limit himself to an early date. He was not primarily interested in small American pamphlet children's books, although he obtained the Harry Stone collection which contained fine small books. His collection had rare expensive children's books of which he often had duplicate copies. He bought the Wilbur Macey Stone collection of *Goody Two-Shoes*, with its rare American editions. Brigham lists nineteen editions of *Robinson Crusoe* belonging to Dr. Oppenheimer. Dr. Oppenheimer's collection of English children's books must be extensive. It included the entire collection of the *Good Housekeeping Magazine* which formerly belonged to the late F. R. Bussell and which made up most of the National Book League's Exhibition of Children's Books in 1945.

The Welch collection, now at the American Antiquarian Society, is represented by over eight hundred books in this bibliography. The major portion of it consists of books printed between 1800 and 1820. There are twenty-eight miniature Bibles, of which John Taylor's *Verbum Sempiternum*, Boston, 1786, is the only known complete copy. Of the twenty-one editions of *Robinson Crusoe*, the Boston: Bible And Heart [*ca.* 1792] is unique. *The History Of The Holy Jesus* is represented by fourteen editions, two of which, the Boston, 1748, and the Suffield, 1803, are each one of two known copies. There are also imperfect copies of Perrault's *Fairy Tales Or Histories Of Passed Times*, Haverhill, 1794; *The History of Goody Two-Shoes*, New York, Hugh Gaine, 1774; *Tom Thumb's Play Book*, Worcester, 1794; *The House That Jack Built*, Boston, 1790; and a complete edition with the imprint: New York: Printed by W. Durell [*ca.* 1793]. Representative books include *The Affecting History of The Children In The Wood*, First Newport Edition, 1799; also the Second Newport Edition, 1803; *The Holy Bible In Verse*, 1717; *Little Red Riding Hood*, Philadelphia, MDCCXCVII; Richard Johnson's *The History Of A Little Child Found Under A Haycock*, Boston, 1794, which contains *Mother Goose Rhymes*, *Mother Goose's Melody*, Third Worcester Edition, Worcester, 1799. Besides this, there are about one hundred or more books which are either unique, one of two known copies, or the best known copy of the book.

Institutional collections of American children's books can be grouped into six classes in order of magnitude based on the number of books used in this bibliography. The classes are: (1) 2000–2500; (2) 450–600; (3) 350–450; (4) 250–350; (5) 100–250; (6) under 100.

The American Antiquarian Society is the only library in class 1. It has by far the largest and most interesting collection of children's books seen. Clarence Brigham, building on a handful of books left by Isaiah Thomas and added to by Dr. Nichols and others, built up the greatest collection of American juveniles ever assembled. The collection got its impetus in the days when children's books were not being collected and were not at a premium. Under Brigham's infectious enthusiasm, collectors, friends, and booksellers either gave or sold books to the Society. Few men have Brigham's peculiar gift of picking out a person and building him into a collector or bibliographer. When I first met him, and expressed my interest in writing a bibliography, he made me feel that my project was the most important one in the world. Soon after my first trip to Worcester, microfilming books and collecting data, I received books lacking title pages and other pages with a note asking me to please identify them. I did not have one-tenth the knowledge of this dean of bibliographers, but because he led me to believe I knew something, I had to live up to his opinion of me. My trips to Worcester over the past 20 years have been particularly pleasant because of his advice and interest in this project. Every once in a while I would get a letter with a duplicate enclosed or a package of books. Some were perfect, others cripples, or fragments of children's books, with a note telling me I could have these duplicates if they were of interest. They were always of unbelievable interest, some being the only other known copy of the book. He did this not only to me, but to other collectors. The Rosenbach collection is rich in books which were formerly duplicates of the American Antiquarian Society. Some of these I know were gifts to Dr. Rosenbach and are among the very prized books of that collection. With such treatment, collectors have reciprocated by gifts to the American Antiquarian Society. Each book has a note in Brigham's handwriting, giving the name of the donor and the year it was acquired. Going through the collection is like reading a "Who's Who" of collectors of children's books. Wilbur Macey Stone gave his superb collection of Isaac Watts' *Divine Songs,* and a select number of very rare books. Miss Edith Whitmore, of Newport, was most generous with a group of choice books. Dr. Rosenbach and many others are among those immortal collectors who have enriched this collection.

When making a study of the books and reading the notes by scholars over the past fifty years, one feels in close contact with the best bibliographers of juvenile literature because all of them have left their mark of learning upon the collection. There are notes by Charles Evans, Wilbur Macey Stone, P. K. Foley, Charles Goodspeed, and Albert C. Bates. Brigham's knowledge of children's books, gained through fifty years of collecting and study, was outstanding. The collection's value has been increased by his notes.

Nearly every important bookseller has at some time sold books to Brigham and has his name or that of his company written in each book where he will be remembered for many a day. Some I knew, such as Benjamin Tighe, Richard Whittemore, Goodspeeds, Isaac Mendosa, Seven Gables Bookshop, Walter Schatzki, and Ernest Wessen.

The collection has the first American edition of James Janeway's *Token For Children,* Boston, 1700; Thomas White's *A Little Book For Little Children,* Boston, 1702. There are more editions than in any other library of *The History*

Of The Holy Jesus, The House That Jack Built, The School of Good Manners, Robinson Crusoe, Watts' *Divine Songs, The Holy Bible in Verse, Mother Goose's Melody,* and books containing *Mother Goose Rhymes.* Since the collection contains almost two-thirds of all extant American children's books, it is not possible to enumerate the large number of top-notch books. It is needless to say that it contains more unique copies than any other library.

The Library of Congress is the next largest collection being the only one in class 2. There are approximately 100 unique books. It has a fine copy of *The Children's Bible,* Philadelphia, 1763; *The Child's New Plaything,* Philadelphia, 1763; four editions of *The History of the Holy Jesus; The Mother's Gift,* Philadelphia, 1791; and numerous other outstanding books.

There are two collections in class 3. The Free Library of Philadelphia with its famous Rosenbach Collection, has a complete copy of *The History Of Little Goody Two-Shoes,* New York, Hugh Gaine, 1775, and fine copies of *Robinson Crusoe,* New-York, 1774; *Mother Goose's Melody,* Worcester, 1794 (a gift from Brigham to Rosenbach); nine editions of Moody's *School of Good Manners,* including the unique New London one of 1754, two editions of *Tom Thumb's Play Book,* 1771; an imperfect copy of *The Children's Bible,* Philadelphia, 1763; early copies of John Taylor's *Verbum Sempiternum;* Ridley's *Adventures of Urad,* Boston, 1767; *Tom Thumb's Folio,* Boston, [ca. 1780]; Swift's *The Adventures of Captain Gulliver,* Philadelphia, 1787; and wonderful examples of early colonial printing in America. Since Ellen Shaffer became head of the rare book room, the collection has increased a great deal. It now boasts a copy of *The Holy Bible In Verse,* 1717, one of only two known copies with paper covers, and Berquin's *The Family Book,* Detroit, 1812, to mention only a few.

The other library in class 3 is the Connecticut Historical Society. The general collection, rich in Connecticut imprints, has been enlarged by the addition of the Caroline M. Hewins and the priceless Albert C. Bates collections. The Bates collection has 19 editions of *The History of The Holy Jesus* including a unique Boston one of 1747; *Mother Goose's Melody,* Boston, S. Hall, 1800; *The Renowned History of Giles Gingerbread,* Boston, 1768; *The History of Goody Two-Shoes,* Boston, 1783; Johnson's *The History of A Little Boy Found Under A Haycock,* Boston [ca. 1796]; the 1717 and 1729 editions of *The Holy Bible in Verse; Tom Thumb's Folio,* Boston, [ca. 1780]; and the Hartford, 1789 edition.

The three libraries in class 4 are The New York Public Library, the University of California at Los Angeles, and Yale University. The former has mostly books bound in boards. Among them are some very choice items such as *The Child's New Plaything,* Boston, 1750; *The History Of The Holy Jesus,* New-

London, 1754; and early editions of John Taylor's *Verbum Sempiternum*. The University of California at Los Angeles is rapidly growing in size. It now owns the Oliver Percival, Bernard Meeks, and Mrs. Elvah J. Karshner collections. The collection is rich in English children's books, but has some fine American ones such as *The London Cries*, Philadelphia, W. Spotswood, 1791, one of the few known small paperbound books issued by this publisher; *The Royal Alphabet*, Boston, 1802; and the other *Holy Bible in Verse*. Yale has a superb collection of English abridged editions of *Robinson Crusoe*. Most of the English source books of American editions are located in this collection. This library also has a nice group of American children's books. Among the top-notch items is the first abridged American edition of *Robinson Crusoe*, New-York, Hugh Gaine, 1774, and a unique copy of *The History Of The Holy Jesus*, New-London, 1769.

There are six libraries in class 5. The largest of these is the Essex Institute with its famous perfect earliest known copy of *The History Of The Holy Jesus*, Boston, 1746. Thanks to Mr. Frederic G. Melcher of R. R. Bowker and Co., a collotype facsimile is now available of this rarity. This library also has a perfect copy of the first American edition of Perrault's *Tales of Passed Times*, Haverhill, 1794, the other complete copy being in the Haverhill Public Library. Harvard University, next in size, owns the earliest American edition of Moody's *School Of Good Manners*, New-London, 1724; fine early editions of John Taylor's *Verbum Sempiternum;* and a copy of Perrault's *Tales of Passed Times*, New-York, 1795, with the plates by A. Anderson. Brown University has five editions of *The History of The Holy Jesus*, and [*The Renowned History of Giles Gingerbread*, Providence?, 1770?]. The three collections at Columbia University are: (1) Teacher's College Library has the Annie Moore Collection and the Harvey Darton Collection of English children's books, a gift of Mr. Carl H. Pforzheimer; (2) the collection in The Library School; (3) The George A. Plimpton Collection in Special Collections. The last one has a group of fine William Charles imprints with beautiful plates, and a perfect copy of *The House That Jack Built*, Boston, 1790. Due to the selective, careful collecting and generosity of Sinclair Hamilton, Princeton University has a choice collection in fine condition, which contains more rarities in proportion to its size than any other collection. Some outstanding items are early editions of *The Prodigal Daughter;* Benjamin Sands' *Metamorphosis; Mother Goose's Melody*, Worcester, 1794, and *The Renowned History Of Giles Gingerbread*, Boston, 1768. Another in this group is The Boston Public Library with its early source book of *Mother*

Goose Rhymes, namely *The Famous Tommy Thumb's Little Story Book,* Boston, 1771, and a copy of Sarah Fielding's *The Story Of The Cruel Giant Barbarico,* Boston, 1768.

Libraries in class 6, while smaller than the above, have some extremely rare books. The Henry E. Huntington Library owns the earliest small American narrative child's book known, exclusive of *The History of The Holy Jesus.* It is *A New Gift For Children, Boston,* D. Fowle [*ca.* 1756]. The New-York Historical Society has a unique copy of both Cowper's *John Gilpin,* Philadelphia, 1794, and *The History Of A Schoolboy,* New-York, 1792. The Massachusetts Historical Society has a fine copy of *The History Of The Holy Bible,* Boston, 1790, and the best copy of Sarah Fielding's *The Story Of The Cruel Giant Barbarico,* Boston, 1768. The Historical Society of Pennsylvania's *A New Gift For Children,* Boston, 1762, is outstanding.

In England, the British Museum Library has by far the largest institutional collection. There is a fable that the British Museum has a large mass of uncatalogued early children's books. This is completely untrue. Those in charge of cataloguing at the British Museum are very efficient and all early children's books are catalogued. That collection is surely an impressive one. In the Roscoe catalogue about a fourth of all the books contained in it are located in the British Museum. It is without doubt one of the most wonderful libraries in the world to work in because everybody is very helpful. The Victoria and Albert Museum Library is another important deposit of English children's books. The largest part of their collection was assembled by Guy Little. The Bodleian has extensive collections of English children's books. Of these I saw only the Douce collection which contains marvelous books in lovely condition. It is housed in a beautiful new air-conditioned library. The Constance Mead Johnson collection at the Oxford University Press, in Oxford, is a delightful experience. The library has an old world atmosphere and is full of rare items.

English private collectors have important holdings. The largest and finest of these is that of Roland Knaster. I went to his home a number of times and was amazed at the number of choice books he produced to show me. Mr. and Mrs. F. G. Renier have a large collection rich in all kinds of fine books. Peter and Iona Opie have a delightful house packed with children's games and books. Sydney Roscoe has a beautiful lot of books, among which is the earliest known edition of *Tom Thumb's Play Book.* Dr. L. A. E. Bell has a small but very choice collection which contains books in extraordinarily fine condition. Percy Muir has a fine lot of haloquinades and books with inserted paper dolls.

It is not possible to enumerate rare books in every collection. I have mainly tried to list the largest holdings of children's books, to mention a few of the smaller ones, and some outstanding books in them. I unfortunately have to omit a good many smaller libraries which have exceedingly interesting material. They are noted in the text of the bibliography.

Works Consulted

THE last name of the author is used in referring to a publication. If an author has several papers or books, the last name is followed by the date of publication. The compiler, or editor, of a catalogue, or bibliography, will not be referred to by name when it is more convenient to use a symbol for the work. This symbol is given preceding the title of the publication in the list of books below.

AAA Sale 1928
 An Unusual Collection of Miniature Books Formed by A Lady. To be sold Wednesday evening February 15, 1928, at 8:15. (New York American Art Association. 1928).

Alden, John Eliot   1949
 Rhode Island Imprints 1727–1800 (New York, R. R. Bowker, 1949).

AII Kentucky   1939
 American Imprints Inventory No. 5. *Check List of Kentucky Imprints 1787–1810.* By Douglas C. McMurtrie and Albert H. Allen (Louisville, 1939).

AII Michigan   1942
 ——— No. 52. *Preliminary Check List of Michigan Imprints 1796–1850* (Detroit, 1942).

AII Ohio   1941
 ——— No. 17. *Check List of Ohio Imprints 1796–1820* (Columbus, 1941).

Andreae, G.   1925
 The Dawn Of Juvenile Literature In England (Amsterdam, H. G. Paris, 1925).

Ashton, John   1882
 Chap-Books of the Eighteenth Century with Facsimiles, Notes, and Introduction (London, Chatto and Windus, 1882).

Barchilon, Jacques and Henry Pettit   1960
 The Authentic Mother Goose Fairy Tales and Nursery Rhymes (Denver, Allan Swallow, 1960).

Barry, Florence V.   [1922]
 A Century of Children's Books (London, Methuen & Co., 1922).

Bates, Albert C.   1911
 The History Of the Holy Jesus (Hartford, 1911).

Bobbitt, Mary Reed   1947
 A Bibliography of Etiquette Books Published in America before 1900 (New York, N.Y. Public Library, 1947). Reprinted from N.Y.P.L. *Bulletin,* Dec. 1947.

Bowe, Forrest   1952
 List of Additions and Corrections to Early Catholic Americana (New York, 1952).

Bowe, Forrest   mss.
  French Literature in early American Translation. A Bibliographical Survey of Books and Pamphlets printed in the U.S. from 1768 to 1820 (typescript).

Brigham, Clarence S.   1958
  Bibliography of American Editions of Robinson Crusoe to 1830 (Worcester, American Antiquarian Society, 1958). Reprinted from A.A.S. *Proceedings*, Oct. 1957.

Bristol, Roger P.   1962
  Evans' American Bibliography Supplement (Checking Edition) (Charlottesville, Virginia, Bibliographical Society of the University of Virginia, 1962).

Brown, H. Glenn and Maud O.   1950
  Directory of the Book-Arts and Book Trade in Philadelphia to 1820 (New York, N.Y. Public Library, 1950). Reprinted from N.Y.P.L. *Bulletin*, May 1949–Mar. 1950.

Brown, Rev. John   1890
  A Book for Boys and Girls; or, Country Rhymes for Children. By John Bunyan. Being a Facsimile of the Unique First Edition, Published in 1686, Deposited in the British Museum. With an Introduction, Giving an Account of the Work (London, Elliot Stock, 1890).

Cahoon, Herbert   1954
  Children's Literature Books and Manuscripts on Exhibition November 19, 1954 through February 28, 1955 (New York, The Pierpont Morgan Library, 1954).

CBEL
  The Cambridge Bibliography of English Literature. Edited by F. W. Bateson. 1660–1800 (New York, Macmillan Co. Cambridge, England, University Press, 1941), 3 vols.

CTO
  Catalogue of the C. T. Owen Collection (typescript).

Darton, F. J. Harvey   1932
  Children's Books in England Five Centuries of Social Life (Cambridge, England, University Press, 1932).

Darton Cat.
  A Note On Old Children's Books (The Harvey Darton Collection) (typescript). A catalogue of books in The Harvey Darton Collection given to Teacher's College Library, Columbia College, N.Y. by Mr. Carl H. Pforzheimer. It was written by F. J. Harvey Darton.

DNB
  Dictionary of National Biography. Edited by Leslie Stephen (New York, Macmillan & Co., 1885).

Doheny
  Catalogue of Books & Manuscripts in the Estelle Doheny Collection. Part XIV. Children's Books (Los Angeles, 1940).

E.A.I. Early American Imprints 1639-1800 Dr. Clifford K. Shipton, Editor. Evans Numbers 1-39162 American Antiquarian Society, Worcester, Mass. A Readex Microprint reproduction.

Earle, Alice Morse   1932
   Child Life in Colonial Days (New York, Macmillan Co., 1932).
Emery, Alice Nancy Sproat   1951
   "Nancy Sproat and her Little Books for Good Children," New York Public
   Library *Bulletin,* LV (Aug. 1951).
Esdaile, Arundell   1912
   A List of English Tales and Prose Romances Printed before 1740 (London,
   Printed for the Bibliographical Society By Blades, East & Blades, Dec. 1912).
Evans, Charles
   *American Bibliography; A Chronological Dictionary of all Books Pamphlets
   and Periodical Publications Printed in the U.S.* (Chicago, 1903–34). Vol. I
   (1639)–Vol. 12 (letter N. 1799); completed by Clifford K. Shipton Vol. 13
   (1799–1800); index compiled by Roger Patrell Bristol, Vol. 14.
      Note: All Evans' numbers are omitted when no copy or advertisement of
      the book has been located.
Evans—MWA Ann.
   The annotated copy of Charles Evans' *American Bibliography* at the American
   Antiquarian Society, Worcester, Mass.
Field, E. M.   1891
   *The Child and his Book. Some Account of the History and Progress of Chil-
   dren's Literature in England* (London, Wells Gardner, Darton & Co., 1891).
FOB
   *Festival of Britain Exhibition of Books Arranged by the National Book League
   at the Victoria & Albert Museum* (London, Published for the National Book
   League by the Cambridge University Press, 1951).
Ford, Paul Leicester   1889a
   *Franklin Bibliography. A List of Books Written by or Relating to Benjamin
   Franklin* (Brooklyn, N. Y., 1889).
—— 1889b
   *The New-England Primer. A Reprint of the Earliest Known Edition, With
   Many Facsimiles and Reproductions, and Historical Introduction* (New York,
   Dodd, Mead and Co., 1899).
GHC—Muir, Percy   1949
   The Good Housekeeping Collection Children's Books Of Yesterday (New
   York, Hearst Magazines Inc., Publishers of Good Housekeeping, 1949).
Greenly, Albert H.   1955
   A Bibliography of Father Richards Press in Detroit (Ann Arbor, Michigan, W.
   L. Clements Library, 1955).
Groce, George C. and David H. Wallace   1957
   The New York Historical Society's Dictionary of Artists in America 1564–1860
   (New Haven, Yale University Press, London, Oxford University Press, 1957).
Gumuchian & Cie   1930
   Les Livres De L'Enfance due XVe au XIXe Siècle (Paris, 1930), 2 vols. Only a
   few Gumuchian numbers for selected works are included in this book.

Halsey, Rosalie V.   1911

Forgotten Books of the American Nursery. A History of the Development of the American Story-Book (Boston, Charles E. Goodspeed & Co., 1911).

Hamilton, Sinclair   1958

Early American Book Illustrators and Wood Engravers 1670–1870 (Princeton, N. J., Princeton University Library, 1958).

Heartman, Charles F.   1934

The New England Primer Issued Prior to 1830. A Bibliographical Check-List for the more easy attaining the true Knowledge of this Book (New York, R. R. Bowker Co., 1934).

Hugo, Thomas   1866

The Bewick Collector. A Descriptive Catalogue of the Works of Thomas and John Bewick (London, Lovell Reeve And Co., 1866).

Hugo, Thomas   1868

The Bewick Collector. A Supplement to a Descriptive Catalogue of the Works of Thomas and John Bewick (London, L. Reeve And Co., 1868).

James, Philip   1933

Children's Books of Yesterday. Edited by C. Geoffrey Holme (London, Special Autumn Number of *The Studio*, 1933).

Jordan, Philip D.   1935

"The Juvenilia of Mary Belson Elliot a List with Notes," New York Public Library *Bulletin*, xxxix (Nov. 1935).

Jordan, Philip D.   1936

The Juvenilia of Mary Belson Elliot. A List Compiled by Philip D. Jordan. With Additions and Revisions by Daniel C. Haskell (New York, N.Y. Public Library, 1936). Reprinted with revisions from N.Y.P.L. *Bulletin*, Nov. 1935.

Kiefer, Monica   1948

American Children through their Books 1700–1835 (Philadelphia, University of Pennsylvania Press, Oxford University Press, 1948).

Lane, William Coolidge   1905

Bibliographical Contributions. No. 56. Catalogue of English and American Chap-Books and Broadside Ballads in Harvard College Library (Cambridge, Mass., Library of Harvard College, 1905).

Littlefield, George Emery   1904

Early Schools and School-Books of New England (Boston, The Club of Odd Volumes, 1904).

Lowndes, William Thomas   1869

The Bibliographer's Manuel of English Literature (London, 1869).

McCorison, Marcus H.   1963

Vermont Imprints, 1778–1820 (Worcester, American Antiquarian Society, 1963).

McKay, George   1942

A Register of Artists, Engravers, Booksellers, Bookbinders, Printers & Publishers in New York City, 1633–1820 (New York, N.Y. Public Library, 1942). Reprinted from N.Y.P.L. *Bulletin*, 1939–41.

Meigs 1953

A Critical History of Children's Literature. A Survey of Children's Books in English from Earliest Times to the Present, Prepared in Four Parts Under the Editorship of Cornelia Meigs. By Cornelia Meigs, Elisabeth Nesbitt, Ann Eaton, Ruth Hill Viguers (New York, Macmillan Co., 1953).

Mikrobiblion

Mikrobiblion Das Buch Von den Kleinen Büchern. (Berlin, 1929. Horodisch & Marx, Verlag) [written by Kurt Freyer & Robert W. Petri] [a bibliography of the collection of Vera von Rosenberg].

More, Hannah 1835

The Works of Hannah More. Complete in Seven Volumes. (New York, Harper & Bros., 1835), Vol. 1.

Muir, Percy 1954

English Children's Books 1600 to 1900 (London, B. T. Batsford Ltd., 1954).

NBL—Muir, Percy 1945

Children's Books of Yesterday With Foreword by the Poet Laureate John Masefield (London, National Book League, 1945).

NNGR. Cat.

A Short List Of Microscopic Books In The Library Of The Grolier Club Mostly Presented By Samuel P. Avery. (New York, 1911).

Newton, A. Edward 1925

The Greatest Book in the World and Other Papers (Boston, Little Brown & Co., 1925).

Nichols, Charles L. 1918

Bibliography of Worcester. A List of Books, Pamphlets, Newspapers and Broadsides, Printed in the Town of Worcester, Massachusetts, from 1775 to 1848. Second Edition (Worcester, 1918).

Nichols, Charles L. 1926

The Holy Bible In Verse (Worcester, American Antiquarian Society, 1926). Reprinted from A.A.S. Proceedings, Apr. 1926.

ODNR—Opie, Iona and Peter 1952

Oxford Dictionary of Nursery Rhymes (London, Oxford University Press, 1952).

Prideaux, Col. W. F. 1904

Mother Goose's Melody a Facsimile Reproduction of the Earliest Known Edition (London, A. H. Bullen, 1904).

Roscoe, S. mss.

Books Published in England by John Newbery, Francis Newbery and Thomas Carnan, Francis Newbery, Thomas Power, Elizabeth Newbery.

Rosenbach, Abraham Simon Wolf 1933

Early American Children's Books (Portland, Maine, Southworth Press, 1933).

Sabin, Joseph

A Dictionary of Books relating to America, from its Discovery to the Present Time, Begun by Joseph Sabin, Continued by Wilberforce Eames, and completed by R. W. G. Vail (New York, 1868–1936), 29 vols. Only a few Sabin numbers for selected works are included in this book.

Shaw, John Mackay   1959
    *Childhood In Poetry. Memorandum prepared by John Mackay Shaw for the
    Confidential Use of College Libraries* (July 15, 1959) (typescript). This is a
    catalogue of the Shaw Collection now deposited at Florida State University,
    Tallahassee, Fla.
— —   1960
    *The Parodies of Lewis Carroll and their Originals. Catalogue of an Exhibition
    with notes* (Florida State University Library, 1960).
Shaw, Ralph R. and Richard H. Shoemaker 1958, 1961
    American Bibliography. A Preliminary Checklist for 1801–1819 (New York,
    Scarecrow Press, 1958–1963). 19 vols.
Shoemaker, Richard H.   1964
    A Checklist of American Imprints for 1820. (New York & London, the Scare-
    crow Press, Inc., 1964).
Silver, Rollo G.   1949
    The Boston Book Trade. 1800–1825 (New York Public Library, 1949). Re-
    printed from N.Y.P.L. *Bulletin,* Oct.–Dec. 1948.
— —   1953
    The Baltimore Book Trade. 1800–1825 (New York Public Library, 1953), Re-
    printed from N.Y.P.L. *Bulletin,* Mar.–July 1953.
Slade, B. C.   1937
    Maria Edgeworth, 1767–1849. A Bibliographical Tribute (London, Constable,
    1937).
Sloane, William   1955
    Children's Books in England & America in the Seventeenth Century (New York,
    King's Crown Press, Columbia University, 1955).
Smith, Elva S.   1937
    The History of Children's Literature. A Syllabus with Selected Bibliographies
    (Chicago, American Library Association, 1937).
Spielmann
    *Catalogue Of The Library Of Miniature Books collected by Percy Edwin Spiel-
    mann.* (London, Edward Arnold. 1961).
Spinney, Gordon Harold   1939
    "Cheap Repository Tracts: Hazard and Marshall Edition," *The Library,* XX
    (Dec. 1939).
St. John, Judith   1958
    The Osborne Collection of early Children's Books. 1566–1910. A Catalogue (To-
    ronto, Ont., Toronto Public Library, 1958).
Stone, Wilbur Macey   1918
    The Divine and Moral Songs of Isaac Watts (New York, The Triptych, 1918).
— —   1926
    A Snuff-Boxful of Bibles (Newark, N. J., Carteret Book Club, 1926).
— —   1928
    The Thumb Bible of John Taylor (Brookline, Mass., The LXIVMOS, 1928).

—— 1933
The Gigantic Histories of Thomas Boreman (Portland, Me., Southworth Press, 1933).

—— 1934
The Holy Bible In Verse, 1698 (Worcester, American Antiquarian Society, 1935). Reprinted from A.A.S. *Proceedings*, Apr. 1934.

—— 1940
The History of Little Goody Two-Shoes (Worcester, American Antiquarian Society, 1940). Reprinted from A.A.S. *Proceedings*, Oct. 1939.

Thomas, Isaiah 1874
The History of Printing in America, with a Biography of Printers, and an Account of Newspapers. (Worcester, American Antiquarian Society, 1874). 2 vols.

Tuer, Andrew W. 1898–9
Pages and Pictures from Forgotten Children's Books (London, Leadenhall Press, 1898–9).

—— 1899–1900
Stories from Old Fashioned Children's Books (London, Leadenhall Press, 1899–1900).

ULS
Union List of Serials in Libraries of the United States and Canada. 2nd ed. Edited by Winifred Gregory (New York, H. W. Wilson, 1943).

Vail, R. W. G. 1942
Moody's School of Good Manners: A Study in American Colonial Etiquette. Studies in the History of Culture. Published for the conference of Secretaries of the American Council of Learned Societies (Menasha, Wisconsin, George Banta, 1942).

Watt, Robert 1824
Bibliotheca Britannica; or a General Index to British and Foreign Literature (Edinburgh, Archibald Constable & Co., and Longman, Hurst, Rees, Orme, Brown & Green, and Hurst Robinson & Co., London, 1824), 4 vols.

Weedon, M. J. P. 1949
"Richard Johnson and the Successors to John Newbery," *The Library*, IV (June 1949).

—— 1951
"Mother Goose's Melody", *The Library*, VI (Dec. 1951).

Weiss, Harry B. 1932a
William Charles Early Caricaturist, Engraver and Publisher of Children's Books (New York, N. Y. Public Library, 1932). Reprinted from N.Y.P.L. *Bulletin*, Dec. 1931.

—— 1932b
Joseph Yeager Early American Engraver Publisher of Children's Books Railroad President New York, N. Y. Public Library, 1932). Reprinted from N.Y.P.L. *Bulletin*, Sept. 1932.

—— 1932c
"Three Hundred Years of Tom Thumb," *Scientific Monthly*, XXXIV (1932).

—— 1932d

"Metamorphoses and Harlequinades," *American Book Collector* (Metuchen, N. J.) (Aug.–Sept. 1932).

—— 1934

"John Norman, Engraver, Publisher, Bookseller; John Walters, Miniaturist, Publisher, Bookseller; And The "World Turned Upside-Down Controversy," New York Public Library, *Bulletin*, XXXVIII (Jan. 1934).

—— 1936

A Catalogue of the Chapbooks in the New York Public Library (New York, N.Y. Public Library, 1936). Reprinted from N.Y.P.L. *Bulletin*, Jan.–Mar., Oct. 1935.

—— 1938a

American Chapbooks (Trenton, N.J., 1938).

—— 1938b

"American Editions of 'Sir Richard Whittington and his Cat'," New York Public Library, *Bulletin*, XLII (June, 1938).

—— 1939

"The Entomology of Thomas Boreman's Popular Natural Histories," New York Entomological Society *Journal*, XLVII (Sept. 1939).

—— 1942

"Samuel Wood & Sons early New York Publishers of Children's Books" New York Public Library, *Bulletin*, LXVI (Sept. 1942).

—— 1946

Hannah More's Cheap Repository Tracts in America (New York, N.Y. Public Library, 1946). Reprinted from N.Y.P.L. *Bulletin*, July and Aug. 1946.

—— 1948

"The Printers and Publishers of Children's Books in New York City, 1698–1830," New York Public Library *Bulletin*, LII (Aug. 1948).

Welsh, Charles 1881

Goody Two-Shoes A Facsimile Reproduction of the Edition of 1766 With an Introduction by Charles Welsh (London, Griffith & Farran, 1881).

—— 1885

A Bookseller of the Last Century (London, Griffin, Farran, Okeden & Welsh; New York, E. P. Dutton & Co., 1885).

Whitmore, William H. 1892

The Original Mother Goose's Melody, as Issued by John Newbery, of London, circa 1760; Isaiah Thomas, of Worcester, Mass., circa 1785; And Munroe & Francis, of Boston, circa 1825 (Boston, Damrell & Upham; London, Griffith, Farran & Co., 1892).

Wing, Donald 1945

A Short-titled Catalogue of Books in England, Scotland, Ireland, Wales, and British America and of English Books Printed in other Countries 1641–1700 (New York, Printed for the Index Society, Columbia University Press, 1945).

Wolf, Edwin 2nd, with John Fleming 1960

Rosenbach. A Biography (Cleveland And New York, World Publishing Co., 1960).

Method of the Work

SCOPE

THIS BIBLIOGRAPHY is primarily concerned with narrative books written in English, designed for children under fifteen years of age. They should be the type of book read at leisure for pleasure. The book must have been originally written for children or abridged for them from an adult version. Defoe's *Robinson Crusoe*, Swift's *Gulliver's Travels*, Richardson's *Pamela* were all specially shortened and rewritten for children.

Books written about or by children, treatises on education or how to rear children are avoided. Exceptions are Moody's *School of Good Manners* and other books similar to it. Books recommended for children are not necessarily children's books. Sloane points out that Foxe's *Book Of Martyrs* was considered excellent reading material for children during the 18th century, but by no stretch of the imagination could it be considered a child's book. However, I include a small book entitled *Martyrology, Or, A Brief Account Of The Lives, Sufferings and Deaths . . . Martyrs, viz. Mr. John Rodgers, and Mr. John Bradford . . .* (Boston, 1736) because of its size and format, and because the subject matter was reprinted many times in the *New England Primer*. While size and format are not invariable guides to classifying children's books, they are extremely useful ones. A good number of eighteenth century adult books are diminutive in size.

Typical chapbooks are often merely referred to in works on children's books. Many a nursery favorite such as *The Babes in the Wood* and Watts' *Divine Songs* came out in such unbound editions, being merely a sheet of paper folded in eight and held together by a thread. *The Prodigal Daughter* and *The Delightful History Of The King And The Cobbler* are only known by chapbook editions. They were probably written for adults, but undoubtedly read by children, and have been traditionally considered juveniles by most collectors.

There is a large assortment of pleasurable non-narrative books written for children. They consist of books of poetry, jokes, riddles, natural history—including accounts of insects, fish, birds, mammals, plants, and minerals; also books describing trades, objects, street cries, peoples of all nations, games, and sports.

Broadsides, sermons, books of advice, catechisms, primers, and school books are excluded. If anywhere in the preface or on the title page the words, "for the use of schools," appear, the book is automatically rejected, unless it says that it was also designed "for children before they go to school." Even in this case only selected books have been entered. Alphabet books and selected preschool books are often very choice pieces of juvenile literature prized by the collector of non-educational books. Since this bibliography is written from a collector's view point, it is natural that such books be given priority.

It is often difficult to decide whether a book is a school book or not. Many 18th century books were definitely intent on teaching the child something while he was being diverted. The bibliographer must use his judgment in selecting which books were recreational and which were probably school books in disguise. Some consider *Aesop's Fables* a school book. Certainly H. Clarke's *Fabulae Aesopae Selectae* is definitely a school book, but the translations of Croxall, Dodsley and the like were advertised as children's books and are considered as such. *The New England Psalter* is such an interesting early American book that, although it is classed a reader by Littlefield, I am including it.

While most children's books can easily be identified, a good number are borderline and can be classed as either juveniles or books for adults or youths over fifteen years of age. I have seen many publishers' listings of children's books that contain books I do not consider children's books. In like manner, I am sure many people will think I erred in including certain titles and will object to my excluding others. The listing of certain books must therefore be left to the individual compiler's discretion. One rule of thumb has been to put in books that had somewhere in the preface or title page the phrase, "for the instruction of youth" or "for the benefit of the rising generation," "for the use of children," or the like; even if the format would lead one to suppose otherwise. Such phrases were used in storybooks to entice the parents to buy the books for the children. Among these is *The History of the Seven Wise Masters of Rome,* which states in the preface that the book "encourages and allures children and youth to learn to read English."

The majority of American children's books are reprinted from English editions. Under the first of a series of editions, such as Barbauld's *Hymns In Prose,* or under a book known by a single title, the earliest English edition located is listed.

No attempt has been made to include children's books written in languages other than English. A few selected German books are included because they caught my fancy or because they were German translations of popular English stories such as *Robinson Crusoe, The Children in The Wood,* or Benjamin Sands' *Metamorphosis.* Children's books written in French or other languages are omitted unless they have an accompanying English text.

ENTRY FORM

The authors of many children's books are unknown and the books have to be listed under title. Whenever known, the name of the author is given and his works listed alphabetically. Rewritten works of an author are placed under the original writer's name, e.g., all abridgments of *Robinson Crusoe* are put under Defoe. In like manner, rewritten versions of *Blue Beard, Cinderella,* etc. are put under Perrault. I have followed Forrest Bowe in the identification of the French authorship of many juveniles. Both he and I have found a number of stories written by Berquin, which were taken from the *Children's Friend* and issued separately under different titles. These stories, even when rewritten and the names of characters changed, are included under Berquin.

The titles of unknown authorship are placed in alphabetical sequence. When the author's name is known it is put in "hanging form," i.e., it is placed to the left of the title. Books having the same author will have an author ditto (a one-em dash —) placed before the title of all editions. If the author is anonymous and the name has been supplied, brackets will surround the author's name or author ditto.

An anonymous book like *Aesop's Fables* is listed under *Aesop's Fables,* followed by the name of the translator or probable translator, with the title of the first American edition coming next. Subsequent editions will have an author ditto (a one-em dash —) which stands for the general title *Aesop,* and the name of the translator. Editions of original works, such as *The Children's Friend* by Berquin, are followed by collections of the work, and finally separate works or selections. Some selections have entirely new titles. If a book of stories is predominantly the work of one author, it is placed under that author's name even though the title of the book may be entirely different.

Each book with a separate title has a number, which is placed before the title. Where the book has an author ditto, the number will be placed in front of the first ditto. Books having the same title are listed chronologically under title or author. The earliest title is given in its entirety. The first letter of each word is capitalized when it is so printed in the original, regardless of whether it is printed in large or small capital letters. Some words on the original title page are entirely in capitals. In these cases only the first letter is capitalized. Succeeding editions with the same worded title have a title ditto (a three-em line ———) meaning that the first title is repeated, although the punctuation and capitalization may be different. When any word variation occurs in the title, the title ditto is used up to the point where the word change occurs, then the remainder of the title is copied.

The earliest edition of a series of similar titles is given the separate title number followed by a period and number one (".1"). The next edition is placed under the same title number followed by a period and number two (".2"), and so on. When two or more imprints of a particular title are issued in the same year, but in different cities, the imprints are arranged alphabetically by the name of the city in which the book was published. For example, an edition published in 1820 in Baltimore would come before one published in the same year in New York. The complete imprint is given as it appears on the title page. Nothing is left out, even a signature is copied if present.

COLLATION

The DLC method of collation is not used in this book. From the standpoint of a collector of juveniles, the DLC method does not give the wanted information. Many juveniles offered for sale are incomplete. They lack a frontispiece, or advertisements at the rear which may not be part of the pagination. After buying a book it is most disconcerting to discover that what you thought was a complete book wants two pages of advertisements at the rear. The DLC method, depending on who follows it, usually omits to mention the pages of advertisements at the rear or an unnumbered page with a woodcut on it. Some cataloguers are kind enough to put in brackets "[1]" meaning an extra page coming after the last numbered page. However, it may mean an extra leaf.

In addition to the usual information, such as number of pages, size, and illustrations when present, one wants to know whether the book has printed and illustrated paper covers, or whether the covers are marbled paper, Dutch paper, or wallpaper. Over the years I have collected such data and devised my own system of collation for my own personal use. I now hope it will be of use to others. I never count the covers of any book as part of the collation, even when the only title is the cover title and the first and last pages are glued to the covers. I hope my method is sufficiently clear so that a person will not have to write busy librarians letters trying to correctly collate a book to determine whether the book is complete or not. If I can do this for somebody, I will be richly rewarded for my efforts.

My system is as follows:

1. All books are paged continuously. Every unnumbered page is included,

even if it has only an illustration, an advertisement, printer's address, colophon, or copyright on it.

2.   The first and last Arabic numbered pages are given. The unnumbered printed pages preceding the first Arabic numbered page and the last numbered page are put in brackets.

fr.[2], t.[3], [4–5], 6–30, [31] p. illus. size

In paperbound books, especially 10 cm. books of 31 pages, the blank recto of the illustrated page opposite the title, the frontispiece, or p. "fr." is often glued to the inside of the front cover, and the blank verso of p. [31], the last page, to the inside of the rear cover. The blank recto of the former and the blank verso of the latter are never counted even when the first and last leaves have come unglued from the covers. Blank fly leaves are not noted.

3.   Very often the page facing the title page is not a typical frontispiece or page having an illustration. If this unnumbered page has only the alphabet, a verse, or prose, the page is entered fr.[2, alphabet], fr.[2, verse], fr.[2, prose]. The last unnumbered pages may contain an advertisement of some sort, such as rags, pens, and general advertisements of books without listing them. In this case p. [31] is noted p. [31, adv.]. If a list of books is given, or the last page is an illustration, or the alphabet, it is described p. [31, adv. list of books], p. [31, illus.], p. [31, alphabet].

4.   Preliminary pages or pages at the beginning or end of the text in Roman numerals are paged continuously as well as the Arabic ones. If the frontispiece is not part of the pagination, the page is designated by a lower case Roman numeral two in brackets, "[ii]". Unpaginated pages are given Arabic or Roman numerals similar to other pages in a particular section. Blank leaves or pages which are part of the pagination are included in the section following them.

fr.[ii], t.[i], [ii–iv], v–vii, [viii–ix], [10], 11–250 p.

Pages [ii], [viii–ix] may be blank pages. In books with complex pagination, the symbol "bl." stands for "blank" after the number of the blank page. Thus, if page [ii] is blank, it is written p. [ii, bl.]. If a blank leaf comes at the end of a book and separates it from another book bound with a preceding one, the words "1 leaf" are used instead of adding numbers to the end of the preceding book. When giving numbers to unnumbered pages, no pretense is made that these are the numbers the printer would have given them if he had numbered them. All that is attempted is to conveniently give the pages numbers by which the sequence of the pages can be shown in order of occurrence.

Many children's books are bound in Dutch paper. This is a paper stamped with various ornamental designs, gold foil, and daubed with bright colors. The embossed design may show outlines of flowers, animals, stars, a mixture of ornaments, or the repetition of a single ornament. The background color may be a solid color with designs in silver or gold. This paper was expensive to make and was used mostly prior to 1800, although a few books had covers of it as late as 1819. Usually, the gold has worn off.

ABBREVIATIONS

abr.	abridged, or abridger.
adv.	advertisement, -s.
ann.	annotated.
bds.	cardboard boards used for book covers.
b. l.	black letter.
bl.	blank page.
bpl.	bookplate or library label.
ca.	circa.
col.	colored.
coll.	collection.
comp.	compiler.
ed.	edition.
emb. st.	embossed library stamp or seal.
engr.	engraved.
fac.	facsimile, -s.
fr.	any printed page opposite the title page. It may or may not be an illustration and therefore not a frontispiece in the strict sense of the word. The symbol is used only in the paging of a book.
front.	frontispiece. The symbol is used everywhere except in the paging of a book.
i.e.	that is.
illus.	illustration, or illustrated.
imp.	imperfect.
i. st.	ink library stamp.
iss.	issue.
mss.	manuscript.
mut.	mutilated.
n.d.	no date of publication.
n.p.	no place of publication.

no.	number.
nos.	numbers.
opp.	opposite.
p.	page, -s.
pam.	pamphlet, -s.
per. st.	perforated stamp or seal.
pl.	plate, -s.
pref.	preface.
pseud.	pseudonym.
pt.	part, -s.
sel. p.	selected pages.
ser.	series.
sic.	thusly (precisely reproduced).
sig.	signature.
sigs.	signatures.
t. or t. p.	title page.
tr.	translator or translated.
vari.	variant.
ver.	version.
vol.	volume.
vols.	volumes.
w.bds.	wooden boards used for book covers.

LOCATIONS OF THE BOOKS

An asterisk is used in the bibliography after the first location symbol to denote the place of the described copy. All other locations follow in alphabetical order.

PRIVATE COLLECTORS

Adomeit	Miss Ruth Elizabeth Adomeit, Cleveland, Ohio.
Ball	Miss Elisabeth Ball, Muncie, Indiana.
Bowe	Forrest Bowe, New York, New York.
Carson	Mrs. Joseph Carson, Philadelphia, Pennsylvania.
Fitzhugh	Wm. M. Fitzhugh, Jr. M.D., Pebble Beach, California.
France	Mrs. A. W. France, Wyncote, Pennsylvania.
Gardner	Frederick R. Gardner, Amityville, New York.
Greenaway	Emerson Greenaway, Philadelphia, Pennsylvania.
Greenwood	Mrs. Arthur Greenwood, Smithsonian Institution, Washington, D. C.

Griffin	Gillett Griffin, Princeton University Library.
Hopkins	Ross Hopkins, Eastlake, Ohio.
Massman	Robert Massman, New Britain, Conn.
Oppenheimer	Edgar S. Oppenheimer, New York, New York.
Ries	Ludwig Ries, Forest Hills, New York.
Walcott	Mrs. Elizabeth S. Walcott, Brattleboro, Vermont.
Warren	Miss Virginia Warren, Washington, D.C.
Whittemore	C. Richard Whittemore, Westborough, Mass.
Wightman	Miss Julia P. Wightman, New York, New York.

LIBRARIES

NOTE: Symbols of libraries used by Evans and other authors when quoted have been changed to these below, for the sake of uniformity. Most of them are taken from: *Symbols used in the National Union Card Catalogue of the Library of Congress.* 7 ed. Lib. of Congress. Washington, 1959.

CALIFORNIA

CCC	The Claremont Colleges.
CCamarSJ	St. John's Seminary, Carmarillo (Doheny Coll.).
CLSU	University of Southern California, Los Angeles.
CLU	University of California at Los Angeles. (Percival, Meeks, Karshner Coll.).
CSmH	Henry E. Huntington Library, San Marino.
CSt	Stanford University Libraries, Palo Alto.

COLORADO

CoU	University of Colorado, Boulder.

CONNECTICUT

Ct	Connecticut State Library, Hartford.
CtH	Hartford Public Library.
CtHC	Hartford Seminary Foundation.
CtHi	Connecticut Historical Society, Hartford. (Bates, Hewins Coll.).
CtHT	Trinity College, Hartford.
CtSoP	Pequot Library Association, Southport.
CtSu	Kent Memorial Library, Suffield.
CtW	Wesleyan University, Middletown.
CtY	Yale University, New Haven.
CtY (Pequot)	Pequot Library Association, Southport, part of whose collection is deposited at Yale.

DISTRICT OF COLUMBIA
DCU	Catholic University.
DFo	Folger Shakespeare Library.
DLC	U.S. Library of Congress.
DNLM	U.S. National Library of Medicine.
DS	U.S. Department of State Library.

DELAWARE
DeHi	Historical Society of Delaware, Wilmington.
DeU	University of Delaware, Newark.
DeWi	Wilmington Institute and New Castle County Free Library.
DeWint	Henry Franics DuPont Winterthur Museum.

FLORIDA
FTaSU	Florida State University, Tallahassee. (John Mackay Shaw Coll.).
FTU	University of Tampa.

ILLINOIS
ICMILC	Midwest Inter-Library Center, Chicago.
ICN	Newberry Library, Chicago.
ICU	University of Chicago (Friedman—Encyclopedia Britannica Coll.).
IU	University of Illinois, Urbana.

IOWA
IaB	Burlington Free Public Library.
IaDmD	Drake University, Des Moines.
IaU	State University of Iowa, Iowa City.

INDIANA
InNd	University of Notre Dame, South Bend.
InU	Indiana University, Bloomington.

KANSAS
KU	University of Kansas, Lawrence.

KENTUCKY
KyHi	Kentucky Historical Society, Frankfort.
KyLx	Lexington Public Library.

MASSACHUSETTS
MB	Boston Public Library.
MBAt	Boston Athenaeum.
MBC	Congregational Library, Boston.
MBChM	Children's Museum, Boston.
MBSi	Simmons College, Boston.

MBSpnea	Society for the Preservation of New England Antiquities, Boston.
MBU	Boston University.
MDeHi	Dedham Historical Society.
MH	Harvard University, Cambridge.
MHa	Haverhill Public Library.
MHi	Massachusetts Historical Society, Boston.
MIpHi	Ipswich Historical Society.
MLe	Leominster Public Library.
MLuHi	Lunenburg Historical Society.
MLxHi	Lexington Historical Society. (Hancock-Clarke House).
MNBedf	Free Public Library, New Bedford.
MNF	Forbes Public Library, Northampton.
MNS	Smith College Library, Northampton.
MNe	Newburyport Public Library.
MNeHi	The Historical Society of Old Newbury, Newburyport.
MPlyA	The Plymouth Atheneum.
MSaAt	Salem Atheneum.
MSaE	Essex Institute, Salem.
MSaP	Peabody Museum of Salem.
MShM	Mount Holyoke College, South Hadley.
MShr	Shrewsbury Public Library.
MWA	American Antiquarian Society, Worcester.
MWA-T	——Benjamin Tighe Coll.
MWA-W	——d'Alté A. Welch Coll.
MWHi	Worcester Historical Society.
MWM	Worcester Art Museum.
MWelC	Wellesley College.
MWiW	Williams College, Williamstown.
MARYLAND	
MdBE	Enoch Pratt Library, Baltimore.
MdBJ	Johns Hopkins University, Baltimore.
MdBP	Peabody Institute, Baltimore.
MdHi	Maryland Historical Society, Baltimore.
MAINE	
Me	Maine State Library, Augusta.
MeB	Bowdoin College, Brunswick.
MeBa	Bangor Public Library.
MICHIGAN	
MiD	Detroit Public Library.

MiDM	Marygrove College, Detroit.
MiDSH	Sacred Heart Seminary, Detroit.
MiDW	Wayne State University, Detroit.
MiU	University of Michigan, Ann Arbor.

MINNESOTA

MnU	University of Minnesota, Minneapolis.

NEW YORK

N	New York State Library, Albany.
NB	Brooklyn Public Library. (Vail Coll.).
NBuG	Grosvenor Reference Division, Buffalo and Erie County Public Library, Buffalo.
NCooHi	New York State Historical Association, Cooperstown.
NEh	Easthampton Free Public Library.
NHi	New York Historical Society.
NIC	Cornell University, Ithaca.
NN	New York Public Library.
NN-C	——Children's Room.
NNC	Columbia University, New York.
NNC-LS	——Library School.
NNC-Pl	——Plimpton Collection.
NNC-Sp	——Special collections.
NNC-T	——Teacher's College Library.
NNCoo	Cooper Union Library, New York.
NNG	General Theological Seminary of the Protestant Episcopal Church, New York.
NNMM	Metropolitan Museum of Art Library, New York.
NNNAM	New York Academy of Medicine.
NNPM	Pierpont Morgan Library, New York.
NNS	New York Society Library.
NNUT	Union Theological Seminary, New York.
NP	Adrience Memorial Library, Poughkeepsie.
NPV	Vassar College, Poughkeepsie.
NRU	University of Rochester. (Davis Coll.).
NSh	John Jermain Memorial Library Public Library, Sag Harbor.
NUt	Utica Public Library.
NWebyC	Children's Library, Westbury Public Library.

NORTH CAROLINA

NcD	Duke University, Durham.

NcU	University of North Carolina, Chapel Hill.
NEW HAMPSHIRE	
Nh	New Hampshire State Library, Concord.
NhD	Dartmouth College, Hanover.
NhHi	New Hampshire Historical Society, Concord.
NEW JERSEY	
NjI	Irvington Free Public Library.
NjMoW	Washington Headquarters Library, Morristown.
NjN	Newark Public Library.
NjP	Princeton University.
NjR	Rutgers University, New Brunswick.
OHIO	
OC	Public Library of Cincinnati.
OCH	Hebrew Union College, Cincinnati.
OCHP	Historical and Philosophical Society of Ohio, Cincinnati.
OChRHi	Ross County Historical Society, Chillicothe, Ohio.
OCl	Cleveland Public Library.
OClJC	John Carroll University, Cleveland.
OClW-LS	Western Reserve University Library School, Cleveland.
OClWHi	Western Reserve Historical Society, Cleveland.
ODW	Ohio Wesleyan University, Delaware.
OO	Oberlin College.
OOxM	Miami University, Oxford. (Edward W. King Coll.).
PENNSYLVANIA	
P	Pennsylvania State Library, Harrisburg.
PBL	Lehigh University, Bethlehem.
PCC	Crozer Theological Seminary, Chester.
PHC	Haverford College.
PHi	Historical Society of Pennsylvania, Philadelphia.
PHuJ	Juniata College, Huntington.
PMA	Allegheny College, Meadville.
PNortHi	Historical Society of Montgomery County, Norristown.
PP	Free Library of Philadelphia. (Rosenbach Coll.).
PPAmS	American Sunday School Union, Philadelphia.
PPF	Franklin Institute, Philadelphia.
PPG	German Society of Philadelphia.
PPL	Library Company of Philadelphia.
PPPrHi	Presbyterian Historical Society, Philadelphia.
PPRF	Rosenbach Foundation, Philadelphia.

PPeSchw	Schwenckfelder Historical Library, Pennsburg.
PPi	Carnegie Library of Pittsburgh.
PPiU	University of Pittsburgh.
PSC	Swarthmore College.
PSt	Pennsylvania State University, University Park.
PU	University of Pennsylvania, Philadelphia.
PWcHi	Chester County Historical Society, West Chester.

RHODE ISLAND

RHi	Rhode Island Historical Society, Providence.
RNHi	Newport Historical Society.
RP	Providence Public Library.
RPB	Brown University, Providence. (Dorr and Harris Coll.).
RPJCB	John Carter Brown Library, Providence.
RWe	Westerly Public Library.

SOUTH CAROLINA

ScU	University of South Carolina, Columbia.

TENNESSEE

T	Tennessee State Library, Nashville.
TC	Chattanooga Public Library.
TNJ	Joint University Libraries, Nashville.
TU	University of Tennessee, Knoxville.

TEXAS

TxF	Fort Worth Public Library.
TxU	University of Texas, Austin.

VIRGINIA

Vi	Virginia State Library, Richmond.
ViAl	Alexandria Public Library.
ViLxW	Washington & Lee University, Lexington.
ViU	University of Virginia, Charlottesville.
ViW	College of William and Mary, Williamsburg.

VERMONT

Vt	Vermont State Library, Montpelier.
VtHi	Vermont Historical Society, Montpelier. (Harold Rugg Coll.).
VtMiS	Sheldon Art Museum, Middlebury.
VtNN	Norwich University, Northfield.
VtU	University of Vermont and State Agricultural College, Burlington.
VtWinoS	Saint Michael's College, Winooski Park.

WASHINGTON
WaPS   State College of Washington, Pullman.
WaU   University of Washington, Seattle.

CANADA
CaNSWA   Acadia University, Wolfville, Nova Scotia.
CaOTP   Toronto Public Library.

ENGLAND
BM   British Museum, London.

A Bibliography of
American Children's Books
Printed Prior to 1821

A

1.1 AN ABRIDGEMENT OF THE HISTORY OF THE HOLY BIBLE. Adorned With Cuts. Printed at Hudson (New-York) By Ashbel Stoddard, And sold, wholesale and retail, at his Printing-Office. M, DCC,XCIII.
    fr.[2], t.[3], [4], 5–31 p.; illus.; 8.5 cm.
    English ed. London: adv. by J. Downing in *The Young Christian's Library*, 1710.
    PP°; Evans 46698.

1.2 ——— New-York: Printed by H. Gaine, in Hanover-Square, 1794.
    fr. 2, t.[3], [4], 5–30, [31] p.; illus.; 10 cm.; green Dutch paper covers.
    NN (t.[3], p.[4] wanting, p. 5–6, 21–30 mut., p.[31] mut. with the page number torn away; rebound & mounted on silk); Evans 46984.

1.3 ——— Printed at Hudson (New-York) By Ashbel Stoddard, And sold, wholesale and retail, at his Printing-Office & Book-Store, M,DCC,XCVI.
    fr.[2], t.[3], [4], 5–29, [30–31] p.; illus.; 9.5 cm.; Dutch paper covers.
    CtHi° (top corner of p. [30–31] wanting); Evans 47723.

1.4 ——— Hudson [N.Y.], Printed and sold by Ashbel Stoddard, At his Book-Store and Printing-Office Corner of Warren and Third Streets. 1804.
    fr.[2], t.[3], [4–5], 6–29, [30–31, adv. list of books] p.; illus.; 10.5 cm.; illus. blue-gray paper covers.
    NCooHi°; Shaw 50404.

ACASTO *pseud.* See Miltmore, James, no. **854.**

2 AN ACCOUNT OF A GIRL, OF TWELVE YEARS OF AGE, Who lived on Lord Collier's Manor, in the Province of Lower Canada; who was converted to the love of God in a wonderful manner, and it proved to be a hopeful conversion of the whole family and a great many of the neighbors in the town. Printed For The Purchaser. 1815.
    t.[1], [2–3], 4–11 p.; 14 cm.
    MWA°; Shaw 33768.

3.1 AN ACCOUNT OF THE REMARKABLE CONVERSION OF A LITTLE BOY AND GIRL. Boston: Printed and Sold by Fowle and Draper, in Marlboro'-street. 1762. < Price 5d. >
    t.[1], [2–3], 4–24 p.; illus.; 16 cm.
    MB° (per. st. on t.[1]); MWA (t.[1], p.[2], 5–8 wanting); PP (p. 23–24 mut.); Evans 41253.

3.2 ——— New-London Printed. Dover [N.H.]: Re-printed For, And To Be Sold By Anthony Nelson. < Price Sixpence. > M,DCC,XCII.
    t.[1], [2], 3–14 p.; 18 cm.
    MWA° (t.[1] mut., all after p. 14 wanting); CtHi (all after p. 14 wanting).

3.3 ——— Bennington [Vt.]: Printed by Anthony Haswell, M,CCD,XCIV, [*sic.*].
    t.[1], [2], 3–18 p.; 15 cm.
    MWA°; Evans 46954.

4 AN ACCOUNT OF THE REMARKABLE CONVERSION OF A LITTLE GIRL. Also A Song For My Brother Sailor. Palmer [Mass.]: Printed by E. Terry. 1814.
    t.[1], [2–3], 4–12 p.; 15 cm.
    RPB°; Shaw 30615.

5 ACCOUNTS OF THE HAPPY DEATHS OF TWO YOUNG CHRISTIANS. Boston: Printed For Nathaniel Willis, Congress-Street. 1819.
    fr.[2], t.[3], [4], 5–22, [23, illus.] p.; illus.; 12.5 cm.; buff paper covers.
    MWA°; CCamarSJ; Shaw 46918.

THE ADVENTURES OF A PINCUSHION. *See* Kilner, Mary Ann, no. **733.**

6 ADVENTURES OF A SCHOOL BOY. Boston. 1812.
    16 mo. orig. cl. with paper label.
    Shaw 24571.

7 THE ADVENTURES OF AN ILLNATURED [*sic. i.e.* Ill-Natured] BOY. And The Sory [*sic. i.e.* Story] of Ants and Flies. Boston: Printed by I. Wh[ite.] 1796.
    t.[3], [4–5], 6–30 p.; illus.; 8.7 mm.
    PP° (fr.[2]?, p. [31]? and covers wanting; p. 29–30 torn and mut.).

8 THE ADVENTURES OF JACK THE BROOM BOY. Philadelphia. Published by Johnson & Warner, No. 147, Market Street. 1809.

    fr.[1], t.[2], [3–16] p. engr. on one side only of 16 leaves; illus.; 14 cm.; pr. yellow paper covers. Cover title imprint: Philadelphia. Published by Benjamin Warner No. 171 Market Street 1821.

    English ed. London: T. & R. Hughes, Jany 14, 1807.

    PP° (col. illus.).

THE ADVENTURES OF MUSUL OR THE THREE GIFTS. *See* Kendall, E. A., no. **722.1.**

9.1 ADVENTURES OF OLD DAME TRUDGE AND HER PARROT. Illustrated With Whimsical Engravings. Philadelphia: Published and sold Wholesale by Wm. Charles, and may be had of all the Booksellers. Price 12 1-2 Cents. 1811. W. M'Culloch, Printer. [cover title].

    [1–8] p. engr. on one side only of 8 leaves; illus.; 13 cm.; pr. yellow paper covers.

    English ed. London: *The Talking Bird: Or, Dame Trudge And Her Parrot.* J. Harris, 1806.

    DLC° (rear cover mut.); Shaw 22660.

9.2 —————— Part I. Illustrated with Whimsical Engravings. Philadelphia: Published and sold Wholesale by Wm. Charles, No. 32, South Third street, and may be had of all the Booksellers. Prince 18¾ cents. 1817. [cover title].

    [1–8] p. engr. on one side only of 8 leaves; illus.; 12.5 cm.; pr. yellow paper covers.

    MWA°; PP (rear cover wanting; differs from MWA copy by not having *Part I.* on cover title); Shaw 39944.

    See also The Continuation of Old Dame Trudge and Her Parrot, no. **230.**

ADVENTURES OF PHILIP QUARLE. *See* Longueville, Peter, no. **793.1.**

10 THE ADVENTURES OF ROBERT EARL OF HUNTINGTON, COMMONLY CALLED ROBIN HOOD, THE FAMOUS ENGLISH ARCHER. Being a complete History of all the merry Adventures and valiant Battles, which he, Little John, and his bold Bowmen, performed and fought at divers Times and on various Occasions. Baltimore: Printed And Sold By William Warner. 1812.

    t.[1], [2–5], 6–110, [111] p.; title vignette only

illus.; 13.5 cm.; bound in ornamented paper covers over bds.; verse.

    PP°; ViU; Shaw 26640.

THE ADVENTURES OF ROBINSON CRUSOE. *See* Campe, Joachim Heinrich von, no. **158.6.**

11 THE ADVENTURES OF THE INDUSTRIOUS COBLER, His Scolding Wife, And Their Affectionate Daughter. Philadelphia; Published and Sold Wholesale by Wm. Charles and may be had of all Booksellers. Price, plain, 12 1-2 Cents—Colored, 18 3-4 Cents. 1814. [cover title].

    [1–8] p. engr. on one side only of 8 leaves; illus.; 13.5 cm.; pr. buff paper covers.

    English ed. London: Didier & Tebbett, 1808.

    NNC-Pl°; MWA (date worn off the front cover); Shaw 33795.

12 THE ADVENTURE OF THE INN: Or The Affecting History Of Emerton, With A Laughable Description Of Dermot O'Dogherty, And Arthur Boarspeg.—Calculated To Amuse, Entertain, And Instruct The Youth Of Both Sexes. Printed And Sold In Danbury [Conn.], By Douglas And Ely. M,DCC,XCII.

    t.[1], [2], 3–22 p.; 20.5 cm.

    CtHi° (p. 21–22 three fourths wanting).

THE ADVENTURES OF TOMMY TITMOUSE. *See* History of Tommy Titmouse, no. **594.1.**

THE ADVENTURES OF URAD. *See* Ridley, James, no. **1113.**

THE ADVENTURES OF VALENTINE AND ORSON. *See* Valentine and Orson, no. **1371.5.**

ÆSOP

13.1 — AESOP'S FABLES [2 lines quot.] Job, xii. 7. New-York: Printed And Sold By S. Wood, at the Juvenile Book-store, No. 357, Pearl-Street. 1811.

    t.[1], [2–5], 6–45 p.; illus.; 12.5 cm.; pr. & illus. brownish-buff paper covers.

    MWA°; NNC-T (p. 45 and rear cover wanting); Shaw 22156.

13.2 — —————— New-York: Printed And Sold By S. Wood, At the Juvenile Book-Store, No. 357, Pearl-street. 1812.

t.[1], [2–5], 6–45 p.; illus.; 12 cm.; pr. & illus. yellow paper covers; cover title dated 1811. NHi°.

13.3 — —— New-York: Printed And Sold By Samuel Wood, At The Juvenile Book-Store, No. 357, Pearl-Street. 1814.
t.[i], [ii-iii], iv, [5], 6–45 p.; illus.; 13 cm.; illus. buff paper covers.
MWA-W° (front cover wanting); CtY (bound with other books); MSaE (p. 45 mut.); PP (covers wanting); Shaw 30639; Weiss 1942.

13.4 — —— [2 lines quot.] New-York: Printed And Sold By S. Wood & Sons; At The Juvenile Book-Store, No. 357, Pearl-Street. 1815.
t.[1], [2–5], 6–44 p.; illus.; 12 cm.; pr. & illus. paper covers; cover title undated.
BM°.

13.5 — —— New-York: Printed And Sold By S. Wood & Sons, At The Juvenile Book-Store, No. 357, Pearl-Street. 1816.
t.[1], [2–5], 6–44 p.; illus.; 12.5 cm.; pr. and illus. brownish-buff paper covers; cover title undated.
MWA° (p. 13–14 mut.); PP (p. 5–6, 29–30, 43–44, torn or mut.); Shaw 36686.

13.6 — —— New-York: Published By Samuel Wood & Sons, No. 261, Pearl-Street, And Samuel S. Wood & Co. 212, Market-st. Baltimore. 1818.
t.[1], [2–5], 6–44 p.; illus.; 13 cm.; pr. & illus. buff paper covers; cover title undated.
MWA-W°; CLU; NNC-LS; Shaw 51731.

ÆSOP. Crouch, Nathaniel, 1632–1725? [Robert Burton (*pseud.*)] ed.
14 — Aesop's Fables, With His Life. Hartwick [N.Y.]: From The Press of L. & B. Todd. 1816.
t.[1], [2–9], 10–95 p.; 13 cm.; bound in blue paper over w. bds.; Otsego Co., New York imprint. Bethel & Lemuel Todd were publishers and printers of the Otsego Co. *Cherry Valley Gazette* from 1818–21.
English ed.: *Aesop's Fables With His Life, Morals And Remarks, Fitted For The Meanest Capacities.* London: A. Bettesworth, and C. Hitch; R. Ware; J. Hodges, 1737.
Welch° (rear cover wanting); MWA; NCooHi (t.[1], p. 95 mut.); Shaw 36685.

15.1 — Aesop's Fables: With His Life, Morals And Remarks. Amusement blended with Instruction. A New Edition. From Sidney's Press, For Increase Cooke & Co. New-Haven. 1806.
t.[1], [ii–iii], iv–viii, [9], 10–142 p.; illus.; 12.5 cm.; bound in wallpaper over bds.
English ed. London: 6 ed. A. Bettesworth, and C. Hitch; R. Ware; J. Hodges, 1737.
MWA° (wallpaper mostly wanting from bds.); IU (mut.); RWe; Shaw 9812.

15.2 — —— From Sidney's Press, New-Haven; For Increase Cooke & Co. 1807.
t.[i], [ii–iii], iv–vi, [vii], viii, [9], 10–142 p.; illus.; 14 cm.; bound in blue-gray paper over w.bds.
Welch°; MWA; NN-C; NjP; PP; Hamilton 236; Shaw 11949.

16.1 The Fables Of Aesop, With His Life, To Which are Added, Morals And Remarks, Accomodated To The Youngest Capacities. By Robert Burton Of London. [2 lines quot.] The Shepherd and the Philosopher, by Gay. Philadelphia: Printed by Robert Bell, in Third-Street. MDCC-LXXVII.
t.[1], [2–3], 4–141, [142–143], [144, adv.] p.; 19 cm.
English ed. London: 6 ed. A. Bettesworth, and C. Hitch; R. Ware; J. Hodges, 1737.
PPL° (rebound); MWA (p. 137–[143] wanting); Evans 15231.

16.2 — —— To which Is Added, —— [same as **16.1**] [2 lines quot.] Alexandria [D.C.] Printed 1802.
t.[1], [2–3], 4–164 p.; 15.5 cm.; bound in leather. Alexandria was Alexandria Va. 1749–1790, Alexandria D.C. 1791–1845, Alexandria Va. 1846. (MWA cat.).
MWA°; DLC (per. st. on t.[1]); Shaw 1723.

ÆSOP. Croxall, Samuel, *tr.* d.1752
17 — An Abridgement Of Aesop's Fables: With Instructive Applications, And A Print Before Each Fable. By Samuel Croxall D.D. Late Archdeacon of Hereford. New-York: Published by Evert Duyckinck, No. 162 Pearl-Street. George Long, Printer. 1813.
t.[i], [ii–iii], iv, [1], 2–108 p.; illus.; 14 cm.
MH° (p. 107–108 mut.); Shaw 51261.

18.1 — FABLES OF AESOP AND OTHERS, Translated Into English. With Instructive Applications; And A Print Before Each Fable. By Samuel Croxall, D.D. Late Archdeacon Of Hereford. The First American Edition, Carefully Revised, And Improved. Philadelphia: Printed And Sold By R. Aitken, Bookseller, Opposite The London Coffee-House, Front-Street, M DCC LXXVII.

fr.[ii], t.[i], [ii–xvi], [1], 2–318, [319–331] p.; illus.; 16.5 cm.; bound in leather; front. signed *Aitken Sculp.*; 11 illus. signed *J. Poupard.*
English ed.: *Fables of Aesop and Others, Newly done into English. With An Application To Each Fable.* [By S. Croxall] . . . London: J. Tonson and J. Watts, 1722.
PHi° (p.[127]–131 worm-eaten); MdBJ; MWA (p. 311–[331] wanting, fr.[ii] mut.).

18.2 — ———— The Second American Edition, Carefully Revised And Improved. Philadelphia: Printed And Sold By R. Aitken, At Pope's Head, In Market Street, Near The Coffee House, M DCC LXXXIII.

fr.[ii], t.[i], [ii–xxiv], [1], 2–318, [319–324] p.; illus.; bound in leather; front. signed *Aitken*; 11 illus. signed *J. Poupard.*
MWA° (i. st. on p.[iii] I. Thomas bookplate); NjP; Evans 17810.

18.3 — ———— The Third American Edition, Carefully Revised And Improved. Philadelphia: Printed And Sold By R. Aitken & Son, At No. 22 Market Street. M,DCC,XCII.

t.[i], [ii–xviv], 1–316, [317–320], p.; illus.; 17 cm.; bound in leather.
MWA° (fr.[ii] wanting); Evans 46370.

18.4 — ———— Croxall, D.D. New-York: Printed by William Durell, For T. B. Jansen and Co. 1800.

fr.[2], t.[3], [4], 5–63 p.; illus.; 10 cm.
PP° (covers wanting); Evans 48999.

18.5 — ———— The Fourth American Edition, Carefully Revised And Improved. Philadelphia: Printed And Sold By R. Aitken, No. 20, North Third Street. 1802.

t.[i], [ii–xx], [1], 2–316, [317–321] p.; illus.; 17 cm.; 11 illus. signed *J. Poupard.*
MWA° (rebound); NjP; Shaw 1724.

18.6 — ———— First Wilmington Edition. Wilmington (Del.): Printed And Sold By Peter Brynberg. 1802.

t[i], [ii–xvi], 1–316, [317–320] p.; illus.; 17 cm.; bound in leather.
DeWi (per. st. on p. 1); CtY; DLC; ICU; MdBJ; PP (covers wanting); PPL; PU; Shaw 1725.

18.7 — ———— New-York: Published By Evert Duyckinck. No. 102 Pearl-Street. G. Long, printer. 1813.

t.[iii], [iv–v], vi–xxiv, [1], 2–336 p.; illus.; 15 cm.; bound in leather.
MWA°; PPL; PU (310 p. only); Shaw 27676.

ÆSOP. Dodsley, Robert, *tr.* 1703–1764

19.1 — SELECT FABLES OF AESOP AND OTHER FABULISTS. In Three Books. Containing, I. Fables From The Antients. II. Fables From The Moderns. III. Original Fables Newly Invented. By Robert Dodsley. [7 lines quot.] Philadelphia: Printed and Sold by Robert Bell, in Third-Street. MDCCLXX VII.

½t.[i], [ii–iii, bl.], fr.[iv], t.[i], [ii–iii], iv–xxviii, [pl. opp. p. [29]], [29], 30–371, [372] p.; 16 pl. engr. including front.; 20 cm.; bound in leather; front. & pl. opp. p. 31, 47 signed *I. Norman Sc.* Page [372] near the middle of the page of contents: Six Oriental Stories, Entertaining and Instructive, to please, and form, the mind of youth.
English ed.: Birmingham: John Baskerville for R. and J. Dodsley, 1761.
PHi°; MWA (½t.[i] wanting); PPL; RNHi; Evans 15232.

19.2 — SELECT FABLES OF ESOP ———— [same as **19.1**] A New Edition. Philadelphia: Printed And Sold By Joseph Crukshank, In Market-Street, Between Second And Third-Streets. MDCCLXXX VI.

fr.[ii], t.[i], [ii–iii], iv, [5], 6–228, [229–230] adv. list of books] p.; front. only illus.; 17 cm.; bound in leather; front. signed *Jas Thackara Sculpt.*
MWA°; DLC (rebound, fr.[ii] wanting); MH; NN; PHi; RPJCB; Evans 19455.

19.3 — ———— Philadelphia: Printed And Sold By Peter Stewart, in Second-street, ninth Door above Chesnut-street. M,DCC,LXXXIX.

t.[i], [ii–iii], iv, [5], 6–215, [216] p.; 13.5 cm.; bound in leather.
MWA°; CSmH.

19.4 —⸻ A New Edition. Philadelphia: Printed By Joseph James, Chesnut-Street. [1790?].
t.[i], [ii–iii], iv–ix, ½t.[1], [2], 3–218, [219–242] p.; illus.; 17 cm.; bound in leather; illus. signed *V.*, *J. V.*, *I.V.* [John Vallance] and *T.*, *I.T.* [James Thackera], or unsigned. Illus. are copied from those in London: J. Dodsley, 1789. ed., which has the illus. on p. 3 signed *T. Gilbert del et sculp: 1777.*
MWA°; CLU.

19.5 —⸻ Printed And Sold By Benjamin Johnson, High-Street, Philadelphia. M,DCC,XCII.
t.[1], [2–3], 4–209, [210–216] p.; illus.; 17 cm.; bound in leather; same illus. as no. **19.4**.
MWA°; NjP; RPJCB; Evans 24027; Hamilton 142 (1).

19.6 —⸻ Philadelphia:—Printed and Sold By William Gibbons, No. 144, North Third Street. M.DCC.XCIV.
t.[1], [2–3], 4–209, [210–216] p.; illus.; 17.5 cm.; bound in leather; same illus. as no. **19.4**.
MWA°; NN (rebound); Evans 26539.

19.7 —⸻ Auserlesene Fabeln des Esop und andrer vorzüglichen Fabeldichter, Zur Bildung des Verstandes und Herzens. Nach der neuesten Englischen Ausgabe des Herrn R. Dodsley. Eine freye Uebersetzung von Gustav Fr. Gortz. In drey Theilen. Philadelphia: Gedruckt bey Steiner und Kammerer, 1794.
t.[i], [ii], [1], 2–214, [215–220] p.; illus.; 16.5 cm.; bound in paper over bds., leather spine; same illus. as no. **19.4**.
MWA°; PPL; Evans 26538.

19.8 —⸻ [same as **19.2**] Philadelphia: Printed For, And Sold By, Joseph And James Crukshank, No. 87, High-Street. 1798.
t.[i], [ii–iii], iv, [5], 6–208, [209–228] p.; 17.5 cm.; bound in leather.
MWA°; MB; MiU; NN (rebound); PSt; Evans 33274.

19.9 —⸻ Aesop, And Other Fabulists. In Three Books. By R. Dodsley. [7 lines of verse]

Montreal [Canada]: Printed by E. Edwards, No. 135, St. Paul-Str[eet] 1800.
t.[1], [2–3], 4–96 p.; 17 cm.
Adomeit° (all after p. 96 wanting).

19.10 —⸻ Esop —⸻ [same as **19.4**] A New Edition. Philadelphia: Printed By R. Cochran, For Mathew Carey, 118, Market-street. March, 1802.
t.[1], [2, bl.], ½t.[3], [4–5], 6–240 p.; illus.; 17.5 cm.; bound in leather; oval illus.
MWA°; PP; Shaw 1727.

19.11 —⸻ Philadelphia: Printed for Mathew Carey, 122, Market-Street. R. Cochran, Printer. 1807.
t.[1], [2], ½t.[3], [4–5], 6–240 p.; illus.; 17 cm.; bound in leather; illus. same as no. **19.4**.
P° (front cover detached); Shaw 12455.

19.12 —⸻ Philadelphia: Printed for Mathew Carey, 122, Market-street. 1811.
t.[1], [2], ½t.[3], [4–5], 6–240 p.; illus.; 17.5 cm.; bound in gray paper over bds.; same illus. as no. **19.4**.
MWA-W°; DLC; MH; MWA; NjP; OOxM; PP; PPL; Hamilton 142.(2); Shaw 22158.

19.13 — Seventy-Four Select Fables Of Aesop And Other Fabulists, By R. Dodsley. In Two Parts. Philadelphia: Published By M. Carey. 1812.
t.[1], [2], [3, contents], 4 [contents], ½t.[3], [4–5], 6–96 p.; illus.; 17.5 cm.; bound in marbled paper over bds., red leather spine. The book is part of a remainder or printed from standing type of p.[3]–96 of the above no. **19.12**. To these pages 2 leaves have been added containing a new title page and 2 p. of contents; the last p. being numbered 4.
PP°; Shaw 24573

ÆSOP. L'Estrange, *Sir* Roger, *tr.* 1616–1704
20.1 — A History Of The Life Of Aesop. According To Sir Roger L'Estrange. To Which Is Added, A Choice Collection Of Fables, With Instructive Morals. For The Benefit of Youth. Taken From The Most Eminent Mythologists. Philadelphia: Printed At The Southwark Office, No. 289, South-Front-Street. 1798.
t.[1], [2–3], 4–136, [137] p.; illus.; 14 cm.; bound in marbled paper over bds., leather

spine. Printed by Timothy Mountford. (MWA cat.).

English ed.: *Fables of Aesop And Other Eminent Mythologists, with Morals and Reflections.* London: R. Sare, T. Sawbridge [and others], 1692.

PP° (p. 9–10 trimmed); DLC (p. 9–10, 27–28, 33–34, 43–48, 59–68, 81–82, 99–100, 113–122 wanting); MWA-T; NN (p. 111–112, 115–118, 123–124 wanting); Evans 33272.

20.2 ———— Portsmouth, N.H. Printed For Thomas And Tappan. From the press of S. Sewall, 1808.

t.[1ͦ], [2–3], 4–120 p.; 15 cm.; bound in blue paper over bds., leather spine.

MWA°; DLC (i. st. on t.[1]); MH; NhD; Shaw 4519 (dated 1803) and 15416.

21 THE AFFECTING HISTORY OF FATHER NICHOLAS. To Which Is Added, Memoirs Of The Count D'Alverez. And The Story of Frederic Wooton: An English Moral Tale. Hartford: Printed By Lincoln & Gleason. 1804.

t.[1], [2–3], 4–70 p.; 13 cm.; ornamental yellow paper covers.

MWA-W°; Shaw 5668.

THE AFFECTING HISTORY OF THE CHILDREN IN THE WOOD. *See* Children in The Wood, no. **173.1** and English, Clara, no. **349.1.**

22 (No. 12.) THE AFRICAN WIDOW. An Interesting Narrative. By A Clergyman. Published By The Philadelphia Female Tract Society. [caption title].

Printed by Lydia R. Bailey, No. 10, North Alley. Philad. [1816] [colophon p. 8].

[1], 2–8 p.; 14 cm. Written by Joseph Dixon. *See also* no. **291.**

English ed. London: J. Evans [1800?].

MWA° (bound with other tracts, with which *The First Annual Report Of The Philadelphia Female Tract Society For The Year 1816* was originally bound); Shaw 37452.

AIKIN, JOHN 1747–1822
23 — THE ARTS OF LIFE: 1. Of Providing Food, 2. Of Providing Cloathing, 3. Of Providing Shelter; Described In A Series Of Letters: For The Instruction Of Young Persons: By Dr. Aikin. Bos-

ton: Printed By Hosea Sprague, For Samuel H. Parker, Court-Street. 1803.

t.[1], [2–3], 4–144 p.; 15 cm.; bound in leather. English ed. London: J. Johnson, 1802.

CtHi°; CLU; CtY; DLC; DNLM; MB; MH; MHi; MSaE; MWA; NNC-T (emb. st. on p. 143); ODW; Shaw 3642.

24 [—] THE CALENDAR OF NATURE; Designed For The Instruction And Entertainment Of Young Persons. New-York: Printed And Sold By Samuel Wood & Sons, At The Juvenile Book-store, No. 357, Pearl-Street. 1815.

t.[i], [ii–iii], iv–v, [vi, bl.], [7], 8–112, [113] p.; illus.; 14 cm.; bound in pr. buff paper over bds.; leather spine; illus. signed A [Alexander Anderson]. Adv. by S. Wood, 1816 in **1188.7**, and 1819 in **1188.8.**

For a rewritten and abridged version *see* nos. **147.1** and **1472.1.**

English ed. Warrington: W. Eyres, for J. Johnson, 1784.

MWA°; CLU (p.[113] wanting); MB; NB (i. st. on t.[1]); NNC-T (emb. st. on t.[1]); NjP; Hamilton 256; Shaw 33806, 33807 and 34270.

AIKIN, JOHN 1747–1822, and ANNA LETITIA (AIKIN) BARBAULD 1743–1845
25.1 [—] EVENINGS AT HOME; Or, The Juvenile Budget Opened. Consisting of A Variety Of Miscellaneous Pieces, For The Instruction And Amusement Of Young Persons. Vol. I (II.–VI.] Second Edition. Philadelphia: Printed By T. Dobson, At The Stone House, No. 41 S. Second Street. 1797.

vol. I.: t.[i], [ii–iii], iv, [1], 2–106 p.; vol. II.: t.[107], [108–109], 110–214 p.; vol. III.: t.[215], [216–217], 218–330, [1], 2 p.; p.[1]–2 at end adv. of books; bound in 1 vol.; vol. IV.: t.[i], [ii–iii], iv, [1], 2–107, [108, bl.] p.; vol. V.: t.[109], [110–111], 112–212 p.; vol. VI.: t.[213], [214–215], 216–314, [315–316, adv. list of books] p.; bound in 1 vol.; 6 vols. in 2; 18 cm.; bound in leather.

English ed. London: J. Johnson, vol. I–II, 1792; vol. III, 1793; vol. IV, 1794; vol. V–VI, 1796.

MWA-W°; CSt; MWiW; OOxM; PHi; PP; PPL; PSC; Evans 31698.

25.2 [—] ———— Vol. I. [II–VI.] Printed In London: Reprinted At Salem, By Thomas C. Cushing; And Sold At The Bible And Heart. 1797.

[probably a misprint for 1799, vols. II–VI dated 1799].

　vol. I.: t.[i], [ii], [1], 2–144 p.; vol. II.: t.[i], [ii–iv], [1], 2–146 p.; bound in 1 vol.; 16.5 cm.; vol. III.: t.[i], [ii–iv], [1], 2–163 p.; vol. IV.: t.[i], [ii–vi], [1], 2–156 p.; bound in 1 vol.; 15 cm.; vol. V.: t.[i], [ii–iv], [1], 2–151, [152, bl.] p.; vol. VI.: t.[i], [ii–iv], [1], 2–150 p.; bound in 1 vol.; 15.5 cm.; 6 vols. in 3. bound in leather. The imprints of vols. II–VI: Reprinted At Salem For Thomas C. Cushing; ——— [same as imprint of vol. I.].
　MWA° (vol. III.–IV. wanting); KU (2 copies vol. III.); MH (vol. V. p. 4–6 wanting); MSaE; OOxM; Evans 31699 and 35087.

25.3 [—] ——— Young Persons. An Abridgement Of the London Edition. Philadelphia: Printed By R. Davison. 1799.
　t.[1], [2–3], 4–143, [144] p.; 13.5 cm.; bound in marbled paper over bds., leather spine.
　MWA°; Evans 48770.

25.4 [—] ——— Vol. I. [II.] Second Edition. Philadelphia: Printed By A. Bartram. 1802.
　vol. I.: t.[i], [ii–iii], iv, [vol. I.], [1], 2–106; [vol. II.], [109], 110–214; [vol. III.], [217], 218–330; Vol. II. t.[i], [ii, bl.]; [vol. IV.]; [vol. V.]; [vol. VI.]–314 p.; 6 vols. in 2; 17 cm.; bound in leather.
　MWA°; CtY (vol. II. p. 111–120 follow p. [iii] and are repeated in the proper place); RPB (vol. I.); Shaw 1732.

25.5 ——— Persons. By Mrs. Barbauld And Dr. Aikin. In Two Volumes. Vol. I. [II.] Boston: Published By Cummings And Hilliard. 1813. Cambridge: Hilliard & Metcalf.
　vol. I.: t.[i], [ii–iii], iv, [i], ii, 3–348 p.; vol. II.: t.[iii], [iv–v], vi, 1–330 p.; 2 vols.; 14.5 cm.; bound in leather.
　MWA°; MeB; MH; MHi (vol. I., t.[i] mut.); MSaE; OClW-LS; PP (vol. I.); RPB; Shaw 27681.

25.6 ——— Vol. II. Boston: Published By Cummings And Hilliard. 1813. Cambridge:::Hilliard & Metcalf.
　fr.[ii], t.[iii], [iv–v], vi, 1–330 p.; 16.5 cm.; varied issue of vol. II. with 6 pl. including front. & a larger book than no. **25.5**.
　MWA°; NNC-T (fr.[ii], wanting but has a pl.

opp. p. 80; p. 15–74, 330–347 mut., emb. st. on t.[iii]); Shaw 27682.

25.7 ——— Persons. Vol. I [II.–IV.] Third Edition. Published By Johnson & Warner, And Sold At Their Bookstores, Philadelphia, And Richmond, Virginia. A. Fagan, Printer. 1813.
　vol. I.: t.[i], [ii–iii], iv, [5], 6–105, [106, bl.]; vol. II.: t.[107], [108–109], 110–209, [210 bl.] p.; vol. III.: t.[211], [212–213], 214–324 p.; illus.; bound in 1 vol.; vol. IV.: t.[i], [ii–iii], iv, [5], 6–105, [106 bl.] p.; vol. V.: t.[107], [108–109], 110–202 p.; vol. VI.: t.[203], [204–205], 206–299, [300] p.; illus.; bound in 1 vol.; 6 vols. in 2; 14 cm.; bound in leather.
　MWA° (vol. IV. p.[iii]–iv wanting, i. st. on t.p. of vol. I.); Shaw 27683 and 28461–62.

26.1 [—] The Farm-Yard Journal, Also, The Histories Of The Dog . . . Cat . . . Mouse . . . Martin . . . And Squirrel. Ornamented With Plates. New York, Published By T. B. Jansen, Bookseller, 116 Broadway, opposite the City-Hotel. L. Nichols, Print. 1806. Price 12 . . . 12 1–2 Cents.
　t.[1], [2–3], 4–36 p.; illus.; 13.5 cm.; blue marbled paper covers.
　MWA-T°.

26.2 [—] ——— Journal, Also, The Histories Of The Cat And Mouse. Ornamented With Plates. New-York: Published By Thomas Powers, Book-Seller, 116 Broadway, opposite the City-Hotel. 1810.
　fr.[ii], t.[1], [2–3], 4–36 p.; illus.; 14 cm.; pr. & illus. paper covers; front. signed *Anderson* [Alexander Anderson]. The story is taken from *Evenings At Home*, but has the preliminary letter to "Dear Tom" p. [3]–4, signed *Richard Markwell. Mr. Thomas Broadstreet, New York,* and dated *Springfield, June 1, 1810*, American cities rather than English ones.
　MWA°; Shaw 20080.

26.3 [—] ——— Journal. Also The History of the Mouse And Marten. Adorned With Cuts. Sidney's Press New-Haven. 1817.
　fr.[2], t.[3], [4–5], 6–31 p.; illus.; 10.5 cm.; illus. yellow-buff paper covers. The preliminary letter to "Dear Tom" p. [5]–6 signed *Richard Markwell* is dated Westchester, July 1, 1805.
　MWA° (front. mut.); CLU; CtY; NB (illus. green paper covers); Shaw 39955.

26.4 [—] ——— Journal. For The Amusement And Instruction Of Children. Cooperstown [N.Y.]: Printed and sold wholesale and retail by H. & E. Phinney. 1819.

fr.[2], t.[3], [4–5], 6–30, [31, adv.] p.; 9.5 cm.; pr. & illus. yellow paper covers. The preliminary letter to "Dear Tom" p. [5]–6 signed *Richard Markwell* is dated Westchester July 4, 1807.

CSmH° (fr.[2], & front cover worm-eaten); Shaw 46945.

26.5 [—] ——— Journal, Also The History Of The Marten. Adorned With Cuts. New-Haven: Sidney's Press. For J. Babcock & Son. 1819.

fr.[2], t.[3], [4–5], 6–30, [31] p.; illus.; 10.5 cm.; illus. buff paper covers, printed in pink ink. MH°; CtHi (Bates, pr. & illus. brown paper covers, cover title dated 1822); Shaw 46946.

THE TRANSMIGRATIONS OF INDUR. [By J. Aikin & Mrs. A. L. Barbauld]. *See* no. **1330.1.**

ALI BABA (arranged chronologically)

27.1 THE STORY OF ALI BABA, AND THE FORTY THIEVES. An Eastern Tale. Embellished With Engravings. Boston: Published By Thomas Wells, No. 3, Hanover-Street. 1813.

fr.[ii], t.[1], [2–3], 4–36, [37] p.; illus.; 14 cm.; pr. & illus. yellow paper covers; front. & illus. p. 5 & 9 signed *Dearborn* [Nathaniel Dearborn], illus. p. 24 signed *B*. Colophon p. 36: Watson & Bangs, Printers, No. 7, State-Street, Boston.; p. 37: < Copy-right of these engravings secured. >; cover title imprint same as title but dated 1814.

English ed. title 1: *Ali Baba Or The Forty Thieves*. London: Tabart and Co. 1804.

English ed. title 2: *The Forty Thieves; Or The Story Of Ali Baba And His Female Slaves*. London: J. Bailey [ca. 1816].

MWA°; Shaw 27690.

27.2 ——— Second Edition. Boston: Published By Thomas G. Bangs, No. 7, State-Street. 1814.

fr.[ii], t.[1], [2–3], 4–36, [37] p.; illus.; 14 cm.; pr. & illus. buff paper covers; reprint of no. **27.1**; Colophon p. 36: Thomas G. Bangs, Printer, 7, State-Street. Boston.; p. 37: same as no. **27.1**; cover title imprint same as title page. MWA-W°; MSaE; NjP; Hamilton 689a; Shaw 51353.

27.3 ——— Engravings. Boston: Published By Charles Callender No. 11, Marlboro' Street. 1814.

fr.[ii], t.[1], [2–3], 4–36, [37] p.; illus.; 14 cm.; pr. & illus. paper covers; reprint of no. **27.1**. Colophon p. 36: Watson & Bangs, Printers, No. 7, State-Street. Boston.; cover title imprint same as title page; p. [37] same as no. **27.1**.

RPB° (top of all p. worm-eaten); Shaw 30701.

27.4 ——— Boston: Published By Watson & Bangs, No. 7, State-Street. 1814. [cover title].

fr.[ii], [3], 4–36, [37] p.; illus.; 14.5 cm.; pr. & illus. paper covers; reprint of no. **27.1**. Colophon p. 36: Watson & Bangs, Printers, No. 7, State-Street, Boston.; p. [37] same as no. **27.1**.

MB° (t.[1] & p.[2] wanting); CtY (t.[1], p.[2], wanting, fr.[ii], p.[3]–4, & covers mut., date wanting from front cover); Shaw 51352.

27.5 ——— Oxford [N. Y.]: Printed and sold by C. Morgan and A. D. Pier. 1815. [cover title].

[1], 2–24 p.; 12.5 cm.; pr. blue-gray paper covers.

MWA-T°.

27.6 ——— Third Edition. Boston: Published By Thomas Wells, Hanover-Street. 1816.

fr.[ii], t.[1], [2–3], 4–36, [37] p.; illus.; 15 cm.; pr. & illus. buff paper covers; cover title dated 1816; reprint of no. **27.1**. Colophon p. 36: Thomas G. Bangs, Printer, 7, State-Street, Boston.; p.[37] same as no. **27.1**.

MWA° (t.[1], p. [2]–4 mut.); PP; Shaw 36706.

27.7 THE FORTY THIEVES: And The Overthrow Of Their Protector, Orcobrand, The Evil Genius of the Forest. Philadelphia: Published and sold Wholesale by Wm. Charles, No. 32, South Third street, and may be had of all the Booksellers. Price 18 3–4 cents. 1817. [cover title].

fr.[1], t.[2], [3–12] p.; engr. on one side only of 12 leaves; illus.; 13 cm.; pr. buff paper covers.

Cover title: The Entertaining & Interesting Story, of Alibaba the Wood Cutter with the Death of the Forty Thieves, and the Overthrow of Protector Orcobrand, the Evil Genius of the Forest.

MWA°; Shaw 39961.

27.8 ALI BABA; OR, THE FORTY THIEVES. A Tale For The Nursery. With three Copper-plates. From A Late London Edition. New-York: Published by

L. & F. Lockwood, No. 110 Chatham-Street. Birch & Kelley, Printers. 1818.

>fr.[ii], t.[1], [2–3], 4–24 p.; 3 col. pl. including front.; 13 cm.; pr. pink paper covers; cover title imprint adds: And By L. Lockwood, Bridgeport, Con. [*sic. i.e.* Conn.].
>English ed. London: Tabart & Co., 1807. pl. dated 15 May 1805.
>MWA°; CtHi (p. 23–24 & rear cover wanting, p. 22 mut.); Shaw 43047.

27.9 THE STORY OF ALI BABA AND THE FORTY THIEVES. New-Haven: Printed For John Babcock And Son. Sidney's Press. 1820.

>fr.[2], t.[3], [4, adv.–5], 6–31 p.; illus.; 15 cm.; pr. & illus. green paper covers; title page vignette shows a kneeling negro slave in chains.
>MWA°; CtHi; DLC; NN (front cover wanting, fr.[2] mut.); Bowe mss.; Shoemaker 72.

ALLADIN (arranged chronologically)

28.1 THE HISTORY OF ALLADIN; Containing A True And Wonderful Account Of An Enchanted Lamp; Found In a Subterraneous Cave, In China. Northampton [Mass.] 1804.

>t.[1], [2], 3–24 p.; 17 cm.
>MWA° (covers wanting); Shaw 5672.

28.2 —— Alladin; Or, The Wonderful Lamp. Philadelphia: Published and Sold By Thomas DeSilver, No. 220 Market, and 152, S. Sixth. 1813.

>t.[i], [ii], [1], 2–126 p.; 13 cm.; pr. paper covers.
>English ed. London: Tabart and Co. 1805.
>MSaE°; Shaw 51263.

29 ALLEGORIES. New-York: adv. by Samuel Wood, 1816 in **1188.7**, and 1819 in **1188.8**.

>This may be an American reprint of the English ed. entitled: Allegories and visions selected from eminent writers. Intended for the amusement and instruction of youth. London. R. Harrild, 1814.

ALLGOOD, NURSE *pseud.*

30.1 —— THE WHITSUNTIDE PRESENT, For Little Masters and Misses; Or, The History of Master George and Miss Charlotte Goodchild. To which is added, Rules for Behavior, And The Reward Of Virtue, An Instructive Story. By your old Friend Nurse Allgood. Sidney's Press. New-Haven, 1813.

>fr.[2], t.[3], [4], 5–30, [31 adv.] p.; illus.; 10.5 cm.; pr. & illus. buff paper covers.
>English ed. London: [*ca.* 1780].
>Welch°; CtHi (Bates, 2 copies varied covers); DLC (p. 29–30 wanting); MH; MWA; PP (fr.[2], p. [31] wanting); Shaw 30531.

30.2 —— Virtue. Adorned With Cuts. Sidney's Press. New-Haven. 1815.

>fr.[2], t.[3], [4], 5–30, [31, adv.] p.; illus.; 10 cm.
>CtHi°; MWA (fr.[2] & p.[31] & covers wanting); Shaw 36569.

30.3 —— Sidney's Press New-Haven. 1817.

>fr.[2], t.[3], [4], 5–30, [31, adv.] p.; illus.; 10.5 cm.; illus. buff paper covers.
>MWA-W°; Shaw 51642.

31.1 AN ALPHABET IN PROSE, Containing Some Important Lessons In Life, For The Use And Edification Of All Great And Small Children In NEW-ENGLAND. To Which Is Added Tom Noddy and his Sister Sue, A Lilliputian Story. Also, Some Account of the Society of Cuzes. First American Edition. Worcester: Printed By Isaiah Thomas, Jun. Sold Wholesale and Retail at his Bookstore. July 1798.

>fr.[2], t.[3], [4–5], 6–31 p.; illus.; 10 cm.; green Dutch paper covers. The word New England on the title page spelt as one word "NEW-ENGLAND" with all the letters in caps.
>Welch° (t.[3], & p.[4] mut., lower half of the page wanting); MWA (wallpaper covers); Evans 48335.

31.2 —— Second Worcester Edition. Worcester: Printed by Isaiah Thomas, Jun. Sold Wholesale and Retail by Him. 1800.

>fr.[2], t.[3], [4–5], 6–31 p.; illus.; 10.5 cm.; yellow wallpaper covers.
>MWA°; Evans 36805.

32 THE ALPHABET IN VERSE. New-York: Sold By T. B. Jansen. No. 11 Chatham-street. 1814.

>t.[1], [2–16] p.; 6.5 cm.
>CtY° (covers wanting); Shaw 51355.

33 T[HE] ALP[HABET] IN V[ERSE] To induce child[ren] [to learn their] Lett[ers] and for the entert[ainment of good] little boy[s] [and] girl[s]

Haverhill, Mass. Printed And Sold By The Hundred, Dozen Or Single By William B. Allen. 1812.
fr.[2], t.[3], [4], 5–28 p.; illus.; 10 cm.; illus. blue paper covers.
MWA-W° (fr.[2], t.[3], & p. 5–8, 25–26 mut., lower half of p. 27–28 wanting, p. 29–31 and rear cover wanting); Shaw 51155.

34 THE ALPHABET IN VERSE; Together, with a choice collection of Stories, Histories, &c. For the amusement of small Children. Adorned with Cuts. Printed by Stiles Nichols. Danbury [Conn.]. 1804.
fr.[2], t.[3], [4], 5–30 p.; illus.; 9.5 cm.; wallpaper covers.
CtHi° (rear cover & p.[31] wanting); Shaw 50405–6.

35 THE ALPHABET OF GOODY TWO SHOES Philadelphia: Published by Johnson and Warner. No. 147 Market Street. 1809.
t.[1], [2–27] p. engr. on one side only of 27 leaves; illus.; 11 cm.; bound in pr. & illus. pink paper over thin bds.; rear cover unprinted; cover title dated 1810.
English ed. London: J. Harris, 1808.
MH° (t.[1] & front cover torn); MWA (t.[1], p.[2] & front cover ½ wanting); OOxM; PP (imp); Shaw 16832 (dated 1809), and 19342 (dated 1810).

36.1 THE ALPHABETICAL TATTOO, Or, Assembly Of The Great and Little Letters, At The Critic's Palace, In Hartford. Hartford: Printed by Hale & Hosmer. 1813.
fr.[2], t.[3], [4–5], 6–31 p.; front. only illus.; 9.5 cm.; pr. & illus. yellow paper covers.
CtHi°; Ct (fr.[2], p. 31, and covers wanting, i. st. on t.[3], & p.[4]); MWA (fr.[2], p. 31, and covers wanting); Shaw 27702.

36.2 ———— Hartford: Printed by Hale & Hosmer. 1814.
fr.[2], t.[3], [4–5], 6–31 p.; front. only illus.; 10 cm.; pr. & illus. blue-gray paper covers.
CtHi°; MWA-T; Shaw 30662.

36.3 ———— Hartford: Published by J. & W. Russell. [1818?].
fr.[2], t.[3], [4–5], 6–31 p.; front. only illus.; 10 cm.; pr. & illus. pink paper covers.
MWA-W° (fr.[2], p. 31, & covers slightly worm-eaten); Shaw 51461.

ALWAYS HAPPY: Or, Anecdotes Of Felix, And His Sister Serena. *See* [Budden, Maria E. (Halsey)], no. **129.**

THE AMBITIOUS SHEPHERD. *See* Sommerville, Elizabeth, no. **1226.1.**

AMBROSE AND ELEANOR. *See* Ducray-Duminil, Francois Guillaume, no. **300.1.**

AMUSEMENT FOR GOOD CHILDREN. *See* C., G. S., no. **143.**

37 AMUSEMENT FOR INFANT MINDS. Book First. Ornamented with Cuts. Rutland [Vt.]: Printed By Fay & Davison. 1813.
fr.[2], t.[3], [4–5], 6–15 p.; illus.; 10 cm.; buff paper covers.
VtHi°; McCorison 1471; Shaw 27725.

38.1 AMUSEMENT HALL; Or, An Easy Introduction To The Attainment of Useful Knowledge. By A Lady. [6 lines of verse] Philadelphia: Printed by Lang and Ustick, and Sold by T. Ustick, No. 79, North Third Street, M.DCC.XCVI.
t.[i], [ii], [1–3], 4–120 [*sic. i.e.* 102] p.; 17 cm.; bound in scalloped marbled paper over bds. The NN copy has 2 extra leaves: 1st t.[ii], [iii–iv], 2nd t.[1], [2–3], 4–120 [*sic. i.e.* 102]; 1st & 2nd title pages the same. Caption p. [iii]: Review From The Evangelical Magazine.
English ed. London: Gardiner, 1794.
MWA°; NN; PP; PPL.

38.2 ———— Elizabeth-Town [N.J.]: Printed by Shepard Kollock for Cornelius Davis, No. 94, Water-Street, New-York. 1797.
t.[1], [2–5], 6–103 p.; 13 cm.; bound in scalloped red marbled paper over w. bds., leather spine.
CtHi°; NjP; Evans 48039.

39 THE AMUSING COMPANION: Or, Interesting Story Teller. Being A Collection of Moral, Sentimental And Miscellaneous Tales. [4 lines of verse] Charlestown [Mass.]: Printed By John Lamson, For John W. Folsom, No. 30, Union-Street, Boston, MDCCXCVII.
t.[1], [2–3], 4–284, [285–287] p.; 16 cm.
MWA° (covers wanting).

40 THE AMUSING COMPANION: Or, Interesting Story Teller. Being A Collection Of Tales, For the Amusement and Instruction of Youth. Binghamton [N.Y.]: Printed At The Office Of The Phoenix. 1815.

t.[1], [2–3], 4–110 p.; 13.5 cm.; bound in blue and brown marbled paper over w. bds., leather spine.

MWA°; NNC-LS; Shaw 33861.

41 THE ANACONDA. An Eastern Tale. [8 lines of verse] Thomson From Sidney's Press. For I. Cooke & Co. New-Haven. 1813.

t.[1], [2–3], 4–108 p.; 13.5 cm.

PP°.

42 ANECDOTES. Religious Tracts. No. 6. [caption title] Theological Printing-Office, Harrisonburg, Va. 1813. Price 6 Cents single—or $4 per hundred. Lawrence Wartman, Printer. [colophon p. 22].

[1], 2–22 p.; 16 cm.; A Sailor, p. [1]–6; Providence Displayed, p. 6–7; The Christian Drummer, p. 13–18; Illness And Death Of Mrs. Legave, p. 18–22.

MWA°; Shaw 51266.

43 Series of Evangelical Tracts, No. 28. ANECDOTES AND HINTS, Relative To the Prevailing but indefensible Practice of Profane Swearing. [caption title].

Printed and sold by Lincoln & Edmands, No. 53, Cornhill, Boston. [5 lines adv.] 1812. Price 33 cts. doz. 2,25 cts. a hun. [colophon p. 12].

[1], 2–12 p.; 18 cm.; pr. blue-gray paper covers.

MWA°; Shaw 24615.

44.1 ANECDOTES OF A LITTLE FAMILY; Interspersed With Fables, Stories, And Allegories, Illustrated With Suitable Morals For Children Of Different Ages, And Both Sexes. Embellished With A Copperplate. Philadelphia: Printed For Benjamin and Thomas Kite, No. 28, North Third Street, And No. 21 South Fourth Street. 1807.

fr.[ii], t.[i], [ii–iii], iv–v, [vi], [1], 2–66 p.; illus.; 14 cm.; bound in marbled paper over bds., green paper spine.

English ed. London: before 1789.

NNC-Pl°; Shaw 11988.

44.2 ———— Philadelphia: Published By Jacob Johnson, No. 147, Market-Street. 1808.

fr.[ii], t. [i], [ii–iii], iv–v, [vi], [1], 2–66 p.; front. only illus.; 14 cm.; marbled paper covers.

Adv. by Johnson & Warner, 1814 in **1449.2.**

MWA° (rear cover wanting); RPB; Shaw 14362.

ANECDOTES OF A SAILOR. *See* Griffin, John, no. **472.**

45 ANECDOTES OF DOGS. Philadelphia: adv. by B. Johnson, 1808 in **777.**

46 ANIMAL CREATION; Or, Juvenile History Of Beasts and Birds. By A Parent. New-York: Printed And Sold By Samuel Wood & Sons, At The Juvenile Book-Store, No. 357, Pearl-Street. 1817.

t.[1], [2–3], 4–71 p.; illus.; 14 cm.; pr. & illus. yellow paper covers.

NN° (i. st. on p.[2]); DLC; Shaw 40007. Weiss 1942.

47 ANN AND MARY, A True Story. New-York: Sold By T. B. Jansen, No. 11 Chatham-Street. < Price two Cents. > [*ca.* 1815].

t.[1], [2–3], 4–16 p.; illus.; 6.5 cm.; pr. & illus. buff paper covers; rear cover has adv. of 8 "Books At 2 Cents." among which is "The Squirrel" which was printed in 1814.

ANNA, THE TALE BEARER. *See* Sandham, Elizabeth, no. **1153.**

48 ANNE WALSH; A Narrative; Founded On Fact. To Which Is Added, An Address to the Friends of Religion, and to all who are interested in the benevolent purpose of holding Societies for Religious Worship. Philadelphia: Published By The Religious Tract Society of Philadelphia, No. 8, South-Front-Street. William Bradford— Agent. 1819.

t.[1], 2–12 p.; 18 cm.

MWA°; Shaw 47005.

THE ARABIAN NIGHTS. The complete edition is not considered a juvenile. Selections from the work are included and arranged chronologically under Alladin, Ali Baba, and Sinbad The Sailor.

THE ART OF MAKING MONEY PLENTY. *See* Franklin, Benjamin, no. **421.1.**

THE ARTS OF LIFE. *See* Aiken, John, no. **23.**

49.1 THE ATTRIBUTES OF GOD; An Account Of The Creation: And The Story of Joseph and his Brethren, Taken From Scripture. Adorned With Cuts. Sidney's Press. New-Haven, 1818.
> fr.[2], t.[3], [4–5], 6–30, [31, adv.] p.; illus.; 10 cm.; illus. white paper covers pr. in green ink.
> MWA-W°; Ct (i. st. on front cover); CtHi (covers pr. in pink ink); CtY; Shaw 43111.

49.2 ——— New-Haven. Sidney's Press. For J. Babcock & Son. 1819.
> fr.[2], t.[3], [4–5], 6–30, [31, adv.] p.; illus.; 10 cm.; illus. white paper covers pr. in green ink.
> MWA°; Ct (i. st. on fr.[2]); CtHi; Shaw 47025.

AULNOY, MARIE CATHERINE JUMELLE DE BERNEVILLE COMTESSE D' 1650–1705
50.1 [—] THE HISTORY OF FORTUNIO, And His Famous Companions. Also, The Wishes, An Arabian Tale. Adorned With Plates. New-York, Published By T. B. Jansen, Book-Seller, 116 Broadway, opposite the City-Hotel. L. Nichols, Print. 1805.
> t.[1], [2–3], 4–36 p.; illus.; 14 cm.; marbled paper covers.
> CtY°; CtHi (p. 36 torn); NjP; Hamilton 229; Shaw 50498.

50.2 [—] ——— Companions. New-York: Published By Thomas Powers, No. 116 Broadway, opposite the City Hotel. 1810.
> t.[1], [2–3], 4–35, [36] p.; illus.; 13.5 cm.; pr. & illus. paper covers.
> MWA° (covers worn); MSaE (emb. st. on t.[1], pr. & illus. yellow paper covers); Shaw 20341.

50.3 [—] ——— Companions. Boston: Published By Isaiah Thomas, Jun. No. 6, Marlborough-Street. 1812.
> fr.[2], t.[3], [4–5], 6–35 p.; illus.; 14 cm.; pr. & illus. blue paper covers.
> MWA-W°; MB; MWA; NB; PP; Shaw 25656.

51 [—]THE HISTORY OF THE TALES OF THE FAIRIES. Newly Done From The French. Containing I. The tale of Graciosa and Prince Percinet shewing the cruelty of a proud Mother-in-law to an Innocent dutiful Virgin. II. The Blue Bird and Floriana, shewing the Happiness of being good natured in both Sexes. III. The Fair Indifferent, or, the Hobgoblin Prince and Furibon. IV. Prince Avenant and the Beauty With Locks of Gold; shewing what difficulties and dangers love will surmount. V. The King Of The Peacocks and the Princess Rosetta; shewing the Vanity of Covetousness, Pride, and envy. VI. Prince Nonpareil and the Princess Valiant, wherein is shewn, that outward beauty is not the only object that love delights in. VII. The Orange Tree and its beloved Bee; shewing the Happiness of those Lovers, who shall find Constancy in Perfection. Wilmington [Del]: Printed By Peter Brynberg. 1800.
> t.[1], [2–3], 4–141, [142, bl.], [143, adv. list of books] p.; 13.5 cm.; bound in blue marbled paper over bds., leather spine. On p.[143] in the list of "Books Printed and Sold Whole-sale and Retail by Peter Brynberg; Wilmington, Del." *Fairy Tales is* misspelled *Fair Tales.*
> English ed. London: E. Tracy, 1716.
> DeWi° (per. st. on t.[1] & p.[3], p. 23–24 mut., all the blue marbled paper wanting from covers. A fragment remains on the inside of the front cover); MB; Bowe mss.; Evans 36863.

AN AUTHENTIC ACCOUNT OF THE CONVERSION, EXPERIENCE AND HAPPY DEATHS OF TEN BOYS. *See* Hendley, George, no. **502.**

AN AUTHENTIC ACCOUNT OF THE CONVERSION, EXPERIENCE AND HAPPY DEATHS OF NINE GIRLS. *See* Hendley, George, no. **503.**

AUNT MARY'S TALES. *See* Hughs, Mary (Robson), no. **620.**

52.1 AUTUMN. Manhood—The Autumn of Life. Printed & sold by Samuel Wood, at the Juvenile Book-store, No. 357, Pearl-street, New York. 1813.
> t.[1], [2–16] p.; illus.; 8 cm.; pr. & illus. orange pink paper covers; cover title undated. Adv. by S. Wood, 1808 in **643.1** and 1812 in **439.1.**
> MWA°; Shaw 51268.

52.2 ——— New-York: Printed & sold by Samuel Wood, at the Juvenile Book store, No. 357, Pearl street. 1814.
> t.[1], [2–16] p.; illus.; 7.5 cm.; pr. & illus. buff paper covers; cover title undated.
> MWA°; Shaw 30719.

52.3 —————— New-York: Printed And Sold By S. Wood, at the Juvenile Book-store, No. 357, Pearl-street. 1815.

    t.[1], [2–16] p.; illus.; 8.5 cm.; pink paper covers.

    MWA° (p. [13–14] mut.); Shaw 33901.

52.4 —————— Nerve-York [*sic. i.e.,* New York]: Printed And Sold By Samuel Wood & Sons, at the Juvenile Book-store, No. 357, Pearl-street. 1816.

    t.[1], [2–16] p.; illus.; 8 cm.; pr. & illus. yellow-buff paper covers; cover title undated.

    MWA-W° (t.[1], p. [2] mut.); CtHi; N (covers wanting, i. st. on t.[1]); NPV; PP; Shaw 51549.

52.5 —————— Nerve-York [*sic. i.e.* New York]: Published by Samuel Wood & Sons, No. 261, Pearl-street, And Samuel S. Wood & Co. No. 212, Market-st. Baltimore. 1818.

    t.[1], [2–16] p.; illus.; 8.5 cm.; pr. & illus. buff paper covers; cover title undated.

    MWA°; CCamarSJ; MH; Shaw 43118.

53 Awful Death Of An Impious Youth: A Fragment. Philadelphia: Printed By H. Maxwell; For A Dickens, Bookseller, No. 41, Market Street. 1799.

    t.[1], [2–3], 4–12 p.; 18.5 cm.

    MWA°; Evans 35131.

B

BABES IN THE WOOD. *See* Children in the Wood, no. **174.1.**

BAG OF NUTS READY CRACKED. *See* Thumb, Thomas (*pseud.*), no. **1306.1**; or Peter Puzzlewit (*pseud.*), no. **1084.**

BAKER, CAROLINE (HORWOOD) *fl.* 1800
54 — THE BROTHER & SISTER; Or, The Advantages of Good Behaviour. A Companion to little Emma and her Father. Written By Miss Horwood. Philadelphia: Published And Sold By W. Charles, No. 32, South Third-Street. [1819].
   fr.[ii], t.[i], [2–3], 4–15 p.; 4 pl. including front.; 13.5 cm.; pr. buff paper covers; colophon p. 15: H. C. Lewis, Printer, No. 272 Market-St.
   Cover title: The Brother & Sister A Poem. Illustrated With Engravings. Philadelphia. Published and sold by [Wm. Cha]rles. Price Plain 12½ cents—Coloured 18[¾] cents. 1819.
   NNC-Pl° (rear cover wanting); Shoemaker **47044.**

55.1 — THE DESERTED BOY; Or, Cruel Parents. A Tale Of Truth. Calculated to Promote Benevolence in Children. Written By Miss Horwood. Philadelphia: Published and Sold by Wm. Charles, No. 32 south Third-Street. 1816.
   fr.[ii], t.[i], [2–3], 4–12 p.; 13.5 cm.; pr. buff paper covers.
   Cover title: ——— Parents. A Moral Tale. Embellished With Beautiful Engravings. Philadelphia: Published by Wm. Charles, No. 32, South Third-street. Price plain, 12½ cents — Coloured, 18 3/4 cents.
   MWA-T° (2 plates wanting: fr.[ii], & pl. opp. p. 12; 2 pl. those opp. pl. 5 and 10 wrongly inserted).

55.2 — ———; Or, Cruel Parents. A Tale Of Truth. Calculated to Promote Benevolence in Children. Written By Miss Horwood. Philadelphia: Published and Sold by Wm. Charles, No. 32 south Third-street. 1817.
   fr.[ii], t.[1], [2–3], 4–12, [pl. opp. p. 12]; illus.;

pr. on one side of the leaf; 12 cm.; pr. buff paper covers; 4 pl. including front.
   Cover title of DLC copy: ——— Parents. A Moral Tale. Embellished With Beautiful Engravings. Philadelphia: Published by Wm. Charles, No. 32, South Third-street. Price plain, 12½ cents—Coloured, 18¾ cents. n.d.
   NNC-Pl° (uncol. pl.); DLC (2 copies; copy 1, col. pl., rear cover mut.; copy 2, front cover mut.); Shoemaker 40044.

56 — LITTLE EMMA AND HER FATHER. A Lesson for Proud Children. Written By Miss Horwood. Philadelphia: Published & Sold By Wm. Charles. No. 32, South Third street. 1819.
   fr.[ii], t.[1], [2–3], 4–15 p.; 4 pl. including front.; 13 cm.; pr. buff-brown paper covers; colophon p. 15: M'Carty & Davis, printers.
   Cover title: Little Emma And Her Father. Or, The Effects Of Pride. Embellished with beautiful Engravings. Philadelphia: Published And Sold By Wm. Charles, No. 32, South Third street. 1819. Price 12½ cents plain—18¾ cents coloured.
   NNC-Pl° (colored pl.); Shaw 47045.

BAKER, J. *See* MY PONY, no. 919 and MY TIPPO, no. **920.1.**

BALDWIN, EDWARD esq. (*pseud.*). *See* Godwin, William, no. **456.1**

BALDWIN'S FABLES. *See* Godwin, William, no. **455.1.**

BARBAULD, ANNA LETITIA (AIKIN) 1743–1825
57 — EASY LESSONS FOR CHILDREN. By Mrs. Barbauld. Windsor [Vt.]: Printed By Jesse Cockran, And Sold At His Book-Store. 1815.
   fr.[2], t.[3], [4–5], 6–31 p.; illus.; 10.5 cm.; pr. & illus. purple paper covers.
   Cover title: Lessons For Children. Windsor Vt. Printed and sold by Jesse Cochran.
   MWA°; VtHi (p. 29–31 & covers wanting); McCorison 1709; Shaw 33990.

58.1 — Easy Reading Lessons For Children. By Mrs. Barbauld. New-York: Published By Thomas Powers, Book-Seller 116 Broadway, opposite the City-Hotel. 1810.

　t.[1], [2–3], 4–36 p.; illus.; 14.5 cm.; green paper covers.

　MWA°; Shaw 19465.

58.2 — —— New-Haven: For J. Babcock And Son. Sidney's Press. 1820.

　fr.[2], t.[3], [4–5], 6–30, [31, adv.] p.; 11 cm.; pr. paper covers.

　CtY° (fr.[2]? & front cover wanting, rear cover worm-eaten); NjN; Shoemaker 307.

59 — Evening Tales; Consisting of Miscellaneous Pieces For The Amusement and Instruction of Children, Extracted From The Works Of Mrs. Barbauld And Mr. Aiken. [*sic. i.e.* Aikin] Wilmington, (Del.) Printed And Sold By Peter Brynberg. [1800?].

　t.[1], [2–3], 4–106, [107, adv. list of books] p.; 10 cm.; bound in ornamental paper over bds., leather spine.

　See also Evening Tales, no. **374**.

　PP°; MWA; Evans 49015.

60.1 — Hymns In Prose For Children. By Mrs. Barbauld, Author of Lessons For Children. The Fourth Edition Norwich [Conn.]: Printed, By John Trumbull. MDCLXXXVI [*sic. i.e.* MDC-CLXXXVI].

　t.[i], [ii–iii], iv–v, [vi], [7], 8–46, [47–48, adv. list of books] p.; 13 cm.; blue wallpaper covers. English ed. London: J. Johnson, 1781.

　MWA°.

60.2 [—] —— For Children. By The Author Of Lessons For Children. The Fifth Edition. New-Haven: Printed By Abel Morse. M.DCC.LXXXIX.

　t.[i], [ii–iii], iv, [5], 6–48 p.; 12 cm.

　CtY°; Evans 45434.

60.3 — —— For Children. By Mrs. Barbauld. Boston: Printed And Sold By W. Spotswood. 1797.

　t.[i], [ii–iv], [1], 2–29, [30–32] p.; 13 cm.

　MB° (p. 5–6, 31–32, & covers wanting); CLU; RPJCB; Evans 31770.

60.4 — —— For Children. By Mrs. Barbauld. To Which Are Added, Watt's [*sic. i.e.* Watts'] Divine Songs And Smart's Hymns In Verse. Boston: Printed And Sold by W. Spotswood. 1797

　t.[i], [ii–iv], [1], 2–29, [30–32, adv. list of books] p.; illus.; 12 cm.; bound in green Dutch paper over w. bds.

　MWA-W° (bound with no. **1218**, dated 1791).

60.5 — —— For Children. By Mrs. Barbauld, Author Of Lessons For Children. The Fifth American Edition. Worcester: Printed By Isaiah Thomas, Jun. Sold Wholesale And Retail At His Bookstore. June-1798.

　fr.[ii], t.[iii], [iv–v], vi–viii, [9], 10–46, [47–48, adv. list of books] p.; illus.; 13 cm.; Dutch paper covers.

　Welch° (rear cover wanting); MB (per st. on t.[iii]); MSaE (fr.[ii], t.[iii], p.[iv], 45–[48] & covers wanting); MWA (emb. st. on t.[iii]); NjP (rebound); NN (rebound, p. [ii–iv], [47–48], & Dutch paper covers silked; i. st. on p.[iv]); Evans 33372.

60.6 — —— By Mrs. Barbauld. To Which Is Added, Pope's Universal Prayer. Dedham [Mass.]: Printed And Sold By H. Mann. 1799.

　t.[i], [ii–iv], [1], 2–32 p.; 13 cm.; wallpaper covers.

　MWA°; PP; Evans 48795.

60.7 — —— By Mrs. Barbauld, Author Of Lessons For Children. New Edition, Improved. Boston: Printed And Sold By Manning & Loring, No. 2, Cornhill. 1802.

　fr.[ii], t.[iii], [iv–v], vi, [7], 8–35, [36, adv.] p.; illus.; 14 cm.; paper covers.

　MSaE°; Shaw 1837.

60.8 — —— By Mrs. Barbauld. Boston: Printed and sold by S. Hall, No. 53, Cornhill. 1803.

　t.[1], [2–5], 6–35 p.; 14 cm.; blue paper covers.

　MWA° (p. 19–20 mut. or torn in half); CtHi; NNC-T; Shaw 3749.

60.9 [—] —— For Children. By The Author Of Lessons For Children. The Sixth Edition. New-York: Printed By Isaac Collins And Son, No. 189, Pearl-Street. 1804.

　t.[i], [ii–iii], iv, [5], 6–96 p.; 13 cm.; bound in marbled paper over bds., leather spine.

　MWA-W°; Shaw 50409.

60.10 [—] ——— By The Author Of Lessons For Children. Norwich [Conn.]: Printed By Ch: E. Trumbull. MDCCCIV.

t.[2], [3–7], 8–41 p.; 12 cm.; blue marbled paper covers.

MWA°; CtY; Shaw 5802.

60.11 [—] ——— The Seventh Edition. Albany: Printed And Sold By Websters And Skinner [*sic. i.e.* Skinners], At their Bookstore in the White House, corner of State and Pearl-Streets. MDC-CCVI.

t.[i], [ii–iii], iv–vi, [7], 8–84 p.; 13 cm.; bound in marbled paper over bds., leather spine.

N° (per. st. on t.[i]); Shaw 50645.

60.12 ———— For Children. By Mrs. Barbauld. Philadelphia: Printed By Benjamin Johnson, No. 31, Market-Street. 1806.

t.[1], [2–3], 4–36 p.; illus.; 14 cm.; illus. p. 24 signed *A* [Alexander Anderson].

MWA° (covers wanting); Shaw 9917.

60.13 ————. By Mrs. Barbauld. From Sidney's Press, New-Haven. 1808.

fr.[2], t.[1], [2–5], 6–63 p.; illus.; 10.5 cm.; illus. paper covers.

MWA-T°; CtHi (p. 63 wanting); Shaw 50826.

60.14 ———— New York: adv. by L. B. Jansen and G. Jansen, 1808 in **766.**

60.15 [—] ——— For The Use Of Children. [2 lines quot.] Psalm civ. 24. New-York: Printed and Sold by Samuel Wood, No. 362, Pearl-Street. 1808.

t.[1], [2–5], 6–59, [60, adv. of books] p.; illus.; 10.5 cm.; pr. & illus. blue-gray paper covers; illus. p. [5], 8, 20, 25, 29, 51, signed *A* [Alexander Anderson].

MWA°, NHi (front cover wanting); NNC-T; Shaw 3748 (dated 1803, error) and 14447 (dated 1808).

60.16 ———— For Children. By Mrs. Barbauld. Newburyport [Mass.]: Printed By W. & J. Gilman. Sold at their Book and Stationery Store, Middle-Street. 1809.

fr.[ii], t.[iii], [iv–v], vi, [7], 8–36 p.; illus.; 14 cm.; marbled paper covers; front., title vignette, & illus. p. 7, signed *W Gilman*, illus. p. 20, 34 signed *Gilman*.

MWA° (p. 15–16 mut., p. 31–32 torn in half and other pages mut.); MNe; Shaw 16941.

60.17 ———— By Mrs. Barbauld. From Sidney's Press. New-Haven. 1809.

fr.[ii], t.[1], [ii–iii], iv, [5], 6–36 p.; illus.; 13.5 cm.; pr. & illus. blue paper covers, cover title undated.

MWA-W°; MWA (variant copy, mut.); DLC (covers mut.); MNS; Shaw 50910.

60.18 [—] ——— For The Use Of Children. [2 lines quot.] Psalm civ. 24. New-York: Printed and sold by Samuel Wood, at the Juvenile Book-Store, No. 357 Pearl-Street. 1809.

t.[1], [2–3], 4–43, [44, adv. list of books] p.; illus.; 12.5 cm.; yellow pr. & illus. paper covers; title page vignette & illus. above each hymn same as no. **60.15**, with the illus. on p. [3], 5, 11, 14, 18, 21, 29, 34, 37 signed *A* [Alexander Anderson]. The tailpieces differ in the two books.

MWA°; CtHi; Shaw 50911.

60.19 [—] ——— New-York: Printed and sold by Samuel Wood, at the Juvenile Book-Store, No. 357, Pearl-Street. 1810.

t.[1], [2–3], 4–43, [44] p.; 13 cm.; pr. & illus. yellow-buff paper covers.

CtHi°; CLU; MH; MWA-T (covers wanting); Shaw 50976.

60.20 ———— For Children. By Mrs. Barbauld. Philadelphia: Published By Benjamin Johnson. J. Bouvier, Printer. 1810.

t.[1], [2–3], 4–36 p.; illus.; 15 cm.; gray marbled paper covers.

MWA°; CtHi; MSaE; Shaw 19466.

60.21 ———— By Mrs. Barbauld. [2 lines quot.] Windsor [Vt.]: Published By P. Merrifield & Co. John Cunningham, Printer. 1810.

t.[1], [2–5], 6–5, [*sic. i.e.* 35] p.; 14 cm.; black marbled paper covers.

MWA-W°; VtHi; McCorison 1149; Shaw 19467.

60.22 ———— For The Use Of Children. By A. L. Barbauld. New York: Printed And Sold By S. Wood, At The Juvenile Book Store, No. 357, Pearl-Street. 1811.

t.[1], [2–5], 6–69, [70, adv. list of school books]

p.; 14.5 cm.; bound in gray marbled paper over bds. This school book ed. has been included for completeness.
MWA°; Shaw 51058.

60.23 —————— For Children. By Mrs. Barbauld. From Sidney's Press. For I. Cooke & Co. New-Haven. 1812.
fr.[ii], t.[iii], vi, [7], 8–47 p.; illus.; 10.5 cm.; buff paper covers.
MWA°; Shaw 51158.

60.24 [—] —————— For The Use Of Children. [2 lines of quot.] Psalm civ. 24. New-York: Published By Samuel Wood, At the Juvenile Book-Store, No. 357 Pearl-street. 1812.
t.[1], [2–3], 4–43, [44, adv.] p.; illus.; 12 cm.; pr. & illus. yellow-buff paper covers; cover title dated 1812; reprint of no. **60.18**.
NHi°; Shaw 51159.

60.25 —————— Prose, For Children. By Mrs. Barbauld. Newburyport [Mass.], Published by W. & J. Gilman, Printers, No. 2, Middle-Street. Sold at their Book-Store, and by the Booksellers in Boston, at wholesale and retail. 1813.
fr.[2], t.[3], [4–5], 6–34, [35, illus.]; illus.; 15 cm.; pr. & illus. paper covers; cover title undated.
NB° (bpl. on front cover); MSaE; MH; MWA-T; Shaw 27826.

60.26 —————— For The Use Of Children. By A. L. Barbauld. New-York: Printed And Sold By Samuel Wood, At The Juvenile Book-Store, No. 357, Pearl-Street. 1813.
t.[1], [2–5], 6–69, [70, adv. list of school books] p.; illus.; 14 cm.; bound in grey-green paper over bds., leather spine; reprint of no. **60.22**.
Welch°; MH (imp: lacks Hymn 1, part of Hymn 2, many pages torn); MWA; NB (wants p. 63–[70]); Shaw 27825.

60.27 [—] —————— For The Use Of Children. [2 lines quot.] Psalm civ. 24. New-York: Printed And Sold By Samuel Wood, At The Juvenile Book-Store, No. 357, Pearl-Street. 1814.
t.[1], [2–3], 4–43 p.; illus.; 12.5 cm.; pr. & illus. yellowish-brown paper covers; cover title undated; reprint of no. **60.18**.
MWA°; CtY (bound with other books); DLC;

MB (per. st. on t.[1]; original covers wanting); MWA-T; NB; OOxM; PP; Shaw 30798.

60.28 [—] —————— New-York: Printed And Sold By S. Wood & Sons, At The Juvenile Book-Store, No. 357, Pearl-Street. 1816.
t.[1], [2–3], 4–43 p.; illus.; 12 cm.; pr. & illus. yellow-buff paper covers; reprint of no. **60.18**.
Welch°; MWA (pr. & illus. brownish-buff paper covers; cover title undated; p. 13–14 slightly mut.); PHi; RPB; Shaw 37908.

60.29 —————— For The Use Of Children. By A. L. Barbauld. New-York: Printed And Sold By Samuel Wood & Sons, At The Juvenile Book-Store, No. 357, Pearl-Street. 1816.
t.[i], [ii–iii], iv, [5], 6–69, [70, adv. list of books] p.; 14.5 cm.; bound in marbled paper over bds., leather spine; reprint of no. **60.22**.
MWA°; ICU; MHa; MSaE; NHi; NN (per. st. on t.[i], rebound); RNHi (emb. st. on t.[i]); Shaw 36874.

60.30 —————— For Children. By Mrs. Barbauld. Adorned With Cuts. Sidney's Press, New-Haven. 1817.
fr.[2], t.[3], [4–5], 6–47 p.; illus.; 13.5 cm.; illus. buff paper covers.
MWA; MB (per st. on t.[3]); Shaw 40136.

60.31 [—] —————— For Children. By The Author Of "Lessons For Children." The Seventh Edition. New-York: Published by P. W. Gallaudet, at his Theological Bookstore, No. 49 Fulton-st. 1818.
t.[1], [2–3], 4–71, [72, adv.] p.; 12 cm.; pr. & illus. gray paper covers.
Cover title: Hymns In Prose For Children. New-York: Published By P. W. Gallaudet, At the Depository of the Sunday School Union Society, and New-York Religious Tract Society, No. 49 Fulton-st. Birch and Kelley, Printers. 1818.
MWA° (p. 7–10 wanting); Shaw 51741.

60.32 [—] —————— Prose, For The Use Of Children. [2 lines of quot.] Psalm civ. 24. New-York: Published By Samuel Wood & Sons, No. 261, Pearl-Street, And Samuel S. Wood & Co. No. 212, Market-st. Baltimore. 1818.
t.[1], [2–3], 4–43 p.; illus.; 13 cm.; pr. & illus. yellow paper covers; cover title undated; reprint of no. **60.18**.
RPB°; NN (covers worn); Shaw 43231; Weiss 1932, p. 387.

60.33 —————— For The Use Of Children. By A. L. Barbauld. Philadelphia: Printed By William Fry, Walnut Near Fifth Street. 1818.

t.[1], [2–5], 6–30 p.; 17 cm.

MWA° (covers wanting); MH; Shaw 42332.

60.34 —————— For The Use Of Children. By A. L. Barbauld. Boston: Published By Timothy Swan, No. 15, Cornhill. 1819.

t.[1], [2–5], 6–32 p.; 13.5 cm.; blue-gray paper covers. p. [2]: Parmenter And Balch, Printers.

MWA°; MH; MSaE; NN (covers wanting, i. st. on p. [2], [4]); PP; RPB; Shaw 47158 and 47157.

60.35 [—] —————— For Children. By The Author Of Lessons For Children. From the Seventeenth London edition, much enlarged. Boston: Published By Wells And Lilly. 1819.

t.[i], [ii–iii], iv–vi, [7], 8–108 p.; 12.5 cm.; red & blue marbled paper covers. Cover label: Barbauld's Hymns for Children.

MNeHi° (p. 107–108 torn); Shaw 51855.

60.36 —————— For Children. By Mrs. Barbauld. Adorned With Cuts. New-Haven: Printed For John Babcock And Son. Sidney's Press. 1819.

fr.[ii], t.[1], [2–3], 4–36 p.; illus.; 13.5 cm., marbled paper covers; p. 34 misprinted p. "54." CtY° (p. 35–36 mut.); CtHi (2 copies with varied covers, & different front., p. 34 is printed correctly in both); Shaw 47156.

60.37 [—] —————— For The Use Of Children [2 line quot.] Psalm civ. 24. New-York: Published By Samuel Wood & Sons, No. 261, Pearl-Street; And Samuel S. Wood & Co., No. 212, Market-st. Baltimore. 1819.

t.[1], [2–3], 4–43 p.; illus.; 13 cm.; pr. & illus. buff paper covers; cover title undated; reprint of no. **60.18.**

MWA°; Shaw 47159.

60.38 —————— For The Use Of Children. By A. L. Barbauld. Auburn [New York]: Printed And Sold By U. F. Doubleday, At his Bookstore, nearly opposite the Bank. 1820.

t.[1], [2–5], 6–43 p.; tailpiece p. 43; 12.5 cm.; buff paper covers.

MWA° (p. 9–12 wanting); Shoemaker 308.

60.39 — Mrs. Barbauld's Hymns In Prose, For The Use Of Children; To Which Is Added A Few Selected Hymns, In Verse, For the use of Sunday Schools. [2 lines quot.] Psalm civ. 24. Printed, Published & Sold, (in large and small quantities), by Denio & Phelps, at their Bookstore, Greenfield, Mass. 1820.

fr.[2], t.[3], [4–5], 6–36 p.; illus.; 13.5 cm.; pr. & illus. brick-red paper covers.

MWA° (covers wanting); PP; RPB; Shoemaker 313.

60.40 —————— For Children. By Mrs. Barbauld. New Haven: Printed For J. Babcock And Son. Sidney's Press. 1820.

fr.[2], t.[3], [4–5], 6–31 p.; illus.; 15 cm.; pr. & illus. blue-gray paper covers.

MWA°; Ct; MiD; MSaE; Shoemaker 309.

60.41 — —————— Philadelphia: Benjamin Johnson. 1820.

Shoemaker 311.

61.1 [—] Lessons For Children, From Two To Four Years Old. Philadelphia: Printed By B. F. Bache. 1788.

t.[1], [2–8], 9–109 p.; 9 cm.; blue-gray paper covers; p. [2], and all even numbered pages from [8]–[108] are blank and not numbered.

English ed. entitled: —————— From Two To Three Years Old. Part I. 1778.

MWA°; DLC; CtHi; N; NHi; NNC; PHi (2 copies); PP; PPL (rebound); Evans 20946.

61.2 [—] Lessons For Children Of Four Years Old. Part I. [II.] Philadelphia: Printed By B. F. Bache. 1788.

pt. I.: t.[1], [2–3], 4–83 p.; pt. II.: t.[1], [2–3], 4–96 p.; 2 vols.; 9.5 cm.; blue-gray paper covers.

English ed. London, entitled: —————— Children Of Three Years Old. Part II. [III.] [text same as above pt. I. [II.]. J. Johnson, 1791.

NNC-Pl.° (pt. I., II.); CtHi (pt. I.); MWA-T (pt. II.); NN (pt. I.); PHi (pt. I., II.); PP (pt. I., II.); PPL (pt. I., II.); Evans 20947 (pt. II.).

61.3 [—] Lessons For Children From Four To Five Years Old. Philadelphia: Printed By B. F. Bache. 1788.

t.[1], [2–3], 4–107 p.; 10 cm.; blue-gray paper covers.

English ed. London, entitled: —————— From

Three To Four Years Old. Part IV. J. Johnson, 1788.

PP°; DLC; PHi; PPL; Evans 20948.

61.4 [—] LESSONS FOR CHILDREN, From Two To Four Years Old. Part I. Portland [Me.]: Printed By Thomas B. Wait. 1793.

t.[1], [2–8], 9–95 p.; 9.5 cm.; marbled paper covers; p. [2] and even numbered pages from [8]–80 blank and unnumbered.

PP°; Evans 46693.

61.5 [—] LESSONS FOR CHILDREN OF FOUR YEARS OLD. Part II. Portland [Me.]: Printed By Thomas B. Wait. 1793.

t.[1], [2–3], 4–96 p.; 9 cm.; marbled paper covers.

PP°; Evans 46695.

61.6 [—] LESSONS FOR CHILDREN, From Four To Five Years Old. Part III. Portland [Me.]: Printed By Thomas B. Wait. 1793.

t.[1], [2–3], 4–107 p.; 9 cm.; marbled paper covers.

PP° (front marbled paper cover wanting); Evans 46694.

61.7 [—] LESSONS FOR CHILDREN, From Five To Six Years Old. Volume II. Boston: Printed and Sold by S. Hall, No. 53, Cornhill. 1800.

t.[3], [4–5], 6–118 p.; 11.5 cm.

MB°; Evans 36891.

61.8 [—] LESSONS FOR CHILDREN, PART II. From Four To Five Years Old. Wilmington, Del. Printed and Sold Wholesale and Retail by James Wilson, At the Mirror Book-Store and Printing Office. 1800.

t.[1]. [2–3], 4–44 p.; illus.; 14 cm.; illus. blue-gray paper covers, p. 43–44 adv. list of books.

MWA°; Evans 36890.

61.9 [—] LESSONS FOR CHILDREN FROM FOUR TO FIVE YEARS OLD. Wilmington, (Del.) Printed and Sold by P. Brynberg. 1801.

t.[1], [2–3], 4–67, [68, adv. list of books] p.; 9.5 cm.; buff paper covers ornamented with design in brown.

MWA-W°; CSmH; CtHi; CtY; DLC (2 copies); DeWi (per. st. on t. [1]); NHi; NN-C; NNC-Pl (2 copies); NNMM; NRU; OOxM; PHi; PP; PPL; PU; Shaw 131; Weiss 1936.

61.10 [—] LESSONS FOR CHILDREN, From Two To Five Years Old. Adorned with-Cuts-Engraved by James Akin [last seven words in a vignette] Part I. From Two to Four Years Old. Wilmington, Del. Printed and Sold Wholesale and Retail by James Wilson, At the Mirror Book-Store and Printing-Office. 1803.

pt. I.: t.[1], [2–4], 5–36 p.; illus.; pt. II.: t.[1], [2–3], 4–44 p.; illus.; p. 43–44 adv. of books; 2 pts. in one vol.; 14 cm.; pinkish-buff paper covers.

Title to Pt. II.: Lessons For Children, Part II. From Four To Five Years Old. Adorned with-Cuts-Engraved by James Akin. [last seven words in a vignette.] Wilmington, Del. Printed and Sold Wholesale and Retail by James Wilson, At the Mirror Book-Store and Printing-Office. 1803.

The words "Adorned with Cuts. Engraved by James Akin" cannot be clearly made out on the heavily printed title vignette on the first title page, but are clear on the second title page which has a lighter impression of the same vignette. The DeHi copy of both parts have a light impression of the vignette and the words are sharp and easy to read.

NN-C°; CtHi (pt. II.); DeHi (pt. I bound in illus. yellow paper covers; pt. II. a separate book bound in illus. light blue-gray paper covers.); DeWi (both pts. bound in one vol., emb. st. on 1st t.[1] & p.[3] of pt. I.); MWA (pt. II.); NjP (pt. II.); PHi (pt. II.); PP (pt. II.); PPL (pt. II.); Hamilton 204; Shaw 3750.

61.11 — MRS. BARBAULD'S LESSONS, Admirably Adapted To The Capacities Of Children. To which is added, Two Elegant Tales, entitled, The Basket Maker: And The Earthquake. New-York: Printed For D. Bliss, No. 56. Maiden-Lane, 1806.

t.[1], [2–3], 4–105 p.; 13.5 cm.; bound in marbled paper over bds., leather spine.

English ed. "The Basket Maker" appeared in *The Amusing Instructor. London, F. Newbery, 1777.*

MWA°; Shaw 9918.

61.12 — LESSONS FOR CHILDREN. Part I. For Children From Two To Three Years Old. By Mrs. Barbauld. Charleston [S.C.]: Printed And Sold By J. Hoff, No. 6, Broad Street. 1807.

1st t.[1], [ii–iii], iv, [5], 6–32, [24, bl.] p.; 2nd t.[1], [2–3], 4–26 p.; 3rd t.[1], [2–3], 4–27, [28, bl.] p.; 4th t.[1], [2–3], 4–28 p.; 4 pts. in

1 vol.; 14.5 cm.; bound in blue marbled paper over bds., leather spine.

2nd title: Lessons For Children. Part II. Being The First For Children Of Three Years Old. By Mrs. Barbauld. Charleston [S.C.]: Printed And Sold By J. Hoff, No. 6, Broad-Street. 1807.

3rd title: ——— Part III. Being The Second For Children Of Three Years Old. By Mrs. Barbauld. Charleston [S.C.]: Printed And Sold By J. Hoff, No. 6, Broad Street. 1807.

4th title: ——— Part IV. For Children From Three To Four Years Old. By Mrs. Barbauld. Charleston [S.C.]: Printed And Sold By J. Hoff, No. 6, Broad Street. 1807.

MWA°; Shaw 12077.

61.13 — LESSONS FOR CHILDREN. By Mrs. Barbauld. Baltimore: Printed And Sold By A. Miltenberger, No. 10, North Howard Street. 1813.

t.[3], [4–5], 6–38 p.; illus.; 12 cm.; paper covers.

MSaE°; Shaw 27827.

61.14 — LESSONS FOR CHILDREN. In Four Parts. Part III. [IV.] Being The Second For Children Of Three Years Old. Boston: Published By Wells and Lilly. 1818.

pt. III: t.[1], [2–3], 4–157 p.; 13.5 cm.; orange-red marbled paper covers. Label on the front cover: Barbauld's Lessons for Children. Part III. Caption title pt. IV. p.[3]: Lessons For Children From three to four years old [followed by 5 lines of text]. pt. IV: p. [3], 4–168 p.; 13 cm.; brownish marbled paper over bds., red leather spine; bound with pt. III.

MWA° (pt. III rebound); NCooHi° (pt. III.) bound with pt. IV.; t.[1] to pt. IV. wanting); Shaw 43233.

61.15 — LESSONS FOR CHILDREN. In Four Parts. By Mrs. Barbauld. Improved By Cuts, Designed By S. Pike, And Engraved By Dr. Anderson. Philadelphia: Published By Benjamin Warner, No. 147, Market Street. Lydia R. Bailey, Printer. 1818.

t.[1], [ii–iii], iv, [5], 6–102 p.; 15 cm.

MWA-W copy A—gray paper covered boards with a label pasted on the front cover: Barbauld's Lessons. In Four Parts. [Engraving of Munroe and Francis' Bookstore] Boston: Munroe And Francis, 4 Cornhill.

MWA copy B—bound in pr. & illus. buff paper over bds. Imprint on the front cover: Philadel-

phia: Published by Benjamin Warner, No. 147, Market Street. 1819. Adv. by Johnson & Warner, 1811 in **340** and 1813 in **971**. In the above edition of 1818 on p.[ii] is stated that this title was deposited in the Clerk's Office of the District of Pennsylvania, May 10, 1810. All other copies located are bound in gray paper over bds.

MWA-W° (A); CtHi; CtY (2 copies); DLC (2 copies); MWA (B); NjP (also orig. wood block of cut on p. 21); NN (t.[i], & covers wanting, bound with other pamphlets); PHi; PP (A); PPL; PU; Hamilton 265; Shaw 43234.

61.16 — MRS. BARBAULD's LESSONS; Admirably adapted to the capacities of Children. To which is added, two elegant Tales, entitled, The Basket-Maker: And The Earthquake. New-York[:] Published By Daniel D. Smith, At the Franklin Juvenile Book-Store, No. 190 Greenwich-Street. 1819.

t.[1], [2–3], 4–108 p.; 13.5 cm.; pr. pink paper covers.

NN° (front cover wanting, bound with other books); MWA; Shaw 47160.

61.17 — LESSONS FOR CHILDREN. In Four Parts. By Mrs. Barbauld. [1 line quot.] Boston: Printed And Sold By James Loring, No. 2, Cornhill, Washington's Head. 1820.

t.[1], [2–5], 6–108 p; t. [1] 14.5 cm.

MWA° (rebound); Shoemaker 314.

62.1 — A SUMMER's WALK, To View The Beauties Of Nature. Extracted from Mrs. Barbauld's Hymns in Prose. Boston: Printed By Nathaniel Willis, No. 76, State-Street. 1816.

fr.[2], t.[3], [4], 5–14, [15] p.; illus.; 11 cm.; yellow paper covers.

MWA°; Shaw 36874.

62.2 ———— Boston: Printed By Nathaniel Willis, Congress-Street. 1819.

fr.[2], t.[3], [4], 5–14, [15] p.; illus.; 10.5 cm.; black paper covers.

MWA°; Shaw 47161.

BARBER, JOHN WARNER 1798–1885

63 — THE PILGRIM's PROGRESS, Exhibited In A Metamorphosis, Or A Transformation Of Pictures, For The Entertainment And Instruction Of Youth. Designed and Published By J. W. Barber. Hartford: Printed by Loomis & Barnes. 1819. Copy Right secured according to law.

5 folded leaves printed on both sides of the leaf; illus.; 13.5 cm. The top and bottom of each leaf is folded so that the folds form an illus.

MWA°; DLC; MB; NHi; NjP; NPV; RPB; Hamilton 360; Shaw 47461 and 47462.

64 [—] THE BASKET-MAKER, AND THE BROTH-ERS. Adorned with Cuts. New-Haven: For J. Babcock And Son. Sidney's Press. 1820.

Caption p. [5]: The Basket-Maker, A Peruvian Tale.

fr.[2], t.[3], [4–5], 6–30, [31, adv.] p.; illus.; 11 cm.; pr. paper covers.

Cover imprint: Published by J. Babcock & Son. New-Haven, And S. and W. R. Babcock, Charleston.

English ed. 1, contained in: *The Amusing Instructor*. London: F. Newbery, 1777, p. 9–20.

English ed. 2. contained in[Mrs. Ann Fisher Slack's] *The Pleasing Instructor Or Entertaining Moralist consisting of Select Essays, Relations, Visions, and Allegories collected from the most Eminent English Authors*. London: G. G. & J. Robinson and S. Hodgson, Oct. 1, 1785, p. 19–23. In the table of contents the story is given as being taken from the *Gentleman's Magazine*.

The story appeared in no. **1040.2**, *The Paternal Present . . . Chiefly Selected From the Writings of Mr. Pratt*. [S. J. Pratt] Philadelphia, 1807, on p. 98–107. On p. 98 the caption reads: "The Basket Maker. A Peruvian Tale From Pratt's *Gleanings*." Since *The Paternal Present* did not appear in England until 1802, and Pratt's *Gleanings Through Wales, Holland, and Westphalia* was not published until 1795, Pratt surely was not the author of this story. A search through Pratt's *Gleanings* has not located the story, though volume 4, entitled *Gleanings in England*, London, 1795, was not seen.

MWA° (2 copies, varied covers with different illus. on the front cover. Copy 1 rear cover has 2 illus.; copy 2 rear cover has adv.); Shoemaker 336.

THE BASKET-WOMAN. *See* Edgeworth, Maria, no. **308.**

BATES, JOSHUA 1776–1854

65.1 — A BRIEF ACCOUNT OF THE HAPPY DEATH OF MARY ANN CLAP, Daughter Of Mr.

Jesse And Mrs. Betsey Clap, Who Died July 15, 1816, In The Eleventh Year Of Her Age; Exhibiting An Example Of Meekness And Submission; Furnishing The Clearest Evidence Of Early Piety; And Imparting The Sweetest Consolation To Pious Friends. By Joshua Bates, A.M. Pastor of the First Church in Dedham [2 lines quot.] Dedham [Mass.]: Published By Abel D. Alleyne. 1816.

t.[1], [2–3], 4–36 p.; 17.5 cm.; blue-gray paper covers. This is the first edition of this work printed in Dedham, Mass. p. [2]: Printed And Sold By A. D. Alleyne.

CtHi° (p. 21–24, 27–30, & front cover wanting); Shaw 51550.

65.2 ——— [2 lines of quot.] Second Edition. Dedham [Mass.]: Published By Abel D. Alleyne. 1816.

t.[1], [2–3], 4–36 p.; 17.5 cm.; blue-gray paper covers; p. [2]: Printed And Sold By A. D. Alleyne.

MWA°; Shaw 36892.

65.3 ——— Third Edition. Boston: Printed by Nathaniel Coverly, Jr. Milk Street. 1816.

fr.[ii], t.[1], [2], 3–24 p.; front. only illus.; 17.5 cm.; front. signed *N.D.* [Nathaniel Dearborn].

MWA° (t.[1] mut. imprint torn away, covers wanting, p. [2], 3–4 and other pages mut.); NN; Shaw 36893.

65.4 ——— [Same as Second Dedham Edition] Third Edition. Dedham [Mass.] Published By Abel D. Alleyne. 1816.

t.[1], [2–3], 4–36 p.; 17.5 cm.; blue-gray paper covers; p. [2]: Printed And Sold By A. D. Alleyne.

MWA°; BM; NN (rear cover wanting, bound with other pams.); Shaw 36894.

65.5 ——— Fourth Edition. Boston: Printed by Nathaniel Coverly, Jr. 1816.

NjP°; Hamilton 1968, 1636.

65.6 ——— Fifth Edition. Boston: Printed By Nathaniel Coverly, Jr. Milk-Street. 1816.

fr.[ii], t.[1], [2], 3–24 p.; 18 cm.; pr. & illus. blue paper covers; front. signed *N D* [Nathaniel Dearborn].

MWA°; Shaw 36895.

65.7 —— —— [same as **65.2**] Church in Dedham. [Mass.] [1 line quot.] [caption title] [*ca.* 1816].

    [1], 2–24 p.; 17.5 cm.
    MWA°; Shaw 36891.

65.8 [—] No. 18. MARY ANN CLAP. List of Tracts Published By The Hartford Evangelical Tract Society. [list of 20 tracts] [1817].

    t.[1], 2–24 p.; 17 cm.; pr. gray-green paper covers.
    MWA°; Shaw 40145.

66 [Battledore] A B C D E F G [cut] H I K L M N O [vignette] Sold by B. Johnson, No. 31, Market St. [*ca.* 1817] [front cover title].

    [1–2] p.; illus. letters of the alphabet A-Z; 16.5 cm.; pr. & illus. gray-green paper covers. *See* nos. **187.1**, **187.2**, and **1363**.
    MWA-T°.

BE MERRY AND WISE. *See* Trapwit, Tommy (*pseud.*) no. **1317.1**.

BEAR YE ONE ANOTHER'S BURDENS. *See* Cheap Repository, no. **169.27**.

67 BEAUTIES OF THE ECONOMY OF HUMAN LIFE Illustrated with Emblematical Plates Part I. [II.] Philadelphia Published & sold wholesale, by Wm. Charles, and may be had of all the Booksellers Price 12½ cents. [1815?].

    pt. I.: [1–12] p. engr. on one side only of 12 leaves; illus.; pt. II.: [1–12] p. engr. on one side only of 12 leaves; illus.; 2 vols.; 13.5 cm.; pr. buff paper covers. Adv. by Wm. Charles, 1815 in **748**.
    MWA-W° (rear cover of both vols. mut.); Weiss 1932a.

68 THE BEGGARLY BOY Published by B Johnson No. 247 Market St Philadelphia [1807].

    t.[i], [ii], [1], 2–26 p.; title vignette only illus.; 14.5 cm.; buff paper covers; engr. title page. Caption title p. [1]: The History Of The Beggarly Boy. Published as No. 30 in The Cheap Repository. Philadelphia. 1800. *See* no. **169.21** English ed. London: J. Marshall (Printer to the Cheap Repository), R. White, S. Hazard at Bath. [June 1, 1795].
    MWA-W° (t.[i], p. [1]–mut.); CLU; NNC-Sp (bound in vol. 2 [*Cheap Repository* 1807]);

PP (covers wanting, p. [2] is unnumbered); Shaw 13121.

THE BEGGARLY GIRL. *See* The Little Beggar Girl, no. **762**.

BELSON, MARY. *See* Elliott, Mary (Belson).

69.1 THE BENEVOLENT OLD MAN OF THE ROCK: An Entertaining Story For Youth. Boston: Published By Thomas B. Wait And Co. And Charles Williams. [1812].

    fr.[2], t.[3], [4–5], 6–35 p.; illus.; 14 cm.; pr. yellow paper covers. Adv. by Thomas B. Wait & Charles Williams, 1812 in **396**.
    MSaE°; DLC; NB; NN (p. 33–34 wanting, i. st. on p. 35); PPL; Shaw 19503.

69.2 —— —— Montpelier [Vt.]: Published By E. P. Walton. 1819.

    t.[1], [2–3], 4–30 p.; illus.; 10.5 cm.; pr. & illus. buff paper covers.
    MWA°; McCorison 2089; Shaw 47196.

BENNETT, MARY E.
70 THE COTTAGE GIRL; Or An Account Of Ann Edwards, A Sunday School Scholar. By the Author Of the Retrospect, Village Observer, &c. &c. Portland [Me.]: Published By William Hyde. A. Shirley, Printer. 1820.

    fr.[ii], t.[iii], [iv–v], vi, [7], 8–54 p.; front. only illus.; 14 cm.; pr. blue-gray paper covers.
    MWA°; CLU; MWA-W; PP; Shoemaker 394 and 877.

BERQUIN, ARNAUD 1749–1791
71.1 — THE CHILDREN'S FRIEND. Translated From The French Of M. Berquin. Vol. I. Boston: Printed By John W. Folsom, And Sold By Him, And Benjamin Larkin. [1790?].

    ½t.[i], [ii, bl.], t.[iii], [iv, bl.-ix], x–xii, [13], 14–361, [362, bl.], [i], ii–iii, [iv, bl.], [i], ii–iv p.; 17 cm.; bound in leather; p. 213, 214, 216, 232 wrongly numbered 113, 114, 116, 132. English ed. London: translated by the Rev. M. A. Meilan, 6 vols., T. Cadell & P. Elmsley, 1783–86.
    MWA°; MHi; MSaE; Bowe mss.; Evans 21676 (dated 1789) and 22344 (dated 1790).

71.2 —— —— Vol. I. [II.–IV.] Newburyport [Mass.]: Printed By John Mycall, For The Proprietor Of The Boston Book-Store, No 59, Corn-hill, Boston. [1790?].

vol. I.: ½t.[1], [2], t.[3], [4–7], 8–317, [318, bl.], [i], ii–iv, [v. adv.] p.; vol. II.: ½t.[1], [2], t.[3], [4–5], 6–287 p.; vol. III.: t.[3], [4–5], 6–276 p.; vol. IV.: ½t.[1], [2], t.[3], [4–5], 6–340, [341–343] p.; 4 vols.; 16–17 cm.; bound in leather.

MWA° (vol. I., II., IV.); DLC (vol. I., p. [5]–8, & iii–iv at end wanting); KU (vol. I.); MSaE; MShr (vol. I.–IV., vol. I. & III. ½t.[1] wanting); PP (vol. I., ½t.[1], p. 15–24 want-ing; vol. II., p. [1]–12, 15–22, 161–164, 253–256, 277–278, 287 wanting); RPB (vol. I.); Bowe mss.; Evans 25163.

71.3 ——— Vol. II. [III.] Newburyport [Mass.]: Printed By John Mycall, For William Blake, At The Boston Book-Store, No. 59, Corn-hill, Boston. [1790?].

vol. II.: t.[1], [2–3], 4–285, 1–2 p.; vol. III.: t.[1], [2–3], 4–274, [275–276] p.; 2 vols.; 17–17.5 cm.; bound in leather. The text of vol. II., no. 71.2 is identical with vol. II., no. 71.3 except for page numbers and signatures. The text of vol. II., no. 71.2 starts on p. [5], while that of no. 71.3 starts on p. [3]. Sig. [A] in both editions is in 6. In no. 71.3 sig. A₂ is printed "A₃". The text of p. 13 sig. B₁ in no. 71.2 is the same as p. 11 sig. [A₆], no. 71.3.

MWA° (vol. II., III.); MH (vol. II.); RPB (vol. II. III.); Bowe mss.; Evans 25163.

71.4 ——— Newburyport [Mass.]: Printed By J. Mycall, For Benjamin Larkin, Cornhill, Boston. [1793?].

vol. I.: t.[1], [2–3], 4–341, [342], [i], ii–iii p.; 16.5 cm. This is a different edition than no. **71.2**.

MH°; MWA-T; Bowe mss.

71.5 ——— Mr. Berquin. Newbury-Port [Mass.]: Printed and Sold by John Mycall; Sold also by Isaac Beers in New-Haven. [1794?].

t.[i], [ii–iii], iv–vi, [1], 2–354 p.; 16.5 cm.; bound in leather. The MBAt copy has on the page opposite the title, a holograph inscription: *Josiah Williams July 1789.*

MWA°; MBAt; MBSpnea; MSaE; NN (t.[i], cut away at the top affecting the first word *The*); PP; Bowe mss.; Evans 26643.

71.6 ——— M. Berquin. [Vol. I.] [II.] Printed At Boston; By Thomas Hall, State Street. 1795.

vol. I.: t.[1], [2–3], 4–274, [275–276] p.; vol. II.: t.[3], [4–5], 6–340, [341–343] p.; 2 vols.; 17 cm.; bound in olive paper over bds., leather spine. The text of vol. I., no. 71.6 has the same page numbering as vol. III., no. 71.3 and may be a remainder of 71.3 with a new title page. Evans considered vols. I. & II. of no. 71.6 a "clumsy attempt, by some dealer in remainders, to deceive." He wrongly ascribes them to be part of a remainder printed by "John W. Folsom, for E. Larkin Junior in Boston, in 1790", possibly no. 71.1. Vol. I. of 71.6 has the same type set up as vol. IV., no. 71.7 with the floral type ornaments above the caption p. [55] and the line below the page number "17" and other variations. These variations do not appear in vol. IV, no. 71.2 which presumably had a similar type set up to vol. IV., no 71.3 of which no copy has been located.

NN°; MSaE; Bowe mss.; Evans 28266.

71.7 ——— Vol. IV. Printed At Boston, By Thomas Hall, State Street, For William P. Blake, At The Boston Bookstore, No. 59, Cornhill. 1795. ½t.[1], [2], t.[3], [4–5], 6–340, [341–342, adv. list of books], [343, bl.], [344, adv. list of books], [345–347, contents] p.;17.5 cm. The adv. of books are inserted out of place. The commencement of the list is on p. 342 instead of 341 and p. [343], which should follow p. [342], is turned around so that it is [344]. The RPB copy has p. [341–343, contents], [344, bl.], [345–347, adv. list of books]. The type set up of vol. IV., no. 71.7 is identical with vol. IV., no. 71.2, and Vol. I., no. 71.6.

MWA°; RPB; Bowe mss.

71.8 ——— M. Berquin. Vol. I. From the latest London Edition. Middletown [Conn.]: Printed By T. & J. B. Dunning. 1801.

t.[i], [ii, bl.], [ii, adv.], [iii, bl.–iv], v–ix, [x, bl.–xi, contents], [1], 2–144 p.; 16.5 cm.; bound in blue-gray paper over w. bds.; p. 104 wrongly numbered "194," p. 106 wrongly numbered "107," & p. 107 wrongly numbered "106"; pref-ace dated Dec. 22, 1786.

Welch° (p.[1]–4, 12–14 mut.); CtHi; FTaSU; MWA; NNC; PP; Bowe mss.; Shaw 164.

72.1 — THE CHILDREN'S FRIEND, And Youth's Monitor. Consisting Of Tales And Stories, Equally Adapted For Instruction, And Entertainment. Translated From The French Of M. Berquin. [two lines quot.] Gay. Philadelphia: Printed By Johnson & Justice, At Franklin's Head, No. 41, Chestnut-Street. M.DCC.XCIII.

t.[i], [ii–iii], iv, [5], 6–160 p.; 17 cm.; bound in leather.

MWA°; DLC (p. 113–114, 159–160 mut.); MH; Bowe mss.; Evans 25164.

72.2 — ——— Philadelphia: Printed By Lang And Ustick, For Selves And C. Davis, New-York. 1796.

t.[1], [2-3], 4–179, [180, bl.], [181–184, adv. of books, for sale by W. M'Culloch] p.; 14 cm.; bound in leather.

MWA°; PU; Bowe mss.; Evans 30061.

72.3 — ——— Wilmington [Del.]: Printed By Joseph Johnson, In Market-Street, Opposite The Bank. 1796.

t.[1], [2-3], 2 [*sic. i.e.* 4], 5–108 p.; 15.5 cm.; bound in marbled paper over bds., leather spine; p. 93–96 wrongly numbered 92–95.

MWA°; Bowe mss.

72.4 — ——— New-Haven: Printed By George Bunce. M.DCC.XCVIII.

t.[1], [2-3], 4–143 p.; 14 cm.; bound in marbled paper over w. bds., leather spine; the "1" of no. "106" not struck.

MWA°; CtHi; Bowe mss.; Evans 48365.

72.5 — ——— [same as **72.4**] New-Haven: Printed By George Bunce, For C. Davis, New-York. M.DCC.XCVIII.

t.[1], [2-3], 4–143 p.; 13.5 cm.; bound in paper over w. bds.

MWA°

72.6 — ——— Philadelphia. Printed by David Hogan, No. 222. South Third street. 1799.

t.[3], [4–9], 10–120 p.; 12.5 cm.; bound in brown paper over w. bds.; p. 74 wrongly numbered "64."

MWA°; Bowe mss.; Evans 48800.

72.7 — ——— Elizabethtown [N.J.]: Printed By John Woods, For Evert Duyckinck, New-York. 1802.

t.[1], [2–3], 4–140, [141, has wallpaper pasted over most of the page including the page no.] p.; 13 cm.; w. bds., leather spine, binding covered over by wallpaper.

MWA° (p. 25–26 mostly wanting, p. 19–24 mut.); MWA-T; Bowe mss.; Shaw 2027.

73 — THE FAMILY BOOK, Or Children's Journal. Consisting of moral & Entertaining Stories, with instructive Conversations on those Subjects which daily occur in Nature & Society. From the French of M. Berquin. To serve as a Continuation to the Children's & Youth's Friend, of the same Author. I. [II.] Part [3 lines quot.] New Edition. Detroit [Mich.]. Printed by Theophilus Mettez. 1812.

pt. I.: ½t.[1], French t.[2], English t.[3], [4–5], 6–252 p.; pt. II: ½t.[1], French t.[2], English t.[3], [4–5], 6–232 p.; 2 vols. in 1; 18.5 cm.; pt. II., t.[3] line 4 has "M" in "Moral" in caps, a period after "Part.", line 10, and after "Mettez.", line 16; [4 line quot.] lines 11–14. There is a publisher's remainder of this book so that it is relatively common.

English ed. London: entitled ——— [same as above Detroit ed.] stories. From the French of M. Berquin. Interspersed with poetical pieces, written by the translator, Miss Stockdale. 1798. PP°; MWA; MiD; MiU; Bowe mss.; Shaw 24811.

BERQUIN, ARNAUD 1749–1791 [M. A. Meilan] *tr.*

74 — THE FRIEND OF YOUTH. Translated From The French Of M. Berquin; Complete In Two Volumes. Vol. I. [II.] Newburyport [Mass.]: Printed By John Mycall, For The Proprietor Of The Boston Bookstore, No. 59, Cornhill, Boston. [1789?].

vol. I.: t.[i], [ii–iii], iv–vii, [viii, bl.], [9], 10–336 p.; vol. II.: t.[i], [ii], iii, [iv, bl.], [5], 6–359 p.; 2 vols.; 17.5 cm.; bound in leather.

English ed. London: 2 vols. C. Dilly, J. Stockdale, T. and J. Egerton, and W. Creech, Edinburgh, 1788, front. dated Oct. 25th 1787.

MWA°; DLC; MSaE; NN (vol. I. dated [1800]); RP; ViU; Bowe mss.; Evans 45437.

75 [—] THE FRIEND OF YOUTH. Containing Jasper and Emilius, The Fickle Youth, The Peasant, his Country's Benefactor, The Lawsuit, Lost Time recovered, Punishment of Pride, The Increase of Family, The Humorous Engagement,

Little Grandison. Philadelphia: Printed By Budd And Bartram. For Benjamin & Jacob Johnson, No. 147, Market Street. 1796.

> t.[1], [2–3], 4–120 p.; 11.5 cm.; bound in ornamented brown paper over w. bds.
> MWA-W°; Evans 47722.

BERQUIN, ARNAUD 1749–1791 [Johnson, Richard], *comp.* 1734–1793

76.1 [—] THE LOOKING-GLASS FOR THE MIND; Or Intellectual Mirror. Being An Elegant Collection Of The Most Delightful Little Stories, And Interesting Tales, Chiefly translated from that much admired Work, L'Ami Des Enfans. A New Edition, Ornamented With Cuts. America: Printed At Providence (R. Island) By Carter And Wilkinson, And Sold At Their Book And Stationery Store, Opposite The Market. M,DCC,XCIV.

> fr.[ii], t.[i], [ii, bl.], [iii–viii], [1], 2–252 p.; illus.; 17.5 cm.; bound in leather; front. signed *S. Hill Boston.*
> Richard Johnson in his day book has this entry "*1787 March. Mr. Badcock*—[E. Newbery's agent] *To compiling The Looking Glass—18 Half Sheets—£ 18. 18 s.*"
> Whether Johnson did translate and adapt this work from Berquin's *L'Ami des Enfans* (1782–3) is uncertain; his was not the first English version, so perhaps this also was partly borrowed from his predecessors . . . This work was ascribed to the Rev. Mr. Cooper in the list on *The Oriental Moralist* (1791/2). (Weedon 1949).
> English ed. London: E. Newbery, 1787.
> MWA°; DLC (2 copies, copy 2 rebound); NjP (rebound); NcD; RHi; RPB; Bowe mss.; Evans 26645; Hamilton 152.

76.2 [—] ———— A New Edition, With Thirty-Six Cuts, Elegantly Engraved. New-York: Printed By W. Durell, No. 208, Pearl-Street, Near The Fly-Market. M,DCC,XCV.

> fr.[ii], t.[i], [ii–iv], [1], 2–259 p.; illus.; 17 cm.; front. engr. signed *Rollinson fc.*, 36 woodcuts by Alexander Anderson. The woodcut illus. are copies in reverse of those by John Bewick in the English ed. London: E. Newbery, 1794.
> MWA° (fr.[ii], wanting, p. [1]–10, 243–250 and other pages mut.); NjP (sig N (p. 133–144) is repeated, p. 259 wanting); Hamilton 210.

76.3 [—] ———— New-York. Printed By W. Durell, For Robert M'Gill, Book-Seller, No. 105, Maiden-Lane. M,DCC,XCV.

> Same as no. **76.2**, but with a varying imprint. RPJCB°; Bowe mss.

76.4 [—] ———— New-York: Printed By W. Durell, For Edward Mitchell, Book-Seller, No. 9, Maiden-Lane. M,DCC,XCV.

> Same as no. **76.2**, but with a varying imprint. NN°; NjP; Hamilton 210.

76.5 [—] Youth's Library. Vol. I. THE LOOKING GLASS—Ornamented With Seventy-Five Wood Cuts. New-York, Printed and Published By D. Longworth. At the Shakespeare Gallery. MDCCC.

> t.[3], [4–7], 8–255 p.; illus.; 17.5 cm.; bound in leather.
> NN° (i. st. on t.[3], t.[3] mut. and crudely repaired, p. [5–6] mut.); NHi; Bowe mss.; Evans 36947.

76.6 [—] ———— [same as **76.1**] L'Ami Des Enfans. With elegant Engravings on Wood, By Anderson. New-York: Printed For S. Campbell, E. Duyckinck, J. Tiebout, G. & R. Waite, D. Smith, S. Stephens, J. Ronalds, J. C Totten. L. Nichols, printer. 1804.

> t.[i], [ii–iv], [1], 2–203 p.; illus.; 18 cm.; bound in leather; illus. by Alexander Anderson. Illus. p. 6, 12, 29, 98 signed *A.* Most of the illus. are copies in the reverse of those by John Bewick in the English ed. London: E. Newbery, 1794. The illus. are redrawn although similar to no. **76.3**.
> MWA-W°; Shaw 50411.

76.7 [—] ———— [same as **76.6**] New-York: Printed for Evert Duyckinck. Bookseller & Stationer, By L. Nichols. 1804.

> Same as no. **76.6** but with a varying imprint. CtY°; Shaw 5840.

76.8 [—] ———— New York: Printed For Campbell And Mitchell, Book-Sellers & Stationers, 124 Pearl-Street. M'Farlane and Long, print. 1807.

> t.[i], [ii–iii], iv, [1], 2–203 p.; illus.; 17.5 cm. NNNAM; Shaw 50758.

76.9 [—] ———— New-York: Printed For Evert Duyckinck, Bookseller & Stationer. M'Farlane and Long, Printers. 1807.

t.[i], [ii–iii], iv, [1], 2–203 p.; illus.; 18 cm.; bound in leather. Woodcut illus. by Alexander Anderson.

NNC-LS°; NjP (orig. covers wanting); NN rebound pp. [i–ii], 73–74 mut.); Bowe mss.; Hamilton 237; Shaw 12112.

76.10 [—] ——— New-York: Printed By M'Farlane And Long, No. 308 Broadway. 1807.

t.[i], [ii–iii], iv, [1], 2–203 p.; illus.; 18 cm.; bound in leather. Some of the wood cut illus. by Alexander Anderson are the same as those in no. **76.6**.

DLC°; Shaw 50759.

76.11 [—] ——— New-York: Printed By George Long, For R. Johnston, No. 33 Maiden-Lane. 1810.

t.[i], [ii–iii], iv, [1], 2–203 p.; illus.; 17.5 cm.

Bowe°, Bowe mss.; Shaw 50979.

76.12 [—] ——— New-York: Published By Evert Duyckinck, No. 102 Pearl-Street. G. Long, Printer. 1815.

t.[i], [ii–iii], iv, [1], 2–203 p.; illus. 18.5 cm.; bound in leather.

MWA-T°.

76.13 [—] ——— New York: Published By William B. Gilley, No. 92 Broadway. G. Long, Printer. 1815.

t.[i], [ii–iii], iv, [1], 2–203 p.; illus.; 18.5 cm.; the illus. at the beginning of each chapter are signed *A* [Alexander Anderson] and the same as those used in no. **76.6**. The tailpieces however are different than no. **76.6**.

MBAt (12 p. adv. list of books following p. 203; rebound); MWA-T; Shaw 33863, 35132 and 51465.

76.14 [—] ——— New-York: Printed And Published By George Long, No. 71 Pearl-Street. 1815.

t.[i], [ii–iii], iv, [1], 2–203 p.; illus.; 18 cm.; bound in leather. Woodcuts by Alexander Anderson.

MWA°; DLC; MSaE; Shaw 34048.

76.15 [—] ——— New-York: Printed And Published By George Long, No. 71 Pearl-Street. 1816.

t.[i], [ii–iii], iv, [1], 2–203 p.; illus.; t.[i] 18 cm.; woodcut illus. by Alexander Anderson.

MWA° (rebound); Bowe mss.; Shaw 36935 and 38093.

76.16 [—] ——— New-York: Published By Evert Duyckinck, No. 68 Water-Street. 1818.

t.[i], [ii–iii], iv, [1], 2–203 p.; illus.; 18 cm.; some of the woodcut illus. by A. Anderson are the same as those in no. **76.6**.

DLC°; Bowe mss.; Shaw 43289 and 44611.

76.17 [—] ——— Tenth New-York Edition. New-York: Printed And Published By George Long, No 71, Pearl-Street. 1819.

t.[i], [ii–iii], iv, [1], 2–203 p.; 18.5 cm.; bound in leather.

OCIW-LS°; N (top of t. p. mut. with the first word "The" wanting); NBuG; Shaw 51859.

76.18 [—] ——— Tenth New-York Edition. New-York: Printed And Published By G. Long, No 71, Pearl-Street. 1820.

t.[i], [ii–iii], iv, [1], 2–203 p.; illus.; 18.5 cm.

NN° (rebound); MH; MWA-T; Bowe mss.; Shoemaker 400.

77.1 [—] THE LOOKING-GLASS FOR THE MIND, Or The Juvenile Friend; Being A Valuable Collection Of Interesting And Miscellaneous Incidents, Calculated To Exhibit To Young Minds The Happy Effects Of Youthful Innocence and Filial Affection. In Prose And Verse. Designed To Improve And Amuse The Rising Generation. Reading Improves The Mind [last 4 words in a vignette]. Embellished With An Elegant Frontispiece And Seventy-Three Cuts. Philadelphia: Printed for John Ormrod, No. 41, Chestnut-street, By Ormrod & Conrad. 1798.

fr.[ii], t.[i], [ii–iv], [1], 2–271, [272, adv.] p.; illus.; 16.5 cm.; bound in leather; frontispiece signed *Thackara* [James Thackara 1767–1848 engraver], woodcut illus. drawn in the reverse of the Anderson ones in no. **76.2**.

MWA° (p. iii–iv), 235–236 torn in half, [1]–2 mut.); PHi (fr. [ii], & other p. wanting, other p. mut.); PP; PPL; Bowe mss.

77.2 [—] ——— Philadelphia: Printed And Sold By John Bioren, No. 88, Chestnut-Street. 1803.

fr.[ii], t.[i], [ii–iv], [1], 2–271, [272, adv.] p.; illus.; t.[i]; 16.5 cm.; front unsigned and different than **77.1**, illus. p. [1] same as **77.2**.

NIC° (bound in tree calf with a red label); Shaw 50335.

77.3 [—] —— Philadelphia: Printed And Sold By John Bioren, No. 88, Chestnut-Street. 1805.
fr.[ii], t.[i], [ii–iv], [1], 2–271, [272, adv.] p.; illus.; t.[i] 16.5 cm.; front. signed *Thackara Sc.,* illus. same as no. **77.1.**
NN° (rebound); PPL; Shaw 7977 and 8799.

77.4 [—] —— Philadelphia, Printed and Sold by John Bioren, No. 88 Chestnut street. 1810.
fr.[ii], t.[i], [ii–iii], iv, [1], 2–271, [272] p.; illus.; 17.5 cm.; bound in leather; front. signed *Thackara.*; illus. same as no. **77.1.**
MWA° (t.[i], p.[ii–iv mut., [1]–6 torn); MSaE; OOxM; PP; RPB; Bowe mss.; Shaw 19508, 19856 and 20589.

77.5 [—] —— Philadelphia: Printed and sold by J. Bioren, No. 88, Chestnut-street. 1813.
fr.[ii], t.[i], [ii–iii], iv, [1], 2–271, [272, adv.] p.; illus.; 17 cm.; bound in leather; illus. same as no. **77.1.**
MWA° (fr.[ii], p. 19–20, 241–244 wanting); PPL; Bowe mss.; Shaw 27878.

77.6 [—] —— Philadelphia: Printed And Sold By John Bioren, No. 88, Chestnut-street. 1815.
fr.[ii], t.[i], [ii–iii], iv, [1], 2–271, [272, adv.] p.; illus.; 18 cm; leather.
CSmH; MH (fr.[ii] wanting); PP; Shaw 34440 and 51466.

77.8 [—] —— Philadelphia: Printed And Published By John Bioren, No. 88, Chestnut Street. 1819.
fr.[ii], t.[i], [ii–iii], iv, [1], 2–271, [272] p.; illus.; 18 cm.; bound in leather; illus. same as no. **77.1.**
MWA° (fr.[ii] wanting); CLU; DLC (fr.[ii] wanting); MB (emb. st. on t.[i]); PP; PSC; Bowe mss.; Shaw 47205.

BERQUIN, ARNAUD 1749–1791
Selections from *The Children's Friend* or adaptations from R. Johnson's version in *The Looking Glass For The Mind* or *Blossoms of Morality.*

78 — Amusing Tales, For Little Children. From the French of M. Berquin. Containing, The

Rose-Bush, The Four Seasons—and The Bird's Nest. Printed and sold by W. & J. Gilman, Newburyport [Mass.]. [*ca.* 1805].
t.[1], [2–3], 4–16 p.; 10.5 cm.; pr. & illus. buff paper covers. Colophon p. 16: The various branches of Letter-Press Printing executed with neatness, By W. & J. Gilman, West end of Middle-Street, Newburyport, Mass. This book was advertised by W. & J. Gilman in *The Graduate in Vice.* Newburyport. 1805. The first story is reprinted from Berquin's *The Children's Friend,* no. **77.1.** The second, "The Four Seasons," is adapted from *The Children's Friend.* "The Bird's Nest" is a poem.
MNe°; NNC-T; Shaw 50500.

79.1 [—] Biography For Boys, Or Interesting Stories For Children. From Sidney's Press, New-Haven. 1808.
fr.[ii], t.[1], [2–3, bl.], 4–63 p.; illus.; 10.5 cm.; pr. & illus. paper covers. All but the last story, "Filial Duty Rewarded," are reprinted from Berquin's *The Looking Glass For The Mind,* no. **76.1.**
MSaE° (p. 63 and rear cover wanting); NhD (fr.[ii], p. 63 & covers wanting); Shaw 50830.

79.2 [—] —— From Sidney's Press, New-Haven. 1809.
fr.[ii], t.[1], [2–3], 4–36 p.; illus.; 13.5 cm.; pr. & illus. buff paper covers.
CtHi°; MB (per. st. on t.[1]); MHi; Shaw 50914.

79.3 [—] —— From Sidney's Press, For I. Cooke & Co. New-Haven. 1812.
fr.[2], t.[3], [4–5], 6–47 p.; illus.; 11 cm. pr. & illus. purple paper covers.
MWA°; Shaw 51160.

79.4 [—] —— From Sidney's Press, For I. Cooke & Co. New-Haven. 1813.
fr.[2], t.[3], [4–5], 6–47 p.; illus.; 11 cm. pr. & illus. buff-yellow paper covers.
MWA-W°; Shaw 51271.

80.1 [—] Biography For Girls, Or Pleasing Stories For Children. From Sidney's Press, New-Haven. 1808.
fr.[ii], t.[1], [2–3], 4–63 p.; illus.; 10.5 cm.; yellow paper covers. Reprinted from Berquin's

The Looking Glass For The Mind, no. **76.1.**
MWA°; CtY (illus. paper covers, rear paper cover mostly wanting, front cover wanting); Shaw 50851.

80.2 [—] ——— From Sidney's Press, New-Haven. 1809.
fr.[ii], t.[1], [2–3], 4–34 p.; illus.; 13.5 cm.; pr. & illus. paper covers; cover title imprint: Published by I. Cooke & Co. New-Haven. [4 lines].
CtHi°; MSaE (2 copies with varying front.); Shaw 50915 and 50916.

80.3 [—] BIOGRAPHY FOR GIRLS, Or, Stories For Children. From Sidney's Press, For I. Cooke & Co. New-Haven. 1812.
fr.[2], t.[3], [4–5], 6–47 p.; illus.; 11 cm.; pr. & illus. yellowish-buff paper covers.
MWA°; MNF; Shaw 51161.

80.4 —— ——— Girls. Philadelphia: adv. by Johnson & Warner, 1814 in **1322.2.**

81 [—] THE BIRD'S EGG, An Instructive Story. Ornamented With Cuts. First Windsor Edition. Printed At Windsor [Vt.]: By Farnsworth & Churchill. 1810.
fr.[2], t.[3], [4–7], 8–28, [29, adv.], [30–31, illus.] p.; illus.; 9.5 cm.; pr. & illus. buff paper covers. Reprinted from Berquin's *The Looking Glass For The Mind,* no. **76.1.** The lower cut p.[30] is printed upside down.
MWA-W°; CtHi; MWHi; NB (i. st. on t.[3]); VtHi; McCorison 1151; Shaw 19570.

82 [—] CAROLINE, Or, A Lesson To Cure Vanity. Also, The Young Gardener's Gift, And The Fable Of The Mouse. Adorned with Cuts. New-Haven. Sidney's Press. For John Babcock & Son. 1819.
fr.[2], t.[3], [4–5], 6–30, [31, adv.] p.; 10.5 cm.; illus. buff paper covers; pr. in green ink. Reprinted from Berquin's *The Looking Glass For The Mind,* no. **76.1.**
See also The History Of Caroline, no. **87.1.**
NN° (i. st. p. 30); Shaw 51858.

83.1 [—] CECILIA AND MARIAN, Or, The New Entertainer. Consisting Of Select Conversations On The Means Of Doing Good. By A Young

Lady. New-Haven: Printed By William W. Morse. 1802.
t.[3], [4–5], 6–30 p.; illus.; 10.5 cm.; green & gold Dutch paper covers. Reprinted from Berquin's *The Children's Friend,* no. **71.1.**
MWA°; Shaw 50274.

83.2 [—] ——— Hartford: Printed by Charles Hosmer. 1815.
fr.[2], t.[3], [4–5], 6–31 p.; 10 cm.
MWA° (fr.[2], & p. 31 & covers wanting, p. 29–30 mut.); Ct° (i. st. on front cover, pr. & illus. buff paper covers); Bowe mss.; Shaw 34305.

84 [—] THE GRADUATE IN VICE: Or, History Of Pascal. [4 lines quot.] Newburyport [Mass.], From the Press of W. & J. Gilman, Sold at their Office, No. 4, Middle-Street. 1805.
t.[1], [2–5], 6–31, [32, adv.] p.; illus.; 11 cm.; blue-gray paper covers. The MWA copy has a preliminary page with 2 illus. (one of a horse, the other of a bird) pasted to the inside of the front cover, followed by a blank leaf, then t.[1]. These illus. are not in other copies. Reprinted from Berquin's *The Children's Friend,* no. **71.1.**
MWA° (p. 31–[32] wanting, pr. & illus. buff paper covers); MSaE; Shaw 7976.

85 [—] THE HAPPY VILLAGER; A Moral Tale. Adorned with Cuts. New-Haven: For J. Babcock & Son. Sidney's Press. 1820.
fr.[2], t.[3], [4–5], 6–30, [31, adv.] p.; illus.; 10.5 cm.; pr. & illus. buff paper covers. Reprinted from R. Johnson's *Blossom's Of Morality,* no. **669.1** adapted from Berquin's "The Peasant, his Country's Benefactor," published in *The Friend Of Youth,* no. **75.**
MWA-W°; CtHi; CtY (covers wanting); MWA; Bowe mss.; Shoemaker 399.

86.1 [—] THE HISTORY OF BERTRAND, A Poor Laborer, And His Little Family. Montpelier [Vt.]: Published by Wright & Sibley. 1812.
t.[1], [2–3], 4–14 p.; 10 cm.; buff paper covers. Reprinted from Berquin's *The Looking Glass For The Mind,* no. **76.1.**
VtHi°; MWA (covers wanting, bound with *The History of Cleopatra,* no. **88**; Bowe mss.; McCorison 1364; Shaw 24812.

86.2 [—] —— Montpelier [Vt.]: Published by E. P. Walton. 1818.

t.[1], [2–3], 4–32 p.; illus.; 10.5 cm.; pr. & illus. brownish-buff paper covers.

PP°; Bowe mss.; Shaw 43287.

87.1 [—] THE HISTORY OF CAROLINE; Or, A Lesson To Cure Vanity. Adorned With Cuts. Sidney's Press. New-Haven. 1817.

fr.[2], t.[3], [4–5], 6–30, [31, adv.] p.; illus.; 10.5 cm.; pink Dutch paper covers. Reprinted from Berquin's *The Looking Glass For The Mind*, no. **76.1**.

MWA-W°; CtHi (covers wanting); CtY (covers, fr.[2], & p.[31] wanting); PP (fr.[2], p.[31], & covers wanting); Bowe mss.; Shaw 40188 and 41050.

87.2 [—] —— Sidney's Press. New-Haven, 1818.

fr.[2], t.[3], [4–5], 6–30, [31, adv.] p.; illus.; 10.5 cm.; illus. white paper covers printed in green ink.

MWA-W°; CtY (covers poor, rest of book foxed but complete); Bowe mss.; Shaw 43288.

88 [—] THE HISTORY OF CLEOPATRA. [caption title] [Montpelier [Vt.]: Published by Wright and Sibley. 1812.] [imprint taken from *The History Of Bertrand*, no. **86.1**].

[3], 4–16 p.; 10 cm.

MWA° (t.[1], p.[2] wanting except for a fragment with the letter *P* on it, all that remains of the word *Published;* bound with *The History Of Bertrand*, no. **86.1**); Shaw 24813.

89.1 [—] THE MOUNTAIN LUTE, Or, The Happy Discovery. Ornamented With Cuts. Litchfield [Conn.]: Printed By Hosmer & Goodwin. 1808.

fr.[2], t.[3], [4–5], 6–31 p.; illus.; 10 cm; orange Dutch paper covers. A version adapted from Berquin's "The Mountain Piper" published in *The Children's Friend*, no. **71.1**.

MWA°; Ct (p.[2] & 31 wanting); CtHi; CtY (p. 29–31, & rear cover wanting); PP (p. 29–30 mut.); Bowe mss.; Shaw 15666.

89.2 [—] —— Hartford: Printed By Hale & Hosmer. 1812.

fr.[2], t.[3], [4–5], 6–31 p.; illus.; 9.5 cm.; pr. & illus. buff paper covers; cover title dated 1813.

MWA-W°; CLU; CtHi; DLC; PP (front cover mut.); Bowe mss.; Shaw 26148.

89.3 [—] —— Adorned with Cuts. Hartford: Printed by Hale & Hosmer. 1814.

fr.[2], t.[3], [4–5], 6–31 p.; illus.; 10 cm.; pr. & illus. buff paper covers.

MWA-W°; CtHi (cover wanting); Bowe mss.; Shaw 30853.

89.4 [—] —— Ornamented With Cuts. Hartford: Printed by Sheldon & Goodwin. < Stereotyped by J. F. & G. Starr. > [1815].

fr.[2], t.[3], [4–5], 6–31 p.; illus.; 10 cm.; pr. & illus. buff paper covers.

Welch°; CtHi; MWA; PP; Bowe mss.; Shaw 35336.

89.5 [—] —— Ornamented With Cuts. Hartford: Published by J. & W. Russell. [1818?].

fr.[2], t.[3], [4–5], 6–31 p.; illus.; 10 cm.; pr. & illus. paper covers.

CtY°; Bowe mss.; Shaw 51467.

90.1 [—] THE MOUNTAIN PIPER; Or, The History Of Edgar And Matilda. To Which Is Added, A Journey To London, A Moral Tale. The First Worcester Edition. Printed at Worcester, Massachusetts, By Isaiah Thomas, And Sold, Wholesale and Retail, at his Book-store. MDCCXCIV.

fr.[2], t.[3], [4–7], 8–96 p.; illus.; 10.5 cm.; green Dutch paper covers. Recorded by Richard Johnson " *1787 June 22, Mr. Badcock* [E. Newbery's agent.]—*to writing The Mountain Piper. £3. 3s.*" Johnson's day-books nowhere mention *A Journey To London* but *The Mountain Piper* alone is hardly long enough to be valued at £3. 3s. . . . (Weedon, 1949). Johnson obtained the story from Berquin's "The Mountain Piper" in *The Children's Friend* translated by M. A. Meilan and published in London 1783–84.

English ed. adv. in the *London Chronicle Dec. 27–29, 1787*.

MWA° (fr.[2], t.[3] mut., back cover wanting).

90.2 [—] —— Matilda. Embellished with Cuts. Hartford: Printed By J. Babcock. 1796.

fr.[2], t.[3], [4–5], 6–31 p.; illus.; 10.5 cm.; green Dutch paper covers.

MWA°; CtHi; RPJCB; Bowe mss.; Evans 30831.

90.3 [—] ——— Hartford: Printed By John Babcock. 1798.
fr.[2], t.[3], [4–5], 6–29, [30, adv.–31, illus.] p.; illus.; 11 cm.; Dutch paper covers.
MWA°.

90.4 [—] ——— The First Newport Edition. Newport [R.I.]: Printed by H. & O. Farnsworth. 1799.
fr.[2], t.[3], [4–5], 6–30, [31, adv.] p.; illus.; 11.5 cm.; Dutch paper covers.
MWA°.

90.5 [—] ——— Matilda. To Which Is Added, The History of Charles Stockwell. Second Worcester Edition. Printed At Worcester, By Isaiah Thomas, Jun. Sold Wholesale and Retail by him July—1802.
fr.[2], t.[3], [4–7], 8–63 p.; illus.; 10 cm.; green Dutch paper covers.
MWA° (fr.[2] and front cover wanting, p. 55–56 mut.); CtHi (p. 57–63 mut.); PP; Shaw 2705.

90.6 [—] ——— Matilda. First Windsor Edition. Windsor, (Vt.) Printed by Farnsworth & Churchill. 1810.
fr.[2], t.[3], [4–5], 6–30, [31, alphabet] p.; illus.; 9 cm.; pr. & illus. paper covers.
MWA°; MH; McCorison 1152; Shaw 20795.

90.7 [—] THE MOUNTAIN PIPER, OR ADVENTURES OF AUVERNGE [sic]. Adorned With Cuts. Sidney's Press. New Haven. 1813.
fr.[2], t.[3], [4–5], 6–31 p.; illus.; 10 cm.; pr. & illus. brown paper covers.
MWA°; Bowe mss.; Shaw 29231.

90.8 [—] ——— Windsor, (Vt.) Printed by Jesse Cochran. And Sold Wholesale and retail at his Book-store. 1814.
fr.[2], t.[3], [4–5], 6–31 p.; illus.; 10 cm.; pr. & illus. buff paper covers.
MWA° (p. 11–12 mut.); VtHi (covers mut.); McCorison 1586; Shaw 30854.

90.9 [—] ——— Windsor, (Vt.) Printed By Jesse Cochran, 1815.

fr.[2], t.[3], [4–5], 6–29 p.; illus.; 10.5 cm.; pr. & illus. buff paper covers.
MWA°; VtHi (t.[3] mut.); McCorison 1712; Shaw 34049.

90.10 [—] THE MOUNTAIN PIPER. Woodstock [Vt.]: Printed By David Watson: 1818.
fr.[2], t.[3], [4–5], 6–31 p.; illus.; 9.5 cm.; pr. & illus. buff paper wrappers; cover date 1819.
MWA°; VtHi; McCorison 1999; Shaw 44915.

90.11 [—] ——— Woodstock [Vt.]: Printed By David Watson: 1820.
fr.[2], t.[3], [4–5], 6–31 p.; illus.; 10 cm.; pr. & illus. buff paper covers.
VtHi°; McCorison 2188; Shoemaker 401.

91.1 [—] THE PEASANT'S REPAST: Or, The Benevolent Physician. Embellished With Three Copper-Plate Engravings. Philadelphia: Published by Jacob Johnson, No. 147, Market-Street. 1808.
fr.[ii], t.[1], [2–3], 4–36 p.; 3 pl. including front.; 13.5 cm.; pr. & illus. blue-gray paper covers; cover title undated; p.[2]: Adams, Printer, Philadelphia. Adapted from Berquin's "The Story of Bertrand" in *The Looking Glass For The Mind*, no. **76.1**, which may have been rewritten from "Arthur" in *The Children's Friend*, no. **71.1**.
English ed. London: J. Harris, pl. dated Dec^r., 1804.
MWA° (upper half of p. 35–36 wanting, fr.[ii]; p. 33–34 & covers torn); MH; PP; Bowe mss.; Shaw 14482 and 15858.

91.2 [—] ——— Physician. New-Market [Va.]: Printed: by Ambrose Henkel and Comp. Shenandoah County, Va. 1811.
t.[1], [2–3], 4–32 p.; illus.; 11.5 cm.; marbled paper covers.
MWA° (covers worn); Shaw 23645.

92 [—] SIR JOHN DENHAM, And His Worthy Tenant. With A Mirror. Adorned With Cuts. Sidney's Press. New-Haven. 1817.
fr.[2], t.[3], [4–5], 6–30, [31, adv.] p.; 10 cm.; illus. yellow-buff paper covers. Reprinted from Berquin's *The Looking Glass For The Mind*, no. **76.1**.
MWA°; CLU; CtHi; CtY; NB (bpl. on t.[3]); Shaw 42120.

93 [—] The Two Apple-Trees, And The Two Boys: Also, The History Of Little Emma. Adorned with Cuts. New-Haven. Sidney's Press. For J. Babcock & Son. 1819.

  fr.[2], t.[3], [4–5], 6–30, [31, adv.] p.; illus.; 11 cm.; illus. white paper covers pr. in green ink. Reprinted from Berquin's *The Children's Friend*, no. 71.1.

  MWA°; CtHi (fr.[2], p.[31], & covers wanting); CtY (t.[3] torn); NNC-T; PP; Shaw 49654.

Betty Brown, The St. Giles Orange Girl. *See* More, Hannah, no. 879.

BEWICK, THOMAS 1753–1828
94 — A History, And Description Of Water Birds; Consisting chiefly of the most rare and singular kinds; with accurate drawings and engravings of each; copied precisely from Bewick's celebrated Birds. Weathersfield, Vt. Printed And Sold By Eddy And Patrick. 1815.

  t.[1], [2], 3–24 p.; illus.; 15.5 cm.; pr. & illus. blue-gray paper covers.

  MWA°; CSmH; DLC (covers wanting); NN; VtHi; McCorison 1713; Shaw 34051.

BIBLE—All excerpts, abbreviations and stories taken from the Bible are listed by title. Miniature or Thumb Bibles under 7.5 cm. are put under Miniature Bibles. The *Verbum Sempiternum* of John Taylor is listed under the author's name. *A Short History of The Bible And Testament* is put under Mills, Alfred.

95 Bible Atlas [engraving] [2 lines quot.] New-Haven: Published By N. & S. S. Joceyln. 1819. Copy-Right Secured.

  t.[1], [2–10, col. pl.], [11–12, Explanations.] p. engr. or pr. on one side only of 12 leaves; 13 cm.; pr. green or tan paper covers; title and 9 pl. engr. & col.

  Cover title: Bible Atlas; Consisting Of Nine Maps, With Explanations: Illustrative Of Scripture History. Designed For The Use of Children and Youth. Price, 37½ Cents. New-Haven: Published By N. & S. S. Jocelyn. 1819.

  MWA° (2 copies); CtHi; PP; Shaw 47348 and 47349.

Bible History. *See* no. 856.1.

96 The Bible In Miniature; Or, A Concise History Of The Old And New Testaments. Burlington, Vt. Printed By S. Mills. 1814.

  t.[1], [2–3], 4–64 p.; 10.5 cm.; blue paper covers. The form of the book is not that of a miniature Bible. *See* no. 857 for miniature Bibles with this title.

  VtHi°; McCorison 1587; Shaw 30856.

Bible Stories. *See* Scolfield, William, no. 1167.1.

97 Bible Stories With Suitable Pictures. Hartford: Oliver D. Cooke. 1820.

  t.[1], [2], 3–16 p.; illus.; 10.5 cm.; pr. & illus. green paper covers.

  Welch°; CtHi; CtY (illus. white paper covers pr. in blue ink; t.[1], p.[2], & covers mut.); MWA; Shoemaker 457.

98.1 The Big Puzzling-Cap: A Choice Collection Of Riddles, In Familiar Verse; With A Curious Cut To Each. The First Worcester Edition. Worcester (Massachusetts), Printed By Isaiah Thomas, And Sold At His Book-Store. MDCC-LXXXVI.

  fr.[2], t.[3], [4–7], 8–90, [91–92, adv. of books] p.; illus.; 10 cm.; green Dutch paper covers. *Mother Goose's Melody* adv. on p. [91].

  MWA° (rear cover wanting, and possibly 2 leaves, sig. F⁷, F⁸ or p. 93–95); Evans 45434.

98.2 ———— Boston: adv. by S. Hall, 1791 in 408.3, 1792 in 673.3, and 1794 in 673.8. Evans 25193 lists an S. Hall 1793 edition probably obtained from an advertisement.

BINGHAM, CALEB 1757–1817
99 [—] The Hunters, Or The Sufferings Of Hugh and Francis, In The Wilderness. A True Story. Boston: Printed By Samuel T. Armstrong, For Caleb Bingham, No. 44, Cornhill, 1814.

  fr.[ii], t.[iii], [iv–v], vi, [7], 8–34 p.; illus.; 14 cm.;

  MHi°; MH; Shaw 31774.

100.1 — Juvenile Letters; Being A Correspondence, Between Children, From Eight To Fifteen Years Of Age. By Caleb Bingham, A.M. Author of the Child's Companion, Young Lady's Accidence, American Preceptor, &c. Published According To Act Of Congress. Boston: Printed

By David Carlisle, For Caleb Bingham, No. 44, Cornhill. 1803.

    t.[i], [ii–iii], iv, [5], 6–108 p.; 14 cm.; Dutch paper over w. bds.

    MWA°; BM; CtHi (covers wanting); PP; Shaw 3830.

100.2 —––––– Second Edition. < Published according to Act of Congress. > Boston: Printed By David Carlisle, For Caleb Bingham, No. 44, Cornhill. 1803.

    t.[1], [2–3], 4–108 p.; 14 cm.; marbled paper over w. bds., leather spine.

    MWA°; BM; DLC; MSaE; NHi; OCIWHi (front cover ½ wanting); PP (rebound); PPL; MnU; Shaw 3831.

100.3 —––––– Third Edition. < Published according to Act of Congress. > Boston: Printed By David Carlisle, For Caleb Bingham, No. 44, Cornhill. 1805.

    t.[1], [2–3], 4–108 p.; 14 cm.; pink Dutch paper over w. bds.

    MWA°; BM; CLU; CtY; MH; Shaw 8034.

100.4 —––––– Fourth Edition. < Published according to Act of Congress. > Boston: Printed By David Carlisle, For Caleb Bingham. No. 44, Cornhill. 1807.

    t.[1], [2–3], 4–108 p.; 14 cm.; green Dutch paper over w. bds.; p. 35 not numbered.

    MWA°; Shaw 12153.

100.5 —––––– Fifth Edition. Boston: < Published according to Act of Congress. > Printed By Lincoln & Edmands For Caleb Bingham, No. 44, Cornhill. 1809.

    t.[1], [2–3], 4–108 p.; 13 cm.

    MSaE°; DLC; MWA-T; Shaw 17042.

100.6 —––––– Preceptor, &c. First Western, From the Second Boston Edition. < Published according to Act of Congress. > Cincinnati: Printed by Mason and Palmer, For Cornelius Wing. 1819.

    t.[1], [2–3], 4–80 p.; 13.5 cm.; bound in blue-gray paper over bds., cloth spine.

    OCIWHi°; Shaw 47361.

BIOGRAPHY FOR BOYS. *See* Berquin, A., no. **79.1**.

BIOGRAPHY FOR GIRLS. See Berquin, A., no. **80.1**.

BIOGRAPHY OF EMINENT PERSONS. *See* Mills, Alfred, no. **846**.

101.1 A BIRTHDAY PRESENT; Or A New Year's Gift. Being Nine Day's Conversation Between A Mother And Daughter, On Interesting Subjects: For The Use Of Young Persons, From Ten to Fifteen Years Of Age. First American, from the fourth London Edition. Boston: Printed By David Carlisle, For Caleb Bingham, No. 44, Cornhill. 1803.

    t.[i], [ii–iv], [1], 2–104 p.; 14.5 cm.; bound in leather. The editor of this edition was probably Caleb Bingham as the book was printed for him and the preface is dated Boston Jan. 1, 1803. (MWA. cat.).

    English ed. 1788.

    MWA°; MB; ICU; MH; MSaE; NNC-T; OOxM; PP (rear cover mostly wanting); Shaw 5078.

101.2 —––––– Second American Edition. Hartford: Printed By Lincoln & Gleason. 1804.

    t.[1], [2–5], 6–106, [107] p.; 12.5 cm.; gray paper over w. bds., leather spine.

    MWA°; CtHi (front cover wanting); Shaw 5879.

101.3 —––––– Second American, from the fourth London Edition. Boston: Printed By David Carlisle, For John West, No. 75, Cornhill. 1805.

    t.[i], [ii–iv], [1], 2–104 p.; 15 cm.; Dutch paper over w. bds.

    MWA°; MH; MSaE; NcD; NNC-LS; Shaw 8030 and 8036.

101.4 —––––– Third American, from the last London Edition. Boston: Printed And Published By E. G. House, No. 100, Court-street. 1814.

    t.[i], [ii–iv], [1], 2–102, [103] p.; 14 cm.; pr. light-violet paper covers.

    OOxM°; MSaE (covers wanting); KU (2 copies, copy 2 has a semicolon after *E. G. House*; in the imprint); Shaw 30924.

BLACK GILES THE POACHER. See Cheap Repository, no. **169.11, 169.12**, and Hannah More, no. **882.1**.

THE BLACK PRINCE. *See* Cheap Repository, no. **169.28**, and Hannah More, no. **880**.

102.1 THE BLACK PRINCE; A True Story: Being An Account Of The Life And Death Of Naimbanna, An African King's Son, Who arrived in England in the year 1791, and set sail on his return in June, 1793. Philadelphia: Printed For Benjamin Johnson, No. 22, North Second street, next door to the church. 1813.

t.[1], [2–3], 4–23, [24, adv. list of books] p.; 13.5 cm.; green paper covers.
MWA°; Shaw 27956.

102.2 ——— Story. [caption p. [3]] [Philadelphia: Published by Benjamin Johnson, No. 31, Market-st. 1818.] [imprint from **902.3**, Sarah More's *Sorrowful Sam*].

[2, illus.], [3], 4–24 p.; one illus. only; 14 cm. The book was originally bound with no. **902.3**, Sara More's *Sorrowful Sam,* another Cheap Repository Tract. The illustrations in **102.2** and **902.3** look as if they were by the same artist.
MWA° (p. 5–20 & title page wanting); Shaw 44470.

103.1 BLACKBEARD, Or The Captive Princess. A Present For The New-Year, 1815. [engraving] The Prince and Princess. [cover title].

1–16 p. engr. on one side only of 16 leaves; illus.; 12 cm.; pr. & illus. yellow paper covers; p. 2–3 are numbered with mirror images of numbers "2" and "3."
English ed. London, entitled: [*The Pirate Blackbeard.*] Darton, Harvey & Darton, n.d.
MWA°; Shaw 34135.

103.2 ——— New-Year 1817. [engraving] The Prince and Princess. [cover title].

1–16 p. engr. on one side only of 16 leaves; illus.; 12 cm.; pr. & illus. buff paper covers.
MWA°; MB (per. st. on cover title); RPB; Shaw 40260.

103.3 ——— New-Year, [engraving] The Prince and Princess. [*ca.* 1820].

1–16 p. engr. on one side only of 16 leaves; illus.; 12.5 cm.; pr. & illus. buff paper covers.
MB° (per. st. on t.[1]; NcU.

104.1 THE BLACKBIRD'S NEST A Tale. Philadelphia Published by Johnson & Warner. 1812.

t.[1], [2–4], 5–36 p.; illus.; 12.5 cm.; pink marbled paper covers; copy A.
Copy A has a clear unblurred imprint on the title page, and is not part of a remainder. Only one copy is known.
Copy B cover title: The Black Bird's Nest. A Tale For Youth. Philadelphia: Published by Johnson and Warner, No. 147, Market Street. 1812. The imprint on the title page is blurred; 12 cm.; pr. & illus. buff paper covers. Part of a large publisher's remainder represented in all the locations given below.
English ed. London; entitled: ——— A Tale For Children. Darton, 1809.
MWA-W° (A); CCamarSJ; CLU; CSmH; CtY; IU; MWA (B); NHi; NN (2 copies); NNC-Pl; NRU; PHi; PP; PPL; Shaw 24883.

104.2 ———A Tale, For Children. New-York: Printed And Published By J. Robinson, 121 Water-Street. 1818.

t.[1], [2–4], 5–36 p.; illus.; 14 cm.; pr. & illus. buff paper covers.
NjR; Shaw 51745.

104.3 ——— A Tale, To which is added, The Fruits Of Disobedience, &c. New-York: Published At The Juvenile Library, 276 Greenwich-street. Thompson & Farrand, Printers. 1819.

t.[1], [2–3], 4–36 p.; illus.; 14 cm.; pr. & illus. paper covers.
RPB°; PP (original covers wanting); Shaw 47368.

104.4 ——— Nest. New-Haven: For J. Babcock And Son. Sidney's Press. 1820.

fr.[2], t. [3], [4–5], 6–31 p.; front. & title vignette only illus.; 11 cm.; pr. & illus. paper covers.
CtHi°; Shoemaker 498.

104.5 ——— A Tale, For Children. Newark, N.J. Published By Benjamin Olds. D. McDuffee, Printer, New-York. 1820.

t.[1], [2–4], 5–32 p.; illus.; 14 cm.; pr. & illus. buff-yellow paper covers; illus. p. [4], [6] signed A [Alexander Anderson].
MWA-W°; CtHi; MWA; PP; Shoemaker 499.

THE BLIND CHILD. *See* Pinchard, Mrs., no. **1006**.

BLOOMFIELD, ROBERT 1766–1823

105 THE FAKENHAM GHOST a true Tale. Taken from Bloomfield's admired Rural Poems. Published by Johnson & Warner. Philadelphia. [*ca.* 1810].

> t.[i], 1–16, [17] p.; engr. on one side only of 18 leaves; illus.; 13 cm.; pr. & illus. pink paper covers. Outside cover pasted to a gray filler to make stiff covers. Front cover title same as title, rear cover a repeat of the plate on p.[17]. This edition is characterized by having the thick portion of each letter of the word "Fakenham" on the title page made up of a column of diagonal lines, another of horizontal lines, and a thick black rule. The verse at the bottom of p.[17] is in 4 lines. Adv. by Johnson & Warner, 1814 in **1449.2**.
> English ed. London: W. Darton, April 4, 1806. MWA-W°; CtY (t.[i], & p.[17] wanting, p.[1] & 16 pasted to the inside of the covers); PP (pr. & illus. pink paper covers wanting, but has green unprinted paper covers); RPB; Shaw 19581.

106 — THE HISTORY OF LITTLE DAVEY'S NEW HAT. By Robert Bloomfield, Author of the "Farmer's Boy" &c. With Engravings. Philadelphia: Published By E. and R. Parker, No. 178, Market Street. J. R. A. Skerrett, Printer. 1818.

> fr.[ii], t.[i], [ii–iii], iv–ix, [1], 2–80 p.; 4 pl.; 14 cm.; bound in marbled paper over bds. Preface p. vi. dated: Shelford, Bedfordshire, February 27th, 1817.
> English ed.: 1815.
> MWA-T°; Shaw 43399.

BLOSSOMS OF MORALITY. *See* Johnson, Richard, no. **669.1**.

BLUE BEARD, And Little Red Riding Hood. *See* Perrault, Charles, no. **986.31**.

THE BOARDING SCHOOL. *See* Foster, Hannah Webster, no. **420**.

107 THE BOOK OF BOOKS, For Children, To teach all good boys and Girls to be wiser than their school-fellows. Adorned with Cuts. Printed at Salem by N. Coverly, 1801.

> t.[1], [2], 3–16 p.; illus.; 9.5 cm.; buff paper covers ornamented with red zigzag lines.
> MWA°; MSaE; PP (t.[1], p.[2] mut.); Shaw 208.

108 THE BOOK OF FABLES, For The Amusement And Instruction Of Children. Hartford. Oliver D. Cooke. 1820.

> t.[1], [2–3], 4–16 p.; illus.; 10.5 cm.; graygreen paper covers.
> MWA°; CtY; DLC; Shoemaker 522.

109 THE BOOK OF GAMES; Or, A History Of The Juvenile Sports Practiced At The Kingston Academy. Illustrated With Twenty-Four Copperplates. Philadelphia, Published By Johnson & Warner, 147 Market Street. A Fagan, Printer. 1811.

> t.[1], [2–5], 6–108 p.; 24 plates; 14 cm.; bound in marbled paper over bds., red leather spine.
> English ed. London: J. Adlard, for Tabart & Co., 1805.
> MWA-W° (p. 41–44, 53–56, 3 pl. wanting); MB (per. st. on t.p., i. st. on all plates); N (imperfect); PP; Shaw 22427.

110.1 THE BOOK OF LETTERS. New York: adv. by Samuel Wood, 1808 in **643.1**.

110.2 THE BOOK OF LETTERS. Printed & sold by Samuel Wood, at the Juvenile Book-store. No. 357, Pearl-Street, New-York. 1809.

> t.[1], [2–16] p.; 7.5 cm.; title vignette & illus. p. [16] only illus.; 7.5 cm.
> OClW-LS° (covers wanting); Shaw 50918.

110.3 ——— Printed & Sold by Samuel Wood, at the Juvenile Book-store, No. 357 Pearl-Street, New-York. 1811.

> t.[1], [2–16] p.; 8 cm.; title vignette & illus. p. [16] only illus.; 8 cm.
> NB° (covers wanting); Shaw 51064.

110.4 ——— New-York: Printed & sold by Samuel Wood, at the Juvenile Book-store, No. 357, Pearl-street, 1814.

> t.[1], [2–16] p.; illus.; 8.5 cm.
> MWA-W° (bound with other books in no. 637.1); Shaw 51366.

110.5 ——— Nerv-York [*sic. i.e.* New York]: Printed And Sold By Samuel Wood & Sons, at the Juvenile Book-store, No. 357, Pearl-street. 1816.

> t.[1], [2–16] p.; title vignette & illus. p. [16

only illus.]; 8 cm.; pr. & illus. yellow-buff paper covers; cover title undated.
NNC-LS*; Shaw 51557.

110.6 ——— New York: Published by Samuel Wood & Sons, at the Juvenile Book-store, No. 357, Pearl-street. 1818.
Shaw 43411.

111 THE BOOK OF NATURE. New-Haven: For J. Babcock & Son. Sidney's Press. 1820.
fr.[2], t.[3], [4–5], 6–30, [31, adv.] p.; illus.; 10.5 cm.; pr. and illus. pink paper covers. Copy 1 cover title imprint: Published by John Babcock and Son, New-Haven, and S. and W. R. Babcock, Charleston. Copy 2 cover title imprint: Published by John Babcock & Son ——— [same as copy 1.]. The book is reprinted from R. Johnson's *Blossoms Of Morality*, no. **669.1**.
MWA-W* (copy 1); CtHi; CtY (2 copies); MWA (copy 1, 2); Shoemaker 523 and 524.

112.1 THE BOOK OF NOUNS, Or Things which may be seen. Philadelphia: Published by J. Johnson, No. 147, Market-street. 1802.
t.[1], [2–3], 4–125, [126, illus.] p.; illus.; 6 cm.; bound in marbled paper over bds., leather spine.; one leaf probably wanting, or p. [127–128?].
English ed. London: Darton & Harvey, 1800.
MWA-W*; Shaw 1924.

112.2 ——— Philadelphia: Published by Jacob Johnson No. 147, Market-street. 1804.
t.[1], [2], 3–64 p.; 6 cm.; green paper covers.
MWA*; CLU; CtHi; DLC; MdHi; NHi; PHi; PP; Shaw 5891.

113 THE BOOK OF PICTURES. Concord, N.H. Published by Daniel Cooledge. Sold at his Book-Store. Geo. Hough, Printer. 1811.
t.[1], 2–16 p.; illus.; 8.5 cm.; pr. & illus. blue-gray paper covers.
Cover title: Concord Toy. No. 1. Book Of Pictures. [illus.].
MWA*; Shaw 22428.

114.1 THE BOOK OF PICTURES. New-York: adv. by S. Wood 1808 in **643.1**, and 1812 in **439.1**. This is a different book from no. **113**.

114.2 THE BOOK OF PICTURES. New-York: Printed & sold by Samuel Wood, at the Juvenile Book-store, No. 357, Pearl-street. 1814.
t.[1], [2–14] p.; illus.; 11.5 cm. Adv. by S. Wood, 1816 in **1188.7**, and 1819 in **1188.8**.
MWA-W* (bound with other books in no. **637.1**); Shaw 51367.

114.3 ——— Nerv-York [*sic. i.e.* New-York]: Printed And Sold By Samuel Wood & Sons, at the Juvenile Book-store, No 357, Pearl-street. 1816.
t.[1], [2–16] p.; illus.; 8.5 cm.
MWA-T* (bound with other books in no. **637.2**).

115.1 THE BOOK OF RIDDLES. New-York: Printed And Sold By S. Wood, At The Juvenile Book-Store No. 362, Pearl-Street. 1808.
fr.[ii, alphabet], t.[1], [2–3], 4–28, [29] p.; illus.; 10.5 cm.
CtY* (fr.[ii], p.[29] & covers wanting); CLU (fr.[ii], p.[29], & covers mut.); Shaw 50833.

115.2 ——— New-York: Printed And Sold By S. Wood, at the Juvenile Book-store, No. 357, Pearl-Street. 1811.
fr.[ii, alphabet], t.[1], [2–3], 4–28, [29, adv. list of books] p.; illus.; 10 cm.; pr. & illus. yellow paper covers; cover title dated 1811. Adv. by S. Wood, 1812 in **439.1**.
MH* (i. st. p. [2]; Shaw 50165.

115.3 ——— Concord [N.H.]: Published and sold by Daniel Cooledge, at his Book-Store. Geo. Hough, Printer. 1812.
fr.[2], t.[3], [4–6], 7–23 p.; illus.; 10 cm.; pr. purple paper covers.
Cover title MH copy: Concord Toy. No. 2. The Book of Riddles.
MWA* (p. 17–22 mut., covers wanting); MH; NhD (front cover mut., blue-gray paper covers); Shaw 24897.

115.4 ——— New-York: Samuel Wood. 1813.
Shaw 27981.

115.5 ——— Baltimore [Md.]: Printed And Sold By W. Warner, Corner of S. Gay & Market-Streets. 1814.
fr.[2, alphabet], t.[3], 4–29 p.; illus.; 10.5 cm.; paper covers.
MdHi*; Shaw 51368.

115.6 ——— New-York: Printed And Sold By Samuel Wood, At The Juvenile Book-Store, No. 357, Pearl-Street. 1814.

> t.[1], [2–3], 4–28 p.; illus.; 10 cm.
> MWA° (covers, fr.[ii] wanting, p.[3]–4 mut.); Shaw 51369.

115.7 ——— New-York: Printed And Sold By S. Wood & Sons, At The Juvenile Book-Store, No. 357, Pearl-Street. 1815.

> fr.[ii, alphabet], t.[1], [2–3], 4–28 p.; illus.; 10 cm.; pr. & illus. brownish-puff paper covers; cover title undated.
> MWA°; Shaw 34162.

115.8 ——— New-York: Printed And Sold By S. Wood & Sons, At The Juvenile Book-Store, No. 357, Pearl-Street. 1816.

> fr.[ii, alphabet], t.[1], [2–3], 4–28 p.; illus.; 10 cm.; pr. & illus. buff paper covers; cover title undated.
> NNC-LS°; DLC (fr.[ii], & covers wanting, p. 5–6 mut.); MWA; Shaw 37040.

115.9 ——— Nerv-York [*sic. i.e.* New York]: Printed And Sold By S. Wood & Sons, At The Juvenile Book-Store, No. 261, Pearl-Street. 1817.

> fr.[ii, alphabet], t.[1], [2–3], 4–28 p.; illus.; 9.5 cm.; green Dutch paper covers.
> MWA-W°; Shaw 51647.

115.10 ——— New-York: Published By Samuel Wood & Sons, No. 261, Pearl-Street, And Samuel S. Wood & Co. No. 212, Market-st., Baltimore. 1818.

> fr.[ii, alphabet], t.[1], [2–3], 4–28 p.; illus.; 10.5 cm.; green Dutch paper covers.
> MWA°; CLU; NWebyC; Shaw 43412.

115.11 ——— New-York: Published By Samuel Wood & Sons, No. 261, Pearl-Street; And Samuel S. Wood & Co No. 212, Market-st., Baltimore. 1820.

> fr.[ii, alphabet], t.[1], [2–3], 4–28 p.; illus.; 10.5 cm.; lilac Dutch paper covers.
> MWA°; MH; Shoemaker 525.

116 THE BOOK OF TRADES, Or Library Of The Useful Arts. Part I. [II.–III.] Illustrated With Twenty-Three Copper-Plates. First American Edition. White-Hall [Pa.]: Published By Jacob Johnson, And For Sale At His Bookstore in Phil-

adelphia, And In Richmond, Virginia. 1807. Dickinson, Printer.

> vol. I.: fr.[ii], t.[i], [ii–iv], [1], 2–140 p.; 23 pl. including front. signed *WR fc* or *sc*. [William Ralph]; vol. II.: fr.[ii], t.[i], [ii–iv], [1], 2–139 p.; 24 pl. including front. nearly all signed *WR Sc* or *W fc*.; t.[1] same as vol. I. except: Part II. Illustrated With Twenty-Four Copper-Plates.; vol. III.: fr. [ii], t.[i], [ii–iv], [1], 2–137 p.; 19 pl. mostly initialed by William Ralph, fr.[ii] signed *I. Bowers Sc*; there is no pl. for the "Watchmaker" or "Needle Maker"; t.[i] same as vol. I. except: Part III. Illustrated With Twenty Copper-Plates; 3 vols.; 14 cm.; bound in marbled paper over bds. Adv. by Johnson & Warner, 1814 in **1449.2**.
> English ed. London: 1st ed. pt. I., II. only Tabart & Co. 1804.
> MWA°; BM (vol. III); DLC (vol. I. t.[1] wanting); MB (vol. I. emb. st. on t.[1]; PHi; PP; Shaw 12173 and 12846.

117 THE BOOKSELLER'S SHOP; Or, The Youth's Library. Compiled By The Printer's Youngest Apprentice, Who waits upon Authors with proof-sheets, and who is vulgarly called "The Printer's Devil." Read, mark, and understand.—Common Sense. Philadelphia: Printed For Messrs. Every-Body. 1813.

> t.[i], [ii–v], vi–xii, [13], 14–108 p.; illlus.; 13 cm.; bound in brown marbled paper over bds., red leather spine.
> MWA-W° (rebound); Shaw 27983.

[BOUDINOT, ELIAS] *ca.* 1803–1839
118 [—] THE HISTORY OF AN INDIAN WOMAN; Or Religion Exemplified In The Life of Poor Sarah. Founded On Fact. Boston: Printed For Samuel T. Armstrong, By Crocker And Brewster, No. 50, Cornhill. 1820.

> t.[1], [2–3], 4–22, [23–24] p.; illus., 13.cm.; pr. & illus. green paper covers.

Boudinot, was a Cherokee Indian who was sent by the missionaries to the school at Cornwall, Conn. While he was there he took the name of Elias Boudinot, the name of the benefactor of the school. In 1828 he was the editor of the *Cherokee Phoenix* mostly printed in English but about a fourth was in Cherokee. In 1833 he translated a book entitled *Poor Sarah or the Indian Woman* into Cherokee. This probably was a translation of the above pamphlet which he may have written and published in 1820 when he was at school in Cornwall, Conn. (Dict. of Amer. Biog.). *See* no. **119.2** for a note on who Poor Sarah may have been.

MWA-W°; MWA (front cover wanting); Shoemaker 552.

119.1 [—] THE PIOUS INDIAN: Or, Religion Exemplified In The Life of Poor Sarah. Newburyport [Mass.], Printed By W. & J. Gilman, Booksellers And Stationers, No. 2, Middle-Street. 1820.

t.[1], [2–3], 4–12 p.; 17.5 cm.

MNe°; MH; RPB; Shoemaker 555.

119.2 [—] —————— Newburyport [Mass.], Printed by W. & J. Gilman, For Charles Whipple, Bookseller, No. 4, State-Street. 1820.

t.[1], [2–3], 4–12 p.; 17.5 cm.; no original covers; p. [3]: < The *Connecticut Mirror,* states that the subject of it was undoubtedly old Sarah Rogers, who lived in a little hut at the head of Snipsick Pond, which lies between the towns of Ellington and Tolland. >

MWA°; Shoemaker 556.

119.3 [—] —————— Newburyport [Mass.], Printed By W. & J. Gilman, 1820.

23 p.

Shoemaker 554.

120.1 [—] POOR SARAH, Or, The Benefits Of Religion Exemplified In The Life And Death Of An Indian Woman. caption p. [1] [n. p. 1820?].

t.[1], 2–11 p.

MWA°; Shoemaker 558.

120.2 [—] POOR SARAH; Or, Religion Exemplified In The Life And Death Of A Pious Indian Woman. Philadelphia: Published by "The Religious Tract Society of Philadelphia," and for sale at their Depository, No. 8, South Front Street. February, 1820. William Bradford, Agent.

t.[1], [2], 3–12 p.; title vignette only illus.; 17 cm.

MWA°; PP; Shoemaker 557.

BOUILLY, JEAN NICOLAS 1763–1842
121 — A FATHER'S TALES TO HIS DAUGHTER. By J. N. Bouilly, Member Of The Philotechnical Society, Of The Academy Of Arts And Sciences, Of Tours, &c. &c. Translated From The French. Two Volumes In One. New-York: Published By

Butler And White, Corner Of Wall And William Streets. 1811.

t.[i], [ii–iii], iv–vii, [viii, bl.–ix], [x, bl.], [1], 2–287 p.; 18 cm.; bound in leather.

MWA°; PPL; RPB; Shaw 22443.

122 THE BOY TEACHER. Published for & sold by J. Lothrop. Meredith, N.H. 1814.

t.[1], [2–29] p. pr. one side only of 29 leaves; 4 cm.; pr. blue-gray paper covers.

MWA° (covers worn); Shaw 51370.

123.1 BOY WITH A BUNDLE, And The Ragged old Woman. A Tale. Ornamented with Cuts. Windham [Conn.]: Printed by Samuel Webb. 1813.

t.[3], [4–5], 6–22 p.; illus.; 9.5 cm.

MWA-W° (fr.[2]?, p. 23? & covers wanting); CLU; Shaw 51275.

123.2 BOY WITH A BUNDLE. Philadelphia: adv. by Johnson & Warner, 1814 in **1449.2**. The story was published with other stories by Johnson & Warner, 1809 in **1288**.

124 THE BRAZIER, A Pathetic Tale; Embellished With Engravings. Albany: Printed By G. L. Loomis & Co., corner of State and Lodge Streets. 1816.

fr.[2], t.[3], [4–5], 6–47 p.; illus.; 13 cm.; pr. yellow paper covers.

MB° (emb. st. on t.[3]); Shaw 37078.

BREWER, GEORGE 1766–
125 — THE JUVENILE LAVATER; Or, A Familiar Explanation Of The Passions Of Le Brun, Calculated For The Instruction and Entertainment of Young Persons; Interspersed With Moral And Amusing Tales, Illustrating The Benefit And Happiness Attendant On The Good Passions, And The Misfortunes Which Ensue The Bad In The Circumstances Of Life. By George Brewer, Author of Hours of Leisure, Siamese Tales, &c. &c. New-York: Published By R. M'Dermut & D. D. Arden, No. 1 City-Hotel, Broadway. 1815.

fr.[ii], t.[iii], [iv–viii], [1], [2], 3–171 p.; fr. [ii] and text pl.; 16cm.

CLU°; MWA; Shaw 34207.

126 [—] THE SIAMESE TALES: Being A Collection Of Stories Told To The Son Of The Mandarin Sam-Sib, For The Purpose Of Engaging His Mind

In The Love Of Truth And Virtue. With An His-
torical Account Of The Kingdom Of Siam. To
Which Are Added The Principal Maxims Of The
Talapins. Translated From The Siamese. [2 lines
of verse] Thompson. Baltimore: Printed For Henry
S. Keating's Book-Store, By T. E. Clayland & T.
Dobbin. 1797.

   t.[i], [ii–iii], iv, [5], 6–178, [179, Contents],
[180, adv.] p.; 17.5 cm.; bound in leather.
These stories were not translated from the Si-
amese, but the scene was laid in Siam to make
the story more interesting to young people.
English ed. London: Vernor and Hood, 1796.
NN° (last leaf wanting); CtY; MH; MWA;
PPL; RPJCB; ViU; Evans 32836.

A Brief Account Of The Happy Death Of
Mary Ann Clap. *See* Bates, Joshua, nos. **65.1–6.**

A Brief Memoir of the Life of William Penn.
See Wakefield, Priscilla, no. **1394.1.**

Brother and Sister. *See* Baker, Mrs. Caroline
(Horwood), no. **54.**

127. The Brother's Gift, Or Pleasing Stories
For Children. Boston: Printed By N. Coverly, Jun.
Corner Of Theatre Alley. 1812.

   fr.[2], t.[3], [4–15] p.; illus.; 10 cm.; yellow
wallpaper covers.
MWA° (p.[15] mut.); Shaw 24942.

128.1 The Brother's Gift: Or, The Naughty
Girl Reformed. [4 lines of verse.] The First
Worcester Edition. Worcester, (Massachusetts)
Printed By Isaiah Thomas, And Sold At His Book
Store. MDCCLXXXVI.

   fr.[2], t.[3], [4–5], 6–30, [31, illus.] p.; illus.;
10 cm.; Dutch paper covers.
English ed. London: adv. by Francis Newbery
in *Mother Bunch's Fairy Tales.* 1773.
MWA°; PPL; Evans 19524.

128.2 ———— Hartford: Printed by Nathaniel
Patten D,DCC,LXXX,IX [*sic. i.e.* M,DCC,-
LXXX,IX].

   fr.[2], t.[3], [4–5], 6–30, [31, illus.] p.; illus.;
10 cm.; dark blue paper covers.
NNP°.

128.3 ———— New York: adv. by William
Durell, 1790 in **612.5.**

128.4 ———— Boston: adv. by S. Hall, 1791 in
408.3 and 1792 in **1408.32.**

128.5 ———— Philadelphia: adv. by F. Bailey,
1792 in **358.**

128.6 ———— Hudson, N.Y. adv. by Ashbel
Stoddard, 1794 in **1220.1.**

128.7 ———— Boston: Printed and sold by S.
Hall, in Cornhill. 1794.

   fr.[2], t.[3], [4–5], 6–31 p.; illus.; 10 cm.;
Dutch paper covers. No letters $\frac{\text{"M"}}{\text{M}}$ on the
recto of the front. A printer's ornament of an
angel's head is on t.[3] & p.[5].
MWA°; MB (per st. on t.[3]); Evans 26705.

128.8 ———— [same as **128.1**] The Third
Worcester Edition. Printed at Worcester, Massachusetts, By Isaiah Thomas jun. For Isaiah
Thomas, Sold at their respective Bookstores an
by Thomas and Andrews in Boston.—MDCCXCV.

   fr.[2], t.[3], [4–5], 6–31 p.; illus.; 10 cm.; illus.
blue-gray paper covers.
MWA-W°; CLU; MWA (2 copies with varying
covers); NjP; PP; Evans 28353.

128.9 ———— New-York: Printed by W. Durell
& Co. No. 15, Little Dock-Street. [1789?].

   fr.[2], t.[3], [4], 5–30, [31, illus.] p.; illus.; 9.5
cm.; illus. paper covers.
The above edition was published prior to 1800,
because the illus. on p. 9, 14, 19, 22, have sharp
rule borders and do not show the nicks that
appear in the Durell 1800 edition of *The Brother's Gift.* The New York Directory for 1789
lists William Durell, China Merchant, 15 Little
Dock Street. (MWA cat.). The book was advertised in *The Holy Bible Abridged New York:
W. Durell 198, Queen Street. 1790,* which address is probably a misprint for 19 Queen Street.
NRU°; Evans 48070.

128.10 ———— Reformed. The First Hudson
Edition. Printed At Hudson, New-York, By Ashbel
Stoddard, and Sold at his Book-Store. M,DCCC.

fr.[2], t.[3], [4–5], 6–31 p.; illus.; 9.5 cm.; green Dutch paper covers.
NB° (fr.[2] mut., i. st. on t.[3]); Evans 49039.

128.11 ——— [6 lines of verse.] New-York: Printed By William Durell, For John Scoles. 1800.
fr.[2], t.[3], [4–5], 6–31 p.; illus.; 10 cm.; green Dutch paper covers.
MWA-W°; Evans 37051.

128.12 ——— New-York: Printed By William Durell, [F]or T. & J. Swords. 1800.
fr.[2], t.[3], [4–5], 6–31 p.; illus.; 10 cm. Dutch paper covers.
MWA° (p. 27–28 wanting); Evans 37052.

128.13 ——— New-York: Printed By William Durell, No. 106, Maiden Lane. 1801.
[ii, illus.], [1, bl.], fr.[2], t.[3], [4–5], 6–31, [32, bl.], [33, illus.] p.; illus.; 10 cm. The illus. on p. [ii] and [33] probably belong to another book.
MWA° (covers wanting); Shaw 235.

128.14 ——— Reformed. To Which Is Added, The Employments of Mankind. Ornamented with Cuts. Hartford: Printed by Lincoln & Gleason. 1803.
fr.[2], t.[3], [4–5], 6–30, [31] p.; illus.; 10.5 cm.
CtY° (fr.[2], p.[31], & covers wanting); MSaE (original covers wanting); Shaw 3879.

128.15 ——— Reformed. Hudson (N.Y.): adv. by A. Stoddard, 1804 in **615.2**; Shaw 50412.

128.16. ——— [4 lines of verse] Worcester: Printed by I. Thomas, Jun. Sold Wholesale and Retail at his Book-Store. 1805.
fr.[2], t.[3], [4–5], 6–30, [31, illus.] p.; illus.; 10.5 cm.; buff paper covers.
Welch°; MWA (blue paper covers); PP; Shaw 8085.

128.17 ——— [same as **128.14**] Hartford: Printed By Lincoln & Gleason. 1806.
fr.[2], t.[3], [4–5], 6–30, [31, adv. list of books] p.; illus.; 10 cm.; green Dutch paper covers.
MWA-W°; CtHi; PP; VtHi; Shaw 10039.

128.18 ——— Hartford: Printed By Peter B. Gleason & Co. 1811.

fr.[2], t.[3], [4–5], 6–30, [31, adv.] p.; illus.; 10.5 cm.; pr. & illus. paper covers; cover title dated 1824.
CtHi; DLC (cover title dated 1811); NB (fr. [2] mut., yellow unprinted paper covers); Shaw 22407.

[BUDDEN, MARIA E. (HALSEY)] 1780–1832
129 [—] ALWAYS HAPPY: Or, Anecdotes Of Felix, And His Sister Serena. A Tale. Written For Her Children, By A Mother. From the Second London Edition. New-York: Published By William B. Gilley. Van Winkle & Wiley, Printers. 1816.
fr.[ii], t.[i], [ii–v], vi–vii, [viii], [1], 2–142 p.; illus.; 14 cm.; bound in buff paper over bds., green leather spine; illus. on p. 109 signed *Anderson* [Alexander Anderson].
English ed. London: J. Harris, 1814.
RPB°; MH; MWA-T; NjP; NN (fr.[ii] & front cover wanting, p. 47–48 mut.); Hamilton 258; Shaw 36718.

130.1 A KEY TO KNOWLEDGE; Or, Things In Common Use. Simply And Shortly Explained, In A Series Of Dialogues. Written By A Mother, Author of "Alway's happy,"—"First Book for Children." &c. &c. [4 lines quot.] More. New-York: Published By W. B. Gilley, No. 92 Broadway. T. & W. Mercein, Printers. January 1816.
fr.[ii], t.[i], [ii–v], vi–viii, [1], 2–154 p.; front. only illus.; 14.5 cm.; bound in buff paper over bds., green leather spine; front. signed *Hoogland Sculpt.* Written by Maria Halsey Budden.
English ed. London: J. Harris and Son, 1814.
MWA°; DLC; MdHi; Shaw 38001.

130.2 [—] ——— [4 lines quot.] New-York: Published By W. B. Gilley, 92 Broadway, J. Van Riper & Co. Print. 1819.
fr.[ii], t.[1], [2–5], 6–8, [9], 10–144 p.; front. only illus.; 14.5 cm.; bound in blue-gray paper over bds., leather spine.
MWA°; Shaw 48422.

131 THE BUDGET; Consisting Of Pieces, Both Instructive And Amusing, For Young Persons. Published By Johnson & Warner, And Sold At their Bookstores, Philadelphia, And Richmond, Virginia. A. Fagan, Printer. 1813.
fr.[2], t.[3], [4–5], 6–72 p.; illus.; 14 cm.; yellow paper covers. Adv. by Johnson & Warner, 1812 in **497**.
PP°; MH; Shaw 28041.

132 THE BUDGET, Or Moral And Entertaining Fragments. Representing The Punishment Of Vice, And The Reward Of Virtue. First American Edition. Wilkesbarre—Pennsylvania: Printed By Asher Miner,—For Mathew Carey, Philadelphia. October, 1801.

> t.[1], [2–5], 6–140, [141] p.; 14 cm.; bound in dark blue paper over bds., leather spine.
> English ed. London: E. Newbery 1799.
> MWA* (p. 9–10 mut.); Shaw 250.

133 THE BUDGET; Or Three Evenings' Amusement, For Children Of 10 To 12 Years Of Age. Philadelphia: Published By Johnson & Warner: A. Fagan, Printer. 1813.

> t.[1], [2–3], 4–71 p.; illus.; 13.5 cm.; pr. & illus. pink paper covers. Adv., under the cover title, by Johnson & Warner, 1814 in **1449.2**
> Cover title: Three Evenings Amusement For Children, Of Ten To Twelve Years Of Age. Philadelphia: Published by Johnson & Warner, No. 147 Market Street. 1813.
> NNC-Pl*.

BUNYAN, JOHN 1628–1688

134.1 [—] THE CHRISTIAN PILGRIM: Containing An Account Of The Wonderful Adventures And Miraculous Escapes Of A Christian, In His Travels from the Land of Destruction to the New Jerusalem. First American Edition. Worcester: Printed by Isaiah Thomas, Jun. Sold Wholesale and Retail at his Book-Store. October, 1798.

> vol. I.: fr.[2], t.[3], [4–7], 8–112 p.; illus.; vol. II.: fr.[ii], t.[113], [114–115], 116–219, [220, bl. 221, adv.] p.; illus.; 2 vols.; 10 cm.; bound in silver paper over w. bds.; vol. I, has "Volume I." above the front.; vol. II. t.[113] has Adventures spelt "Adventure; First American Edition, —Vol. II."; the date 1798 misprinted "1789."; and "Volume II." printed above the front., a duplicate of the front. of vol. I.
> English ed. *Pilgrim's Progress* 1st ed. pt. I. 1678, pt. II. 1684, pt. III 1693.
> Welch* (fr.[112], vol. II. wanting); CLU (vol. I., t.[3], p.[4–6] wanting, several p. torn); CtY (fr. [ii] vol. II. wanting); DLC; MH; MWA (pink Dutch paper covers); MWHi (fr. [ii], vol. II. wanting); NjP (fr.[112], vol. II. wanting); NNC-Pl; PP (emb. st. on t.[3], and t.[113]); Evans 33473; Hamilton 177.

134.2 [—] —— New Jerusalem. < Two volumes In One> Second American Edition. Volume I. [II.] Hartford: Printed By John Babcock. 1802.

> 1st t.[1], [2–3], 4–44 p.; 2nd t.[45], [46–47], 48–107 p.; 2 vols. in 1; 15 cm.; bound in marbled paper over w. bds.
> OClWHi* (p. 5–8 wanting); Shaw 1959.

134.3 [—] —— Second American Edition. Printed At Worcester For Isaiah Thomas, Jun. Sold Wholesale and Retail at his Bookstore, and by Thomas Whipple, Newburyport [Mass.], and by Thomas & Tappan, Portsmouth, [N.H.]. 1807.

> fr.[2], t.[3], [4–7], 8–216 p.; illus.; 11 cm.; bound in leather.
> Welch* (p. 59–60, 193–194 mut.); MWA (i. st. on t.[1], I. Thomas' bookplate in book); PP; Shaw 12232.

134.4 [—] —— New Jerusalem. Vol. I. [II.] Boston: Published By Hastings, Etheridge And Bliss. 1808.

> vol. I.: t.[3], [4–7], 8–101, [102, bl.]; vol. II.: t.[103], [104–105], 106–198 p.; illus.; 2 vols. in 1; 11 cm.; bound in leather; p.[4]: Charlestown, (Mass.) Printed By S. Etheridge.
> MWA* (p. [5]–16, 141–142 mut.); Shaw 14607.

134.5 [—] —— Boston: Printed and published by Samuel Avery, No. 29, Marlboro'-Street, opposite the Old South Meeting-house. 1810.

> fr.[2], t.[3], [4–5], 6–224 p.; illus.; 10.5 cm.; bound in leather.
> MWA*; PP; Shaw 19675.

134.6 [—] —— Windsor [Vt.]: Published By P. Merrifield, & Co. 1811. T. M. Pomroy, Printer.

> fr.[2], t.[3], [4–5], 6–156 p.; illus.; 13 cm.; bound in leather; front.: P. Merrifield & Co's [illus.] First Vermont Edition.
> MWA*; CLU; DLC; OOxM; PP; VtHi (rear cover wanting); McCorison 1265; Shaw 22431.

134.7 [—] —— Montpelier [Vt.]: Published by Wright & Sibley. 1812.

> fr.[2], t.[3], [4–5], 6–142 p.; illus.; 13 cm.; bound in blue marbled paper over w. bds., leather spine; front.: Wright & Sibley's [cut] First Edition.
> MWA*; VtHi; McCorison 1369; Shaw 24982.

134.8 [—] ———— Boston: Printed & Published By Lincoln & Edmands, At their Bible Warehouse & Theological & Miscellaneous Book-store 53 Cornhill. 1818.
> fr.[2], [5], 6–52, [53] p.; illus.; 14 cm.; pr. & illus. blue paper covers.
> MWA°; MB (p.[3–4] wanting); MWHi; Shaw 43477.

134.9 [—] ———— Boston: 1819.
> Shaw 47600.

134.10 [—] ———— Montpelier [Vt.]: Published by E. P. Walton, 1819.
> t.[1], [2–3], 4–141, [142, bl.], [143–144, adv. list of books] p.; illus.; 13.5 cm.; bound in blue paper over w. bds., leather spine.
> Welch°; MiU; MWA; PP; Vt (covers wanting, p. 121–[144] mut.); McCorison 2097; Shaw 47459.

134.11 [—] ———— Boston: Printed & Sold By Lincoln & Edmands, At their Bible Warehouse & Theological & Miscellaneous Bookstore, 53 Cornhill. 1820.
> fr.[2], t.[3], [4–5], 6–52, [53] p.; illus.; 14 cm. CtHi° (top ¼ of t.[3] torn away, covers wanting); MH; Shoemaker 620.

134.12 [—] ———— Who Travels From The Land Of Destruction To the New Jerusalem. Vol. I. [II.] Salem [Mass.]: Published By Thomas Carey. 1820.
> fr.[2], t.[3], [4–7], 8–103, [104, bl.] p.; 2nd t.[105], [106–107], 108–192 p.; illus.; 2 vols. in 1; 11 cm.; bound in black paper over bds., leather spine; p.[4]: J. D. Cushing, Printer.
> MWA°; CLU; DLC; MB (imp.); MH; PP; Shoemaker 621.

135.1 — Divine Emblems: Or, Temporal Things Spiritualized. Fitted For The Use Of Boys And Girls. By John Bunyan. New-York. Printed By James Carey, For Mathew Carey, Philadelphia. n.d. [1794].
> t.[i], [ii–iii], iv–vi, [7], 8–84, [85–90, adv. list of books] p.; illus.; 14 cm.; bound in marbled paper over w. bds., leather spine. The OClW-LS copy seems to have been issued without the 6 pages of adv. or p.[85–90].
> English ed. London: *A Book For Boys And Girls: Or, Country Rhymes For Children. By J. B. . . . London, Printed for N. P. and Sold by the Booksellers in London. 1686.*
> MWA° (p. 9–16 wanting); CtY (imp.); OClW-LS; Evans 26712.

135.2 — ———— By John Bunyan. Philadelphia: Printed For Mathew Carey, No. 118, Market-Street. 1796.
> t.[i], [ii–iii], iv–vi, [7], 8–90 p.; illus.; 14 cm.; bound in green wallpaper over bds.
> MWA°; PHi (p. 89–90 mut.); Evans 30138.

135.3 — ———— Embellished With 49 Cuts. Philadelphia: Printed For Mathew Carey, No. 122, High-Street. R. Cochran, Printer. 1808.
> fr.[ii], t.[iii], [iv–v], vi–viii, [9], 10–108 p.; illus.; 14 cm.; bound in blue marbled paper over bds., red leather spine.
> MWA-W°; MBAt; MiU; NN; PHi; PP; Shaw 14608.

Bunyan's Pilgrim's Progress Exhibited In a Metamorphosis. *See* Barber, J. W., no. **63**.

BURDER, GEORGE 1752–1832
136.1 — Bunyan's Pilgrim's Progress, Versified: For The Entertainment And Instruction Of Youth. By George Burder, Author Of Village Sermons, &c. Burlington, N.J. Printed And Published By Stephen C. Ustick, 1807.
> t.[i], [ii–iii], iv, [5], 6–71, [72] p.; 14.5 cm.; bound in reddish-brown marbled paper over bds., dark green leather spine.
> English ed. London: C. Whittingham, and sold by T. Williams, 1804.
> FTaSU°; CLU; MWA; NN (em. st. p. [5]–6); PPL; Shaw 12238.

136.2 — ———— Burlington, N.J. Printed And Published By Stephen C. Ustick, 1807.
> fr.[ii], t.[i], [ii–iii], iv, [5], 6–71, [72] p.; illus.; 15 cm.; Same as preceding edition, but with 7 plates including front.
> MWA-W°; Shaw 12238.

136.3 — ———— Hanover, N.H. Printed By Moses Davis. 1807.
> t.[i], [ii–iii], iv, [5], 6–60 p.; 18 cm.
> MWA°; CLU; PP; Shaw 12239.

136.4 —————— Village Sermons, &c. With Other Poems Subjoined. Philadelphia: Published By Joseph Sharpless. Merritt Printer, 1814.
  t.[i], [ii–iii], iv, [5], 6–107 p.; 14.5 cm.; bound in leather.
  RPB°; MWA (bound at the rear of the book with Joseph Sharpless' *The Story of Joseph. Philadelphia. 1814.*); PP (p. 81–84 wanting); Shaw 31031.

136.5 —————— Of Village Sermons, &c. Hartwick [N.Y.]: Printed At The Office Of L. & B. Todd. 1818.
  t.[i], [ii–iii], iv, [5], 6–71, [72] p.; 17 cm.; bound in blue paper over bds., leather spine.
  PP°; NCooHi (3 copies); NN; Shaw 43481.

137.1 — EARLY PIETY; Or Memoirs Of Children Eminently Serious Interspersed With Familiar Dialogues, Prayers, Graces And Hymns. By G. Burder. [3 lines of verse] Matt. xxi. 16. The first American from the seventh London Edition. From Sidney's Press, New-Haven, For Increase Cooke & Co. 1806.
  fr.[2], t.[3], [4–7], 8–72 p.; front. only illus.; 13.5 cm.
  English ed. London: Sold by H. Trapp; and Vallance and Simons, 1777.
  MWA° (covers wanting); CtY (fr.[2] mut.); DLC (buff paper covers); Shaw 10061.

137.2 [—] —————— Hymns; To Which Is Added The Gallery of Pictures—the Museum—the History of Edward VI. king of England, and the remarkable conversion of several children at the Orphan house in Georgia. Windsor [Vt.]: Printed And Published By Jesse Cochran, 1812.
  t.[1], [2–4], 5–32 p.; 12 cm.; blue marbled paper covers.
  MWA°; VtHi; McCorison 1370; Shaw 24988.

137.3 [—] —————— Serious. Interspersed With Familiar Dialogues, Emblematical Pictures, And Hymns, Upon Various Occasions. [1 line quot.] Prov: viii. 17. New-York: Printed And Sold By T. and J. Swords, No. 160 Pearl-street. 1817.

fr.[ii], t.[1], [2–5], 6–85 p.; 8 pl. including front.; 10.5 cm.; green Dutch paper covers.
  MWA°; MH; NB (p. [3–4], 13–14 wanting); NNUT; PP; Shaw 40348 and 40713.

138 — THE HERMIT, Exhibiting a Remarkable Instance of the Providence Of God: The Stories of a Good Child, And A Wicked Child. Selected From The Rev. G. Burder's "Early Piety." Adorned with Cuts. Sidney's Press. New-Haven. 1818.
  fr.[2], t.[3], [4–5], 6–30, [31, adv.] p.; illus.; 10.5 cm.; illus. ivory paper covers printed in pink ink.
  MWA-W°; Shaw 51747.

139 — THE HISTORY OF MASTER BILLY & MISS BETSEY GOODCHILD. Story Of The Prodigal Son: And Hymns For Children. Selected From The Rev. G. Burder's "Early Piety." Adorned With Cuts. Sidney's Press. New-Haven, 1818.
  fr.[2], t.[3], [4–5], 6–30, [31, adv.] p.; illus.; 10 cm.; illus. buff paper covers pr. in blue ink.
  CtHi°; PP (illus. buff paper covers pr. in pink ink); Shaw 43483.

BURTON, RICHARD. *See* Nathaniel Crouch, no. **252**, and Aesop, no. **16.1.**

BUTCHER, EDMUND 1757–1822
140 — THE NEW YEAR'S GIFT; Or, Moral Tales: Designed To Instruct And Improve The Minds Of Youth. By The Rev. Edmund Butcher. [3 lines of verse] Beattie's Minstrel. From The London Edition. Boston: Published By Leonard C. Bowles, No. 59, Cornhill. 1819. E. G. House, printer.
  fr.[ii], t.[i], [ii–iii], iv, [7], 8–123 p.; front. only illus.; 14.5 cm.; bound in buff paper over bds., leather spine.
  English ed. London: Vernor And Hood, E. Newberry, 1801.
  MWA-W°; (fr.[ii] wanting; the stain of the fr.[ii] shows on the title page, p. 45–46 mut.); Shaw 47477.

THE BUTTERFLY'S BIRTH-DAY. *See* M., A. D., no. **808** and Roscoe, William, no. **1130.1.**

C

C., C.

141 —— First Published By The Christian Tract Society. Nº. XIX. Boston: Wells And Lilly, Court-Street. 1820.

t.[1], [2–3], 4–16 p.; t.[1] 15.5 cm.; end of tract p. 16 signed *C.C.*

MWA° (bound with other tracts); Shoemaker 3230.

C., E.

142.1 [—] Instructive Hints In Easy Lessons For Children. Philadelphia: Published By Jacob Johnson, No. 147, Market Street. 1808.

t.[1], [2–5], 6–54, [55–56, adv. list of books] p.; illus.; 16 cm.; pr. buff paper covers; colophon p. 54: Lydia R. Bailey, Printer, No. 84, Crown Street. The text is the same as the Utica [N.Y.]; Seward & Williams 1810 ed. by E°°°° C°°°°°. Adv. by Johnson & Warner, 1812 in **263**, and 1814 in **1449.2**. *See* no. **645** for Philadelphia 1802 ed.

English ed. London: Darton And Harvey, 1800. MWA° (t.[1], torn, p. [3–4] mut., other p. torn or mut.); Shaw 15306.

142.2 —— For Children. By E°°°° C°°°°° Utica [N.Y.]: Printed By Seward & Williams. 1810.

t.[1], [2–3], 4–62, [63] p.; 10 cm.; blue-gray paper covers.

MWA°; Shaw 19698.

C., G. S.

143.1 — Amusement For Good Children, By G. S. C. Or, An Exhibition of Comic Pictures, By Bob Sketch. Be Merry And Wise. Printed at the Bible and Heart Office, By And For Warner And Hanna, And Sold By Them And J. Vance & Co. Baltimore. 1806.

t.[1], [2–3], 4–43, [44, adv. list of books] p.; illus.; 16 cm.; marbled paper covers.

English ed. London: H. Ireton. [n.d.].

Welch°; DLC; MdHi; MWA; NN; PP; Shaw 9840 and 10079.

143.2 —— Wise. (Second Edition.) Baltimore: Printed & Sold By Warner & Hanna, at the Bible and Heart Office. 1808.

t.[1], [2–3], 4–51, [52, adv. list of books] p.; illus.; 16 cm.; marbled paper covers.

MdHi°; MWA (title page mut.); Shaw 14352.

C., H. A.

144 The History Of Mother Twaddle,—and the—Marvellous Atchievments [*sic*] Of Her Son Jack, by H. A. C. Philadelphia: Published and Sold Wholesale by Wm. Charles. 1809.

fr.[2], t.[3], [4–17] p. engr. on one side only of 16 leaves; illus.; 13 cm.; pr. buff paper covers. Cover title has an added caption "Jack and the Bean Stalk." and the words "Illustrated With Fifteen Engravings." with the imprint: Philadelphia: Published and sold Wholesale by Wm. Charles, and may be had of all the Booksellers. 1809. Price 25 Cents.

English ed. London: entitled: —— [same as above] by B. A. T. J. Harris, April 25th, 1807.

MWA° (paper of rear cover torn away); NN; PHi (covers defective, lacking t. & [3]; PP (cover title dated 1814); Shaw 17757.

145 The Cabinet, Containing A Variety Of Useful Instruction, Adapted To The Capacities Of Young And Aged of Both Sexes. By The Printer's Boy. [3 lines of verse.] Thomson. Philadelphia: Published By John Fordyce, No. 368, North Third Street. 1813.

t.[i], [ii–iii], iv–viii, [9], 10–108 p.; 13.5 cm.

OClWHi° (covers wanting); Shaw 51276.

146 The Cabinet; Containing An Elegant Collection Of Entertaining Stories, Designed for the Amusement of Boys And Girls. By Mrs. Opie, Madame De Montollieu and others. Poughkeepsie [N.Y.]: Printed By Paraclete Potter. [1818?].

t.[i], [ii], [1], 2–28, [1], 2–32, [1], 2–24, [1], 2–59 p.; 13 cm.; bound in marbled paper over bds. Captions of stories are: "The Black Velvet Pelisse.", p. [1]–28; "Marcel; Or, The Cobbler Of The Cottage.", p. [1]–25; "The Duel.", p. 25–32; "The Lady Among Murderers.", p. [1]–9; "The Captain Of Banditti.", p. 9–24; "Conradine, Or Innocence Triumphant.", p. [1]–39; "The Sport Of Fortune.", p. 40–59.

MWA-W° (p. 27–28 of "The Black Velvet Pelisse" wanting); CLU front leather cover wanting), CtHi (imp.); Shaw 43519.

147.1 THE CABINET OF NATURE, For The Year; Containing, Curious Particulars Characteristic Of Each Month. Intended To Direct Young People To the Innocent And Agreeable Employment Of Observing Nature. [6 lines of verse] New-York: Printed And Sold By Samuel Wood & Sons, At The Juvenile Book-Store, No. 357, Pearl-Street. 1815.

t.[1], [2–3], 4–48 p.; illus.; 14 cm.; pr. yellow paper covers. This title was originally *The Youth's Cabinet of Nature* 1811–1814, *see* no. **1471.1–3.** The book is a rewritten and abridged version of John Aikin's *The Calendar Of Nature*, no. **24.**

N°; NjR; Shaw 51475.

147.2 ———— New-York: Printed And Sold By Samuel Wood & Sons, At The Juvenile Book-Store, No. 357, Pearl-Street. 1817.

t.[1], [2–3], 4–48 p.; illus.; 13.5 cm.; pr. & illus. buff-yellow paper covers.

MWA° (2 copies varying covers); CLU; PP; RPB; Shaw 40376 and 40377.

THE CALENDER OF NATURE. *See* Aikin, John, no. **24.**

[CAMERON, LUCY LYTTELTON (BUTT)] 1781–1858

148 [—] THE HISTORY OF FIDELITY AND PROFESSION. An Allegory. By The Author Of 'The Raven and the Dove,' 'The Two Lambs,' &c. &c. New-York: Published By Samuel Wood & Sons, No. 261, Pearl-Street; And Samuel S. Wood & Co. No. 212, Market-street, Baltimore. 1820.

t.[1], [2–3], 4–34 p.; 14 cm.; pr. & illus. brown paper covers; cover title undated.
English ed. Wellington, Salop: F. Houlston And Son, Scratcherd and Letterman, 1819.
MWA°; MSaE; RPB (covers wanting); Shoemaker 650.

149 [—] THE NOSEGAY OF HONEY SUCKLES. By the Author of "The Two Lambs." &c. Portland [Me.]: Published By William Hyde, And for sale at his Book-store, No. 3, Mussey's-Row Middle-street. 1820.

fr.[2], t.[3], [4–5], 6–30, [31] p.; illus.; 14 cm.; pr. & illus. blue paper covers.

NNC-T°; MSaE; MWA; OClWHi; RPB; Shoemaker 651.

150 [—] THE POLITE LITTLE CHILDREN. By The Author Of "The History Of Margaret Whyte," "The Two Lambs," &c. First American Edition. Andover [Mass.]: Published By Mark Newman. 1820.

t.[1], [2–3], 4–17 p.; 14.5 cm.; pr. buff paper covers.
Welch°; MWA; MSaE; NN (covers wanting); PP; Shoemaker 652.

151.1 [—] THE TWO LAMBS. An Allegorical history. By The Author Of Margaret Whyte, &c. First American Edition. Burlington, N.J. Printed And Sold, By David Allinson. 1816.

t.[1], [2–3], 4–32 p.; 10.5 cm.; pink paper covers. Written in 1803. (DNB).
MWA°; PP; Shaw 37156.

151.2 [—] ———— Second American Edition. Windsor, Vt. Printed And Published By Pomroy & Hedge. 1816.

t.[1], [2–3], 4–32 p.; 10 cm.; yellow paper covers.
VtHi°; DLC; MSaE; McCorison 1830; Shaw 37157.

151.3 [—] ———— No. 19. THE TWO LAMBS. List Of Tracts Published By The Hartford Evangelical Tract Society. [a list of 20 tracts] [cover title].

Published for gratuitous distribution by The Hartford Evangelical Tract Society. March, 1817. 5000 Hudson and Co. Printers. [colophon p. 12].
[1], 2–12 p.; 16.5 cm.; pr. blue paper covers. The verso of the front cover has caption: Happy Poverty, Or The Story Of Poor Blind Ellen.
MWA°; Shaw 40384.

151.4 [—] ———— Margaret Whyte, &c. Second Newburyport Edition, Printed And Sold By W. & J. Gilman, No. 2, Middle-Street. [1817?].

fr.[ii], t.[1], [2–3], 4–21 p.; illus.; 13 cm.; pr. & illus. buff paper covers.
The Third Newburyport edition is dated 1818, and the Burlington, N.J. 1816 edition is called "The First American Edition." (MWA cat.).
MWA°; Shaw 40385.

151.5 [—] ———— Third Newburyport Edition: Published By W. & J. Gilman, Printers, Booksellers, and Librarians, No. 2, Middle-street. 1818.
fr.[2], t.[3], [4–5], 6–23 p.; illus.; 13.5 cm.; pr. & illus. buff paper covers. Cover title, copy 1, has vignette of a shepherd and two lambs. Copy 2 has vignette of a lamb and flying birds. Cover title, copy 3, has a vignette of two standing sheep facing each other.
MWA° (copy 1, 2, 3); MH; PP; Shaw 43522.

151.6 [—] ———— Fourth Newburyport Edition: Published By W. & J. Gilman, Printers, Booksellers, & Librarians, No. 2, Middle-Street. 1820.
fr.[2], t.[3], [4–5], 6–23 p.; illus.; 13.5 cm.; pr. & illus. buff paper covers.
MWA°; MB; MSaE; Shoemaker 654.

151.7 [—] ———— An Allegorical History. New-York: Published By D. H. Wickham, At the General Depository of the Sunday School and Religious Tract Societies, and the New-York and Marine Bible Societies, No. 59 Fulton-street. Printed by G. L. Birch & Co. 39½ Frankfort-st. 1820.
t.[1], [2–3], 4–24 p.; 12.5 cm.; pr. gray paper covers.
MWA°; CtHi; Shoemaker 653.

CAMPBELL, JOHN 1766–1840
152.1 — ALFRED AND GALBA: Or The History Of Two Brothers, Supposed To Be Written By Themselves. For the Use of Young People. By John Campbell, Author of Worlds Displayed, &c. Boston: Printed And Sold By Lincoln & Edmands, No. 53 Cornhill. [5 lines adv.] 1812. Price 3 dolls. a dozen.
fr.[2], t.[3], [4–7], 8–143, [144, adv. list of books] p.; 14.5 cm.; bound in pr. yellow-buff paper over w. bds.; advertisement p. 8 signed: J. C. [John Campbell] Kingsland, April 5, 1805. English ed. London: William Smith, 1805.
MWA°; ICU; MB; Shaw 25018.

152.2 — ———— Newburyport: adv. by W. & J. Gilman, 1813 in 490.2.

152.3 — ———— Worlds Displayed. &c. [3 lines quot.] Northhampton [Mass.]: Published By Simeon Butler. J. Metcalf Printer. 1817.
t.[1], [2–5], 6–141 p.; 14 cm.; bound in blue marbled paper over w. bds., leather spine.

MWA°; DLC; MH; NNC (t.[1] & p. 141 mut.); Shaw 40389.

153.1 — WALKS OF USEFULNESS IN LONDON AND ITS ENVIRONS. By John Campbell, Kingland, near London. Boston: Printed & Published By Lincoln & Edmands, No. 53 Cornhill, [4 lines adv.] 1812. Price 25 cts. 2.40 a dozen.
fr.[2], t.[3], [4–5], 6–108 p.; 15 cm.; pr. buff paper covers over w. bds.
English ed. London: J. Burditt, 1808.
MWA° (rear cover wanting); CSt; Shaw 25019.

153.2 — ———— New-York: Published by Whiting & Watson, Theological And Classical Booksellers, No. 96, Broadway. J. Seymour, print. 1812.
t.[1], [2–3], 4–136 p.; 14 cm.; bound in leather.
MWA°; CtY (front cover wanting); N; NN (rebound, i. st. on t.[1]); Shaw 25020.

153.3 — ———— London. [1 line quot.] Newburyport [Mass.]: Printed By William B. Allen & Co. Who do all kinds of Printing on the most reasonable terms—particularly for charitable distribution. 1813.
t.[1], [2–3], 4–120 p.; 13 cm.
MWA° (covers wanting, t.[1] mut.); DLC (covers wanting); MNe; Shaw 28069.

153.4 — ———— Newburyport: adv. by W. & J. Gilman, 1813 in 490.2.

153.5 — ———— Andover [Mass.]: Printed And Published By Flagg & Gould. 1815.
t.[i], [ii–iii], iv–viii, [9], 10–144 p.; 12 cm.; bound in brown paper over bds., green leather spine.
MWA°; Shaw 34273.

153.6 — ———— Author of Worlds Displayed, Alfred & Galba, &c. Boston: Printed and published at No. 53 Cornhill, by Lincoln & Edmands, [3 lines adv.] 1816.
t.[3], [4–5], 6–108 p.; 14.5 cm.; bound in pr. buff paper over bds.; cover title dated 1817.
MWA° (fr.[2] wanting); Shaw 37162.

153.7 — ———— Boston: Printed and published at No. 53 Cornhill, by Lincoln & Edmands, [3 lines adv.] 1817.

fr.[2], t.[3], [4–5], 6–108 p.; illus.; 14.5 cm.; bound in pr. buff paper over bds.
MWA°; MHi; Shaw 40390.

153.8 — —— [same as **153.1.**] Albany: Printed By Websters And Skinners, At Their Bookstore, Corner Of State and Pearl-Streets. 1818.
t.[i], [ii–iii], iv–vi, [7], 8–106 p.; t.[i]; t.[1] 13.5 cm.
MWA° (rebound); Shaw 43524.

153.9 — —— Auburn [N.Y.], Printed by David Rumsey. 1819.
t.[5], [6–8, bl.], [9], 10–136 p.; 13 cm.; bound in leather.
MPlyA°.

153.10 — —— [same as **153.6**] Galba, &c. Northhampton [Mass.]: Published By Simeon Butler. J. Metcalf, Printer. 1819.
t.[1], [2–3], 4–108 p.; 14 cm.; bound in buff paper over w. bds., leather spine.
MWA°; Shaw 47499.

153.11 — —— Boston: Printed and published at No. 53 Cornhill, by Lincoln & Edmands. [4 lines adv.] 1820.
fr.[2], t.[3], [4–5], 6–108 p.; 15 cm.; front. only illus.; bound in original pr. blue-gray paper pasted on new cloth binding.
MWA° (rebound foxed copy); Shoemaker 656.

153.12 — —— Alfred and Galba, &c. To Which Is Added A Set Of Pictures, For the Amusement of Children. Hartford: Published By Oliver D. Cooke. P. B. Goodsell, Printer. 1820.
fr.[2], t.[3], [4–6], 7–32 p.; illus., 14 cm.; pr. & illus. paper covers.
MWA° (2 copies varying covers); CtHi (2 copies); ICU; PP; Shoemaker 657 and 658.

154.1 [—] WORLD'S DISPLAYED, For The Benefit Of Young Persons, By A Familiar History Of Some Of Their Inhabitants. [4 lines quot.] First American Edition. New-York: Printed By James Oram, 102 Water-Street, For Cornelius Davis, Book-Seller, 167, Water-Street. 1801.
t.[i], [ii–iii], iv, [5], 6–120 p.; 10 cm.; marbled paper covers, leather spine.
CtY°; MSaE (poor copy).

154.2 [—] —— [3 lines quot.] Second American Edition. Newbury-port [Mass.]: Printed By A. March, South-Side Market-Square, 1802.
t.[i], [ii–iii], iv, [5], 6–96 p.; 12.5 cm.; bound in blue-gray paper over w. bds.
MWA°; MSaE (front cover wanting); Shaw 1985.

154.3 [—] —— [same as **157.1**] New-York: Printed by James Oram, No. 102, Water-Street. [*ca.* 1803].
t.[i], [ii–iii], iv, [5], 6–128 p.; 10.5 cm.; bound in marbled paper over bds., leather spine. James Oram was at 102 Water-Street, 1800–1803, 1814–1816. The book has been dated [*ca.* 1803] because the only children's books seen printed by Oram were printed between 1796 and 1801. Oram published the first edition of this popular work in 1801. *See* no. **154.1**.
MWA°; Shaw 50340.

154.4 — —— Inhabitants [2 lines quot.] [1 line quot.] Isa. iii II. By The Rev. J. Campbell. The Fifth Edition, Wilmington [Del.]: Printed by Bonsal & Niles, for the Rev. Daniel Dodge. 1803.
t.[i], [ii], iii–iv, [5], 6–128 p.; 10 cm.; bound in leather.
DeWi° (i. st. on t.[i], & p.[5]); Shaw 3927.

154.5 [—] —— [4 lines quot.] Boston: Printed and sold at No. 53, Cornhill, By Lincoln & Edmands. 1807.
t.[i], [ii–iii], iv, [5], 6–123, [1], 2–5 p.; 10 cm.; blue marbled paper covers. Caption p.[1]: Pious Meditations.
Welch°; MHi; MSaE (poor copy); MWA (front cover wanting); PP; Shaw 12263.

154.6 [—] —— [4 lines quot.] Second American Edition. Corrected and Improved. Windsor, (Vt.) Published By H. H. Cunningham. 1808. C. Spear, Printer.
t.[i], [ii–iii], iv, [5], 6–69, 1–2 p.; 14 cm.; gray marbled paper covers.
VtHi°; McCorison 977; Shaw 14635.

154.7 [—] —— [4 lines quot.] Second American Edition. Hudson [N.Y.]: Published By Hez. Steele, No. 118 Warren Street. N. Elliot, Printer, Catskill [N.Y.] 1809.
t.[i], [ii–iii], iv, [5], 6–89, [90, bl.–91, adv.] p.; 14 cm.; bound in brown paper over bds., leather spine.
MWA°; Shaw 17142.

154.8 [—] ———— [4 lines quot.] Newark, (N.J.) Printed By John Austin Crane. 1809.

   t.[i], [ii–iii], iv, [5], 6–128 p.; 10.5 cm.; bound in marbled paper over bds., leather spine.

   MWA°; NjI; NjP; Shaw 17141.

154.9 [—] ———— Boston: Printed and sold at No. 53, Cornhill, By Lincoln & Edmands. [4 lines adv.] 1811. Price, 1,20 cts. a doz. 9 dols. a hundred.

   fr.[2], t.[3], [4–5], 6–70, [71, illus.] p.; illus.; 13.5 cm.; blue marbled paper covers; p. 20 numbered "21"; p. 22 numbered "20"; p. 31 numbered "13."

   MWA-W; CLU; DLC; ICU; MB; MSaE (3 copies), MWA; NNC-T; NcD; PP; Shaw 22435 and 22468.

154.10 [—] ————Newburyport: adv. by W. & J. Gilman, 1813 in **490.2.**

154.11 [—] ———— [3 lines quot.] Andover [Mass.]: Published And Sold By Mark Newman. Flagg And Gould, Printers, 1814.

   t.[1], [2–3], 4–71 p.; 13.5 cm.; blue-gray paper covers.

   MWA°; MSaE; Shaw 31075.

154.12 [—] ———— [3 lines quot.] Isa. iii. 11. Boston. Printed & published by Lincoln & Edmands, Sold at their Bible Warehouse, And Theological & Miscellaneous Bookstore, No. 53 Cornhill. 1815. Price, 1, 12 cts. a doz. 8 dols. a hundred.

   fr.[2], t.[3], [4–5], 6–70, [71, illus.] p.; illus.; 14 cm.; pr. and illus. buff paper covers; cover title dated 1816.

   MWA° (p. 69–70 wanting); DLC; MNF (p. 60–[71] wanting); Shaw 34274.

154.13 [—] ———— Boston: Printed and published by Lincoln & Edmands, Sold at their Bible Warehouse, And Theological & Miscellaneous Bookstore, No. 53 Cornhill. 1819.

   fr.[2], t.[3], [4–5], 6–52, [53, illus.] p.; illus.; 14.5 cm.; pr. & illus. violet paper covers.

   MWA° (2 copies varied covers); MHi; NN; NcD; PP; TxU; Shaw 47500 and 50172.

154.14 [—] ———— [1 line quot.] Eccles. viii. 12. [1 line quot.] Isa. iii. 11. Published By The Philadelphia Female Tract Society, And For Sale At Their Depository, No. 20, Walnut Street. 1819. Lydia R. Bailey, Printer.

   t.[1], [2–3], 4–52 p.; 14 cm.; pr. blue-gray paper covers.

   MWA°; CCamarSJ; CLU; CSmH; CtHi; CtY; DLC (2 copies); IU; MSaE; NHi; NN; NNC-Pl; NNC-T; OOxM; PHi; PP; PPL; PU; Shaw 47501 and 50173.

[CAMPE, JOACHIM HEINRICH von] 1746–1818

155 [—] An Abridgement Of The New Robinson Crusoe; An Instructive And Entertaining History, For The Use Of Children Of Both Sexes. Translated From The French. Embellished with Thirty-two Cuts. New-York: Printed and published by I. Riley. 1811.

   t.[i], [ii–iii], iv, [1], 2–222 p.; illus.; t.[i] 16 cm.; 31 full p. illus. The text is the same as no. **157.1.** The preface is abridged by omitting portions and rewriting some sentences.

   MWA° (rebound, p. 61–62, 133–134 mut.); MH; MiU; NN (bound in yellow paper over bds., leather spine, t.[i] mut.); NNC-Pl; PP; PPL; Brigham 74; Shaw 22474.

156 — Columbus Or The Discovery Of America: as related by a father to his children, and designed for the instruction of Youth. Translated from the German of J. H. Campe by Elizabeth Helm. Boston:, New-York, Munroe & Francis, and S. Francis, 1818.

   English ed. title 1: *Columbus or the Discovery of America.* [translated by] Elizabeth Helme. London: Sampson Low And Sold By C. Law; E. Booker, And R. And L Peacock, 1799.

   English ed. title 2: *The Discovery Of America.* [anon. version]. London: J. Johnson, 1799.

   Shaw 43525.

157.1 [—] The New Robinson Crusoe: An Instructive And Entertaining History. For The Use Of Children Of Both Sexes. Translated From The French. Printed At Boston, By Thomas And Andrews, at Faust's Statue. Sold at their Bookstore, No. 45, Newbury Street, and by said Thomas at his Bookstore in Worcester.—Also by J. Boyle and D. West, in Marlborough Street, and B. Guild, B. Larkin, and E. Larkin, jun. in Cornhill, Boston. MDCCXC.

   fr.[ii], t.[i], [ii–iii], iv–viii, [9], 10–270 p.; illus.; 18 cm.; bound in leather. Front. signed *Hill Sc.*

English ed. London: 4 vols in 2, John Stockdale, 1788.

MWA° (cmb. st. on t.[i]); CSt; CtY; DLC (fr.[ii] wanting, rebound); MB (p. 191–270 wanting); MiU; PP; Brigham 13; Evans 22389.

157.2 [—] ——— Translated From The French. In Two Volumes. Vol. I. [II.] Philadelphia: Printed and Sold by W. Woodhouse, at the Bible, No. 6, South Front-street. M.DCC.XCII.

vol. I.: fr.[ii], t.[i], [ii–iii], iv–ix, [x], [11], 12–172 p.; vol. II.: t.[1], [2–3], 4–163, [164, adv. list of books] p.; 17.5 cm.; 2 vols. in 1.

MWA° (fr.[ii] wanting, rebound); MiU; PHi (vol. I. p. 147–148 mut.); RPB; Brigham 22; Evans 24171.

[CAMPE, JOACHIM HEINRICH von] 1746–1818 [Johnson, Richard], *abr.* 1734–1793

158.1 [—] THE NEW ROBINSON CRUSOE, Designed For The Amusement and Instruction Of The Youth of both Sexes. Translated from the original German. Embellished with Cuts, Hartford: Printed By John Babcock. 1800.

fr.[2], t.[3], [4–5], 6–108 p.; illus.; 13.5 cm.; bound in white paper ornamented with green and black circles and black dots, over w. bds., leather spine.

An entry in Richard Johnson's account book reads: "*1790 Mr. Babcock [E. Newbery's agent] —To translating The New Robinson Crusoe— £5. 5s. [Paid 1791, Jan. 18.]*" Probably E. Newbery's 1790 ed. and (in spite of the title page) not necessarily translated from German direct, as the author had himself translated it into French, E. Newbery's List, 1800, included versions at *6d.* and *4s.* (Weedon, 1949).

Johnson abridged and adapted the story from Campe's work first published in England in 1788 by Stockdale, 4 vols. in 2. In the Johnson version Robinson Crusoe was born in Hamburgh.

English ed. London: E. Newbery, 1790.

MWA-W° (orig. front. cover wanting); CtHi; CtY; MB; MWA; NN (rebound, p. 5–8 wanting); OOxM; PP; Brigham 41; Evans 38071.

158.2 [—] THE NEW ROBINSON CRUSOE. Designed For Youth. Ornamented With Plates. New-York, Published By T. B. Jansen, Book-Seller, 116 Broadway, opposite the City-Hotel. M'Farlane & Long, print. 1806. Price 12 1-2 Cents.

t.[1], [2–3], 4–35, [36, adv. list of books] p.; illus.; 13.5 cm.; marbled paper covers.

This American edition may have been copied from the 6d ed. adv. in 1800 by E. Newbery, and in *The Triumph of Goodnature. London: E. Newbery, [ca. 1800]*.

PP° (p. 15–17 mut.); Shaw 50656.

158.3 [—] [THE NEW ROBINSON CRUSOE, designed for the instruction and amusement of the Youth of both sexes. Translated from the German. . . . Just published and for sale the New Printing Office, Union Street, Portland.] [taken from an adv. in the Portland, Me. *Eastern Argus, Feb. 14, 1806*].

fr.[2], 23–130 p.; illus.; 12.5 cm.; bound in brown paper over w. bds. Colophon p. 130: Printing, In Its Variety, executed with Neatness or Elegance, By J. McKown, At The New Printing Office, Over Munroe & Tuttle's store, Portland [Me.]. The text is the same as the Hartford 1800 ed., but differs in having the captions on each page read "New Crusoe" instead of Robinson Crusoe.

MWA° (all between fr.[2] and p. 23 wanting); Brigham 58; Shaw 10992.

158.4 [—] THE NEW ROBINSON CRUSOE. Designed For Youth. Ornamented With Plates. New-York: Published By Thomas Powers, Book-Seller, 116 Broadway, opposite the City-Hotel. 1810.

t.[1], [2], 3–36 p.; illus.; 14.5 cm.; pr. & illus. yellow-buff paper covers. The above follows "the abridged version of the Campe narrative except for the notable insertion of calling Crusoe an American and the city of New York 'the place of his nativity'." Brigham p. 142. The text follows the Richard Johnson version with variations.

MWA°; CLU; CtY; Brigham 72; Shaw 20882.

158.5 [—] THE NEW ROBINSON CRUSOE: Designed For Youth. Adorned With Cuts. New-Haven. Printed For J. Babcock & Son. Sidney's Press. 1819.

t.[1], [2–3], 4–36 p.; illus.; 14 cm.; pr. & illus. pink paper covers; cover title undated. The text is the same as no. **158.1**. Cover title imprint: Published By J. Babcock & Son, Booksellers, Stationers and Printers, adjoining the Post-Office, New-Haven. Sold by S. & W. R. Babcock, Booksellers and Stationers, Charleston, S.C.

CtY°; CtHi; RPB; Brigham 93; Shaw 47503 and 47805.

158.6 [—] THE ADVENTURES OF ROBINSON CRUSOE. New Haven: Printed For J. Babcock And Son. Sidney's Press. 1820.

fr.[2], t.[3], [4–5], 6–31 p.; illus.; 14.5 cm.; pr. & illus. orange-buff paper covers. A rewritten version of Richard Johnson's abridgement of Campe's *New Robinson Crusoe*.
Cover title: Robinson Crusoe. Published and sold by John Babcock and Son, New-Haven, and S. & W. R. Babcock, Charleston.
MWA°; CtHi; CtY; CSmH; Brigham 97; Shoemaker 982.

THE CANARY BIRD. *See* Kendall, E. A., no. **722.1**.

159 CANINE BIOGRAPHY: Or, Curious And Interesting Anecdotes Of Dogs. Designed For Youth. Sidney's Press. Published by John Babcock & Son. New-Haven, S. & W. R. Babcock. No. 163 King-Street, Charleston and M'Carty & Davis, Philadelphia, 1820.

fr.[2], t.[3], [4–5], 6–31 p.; illus.; 14.5 cm.; pr. & illus. red paper covers.
CtHi°; DLC; MdHi; MH; MSaE; MWA-T; NNC-Pl (pr. & illus. blue paper covers); Shoemaker 668.

CARELESS ISABELLA; Or, The Dangers Of Delay. *See* Sandham, Elizabeth, no. **1154.1**.

CAROLINE, OR A LESSON TO CURE VANITY. *See* Berquin, Arnaud, no. **82**.

160.1 THE CASKET: Or The Orphan's Portion. Philadelphia: Published By B. & T. Kite, No. 20, North Third Street. J. Bouvier, Printer. 1810.

fr.[ii], t.[1], [2–3], 4–33 p.; 12.5 cm.; pr. blue paper covers; 3 engr. pl. including front.; cover title dated 1811.
PP°; MH (fr.[ii] wanting); MWA-T; Shaw 22487.

160.2 —— Portion, Together With Divine Hymns. Adorned With Cuts. From Sidney's Press. New-Haven. 1817.

fr.[2], t.[3], [4–5], 6–46, [47, adv.] p.; illus.; 12.5 cm.; illus. buff paper covers.
OClWHi°; Shaw 40414.

160.3 —— New-Haven: Printed For J. Babcock And Son. Sidney's Press. 1819.

fr.[ii], t.[1], [2, adv.–3], 4–35 p.; illus.; 13.5 cm.; pr. & illus. red paper covers; front. signed A [Alexander Anderson].
Cover title: The Casket. Published By J. Babcock & Son, Booksellers, Stationers and Printers, adjoining the Post-Office, New-Haven. Sold by S. & [W.] R. Babcock, Booksellers [and] Stationers, Charleston, S.C.
CtHi°; Shaw 47522.

THE CATERPILLARS & THE GOOSEBERRY BUSH. *See* Clowes, John, no. **207.1**.

CATHERINE HALDANE. *See* Haldane, James Alexander, no. **481.1**.

161 CATHERINE AND HER LITTLE LAMB. Entered according to Act of Congress. Sept. 26, 1814. New-York: Sold By T. B. Jansen, No. 11 Chatham-street. 1814.

t.[1], [2], 3–16 p.; 7 cm. Rewritten from A. Berquin's "The Lamb" in *The Children's Friend*, no. **71.1**.
NNC-LS° (front and most of rear cover wanting); MWA (p. 13–16 wanting); Shaw 51374.

162 THE CATS CONCERT. [2 lines of verse] Philadelphia. Pubd. and Sold wholesale by Wm Charles, and may be had of all the Booksellers. 1809. Price Twenty-Five Cents.

fr.[2], t.[3], [4–16] p. engr. on one side only of 15 leaves; illus.; 15 cm.; pr. yellowish-buff paper covers. Adv. by Wm. Charles, 1814 in **356**, and 1815 in **748**.
Cover title: The Cat's Concert; Or The Disasters Of Grimalkin. Illustrated With Elegant Engravings. Philadelphia: Published and Sold wholesale by Wm Charles, and may be had of all the Booksellers. 1809. Price Twenty-Five Cents.
English ed. London: C. Chapple. n.d.
Carson°; Shaw 17170.

CEBES
163 —— THE CIRCUIT OF HUMAN LIFE: A Vision. In Which Are Allegorically Described, The Virtues And Vices. Taken from the Tablature of Cebes, a Disciple of Socrates. For the Instruction of Youth. The Third Edition, Corrected. Philadelphia: Printed By Joseph Crukshank, In Market-

Street, Between Second And Third-Streets.
MDCCXC.

   t.[1], [2–3], 4–88 p.; 13 cm.; green Dutch
paper covers.

   English ed. London: T. Carnan, 1774.

   DLC° (rebound, i. st. on t.[1]).

CECIL, SABINA.
164 — Little Charlotte; Or, The Picture-
Book. By Sabina Cecil, Author Of Little Eliza,
Little Caroline, Little Charles, &c. Philadelphia:
Published By E. And R. Parker, No. 178, Market
Street. J. R. A. Skerrett, Printer. 1819.

   t.[1], 2–11, [12, adv.] p.; illus.; 12 cm.; pr.
orange paper covers; 10 col. pl.

   English ed. London: J. Marshall. [*ca.* 1818],
engr. pl. dated 1800.

   MWA°; ICU (a poor copy, date worn off);
Shaw 47532.

165.1 — Little Jane; Or, The Picture-Book.
By Sabina Cecil, Author Of Little Eliza, Little
Caroline, Little Charles, &c. Philadelphia: Published By E. And R. Parker, No. 178, Market
street. J. R. A. Skerrett, Printer. 1818.

   t.[1], 2–15, [16] p.; 10 pl.; 11.5 cm.; pr. yellow
paper covers.

   English ed. London: J. Marshall, 1822.

   MB°.

165.2 — ——— Philadelphia: Published By E.
And R. Parker, No. 178, Market Street. J. R. A.
Skerrett, Printer. 1819.

   t.[1], 2–15, [16, adv.] p.; 10 pl.; 12 cm.; pr.
buff paper covers.

   MWA° (rear cover ½ wanting); Shaw 47533.

166.1 — Little Mary; Or, The Picture-
Book. By Sabina Cecil. Author Of Little John,
Little Jane, Little Charlotte, &c. Philadelphia:
Published By E. And R. Parker. No. 178, Market
street. J. R. A. Skerrett, Printer. 1818.

   t.[1], 2–11, [12, adv.] p.; 10 pl.; 12 cm.; pr.
yellowish paper covers.

   English ed. London: J. Marshall, 1818. engr.
pl. dated Dec. 1st, 1800.

   MWA°; CLU; MSaE; Shaw 43559.

166.2 — ——— Philadelphia: Published By E.
And R. Parker, No. 178, Market Street. Price
coloured, 31 cts. Plain, 25 cts. 1819. [cover title].

   [pl. 2, opp. p. 3] 3–10, pl.[9–10] p.; 12 cm.;

pr. paper covers. Only 9 pl., of the former probable 10, are present. pl.[1] opp. p. 2 is the
probable missing pl.; pl.[2] pr. on one side of
the leaf; pl. 3–10 pr. on both sides of the leaf;
pl. [9] opp. p. 10 & pl.[10] opp. missing p. 11.
pr. on one side of the leaf.

   CtY° (t.[1], p. 2, all text p. following p. 10, &
pl.[1], wanting); Shaw 47534.

167.1 — Little Sophia; Or, The Picture-Book.
By Sabina Cecil, Author Of Little Mary, Little
Joseph, Little Charles, &c. Philadelphia: Published
By E. And R. Parker, No. 178, Market street.
J. R. A. Skerrett, Printer, 1818.

   t.[1], 2–11, [12, adv.] p.; 10 pl.; 12 cm.; pr.
paper covers.

   PP°; OClWHi (pr. orange paper front cover;
rear cover wanting).

167.2 — ——— Philadelphia: Published By E.
And R. Parker. No. 178, Market Street. J. R. A.
Skerrett, Printer. 1819.

   t.[1], 2–11, [12, adv.] p.; 10 pl.; 11 cm.; green
printed paper covers.

   MWA-T°; PP.

Cecilia and Marian. *See* Berquin, Arnaud, no.
83.1.

Charlotte or The Pleasing Companion. *See*
Somerville, E., no. **1227.1.**

168 Charlotte The Vain Little Girl; And
Poems For Children. Adorned with Cuts. New-
Haven. Sidney's Press. For J. Babcock & Son. 1819.

   fr.[2], t.[3], [4–5], 6–30, [31] p.; illus.; 10.5
cm.; illus. paper covers pr. in blue ink.

   MWA-W°; Ct; CtHi; DLC; NPV; Shaw 47568.

CHEAP REPOSITORY
   The following *Cheap Repository* tracts no. 1–42
are all 13.5–14.5 cm. with the same imprint. The
title vignette is the only illus. and differs in each
book. The title and location of the tracts are listed
without the name and address of the publisher.
Many of these tracts surely were meant for or
read by children. Others do not seem to be children's fare. For completeness the list of 42 tracts
is given. A complete set is in DLC, bound in
leather; CtY copy lacks no. 17, 32–39.

   The *Cheap Repository* tracts were first produced in England to bridge over the gulf "which

seperated the pious and improving books which the uneducated poor were expected to read from the loose ballads which they not only read, but sang aloud in the alehouses." (Spinney). The originator of this scheme was Hannah More, who not only guided the scheme, but wrote extensively for it. Her sister Sarah More was also a contributor. "The printers first associated wih the scheme were Samuel Hazard of Bath and John Marshall of London, who printed the tracts from March 3, 1795 to November 1797. After November, 1797 Evans & Hatchard became the publishers and some tracts were issued by H. More and F. C. Rivington." (Weiss 1946). On the back of a tract entitled *The Fall Of Adam. London. J. Evans, (Printer to the Cheap Repository for Moral and Religious Tracts,)* . . . *J. Hatchard, S. Hazard, Bath.* n.d. there is a notice dated Dec. 6, 1791 which states that John Marshall had refused to continue to print or sell the tracts for the conductors of the *Cheap Repository* unless he be given the copyright. The conductors of the *Cheap Repository* made certain conditions which Marshall did not choose to comply with so the rights of publication passed to J. Evans. The date 1791 in the MWA copy of *The Fall Of Adam* is undoubtedly a misprint for 1797 because Spinney, who had access to Hannah More's original letters, says that the break with Marshall occurred in November 1797 when the "right to publish reprints of the 1795-7 tracts was sold outright to Evans, Hatchard and Rivington, and the distributing organization of the Repository disbanded" (Spinney). The tracts were exceedingly successful. Between March 3, 1795–March 1796 over 2,000,000 were sold (Spinney). They were so lucrative that John Marshall continued to publish them until November 1799, even though he no longer had the right to. What was even worse he added new tracts such as the *Centered Cobler, The Baker's Dream,* "and other tracts of dubious moral value" (Spinney). Spinney states that Marshall kept the original woodblocks, and raises the question of who was the printer of the Evans, Hatchard, and Hazard Versions.

The imprints on the English ed. of the *Cheap Repository* vary. The title (Printer to the Cheap Repository) follows either or both the names of John Marshall of London, and Samuel Hazard of Bath, the tracts being sold by them as well as R. White of London and J. Elder of Edinburgh. The title (Printer to the Cheap Repository) will be abbrevi-

ated in all entries in this bibliography to "(pr.)". The abbreviations of the imprints used in citing the English source books of each tract and the dates of their appearance taken from Spinney are: Mar. 3, 1795–May 1795; Hazard (pr.), Marshall, White; May 1795–Jan. 1796: Hazard (pr.), Marshall (pr.), White; or Marshall (pr.), White, Hazard (pr.); Feb.–Dec. 1796: Marshall (pr.), White, Hazard; Jan.-July 1797; Marshall (pr.), White, Hazard, Elder; Aug.–Nov. 1797: Marshall (pr.), Hazard, Elder.

169.1 < Cheap Repository. > [No. I.] The Shepherd of Salisbury Plain, Part I. Philadelphia: Printed By B. & J. Johnson, No. 147 High-Street. 1800. < Price 4d, Or 2s. 9d. per doz. > [1800].
t.[1], [2], 3–36 p. Written by Hannah More.
English ed. Bath: Hazard (pr.); Marshall, White. [1795].
MWA°; CtY; DLC; PHi; Evans 37128; Weiss 1946.

169.2 < ——— > [No. II.] ——— Plain. Part II. To Which Is Added The Sorrows Of Yamba, A Poem. Philadelphia. ——— [1800].
t.[1], 2–36 p. Written by Hannah More.
English ed. Bath: Hazard (pr.), Marshall (pr.), White. [1795]. Sorrows Of Yamba. London: Marshall (pr.), White, Hazard (pr.) [collected vol. 1795].
MWA°; CtY; DLC; PHi; Evans 37129; Weiss 1946.

169.3 < ——— > [No. III.] Sunday Reading. The Parable Of The Labourers in the Vineyard. Philadelphia: ——— 1800.
t.[1], [2], 3–36 p.
English ed. London: Marshall (pr.), White, Hazard. [collected vol. 1795].
MWA°; CtY; DLC (p. 33–34 cropped, [35]–[36] cropped with page numbers wanting); PHi; Evans 37130; Weiss 1946.

169.4 < ——— > [Number IV.] The Wonderful Advantages of Adventuring In The Lottery!!! To Which Is Added The Happy Waterman. Philadelphia: ——— 1800.
t.[1], [2], 3–36 p.
English ed. London: Marshall (pr.), White, Hazard, Elder [1797]. The Happy Waterman. Bath: Hazard (pr.), Marshall (pr.), White. [1795].

MWA°; CtY; DLC; OOxM; Evans 37131; Weiss 1946.

169.5 < ———— > < No. V.> [VI.–IX.] The Two Wealthy Farmers; Or the History of Mr. Bragwell. Part I [II.–V.] Philadelphia: ———— 1800. < Price 4 Cents Or 2s. 4d. per doz. >
pt. I., II., III., IV. each have: [1], [2], [3], 4–36 p. Written by Hannah More.
English ed. Bath: Hazard (pr.), Marshall (pr.), White. [1795].
MWA°; CLU; CtY; DLC; OOxM; PHi; Evans 37132–37136; Weiss 1946.

169.6 < ———— > < No. X. > Sorrowful Sam; Or, the History of the Two Blacksmiths. Philadelphia: ———— 1800. < ———— >
t.[1], [2], 3–36 p. Written by Sarah More.
English ed. Bath: Hazard (pr.), Marshall (pr.), White. [collected vol. 1795].
MWA°; CtY; DLC; OOxM; PHi; Evans 37137; Weiss 1946.

169.7 < ———— > < No. XI. > The History Of Tom White, The Postilion. Philadelphia: ———— 1800. < ———— >
t.[1], [2], 3–36 p. Written by Hannah More.
English ed. Bath: Hazard (pr.), Marshall, White. [1795].
MWA°; CLU; CtHT; CtY; DLC; Evans 37138; Weiss 1946.

169.8 < ———— > < No. XII. > The Way To Plenty, Or, The Second Part Of Tom White. Philadelphia: ———— 1800. < ———— >
t.[1], [2], 3–36 p. Written by Hannah More.
English ed. London: Marshall (pr.), White, Hazard (pr.) [1795].
MWA°; CLU; CtHT; CtY; DLC; Evans 37139; Weiss 1946.

169.9 < ———— Number 13. > The Cheapside Apprentice; Or, The History of Mr. Francis Hˣˣˣ. Fully setting forth the Danger of Playing with Edge Tools. Shewing also, how a gay Life may prove a short one; and that a merry Evening may produce a sorowful Morning. Philadelphia: ———— 1800. < Price 4 Cents. > [< price 6 cents >] [DLC copy].
t.[1], [2], 3–35, [36, adv.] p. Written by Sarah More.

English ed. London: Marshall (pr.), White, Hazard. [1796].
MWA°; CtHT; CtY (p. 3–34 wanting); DLC; PHi; Evans 37140; Weiss 1946.

169.10 < ———— Number 14. > Husbandry Moralized; Or, pleasant Sunday Reading for a Farmer's Kitchen. Philadelphia. ———— 1800. < ———— > [< price 6 Cents. >] [DLC copy].
t.[1], [2], 3–35, [36, adv.] p.
English ed. Bath: Hazard (pr.), Marshall, White. [1795].
MWA°; CtHT; CtY; DLC; PHi; Evans 37141; Weiss 1946.

169.11 < ———— Number 15. > Black Giles the poacher; With some account of a Family who had rather live by their Wits than their Work. Philadelphia: 1800. < ———— > [< Price 6 Cents. >] [DLC copy].
t.[1], [2], 3–36 p. Written by Hannah More.
English ed. London: Marshall (pr.), White, Hazard. [1796].
MWA°; CtHT; CtY; DLC; NN; PHi; PP; RPJCB; ViU; Evans 37142; Weiss 1946.

169.12 < ———— Number 16. > poacher; With The History of Widow Brown's Apple-Tree. Philadelphia: ———— 1800. < ———— > [< Price 6 Cents. >] [DLC copy].
t.[1], [2], 3–35, [36] p.; caption p. 3: Tawny Rachel, &c. Written by Hannah More.
English ed. London: Marshall (pr.), White, Hazard. [1796].
MWA°; CtHT; CtY; (p. 35–[36] wanting); DLC; NN; PHi; PP; RPJCB; ViU; Evans 37143; Weiss 1946.

169.13 < ———— Number 17. > The History of Tawny Rachel, The Fortune Teller, Black Giles' wife. Philadelphia: ———— 1800. < ———— > [< Price 6 Cents. >] [DLC copy].
t.[1], [2], 3–35, [36, adv.] p. Written by Hannah More.
English ed. London: Marshall (pr.); White, Hazard, Elder. [1797].
MWA°; CtHT; DLC; NN; PHi; PP; RPJCB; ViU; Evans 37144; Weiss 1946.

169.14 < ——— Number 18. > [19.–21.] The History of the Two Shoemakers. Part I. [II–IV.] Philadelphia: ———— 1800. < Price 4 Cents. >

pt. I., II., III., IV. each have: t.[1], [2, bl.], [3], 4–36 p. Written by Hannah More.

English ed. Bath: pt. I. Hazard (pr.), Marshall, White. [1795].

MWA°; CLU (pts. I–III); CtHT (pts. I.–III.); CtY; DLC; NN (pt. IV.); PHi; PP (pt. I–IV); PPL (pt. IV.); Evans 37145–48; Weiss 1946.

169.15 < ——— Number 22. > Sunday Read-ing. The Harvest Home. Philadelphia: ——— 1800. < ——— >

t.[1], [2–3], 4–36 p.

English ed. London: Marshall (pr.), White, Hazard (pr.) [1795].

MWA°; CtY; DLC; NN; PHi; PP; PPL; Evans 37149; Weiss 1946.

169.16 < ——— Number 23. > The History Of The Plague In London, In 1665. Philadel-phia: ——— 1800. < ——— >

t.[1], [2–3], 4–36 p. Written by Daniel Defoe.

English ed. Bath: Hazard (pr.) Marshall, White. [1795].

MWA°; CtY; DLC; NN; PHi; PP; PPL; Evans 37150; Weiss 1946.

169.17 < ——— Number 24. >, [25.–26.] Sunday Reading. The Story Of Joseph And His Brethren. Part I. [II.–III.] Philadelphia: ——— 1800. < ——— >

pt. I., II., III. all have: t.[1], [2–3], 4–36 p.; bound in green Dutch paper.

English ed. London: pt. I.–III. Marshall (pr.), White, Hazard, Elder. [1797].

Welch°; CLU; CtY; DLC (3 pts. bound in green Dutch paper in a vol. of tracts); MWA; NN; PHi; PP; PPL; OOxM (pt. II.); Evans 37151–37153; Weiss 1946.

169.18 < ——— Number 27. > The Game-ster. Philadelphia: ——— 1800. < ——— >

t.[1], [2, bl.], [3], 4–36 p.

English ed. London: Marshall (pr.), White, Hazard. [1796].

CtHi°; CtY; DLC; MWA; NN; PHi; PP; PPL; Evans 37154; Weiss 1946.

169.19 < ——— Number 28. > The Fall Of Adam. Philadelphia: ——— 1800. < ——— >

t.[1], [2–3], 4–36 p.

English ed. London: J. Evans (pr.) J. Hatchard, & S. Hazard, Bath. n.d. adv. p. [16] dated Dec.

6, 1791. The date 1791 is probably a misprint for 1797.

MWA°; CtY; DLC; NN; PHi; PP; PPL; Evans 37155; Weiss 1946.

169.20 < ——— Number 29. > The Life of William Baker. Philadelphia: ——— 1800. < ——— >

t.[1], [2–3], 4–36 p. Written by the Rev. Mr. Gilpin.

English ed. Bath: Hazard (pr.), Marshall, White. [1795].

MWA°; CtHT; CtY; DLC; NN; PHi; PP; PPL; Evans 37156; Weiss 1946.

169.21 < ——— Number 30. > The History Of The Beggarly Boy. Philadelphia: ——— 1800. < ——— >

t.[1], [2–3], 4–36 p.

English ed. London: Marshall (pr.), White, Hazard (pr.). [1795].

PPL°; CtY (p. 17–20 wanting); DLC; NN; OOxM; PP; PPL; Evans 37157; Weiss 1946.

169.22 < ——— Number 31. > The Shop-keeper turned Sailor; To which is prefixed, A True Story Of A Good Negro Woman. Philadel-phia: ——— 1800. [no price given in no. 31–42].

t.[1], [2–3], 4–36 p. Written by Hannah More.

English ed. London: pt. I. Marshall (pr.), White, Hazard (pr.). [1796].

NN° (p. 29–30 mut.); CtY; DLC; PP; PPL; Evans 37158; Weiss 1946.

169.23 < ——— Number 32. > The Troubles Of Life. To which is prefixed, Patient Joe, Or The New-Castle Collier. Philadelphia: Printed ——— 1800.

t.[1], [2], 3–36 p.

English ed. London: broadside, Marshall (pr.), White, Hazard. [1795]. Patient Joe. London: Hazard (pr.), Marshall (pr.), White. [1795].

CtHi°; DLC; MH; MWA; NN; PP; PPL; Evans 37159; Weiss 1946.

169.24 < ——— Number 33. > The History of Mary Wood, The Housemaid; Or the Danger of False Excuses. Philadelphia: ——— 1800.

t.[1], [2–3], 4–36 p.

English ed. Bath: Hazard (pr.), Marshall (pr.), White. [1796].

MWA°; DLC; MH; NN; PP; PPL; Evans 37160; Weiss 1946.

169.25 < —— Number 34. > THE HISTORY
OF MR. FANTOM, The New Fashioned Philosopher. And His Man William. Philadelphia: ——
1800.

t.[1], [2], 3–36 p. Written by Hannah More.
English ed. London: Marshall (pr.), Hazard,
Elder. [1797].
MWA°; CtHi; DLC; MH; NjR; NN; PP; PPL;
Evans 37161; Weiss 1946.

169.26 < —— Number 35. > THE HUBUB;
Or, The History Of Farmer Russel, The Hard-
Hearted Overseer. Philadelphia: —— 1800.

t.[1], [2, bl.], [3], 4–36 p. *The Hubub* is signed
S [Sarah More] and followed by *The Lady and
the Pye*, in verse, signed Z [Hannah More].
English ed. London: Marshall (pr.), White,
Hazard, Elder. [1797].
MWA°; CtHi; DLC; MH; NjR; NN; PP; PPL;
Evans 37162; Weiss 1946.

169.27 < —— Number 36. > BEAR YE ONE
ANOTHER'S BURDENS; Or, The Valley Of Tears;
A Vision. Philadelphia: —— 1800.

t.[1], [2–3], 4–36 p. Written by Hannah More.
English ed. London: Marshall (pr.), White,
Hazard. [1796].
Welch°; MWA; CtHi; DLC; NN; PP; PPL;
Evans 37163; Weiss 1946.

169.28 < —— Number 37. > THE BLACK
PRINCE, A True Story; Being An Account of the
Life and Death Of Naimbanna, an African King's
Son, Who arrived in England in the Year 1791,
and set Sail on his Return in June 1792. Philadel-
phia. —— 1800.

t.[1], [2–3], 4–34, [35–36, adv.] p.
CtHi°; DLC; MWA; NN; PP; PPL; Evans
37164; Weiss 1946.

169.29 < —— Number 38. > BETTY BROWN,
THE ST. GILES'S ORANGE GIRL; With Some Account Of Mrs. Sponge, the Money-Lender. Philadelphia: —— 1800.

t.[1], [2–3], 4–36 p. Written by Hannah More.
English ed. London: Marshall (pr.), White,
Hazard. [1796].
MWA°; CtHi; DLC; MH; NN; PP; PPL; Evans
37165; Weiss 1946.

169.30 < —— Number 39. > THE COCK-
FIGHTER. A True History. Philadelphia: ——
1800.

t.[1], [2, bl.], [3], 4–36 p.
English ed. Bath: Hazard (pr.), Marshall,
White. [1795].
CtHi°; DLC; MH; MWA; NN; PP; PPL; Evans
37166; Weiss 1946.

169.31 < —— Number 40. > ONESIMUS; Or
The Run-Away Servant Converted. A True Story.
Philadelphia: —— 1800.

t.[1], [2, bl.], [3], 4–36 p.
English ed. London: Marshall (pr.), White,
Hazard. [1796].
CtHi° (p. 31–32, 35–36 mut.); DLC; MH;
MWA; NjR; NN; PP; PPL; Evans 37167; Weiss
1946.

169.32 < —— Number 41. > THE HISTORY
OF CHARLES JONES, The Footman; Written By
Himself. Philadelphia: —— 1800.

t.[1], [2–3], 4–36 p.
English ed. London: Marshall (pr.), White,
Hazard. [1796].
NN°; DLC; MH; MWA; PP; PPL; Evans
37068; Weiss 1946.

169.33 < —— Number 42. > SOME NEW
THOUGHTS FOR THE NEW YEAR. Philadelphia:
—— 1800.

t.[1], [2–3], 4–36 p.
English ed. London: Marshall (pr.), White,
Hazard (pr.). [1796].
CtHi° (t.[1], & p.[2] wanting); DLC; MWA;
NN; PP; PPL; Evans 37169; Weiss 1946.

170.1 CHEAP REPOSITORY TRACTS; Entertaining,
Moral, And Religious. Consisting Of A Great Va-
riety Of Separate Performances, Written In A
Neat, Yet Simple Style, And Eminently Calcu-
lated For The Amusement And Instruction Of The
Youth Of Both Sexes. Vol. I. The First Boston,
From The Latest English, Edition. Boston: Printed
And Sold By E. Lincoln, Water-Street. 1802.

t.[i], [ii, bl.—iii], [iv, bl.], [1], 2–380 p.; 17.5
cm.; bound in leather.
MBC° (top of p. 379–380 wanting); MB; MH
(t.[i] wanting); Shaw 2689; Weiss 1946.

170.2 —— Vol. II. The First Boston, From
The Latest English, Edition. Boston: Printed And
Sold By E. Lincoln, Water-Street, 1803.

t.[i], [ii–iii], iv, [5], 6–432 p.; 18 cm.; bound in leather.
MWA°; MBC (t.[1], p. 403–432 & covers wanting); KU; Weiss 1946.

170.3 ——— Vol. III. The First Boston, Edition. Boston: Printed And Sold by E. Lincoln, Water-Street. 1803.
1st t.[1], [2–5], 6–184; 2nd t.[185], [186–187], 188–352 p.; 17 cm.; bound in leather.
2nd title: Cheap Repository Tracts; ——— [same as 1st t.] Religious. A Monument To Praise Of The Lord's Goodness, And To The Memory Of Eliza Cunningham. [1 line quot.] I Cor. xv. 55. Boston: Printed And Sold By E. Lincoln, Water-Street.
The tract *A. Monument &.*, p. 212, is signed *John Newton, Charles's Square, Hoxton, October 13, 1785.*
MWA° (p. 109–110 mut.); KU; MBC; MH (p. 351 torn; text missing); NjP; NNC (rebound, t.[1], p. 351–352 mut.); Shaw 4678; Weiss 1946.

THE CHEAPSIDE APPRENTICE. *See* Cheap Repository, no. **169.9**, and More, Sarah, no. **900.1**.

THE CHERRY ORCHARD. *See* Edgeworth, Maria, no. **311**.

171.1 CHILDHOOD. New-York: adv. by S. Wood, 1812 in **439.1**.

171.2 CHILDHOOD. [3 lines quot.] Printed & sold by Samuel Wood, at the Juvenile Book-store, No. 357, Pearl-street. New York. 1813.
t.[1], [2–16] p.; illus.; 8 cm.; pr. & illus. paper covers; cover title undated.
MH°; Shaw 28125.

171.3 ——— New-York: Printed & sold by Samuel Wood, at the Juvenile Book-store, No. 357, Pearl-street, 1814.
t.[1], [2–16] p.; illus.; 8.5 cm.
MWA-W° (bound with other books in no. **637.1**).

171.4 ——— New-York: Printed And Sold by S. Wood, at the Juvenile Book-store, No. 357, Pearl-street. 1815.
t.[1], [2–16] p.; illus.; 8.5 cm.; pr. & illus. buff paper covers; cover title undated.
MWA°; Shaw 34334.

171.5 ——— Nerv-York [*sic. i.e.* New York]: Printed And Sold By Samuel Wood & Sons, at the Juvenile Book-store, No. 357, Pearl-street. 1816.
t.[1], [2–16] p.; illus.; 8 cm.; pr. & illus. buff paper covers; cover title undated.
MWA-W°; MWA; Shaw 51560.

171.6 ——— Nerv-York [*sic. i.e.* New York]: Published by Samuel Wood & Sons, No. 261, Pearl-street, And Samuel S. Wood & Co. No. 212, Market-st. Baltimore. 1818.
t.[1], [2–16] p.; illus.; 8 cm.; pr. & illus. buff paper covers; cover title undated. Adv. by S. Wood, 1819 in **1188.8**.
MWA°; MWA-W; PP; Shaw 43601.

THE CHILDREN IN THE WOOD (arranged chronologically)

172 THE AFFECTING HISTORY OF THE BABES IN THE WOOD. Embellished With Cuts. [2 lines of verse] New-York: Printed by J. Harrison, Peck-Slip. < Price three cents. > [*ca.* 1803].
t.[3], [4–5], 6–30 p.; illus.; 9 cm. John Harrison used the address "3 Peck-Slip" from 1801–1804. He died in 1804. The address at "Yorick's Head, 3 Peck Slip" was used from 1791–1800.
MWA-W° (covers, and 2 leaves, p.[2], [31] wanting); Shaw 50343.

173.1 THE AFFECTING HISTORY OF THE CHILDREN IN THE WOOD. Embellished with Cuts. [4 lines of verse] Hartford: Printed By J. Babcock. 1796.
fr.[2], t.[3], [4–5], 6–30, [31, adv.] p.; illus.; 10 cm.; orange Dutch paper covers.
MWA°; DLC (p. 29–30, & covers wanting, p.[2–4] mut., 13–28 torn); MB (per. st. on t.[1]); MiU (p. 29–30 wanting); NjP; PP (fr. [2] & front cover mut.).

173.2 ——— Hartford: Printed By John Babcock. 1798.
fr.[2], t.[3], [4–5], 6–29, [30–31, illus.] p.; illus.; 11 cm.
OOxM (t.[3], p.[4], 27–[30] wanting).

173.3 ——— First Newport Edition. Newport [R.I.]: Printed by H. & O. Farnsworth. 1799.
fr.[2], t.[3], [4–5], 6–27, [28, adv.], [29–31, illus.] p.; illus.; 11.5 cm.; gold Dutch paper covers.
MWA-W°; CtHi (poor copy); NjP; Evans 35086.

173.4 ———— [3 lines of verse] Stonington-Port [Conn.], Printed By S. Trumbull. 1800.

> fr.[2], t.[3], [4–5], 6–23 p.; illus.; 12 cm.; ornamented paper covers.
> PP*; Evans 36778.

173.5 ———— [4 lines of verse] Second Rhode Island Edition. Newport [R.I.]; Printed by Oliver Farnsworth. 1803.

> fr.[2], t.[3], [4–5], 6–29, [30–31, alphabets] p.; illus.; 11 cm.; ornamented gray wallpaper wrappers.
> MWA-W*; RNHi; Shaw 50344.

173.6 ———— Ornamented with Cuts. Providence [R.I.]: Printed By Heaton & Williams. [1804].

> illus. [1], [2, bl.] t.[3], [4–5], 6–31, [32 illus.] p.; illus.; 11 cm.; no separate covers; p. [1] & [32] serve as the covers.
> MWA*; CLU; Shaw 50416.

173.7 ———— [3 lines verse] First Vermont Edition. Windsor [Vt.], Printed By O. Farnsworth. Sold wholesale and retail at the Windsor Bookstore. 1809.

> fr.[2], t.[3], [4–5], 6–28, [29, bl.], [30, illus.], [31, alphabet] p.; illus.; 10 cm.; green paper covers.
> MWA*; RPB (p. 27–[31] wanting, t.[3], p. [4]–8 mut.); VtHi; McCorison 1052; Shaw 17201.

173.8 ———— Wood. [3 lines quot.] (Adorned with Cuts.) Windsor [Vt.], Printed By Jesse Cochran. And sold whole-salc [*sic. i.e.*—sale] and retail at his Book-store. 1814.

> fr.[2], t.[3], [4–5], 6–31 p.; illus.; 10 cm.; pr. & illus. yellowish-buff paper covers.
> Cover title of copy 1: Children In The Woods. Windsor, Vt. Printed and Sold by Jesse Cochran. Cover title of copy 2: The Children In The Wood. Windsor: Printed And Sold By Jesse Cochran, 1814. In this copy "whole-sale" is correctly printed on the title page.
> MWA* (copy 1); VtHi (copies 1 and 2); McCorison 1562; Shaw 31142.

173.9 ———— [2 lines of verse] (Adorned With Cuts.) Windsor, Vt. Printed By Jesse Cochran, And sold whole-sale and retail at his Book Store. 1815.

> fr.[2], t.[3], [4–5], 6–31 p.; illus.; 10.5 cm.; pr. & illus. buff paper covers.

Cover title: Children In The Woods. Windsor, Vt. Printed and Sold by Jesse Cochran.
See also English, Clara, no. **349.1.**
MWA* (p. 31 mut.); DLC; RPB (covers wanting, t.[3] mut.); McCorison 1693; Shaw 34335.

174.1 The Babes In The Wood. Their Death And Burial. Philadelphia: Printed in the year 1791.

> t.[1], 2–8 p.; 15.5 cm.
> PP*; Evans 46135.

174.2 The Babes In The Wood. To which is [added] The Bonny Sailor. [S]old at the Printing-Office in State-street, Albany, where may be had a great variety of entertaining Pamphlets, Songs, Picture Books, large Sheet-Pictures, &c. &c. [*ca.* 1799].

> t.[1], 2–8 p.; title vignette only illus.; 14 cm. A chapbook or ballad version.
> *See also* nos. **180–181.2.**
> An English ballad edition of *The Children In The Wood* was printed as early as 1593 according to the *Stationer's Register* and was included by Thomas Percy in his *Reliques*. 1765. Ashton records chapbook versions of 1640, 1700, 1720.
> MWA* (entire book torn in half).

THE CHILDREN IN THE WOOD (German editions)

175.1 Die Kinder Im Wald. Ephrata [Pa.]: Gedruckt bey Benjamin Mayer, 1797.

> t.[1], [2–3], 4–14, [15] p.; 12.5 cm.
> MWA*; P (rebound); PPL.

175.2 ———— Wald. Ephrata [Pa.]: Gedruckt bey John Baumann, 1807.

> t.[1], [2–3], 4–14 p.; title vignette only illus.; 13 cm.
> PP*; P; Shaw 12295.

175.3 ———— Libanon [Pa.] J. Schnee. 1809. Shaw 50922.

175.4 ———— Wald. Welche sehr bedauerlich auf mäuchelmerderische Art zu ihrem Ende gebracht worden sind. [Cut] Libanon [Pa.], Gedruckt bey Jacob Schnee, 1810.

> t.[1], [2], 3–12 p.; title vignette only illus.; 13 cm.; pr. 3 & illus. blue-gray paper covers.
> MWA* (rear cover wanting); PP; Shaw 19765.

THE CHILDREN IN THE WOOD, An Instructive Tale. *See* English, Clara, no. **350.1.**

176 THE CHILDREN IN THE WOOD. Or, The Norfolk Tragedy. Albany: Printed And Sold By Churchill & Abbey, No. 95, State-street, five doors east of the Episcopal Church. 181[5?].
t.[1], [2–3], 4–12 p.; illus. p. 12 only illus.; 11 cm; the last number of the date obliterated. Churchill & Abbey were in business together only in 1815 and the first two months of 1816. (MWA cat.).
MWA° (p. 11–12 mut.); Shaw 34336.

THE HISTORY OF THE CHILDREN IN THE WOOD, An Affecting Tale. *See* English, Clara, no. **349.1.**

177 THE HISTORY OF THE CHILDREN IN THE WOOD. Interspersed With Instructive Morals. Embellished With Cuts. Printed And Sold By Hosea Sprague, No. 88, Newbury-Street, Boston. 1804. < Price six cents. >
fr.[2], t.[3], [4–5], 6–64 p.; illus.; 11 cm.; Dutch paper covers. Same text as *The Tragical History Of The Children In The Wood*, no. **179.1.**
MWA° (rear cover wanting); MB (fr.[2] wanting; Shaw 6476.

178 THE HISTORY OF THE TWO BABES IN THE WOOD; Or, Murder Revenged: Containing, The sad and lamentable story of the death of two children of a Gentleman, who after the decease of their parents, were delivered by their uncle, to two ruffians to be murdered for their estates; but in the end they were left in an unfrequented wood, and there starved to death, and covered over by a Robin-red-breast. Together with the relation of the heavy judgements which befel their unnatural uncle, who died miserable in prison; & how it came to be discovered by one of the ruffians, upon his being condemned for a notorious robbery. With many other circumstances at large. [n.p.] [*ca.* 1809].
t.[1], [2, bl.], [3–4], 5–39 p.; 9.5 cm.; buff paper covers.
p.[3] has the holograph inscription *Sally Savage's Property Francestown*, [N.H.,] 1809.
CtHi°; MWA-T.

179.1 THE TRAGICAL HISTORY OF THE CHILDREN IN THE WOOD. Containing A True Account Of Their Unhappy Fate, With The History Of Their Parents, And Their Unnatural Uncle. Interspersed With Instructive Morals. Embellished With Cuts. Boston: Printed and sold by S. Hall No. 53, Cornhill. [1798].
fr.[2], t.[3], [4–5], 6–91 p.; illus.; 10 cm.; pr. buff paper covers; front cover imprint of MWA copy: Boston: Sold at Lincoln & Edmands' Bookstore, No. 53 Cornhill. 1815. The MH copy has Dutch paper covers, which was probably the way the book was originally issued. Lincoln & Edmands bought out Samuel Hall and moved to 53 Cornhill Sept. 14, 1807. The MWA & Welch copies are probably part of a remainder which Lincoln & Edmands rebound for sale in 1815.
English ed. York: T. Wilson and R. Spence, 1802.
Welch° (covers worn most of imprint wanting, p. 27–28 mut.); DLC; MH (rear Dutch paper cover wanting, fr.[2], t.[3] and other p. mut.); MWA; Evans 34677 (dated [1798]).

179.2 ———— Embellished with Twenty-Eight Engravings. Boston: Printed and Sold By Manning & Loring, No. 2, Cornhill. 1802.
fr.[2], t.[3], [4–5], 6–92, [93, adv.] p.; illus.; 11 cm.; Dutch paper covers.
MWA° (front mut.); Shaw 3176.

179.3 ———— Boston: Printed And Sold By Manning & Loring, No. 2, Cornhill. 1804.
fr.[2], t.[3], [4–5], 6–92, [93, adv.] p.; illus.; 11 cm.; yellow wallpaper covers ornamented with blue spots.
MWA°; Shaw 7381.

179.4 ———— Ornamented with Cuts. From Sidney's Press, New-Haven. For Increase Cooke & Co. 1806.
fr.[2], t.[3], [4–5], 6–71 p.; illus.; 13.5 cm.; buff paper covers.
CtHi°; MH; MShM; MWA-W (p. [2]–10, 57–71 wanting); Shaw 50657.

179.5 ———— Morals. Catskill [N.Y.]: Printed By Nathan Elliot. 1807.
t.[1], [2], 3–48 p.; 13 cm.; bound in marbled paper over bds., leather spine.
MWA°; Shaw 12296.

179.6 ——— Embellished with Twenty-Eight Engravings. Boston: Printed And Sold By Manning & Loring, No. 2, Cornhill. 1808.

  fr.[2], t.[3], [4–5], 6–95 p.; illus.; 11 cm.; blue marbled paper covers.

  Welch° (p. 49–50 mut.); CtHi (p. 89–95 wanting); MB (per. st. on t.[3]); MH (1st and last leaf torn); MWA (front cover wanting); Shaw 14684.

179.7 ——— [same as **179.1**]. Morals. Ornamented with Cuts. Wilmington [Del]: Printed By P. Brynberg; For Mathew R. Lockerman. 1809.

  fr.[2], t.[3], [4–5], 6–57 p.; illus.; 13.5 cm.; paper covers.

  DeWint°.

179.8 ——— Morals. Pittsburgh, Printed and Published By Cramer, Spear And Eichbaum, 1814.

  fr.[2], t.[3], [4–5], 6–108 p.; illus.; 13.5 cm.

  MWA° (covers wanting); Shaw 51376.

180 THE TWO BABES IN THE WOOD: Or, The Norfolk Gentleman's Last Will and Testament. To which is added, Mary's Dream, or Sandy's Ghost. New-York: Printed for the United Company of Flying Stationers. [1795?].

  t.[1], [2], 3–8 p.; title vignette only illus.; 16 cm. This is a chapbook version. The date is conjectural.

  MWA-W°; Evans 47382.

181.1 THE TWO BABES IN THE WOOD: Together With Divine Songs For Children. Poughkeepsie [N.Y.]; Printed By Nathan Douglas. 1796.

  t.[1], [2–3], 4–12 p.; 15 cm.

  MWA° (p. 11–12 mut.); PP (rebound); Evans 31326.

181.2 ——— Poughkeepsie—Printed, For the Travelling Booksellers. [*ca.* 1798].

  t.[1], [2–3], 4–12 p.; 20 cm.; text pr. on blue-gray paper.

  CtHi°; Evans 48391.

182 CHILDREN'S AMUSEMENTS. [2 lines of verse] New-York: Published By Samuel Wood & Sons, No. 261, Pearl-street; And Samuel S. Wood & Co. No. 212, Market-Street. Baltimore. 1820.

  t.[1], [2], 3–30 p.; illus.; 13 cm.; pr. & illus. buff paper covers. Adv. by S. Wood, 1819 in **1188.8**.

  MWA°; RPB; Shoemaker 732.

183 THE CHILDREN'S BIBLE: Or, An History of the Holy Scriptures. In which, the several Passages of the Old and New Testament are laid down in a Method never before attempted; being reduced to the tender Capacities of the Little Readers, by a lively and striking Abstract, so as, under God, to make those excellent Books take such a firm Hold of their young Minds and Memories, and leave such Impressions there, both of Moral and Religious Virtue, as no Accidents of their future Lives will ever be able to blot out. To which is added, The Principles of the Christian Religion, adapted to the Minds of Children: with a small Manual of Devotions fitted for their Use. By a Divine of the Church of England. Adorned with Cuts. London: Printed, And, Philadelphia: Re-Printed and sold by Andrew Steuart, at the Bible in Heart in Second-street, M,DCC,LXIII.

  fr.[ii], t.[iii], [iv–v], vi–xiv, [15], 16–127, fr.[128], 2nd t.[129], [130], 131–158, [159, bl.], fr.[160], 3rd t.[161], [162–163], 164–224 p.; 3 front. only illus.; 12.5 cm.; bound in leather.

  Second title: The Principles Of The Christian Religion, Adapted to the Minds of Children: With a small Manual of Devotions Fitted for their Use. London: Printed, And, Philadelphia: Re-Printed and sold by Andrew Steuart, at the Bible in Heart in Second-Street, M,DCC,LXIII.

  Third title: An History Of The New Testament. London: Printed, And, Philadelphia: Re-Printed and sold by Andrew Steuart, at the Bible in Heart in Second-Street, M,DCC,LXIII.

  English ed. London: J. Wilkie, 1759.

  PP° (all before p. 33 wanting); DLC (p.[v]–vi want); NN (copy 1., 1st t.[iii] wanting, 3rd t.[161] largely torn away; copy 2., all 3 title pages mut., everything below first line of imprint cut away).

THE CHILDREN'S FRIEND. *See* Berquin, Arnaud, nos. **71.1–8**.

THE CHILDREN'S FRIEND, And Youth's Monitor. *See* Berquin, Arnaud, nos. **72.1–7**.

184 A Premium For Sabbath Schools. CHILDREN'S HYMN BOOK; Being A Selection of Hymns, From Various Authors. [4 lines of verse] Newark, N. J. Published By William Tuttle, And For Sale at his Book & Stationary Store 1819.

fr.[2], t.[3], [4–5], 6–35 p.; front. only illus.; 13.5 cm.; pr. yellow paper covers. MWA*; Shaw 47582.

185 THE CHILDREN'S MAGAZINE; Calculated For The Use Of Families And Schools For January 1789. Hartford: Printed By Hudson And Goodwin With Privilege of Copy-Right.

[No. 1] January 1789: t.[1], [ii–iii], iv, 5–48 p.; 18 cm.

[No. 2] The Children's Magazine; For February 1789. [caption title] p. 49–96 p.; 18.5 cm.

[No. 3] ———— For March 1789. Contents [2 columns of 13 lines.] Hartford: Printed And Sold By Hudson and Goodwin. [cover title] 97–144 p.; 18.5 cm.; pr. blue-gray paper covers.

[No. 4] ———— For April 1789. Contents. [2 columns of 13 lines] Hartford: Printed and Sold by Hudson and Goodwin. [cover title] 145–192 p.; 18.5 cm.; pr. blue-gray paper covers.

MWA* ([No. 1] p.[1]–12, and covers wanting; [No. 2] covers wanting; [No. 3] rear cover wanting; [No. 4] p. 181–192, and rear cover wanting, p. 145–148 mut.); [DLC [No. 4]; MCB (complete); N (No. 1–4, 4 incomplete); RPJCB ([No. 3], p. 139–144 wanting); Evans 21734.

186 THE CHILDREN'S MISCELLANY: In Which Is Included The History Of Little Jack; By Thomas Day, Esq., Author Of The History Of Sandford And Merton. [4 lines of quot.] Dryden. First American Edition; Embellished with Thirty-Five Cuts and Frontispieces. Boston: Printed And Sold By William Spotswood. 1796.

fr.[ii], t.[i], [ii–iv], [1], 2–331, [332, adv. list of books] p.; illus.; 17.5 cm.; bound in leather. fr.[ii] signed *Trenchard;* illus. p.[278] signed *J. G. Weston,* p. 79 pr. 97.

English ed. London: 1787.

MWA* (p. 283–288 mut.); NjP; NN (fr.[ii], p. 59–60, 289–290, 299–300 wanting, other p. ½ wanting or mut.); Evans 30190; Hamilton 168.

187.1 THE CHILD'S BATTLEDOOR. Nerv-York [*sic. i.e.* New York]: Printed And Sold By Samuel Wood & Sons, No. 261, Pearl-Street. 1817. [cover title].

[1–4] p. pr. on one side only of 8 leaves; illus.; 17 cm.; pr. & illus. yellow paper covers. MWA* (p. [3] slightly mut.); Shaw 40466.

187.2 ———— Nerve-York [*sic. i.e.* New-York]: Printed And Sold By Samuel Wood & Sons, No. 357 Pearl-Street. 1817. [cover title].

[1–4] p.; illus.; 18 cm.; yellow pr. & illus. paper covers. The book is the same as no. **187.1**, which also has "New York" spelled "Nerve York" except for the address which is "261" Pearl-Street instead of "357".

MWA-T* (all pages slightly mut.).

188 THE CHILD'S BIRTHDAY HISTORY OF SAMUEL DANIEL; and Little Nancy. Philadelphia: Published by the Sunday and Adult Sunday School Union. Clark & Raser Printers. 1818.

t.[1], [2–3], 4–32 p.; 10 cm.

Oppenheimer*.

189 THE CHILD'S CABINET. New-York: Printed And Sold By S. Wood & Sons, At The Juvenile Book-Store, No. 357, Pearl-Street. 1815.

One volume of twelve books. All twelve were issued separately by Samuel Wood, the collation of which will be found under each title. The two books present are: *The Pleasing Toy,* no. **1025.5,** and *The Cries Of London,* no. **249.20.** The remaining missing books, but listed on p. [iii], are: *Little Poems For Little Readers,* **441.4;** *Hymns for Little Children,* **439.3;** *Beauties of the New England Primer; The Medley,* **829.2;** *The History Of Beasts,* no 1815 edition known; *The History of Birds,* **534.9;** *The History Of Fish,* **539.5;** *The History Of Insects,* no 1815 ed. known; *The Book of Riddles,* **115.7;** *New-Year's Gift,* **944.8.** Adv. by Samuel Wood & Sons, 1816 in **1188.7,** and 1819 in **1188.8.** MWA-T.

190.1 THE CHILD'S COMPANION; No. I [II]. Being A Collection Of Easy Pieces In Prose And Poetry, For Young Readers. Auburn [N.Y.]: Printed for the Union Tract Association of Friends in the western counties of the state of New-York, By J. Beardslee and Co. 1818.

No. I.: t.[1], [2], 11–14 p.; 15 cm.; covers wanting; No. II.: t.[1], [2–3], 4–18 p.; 13.5 cm.; 2 vols.; blue-gray paper covers; caption p. [3]: The Child's Companion. < No. II First Month, 1819.

PHC* (No. I.: p.[3]–10, 15–18, & covers wanting; i. st. on t.[1]; No. II.); MWA (No. II.); Shaw 43603.

190.2 ———— Auburn [N.Y.]; Printed for the Union Tract Association of Friends in the western counties of the state of New-York, by D. Rumsey. 1819.

t.[1], [2–3], 4–18 p.; 15.5 cm. Caption p.[3]: The Child's Companion. <No. III. Third Month, 1819.

PHC° (emb. st. on t.[1]); Shaw 51866.

191 THE CHILD'S MAGAZINE. In Two Volumes. Vol. I. [II.] New-York: Printed And Sold By Samuel Wood, At The Juvenile Book-Store, No. 357, Pearl-Street. 1815.

vol. I.: t.[i], [ii–iv] p.; followed by six books bound together which were issued separately by Samuel Wood, the collation of which will be found under each title. They are: The Cries Of New York. 1816; Poetic Tales. 1815; Garden Amusements. 1815; History Of Alexander Selkirk. 1815; Select Fables, In Prose And Verse. 1815; The Olio. 1815; 13.5 cm.

vol. II.: t.[i], [ii–iv] p.; followed by a series of six books bound in this volume, which were issued separately by Samuel Wood, the collation of which will be found under each title. They are as follows: [Parnell, Thomas] *The Hermit and The Traveller. 1814; The Life Of That Wonderful and Extraordinarily Heavy Man, Daniel Lambert. 1814;* Colles, Christopher. *An Account of the Astonishing Beauties And Operations of Nature. 1815; The Youth's Cabinet Of Nature. 1814;* [More, Hannah] *The Pilgrims And Parley The Porter. 1815; The Wonderful Advantages of Adventuring in the Lottery.* [1815]; 13.5 cm.

NHi° (vol. I. Poetic Tales [n.d.]); MWA (vol. II.); NWebyC (vol. I. contains same books as NHi copy with Poetic Tales dated 1815); PHi; PP (vol. I.); Shaw 51476.

192 THE CHILD'S MANUAL. Montpelier [Vt.]: adv. by E. P. Walton, 1819 in **134.10.**

193.1 THE CHILD'S MUSEUM; Containing A Description Of One Hundred and eight Interesting Subjects. With Plates. Philadelphia: Published By Jacob Johnson, No. 147, Market-street. 1804. < J. Rakestraw, Printer. >

t.[1], [2–3], 4–72 p.; 18 pl; t.[1]; 14 cm.; pl. I–XVIII are reprints of pl. XIX–XXXV in *A Mother's Remarks On A Set Of Cuts. Philadelphia.* 1803. *See no.* **909.**

English ed. London: the plates first appeared in

[Mrs. Lovechild's Book of Three Hundred & Thirty-six Cuts.] title page wanting, pl. III signed *Will.ͫ Darton & Jos.ʰ Harvey, . . . Dec.ͬ 31, 1799.*

MWA-W° (rebound); PP (bound in marbled paper over bds.); Shaw 50417.

193.2 ———— Philadelphia: Published By Johnson & Warner, No. 147, Market Street. 1809. Lydia Bailey, Printer.

t.[1], [2–3], 4–72 p.; illus.; 15 cm.; bound in blue marbled paper over bds.; 16 pl. Adv. by Johnson & Warner, 1814 in **1449.2.**

MDeHi°; CLU; NN (p. 69–72 and covers wanting); Shaw 17204.

194.1 THE CHILD'S NEW PLAY-THING: Being A Spelling-Book Intended To make the Learning to Read a Diversion instead of a Task. Consisting of Scripture-Histories, Fables, Stories, Moral and Religious Precepts, Proverbs, Songs, Riddles, Dialogues, &c. The Whole adapted to the Capacities of Children, and Divided into Lessons of one, two, three, and four Syllables. The Fourth Edition. To which is added Three Dialogues; 1. Shewing how a little Boy shall make every body love him. 2. How a little Boy shall grow wiser than the rest of his School-fellows. 3. How a little Boy shall become a great Man. Designed for the Use of Schools, or for Children before they go to School. Boston: Printed by J. Draper, J. Edwards in Cornhill. 1750.

t.[1], [2], 3–120 p.; 14.5 cm.; yellow paper covers. The Boston edition is the first American child's book with folk tales such as "St. George and the Dragon", "Fortunatus", "Guy of Warwick", "Reynard the Fox", and "Riddles". English ed. London: T. Cooper, 1743. This edition preceded Mary Cooper's ed. of 1743.

NN° (p. 5–8, 23–24, wanting, p. 25–26 half wanting, t.[1], p.[2]–14 and other p. mut.); Evans 6477.

194.2 ———— Consisting Of A new-invented Alphabet for Children. A Variety of Lessons in Spelling, of one, two, three, four, five, six, and seven Syllables, with Scripture-Histories, Fables Stories, Moral and Religious Precepts, Riddles, &c. With entertaining Pictures to each Story and Fable. The Whole adapted to the Capacities of Children, and designed for the Use of Schools, or for Children before they go to School. To which is added,—Three Dialogues, shewing, First, How a little Boy shall make every Body love him. Second, How he shall grow wiser than the rest of his School-fellows. And, Third, How he shall become a great Man. Philadelphia: Printed by W. Dunlap, at the Newest-Printing-Office, on the South Side of the Jersey Market. M,DCC,LXIII.

t.[1], [ii, bl.–iii], iv–v, 6–136 p.; illus.; 13.5 cm.; bound in buff paper over w. bds., leather spine.

DLC° (p. 85–86 wanting); Evans 41334.

195 THE CHILD'S OWN BOOK, Containing the Alphabet, and easy Lessons, in Verse and Prose; with the History of Polly Pleasant and Betsey Thoughtless. Boston: Adv. by S. Hall, 1792 in **1408.32.**

English ed. London: J. Marshall. [*ca.* 1787].

196 THE CHILD'S PICTURE-BOOK. New-York: Printed And Sold By John C. Totten, No. 9, Bowery. 1820.

fr.[2], t.[3], [4–7], 8–34 p.; illus.; 13.5 cm.; pr. & illus. buff paper covers.

MWA-W° (rear cover & p. [35]? wanting); Shoemaker 734.

197.1 THE CHILD'S PLAIN PATH-WAY TO ETER- NAL LIFE; Or An Heavenly Messenger. Being A most wonderful Relation How one Mr. James Worthy, a pious Gentleman of Titbury in [Staf- fordshire] had Twelve Sons, whom [h]e baptized after the Names of Jacob's Twelve Sons.—How they all died in their Childhood, but Benjamin the younger: Of this Youths early Piety, and godly Discourses betwixt him and his Father, when but nine Years Old. How he made a Prayer to God for Grace, and was answered by an invisible Voice, That he was a Child of God. How he was taken ill of a Fever, August 22, 1745. Of his pious Be- havior during his Sickness, and the holy Expres- sions he used at the Hour of Death.—With the Manner of the Apparition of this blessed Youth, his Eleven Brothers and Mother cloathed in White, with Crowns of Gold on their Heads, and Instruments of Music in their Hands, appeared to his Father, and the Reverand Mr. Jones, rector of the Parish, to whom they gave a wonderful Ac- count of Heaven and Hell, and of the glorious State of the Blessed, and miserable Torments of the Wicked. The Truth is attested by Mr. Jones, Rector of Titbury's Parish, Richard King, Gent.

James Clark and John Rogers, Church-Wardens. New London: T. Green. 1765.

t.[1], [2], 3–8 p.
RPJCB.

197.2 ———— New-Haven: Printed and Sold by T. & S. Green. [*ca.* 1775].

t.[1], [2], 3–8 p.; 21 cm.
CtHi°; Evans 42790.

197.3 ———— efter [*sic. i.e.:* after] the Names of Jacob's ———— nine Year's old. —How he was taken ill of a Fever, August 22d. 1745 ———— ap- pear'd to his Father ———— [same as New-Haven [*ca.* 1775] ed.] Printed and sold in New-London. [*ca.* 1790].

t.[1], [2], 3–11, 24[sic. 12] p.; 15 cm.
NN° (rebound, i. st. on p.[2]); DLC (blue- gray paper covers wanting except for a frag- ment); RPJCB.

197.4 ———— Norwich, [Conn.]. Printed by J. Trumbull. 1791.
NhD.

197.5 ———— Messenger. Containing, A True Account of one Mr. James Worthy, a pious Gentle- man of Titbury in Staffordshire, who had twelve Sons, whom he baptized after the names of Jacob's ———— Discourses between him and his Father, ———— How he made a Prayer to God for Grace, and was answered by a voice, That he was a Child of God. How he was taken ill ———— appearing to his Father, and the Rev. Mr. Jones, Minister of the Parish, to whom he gave a wonderful Relation ———— [same as New-London *ca.* 1790 ed.]. Newburyport [Mass.]: Printed In The Year, M, DCC,XCIII.

t.[1], [2, bl.–3], 4–12 p.; 19.5 cm.
MWA°; Evans 26512.

197.6 ———— [same as **197.5**] Jacob's twelve Sons. How ———— [same as **197.1**] Of this Youth's early Piety, and good Discourse between him ———— and was answer'd by a Voice, ———— at the Hour of Death. With the Manner ———— to whom he gave a wonderful Relation of Heaven and Hell, ———— Mr. Jones, Rector of Titbury Parish, Richard King, Gentleman, ———— Church- Wardens. Sold at the Bible & Heart in Cornhill, Boston. [*ca.* 1793].

t.[1], 2–8 p.; 15.5 cm.; blue wallpaper covers.

The old form of the letter "s" is used. On p. 8 is a mss. date "*1801*". The text follows the version of no. **197.5**. The book is being tentatively dated [*ca.* 1793].
MWA-T°.

198 THE CHILD'S PLAY BOOK. To Teach Children Their Letters As Soon As They Can Speak. Windsor, Vt. Printed By E. Brooks. 1811.
   t.[3], 4–31 p.; 6 cm.; marbled paper covers.
This is an edition of *Tom Thumb's Play Book* with a new title.
MWA° (covers and first leaf wanting); Shaw 22521.

CHILD'S SPELLING BOOK. *See* Walton, Eliakim Persons, no. **1403**.

199 THE CHILD'S TRUE FRIEND. A Series Of Examples For The Proper Behavior Of Children. With Five Beautiful Engravings. Philadelphia: Published By Johnson & Warner, No. 147, Market-Street. 1811.
   t.[i], [ii–iii], iv, [5], 6–108 p.; 5 pl.; 14 cm.; bound in pr. pink paper over bds.
English ed. London: Tabart And Co. 1808.
NNC-Pl°; Shaw 22522.

THE CHIMNEY-SWEEPER'S COMPLAINT. *See* Holloway, William, no. **611.1**.

200 A CHOICE COLLECTION OF HYMNS, And Moral Songs; Adapted to the Capacities of Young People, on the several Duties and Incidents of Life. Adorned with Cuts, to impress more lasting ideas of each Subject upon the Mind, than can be attained by those in common use. To which is added, Specimens Of Divine Poetry. By Several Authors. Hartford: Printed By John Babcock. 1801.
   t.[3], [4–5], 6–111 p.; 13 cm.; bound in buff paper over bds., leather spine.
English ed. Newcastle: T. Saint; W. Charnley; and J. W. Whitfield. MDCCLXXXI.
MWA°; Ct; Shaw 304.

201.1 A CHOICE COLLECTION OF RIDDLES: For the Improvement of Young Minds. Chiefly From The Big Puzzling Cap. Printed at Worcester: Massachusetts, By Isaiah Thomas, Jun. Sold Wholesale and Retail by Him 1793.

fr.[2], t.[3], 4–31 p.; illus.; 11 cm.; Dutch paper covers.
MWA° (rebound); Evans 25194.

201.2 ———— Printed at Worcester: Massachusetts, By Isaiah Thomas, Jun. Sold Wholesale and Retail by Him. 1799.
   fr.[2], t.[3], 4–31 p.; illus.; 10.5 cm.; ornamented buff paper covers.
CtHi°; MWA-W (p. [2]–6, 27–31 & covers wanting); Evans 48820.

CHOICE EMBLEMS FOR CHILDREN. *See* Smart, Christopher, no. **1217**.

CHOICE EMBLEMS FOR THE IMPROVEMENT AND PASTIME OF YOUTH. *See* Wynne, John Huddlestone, no. **1456.1**.

CHOICE EMBLEMS, NATURAL, HISTORICAL, FABULOUS, MORAL AND DIVINE, For The Improvement and Pastime Of Youth. *See* Wynne, John Huddlestone, no. **1457.1**.

202 CHOICE TALES; Consisting Of An Elegant Collection Of Delightful Little Pieces For The Instruction & Amusement Of Young Persons. Philadelphia, Printed By Joseph Charless, For Mathew Carey, No. 118, Market Street. 1800.
   t.[1], [2–3], 4–170, [171–172] p.; 14 cm.; bound in brown paper over bds., leather spine.
English ed. London: Vernor & Hood, 1799.
Welch°; CLU; DLC (rebound, i. st. on t.[1]); ICU; MWA; PP; PU; Evans 37180.

CHOICE TALES, For The Improvement Of Youth Of Both Sexes. *See* Somerville, Elizabeth, no. **1228**.

203.1 No. 11. THE CHRISTIAN DRUMMER: A True Interesting Story. Published By The Philadelphia Female Tract Society. [caption title]. Printed by Lydia R. Bailey, No. 10, North Alley, Philad. [1816].
   [1], 2–8 p.; 14 cm.; [colophon p. 8].
MWA° (bound with other tracts with which *The First Annual Report Of The Philadelphia Female Tract Society For The Year 1816* was originally bound); Shaw 37146.

203.2 CHRISTIAN DRUMMER. Published For The Hartford Evangelical Tract Society, And To Be

Had Of Their Agent, Mr. James R. Woodbridge, In Hartford, And At Their Depository In The Principal Towns In This State. Price, 1 cent, or $1 per 100. Hartford, Conn. 1820.

t.[1], 2–4 p.; 16 cm.; pr. blue-gray paper covers; signed *J. C.* on p. 4.

MWA* (per. st. on front cover); Shoemaker 741.

204 EIN CHRISTAGS-GESCHENK FÜR KLEINE KNABEN; oder eine Sammlung von verschiedenen Unterretungen. Das 3te Virginische Kinderbuch. Neumarket: Schenandoah Caunty, Virg. Gedruckt für Salmon Henkel, 1809.

t.[1], [2–3], 4–36 p.; illus.; 13.5 cm.; paper covers; p. 36: Andreas N. Henkel, Drucker: Neumarket.

MWA*; PPL; Shaw 17209.

205 CHRISTMAS-GIFT TO CHILDREN WHO DELIGHT IN THE PRAISES OF THE INCARNATE SAVIOR. [n.p.] [*ca.* 1790].

t.[1], [2–8] p.; 14 cm.; verse.

CtHi*.

CHRISTMAS TALES. *See* Sobersides, Solomon, no. **1220.1.**

CINDERELLA. *See* Perrault, Charles, no. **987.1.**

CITY SCENES. *See* Gilbert, Ann (Taylor), no. **436.**

206 CLARA OR THE REFORM. New York: adv. by T. B. Jansen, [*ca.* 1815] in **47.**

207.1 CLARISSA DORMER: Or, The Advantages Of Good Instruction. Philadelphia. Published By B. And T. Kite. No. 20, North Third-street. 1810.

fr.[ii], t.[1], [2–3], 4–36 p.; 3 pl. including front.; 13 cm.; gray-green paper covers. Label on the front cover: History Of Clarissa Dormer, Or The Advantages Of Good Instruction. With Engravings. Boston. Sold By Munroe & Francis, No. 4 Cornhill, Corner of Water-Street; And David Francis Five doors North of Boylston [Market].

English ed. London: J. Harris, 1808

MWA*; CLU; PPL; Shaw 19783.

207.2 ——— Philadelphia. Printed For Johnson And Warner, No. 147, Market Street. 1810. Lydia R. Bailey, Printer, No. 10, North-Alley.

fr.[ii], t.[1], [2–3], 4–36 p.; 3 pl. including front.; 13.5 cm.; paper covers.

MSaE*; Shaw 50990.

[CLOWES, JOHN] 1743–1831

208.1 [—] THE CATERPILLARS AND THE GOOSEBERRY BUSH; Or A True Figure Of The Bad Passions And Their Mischievous Effects; Together With A Brief Account Of Their Origin And Cure. In Three Dialogues, Between A Father And Son. Designed For The Instruction Of Youth. [1 line quot.] Hosea xii. 10. Printed In London: Reprinted At Salem, By Thomas C. Cushing. 1802.

t.[1], [2–3], 4–32 p.; 14.5 cm.; blue-gray paper covers; p. [2] signed *J. Clowes. St. John, Jan.* 20, 1800.

English ed. Manchester: C. Wheeler & Son. 1807.

MWA* (rear cover wanting); CLU; KU; MSaE; OClWHi; Shaw 2004.

208.2 ——— Effects. To Which Is Added, The Rain-Bow, Or The Token Of God's Covenant With His People. By Way Of Dialogue, Between A Father And His Son. By The Rev. John Clowes. [1 line quot.] Hosea xii. 10. Baltimore: Printed By John West Butler, Corner Of Gay & Water Streets, Near The Custom-House. 1808.

t.[1], [2–3], 4–60 p.; 13.5 cm.

NcD* (covers wanting); MdBJ; Shaw 14711.

208.3 [—] ——— Account Of Their Orig [*sic. i.e.* Origin] ——— [same as **208.1**] Philadelphia: Published by Jacob Johnson. No. 147, Market street. 1808. W. M'Culloch, Printer.

t.[1], [2–5], 6–35 p.; 13 cm.; marbled paper covers.

MWA*; DLC; NcD; Shaw 14712.

208.4 [—] ——— [same as **208.1**] From The Halcyon Press. New-York: Printed And Published By S. Woodworth & Co. No. 468 Pearl-Street. 1811.

t.[1], [2–5], 6–33 p.; 15 cm.; bound with *A Picture Of The Broad And Narrow Way . . . From The Halcyon Press. New-York: Printed And Published By S. Woodworth & Co., No. 468 Pearl-street. 1811.*

CtY*; Shaw 51073.

208.5 [—] ——— Effects. In Two Dialogues between a Father and Son. Boston: Printed By Nathaniel Willis. 1816.

fr.[1], t.[2], 3–21, [22, illus.] p.; illus.; 12 cm.; illus. blue-gray paper covers.

MWA-W° (front cover wanting); OOxM (front cover present); Shaw 37276.

208.6 [—] ——— [same as **208.1**] Hallowell [Me.]: Printed By Ezekiel Goodale. 1816.

t.[1], [2–3], 4–35 p.; 14.5 cm.; pr. blue paper covers. Cover title imprint: Hallowell: Sold By Glazier & Co. 1826.

MWA°; CLU; DLC; ICU; MBAt; MeBa; MSaE; PP; Shaw 37277.

208.7 [—] ——— Father and Son. Boston: Printed By N. Willis. 1818.

fr.[1], t.[2], 3–21 p.; front. only illus.; 12 cm. MWA° (fr.[1], p.[22] and covers wanting); NB (2 copies sewn together, both want p. [22] and rear cover, copy 1 has a bookplate pasted over fr.[1], copy 2 wants front pink paper cover); PP (p.[22], and rear cover wanting); Shaw 43648.

209 [—] THE GOOSEBERRY-BUSH, AND CATER-PILLARS: Or, A True Figure of the bad Passions, And Their Mischievous Effects. In Two Dialogues Between A Father And Son. Printed and sold by Lincoln & Edmands, No. 53 Cornhill, Boston. 1818.

t.[1], [2–3], 4–23, [24, adv. list of books] p.; illus.; 13 cm.; pr. & illus. brick-red paper covers. Cut of a tree on the front cover.

MWA°; CLU; MSaE (emb. st. on t.[1]); OOxM; PP; Shaw 44184.

210 [—] Sacred Histories, selected from the Old Testament. Philadelphia, printed by Lydia R. Bailey, for William Schlatter, 1818.

Shaw 43649.

COBWEBS TO CATCH FLIES. *See* Fenn, *Lady Eleanor*, no. **397**.

THE COCK-FIGHTER. *See* Cheap Repository, no. **169.30**.

COCK ROBIN (arranged chronologically)

211 COCK ROBIN'S DEATH AND FUNERALS. Sold at the Bible & Heart in Cornhill, Boston. [*ca.* 1780].

t.[1], 2–32 p.; illus.; 9.5 cm.; orange Dutch paper covers.

On p. 3 is an alphabet cut used for "N. Nightingales Sing" in *The New England Primer* for an edition earlier than the Boston 1727 edition of *The New England Primer,* which has this cut in the reverse. This early primer cut and more of the same series were used by Thomas and John Fleet in *Tom Thumb's Folio,* [*ca.* 1789], no. **1315.1**. Still earlier these same cuts were used in Harris' *The Holy Bible In Verse,* 1717 in **492.1** and 1724 in **492.3,** printed by John Allen. The 1729 edition of *The Holy Bible In Verse,* no. **492.4,** probably printed by Thomas Fleet, again has these old primer cuts and a new one.

English ed. London: 1st four verses only: *Tommy Thumb's Pretty Song Book. M. Cooper* [*ca.* 1744].

DLC°; MWA (t.[1], p. 2, 29–30 wanting); PP; Evans 43778.

212.1 THE COURTSHIP & MARRIAGE OF COCK ROBIN, And Jenny Wren. Illustrated with Elegant Engravings. Philadelphia: Published and sold wholesale by Wm. Charles And may be had of all the [Book]sellers. 1808. Price twenty-five Cents. [cover title].

[1–13] p.; engr. on one side only of 13 leaves; illus.; 12.5 cm.; pr. yellow paper covers. The text and illus. (in the reverse) are copied from the first half, p. [1]–15, of the English ed. below.

English ed. London, entitled: *The Happy Court-ship, Merry Marriage, And Pic Nic Dinner, Of Cock Robin, And Jenny Wren. To which is added, Alas! The Doleful Death Of The Bride-groom.* J. Harris, 1806.

MWA°; Shaw 14717.

212.2 ——— Philadelphia: Published and sold By Johnson & Warner, And may be had of all the Book-sellers. 1809. Price 18 Cents. [cover title].

[1–13] p. engr. on one side only of 13 leaves; illus.; 12 cm.; pr. brown paper covers; rear cover had adv. of 9 titles; pl.[8] "Jenny And Attendants", and pl.[9] "Robin And The Bul-finch" in wrong order in MWA copy.

The plates used in **212.1** and **212.2** appear in a book without a title page and having brown paper covers. The book is part of a publisher's remainder which was considered to be printed after 1820. While the date is still in question it

is possible that the book is part of a remainder printed by Johnson and Warner in 1809.
MWA°; MBSpnea; OOxM; Shaw 50925.

213.1 THE DEATH AND BURIAL OF COCK ROBIN; With The Tragical Death Of A, Apple Pye: The Whole Taken From the original Manuscript In The Possession of Master Meanwell. First Worcester Edition. Printed at Worcester, Massachusetts, By Isaiah Thomas, And sold Wholesale and Retail at his Book-Store. MDCCLXXXVII.
fr.[2], t.[3], [4–5], 6–31 p.; illus.; 10 cm.; gold Dutch paper covers.
English ed. London: adv. by John Marshall with the title *The Life, Death, and Burial Of Cock Robin* in *The Wisdom Of Crop The Conjurer* [1787?].
MWA° (2 copies, copy 1 p.[3–4], 29–30 wanting but supplied from copy 2; copy 2 wants p.[2]–6, 29–31 and covers); NjP (Hamilton, illus. gray-green paper covers fr.[2], p. 31 & covers wanting, but supplied from MWA copy 2); OOxM (p. 29–30 wanting); Evans 20319.

213.2 [——— Boston: Printed and sold by S. Hall, No. 53 Cornhill.] [1789?].
[5], 6–26 p. only; illus.; 10 cm. Adv. by S. Hall [1789?] in **568.2**, **673.1**, and **729.1**, and 1790 in **1406.3**.
MWA° (all before p.[5], 27–end, & covers wanting); Evans 45462.

213.3 ——— Boston: Printed and sold by Samuel Hall, No. 53, Cornhill. 1791.
t.[3], [4–5], 6–30 p.; illus.; 10.5 cm.; p. 20 printed "25." Adv. by S. Hall, 1792 in **1408.32**, 1794 in **673.8**, and 1796 in **587.37**.
MWA° (fr.[2], p. 31 & covers wanting); CtHi (fr.[2], p. 29–31 wanting); Evans 46138.

213.4 ——— The Second Worcester Edition. Printed at Worcester, Massachusetts. By Isaiah Thomas, And sold Wholesale and Retail, at his Book-Store. 1794.
fr.[2], t.[3], [4–5], 6–31 p.; illus.; 10 cm.; green Dutch paper covers.
MWA°; Evans 47011.

213.5 ——— Boston: Printed and sold by S. Hall. No. 53, Cornhill. 1798.
fr.[2], t.[3], [4–5], 6–31 p.; illus.; 10.5 cm.; pink and green Dutch paper covers.
DLC°; Evans 33614.

213.6 ——— Boston: adv. by John W. Folsom, 1798 in **672.2**.

213.7 ——— Cock Robin: With The Story Of The Farmer's Daughters. Embellished with Cuts. Baltimore [Md.]: Printed by Warner & Hanna. 1801.
fr.[2], t.[3], [4–5], 6–31 p.; illus.; 10 cm.; green and buff Dutch paper covers.
MWA°; Shaw 321.

213.8 ——— Exeter [N.H.]: adv. by Henry Ranlet, 1801 in **558.2**.

213.9 ——— Wilmington, Del. adv.: ". . . may be had at James Wilson's Book-Store, at the Sign of Shakespear, in Market Street", 1803 in **1081**.

213.10 ——— Farmer's Daughters. To which is added, The Tragical Death Of An Apple-Pye. Embellished with Elegant Cuts, Hartford; Printed by John Babcock. 1802.
fr.[2], t.[3], [4–5], 6–31 p.; illus.; 11 cm.
CSmH° (p.[5]–6, 29–31 mut.); MShM (fr.[2] & covers wanting); Shaw 50283.

213.11 ——— The First Hudson Edition. Hudson [N.Y.]: Printed By Ashbel Stoddard, And sold Wholesale and Retail, at his Book-Store. 1803.
fr.[2], t.[3], [4], 5–29, [30, alphabets], [31, adv. list of books] p.; illus.; 11.5 cm.; buff and green Dutch paper covers.
MWA-W°; Shaw 50345.

213.12 ——— Embellished with Elegant Cuts. From Sidney's Press, New-Haven. 1805.
fr.[2], t.[3], [4–5], 6–31 p.; illus.; 105 cm.; orange Dutch paper covers.
Welch°; CtHi; MWA; Shaw 8204.

213.13 ——— Apple-Pye. Albany: Printed By E. & E. Hosford. 1806.
fr.[2], t.[3], [4–5], 6–31 p.; illus.; 11 cm.; yellowish-orange Dutch paper covers.
MWA-W; PP.

213.14 ——— Apple-Pye. Ornamented with Cuts. From Sidney's Press. New-Haven. 1806.
fr.[2], t.[3], [4–5], 6–31 p.; illus.; 10.5 cm.
MWA°.

213.15 COCK ROBIN. Philadelphia: adv. by B. & T. Kite, 1807 in **611.1**.

213.16 ———— Apple-Pye. Albany: Printed By E. And E. Hosford. 1808.

> fr.[2], t.[3], [4–5], 6–30, [31] p.; illus.; 11 cm.; pr. & illus. paper covers.
> OClWHi° (p.[31] & rear cover mut., all printing rubbed off from covers); MWA (fr.[2], p.[5]–28, [31] & covers wanting); Shaw 14718.

213.17 ———— [same as **213.1**] Master Meanwell. Exeter [N.H.]. Printed and Sold by Norris & Sawyer. 1808.

> fr.[2], t.[3], [4–5], 6–31 p.; illus.; 10 cm.; illus. yellowish-buff paper covers.
> NN° (i. st. on p. 31); Shaw 14719; Weiss 1936, p. 144.

213.18 ———— [same as **213.10**] Apple-Pye. Ornamented With Cuts. Litchfield [Conn.]: Printed by Hosmer & Goodwin. 1808.

> fr.[2], t.[3], [4–5], 6–31 p.; illus.; 10 cm.; yellow paper covers.
> MWA° (p. 17–20, 29–31, closely trimmed affecting text); DLC (fr. [2], p.[31] & covers wanting); Shaw 14720.

213.19 ———— Adorned with Cuts. From Sidney's Press, New-Haven. 1808.

> fr.[2], t.[3], [4–5], 6–31 p.; illus.; 10.5 cm.; paper covers.
> RNHi (yellow paper covers); Shaw 50839.

213.20 ———— Ornamented with Engravings. Albany: Printed By E. And E. Hosford. 1809.

> fr.[2], t.[3], [4–5], 6–31 p.; illus.; 11 cm.; wall-paper covers.
> MiD°; Shaw 7242.

213.21 ———— Adorned With Cuts. Hallowell, Maine. Published by Ezekial Goodale. N. Cheever, Printer. 1809.

> t.[3], [4–5], 6–30, [31, adv.] p.; illus.; 9.5 cm.; pr. blue-gray paper covers.
> MWA-W° (front cover & fr.[2] wanting); Shaw 17243.

213.22 ———— Adorned with Cuts. From Sidney's Press, New-Haven, 1809.

> fr.[2], t.[3], [4–5], 6–30 p.; illus.; yellow paper front cover.
> MWA-T° (imp.).

213.23 ———— Ornamented with Engravings. Albany: Printed By E. & E. Hosford. 1810.

> fr.[2], t.[3], [4–5], 6–31 p.; illus.; 10 cm.; pr. & illus. buff paper covers; cover title undated.
> MWA°; NN (covers wanting); Shaw 19793; Weiss 1936, p. 143.

213.24 ———— Albany: Printed By E. And E. Hosford. 1810.

> Same as no. **213.23** but with "E. And E. Hosford" in the imprint instead of "E. & E. Hosford." MWA-W° (p. 19–20, 31 & rear cover wanting, p. 27–30 mut.); DLC (t.[3], p.[4], 31 & covers mut., remaining p. torn. t.[3] bound between p. 30–31).

213.25 ———— Adorned With Cuts. From Sidney's Press, New-Haven, 1810.

> t.[3], [4–5], 6–31 p.; illus.; 11 cm.; yellow paper covers.
> MWA-T°; Shaw 50991.

213.26 ———— Ornamented with Engravings. Albany: Printed By E. And E. Hosford. 1811.

> fr.[2], t.[3], [4–5], 6–31 p.; illus.; 10 cm.; pr. & illus. buff paper covers; cover title undated.
> MWA°; PP (fr.[2], p. 31 & covers mut.); Shaw 51074.

213.27 ———— [same as **213.1**] Meanwell. C. Morris & Co. Printers, Exeter. 1812.

> fr.[2], t.[3], [4–5], 6–31 p.; illus.; 10 cm.; illus. buff paper covers.
> MWA-W°; NhHi; Shaw 51174.

213.28 ———— Meanwell. The Second Hudson Edition. Hudson [N.Y.]: Printed By Ashbel Stoddard, And sold Wholesale and Retail, at his Book-Store. 1812.

> fr.[2], t.[3], [4], 5–30 p.; illus.; 11.5 cm.; pr. & illus. blue-gray paper covers.
> MWA° (p. 31 and covers wanting); DLC (p. 31 and covers wanting); Shaw 51175.

213.29 ———— [same as **213.10**] Apple-Pye. Ornamented With Engravings. New-York: Printed and sold by Smith & Forman, At The Franklin Juvenile Bookstores. 195 and 213 Greenwich-street. 1812.

> fr.[2], t.[3], [4–5], 6–31 p.; 9.5 cm.; yellow paper covers.
> MB°; Shaw 51176.

213.30 ——— Albany: Printed By E & E. Hosford. 1813.
 fr.[2], t.[3], [4–5], 6–31 p.; illus.; 10.5 cm.; pr. & illus. paper covers.
 PP*; Shaw 51282.

213.31 ——— Jaffrey, N.H. Printed By Saimon [*sic., i.e.* Salmon] Wilder. 1813.
 fr.[2], t.[3], [4–5], 6–31 p.; illus.; 11 cm.; pr. & illus. buff paper covers; cover title undated; p. 29 incorrectly printed "39."
 Cover title, copy 1: Cock Robin, Printed by S. Wilder. Rear cover has a cut of the U.S. emblem and one of an owl.
 Cover title, copy 2: Cock Robin. Jaffrey Printed By Salmon Wilder. 1813. The rear cover has cuts of two birds.
 MWA* (copy 1, complete; copy 2, covers only of another copy); NhHi (copy 2, rebound); Shaw 28168.

213.32 ——— Adorned with Cuts. Sidney's Press. New-Haven, 1813.
 fr.[2], t.[3], [4], 7–31 p.; illus.; 10.5 cm.; illus.; paper covers.
 MWA* (p. [5]–6, 17–18 wanting, p. 15–16 mut.).

213.33 ——— Albany: Printed By E. & E. Hosford. 1814.
 fr.[2], t.[3], [4–5], 6–31 p.; illus.; 10 cm.; pr. & illus. yellow-buff paper covers; cover title undated.
 MWA*; CtHi (front cover and fr.[2] wanting); CtY (pr. & illus. yellow-buff paper covers); PP; Shaw 31187.

213.34 ——— Embellished With Cuts. Hartford Printed by Sheldon & Goodwin. < Stereotyped by J. F. & C. Starr. > [1815].
 fr.[2], t.[3], [4–5], 6–31 p.; illus.; 10 cm.; pr. & illus. buff paper covers.
 MWA-W*; CtHi; MB (per st. on t.p.); Shaw 34381.

213.35 ——— Ornamented with Engravings. Albany: Printed By E. & E. Hosford. 1816.
 fr.[2], t.[3], [4–5], 6–31 p.; illus.; 10.5 cm.; pr. & illus. yellow-buff paper covers; cover title undated.
 NB*; PP; Shaw 51562.

213.36 ——— Ornamented With Cuts. Boston: Printed By N. Coverly, Milk-Street, 1817.
 t.[1], [2–16] p.; illus.; 10 cm.; silver and blue Dutch paper covers.
 MWA*; Shaw 40501.

213.37 ——— Ornamented With Engravings. Albany: Printed By E. & E. Hosford. 1818.
 fr.[2], t.[3], [4–5], 6–31 p.; illus.; 10.5 cm.; pr. & illus. paper covers.
 MWA* (covers wanting and p. 31 mut.); Shaw 43655.

213.38 ——— Ornamented With Cuts. Boston: For N. Coverly. Milk Street. 1820.
 t.[1], [2–16] p.; illus.; 9.5 cm.; marbled paper covers.
 MWA* (covers wanting); Shoemaker 802.

214 An Elegy On The Death And Burial Of Cock Robin. With The Story Of The Farmer's Daughters. To which is added, The Tragical Death Of An Apple-Pye. [4 lines of Verse] Embellished with Elegant Cuts. Philadelphia: Printed By John Adams. 1805.
 fr.[2], t.[3], [4–5], 6–30 p.; illus.; 10.5 cm.; purple paper covers; p. 29–30 adv. of books.
 PP*; PHi; Shaw 8380.

215 The Tragi-Comic History Of The Burial Of Cock Robin; With The Lamentation Of Jenny Wren; The Sparrow's Apprehension; And The Cuckoo's Punishment. Being A sequel To The Courtship, Marriage, And Picnic Dinner Of Robin Red-Breast And Jenny Wren. Philadelphia, Published By Johnson And Warner, No. 147, Market Street. J. Bouvier, Printer. 1811.
 fr.[ii], ½t.[1], [2], t.[3], [4–5], 6–16, [pl. opp. p. 16] p.; 8 pl. including front; 12 cm.; pr. buff paper covers.
 English ed. London: J. Harris, 1808.
 MWA*; CLU; NNC-T; PHi; PP; PPL; Shaw 24052.

216 The Wedding Dinner Of Cock Robin And Jenny Wren; With The Tragical Death Of Cock Robin. Philadelphia: Published By Benjamin Johnson, No. 249, Market Street. 1809. [cover title].
 [1–13] p. engr. on one side only of 13 leaves; illus.; 12.5 cm.; pr. yellow paper covers. The text and illus. (in reverse) are copied from the

last half, p. 16–28, of the English ed. *See* no. **212.1.**

MWA° (p. [1], rear cover wanting); NjR (13 pl.) covers wanting); Shaw 17244.

COCKLE, MARY

217　THE FISHES GRAND GALA. A Companion To The "Peacock At Home," &c.&c. By Mrs. Cockle, Author Of The Juvenile Journal, &c. Part I. [II.] [2 lines of verse] Philadelphia: Published By Benjamin C. Busby, At His Juvenile Book-Store, No. 2, North Third Street. 1809.

pt. I: fr.[ii], t.[1], [2–3], 4–16 p.; 6 pl. including front.; 12.5 cm.; pr. & illus. paper covers. Colophon at End Of Part First, p. 14: Joseph Rakestraw, Printer.; pt. II: fr.[ii], t.[1], [2–3], 4–16 p.; 6 pl. including front.; 12 cm.; pr. buff paper covers; 2 vols. The text in each pt. is not enough to fill up all 16 p. In pt. I, p. 15–16 has: Note First—Note III on the "Papar [*sic. i.e.* Paper] Nautilus", the "Flying Fish" and "White Water Lilly". Pt. II, p. 12–16 has: NOTE IV—Note VIII—Note The Last which deal with "Sea Anemone"; "The Broadfinned Sword Fish"; "Shooting Fish"; "Maids. This fish is caught with a red cloth."; "The Dolphin."; "Sea Pens". English ed. London: 1808.

NjN°; MB (pt. II); MWA (pt. II); PP (pt. I. fr.[ii]& covers wanting; p. 9–12 mut.); Shaw 17245.

218　A COLLECTION of EASY AND FAMILIAR DIALOGUES For Children. The Fifth Edition. Windsor, (Vermont) Re-printed and sold, Wholesale and Retail, at the Printing-Office of Alden Spooner. [179—?].

t.[1], [2–3], 4–56 p.; 18.5 cm.; bound in beige paper.

Vt° (per. st. on t.[1]); McCorison 2254; Evans 45757.

219　A COLLECTION Of MORAL AND ENTERTAINING STORIES, Calculated for the Instruction and Entertainment of Youth. Containing I. Story Of Frank Leeson. II. Florio.—An Affecting Story. III. Story of Edward and Maria. IV. The Generosity of an Injured Daughter. V. Fraternal Affection. VI. The Remarkable Duel. Printed At Northhampton [Mass.], MDCCXCVIII.

1st t.[1], [2–3], 4–34; 2nd t.[35], [36–37], 38–80 p.; 13 cm.

The 2nd t.[35]: The New Pygmalion. A Novel.

To Which Is Added, Amelia: Or, The Faithless Briton. An American Tale. Northhampton [Mass.], Printed By Andrew Wright. 1798.

MWA° (p. 69–76, 81 & covers wanting); NcU; Evans 33533.

220　A COLLECTION Of SELECT FABLES, Consisting of Words not exceeding two Syllables. Wrentham [Mass.]: Printed by N. Heaton, Jun. n.d. [*ca.* 1802].

t.[1], [2], 3–32 p.; illus.; 10 cm. Nathaniel Heaton, Jr. printed at Wrentham from 1800–1802.

MWA-W° (covers wanting); Shaw 50284.

COLLES, CHRISTOPHER 1738–1816

221.1　— AN ACCOUNT Of THE ASTONISHING BEAUTIES AND OPERATIONS OF NATURE IN THE MINUTE CREATION, Displayed By The Solar Microscope. By Christopher Colles New-York: Printed And Sold By Samuel Wood, At The Juvenile Book-Store, No. 357, Pearl-street, 1813.

t.[1], [2–3], 4–44, [45, adv.] p.; illus.; 13.5 cm.; pr. & illus. paper covers.

MSaE°; MH; MWA; Shaw 28183 and 51283.

221.2　————— Solar Microscope By Christopher Colles. New-York: Printed And Sold By Samuel Wood, At The Juvenile Book-Store, No. 357, Pearl-Street. 1815.

t.[1], [2–3], 4–44, [45, adv.] p.; illus.; 13 cm.

MWA° (bound with other books in no. **191**); DLC; ViW; Shaw 34392.

221.3　————— New-York: Printed And Sold By Samuel Wood & Sons, At The Juvenile Book-Store, No. 357, Pearl-Street. 1816.

t.[1], [2–3], 4–44, [45, adv.] p.; illus.; 13.5 cm.; pr. & illus. yellow-buff paper covers; cover title undated.

MWA°; NN; PP; Shaw 37296.

COLUMBUS, CHARLEY *pseud.*

222　THE NATURAL HISTORY Of BEASTS, Which are to be met with In the Four Quarters of the Globe. By Charley Columbus. Embellished With Pictures. The First Worcester Edition. Printed at Worcester, Massachusetts, By Isaiah Thomas. Sold Wholesale and Retail at his Bookstore in Worcester, and by him and Company in Boston. MDCCXCIV.

fr.[ii], t.[i], [ii–iii], iv–vi, [7], 8–158 p.; illus.; 10 cm.

Most of the book is reprinted from the English edition entitled: *The Natural History Of Four-Footed Beasts. By T. Telltruth, London: E. Newbery. 1781.* Adv. by F. Newbery in Richardson's *The History of Pamela, 1769.*
MWA °(rebound in leather, I. Thomas' bookplate); CLU; MSaE; PP (i. st. on t.[i]); Evans 26797.

COLUMBUS, CHRISTOPHER *pseud.*
223 THE DISCOVERY OF AMERICA. By Christopher Columbus. To Which Is Added, His Two Three [*sic. i.e.* Last] Voyages. Philadelphia. Printed And Sold By Joseph & James Crukshank, No. 87, High-Street. 1801.
t.[1], [2–3], 4–107, [108, adv. list of books] p.; 14.5 cm.; bound in gray-green paper over bds. PP°; MWA; NN (rebound); Shaw 418.

THE COMIC ADVENTURES OF OLD MOTHER HUBBARD. *See* Martin, Sarah Catherine, no. **776.2.**

224.1 THE COMICAL HOTCH POTCH Or The Alphabet turn'd Posture Master. [cut] Do but see this comic Set Of Fellows form the Alphabet. Published & Sold by J. Webster No 91 South 6th Street Philadela. [1814].
t.[1], [2–16] p.; engr. on one side only of 16 leaves; illus.; 11.5 cm. James Webster, paper stainer, bookseller, publisher was at 91 South 6th street only in 1814. On the verso of p.[2] is a holograph inscription: *Howard M. Huntington from G. W. H. 1816.*
CtHi°; Shaw 51378.

224.2 ——— form the Alphabet. [n.d. no imprint] [*ca.* 1814].
t.[1], [2–16] p.; engr. on both sides of 8 leaves; illus.; cm.; blue marbled paper covers.
CtHi°.

225 THE COMMERCE OF ENGLAND! With The Principal Nations In Europe. For The Instruction Of Youth. [4 lines of verse] Philadelphia: Published By Benjamin And Thomas Kite, No. 20, North Third Street. 1810.
t.[1], [2–3], 4–32 p.; illus.; 11.5 cm.; pr. & illus. yellow-buff paper covers; colophon p. 32; J. Rakestraw, Printer.
English ed. London, entitled: *The Commerce of Albion!* ——— *Intended To Imprint On The*

Youthful Mind, The Honour, Consequence, And Riches Of Old England. J. Harris, 1809.
CtHi°; Shaw 50992.

226 A COMPENDIOUS HISTORY OF THE WORLD, From The Creation to the Dissolution of the Roman Republic. Compiled for the use of young Gentlemen and Ladies. Embellished with Variety of Copperplates. In Two Volumes. Vol. I. [II.] Philadelphia: Printed And Sold By R. Aitken Bookseller, Opposite The London Coffee-House, Front-Street. M.DCC.LXXIV.
vol. I.: fr.[ii], t.[1], [2–4], 5–217 p.; 7 pl. including front.; vol. II.: fr.[ii], t.[1], [2–3], 4–176 p.; 7 pl. including front.; 2 vols.; 10 cm.; bound in Dutch paper over w. bds.
English ed. London: vol. II. John Newbery, 1763.
MWA° (2 vols., 1 pl. wanting vol. I.), CtHi (vol. I.), CtY (vol. I., all pl. wanting); MB (t.[1], final leaf & 1 plate wanting from vol. II., p. 7–10 slightly mut.), NjMoW; PP (3 sets of 2 vols., varying numbers of pl.).

227 A CONCISE NATURAL HISTORY OF BIRDS. [cut.] With numerous Engravings. Boston: Published By Thomas B. Wait And Co. And Charles Williams. Price 12½ cents. [*ca.* 1812].
fr.[2], t.[3], [4–5], 6–35 p.; illus.; 15 cm.; pr. & illus. buff paper covers.
CtHi°; Shaw 51178.

228 A CONCISE NATURAL HISTORY OF QUADRUPEDS. With Numerous Engravings. Boston: Published By Charles Williams. 1813.
fr.[2], t.[3], [4], 5–35 p.; 13.5 cm.; pr. & illus. buff paper covers.
Cover title: A Concise Natural History Of Beasts. With Numerous Engravings. Boston: Published by Charles Williams. 1813.
CtHi°; MH (copy 1, front cover wanting; copy 2, fr.[2], p. 35 & covers wanting); MWA (covers, fr., p. 35 wanting); NB; Shaw 51284.

CONDIE, THOMAS G.
229 ——— THE JUVENILE PORT-FOLIO, And Literary Miscellany; Devoted To the Instruction And Amusement Of Youth. Conducted by Thomas G. Condie, jun. [two lines of verse] Vol. I. [II.–IV.]. Philadelphia. Printed By John Bioren, No. 88, Chesnut-Street, For The Editor, No. 22, Carter's Alley. 1813. [1814], [1815], [1816].

vol. I.: t.[1], [2–3], 4, [v], vi–viii, [1], 2–248 p.; 23 cm.; bound in leather; 61 no. from Oct. 17, 1812—Dec. 11, 1813; vol. II.: t.[i], [ii–iii], iv, [1], 2–199, [200–204, subscribers] p.; 23 cm.; bound in leather; 49 no. from Jan. 8—Dec. 10, 1814; vol. III.: t.[i], [ii–iii], iv, [1], 2–204 p.; 22.5 cm.; bound in leather; 49 no. from Jan. 7—Dec. 9, 1815; vol. IV.: t.[i], [ii–iii], iv, [1], 2–203 p.; 22.5 cm.; bound in leather; 49 no. from Jan. 6—Dec. 7, 1816. On t.[i], vol. IV. the "B" of "By Thomas G. Condie" is capitalized. On t.[i], vol II., IV. "jun." is omitted and "Condie" is followed by a period.

MWA° (vols. I.–IV., vol. III. p. [1–4], 203–204 wanting, 201–202 ½ wanting, 193–194 mut.); CtHT; CtY; DLC; MB; MH; MdBE; NN; NHi; OClWHi; PHi; PHuJ; PP; PPL; Shaw 25767 and 28858.

230 THE CONTINUATION OF OLD DAME TRUDGE AND HER PARROT. Illustrated With Whimsical Engravings. Philadelphia: Published and sold Wholesale by Wm. Charles, and may be had of all the Booksellers. Price 12 1–2 Cents. 1812. W. M'Culloch, Printer. [cover title].

[1–8] p.; engr. on one side only of 8 leaves; illus.; 12.5 cm.; pr. yellow-buff paper covers.

PP° (rear cover mut. mostly wanting); NNC-Pl (p.[8] slightly mut., rear cover wanting); Shaw 51182.

THE CONTINUATION OF THE COMIC ADVENTURES OF OLD MOTHER HUBBARD AND HER DOG. *See* Martin, Sarah Catherine, no. **818.1.**

231.1 A CONTINUATION. OF TOM THE PIPER'S SON. Illustrated With Eight Whimsical Engravings. Part The Second. Philadelphia: Published and sold wholesale, by Wm. Charles, And may be had, of all the Booksellers. 1808. Price 12½ cents. [cover title].

[1–8] p. engr. on one side only of 8 leaves; illus.; 13 cm.; pr. yellow paper covers.

MWA° (col. illus.); Shaw 14773.

231.2 —— Part The Second. Philadelphia: Published And Sold Wholesale By Wm. Charles, And May Be Had Of All The Booksellers. 1810. Price 12 1–2 Cents. [cover title].

[1–8] p.; engr. on one side only of 8 leaves; illus.; 12.5 cm.; pr. brownish-buff paper covers.

DLC° (rear cover mut. mostly wanting); Shaw 21505 and 50993.

CONUNDRUM, CHRISTOPHER *pseud.*

232 A PRETTY RIDDLE BOOK, For Little Children. By Christopher Conundrum. Newburyport [Mass.]—Printed for the purchasers. 1805.

t.[1], [2–3], 4–16 p.; illus.; 10 cm.; wallpaper covers.

DLC° (rear wallpaper cover wanting); MSaE; PP (rebound); Shaw 8247.

233.1 CONVERSATION IN A BOAT BETWEEN TWO SEAMEN. Written By A Clergyman, Formerly A Lieutenant In The Royal Navy. [caption title]. Andover [Mass.]: Printed For The New England Tract Society. 1818.

Shaw 43722.

233.2 —— The Royal Navy. [caption title]. Published For The Hartford Evangelical Tract Society. March, 1818. 5000 [colophon p. 24].

[1], 2–24 p.; 13.5 cm.

CtHi°; MWA; Shaw 43723.

233.3 < 87. —— [caption p. [1]]. Andover [Mass.]: Printed For The New England Tract Society By Flagg and Gould, [1819] < 2 ed. edit. 6,000. [colophon p. 8].

t.[1], 2–8; 16.5 cm.; also paged [25], 26–32 p.

MB° (bound with other tracts in *The Publications Of The New England Tract Society. Vol. V. Andover [Mass.] Published By Flagg And Gould, 1820*); Shaw 47719.

CONVERSATIONS OF EMILY. *See* Épinay, Louise Florence de la Live d', no. **369.**

234 CONVERSATIONS ON NATURAL HISTORY, For The Use Of Children And Youth. Boston: Published By Timothy Swan, No. 15, Cornhill. 1820.

t.[i], [ii–iv], [1], 2–140 p.; 15 cm.; p. 108 wrongly numbered "109"; bound in buff paper over bds., dark green spine.

MWA°; CLU; MH (bound in green paper over bds., red spine); MHi; Shoemaker 862.

235 THE CONVERSION OF AN ATHEIST, By His only Daughter. Massachusetts' Edition. Printed for Josiah Wilcox. 1810.

t.[1], [2–3], 4–12 p.; 18.5 cm.; in Verse.

DLC° (rebound); Shaw 19852.

[CORRY, JOHN] fl. 1825

236.1 [—] BIOGRAPHICAL MEMOIRS OF THE IL-

LUSTRIOUS GENERAL GEORGE WASHINGTON, Late President Of The United States Of America, And Commander in Chief of their Armies, during the Revolutionary War. Dedicated To The Youth Of America. Philadelphia: Published And Sold By David Hogan, No. 51, South Third-Street. 1808. Stiles, Printer.

t.[3], [4–5], 6–108 p.; t.[3] 13.5 cm.

This has been attributed to Thomas Condie who wrote a similar title, but this text begins with the words "In the history of man . . ." which does not appear in Condie's work but does in the *Life of George Washington* with Corry's name on the title, particularly the Philadelphia 1801 edition which has a dedication signed by Corry. (MWA cat.).

MWA° (rebound); CSmH; Sabin 101778; Shaw 14783.

236.2 [—] ———— From Sidney's Press. For I. Cooke & Co. Book-Sellers, N. Haven. 1809.

fr.[2], t.[3], [4–5], 6–144 p.; front only illus.; 14 cm.; bound in blue paper over bds.

MWA°; CSmH; CtHi; CtY (orig. covers wanting); DLC; ICU; KU; MB; MBAt; MH; PHC; PHi; Shaw 17273.

236.3 [—] ———— From Sidney's Press. For I. Cooke & Co. Book-Sellers, N. Haven. 1810.

fr.[2], t.[3], [4–5], 6–144 p.; front. and title vignette only illus.; 14.5 cm.; bound in buff paper over bds.

Welch°; CSmH; CtHi; CtY; MB; MWA; MiU; N; NN (2 copies rebound, copy 2 wants p. 143–144); NjP; NjR; OOxM; PHi; PP; Shaw 19832 and 19869.

236.4 [—] ———— Wilmington [Del]: Published And Sold By Peter Brynberg. 1810.

t.[1], [2–3], 4–108 p.; 13.5 cm.

CtY°; CSmH; DS; PWcHi; Shaw 19870.

236.5 [—] ———— From Sidney's Press. For I. Cooke & Co. Book-Sellers, N. Haven. 1811.

fr.[2], t.[3], [4–5], 6–144 p.; front. only illus.; 13.5 cm.; bound in marbled paper over bds., leather spine.

MWA°; CSmH; CtHi; CtY (bound in marbled paper over bds., leather spine); DLC; MB; MBAt; PP; Shaw 22625.

236.6 [—] ———— Biographical Memoirs Of The Illustrious General George Washington, Late

President Of The United States. Containing A History Of The Principal Events Of His Life, With His Speeches To Congress, And Public Addresses: To Which Is Added, An Oration Upon His Death, By The Reverand Samuel Stanhope Smith, President of the College of New-Jersey. A New Edition, Improved. Trenton [N.J.]: Printed And Published By James Oram. 1811.

fr.[228], t.[229], [230–231], 232–371 p.; front. & tailpiece p. 344, 371 only illus.; 18.5 cm.

MWA° (rebound); Shaw 22626.

236.7 [—] ———— Washington, First President Of The United States Of America, And Commander in Chief of their Armies, during the Revolutionary War. Dedicated to the Youth of America. Baltimore: Printed And Sold By William Warner. 1812.

t.[1], [2–3], 4–103, [104, bl.], [105–107 adv. list of books] p.; title vignette only illus.; t.[1] 13 cm.

MWA° (rebound); CSmH; DLC; MB; NN (2 copies rebound, both have a per. st. on t.[1]); PHi; Shaw 25167.

236.8 [—] ———— Gen. George Washington, Late President ———— [same as **236.1**] Barnard, Vt. Published By Joseph Dix. 1813. I. H. Carpenter, printer.

fr.[ii], t.[1], [2–3], 4–160 p.; 13.5 cm.; front only illus.; bound in leather; fr[ii.] signed *A Reed sc E. W. Con.*

MWA°; CSmH; DLC; ICU; MB; MBAt; MH; MiU; NBuG; NN; OC; OClWHi; PHi; PP; Shaw 28231.

236.9 [—] ———— Pittsburgh, Printed By Cramer, Spear, And Eichbaum, Market-Street, Between Front And Second Streets. 1813.

t.[3], [4–5], 6–104 p.; t.[3] 14 cm.

MWA° (rebound); OClWHi (p. 93–94 & marbled paper covers wanting, t.[3] mut.); Shaw 28232.

236.10 [—] BIOGRAPHISCHE SKIZZEN DES DURCHLAUCHTIGSTEN GENERALS GEORGE WASCHINGTON [*sic. i.e.* WASHINGTON], gewesenen Presidenten der Vereinigten Staaten von America, und Ober-Befehlshaber ihrer Armeen, während den Revolutions-Kriege. Der Jungend von America gewidmet.

Aus dem Enlischen [*sic*] übersetzt. Libanon [Pa.], Gedruckt und zu haben, bey J. Hartman. 1815.

> t.[1], [2–3], 4–131 p.; 16.5 cm.; bound in blue-gray paper over bds., leather spine.
> MWA°; CtY; Shaw 34453.

236.11 [—] —— [same as **236.1**] New-York: Published By Evert Duyckinck, No. 102 Pearl-Street. J. C. Totten, printer. 1815.

> t.[1], [2–3], 4–108 p.; 14 cm.; title vignette only illus.; bound in brown paper over bds., leather spine.
> Welch°; CSmH; DLC; MB; MBAt; MiU; MWA; N; NHi; Nh; NN; PHi; PP; Shaw 34451.

236.12 [—] —— Pittsburgh: Published By R. Paterson. S. Engles, Printer. 1815.

> t.[1], [2–3], 4–107 p.; 14.5 cm.; bound in ornamented buff paper over bds.
> CtY°; Shaw 34452.

236.13 [—] —— Pittsburgh, Pa.: Eichbaum and Johnson. 1818.

> Shaw 43367.

237.1 [—] Life Of General George Washington, Late President Of The United States Of America. And Commander In Chief Of Their Armies; During The Revolutionary War. Dedicated to the Youth of America. Poughkeepsie [N.Y.]: Printed By Paraclete Potter, Main Street. 1812.

> fr.[ii], t.[1], [2–3], 4–143, [144, adv.] p.; 13 cm.; bound in leather; MWA copy does not have fr.[ii] and appears never to have had one. The NN copy has fr.[ii].
> MWA°; MB; NN (rebound); NPV; PHi; PP; PPL; Shaw 25168.

237.2 [—] —— Boston: Published By Isaiah Thomas, Jun. 1815.

> t.[1], [2–3], 4–144 p.; 13.5 cm.; bound in leather; front. eng. *J. R. Smith*.
> MWA°; Shaw 34454 and 35103.

237.3 [—] —— Bridgeport [Conn.]: Printed And Sold By Lambert Lockwood. 1815.

> t.[1], [2–3], 4–107, [108, adv.] p.; 14 cm.; bound in buff paper over w. bds., leather spine.
> MWA°; PHi; PPL; Shaw 34455 and 35102.

Costumes Of Different Nations. *See* Mills, Alfred, no. **847**.

238 The Cottage Boy, Or, The History Of Peter Thomson. Philadelphia: Published by the Sunday & Adult School Union, And for Sale at their Depository, 78 Arch Street. Clark & Raser, Printers. 1819.

> t.[i], [ii–iii], iv, [5], 6–48 p.; title vignette only illus.; 13 cm.; pr. & illus. blue-gray paper covers.
> PP°; MiD; Shaw 51872.

The Cottage Girl: Or An Account Of Ann Edwards. *See* Bennett, Mary E., no. **70**.

239.1 The Cottager's Wife. [1 line quot.] Annapolis [Md.]: Published By George Shaw. J. Green, Printer. June, 1815.

> t.[1], [2–3], 4–56 p.; 14.5 cm.; pr. buff paper covers.
> MWA°; Shaw 34457.

239.2 —— A Narrative . . . Ed. 4. Andover, Mass. Pr. by Flagg & Gould. 1819.

> 24p.
> Shaw 47733.

[COTTON, NATHANIEL] 1705–1788

240.1 [—] Visions, For The Entertainment And Instruction Of Young Minds, Concerning Slander, Pleasure, Health, Content, Happiness, Friendship, Marriage, Life, and Death. [1 line quot.] Printed At Exeter [N.H.], By Henry Ranlet, And Sold At His Office. MDCCXCIV.

> t.[1], [2–3], 4–121, [122, bl.–123] p.; 13.5 cm.; bound in green Dutch paper over w. bds.; poetry.
> English ed. London: R. Dodsley; M. Cooper. 1751.
> MWA°; CtY; NN; NhD; PHi; PP; PPL.

240.2 [—] Visions For The Instruction Of Younger Minds. [1 line quot.] Brunswick [Me.]: Published By Griffin & Haselton. 1820.

> t.[i], [ii–iii], iv–xiii, [1], 2–108 p.; 14.5 cm.; bound in marbled paper over bds., leather spine.
> MWA°; CSmH; DLC; MeB; PHi; Shoemaker 881.

241 The Council Of Dogs. Illustrated With Suitable Engravings. Philadelphia: Published By Johnson & Warner, No. 147, Market-Street. Brown & Merritt Printers, 24, Church-alley. 1809.

fr.[ii], t.[1], [2–3], 4–16 p.; 8 pl. including front.; 13 cm.; pr. & illus. yellow paper covers; cover title dated 1809.

English ed. London: J. Harris. 1808.

PP°; CCamarSJ; CLU; CSmH; DLC (2 copies); FTaSU; MH (not a remainder); MWA; MiD; NB; NHi; NNC-Pl; NRU; OOxM; PHi; PU; ViU; Shaw 17313.

242 COUNTRY SCENES. Illustrated with Emblematical Prints. Philadelphia Published and sold by Wm Charles N° 32 South Third St Price 6½ cents. [cover title] [prior to 1814].

Printed covers pasted to the inside of the covers of *The Entertaining History Of Jobson & Nell.* *See* no. **357.**

MWA-T°.

243 THE COUNTRY SCHOOL-MASTER AND HIS NEPHEW; Or The Interesting Narrative Of George Ferguson. Intended to do good. Hartford: Published By Oliver D. Cooke. Roberts & Burr, Printers: 1820.

fr.[2], t.[3], [4], 5–32 p.; illus.; 13 cm.; pr. & illus. green paper covers.

MWA° (front cover & fr.[2] wanting); CtHi (complete); PP; Shoemaker 882.

COURTSHIP & MARRIAGE OF COCK ROBIN, And Jenny Wrenn. *See* Cock Robin, no. **212.1.**

COWPER, WILLIAM 1731–1800

244 [—] THE DISASTROUS JOURNEY OF JOHNNY GILPIN TO EDMONTON, In Which Is Shown The Wonderful Prowess Of The Calendrer's Horse, On Sixteen Elegant Engravings. New-York: Published By I. Riley, No. 4, City-Hotel. 1813. Price 25 cents. [cover title].

[1–16] p. engr. on one side only of 16 leaves; illus.; 11.5 cm.; pr. yellow-buff paper covers.

English ed. London: pr. in *Public Advertizer.* *Nov.* 14, 1782.

DLC°; Shaw 51290.

245.1 [—] THE DIVERTING HISTORY OF JOHN GILPIN Shewing How He Went Farther Than [He] Intended And Came Safe Home Again. Printed At Osborne's Press, Market-Square, Newburyport [Mass.]. MDCCXCIII.

t.[1], [2–3], 4–12 p.; 15 cm.

OClWHi°; Evans 46719.

245.2 [—] ——— Printed At Osborne's Office, Guttemberg's Head, In Market-Square, Newburyport [Mass.]. MDCCXCIII.

t.[1], [2–3], 4–11 p.; 15.5 cm.

MSaE°; Evans 25354.

245.3 [—] ——— again. From Park's Press, Montpelier, Vt. 1808.

t.[1], [2–3], 4–14 p.; 10 cm.; pr. paper covers.

MWA°; McCorison 981; Shaw 14788.

245.4 [—] ——— Illustrated With Humorous Engravings On Copperplate. Philadelphia: Published and Sold wholesale by Wm. Charles, and may be had of all the Booksellers. 1809. W. M'Culloch, Printer.

fr.[2], t.[3], [4–5], 6–31 p.; 8 engr. pl. including front.; 13 cm.; pr. paper covers. Adv. by Wm. Charles, 1808 in **1312.**

English ed. London: J. Harris. 1808.

MWA° (p. 31 & front cover mut.); Shaw 17315.

245.5 [—] ——— Philadelphia: Published and sold wholesale by Wm. Charles, and may be had of all the Booksellers. 1815.

fr.[2], t.[3], [4–5], 6–31 p; 8 engr. illus. including front.; 12 cm.; pr. buff paper covers. Cover title imprint: Philadelphia: Published And Sold Wholesale By Wm. Charles, And May Be Had Of All The Booksellers. 1810. Price 25 Cents.

MWA-W°; CLU; CtY; PHi; PP (illus. p. 14 wanting); Shaw 34462.

246.1 [—] THE FACETIOUS HISTORY OF JOHN GILPIN: Shewing, How he went farther than he intended, and came safe home again. To Which is Added, The Hunting In Chevy Chase. Both adorned with Cuts. W. & J. Gilman, Printers, Middle-Street, Newburyport [Mass.]. 1806.

1st t.[1], fr.[2]; 2nd t.[3], [4–5], 6–18; 3rd t.[1], [2, illus.–3], 4–15, [16, adv.–17, illus.] p.; illus.; 15 cm.; blue paper covers.

2nd title: The Facetious History of John Gilpin; Shewing, How he went farther than he intended, and came safe home again. W. & J. Gilman, Printers, Middle-street.

3rd title: The Hunting In Chevy Chase. W. & J. Gilman, Printers, Middle-street, Newburyport.

MNe° (rear cover wanting); Shaw 10381.

246.2 [—] ——— Gilpin. To Which Is Added, Juvenile Sports And Amusement. Newburyport

[Mass.]: Printed By W. & J. Gilman. Sold at their Book and Stationery Store, Middle-Street. 1809.
　　fr.[2], t.[3], [4–5], 6–36 p.; 12.5 cm.; pr. & illus. buff paper covers; cover title undated.
　　MH°; Shaw 50929.

247 [—] The Facetious Story Of John Gil-pin; His Going Farther Than He Intended, And Returning Home Safe At Last. To Which Is Added, A Second Part; Containing An Account Of The Disasterous Accidents Which Befel His Wife, On Her Return To London. Also A Third Part; Containing John Gilpin's Second Holiday; Or A Voyage To Vaux-Hall. Philadelphia: Printed By Wrigley & Berriman, For Thomas Stephens, No. 57, South-Second-street, and Alexander M'Kenzie, No. 126, South Front-street. M.DCC.-XCIV.
　　1st title: t.[1], [2–3], 4–12; 2nd t.[13], [14–15], 16–24; 3rd t.[25], [26–27], 28–36 p.; t.[1] 17 cm.
　　2nd title: An Historical Account of the Disasterous Accidents which Befel Mrs. Gilpin, on her Return to London. Hart [*sic i.e.* Part] the Second. —— [imprint, as on 1st title-page].
　　3rd title: A Second Holiday for John Gilpin, or, A Voyage to Vaux-Hall, where Though he had Better Luck than Before, he was far from being Contented. Part the Third. —— [imprint, as on 1st title page].
　　NHi° (rebound); Evans 26826.

248 [—] The History of John Gilpin of Cheapside, A Droll Story. And The Historical Ballad, of the Children in the Wood. Philadelphia: Published By Jacob Johnson, No. 147 High Street. 1807.
　　fr.[ii], t.[1], [2–3, bl.], [4, illus.–5], 6–52 p.; 11 engr. p. including front. [ii], t.[1], & 9 illus.; 13.5 cm.; colophon p. 52: Joseph Rakestraw, Printer.
　　MWA° (fr.[ii], 2 engr. illus. & covers wanting); PP (3 engr. illus. & p. 51–52 wanting); Shaw 12361.

The Cowslip. *See* Turner, Elizabeth, no. **1354**.

THE CRIES OF LONDON (arranged chronologically)

249.1 The Cries of London. Worcester, (Mass.): adv. by Isaiah Thomas, 1786 in **395.1**.

249.2 The London Cries. For The Amusement of all good Children throughout the World. Philadelphia, Printed by Young and M'Culloch, the Corner of Chesnut and Second-streets. 1787.
　　t.[3], [4], 5–29, [30, adv. list of books] p.; illus.; 10 cm.
　　English ed. London: T. Carnan, 1770.
　　MWA° (fr.[2], p. 31 and covers wanting); Evans 45087.

249.3 —— Of All The Good Children Throughout the World. Taken from the Life. Philadelphia: Printed By W. Spotswood. 1791.
　　t.[1], [2], 3–31 p.; illus.; 9.5 cm.; green Dutch paper covers.
　　CLU°; Evans 46203.

249.4 The London Cries. Philadelphia: adv. by William Young, 1794 in **287**.

249.5 The Moving Market, or New London Cries. Boston: adv. by William Spotswood 1795 in **1006.2**.

249.6 The Cries Of London, As They Are Daily Exhibited In The Streets; With An Epigram In Verse, Adapted To Each. Embellished With Elegant Characteristic Engravings. [3 lines of verse.] Philadelphia: Printed For Benjamin Johnson, Jacob Johnson, And Robert Johnson. 1805.
　　Issued in four separate parts or vols. Each part has a label on the front cover which reads: "London Cries. Part. I. [2–4]." The engraved illus. or plates are engraved on one side only of the leaf. The blank side of the leaf as well as the engr. illus. are unnumbered, but part of the pagination. An exception to this is the blank verso of illus. [13] and blank recto of illus. [14] pt. I.
　　pt. I.:t.[1], [2, bl.–3], 4–6, [9, bl.], [10, illus.], [11], 12–40, [41, illus.] p.; 12 engr. illus.; 17 cm.; bound in pink paper over bds., green paper spine; illus. not initialed by William Ralph, but probably drawn by him. First illus. p.[10] entitled "Any Knives Scissars Or Razors To Grind."; last illus. p.[41] entitled "Any Milk Maids Above Or Below." At the end of the MWA copy is an engraved plate showing St. Paul's Church and Johnson's Juvenile Library in the foreground. An English ed. London: J. Harris, 1804, has the original of this engraving, used as a frontispiece, with a similar picture of

the bookstore in the foreground entitled: J. Harris' Juvenile Library. The American ed. is reprinted from the English one with the plates redrawn in the reverse and the text of one vol. of the English one broken up into two parts. The English ed. has on p. 7–8 a poem entitled "A Song On The City Of London." Both the frontispiece and poem are omitted in pt. I of the Philadelphia 1805 ed. Where the engraving of St. Paul's Church and Johnson's Juvenile Library belongs is not known. In the Philadelphia 1813 ed., no. **249.16**, the engraving is inserted opposite page 5.

pt. II.: t.[1], [2, bl.–5], 6–36, [37, bl.–38, illus.] p.; 12 engr. illus.; 16.5 cm.; marbled paper covers, pink paper spine; illus. signed *W. R. fc* [William Ralph]; first illus. p. [3] entitled "Choice Fruit Madam. Fine Pippins."; last illus. p. [38] entitled "Come Buy My Water Cresses." pt. III.: t.[1], [2, bl.–4], 5–36, [37, illus.] p.; 12 engr. illus.; 17 cm.; illus. signed *WR. fc* [William Ralph]; first illus. p. [4] entitled "Hot Spice Gingerbread Hot"; last illus. p. [37] entitled "Past Twelve O'Clock, & A Cloudy Morning."

pt. IV.: t.[1], [2, bl.–6], 7–37 p.; 11 engr. illus.; 17 cm.; marbled paper covers, brown paper spine; illus. not initialed by W. Ralph, but probably drawn by him; first illus. p. [6] entitled "Mackarel, New Mackarel"; last illus. p.[35] entitled "Green and Large Cucumbers." English ed. London: J. Harris, 1804. The Harris ed. was taken in part from an earlier Newbery ed. illustrated with woodcuts instead of engraved plates. Earlier English ed. London: F. Newbery, 1775.

MWA-W° (pt. I); CLU (pt. II); MWA (pts. I, II, III, IV); OOxM; PNorthHi; PP; Shaw 8262 and 8263.

249.7 ———— Philadelphia: Printed For Benjamin Johnson, Jacob Johnson, And Robert Johnson, 1805.

t.[1], [2,bl.–5], 6–36, [37, illus.] p.; 12 engr. illus.; 17 cm.; pr. pink paper covers; illus. signed *WR. sc* [William Ralph]; first illus. p.[4] entitled "Choice Fruit Madam, Fine Pippins."; last illus. p. [37] entitled "Come Buy My Water Cresses."; cover title imprint: Philadelphia: Published By Johnson & Warner, No. 147, Market Street. 1813. Part IV. An 1813 issue of The Cries of London with the title

page of the 1805 ed., no. **249.6**. The text is reprinted from pt. II of **249.6** with *s* not printed *f*.

NN°; CLU; Shaw 8262 and 8263; Weiss 1936, p. 134.

249.8 ———— daily exhibited in that City; Represented by Characteristic Engravings. [two lines of verse] Hartford: Published by A. Reed. 1807.

t.[1], [2–16] p. engr. on one side only of 16 leaves; illus.; 9.5 cm.; green Dutch paper covers; title vignette signed *W. M sc* [William Morgan]. The illus. are copied from the Philadelphia 1805 ed., no. **249.6** mostly from pts. 2., 3. The 15 engr. text illus. are reprinted in the Litchfield 1808 ed., no. **249.11** which has 16 p. of text as well, and uses the same engr. title page with the imprint changed.

PP°; Shaw 12370.

249.9 THE LONDON CRIES, For The Amusement Of All The Good Children Throughout the World. Embellished with Cuts taken from Life. Philadelphia: Printed By John Adams. 1807.

fr.[2], t.[3], 4–31 p.; illus.; 10.5 cm.; pr. & illus. paper covers; p. 30–31 adv. list of books. The cuts p. 4–29 are from the same blocks used by W. Spotswood in the Philadelphia 1791 ed., no. **249.3**.

Cover title: Toy-Book. Philadelphia: Printed & sold by John Adams. 1808.

PP°; Shaw 15448.

249.10 LONDON CRIES. Philadelphia: adv. by B. & T. Kite, 1807 in **611.1**.

249.11 THE CRIES OF LONDON. As they are daily exhibited in that City: Represented by Characteristic Engravings. [2 lines of verse] Published by Hosmer & Goodwin. Litchfield [Conn.] 1808.

t.[1], [2–5], 6–31, [32] p.; engr. t.[1] & 15 engr. illus.; 10 cm.; green Dutch paper covers; p.[2] adv. of 11 books.

CtHi°; Shaw 50844.

249.12 LONDON CRIES FOR CHILDREN. With Twenty Elegant Wood Cuts. [Cut of a boy holding a hat outstretched in one hand and a broom in the other] Philadelphia: Published by Johnson & Warner, No. 147, Market Street. John Bouvier, Printer. 1810.

fr.[2], t.[3], [4], 5–40 p.; illus.; 14 cm.; pink paper covers. Part of a large publisher's remainder.

OClW-LS°; CCamarSJ; CLU; CSmH; DLC; InU; IU; MB; MWA; NHi; NN (2 copies); NRU; PHi; PP; PPL; Shaw 19892 and 20586.

249.13 THE CRIES OF LONDON. New York: Printed And Sold By S. Wood, At the Juvenile Book-Store, No. 357, Pearl-street. 1811.

t.[1], [2–5] 6–29 p.; illus.; 10 cm.

DLC° (covers wanting); Shaw 51078.

249.14 THE MERRY CRIES OF LONDON CITY, As They Are Exhibited Every Day. With Fifteen Prints Of Living Characters. [6 lines of verse] Boston: Published By Thomas B. Wait And Company And Charles Williams. Price 12½ Cents. [1812].

fr.[2], t.[3], [4–5], 6–35 p.; illus.; 14 cm.; pr. purple paper covers; cover title same as title, rear cover has a list of books. Thomas B. Wait And Company and Charles Williams were both in business under their above names from 1811-1813. On the recto of the front. of the MB copy is the inscription: *Sukey Rogers' 1815.* Adv. by above publishers in *Felix The Woodcutter. 1812. See* no. **396.**

MWA°; MB (per. st. & i. st. on t.[3]; MH; Shaw 20725 (dated [181–?] in 1810 vol.) and 51218.

249.15 THE CRIES OF LONDON. New York: Printed And Sold By Samuel Wood, At the Juvenile Book-store, No. 357, Pearl-street. 1813.

fr.[ii], t.[1], [2–5], 6–29 p.; illus.; 10 cm.; pr. paper covers; cover dated 1814.

NjR° (p. 29, pr. covers wanting); Shaw 51293.

249.16 ———— London, As They Are Daily Exhibited In The Streets; With An Epigram In Verse, Adapted To Each. Embellished With Elegant Characteristic Engravings. [3 lines of verse]. Philadelphia: Printed for Benjamin Johnson, No. 22, North Second Street, and Johnson and Warner, No. 147, Market Street. 1813.

pt. I.: t.[1], [2, bl.–3], 4, [pl. opp. p. 5], 5–6, [pl. opp. p. 7], 7–37 p.; 2 engr. pl. & 10 engr. illus.; 16.5 cm.; pr. pink paper covers; first pl. opp. p. 5, a picture of St. Paul's Church with Johnson's Juvenile Library in the foreground, redrawn from the English ed. London: J. Har-

ris, 1804.; second pl. opp. p. 7 entitled "Mackarel, New Mackarel"; last illus. p. [36] entitled "Green And Large Cucumbers"; t.[1] & text p. [3]–6 same as pt. 1 of **249.6,** and p. 7–37 same as pt. 4 of **249.6.**

pt. II.: t.[1], [2, bl.–4, illus.], 5–36, [37, illus.] p.; 12 engr. illus.; 17 cm.; pr. paper covers; illus. signed *WR.sc;* first illus. p. [4] entitled "Hot Spice Gingerbread Hot."; last illus. p. [37] entitled "Past Twelve O'Clock, & A Cloudy Morning."; text & illus. same as pt. 3. of **249.6.**

pt. III.: [all before p.[10] wanting]; [10, illus.], [11], 12–40, [41, illus.] p.; 12 engr. illus.; 17.5 cm.; first illus. p. [10] entitled "Any Knives Scissars Or Razors To Grind."; last illus. p. [41] entitled "Any Milk Maids Above Or Below."; text and illus. same as pt. 1.; no. **249.6.**

pt. IV.: t.[1], [2, bl.–4, illus.], [5], 6–36, [37, illus.] p.; 12 engr. illus.; 16.5 cm.; pr. paper covers; illus. signed *WR. sc* [William Ralph]; first illus. p. [4] entitled "Choice Fruit Madam, Fine Pippins."; text & illus. same as pt. 2 of **249.6** and pt. IV of **249.7.** The cover title imprint when present: Philadelphia: Published By Johnson & Warner, No. 147, Market Street. 1813. Part I. [II., IV.]. The use of the letter *f* for *s* does not occur in the 1813 edition.

MWA° (pt. I.; pt. II. p.[27]—[34] [37] wanting); MB° (pt. I. covers, p.[3–4] [29]–37 wanting, p. 37 half wanting, bound out of place; pt. II.; pt. III. front cover and all before p.[10] & p. 15–16 21–22 wanting, p. 39–40 mut.); MSaE° (pt. IV. p. 35–36 upper half wanting; illus. p.[37] & rear cover wanting); Shaw 28245.

249.17 ———— [same as **249.16**] Philadelphia: Printed for Benjamin Johnson No. 22, North Second Street and Johnson and Warner, No. 147 Market Street. 1813.

t.[1], [2–4], 5–36, [37, illus.] p.; 12 engr. illus.; 16 cm.; pr. paper covers; illus. signed *W. R. sc.* [William Ralph] which are the same as those in pt. 3, no. **249.6.** Cover title imprint: Philadelphia: Published By Benjamin Johnson No. 21, North Second Street. 1813. Part III. MWA° (pt. III., p. 5–6, [9]–[14], 23–24, and lower fourth or half of p. 17–18, 35–36 wanting, illus. p.[34], [37] repeated); Shaw 28246.

249.18 ———— As They Are Exhibited Every Day; With Copperplate Engravings Of Living Characters, Affixed To Each Letter Of The Alphabet. Engraved For, And Published By Thomas Wells, No. 3, Hanover-St. Boston, 1814.

fr.[ii], t.[i], [ii–iii], iv–vi, [1–6, pl.] p.; front., title page vignette, and 6 pl., each pl. divided into 4; 11 cm.; pr. & illus. buff paper covers; cover title dated 1814. Copy A: The cover title same as cover title of copy B below, except for the vignette, which shows a coach, coachman and four white horses, below which is another coach, without horses, with a man in front of it. The frontispiece shows a black horse in the foreground, with a fence and a man running along side of a horse in the background. The cut is a redrawn version of the illustration on the rear cover of *The Uncle's Present, A New Battledore*, no. **1363**. The title page vignette includes a ship, a woman seated on bales on a wharf, holding in her left hand a caduceus. In the foreground are three barrels on the left, and a bale on the right with the letters "D B" on it. The alphabet plates p. [1–6] show a cry for each letter of the alphabet. There are four cries to a plate. They are redrawn versions of those in *The Uncle's Present*, no. **1363**. Copy B: The Cries Of London, As They Are Exhibited Every Day; With copperplate engravings of living characters, affixed to each letter of the alphabet. Engraved For, And Published By Thomas Wells, No. 3, Hanover-St. Boston, 1814. [cover title]. The cover title vignette is the same cut used on the title page of copy A. The frontispiece is different from copy A. It is rectangular, and shows a man holding a saddled white horse under a two trunked tree. Above the cut is a bow-like ornament with a leafy vine coming off of each end. The plates are the same as in copy A.

Warren* (copy A; copy B, t.[i], p. [ii]–vi wanting); Shaw 51381.

249.19 THE CRIES OF LONDON. New-York: Printed And Sold By Samuel Wood, At The Juvenile Book-Store, No. 357, Pearl-Street. 1814.

fr.[ii, alphabet], t.[1], [2–5], 6–29 p.; illus.; 10 cm.; pr. & illus. buff paper covers.
MWA*; Shaw 31265.

249.20 ———— London. Nerve-York [*sic: i.e.* New York]: Printed And Sold By S. Wood & Sons, At The Juvenile Book-Store, No. 357, Pearl-Street. 1815.

fr.[ii, alphabet], t.[1], [2–5], 6–29 p.; illus.; 10 cm.
MWA* (fr.[ii] & covers wanting); NN (has fr.[ii] & pr. & illus. buff paper covers); PPL; Shaw 34475.

249.21 ———— New-York: Printed And Sold By S. Wood & Sons, At The Juvenile Book-Store, No. 357, Pearl-Street. 1816.

fr.[ii, alphabet], t.[1], [3–5], 6–29 p.; illus.; 10.5 cm.; pr. & illus. buff paper covers.
Warren*; Shaw 37360.

249.22 ———— Cooperstown [N.Y.]; Printed and sold by H. & E. Phinney. 1817.

fr.[ii, alphabet], t.[1], [2–5], 6–29 p.; illus.; 10.5 cm.; pr. & illus. buff paper covers.
MWA*; Shaw 40593.

249.23 ———— Cooperstown [N.Y.]: Printed and sold by H. & E. Phinney. 1819.

fr.[ii, alphabet], t.[1], [2–5], 6–29 p.; illus.; 10 cm.; pr. & illus. buff paper covers.
Cover title: London Cries. Cooperstown: Printed And Sold Wholesale And Retail By H. & E. Phinney. 1819.
MWA*; Shaw 47750.

249.24 ———— New-York: Published By Samuel Wood & Sons, No. 261, Pearl-Street; And Samuel S Wood & Co. No. 212, Market-st. Baltimore. 1820.

fr.[ii, alphabet], t.[1], [2–5], 6–29 p.; illus.; 10.5 cm.; Dutch paper covers.
MWA*; NN (front cover & fr.[ii] wanting); Shoemaker 914; Weiss 1936, p. 133.

250.1 THE CRIES OF NEW-YORK. New York: Printed And Sold By S. Wood, At The Juvenile Book-Store, No. 362, Pearl-Street. 1808.

t.[3], [4–5], 6–47 p.; illus.; 13 cm.; pr. & illus. yellowish-buff paper covers. On p. 4 is a description of New York which in later editions is placed opposite the title page.
MWA-W*; CtHi; NN (i. st. p. 47); Shaw 14800; Weiss 1936, p. 137.

250.2 ———— New-York: Printed And Sold By S. Wood, At The Juvenile Book-Store, No. 357, Pearl-Street. 1809.

fr.[2, prose], t.[3], [4–5], 6–47 p.; illus.; 12.5

cm.; pr. & illus. yellow-buff paper covers; fr.[2] is a description of New York.

MWA°; MH (fr.[ii] & p. 47 wanting); Shaw 50931.

250.3 ———— New-York: Printed And Sold By S. Wood, At The Juvenile Book-Store, No. 357, Pearl-Street. 1810.

fr.[ii, prose], t.[1], [2–3], 4–45 p.; illus.; 12.5 cm.; pr. & illus. yellow-buff paper covers; fr.[ii] same as no. **250.2**.

OClWHi° (front cover mut. date torn away); MWA (fr.[ii] and front cover wanting); Shaw 19893.

250.4 ———— New-York: Printed And Sold By S. Wood, At The Juvenile Book-Store, No. 357, Pearl-street. 1812.

fr.[ii, prose], t.[1], [2–3], 4–45 p.; illus.; 13 cm.; pr. & illus. buff paper covers; fr.[ii] same as no. **250.2**.

MWA°; NHi; Shaw 25183.

250.5 ———— New-York: Printed And Sold By Samuel Wood, At The Juvenile Book-Store, No. 357, Pearl-Street. 1814.

fr.[ii, prose], t.[1], [2–3], 4–45 p.; illus.; 13 cm.; pr. & illus. yellow-buff paper covers; fr.[ii] same as no. **250.2**.

MWA° (covers worn, fr.[ii] mut.); CLU; CtY (bound with other books); NHi; NN; PP (covers wanting); Weiss 1936, p. 136; Shaw 31266.

250.6 ———— New-York: Printed And Sold By S. Wood & Sons, At The Juvenile Book-Store, No. 357, Pearl-Street. 1816.

fr.[ii, prose], t.[1], [2–3], 4–45 p.; illus.; 12.5 cm.; fr. [ii] same as no. **250.2**.

MWA° (paper pasted over covers, fr.[2] mut.); MH; NHi (bound with other books in no. **191**); NN (pr. & illus. buff paper covers); Shaw 37361.

250.7 ———— New-York: Published By Samuel Wood & Sons, No. 261, Pearl-Street, And Samuel S. Wood & Co. No. 212, Market-st. Baltimore. 1818.

fr.[ii], t.[1], [2–3], 4–45 p.; illus.; 13 cm.; pr. &

illus. yellow-buff paper covers; fr.[ii], as in no. **250.2**; cover title undated.

MWA° (p. 45 torn); Shaw 43771.

THE CRIES OF PHILADELPHIA (arranged chronologically)

251.1 The Moving Market: or Philadelphia Cries. Embellished with thirty-one elegant Engravings. Price three-pence. Philadelphia: adv. by Young and M'Culloch, 1787 in **249.2**; and by W. Young, 1794 in **305** and 1795 in *Sermons For Children*.

251.2 Philadelphia Cries. Philadelphia: adv. by B. & T. Kite, 1807 in **611.1**.

251.3 The Cries Of Philadelphia: Ornamented With Elegant Wood Cuts. Philadelphia: Published By Johnson And Warner, No. 147, Market Street. John Bouvier, Printer. 1810.

t.[1], [2–3], 4–36 p.; illus.; 13 cm.; pr. paper covers.

Cover title: Johnson & Warner's Juvenile Library. The Cries Of Philadelphia. Embellished With Cuts. No. 147, Market-Street, Philadelphia.

PP°; DLC (per. st. on t.[1], unprinted paper covers); MB (emb. st. on t.[1]); MWA-T (covers wanting); PHi; Shaw 19894.

[CROUCH, NATHANIEL] 1632?–1725? Richard Burton *pseud*.

252 [—] Some Excellent Verses For the Education of Youth, Taken from Eccles. 12. I. Remember thy Creator in the Dayes of thy Youth, &c. To which are added Verses for Little Children. By a Friend. Boston, Printed by Bartholomew Green. Sold at the Printing House. 1708.

t.[1], [2], 3–12 p.; 14 cm.; p. 4–7 also numbered 3, 6, 9, 12 in succession.

PP°.

A Curious Account of The Comic Adventures of Old Mother Hubbard and Her Dog. *See* Martin, Sarah Catherine, no. **817.1**.

A Curious Hieroglyphic Bible. *See* Hieroglyphic Bibles, no. **510**.

D

THE DAIRYMAN'S DAUGHTER. *See* Richmond, Legh, no. **1107.1**.

THE DAISY. *See* Turner, Mrs. Elizabeth, no. **1355.1**.

253.1 DAME PARTLET'S FARM; Containing An Account Of The Great Riches She Obtained By Industry, The Good Life She Led, And Alas, Good Reader! Her Sudden Death; To Which Is Added, A Hymn, Written By Dame Partlet, Just Before Her Death, And An Epitaph For Her Tomb Stone. [illus. of a tomb stone with the word *Johnson* on it.] Philadelphia: Published And For Sale By J. Johnson, 147, Market Street, And At His Book-Store In Richmond, Virginia. 1806.
> t.[1], [2–5], 6–59 p.; illus.; 16 cm.; pr. & illus. blue-gray paper covers; illus. p. 9, 47 signed A [Alexander Anderson].
> English ed.; holograph note p.[3]: "This book was written by Dr. James Hodson." London: J. Harris, 1804.
> MWA*; CtHi (p.[5]–6 wanting); MiD; PHi; RPB; Shaw 10247.

253.2 ——— Philadelphia: Published and for Sale by Johnson and Warner, No. 147, Market Street, and at their Bookstore in Richmond, Virginia, and Lexington, Kentucky. J. Bouvier, Printer. 1810.
> t.[1], [2–5], 6–59 p.; illus.; 17.5 cm.; pr. & illus. olive-gray paper covers; illus. p. 9, 19, signed A [Alexander Anderson]. (copy 2).
> Cover title (probably 1810 ed.): ——— She Led. From The Juvenile Library, 147 Market Street, Philadelphia. (copy 1).
> Cover title (reissue): ——— She Led. From The Juvenile Library, No. 171, Market Street, Philadelphia. 1819. Griggs & Co. Printers. (copy 2).
> MWA* (copy 2); CtHi (copy 2); MiD; MSaE; N; NcD; NHi (copy 2); NNC-Pl* (copy 1, 2); PHi; PP (copy 2); PU (copy 2); Shaw 19912.

254.1 DAME TROT, AND HER COMICAL CAT. Illustrated With Sixteen Elegant Engravings. Philadelphia: Published and sold wholesale by Wm. Charles, and may be had of all the Booksellers. 1809. [cover title].
> Cover title & rear cover originally pasted on inside of front & rear covers of Dorsets' *The Peacock "At Home"*, no. **296.2**.
> English ed. London: J. Harris, 1808, pl. dated Oct. 1, 1806.
> DLC*.

254.2 ——— Philadelphia: Published and sold by Wm. Charles, No. 32, S. Third-st. 1817. [cover title].
> [1–16] p. engr. on one side only of 16 leaves; illus.; 12.5 cm.; pr. buff paper covers. The plates are copied in the reverse from the London, J. Harris plates dated 1806.
> PP* (rear cover wanting); CSmH ([8]p. only); DLC (rear cover mostly wanting); Shaw 40611; Weiss 1932a.

DAME TRUDGE. *See* Adventures Of Old Dame Trudge, no. **9.1**.

255 DAME TRUELOVES TALES. Philadelphia: adv. by E. & R. Parker, 1818 in **704.1**.

DANIEL LAMBERT. *See* The Life Of That Wonderful and Extraordinarily Heavy Man, Daniel Lambert, no **757.1**.

256 THE DANGERS OF THE STREET, and other tales. Embellished with three copper plate engravings. [Philadelphia] Jacob Johnson, 1808.
> Adv. by Johnson and Warner, 1814 in **1449.2**.
> This is the English version of the German book *Die Gefar in den Strassen*, no. **431**.
> English ed. London, entitled: *Tales uniting Instruction with Amusement: consisting of The Dangers of the Streets; and Throwing Squibs*. J. Harris. n. d.
> Shaw 14828.

DARTON, WILLIAM 1755–1819
257.1 [—] THE FIRST CHAPTER OF ACCIDENTS, And Remarkable Events: Containing Caution And Instruction For Children. Philadelphia: Published By Jacob Johnson, No. 147, Market-Street. 1802.

t.[1], [2–48] p.; illus.; 12.5 cm.; marbled paper covers. Colophon p. [48]: Published by Jacob Johnson. John W. Scott, Printer, No. 27, Bankstreet.
OOxM°; Shaw 2227.

257.2 [—] ——— Philadelphia: Published By Jacob Johnson, No. 147, Market-Street. 1804.
t.[1], [2–48] p.; illus.; 12.5 cm.; marbled paper covers.
PP°; CtY; MHi; NNC-Pl.

258.1. [—] THE SECOND CHAPTER OF ACCIDENTS And Remarkable Events: Containing, Caution & Instruction For Children. Philadelphia: Published By Jacob Johnson, Market-Street. 1803.
t.[1], [2–48] p.; illus.; 13 cm.; blue-gray marbled paper covers.
English ed. London: Darton and Harvey, 1801.
MWA-T°.

258.2 [—] ——— Philadelphia: Published By Jacob Johnson, Market-Street 1807.
t.[1], [2–48] p.; illus.; 13 cm.; blue-gray marbled paper covers; colophon p.[48]: Robert Bailey, Printer, No. 84 Crown-street.
MWA-W°; CaOTP; CLU; CSmH; CtHi; CtY; DLC; NHi; NNC-Pl; PHi; PP; PPL; Shaw 12394 and 13561.

259.1 [—] THE THIRD CHAPTER OF ACCIDENTS And Remarkable Events: Containing Caution And Instruction For Children. Philadelphia: Published By J. Johnson, Market-Street. 1803.
t.[1], [2–48] p.; illus.; 13 cm.; blue-gray marbled paper covers.
English ed. London: Darton & Harvey, 1801.
CtHi°; CtY; OOxM.

259.2 [—] ——— Philadelphia: Published By J. Johnson, Market-Street. 1807.
t.[1], [2–48] p.; illus.; 13 cm.; blue-gray marbled paper covers; p. [16] shows an illus. of an air balloon. The Chapter Of Accidents, 3 parts. Adv. by Johnson and Warner, 1814 in **1449.2**.
Welch°; CSmH; CtHi; CtY; DLC; MSaE; MWA; NHi; NNC-Pl (2 copies); PHi; PP; PPL; Shaw 12394 and 13685.

260.1 [—] JACK OF ALL TRADES, Philadelphia: Published By Jacob Johnson, No. 147, Market-Street. 1808.

t.[1], [2–3], 4–48 p.; illus.; 16 cm.; pr. paper covers.
Verso of title page: Adams, Printer, Philadelphia. Colophon p. 48. The text is the same as *Little Jack Of All Trades*, no. **261.1**. written by Wm. Darton. *See* Darton Cat. no. 333.
Cover title: Jack Of All Trades, For The Use Of Good Little Boys. Ornamented With Engravings. Philadelphia: ——— 1808.
MWA-W°; MdHi (upper half of t.[1] wanting, p. 47–48 mut.); NNC-Pl (p. 24–48 & covers wanting); OOxM; RPB (t.[1] & rear cover wanting, p. 5–6, 9–10, 37–38 three-fourths wanting); Shaw 15312.

260.2 [—] ——— Philadelphia, Published By Johnson And Warner, No. 147, Market-Street. 1815.
t.[1], [2–3], 4–48 p.; illus.; 16.5 cm.; pr. pink paper covers; cover title same as no. 260.1 with imprint: Philadelphia: Published By Johnson And Warner. ——— 1815.
NNC-Pl°; Shaw 35006.

261.1 [—] LITTLE JACK OF ALL TRADES, With Suitable Representations. Part I. Boston: Published By Thomas B. Wait And Co. And Charles Williams. [1813].
t.[3], [4], 5–71 p.; illus.; 14 cm.; title vignette & illus. p. [4], [8], [54], [57], [63], [70] signed [Nathaniel Dearborn]. Pt. II. was published in 1813, *see* no. **261.2** below. The book was published in 1808 under the title: *Jack of all Trades*. *See* no. **260.1**.
English ed. London: 2 vols. Darton & Harvey & Harris, 1804–05.
MWA° (covers wanting); Shaw 28962.

261.2 [—] ——— Part II. Charles Williams Bookseller Boston [in the title vignette] Boston: Published By Thomas B. Wait And Co. And Charles Williams. 1813.
t.[1], [2–3], 4–69 p.; illus.; 14.5 cm.; pr. & illus. buff paper covers; list of books on the rear cover.
CtHi° (covers mut.); MWA; NNC-T (2 copies varying covers); Shaw 28963.

262.1 [—] LITTLE TRUTHS BETTER THAN GREAT FABLES: In Variety of Instruction for Children from four to eight years old. Volume I. Philadelphia: Printed And Sold By Joseph Crukshank, In

Market-Street, Between Second And Third-Streets. MDCCLXXXIX.

   fr.[i], [ii, bl.], t.[i], [ii], iii–v, 6–56 p.; 3 engr. pl. including front.; 11.5 cm.; wallpaper covers. Bottom of p. 56: End of the First Volume. Top of fr.[i] has "Frontispiece."; pl. opp. p. 17 is numbered "Page 17"; pl. opp. p. 53 is numbered "Page 53".

   English ed. London: William Darton, MDCC-LXXXVII.

   NjR°; Evans 21785.

262.2   [—] LITTLE TRUTHS: Containing Information on divers Subjects, for the Instruction of Children. [5 lines quot.] Winter Evenings. Volume II. With Copper-Plate Cuts. Philadelphia: Printed And Sold By Joseph Crukshank, In Market-Street, Between Second and Third-Streets. M DCC LXXXIX.

   fr.[ii], t.[1], [2], 3–64 p.; 4 pl. including front.; 11 cm.; Dutch paper covers. At the top of p. 3 is a double rule, ornamented at the ends with a crozier-like ornament.

   Irish ed. Dublin: 1796.

   MWA° (vol. II.); PP (vol. II., rear cover & pl.[2] wanting); Evans 21785.

262.3   [—] LITTLE TRUTHS BETTER THAN GREAT FABLES: Containing Information on divers Subjects, for the Instruction of Children. Vol. I. Illustrated With Cuts. The Sixth Edition, With Many Alterations And Additions. Boston: Printed and sold by Samuel Hall, No. 53, Cornhill. 1794.

   vol. I.: t.[iii], [iv], v–vi, [7], 8–71 p.; illus.; 12 cm.; Dutch paper covers; vol. II.: t.[3], [4–5], 6–70, [71–72, adv. list of books]; illus.; 11 cm. Title to vol. II.: —— Truths; Containing Information on divers Subjects, For The Instruction Of Children. Vol. II. Illustrated With Cuts. [4 lines quot.] Boston: Printed and sold by Samuel Hall, No. 52, Cornhill. 1794.

   MWA° (vol. II., p.[71–72] & covers wanting, t.[3] mut.); CtHi (vol. II. p.[71–72] wanting, t.[3], p. 69–70 & covers mut.); MB° (vol. II., per. st. on t.[3]); NN (vol. II.), RPJCB (vol. II.); Evans 26848 (vol. I.) and 26849 (vol. II.)

262.4   [—] —— Fables: Containing Information on divers Subjects, for the Instruction of Children. [4 lines quot.] Winter Evenings. Volume I. [II.] Illustrated With Copper-Plates. Philadelphia: Printed For, And Sold By, J. And J. Crukshank, No. 87, High-Street. 1800.

vol. I.: fr. [ii] t.[1], [ii–iii], iv–v, [6], 7–56 p.; 4 pl. including front.; illus. blue-gray paper covers; vol. II.: fr.[ii], t.[1], [2–3], 4–64 p.; 4 pl. including front.; illus. buff paper covers; 2 vols.; 10 cm.

   MWA°; CCamarSJ; CLU (vol. I.–II.); CSmH; CtHi; DLC; IU; MH; NB; NHi; NN-C; NNC-Pl; NRU; PP; PPL (vol. I.); PU (vol. I.); Evans 37291.

263   [—] LITTLE TRUTHS FOR THE INSTRUCTION OF CHILDREN. Vol. I. [II.] Philadelphia. Published by Johnson & Warner. 1812.

   vol. I.: t.[i], [ii–iii], iv, [5–48] p.; illus.; 16 cm.; pr. & illus. pinkish-buff paper covers; vol. II.: t.[2], [3–5], 6–48 p.; illus.; 16.5 cm.; pr. & illus. white paper covers; cover title of both vols. dated 1812.

   Title page vol. II.: —— Philadelphia, Published by Johnson & Warner, No. 147. Market Street. [1812]. Vignette on cover title of Vol. II. signed M [William P. Morgan], one of Anderson's four pupils. MWA copy has an adv. of Munroe & Francis on p. opp. t.[i].

   English ed. London: vols. I–II. Darton And Harvey. 1802.

   MWA-W° (vols. I.–II.); CLU (vols. I.–II.); CtHi (vol. II.); CtY (vols. I.–II.); DLC (vol. II.); MSaE (vol. II.); MWA (vols. I.–II.); NHi (vol. II.); NN (vol. II.); NNC-Pl (vol. II.); PHi (vol. II.); PP (vols. I.–II.); Shaw 25216–7 and 25870.

264.1   [—] A PRESENT FOR A LITTLE BOY. [2 lines quot.] Cotton. A New Edition Enlarged. Philadelphia, Published By Jacob Johnson, High-Street. 1802.

   t.[1], [2–58] p.; illus.; 16 cm.; scalloped marbled paper covers, pink paper spine; p. [57–58] adv. list of books; illus. p. [24] signed *W. R. sc.* [William Ralph]; no colophon.

   English ed. London: Wm. Darton, 1798.

   MWA°; CoU; NPV; Shaw 2930.

264.2   [—] —— Cotton. Philadelphia: Published By Jacob Johnson, No. 147, High-Street. 1804.

   fr.[2], t.[3], [4–60] p.; illus.; 17 cm.; marbled paper covers; p.[59–60] adv. list of books; reprint of no. **264.1**. Colophon p. [58]: A. & G. Way, Printers.

   MWA-W°; NjR° (fr.[2], p. [27–28], [33–34] & covers wanting); Shaw 50421.

264.3 [—] ——— Philadelphia: Published By Johnson And Warner, No. 147 Market Street. A. Fagan, Printer. 1815.

fr.[2], t.[3], [4–60] p.; illus.; 16 cm.; gray paper covers. p. [59–60] adv. list of books; reprint of no. **264.1**; no colophon.

MWA°; NHi; NNC-Pl.

265.1 [—] A PRESENT FOR A LITTLE GIRL. Philadelphia: Published By Jacob Johnson, No. 147, Market-Street. Samuel Akerman, Printer. 1804.

t.[1], [2–48] p.; illus.; 17.5 cm.; blue marbled paper covers. Title vignette and woodcuts p. [6], [39] signed *A* [Alexander Anderson].

English ed. London: Wm. Darton & Josh. Harvey, Decr. 26, 1797.

CLU°; CtY (p. [29–32] wanting); MiDSH; RPB; Shaw 7113.

265.2 [—] ——— Baltimore: Printed by Warner & Hanna, And Sold By Them And J. Vance & Co. 1806.

fr.[2], t.[3], [4], 5–60 p.; illus.; 16 cm.; blue marbled paper covers; fr.[2] & illus. p. 20 signed *C, G.*, title vignette & illus. p. 10, 22 signed *G.*, illus. p. 47 signed *Gobrecht* [Christian Gobrecht]. Adv. by Johnson & Warner. Philadelphia. 1814 in **1449.2.**

MWA° (i. st. on. t.[3]); NjP (Hamilton, front cover wanting); Shaw 11212.

[DAWES, JUDGE] *See* Juvenile Vice & Piety Contrasted, no. **720.1.**

[DAY, THOMAS] 1748–1789
266.1 [—] THE FORSAKEN INFANT Or Entertaining History of Little Jack. Embellished with Eight Elegant Copper Plate Prints. Philadelphia; Published By R. Johnson. No.–2 North–3rd. Street. 1806.

fr.[ii], t.[1], [2–3], 4–37 p.; engr. t.[1] & 7 engr. pl. including front.; 13 cm.; scalloped marbled paper covers; title vignette signed *G Love;* Colophon p. 37: Abel Dickinson, Printer. English ed. first printed in *The Children's Miscellany*, Stockdale, 1788.

MWA°; NNMM (pr. & illus. yellow paper covers dated 1811); Shaw 10262.

266.2 [—] ——— Little Jack. New-York: Printed And Sold By C. Totten, No. 155 Chatham-street. 1811.

t.[1], [2–3], 4–52 p.; illus.; 14 cm.; pr. & illus. brown paper covers.

MWA° (front cover wanting, t.[1], p. [2]–4, 51–52 & rear cover mut.); CLU; NNC-Pl; Shaw 22669.

266.3 [—] ——— Embellished with Eight Elegant Copper Plate Prints. Philadelphia: Published By J. Pounder No 352 North 3rd. Street. 1813.

fr.[ii], t.[1], [2–3], 4–38, [pl. opp. p. 38] p.; engr. t.[1] & 7 engr. pl. including front.; 14 cm.; illus. blue-gray paper covers; title vignette signed *G. Love.*

Cover title imprint: Philadelphia: Sold By Jonathan Pounder, No. 352, North Third Street. 1813.

MWA° (t.[1] torn affecting 1st two lines, 1 pl. wanting); NHi (cover title dated 1815); NjR; NNC-LS (unprinted gray paper covers); PP; Shaw 28542.

266.4 [—] ——— [same as **266.2**] New-York: Printed And Sold By J. C. Totten, No. 9 Bowery. 1819.

fr.[2], t.[3], [4–5], 6–46 p.; illus.; 14.5 cm.; pr. & illus. buff paper covers.

MWA° (fr.[2] mut.); CLU; CtHi (2 copies); CtY; DLC; NHi; NN; NNC-Pl; PHi; PP; PPL; Shaw 47797.

267 [—] [THE] GRATEFUL TURK. Or The Advantages Of Friendship. Boston: Printed by J. White. 1796.

t.[3], [4–5], 6–30, [31] p.; illus.; 9 cm.; the rear paper cover has a cut of Robinson Crusoe. An abridged version of "The Story Of The Grateful Turk," which first appeared in vol. 1 of Day's *Sandford And Merton* first published in London, 1783.

Griffin° (fr.[2] & front cover wanting, top of t.[3] trimmed so that the word [The] may be wanting); Evans 47764.

268.1 [—] THE HISTORY OF LITTLE JACK. Embellished With A Number Of Engravings. To Which Is Added, The Little Queen, A Moral Tale. Natural History Of The Bee. Natural History Of The Silkworm. Epistle To A Friend On His Return From The Army. And The Universal Prayer, By A. Pope, Esq. Boston: Printed And Sold By William Spotswood. 1795.

t.[i], [ii], [1], 2–94 p.; illus.; 17 cm.; bound in

blue-gray paper over bds., leather spine.
English ed. London: Published in Stockdale's *Children's Miscellany*. *1788* and reprinted separately in the same year.
MWA-W° (p. 1–12, 23–28 slightly mut.); Evans 28539.

268.2 [—] ——— Philadelphia: Printed And Sold By H. and P. Rice; Sold Also By James Rice And Co. Baltimore. 1795.
t.[i], [ii, bl.], [1], 2–94 p.; illus.; t.[1] 8 cm. The same illus., type & type set up as no. **268.1.**
NN° (rebound, poor copy, title & many other leaves repaired, covered with tissue paper, p. 5–6 wanting, other p. mut.); Evans 47396; Weiss 1936, p. 336.

268.3 [—] ——— New York: adv. for twelve cents by Thomas B. Jansen, 1805 in **1373.**

269.1 [—] THE HISTORY OF SANDFORD AND MERTON. A Work Intended for the Use of Children. [2 lines quot.] In Two Volumes. Vol. I. [II.] The Fifth Edition Corrected. Philadelphia: Printed by W. Young, Bookseller and Stationer, at the Corner of Second and Chesnut-Streets. M,DCC, LXXXVIII.
vol. I.: t. [i], [ii–iii], iv–vi, [13], 14–127, [128, bl.] p.; vol. II.: t.[129], [130–131], 132–257, [258, adv. list of books] p.; 2 vols. in 1; 17.5 cm.; bound in leather. A third volume was published by William Young, Philadelphia. 1791. On t. [129] Vol. II. there is a comma after "Merton,".
English ed. London: J. Stockdale, vols. 1–2, 1783, 1786.
MWA° (i.st. on t.–p.); MH; NNC; NjR; PP; PPL; Evans 21043.

269.2 [—] ——— Use of Children. [8 lines of verse.] Vol. III. Philadelphia: Printed for William Young, Bookseller, Second-Street, No. 52, the corner of Chesnut-Streets. M,DCCXCI.
t.[1], [2–3], 4–132 p.; t.[1]; 16.5 cm.
NN° (rebound, all after p. 120 wanting, p. 119–120 mut.); PHi; Evans 23315.

269.3 [—] ——— Use of Children. [2 lines quot.] In Three Volumes. Vol. I. [II.–III.] The Sixth Edition. Philadelphia: Printed By William Young, Bookseller, No. 52, Second-Street, The Corner Of Chesnut-Street. M,DCC,XCIII.

vol. I.: t.[i], [ii–iii], iv–vi, [13], 14–127, [128, bl.] p.; vol. II.: t.[129], [130–131], 132–257, [258, bl.] p.; vol. III.: [no title page, a bl. leaf or p. 259–60], [261], 262–391, [392. adv. list of books] p.; 3 vols. in 1; 17.5 cm. bound in leather. Vol. II. t.[129]: ——— [6 line quot.] Ld. Monboddo. In Three Volumes. Vol. III. ——— [same as vol. I.]; vol. I. p. 95 numbered "59", vol. II. p. 245 numbered "145"; p. 248 numbered "148".
MWA°; MBC; MiU; MNF; NN; PHi; RPJCB; Evans 25380.

269.4 [—] ——— In Three Volumes. Vol. I. [II.–III.] The Sixth Edition. Philadelphia: Printed By William Young, Bookseller, No. 52, Second-Street, The Corner Of Chesnut-Street. M,DCC, XCIII.
vol. I.: t.[i], [ii–iii], iv–vi, [13], 14–127, [128, bl.] p.; vol. II.: [no title page, p. [129–130] wanting but sigs. correct], [131], 132–257, [258, bl.]; vol. III.: t.[1], [2–3], 4–132 p.; 3 vols. in 1; 17.5 cm.; bound in leather. A varying ed. of no. **269.3**, with same pages wrongly numbered in vols. I. and II.
The title page of vol. III.: ——— Use of Children. [8 lines of quot.] vol. III. Philadelphia: Printed for William Young, Bookseller, Second-street, No. 52, The Corner Of Chesnut-Street. M,DCC,XCI.
MWA°; CtY; N; NjR; PPL; RPB.

269.5 [—] ——— A Work Intended For The Use Of Children. [2 lines quot.] The Seventh Edition. Whitehall [Pa.]: Printed For William Young, Bookseller And Stationer, No. 52, South Second-Street, Philadelphia. M,DCC,XCVIII.
t.[1], [2–3], 4–8, [13], 14–233, [234, bl.], 2nd t.[235], [236–237], 238–470, 3rd t.[469], [470–471], 472–697, [698 adv., list of books] p.; 17 cm.; bound in leather.
2nd & 3rd titles ——— [same as 1st title] Children. [4 lines of quot.] Ld. Monboddo. In Three Volumes. Vol. II. [III.] The Seventh Edition. White-Hall [Pa.]: Printed By William Young, Bookseller And Stationer, No. 52, South Second-Street, Philadelphia. M,DCC,XCVIII.
CtY°; MiU; MWA-T.

269.6 [—] ——— [4 lines of verse] Ld. Monboddo. In Two Volumes. Vol. I. [II.] The Seventh Edition. Whitehall [Pa.]: Printed For William

Young, Bookseller And Stationer, No. 52, South Second-Street, Philadelphia. M,DCC,XCIX.

vol. I.: t.[1], [2–3], 4–342 p.; vol. II. t.[i], [ii], 343–697, [698, adv. list of books] p.; 2 vols.; 17 cm.; bound in leather.

title vol. II.: —— [8 lines of verse] In Two Volumes. Vol. II. Commencing with the interesting Story of Leonidas King of Sparta. The Seventh Edition. —— [same as vol. I.]. PU°.

269.7 —— —— Children. [2 lines quot.] III Volumes In One. By Thomas Day, Esq. Baltimore: Printed by Warner & Hanna, No. 37, Market-street, corner of South Gay-street. 1801.

vol. I.: t.[i], [ii–iii], iv–vi, [7], 8–128, [129, caption title vol. II.], 130–264, [265, caption title vol. III.], 266–403 p.; 3 vols. in 1; 17.5 cm.; bound in leather.

MWA°; DLC; MdBP; OC; PP (covers wanting); Shaw 389.

269.8 [—] —— New York: adv. by Thomas B. Jansen, 1805 in **1371.5**.

269.9 —— —— Children. [2 lines quot.] (Second Baltimore Edition) Three Volumes In One. By Thomas Day, Esq. Baltimore: Printed And Sold By Warner & Hanna. 1809.

t.[i], [ii, bl.–iii], iv–vi, [7], 8–128, [129, caption title vol. III.], 130–264, [265, caption title vol. III.], 266–403, [404, bl.], [405–406 adv. list of books] p.; 3 vols. in 1; 17 cm.; bound in leather.

MWA°; OOxM; PP; Shaw 17349.

269.10 [—] —— Baltimore: Printed By Warner & Hanna, For John Vance & Co. No. 178, Market-Street. 1809.

t.[i], [ii–iii], iv–vi, [7], 8–128, [129, caption title vol. II.], 130–264, [265, caption title vol. III.], 266–403, [404], [405 adv. list of school books] p.; 3 vols. in 1; 17 cm.; bound in leather.

MWA-W°; DLC; MH; MHi (top of t.[i] cut away).

269.11 —— —— Merton, A Work Intended For The Use Of Schools. [2 lines of quot.] Third Baltimore Edition. Three Volumes In One. By Thomas Day, Esq. Baltimore: Printed By William Warner. 1816.

t.[i], [ii–iii], iv–v, [vi], [7], 8–365 p.; 17 cm.; bound in leather.

MWA°, MdBE; MWiW; PPL; Vi; Shaw 37407.

269.12 —— —— [same as **269.1**] Three Volumes In One. By Thomas Day, Esq. New-York: Printed By Evert Duyckinck, No. 68, Water-Street. J. & J. Harper, printers. 1818.

t.[i], [ii–iii], iv, [5], 6–70, [71, caption title vol. II.], 74 [*sic.* 72], 73–147, [148, bl.], [149, caption title vol. III.], 150–256 p.; 19 cm.; bound in leather.

MWA°; MH; Shaw 43819.

THE HISTORY OF SANDFORD AND MERTON. Abridged ed.; not compiled by R. Johnson.

270.1 [—] —— and Merton. A Work Intended For The Use Of Children. New-York: Published By John C. Totten, N. 155, Chatham-street. 1810.

t.[1], [2–3], 4–48 p.; illus.; 13.5 cm.; pr. brownish-buff paper covers. Rear cover has adv. list of books. A different abridgement than no. **271.1**. *See* same title in *The Juvenile Library*, no. **705**.

DLC° (t.[1] mut., front cover wanting).

270.2 [—] —— & Merton. A Work Intended For The Use Of Children. New-York: Published By John C. Totten, No. 9 Bowery. 1815.

t.[1], [2–3], 4–48 p.; illus.; 14 cm.; marbled paper covers.

CtY°; MWA; NjN.

[DAY, THOMAS] 1748–1789 [JOHNSON, RICHARD], *abr.* 1734–1793

271.1 [—] THE HISTORY OF SANDFORD AND MERTON. Abridged From The Original. Embellished With Elegant Plates. For the Amusement and Instruction of Juvenile Minds. Printed For The Booksellers. M,DCC,XCII.

t.[1], [2–3], 4–107 p.; no illus.; 14 cm.; bound in leather. Page numbers 106–107 printed on the inside of the page.

Entered in Richard Johnson's day book as follows: "*1790 April. Mr. Badcock* [E. Newbery's manager]—*To writing the History of Sandford and Merton*—£ *10. 10 s.*" Apparently first published by John Wallis, with engravings dated 22 May 1790. The same plates used for later editions. (Weedon).

English ed. London: J. Wallis. [1790].
DLC°; Evans 46423.

271.2 [—] ——— Original. For the Amusement and Instruction of Juvenile Minds. New-York: Printed And Sold By William Durrell At His Book Store And Printing-Office, No. 19, Queen Street. M,DCC,XCII.

fr.[2], t.[3], [4–5], 6–133 p.; front. only illus.; 13.5 cm.; bound in greenish-gray paper over w. bds., leather spine.
MWA°; Evans 24249.

271.3 [—] ——— [same as **271.1**] Boston: Printed By Samuel Etheridge, And Sold By The Booksellers. 1796.

fr.[ii], t.[1], [2–3], 4–110 p.; 6 pl. including front.; 14.5 cm.; bound in Dutch paper over w. bds.
MWA°; DLC (t.[1] pasted to inside of front cover, fr.[ii], & p. [3]–4 wanting); MB; MH; NN (bound in leather); PHi; PP; Evans 30316.

271.4 [—] ——— Embellished With Cuts. [8 lines of verse]. The Third Edition. To Which Is Prefixed, A Sketch Of The Author's Life, From Seward's Life Of Dr. Darwin. Carlisle [Pa.]: From The Press Of A. Loudon, (Whitehall.) [Pa.] 1809.

t.[1], [2–3], 4–186 p.; illus.; 14.5 cm.; bound in leather.
MWA°; CtY; NN (p. 185–186 wanting); PPL; Shaw 14350.

271.5 ——— ——— Merton, Embellished With Elegant Plates, For The Amusement And Instruction Of Juvenile Minds. By Thomas Day, Esq. New-York. Published By Richard Scott, Bookseller, No. 243 Pearl-Street. Walker, Printer, New Brunswick, N. J. 1809.

fr.[2], t.[3], [4–5], 6–206 p.; 8 pl. including front.; 18.5 cm.; pr. & illus. violet-gray covers.
MWA°; Shaw 17351.

272 A Day's Ramble In Derbyshire; Or, The Travels Of Tommy Wilson And Billy Passmore; Interspersed With Observations And Anecdotes. Ornamented with Six Beautiful Copper-Plates. Philadelphia: Published By Benjamin Johnson, No. 249, Market Street. 1806.

t[1], [2–3], 4–23 p.; 6 engr. pl.; 16.5 cm.; marbled paper covers. Adv. by. Johnson & Warner, 1814 in **1449.3**.
NNC-Pl°; CLU; Shaw 10263.

DAYTON, EBENEZER

273.1 — A Serious Poem On Various Subjects, Written for the Perusal of Children. By Ebenezer Dayton, School-Master in Newport, Rhode-Island. Printed For The Author. 1769.

t.[1], [2], 3–16 p.; 11.5 cm.
CSmH°; RHi (blue paper covers); RPB.

273.2 ——— ——— The Second Edition. Printed For The Author. 1769.

t.[1], [2], 3–16 p.; 12 cm.
CSmH° (rebound in red morocco); RHi (brown paper covers); Evans 11233.

The Death And Burial Of Cock Robin. *See* Cock Robin, no. **213.1**.

274.1 The Decoy; Or, An Agreeable Method Of Teaching Children The Elementary Parts Of English Grammar, By Conversations And Familiar Examples. New-York: Printed And Sold By Samuel Wood & Sons, At The Juvenile Book-Store, No. 357, Pearl-Street. 1816.

fr.[ii], t.[1], [2–5], 6–62 p.; illus.; 13.5 cm.; pr. & illus. yellow paper covers; cover title undated.
English ed. London: adv. by Darton And Harvey in *A Present For A Little Boy*. 1813.
MWA°; NN (covers wanting); RP; RPB; Shaw 37413; Weiss 1942.

274.2 ——— New-York: Published By Samuel Wood & Sons, No. 261, Pearl-Street; And Samuel S. Wood & Co. No. 212, Market-St. Baltimore. 1820.

t.[1], [2–3], 4–32+ p.; illus.; 18 cm.; pr. & illus. buff paper covers.
MWA-W° (fr. [ii] & all after p. 32 wanting).

DEFOE, DANIEL 1661?–1731

ROBINSON CRUSOE (arranged chronologically)

275.1 [—] The Wonderful Life, And Surprising Adventures Of that Renowned Hero, Robinson Crusoe: Who lived Twenty-Eight Years On An Uninhabited Island, Which he afterwards colonized. New-York: Printed by Hugh Gaine, at his Book-Store in Hanover-Square, where may be had a great Variety of Little Books for Young Masters and Misses. M,DCC,LXXIV.

fr.[2], t.[3], [4–5], 6–138, [139–142 adv. list of books] p.; illus.; 10 cm.; Dutch paper covers.

The title page of the PP copy differs in having, "The Renowned Hero". Life and Adventures p. [5]–138. English version 3.

English ed. 1st unabridged ed. London: W. Taylor. 1719.

Abridged ed., English version 3, [London]: Printed for the inhabitants of his Island, and Sold by all the Booksellers in the World. Price Six-pence bound. [*ca.* 1768]. Probably published in London by F. Newbery and T. Carnan [*ca.* 1768]. Cahoon's imprint [Newbery 1760] is open to question since John Newbery was the only member of the family publishing in 1760. No advertisement of *Robinson Crusoe* has been located in any John Newbery list. London: adv. by Newbery and Carnan in *The History Of Little Goody Two-Shoes.* 1768.

English version 3. Portion of the first and last sentences of the first and last paragraphs of the [*ca.* 1768] ed.: *I was born of a good family . . . persuaded me to go with him. . . . Arrived at London . . . ending my days in peace, and in true worship of my Almighty Deliverer.*

CtY°; MWA (rebound, fr.[ii], p. 15–18, 31–34, 47–50, 63–66, 79–82, 95–98, 111–114, 127–130 wanting); PP; Brigham 1; Evans 42582.

275.2 [—] The Wonderful Life, And Surprising adventures of that Renowned Hero, Robinson Crusoe, Who Lived Twenty-Eight Years On An Uninhabited island, [a row of "x" like type ornaments] Written by Himself, [a row of x-like type ornaments] Boston Printed and sold by N. Coveely [*sic. i.e.* Coverly].₀°₀ Price Three Pence. [*ca.* 1784].

illus.[1], fr. [2], t.[3], [4], 5–32 p. illus.; 10 cm. The last *t* of the word *that* on t.[3] is higher than the other letters; the three stars before the word *Price* are in the form of a triangle; no punctuation after *Boston.* The lower illus. of the front., and illus. p. 13, 28 were used by N. Coverly, in his 1783 ed. of *Goody Two-Shoes,* no. **463.2**, p. 14, 60, 64 respectively. These illus. are drawn in the reverse from both the 3rd London, J. Newbery, 1766 ed. and the New York, Hugh Gaine, 1775 ed., no. **463.1** of *Goody Two-Shoes.* The woodcut illus. of the "Statute of a Man" on p. 64 of Coverly's 1783 ed. of *Goody Two-Shoes* has the thick ruled borders in perfect condition. In the above ed. of *Robinson Crusoe,* no. **275.2**, the same cut on p. 28 the cut has been damaged and there is an identation in

the upper left border. This defect must have occurred after 1783 and for this reason the book is dated [*ca.* 1784]. Wonderful Life &c.; p. [4]–32. English version 4 with textual variations. The first portion of the last paragraph: *I cannot express the agony it now causes in me.* All American ed. of English version 4 have the extra word *now* in the beginning of the last paragraph.

Abridged ed., English version 4, entitled: *The Wonderful Life and Adventures Of Robinson Crusoe. Written by Himself.* Exeter: M'Kenzie and Son, 1797. This is the earliest dated English ed. of English version 4 from which nos. **275.2, 275.3,** and **275.4** were also taken. An English ed. earlier than the American ones has yet to be located.

English ed. of English version 4, London, entitled: *The Life And Adventures Of Robinson Crusoe. Written by Himself.* T. Evans, Long Lane, West Smithfield. Price 1d.; T. Evans fl. 1800; York: J. Kendrew [*ca.* 1820].

English version 4. portion of the first and last sentences of the first and last paragraphs of the [*ca.* 1820] ed.: Life and Adventures, *With permission, reader, I will relate to you . . . in my power to entertain you. I cannot express the agony it causes in me; . . . the most miserable object living, and heartily I repent giving way to that restless disposition which made me leave my parents, as from that hour I date all the subsequent misfortunes of my life.*

MWA°; Brigham 4 (dated [*ca.* 1779]); Evans 43621.

275.3 [—] The Wonderful Life And Surprising Adventures of that Renowned Hero, Robinson Crusoe, Who Lived Twenty-Eight Years On An Uninhabited Island. [a row of scroll-like printer's ornaments] Written by Himself. [a row of scroll-like printer's ornaments, also a rule which is thicker in the middle and tapering at the ends] Boston: Printed and sold by N. Coverly °₀° Price Three Pence. [*ca.* 1784].

t.[3], [4], 5–30 p.; illus.; 11 cm. A varying issue of the preceding no. **275.2**. Same title, but *Adventures* and *Island* are capitalized; the row of type ornaments above and below *Written by Himself* are different; there is a colon after *Boston:;* an inverted triangle of asterisks °₀° before *Price;* and *Coverly* is spelled correctly. MWA° (illus. [1]?, fr.[2]?, p. 31–32 & covers wanting); Brigham 5 (dated [*ca.* 1779]); Evans 43621.

275.4 [—] TRAVELS OF ROBINSON CRUSOE. Written By Himself. Worcester (Massachusetts) Printed By Isaiah Thomas, And Sold At His Book-Store, MDCCLXXXVI: Where may be had a Variety of little Books for Children.
  fr.[2], t.[3], [4], 5–31 p.; illus.; 10 cm.; illus. buff paper covers. Travels, p. 5–23, English version 4, no. **275.2**; to this is added a new paragraph: *Now as many of my readers,* . . . p. 23–24; Of taking our Parents Advice, p. 25–27; A Dialogue, p. 28–30; [cut of ship & 4 lines of verse], p. 31.
  MWA°; NjP; Brigham 6; Evans 19599.

275.5 [—] ——— [same as **275.1**] London, Printed: Philadelphia, Reprinted By Charles Cist, In Race-Street, Between Front And Second-Streets, 1787.
  t.[3], [4–5], 6–160 p.; illus.; 10 cm.; 6 full page illus. Life and Adventures, p. [5]–160. English version 3, no. **275.1**.
  PHi° (rebound, p. 103–106, [1]56–[16]0, mut. affecting p. nos.; p. 103–106 bound out of sequence and placed at end after p. [16]0); Brigham 7; Evans 45059.

275.6 [—] DIE WUNDERBARE LEBENSBESCHREI-BUNG, UND ERSTAUNLICHE BEGEBENHEITEN DES BERÜHMTEN HELDEN ROBINSON CRUSOE, Welcher 28 Jahr auf einer Unbewohnten Insel wohnete, die er nachderhand bevölkert hat. Philadelphia: Gedruckt bey Carl Cist, in der Rehs-strasse, zwichen der Front-und Zweyten-strasse. 1788.
  fr.[ii], t.[iii], [iv], [1], 2–154 p.; illus.; 13.5 cm.; bound in green Dutch paper over bds.; 7 full page illus. including front. Below the word *Ende* on p. 154 there is a tailpiece made up of 6 flower-like ornaments grouped in the form of a triangle with the apex pointed towards the bottom of the page. The ornaments are the same as those used in the border of the frontispiece. Das Leben und die Begebenheiten, p. [1]–154. Text is a German translation of English version 3, no. **275.1**.
  MWA°; Brigham 8; Evans 21045.

275.7 [—] ——— [same as **275.6** with variations in type setting].

The page numbers and sigs. are in slightly different positions on certain pages of **275.7**, although many pages are identical with **275.6**. On p. 13 of no. **275.7** the "3" lies above the space and slightly over the *g* of *Ich gab* and the "1" is above the *h*, also sig. "B" is below the *hu* of *unschuldig*. In no. **275.6** the number "13" is above the *ga* of *gab* and sig. "B" is below the *di* of *unschuldig*. Many such variations in type setup occur. The frontispieces are the same in **275.6** and **275.7**. In no. **275.7** there is a group of 6 different type ornaments below the word *Ende* on p. 154. The top one is circular with a central fleur-de-lis, and is the same ornament also used in the corners of the border of the frontispiece. Below this is a column of three small ornaments the same as those below the cut of the frontispiece, and flanked on either side by a large scroll-like ornament. The basal line of 3 ornaments consists of a central squarish checkerboard-like one, the same as those used above the cut of the frontispiece, and flanked on either side by an asterisk-like ornament.
  NN° (bound in green Dutch paper over bds.); Brigham 8; Evans 21045.

275.8 [—] ——— [same as **275.6**] Philadelphia: Gedruckt bey Carl Cist, in der Rehs-strasse, zwichen der Front-und Zweyten-strasse. 1789.
  fr.[ii], t.[iii], [iv], [1], 2–154 p.; 7 illus. including front.; 13.5 cm.; illus. p. 122 [*sic i.e.* 130]. Text same as no. **275.6**.
  MWA° (rebound, fr.[ii], p. 149–154 wanting); PP; Brigham 9; Evans 45465.

275.9 — THE LIFE AND MOST SURPRISING ADVENTURES OF ROBINSON CRUSOE, Of York, Mariner. Containing a full and particular Account how he lived twenty-eight years in an uninhabited Island on the coast of America: How his ship was lost in a storm, and all his companions drowned; and how he was cast upon the shore by the wreck: With a true Relation how he was at last miraculously preserved by Pirates. Faithfully epitomized from the Three Volumes, and adorned with cuts, suited to the most remarkable stories. Philadelphia: Printed by Peter Stewart, West side of Second-street, ninth Door above Chesnut-street. M,DCC,LXXXIX.
  fr.[2], t.[3], [4–5], 6–180 p.; illus.; 14 cm.; bound in leather. Preface p. [4]; Life and Ad-

ventures, p. [5]–93; Further Adventures p. [94]–156; Vision of the Angelic World p. [157]–180; [6 lines of verse] Life's but a snare, . . . p. 180. Variant issue 1 of English version 1. The preface, 1st vol. and the beginning of the 2nd vol. follow English version 1 below with many textual changes. The last sentences of the 1st two vols. end: [1st vol.], . . . *year 1689 . . . my island. An account of which you shall have in the second volume.;* [2nd vol.], . . . *England, where I hope to have the blessing of ending my days in peace.* The last part of the 2nd vol. p. 153–155 follows p. 212–214 of the Worcester 1794 ed., English version 2, no. **275.27** with variations. The 3rd vol. is a mixed abridgement of English version 1 and 2 with the last paragraph and closing 6 lines of verse the same as English version 1.

English ed. of the 1st abr. ed. London: 1st t. T. Cox. 1719, 2nd t. E. Smith, 1719. This abr. ed. or English version 1a was not printed in America, but rewritten English version 1 may have been based on it.

English ed. of English version 1, London: Edw. Midwinter. [172?]. A. Bettesworth and C. Hitch; J. Osborn, R. Ware, J. Hodges, 1734. English version 1. Portion of the first and last sentences or the last two sentences of the first and last paragraphs of the preface and each volume of [172?] ed.: Preface, *In this new epitome, . . . in this edition. . . . Let this epitome, . . . to his perusal.* Life and Adventures [Vol. I.], *He that pretends . . . the following narration. . . . Having cast my Anchor, . . . did in the year, 1649* [*sic. i.e.* 1694] *and in my passage, visited my island. A full and . . . the subject of the second and third volume* [*sic. i.e.* volumes] *of my narrative;* Farther Adventures, Vol. II., *My new Kingdom . . . death of my wife . . . After we had passed the River Kirtza, . . . ten years and nine months absence;* Vision of the Angelick World, Vol. III., *Solitude is a noble refiner . . . with an enemy. . . . It would be too long to inform . . . this side the Angelick World.* [6 lines of verse] *Life's but a snare, . . . trembling from the stage.*

English and American ed. follow the text of English version 1 with changes. The Preface and 3rd vol. may be omitted. Sentences, words, dates, and the spelling of words are changed. "Angelick" may be spelled "Angelic" as in most editions. The end of 3rd vol. shows the great-

est variation. The lines of verse are often omitted and different parts of the prose abridged. In the English ed. the date near the end of the 1st vol. is "1649" [*sic i.e.* 1694] in [172?], 1734 ed.; "1696" in 1772 ed.; and "1689" in the remaining ones. The American ed. show the greatest diversity, often mixing English version 1 with 2 or 2a. In this respect the J. Hollis [1796] ed. resembles an American mixture. The preface and the beginning of the 1st vol. are similar to English version 2a, no. **275.50**, while the end of the 1st vol. and 2nd and 3rd vols. follow English version 1. Because of the great variation in American ed. close to English version 1, those having characteristic endings to the 1st and 2nd vols. are called variant issues, numbers 1, 2, 3, and described in order under nos. **275.9**, **275.10** and **275.23**.

MWA° (p. 4–8, 71–72, 159–160, 179 mut.); Brigham 10; Evans 21787.

275.10 [—] The Most Surprising Adventures, And Wonderful Life Of Robinson Crusoe, Of York, Mariner. Containing A Full And Particular Account How His Ship Was Lost In A Storm, And All His Companions Were Drowned, And He Only Was Cast Upon The Shore By The Wreck; And How He Lived Eight And Twenty Years In An Uninhabited Island, On The Coast Of America, &c. With A True Relation How He Was At Last Miraculously Preserved By Pirates &c. &c. &c. Portland [Me.]: Printed And Sold By Thomas B. Wait. MDCCLXXXIX.

fr.[2], t.[3], [4–5], 6–130, [131, illus.] p.; illus.; 15.5 cm.; bound in leather. Preface, p. [4]; Life and Adventures, p. [5]–82; Further Adventures, p. [83]–130. Variant issue 2 of English version 1. The text is close to English version 1, no. **275.9**, with the following variations: the first line of the preface: *In this new abridgement . . . ;* end of the last paragraph of the 1st vol.: *. . . year 1689, . . . A full and particular account of which I intend shall be the subject of the subsequent parts of my narrative.*

MWA° (fr. [2] mut.), CtY (p. 61–62, 69–72, 83–84 wanting; fr. [2] mut.); MiU (p. 5–8, 65–68, 77–80. 123–131 wanting); NN (copy 1, p. [2–4]; [131] wanting, p. [5]–14 slightly mut.; copy 2, p. [2]–8 mut., front cover broken); NjP (bound in blue-gray paper over w. bds.); Brigham 11; Evans 21788; Hamilton 126.

275.11 [—] Travels Of Robinson Crusoe. Written By Himself. The Second Worcester Edition. Printed at Worcester, Massachusetts. By Isaiah Thomas, Sold at his Bookstore, and by Thomas and Andrews in Boston. MDCCLXXXIX.
  fr.[2], t.[3], [4], 5–31 p.; illus.; 10 cm.; Dutch paper covers. Travels, p. 5–24, English version 4, no. **275.2**; Of taking our Parent's Advice, p. 25–27; A Dialogue, p. 28–30; [cut of a ship & 4 lines of verse], p. 31. Entire text same as no. **275.4**.
  MWA°; CtY (fr.[2] mut. & ¾ths wanting, t.[3] trimmed, p. 29–31 & covers mut.); Brigham 12; Evans 45464.

275.12 [—] The Wonderful Life —— [same as **275.1**]. Albany: Printed by C. R. & G. Webster, at their Office, in State-street, where Printing in general, in the English and German Languages, is performed with Expedition and on reasonable Terms. M.DCC.XC.
  t.[3], [4–5], 6–138 p.; illus.; 11.5 cm.; bound in buff paper stripped with black & red; 6 full p. illus. Life and Adventures, p. [5]–138. English version 3, no. **275.1**.
  MWA°; Brigham 14; Evans 45858.

275.13 [—] Travels Of Robinson Crusoe. Written By Himself. Boston: Printed by Samuel Hall, at No. 53, Cornhill. 1790.
  fr.[2], t.[3], [4–5], 6–31 p.; illus.; 10 cm.; illus. buff paper covers pr. in. red ink. Travels, p. 5–25, English version 4, no. **275.2**; Of taking our Parents' Advice, p. 26–27; A Dialogue p. 28–30; [cut of a ship and four lines of verse], p. 31. Entire text same as no. **275.4**.
  DLC°; Brigham 15; Evans 45859.

275.14 [—] Travel [*sic. i.e.* Travels] Of Robinson Crusoe. Written By Himself. Boston: Printed by J. White and C. Cambridge, near Charles' River Bridge. [1790?].
  t.[3], [4–5], 6–30+ p.; illus.; 9 cm. Travels, p. [5]–30. English version 4, no. **275.2**, with the additional paragraph of no. **275.4**.
  MWA° (fr.[2] p. [31] & covers wanting), PP (fr.[2], p. 29–30 [31], & covers wanting, p. 27–28 mut., 8.5 cm.); Brigham 16; Evans 45860.

275.15 [—] Travels Of Robinson Crusoe Who was twenty-eight Years on a desolate Island. Written By Himself. Boston: Printed by J. White &

C. Cambridge, near Charles' Rive [*sic. i.e.* River] Bridge. 1791.
  fr.[2], t.[3], [4–5], 5–29 p.; illus.; 10 cm.; buff paper covers. Travels, p.[5]–26, English version 4, no. **275.14**, the additional paragraph has: *will* [*sic. i.e.* wild] *inclination;* A Dialogue, p. 27–29. Text follows no. **275.4**.
  MiU°; Evans 46147.

275.16 [—] The Wonderful Life —— [same as **275.1**]. Boston: Printed and Sold by J. White and C. Cambridge, near Charles-river Bridge. 1791.
  fr.[2], t.[3], [4–5], 6–72 p.; illus.; 13.5 cm.; bound in buff paper over w. bds., leather spine. Life and Adventures, p. [5]–72. English version 3, no. **275.1**.
  MWA-W°; CLU (fr.[2] & covers wanting), CtY, NjP; Hamilton 137; Evans 46148.

275.17 [—] The Life and Most Suprising [*sic. i.e.* Surprising] Adventures of Robinson Crusoe, of York, Mariner. Containing a Full and Particular account How he lived twenty-year years in an Uninhabited Island on the Coast of America: How His Ship was lost in a Storm, and all His Companions Drowned; and How he was cast upon the Shore By the Wreck: With A true Relation How he was at Last Miraculously Preserved By Pirates. Faithfully Epitomized From the three Volumes. Philadelphia: Printed and sold by W. Woodhouse, at the Bible, No. 6, South Front-street. 1791.
  MWA° [3], 4–157, [158 adv.]; (title page and pages preceding 3, 11–12, 25–26, 35–36 wanting); Evans 23320.

275.18 [—] The Wonderful Life And most Surprising Adventures Of Robinson Crusoe, Of York, Mariner. Containing, A full and particular Account how his Ship was lost in a Storm, and all his Companions were drowned, and he only was cast upon the Shore by the Wreck; and how he lived Eight and Twenty Years in an uninhabited Island, on the Coast of America, &c. With A True Relation how he was at last miraculously preserved by Pirates, &c, &c &c. Boston: Printed and sold at the Bible & Heart, in Cornhill. [*ca.* 1792].
  t.[3], [4–6], 9–114, [115–118 wanting], [119, illus.] p.; illus.; 15.5 cm.; bound in brownish-buff paper over w. bds., leather spine. Preface,

p. [5]–6; [Life and Adventures] p. [7]–68; Farther Adventures, p. 69–109; Vision of the Angelic World, p. 110–[118?]; illus. of Robinson Crusoe, p. [119]. Variant issue 2 of English version 1. The text is close to no. **275.10,** but differs in the 2nd vol. p. 88–97 by having a more extensive account of A Continuation of the Life of Robinson Crusoe. The beginning of the 3rd vol. follows English version 1, no. **275.9.**
MWA-W° (fr. [2], p. [7–8], [115–118] wanting, p. 35–36 mut.); Brigham 19; Evans 46425.

275.19 [—] THE WONDERFUL LIFE ——— [same as **275.1**]. Boston: Printed and Sold by J. White and C. Cambridge, near Charles-river Bridge. 1792.
fr.[2], t.[3], [4–5], 6–72 p.; illus.; 13.5 cm.; bound in blue-gray paper over w. bds., cloth spine. Life and Adventures, p.[5]–72. English version 3, no. **275.1.**
Welch°; CLU (p. 49–52, 57–60 wanting, p. 53–56 trimmed part of text destroyed); MB; MWA; NN (t.[3] wanting, fr.[2] mut.); PP; Brigham 20; Evans 24253.

275.20 [—] THE WONDERFUL LIFE ——— [same as **275.1**]. London, Printed: Philadelphia, Reprinted by Charles Cist, No. 104 in Second-street, near Race-street, M,DCC,XCII.
fr.[2], t.[3], [4–5], 6–160 p.; illus.; 10.5 cm.; violet Dutch paper covers; 6 full page illus. including front. Adventures, p.[5]–160. English version 3, no. **275.1.**
Carson° (p. 99–111 trimmed affecting p. nos. and heading); Brigham 21; Evans 24254.

275.21 [—] TRAVELS OF ROBINSON CRUSOE. Written By Himself. Windham [Conn.]: Printed By John Byrne. M,DCC,XCII.
fr.[2], t.[3], [4], 5–31 p.; illus.; 10.5 cm. Travels, p.[4]–31. English version 4, text same as no. **275.14.** The second from the last paragraph ends . . . *the most miserable object living.* The final portion of the sentence . . . *and heartily I repent . . . misfortunes of my life.* is omitted.
CtHi°; PP (browned copy all p. mut.; illus. buff paper covers); Brigham 23; Evans 46424.

275.22 [—] THE MOST SURPRISING ADVENTURES ——— [same as **275.10**]. Preserved By Pirates, &c. &c. Printed At Osborne's Office, Market-Square, Newburyport [Mass.]. MDCCXCIII.

t.[1], [2–3], 4–118 p.; 14 cm. Life And Adventures, p.[3]–75; Further Adventures, p. 75–118. Text same as variant issue 2 of English version 1, no. **275.9.**
MWA° (rebound, p. 41–44 wanting; p. 117–118 slightly mut.); MNe; MSaE (bound in blue-gray paper over w. bds., leather spine; p. 117–118 mut.); NN (p. 5–8 supplied from another copy); Brigham 24; Evans 46724.

275.23 [—] THE WONDERFUL LIFE AND MOST SURPRISING ADVENTURES OF ROBINSON CRUSOE of York, Mariner: Containing A full and particular Account how he lived eight and twenty years in an uninhabited Island on the Coast of America; how his ship was lost in a storm, and all his Companions drowned; and how he was cast upon the shore by the wreck. With a true Relation how he was at last miraculously preserved by Pirates. Faithfully Epitomized from the three Volumes, & adorned with Cuts suitable to the most remarkable Stories. New-York: Printed and Sold by W. Durell, at his Book Store & Printing Office; No. 19 Queen Street. [ca. 1793].
fr. [2], t.[3], [4–7], 8–148 p.; illus.; 13.5 cm.; bound in blue-gray paper over w. bds., leather spine. On p. "9" the lower part of the number "9" is not struck. Preface, p. [5–6]; Life and Adventures, p. [7]–90; Farther Adventures, p. [91]–148; [6 lines of verse] Life's but a snare, . . . p. 148. Variant issue 3 of English version 1. The text is rewritten but resembles English version 1. no. **275.9,** with the 1st vol. ending . . . *subject of the second and third volumes of my narrative.* The third from the last paragraph of the 2nd vol. ends. . . . *ten years and nine months absence.,* the closing lines of the 2nd vol. English version 1. The last two paragraphs of the same vol. and the closing six lines of verse are taken from the 3rd vol. of English version 1.
MWA-W°; MiU; PP (t.[3], p. 29–30, 105–106, 133–134, 147–148 mut.); Brigham 25; Evans 25386.

275.24 [—] THE LIFE AND ADVENTURES OF ROBINSON CRUSOE. Written by Himself. Embellished With Cuts. Baltimore [Md.]: Sold by George Keating, Bookseller, Bookbinder and Stationer, Second Street. 1794.
fr.[2], t.[3], [4–5], 6–30 p.; illus.; 9.5 cm.;

Dutch paper covers. Life and Adventures, p.
[5]–30. English version 4, no. **275.2**.
MWA°; MiU; Brigham 26; Evans 26864.

275.25 [—] The Wonderful Life ———
[same as **275.1**]. Boston: Printed and Sold by
Samuel Hall, No. 53, Cornhill. MDCCXCIV.
fr.[2], t.[3], [4–5], 6–116 p.; 7 full page illus.
including front.; 13.5 cm.; bound in Dutch
paper over w. bds.; illus. p. 92 repeated on p.
96. Adventures p. [5]–116. English version 3,
no. **275.1**.
CtY° (front cover & fr.[2] wanting); CtHi;
DLC; MWA-T; NN (bound in Dutch paper
over w. bds.); Brigham 28; Evans 26865.

275.26 [—] [Travels Of Robinson Crusoe
———] [probably the same as **275.13**] [Boston:
Printed by Samuel Hall, at No. 53, Cornhill.
1794].
fr.[2], t.[3], [4–5], 6–31 p.; illus.; 10 cm.;
Dutch paper covers. Travels, p. [5]–25, English
version 4, no. **275.2**; Of Taking our Parent's
Advice, p. 26–27; A Dialogue, p. 28–[30?];
[cut of a ship and 4 lines of verse], p. 31. Text
same as no. **275.4**. It is believed that this book
is Samuel Hall's Boston edition of 1794, because
of the two large letters $\begin{smallmatrix}M\\M\end{smallmatrix}$ on the recto of the
frontispiece, which are only found in S. Hall's 10
cm. type books printed in 1794. At the bottom
of p. 25 S. Hall's address is printed. The printer's ornaments of a crown and angel's head were
used extensively by S. Hall in his 10 cm. type
books printed in 1794, although they were also
used as early as 1793 and later. Adv. by S. Hall,
1794 in **673.8**.
MWA° (t.[3] & p. 29–30 wanting); Brigham
37; Evans 47626.

275.27 [—] The Life And Most Surprising
Adventures Of Robinson Crusoe, Of York,
Mariner; Who Lived Eight and Twenty Years in
an uninhabited Island, on the Coast of America,
lying near the Mouth of the great river of Oroonoque: Having been cast on Shore by Shipwreck,
wherein all the men were drowned but himself:
As Also, A Relation how he was wonderfully delivered by Pirates. The whole Three Volumes
faithfully abridged. Printed At Boston, By I.
Thomas And E. T. Andrews, Faust's Statue No
45 Newbury Street. M.DCC.XCIV.
t.[i], [ii–iii], iv, [5], 6–231 p.; 17.5 cm.; bound

in leather. Preface p.[iii]–iv; Life and Adventures, p.[5]–125; Farther Adventures, p.[126]–
214; Angelic World, p.[215]–231. English version 2.
English ed. of English version 2, London: E.
Midwinter, A. Bettesworth, J. Brotherton, W.
Meadows, M. Hothan, 1722. The title page of
the above English ed. starts: *The Life And Most
Surprising Adventures Of Robinson Crusoe, . . .*
Portion of the first and last sentences of the
first and last paragraphs of the preface and each
vol. of the 1722 ed.: Preface, *It is very well
known what universal reception . . . knowledge
of the divine blessings. . . . Needless therefore
is it to enlarge any farther . . . to render this
history delightful, instructive and entertaining.;*
[vol. I.] *In the year, 1632. I was born at York,
of a reputable family . . . . by the name of
Crusoe. . . . One might reasonably imagine, . . .
great Creator shewen, one way or other, over
the face of the whole earth.;* Vol. II., *When we
consider the puissant force of nature, . . . is
all that I desire. . . . All that night we worked
hard. . . . January, 1705, after ten years and
nine months absence from England.;* [Vol. III]
*However solitude is look'd upon as a restraint
. . . everlasting happiness in Heaven. . . . Some
people make a very ill use . . . for the general
good and benefit of the world.* English and
American editions follow this 1722 ed. with
textual variations; the preface, vol III., paragraphs and sentences may be omitted. The
prefaces of the [175?] & 1777 ed. have 10 or
more lines omitted from the first paragraph.
See also English version 2a, no. **275.50**.
Welch° (p. [iii]–iv, 209–210 mut.), CtY (p.
231 mut.); MWA (i. st. on t.[i]); Brigham 27;
Evans 47024.

275.28 [—] The Life And Most Surprising
Adventures ——— lived twenty-eight years
——— [same as **275.23**] Philadelphia: Printed
by Stewart & Cochran, No. 34, South Second-
street. M,DCC,XCIV.
fr.[2], t.[3], [4–5], 6–179 p.; illus.; 13.5 cm.;
bound in gray paper over bds. Preface, p. [4];
Life and Adventures, p. [5]–91; Farther Adventures, p. [92]–153; Vision of the Angelick
World, p. [154]–176; [6 lines of verse] Life's
but a snare . . . , p. 176. Text close to variant
issue 1 of English version 1, no. **275.9**.
PP°.

275.29 [—] THE WONDERFUL LIFE AND SUR-
PRISING ADVENTURES OF ROBINSON CRUSOE,
———— [same as **275.43**] miraculously preserved.
Adorned with Cuts. Philadelphia: Printed and
sold by John M'Culloch, No. 1, North Third-
street. 1794.

fr.[2], t.[3], [4–5], 6–144 p.; illus.; 13.5 cm.;
bound in brown paper speckled with black, p.
65 wrongly numbered "23". Life And Adventures, p. [5]–88; Farther Adventures, p.[89]–
144; [6 lines of verse] Life's but a snare . . .
p. 144. Variant issue 3 of English version 1.
The text is the same, with minor variations, as
no. **275.43**.
MWA-W°.

275.30 [—] TRAVELS OF ROBINSON CRUSOE.
Written By Himself. The Third Worcester Edition. Printed at Worcester, Massachusetts, By
Isaiah Thomas. And Sold Wholesale and Retail,
at his Bookstore. MDCCXCIV.

fr.[2], t.[3], [4–5], 6–31 p.; illus.; 9.5 cm.;
green Dutch paper covers. Travels, p. [5]–24,
English version 4, no. **275.2**; Of Taking our
Parents Advice, p. 25–27; A Dialogue, p. 28–
30; [cut of a ship & 4 lines of verse], p. 31.
Text same as no. **275.4**.
MWA° (i. st. on fr.[2]); PP (illus. blue-gray
paper covers); Brigham 29; Evans 47027.

275.31 [—] THE WONDERFUL LIFE ————
[same as **275.1**] Haverhill [Mass.]: Printed by
Peter Edes. 1795.

Evans 28554 (no location). Probably taken
from an advertisement.

275.32 [—] THE WONDERFUL LIFE AND MOST
SURPRISING ADVENTURES OF THAT RENOWNED
HERO, ROBINSON CRUSOE, Who lived Twenty-
eight Years On An Uninhabited Island. Which
he afterwards Colonized. New-York: Printed by
Hurtin & Commardinger, for E. Duyckinck, &
Co. 1795.

fr.[2], t.[3], [4–5], 6–143 p.; illus.; 13.5 cm.;
copy 1 bound in buff paper, ornamented with
a red rule lines, over w. bds.; copy 2 bound in
green Dutch paper over w. bds. Life and Adventures, p. [5]–121; Farther Adventures, p.
122–143. An abridged ed. of English version
1a, below, with the preface and 6 lines of verse
at the end of the 2nd vol. omitted. The 1st
vol. starts with the 2nd paragraph, *I was born*

at York, . . . after her maiden name. The last
paragraph of the 1st vol., *Having cast my anchor, . . . 1694, and in my passage visited my
island.,* is the same as English version 1, no.
275.9. The first sentence of the last paragraph
of the 2nd vol. differs from English version 1a
by being contracted to, *We arrived at Nanquin,
when* . . . The remainder of the paragraph is
the same in both books.

English ed. of English version 1a, London: Sold
By The Booksellers In Great-Britain, Ireland
And America. 1791.

English version 1a. Portion of the first and last
sentences of the first two and last paragraphs of
the preface and each vol. of the 1791 ed.:
Preface, *In this new epitome . . . the history
entire and correct. . . . Let this epitome, . . . to
his perusal.*; Life and Adventure, [1st para.]
He that pretends . . . following narration. [2nd
para.], *I was born at York, . . . maiden name.
. . . Having cast my anchor, . . . year 1694, . . .
second and third volumes of my narrative.*;
Farther Adventures, *My new Kingdom . . .
death of my wife. . . . We left the bay the next
morning, and sailed to Nanquin, when to our
great joy, . . . in true worship of my Almighty
Deliverer.* [6 lines of verse] *Life's but a snare,
. . . from the stage.* English version 1a follows
English version 1 with changes and abridgements. The preface of version 1a is abridged.
The end of the 3rd vol. resemble English
version 3, no. **275.1**. The 6 lines of verse, when
present, come at the end of the 3rd vol. in
English version 3.
Welch° CLU; CtY (covers wanting, p. 143
mut.); MWA (p. 143 mut.); PP; Evans 28555.

275.33 [—] ———— [same as **275.32** but with
a different imprint] New-York: Printed by Hurtin
& Commardinger, for Benjamin Gomez. 1795.

fr.[2], t.[3], [4–5], 6–143 p.; illus.; 13 cm.;
bound in blue-gray paper over bds. English
version 1a same as no. **275.32**.
MWA° (i. st. on fr.[2]); NjP; PP (2 leaves
sig. B. wanting, worm holes p. 137–143, covers
half wanting, 4 leaves sig. A. repeated); Brigham 32; Evans 28555.

275.34 [—] THE MOST SURPRISING ADVENTURES
———— [same as **275.10**] Printed at Worcester,
Massachusetts, And Sold at the Worcester Book-
store. 1795.

fr. [2], t.[3], [4–5], 6–144 p.; illus.; 14.5 cm.; bound in leather. Printed by Isaiah Thomas. Preface, p.[4]; Life and Adventures, p. [5]–85; Farther Adventures, p. 86–132; Vision of the Angelic World, p. 133–144. Variant issue 2 of English version 1. The Preface and the 1st vol. through p. 9 has the same text as no. **275.10**. The last part of the 1st vol. and all of the 2nd vol. are closest to the London 1775 ed. English version 1, no. **275.9**. The 3rd vol. follows the Boston 1794 ed. English version 2, no. **275.27**. Chapters I. and II. are the same in both books. Chapters III. and VI. of **275.27** are omitted and chapters IV. and V. are renumbered III. and IV. in **275.34**. The book terminates with the last paragraph of chapter IV., *When the negative man . . . Fœlix this negative man tremble.* MWA° (i. st. on t.[3]); BM (p. 5, 25, & 41 mut.); CtY; MB (fr.[2], & covers wanting; p. 111–114 mut.); MH; MiU; NHi; NN; PHi (i. st. on t.[3]; p. 133–144 wanting); PPi (i. st. on t.[3]; fr.[2] & covers wanting); Brigham 33; Evans 28552.

275.35 [—] The Wonderful Life, And Most Surprising Adventures Of that renowned Seaman, Robinson Crusoe, Who lived Twenty-eight Years on an Uninhabited Island, And was afterwards relieved by Pirates. Together with some Account of his Man Friday. Fairhaven [Vt.]: Re-printed and sold by J. P. Spooner. [1796].
fr.[2], t.[3], [4], 5–46, [47, illus. & adv. of books] p.; illus.; 13 cm. Life and Adventures, p. [4]–46; [cut of a ship, 4 lines of verse, and an adv. of 8 books one of which, Sterling's *Child Instructor*, was printed in 1796 according to Brigham]. An abridged ed. of English version 3, no. **275.1**.
PP° (covers wanting); Brigham 34; McCorison 385.

275.36 [—] The Life And Most Surprising Adventures, ———— [same as **275.9**] Faithfully Epitomized From The Three Volumes. Wilmington [Del.]: Printed & Sold By Peter Brynberg. 1796.
t.[i], [ii-iii], iv, [5], 6–144 p.; t. [i] 13.5 cm. Preface, p. [iii]–iv; Life and Adventures, p. [5]–86; Farther Adventures, p. [87]–144. Close to variant issue 1 English version 1. The text is an abridged form of no. **275.9**. The end of the

last paragraph of the 1st vol. ends, . . . *year 1694, . . . visited my island.* The 2nd vol. starts out similarly to English version 1, but the last 4 pages appear to be an abridged form of English version 2, no. **275.27**, with the last paragraph ending . . . *nine months absence from England, where I hope to have the blessing of ending my days in peace;* the same as variant issue 1, no. **275.9**.
MWA° (rebound); DeHi (bound in brown paper over bds. speckled with black & brown); Brigham 35; Evans 30325.

275.37 [—] Travels Of Robinson Crusoe. Written By Himself. Windham, (Connecticut), Printed By John Byrne, MDCCXCVI.
fr.[2], t.[3], [4–5], 6–31 p.; illus.; 10 cm.; marbled paper covers. Travels, p.[5]–28, English version 4, no. **275.2**; A Dialogue, p. 29–31. Text the same as no. **275.4** with omissions.
MWA°; CtHi (fr.[2] mut.); PP; Brigham 36; Evans 47765.

275.38 [—] ———— Boston: Printed and sold by Samuel Hall, No. 53, Cornhill. 1798.
fr.[2], t.[3], [4–5], 6–30 p.; illus.; 10.5 cm.; Dutch paper covers; t.[3] has a printer's ornament of a crown, p. 29 printer's ornaments of a crown and angel's head. Travels, p.[5]–24, English version 4, no. **275.2**; Of taking our Parent's Advice, p. 25–26; A Dialogue, p. 27–29; [cut of a ship & 4 lines of verse], p. 30. Text same as no. **275.4**.
MWA° (i. st. on fr.[2]); Brigham 37; Evans 33617.

275.39 [—] ———— First Newport Edition. Newport [R.I.]: Printed by H. & O. Farnsworth. 1799.
[ii, illus.], [1, 3 cuts], fr. [2], t.[3], [4–5], 6–26, [27, adv.], [28, 2 cuts], [29, illus.] p.; illus.; 11 cm.; Dutch paper covers; p. [ii] has a cut of a goose, p. [29] a cut of a pelican. Travels, p. [5]–25; cut of a ship and 5 lines of verse, p. 26. Text same as no. **275.4** with omissions.
PP°; MWA (p. [ii]– fr.[2], [29], and covers wanting); RNHi (p.[27–29] & covers wanting); RPJCB; Brigham 38; Evans 36445.

275.40 [—] Life And Surprising Adventures Of The Renowned Robinson Crusoe, Who lived

Twenty-Eight Years on an Island Inhabited by no Human Creature but Himself, And which he afterwards Lived to Colonize. <First American, from a much admired London Edition.> Dedham [Mass.]: Printed And Sold By Herman Mann. 1800.

    fr.[2], t.[3], [4–5], 6–136 p.; illus.; 13.5 cm. bound in blue marbled paper over w. bds., leather spine. Life and Adventures, p. [5]–131, English version 3, no. **275.1**; An Account of the Island of Juan Fernandes, p. [132]–133; Verses Supposed to be Written by Alexander Selkirk [*I am the monarch of all I survey, . . . reconciles man to his lot.* Cowper.], p. [134]–136. The text of Robinson Crusoe, as in no. **275.1**, ends on p. 131, . . . *of my Almighty Deliverer.* This is followed by an additional paragraph, *Mr. Crusoe lived . . . a monument was placed over his remains.* The entire text including the additional paragraph and illustrations on p. 20, 42, 51, 53, 54, 78, 92, 110 copied in the reverse, are taken from the London [1796?] ed. below. English ed. of English version 3 variant issue 1, London: S. Jewkes and Co. [1796?]. This English ed. ends on p. 125 with the additional paragraph above.

    MWA-W°; DLC (fr.[2], t.[3], p. 77–78 mut.); PP (p. 25–26, 71–72 slightly mut.); Brigham 39; Evans 37303.

275.41 [—] THE WONDERFUL LIFE AND ADVENTURES OF ROBINSON CRUSOE. Ornamented with Cuts. Hartford: Printed by John Babcock. 1800.

    fr.[2], t.[3], [4–5], 6–31 p.; illus.; 11 cm.; orange & green Dutch paper covers. Alphabets, p. [4], History, p.[5]–31. English ed. of English version 5, York: Wilson, Spence & Mawman. (Price One Penny) [1797]. Adv. by Wilson, Spence, & Mawman in Don Stephano Bunyano's (*pseud.*) *The Prettiest Book For Children.* 1797. Adv. among *Penny Books* by T. Wilson and R. Spence in Defoe's *The Wonderful Life And Surprising Adventures Of Robinson Crusoe.* 1802.

    English version 5. Portion of the first and last sentences of the first and last paragraphs of the [1797] ed.: *The life of this surprising Adventurer . . . before their eyes. . . . In this situation, . . . the place of his master's nativity.*

    MWA° (i. st. on fr.[2]); CtHi; CtY (fr.[2] & front cover wanting; p. 31 mut.); MB; Brigham 40; Evans 37305.

275.42 [—] THE WONDERFUL LIFE ——— [same as **275.1**] New-York: Printed By John Tiebout, No. 246, Water-Street, June, 1800.

    fr.[2], t.[3], [4], 5–134 p.; illus.; 13 cm. Preface, p. [4]; Life and Adventures, p. 5–89; Farther Adventures [*sic i.e.* Adventures], p. [90]–134; [6 lines of verse] Life's but a snare, . . . , p. 134. English version 1a, no. **275.32**. The end of the 1st vol. differs from no. **275.32** by ending, . . . *the subject of the second volume of my narrative.*

    MWA° (rebound); CtY (covers wanting); NjP (rear cover wanting); Brigham 42; Evans 37306.

275.43 [—] THE WONDERFUL LIFE AND SURPRISING ADVENTURES OF ROBINSON CRUSOE, Of York, Mariner: Containing, A full and particular Account how he lived eight and twenty years upon an uninhabited island on the coast of America: With a true Relation how he was at last miraculously [*sic. i.e.* miraculously] preserved. Adorned with Cuts. Philadelphia: Printed and sold by John M'Culloch, No. 1, North Third-street. 1800.

    t.[3], [4–5], 6–144 p.; 8 illus.; 13.5 cm.; bound in marbled paper over bds., leather spine; p. 25 wrongly numbered "67"; p. no. 67 wrongly numbered "25". Life and Adventures, p. [5]–88; Further Adventures, p. [89]–144; [6 lines of verse] Life's but a snare . . . p. 144. Variant issue 3 of English version 1. The text is rewritten but close to no. **275.23**. The ending of the fourth from the last paragraph of the 2nd vol., . . . *20th of April, and landed in London the 12th of September.*, is changed from the ending of no. **275.23**. The third from the last paragraph of no. **275.23** is omitted. The last two paragraphs and the closing 6 lines of verse are the same in both books and are taken from the 3rd vol. of English version 1, no. **275.9**.

    DLC° (fr.[2] wanting); Brigham 43; Evans 37307.

275.44 [—] THE WONDERFUL LIFE ——— [same as **275.41**] Hartford: Printed by John Babcock. 1802.

    fr.[2], t.[3], [4–5], 6–31 p.; illus.; 11 cm. Alphabets, p. [4]; History, p. [5]–31. English version 5, no. **275.41**.

    MiU° (fr.[2] mut.); Brigham 44; Shaw 50287.

275.45 [—] THE WONDERFUL LIFE AND SURPRISING ADVENTURES ——— [same as **275.1**]

Philadelphia: Printed By B. Johnson, No. 31, High Street. 1802.

> folded fr.[ii], t.[1], [2–3], 4–128 p.; front. only illus.; 11 cm.; bound in buff paper over bds., red leather spine. Life and Adventures, p. [3]–128. English version 3, no. **275.1**.
> MWA°; Brigham 45; Shaw 2126.

275.46 [—] THE WONDERFUL LIFE AND SURPRISING ADVENTURES OF ROBINSON CRUSOE; Containing A full and particular Account how he lived 28 Years in a uninhabited Island on the Coast of South America; how his Ship was lost in a Storm, and all his companions drowned; and how he was cast upon the Shore, and miraculously preserved, &c. Epitomized From The Large Work. Baltimore [Md.]: Printed For G. Douglas, Bookseller. 1803.

> t.[i], [ii, bl.–iii], iv, [5], 6–141, [142, adv. list of books] p.; 2 vols. in 1; 13.5 cm.; bound in blue paper over bds., leather spine. Preface, p.[iii]–iv; Adventures, p.[5]–90; Adventures, Part II., p. 91–141; Books now selling by the printer, p. 142. Variant issue 1, English version 1. The text is close to no. **275.36** with word changes and abridgements. The last sentences of the 1st and 2nd parts have similar endings to the 1st and 2nd vols. of no. **275.36**.
> MWA-W°; Brigham 46; Shaw 4060.

275.47 [—] THE WONDERFUL LIFE AND ADVENTURES OF ROBINSON CRUSO[E.] Adorned with Cuts. From Sidney's Press, New-Haven. 1803.

> fr.[2], t.[3], [4–5], 6–31 p.; illus.; 10.5 cm.; green Dutch paper covers. Alphabets, p. [4]; History, p. [5]–31 English version 5, no. **275.41**.
> CtHi° (fr.[2], & t.[3] cropped or torn along right margin, covers mut.); Brigham 48; Shaw 50351.

275.48 [—] THE WONDERFUL LIFE AND ADVENTURES OF ROBINSON CRUSO. [*sic. i.e.* Crusoe]. Ornamented with Cuts. Second Rhode Island Edition. Newport [R.I.]: Printed by Oliver Farnsworth. 1803.

> fr.[2], t.[3], [4], 5–31 p.; illus.; 11.5 cm.; blue-gray wallpaper covers. History, p. [4]–31. English version 5, no. **275.41**.
> MWA°; Brigham 49.

275.49 [—] THE LIFE AND MOST SURPRISING ADVENTURES ——— [same as **275.9**] Faithfully

Epitomized From the three Vols. Philadelphia: Printed By Thomas & William Bradford, Booksellers And Stationers, No. 8, South Front Street. 1803.

> t.[3], [4–5], 5–158 p.; 14 cm.; bound in blue-gray paper over bds., leather spine. Life and Adventures, p. [5]–94; Farther Adventures, p. [95]–158. Variant issue 1 of English version 1. Close to no. **275.36** with textual variations. The last sentence of the 1st vol. ends, . . . *year 1689, and in my passage visited my island*.
> MWA°; Brigham 50; Shaw 4058.

275.50 [—] LIFE AND MOST SURPRISING ADVENTURES ——— [same as **275.36**] of America, Near The Mouth Of The Great River Oroonoko. With An Account Of His Deliverance Thence, And His After Surprising Adventures. Embellished With Copperplates. Philadelphia: Printed For William Woodhouse, No. 6, South-Front-Street. 1803.

> fr.[ii], t.[i], [ii–iii], iv, [5], 6–250 p.; 4 pl. including front.; 17 cm.; bound in leather. Preface, p. [iii]–iv; Life and Adventures, p. [5]–145; Further Adventures, p. [147]–250. English version 2a. British and Irish ed. of English version 2a, Edinburgh: 8 ed. A. Donaldson and J. Reid, For Alexander Donaldson, 1765. English version 2a. This version follows the text of English version 2, no. **275.27**, except for a new preface and other variations. Portions of the first and last sentences of the first and last paragraphs of selected sections of the Edinburgh 1765 ed.: Preface, *If ever a story of any private man's adventures . . . thinks this will be so. . . . The editor believes, . . . a great service in the publication.*; Life and Adventures, *I was born at York, . . . name of Crusoe. . . . One might reasonably imagine, . . . over the face of the earth, if duly averted to.* The 2nd and 3rd vols. are the same as English version 2.
> English and American editions follow this text of the 1765 ed. with textual variations. The words *if duly averted to* at the end of the 1st vol. may be omitted.
> MWA°; Brigham 51; Shaw 4057.

275.51 [—] THE WONDERFUL LIFE ——— [same as **275.41**]. Providence [R.I.]: Printed By Heaton & Williams. [1804?].

> illus.[1], fr.[2], t.[3], [4], 5–32 p.; illus.; 11

cm.; no covers. History, p.[4]–32. English version 5, no. **275.41**.
MWA*, Brigham 52; Shaw 6138.

275.52 [—] The Life And Most Surprising Adventures ——— [same as **275.9**]. Faithfully Epitomized From The Three Volumes. Baltimore —Printed by Warner & Hanna No. 37, Corner of South Gay & Market-streets. 1805.
½t.[1], fr.[2], t.[3], [4–5], 6–144 p.; illus.; 14 cm.; bound in ornamental paper over bds. Life And Adventures, p. [5]–86; Farther Adventures, p. 87–144. Variant issue 1 of English version 1, no. **275.9**, with textual variations. The last sentence of the 1st vol. ends, . . . *year 1694, . . . An account of which you shall have in the second volume.*
MWA*; CLU (t.[3] torn, p. 65 mut.); CtY (p. [1–2] wanting, top of p. [5]–6 torn away); DLC (rear cover wanting); MdBE; MiU; Brigham 53; Shaw 8310.

275.53 [—] The Wonderful Life And Adventnres [*sic. i.e.* Adventures] Of Robinson Crusoe. Adorned with Cuts. From Sidney's Press, Hew-Haven [*sic. i.e.* New-Haven]. 1805.
t.[3], [4–5], 6–30 p.; illus.; 10.5 cm., fr.[2], p. [31, adv.], and illus. white paper covers pr. in green ink belong to another book; fr.[2] & p. [31] match those in Sommerville's *Maria, Or The Ever-Blooming Flower. New Haven: Sidney's Press. For J. Babcock & Son.* 1819. Alphabets, p. [4]; History, p. [5]–30. English version 5, no. **275.41**. It is interesting that *The Life And Death of Tom Thumb. Sidney's Press. 1805,* no. **1314.3**, also has New-Haven misspelled "Hew-Haven."
Gardner* (fr.[2], p. 31 & covers wanting); Shaw 50525.

275.54 Life And Adventures Of Robinson Crusoe. With Cuts, 12 cents. New-York: adv. by Thomas B. Jansen, 1805 in **1371.5**.

275.55 [—] The Wonderful Life and Adventures Of Robinson Crusoe. Embellished with elegant Cuts. Philadelphia: Printed By John Adams. 1805.
fr.[2], t.[3], [4–5], 6–32 [*sic. i.e.* 31] p.; illus.; 10.5 cm.; blue marbled paper covers; last 2 p. have adv. list of 22 books. Alphabets, p. [4]; History, p. [5]–29; adv. list of books, p. 32

[*sic. i.e.* 31]. English version 5, no. **275.41**.
MWA*; Brigham 54; Shaw 8311.

275.56 [—] The Wonderful Life And Adventures Of Robinson Crusoe. Ornamented with Cuts. Albany: Printed And Sold By The Gross Or Dozen, By E. And E. Hosford. 1806.
fr.[2], t.[3], [4–5], 6–31 p.; illus.; 10.5 cm.; black Dutch paper covers. Alphabets, p. [4]; History, p. [5]–28; English version 5, no. **275.41**; Virtue Rewarded, p. 29–31.
PP*.

275.57 [—] ——— [same as **275.56** but with a varied imprint]. Albany: Printed By E. And E. Hosford. 1806.
fr.[2], t.[3], [4–5], 6–31 p.; illus.; 10 cm.; blue marbled paper covers. Text same as no. **275.56**.
MWA*; Brigham 55; Shaw 10269.

275.58 [—] ——— Adventurs [*sic. i.e.* Adventures] Of Robinson Crusoe. Adorned with Cuts. From Sidney's Press, New-Haven. 1806.
fr.[2], t.[3], [4–5], 6–31 p.; illus.; 10.5 cm.; Dutch paper covers. Alphabets, p. [4]; History p. [5]–31. English version 5, no. **275.41**.
MWA-W*; MB (per. st. on t.[3], p. 7–8 mut.); MWA; Brigham 56; Shaw 50666.

275.59 [—] ——— [same as **275.56**]. Embellished With Cuts. Newtown [Pa.]: Printed by William Coale. [*ca.* 1806].
fr.[2], t.[3], [4–5], 6–30 p.; illus.; 10 cm. Alphabets, p. [4]; History, p. [5]–30. English version 5, no. **275.41**. "The date of imprint is conjectural, as William Coale printed under his name at Newtown, Penn., from 1802 to 1810." Brigham.
Brigham 57.

275.60 [—] The Life And Wonderful Adventures Of Robinson Crusoe. From Parks' Press, Montpelier, Vt. 1807.
t.[2], [3], 4–31 p.; illus.; 9 cm.; t.[2] on verso of 1st leaf facing p. [3]. History, p. [3]–31. English version 5, no. **275.41**.
VtHi* (covers wanting); Brigham 59; McCorison 913; Shaw 12412.

275.61 [—] The Wonderful Life ——— [same as **275.47**]. From Sidney's Press, New-Haven. 1807.

fr.[2], t.[3], [4–5], 6–31 p.; illus.; 10 cm.; pink & green Dutch paper covers. Alphabets, p. [4]; History, p. [5]–31. English version 5, no. **275.41**.

MWA° (emb. st. on t.[3]); Brigham 60; Shaw 12413.

275.62 [—] THE WONDERFUL LIFE AND SURPRISING ADVENTURES ——— [same as **275.45**]. From Sidney's Press, For Increase Cooke & Co. New-Haven 1807.

t.[1], [2–3, bl.], [4, illus.], [5], 6–144 p.; illus.; 14 cm.; bound in Dutch paper over bds. Life And Adventures, p. [5]–98. English version 3, no. **275.1**; The Youth's Amusement [short stories and anecdotes], p. [99]–144.

CtY°; Shaw 50768.

275.63 [—] THE LIFE AND SURPRISING ADVENTURE's OF ROBINSON CRUSOE, of York, Mariner. With Plate's G. Love. sc. Philadelphia, Published By B. C. Buzby. 1807.

fr.[2], t.[3], [4–5], 6–52 p.; 8 engr. p. or illus. including fr.[2] & t.[3]; 13.5 cm.; buff paper covers. Colophon p. 52: Joseph Rakestraw, Printer, No. 190, North Third street. Adventures, p. [5]–52. An abridged edition of English version 3, no. **275.1**.

MWA° (rebound, front cover mut.); CtHi (marbled paper covers); MWA-W° (p. [24] mut., blue paper covers); Brigham 61; Shaw 12411.

275.64 [—] THE WONDERFUL LIFE AND ADVENTURES OF ROBINSON CRUSOE. Ornamented with Engravings. Albany: Printed By E. And E. Hosford. 1808.

fr.[2], t.[3], [4–5], 6–31 p.; illus.; 10.5 cm.; pr. & illus. buff paper covers. Alphabets, p. [4]; History, p. [5]–28, English version 5, no. **275.41**; Virtue Rewarded, p. 29–31. Text same as no. **275.56**.

Welch° (p. 23–24 wanting); MWA; Brigham 62; Shaw 14844.

275.65. [—] ——— Adorned with Cuts. From Sidney's Press, New-Haven. 1808.

fr.[2], t.[3], [4–5], 6–31 p.; illus.; 10.5 cm.; yellow paper covers. Alphabets, p. [4]; History, p. [5]–31. English version 5, no. **275.41**.

Welch°, MWA; Brigham 63.

275.66 [—] THE WONDERFUL LIFE AND SURPRISING ADVENTURES ——— [same as **275.1**]. Philadelphia: Published By Johnson & Warner, No. 147, Market Street. 1808.

t.[1], [2–3], 4–143 p.; 13 cm.; bound in marbled paper over bds. Colophon p. 143: Lydia R. Bailey, Printer, No. 10, North-Alley. Life and Adventures, p.[3]–105, English version 3, no. **275.1**; The Youth's Amusement [short stories and anecdotes] p. 107–143. Text same as no. **275.62**.

MWA° (new front cover & spine p. 113–116, 125–128 wanting); CtY (rebound); MiU; Brigham 64; Shaw 14845.

275.67 [—] THE WONDERFUL LIFE ——— [same as **275.64**]. Ornamented with Cuts. Albany: Printed By E. And E. Hosford, 1809.

fr.[2], t.[3], [4–5], 6–31 p.; illus.; 10.5 cm.; pr. & illus. buff paper covers; cover title undated. Alphabets, p. [4]; History, p. [5]–28, English version 5, no. **275.41**; Virtue Rewarded, p. 29–31. Text same as no. **275.56**.

ICU° (front cover mut.); Brigham 65.

275.68 [—] ——— [same as **275.47**]. From Sidney's Press, New-Haven. 1809.

fr.[2], t.[3], [4–5], 6–31 p.; illus.; 10.5 cm.; green Dutch paper covers.

Alphabets, p. [4]; History, p. [5]–31. English version 5, no. **275.41**.

MWA°; NRU; PP; Brigham 66; Shaw 17361.

275.69 [—] ——— [same as **275.50**]. New-York: Printed And Sold By George Forman, No. 178, Greenwich-Street. 1809.

fr.[ii], t.[i], [ii–iii], iv, [5], 6–250 p.; 4 pl. including front.; 17.5 cm.; bound in leather. Preface p. [iii]–iv; Life and Adventures, p. [5]–145; Further Adventures, p. [147]–250. English version 2a, no. **275.50**.

MWA°; CtY; Brigham 68; Shaw 17359.

275.70 [—] ——— New-York: Printed By Geo: Forman, No. 178, Greenwich-St. For M. Carey, Philadelphia. 1809.

fr.[ii], t.[i], [ii–iii], iv, [5], 6–250 p.; 4 pl. including front.; 18.5 cm.; bound in leather. Text same as no. **275.69**.

NN° (fr.[ii], & pl. opp. 89 wanting); Brigham 67; Shaw 17360.

275.71 [—] Die wunderbare Lebensbe-schreibung und Erstaunliche Begebenheiten des berühmten Helden Robinson Crusoe, welcher acht und zwanzig Jahr auf einer unbewohnten Insel lebte, die er nachher bevölktert hat. Philadelphia: Gedruckt bey Conrad Zentler, in der Zweyten-, nahe bey der Rehs-Strasse. 1809.

fr.[ii], t.[i], [2–3], 4–141 p.; illus.; 14.5 cm.; bound in blue-green marbled paper over bds. leather spine. Text same as **275.6**, a German translation of English version 3, no. **275.1**.

MWA-W°; MH; MWA; MiU; P; PP (3 copies); PPG; PPL; Brigham 69; Shaw 17362.

275.72 [—] The History Of Robinson Crusoe. [caption title p.[3]] Windsor [Vt.]: Printed for Farnsworth & Churchill, and sold at the Windsor Book-Store. 1809. J. Cunningham. Printer. [imprint under frontispiece p. [2]].

fr.[2], [3], 4–31 p.; illus.; 10 cm.; blue paper covers. History, p. [3]–31. English version 5, no. **275.41**.

MWA°; Brigham 70; McCorison 1070; Shaw 17357.

275.73 [—] The Wonderful Life ——— [same as **275.64**]. Albany: Printed By E. And E. Hosford. 1810.

fr.[2], t.[3], [4–5], 6–31 p.; illus.; 10 cm.; pr. & illus. buff paper covers. Alphabets, p. [4]; History, p. [5]–28, English version 5; Virtue Rewarded, p. 29–31. Text same as no. **275.56**. The last word in the 1st line p. [5] is "surprizing." It may be spelled "surprising."

MWA-W°; CtY; MiU; N; NN; NN–C; PP; Brigham 71; Shaw 19941.

275.74 [—] ——— Adorned with Cuts. From Sidney's Press. New-Haven. 1810.

fr.[2], t.[3], [4–5], 6–31 p.; illus.; 11 cm.; pr. & illus. buff paper covers.

Cover title: Robinson Crusoe. Published by I. Cooke & Co. Universal Book-Store, Church-Street, New-Haven. Alphabet p. [4]; History, p. [5]–31. English version 5, no. **275.41**.

OOxM° (rear cover wanting); Shaw 19942.

275.75 [—] ——— Ornamented with Engravings. Albany: Printed By E. & E. Hosford. 1811.

fr.[2], t.[3], [4–5], 6–31 p.; illus.; 10 cm.; pr. & illus. buff paper covers. Alphabets, p. [4]; History, p. [5]–28, English version 5, no.

275.41; Virtue Rewarded, p. 29–31. Text same as no. **275.56**.

MWA°; N; Brigham 73.

275.76 [—] ——— Albany: Printed By E. And E. Hosford. 1811. Same as no. **275.75** but with the "And" spelled out in "E. And E. Hosford."

NN-C (i. st. on t.[3]).

275.77 [—] ——— Adorned with Cuts. From Sidney's Press. New-Haven, 1812.

fr.[2], t.[3], [4–5], 6–31 p.; illus.; 10.5 cm.; yellow paper covers. Alphabets, p. [4]; History, p. [5]–31. English version 5, no. **275.41**.

MWA° (p. [2]–10 mut., i. st. on fr.[2]); CtY (covers wanting); DLC; MWHi; Brigham 75; Shaw 25235.

275.78 [—] The Wonderful Life And Surprising Adventures ——— [same as **275.1**]. Philadelphia: Published By Benjamin Johnson, No. 22, North Second Street, Next Door To The Church. 1813.

fr.[ii], t.[1], [2–3], 4–96 p.; front. only illus.; 13.5 cm. Life and Adventures, p. [3]–96. English version 3, no. **275.1**.

MWA° (rebound); MH (p. 7–10 wanting, p. 5–6, 11–12 torn and part of text wanting; bound in pr. & illus. gray-green paper over bds.); Brigham 77; Shaw 28290.

275.79 [—] The Wonderful Life ——— [same as **275.64**]. Albany: Printed By E. & E. Hosford. 1814.

fr.[2], t.[3], [4–5], 6–31 p.; illus.; 9.5 cm.; pr. & illus. buff paper covers. Alphabets, p. [4]; History, p. [5]–28, English version 5; Virtue Rewarded, p. 29–31. Text same as no. **275.56**.

MWA° (i. st. on fr.[2]); CtHi (fr.[2], p. 29–31, & covers wanting; p. 25–26 mut.); CtY; Brigham 78; Shaw 31310.

275.80 [—] ——— Crusoe. Cooperstown [N.Y.] Printed By H. & E. Phinney. And Sold By Them Wholesale And Retail. 1814.

t.[3], [4–5], 6–23 p.; illus.; 10 cm.; pr. & illus. gray paper covers. Alphabets; p. [4]; History, p. [4]; History, p. [5]–21, English version 5, no. **275.41**; Virtue Rewarded, p. 22–23. Text same as no. **275.56**.

MWA°; Brigham 80; Shaw 31311.

275.81 [—] THE HISTORY OF R. CRUSOE, Of York, Mariner. First American From Second London. Philadelphia: Printed by H. B. 1814.

t.[1], [2–3], 4–103 p.; 4 cm. H. B. may stand for "Henry Brickley, editor, publisher. N. W. cor. Walnut and Second, and 96 S. Third, 1814; or Henry Brackin, printer 7 Cressons Alley, 1814, 1816–1820; or Horatio Boate, printer 93 N. Fifth, 1808–11, 1813–14, 1816–19." Brown. History Of R. Crusoe, p. [3]–103. Portions of the first and last sentences of the first and last paragraphs: *Robinson Crusoe was born at York in 1632, and was named Robinson . . . took shipping, Sept. 1, 1651. . . . But greater were the emotions . . . 1705, after a 2nd absence of 10 years, sufficiently wearied of rambling.* CtY°; Brigham 81.

275.82 [—] THE HISTORY OF ROBINSON CRUSOE. [cover title] Windsor, Vt. Printed and Sold By Jesse Cochran. 1814. [Imprint date at foot of front. [2].]

fr.[2], [3], 4–31 p.; illus.; 10 cm.; pr. & illus. buff paper covers. History, p. [3]–31. English version 5, no. **275.41**.

MWA-W°; Brigham 82; McCorison 1595; Shaw 31309.

275.83 [—] LIFE AND MOST SURPRISING ADVENTURES —— [same as **275.83**]. Faithfully Epitomized From The Three Volumes. Baltimore.— Printed By William Warner. Corner of South Gay & Market-streets. 1815.

½t.[1], fr.[2], t.[3], [4–5], 6–144 p.; front. only illus.; 13.5 cm. Life and Adventures, p.[5]–86; Farther Adventures, p. 87–144. Close to variant issue 1 of English version 1, no. **275.9** with textual variations.

MWA° (rebound); PP; Brigham 83; Shaw 34548.

275.84 [—] THE LIFE AND MOST SURPRISING ADVENTURES —— [same as **275.50**]. New-York: Published By E. Duyckinck, No. 102 Pearl-Street. G. Long, print. 1815.

fr.[ii], t.[i], [ii–iii], iv, [5], 6–250 p.; 4 pl. including front.; 18 cm.; bound in leather. Preface, p. [iii]–iv; Life And Adventures, p. [5]–145; Further Adventures, p. [147]–250. English versions 2a, no. **275.50**, with textual variations. The first sentence of the last paragraph of [vol.

II.] varies as follows: *All that night we wrought hard, . . .*

PP°; MB; NjR; OClW; Brigham 84.

275.85 [—] —— [same as **275.50**]. New-York: Printed And Published By George Long, No. 71 Pearl-Street. 1815.

fr.[ii], t.[i], [ii–iii], iv, [5], 6–250 p.; 4 pl. including front.; 18 cm.; bound in leather. Text same as no. **275.84**.

MWA° (i. st. on t.[i]); CtY (fr.[ii], p.[iii]–10 wanting); MiU; MSaE; NHi (fr.[ii], t.[i] crudely repaired & covered by transparent tissue paper); NjP (emb. st. on t.[i], fr.[ii] wanting); NjR (2 copies; copy 2 fr.[ii] wanting); Brigham 85; Shaw 34549 and 34550.

275.86 HISTORY OF ROBINSON CRUSOE. Windsor, Vt. Printed & Sold by Jesse Cochran. [cover title] Windsor, Printed And Sold By Jesse Cochran. 1815. [imprint under front. p. [2]].

fr.[2], [3], 4–31 p.; illus.; 10.5 cm.; pr. & illus. gray paper covers. History p. [3]–31. English version 5, no. **275.41**.

MWA°; Brigham 88; McCorison 1728; Shaw 34547.

275.87 [—] THE WONDERFUL LIFE —— [same as **275.64**]. Albany: Printed By E. & E. Hosford. 1816.

fr.[2], t.[3], [4–5], 6–31 p.; illus.; 10 cm.; pr. & illus. buff paper covers. The illus. p. 22 printed upside down in NB & NHi copies, but not in MWA copy. Alphabets, p. [4]; History, p. [5]–28, English version 5, no. **275.41**; Virtue Rewarded, p. 29–31. Text same as no. **275.56**.

MWA°; (i. st. on front.); NB; NHi; NNC-LS; Brigham 89; Shaw 37416.

275.88 [—] THE WONDERFUL LIFE. —— [same as **275.1**]. New-York: Published By Evert Duyckinck, No. 102 Pearl-Street. 1816. J. C. Totten, printer.

fr.[2], t.[3], [4–5], 6–144 p.; illus.; 11 cm.; bound in blue-gray paper over bds., leather spine. Adventures, p. [5]–106; English version 3, no. **275.1**; Verses . . . By Robinson Crusoe [*I am the monarch of all I survey. . . .*], p. [107]–109; The Youth's Amusement [short stories and anecdotes], p. [110]–144. Text same as **275.62**, with the added *Verses . . . By Robinson Crusoe*, found in **275.40**.

MWA° (rebacked); PP; Brigham 90; Shaw 37417.

275.89 [—] THE WONDERFUL LIFE ——— [same as **275.64**]. Albany: Printed By E. & E. Hosford. 1818.

fr.[2], t.[3], [4–5], 6–31 p.; illus.; 9.5 cm.; pr. & illus. paper covers. Alphabets, p. [4]; History, p. [5]–28, English version 5, no. **275.41**; Virtue Rewarded, p. 29–31. Text same as no. **275.56**. MWA°; N (2 leaves only, t.[3] & p.[4], 29–30, bound in *The History of the Birds*, Albany, 1818.); Brigham 91; Shaw 43826.

275.90 [—] THE LIFE AND MOST SURPRISING ADVENTURES OF ROBINSON CRUSOE, of York Mariner. Dublin: John Jones, 1819.

fr.[2], t.[3], [4–5], 6–180 p.; illus.; 14 cm.; bound in pr. & illus. light brown paper over bds.; 6 full page illus. including front.; tailpiece p. 177.
Cover title: Adventures of Robinson Crusoe. Illustrated with cuts. Boston: Sold by Munroe and Francis, No. 4, Cornhill. Life and Adventures, p. 5–174; verses by Selkirk, p. 175–177; Family maxims, p.[178]–180.
"The Munroe & Francis cover title entitles this edition to an entry in this bibliography. The Munroe & Francis firm frequently sold British publications with a foreign imprint, but using a cover title indicating that the book was sold by them. In this way, they issued *Poems selected from the works of approved authors*, printed at Dublin by William Espy in 1818." Brigham.
PPRF°; Brigham 92.

275.91 — THE LIFE AND MOST SURPRISING ADVENTURES ——— Who Lived Twenty-Eight Years ——— [same as **275.69**]. Great River Oroonoque. With An Account Of His Deliverance Thence, And His After Surprising Adventures. By Daniel De Foe, [*sic. i.e.* Defoe] Author Of Religious Courtship And Various Other Works. A new Edition. Embellished with Four Beautiful Copperplate Engravings. New-York: Printed And Published By George Long, No. 71, Pearl-Street. 1819.

fr.[2], t.[1], [2–5], 6–246 p.; illus.; 4 engr. pl. including front. which are the same ones used in G. Long's N.Y. 1815 ed., no. **275.85**; 18 cm.; bound in leather. Adventures, p. [5]–133; Fur-

ther Adventures, p. 134–246. English version 2a, no. **275.50**, with textual variations. First sentence of [vol. I.] varies as follows: *In the year 1632 I was born at York, . . .* and is the same as English version 2, no. **275.27**.
Welch°; CtY (rebound); DLC; MB; MWA; PP; Brigham 95; Shaw 47804 and 43825.

275.92 [—] THE LIFE AND ADVENTURES OF ROBINSON CRUSOE. Written By Himself. Philadelphia: Published by R. Desilver No. 110 Walnut St. and T. Desilver No. 2 Decatur St. n.d. [1819].

[vol. I]: fr.[ii], t.[i], [ii–iii], iv–v, [vi], [1], 2–263 p.; engr. front. and title vignette only illus.; p. 263; "End of Vol. I."; [vol. II]: t.[i], [ii], [1], 2–244 p.; engr. title vignette only illus.; p.[1] at the bottom of the page: "Vol. II."; colophon p. 214, "G. Goodman, Printer, 24, Cherry-st."; 2 vols.; 17 cm.; bound in leather. Thomas Desilver was at No. 2 Decatur St. only in 1819 and George Goodman was at 24 Cherry Street from 1819–1820. (MWA cat.). Vol. I., Life of the Author, p. [iii]–v; Robinson Crusoe, p. [1]–263; Vol. II., Robinson Crusoe, p. [1]–244. The text does not match any of the preceding abridgements and may be one based on an unabridged or more complete ed. It is open to question whether this is a children's edition.
MiU°; MWA (vol. II); Brigham 99.

275.93 [—] THE HISTORY OF ROBINSON CRUSOE. Woodstock [Vt.]: Printed By David Watson. 1819.

fr.[2], t.[3], [4–5], 6–31 p.; illus.; 9.5 cm.; pr. & illus. paper covers. History, p. [5]–31. English version 5, no. **275.41**, with an extra final paragraph: *Robinson, on his arrival in England, . . . and esteem of all his acquaintances.*
MWA° (p.[3–4], 29–30 wanting); Brigham 96; McCorison 2106; Shaw 47803.

ADVENTURES OF ROBINSON CRUSOE. New-Haven. 1820. *See* Campe, Joachim Heinrich von, no. **158.6**.

275.94 [—] [THE HISTORY] OF ROBINSON CRUSOE. Woodstock [Vt.]: Printed By David Watson. 1820.

Title page only, printed upside down on the recto of the yellow paper back cover, originally pasted to p. [31] of Berquin's *The Mountain Piper,* no. **90.11.**

VtHi°; McCorison 2197; Shoemaker 983.

276.1 — The Voyages, Travels, And Surprising Adventures Of Captain Robert Singelton. Containing An Account of his being set on Shore in the Island of Madagascar; of his Passage from thence, and Travels through the Desarts [*sic. i.e.* Deserts] of Africa; his various Encounters with Savages and wild Beasts; his acquiring great Riches in Gold-Dust and Elephants' Teeth, and Return to England. By Daniel Defoe, Author of Robinson Crusoe, &c. New-York: Printed For Christian Brown, No. 70, Water-Street. 1802.

fr.[2], t.[3], [4–5], 6–102 p.; front. only illus.; 13.5 cm.; bound in buff paper over bds., leather spine; front. signed *Anderson* [Alexander Anderson].

MWA-W°; NjP (rebacked); Hamilton 220; Shaw 2125.

276.2 — ——— Baltimore: Printed By William Warner. At the Corner of South Gay and Market Streets. [1815].

fr.[2], t.[3], [4–5], 6–107 p.; front. only illus.; 13.5 cm.; bound in brown paper over bds. Originally the color of the paper was pink, as can be seen by lifting up the fly leaf pasted to the inside of the front cover. William Warner's address in 1815 was Corner of South Gay & Market-streets. *See* his 1815 edition of Robinson Crusoe, no. **275.83.**

MWA-W°.

276.3 — ——— Travels thro' the Deserts of Africa ——— New-York: Published By Evert Duyckinck, 102 Pearl-Street. George Long, Printer. 1815.

fr.[2], t.[3], [4–5], 6–102, [103–104, adv. list of books] p.; 13 cm.; bound in brown paper over bds., leather spine.

MWA°; CtHT-W; DLC (covers wanting); N; PP (covers wanting); OOxM; Shaw 34551.

DEPPING, GEORGE BERNARD
277.1 — Evening Entertainments; Or Delineations Of The Manners And Customs Of Various Nations, Interspersed With Geographical Notices, Historical And Biographical Anecdotes, And Descriptions In Natural History. Designed For The Instruction And Amusement Of Youth. By J. B. Depping [1 line quot.] Philadelphia: Published And Sold By David Hogan, No. 249, Market-street. < From The London Edition > 1812.

t.[v], [vi–vii], viii–xii, [13], 14–424 p.; 19 cm.; bound in leather; p.[vi]: Stiles, printer.

English ed. London: Henry Colburn, 1811.

MWA°; PP; PPL; Shaw 25262.

277.2 — ——— Philadelphia: Second Edition Published And Sold By David Hogan, No. 249, Market-street. D. Dickinson, Printer. 1817.

t.[i], [ii–v], vi–vii, [vii, bl.], [9], 10–384 p.; 18.5 cm.; bound in marbled paper over bds., leather spine.

MWA°; PP; Shaw 40649.

278 A Description Of Animals, Of Different Countries. For the amusement of Children. Adorned with Cuts. Haverhill [Mass.]: Printed And Sold By Wm. B. Allen. 1809.

fr.[2], t.[3], [4–7], 8–16 p.; illus.; 10.5 cm.; illus. gray paper covers.

MWA°.

279 A Description Of Birds And Beasts, To Which Is Added, A Short Account Of A Sailor's Life, For The Information Of Children In The Country. York-State [*i.e.* N.Y.] Printed for the Book-Sellers. M.DCCC.IV.

fr.[2], t.[3], [4], 5–30 p.; illus.; 10.5 cm.; marbled paper covers. "Printed at Stanfordville, Duchess [*sic. i.e.* Dutchess] Co. N.Y."

MWA°; CtHi (fr.[2] & covers wanting; p. 29–30 mut.); NPV; PP; Shaw 6157.

280 A Description Of The Geographical Clock: Which Contains The Names And Situations Of The Most Remarkable Places In the World; And Exhibits At One View The Time Of Day Or Night At All Those Places Round the Globe: With A Copious Index; Intended For The Instruction And Amusement Of Youth. Philadelphia: Printed For Joseph Scott, And Sold By Francis Bailey, No. 116, High-Street, And Peter Stewart, No. 34, South-Second-Street, M,DCC, XCII.

t.[1], [2–3], 4–24 p.; 19 cm.

English ed. London: Printed for the Author, 1791.

PP°; Evans 46429.

281.1 A Description Of The Most Remarkable Beasts, For The Entertainment Of Children. First Newport Edition. Newport [R.I.]:
Printed by Oliver Farnsworth. 1800.
    t.[3], [4], 5–30 p.; illus.; 11.5 cm.
    RHi° (fr.[2] & p.[31] probably wanting, covers
wanting, p. 15–16 mut.).

281.2 ———— Second Rhode Island Edition.
Newport [R.I.]: Printed by Oliver Farnsworth.
1803.
    fr.[2], t.[3], [4], 5–30, [31, alphabet] p.; illus.;
11 cm.; paper covers.
    RNHi°.

281.3 ———— First Vermont Edition. Windsor
[Vt.], Printed By O. Farnsworth, Sold wholesale
and retail at the Windsor Book-Stor[e.] 1809.
    fr.[2], t.[3], [4], 5–30, [31, illus.] p.; illus.; 9.5
cm.; scalloped marbled paper covers.
    MWA° (fr.[2], t.[3] & p. 29–[31] mut.); Mc-
Corison 1071; Shaw 17377.

282 A Description Of The Most Remarkable
Birds. For The Entertainment Of Children. Hart-
ford: Printed By John Babcock. 1798.
    fr.[2], t.[3], [4], 5–31 p.; illus.; 11 cm.; green
Dutch paper covers.
    MWA° (fr.[2], p. 31, & covers mut.); CtHi;
Evans 33629.

283.1 A Description Of Various Objects.
Vol. I. Philadelphia: Published by J. Johnson.
1803. (B. Graves, Printer).
    t.[1], [2], 3–30 p.; 5 cm.; bound in marbled
paper over bds.
    English ed. London: John Marshall [1801].
2 vols. with a set of 28 col. engr. cards dated
June 29 1801, all of which are in the original
wooden box. The sliding lid of the box has a lid
title page: The Infant's Library Of Various Objects. Made and Sold by John Marshall . . .
Vols. I. and II. are the same as **283.1** and **283.2**.
PP°; DLC; NN-C; PHi; PPL; OOxM; Shaw
4073.

283.2 ———— Vol. II. Phila. printed: by B.
Graves, for J. Johnson. 1803.
    t.[1], [2], 3–30 p.; 6 cm.; bound in marbled
paper over bds.
    MWA°; DLC; NB (i. st. on t.[1]); NN; NN-C;

NNC-LS, NNC-Pl, PHi, PP; PPL; Shaw 4073;
Weiss 1936, p. 148.

The Deserted Boy. *See* Baker, Caroline (Horwood), no. **55.2**.

284 No. XX. A Dialogue Between a Father
and his Son. [caption title.] From Sidney's Press
For The Connecticut Religious Tract Society, And
Deposited For Sale At The Bookstores Of Increase
Cooke & Co. New • Haven, And Oliver D. Cooke,
Hartford. Price two and a half cents each, by the
large or small quantity. Jan. 1809. 1st. Edition
3000. [colophon p. 24].
    t.[1], 2–24 p.; 17 cm.
    Welch°; MWA; PP; Shaw 17382.

285 (No. 7.) A Dialogue Between A Father,
And His Son George, About Cannibals in India.
Published By The Philadelphia Female Tract So-
ciety. And for sale at their Depository, No. 77,
South Second Street. [caption title]. Printed by
Lydia R. Bailey, No. 10, North Alley, Philad.
[1816]. [colophon p. 12].
    [1], 2–12 p.; 14 cm.
    English ed. London, entitled: *A Dialogue Be-
tween Farmer Trueman And His Son George,
About The Cannibals In India.* J. Evans and
Son, F. Collins, J. Nesbet [*ca.* 1809].
    MWA° (bound with other tracts, with which
*The First Annual Report Of The Philadelphia
Female Tract Society For The Year 1816* was
originally bound); Shaw 37442.

286.1 Dialogue, Between A Fond Father
and his little Son. Designed to amuse and instruct Children. Norwich [Conn.]: Printed By
John Trumbull, 1798.
    1st t.[1], [2–5], 6–29, [30]; 2nd t.[31], [32],
33–36 p.; 12.5 cm.; blue paper covers.
    The 2nd title: Entertaining Extracts, From vari-
ous Authors. Worthy the perusal of every good
Child. Learning advances men of mean degree,
To high attainments, wealth, and dignity.
Printed February, 1798.
    CtHi°; Evans 48411.

286.2 ———— Norwich [Conn.]: Printed By
Henry Trumbull, 1804.
    t.[1], [2–5], 6–32 p.; 11 cm.; blue marble paper
covers.
    MWA°; DLC; Shaw 6161.

287.1 A Dialogue Between Two Seaman After A Storm. [caption, p.[1]] Printed & Published By Lincoln & Edmands, No. 53 Cornhill, Boston, [4 lines adv.] 1813. Price 25 cts. doz. 1,75 per hun. [colophon p.[8]].

t.[1], 2–7, [8] p.; 17 cm.; above the caption p.[1]: Series of Evangelical Tracts, No. 33. English ed. London: Religious Tract Society. [*ca.* 1810].
MWA°; Shaw 28324.

287.2 No. 6. Dialogue Between Two Seaman. List Of Tracts Published By The Hartford Evangelical Tract Society. March 1816. [list of 9 tracts]. [cover title].

[1], 2–7, [8] p.; 16.5 cm.; pr. blue-gray paper covers; last line p. 7: Hudson & Co. Printers. 5000 March 1816.
MWA°.

287.3 A Dialogue Between Two Seaman, After A Storm; The Wonderful Cure Of General Naaman; The Blind Irishman Restored To Sight; An Account Of Some Seamen In The Battle Of The Nile; Hymns, &c. Suitable For The Sabbath-School Premiums. New-York: Printed And Sold By Mahlon Day, No. 84, Water-street. 1820.

fr.[ii], t.[1], [2–3], 4–43 p.; illus.; 13 cm.; green paper covers.
DLC° (covers wanting, fr.[ii], t.[1] mut.).

288.1 Dialogue For The Amusement And Instruction Of Youth. From Sidney's Press. For I. Cooke & Co. Newhaven. 1812.

fr.[2], t.[3], [4–5], 6–47 p.; illus.; 11 cm.; pr. & illus. paper covers.
CtY°; Shaw 51189.

288.2 —— From Sidney's Press. For I. Cooke & Co. New-Haven. 1813.

fr.[2], t.[3], [4–5], 6–47 p.; illus.; 11 cm.
MH° (covers wanting); Shaw 51295.

289 A Dictionary, Or Index To A Set Of Cuts For Children. Philadelphia: Published By Jacob Johnson, No. 147, Market-Street. 1804. < J. Rakestraw, Printer. >

t.[1], [2–32] p.; 10.5 cm.; brown marbled paper covers, green paper spine. This is an index to the cuts issued with *The Mother's Remarks On A Set of Cuts For Children. See* no. **909**.

Welch°; CtHi; DLC; MWA; NNC-Pl; PHi; PP; PPL; Shaw 6165.

The Disasterous Events Which Attended Joe Dobson. *See* T., B. A., no. **1284**.

The Discovery Of America. *See* Columbus, Christopher (*pseud.*), no. **223**.

290 The Disobedient Son. New-York: adv. for 2 cents by T. B. Hansen, [*ca.* 1815] in **47**.

Divine Emblems. *See* Bunyan, John, no. **135.1**.

DIXON, JOSEPH
291 —— The African Widow. An Interesting Narrative. By Joseph Dixon. Dedham [Mass.]: Printed By H. & W. H. Mann. 1817, [*sic. i.e.* "."]

t.[1], [2–3], 4–12 p.; 16.5 cm. *See* no. **22**.
RPB°; MWA; Shaw 40672.

DOBSON, THOMAS
292.1 [—] —— First Lessons For Children. Philadelphia: Printed by T. Dobson, No. 41, So. Second Street. 1797. < Copy Right Secured. >

t.[1], [2], 3–36 p.; illus.; 13 cm.; buff paper covers; p. 3–28 have the alphabet with illus. In the DLC title page collection the above t.[1] is the same except "Copy Right Secured" is omitted. On the verso of the t.[1] is written in mss.: *deposited 6. March 1797 by T. Dobson as Author.*
PP°; DLC (title page coll.); PHi; Evans 32054.

292.2 [—] —— Children. Volume Second. Philadelphia: Printed by T. Dobson, No. 41, So. Second Street. 1797.

title page 14 cm. On the verso of the title page is written in mss.: *Deposited 6. March 1797 by T. Dobson Author.*
DLC° (title page coll.).

293 [—] The Holiday, Or Children's Social Amusement. Philadelphia: Printed by Thomas Dobson, No. 41, So. Second Street. 1797. < Copy Right Secured. >

title page 14 cm.
DLC° (title page coll.); on the verso of the title page is a holograph inscription: *deposited by Thomas Dobson as Author 23 March 1797.*; Evans 32055.

294 [—] PLEASING INSTRUCTIONS FOR YOUNG MINDS. Philadelphia: Printed by T. Dobson, No. 41, So. Second Street. 1797. < Copy Right Secured. >

t.[1], [2–3], 4–68 p.; illus.; 13.5 cm.; blue-green paper covers. In the DLC title page collection on the verso of t.[1] is written in mss.: *No 180. Title page deposited by T. Dobson as Author. May 20, 1797.*

DeWint° (p. 5–8 wanting); DLC (title page coll.); Evans 32055.

DODSLEY, ROBERT. See Æsop. Dodsley, Robert, tr., no. **197**.

DODD, W.

295.1 — THE BEAUTIES OF HISTORY; Or Pictures of Virtue and Vice: Drawn From Examples of Men eminent for their Virtues, or infamous for their Vices. Selected For The Instruction And Entertainment Of Youth. By The Late W. Dodd, LL.D. Considerably Enlarged. Boston: Printed For Joseph Bumstead. Sold By Him, No 20, Union-Street; By E. Larkin, Cornhill; By D. West, Marlboro' Street, And By Other Booksellers In Boston. 1796.

t.[i], [ii–iii], iv, [5], 6–215, [216] p.; 17.5 cm.; bound in leather.

English ed. London: Vernor And Hood, E. Newbery, 1795.

Welch°; DLC; MB; MBAt; MWA; NNC-Pl; PPL; Evans 30355.

295.2 —— Philadelphia: Printed For B. And T. Kite, No. 28, North Third Street, And No. 21, South Fourth Street. 1807. John Adams, Printer.

t.[1], [2–3], 4–244, [i], ii–viii p.; 17.5 cm.

MWA° (i. st. on. t.[1], rebound); DLC (i. st. on t.[1]); PP (rear cover wanting); PPL; Shaw 12443.

THE DOLEFUL DEATH OF POOR OLD ROBIN. See Prim, Peter, no. **1063**.

DORSET, CATHERINE ANN (TURNER) 1750?–1817?

296.1 [—] THE PEACOCK "AT HOME:" A Sequel To The Butterfly's Ball. Written By A Lady. New York: Published By David Longworth, At the Dramatic Repository, Shakspeare Gallery. 1808.

fr.[2], t.[3], [4–5], 6–20 p.; 4 pl. including front. signed *AA* [Alexander Anderson]; 14 cm.; pr. yellow paper covers.

Cover title: No. 1 Of The Substitute, Containing The Peacock At Home. Being A Sequel To "The Butterfly's Ball" Written by a Lady. To Which Is Added The Butterfly's Ball. New-York: Published By David Longworth. 1808. In The London 1816 ed. of Hofland's *The Blind Farmer*, no. **602.1**, on the third page of adv. at rear of the book, J. Harris states that 25,000 copies of *The Peacock at Home* had been sold. This is the first American ed. of Catherine Ann Dorset's *The Peacock "At Home"*. It is a sequel to *The Butterfly's Ball* by William Roscoe, the first American ed. of which also appears in this book. *See* Roscoe, William, no. **1129** and *The Butterfly's Birthday* by the same author, no. **1130.1**.

English ed. London: J. Harris January 1st 1807.

MWA-W° (rear cover wanting); CLU; CtHi (paper pasted over covers); NN (covers wanting, i. st. on t.[3]); Shaw 14885.

296.2 [—] —— "AT HOME:" Or Grand Assemblage Of Birds. Written By Roscoe. Illustrated With Elegant Engravings. Philadelphia: Published and sold Wholesale by Wm. Charles, and may be had of all the Booksellers. 1814. W. M'Culloch, Printer.

fr.[ii], t.[1], [2, bl.], [pl. opp. p. [3]], [3], 4–16 p.; 7 full page plates including front.; 13.5 cm.; pr. yellow paper covers. Page "11" printed "14," p. "14" printed "11." Cover title is almost same as title except that "Illustrated with Eight Plates" is substituted for "Illustrated With Elegant Engravings." This is an error because there are only 7. The statement "Written By Roscoe" is on the title page wrong because the author was Mrs. Dorset.

MWA°; CtHi; NNC-Pl (rear cover partly torn away); PHi; PP; Shaw 31352; Weiss 1932b.

296.3 [—] —— [same as **296.2** but has cover title]: THE PEACOCK "AT HOME:" Or Grand Assemblage Of Birds. Written By Roscoe. Embellished with beautiful Engravings. [4 lines of verse]. Philadelphia: Published By Morgan & Yeager, At Their Juvenile Bookstore. Price 25 cents Colored, 18 cents plain. n.d. [*ca.* 1825].

A reprint of no. **296.2**.

CtHi°; DLC; PP; Weiss 1932a.

297.1 [—] THINK BEFORE YOU SPEAK: Or, The Three Wishes. A Tale. By The Author Of The Peacock At Home. Philadelphia: Published By Johnson & Warner, No. 147, Market Street. J. Bouvier, Printer. 1810.

fr.[ii], t.[1], [2–5], 6–32 p.; 6 pl. including front.; 12 cm.; pr. buff paper covers; cover title dated 1811 (copy 1). Copy 2 may have duplicate frontispieces; one pasted to the inside of the front cover, followed by the second facing the title. At the rear there are two leaves of gray paper, one a fly leaf and one pasted to the inside of the rear cover.

English ed. London: M. J. Godwin, 1809.

MWA-W° (copy 1); MWA (copy 2); CCamar-SJ; CLU (copy 1); CtY (copy 2); DLC (copy 1, front cover wanting; copy 2); IU; KU; MB (copy 1, per. st. on t.[1]); MH (copy 1); MiD; MiU; NN (copy 2); NNC-Pl (copy 1); NRU (copy 1); OOxM; PHi (copy 2); PP (copy 2); PPL; PU; Shaw 19992, 21480, 22717 and 24026; Weiss 1932a.

297.2 [—] ——— Wishes, A Poetic Tale. First American From The Second London Edition. Philadelphia: Published And Sold Wholesale By Wm. Charles, And May Be Had Of All The Booksellers. 1810. W. M'Culloch, Printer.

fr[ii], t[1], [2–5], 6–32 p.; 6 engr. pl. including front.; 12 cm.; pr. yellow paper covers; cover title same as t.[1].

NNC-Pl° (rear cover mostly wanting); Shaw 19993.

DOW, HENDRICK 1761–1814
298.1 — A WARNING TO LITTLE CHILDREN, From the Dying Words of Jane Summer, Of Ashford: Who died February 19th, 1783. Ætat. 12. Written nearly verbatim: To Which Is Added An Acrostick, By Hendrick Dow. New-London [Conn.]: Printed by T. Green and Son. M,DCC, XCII.

t.[1], [2–3], 4–15 p.; 13 cm.; paper covers. CtHi.°.

298.2 ——— Windsor [Vt.]: adv. by Alden Spooner, 1795 in **810.14**.

298.3 ——— New-London [Conn.]: Printed and sold by James Springer. 1796.

t[i], [ii], iii, [4], 5–16 p.; 15.5 cm. CtHi°; RPB; Evans 47769.

298.4 ——— verbatim. Bridgeport. [Conn.] 1816.

t.[i], [2–3], 4–8 p.; 17 cm.; wallpaper covers. PP°.

299 A DRAWING BOOK OF LANDSCAPES. Philadᵃ Pubᵈ by Johnson & Warner, Nᵒ 147 Market Street 1810.

t.[1], [2–4] p.; illus.; 15 x 23.5 cm.; pr. paper covers.

MWA°; NN; PP; Shaw 19995.

[DUCRAY-DUMINIL, FRANCOIS GUILLAUME] 1761–1819
300.1 [—] AMBROSE AND ELEANOR, Or The Adventures Of Two Children Deserted On an Uninhabited Island. (Translated From The French) [1 line quot.] To Which Is Added Auguste and Madelaine, A Real History, By Miss Helen Maria Williams.—Baltimore:—Printed For Thomas, Andrews, And Butler, No. 184, Market Street. By Warner And Hanna, Harrison Street. 1798.

t.[1], [2–5], 6–215 p.; 17 cm.; bound in leather. English ed. London: R. & L. Peacock, 1796. MdHi; Bowe mss.; Evans 48336.

300.2 [—] ——— —Baltimore:—Printed For Thomas, Andrews, And Butler, No. 184, Market Street. By Warner And Hanna, Harrison Street. 1799.

t.[1], [2–5], 6–215 p.; 17 cm.; bound in leather. MWA° (i. st. on t.[1]); OOxM; PP; Evans 35098.

E

E., H.
301 — A Short View Of The Natural History Of The Earth. Designed For The Instruction [sic. i.e. Instruction] & Amusement Of Young Persons. By H. E. Boston—Printed By Hosea Sprague, No. 4, West-Street. 1803.

> t.[1], [2], 3–87 p.; 10 cm.; bound in Dutch paper over w. bds.
> MWA*; MB (p. 87 wanting); MSaE (emb. st. on t.[1], p. 87 wanting); Shaw 5048.

Early Instruction Recommended In A Narrative Of The Life Of Catherine Haldane. *See* [Haldane, James Alexander], no. **481.1**.

Early Piety; Or Memoirs Of Children Eminently Serious. *See* Burder, George, no. **137.1**.

Early Piety Exemplified In Elizabeth Osborn. *See* Raymond, Jane (Osborn), no. **1088**.

302 The Easter-Gift. Philadelphia: adv. by Francis Bailey, 1793 in **773.1**.

303 Easy And Instructive Lessons for Children. Also, The Ladder to Learning; Or, A Selection Of Fables. Consisting Of Words Of Only One Syllable, Being An easy Introduction to the useful Art of Reading. Boston: Printed by Manning & Loring, For Ezekiel Goodale. Bookseller, Hallowell [Me.]. 1804.

> fr.[2], 1st t.[3], [4–7], 8–28; 2nd t.[29], [30–31], 32–64 p.; illus.; 13.5 cm.
> The 2nd title: The Ladder to Learning; Or, A Selection Of Fables. Consisting Of Words Of Only One Syllable, Being An easy Introduction to the useful Art of Reading. B₃
> MHi* (t.[3] mut., rear cover & lower half of p. 5–6 wanting); DLC; MiU.

304 An Easy And Pleasant Guide To The Art Of Reading. Adorned With Cuts. To which is added Songs And Lessons, For the amusement of Children. Windsor [Vt.]: Printed by J. Cunningham. 1812.

> fr.[2], t.[3], [4], 5–15 p.; illus.; 10 cm.; pr. & illus. pink paper covers.

Cover title: Art of Reading. Printed At Windsor By John Cunningham. June, 1812.
VtHi*; McCorison 1381; Shaw 25315.

Easy Lessons For Children. *See* Barbauld, A. L. (Aikin), no. **57**.

305 Easy Lessons For Young Children. Philadelphia: Printed by W. Young, No. 52, South Second the Corner of Chesnut-street. M,DCC,XCIV.

> t.[1], [2–3], 4–108, [109–111, adv. list of books] p.; 10.5 cm.; ornamented paper covers.
> PP* (rear cover wanting); Evans 47037.

EDGEWORTH, MARIA 1767–1849
306 — Angelina: Or, The Unknown Friend. By Maria Edgeworth. Philadelphia: Published By Bennett & Walton, No. 31, Market Street. J. Bouvier, Printer, Bellavista: Hamiltonville. 1811.

> t.[1], [2–3], 4–131 p.; 14.5 cm.; bound in green paper over bds., leather spine. Reprinted from *Moral Tales*.
> MWA*; CtY; PP; Shaw 22743.

307.1 — The Barring Out; Or, Party Spirit. By Maria Edgeworth, Author Of Practical Education, And Letters For Literary Ladies. First American Edition. Philadelphia: Published By Jacob Johnson, No. 147, Market-Street. 1804.

> t.[1], [2–3], 4–108 p.; 15 cm.; bound in black paper over bds., pink paper spine. Reprinted from *The Parent's Assistant*.
> P*; Shaw 6218.

307.2 ——— Second American Edition. Philadelphia: Published By Johnson & Warner. No. 147, Market-Street. 1809. W. M'Culloch, Printer.

> fr.[ii], t.[1], [2–3], 4–105, [106–108, adv. list of books] p.; 14 cm.; bound in marbled paper over bds., leather spine.
> MWA*; CLU (fr.[ii], p.[1]–10 wanting); CtY; DLC (per. st. on t.[1]); NNC-LS; NNC-Pl; PHC; PHi; PP; ViLxW; Shaw 17424.

307.3 — No. 16. The Barring Out: Or, Party Spirit. By Miss Edgeworth. Boston: Published by Wells and Lilly. Price 25 cents. 1816. [cover title].

pl.[ii], [219], 220–315 p.; pl. only illus.; 15 cm.; pr. & illus. brown paper covers; duplicate front cover & text pl. signed *Anderson* [Alexander Anderson]. Adv. by Wells and Lilly, 1815 in **326.1.** Reprinted from *The Parent's Assistant.* Wells and Lilly appear to have published the entire work and then bound and issued each story or play separately, in 1815, 1816 and 1819 as in the 1818 ed. *See no.* **328.3.**
MWA-W°; Shaw 51570.

308 [—] THE BASKET-WOMAN, And The Orphans. Adorned With Cuts. New-Haven. Printed For J. Babcock & Son. Sidney's Press. 1819.
fr.[ii], t.[1], [2–3], 4–35, [36, adv.] p.; illus.; 14 cm.; pr. & illus. yellow-buff paper covers.
Cover title: The Basket-Woman. Published By J. Babcock & Son. Booksellers, Stationers and Printers, adjoining the Post-Office, New-Haven. Sold By S. & W. R. Babcock, Booksellers and Stationers, Charlestown, S.C.
MWA° (p. [36] was hidden by the publisher in this copy by pasting it to the inside of the rear cover); NN (fr. [ii] & front cover wanting, rear cover mostly wanting; i. st. on t.[1]; rebound with other books); Shaw 47173.

309.1 — No. 4. THE BIRTH-DAY PRESENT. By Miss Edgeworth: Boston: Published by Wells and Lilly. Price 12 1-2 Cents. 1816. [cover title].
pl.[ii], [167], 168–203 p.; pl. only illus.; 14.5 cm.; pr. & illus. brown paper covers; duplicate front cover and text pl. signed *A* [Alexander Anderson]. Adv. by Wells and Lilly, 1815 in **326.1.** Reprinted from *The Parent's Assistant.*
MWA-W°; Shaw 51571.

309.2 — THE BIRTH DAY PRESENT. By Miss Edgeworth. Boston: Published by Wells and Lilly. 1819 [cover title].
pl.[ii], [1], 2–31 p.; pl. only illus.; 13 cm.; pr. & illus. yellow-buff paper covers; duplicate front cover and text pl. signed *A* [Alexander Anderson].
MWA°; PP; Shaw 47876.

310.1 — THE BRACELETS. By Maria Edgeworth, Author Of Practical Education, And Letters For Literary Ladies. First American Edition. Philadelphia: Published By Jacob Johnson, No. 147, Market-Street. Brown & Bowman, Printers. 1804.
t.[1], [2–3], 4–67 p.; 14 cm.; bound in marbled

paper over bds. Reprinted from *The Parent's Assistant.*
MWA°; CtY; PHi; PP; Shaw 6219.

310.2 ———— By Miss Edgeworth. Boston: adv. by Wells and Lilly, 1815 in **326.1**; 1816 in **332**; 1819 in **321.3.** *See no.* **307.3.**

311 [—] THE CHERRY-ORCHARD: Also, A Description Of The Tiger. Sidney's Press. Published by John Babcock & Son, New-Haven, S. & W. R. Babcock, Charleston, S. C. and M'Carty & Davis, Philadelphia. 1820.
fr.[2], t.[3], [4–5], 6–31 p.; front. & title vignette only illus.; 14.5 cm.; pr. & illus. blue paper covers. The Cherry-Orchard is printed in *Harry And Lucy,* . . . Boston, 1818. p.[90]–105, no. **317.2.**
MWA°; CtHi; CtY; DLC; MiD; NNC-Pl; PHi; PP; Shoemaker 1076.

312.1 — CONTINUATION OF EARLY LESSONS. In Two Volumes. By Maria Edgeworth. Vol. I. Containing Frank, And The Beginning Of Rosamond. [4 lines verse]. Boston, Published By Bradford And Read. 1815.
1st t.[i], [ii–iii], iv–xxviii, xxxix [*sic. i.e.* xxix], [xxx, bl.], [1], 2–178; 2nd t.[1], [2–3], 4–72, 3rd. t. [73], [74–75], 76–216 p.; 2 vols. in 1; 14.5 cm.; p.[ii]: Boston, Printed by J. Belcher; p. 216: Munroe, Francis & Parker, Print.
Second title: ———— Edgeworth. Vol. II. Containing The Conclusion Of Rosamond, And Harry And Lucy. [4 lines of verse] Boston, Published By Bradford And Read. 1815.
Third title: Harry And Lucy. By Richard Lovell Edgeworth, And Maria Edgeworth. [6 line quot.] Boston, Published By Bradford & Read. 1815.
English ed. London: J. Johnson, 1814.
CLU; MH; Shaw 34618.

312.2 ———— Edgeworth. Vol. II. Containing The Conclusion Of Rosamond, And Harry And Lucy. [4 lines of verse] Boston, Published By Bradford And Read. 1815.
t.[1], [2–3], 4–178 p.; 14 cm.; bound in blue marbled paper over bds., red leather spine; p. 178: End Of Vol. I. This edition is different than Vol. II., no. **311**. Pages [73]–104 are omitted. Pages [105]–178 contain 5 chapters of

Rosamond, and not *Harry And Lucy* as in no. **311.**
MWA*.

313.1 — No. 17. Eton Montem. By Miss Edgeworth. Boston: Published By Wells And Lilly. 1815. [cover title].
pl.[ii], [317], 318–412 p.; pl. only illus.; 15 cm.; bound in pr. & illus. yellow paper over bds.; duplicate front cover and text pl. signed *A* [Alexander Anderson]. Reprinted from *The Parent's Assistant.*
MWA* (p. 413 & rear cover wanting); Shaw 34619.

313.2 — ——— Boston: Published by Wells and Lilly. Price 25 cents. 1816. [cover title].
pl.[ii], [317], 318–413 p.; pl. only illus.,; 15 cm.; pr. & illus. brown paper covers; duplicate front cover and text pl. signed *A* [Alexander Anderson].
CtY.

313.3 — Eton Montem. By Miss Edgeworth. Boston: Published by Wells and Lilly. 1819. [cover title].
pl.[ii], [397], 398–430 p.; pl. 1. only illus.; 13.5 cm.; pr. & illus. buff paper covers; duplicate front cover and text pl. signed *A* [Alexander Anderson].
MH*.

314.1 — No. 3. The False Key. By Miss Edgeworth. Boston: Published by Wells and Lilly. 1815. [cover title].
pl. [ii], [109], 110–165 p.; pl. only illus.; 14.5 cm.; printed and illus. paper covers, duplicate front cover and text pl. signed *A* [Alexander Anderson]. Reprinted from *The Parent's Assistant.*
PP*.

314.2 — ——— Boston: Published by Wells and Lilly. 1819. [cover title].
pl.[ii], [113], 114–158 p.; pl. only illus.; 13.5 cm.; pr. & illus. paper covers; duplicate front cover and text pl. signed *A* [Alexander Anderson]. Adv. by Wells and Lilly, 1815 in **326.1** and 1816 in **332.** Reprinted from *The Parent's Assistant. See* no. **307.3.**
MH* (p. 131–132, 141–142, and all after p. 158 wanting); MWA-T; PP.

315 — No. 15. Forgive And Forget. By Miss Edgeworth. Boston: Published by Wells and Lilly. Price 12 1–2 cents. 1816. [cover title].
pl.[ii], [181], 182–217 p.; pl. only illus.; 15 cm.; pr. & illus. brown paper covers; duplicate front cover & text pl. signed *A* [Alexander Anderson]. Adv. by Wells and Lilly, 1815 in **326.1** and 1819 in **321.3.** Reprinted from *The Parent's Assistant. See* no. **307.3.**
DLC*.

316.1 [—] Frank, Part I. [II.] By The Author Of The Parent's Assistant, Six Volumes. Philadelphia: Published By Jacob Johnson, No. 147, Market-Street. 1808.
pt. I.: t.[1], [2–3], 4–108 p.; pt. II.: t.[1], [2–3], 4–113 p.; 2 vols.; 13.5 cm.; bound in marbled paper over bds., leather spine. On p.[2] of both vols.: Adams, Printer, Philadelphia.
English ed. issued in 4 pts. or pts. 6–9 of *Early Lessons,* London: J. Johnson, by H. Bryer, 1801.
MWA* (pt. I., II.); ICN (pt. I., II.); IU; MBAt (pt. I.); MH (pt. I.); MSaE (pt. I., II., emb. st. on t.[1]); PP (pt. II.); Shaw 14915.

316.2 [—] Frank, Part I. By The Author Of The Parent's Assistant. Boston: Published By Cummings And Hilliard, No. 1, Cornhill. 1813.
t.[1], [2–3], 4–144 p.; 14.5 cm.; bound in green paper over bds., leather spine.
MWA*; Shaw 28402.

316.3 — Frank. By Maria Edgeworth. [4 lines of verse.] Boston: Published By Ezra Read 23, School-Street. January 1817.
fr.[ii], t.[i], [ii–iii], iv–xxxix [*sic. i.e.* xxix], [xxx], [1], 2–103 p.; 15 cm.; bound in olive paper over bds., leather spine; fr. signed *Anderson.*
MH* (ft.[ii] mut.); CtY (fr.[ii] wanting); Shaw 40728.

317.1 [—] Harry And Lucy, Part I. [II.] Being The First Part Of Early Lessons, By The Author Of The Parent's Assistant, Six Volumes. Philadelphia: Published By Jacob Johnson, No. 147, Market-Street. 1805.
pt. I.: ½t.[1], [2], t.[3], [4–5], 6–96 p.; pt. II.: ½t.[1], [2], t.[3], [4–5], 6–95 p.; 2 vols.; 10.5 cm.; blue marbled paper covers. Part II. is part of a large publisher's remainder. *Harry and Lucy* was written by Maria Edgeworth's father, Richard Lovell Edgeworth, with the assistance

of his second wife Honora Sneyd. It was published under the title: *Practical Education: Or, The History Of Harry And Lucy.* Vol. II. . . . Litchfield: Printed By J. Jackson, And Sold By J. Johnson. . . . MDCCLXXX.

English ed. (under Maria Edgeworth's authorship) London: 1st ed. 1st issue, J. Johnson, By G. Woodfall, 1801.

MWA° (pt. I., II.); CLU (pt. II.); CSmH (pt. II.); CtHi (pt. I., II.); CtY (pt. II.); DLC (pt. II.); ICU; NHi (pt. II.); NNC-Pl (pt. I., II.); NPV; PHi; PP (pt. I., II.); PPL (pt. I.); Shaw 8372.

317.2 — —— Lucy, Being The First Part Of Early Lessons. By Maria Edgeworth. Boston: Published By Cummings And Hilliard, No. 1, Cornhill. 1813.

t.[1], [2–3], 4–132, [133, pl.] p.; 6 pl.; 14.5 cm.; bound in brown paper over bds., green leather spine.

MWA°; MH; MHi; Shaw 28403.

317.3 — —— Lucy. By Richard Lovell Edgeworth, And Maria Edgeworth. [Six lines of quot. in French] Boston, Published By Bradford & Read. 1815.

fr.[72], t.[73], [74–75], 76–216 p.; front. only illus.; 15 cm.; bound in olive paper over bds., red leather spine; colophon p. 216: Munroe, Francis & Parker, Print.

MH°.

317.4 — —— Lucy, Being The First Part Of Early Lessons. By Maria Edgeworth. Poughkeepsie [N.Y.]: Published By Paraclete Potter. P. & S. Potter, Printers. 1815.

t.[1], [2–3], 4–131 p.; 14.5 cm.; bound in blue-gray paper over bds., leather spine.

MWA°, NPV; Shaw 34620.

317.5 — —— Boston: Published By Cummings And Hilliard, No. 1, Cornhill. Printed by Hilliard & Metcalf. 1818.

t.[1], [2–3], 4–105 p.; 15 cm.; bound in marbled paper over bds., red leather spine.

Welch°; MH (p. 83–84 mut.); MHi; MWA; Shaw 43914.

318.1 [—] Idleness And Industry Exemplified, In The History Of James Preston And Lazy Lawrence. Philadelphia: Published by J. Johnson, No.

147, Market Street. 1803. < B. Graves, Printer. > fr.[ii], t.[1], [2–3], 4–72 p.; front. only illus.; t.[1]; 13.5 cm.

MWA° (rebound); CLU; DLC (bound in marbled paper over bds.); Shaw 4129.

318.2 [—] —— Philadelphia: Published By J. Johnson, No. 147, Market Street. 1804. Archibald Bartram, Printer.

fr.[ii], t.[1], [2–3], 4–70, [71–72, adv. list of books] p.; 14.5 cm.; bound in orange paper over bds., leather spine.

MWA°; CLU; PP; Shaw 6220.

318.3 [—] —— Industry. Philadelphia: adv. by B. & T. Kite, 1807 in **611.1**.

318.4 [—] —— To Which Is Added, The Shepherd Of Salisbury Plain. By Hannah More. Philadelphia: Published By Johnson And Warner, No. 147, High Street. 1811.

t.[1], [2–3], 4–108 p.; 13.5 cm.; bound in pr. blue-gray paper over bds.; text printed on gray paper. Adv. by Johnson And Warner, 1814 in **1449.3**.

Cover title: Lazy Lawrence, Or Idleness And Industry Exemplified By Eliza Edgeworth. To Which Is Added The Shepherd Of Salisbury Plain, By Hannah More. Philadelphia: Published By Johnson & Warner, No. 147, Market Street. 1811.

MWA°; DLC; PP; Shaw 22744, 23082; and 23424.

319 — Lame Jervas; A Tale. By Maria Edgeworth. Pittsburgh: Published By Cramer & Spear, Franklin Head, Wood Street. 1818.

t.[1], [2–3], 4–108 p.; 13.5 cm.; bound in pr. blue-gray paper over bds.

OOxM°; TxU; Shaw 43915.

320.1 — Lazy Lawrence, An Interesting Story For Children. By Maria Edgeworth. From Sidney's Press, New-Haven, 1808.

fr.[ii], t.[1], [2–3], 4–63 p.; front. only illus.; 10.5 cm.; yellow paper covers. Reprinted from *The Parent's Assistant.*

MWA-T°; CtHi (front cover, fr.[ii], wanting, bound with other books); Shaw 14916.

320.2 — —— From Sidney's Press, New-Haven. 1809.

t.[1], [2–3], 4–36 p.; t.[1]; 13.5 cm.; bound in pr. & illus. blue-gray paper covers.
NN° (rebound; i. st. on t.[1]; front cover wanting); Shaw 17425.

320.3 — ——— Lawrence. By Miss Edgeworth. Boston: adv. by Wells and Lilly, 1815 in **326.1**, 1816 in **332**, and 1819 in **321.3**. *See* no. **307.3**.

321.1 — THE LITTLE MERCHANTS, Or Honesty And Knavery Contrasted. By Maria Edgeworth, Author of Practical Education. From Sidney's Press, New-Haven, 1808.
t.[1], [2–3], 4–46, [47–48, adv. list of books] p.; 11.5 cm.; buff paper covers. Reprinted from *The Parent's Assistant*.
MWA-W°; Ct (pr. & illus. yellow paper covers); CtHi; CtY; DLC (pr. & illus. buff paper covers, p. 47–48 & rear cover wanting); PP; Shaw 14917.

321.2 — ——— Merchants. by Maria Edgeworth. Baltimore: Published by F. Lucas, Jr. J. Vance & Co. and Anthony Miltenberger. A. Miltenberger, Printer. 1811.
t.[1], [2–3], 4–107 p.; 13.5 cm.; bound in wallpaper over bds.
MWA°; DLC (bound in buff paper over bds., leather spine); Shaw 22745.

321.3 — ——— By Miss Edgeworth. Boston: Published by Wells and Lilly. 1819. [cover title].
pl.[ii], [385], 386–500 p.; pl. only illus.; 14 cm.; pr. & illus. yellow paper covers; duplicate front cover and text pl. signed A [Alexander Anderson]. Adv. by Wells and Lilly, 1815 in **326.1** and 1816 in **332**. Reprinted from *The Parent's Assistant. See* no. **307.3**.
MWA° (rebound); MSaE (p. 499–500 wanting); Shaw 47877.

322 — No. 10. MADEMOISELLE PANACHE. By Miss Edgeworth. Boston: Published By Wells And Lilly. 1815. [cover title].
316–374 p.; 14.5 cm.; bound in pr. & illus. yellow paper over bds.; front cover illus. signed A [Alexander Anderson]. Adv. by Wells and Lilly, 1816 in **332** and 1819 in **321.3**. Reprinted from *The Parent's Assistant. See* no. **307.3**.
MWA° (pl.[ii] wanting); Shaw 34621.

323 — THE MIMIC. By Miss Edgeworth. Boston: adv. by Wells and Lilly, 1815 in **326.1**, 1816 in

332, and 1819 in **321.3**. Reprinted from *The Parent's Assistant. See* no **307.3**.

324.1 — MORAL TALES For Young People. By Maria Edgeworth, Author Of Practical Education, &c. Vol. I. [II.–III.] Containing Forester, And The Prussian Vase. Published By Johnson & Warner, And For Sale At Their Bookstores In Philadelphia, Richmond (Vir.), And Lexington (Kty). John Bouvier, Printer. 1810.
vol. I.: fr.[ii], t.[1], [2–3], 4–264 p.; front. only illus.; vol. II.: t.[1], [2–3], 4–256 p.; vol. III.: t.[1], [2–3], 4–284 p.; 3 vols.; 14.5 cm.; bound in leather.
Title to vol. II.: ——— Vol. II. Containing The Good Aunt, And Angelina. ——— [same as imprint of vol. I.].
Title to vol. III.: ——— Education, Vol. III. Containing The Good French Governess, Mademoiselle Panache, And The Knapsack. ——— [same imprint as vol. I.].
English ed. London: [1 ed.] 5 vols. Vol. I., IV. J. Johnson, By G. Woodfall, 1801; Vol. II., V. J. Johnson, By H. Bryer, 1801; Vol. III. J. Johnson, By T. Bensley, 1801.
MWA° (vols. I., III.; vol. I., i. st. on t.[1], fr. [ii] wanting; vol. III.; t.[1] mut.); CtY (vol. II. rebound); MH (vols. I. & III.); PP; ViU (vol. II.); Shaw 20031.

324.2 — ——— Maria Edgeworth. Author Of The Parent's Assistant, Tales Of Fashionable Life, &c. In Three Volumes. Vol. III. George Town: Published By Joseph Milligan. 1811.
t.[1], [2–3], 4–234 p.; 14.5 cm.; bound in leather.
NNC-T° (emb. st. on t.[1]).

324.3 — ——— Life, &c. In Three Volumes. Vol. I. New-York; Published By W. B. Gilley, 96 Broadway. E. B. Gould, Printer. 1818. [2nd title page].
fr.[ii], 1st t.[iii], [iv], 2nd t.[1], [2–3], 4–222 p.; fr.[ii] & vignette on 1st t.[iii] only illus.; 14.5 cm.; bound in green paper over bds., green leather spine; fr.[ii] signed *Anderson*, vignette on 1st t.[iii] signed A [Alexander Anderson].
1st or added title: Moral Tales; By Maria Edgeworth. In Three Volumes. [vignette] vol. I. p. 98. Vol. I. New-York: Published By W. B. Gilley, No. 92 Broadway. 1818.

CLU°; DLC; PPL; TNJ (fr.[ii], 1st t.[iii], pp. 4–34 wanting); ViU; Shaw 43916.

324.4 ———— Fashionable Life, Etc. In Three Volumes. Vol. II. New York: Published By W. B. Gilley, 92 Broadway. Abraham Paul Printer. 1818. [2nd title page].

fr.[ii], 1st t.[iii], [iv], 2nd t.[1], [2–3], 4–115 [*sic. i.e.* 215] p.; fr.[ii] & vignette on 1st t.[iii] only illus.; 14.5 cm.; bound in marbled paper over bds., black leather spine. 1st or added title: ——[same as **324.3**] [vignette] vol. II. p. 54. Vol. II. New-York: Published By W. B. Gilley, No. 92 Broadway. 1818.
MB°; PPL.

324.5 ———— Vol. III. New-York: Published By W. B. Gilley, 92 Broadway. 1818. [2nd title page].

fr.[ii], t.[iii], [iv], 2nd t.[1], [2–3], 4–233 p.; fr.[ii] & 1st t.[iii] vignette only illus.; 14.5 cm.; bound in marbled paper over bds., black leather spine.

1st title or added title: ——— [same as **324.3**] [vignette] vol. III. p. 212. Vol. III. New-York: Published By W. B. Gilley, No. 92 Broadway. 1818. Nos. **324.3–324.5** probably made up the 3 vol. set of Gilley's 1st ed. He appears to have had a remainder of vol. I., no. **324.3**, with which he made up sets with later dated vols. such as vols. II. & III. printed in 1819. *See* no. **324.6**.
MB°; MWA-T; PP.

324.6 ———— In Three Volumes. Vol. I. [II.] New-York: Published By W. B. Gilley, 96 Broadway. J. C. Totten, printer. 1819. [2nd title page]. vol. I.: fr.[ii], 1st t.[iii], [iv], 2nd t.[i], [ii–iii], iv–viii, [9], 10–222 p.; fr.[ii] & 1st t.[iii] vignette only illus.; vol. II.: fr. [ii], 1st t.[iii] [iv], 2nd t.[1], [2–3], 4–206 p.; fr.[ii] & 1st t.[iii] vignette only illus.; 2 vols.; 15 cm.; Vol. I. bound in blue-gray paper over bds., black leather spine; Vol. II. bound in buff paper over bds., black leather spine; in both vols. fr.[ii] signed *Anderson* & 1st t.[iii] vignette signed *A* [Alexander Anderson]; 2nd t.[1] address in vol. II.: 92 Broadway.

1st or added title pages for vols. I. & II. are the same as **324.3** and **324.4** with the address and date, 92 Broadway. 1818. Gilley uses the 1st or added title page [iii] of the 1818 ed. with the 1819 text. Since no copy of the 1819 ed. of vol.

III with the 1st t.[iii] dated 1818 is available, the collation is not given under **324.6**, but *see* **324.7** for the 1819 ed. with the 1st t.[iii] dated 1826.

NNC-LS° (vols. I., II.); MB (vol. I.); MWA (vol. I); NN (vol. I.); PP; ViU (vol. II., vol. III.: fr.[ii], 1st t.[iii] & p. 231 wanting and could be a defective copy of no. **324.7**); Shaw 47878.

324.7 ———— In Three Volumes. Vol. III. New-York: Published By W. B. Gilley, 92 Broadway. J. C. Totten, printer, No. 9 Bowery. 1819. [2nd title page].

fr.[ii], 1st t.[iii], [iv], 2nd t.[1], [2–3], 4–231 p.; fr.[ii] & 1st t.[iii] vignette only illus.; 14.5 cm.; bound in green paper over bds., red leather spine; fr.[ii] signed *Anderson*, 1st t.[iii] vignette signed *AA* [Alexander Anderson].

1st title: Moral Tales, By Maria Edgeworth. In Three Volumes. [vignette] vol. III. p. 212. Vol. III. New-York: Published By W. B. Gilley, No. 94 Broadway. 1826.
DLC° (vol. III.).

324.8 ———— Author of the Parent's Assistant, Tales of Fashionable Life, &c. In Three Volumes. Vol. I. [II.–III.] New-York: Published By W. B. Gilley, 96 Broadway. J. C. Totten, printer. 1819. [2nd title].

vol. I.: fr.[ii], 1st t.[iii], [iv], 2nd t.[i], [ii–iii], iv–viii, [9], 10–222 p.; fr. [ii] & 1st t.[iii] vignette only illus.; fr.[ii] signed *Anderson*, 1st t.[iii] vignette signed *AA* [Alexander Anderson]; vol. II.: fr.[ii], 1st t.[iii], [iv], 2nd t.[1], [2–3], 4–206 p.; fr.[ii] & 2nd t.[1] vignette only illus.; fr.[ii] signed *Anderson*, 2nd t.[1] vignette signed *A.* [Alexander Anderson]; vol. III.: fr. [ii], 1st t.[iii], [iv], 2nd t.[1], [2–3], 4–231 p.; fr.[ii] & 2nd t.[1] vignette only illus.; fr.[ii] signed *Anderson*, 2nd t.[1] vignette signed *AA.* [Alexander Anderson]; 3 vols.; 14 cm.; bound in green cloth leather spine; imprint in vols. II. & III.: New-York: Published By W. B. GILLEY, 92 Broadway. J. C. Totten, printer, No. 9 Bowery. 1819.

1st title vol. I. [II.–III.]: Moral Tales; By Maria Edgeworth. In Three Volumes. [vignette] Vol. I. p. 98. Vol. I. [[vignette] Vol. II. p. 54. Vol. II.]] [[vignette] Vol. III. p. 212. Vol. III.] New-York: W. B. Gilley 94 Broadway. 1829.

PP° (vols. I.–III. bound in green cloth; copy 1

of vol. II., fr.[ii] wanting; copy 2 of vol. II. complete, bound in gray paper over bds., leather spine); OOxM (vol. I., fr.[ii] wanting).

325 — MURAD, THE UNLUCKY. A Tale. By Maria Edgeworth. Pittsburgh: Published By Cramer & Spear, Franklin Head, Wood Street. 1818.

t.[1], [2–3], 4–71 p.; 12 cm.; pr. blue-gray paper covers.

MWA-W*; CSmH; CtY; ICU; PP; PPi; Shaw 43917.

326.1 — No. 8. OLD POZ. By Miss Edgeworth. Boston: Published By Wells And Lilly. 1815. [cover title].

pl.[ii], t.[205], 206–233 p.; pl. only illus.; 14 cm.; pr. & illus. yellow paper covers; duplicate front cover & text pl. signed A [Alexander Anderson]. Reprinted from *The Parent's Assistant*. *See* no. **307.3**.

MWA* (rebound); Shaw 34622.

326.2 — ——— Boston: Published by Wells and Lilly. Price 12 1-2 Cents. 1816. [cover title].

pl.[ii], [205], 206–233 p.; pl. only illus.; 14.5 cm.; pr. & illus. brown paper covers; duplicate front cover & text pl. signed A [Alexander Anderson]. Adv. by Wells and Lilly, 1819 in **321.3**.

DLC*.

327 — THE ORPHANS. By Miss Edgeworth. Boston: Published by Wells And Lilly, 1819.

pl.[ii], p. [161], 162–205; pl. only illus.; 14.5 cm.; pr. & illus. paper covers; duplicate front cover and text pl. signed A [Alexander Anderson]. Adv. by Wells and Lilly, 1815 in **326.1**, 1816 in **332**, 1819 in **321.3**. Reprinted from *The Parent's Assistant*. *See* no. **307.3**.

MWA*.

328.1 — THE PARENT'S ASSISTANT; Or, Stories For Children. By Maria Edgeworth. Author Of Practical Education, And Letters For Literary Ladies. In Three Volumes. Vol. I. [II.–III.] First American Edition. George Town: Published By Joseph Milligan. Dinmore & Cooper, Printers. 1809.

vol. I.: fr.[ii], t.[i], [ii–iii], iv–xii, [1], 2–276 p.; fr.[ii] signed *Kneass*; vol. II.: fr.[ii], t.[1], [2–3], 4–287 p.; fr.[ii] signed *Knease*; vol. III.: fr.[ii], t.[1], [2–3], 4–318, [319, adv.] p.;

3 vols.; 14.5 cm.; bound in leather.

English ed. London: adv. by J. Johnson 1795 in Maria Edgeworth's *Letters For Literary Ladies*.

MWA* (vols. II., III.); CtY (vols. I., II., III.); PP (vol. I., all after p. 276 wanting); Shaw 17426.

328.2 — ——— Children. In Three Volumes. By Maria Edgeworth, Author of Practical Education, and Letters for Literary Ladies. Volume I. [II.–III.] Published by W. Wells, and T. B. Wait, and Co. Boston: Eastburn, Kirk and Co. New York: M. Carey, Moses Thomas, and Edward Parker, Philadelphia. [1814].

vol. I.: t.[i], [ii–iii], iv–x, [1–2, bl.], [3], 4–359 p.; vol. II.: t.[1], [2–3], 4–374 p.; 5 pl.; vol. III.: t.[1], [2–4], 5–413 p.; 7 pl.; 3 vols.; 15 cm.; bound in leather. The pl. in all 3 vols. signed *Anderson* [Alexander Anderson]. Adv. by Eastburn, Kirk and Co., 1814 on the rear cover of Mrs. Hofland's *Son Of A Genius*.

PP* (vol. I. pl. opp. p. 184 mut., on t.[i] is a holograph signature *Rebecca Bap Miller 25 December 1814*); MH (vols. II., III. dated *ca.* 1810); PPL (vol. I); Shaw 20032 and 28404 (Boston, 1813. A ghost and error for no. **328.2**.)

328.3 — ——— Children. In Two Volumes. By Maria Edgeworth, Author of Practical Education, and Letters for Literary Ladies. Volume I. [II.] Boston: Published By Wells And Lilly. 1818.

vol. I.: t.[i], [ii–iii], iv–xii, [3], 4–480 p.; 6 full page illus. on p. [56], [94], [126], [306], [338], [396], 2 pl. opp. p. [257], [277]; vol. II.: t.[1], [2–3], 4–500 p.; 3 full page illus. on p. [60], [206], [274], 4 pl. opp. p. [113], [161], [359], [385]; 2 vols. 13.5 cm.; bound in leather. vol. I.: preface, p. [iii]–xii; Lazy Lawrence, p. [3]–55, Tarlton, p. [57]–93; The Birth-Day Present, p. [95]–125; Simple Susan p. [127]–256; The White Pigeon, p. [257]–276; The Basket Woman, p. [277]–305; Forgive And Forget p. [307]–337; Waste Not, Want Not, p. [339]–395; Eton Montem, [397]–480; vol. II., The Bracelets, p. 3–59; Mademoiselle Panache, p. [61]– 112; The False Key, p. [113]–160, The Orphans, p. [161]–205; The Mimic, p. [207]– 273; The Barring Out, p. [275]–358; Old Poz, p. [359]–384; The Little Merchants, Chapter I, [385]–414, Chapter II, [415]–447, Chapter III, [449]–469, Chapter IV, p. [471]–500.

Plates signed *A* or *Anderson* [Alexander Anderson].

MWA-T° (vol. I., p. 95–98 mut.).

328.4 —　——— Children. In Two Volumes. By Maria Edgeworth ——— [same as **328.1**] Vol. I. [II.] New-York: Published By E. Duyckinck, No. 68 Water-Street. G. Long, Printer. 1820.

vol. I.: fr.[ii], t.[iii], [iv–v], vi–xi, [xii], [13], 14–252 p.; illus.; t.[1] 14 cm.; vol. II.: fr.[2], t.[3], [4–5], 6–247 p.; illus.; 14.5 cm. In both vols. front. signed *Anderson,* and all the illus. signed *A* [Alexander Anderson].

MWA° (vol. II.); NjP (vols. I., II. rebound); Shoemaker 1077.

329 — THE PRUSSIAN VASE; Or, The History Of Sophia Mansfield. By Maria Edgeworth. Philadelphia: Published By Bennett & Walton. No. 31, Market Street. John Bouvier Printer, Bellavista Hamilton-ville. 1811.

t.[1], [2–3], 4–103 p.; 13.5 cm.; pr. blue-gray paper covers; cover title dated 1812.

DLC°; Shaw 22746.

330.1 [—] ROSAMOND, Part I; Containing The Purple Jar,—The Two Plums,—The Day Of Misfortunes—Rivuletta: By The Author Of The Parent's Assistant, Six Volumes. Philadelphia: Published By Jacob Johnson, No. 147, Market-Street. 1808.

Part I.: t.[1], [2–3], 4–114 p.; 13 cm.; Part II.: t.[1], [2–3], 4–91 p.; 2 vols.; 13.5 cm.; bound in marbled paper over bds., leather spine. Page 2 of both vols.: *Adams, Printer, Philadelphia.* The text is taken from *Early Lessons.* The title of Part II.: Rosamond, Part II; Containing The Thorn,—The Hyacinths,—The Story Of The Rabbit: By The Author Of The Parents Assistant, Six Volumes. Philadelphia: Published By Jacob Johnson, No. 147, Market-Street. 1808.

English ed. issued in 3 pts. or pts. 3–5 of *Early Lessons,* London: J. Johnson, by H. Bryer, 1801. MWA° (vols. I., II.); CtY (vols. I., II.); DLC (vols. I., II.); MSaE (vol. I., emb. st. on t.[1]); Shaw 14918.

330.2 [—] ROSAMOND, Part I. Containing The Purple Jar—The Two Plums—The Day Of Misfortunes—Rivuletta. By The Author Of The Parent's Assistant. Boston: Published By Cummings And Hilliard, No. 1, Cornhill. 1813.

t.[1], [2–3], 4–106 p.; 14.5 cm.; bound in marbled paper over bds., black leather spine.

Cover title of MWA copy: Rosamond. By The Author Of The Parent's Assistant. Boston: Published By Cummings And Hilliard, No. 1, Cornhill. 1813.

Part II.: caption title p.[61]: Rosamond, Part II. Containing The Thorn—The Hyacinth—The Story Of The Rabbit.

Welch°; MWA (bound in pr. yellow paper over bds.); PP; Shaw 28406.

330.3 — ROSAMOND. By Maria Edgeworth. [4 lines of verse] Boston: Published By Ezra Read 23, School-Street. January 1817.

vol. I.: fr. [102], t.[103], [104–105], 106–178 p.; vol. II.: [3], 4–72 p.; front. only illus.; 2 vols. in 1; 15 cm.; bound in olive paper over bds., leather spine.; front. by Alexander Anderson; no title page for vol. II., p. 6 of vol. II. wrongly numbered 9.

MWA° (wants fr.[102]); MH (has fr.[102]); Shaw 40732.

331.1 — SIMPLE SUSAN. By Miss Edgeworth. Boston: adv. by Wells and Lilly, 1815 in **326.1** and 1816 in **332**. Reprinted from *The Parent's Assistant. See* no. **307.3**.

331.2 — SIMPLE SUSAN. By Miss Edgeworth. Boston: Published by Wells and Lilly. 1819. [cover title].

pl.[ii], [127], 128–256 p.; pl. only illus.; 13.5 cm.; pr. & illus. paper covers; duplicate front cover & text pl. signed *A* [Alexander Anderson]. NNC-T° (per st. on pl.[ii]; emb. st. on p.[127]); CLU; Shaw 43918.

332 — No. 2. TARLTON. By Miss Edgeworth. Boston: Published by Wells and Lilly. Price 12 1–2 cents. 1816. [cover title].

pl.[ii], [65], 66–108 p.; pl. only illus.; 14.5 cm.; pr. & illus. brown paper covers; duplicate front cover & text pl. signed *Anderson* [Alexander Anderson]. Adv. by Wells & Lilly, 1815 in **326.1** and 1819 in **321.3**. Reprinted from *The Parent's Assistant. See* no. **307.3**. MWA-W°; Shoemaker 51576.

333 [—] THREE STORIES FOR YOUNG CHILDREN: 1. The Little Dog Trusty. 2. The Orange Man. 3. The Cherry Orchard. By The Author Of The

Parent's Assistant, Six Volumes. Philadelphia: Published by Jacob Johnson, No. 147, Market-street. 1805.

    t.[1], [2–3], 4–84 p.; 10 cm.; blue marbled paper covers.

    English ed. pt. 10 of *Early Lessons*, London, entitled: *The Little Dog Trusty; The Orange Man; And The Cherry Orchard*. J. Johnson, By H. Bryer, 1801.

    NNC-Pl°; Shaw 9480.

334 — No. 14. WASTE NOT, WANT NOT: Or, Two Strings To Your Bow. By Miss Edgeworth. Boston: Published by Wells and Lilly. Price 20 cents. 1816. [cover title].

    pl.[ii], [115], 116–180 p.; pl. only illus.; 14.5 cm.; pr. & illus. brown paper over bds.; duplicate front cover & text pl. signed *Anderson* [Alexander Anderson]. Adv. by Wells and Lilly, 1815 in **326.1** and 1819 in **321.3**. Reprinted from *The Parent's Assistant. See no.* **307.3.**

    MWA-W°; MiD; Shaw 51575.

335.1 — No. 12. THE WHITE PIGEON. By Miss Edgeworth. Boston: Published by Wells and Lilly. Price 12 1-2 cents. 1816.

    pl.[ii], [37], 38–60 p.; pl.[ii] only illus.; 15 cm.; pr. & illus. dark-brown paper covers; duplicate front cover & text pl. signed A [Alexander Anderson]. Reprinted from *The Parent's Assistant.*

    MWA°.

335.2 — ———— Boston: Published by Wells and Lilly. 1819. [cover title].

    pl.[ii], [1], 2–20 p.; pl. only illus.; 13 cm.; pr. & illus. yellow-buff paper covers; duplicate front cover & text pl. signed A [Alexander Anderson]. Adv. by Wells and Lilly, 1815 in **326.1** and 1816 in **332**. Reprinted from *The Parent's Assistant. See no.* **307.3.**

    ICU°; MH (pl.[ii] ¾ wanting); Shaw 47880.

EDWARD AND GEORGE. New-York: adv. for 2 cents by T. B. Jansen, [*ca.* 1815] in **47**.

336 THE EFFECTS OF OBEDIENCE & DISOBEDIENCE: Or The History Of A Good Boy & Bad Girl; Being A Pleasing Account Of Henry And Caroline, To Which Is Added, The Histories of Benjamin Goodwin, and William Trueman. Being A Valuable Collection, For Little Masters And Misses. New-York, May, 1798.

fr.[2], t.[3], [4–5], 6–60 p.; illus.; 10 cm.; green Dutch paper covers.

    MWA° (fr.[2], t.[3] mut.); Evans 48416.

337 THE ELEMENTS OF ANCIENT AND UNIVERSAL HISTORY, Illustrating The Most Remarkable Events Which Have Occurred During the Lives Of Distinguished Warriors, Kings, Legislators, And Philosophers, Recorded In Sacred And Profane History. [3 lines quot.] Boston: Published By Munroe & Francis, No. 4, Cornhill, And David Francis, No. 90, Newbury-Street. 1818.

    t.[3], [4–5], 6–216 p.; illus.; 14.5 cm.; bound in leather. This is one of the few books of *Juvenile Classicks* which was not published later than 1820.

    MWA°.

338.1 ELLEN: A Tale—In Three Parts. By An American Lady. Philadelphia: Published By The Sunday and Adult School Union. Clark & Raser, Printers. 1819.

    t.[1], [2–3], 4–36 p.; title vignette only illus.; 12.5 cm.; pr. & illus. blue paper covers.

    MWA°; Shaw 47891.

338.2 ———— Second Edition. Philadelphia: Published by the Sunday & Adult School Union, And for sale at their Depository, 29 N. Fourth Street. Clark & Raser, Printers. 1820.

    t.[1], [2–3], 4–36 p.; title vignette only illus.; 13.5 cm.; pr. & illus. blue paper covers.

    CtHi°; PP.

ELLIOTT, MARY (BELSON) 1794?–1867?
339 [—] GRATEFUL TRIBUTES; Or Recollections Of Infancy. By M. Belson, Author of "Industry and Idleness;" "Innocent Poetry;" "Baby's Holiday;" "Precept and Example;" &c.&c.&c. New-York: Published By Samuel Wood & Sons, No. 261, Pearl-Street; And Samuel S. Wood & Co. No. 212, Market-st. Baltimore. 1819.

    t.[i], [ii–iii], iv, [5], 6–46 p.; illus.; 13 cm.; pr. & illus. buff paper covers; cover title undated; illus. signed A [Alexander Anderson].

    English ed. London: Darton. 1811.

    MWA°; CLU; Shaw 47893.

340 [—] INDUSTRY AND IDLENESS, A Pleasing And Instructive Tale, For Good Little Girls, In Words Not Exceeding Two Syllables. Philadelphia: Published By Benjamin Warner, No. 147, Market Street. 1816.

folded fr.[ii], t.[1], [2–3], 4–47 p.; front. only illus.; 16.5 cm.; pr. green paper covers; cover date 1817. Adv. by Johnson & Warner, 1817 in **1355.3**.

English ed. London: William Darton Jun. 1816, with the author's name, Mary Belson. Front. dated January 27th. 1811.

MWA° (copy 1, green paper covers; copy 2, bound with *Dame Partlet's Farm*. Johnson & Warner, 1810); MBAt; MiD; MSaE; NNC-Pl; Shaw 37504.

341 [—] INNOCENT POETRY. Philadelphia: Published By Johnson & Warner, No. 147, Market Street. William Brown, Printer, No. 24, Church-alley. 1811.

fr.[1], [2, bl.], t.[3], 4–9, 10–69 p.; illus.; 15.4 cm.; pr. & illus. pink paper covers; 9 pl. including front. Adv. by Johnson & Warner, 1814 in **1449.3**.

English ed. London: adv. by W. Darton Jun. in *Grateful Tributes*. 1811.

MWA-W° (t.[3] 99% wanting, front cover half wanting); NWebyC (fr.[2] faces t.[3], fr.[2] & covers mut.; per. st. on p.[5], 69); PPL; Shaw 23094.

342.1 [—] MY BROTHER. A Poem for Children. [1 line quot.] New York: Published by Samuel Wood & Sons, No. 357, Pearl Street. [1816].

t.[1], [2–5] p. engr. on one side only of 5 leaves; illus.; 13 cm.; pr. & illus. olive-green paper covers; title page vignette signed *Scoles sculp.* The firm of Samuel Wood & Sons was at 357 Pearl Street from 1815–1816.

Cover title —— [illus. of a woodpecker] New-York: Published By Samuel Wood & Sons, No. 261, Pearl-Street. 1817.

English ed. London: p. 13–16 in *Grateful Tributes*. W. Darton Jun. 1811.

MWA° (p.[6] & rear cover wanting); Shaw 40745 (dated [1817]).

342.2 [—] —— A Poem Illustrated With Engravings. Philadelphia, Published and sold by Wm. Charles. Price Plain 12½ cents Coloured 18¾ cents. 1817. [cover title].

[1–6] p. engr. on one side only of 6 leaves; illus.; 14.5 cm.; pr. olive-buff paper covers.

NNC-Pl° (rear pr. paper cover torn away);

MWA (p.[5–6] wanting, entire book has a central tear); Shaw 40746 and 41537.

342.3 [—] —— Philadelphia, Published and sold by Wm Charles. Price Plain 12½ cents—Coloured 18¾ cents. 1819. [cover title].

[1–6] p. engr. on one side only of 8 leaves; illus.; 13 cm.; pr. gray paper covers.

MWA°; Shaw 47894.

343.1 [—] MY FATHER. [Engraved full page illus.] The tears would trickle down thy face,—My Father. Published March 1st 1817. by W. Hooker, Engraver, 202 Water. Street. Corner of Fulton Street. New York.

t.[1], [2–4] p. engr. on one side only of 4 leaves; t.[1] only illus.; 14.5 cm.; pr. yellow paper covers. Either a remainder issued with new covers in 1843 or a reprinting of the 1817 pl. Cover title: My Father Portland: S. H. Colesworthy. 1843.

MWA-W°.

343.2 [—] MY FATHER. A Poem for Children. [1 line quot.] Prov. New York: Published by Samuel Wood & Sons. No. 261, Pearl Street. n.d. [1817].

t.[1], [2–6] p. engr. on one side only of 6 leaves; illus.; 13 cm.; pr. & illus. paper covers.

Cover title: My Father. A Poem for Children. [cut of a beehive and a rose] New-York: Published By Samuel Wood & Sons, No. 261, Pearl-Street. 1817.

English ed. London: p. 5–8 in *Grateful Tributes*. W. Darton Jun. 1811.

PP°; DLC (1 leaf bound out of order before t.[1], 1 leaf mut. ½ wanting); Shaw 40747 (error, not in MWA).

343.3 [—] —— same as **342.2** but with different covers and cover imprint.

t.[1], [2–7] p. engr. on one side only of 7 leaves; illus.; 13.5 cm.; pr. & illus. paper covers.

Cover title: My Father. A Poem For Children. [cut of a bird] New-York: Published By Samuel Wood & Sons, No. 261, Pearl-Street, And Samuel S. Wood & Co. No. 212, Market Street. Baltimore. This was probably an edition issued [*ca.* 1818] or later using the [1817] plates. Another variant in NHi has the cover title surrounded by a thick border, the same cover imprint as the above CtHi copy, but lacks a vignette. It was probably printed *ca.* 1820 or later.

CtHi°; NHi.

343.4 [—] ——— A Poem Illustrated With Engravings. Philadelphia, Published and sold by Wm. Charles. Price Plain 12½ cents Coloured 18¾ cents. 1817. [cover title].

[1–6] p. engr. on one side only of 8 leaves; illus.; 13.5 cm.; pr. olive-green paper covers.

MWA° (pr. rear cover torn away); Shaw 40748.

343.5 [—] ——— Philadelphia, Published and sold by Wm. Charles. Price Plain 12½ cents Coloured 18¾ cents. 1818. [cover title].

[1–6] p. engr. on one side only of 6 leaves; illus.; 12.5 cm.; pr. yellow-buff paper covers.

NN°; MWA (pr. paper covers only, remainder of book wanting); Weiss 1932a.

344 — MY SISTER. A Poem by Mary Belson. Illustrated With Elegant Engravings. Philadelphia, Published and sold by Wm Charles Price plain 12½ cents Coloured [bl. space] cents. 1816. (cover title).

[1–6] p. engr. on one side only of 6 leaves; illus.; 13.5 cm.; pr. yellow paper covers; the price on the cover title is not printed after the word "Coloured."

English ed. London: W. Darton. n.d. [1818].

MWA-W°; NNC-Pl (rear cover wanting); RPB (covers wanting, may be this ed.); Shaw 37505.

345.1 — THE ORPHAN BOY; Or, A Journey To Bath. Founded On Fact. By Mary Belson, Author Of The Mice And Their Pic Nic—Precept And Example—Industry And Idleness—Innocent Poetry—Grateful Tributes—Baby's Holiday—Simple Truths, &c. &c. New-York: Published By W. B. Gilley, No. 92 Broadway. T. & W. Mercein, print. 1816.

[fr.[ii], t.[1], [2–3], 4–143 p.; front. only illus.; 14 cm.; bound in red marbled paper over bds., green leather spine; front. signed *Scoles sculp.*

English ed. London: adv. by W. Darton Jun. in Elliott's *The Baby's Holiday. 1812.*

Welch°; DLC; MSaE; MWA; NN; PP; Shaw 36924.

345.2 ——— New-York: Published By W. B. Gilley, 92 Broadway. N. Van Riper, Printer. 1819.

fr.[ii], t.[1], [2–3], 4–143 p.; front. only illus.; 14.5 cm.; bound in buff paper over bds., black leather spine; front. signed *Scoles sculp.*

MWA°; MH; NN (bound in yellow paper over bds., black leather spine); PP; Shaw 47895.

345.3 [—] ——— Boy. New-York: Printed by D. H. Wickham, At the Sunday School Depository, No. 59 Fulton-street. 1820. [cover title].

[1], 2–24 p.; cover title vignette only illus.; 13 cm.; pr. & illus. buff paper covers.

MWA-T°.

346 — SIMPLE TRUTHS IN VERSE. For the Amusement And Instruction Of Children, At An Early Age. By Mary Belson, Author Of "Innocent Poetry,"—"Grateful Tributes,"—"The Orphan Boy,"—"Precepts and Example,"—"Industry and Idleness," &c.&c. Morris-Town [N.J.]: Printed By Henry P. Russell, 1815.

t.[i], [ii–iii], iv, [I], II–IV, [5], 6–84 p.; 14 cm.; green and pink marbled paper covers.

English ed. London: W. Darton, 1812.

CtHi°; Shaw 51490.

ELMINA; OR, THE FLOWER THAT NEVER FADES. *See* Masson, Charles F. P., no. **823.1**.

EMBLEMS AND FABLES, NATURAL, HISTORICAL, MORAL, FABULOUS AND DIVINE. *See* Wynne, John Huddlestone, no. **1458**.

EMBLEMS, NATURAL, HISTORICAL, MORAL AND DIVINE. *See* Wynne, John Huddlestone, no. **1459**.

347.1 EMBLEMS OF MORTALITY; Representing, In Upwards Of Fifty Cuts, Death Seizing All Ranks And Degrees Of People; Imitated from a Painting in the Cemetery of the Dominican Church at Basil, in Switzerland; With an Apostrophe to each; Translated from the Latin and French. Intended as well for the Information of the Curious, as the Instruction and Entertainment of Youth. To Which Is Prefixed, A Copious Preface, Containing an historical Account of the above, and other Paintings on the Subject, now or lately existing in divers Parts of Europe. To Which Is Added, The Death of Adam, and the Bird of Paradise. First American Edition. Hartford: Printed By John Babcock. 1801.

fr.[ii], t.[iii], [iv–v], vi–xxxix, [xl, bl.], 41–108 p.; illus.; 14.5 cm.; bound in marbled paper over bds., leather spine; p. 107–108 adv.
English ed. London: T. Hodgson, 1789.
MWA° (emb. st. on t.[iii]); CtHi (t.[iii] mut.); CtY (p. 45–46 mut., front cover wanting); MB; MSaE; PP; Shaw 443.

347.2 ———— Translated from the Latin. Intended as well for the information of the Curious, as the Instruction and Entertainment of Youth. To Which Are Added, The Death of Adam, and the Bird of Paradise. Sidney's Press, New-Haven. 1810.
fr.[2], t.[3], [4], 5–69 p.; illus.; 13.5 cm.; pr. & illus. buff paper covers.
CtHi°; CtY; MWA; NjP; Hamilton 247; Shaw 20049.

THE ENCHANTED PLANTS; Fables In Verse. *See* Montollieu, Mrs., no. **870.**

348 THE ENCHANTED MIRROR. A Moorish Romance. First American Edition. Hartford: Printed And Sold By B. & J. Russell, jr. State-Street. 1814.
t.[1], [2–3], 4–93, [94–95, index, 96, adv.] p.; title page vignette & tailpiece p. 93 only illus.; 12 cm.; bound in blue paper over bds., pink paper spine.
English ed. Salisbury: J. Easton, E. Newbery, 1799.
MWA-W°; DLC; Shaw 31416.

THE ENGLISH HERMIT. *See* Longueville, Peter, no. **793.1.**

ENGLISH, CLARA
349.1 — THE AFFECTING HISTORY OF THE CHILDREN IN THE WOOD. By Clara English. New-York: Printed And Sold By John C. Totten, No 155 Chatham-street. 1809.
1st t.[1], [2–4], 5–47, [48], 2nd t.[1], [2], 3–12 p.; illus.; 14 cm.; illus. blue paper covers.
2nd title: The Children In The Wood. A Favorite Ballad. New-York: Printed By John C. Totten, No. 155 Chatham-street. 1809.
CtHi°.

349.2 — ———— Hartford: Printed By Charles Hosmer. 1811.
t.[1], [2–3], 4–54 p.; illus.; 13 cm.; pr. yellow paper covers; cover title imprint: Hartford: Published By Hale & Hosmer 1811.
MWA°; Shaw 22767.

349.3 [—] ———— Wood. [4 lines of verse] Hallowell [Me.]: Printed For E. Goodale And N. Cheever. Sold at their respective Bookstores. 1813.
t.[1], [2–3], 4–48 p.; illus.; 14 cm.; pr. & illus. buff paper covers; copy 1.
Cover title copy 1: The History Of The Children In The Wood. [cut of 2 children, The Uncle and 2 ruffians] Hallowell: Published By E. Goodale And N. Cheever. 1813. [2 woodcuts on rear cover.].
Cover title copy 2: ———— [cut of an eagle above a woodcut device] Published And Sold By [Eze]kiel Goodale [at the Hal]lowell Bookstore. [rear cover has a list of books; green paper covers].
Cover title copy 3: ———— [cut of a woman looking at 2 reclining children] Hallowell: Printed By N. Cheever, And Sold At His Bookstore. 1817. [blue-gray paper covers, rear cover has an adv.].
MWA-W° (copies 1, 2, 3, with varient covers); MWA (copy 4, rear cover wanting, also p. 21–22); MH; MSaE (covers mut.); Shaw 28126.

349.4 — ———— By Clara English. Hartford: Printed by Charles Hosmer. 1815.
t.[1], [2–3], 4–54 p.; illus.; 13.5 cm.; pr. buff paper covers dated 1815.
CtHi°.

349.5 [—] ———— Hallowell [Me.]: Published by E. Goodale. Sold at his Bookstore. 1816.
t.[1], [2–3], 4–44 p.; illus.; 14 cm.; pr. & illus. blue-gray paper covers.
Cover title: The History Of The Children in the Wood. Hallowell: Printed By E. Goodale. 1817.
MWA-W° (cover title vignette, 2 children, 2 ruffians & the uncle); MWA (cover vignette, a man walking with a boy & girl); NNC; Shaw 37225.

349.6 [—] ———— Wood. Adorned With Cuts. [4 lines verse] From Sidney's Press New-Haven. 1817.
fr.[2], t.[3], [4–5], 6–46, [47, adv.] p.; illus.; 12.5 cm.; illus. buff paper covers.
MWA°; Shaw 40465.

349.7 — ———— Clara English. Hartford: Published by George Goodwin & Sons. 1819.
t.[1], [2–3], 4–54 p.; illus.; 13.5 cm.; marbled paper covers.
CtY° (front cover wanting); Ct; CtHi (p. 52–53 wanting); MH; Shaw 47906.

350.1 — THE CHILDREN IN THE WOOD An Instructive Tale by Clara English Philadelphia Publish'd by J. Johnson. 1803.
t.[1], [2–63] p.; illus.; 16 cm.; bound in leather; colophon p. [63]: Printed by Budd & Bartram. English ed. London: Darton and Harvey, 1801.
MWA°; Shaw 4165.

350.2 — ———— Philadelphia Publish'd by J. Johnson. 1803.
t.[1], [2–63] p.; illus.; 16 cm.; bound in marbled paper over bds.; no colophon p.[63].
MWA°; OOxM; Shaw 8397.

350.3 — ———— Baltimore: Printed at the Bible and Heart Office, By And For Warner And Hanna, And Sold By Them And John Vance And Co. 1806.
t.[1], [2–3], 4–60 p.; illus.; 16 cm.; title vignette signed *C. Gobrecht*, illus. p. 5 signed *C. B.*, that on p. 12 *Gobrecht* [Christian Gobrecht].
RPB°; MSaE (emb. st. on t.[1]; marbled paper covers); NjR; NN; Weiss 1936, p. 82; Shaw 10359.

350.4 — ———— [same as **350.1**] Philadelphia Publish'd by J. Johnson. 1807.
t.[1], [2–63] p.; illus.; 16 cm.; bound in marbled paper over bds.; p.[3] has a thick and thin rule above the caption: The Children In The Wood.; and a printer's ornament 2.8 cm. long below the caption; colophon p.[63]: Joseph Rakestraw, Printer.
Front cover label: Children In The Wood. Sold at Munroe & Francis' Juvenile Library, 4 Cornhill, Boston.
MWA-W° (the lower half of p. 25–26 wanting); CLU; CtHi; MWA; PP; RPB (p. [3–18] wanting; t. [1] mut.); Shaw 12505.

350.5 — ———— Philadelphia Publish'd by J. Johnson. 1807.
t.[1], [2–63] p.; illus.; 16 cm.; bound in brown marbled paper over bds. A variant of no. **350.4**.

There is no double rule above the caption on p.[3], the printer's ornament below the caption is 1 cm. long, and p.[63] has no colophon.
MWA°; CtY (Pequot); NNC-Pl.

350.6 — ———— [same as **350.3**] Philadelphia: Printed By Jacob Meyer, 1813.
t.[1], [2–47] p.; illus.; 16.5 cm.; buff paper covers. Part of a large publisher's remainder.
MWA-W°; CtHi; DLC (bound in marbled paper over bds., not a remainder); NHi; NN; NNC-Pl; PP; Shaw 28433.

350.7 — ———— Clara English. To Which Is Added Little Charles, Or The Good Son. Baltimore: Printed And Sold By William Warner, Corner of South Gay and Market-streets. 1814.
t.[1], [2–3], 4–71 p.; illus.; 14 cm.; pr. & illus. paper covers; title vignette signed *C. Gobrecht*, illus. p. 11 signed *Gobrecht*, & illus. p. 53 signed *C. G.* [Christian Gobrecht].
MWA°, Shaw 31419.

350.8 — ———— Clara English. Philadelphia: Printed And Sold By Joseph Rakestraw, No. 256, North Third street. 1818.
t.[1], [2–3], 4–47 p.; illus.; 14.5 cm.; pr. & illus. paper covers.
MWA°; PHi; Shaw 43945.

351.1 — THE HISTORY OF THE CHILDREN IN THE WOOD. An Affecting Tale, By Clara English. New-York: Stereotyped and Published, by Charles Starr, For the Booksellers. 1818.
fr.[ii], t.[1], [2–3], 4–5 p.; illus.; 13.5 cm.; pr. pink covers.
DLC°; NN; Shaw 43946.

351.2 — ———— Published by Robert De Silver, No. 110 Walnut-st. Philadelphia. 1818.
fr.[ii], t.[1], [2–3], 4–45 p.; illus.; 13 cm.; pr. yellow paper covers; cover title dated 1819.
CSmH°.

351.3 [—] ———— New-York: Printed And Sold By J. C. Totten, No. 9 Bowery. 1819.
fr.[2], t.[3], [4–5], 6–46 p.; illus.; printed and illus. buff paper covers.
MWA°.

351.4 [—] ———— Tale. Cooperstown [N.Y]: Printed And Published By H. & E. Phinney, And Sold At Their Book-Store. 1820.

fr.[2], t.[3], [4–5], 6–59 p.; illus.; 12.5 cm.; pr. & illus. buff paper covers.

MWA°; CtHi; Shoemaker 1105.

352 ENTERTAINING AND DIVERTING STORIES, On Various Subjects, For the Instruction Of Children. Adorned with Cuts. Printed for, and sold by the Booksellers. 1800.

t.[1], [2–3], 4–16 p.; illus.; 9.5 cm.; the wood cut illus. on p. [3], 7, 8, 12, [15] were used by N. Coverly [1787] in **616.3**; those on p. [3], 13, 16 were used by N. Coverly, 1794 in **676**; those on p. 6, 8, 11, [14], [15] were used by [J. White] 1790 in **616.5**.

MWA°, MSaE; Evans 37373.

353 ENTERTAINING FABLES FOR CHILDREN. Philadelphia: adv. by William Young, 1794 in **305**. This may be an adv. for no. **354.1**.

354.1 ENTERTAINING FABLES FOR THE INSTRUC- TION OF CHILDREN. Embellished with cuts. To which is added, The trial of an ox for killing a man. Philadelphia: Printed by Young and M'Cul- loch, the corner of Chesnut and Second-streets. 1787.

[3]–28, [2] p.; 14.5 cm.

English ed. London: adv. price 3d by Newbery and Carnan in *The History Of Little Goody Two-Shoes*. 1768.

Greewood°; Evans 45062.

354.2 —— Children. [4 lines quot.] Gay. The Second Worcester Edition. Printed at Worces- ter, Massachusetts, By Isaiah Thomas. Sold Wholesale and Retail at his Bookstore. MDCC- XCIV.

fr.[2], t.[3], [4–8], 9–27, [28–31, adv. of books] p.; 10 cm.; green Dutch paper covers.

MWA°; PP (rebound); Evans 26947.

355 ENTERTAINING HISTORIES for young Masters and Misses. [running title at the top of p. 10–11 and others] [Hudson [N.Y.]: Printed by Ashbel Stoddard, And Sold Wholesale and Retail at his Book-store. 1804?] [taken from A. Stoddard's ed. of *The Hermit Of The Forest*, no. **673.21**].

fr.[2], [5], 6–126, [127] p.; illus.; 10.5 cm.; adv. caption p.[127]. The entire p.[127] is identical, both in context and type set up, with

p.[31] of Johnson's *Hermit Of the Forest. Hud- son: A. Stoddard, 1804.*, no. **673.21**, except that the 11th book advertised in **355** is "The Hermit Of The Forest, and the Wandering Infants" which is omitted in **673.21**. Since the advertisement caption varies in different years it is probable that the above caption used in both books was printed in the same year or 1804. The text is the same and most of the woodcut illus. are from the same blocks used by A. Stoddard in his 1794 ed. of Solomon Sobersides' *Christmas Tales*, no. **1220.1**. The type setup differs in both books as well as the running title at the top of the pages of the text. In **355** the following woodcut illus. on p. 31, 54, 61 show breaks or the loss of small portions of the border of the cuts which are present in **1220.1**. These imperfections in the cuts are added evidence that **355** must have been printed later than **1220.1**.

OChRHi° (t.[3], p. [4], 7–8 wanting).

356 THE ENTERTAINING HISTORY OF HONEST PETER, By Miss D———Y. [2 lines of verse] Ornamented By Six Beautiful Descriptive Pictures. Boston: Printed and sold by S. Hall, No. 53, Corn- hill. 1794.

fr.[2], t.[3], [4–5], 6–48, [49–51, adv. list of books] p.; illus.; 10.5 cm.; blue marbled paper covers; advertisement caption p. [49] same as that on p. [29], no. **408.4**.

English ed. London: Published for the author, W. Heffer. [*ca.* 1792?].

RPB°; Evans 47038.

357 T[HE] ENTERTAINING HISTORY OF JOBSON & Nell. Illustrated With Humerous Engravings. Philadelphia: Published and sold Wholesale by Wm. Charles, and may be had of all the Book- sellers. 1814. Price 18 3/4. Cents. [cover title].

[1–12] p. engr. on one side only of 12 leaves; illus.; 13.5 cm.; pr. buff paper covers.

English ed. London: G. Martin. n.d.

MWA°; Shaw 31421; Weiss 1932b.

358 THE ENTERTAINING HISTORY OF LITTLE JACK. Designed to edify and instruct Youth of both sexes. Stonington-Port [Conn.]: Printed By Samuel Trumbull, And sold at his Office by the Thousand, Gross, Dozen or single. [1801].

fr.[2], t.[3], [4–5], 6–23 p.; illus.; 12 cm.; bound in Dutch paper over bds.; on p.[3] is a

holograph inscription: *Joseph Palm's book bought July 13, 1801.*
CtY° (front cover wanting, p. 23 mut.); CtHi (covers intact except for a small piece of Dutch paper wanting from rear cover); Shaw 454.

359 THE ENTERTAINING HISTORY OF POLLY CHERRY, And Her Golden Apple. To Which Are Added, The Adventures Of Prince George. Adorned With Cuts. Philadelphia: Printed by F. Bailey, at Yorick's-head, No. 116. High-street. 1792.

fr.[2], t.[3], [4–5], 6–30, [31, adv. list of books] p.; illus.; 11 cm.; reddish-brown Dutch paper covers.
English ed. is entitled: *The New Entertaining History Of Polly Cherry . . .* London: [John Marshall, n.d. *ca.* 1783].
MWA°; Evans 46439.

THE ENTERTAINING HISTORY OF TOMMY GINGER-BREAD. *See* Tommy Gingerbread, no. **453.1.**

360 AN ENTERTAINING HISTORY OF TWO PIOUS TWIN CHILDREN, Who were stolen from their Christian Parents By A Jew, And Sold To The Turks As Slaves; And with their Father, were marvelously saved from death. First Edition. Translated from the German. To Which Is Added Little Charles, Or The Good Son. New-Market [Va.]: Printed in S. Henkel's Printing-Office. 1816.

fr.[2], t.[3], [4–5], 6–36 p.; illus.; 14 cm.; ornamented buff paper covers.
MWA°; DLC; PP; Shaw 37519.

361.1 THE ENTERTAINING, MORAL, AND RELIGIOUS REPOSITORY; Written in a simple yet pleasing Stile, Emmently Calculated For The Amusement and Instruction Of The Youth Of Both Sexes. Published by a Society in Great Britain, instituted for the beneficent purpose of aiding the intention of His Majesty, as expressed in his royal proclamation for the suppression of vice and immorality. Vol. I. Elizabeth-Town [N.J.]: Printed By Shepard Kollock For Cornelius Davis, No. 94, Water-Street, New-York. 1798.

t.[1], [2–3], 4–96 p.; 16 cm.; bound in blue-gray paper over w. bds., leather spine. The book contains the first appearance in America of some of the *Cheap Repository* tracts. In this volume are: The Shepherd Of Salisbury Plain; The History Of Tom White, The Postillion. [both by Hannah More]; The Life Of William Baker By The Rev. Mr. Gilpin.; A Funeral Sermon; The Two Soldiers.
English ed., *see Cheap Repository*, no. **169.1**; **169.7–8** and **169.20**; also London, entitled: *The Two Soldiers.* Evans And Co., J. Hatchard; S. Hazard, Bath. [*ca.* 1799].
MWA°; PP; Evans 35296; Weiss 1946.

361.2 ——— Repository; Containing Upwords Of Three Score Separate Performances, All Of Which Are written in a simple yet pleasing Stile, And Are Eminently Calculated For The Amusement and Instruction Of The Youth Of Both Sexes. Published by a Society in Great Britain, instituted for the beneficent purpose of aiding the intention of His Majesty, as expressed in his royal proclamation for the suppression of vice and immorality. In Two Volumes. Vol. II. Elizabeth-Town [N.J.]: Printed By Shepard Kollock For Cornelius Davis, No. 94, Water-Street, New-York. 1798.

t.[1], [2–3], 4–324 p.; 17 cm.; bound in leather. Since this volume contains the earliest appearance of certain *Cheap Repository* tracts in America, the contents of Vol. II are listed as follows: The History Of Charles Jones, p. [3]–17; The Cheapside Apprentice, p. [18]–29; The Story Of Poor Tricket, The Gamester, p. [30]–40; Betty Brown, The St Giles Orange Girl, p. [41]–52; Black Giles, The Poacher, p. [53]–77; Some New Thoughts For The New Year, p. 77–96; A True Example Of The Interposition Of Providence, p. 96–98; The Touchstone, p. [99]–111; Onisimus, p. [112]–125; Look At Home, p. 125–134; The Grand Assizes, p. [135]–143; Bear Ye One Another's Burdens, Or, The Valley Of Tears, p. 143–149; The Strait and the Broad Way, Being The Second Part Of Valley Of Tears, p. 149–160; The Cottage Cook, p. [161]–173; The Sunday School, p. [174]–187; The History Of Hester Wilmot, p. [198]–210; On The Sacrament [211]–219; The History Of Mr. Fantom, [220]–238; The Hubbub, p. [239]–250; Tawney Rachel, p. [251]–262; The Explanation Of The Ten Commandments, p. 262–289; The Servant Man turned Soldier, p. 289–290; The General Insurrection, p. [300]–305; Prayers, p. [306]–324. A True Example Of The Interposition Of Providence appears in both **361.3** and **361.2**.

English ed. *See Cheap Repository*, no. **169.9** and other nos.

MWA° (I. Thomas copy, i. st. on t.[1]); Evans 35296; Weiss 1946.

361.3 ——— [same as **361.2**] In Two Volumes. Vol. I. Elizabeth Town: Printed By Shepard Kollock For Cornelius Davis, No. 94, Water-Street, New-York.

t.[1], [2–3], 4–396 p.; 16.5 cm.; p. 96. The title page follows no. **361.2** and is probably the first volume of the set. No. **361.1** is a variant edition with a differently worded title page and only the first 96 pages. Both books have the same contents through p. 96, and both have on p. 96 "The End Of Volume I." In no. **361.3**, p. [97]–396 are present, but no word signifying the end of the volume occurs at the bottom of p. 396. The contents are: The Shepherd Of Salisbury Plain, p. [3]–30; The History Of Tom White, p. [31]–63; The Life Of William Baker, p. [64]–74; Funeral Sermon, p. 74–83; The Two Soldiers, p. [84]–96; The Two Shoemakers, pt. I–IV, p. [97]–165; The History Of The Plague In London, In 1665, p. 165–177; The Lancashire Collier Girl, p. 177–185; The Happy Waterman, p. 185–192; The Two Wealthy Farmers, pt. I–V, 193–266; The Good Mother's Legacy, [261]–274; Sorrowful Sam, p. 274–289; Wonderful Escape From Shipwreck, p. [290]–298; Babay, p. 298–300; The Comforts Of Religion, p. 300; A True Account Of A Pious Negro, p. [301]–304; The Beggarly Boy, p. [305]–315; The Wonderful Advantages Of Adventuring in the Lottery, p. [316]–328; Daniel In The Den Of Lions, p. 328–340; Noah's Flood, p. [341]–351; The Harvest Home, p. 351–361; The Parable Of The Laborers In The Vineyard, p. [362]–378; The Trouble Of Life, p. 378–394; A True Example Of Interposition Of Providence, p. [395]–396.

MWA-T°.

361.4 ——— immorality. Elizabeth-Town [N.J.]: Printed by Shepard Kollock, for Cornelius Davis, No. 94, Water-Street, New-York. 1799.

t.[i], [ii], [1, contents–2, bl.], [3], 4–324 p.; 16.5 cm.; bound in leather.

MWA°; CtY (rebound); DLC; NjP; NN; PP; PPL; RPJCB; Evans 35298; Weiss 1946.

361.5 ——— New York: Printed by George Forman, for Cornelius Davis, no. 94, Water-Street. 1799.

t.[1], [2–3], 4–396 p.; 17 cm.; bound in leather. The CtY & NN copies have an added leaf, which lies between p.[2] and [3], and has the table of contents pr. on the recto.

MWA° (i. st. on. t.[1], p. 1–2 wanting); CtY; DLC; NN; PPL; Evans 35297; Weiss 1946.

361.6 ——— Repository; Containing, The Two Wealthy Farmers, page 193; The Sad Adventures of Miss Bragwell, 247; The Good Mother's Legacy, 261; Sorrowful Sam, 274; Wonderful Escape from Shipwreck, 290; Baybay, 298. All Of Which Are written ——— [same as **361.2**] New-York: Printed for Cornelius Davis, No. 94, Water-street. 1799.

t.[191], [192–193], 194–299, [300] p.; t.[191]; 16.5 cm.

MWA° (rebound); Evans 35298 and 48845.

361.7 ——— [same as **361.2**] Elizabeth-Town [N.J.]. Printed by Shepard Kollock, for C. Davis, No. 167 Water-Street, New-York. 1800.

t.[i], [ii, bl.], [1, bl.–3], 4–324 p.; 17 cm.; bound in leather.

MWA°; CtY; NjN; OOxM; TU; Evans 37374.

361.8 ——— Containing, Many Performances, All Of Which Are written ——— [same as **361.2**] New-York: Printed by Johnson & Stryker, For Cornelius Davis, No. 167 Water-Street. 1801.

t.[i], [ii–iii], [iv, bl.], [1], 2–305 p.; t.[i] 16.5 cm.

MWA° (rebound); CtY (rebound & bound with no. **361.9**); Shaw 456.

361.9 ——— Moral & Religious Repository; Containing Many Separate Performances, All Of Which Are Written ——— [same as **361.2**] immorality. New-York: Printed by G. & R. Waite, for Cornelius Davis, No. 167, Water-street. 1801.

t.[1], [2–3], 4–106, [107, contents] p.; t.[1] 16 cm.

MWA° (rebound); CtY (rebound & bound with no. **361.8**); Shaw 455.

362 ENTERTAINING PIECES FOR CHILDREN AND OTHERS. n.p. [1810?].

t.[1], [2–3], 4–16 p.; illus.; 13 cm.

CtHi°.

363 ENTERTAINING POEMS AND FABLES FOR CHILDREN. Newburyport [Mass.], Printed By W. & J. Gilman. Sold at their wholesale and retail Book-Store, No. 2, Middle-Street. [1820?].

fr.[2], t.[3], [4–5], 6–35 p.; illus.; 17.5 cm.; pr. & illus. paper covers; illus. p. 23 signed *Gilman*.

MB°; MWA-T; RPB; RPJCB.

364.1 ENTERTAINING STORIES For Little Children. Ornamented With Cuts. Boston: Printed For And Sold By The Book-Sellers. 1810.

fr.[2], t.[3], [4–5], 6–15 p.; illus.; 10.5 cm.; purple paper covers; looks as if it were printed by N. Coverly.

MWA° (t.[3] mut.); Shaw 20058.

364.2 ———— Leominster [Mass.]: Printed By Salmon Wilder, 1811.

fr.[ii], t.[1], [2–3], 4–13 p.; 10.5 cm.; pr. & illus. yellow paper covers.

Cover title: Stories For Children.

MWA-W°; MWA (fr.[ii] & p. 13 worm-eaten; 9.5 cm.; different front. than MWA-W copy, covers unprinted); MLe; PP; Shaw 22769.

365 THE ENTERTAINING STORIES OF KING LEAR AND HIS DAUGHTERS, And Florio & Florella. Published With Curious Cuts. Hartford: Printed by Charles Hosmer. 1815.

fr.[2], t.[3], [4–5], 6–31 p.; illus.; 10 cm.; pr. & illus. buff paper covers.

English ed. London: published in *The Sugar Plumb*. Printed for The Booksellers. [*ca.* 1796].

CtHi°; Shaw 34646.

366.1 [AN] ENTERTAINING STORY BOOK For Little Boys and Girl's, Containing a Number of Jests, And Divertin[g] Stories, Together with some P[leasant] Jokes For The Amusement of Children. Adorn'd vvith Cuts. Boston: Printed and sold b[y] N. Coverly in Newbury-Street. MDCCLXXIX. Price Five Shillings.

t.[1], [2–3], 4–31, [32] p.; illus.; 9.5 cm.

The "w" in "Adorn'd with Cuts" on the title page is made up of two "v's." On page [3], there is a row of printers ornaments at the top of the page and another row a little above the center of the page. Many pages are cropped at the top of the book. However when the top of the page

is present the heading on the recto of each text leaf is usually "Be Merry and Wise, or," while on the verso it is "The Cream of the Jest." "w" is printed "vv" in "Dr. Swift," p. 19, and throughout p. 26. The page numbers are on the inner margin of the page.

MWA°; Evans 43626.

366.2 ———— [same as **366.1**] Children. [A]dorned with cuts. Boston: Printed and sold by N. Coverly in Newbury-Street. MDCCLXXIX. Price Six Shillings.

t.[1], [2–6], 7–26, [27–32] p.; illus.; 10 cm.

In this six shilling edition "w" in "Adorned with cuts" is printed with a "w." The heading "The Cream of the Jests" usually occurs on the recto of each leaf of the text, "Be Merry and Wise or" on the verso of each leaf. On p. 19 the "w" in "Dr. Swift" is a "w" & not 2 "v's." On p. 26 all the words beginning with "w" are printed with the letter "w" except "was" line 1 which has 2 "v's" for a "w." The page numbers are on the outer margin of the page.

MWA° (p. 29–30 wanting, t.[1] mut.); Evans 43627.

367 ENTERTAINING TALES. Mother Shipton: The Justice Of Providence, No Friendship; And The Rights Of Hospitality. [2 lines verse] Printed and Published at New York. 1815.

fr.[2], t.[3], [4–5], 6–132 p.; illus.; t.[3] 16 cm.; 6 very crude full page illus. including front.

MWA° (rebound); Shaw 34647.

368 ENTERTAINING TALES FOR YOUTH, Containing The Unfortunate Shepherd Boy, And The Faithful Steward. Embellished With Many Engravings. Boston: Published By Thomas B. Wait And Co. And Charles Williams. Price 12½ cents. [1812].

fr.[2], t.[3], [4–5], 6–34 p.; illus.; 14.5 cm.; adv. by Thomas B. Wait & Co. And Charles Williams, 1812 in **396**.

English ed. London: adv. under sixpenny books by R. Harrild, 1807 in *The Youth's Guide To Wisdom*.

MHi°, RPB (bound with other books).

THE ENTERTAINING TRAVELLER. *See* Johnson, Richard, no. **670.2**.

[ÉPINAY, LOUISE FLORENCE PÉTRONILLE DE LA LIVE D'] 1725–1783

369 [—] THE CONVERSATIONS OF EMILY. Abridged From The French. Philadelphia: Published By M. Carey & Son, No. 121, Chestnut-Street. 1817.

t.[i], [ii–iii], iv, [1], 2–200 p.; t.[i] 13.5 cm.; colophon p. 200: Asher Miner, Printer, Doylestown, Pa.

English ed. London: J. Marshall and Co. 1787. MWA* (rebound); KU; PPi (15.5 cm.; bound in blue-gray paper over bds.); Show 40761.

370.1 EPITAPHS AND ELEGIES. [4 lines of verse] New-York: Printed And Sold By Samuel Wood, At The Juvenile Book-Store, No. 357, Pearl-Street. 1814.

t.[i], [ii–iii], iv, [5], 6–72 p.; illus.; 13.5 cm.; pr. & illus. yellow-buff paper covers. Adv. by S. Wood, 1819 in **1188.8**.

DLC* (2 copies); MB; MWA; Shaw 31423.

370.2 ——— New-York: Printed And Sold By Samuel Wood & Sons, At The Juvenile Book-Store, No. 357, Pearl-Street. 1816.

t.[i], [ii–iii], iv, [5], 6–72 p.; illus.; 14 cm.; pr. & illus. yellow paper covers.

Cover imprint copy 1: Printed And Sold By Samuel Wood & Sons At The Juvenile Book-Store, No. 357 Pearl-Street, New-York.

Cover imprint copy 2: ——— [same as copy 1] No. 261, Pearl-Street, New-York.

Cover imprint copy 3: New-York: Published By Samuel Wood & Sons, No. 261, Pearl-Street; And Samuel Wood & Co. No. 212 Market-street, Baltimore.

MWA* (copy 1, 3); DLC* (copy 2); MiD (covers wanting); Shaw 37522 (copy 1) and 37523 (copy 3).

371 ERRORS OF YOUTH. Illustrated With Engravings. Philadelphia: Published and sold Wholesale by Wm. Charles, and may be had of all the Booksellers. Price 13 3–4 cents. 1812. W. M'Culloch, Printer. [cover title].

[1–8] p. engr. on one side only of 8 leaves; illus.; 13.5 cm.; pr. paper covers.

NNC-Pl* (colored illus.); Shaw 25352.

ESOP. *See* Æsop.

372 EVENING AMUSEMENTS FOR THE LADIES; Or, Original Anecdotes, Intended To promote a Love of Virtue In Young Minds. A Series of Letters. [3 lines of quot.] Boston: Printed by Manning & Loring, For Ebenezer Larkin, No. 47, Cornhill. MDCCXCVI.

t.[i], [ii–iii], iv–vi, [vii, contents], [viii, bl.], [9], 10–135 p.; 14.5 cm.; bound in leather.

MWA*; DLC (2 copies); MB; Evans 30397.

EVENINGS AT HOME; Or, The Juvenile Budget Opened. *See* Aikin, John & Barbauld, Mrs. Anna Letitia (Aikin), no. **25.1**.

373.1 EVENING RECREATIONS; A Collection Of Original Stories, Written By A Lady, For The Amusement Of Her Young Friends. New-York: Printed For T. B. Jansen & Co. Booksellers, No. 248, Pearl-Street. 1802.

fr.[ii], t.[1], [2–3], 4–144 p.; 8 pl. including the front. title page vignette and tailpieces; title page 13.5 cm.; 3 pl. signed *Anderson*; 1 pl. *Anderson F.*; 1. pl. *Anderson S.*; 2 pl. *A.* [Alexander Anderson].

MWA-T*; PP.

373.2 ——— New-York: Printed For T. B. Jansen & Co. Booksellers, No. 248 Pearl-Street. 1802.

fr.[ii], t.[1], [2–3], 4–31 p.; title page vignette, and tailpieces; 13.5 cm.; marbled paper covers. The text is the same as no. **373.1**, but the plates are wanting and all after p. 31 is omitted.

PP*.

373.3 ——— Keene, N. H. Printed By John Prentiss, And Sold At His Book-Store. 1809.

t.[1], [2–3], 4–144 p.; 13 cm.; bound in blue marbled paper over bds., leather spine.

OClWHi*; DLC (rebound, i. st. on t.[1]); MB; Shaw 17467.

374 EVENING TALES; Consisting Of Miscellaneous Pieces. For The Amusement And Instruction Of Children. Extracted From The Works Of Mrs. Barbauld And Mr. Aiken. Philadelphia: Printed by W. Young, No. 53 South Second the Corner of Chesnut-street. M,DCC,XCV. Price 18¼ Cents.

t.[1], [2–3], 4–160 p.; 10.5 cm.

See also Barbauld, Anna Letitia, no. **59**.

PPL*; Evans 47357.

375 EVENING TALES; Or Amusements For Youth. Published By Johnson & Warner, And Sold At

Their Bookstores, Philadelphia, And Richmond, Virginia. A. Fagan, Printer. 1813.

fr.[2], t.[3], [4–5], 6–70 p.; illus.; 14 cm.; pr. & illus. pink paper covers.

MWA*; MH; NNC-LS; NNC-Pl; Shaw 28460.

EYTON, JOHN
376 (No. 9) ACCOUNT OF HANNAH BEECH. By The Rev. John Eyton, A.M. Rector of Eyton and Vicar of Wellington, Salop. Published By The Philadelphia Female Tract Society. [caption title]. Printed by Lydia R. Bailey, No. 10, North Alley, Philad. [1816] [colophon p. 12].

[1], 2–12 p.; 14 cm.

MWA* (bound with other tracts with which *The First Annual Report Of The Philadelphia Female Tract Society For the Year 1816* was originally bound); Shaw 37553.

F

377 THE FABLE OF THE BEAR AND BEES, In Hieroglyphics. For The Amusement Of Children. Hartford: Sold By Cooke And Hale. < Copyright secured. > [1816].

t.[1], 2–16 p.; illus.; 6 cm. Oliver D. Cooke and Horatio G. Hale were as a booksellers firm in Hartford only from 1816–1819. (MWA cat.). MWA-W° (covers wanting).

FABLES ANCIENT AND MODERN. Adopted For The Use Of Children. By Edward Baldwin Esq. *See* Godwin, William, no. **456.1.**

378 FABLES FOR CHILDREN. Ornamented With Cuts. With Select Pieces In Prose And Verse. Published And Sold By Thomas & Whipple, Newburyport, — And Henry Whipple, Salem, Mass. 1814.

fr.[2], t.[3], [4–5], 6–35 p.; illus.; 14.5 cm.; pr. paper covers. Both covers have lists of books for sale. NB° CtHi (fr.[2], p. 35 & covers wanting); MB; MSaE.

379 FABLES, MORAL AND ENTERTAINING, Illustrated With Cuts. Philadelphia: Published By Jacob Johnson, No. 147, Market Street. 1807.

t.[1], [2–3], 4–48 p.; illus.; 16 cm.; yellow paper covers; colophon p. 48: Robert Bailey, Printer, No. 84, Crown Street. *See* no. **872** for the same book with a different title. MWA-W° (top of title page above the vignette torn away).

380 FABLES WITH INSTRUCTIVE APPLICATIONS. Embellished With Cuts. Printed and sold by Hosea Sprague, No. 88 Newbury-Street, Boston. 1807.

fr.[2], t.[3], [4–5], 6–21, [22, bl.], [23, adv. of The Bible In Miniature] p.; illus.; 11 cm.; blue marbled paper covers. MWA-W°.

THE FACTORY GIRL. *See* Savage, Sarah, no. **1164.**

381 THE FAIRING: Or, A Golden Toy For Children Of All Sizes And Denominations. In which they may see all the fun of the Fair, And at home be happy as if they were there. Adorned With A Variety Of Cuts From Original Drawings. The First Worcester Edition. Printed at Worcester, Massachusetts, By Isaiah Thomas. Sold at his Bookstore. MDCCLXXXVIII.

t.[1], [2], 3–86, [87–90] p.; illus.; t.[1] 10 cm.; p. 71–73, A New Love Song. There was a little Man, Who Wooed a little Maid. English ed. London: adv. by John Newbery, 1764, for 2d. in *A Present and Useful Companion to the Church of England, Or . . . Exposition Of The Book Of Common Prayer.* MWA° (rebound, fr.[ii] and all after p.[90] wanting; p. [87–90] are dog-eared or mut. so that the pagination is wanting); Evans 21079.

THE FAKENHAM GHOST. *See* Bloomfield, Robert, no. **105.**

THE FALL OF ADAM. *See* Cheap Repository, no. **169.19.**

382 THE FALL OF ADAM. Philadelphia: Printed For Johnson & Warner, No. 147, Market-Street. 1811.

t.[1], [2–3], 4–103 p.; title vignette only illus.; 14.5 cm.; bound in pr. blue-gray paper over bds. Cover title: The Fall Of Adam, To Which Is Added The Book Of The Martyrs. An Account of Holy Men Who Died For The Christian Religion. Philadelphia: Published By Johnson And Warner, No. 147, Market Street. 1811. Contents: The Fall of Adam; p. [3]–23; Book Of Martyrs, p. 24–34; The Martyr's Hymn, p. 35–36; The History Of Mr. Fantom, p. [37]–68; The Last Words, Confession, and Dying Speech Of William Wilson, p. [69]–72; The Troubles Of Life, p. [73]–103. MWA° (p. 101–102 mut. affecting the last 6 lines on each page); MB (per. st. on t.[1]); Shaw 22799.

FALSE ALARMS; Or The Mischievous Doctrine Of Ghosts And Apparitions. *See* Johnson, Richard, no. **671.1.**

383.1 FALSE STORIES CORRECTED. [1 line quot.] New-York: Printed And Sold By S. Wood, At the

Juvenile Book-Store, No. 357, Pearl-street. 1813.
  t.[1], [2–3], 4–44, [45, adv.] p.; illus.; 12 cm.;
  pr. & illus. yellow paper covers; cover dated
  1812.
  NHi*.

383.2 ——— [2 line quot.] New-York: Printed
And Sold By Samuel Wood, At The Juvenile
Book-Store, No. 357, Pearl-Street. 1814.
  t.[1], [2–3], 4–44, [45, adv.] p.; illus.; 13 cm.
  OChRHi*; CtY (bound with other books); PP
  (bound with other books); Shaw 31450.

383.3 ——— New-York: Printed And Sold By
S. Wood & Sons, At The Juvenile Book-Store, No.
357, Pearl-Street. 1815.
  t.[1], [2–3], 4–41, [42, adv.] p.; illus.; 12 cm.;
  pr. & illus. yellowish-buff paper covers; cover
  title undated. Adv. by S. Wood & Sons, 1816
  in **1188.7**.
  MWA*; PP; Shaw 34670.

383.4 ——— [cut] "Learn To Unlearn What
You Have Learned Amiss." New-York: Printed
And Sold By S. Wood & Sons, At The Juvenile
Book-Store, No. 357, Pearl-Street. 1817.
  t.[1], [2–3], 4–41, [42, adv.] p.; illus.; 12.5 cm.;
  pr. & illus. yellow paper covers.
  MWA-W*; OClWHi; Shaw 40790.

383.5 ——— Nerv-York [*sic. i.e.* New-York]:
Published By Samuel Wood & Sons, No. 261,
Pearl-Street; And Samuel S. Wood & Co. No. 212,
Market-st. Baltimore. 1819.
  t.[1], [2–3], 4–41, [42, adv.] p.; illus.; 12.5 cm.;
  pr. & illus. buff paper covers.
  MWA-W*; MB.

384 A Familiar Description Of Beasts, With
A Picture Of Each. Published for the Instruction
of Youth. Boston: Printed By Lincoln & Edmands.
And sold at their Bookstore, No. 53, Cornhill.
1813.
  t.[1], [2–3], 4–16 p.; illus.; 14 cm.; pr. & illus.
  blue paper covers. The text illus. are the same
  as those used by Samuel Hall in Boston in *Pictures Of Seventy-Two Beasts & Birds*. 1796, no.
  997.
  Cover title: History Of Beasts. Printed by Lincoln & Edmands, Who publish and have for

sale at their Bookstore, No. 53 Cornhill, a great
variety of Instructive and entertaining Books
for Youth.
  MWA*; Shaw 28476.

385 A Familiar Description Of Beasts and
Birds, With A Picture Of Each. Published for the
Instruction of Youth. Boston: Printed By Lincoln
& Edmands. And sold at their Bookstore, No. 53
Cornhill. 1813.
  fr.[2], t.[3], [4–5], 6–71 p.; illus.; 14 cm.; pr. &
  illus. purplish-gray paper covers; illus. the same
  as those used by S. Hall, 1796 in no. 997.
  Cover title: History Of Beasts & Birds. ———
  [same imprint as on cover title of no. **384**].
  MWA*; CSmH (blue marbled paper covers);
  DLC (fr.[2], p. 69–71, & original covers wanting; covers on the book belong to another book
  with a picture of Lincoln & Edmands' Bible
  Warehouse pasted on the inside of the back
  cover, front cover dated 181[?]; title mostly
  wanting); Shaw 28477.

386 A Familiar Description Of Birds, with a
Picture of Each. Published for the Instruction of
Youth. Boston: Printed by Lincoln & Edmands
and Sold at their Bookstore. 1813.
  16 p.; illus.; 14.5 cm.; pr. & illus. paper covers.
  PP*.

387 A Familiar Description Of Horses. Embellished with Coloured Engravings. Philadelphia:
Published By E. And R. Parker, No. 178, Market
Street. J. R. A. Skerrett, Printer. Price coloured,
12 cts.—Plain, 6 cts. 1819.
  fr.[2], t.[3], 4–30, [31, illus.] p.; 8 engr. illus.
  including front. 8.5 cm.; pr. & illus. buff paper
  covers.
  Cover title: A Description Of Horses.
  PP*.

388 (No. 18.) Familiar Dialogues. Published
By The Philadelphia Female Tract Society. [cap-
tion title]. Printed by Lydia R. Bailey, No. 10,
North Alley, Philad. [1817] [colophon p. 8].
  [1], 2–8 p.; 14 cm.
  MWA* (bound with other tracts with which
  *The Second Annual Report of The Philadelphia
  Female Tract Society For The Year 1817* was
  originally bound); Shaw 40791.

FAMILIAR DIALOGUES For The Instruction And Amusement Of Children Of Four And Five Years Old. *See* Kilner, Mary Ann, no. **734.1.**

FAMILIAR DIALOGUES For The Instruction And Amusement Of Little Children From Four To Five Years Old. *See* Kilner, Mary Ann, no. **734.3.**

389.1 FAMILIAR LESSONS For Children, Intended As An Early Introduction To Useful Knowledge. [2 lines of quot.] Philadelphia: Published By Jacob Johnson, Market-street. 1804.
    t.[i], [ii–iii], vi [*sic. i.e.* iv], v–vi, [7–8], 9–48 p.; illus.; 16 cm.; blue marbled paper covers; p. 35 correctly numbered; illus. p. vi signed *W. R. sc* [William Ralph]; colophon p. 48: T. S. Manning, Printer, No. 143, N. Third Street, Philadelphia.
    English ed. London: Darton And Harvey, 1806, with different illus. from no. **389.1.**
    MWA° (p. 23–28 mut.); RPB; Shaw 6278.

389.2 ———— Knowledge. Adorned With Cuts. Sidney's Press. New-Haven. 1815.
    fr.[2], t.[3], [4–5], 6–30, [31, adv.] p.; illus.; 10.5 cm.; illus. yellow-buff paper covers.
    MWA-T; (not in Shaw).

389.3 ———— Philadelphia: Published By Benjamin Warner, High Street. 1816.
    t.[i], [ii–iii], iv–vi, [7–8], 9–48 p.; illus.; 15.5 cm.; the "5" of page "35" not struck; colophon p. 48: Greggs & Co Printers, Whitehall. A reprint of J. Johnson's 1804 ed., no. **389.1,** with same engr. illus.
    MWA° (original covers wanting); MSaE.

390 A FAMILY BOOK, For Children. Containing Part I. The New Testament History of our Lord Jesus And His Apostles; With A Number Of Hymns, By Dr. Watts; Rules And An Admonition To Good Behavior In Children. Hartford: Printed By John Babcock. 1799.
    t.[1], [2–3], 4–48, 2nd t.[49], [50–51], 52–120 p.; illus.; 13.5 cm.; bound in leather.
    2nd title: A Family Book For Children. Containing Part 2. Dr. Watt's Divine and Moral Songs; With a number of Hymns, by other authors. The Shorter Catechism; Dr Watt's Catechism For Little Children, And His Second Catechism For Youth; Morning And Evening

Prayers, &c. Hartford: Printed By John Babcock. 1799.
    MWA° (p. 119–120 mut.); RPB; RPJCB (covers wanting, p. 3–4 mut.); Evans 35458.

THE FAMILY BOOK, Or Children's Journal. *See* Berquin, Arnaud, no. **73.**

THE FAMOUS TOMMY THUMB'S LITTLE STORY BOOK. *See* Tommy Thumb, no. **1320.1.**

391 THE FARM, OR A PICTURE OF INDUSTRY. Philadelphia: adv. by Benjamin Johnson, 1813 in **899.1.**

392 THE FATAL MISTAKE: To which are added, Sophia Lefevre, Or the Poor Blind Girl; Edmund And Maria, Or the Peaceful Villa; The Triumphs Of Sincerity, A Moral Tale, &c. &c. The subjects interesting—The Style engaging. Hartford; Printed By John Babcock. 1801.
    t.[1], [2–3], 4–72 p.; 12.5 cm.
    MWA° (covers wanting).

393 A FATHER'S ADVICE TO HIS CHILD; Or The Maiden's Best Adorning. Exeter [N.H.]: Printed by Henry Ranlet. 1792.
    t.[1], [2–3], 4–8 p.; 14 cm.; verse.
    PP°; Evans 24310.

394 THE FATHER'S GIFT; Containing An Interesting Description Of One Hundred And Eight Objects. With Plates. Philadelphia: Published By Jacob Johnson, No. 147, Market-street. J. Rakestraw, Printer. 1804.
    t.[1], [2–3], 4–72 p.; 108 woodcuts on XVIII engraved plates; 15 cm.; bound in marbled paper over bds. The plates are the same as pl. XXXVIII–LIV in no. **909,** except for the numbering of the plates and cut illustrations. For English ed. of the plates *see* no. **909.**
    CtY° (pl. II. mut.); DLC; NN; PP; Shaw 6288.

395.1 THE FATHER'S GIFT: Or, the Way to be Wise And Happy. Worcester (Massachusetts) Printed By Isaiah Thomas, And Sold At His Book-Store, MDCCLXXXVI: Where may be had a variety of little Books for Children.
    fr.[2], t.[3], [4–5], 6–30, [31, adv. of books] p.; illus.; 10 cm.; Dutch paper covers.
    English ed. London: adv. by F. Newbery in *The Cries Of London,* 1775.
    MWA°; Evans 19641.

395.2 ——— Philadelphia: adv. by F. Bailey, 1792 in **359** and 1793 in **773.1.**

395.3 ——— Boston: [Print]ed and sold by Samuel Hall. [No. 53,] Cornhill. 1794.

fr.[2], t.[3], [4–5], 6–30, [31, adv. list of books] p.; illus.; 10.5 cm.; Dutch paper covers. There are two large M's $\begin{smallmatrix} M \\ M \end{smallmatrix}$ on the recto of the front.; the title page has a printer's ornament of a crown with an angel's head below it; on p. 26 there is a row of 7 angels' heads. Adv. by S. Hall, [1789?] in **568.2**; and 1791 in **408.3.** Advertisement caption p.[31] same as that on p. [29], no. **408.4.**

CtHi°; Evans 47040.

395.4 ——— Philadelphia: adv. by William Young, 1794 in **305.**

395.5 ——— Third Worcester Edition. Printed at Worcester Massachusetts, By Isaiah Thomas. Sold wholesale and Retail in his Bookstore. MDCC-XCIV.

fr.[2], t.[3], [4–5], 6–30 p.; illus.; 10 cm.; illus. paper covers.

MWA° (p. 17–18, 25–31, & rear cover wanting, p. 9–12 mut.); Evans 47041.

395.6 ——— Boston: adv. by John Folsom, 1798 in **672.1.**

395.7 ——— Hartford: adv. by Lincoln and Gleason, 1803 in **673.20.**

395.8 ——— Hallowell, (Maine) Published by Ezekiel Goodale. N. Cheever, Printer. 1809.

fr.[2], t.[3], [4–5], 6–30, [31, adv.] p.; illus.; 10.5 cm.; pr. & illus. blue paper covers.

MWA-W°; MWA; PP; Shaw 17491.

396 FELIX, THE WOODCUTTER, Or Good And Evil. A Moral Tale For Youth. [1 line quot.] Boston: Published By Thomas B. Wait And Co. And Charles Williams. 1812.

fr.[4], t.[5], [6–7], 8–34 p.; illus.; 14 cm.; pr. green paper covers.

Welch°; CLU; MWA; MHi; Shaw 25414.

[FENN, *Lady* ELEANOR (FRERE)] 1743–1813

397 [—] COBWEBS TO CATCH FLIES. In Two Parts. Philadelphia: adv. by Johnson & Warner, 1813 in **430.2** and 1814 in **430.3.**

English ed. London: [1783]; adv. by J. Marshall as written by Mrs. Teachwell in M. A. Kilner's *A Course of Lectures For Sunday Evenings.* [1783].

398 [—] FABLES, by Mrs. Teachwell. . . . Hallowell [Me.] Pr. by N. Cheever, For Ezekiel Goodale, 1809.

English ed. London: John Marshall, [1783].

31 p.

Shaw 17579.

399 [—] FABLES IN MONOSYLLABLES By Mrs. Teachwell, To Which Are Added Morals In Dialogues Between A Mother and Children. [six lines of verse] Rousseau. Philadelphia: Printed For Thomas Dobson, At The Stone House No. 41, South Second Street. 1798.

fr.[ii], t.[iii], [iv, bl.], v–xiv, 15–60, [i. bl.], fr.[ii], 2nd t.[iii], [iv, bl.], v–viii, [ix–x], 11–39 p.; 2 front. only illus.; 17 cm.; yellow and gold Dutch paper covers.

The 2nd title: Morals To A Set Of Fables, By Mrs. Teachwell, The Morals In Dialogues Between A Mother And Children. In Two Sets. Philadelphia: Printed For Thomas Dobson, At The Stone No. 41, South Second Street. 1798.

Lady Fenn wrote her children's books for her nieces and nephews. Most of them were published anonymously or under the pseudonyms of Mrs. Teachwell, Mrs. Lovechild, or Solomon Lovechild.

English ed. London: adv. by J. Marshall as written by Mrs. Teachwell in M. A. Kilner's *A Course Of Lectures For Sunday Evenings.* [1783].

MWA°; DLC (p. v–viii, 39, of *Morals To A Set Of Fables* wanting); Evans 33728.

400 [—] JUVENILE CORRESPONDENCE; Or, Letters, Suited To Children, From Four To Above Ten Years Of Age. In Three Sets. New-Haven: Printed By Abel Morse. M.DCC.XCI.

t.[iii], [iv–v], vi, 7 [*sic. i.e.* vii], viii, [9–12], 13–106 p.; 14 cm.; Dutch paper covers.

English ed. London: adv. by John Marshall in M. A. Kilner's *A Course Of Lectures For Sunday Evenings.* [1783].

CtHi°; Evans 23479.

401.1 [—] RATIONAL SPORTS In Dialogues Passing Among Children Of A Family. Designed As A Hint To Mothers How They May Inform The Minds Of Their Little People Respecting The Objects With Which They are Surrounded. Boston: Published By Cummings And Hilliard, No. 1, Cornhill. 1814.

t.[i], [ii–iii], iv–x, [11–13], 14–70, [71] p.; 14 cm.; gray paper covers; p.[ii]: Andover, Flagg And Gould, Printers.

English ed. London: adv. by J. Marshall in M. A. Kilner's *A Course Of Lectures For Sunday Evenings.* [1783].

MWA°; CtHi; CtY; MHi; NRU; PP; Shaw 32609.

401.2 [—] —— Sidney's Press. Published by John Babcock & Son, New-Haven, S. & W. R. Babcock, No. 163 King-Street, Charleston, and M'Carty & Davis, Philadelphia. 1820.

fr.[2], t.[3], [4–5], 6–31 p.; front. only illus.; 14.5 cm.; pr. & illus. pink paper covers.

MWA-W°; CtHi; DLC; MWA; NN (fr.[2], p. 31 & covers wanting); Shoemaker 2940.

402 [—] REMARKS ON A SET OF CUTS FOR CHILDREN. [4 lines of verse] Philadelphia: Published By Johnson & Warner, No. 147, Market-Street. 1809.

t.[1], [2–3], 4–69, [70, full page illus. numbered XVII]+ p.; 17 pl. illus. no. I–XVII; 15 cm.; bound in blue marbled paper over bds. The book consists of Part I. of the first American edition of 1803, no. **908**, with the plates or "doucers" marked I–XVII, used for illustrations. English ed. title 4: *The Mother's Remarks On A Set Of Cuts For Children.* Part I. [II.] London: Darton and Harvey, 1799. The copy wanting a title page described under no. **909**, English title 3, surely consists of the plates or "doucers" bound in one volume which formerly accompanied the two volumes of this book. The plates are numbered I–LVI and have 6 cuts on each plate which are consecutively numbered 1–336. Signatures A₁, B₁, [C₁], D₁, E₁, F₁ or plates I, XVII, XXV, XXXIII, XLI, XLIX are signed *Willm Darton & Josh^. Harvey, London Decr. 31, 1799.*

FENNELL, JAMES 1766–1816
403 A NEW YEAR'S GIFT; Presented To The Youth Of Both Sexes. By James Fennell. Boston:

Published by John West And Co. No. 75, Cornhill. 1810. E. G. House. Printer.

t.[1], [2–3], 4–72 p.; 12 cm.; pr. blue-gray paper covers. Cover title imprint: Published by West & Richardson, No. 75, Cornhill. 1812.

MB; Shaw 20106.

FENWICK, ELIZA
404 —— INFANTINE STORIES; In Words Of One, Two, And Three Syllables. By E. Fenwick. Illustrated with engravings. Boston: Published By Munroe & Francis, No. 4, Cornhill, (Corner of Water-street;) And David Francis, No. 90, Newbury-Street, (Five doors north of Boylston Market.) 1818.

fr.[ii], t.[1], [2–3], 4–102 p.; front. only illus.; 14 cm.; pr. & illus. yellow paper covers; duplicate front cover & front. signed *AB* [Abel Bowen].

English ed. London: Tabart and Co. 1810.

NNC-Pl°; Shaw 44032.

405 THE FERRY; A Tale For Young Persons, Showing That Humanity To Our Fellow Creatures Is The Sure Road To Happiness. Philadelphia: Published By E. And R. Parker, No. 178, Market Street. J. R. A. Skerrett, Printer. 1818.

½t.[i], [ii, bl.], [1, bl.], fr.[2], t.[3], [4–5], 6–70, [71, adv.] p.; 6 pl. including front.; 13 cm.; pr. purplish-buff paper covers.

MSaE° (col. pl.).

FIELDING, HENRY 1707–1754
406.1 —— THE HISTORY OF TOM JONES, A Foundling. By Henry Fielding, Esq. Norwich, (Connecticut) Printed And Sold By Ebenezer Bushnell. M.DCC.XCI.

t.[i], [ii], [1], 2–194 p.; 12 cm.

English ed. London: adv. by F. Newbery in *The History Of Pamela.* 1769.

CtHi° (covers wanting, p. 125–126 mut.); Evans 46167.

406.2 —— —— A Foundling. By Henry Fielding (Abridged For The Young.) Norwich, Connecticut: Printed by John Trumbull. 1791.

pp. 194; 14 cm.

Evans 23371 (no location).

406.3 —— —— A Foundling. Abridged from the Works of Henry Fielding, Esq. Adorned With Cuts. Boston: Printed and sold by S. Hall, in Cornhill. 1797.

fr.[ii], t.[1], [2–5], 6–131 p.; 6 pl. including front.; 13.5 cm.; bound in marbled paper over w. bds.

MWA°; CtHi; DeWint; MB (bpl. on fr.[ii], emb. st. on t.[1]); NjP; Evans 32128; Hamilton 172.

407 [—] THE HUMOROUS HISTORY OF TOM JONES, A Foundling: Containing An Account Of The Benevolent Mr. Allworthy; And The Fox-Hunting Squire Western, &c. &c. Interspersed with many curious Love-Particulars Between Mr. Jones, And The Beautiful Miss Sophia Western. The whole comprehending such entertaining scenes, both in high and low life, as are seldom met with in any history of the kind. Printed For And Sold By F. Lucas.—Baltimore. 1813.

408.1 [—] THE REMARKABLE HISTORY OF TOM JONES, A Foundling. The First Worcester Edition. Printed At Worcester, Massachusetts, By Isaiah Thomas, And Sold At His Book Store., MDCC-LXXXVII.

fr.[2], t.[3], [4–5], 6–31 p.; illus.; 10 cm.; Dutch paper covers.

MWA°; Evans 20356.

408.2 [—] [————] [1789?].

fr.[2], [5], 6–24, [29] p.; illus.; 9.5 cm.; scalloped marbled paper covers. This fragment, lacking a title page, has illustrations which are crude versions of those which appear in I. Thomas' edition of *The Remarkable History Of Tom Jones Worcester, 1787*, no. **408.1**, and Samuel Hall's edition of 1791, no. **408.3**. The figures in this fragment are thicker than in I. Thomas' 1787 edition. The frontispiece, Mr. Allworthy, talking to Mrs. Deborah Wilkins, in the 1787 edition measures 3.4 cm. by 7 mm. while in the fragmentary copy he is 3.5 cm. by 1 cm. This book copies the 1787 edition by having a rule under each page number. In the 1787 ed. the rule is 9 mm. long, in **408.2** it is 12 mm. long.

MWA-W° (t.[3], p. [4], [25–28] wanting).

408.3 [—] ———— A Foundling. Boston: Printed and sold by Samuel Hall, No. 53, Cornhill. 1791.
fr.[2], t.[3], [4–5], 6–28, [29–31, adv. list of books] p.; illus.; 10 cm.; Dutch paper covers. Advertisement caption p. [29]: *A great Variety of BOOKS,/well calculated for Instruction and*

A-/musement, and suited to Children of all/ Ages and Capacities, are constantly/kept for Sale by S. Hall, No. 53,/Cornhill, Boston; among which are the/following, viz. Adv. by S. Hall, 1792 in **1408.33**.

MWA° (p.[31] & rear cover wanting); N; Evans 46166.

408.4 [—] ———— Boston: Printed and sold by Samuel Hall, No. 53, Cornhill. 1794.
t.[3], [4–5], 6–28, [29–30, adv. list of books] p. illus.; 10 cm.; p. [5] has a crown, 4 angel's heads and other printer's ornaments above the caption title. Advertisement caption p. [29]: *A great Variety of BOOKS,/ designed for Instruction and Amusement,/and suited to Children of all Ages and/Capacities, are constantly kept for Sale/by* S. HALL, *No. 53, Cornhill, Boston;/among which are the following, viz.*
Evans 47042.

408.5 [—] ———— The Third Worcester Edition. Printed at Worcester, Massachusetts, By Isaiah Thomas. Sold Wholesale and Retail at his Bookstore. MDCCXCIV.
fr.[2], t.[3], [4–5], 6–31 p.; illus.; 10 cm.; Dutch paper covers.
MWA°, Ct; Evans 47043.

408.6 [—] ———— Boston: Printed and sold by S. Hall, No. 53, Cornhill. 1798.
fr.[2], t.[3], [4–5], 6–28, [29–31, adv. list of books] p.; illus.; 10 cm.; violet & green Dutch paper covers. Advertisement caption p. [29]: *A great Variety of BOOKS,/suited to Children of all Ages and/Capacities, are constantly kept for/Sale by* S. HALL *No. 53, Corn-/hill, Boston; among which are the/following viz.—/.* This advertisement caption is different from that in no. **673.13**. This is the only year in which S. Hall used different advertisement captions in his 10 cm. books.
MHi°; Evans 48423.

408.7 [—] ———— Salem [Mass.]: Printed and sold by N. & J. Coverly, Faust's Statue, Essex Street. 1799.
fr.[2], t.[3], [4–5], 6–29 p.; front. only illus.; 10 cm.; pink paper covers.
PP° (p. 29 mut.); MSaE; Evans 35481.

408.8 [—] ——— Salem [Mass.]: Printed and sold by N. & J. Coverly, Faust's Head. Essex treet [*sic. i.e.* street]. 1799.

　　t.[3], [4–5], 6–29 p.; 10 cm.
　　MWA-W* (fr.[2] & covers wanting).

408.9 [—] ——— Salem, [Mass.]: Printed and sold at Faust's Head, Essex Street. 1799.

　　fr.[2], t.[3], [4–5], 6–29 p.; front. only illus.; 10 cm.; ornamented brown paper covers.
　　MWA*; Evans 36198.

408.10 [—] ——— The Fourth Worcester Edition. Printed at Worcester, Massachusetts. By Isaiah Thomas, Jun. Sold Wholesale and Retail by Him, 1799.

　　fr.[2], t.[3], [4–5], 6–28, [29–30, adv. list of books], [31, 2 oval cuts] p.; illus.; 10.5 cm.; orange and silver Dutch paper covers.
　　MWA-W*; Evans 35482.

408.11 [—] ——— A Foundling. To Which Is Added, Beneficence Exemplified. Ornamented with Cuts. Hartford: Printed by Lincoln & Gleason. 1803.

　　fr.[2], t.[3], [4–5], 6–31 p.; illus.; 10.5 cm.
　　CtHi* (covers wanting); MWA-W (fr.[2], p. 31 & covers wanting).

408.12 [—] ——— Hartford: Printed By Lincoln & Gleason. 1806.

　　fr.[2], t.[3], [4–5], 6–31 p.; illus.; 10 cm.; green Dutch paper covers.
　　MWA*; CtHi; Shaw 10412.

408.13 [—] ——— Hartford: adv. by Peter B. Gleason, 1811 in **1133.2**.

FIELDING, SARAH 1710–1768

409 [—] The Governess: Or, Little Female Academy. Being The History of Mrs Teachum, And Her Nine Girls. With Their Nine Days Amusement. Calculated For The Entertainment and Instruction of Young Ladies in their Education. By The Author of David Simple. A New Edition. [13 lines of quot.] Shakesp. Midsummer Night's-Dream. Philadelphia: Printed By T. Dobson, At The Stone House, No 41 Second-Street. M,DCC,XCI.

　　t.[i], [ii–iii], iv–xii, [1], 2–228 p.; 12.5 cm.; bound in leather.

English ed. London: Printed for the Author, Sold by A. Millar, 1749.
　　MWA*; MH; NjR; PP; PPL; Evans 23372.

410 [—] The Story Of The Cruel Giant Barbarico, The good Giant Benefico, And the little Pretty Dwarf Mignon. Boston: Printed by Mein and Fleeming, and to be sold by John Mein at the London Book-Store, North-side of King-street. MDCCLXVIII. At which Place may be had, A great variety of Entertaining and Instructive Books for Children.

　　t.[1], [2–3], 4–53, [54, adv.] p.; 11 cm.; paper covers. This is the first fairy story in Sarah Fielding's *The Governess*.
　　MHi*; MB (top of title page cropped, affecting the word *The;* per. st. on t.[1]); NN (p. 19–36 wanting; t.[1] mut.; gray paper covers); Evans 11082.

411 Filial Intrepidity, A Real Incident. Boston: adv. by Lincoln & Edmands, 1819 in **1170**.

412.1 The Fire: Or, Never Despair. Philadelphia: Published By B. and T. Kite, No. 20 North Third Street, J. Bouvier, Printer. 1810.

　　fr.[ii], t.[1], [2–3], 4–32 p.; 3 pl. including the front.; 12.5 cm.
　　English ed. London: W. Darton & F. Harvey, 1808.
　　MWA* (3 pl. and covers wanting); MWA-T* (title page and covers wanting); Shaw 20116.

412.2 ——— Despair. With The History And Adventures Of a Cat. From Sidney's Press, For I. Cooke & Co. New-Haven. 1812.

　　fr.[2], t.[3], [4–5], 6–47 p.; illus.; 11 cm.; pr. & illus. violet paper covers.
　　CtY* (fr.[2], p. 47 and covers wanting); CtHi; MWA-T (covers mut.); PPL; Shaw 25426.

Fire-Side Amusement. *See* Puzzlebrain, Jeffrey (*pseud.*), no. **1082.1**.

The Fisherman. *See* Sandham, Elizabeth, no. **1150**.

First Lessons For Children. *See* Dobson, T., no. **292.1**.

The Fishes Grand Gala. *See* Cockle, Mrs., no. **217**.

[FITZ, DANIEL] 1795–1869?

413.1   [—] ORIGINAL TALES; Never Before Published. Designed As A New-Year's Gift For The Year 1813. [10 lines of verse.] Boston: Published By Charles Callender, No. 11 Marlborough-Street. Jan. 1, 1813.

> t.[1], [2–5], 6–104 p.; 15 cm.; bound in pr. green paper over w. bds.
> MWA°; DLC; Shaw 28511 and 29423.

413.2   [—] ORIGINAL TALES; Written For The Improvement Of Youth. [5 lines of verse.] Second Edition. Boston: Published By Charles Callender, No. 11 Marlboro' Street. 1814.

> t.[1], [2–7] 8–107 p.; t.[1] 14.5 cm.; colophon p. 107: Watson & Bangs, Printers, No. 7, State-Street, Boston. On the title page of MWA copy is a holograph inscription *By Daniel Fitz, Teacher of youth.* This inscription is signed *J. D. Ross.*
> MWA° (rebound); Shaw 32413.

414.1   FLORA'S GALA. Illustrated With Elegant Engravings. [4 lines of verse]. Darwin's Botanic Garden. Philadelphia: Published And Sold By B. C. Buzby, At His Juvenile Book Store, No. 2, North Third Street. 1809.

> fr.[ii], t.[1], [2–3], 4–16, [pl. opp. p. 16]; p.; 6 pl. including front.; 12.5 cm.; pr. & illus. paper covers; front. numbered p. 10, those opp. p. 10, 12, 14, 16 are marked p. *10, 12, 14, 16*; colophon p. 16: Joseph Rakestraw, printer.
> English ed. London: J. Harris, 1808.
> MWA° (pl. opp. p. 13 wanting).

414.2   ——— Philadelphia: Published and Sold wholesale by Wm. Charles, and may be had of all Booksellers. 1809. W. M'Culloch, Printer.

> fr.[ii], t.[1], [2–3], 4–16 [pl. opp. p. 16] p.; 6 plates including front.; 12.5 cm.; pr. buff paper covers. The pl. are the same as in no. 414.1. The text shows variations in type set up, and lacks a colophon. Front. numbered "Pa 10", those opposite p. 10, 12, 13, 14, 16 are marked *Pa. 10, 12, 13, 14, 16.*
> MWA-W°; NNC-Pl (6 pl.); PP (5 pl).

415   FOOD FOR THE MIND: Or, A New Riddle Book. Compiled for the Use of The Great and the Little Good Boys And Girls In America. [2 lines quot.] Homer. The First Worcester Edition. Printed at Worcester, Massachusetts By Isaiah Thomas. Sold Wholesale and Retail at his Bookstore. MDCCXCIV.

> fr.[2], t.[3], [4–5], 6–31 p.; illus.; 10 cm.; green & gold Dutch paper covers. On the title page of the MWA copy the word "First" of "First Worcester Edition" is crossed out and *2d* written above it. This holograph correction according to Nichols is "in handwriting of Isaiah Thomas." No earlier edition has been located even in an advertisement.
> *See* also Food For The Mind, no. **666.**
> English ed. London: 2nd ed. adv. by J. Newbery 1758.
> MWA°; NN-C (fr.[2], p. 31 and covers, wanting); PP; Evans 26985.

416.1   FOOTSTEPS To THE NATURAL HISTORY OF BEASTS. Philadelphia: Published By Jacob Johnson, No. 147, High Street. 1804.

> t.[1], [2–3], 4–46, [47–48, adv. of 9 books] p.; illus.; 17 cm.; bound in marbled paper over bds.; most of the illus. signed *A* [Alexander Anderson].
> English ed. London, entitled: *Footsteps To The Natural History Of Beasts And Birds.* Part I. Darton And Harvey, 1804.
> MWA°; Shaw 6316.

416.2   ——— Baltimore: Printed By Warner And Hanna, And Sold By Them And John Vance & Co. 1807.

> t.[1], [2–3], 4–60 p.; 16.5 cm.; paper covers; title page vignette & illus. p. [3] signed *Gobrecht*, illus. p. 6, 20, 33 signed *G* [Christian Gobrecht]. *See* also no. **655.**
> MdHi°; MH° (p. 57–60 & original covers wanting); OOxM (front cover wanting); PP; Shaw 12580.

416.3   ——— From Sidney's Press, New-Haven. 1808.

> fr.[ii], t.[1], [2–3], 4–62, [63, alphabet], p.; illus.; 10.5 cm.; pr. & illus. buff paper covers. Cover title: History Of Beasts. Published by I. Cooke & Co. N. Haven, 1809.
> MWA°; Shaw 15027.

416.4   ——— From Sidney's Press, New-Haven. 1809.

> fr.[ii], t.[1], [2–3], 4–36 p.; illus.; 13 cm.; pr. & illus. paper covers. Cover title: History Of Beasts. Published by

I. Cooke & Co. New-Haven, Book-Sellers, Stationers and Printers.
MWA*; Shaw 17520.

416.5 —— Wilmington [Del.]: Printed And Sold By J. Wilson, No. 105, Market Street. 1814.
t.[1], [2–3], 4–36 p.; illus.; 13.5 cm.; pr. & illus. blue-gray paper covers.
MWA*; DeHi; Shaw 31499.

417.1 Footsteps To The Natural History Of Birds. Philadelphia: Published By Jacob Johnson, No. 147, Market Street. 1803.
fr.[2], t.[3], [4–5], 6–48 p.; illus.; 15.5 cm.; bound in green marbled paper over bds. Printed on unusually thick paper. Woodcuts signed A [Alexander Anderson]; colophon p. 48: <M'-Laughlin Printer.>
Welch*; MWA (emb. st. on t.[3]); Shaw 4213.

417.2 —— Baltimore: Printed By Warner & Hanna, And Sold By Them And John Vance & Co. 1807.
t.[1], [2–3], 4–60 p.; illus.; 15.4 cm.; green marbled paper covers.
English ed. London, entitled: *Footsteps to The Natural History Of Beasts And Birds.* Part I.[II.] Darton And Harvey, 1806.
Welch*; MWA (i. st. on p.[3]); NjR; PP; Shaw 12581.

417.3 —— From Sidney's Press, New-Haven. 1809.
fr.[ii], t.[1], [2–3], 4–35 p.; illus.; 13.5 cm.; pr. & illus. yellow paper covers; front. signed A [Alexander Anderson].
MWA*; Shaw 17521.

418 The Force Of Example. A Poem, Illustrated With Engravings. Philadelphia: Published and sold Wm. Charles. Price Plain 18 3/8 Cents Coloured 25 Ct. 1819. [cover title].
fr.[ii], t.[1], 2–8, [pl. 8 opp. p. 8] p.; 8 engr. pl. including front.; 13.5 cm.; pr. & illus. orange paper covers; pl. 2–8 are numbered and are opp. p. 2–8.
English ed. London: B. Tarbart & Co., 1810.
NNC-Pl* (rear cover mut.; col. pl.).

The Forsaken Infant. *See* Day, Thomas, no. **266.1**.

[FOSTER, MRS. HANNAH (WEBSTER)] 1759–1840.

419 [—] The Boarding School; Or, Lessons Of A Preceptress To Her Pupils: Consisting of Information, Instruction, And Advice, Calculated to improve the Manners, and form the Character of Young Ladies. To Which Is Added, A Collection of Letters, written by the Pupils, to their Instructor, their Friends, and each other. By A Lady of Massachusetts; Author Of The Coquette. Published according to Act of Congress. Printed At Boston, By I. Thomas And E. T. Andrews. Sold by them, by C. Bingham, and other Booksellers in Boston; by I. Thomas, Worcester; by Thomas, Andrews & Penniman, Albany; and by Thomas, Andrews & Butler, Baltimore. June, 1798
fr.[ii], [2–5], 6–252 p.; 16.5 cm.; bound in leather.
Welch* (fr.[ii] wanting); CtHi; MWA; PHi; Evans 33748.

The Fortune-teller. *See* Hurlothrumbo, Dr. (*pseud.*), no. **626.1**.

The Fortune Teller. *See* More, Hannah, no. **881**.

The Foundling; Or The History of Lucius Stanhope. *See* Johnson, Richard, no. **672.1**.

420 The Four Sisters. To Which Is Added The Power Of Habit, And Other Instructive Lessons. Published By Johnson & Warner, And Sold At Their Bookstores, Philadelphia, And Richmond, Virginia. A. Fagan, Printer. 1813.
fr.[2], t.[3], [4–5], 6–71 p.; 14 cm.; pr. & illus. pink paper covers.
CtHi*; NNC-Pl; Shaw 28548.

FRANKLIN, BENJAMIN 1706–1790
421.1 [—] The Art Of Making Money Plenty. New-York: Sold By Samuel Wood, At the Juvenile Book store, No. 357, Pearl-street. [a double row of dots]. 1811. [cover title].
t.[1], [2–8] p. engr. on one side only of 8 leaves; 13 cm.; pr. & illus. pink paper covers; the words "Pearl-street" on the cover title are printed in the lower case except for the "P." These words are followed by a double row of 13 dots. Adv. by S. Wood, 1812 in **439.1**; 1813–1816 in **430.2–5**; 1819 in **1188.8**.

Title page: [Portrait of Dr Franklin] The Art of Making Money Plenty, in every Man's Pocket, By Dr. Franklin. Pub. & Sold by S. Wood, 357 Pearl St. N.Y.].
English ed. London: Darton, Harvey & Darton; And Wm. Alexander, York, 1817, with different illus.
MWA-W°.

421.2 [—] ——— New-York: Sold By Samuel Wood, At the Juvenile Book-store, No. 357, PEA[RL-]STREET. [one row of dots] 1811. [cover title].
Same as preceding but the words "PEA[RL]-STREET" in the cover title are printed in capitals and followed by a single row of dots. The word "Book-store" is hyphenated, and the cut above the imprint is of a different plant.
MWA° (bottom of t.[1] cropped, cutting off the imprint); MB; Shaw 22846.

Note: All editions of THE WAY TO WEALTH are not children's books. Nos. **422.4–8** were listed under *Juvenile Books* by S. Wood in no. **430.4** and **430.5**.

422.1 — FRANKLIN'S WAY TO WEALTH; Or, "Poor Richard improved." Philadelphia: Published By Jacob Johnson. 1808.
t.[3], [4–7], 8–53 p.; illus.; 14 cm.; p.[4] Dickinson, Printer, Whitehall [Pa.].
English ed. London: W. Darton, Jun. 1805.
RPB° (fr.[2] wanting, p. 7–8 mut.); CtY; PU; Shaw 15041.

422.2 —— ——— New York: Printed And Sold By S. Wood At The Juvenile Book-Store, No. 357, Pearl-Street, 1811.
t.[1], [2–5], 6–44 p.; illus.; 13 cm.; pr. & illus. yellow-buff paper covers.
MWA°; (not in Shaw).

422.3 —— ——— Improved." Industry leads to wealth. New-York: Printed And Sold By S. Wood, At The Juvenile Book-Store, No. 357, Pearl-Street. 1812.
t.[1], [2–5], 6–44 p.; illus.; 12.5 cm.; pr. & illus. yellow-buff paper covers.
MWA°; NHi; PP.

422.4 —— ——— New-York: Printed And Sold By S. Wood, At the Juvenile Book-Store, No. 357, Pearl-street. 1813.
t.[1], [2–5], 4–44 p.; illus.; 12.5 cm.; pr. & illus. buff paper covers.
MWA°; CtY; NN; Shaw 28556.

422.5 —— ——— New-York: Printed And Sold By Samuel Wood, At The Juvenile Book-Store, No. 357, Pearl-Street. 1814.
t.[1], [2–5], 6–44 p.; illus.; 12.5 cm.; pr. & illus. buff paper covers.
Welch°; CtY (bound with other books dated 1814, t.[1] wanting); MWA; ICU; PP; PPL; Shaw 31512.

422.6 —— ——— New-York: Printed And Sold By S. Wood & Sons, At The Juvenile Book-Store, No. 357, Pearl-Street. 1815.
t.[1], [2–5], 6–44 p.; illus.; 12.5 cm.; pr. & illus. buff paper covers, cover title undated.
Adv. by S. Wood, 1816 in **430.5**.
MWA° (3 copies varying covers; copies 1 & 2, cover title undated; copy 3, cover title dated 1814); NHi (cover title undated); Shaw 34722 and 34723.

422.7 —— ——— New-York: Printed And Sold By S. Wood & Sons, At The Juvenile Book-Store, No. 261, Pearl-Street. 1817.
t.[1], [2–5], 6–44 p.; illus.; 13 cm.; pr. yellow paper covers; cover title undated. Copy A: pr. & illus. buff paper covers with a vignette of a boy blowing soap bubbles. Copy B: a vignette of a standing negro holding a gourd in his left hand.
MWA-T° (copy A, B); MH; MWA; Shaw 40850.

422.8 —— ——— New-York: Published By Samuel Wood & Sons, No. 261, Pearl-Street; And Samuel S. Wood & Co. No. 212, Market-St Baltimore. 1820.
t.[1], [2–5], 6–44 p.; 13 cm.
MWA°; DLC (rebound, covers wanting); NN; NPV; PP (pr. & illus. buff paper covers); Shoemaker 1276; Weiss 1942.

423.1 — POOR RICHARD: OR, THE WAY TO WEALTH. By Dr. Franklin. Hartford: Printed By Lincoln & Gleason. 1803.
t.[1], [2–3], 4–30, [31, adv.] p.; 9.5 cm.;

p.[31] has adv. of Watts' *Divine Songs. attempted in easy language . . . A Variety of small books for children—New England Primers, &c.*
MWA-W° (covers wanting).

424.1 — THE WAY TO WEALTH. By Dr. Franklin. [2 lines verse] Walpole, N.H. Printed For Preston Merrifield, At The Press Of Charter & Hale. 1807.
   t.[1], [2-3], 4-34 p.; t.[1]; 13.5 cm.
   MWA° (covers wanting); PPL; Shaw 12592.

423.2 — ——— Middletown [Conn.]: Printed by Hart & Lincoln. 1814.
   t.[1], [2-3], 4-24 p.; 12 cm.
   CtHi° (covers wanting); Shaw 31511.

NOTE: The following editions of THE WAY TO WEALTH are small in size and may have been children's books although some people may consider them purely adult fare.

424.2 — Pride breakfasted with Plenty, dined with Poverty, and supped with Infamy. THE WAY TO WEALTH. By Dr. Franklin. [2 lines of verse] Montpelier, Vt. Printed For Josiah Parks, At The Press Of Walton & Goss. November, 1810.
   t.[1], [2-3], 4-31 p.; 13.5 cm.; buff paper covers.
   MWA°; CtY; DLC; MB; VtU; McCorison 1168; Shaw 20137.

424.3 — ——— Wealth; Or Poor Richard Improved. By Benjamin Franklin. Boston: Wells And Lilly, Court-Street. 1820.
   t.[1], [2-3], 4-20 p.; 16 cm.
   MH° (bound with other tracts); CtY; PP; PPL; Shoemaker 1275.

425 THE FRIAR AND BOY: Or, The Young Piper's pleasant Pastime. Containing the witty Adventures betwixt the Friar and Boy, in relation to his Step Mother, whom he fairly fitted for her unmerciful cruelty. Boston: Printed for, and Sold by A. Barclay, Second Door North of the three King's in Corn-hill. 1767. Price 6 Coppers.
   t.[1], [2], 3-24 p.; 16 cm.; p.[2] has a list of books for sale. While this typical chapbook was not written for children it was undoubtedly read by children and was the type the Puritan parents did not relish having their children read. Because of such books full of earthy, lusty, and vulgar humor, Puritan parents readily bought more moral fare for their children published in England by Thomas Boreman, Mary Cooper, John Newbery and others and so insured the success of publishers of moral childrens books.
   See also Jack The Piper, no. **662** and The Pleasant History Of The Friar And The Boy, no. **1015.**
   English ed. entitled: *The frere and the boy.* Wymkynd de Worde [*ca.* 1512].
   Evans 41710.

THE FRIEND OF YOUTH. *See* Berquin, A., tr. by Meilan, M. A., no. **74** and no. **75.**

426 THE FRIENDS; Or, The History of Billy Freeman And Tommy Truelove. Proper To Be Imitated By All Those, Who Desire To Be Good And Great. Hartford: Printed By John Babcock. 1801.
   t.[1], [2-3], 4-71 p.; illus.; 14 cm.; pink paper covers.
   English ed. London: adv. by John Marshall in *The Wisdom of Crop The Conjurer* [1787?].
   CtY° (p.[2]-4 mut.); Shaw 541.

FULLER, ANDREW 1754-1815
427 A NEW-YEAR'S GIFT FOR YOUTH. By Mr. Andrew Fuller, Kettering. Boston: Printed And Sold By Manning And Loring, No. 2, Cornhill. 1802.
   t.[1], [2-5], 6-23, [24, adv.], 2nd t.[1], [2-3], 4-12 p.; 13.5 cm.; ornamented paper covers.
   2nd title: The Dying Exercises Of Susannah Wright, Of Weekly, Near Kettering, A Child Under Twelve Years Of Age; In A Letter From Her Mother, To Mr. Andrew Fuller, Kettering. Boston: Printed And Sold By Manning And Loring, No. 2, Cornhill. 1802.
   MWA°; NNC-T; Shaw 2294.

428.1 Gaffer Goose['s] Golden Plaything; Being A New Collection Of Entertaining Fables. Intended As a Present for all those Good Girls and Boys who behave according to the following Rules: That Is, Do as they are bid, Come when they are called, and shut the Door after them. Boston: Printed and sold by John W. Folsom, No. 30, Union-Street, 1798.

t.[3], [4–5], [6], 7–28, [29], [30–31, adv. list of books] p.; illus.; 10 cm.; illus. buff rear paper cover.
English ed. London: adv. by John Marshall in *The Wisdom Of Crop The Conjurer.* [1787?].
DLC* (front cover & fr.[2] wanting, p. no. torn away from p. 6, only a trace remains of nos. 7–9); Evans 48450.

428.2 —— Exeter. Printed and Sold by Henry Ranlet. 1801.

fr.[2], t.[3], [4–5], 6–29, [30], [31, adv. of 16 books] p.; illus.; 10.5 cm.; illus. yellowish-buff paper covers.
NNC-T*.

428.3 —— Exeter [N.H.]: Printed and Sold by Norris & Sawyer. 1808.

fr.[2], t.[3], [4–5], 6–29, [30–31, adv. list of books] p.; illus.; 10 cm.; illus. buff paper covers.
MWA*; CtHi (p. 29–[30] wanting); Shaw 15082.

429 Gaping Frog. Philadelphia: adv. by E. & R. Parker, 1818 in **704.1.**

430.1 Garden Amusements, For Improving The Minds Of Little Children. Boston: Published By Thomas B. Wait And Co. And Charles Williams. 1812.

t.[3], [4–7], 8–34 p.; illus.; 14 cm.; pr. paper covers; cover title undated.
English ed. London: Darton & Harvey, 1803.
MWA*; Shaw 25489.

430.2 —— New-York: Published By Samuel Wood, At The Juvenile Book-Store, No. 357, Pearl-Street. 1813.

t.[1], [2–5], 6–44, [45–48, adv. list of books] p.;
illus.; 13.5 cm.; paper covers; colophon p.[48]: Pelsue & Gould, Printers, No. 9 Wall, Corner of Broad-Street.; p.[45–46] list 45 S. Wood publications included in this bibliography; p. [46–48] list 88 Johnson & Warner publications sold by S. Wood.
CtHi*; NjP (pr. & illus. green paper covers, emb. st. on t.[1]); PPL; MWA.

430.3 —— New-York: Printed And Sold By Samuel Wood, No. 357, Pearl-Street. 1814.

t.[1], [2–5], 6–44, [45–48, adv. list of books] p.;
illus.; 13.5 cm.; pr. & illus. yellow paper covers; no colophon; p.[45–46] list S. Wood publications; p.[46–48] list Johnson & Warner publications sold by S. Wood.
MWA*; CtHi; CtY; DLC; NHi; NN; OOxM; PHi; PP (p. 17–18 mut.); Shaw 31558; Weiss 1942.

430.4 —— New-York: Printed And Sold By Samuel Wood & Sons, At The Juvenile Book-Store, No. 357, Pearl-Street. 1815.

t.[1], [2–5], 6–44, [45–47, adv. list of books] p.;
illus.; 14 cm.; p.[45–47] list only S. Wood & Sons publications.
NHi* (bound with other books in no. **191**); DLC; MSaE (pr. & illus. buff paper covers); PP; PPL; Shaw 34760.

430.5 —— New-York: Printed And Sold By Samuel Wood & Sons, At The Juvenile Book-Store, No. 357, Pearl-Street. 1816.

t.[1], [2–5], 6–34 [*sic. i.e.* 44], [45–47] p.;
illus.; 13.5 cm.; yellow paper covers; p.[45–47] list only S. Wood & Sons publications.
Welch*; CLU; MWA (pr. & illus. paper covers, cover title undated); PP; Shaw 37681.

431 Die Gefahr in den Strassen. Nebst eingen andern Erzählungen. Philadelphia: Gedruckt bey Jacob Meyer. Für Johnson und Warner Nro. 147. Markrstrasse. 1810.

t.[1], [2–3], 4–36 p.; illus.; 13.5 cm.; pink paper covers. For English ed. *see* no. **256.**
Welch*; DeWint; IU; MiD; MWA; NHi; NRU; PHi; PP; PPL; PU; Shaw 20192.

GENLIS, STEPHANIE FELICITE DUCREST
DE SAINT-AUBIN, *Comtesse* DE 1746–1830
432 — THE BEAUTY AND THE MONSTER. A
COMEDY. From The French of the Countess De
Genlis. Extracted From The Theatre Of Educa-
tion. Printed at Worcester, Massachusetts, By
Isaiah Thomas, And Sold at his Book-Store:—
Sold also by E. Battelle, Boston. MDCCLXXXV.
  t.[1], [2–3], 4–35 p.; 14.5 cm.; Dutch paper
covers.
  MWA*; PP; RPJCB; Bowe mss.; Evans 19021.

433.1 [—] HAGAR IN THE DESERT. Translated
From The French, For The Use Of Children. The
Fourth Edition. Printed at Worcester, Massachusetts, By Isaiah Thomas. MDCCLXXXV.
  fr.[2], t.[3], [4–5], 6–32 p.; front. only illus.;
11 cm.; Dutch paper covers.
  MWA*; PP; Bowe mss.; Evans 19032.

433.2 [—] ———— Children. Newbury-Port
[Mass.]: Printed And Sold By John Mycall.
[1790?].
  t.[1], [2–3], 4–24 p.; 16.5 cm.
  RPB*; MiU; MNe (t.[1] wanting, p.[3]–4
mut.); Bowe mss.; Evans 22547.

GIBBONS, THOMAS 1720–1785
434 — SELECT PORTIONS OF SCRIPTURE, And
Remarkable Occurrences; Versified For The In-
struction And Entertainment Of Youth, Of Both
Sexes. By Thomas Gibbons, D.D. To Which Is
Added, A Father's Advice To His Son. First
American Edition. Dedham [Mass.]: Printed And
Sold By H. Mann, 1805.
  t.[i], [ii–iii], iv–vii, [viii, bl.], [9], 10–114,
[115–116, adv.] p.; 17.5 cm.; bound in marbled
paper over bds., leather spine.
  Welch*; MB; MWA; NBuG; NNuT; PP; PPL;
PSC; Shaw 8523.

435.1 A GIFT FOR CHILDREN. [2 lines quot.]
Norwich [Conn.]: Printed by Sterry and Co. M,-
DCC,XCVI.
  t.[1], [2–30] p.; 12 cm.; buff-brown paper
covers.
  MWA* (front cover mut.); CtHi; PP (covers
worn & mut.); Evans 30490.

435.2 ———— Norwich [Conn.]: Printed and
sold by John Sterry. M,DCCC.

t.[1], [2], 3–29 p.; 12 cm.; green marbled paper
covers.
  Welch*; MWA; Evans 49075.

GILBERT, ANN (TAYLOR) 1782–1866 and
JANE TAYLOR 1783–1824
436 [—] CITY SCENES; Or A Peep Into London
For Good Children. By the Author of Rural
Scenes. Philadelphia Pub. by James P. Parke No.
119 High St. 1809.
  t.[i], [ii], [1], 2–72, [pl. opp. p. 72] p.; 36 engr.
pl. including engr. t.[i]; 14.9 cm.; bound in
marbled paper over bds., leather spine; colophon p. 72: Brown & Merrit, Printers, No. 24,
Church-Alley.
  This was first written in 1801 by William Darton, who also drew and engraved the copper-
plates. In 1806 it was revised by Jane and Ann
Taylor with the illustrations drawn and engraved by Jane Taylor.
  PP*; Shaw 18724.

437 [—] HYMNS AND SONGS OF PRAISE, For
Children. By The Authors Of 'Hymns For Infant
Minds,' 'Original Poems,' &c. Hartford, Oliver D.
Cooke. 1820.
  t.[1], [2–3], 4–16 p.; illus.; 11 cm.; pr. & illus.
buff paper cover.
  MWA*; Ct; NjR; RPB; Shoemaker 3392.

438.1 [—] HYMNS FOR INFANT MINDS. By The
Author Of Original Poems, Rhymes For The
Nursery, &c. [1 line quot.] Third Edition. Boston:
Printed By Samuel T. Armstrong, Sold by him at
No. 50, Cornhill, Price $7,75 a hundred, 1,20 a
dozen, 12 cts. single. 1811.
  [1–2, adv. of books], t.[3], [4–7], 8–72 p.; 13
cm.; blue marbled paper covers.
  English ed.: 1810.
  MSaE*.

438.2 [—] ———— Boston: Printed & Published
By Lincoln & Edmands, No. 53, Cornhill. Who
publish a great variety of Cheap Religious Tracts.
On cash purchases of 5 dols. a discount of 5 per
cent will be made; over 10 dols. 10 percent. The
orders of charitable distributors, resident in any
part of the United States, promptly answered.
1811. Price, $7,75 a hun. 1.12 cts. a doz. 12 cts.
single.
  fr.[2], t.[3], [4–5], 6–70, [71, illus.] p.; front. &
illus. p.[71] only illus.; 14 cm.; blue marbled

paper covers; above front.: Lincoln & Edmands'
Second Edition.
MSaE* (em. st. on t.[3]).

438.3 [—] ——— Boston: Published By Munroe
And Francis. Shakspeare Bookstore, No. 4, Cornhill. 1811.
    fr.[ii], t.[i], [ii–iii], iv–vii, [viii], [9], 10–108 p.;
14 cm.; bound in pr. & illus. buff paper covers
over w. bds.
    Welch* (p. 107–108, & rear cover wanting);
ICU; MWA (fr. [ii] wanting); OOxM (fr. [ii]
wanting); Shaw 23079.

438.4 [—] ——— Hartford: Printed And Sold
By Peter B. Gleason & Co. 1811.
    fr.[ii], t.[1], [2–3], 4–70, [71–72] p.; front. only
illus.; 14.5 cm.; marbled paper covers.
    MWA-T*; Ct; CtY.

438.5 [—] ——— Boston: Printed & Published
By Lincoln & Edmands, No. 53 Cornhill, Who
publish a great variety of Cheap Religious Tracts.
On cash purchases of 5 dols. a discount of 5 per
cent will be made; over 10 dols. 10 per cent. The
orders of charitable distributors, resident in any
part of the United States, promptly answered.
1812. Price, $8.00 a hun. 1.12 cents. a doz. 12 cts.
single.
    fr.[2], t.[3], [4–5], 6–70, [71, two cuts & verse]
p.; illus.; 14.5 cm; gray wallpaper covers; above
front.: Lincoln & Edmands's Edition.
    Welch*; CtHi; MSaE (bpl. pasted over fr.[2]);
MWA; Shaw 25710.

438.6 [—] ——— Norwich [Conn.]: Printed
By S. Webb. 1812.
    [t.[1], [2–3], 4–70, [71–72] p.; 15 cm.; blue
marbled paper covers.
    DLC*; MiD.

438.7 [—] ——— Fifth Edition. Boston:
Printed By Samuel T. Armstrong, Sold by him,
No. 50, Cornhill. Price $7,75 a hundred, 1,20 a
dozen, 12 cts. single. 1813.
    fr.[2], t.[3], [4–5], 6–91, [92–96, adv. list of
adult books] p.; illus.; 13.5 cm.; paper covers;
above the front.: Armstrong's Second Edition,
Adorned With Twenty-Eight Cuts. Possibly a
reprint from standing type of Armstrong's second edition printed in 1810 since his unillustrated third edition of 72 pages came out in

1811. The DLC copy dated 1810 lacking a title
page matches this ed. in type set up and illustrations, and may be this edition rather than the
1810 one.
    MB* (i. st. on fr.[2], emb. st. on t.[3]); DLC
(dated [1810]; t.[3], p.[4]–6 wanting, blue
marbled paper covers; rebound; i. st. on p.[9]);
MWA (fr.[2] ½ wanting, p. 93–96 & covers
wanting); PP; Shaw 28632.

438.8 [—] ——— Second Hartford Edition.
Hartford: Printed and sold by Peter B. Gleason
& Co. 1813.
    fr.[ii], t.[1], [2–3], 4–70, [71–72] p.; front. only
illus.; 14 cm.; pr. tan paper covers.
    MWA-W* (not in Shaw).

438.9 [—] ——— Newburyport [Mass.]: adv.
by W. & J. Gilman, 1813 in **490.2**.

438.10 [—] ——— London Printed. Stockbridge [in a vignette] Reprinted By H. Willard.
[*ca.* 1813].
    fr.[ii], t.[iii], [iv–v], vi, [7], 8–112 p.; front.
only illus.; 13 cm.; bound in blue marbled paper.
    MWA*; FTaSU (p. 34 mut.; bound over bds.);
Shaw 51303.

438.11 [—] No. 34. HYMNS FOR INFANT MINDS.
caption p. [61] Andover [Mass.]: Printed For The
New England Tract Society By Flagg And Gould.
1814. First edit. 6000. [colophon p. 120].
    [61], 62–120 p.; 17 cm.; blue paper covers.
The book has two sets of page numbers. The
above set occurs at the top center of each page.
The other set of numbers are placed at the
outer top edge of the page.
    [1], 2–60 p.
    NNC-T*; MWA ([61], 62–120 p.; also paged
[1], 2–60 p.); Shaw 31782.

438.12 [—] ——— [same as **438.1**] Nursery, &c.
[1 line quot] Sixth Edition. To Which are added
lines on the Death Of Mrs. Harriet Newell and
The Twins. Boston: Printed By Samuel T. Armstrong, Sold by him, No. 50, Cornhill. Price 7,75
a hundred, 1,20 a dozen, 12 cts. single. 1814.
    fr.[2], t.[3], [4, bl.], [5–6, advertisement], [7],
8–68, [69–70, adv. list of books] p.; front. &
illus. p. 68 only illus.; 12.5 cm.; blue marbled
paper covers.
    MWA*; IU; MB (p. 67–70 wanting); MH;
Shaw 31783.

438.13 [—] ——— Newburyport [Mass.]: Published By W. B. Allen & Co. No. 13 Cornhill. Who do all kinds of Printing on the most reasonable terms—particularly for charitable distribution. Horatio G. Allen—Printer. 1814.
> fr.[2], t.[3], [4–5], 6–71 p.; illus.; 14.5 cm.; pr. & illus. green paper covers; front. & illus. p.[5] signed *Gilman*.
> MSaE°; MB (rebound, per. st. on t.[3]).

438.14 [—] ——— Newburyport [Mass.]: Published By W. & J. Gilman. Sold at their Miscellaneous Bookstore, No. 2, Middle-Street. Horatio G. Allen Printer. 1814.
> fr.[2], t.[3], [4–5], 6–70 p.; 14 cm.; front. & illus. p.[5] signed *Gilman*.
> RPB° (p. 71 & covers wanting).

438.15 [—] ——— From Sidney's Press. New-Haven: 1814.
> fr.[2], t.[3], [4–5], 6–70 p.; front. only illus.; 14 cm.
> MWA° (fr.[2] bound out of place between p.[4] and [5]; covers wanting); CtHi; Shaw 31784.

438.16 [—] ——— Newark: Published By Isaac Meeker. Pelsue And Gould, Printers. 1814.
> t.[3], [4–5], 6–70 p.; 13.5 cm.; blue marbled paper covers.
> MWA-W°; NjR.

438.17 [—] ——— Philadelphia: adv. by Johnson & Warner, 1814 in **430.3.**

438.18 [—] ——— [one line quot.] Boston: Printed & Published By Lincoln & Edmands. Sold at their Bible Warehouse, And Theological & Miscellaneous Bookstore, No. 53 Cornhill. 1815. Price $8.00 a hun. 1,12 cts. a doz. 12 cts. single.
> fr.[2], t.[3], [4–5], 6–70, [71] p.; illus.; 14 cm.; pr. & illus. buff paper covers; cover title dated 1816. Above the front.: Lincoln & Edmands' Fourth Edition. The MSaE copy has "Ware-House" on the title page spelled with a hyphen.
> Welch°; DLC (covers wanting); MSaE; MWA (covers mut.); PP; Shaw 34986.

438.19 [—] ——— [1 line quot.] Newburyport [Mass.]: Published By W. B. Allen & Co. No. 13, Cornhill, Who do all kinds of Printing on the most

reasonable terms—particularly for charitable distribution. 1816.
> fr.[2], t.[3], [4–5], 6–71 p.; illus.; 14.5 cm.; pr. & illus. green paper covers; front. & illus. p.[5] signed *Gilman*.
> MSaE° (emb. st. on t.[3]).

438.20 [—] ——— Newburyport [Mass.]: Published By W. & J. Gilman, Sold at their Miscellaneous Book-Store, No. 2, Middle-Street, 1816.
> t.[3], [4–5], 6–71 p.; illus.; 14 cm.; pr. paper covers.
> MNe° (front cover & fr.[2] wanting, t.[3] & p.[4] mut.); Shaw 37905.

438.21 [—] ——— Greenfield, Mass. Printed & Sold By Denio & Phelps. 1817. Price, $8.00 a hun. 1,12 cts. a doz. 12 cts. single.
> fr.[2], t.[3], [4–5], 6–72 p.; illus.; 13 cm.; pr. & illus. blue paper covers. Above the front.: Denio & Phelps' First Edition.
> MWA°; CLU; CtY (2 copies; copy 1, top of fr.[2] cut away; copy 2, rear cover wanting); Shaw 41118.

438.22 [—] ——— Boston: Printed And Published By Lincoln & Edmands, No. 53 Cornhill. 1818.
> fr.[2], t.[3], [4–5], 6–70, [71] p.; illus.; 14.5 cm.; pr. & illus. blue paper covers; cover title dated 1818. Above the front.: Lincoln & Edmands Fifth Edition.
> MWA°; FTaSU; MSaE; PP; Shaw 41119 and 45838.

438.23 [—] ——— Newburgh [N.Y.]: Published by Benjamin F. Lewis, & Co. 1818.
> fr.[ii], t.[1], [2–3], 4–68 p.; front. & title vignette only illus.; 14 cm.; pr. & illus. green paper covers.
> MSaE°; NB.

438.24 [—] ——— From Sidney's Press, New-Haven. 1818.
> t.[1], [2–4], 5–64 p.; 14.5 cm.; pr. & illus. yellowish-buff paper covers; p. 4 not struck.
> MWA-W°; CtHi (p. 4 struck, covers and all after p. 16 wanting); MnU; Shaw 45839.

438.25 [—] ——— Seventh Edition. To which are added lines on the Death Of Mrs. Harriet Newell, and The Twins. Boston: Published By

Samuel T. Armstrong, Sold by him, No. 50, Corn-hill. Price, 7,75 a hundred, 1,20 a dozen, 12 cts. single. U. Crocker, Printer. 1819.

fr.[2], t.[3], [4–5], 8 [*sic. i.e.* 6], [7–9], 10–71 p.; illus.; 13 cm.; pr. & illus. green paper covers. The leaf containing the Advertisement should be numbered p. [5–6], but, being bound after the leaf of Contents, p. [7]–8, the page number "8" becomes an error and should be "6" and p. [5–6] become [7–8].
Cover title imprint: Boston: Printed For Samuel T. Armstrong, By Crocker And Brewster, No. 50, Cornhill. 1820.
MWA* (2 copies, varied illus. on covers; copy 1, pr. & illus. green paper covers; copy 2, pr. & illus. red paper covers, fr.[2], t.[3], p. [7–8] mut.; rear cover wanting); DLC (fr.[2] follows title page); MH; NHi; PP; Shaw 48315.

438.26 [—] —— Boston: Published By Benjamin Crocker. 1819. Price, 12 cts. single 1,12 cts. a dozen. 8 dolls. a hundred.
t.[3], [4–5], 6–71 p.; 13.5 cm.; pr. & illus. blue-gray paper covers.
DLC*.

438.27 [—] —— Hanover [N.H.]: Printed By Charles Spear. Price 7,00 a hundred, 1,00 a doz., 12 cts. single. 1819.
t.[1], [2–7], 8–72 p.; 11 cm.; blue paper covers.
MWA*; Shaw 48316.

438.28 [—] No. 34. Part I ——. [caption p. [1]. Andover [Mass.]: Printed For The New England Tract Society, By Flagg and Gould. 1820. < 3d. edit. 6,000. >
t.[1], 2–28 p.; 17 cm.; also paged [61], 62–88 p. MB* (bound with other tracts in *The Publications Of The New England Tract Society. Vol. II. Andover [Mass.]: Printed By Flagg And Gould. 1820*).

438.29 [—] —— Canadaigua [N.Y]: Printed by J. D. Bemis & Co. 1820.
t.[1], [2–3], 4–72 p.; 12 cm.; blue marbled paper covers.
MWA*; DLC; Shoemaker 3393.

438.30 [—] —— Greenfield, (Mass.) Printed And Sold By Denio & Phelps. 1820. Price, $8 a hund. $1,12 cts. a doz. 12 cts. single.
fr. [2], t.[3], [4–5], 6–72 p.; front. & illus. p. 33 only illus.; 13 cm.; pr. & illus. blue paper covers. MWA-W*; (not in Shoemaker).

438.31 [—] —— Seventeenth New-England Edition. Hartford: Published By Oliver D. Cooke. Roberts & Burr, Printers. 1820.
t.[1], [2], 3–60 p.; title vignette only illus.; 12.5 cm.; yellow paper covers.
MWA*; CtHi (rear cover wanting); NNC-T; OClWHi; PP; Shoemaker 3396.

438.32 [—] —— Rhymes For The Nursery, &c. To Which Are Added. Original Hymns For Sabbath Schools: By The Same Author. Published And Sold By Samuel G. Goodrich, At The Hartford Sunday-School Repository. Roberts & Burr, Printers. 1820.
t.[1], [2–3], 4–93 p.; 14 cm.
CtHi*; Shoemaker 3397.

438.33 [—] —— Nursery, &c. [1 line quot.] Hartford: Printed by Geo. Goodwin & Sons. 1820.
fr.[2], t.[3], [4–5], 6–69, [70–71]; p.; illus.; 13.5 cm.; pr. & illus. paper covers.
MWA*; CtHi; MB; Shoemaker 3395.

438.34 [—] —— Newburgh [N.Y.]: Printed By Uriah C. Lewis, For Himself, and Junius S. Lewis. Catskill [N.Y.]. 1820.
fr.[2], t.[3], [4–5], 6–70 p.; front. & title vignette only illus.; 14 cm.; pr. & illus. buff paper covers.
PP*; CtY (Pequot); Shoemaker 3399.

438.35 [—] —— New-Haven: Published By J. Babcock And Son. Sidney's Press. 1820.
fr.[2], t.[3], [4–5], 6–71 p.; illus.; 14 cm.; pr. & illus. blue-gray paper covers; cover title vignette & front. signed A [Alexander Anderson].
Cover title imprint: Published And Sold By John Babcock & Son, New-Haven, And S. & W. R. Babcock, Charleston, S. C.
MWA*; CtHi; NjR; Shoemaker 3398.

439.1 [—] Hymns For Little Children. New-York: Printed And Sold By S. Wood. At the Juvenile Book-store, No. 357, Pearl-street, 1812.
fr.[ii, alphabet], t.[1], [2–3], 4–26, [27–28, adv. list of books] p.; illus.; 10 cm.; pr. & illus. buff paper covers.
MWA-W*; CtHi; PP; Shaw 51204.

439.2 [—] ——— New-York: Printed And Sold By Samuel Wood, At The Juvenile Book-Store, No. 357, Pearl-Street. 1814.
　　fr.[ii, alphabet], t.[1], [2, bl.–3], 4–26, [27–28, adv. list of books] p.; illus.; 10 cm.; pr. & illus. buff paper covers.
　　MWA-W*; Shaw 51394.

439.3 [—] ——— New-York: Printed And Sold By S. Wood & Sons, At The Juvenile Book-Store, No. 357, Pearl-Street. 1815.
　　fr.[ii, alphabet], t.[1], [2–3], 4–26, [27–28, adv. list of books] p.; illus.; 10 cm.; pr. & illus. paper covers.
　　MWA*; Shaw 34987.

439.4 [—] ——— New-York: Printed And Sold By S. Wood & Sons, At The Juvenile Book-Store, No. 357, Pearl-Street. 1816.
　　fr.[ii, alphabet], t.[1], [2–3], 4–26 p.; illus.; 10 cm.; pr. & illus. yellow-buff paper covers; cover title undated.
　　MWA*; PP; Shaw 37906.

439.5 [—] ——— Nerv-York [*sic. i.e.* New-York]: Printed And Sold By S. Wood & Sons, At The Juvenile Book-Store, No. 261, Pearl-Street. 1818.
　　fr.[ii. alphabet], t.[1], [2–3], 4–26 p.; illus.; 10 cm.
　　MWA-W* (covers wanting); DLC (fr.[ii] & covers wanting); MH (purple Dutch covers); MSaE (fr.[ii], p. 25–26 & covers wanting); NN-C (fr.[ii] & covers wanting); Shaw 51780; Weiss 1942.

439.6 [—] ——— New-York: Published By Samuel Wood & Sons, No. 261, Pearl-Street. And Samuel S. Wood & Co., No. 212, Market-st. Baltimore. 1818.
　　fr.[ii, alphabet], t.[1], [2–3], 4–26 p.; illus.; 10.5 cm.; green Dutch paper covers.
　　MWA*; MSaE (t.[1] mut., all after p. 24 wanting); CtHi; NN-C (covers & p. 26 wanting; Shaw 44408; Weiss 1942.

439.7 [—] ——— Nerv [*sic. i.e.* New] York: Published By Samuel Wood & Sons, No. 261, Pearl-Street; And Samuel S. Wood & Co. No. 212, Market-st. Baltimore. 1819.
　　fr.[ii, alphabet], t.[1], [2–3], 4–26 p.; illus.; 10 cm.; violet & green Dutch paper covers.
　　MWA-W*; DLC; RPB; Shaw 48317.

439.8 [—] ——— New-York Published By Samuel Wood & Sons, No. 261, Pearl-Street; And Samuel S. Wood & Co. No. 212, Market-st. Baltimore. 1820.
　　fr.[ii, alphabet], t.[1], [2–3], 4–26 p.; illus.; 10.5 cm.; silver paper covers.
　　MWA*; Shoemaker 1730.

440 [—] Limed Twigs To Catch Young Birds. By The Authors Of Original Poems, Rhymes For The Nursery, &c. &c. Part I. Philadelphia: Published By Johnson & Warner, No. 147, Market-Street. 1811.
　　fr.[ii], t.[1], [2–3], 4–44, ½ t.[45], [46–47], 48–105 p.; front. only illus.; 14.5 cm.; bound in pr. & illus. pink paper over bds.
　　Half title: Limed Twigs To Catch Young Birds. Part II.
　　English ed. London: Darton & Harvey, 1808. MWA-W*; MH (rebound); PHi; PP; Shaw 22909, 23226 and 24013.

441.1 [—] Little Poems For Little Readers. New-York: Printed And Sold By S. Wood, At the Juvenile Book-Store, No. 357, Pearl-street. 1811.
　　fr.[ii, alphabet], t.[1], [2–3], 4–28, [29] p.; illus.; 10 cm.; pr. & illus. yellow-buff paper covers; cover title dated 1812. The poems are a selection from *Original Poems and Hymns For Infant Minds.*
　　France*; Shaw 51097.

441.2 [—] ——— New York: Printed And Sold By Samuel Wood. At the Juvenile Book-store, No. 357, Pearl-street. 1813.
　　fr.[ii, alphabet], t.[1], [2–3], 4–28, [29] p.; illus.; 10 cm.; pr. & illus. buff paper covers.
　　Ct*.

441.3 [—] ——— New-York: Printed And Sold By Samuel Wood, At The Juvenile Book-Store, No. 357, Pearl-Street. 1814.
　　fr.[ii, alphabet], t.[1], [2–3], 4–28, [29] p.; illus.; 10 cm.; pr. & illus. brown paper covers.
　　Welch*; DLC (copy 1, fr.[ii], p.[29] & front cover mut.; copy 2, varying covers, p.[29] & rear cover mut.); N; OO; RNHi (covers, fr.[ii]; p.[29] wanting, t.[1] mut.); RPB (i. st. p.[3]; fr.[iii]; p. [29] and covers wanting; Shaw 31943.

441.4 [—] ———— New-York: Printed And Sold By Samuel Wood, At The Juvenile Book-Store, No. 357, Pearl-Street. 1815.
  fr.[ii, alphabet], t.[1], [2–3], 4–28, [29] p. illus.; 10 cm.; pr. & illus. buff paper covers.
  MWA°; CtHi; Shaw 35120; Weiss 1942.

441.5 [—] ———— Nerv-York [*sic. i.e.* New-York]: Printed And Sold By S. Wood & Sons, At The Juvenile Book-Store, No. 357 Pearl-Street. 1816.
  fr.[ii, alphabet], t.[1], [2–3], 4–28 p.; illus.; 10 cm.; pr. & illus. buff paper covers.
  MWA-W°; DLC; N (t.[1], p. 27–28 mut.); PPL; Shaw 51589.

441.6 [—] ———— Nerv-York [*sic. i.e.* New-York]: Printed And Sold By S. Wood & Sons, At The Juvenile Book-Store, No. 261, Pearl-Street. 1818.
  fr.[ii, alphabet], t.[1], [2–3], 4–28 p.; illus.; 10 cm.; Dutch paper covers.
  MWA°; MWHi; PP; PPL; Shaw 44596.

441.7 [—] ———— New-York: Published By Samuel Wood & Sons, No. 261 Pearl-Street. And Samuel S. Wood & Co. No. 212, Market-st. Baltimore. 1818.
  fr.[ii, alphabet], t.[1], [2–3], 4–28 p.; illus.; 10.5 cm.; Dutch paper covers.
  MWA°; Shaw 44597.

441.8 [—] ———— Nerv-York [*sic. i.e.* New York]: Published By Samuel Wood & Sons, No. 261, Pearl-Street; And Samuel S. Wood & Co. No. 212, Market-st. Baltimore. 1819.
  fr.[ii, alphabet], t.[1], [2–3], 4–28 p.; illus.; 10.5 cm.; orange Dutch paper covers.
  Welch°; CtHi; MiU; MWA; NN; NNC-T; RPB; Shaw 48502; Weiss 1942.

442 [—] My Mother A Poem By A Lady. Illustrated With Engravings Philadelphia Published and sold by Wm Charles. Prince Plain 12½ cents Coloured 13¾ cents. 1816. [cover title].
  [1–6] p. engr. on one side only of 6 leaves; illus.; 13.5 cm.; pr. paper covers. Reprinted from *Original Poems*, no. **444.1**. "Original holograph manuscript [of *My Mother*] entirely in the author's hand and with nine original pencil drawings by her brother Isaac. Lady Hamilton is said to have sat for these drawings." NBL 457.

English ed. London: pl.[5] signed *Published 9th. June 1815 by William Darton Junr.*
  RPB° (p.[2–5] slightly mut.); DLC (col. illus.); NNC-Pl; Shaw 37708 and 38349.

443.1 [—] Original Hymns for Sabbath Schools. By The Authors Of "Hymns For Infant Minds," "Original Poems," &c. First American Edition. Boston: Printed For Samuel T. Armstrong, By Crocker & Brewster. No. 50, Cornhill. 1820.
  fr[2], t.[3], [4–5], 6–36 p.; illus.; 14 cm.; pr. & illus. brick-red paper covers.
  English ed., entitled: *Original Hymns for Sunday School.* 1816.
  MWA-W°; ICU; PP (fr.[2] wanting); (not in Shoemaker).

443.2 [—] ———— "Original Poems," &c. Hartford: Published By Oliver D. Cooke. Roberts and Burr, Printers. 1820.
  t.[1], [2], 3–24 p.; t.[1] vignette only illus.; 11 cm.; pr. & illus. gray paper covers.
  MWA°; CCamarSJ; NNC-T (orig. covers wanting); Shoemaker 1382.

444.1 [—] Original Poems, For Infant Minds. By Several Young Persons. [4 lines quot.] [Vol. I.] Vol. II. Philadelphia: Printed And Sold By Kimber, Conrad, & Co. No. 93, Market Street, And No. 170, South Second Street. 1806.
  [vol. I.]: t.[i], [ii], [1–7], 8–112 p.; vol. II.: t.[i], [ii-vi], [1], 2–120 p.; 14 cm.; bound in leather. Vol. I. is not marked [Vol. I.] on the title page and has a semicolon after the word "Philadelphia;". Vol. II. is so marked on the title page and has a colon after "Philadelphia:".
  English ed. London: Darton And Harvey, 1804.
  MWA-W°; DLC (vol. I.); MiD; PP (vol. I.); Shaw 10483.

444.2 [—] ———— [4 lines of verse] Watts. Vol. I. Philadelphia: Printed And Sold By Kimber, Conrad, & Co. No. 93, Market Street, And No. 170, South Second Street. 1807.
  [vol. I.] t.[i], [ii], [1–7], 8–112 p.; 14.5 cm.; vol. II. is same as no. **444.1**.
  MWA°; Shaw 12659.

444.3 [—] ———— [4 lines quot.] Watts. Boston: Printed By E. G. House, No. 5, Court Street. Sold By John West And Co. 75, David West, 56, And Munroe Francis And Parker, 4, Cornhill, Also, By

O. C. Greenleaf, 3, Court Street. 1808.
t.[1], [2–9], 10–180 p.; 14.5 cm.; bound in marbled paper over bds.
MWA*; CLU; FTaSU; NjR; Shaw 15103.

444.4 [—] ——— [4 lines quot.] Vol. I. [II.] Exeter [N.H.]: Printed By Norris & Sawyer, For William Sawyer & Co. Booksellers, Newburyport [Mass.]. 1808.
vol. I.: t.[1], [2–9], 10–108 p.; vol. II.: t[1], [2–7], 8–120 p.; 2 vols. in 1; 15 cm.; bound in leather.
MWA*; DLC; FTaSU; MH; MNS; NN (vol. I., t.[1] wanting; vol. II., p.[3–4] mut., p. 119–120 wanting); PP; RPB; Shaw 15104.

444.5 [—] ——— In Two Volumes. Ornamented With Twenty Elegant Wood Cuts. [4 lines quot.] Volume I. [II.] Philadelphia: Published By Kimber & Conrad, No. 93, Market-Street. Brown & Merritt, Printers, 24 Church-alley. 1809.
vol. I.: t.[i], [ii-iv], [1], 2–120, [121–123] p.; illus.; 14.5 cm.; vol. II.: t.[1], [2–3], 4–134, [135–137] p.; illus.; 14 cm.; 2 vols.; bound in leather.
MWA*; CLU; DLC (title page coll. title of vol. I.); FTaSU; MSaE (vol. II.); PPL; Shaw 17619.

444.6 [—] ——— Persons. [4 lines quot.] Volume I. Philadelphia: Published By Kimber & Conrad, No. 93, Market-Street. 1809. Brown & Merritt, Printers.
t.[i], [ii, bl.–iv], [1], 2–120, [121–123, contents] p.; illus.; t.p. 13.5 cm. A variant of the preceding no. **444.5** not having "Ornamented With Twenty Elegant Wood Cuts," and the address "24 Church-alley" on the title page.
CtY* (rebound in cloth).

444.7 [—] ——— Volume I. Philadelphia: Published By Kimber & Conrad, No. 93, Market-Street. 1809. Brown & Merritt, Printers.
t.[i], [ii–iv], 13–134, [135–137, contents] p.; 14.5 cm.; bound in leather. A varied issue of **444.5** with the same title page of Vol. I. as **444.6**. The text however follows Vol. II. with p.[3]–12 omitted.
NHi*.

444.8 [—] ——— [4 lines quot.] Watts. Boston: Published By West And Richardson, No. 75, Cornhill. 1813. E. G. House, Printer, Court Street.
t.[1], [2–9], 10–810 [*sic. i.e.* 180] p.; 14.5 cm.; bound in leather.
MWA* (t.[1] & p. [9]–10 mut.); DLC (rebound, per st. on t.[1]); MB (per st. on t.[1]); MSaE; NcD; NNC-Pl (p.[3–4] wanting, p. 180 correctly printed); Shaw 28633 and 29918.

444.9 [—] ——— Boston: Published by West & Richardson, No. 75 Cornhill. 1813. E. G. House, Printer, Court Street.
t.[i], [ii-v], vi–vii [*sic. i.e.* viii], [9], 10–810 [*sic. i.e.* 180] p.; 14.5 cm.; bound in leather.
MWA* (t.[i] & p.[9]–10 mut.); Shaw 28634 and 29422.

444.10 [—] ——— [4 lines quot.] From Sidney's Press. For I. Cooke & Co. New-Haven. 1813.
fr.[2], t.[3], [4–5], 6–47 p.; illus.; pr. & illus. green paper covers.
Massman*.

444.11 [—] ——— Persons. In Two Volumes. Ornamented With Twenty Elegant Wood Cuts. [4 lines quot.] Volume I. [II.] Philadelphia: Published By Solomon W. Conrad, No. 87, Market-Street. W. Brown, Printer, 23 Church Alley, 1816.
vol. I.: t.[i], [ii–iii], iv, [5], 6–115, [116–119], [120, bl.] p.; vol. II.: t.[1], [2–3], 4–127, [128–131] p.; illus.; 2 vols. in 1.; 5 cm.; bound in leather.
Welch*; CtY; MWA-T; PP (covers loose, vol. I. p.[5]–6, 77–78 mut.); PPL.

445.1 [—] Poems For Children. New-York: Printed And Sold By S. Wood, At The Juvenile Book-Store, No. 357, Pearl-Street. 1811.
t.[1], [2–3], 4–45 p.; illus.; 12.5 cm.; pr. & illus. yellowish-buff paper covers. The poems are mainly selections from *Original Poems For Infant Minds.*
NN-C*; CCamarSJ; CtHi (covers wanting); Shaw 22910; Weiss 1942.

445.2 [—] ——— New-York: Printed And Sold By S. Wood, At the Juvenile Book-Store, No. 357, Pearl-street. 1813.
t.[1], [2–3], 4–45 p.; illus.; 12.5 cm.; pr. & illus. yellow paper covers.
MWA*; DLC; NHi; PP; Shaw 29534.

445.3 [—] ——— New-York: Printed And Sold By Samuel Wood, At The Juvenile Book-Store, No. 357, Pearl-Street. 1814.

t.[1], [2–3], 4–45 p.; illus.; 13 cm.

CtY° (bound with other books, p. 43–44 wanting); PP (covers wanting); Weiss 1942.

445.4 [—] ——— New-York: Printed And Sold By S. Wood & Sons, At The Juvenile Book-Store, No. 357, Pearl-Street. 1815.

t.[1], [2–3], 4–44 p.; illus.; 12.5 cm.; pr. & illus. paper covers; cover title undated.

MWA° (t.[1], p.[2]–4, & covers worm-eaten); RPB.

445.5 [—] ——— New-York Printed And Sold By S. Wood & Sons, At The Juvenile Book-Store, No. 261, Pearl-Street. 1817.

t.[1], [2–3], 4–44 p.; illus.; 12.5 cm.; pr. & illus. buff paper covers; cover title undated.

Welch° (p. 39–44 & rear cover wanting); ICU; MWA (ornamented yellow & green paper covers); Shaw 41848.

445.6 [—] ——— New-York: Published By Samuel Wood & Sons, No. 261, Pearl Street; And Samuel S. Wood & Co. No. 212, Market-st. Baltimore. 1819.

t.[1], [2–3], 4–44 p.; illus.; 12.5 cm.; pr. & illus. buff paper covers.

Cover title: True Stores Related, undated.

MWA°; Shaw 49142.

446 [—] Poems For Little Children. Suitable For Young Classes in Sabbath Schools. Boston: Printed and sold at No. 53 Cornhill, by Lincoln & Edmonds. 1819.

t.[1], [2], 3–8 p.; illus.; 11.5 cm.; contains a selection of poems from *Original Poems For Infant Minds,* no. **444.1.**

Welch° (covers wanting); MB; MSaE; MWA (orange paper covers).

447.1 [—] Rhymes For The Nursery. By The Authors Of "Original Poems." Hartford: Printed and sold by Peter B. Gleason & Co. 1813.

t.[1], [2–5], 6–68 + p.; 14 cm.; pr. paper covers.

MWA-T° (sigs F₅–F₆ and rear cover wanting; the last 9 lines of the last poem "A very sorrowful Story" are wanting so the text may have ended on page 69); Shaw 28631.

447.2 [—] ——— Utica [N.Y.]: Printed And Sold By Camp, Merrell & Camp, Genesee-street. 1815.

fr.[ii], t.[1], [2–5], 6–70, [71–72] p.; illus.; 14 cm.; bound in marbled paper over bds., leather spine.

English ed.: London: Darton and Harvey, 1806. MWA°; CtY (rebound); Shaw 34786 and 36054.

448.1 [—] Select Rhymes For The Nursery. Philadelphia: Published By Johnson & Warner. 1810.

t.[1], [2–3], 4–48 p.; illus.; 15 cm.; p.[2]: Lydia R. Bailey, Printer. Adv. by Johnson & Warner, 1813 in **430.2**, and 1814 in **430.3**.

English ed. London: Darton and Harvey 1808. MWA° (covers wanting); CLU; DLC (brown paper covers); PP; Shaw 20212.

448.2 [—] ——— Nursery, Sidney's Press. New-Haven, 1813.

t.[3], [4–5], 6–31 p.; illus.; 10 cm.; illus. green rear paper cover.

CtHi° (fr.[2?] and front cover wanting, many pages mut.); MWA (title and covers wanting); Shaw 29766.

448.3 [—] ——— Nursery. Adorned With Cuts. Sidney's Press. New-Haven. 1815.

fr.[2], t.[3], [4–5], 6–31 p.; illus.; 10.5 cm.; illus. buff paper covers; illus. p. 21 signed A [Alexander Anderson].

NjN°; MWA-T; Shaw 35893.

448.4 [—] ——— Sidney's Press. New-Haven. 1818.

fr.[2], t.[3], [4–5], 6–30, [31, adv.] p.; illus.; 10.5 cm.; illus. white paper covers pr. in pink ink.

MWA°; CtHi; Shaw 44159 and 45680.

449.1 [—] The World Turn'd Upside Down; Or, The Wonderful Magic Lantern. Illustrated With Whimsical Engravings. Philadelphia: Published and sold Wholesale by Wm. Charles, and may be had of all the Booksellers. Price 18 3 4 Cents. 1811. W. M'Culloch, Printer.

fr.[2], t.[3], [4–5], 6–32 p.; 8 engr. pl. including front.; 13 cm.; pr paper covers; cover title same as title page, but dated 1814.

English ed. London, entitled: *Signor Topsy-Tur-*

vey's *Wonderful Magic Lantern; Or The World turned upside down*. Tabart & Co. 1810. The American edition is abridged or selected from the English one.
CtHi°.

449.2 [—] ——— Illustrated With Elegant Engravings. Part II. Philadelphia: Published and sold Wholesale by Wm. Charles, and may be had of all the Booksellers. 1814. W. M'Culloch, Printer.
fr.[ii], t.[1], [2], 3–16, [pl. opp. p. 16] p.; 8 engr. pl. including front.; 13.5 cm.; pr. buff paper covers; cover title same except: Illustrated With Whimsical Engravings. Part II.
——— all the Booksellers. Price, 18 3–4 Cents. 1814.
NNC-Pl° (rear paper cover wanting); MWA (p. 15–16 & pl. opp. p. 16 wanting); PP (rear cover mostly wanting); RPB.

GINGERBREAD, GILES (arranged chronologically)

450.1 The Entertaining History Of Giles Gingerbread, A Little Boy, Who Lived Upon Learning. First Hudson Edition. Hudson [N.Y.]: Printed by Ashbel Stoddard, And sold Wholesale and Retail, at his Book Store. 1806.
fr.[2], t.[3], [4–5], 6–31 p.; illus.; 10.8 cm.; purple Dutch paper covers.
NN°; Shaw 10361; Weiss 1936, p. 171.

450.2 ——— Learning. Adorned with Copperplate Engravings. Philadelphia: Published And Sold By George Pryor, No. 2, North Third Street. 1806. Dickinson, Printer.
t.[1], [2–3], 4–18 p.; 4 engr. pl.; 14.5 cm.; green and gold Dutch paper covers.
Welch°; MWA; PTi; Shaw 10362.

450.3 ——— Philadelphia: Published And Sold By B. C. Busby, No. 2, North Third Street. 1810.
t.[1], [2–3], 4–22 p.; 4 engr. pl.; 13.5 cm.; blue paper covers. The 4 engr. pl. are the same as those in no. **450.2**.
DLC°; Shaw 20215.

450.4 ——— [a scalloped line] [a double rule] Adorned With Cuts. [a double rule] [a scalloped line] Sidney's Press. New Haven. 1813.
fr.[2], t.[3], [4–5], 6–31 p.; illus.; 10 cm.; pr. & illus. pink paper covers. The front cover has Gil[es Gingerbread]" and an engraving of 3

boys and a man placed lengthwise on the side of the page. The rear cover has an engraving of a peacock. The title page has a type ornament 11 mm. long above the date 1813.
MWA-W° (front cover mut.); Shaw 51298.

450.5 ——— [a zigzag line] Adorned With Cuts. [a zigzag line] Sidney's Press. New-Haven. 1813.
fr.[2], t.[3], [4–5], 6–31 p.; illus.; 10.5 cm.; pr. & illus. buff paper covers. A variant of no. **450.4**. The front cover has a square cut mostly wanting. Rear cover has an engraving of 3 boys and a man probably the same as the much mutilated cut on the front cover of no. **450.4**. The title page has "Adorned With Cuts" printed in black letters. "New-Haven" is printed in larger type than above; the type ornament above the date 1813 is 9 mm. long.
MWA°; MSaE (p. 29–31 & rear cover wanting; p. 28 mut.); Shaw 51298.

450.6 ——— Learning. Adorned with Copperplate Engravings. Philadelphia: Published And Sold By Benjamin C. Buzby, No. 2, North Third Street. D. Dickinson, Printer. 1815.
t.[1], [2–3], 4–24 p.; 4 engr. pl.; 13 cm.; blue marbled paper covers. The 4 engr. pl. are the same as those in no. **450.2**.
FTaSU° (p. 11–14 wanting).

450.7 ——— Adorned with Cuts. Hudson [N.Y]: Printed by Ashbel Stoddard, And sold Wholesale and Retail at his Bookstore. 1818.
fr.[2], t.[3], [4–5], 6–31 p.; illus.; 10.5 cm.; pr. & illus. paper covers; cover title dated 1821.
Oppenheimer°.

451 The History Of Giles Gingerbread. A Little Boy who lived upon lea[rning] Boston Printed and Sold by Edes & Gill in Queen-Street. Sold also by Cox & Berry, in Cornhill. [1776?].
fr.[2], t.[3], [4], 5–28, [29], [30, alphabet], [31, illus. & verse] p.; illus.; 9 cm.; brown paper covers. Inside of the front cover there is a holograph inscription *William Wilder his book 1778*.
British ed. [Gainborough]: Mozley's Lilliputian Book Manufactory, 1791.
MWA° (fr.[2], t.[3], [4]–6, 13–14, 27–28, 29–30 mut.; remaining p. frayed along the outer edge affecting text).

452.1 THE RENOWNED HISTORY OF GILES GIN-
GERBREAD A Little Boy who lived upon Learning.
<Price Two Coppers.> Boston: Printed by Mein
and Fleeming, and to be sold by John Mein at
the London Book-Store, North-side of King-street.
Boston. MDCCLXVIII. At which Place may be
had, A great variety of Entertaining and Instructive Books for Children.
> fr.[2], t.[3], [4], 5–34, [35], [36] p.; illus.;
> 10 cm.
> English ed. London: adv. by John Newbery in
> *London Chronicle* 27-9, December 1764.
> CtHi°; NjP (fr.[2], t.[3], p. 12, top of page
> cropped affecting top line, p. 29[–36] mut., p.
> 19–28 have a small central tear); Evans 41870;
> Hamilton 49.

452.2 ——— Learning. London, Printed: Newport: Re-Printed And Sold By S. Southwick, In
Queen-Street, 1771.
> t.[1], [2–3], 4–30, [31] p.; illus.; 10.5 cm.;
> paper covers.
> Evans 42239.

452.3 ——— [same as **452.1**] The First Worces-
[ter Edition.] Worcester, (Mass[achusetts)] Printed
By ISAIAH [Thomas] And Sold At His B[ook-
store] MDCC[LXXXVI].
> fr.[2], t.[3], [4–5], 6–30+p.; illus.; 10 cm.
> MWA-T° (p. 31 & covers wanting, fr.[2],
> t.[3], p.[4], 27–30 mut.; manuscript date
> *1786*); Evans 20625.

452.4 ——— Learning. Look at him [illus.]
Philadelphia, Printed by Young and M'Culloch,
the Corner of Chesnut and Second-streets. 1787.
> t.[1], 2–32 p.; illus.; 10 cm.; Dutch paper
> covers.
> MWA°; Evans 45076.

452.5 ——— Philadelphia: adv. by F. Bailey,
1792 in **359** and 1793 in **773.1**.

452.6 ——— Learning. Look at him [vignette]
Philadelphia: Printed by W. Young, No. 52,
Second-street, the corner of Chesnut-street.
M,DCC,XCIII.
> t.[1], 2–31, [32, adv.] p.; illus.; 10 cm.; Dutch
> paper covers.
> PP°.

452.7 ——— Wilmington: adv. by J. Wilson,
1803 in **1081**.

GINGERBREAD, TOMMY (arranged chronologically)

453.1 THE ENTERTAINING HISTORY OF TOMMY
GINGERBREAD: A Little Boy, Who lived upon
Learning. New-York: Printed by James Oram for
the Book-binders Society,—1796.—Price Three
Cents.
> fr.[2], t.[3], [4], 5–31 p.; illus.; 9.5 cm.; green
> Dutch paper covers.
> British ed. Edinburgh: G. Ross, [1815?].
> MWA°; Evans 47772.

453.2 ——— Boston: Printed and sold by John
W. Folsom, No. 30, Union-Street. 1798.
> fr.[2], t.[3], [4–5], 6–31 p.; illus.; 10 cm.; buff
> paper covers, ornamented with a striped design
> in black.
> MSaE°; Evans 48417.

453.3 ——— Exeter [N.H.]: adv. by Henry
Ranlet, 1801 in **558.2**.

453.4 ——— Ornamented With Cuts. Litchfield [Conn.]: Printed By Hosmer & Goodwin.
1808.
> fr.[2], t.[3], [4–5], 6–30, [31, adv.] p.; illus.;
> 10 cm.; pink wallpaper covers, ornamented with
> blue flowers & gold lines.
> CtHi°.

453.5 ——— Hartford: Printed by Hale &
Hosmer. 1812.
> fr.[2], t.[3], [4–5], 6–30 p.; illus.; 10 cm.; pr.
> & illus. yellow paper covers. Adv. by Hale &
> Hosmer, 1814 in **595.3**.
> Cover title: The History of Tommy Ginger-
> bread, dated 1813.
> MWA-W; Shaw 51192.

453.6 ——— Hartford: adv. by Sheldon &
Goodwin, [1815] in **673.31**.

454 THE HISTORY OF TOMMY GINGERBREAD.
Exeter [N.H.] adv. by Norris and Sawyer, 1808
in **428.3**.

THE GODMOTHER'S TALES. *See* Sandham, Elizabeth, no. **1151**.

[GODWIN, WILLIAM] 1756–1836
455.1 [—] BALDWIN'S FABLES: Ancient and
Modern. Designed For Youth. Adorned With

Cuts. New-Haven: Printed For J. Babcock And Son. Sidney's Press. 1819.

fr.[ii], t.[1], [2–3], 4–35 p.; illus.; 14 cm.; pr. & illus. buff paper covers; p. 36 is present in MWA copy, but pasted by the printer to the inside of the rear cover.

CtHi° (2 copies varied covers); MWA (fr.-[ii] and front cover wanting); Shaw 48088.

455.2 [—] ———— New-Haven: Printed For J. Babcock And Son. Sidney's Press. 1819.

A variant of the preceding with 36 p.; illus.; 13.5 cm.

CtY° (rear cover wanting, fr.[ii], t.[1], p. 35–36 mut. but not affecting text; frontispiece, 2 engravings of birds, one above the other); Shaw 48088.

455.3 [—] ———— Sidney's Press. Published by John Babcock & Son, New-Haven, S. & W. R. Babcock, No. 163 King-Street, Charleston, and M'Carty & Davis, Philadelphia. 1820.

fr.[2], t.[3], [4–5], 6–31 p.; illus.; 14.5 cm.; pr. & illus. pink paper covers.

MWA°; CtHi (rear cover wanting); Shoemaker 1399.

455.4 [—] ———— For Youth. New Haven: Printed For John Babcock And Son. Sidney's Press. 1820.

fr.[2], t.[3], [4, adv.–5], 6–31 p.; illus.; 14.5 cm.; pr. & illus. paper covers. Cover title imprint: Published and sold by John Babcock and son New Haven, and S. & W. R. Babcock Charleston.

MWA-T°; CtY (p. 23–24, ½ wanting); PP; RPB.

456.1 [—] Fables Ancient And Modern. Adapted For The Use Of Children. By Edward Baldwin Esq. Adorned With Cuts By Anderson. From Sidney's Press, For Increase Cooke And Co. 1807.

t.[i], [ii–iii], iv–v, [vi], 7–142 p.; illus.; 14 cm.; paper covers.

English ed. London: 2 vols. T. Hodgkins 1805.

CtY°; PP; PPi (i. st. on t.[i]; rebound); Shaw 50777.

456.2 [—] ———— Adorned With Seventy-Three Cuts. First American Edition. Philadelphia: Published By Johnson & Warner. No. 147, Market Street. William Brown Printer, Church-alley. 1811.

½t.[i], [ii], t.[iii], [iv–v], vi–xi, [xii], [1], 2–273 p.; illus.; 17.5 cm.; bound in leather. Most of illus. signed A [Alexander Anderson].

MWA°; NjP (rear cover wanting); WaU; Hamilton 251; Shaw 22921.

456.3 [—] ———— Adorned with Cuts. From Sidney's Press New-Haven. 1817.

fr.[2], t.[3], [4–5], 6–47 p.; illus.; 12.5 cm.

MB°; Shaw 40940.

456.4 [—] ———— Second American Edition. Philadelphia: Published By Benjamin Warner, And Sold At His Book-Stores In Philadelphia And Richmond, Virginia. Wm. Greer, Printer. Harrisburg [Pa.]. 1818.

t.[i], [ii, bl.–iii], iv–ix, [x, bl.], [11], 12–234 p.; illus.; 18 cm.; bound in leather; engravings in text signed A [Alexander Anderson].

NHi°; DLC (rebound); MH; Shaw 43137 and 44167.

457 The Golden Plaything; Being A New Collection Of Entertaining Fables, Intended As a Present for all those Good Boys and Girls who behave according to the following Rules: That is, Do as they are bid, come when they are called, and shut the door after them. Shirley [Mass.]: L. Parker, Printer. 1802.

fr.[2], t.[3], [4–5], 6–27, [28–30, an oval cut per page] p.; illus.; 9 cm.; black paper covers.

MWA°; Shaw 2334.

The Golden Plaything; Or The Way To Be Wise And Happy. *See* Lovechild, Mr. (*pseud.*), no. **800.**

GODWIN, OLIVER 1728–1774

458 — Dr. Goldsmith's Celebrated Elegy, on that Glory of Her Sex, Mrs. Mary Blaize. 1809. Philada. Published by Johnson & Warner No. 147 High Street.

t.[2], [3–14] p.; engr. on one side only of 13 p.; illus.; 13.5 cm.; pr. yellow-buff paper covers.

Cover title: ———— Illustrated, with Twelve Comic Engravings, On Copper Plate. Philadelphia: Published By Johnson And Warner No. 147, Market-Street. Brown & Merritt, Printers, No. 24, Church all[ey.] 1809.

English ed. London: J. Harris. 1808.

PHi°; MWA (t.[1] & covers wanting); NNC-Pl; PP (p.[2–6] mut., col. pl.); Shaw 17638.

GOMEZ, ISAAC, JUN.

459 — SELECTIONS OF A FATHER For The Use Of His Children. In Prose And Verse. By Isaac Gomez, Jun. [6 lines quot.] Anonymous. New York: Printed By Southwick And Pelsue, No. 9 Wall-street. 1820.

t.[i], [ii–v], vi–viii, [9], 10–408 p.; 22 cm.; bound in leather.
MWA*; PP.

460.1 THE GOOD BOY'S SOLILOQUY; Containing His Parents Instructions, Relative To His Disposition And Manners. New-York: Printed And Sold By Samuel Wood & Sons, No. 261, Pearl-Street. 1818.

t.[1], [2–3], 4–28 p.; illus.; 13 cm.; pr. & illus. buff paper covers.
English ed. London: W. Darton, Jun., 1811.
MSaE* (14 leaves only, 2 wanting, probably fr.[ii], p. 29–30, & rear cover wanting).

460.2 ———— New-York: Published By Samuel Wood & Sons, No. 261, Pearl-Street; and Samuel S. Wood & Co. No. 212, Market-st. Baltimore. 1819.

fr.[ii], t.[1], [2–3], 4–30 p.; illus.; 12.5 cm.
RPB*; ICU (pr. & illus. buff paper covers).

THE GOOD CHILD'S DELIGHT. *See* Kilner, Dorothy, no. **726.1.**

461 THE GOOD CHILD'S GOLDEN COMPANION; Full Of Amusement And Instruction. (No. 1.) Adorned With Cuts. First Vermont Edition. Rutland [Vt.]: Printed By William Fay & Co. 1813.

fr.[2], t.[3], 4–31 p.; illus.; 10 cm.; covers.
MWA*.

THE GOOD GIRL'S SOLILOQUY. *See* Sproat, Nancy, no. **1245.1.**

462 A GOOD WIFE; Or, The Character of Elizabeth Markum, First Published By The Christian Tract Society. No. XVI. Boston: Wells And Lilly, Court-Street. 1820.

t.[1], [2–3], 4–14 p.; 15.5 cm.
MWA*.

THE ALPHABET OF GOODY TWO-SHOES. *See* Alphabet, no. **35.**

GOODY TWO-SHOES (arranged chronologically)

463.1 THE HISTORY OF LITTLE GOODY TWO-SHOES; Otherwise called, Mrs. Margery Two-Shoes. With The Means by which she acquired her Learning and Wisdom, and in Consequence thereof her Estate. Set forth at large for the Benefit of those, Who from a state of Rags and Care, And having Shoes but half a Pair, Their Fortune and their Fame would fix, And gallop in a Coach and Six. See the Original Manuscript in the Vatican at Rome, and the Cuts by Michael Angelo; illustrated with Comments of our great modern Critics. New-York: Printed by H. Gaine, at the Bible and Crown, in Hanover-Square. 1775.

t.[1], [2–3], 4–156 p.; illus.; 9.5 cm.
English and Scottish ed. title 1: *The History Of Little Goody Two-Shoes.* London: adv. by J. Newbery, 1764 in *A Pleasant And Useful Companion To The Church Of England; Or, A Short Plain, And Practical Exposition Of The Book Of Common Prayer.* J. Newbery, 1765.
English & Scottish ed. title 2: *The History Of Goody Two-Shoes.* London: Darton And Harvey, 1801. ———— *With the Adventures Of Her Brother Tommy.* Glasgow: J. Lumsden & Son. & Sold by Stoddart & Craigs, Hull. [1816 or later]. Darton, Harvey And Darton, 1817.
English & Scottish ed. title 3: *The Renowned History Of Goody Two-Shoes:* Glasgow: J. Lumsden & Son at their Toy Book Manufactory. [ca. 1810].
PP* (covers wanting); CSmH (t.[1], 145–146 wanting); MWA (p. 145–156 wanting, p. 45–46 mut.); NjP (p. 143–156 wanting); NN (t.[1] mut., p. 155–156 wanting); Evans 14117.

463.2 ———— Boston: Printed and sold by Nathaniel Coverl[y] Near the Sign of the White-Hors[e] 1783.

t.[1], [2–3], 4–62, [63–64] p.; illus.; 9 cm.; green paper covers.
CtHi* (p. [63–64] mut. p. no. wanting, p. 4–6 p. no. wanting, title page worn); CLU (t.[1] & p. 63–64 wanting, some leaves worn and mut.); NjP (complete); Evans 44386.

463.3 ———— Philadelphia: Printed by Young and M. Culloch [*sic. i.e.* M'Culloch], the corner of Chesnut and Second-street 1787.

fr.[2], t.[3], [4–5], 6–158 p.; illus.; 12 cm.
PP; Evans 45077.

463.4 ———— The First Worcester Edition. Printed at Worcester, Massachusetts. By Isaiah Thomas, and sold, Wholesale and Retail, at his Book Store. MDCCLXXXVII.

fr.[2], t.[3], [4–6], 7–158, [159–160 adv. list of books] p.; illus.; 10.5 cm.; Dutch paper covers. The book is relatively common. A publisher's remainder of it was found some years ago. The remainders are either rebound, in uncut sheets, or rebound in an embossed paper that is supposed to resemble Dutch paper. MWA copies 1 & 3 are not part of a publisher's remainder.

MWA* (copy 1, I. Thomas' copy bound in brown leather, copy 2 bound in blue morocco, copy 3 bound in Dutch paper); CCamarSJ; CLU (unbound sheets); CSmH; CtHi; CtHT, bound with other books); CtY (Pequot) (2 copies, copy 1 rebound, copy 2 unbound sheets); DLC (unbound sheets); MB; MH; MiU; NN (2 copies); NNC-LS; NNC-Pl (unbound sheets); NRU; PHi; PP; RPJCB (unbound sheets); Evans 20459.

463.5 ———— Philadelphia: Printed by W. Young. No. 52, Second-street, the corner of Chesnut-street. M,DCC,XCIII.

fr.[2], t.[3], [4–5], 6–136 p.; illus.; 10.5 cm.; bound in Dutch paper over bds. Adv. by William Young, 1794 in **305.**

MWA* (p. 95–96 wanting); Evans 46763.

463.6 ———— her estate. Set forth at large for the benefit of all those pretty little Boys and Girls who wish to be good and happy. Wilmington [Del.]: Printed By Brynberg And Andrews. M,DCC,XCIII.

fr.[2], t.[3], [4–5], 6–127 p.; illus.; 10 cm.; bound in green Dutch paper over bds.

DeWi* (per. st. on. t.[3]; rear cover wanting); Evans 46764.

463.7 ———— Wilmington [Del.]. Printed By Peter Brynberg. 1796.

fr.[2], t.[3], [4–5], 6–127 p.; illus.; 10 cm.; bound in marbled paper over bds., leather spine.

MWA*; DeWint; PHi; PP; Evans 32257.

463.8 ———— Goody Two Shoes. Ornamented With Cuts. Charlestown [Mass.]: Printed by J. Lamson, for Samuel Hall, in Cornhill, Boston, 1797.

fr.[2], t.[3], [4–5], 6–94 p.; illus.; 10.5 cm.; green Dutch paper covers.

MWA* (p. 73–74 slightly mut.); CtHi (fr.[2] wanting; t.[3], p. 93–94 mut.); Evans 32256.

463.9 ———— Of Goody Two-Shoes; otherwise called Mrs. Margery Two-Shoes; With Her Means Of Acquiring Wisdom, Learning, And Riches. Printed in Litchfield [Conn.], by T. Collier. 1798.

t.[1], [2–3], 4–112 p.; illus.; 12 cm.

CtHi (p.[1–2], 7–8, 15–16, 29–30, 33–66, 79–80, 95–98, 111–112 wanting); Evans 48459.

463.10 ———— New York: adv. by Thomas B. Jansen, 1805 in **1371.5.**

463.11 ———— Of Goody Two-Shoes. To Which Is Added, The Rhyming Alphabet, Or Tom Thumb's Delight. Adorned With Cuts. Litchfield [Conn.]: Printed By Hosmer & Goodwin. 1808.

fr.[2], t.[3], [4–5], 6–29, [30], [31, adv. of 12 books] p.; illus.; 10 cm.

Shaw 15136.

463.12 ———— Little Goody Two-Shoes. Ornamented With Twenty-One Original Designs. Philadelphia: Published by Johnson & Warner, No. 147, Market Street. William Brown, Printer, Church-alley. 1811.

fr.[2], t.[3], [4–5], 6–103 p.; illus.; 14.5 cm.; bound in pr. & illus. buff paper over bds.; cover imprint same as title, with "William Brown, Printer, Church-alley" omitted.

Cover label of the PP copy: Little Goody Two-Shoes. Boston: Munroe And Francis, 4 Cornhill. Welch* (p. 25–26, 43–44 mut.); CLU; MWA; PP; Shaw 23012.

463.13 ———— Of Goody Two-Shoes To Which Is Added, The Rhyming Alphabet, Or Tom Thumb's Delight. Hartford: Printed by Hale & Hosmer. 1812.

fr.[2], t.[3], [4–5], 6–28, [29], [30, bl.], [31, adv.] p.; illus.; 9.5 cm.; pr. & illus. pinkish-buff paper covers; cover title dated 1813.

DLC*.

463.14 ———— Embellished with Cuts. Hartford: Printed by Hale & Hosmer: 1814.

fr.[2], t.[3], [4–5], 6–28, [29], [30, bl.], [31, adv. list of 12 books] p.; illus.; 10 cm.; pr. & illus. buff paper covers.

MWA-T°; CtHi (fr. [2], p. [29–31] & covers wanting); OOxM (original covers wanting); Shaw 31602.

463.15 ———— Hartford: Printed for J. & W. Russell. < Stereotyped by J. F. & C. Starr. > [1815?].

fr.[2], t.[3], [4–5], 6–30, [31, adv. list of books] p.; illus.; 10 cm.
MWA° (no date).

463.16 ———— Hartford: Printed by Sheldon & Goodwin. < Stereotyped by J. F. & C. Starr. > [1815].

fr.[2], t.[3], [4–5], 6–29, [30], [31, adv. list of books] p.; illus.; 10 cm.; pr. & illus.; yellowish-buff paper covers.
CtHi°; CtY; DLC; MWA-T (p. 7–16 cropped); NB; Shaw 34800.

The Gooseberry-Bush And Caterpillars. *See* Clowes, John, no. **209.**

464 The Grandmother's Gift, Or, Moral Stories For Children. New-Haven: Printed For John Babcock And Son. Sidney's Press. 1820.

fr.[2], t.[3], [4, adv.–5], 6–31 p.; illus.; 15 cm.; pr. & illus. green paper covers.
MWA°; CtHi; NPV; PP (fr.[2], p. 31 & covers wanting); Shoemaker 1425.

465 A Grandmother's Stories. Hagerstown, Md.: adv. by Jacob D. Dietrick in the Hagerstown *Maryland Herald May 31, 1805.*

466 A Grandmother's Stories. Vol. II. Comprising, The History Of An Old Rat. Francis And Laura. Ingratitude Punished. From Sidney's Press, For I. Cooke & Co. New-Haven. 1813.

fr.[2], t.[3], [4–5], 6–47 p.; illus.; 11 cm.; pr. & illus. green paper covers.
Cover title: Grandmother's Stories. Vol. II.
English ed. London: Vol. I. B. Crosby & Co. And B. Tabart [*ca.* 1812].
MWA-W°; Shaw 51308.

467 The Grateful Return; An Entertaining Story, for Children. Embellished with Cuts. The First Edition. Lansingburgh [N.Y.]: Printed By Luther Pratt, & Co. MDCCIXVI [*sic. i.e.* MDCCXCVI].

fr.[ii], t.[1], [2–3], 4–27 p.; illus.; 10 cm.; wall-paper covers.
PP°; Evans 30507.

Grateful Turk. *See* Day, Thomas, no. **267.**

468 Gratitude A Poem By A Youth Illustrated With Elegant Engravings Philadelphia Published and sold by Wm Charles Price, Plain 12½ cents Coloured 18 3/4 cents 1816. [cover title].

[1–6] p. engr. on one side only of 6 leaves; illus.; 14 cm.; pr. buff paper covers.
English ed. London: pl. signed: *Published October 1st. 1812. by Willm Darton Jun.*
NNC-Pl°; DLC; Shaw 37742 and 39053.

[GREEN, WILLIAM] 1771–1801
469.1 [—] The School Of Good Manners: Containing, I. Rules for children's behavior in every situation in life. II. A brief summary of the doctrines contained in the Holy Scriptures. III. An explanation of many terms used in moral philosophy and divinity. IV. Fourteen short forms of prayer composed for the use of children, particularly for such as attend schools, and academies, for every morning and evening, in the course of a week. By The Preceptor Of The Ladies Academy In New-London. New-London [Conn.]: Printed By Samuel Green. [1801?].

t.[1], [2–3], 4–48 p.; 16.5 cm.; marbled paper covers. This is a different book than Moody's *School of Good Manners,* having been entirely rewritten.
MWA°; MSaE (rebound); Shaw 947 (dated 1801?) and 16152 (dated 1808?).

469.2 [—] ———— Manners. Containing Rules For Children's Behaviour In Every Situation Of Life. Sangerfield, [N.Y.] J. Tenny, Printer. 1814.

t.[1], [2–3], 4–48 p.; 10 cm.; marbled paper covers.
See also The School of Good Manners, no. **871.1.**
CtY°.

GREGORY, RICHARD
470 — My Daughter A Poem, By Mr. R^d Gregory Illustrated With Elegant Engravings. Philadelphia Published and sold by Wm. Charles Price plain 12½ cents Colour'd 18 3/4 cents 1816. [cover title].

[1–6] p. engr. on one side only of 6 leaves; illus.; 13 cm.; pr. paper covers.
MWA*; NNC-Pl; Shaw 37747; Weiss 1932.

471 — MY SON A Poem By Richard Gregory Illustrated With Engravings Philadelphia Published and sold by Wm. Charles Price Plain 12½ cents Coloured 13 3/4 cents 1816 [cover title].
[1–6] p. engr. on one side only of 6 leaves; col. illus.; 13.5 cm.; pr. yellow paper covers.
English ed. London [Wm. Darton, Jun.] July 18, 1812.
MWA* (rear cover wanting); IU (3 leaves wanting); PP; Shaw 37749.

A GREY-CAP FOR A GREEN-HEAD. *See* Puckle, James, no. **1075**.

GRIFFIN, JOHN 1769–1834
472 [—] No. 5 ANECDOTES OF A SAILOR. List Of Tracts Published By The Hartford Evangelical Tract Society. March 1816. [a list of 9 tracts] [cover title].
[1], 2–4 p.; 16.5 cm.; pr. blue paper covers not part of the pagination. The covers are printed on both sides of the leaf; rear cover leaf paged 3 & 4; The text is signed *John Griffin on* p. 4.
MWA*; Shaw 37756.

473.1 — A CHILD'S MEMORIAL: Containing An Account Of The Early Piety And Happy Death Of Miss Dinah Doudney, Of Portsea, Aged 9 Years, Delivered To A Congregation Of Children, In Orange Street Chapel, On New Year's Day, 1805. To Which Is Added An Account Of Miss Sarah Barrow, Who Was Burnt To Death, April the 4th, 1805. First American, from the Seventh English Edition. By John Griffin. Charlestown [Mass.]: Printed by Samuel T. Armstrong, For Rev. Daniel Oliver. 1809.
t.[1], [2–5], 6–54 p.; 15 cm.; pink and blue marbled paper covers.
MWA*; Shaw 17684.

473.2 —————— Utica [N.Y.]: Seward and Williams. 1810
79 p.
MWA-T*.

474 — A CHILD'S MEMORIAL. Exhibiting The Early Piety And Happy Death Of Miss Dinah Doudney, Of Portsia, England. Delivered to a large Congregation of Children, on New-Year's Day, 1805. By John Griffin. Concord [New Hampshire]: Printed By George Hough, July, 1812. [cover title].
[1], 2–24 p.; 17 cm.; pr. gray paper covers.
MWA*; Shaw 25571.

475.1 — A CHILD'S MEMORIAL, Or, New Token For Children: Exhibiting the Early Piety and Happy Death of Miss Dinah Doudney, Of Portsea, Delivered To A Congregation Of Children, In Orange Street Chapel, on New Year's Day, 1805. To Which Is Added, An Account Of Miss Sarah Barrow, Who Was Burnt To Death, April the 4th, 1805. By John Griffin. Second American Edition. With Other Lives, Additions, And Corrections. Charlestown, (Mass.) Printed By Samuel T. Armstrong. 1809.
t.[1], [2–3], 4–72 p.; 15 cm.; blue marbled paper covers.
MWA*; MSaE; Shaw 17685.

475.2 —————— Third American Edition. With Other Lives, Additions, And Corrections. Charlestown, (Mass.) Printed By Samuel T. Armstrong. 1809.
t.[1], [2–3], 4–72 p.; 14 cm.; blue and pink marbled paper covers.
MB*.

475.3 —————— By John Griffin. Fourth American Edition. With Other Lives, Additions, And Corrections. Utica, (N.Y.) Printed By Seward And Williams. 1810.
t.[1], [2–3], 4–79 p.; 13.5 cm.; blue marbled paper covers.
MWA*; CtHi; DLC (rebound, i. st. on t.[1], original covers wanting); Shaw 20260.

476.1 — No. 38. EARLY PIETY, RECOMMENDED In The History Of Miss Dinah Doudney, Portsea Eng. In A Sermon By John Griffin. caption title p.[1] Andover [Mass.]: Printed For The New England Tract Society By Flagg And Gould. 1814. First edit. 6000. [colophon p. 20 [or 189]].
[1], 2–20 p.; 17 cm.; also paged [169], 170–189 p.
MWA* (bound with other tracts in *Twelve Witnesses . . . Boston. N. Willis. 1814*); Shaw 31618.

476.2 — —— [caption title] Andover[Mass.]: Pr. For The New England Tract Society By Flagg And Gould. . . . 1815.

Shaw 34818.

476.3 — No. 38 —— [caption title] Andover: Printed For The New England Tract Society By Flag And Gould. 1816. < 3d Edit. 6000. > [colophon p. 20].

[1], 2–20 p.; 17.5 cm.

MWA-W*; Shaw 51593.

476.4 — No. 38 —— [caption title] Andover: Printed For The New England Tract Society By Flagg And Gould. 1817. [colophon p. 16].

[1], 2–16 p.; 17 cm.

DLC* (bound with other tracts).

476.5 — No. 46. Early —— Griffin. [caption title]. Published By The New-York Religious Tract Society. D. Fanshaw, Printer, No. 241 Pearl-street. < June, 1817.–5000 > [colophon].

[1], 2–20 p.; 17.5 cm.

DLC*.

476.6 — (No. 19.) —— By John Griffin. Published By The Philadelphia Female Tract Society. [caption title p.[1]]. Printed by Lydia R. Bailey, No. 10, North Alley, Philad. [1817] [colophon p. 16].

[1], 2–16 p.; 14 cm.

MWA* (bound with other tracts with which *The Second Annual Report Of The Philadelphia Female Tract Society For The Year 1817* was originally bound); Shaw 40957.

476.7 — (No. 20) ——Doudney (concluded) Published By The Philadelphia Female Tract Society. [caption title p. [17]]. Printed by Lydia R. Bailey, No. 10, North Alley, Philad. [1817] [colophon p. 28].

[17], 18–28 p.; 14 cm.

MWA* (bound with other tracts with which *The Second Annual Report Of The Philadelphia Female Tract Society For The Year 1817* was originally bound); Shaw 40957.

476.8 — No. 38. —— Doudney, Portsea, Eng. In A Sermon By John Griffin. [caption p. [1]]. Andover: Printed For The New England Tract Society By Flagg And Gould. 1820 < 5 Ed. 6000. >

[1], 2–20 p.; 17 cm.; also paged [169], 170–188 p.

MB* (bound with other tracts in *The Publications of The New England Tract Society. Vol. II. Andover [Mass.]: Printed By Flagg And Gould. 1820.*).

GRINDER, GILES *pseud.*

477 — Pleasing And Instructive Lessons On Turning the Grindstone. By Giles Grinder. Who'll Turn Grindstone? [n.p.] [n.d.].

t.[1], [2–3], 4–13 p.; title vignette, a portrait silhouette, only illus.; 11 cm.; pr. & illus. front cover.

Cover title: Lessons On Turning The Grindstone. By Giles Grinder. Who'll Turn Grindstone?. Possibly an apprentice's token printed [*ca.* 1800–1810].

MWA-T*.

478.1 The Guardian, Or Youth's Religious Instructor: A Monthly Publication, Devoted To The Moral Improvement Of The Rising Generation. Vol. I. [1 line quot.] New-Haven: Published By Stephen Dodge, At The Office Of The Religious Intelligencer. 1819.

[ii, Prospectus Of The Guardian], t.[1], [2, bl.], [3, No. 1 January, 1819. Vol. I.], 4–[397, No. 12. December, 1819. Vol. 1.]–429, [430–432, index] p.; 8.5 cm.; bound in one vol.

MWA* (12 numbers bound in one vol. with covers in a separate envelope; covers for Nos. 6 & 12 wanting).

478.2 —— Vol. II. [1 line quot.] New-Haven: Published By Stephen Dodge, At The Office Of The Religious Intelligencer. 1820.

t.[1], [2, bl.], [3, No. 1. January, 1820. Vol. II.], 4– [397, No. 12. December, 1820. Vol. II.], 398–428, [429–32, index] p.; 18.5 cm.

See Union List of Serials.

MWA* (12 numbers bound in one vol. with covers only of No. 3.); PP (Nos. 2, 8, wanting).

479 Guess Again, or Easy Enigmas and Puzzles for Little Folks. Ed. 2. Philadelphia: adv. by Wm. Charles, 1808 in **231.1**.

GUPPY, MRS. *pseud.*

480 — Instructive And Entetaining [*sic. i.e.* Entertaining] Dialogues For Children. By Mrs. Guppy. First American Edition. Philadelphia:

Published By Jacob Johnson. 1808. Dickinson, Printer.

fr.[ii], t.[iii], [iv–ix], x–xii, [13], 14–90 p.; illus.; 14.5 cm.; bound in marbled paper over bds.

MWA*; DLC; PP; RPB; Shaw 15177.

GUY, EARL OF WARWICH. *See* Wonderful Exploit Of Guy Earl Of Warwick, no. **1450.1.**

H

HAGAR OF THE DESERT. *See* Genlis, Stephanie Felicite Ducrest de Saint-Aubin, Comtesse de, no. **433.1.**

[HALDANE, JAMES ALEXANDER] 1768–1851
481.1 [—] EARLY INSTRUCTION RECOMMENDED: IN A NARRATIVE OF THE LIFE OF CATHERINE HALDANE. With An Address To Parents On The Importance Of Religion. [1 line quot.] Proverbs viii. 17. Boston: Printed By Manning & Loring, No. 2, Cornhill. 1806. Price 4 [dols.] per hundred —8 cts. single.
    t.[1], [2–3], 4–14 p.; 16.5 cm.; blue paper covers.
    MWA*; Shaw 10512.

481.2 [—] ——— [2 lines quot.] From Sidney's Press. For I. Cooke & Co. NEWHAVEN. 1812.
    fr.[2], t.[3], [4–5], 6–47 p.; front. & tailpiece p. 47 only illus.; 11 cm.; pr. & illus. yellow paper covers; inscription p. [4] signed *J. A. Haldane.* Cover title undated.
    MWA*; Ct(fr.[2], p. 47 & covers wanting); Shaw 25584.

481.3 [—] ——— From Sidney's Press; For I. Cooke & Co. New-Haven. 1813.
    fr.[2], t.[3], [4–5], 6–47 p.; illus.; 11 cm.
    NB*; Ct.

481.4 [—] ——— From Sidney's Press. New-Haven. 1817.
    fr.[2], t.[3], [4–5], 6–46, [47, adv.] p.; front. only illus.; 12.5 cm.; illus. buff paper covers.
    MWA*; CtY (fr.[2], p. [47] & covers wanting); Shaw 40872.

481.5 [—] ——— Boston: Printed And Sold By Lincoln & Edmands, No. 53 Cornhill. 1819.
    t.[1], [2–3], 4–36 p.; title page vignette only illus.; 13.5 cm.; pr. & illus. red paper covers.
    MWA*; Shaw 48131.

481.6 [—] ——— New-Haven: Printed For J. Babcock And Son, Sidney's Press. 1819.
    fr.[ii], t.[1], [2–3], 4–36 p.; front. only illus.; 13.5 cm.; pr. & illus. buff paper covers.

Cover title: Catherine Haldane. Published by J. Babcock & Son, Booksellers, Stationers and Printers, adjoining the Post-Office, New-Haven. Sold by S. & W. R. Babcock, Booksellers and Stationers, Charleston, S.C.
    MWA*; CtHi; DLC; RPB; Shaw 47866 and 48132.

481.7 [—] ——— Portland [Me.]: Published by William Hyde. A. Shirley, Printer. 1819.
    t.[1], [2], 3–24 p.; 12.5 cm.; pr. & illus. gray paper covers.
    MWA* (p. 9–16 wanting); Shaw 48133.

481.8 [—] ——— No. 115 ——— [probably caption title p. [1]] Andover: Printed For The New England Tract Society By Flagg And Gould. 1820. [probably colophon on last p.].
    Shoemaker 1485.

481.9 [—] ——— New Haven, Printed For J. Babcock & Son. Sidney's Press. 1820.
    fr.[2], t.[3], [4–5], 6–31 p.; front. only illus.; 14 cm.; pr. & illus. pink paper covers; rear cover adv. list of books; front. signed A [Alexander Anderson].
    MWA-W*; CtHi (2 copies); DLC; MWA; NB; NjP; PHi; PP; Shoemaker 1486 and 1487.

481.10 [—] ——— Sidney's Press. For John Babcock And Son. NEW-HAVEN. S. And W. R. Babcock, 163 King-St. Charleston [S. C.], And M'Carty And Davis. Philadelphia. 1820.
    fr.[2], t.[3], [4–5], 6–31 p.; front. only illus.; 14.5 cm.; pr. & illus. green paper covers; front. signed A [Alexander Anderson].
    NNC-Pl*; Shoemaker 1488.

482 [—] (No. 4) THE LIFE OF CATHERINE HALDANE. Written By Her Father, Who Was A Minister Of The Gospel. Published By The Philadelphia Female Tract Society. [1st caption title p. [1]] Printed by Lydia R. Bailey, No. 10, North Alley, Philad. [1816] [colophon p. 12 & 28].
    1st capt. t.[1], 2–12; 2nd capt. t.[13], 14–28 p.; 14 cm. 2nd caption title p. [13]: (No. 5.) The Life Of Catherine Haldane. (Concluded.) Published By ——— [same as 1st caption title].
    MWA*; Shaw 37772.

483 THE HAPPY BOATMAN; A Story For Children. Hartford, Oliver D. Cooke. 1820.

t.[1], [2–3], 4–16 p.; illus.; 10.5 cm.; pr. & illus. pink paper covers.

MWA*; CtHi; Shoemaker 1506.

484.1 THE HAPPY CHILD. Boston: adv. as "just published. And to be Sold by Z. Fowle, at his Printing-Office in Back Street" in *A Golden Chain Of Four Links*. [ca. 1765].

484.2 ——— Child: Or, A Remarkable and Surprising Relation Of a little Girl, Who dwelt at Barnart. Boston: Printed and Sold at the *Heart* and *Crown* in Cornhill, 1767.

t.[1], 2–8 p.; title vignette only illus.; 11 cm.; printed by Thomas and John Fleet. The title vignette is a *New England Primer* cut which accompanied the alphabet verse "Job feels the Rod Yet Blesses God." The cut first appeared in Benjamin Harris' *The Holy Bible In Verse*. 1729, sig. B₁ recto, no. **492.4**. In the above book, the cut has a break 2 mm. wide in the right lower basal border below the picture of the house. The top horizontal border has a break 1 mm. wide at the left side of the cut near or just above the shading of the sky. The same cut was used by the Fleet Brothers in no. **484.3**, but these breaks are not apparent.

MDeHi* (entire book torn in half, with a small portion along the tear mut.); Evans 41720.

484.3 ——— at Barnart. [caption title] *Sold at the* Heart & Crown *in Cornhill,* Boston. [1774?] [colophon p. 8].

t.[1], 2–8 p.; title vignette only illus.; 10.5 cm. Thomas and John Fleet were in business at The Heart & Crown 1757–1776. *The New England Primer* cut, used for the title page vignette, is the same as in no. **484.2** but does not have a break below the house in the right lower basal border, nor the break in the top horizontal border, and looks fresher than in the 1767 edition. It is possible that this ed. is earlier than no. **484.2**, but, until another copy of the 1767 ed. is found, it is not possible to be sure whether the breaks in the borders of the cut are due to poor printing or actual breaks. The copy in the PP is bound in a portion of a newspaper in which one of the advertisements is dated Nov. 26, 1774.

MWA-W*; PP; Evans 42619.

484.4 ——— Child. Printed and Sold in Hudson, 1795.

t.[1], 2–8 p.; 17.5 cm.

DLC*; Evans 28798.

485 (No. 22) THE HAPPY COTTAGERS; Or, The Breakfast, Dinner, and Supper. Published By The Philadelphia Female Tract Society. And for sale at their Depository, No. 20, Walnut Street. [caption title] Printed by Lydia R. Bailey, No. 10, North Alley, Philad. [1817] [colophon p. 8].

[1], 2–8 p.

MWA*; Shaw 40992.

486 THE HAPPY FAMILY or Memoirs of Mr. & Mrs. Norton. Intended to shew the delightful Effects of Filial Obedience. Printed by S. C. Ustick, & sold N⁰ 79 North Third Street Philadelphia. 1799 W. Barker sculp.

engr. fr.[ii], engr. t.[iii], [iv, bl.], [I], II–[IV], [5], 6–90 p.; front. only illus.; 11 cm.; bound in green Dutch paper over bds. The CBEL ascribes the book to Mary Ann Kilner. Although John Marshall lists this book among advertisements of his publications, in *A Course Of Lectures For Sunday Evenings*. [front. dated Dec. 1st 1783], he does not put "S.S.", Mary Ann Kilner's pseudonym, after the title of this book. Since J. Marshall carefully puts "S.S." and "M.P.", Dorothy Kilner's pseudonym, after all their respective publications, this book probably was not written by either of the Kilners.

English ed. London: entered at Stationer's Hall January 23, 1786, by John Marshall & Co.

MWA-W*; Evans 48919.

487.1 THE HAPPY FAMILY; Or, Winter Evenings' Employment. Consisting Of Reading And Conversations, In Seven Parts. By A Friend Of Youth. With Cuts By Anderson. [3 lines quot.] From Sidney's Press. For Increase Cooke & Co. 1803.

fr.[ii], t.[iii], [iv–v], vi, [7], 8–106, [107–108, adv.] p.; illus.; 13.5 cm.; bound in blue paper over w. bds.; front. signed A [Alexander Anderson]. Printed in New-Haven.

English ed. York: T. Wilson, 1800.

MWA-W*; MH (p. 103–104 mut., other p. worn).

487.2 ——— From Sidney's Press, For Increase Cooke & Co. 1804.

fr.[ii], t.[iii], [iv–v], vi, [7], 8–106, [107 adv.] p.; illus.; 14 cm.; bound in illus. blue paper over w. bds.; illus. same as no. 487.1. Printed in New-Haven.
MWA*; CtHi.

487.3 ——— Conversations. To Which Is Added, Select Fables Of Esop. [4 lines of verse]. New-York: Printed and Published by John C. Totten, No. 155, Chatham-street. 1806.
fr.[4], t.[5], [6–7], 8–58 p.; illus.; 14 cm.; illus. paper covers.
CtHi*; ICU (p. 37–48 wanting); MWA; Shaw 10524.

487.4 ——— [same as 487.2] From Sidney's Press, For Increase Cooke And Co. 1807.
fr.[ii], t.[iii], [iv–v], vi, [7], 8–106 p.; illus.; 14 cm.; bound in blue marbled paper over w. bds.; illus. same as no. 487.1. Printed in New Haven.
MWA-W*; BM; DLC; Shaw 12710.

487.5 ——— Youth [4 lines of verse]. New-York: Printed And Sold By J. C. Totten, No. 9 Bowery. 1815.
fr.[2], t.[3], [4–5], 6–48 p.; illus.; 14 cm.; pr. & illus. brown paper covers; front. [2] signed A [Alexander Anderson].
NNC-T* (fr.[2], & covers mut.); MSaE (covers wanting); MWA (fr.[2], and front cover wanting); Shaw 34854.

488.1 < No. 56. HAPPY POVERTY, OR THE STORY OF POOR BLIND ELLEN. A Well Authenticated Narrative. [caption p. [1] Andover [Mass.] Printed For The New England Tract Society By Flagg and Gould. 1815. < First edit. 6000.
t.[1], 2–8 p.; 17 cm.
MWA*.

488.2 ——— Narrative. [caption title p. [1]] Published for gratuitous distribution by The Hartford Evangelical Tract Society. May, 1817. 5000 Hudson and Co. Printers. [colophon p. 12].
[1], 2–12 p.; 16.5 cm.; pr. blue gray paper covers.
Cover title: No. 20. Blind Ellen. List Of Tracts Published By The Hartford Evangelical Tract Society. [list of 20 tracts].
OClWHi; CtHi (covers wanting); Shaw 40993.

488.3 ——— Narrative. To Which Is Added The Highway Of The Cross, And An Address On The Duty Of Private Prayer. Philadelphia: Published by "The Religious Tract Society of Philadelphia," No. 8. South-Front-Street. William Bradford—Agent. 1819.
t.[1], [2], 3–12 p.; title vignette only illus.; 19 cm.
NjR*; Shaw 40993.

489 THE HAPPY SEQUEL, Or, The History Of Isabella Mordaunt. A Tale For Young People. New-York: Published By William B. Gilley, Van Winkle & Wiley, Printers. 1815.
½t.[1], [2, bl.], [i, bl.], fr.[ii], t.[3], [4–7], 8–87 p.; front. only illus.; 15 cm.; bound in marbled paper over bds., leather spine; front. signed *Scoles sculp.* and inserted between ½t.[1] and t.[3]. Half title: The Happy Sequel, &c. &c.
English ed. London: J. Harris, 1815.
MWA*; DLC (½t.[1] & fr.[ii] wanting); MH; NNC-T (per. st. on. t.[3]); PP; Shaw 34856.

THE HAPPY VILLAGER. *See* Berquin, A., no. 85.

THE HAPPY WATERMAN. Philadelphia, 1800. *See* Cheap Repository, no. 169.4.

490.1 THE HAPPY WATERMAN. Published by B. Johnson, No. 247 Market St. Philadelphia n.d. [*ca.* 1807].
t.[i], [ii. bl.], [1], 2–36 p.; title page vignette only illus.; 14 cm.
English ed. London: adv. by John Marshall in *The Beggarly Boy* [1795] "on the 1st of August 1795 will be published."
NNC-SP* (bound in vol. 2. [*Cheap Repository Tracts. Philadelphia, 1807*]); PP (covers wanting); Shaw 13126.

490.2 ——— Waterman: Or, Honesty Rewarded. To Which Is Added, Lines Written On A Blank Leaf Of A Pocket Bible. Newburyport [Mass.], Printed By W. & J. Gilman. Sold at their Book-Store, No. 2, Middle-Street 1813. A variety of Useful Tracts, &c. for charitable distribution, cheap, at wholesale or retail.
t.[1], [2–3], 4–16 p.; p. [3] only illus.; 13.5 cm.; pr. & illus. gray paper covers; cover title dated 1814.
DLC* (rear cover wanting); MWA; Shaw 29207.

490.3 ——— Waterman. Ornamented With Cuts. Philadelphia: Published By Benjamin Johnson, No. 22, North Second Street. 1814.

t.[1], [2–3, bl.], illus. [4], [5], 6–24 p.; illus.; 13.5 cm.; pr. & illus. green paper covers. Adv. by Benjamin Johnson, 1813 in **899.1**.

MWA°; Shaw 31640.

490.4 ——— Philadelphia: Published by Benjamin Johnson, No. 31, Market-st. 1818.

t.[1], [2–3, bl.], illus.[4], [5], 6–24 p.; title vignette & 4 full page illus.; 14 cm.; olive-buff paper covers.

MWA° (covers wanting); NB; NhD; Shaw 44254.

490.5 ——— Waterman; Or, Honesty the best Policy. To which are added, The Boy Of Dundee. And The Gardener and Rose Tree. Suitable for Sabbath-School Readings. Printed & sold by Lincoln & Edmands, No. 53 Cornhill. 1819.

t.[1], [2–3], 4–24 p.; illus.; 13 cm.; pr. & illus. light-violet paper covers; front cover undated. Printed in Boston.

See also The Story Of The Happy Waterman, no. **1271**.

MWA-W°; DLC (pr. & illus. brick-red paper covers); MWA (pr. & illus. blue paper covers); PP; Shaw 48153.

491 THE HARE: Or, Hunting Incompatible With Humanity: Written As A Stimulus To Youth Towards A Proper Treatment Of Animals. [3 lines of verse]. Thomson. Philadelphia: Printed for Benjamin Johnson, No. 31 High-Street And Jacob Johnson No. 147 High-Street. 1802.

1st ½t.[1], [2, bl.], [i, bl.], fr.[ii], t.[3], [4–7], 8–60 p.; 2nd ½t.[61], [62], 64–144 p.; engr. front. illus. and tailpiece p. 144 only illus.; 14 cm.; bound in paper over bds., leather spine; p. 63 omitted. Adv. by Johnson & Warner, 1814 in **1449.2**.

English ed. London: Vernor and Hood, 1799.

DLC° (2 copies. copy 2 has the title mutilated, and wants engraved fr.[ii]); Shaw 2372.

HARRIS, BENJAMIN
492.1 [—] THE HOLY BIBLE IN VERSE. Bible [in a vignette of an open book]. 1717.

fr.[2, verse], t.[3], [4–62] p.; [A]-C$_8$, D$_7$ plus blank leaf D$_8$; illus.; 9 cm.; bound in leather. Page [32] or verso of sig. B$_8$ reads: "The Reader is hereby Caution'd against a little spurious Book, Printed with the same Title as this, and shaped like it, as ignorantly and illiterately as can be, Printed by one *Bradford*, which Book is partly stolen from the Original first printed by *B. Harris*, Senior, partly Corrupted, and perverted in its Sense; and generally the Word of God imposed upon with Nonsense, and Inconsistency: so that the real Design of the Author is Abused by such scandalous Imposition upon the Publick. B. Harris, Junior. March the 15th. 1712."

Page [33] caption: The New Testament.

The author Benjamin Harris, according to I. Thomas, sometimes printed in connection with John Allen in Boston but was not in regular partnership with him. Evans states they were in partnership from 1691–1692. Harris returned to England in 1695. *The Holy Bible In Verse* first appeared in 1698. The 1717 edition for years has been considered an English publication. However John Wyllie, Librarian of the University of Virginia, on seeing the PP copy recognized it to be American, and from the types of John Allen in Boston. If the title page and pages xxii and 1 of Increase Mather's *Some Important Truths About Conversion. Boston, John Allen, 1721*, title page 15 cm., are compared with the title page and D$_2$ verso, and C$_6$ verso of *The Holy Bible in Verse—1717*, some striking similarities are apparent. The clover leaf type ornament often used by John Allen is present in both books. The same font titling black letter "i" and "e" of "Conversion" in the former with "Bible" in the latter is striking. John Allen in these two books and in other books mixed identical italic and Roman types in the text. *The Holy Bible . . .* is printed in 58 (20 line measure) of Roman and italic type, the same as p. xxii of Mather's book. When examining this 58 Roman and italic type under a low powered microscope, with a magnification of twice natural size, the lower case italic "w" is of the closed top variety. The lower case Roman "w" varies in *The Holy Bible . . .* from having serifs in "was" D$_2$ verso line 3, to not having serifs in "likewise" C$_7$ recto line 8. In *Some Important Truths . . .*, p. xxii, the Roman lower case "w" in "would" line 23 is without serifs but "while" line 27 has serifs. The capital Roman "W's" in both books also look as if they came from the same type font. In the upper and lower case "w's" the character is always set off-center on its base. The resulting left set of the type face is unusually wide thus leaving a conspicuous gap between each "w" and the letter that follows it. The type in *The Holy Bible* . . . 1717 is undoubtedly from the same type font as in John Allen's printing of *Some Important Truths,* and therefore printed by John Allen. *The Holy Bible In Verse* was republished in 1724, with the same Allen 58 Roman and italic types in the same format as the 1717 edition without an imprint and with many pages printed from standing type. According to Evans, vol. I., John Allen was in Pudding Lane near the Post Office 1708–1724. Isaiah Thomas in the 1874 edition of his *History Of Printing in America,* p. 92, says that he had seen a number of books after 1711 printed "by Allen alone, the last of which is Whittemore's Almanac, bearing the date 1724." The only edition of Whittemore listed in Evans around 1724 is *The Farmer's Almanac. Boston, Printed by Thomas Fleet.* [1724] The cuts in the 1717 edition are exceedingly interesting. They are *New England Primer* alphabet cuts from an edition which has not survived and antedates the earliest known copy printed in 1727. The cuts are: 1. Bible, p. [3]; 2. Adam, p. [5]; 3. Samuel, p. [12]; 4. Uriah's beauteous Wife, p. [13]; 5. King, p. [14]; 6. Queen Ester, p. [17]; 7. Job, p. [18]; 8. Time, p. [21]; 9. Whale, p. [27]; 10. Peter, p. [50]. In the *New England Primer Boston: S. Kneeland and T. Green, 1727,* and *Boston: S. Kneeland and T. Green, 1735,* crude copies of the above cuts in the reverse are found. The 1729 edition of *The Holy Bible In Verse* is larger, 9 x 6.5 cm. instead of 8.5 x 5.5 cm. It is printed in different type in a new type set up. Cuts 1–6, 8–10 are from the same blocks used by Allen in 1717. Cut 7 of Job however is new. This different cut of Job is used as a title vignette in *The Happy Child. Boston: Printed and Sold at the Heart and Crown in Cornhill, 1767,* no. **484.2.** Thomas and John Fleet were at this address 1757–1776. The same cut also appears on the first page of the Fleet brothers' [1774?] edition of *The Happy Child,* no. **484.3.** The early Allen primer cuts can also be found in *Cock Robin's Death And Funeral,* no. **211,** and in *Tom Thumb's Folio,* no. **1315.1,** both printed at the Bible and Heart [*ca.* 1780]. Thomas and John Fleet according to Isaiah Thomas changed the

crown for a Bible when crowns became unpopular. The cut of The Bible appears in John Taylor's *Verbum Sempiternum. Boston: Thomas Fleet 1801.* These alphabet cuts with the exception of the cut of Job must have been acquired by Thomas Fleet, who also printed Whittemore's *Farmer's Almanac* in [1724]. The cuts furnish further evidence that John Allen published the first American edition of *The Holy Bible In Verse. 1717,* written by his former partner Benjamin Harris. Whether John Allen printed the 1724 edition early in 1724 before his death, or whether a successor did, using Allen's types, is not known. If Evans' and Isaiah Thomas' dates are correct, Allen must have died in 1724 and could have printed the book before his death. After his death the primer alphabet cuts were acquired by Thomas Fleet as well as some of Allen's business. Because of the presence of the cuts it is likely that Thomas Fleet printed the 1729 edition.

English ed. London: B. Harris, 1698.

Welch° (fr.[2] & p. [57–58] mut.); CLU (marbled paper covers); MWA; NN (p. [61–62] or D$_7$ and blank leaf D$_8$ wanting; this copy has on [A]$_2$ verso, "Christian Reader", "Berean" for the first word in line 16, which occurs in all copies of the 1717 edition and in the first English edition, and is not "therein", in this copy); PP (marbled paper covers); Evans 39659.

492.2　[—] The Holy Bible In Verse. [cut of open Bible] 1718. Size 3½ x 2¼, 64 pp. unnumbered. 24 lines to page. Nine cuts in text and one on title page. Ornamental rules at top of pages 52 and 58 same as in 1717 edition.

Lacks first two leaves, title in facsimile from original now lost, lacks a leaf in sig. D. Contains 'Author's caution to Reader.' Typographical errors and changes in use of italic type show this edition to have been reset.

Evans 39679.

492.3　[—] ——— Verse. Bible [in a vignette of an open book] 1724.

t.[3], [4–16], [33–48] p.; [A]$_2$–[A]$_8$, & all of C$_8$ only; 8.5 cm.; unbound.

The Introduction is on p. [4] instead of being opposite the title page, or p. [2], as in no. **492.1,** the 1717 edition. The text is the same as the 1717 edition with some of the pages printed from standing type and others reset. The primer cuts are from the same blocks used in no. 492.1, but portions of the borders are now lacking in certain ones. They are: 1. Bible, wanting the top and bottom rules; 2. Adam, with the same break in the bottom rule and base, but lacks the short thick and thin rules to the right of the base of the cut which appear in the 1717 edition; 3. Samuel, 4. Uriah's . . . wife, both lack the top thin rule; 5. King, only the right third of the top inner rule is present. *See* the discussion about these primer cuts and the evidence that John Allen may have also printed this edition, under no. **492.1**.

Griffin° ([A]₁, all of B & D wanting); Evans 39801.

492.4 [—] ———— Verse. Very pleasant and profitable, and greatly tending to encourage Children & Others to Read, and also to understand what they read in that sacred Book. Bible [in a vignette of an open book] Printed in the Year 1729.

fr.[2, verse], t.[3], [4–62] p.; [A]–C₈, D₇; illus.; 9.5 cm.; marbled paper covers.
The New England Primer woodcut illustrations are again used in this edition with the exception of no. 7, of Job, which is new. This new woodcut is used for the title vignette in *The Happy Child. Boston: Printed and Sold at the Heart and Crown in Cornhill, 1767*, no. **484.2**. Thomas and John Fleet published at this address from 1757–1776. This cut of Job is in the reverse in *The New England Primer. Boston, T. Fleet, 1738*. The illustrations in the 1729 edition of *The Holy Bible In Verse* show the same breaks in the borders observed in the 1724 edition. Cuts no. 1, 3, and 4 were again used by Thomas and John Fleet in *Tom Thumb's Folio* [*ca.* 1780], no. **1315.1**, which contains three additional primer cuts which belong to this series and are also in the reverse of those which appear in the 1727 edition of *The New England Primer*. Because of the presence of this new illustration of Job and its subsequent history, this 1729 edition of *The Holy Bible . . .* was undoubtedly printed by Thomas Fleet in Boston. *See* discussion in no. **492.1**.
MWA°; CtHi; Evans 39904.

492.5 [—] ———— Boston: adv. in Wigglesworth's *Day of Doom* "Books to be sold by T. Fleet." 1751.

492.6 [—] ———— Philadelphia, Printed by James Chattin, 1754.
Evans 7148.

492.7 [—] ———— Boston: adv. by D. Fowle, [*ca.* 1756] in **932**.

493 [—] The Holy Bible epitomized in Verse. Boston: adv. as "Just Re-Printed and to be Sold at the Heart and Crown T. and J. Fleet," 1773 in **1408.13**.

HARRIS, SAMUEL
494 MEMOIRS OF MISS MARY CAMPBELL, Daughter Of Mr. David Campbell, Of Windham, N. H. Who Died July 21, 1819, Aet. 28. Compiled by Samuel Harris, Pastor Of The Church In Windham. Published by request. Haverhill [Mass.]: Burrill And Hersey Printers. 1820.
t.[1], [2–3], 4–107 p.; 14 cm.; blue marbled paper covers.
MWA-W°.

THE HARVEST HOME. *See* The Cheap Repository, no. **169.15**.

495 THE HARVEST HOME REPRESENTING THE PROGRESS OF WHEAT in a series of elegant Engravings. Philada. Pubd. 1809, by Johnson and Warner No. 147, Market Street. [1809].
t.[1], [2–16] p. engr. on one side only of 16 leaves; illus.; 12.5 cm.; pr. paper covers. Adv. by Johnson and Warner, 1814 in **1449.2**.
Cover title: Harvest Home; Representing The Progress of Wheat, In A Series Of Elegant Engravings. Philadelphia: Published and sold by Johnson & Warner, And May be had of all the Book-sellers. 1809. Price 18 Cents.
English ed. London: J. Wallis, Jany. 1, 1807.
RPB°; DLC (pr. pink paper covers); MWA (front cover mut. p. [4–5] bound out of order and follow p. [9]; Shaw 17720; Weiss 1932b.

HAYS, ALICE (SMITH) 1657–1720
496.1 — A LEGACY, OR WIDOW'S MITE; Left By Alice Hays, To Her Children and others. Being a Brief Relation of her Life; With An Account Of Some Of her Dying Sayings. The Second Edition. [2 lines quot.] London, printed: And Philadelphia, Re-printed by Andrew Steuart, at the Bible-in-Heart, in Second-street. MDCCLXVI.
t.[1], [2], 3–48 p.; 15.5 cm.
PHi°; NN (rebound); Evans 10331.

496.2 ———— Sayings. [2 lines quot.] Psalm lxvi. 16. New-York: Printed And Sold By Samuel Wood, No. 362, Pearl-Street. 1807.

  t.[1], [2–3], 4–55 p.; 16.5 cm.
  PPL° (rebound); DLC; PHC; Shaw 12733.

HAYS, S.
497 — Stories For Little Children. By S. Hays. Part I. [II.] Philadelphia, Published by Johnson & Warner 1812.

  vol. I.: t.[1], [2–4], 5–36 p.; illus.; 13 cm.; vol. II.: t.[1], [2–4], 5–36 p.; illus.; 12.5 cm.; pr. pink paper covers; cover titles undated. Part of a large publisher's remainder. The author's name is spelled "Hayes" on the cover titles. There is a period after "Warner." on t.[1] of pt. II. The DLC copy of pt. I has black unprinted paper covers and is not part of the publisher's remainder.

  English ed. London, entitled: *Stories*. by E. Hayes, 2 parts, plates., adv. by Darton, Harvey, and Darton in *The Ancient and Renowned History Of Whittington And His Cat*. 1812.

  MWA°; CSmH (pt. II.); CtHi; CtY (pt. II.); DLC; MB; MHi (pt. II.); NB (pt. II.); NN (pt. II.); NNC-Pl (pt. II.); PHi (pt. II.); PP; PPL.

HELME, ELIZABETH *d.* 1818
498.1 — Instructive Rambles In London, And The Adjacent Villages. Designed to Amuse The Mind, And Improve The Understanding Of Youth. By Elizabeth Helme. [5 lines quot.] Philadelphia: Printed By Budd And Bartram, For Thomas Dobson, At The Stone House, No. 41, South Second Street. 1799.

  ½t.[i], [ii, bl.], [i, bl.], fr.[ii], t.[iii], [iv–v], vi–xii, [13], 14–308 p.; front. only illus.; 18 cm.; bound in leather; front. inserted between ½-t.[i] and t.[iii] is signed *Lawson sc.* [Alexander Lawson].

  English ed. London: 2 vols., E. Newbery, 1798.
  MWA°, OOxM; PPi; Evans 35610.

498.2 ———— [five lines of verse] New-York. 1814.

  ½t.[i], [ii, bl.], [i, bl.], fr.[ii], t.[iii], [iv-v], vi–xii, [13], 14–308 p.; front. only illus.; 18 cm.; bound in leather; front. signed *Lawson sc.* [Alexander Lawson].
  MWA°, OOxM; PPi; Evans 35610.
  PP; Shaw 31685.

499 [—] James Manners, Little John, And Their Dog Bluff, [4 lines of verse] Philadelphia: Printed And Sold by Joseph And James Crukshanks [*sic. i.e.* Crukshank], No. 87, High-Street 1801.

  t.[i], [ii–iii], iv, [5], 6–105 p.; 14 cm.; bound in yellow paper over bds.

  English ed. London: Darton and Harvey, and E. Newbery, 1799.
  MWA°; Shaw 644.

500 [—] Maternal Instruction, Or Family Conversations, On Moral And Entertaining Subjects, Interspersed With History, Biography, And Original Stories. Designed For The Perusal Of Youth. By Elizabeth Helme, Author Of Instructive Rambles In London, &c.&c.&c. First American Edition. New-York: Re-Printed From The London Edition, By James Oram. 1804.

  fr.[ii], t.[i], [ii–vii], viii-xii, [1], 2–231 p.; front. & tailpiece p. 231 only illus.; 18.5 cm.; bound in leather.
  DeWint; Shaw 6466.

HEMMENWAY, MOSES 1735–1811
501.1 — A Discourse To Children. By The Rev. Moses Hemmenway, D.D. Also, The Conversion And Death Of Joseph: An Affecting Story, Founded On Fact. Embellished With Two Elegant Engravings. Published According To Act Of Congress. Printed At Portland [Me.], By Thomas B. Wait. 1792.

  fr.[ii], t.[1], [2–3], 4–23 p.; 2 pl. including front.; 14 cm. The Story of Joseph p. [21]–23. Engr. front. & pl. opp. p. 20 signed S. *Hill, Boston. The Discourse To Children* is a sermon and not within the scope of this bibliography. "The Conversion and Death of Joseph" is a narrative and because of it this book is included.
  MWA°; ICU; NN; RPJCB; Evans 24390.

501.2 ———— Act of Congress. Boston: Printed By Samuel Hall, In Cornhill. 1793.

  fr.[ii], t.[1], [2–3], 4–23 p.; 2 pl. [same as **501.1** with the signatures scratched off both of them]; 14 cm. There is a printer's ornament of a crown on t.[1] and p. 20. At the top of page [3] a decorative bar of printer's ornaments contains six angels' heads. This is the earliest use of these two printer's ornaments by S. Hall. At the end, p. [21]–23, "The Story Of Joseph" is added. It is not the Biblical Story.

Welch° (covers wanting); MB (per st. on t.[1]); MH; MHi (fr.[ii] wanting); MWA; NN (fr.[ii] & pl. opp. p. 21 wanting); RPJCB; Evans 22596.

501.3 —⸻ On Fact. And A New Year's Gift For Youth. By The Rev. Andrew Fuller, D.D. Kettering. Charleston [Mass.]. Printed And Sold By Samuel Etheridge. 1802.
  t.[1], [2], [3], 4–36 p.; 15.5 cm.; gray paper covers. The Story of Joseph p. 22–24.
  MWA° (p.[3]–4 trimmed); CLU; ICU; PP; Shaw 2393.

501.4 —⸻ Founded On Fact. Charleston [Mass.]: Printed And Sold By Samuel Etheridge. 1803.
  t.[1], [2–3], 4–28 p.; 15.5 cm.; gray paper covers.
  MWA°; MHi; Shaw 4361.

501.5 —⸻ Hemmenway, D.D. Johnstown: Printed By Taylor And Andrews For Erastus Frary. 1808.
  t.[1], [2], 3–12 p.; 17 cm.
  CtHi°.

HENDLEY, GEORGE
502 — An Authentic Account Of The Conversion, Experience, And Happy Deaths, Of Ten Boys. Designed For Sunday Schools. Sidney's Press. Published by John Babcock & Son, New-Haven, S. & W. R. Babcock, No. 163 King-Street, Charleston [S.C.] and M'Carty & Davis, Philadelphia. 1820.
  fr.[2], t.[3], [4, adv.], [5], 6–31 p.; front. only illus.; 14.5 cm.; pr. & illus. yellow paper covers.
  Cover title: Biography For Boys.
  MWA° (p. 31 mut.; covers worn & mut.); Ct (i. st. on fr.[2]); CtHi; CtY; DLC; ICU; PP (p. 29–30 torn in half); Shoemaker 1564.

503 — An Authentic Account Of The Conversion, Experience, And Happy Deaths, Of Nine Girls. Designed For Sunday Schools. Sidney's Press. Published by John Babcock & Son, New-Haven, S. & W. R. Babcock, No. 163 King-Street, Charleston [S.C.], and M'Carty & Davis, Philadelphia. 1820.
  fr.[2], t.[3], [4, adv.], [5], 6–31 p.; front. only illus.; 14.5 cm.; pr. & illus. paper covers; front. signed A [Alexander Anderson].

Cover title: Biography For Girls. Published and Sold by John Babcock & Son, [same as t.[3]] Philadelphia. Sidney's Press.
  MWA°; CtHi; CtY; NB (bpl. on front cover); PP; Shoemaker 1563.

504.1 — A Memorial For Children; Being An Authentic Account Of The Conversion, Experience and happy Deaths Of Eighteen Children. Designed As A Continuation Of Janeway's Token. By George Hendley, Minister Of The Gospel. [2 lines quot.] From Sidney's Press, New-Haven. 1806.
  t.[i], [ii–iii], iv, [5], 6–108 p.; 14 cm.; bound in green Dutch paper over w. bds.
  MWA°; CtHi; CtY (covers wanting); MH; MHi; NRU; PP; Shaw 10548.

504.2 —⸻ Ballston Spa [New-York]: Printed By J. Comstock, For Reuben Sears. 1814.
  t.[1], [2–3], 4–108 p.; 13.5 cm.; bound in brownish-buff paper over w. bds., leather spine. The preface p. 4 is signed *Hanley, May 28th, 1805.*
  N° (i. st. p.[3])

505.1 — < No. 34. Part II. A Memorial For Sunday School Boys, Being An Authentic Account Of The Conversions, experience, and Happy Deaths, of Nine Children. By George Hendley, Minister of the Gospel. [caption title p. [1]] Andover [Mass.]: Printed For The New England Tract Society By Flagg And Gould. 1820. < 1st edit. 6,000. [colophon p. 16].
  [1], 2–16 p.; 17.5 cm.
  Shoemaker.

505.2 — A Memorial ⸻ Boys, ⸻ of Twelve Boys. By George Hendley, Minister Of The Gospel. [1 line quot.] Eighth Edition. Boston: Printed For Samuel T. Armstrong, By Crocker And Brewster, No. 50, Cornhill. 1820.
  t.[i], [ii–iii], iv–viii, [9], 10–47, [48] p.; 12.5 cm.; pr. & illus. brick-red paper covers.
  Cover-title: A Memorial For Sabbath School Boys. Boston: . . . 1820. Rear cover adv. list of books.
  MWA°; PP; NCooHi; Shoemaker 1566.

506.1 — A Memorial For Sunday School Boys, Being The First Part Of An Authentic Account Of The Conversion, Experience, and Happy Deaths Of Twenty-Five Children. By George

Hendley, Minister of the Gospel. [2 lines quot.] First American, from the Sixth English Edition. Boston: Published By Samuel T. Armstrong, No. 50, Cornhill. U. Crocker, Printer. 1819.

t.[i], [ii-iii], iv–viii, [9], 10–47, [48] p.; 13 cm. MB (per. st. on t.[i]).

506.2 — —— Deaths of Twenty-Three Children. By George Hendly, Minister of the Gospel. [2 line quot.] Greenfield [Mass.]: Published By Clark & Tyler. H. Graves, Printer. 1820.

t.[i], [ii-iii], iv–v, [vi], [7], 8–48 p.; 12 cm.; pr. & illus. buff paper covers. Preface p. v signed: *January 1, 1816.*
MWA°; DLC; MH; Shoemaker 1567.

507.1 — A MEMORIAL FOR SUNDAY SCHOOL GIRLS, Being The Second Part Of An Authentic Account Of The Converison, Experience, and Happy Deaths Of Twenty-Five Children. By George Hendley, Minister of the Gospel. [2 lines quot.] First American, from the Sixth English Edition. Boston: Published By Samuel T. Armstrong, No. 50, Cornhill. U. Crocker, Printer. 1819.

t.[1], [2–3], 4–48 p.; 12.5 cm.; ornamented orange paper covers.
Welch°; MWA; Shaw 48208.

507.2 — —— Girls, Being An Authentic Account, Of The Conversion, Experience, and Happy Deaths, Of Thirteen Girls. By George Hendley, Minister Of The Gospel. [1 line quot.] Eighth Edition. Boston: Printed For Samuel T. Armstrong, By Crocker And Brewster, No. 50, Cornhill. 1820.

t.[1], [2–3], 4–48 p.; 12.5 cm.; pr. & illus. gray-green paper covers.
Cover title: A Memorial For Sabbath School Girls. Boston: [same as t.[1]] 1820.
MWA-W° (rear cover wanting).

507.3 — —— [same as **507.1**] Greenfield [Mass.]: Published By Clarke And Tyler. J. Metcalf Printer. 1820.

t.[1], [2–3], 4–48 p.; 12.5 cm.; pr. & illus. buff paper covers.
DLC°.

HERBSTER, MRS. (afterwards Metaal Backker, F.)
508.1 [—] THE TWO SISTERS; Or The Cavern. New-Haven, Sidney's Press. 1810.
Shaw 21543.

508.2 — —— The Cavern. A Moral Tale. Translated From The French Of Madame Herbeter [*sic. i.e.* Herbster] New-York: Published By E. Duyckinck, No. 68 Water-Street. N. Van Riper, Printer. 1818.

t.[1], [2–3], 4–128 p.; 11 cm.
MWA° (covers wanting); Bowe mss.; Shaw, 44303 and 44304.

THE HERMIT AND THE TRAVELLER. *See* Parnell, Thomas and Oliver Goldsmith, no. **973.1**.

THE HERMIT EXHIBITING A REMARKABLE INSTANCE OF THE PROVIDENCE OF GOD. *See* Burder, George, no. **138**.

THE HERMIT OF THE FOREST. *See* Johnson, Richard, no. **673.1**.

THE HERMIT OR THE UNPARALLELED SUFFERINGS AND SURPRISING ADVENTURES OF PHILIP QUARLL. *See* Longueville, Peter, no. **793.1** for the rewritten children's version entitled The English Hermit; Or The Adventures Of Philip Quarell.

509.1 HERZLICHE BITTE AN DIE KINDER UND JUGEND. Reading [Pa.]; Gedruckt, bey Gottlob Jungman u Comp. [1796?].
t.[1], [2–8] p.; 9.5 cm.
MWA°; Evans 47804.

509.2 — —— Libanon [Pa.]: Gedruckt und zu haben bey Jacob Schnee [*ca.* 1810].
t.[1], [2–3], 4–12 p.; 12 cm.; pr. & illus. gray paper covers.
PP°.

HIEROGLYPHIC BIBLE (arranged chronologically)

510 A CURIOUS HIEROGLYPHICK BIBLE; Or, Select Passages In The Old And New Testaments, Represented With Emblematical Figures, For The Amusement Of Youth: Designed Chiefly To familiarize tender Age, in a pleasing and diverting Manner, with early Ideas of the Holy Scriptures. To Which Are Subjoined, A short Account of the Lives of the Evangelists, and other Pieces. Illustrated with nearly Five Hundred Cuts. The First Worcester Edition. Printed at Worcester, Massachusetts, By Isaiah Thomas, And Sold, Wholesale and Retail, at his Bookstore. MDCCLXXXVIII.

fr.[ii], t.[iii], [iv–vii], viii, 9–144 p.; illus.; 14

cm.; bound in leather; p. 135 misprinted "235". English and Irish ed. London: T. Hodgson 1783.
Welch° (fr.[ii] wanting, p. 15–16, 143–144 mut.); CtHi (fr.[ii], p. 133–144 wanting many p. mut.); CtY; MWA; MWHi; (rebound); OClWHi (p. [ii-vi], 49–50, 143–144 wanting other p. mut.); PP (rebound, fr.[ii] wanting); Evans 2096.

511 A Hieroglyphical Bible For The Amusement And Instruction Of Children; Being A A [*sic*] Selection Of The Most Useful Lessons And Interesting Narratives: From Genesis To Revelations. Embellished With Familiar Figures And Striking Emblems. New-Ipswich, N. H. Printed By Salmon Wilder. 1820.
 fr.[ii], t.[1], [2–4], 5–108 p.; illus.; 13.5 cm.; wallpaper covers; the front. is numbered p. "100" & repeated on p. 100.
 MWA° (p.[3]–8 torn in half, p. 57–58 mut.); Shoemaker 406.

512.1 The Hieroglyphik [*sic. i.e.* Hieroglyphic] Bible; Or Select Passages In The Old And New Testments, Represented With Emblematical Figures, For The Amusement Of Youth: Designed Chiefly To familiarize tender age, in a pleasing and diverting manner, with early ideas of the Holy Scriptures. To Which Are Subjoined, A short Account of the Lives of the Evangelists, and other pieces. Illustrated with nearly five hundred cuts. Second Edition. Boston: Published By Isaiah Thomas, Jun. No. 6, Marlborough Street. J. T. Buckingham, Printer. 1814.
 fr.[ii], t.[iii], [iv–v], vi–vii, [8–9], 10–144 p.; illus.; 14.5 cm.; bound in printed gray-green paper over bds., red leather spine.
 Cover title copy A: "Thomas' Second Edition. Hieroglyphick Bible. Price 75 cents." Cover title copy B: Thomas's Edition ——— [same as copy A].
 MWA° (copy A, B); CtY (fr.[ii] wanting); MB; MHi (copy A); NN (bound in leather); PP; OOxM; Shaw 30861.

512.2 ——— Third Edition. Plymouth [Mass.]: Published By Joseph Avery, And For Sale At His Book-Store. Printed At George Clark & Cos [*sic. i.e.* Co's] Office. Charleston [Mass.] 1820.

fr.[ii], t.[iii], [iv–v], vi–vii, [8–9], 10–144 p.; illus.; 14.5 cm.; bound in gray-green paper over bds., leather spine.
 MWA°; NjR; Shoemaker 409.

513.1 A New Hieroglyphical Bible For the Amusement & Instruction of Children; Being A Selection of the most useful Lessons; and most interesting Narratives; (Scripturally Arranged) From Genesis to the Revelations. Embellished with Familiar Figures & Striking Emblems Neatly Engraved To the whole is Added a Sketch of the life of Our Blessed Savior, The Holy Apostles &c. Recommended by the Rev.d Rowland Hill M.A. Boston Printed for W. Norman Book & Chartseller [*ca.* 1796].
 engr. folded fr.[ii], engr. t.[iii], [iv. bl.]; [i–ii], iii, [4], 5–144 p.; illus.; 15 cm.; bound in Dutch paper over w. bds. Recommendation p. [i] signed: *R. Hill. Surry Chapel, May 12, 1794.*
 English ed. London: G. Thompson, 1794.
 Welch°; CLU; CSmH; DeWint; ICMILC (t.[iii] wanting); MH; MHi; MiU; MWA; NN (rebound); PP (fr.[ii] follows t.[iii]; RPJCB (front cover wanting); Evans 26651.

513.2 ——— Emblems Elegantly Engraved To the whole is added ——— [same as **513.1**]. New York: Printed for & Published by the Booksellers. MDCCXCVI.
 engr. fr.[ii], engr. t.[iii], [iv. bl.], [i–ii], iii, [4], 5–144 p.; illus.; 14 cm.; bound in leather over w. bds.
 MWA-W°; CLU; CtY; DLC; MH (p. 139–144 wanting); N (soiled worn copy); NHi (p. 143–144 wanting, bound in marbled paper over bds., leather spine); NhHi (p. 143–144 mut.); Evans 30668.

513.3 ——— Striking Emblems. To the whole is added a sketch of the life of Our Blessed Saviour. Recommended by the Rev. Rowland Hill, M.A. From an English Edition: Reprinted at Jaffrey N. H. by Salmon Wilder: Sold at his Printing Office by the gross, dozen or single. 1814.
 t[1], [ii–iv], v, [vi], 7–120 p.; illus.; 16.5 cm.; copy A, bound in gray-green paper over w. bds., leather spine; copy B, wants rear cover bound in pr. yellow-buff paper over w. bds.
 MWA° (copy A, B); CLU; DLC; NhHi (emb. st. on t.[1]); Shaw 30872.

513.4 ────── useful lessons and interesting narratives, from Genesis to the Revelations. Embellished With Familiar Figures And Striking Emblems, Neatly Engraved. To the whole is added, A Sketch Of The Life Of Our Blessed Saviour, And The Holy Apostles, &c. New-York: Printed And Sold By Samuel Wood & Sons, At The Juvenile Book-Store, No. 357, Pearl-Street. 1815.

engr. pl.[ii], engr. pl. [iii], [iv. bl.], t.[1], [2–5], 6–56, [57–72] p.; illus.; 14.5 cm.; bound in pr. buff paper over bds., black leather spine; cover title undated. Adv. by S. Wood & Sons, 1816 in **1188.7** and 1819 in **1188.8**.
MWA-W°; DLC (2 copies); MSaE; MWA; Shaw 34076.

513.5 ────── Embellished With Nearly Two Hundred Emblems, Neatly Engraved. To Which Is Added, A Sketch ────── [same as **513.4**]. Hartford: Published By Cooke And Hale, 8 Rods North Of The State-House. 1818. P. B. Gleason & Co. Printers.

t.[1], [2–5], 6–56, [57–72] p.; illus.; 15 cm.; bound in pr. & illus. yellowish-buff paper over bds., leather spine. Cover title imprint: Hartford: Published By Cook And Hale.
MWA-W°; Ct (p. 7–8, [57–72] wanting, p. 6 mut.); MDeHi; MWA; NPV; RPB (covers worn); Shaw 43311.

513.6 ────── Hartford: Published By Cooke And Hale, 8 Rods North Of The State-House, 1818. Hamlen & Newton, Printers.

t.[1], [2–5], 6–56, [57–72] p.; illus.; 15 cm.; bound in pr. & illus. yellow-buff paper over bds., leather spine; cover title undated.
NN° (p. [71–72] mut.); CtY; MdHi.

513.7 ────── Apostles &c. Printed For Randolph Barnes, Bookseller, Pittsburgh. 1818. Hamlin & Newton, Printers, Hartford, (Con.)

t.[1], [2–5], 6–56, [57–72] p.; illus.; 15.5 cm.; bound in pr. paper over bds., leather spine.
MSaE°(p. 47–50 mut.).

513.8 ────── [same as **513.4**] New-York: Published By Samuel Wood & Sons, No. 261, Pearl-Street, And Samuel S. Wood & Co. No. 212, Market-street, Baltimore. 1818.

engr. pl. [ii], engr. pl. [iii], [iv, bl.], t.[1], [2–5], 6–56, [57–72] p.; illus.; 14.5 cm.; bound in

glossy green marbled paper over w. bds., red leather spine.
MWA°; MSaE; NHi; PP; Shaw 43312.

513.9 ────── [same as **513.5**] Hartford: Published By Oliver D. Cooke, For Sale By Him And Most Booksellers In The United States. 1820. P. B. Goodsell, Printer.

fr.[2], t.[3], [4–5], 6–56, [57–72] p.; illus.; 14.5 cm.; pr. & illus. orange-buff paper over bds., leather spine.
Cover title; Seventh Edition—Price 38 Cents. A New ────── [same as t.[3]] Children. With Nearly 200 Engravings. And The Life Of Our Saviour, And The Apostles. Hartford, Oliver D. Cooke. 1821.
MWA-W°; CtHi; ICU; MWA (gray-green pr. & illus. paper over bds.); NN (i. st. on t.[3], p. [71–72] wanting); OClWHi, RPB; Shoemaker 426.

513.10 ────── Bible For The Instruction and Amusement of Good Children. Embellished With Upwards Of Fifty Emblems, Neatly Engraved. To which is added, A Sketch Of The Life Of our Blessed Saviour, And The Four Evangelists. Hartford: Published By Oliver D. Cooke. P. B. Goodsell, Printer. 1820.

t.[1], [2–3], 4–18, [19–24] p.; illus.; 13.5 cm.; illus. white paper covers printed in pink ink.
Welch°; Ct; CtW; MWA-T; PP; Shoemaker 427.

513.11 ────── Bible In Miniature, For The Instruction and Amusement of Good Children. To which is added, A Sketch Of The Life Of Our Blessed Saviour. Hartford, Oliver D. Cooke, 1820.

t.[1], [2–3], 4–13, [14–16] p.; illus.; 10.5 cm.; copy A, illus. white paper covers pr. in blue-green ink; copy B, pr. & illus. white paper covers pr. in tan ink, cover dated 1820.
MWA° (copy A), ICU (copy B); Shoemaker 424 and 425.

HILL, HANNAH

514 ── A Legacy for Children, Being Some of the Last Expressions, and Dying Sayings, Of Hannah Hill, Junr. Of the City of Philadelphia, in the Province of Pennsilvania [*sic. i.e.* Pennsylvania], in America, Aged Eleven Years and near Three Months. The Third Eddition [*sic. i.e.* Edition] [7 lines quot.] Printed by Andrew Bradford, at the Sign of the Bible in Second Street, in Philadelphia, 1717.

t.[1], [2–4], 5–35 p.; 14 cm.

Irish ed. Dublin: Sam Fairbrother, 1719.

PP*; PPL; Evans 1884.

515 HISTORICAL SKETCHES FOR JUVENILE MINDS, Ornamented with Engravings. Written By A Lady. New-York: Printed For And Sold By T. B. Jansen & Co. No. 248, Pearl-Street. 1802.

fr.[ii], t.[1], [2–3], 4–72 p.; illus.; 14.5 cm.; bound in blue-gray marbled paper over bds., leather spine. Some of the cuts are signed *A*, or *Anderson* [Alexander Anderson].

NHi*; Shaw 2405.

516.1 THE HISTORY AND ADVENTURES OF LIT-TLE ELIZA, A Companion To Little William; Illustrated With A Series Of Elegant Figures. Eliza in the Garden reading a little Book. [12 lines of verse]. Philadelphia: Published and sold Wholesale by William Charles, and may be had of all the Booksellers. 1811 W. M'Culloch, Printer.

fr.[ii], t.[1], [2–8], [pl. opp. p. [8]] p.; 8 pl. including the front.; 12.5 cm.; pr. yellow paper covers.

English ed. London, entitled: *The History Of Little Eliza. A Companion To Little Fanny.* J. Aldis, 1810, with 7 paper dolls.

NNC-Pl* (rear cover torn in half); NN (i. st. p. [1–2]; pl. [1, 2, 3] wanting, other pl. bound out of order); Shaw 23006; Weiss 1932b.

516.2 ———— Philadelphia: Published and Sold Wholesale by William Charles, and may be had of all the Booksellers. J. Bioren, Printer. 1815.

fr.[ii], t.[1], [2–8], [pl. opp. p. [8]] p.; 8 pl. including the front.; 12.5 cm.; pr. tan paper covers.

Copy A, cover imprint: Philadelphia: Published By Morgan & Yeager, At Their Juvenile Bookstore. Price 25 cents coloured, 18 cents plain. Copy B, cover imprint: Philadelphia: Published and Sold Wholesale by Wm. Charles and may be had of all the booksellers. Price plain 18 3-4 Cents—Colored, 25 cents. 1814.

MWA-W* (copy A, col. pl.); DLC (copy B); NN; PP (copy A, B).

517.1 THE HISTORY AND ADVENTURES OF LITTLE HENRY, Exemplified in A Series Of Figures. Boston: Printed By J. Belcher. 1812.

t.[1], [2–3], 4–20 p.; illus. with 7 moveable fig-

ures which lie loose in the book; 11 cm.; blue-gray paper covers. The figures are 8.5 cm. high without the interchangeable head, and show Henry in different costumes which he wore during his adventures: 1 As a child of Wealthy parents, 2. A beggar boy, 3. a chimney sweeper, 4. a drummer, 5. a sailor, 6. a midshipman, 7 a costume worn by Henry when he returns to his parents.

English ed. London: S. & J. Fuller, 1810.

MWA-W* (7 figures; head & hats wanting); CtHi (5 figures; head & hats wanting); MiD (head and 7 figures, 1 cap or hat).

517.2 ———— Figures. Philadelphia: Published and Sold Wholesale by Wm. Charles, and may be had of all the Booksellers, 1812. Price—18 Cents, Plain,—Coloured, 25 Cents. W. M'Culloch, Printer.

fr. [ii], t.[i], [2–3], 4– 16 p.; 7 pl.; 13 cm.; pr. paper covers.

DeWint*.

517.3 ———— New-York: Published by W. B. Gilley, 92 Broadway. 1819.

t.[1], [2–3], 4–20 p.; illus. with 7 moveable figures, which lie loose in the book; 11 cm.; pr. brownish-buff paper covers. The moveable figures are the same as no. **517.1**. There is a moveable hat for figures 3, 4, 6, 7. A ribbon is knotted in the spine so that the book can be closed and tied together.

MWA-W*.

518.1 THE HISTORY AND ADVENTURES OF LIT-TLE WILLIAM, A Companion To Little Eliza; Illustrated With A Series Of Elegant Figures. William at Home with his Parents. [12 lines of verse]. Philadelphia: Printed and sold Wholesale by Wm. Charles, and may be had at all the Booksellers. 1811. W. M'Culloch, Printer.

fr.[ii], t.[1], [2–8] p.; 8 pl. including front.; 13 cm.; pr. buff paper covers.

Cover title: ———— Eliza; Illustrated With Whimsical Engravings. Philadelphia: Published and sold Wholesale by Wm. Charles and be had of all the Booksellers. 1811. W. McCullock, Printer.

The "may" of "may be had of all the Booksellers" is wanting in the cover title.

NNC-PI* (pl. opp. p. [5] wanting, rear cover ¾ wanting).

518.2 ——— Philadelphia: Printed and Sold Wholesale by William Charles, and may be had of all the Booksellers. J. Bioren, Printer. 1815.

fr.[ii], t.[1], [2–8] p.; 8 pl. including front.; 13 cm.; pr. paper covers; cover title same as title but dated 1814. (copy A). Cover title imprint copy B: Philadelphia: Published By Morgan & Yeager, At The Juvenile Bookstore, No. 114, Chestnut Street, first door below the Post-Office. Price, plain 18¾ cents—coloured 25 cents.

MWA° (copy A); DLC (copy A); MiD; PP (copy A, B); Shaw 34904.

THE HISTORY AND DESCRIPTION OF WATER BIRDS. *See* Bewick, Thomas, no. **94.**

519 THE HISTORY AND SUFFERING OF ALEXANDER SELKIRK, Who was left on Juan Fernandez, a desolate island in the Pacific Ocean. Philadelphia: Published by Bennett & Walton, No. 31, Market Street 1814.

t.[1], [2–3], 4–108 p.; 14.5 cm.; bound in pr. gray paper over bds.

See also The History of Alexander Selkirk, no. **527.1.**

MWA°; Shaw 31716.

520.1 HISTORY OF A BIBLE, &c. &c. Ballston Spa [N. Y.]: Printed By James Comstock, For Phinehas Webb. 1811.

t.[1], [2–3], 4–12 p.; t. [1], 17.5 cm.; bound with other tracts in a contemporary binding of blue-gray paper over w. bds., leather spine.

MWA°; Shaw 23007.

520.2 (No. 17.) HISTORY OF A BIBLE. Published By The Philadelphia Female Tract Society. [caption title p. [1]]. Printed by Lydia R. Bailey, No. 10, North Alley, Philad. [1817] [colophon p. 12].

[1], 2–12 p.; 14 cm.

MWA° (bound with other tracts, with which *The Second Annual Report Of The Philadelphia Female Tract Society For The Year 1817* was originally bound); Shaw 41049.

521.1 Boston Series of Cheap Religious Tracts, No. 2. THE HISTORY OF A BIBLE, Describing Its Happy Influence On The Members Of Different Families, Into Whose Libraries it gained Admission. Boston: Printed And Sold By Lincoln & Ed-

mands, No. 53 Cornhill. Who publish a great variety of cheap Religious Tracts. The charitable, resident in any part of the Union, who purchase for distribution, will find their orders answered on the most liberal terms. 1809. Price, 4 cts. single—33 cts. doz.—2,25 cts. a hundred.

t.[1], [2–3], 4–12 p.; 17 cm.; blue paper covers. MWA°; Shaw 17754.

521.2 Boston Series of Cheap Religious Tracts, No. 2. THE HISTORY OF ——— Admission. [caption p. [1]] Boston: Printed And Sold By Lincoln & Edmands, No. 53, Cornhill. Who publish a great variety of Cheap Religious Tracts On cash purchases of 5 dols a discount of 5 pr. cent will be made; over 10 dols. 10 pr. cent. The orders of charitable distributors, resident in any part of the United States, promptly answered. 1811. Price, 2,25 cts. a hundred, 33 cts. a doz. [colophon p. 12].

t.[1], 2–12 p.; t.[1] 16.5 cm.

MWA° (rebound, bound with other tracts in *Evangelical Tracts, Doctrinal, Experimental, And Practical. Vol. I. Boston: Lincoln & Edmands. 1813.*); Shaw 23008.

521.3 ——— Bible . . . Utica, N. Y. Pr. by Ira Merrell, at the Patriot Office, 1812.

[94] p.

NUt (not seen); Shaw 25654.

521.4 < No. 77. THE HISTORY ——— Admission. Part I. [caption title p.[1]]. Andover [Mass.]: Printed For The New England Tract Society By Flagg And Gould. 1818. < 3d edit. 6000 [colophon p. 12].

[1], 2–12 p.; 17.5 cm.

MWA°; Shaw 44325.

521.5 < No. 77. THE HISTORY ——— Admission. Part I. [caption title.] Andover [Mass.]: Printed For The New England Tract Society By Flagg And Gould. 1820. < 4th edit. 6,000. [colophon p. 12].

[1], 2–12 p.; 17 cm.

MWA° (bound with other publications of *The New England Tract Society. vol. IV. Andover: Flagg And Gould. 1820*); MB.

522 THE HISTORY OF A BIBLE, Exhibiting Its Happy Influence Upon Several Of Its Proprietors, And Connected With Anecdotes Of Some Of Its

Possessors. Augusta: (Geo.) Printed And Sold by Hobby & Bunce, At their Book-Store, Broad-Street. 1812.

t.[1], [2–3], 4–35 p.; no illus.; 17 cm.; pr. buff paper covers; front and rear cover titles the same as the title page surrounded by a border of printer's type ornaments.
ICU°:

THE HISTORY OF A DOLL. *See* Johnson, Richard, no. **674.1.**

523   THE HISTORY OF A GOLDFINCH: Addressed To Those Children, Who Are Dutiful To Their Parents, And Humane To Their Fellow Creatures. Philadelphia: Published By B. And T. Kite, No. 20, North Third Street. Fry And Kammerer, Printers. 1807.

fr.[ii], ½t.[1], [2, bl.], t.[3], [4–5], 6–33 p.; 3 pl. including front.; 14 cm.; blue marbled paper covers. Half title: The History Or A Goldfinch. English ed. London: Darton, 1806.
MWA-W°; DLC (per. st. on t.[3]); Shaw **12757.**

THE HISTORY OF A GREAT MANY BOYS AND GIRLS. *See* Kilner, Dorothy, no. **727.1.**

THE HISTORY OF A LITTLE BOY FOUND UNDER A HAYCOCK. *See* Johnson, Richard, no. **675.1.**

HISTORY OF A LITTLE CHILD FOUND under a Haycock. *See* Johnson, Richard, no. **676.**

524   THE HISTORY OF A LITTLE SILVER FISH. A new Tale for Children. Hartford [Conn.]: Published by S. G. Goodrich. Roberts & Burr, Pr's. 1819.

fr.[2], t.[3], 4–16 p.; fr.[2] and illus. p. 16 only illus.; 10.5 cm.; illus. paper covers printed in red ink.
MWA-T°.

525.1   THE HISTORY OF A PIN, As Related By Itself. Interspersed With a Variety Of Anecdotes, Pointing out to the Youth of both Sexes, the Superiority of a generous Mind over one that is narrow and uncultivated. By the author of the Brothers, A Tale for Children, &c. Easton [Pa.]: Printed By Samuel Longcope, For Jacob Johnson, No. 31 High-Street, Philadelphia. 1802. [Written by Miss Smythies of Colchester].

fr.[ii], t.[1], [2–3], 4–64 p.; front. only illus.; 12.5 cm.; blue marbled paper covers. Engr. front. signed *Ralph sc.* [William Ralph]. English ed. London: E. Newbery, 1798.
Welch°; DLC (fr.[ii] wanting, rebound); MWA; PP; Shaw 2406.

525.2   ——— Mind over one that is contacted. Printed and Sold by Whittingham and John Gilman, Middle-street. Newburyport [Mass.]. Feb. 1808.

fr.[2], t.[3], [4–5], 6–34 p.; illus.; 14 cm. MSaE°.

526.1   THE HISTORY OF A SCHOOLBOY. With Other Pieces. New-York: Printed and Sold by W. Durell, at his Book-Store and Printing-Office, No. 19, Queen-Street. MDCC,XCII.

fr.[2], t.[3], [4–7], 8–74 p.; front. only illus.; 13 cm.; bound in blue-gray paper over bds., leather spine. English ed. London: J. Stockdale, 1788.
NHi°; Evans 46464.

526.2   ——— Philadelphia. Printed by Benjamin Johnson, No. 147 High-street. 1794.

t.[1], [2–3], 4–124 p.; 10 cm.; bound in buff paper covers ornamented with red characters. MWA-W°; Evans 47073.

527.1   THE HISTORY OF ALEXANDER SELKIRK, The Real Robinson Crusoe. To which are added, Sketches Of Natural History. New-York: Printed And Sold By Samuel Wood & Sons, At The Juvenile Book-Store, No. 357, Pearl-Street. 1815.

fr.[ii], t.[1], [2–3], 4–45 p.; illus.; 13.5 cm.; pr. yellow paper covers; cover title undated; fr.[ii] and illus. p. 7, 9, 21 signed A [Alexander Anderson]. Adv. by Samuel Wood & Sons, 1816 in **1188.7** and 1819 in **1188.8.**
MWA°; NHi (bound with other books in *The Child's Magazine.* Vol. 1. no. 185); Shaw 34907.

527.2   ——— New-York: Printed And Sold By Samuel Wood, At The Juvenile Book-Store, No. 357, Pearl-Street. 1815.

fr.[ii], t.[1], [2–3], 4–48 p.; illus.; 14 cm.; pr. brownish-buff paper covers; cover title undated; fr.[ii] signed A [Alexander Anderson].
NHi°; MWA; NN (covers mostly wanting, fr[ii] mut.) PP; Shaw 34907.

527.3 ——— The Real Robinson Crusoe. Adorned with Cuts. New-Haven: For J. Babcock & Son. Sidney's Press. 1820.

fr.[2], t.[3], [4–5], 6–30, [31, adv.] p.; illus.; 10 cm.; pr. & illus. paper covers; copy A has a cut of a bird on the front cover; copy B has a cut of a squirrel on the limb of a tree. Cover imprint of both copies A and B: Published by J. Babcock & Son, New-Haven, and S. and W. R. Babcock, Charleston.

MWA° (copy A & B); Ct. (i. st. on fr.[2]); CtHi; MSaE (emb. st. on t.[3]); PP; Shoemaker 1600.

528 THE HISTORY OF ALIBEG, THE PERSIAN. Hartwick [New York]: From the Press of L. & B. Todd. 1815.

t.[1], [2–3], 4–28 p.; 5.5 cm.

English ed. London: J. Lowe, for M. Bassam. [1811?].

MWA° (covers wanting).

THE HISTORY OF ALLADIN [*sic. i.e.* Aladdin]. *See* Alladin, no. **28.1.**

529 THE HISTORY OF ALMIRA. Designed To Show The Advantages Of A Good Education. By A Youth. Meredith [N.H.]: Published by Jason Lothrop. 1815.

t.[i], [ii–iii], iv–v, [vi–viii], [9], 10–68 p.; 8.5 cm.; bound in buff paper over w. bds., leather spine; p. [ii]: George Hough, Printer, Concord [N.H.] Preface p. v. signed: *Meredith, March 13, 1815.*

Welch° (p. 29–30 mut.); DLC; MWA; NjR; PP; Shaw 34909.

530.1 THE HISTORY OF AMELIA, Or an elegant Collection of Entertaining Stories For Boys and Girls, [*sic. i.e.* "."] Boston: Printed and sold by N. Coverly. 1792. Price three Pence.

½t.[1], fr.[2], t.[3], [4], 5–32 p.; illus. 10.5 cm. MWA°.

530.2 ——— Boston: Printed and sold by N. Coverly. 1793. Price Three Pence.

½t.[1], fr. [2], t.[3], [4], 5–32 p.; illus.; 10 cm. This book contains cuts used in the N. Coverly 1793 edition of *The History of Little Goody Two-Shoes*, and the 1789 edition of *The House That Jack Built.* Half title p.[1]: The History Of Amelia.

CtHi°; MWA (½t.[1], fr.[2], & p. 27–32 wanting, t.[3] mut.); Evans 46782.

530.3 ——— Collection of Diverting Stories, For Boys and Girls. Printed for and sold by the Booksellers. 1800.

t.[1], [2–3], [4], 5–14, [15–16] p.; illus.; 10 cm.; pink paper covers.

MWA° (corner of p. [4], [15–16] wanting including pagination); Evans 37618.

531 THE HISTORY OF AMERICA, Abridged For the Use Of Children Of All Denominations. Adorned with Cuts. [1 line quot.] Philadelphia: Printed by Wrigley & Berriman, for John Curtis. 1795.

fr.[ii], t.[iii], [iv–v], vi, [7–8], 9–127, [128 adv. list of books] p.; illus. 11 cm. bound in Dutch paper over bds. The same portrait is used for "Dr. Benjamin Franklin" p. 16 and "Thomas S. Lee, Esq." p. 55.

PP°; NjP (bound in Dutch paper over bds.); PHi; Evans 28831.

THE HISTORY OF AN INDIAN WOMAN. *See* [Boudinot, Elias], no. **118.**

532 [THE HISTORY OF AN OLD WOMAN WHO HAD THREE SONS JERRY, JAMES, AND JOHN.] n.p. [1816?].

[1], 2–16 p. engr. on one side only of 16 leaves; illus.; 13.5 cm.; buff paper covers. The title is taken from the cover title of the English ed. Caption p. [1]: The Old Woman & Her Three Sons. The illustrations are redrawn from the English ed. of J. Harris, 1815. The book was probably published and engraved by John Scoles, in New York City [ca. 1816]. Scoles published another London publication of J. Harris' entitled *The Doleful Death Of Poor Old Robin . . . By Peter Prim.* no. **1063,** which has similar illustrations which are close to the English edition, but redrawn.

MWA-W°.

533.1 THE HISTORY OF BEASTS. Philadelphia: adv. by John Adams, 1806 in **646.3.**

533.2 THE HISTORY OF BEASTS. [2 lines quot.] New-York: Printed And Sold By S. Wood, At The Juvenile Book-Store, No. 362, Pearl-Street. 1808.

fr.[ii, alphabet], t.[1], [2–3], 4–29 p.; illus.;

10 cm.; black Dutch paper covers.
MWA°; CtHi; CtY; PP; Shaw 15241.

533.3 ———— New-York: Printed And Sold By
S. Wood, At The Juvenile Book-Store. No. 357,
Pearl-Street. 1810.
　fr.[ii, alphabet], t.[1], [2–3], 4–29 p.; illus.;
　10 cm.; illus. blue-gray paper covers.
　Adomeit°.

533.4 ———— New-York: Printed And Sold By
S. Wood, at the Juvenile Book-store, No. 357,
Pearl-Street. 1811.
　fr.[ii, alphabets], t.[1], [2–3], 4–29 p.; illus.;
　10.5 cm.; pr. & illus. buff paper covers.
　MWA-T°.

533.5 ———— Beasts. Concord [N.H.]: Published and Sold by Daniel Cooledge, at his Book-
Store. 1812. Geo. Hough, Printer.
　fr.[2], t.[3], [4–5], 6–23 p.; illus. blue-gray
　paper covers; fr.[2] a picture of Daniel Cool-
　edge's Bookstore; preface p. [4] signed: S. W.
　This is a different book from the S. Wood pub-
　lication.
　CtHi° (front cover wanting); NHi (p. 22–23
　& covers wanting); PP (all pages except fr.[2]
　and front cover worm-eaten).

533.6 ———— New-York: Printed And Sold By
Samuel Wood, At the Juvenile Book-Store, No.
357, Pearl-street. 1812.
　fr.[ii, alphabet], t.[1], [2–3], 4–29 p.; illus.;
　10 cm.; pr. & illus. brownish-buff paper covers.
　MWA-T° (p. 9–10 wanting, fr.[ii], t.[1], p.
　[2]–8 & front cover mut.).

533.7 ———— [2 lines quot.] New York: Printed
And Sold by Samuel Wood, At the Juvenile Book-
store, No. 357, Pearl-street. 1813.
　fr.[ii, alphabet], t.[1], [2–3], 4–29 p.; illus.;
　10 cm.; pr. & illus. buff paper covers.
　MWA-T°; NRU; MSaE (fr.[ii], p. 29 & covers
　wanting, emb. st. on t.[1]).

533.8 ———— New-York: Printed And Sold By
Samuel Wood. At The Juvenile Book-Store, No.
357, Pearl-Street. 1814.
　fr.[ii, alphabet], t.[1], [2–3], 4–29 p.; illus.;
　10 cm.; pr. & illus. buff paper covers.
　MWA-T° (covers wanting); CtY.

533.9 ———— New-York: Printed And Sold By
S. Wood & Sons, At The Juvenile Book-Store,
No. 357, Pearl-Street. 1816.
　fr.[ii, alphabet], t.[1], [2–3], 4–29 p.; illus.;
　11 cm.; pr. & illus. buff paper covers.
　DLC (fr.[ii] & covers wanting, t.[1] mut.);
　NWebyC.

533.10 ———— Nerv-York [*sic. i.e.* New-York]:
Printed And Sold By S. Wood & Sons, At The
Juvenile Book-Store, No. 261, Pearl-Street. 1818.
　fr.[ii, alphabet], t.[1], [2–3], 4–29 p.; illus.;
　10.5 cm.; orange Dutch paper covers.
　MWA-W°.

533.11 ———— New-York: Published By Samuel
Wood & Sons, No. 261, Pearl-Street. And Samuel
S. Wood & Co. No. 212, Market-st. Baltimore.
1818.
　fr.[ii, alphabet], t.[1], [2–3], 4–29 p.; illus.;
　10.5 cm.; green Dutch paper covers.
　MH° (i. st. on p. [2]); PP; PPL; Shaw 44326.

533.12 ———— New-York: Published By Samuel
Wood & Sons, No. 261, Pearl-Street; And Samuel
S. Wood & Co. No. 212, Market-st. Baltimore.
1820.
　fr.[ii, alphabet], t.[1], [2–3], 4–29 p.; illus.;
　10.5 cm.; green Dutch paper covers.
　ICU°; DLC (fr.[ii], p. 29 & covers wanting).

THE HISTORY OF BERTRAM. *See* Berquin, A., no.
86.1.

534.1 THE HISTORY OF BIRDS. [2 lines quot.]
New-York: Printed And Sold By S. Wood, At The
Juvenile Book-Store. No. 357, Pearl-Street. 1810.
　fr.[ii, alphabet], t.[1], [2–3], 4–29 p.; illus.;
　10. cm.; illus. gray-green paper covers; last line
　p. 29: See the book of Riddles. Title vignette
　signed A[Alexander Anderson], and in nos.
　534.2–13.
　MWA°; Shaw 20338.

534.2 ———— New-York: Printed And Sold By
S. Wood, at the Juvenile Book-store, No. 357,
Pearl-Street. 1811.
　fr.[ii, alphabet], t.[1], [2–3], 4–29 p.; illus.;
　10 cm.; pr. & illus. yellow-buff paper covers;
　cover title dated 1811. Last line p. 29: See the
　book of Riddles.
　MWA°; NhHi; Shaw 23009.

534.3 ——— Birds. Printed By W. & J. Gilman, Newburyport [Mass.]. Sold at their Book-Store & Printing-Office, with a variety of Children's Books, wholesale and retail. 1812.

fr.[2], t.[3], [4–5], 6–27 p.; illus.; 12.5 cm.; pr. & illus. yellow-buff paper covers. This is a different book from no. **534.2**.
Fitzhugh°.

534.4 ——— [same as **534.2**] New-York: Printed And Sold By Samuel Wood, At The Juvenile Book-Store, No. 357, Pearl-Street. 1813.

fr.[ii, alphabet], t.[1], [2–3], 4–29 p.; illus.; 10 cm.; pr. & illus. buff paper covers. On the frontispiece the alphabet groups are separated by division ornaments. Alphabet group one and two and four and the bottom line are separated by a thick rule, 9 mm. long, which tapers at each end. Alphabet group two and three and three and four are separated by an ornament, 11 mm. long, composed of a central diamond, on either side of which is a club shaped rule tapering at one end. The last line p. 29 printed in italics: *See the Book of Riddles.*
Cover title: ——— Birds. [illus. of three boys playing with a top] [a thick rule tapering at the ends] New-York: ——— S. Wood, At the Juvenile Book-store, No. 357, Pearl-street. [a thick rule tapering at the ends]. 181[3].
OOxM°.

534.5 THE HISTORY OF BIRDS. [illus. of four groups of flowers] [an ornament composed of a central diamond on either side of which is a club shaped rule tapering at one end] New-York: Printed And Sold By Samuel Wood. At the Juvenile Book-store, No. 357, Pearl-street. [a row of 9 dots] 1813. [cover title].

A variant of no. **534.4** with a different type setting for the cover title and differences in the type setting of the frontispiece and p. 29. On the frontispiece the upper three division ornaments have a thick rule with a slightly diamond shaped center, which tapers at each end. The lowest division ornament is thick at the center and tapers at each end. The last line p. **29** printed in italics: *See the book of Riddles,* with the "b" of "book" in the lower case.
MB° (most of the imprint cut off of t.[1]); MWA-T; Shaw 28748.

534.6 ——— [2 lines quot.] New-York: Printed And Sold By Samuel Wood, At the Juvenile Book-store, No. 357, Pearl-street. [a row of 9 dots] 1813. [title page].

The frontispiece and text is the same as no. **534.5**, which is missing the imprint on the title page. The cover title is also the same, but has a different cut. The illustration consists of the upper portion of a plant showing inflorescence, leaves and stem.
MWA-T°.

534.7 ——— New-York: Printed And Sold By Samuel Wood, At The Juvenile Book-Store, No. 357, Pearl-Street. 1814.

fr.[ii, alphabet], t.[1], [2–3], 4–29 p.; illus.; 10 cm.; pr. & illus. yellow-buff paper covers; cover title undated.
MNS°.

534.8 HISTORY OF BIRDS. Newburyport [Mass.], Printed By W. & J. Gilman. And Sold at their Miscellaneous Book-Store, No. 2, Middle-Street. 1814.

fr.[2], t.[3], [4–5], 6–23 p.; illus.; 13.5 cm.; pr. & illus. paper covers. Cover title undated. This is a different book from no. **534.7**.
MWA°; Shaw 31717.

534.9 ——— [same as **534.7**] New-York: Printed And Sold By S. Wood & Sons At The Juvenile Book-Store, No. 357, Pearl-Street. 1815.

fr.[ii, alphabet], t.[1], [2–3], 4–29 p.; illus.; 10 cm.; pr. & illus. brownish-buff paper covers; last line p. 29: See the Book of Riddles. Cover title imprint: New-York: Printed And Sold By Samuel Wood, ——— [same as t.[1]] n.d.
MWA° (fr. ii, t.[1], p. [2] mut.); Shaw 34910.

534.10 ——— New-York: Printed And Sold By S. Wood & Sons, At The Juvenile Book-Store, No. 357, Pearl-Street. 1816.

fr.[ii, alphabet], t.[1], [2–3], 4–29 p.; illus.; 10 cm.; pr. yellow paper covers; cover title undated.
MWA°; DLC (fr.[ii] & covers wanting); MH; NWebyC; PPL; Shaw 37839.

534.11 ——— Nerv-York [*sic. i.e.* New-York]: Published By Samuel Wood & Sons, No. 261, Pearl-Street. And Samuel S. Wood & Co. No. 212, Market-st., Baltimore. 1818.

fr.[ii, alphabet], t.[1], [2–3], 4–29 p.; illus.; 10.5 cm.; blue Dutch paper covers.
MWA-W°; MWA; PP (green Dutch paper covers); Shaw 44327.

534.12 ———— New-York: Printed And Sold By S. Wood & Sons, At The Juvenile Book-Store, No. 261, Pearl-Street. 1818.
fr.[ii], t.[1], [2–3], 4–29 p.; illus.; 10.5 cm.
MWA-W° (p. 29 & covers wanting); NjR; PP; Weiss 1942, p. 766.

534.13 ———— New-York: Published By Samuel Wood & Sons, No. 261, Pearl-Street; And Samuel S. Wood & Co. No. 212, Market-st. Baltimore. 1820.
fr.[ii, alphabet], t.[1], [2–3], 4–29 p.; illus.; 10.5 cm.
MH° (i. st. p. [2]).

535 THE HISTORY OF BIRDS AND BEASTS. New-York: adv. by William Durell, 1790 in **612.5**.

THE HISTORY OF BLACK GILES. *See* More, Hannah, no. **882.1**.

THE HISTORY OF CAROLINE. *See* Berquin, A., no. **87.1**.

536 THE HISTORY OF CHARLES AND JOHN SPENCER. Hartford: adv. by Lincoln & Gleason, 1803 in **571.1** and 1806 in **571.2**.

THE HISTORY OF CLEOPATRA. *See* Berquin, A., no. **88**.

537 THE HISTORY OF FANNY. To Which Are Added, Serious Considerations, And Hymns. New-buryport [Mass.], Printed By W. & J. Gilman. Sold at their Book-Store, No. 2, Middle-Street. 1813. A variety of Useful Tracts, &c. for charitable distribution, cheap, at wholesale or retail.
t.[1], [2–3], 4–16 p.; illus.; 15 cm.
MSaE° (original covers wanting).

538 THE HISTORY OF FANNY BEVERLY, And Her Dog Fido. Adorned with Cuts. New-Haven. Sidney's Press. For J. Babcock & Son. 1819.
fr.[2], t.[3], [4–5], 6–31 p.; illus.; 10 cm.; illus. buff paper covers printed in pink ink.
MWA (p. 7–10, 29–30 mut.; remaining p. torn); DeWint; NCooHi; Shaw 48229.

THE HISTORY OF FIDELITY AND PROFESSION. *See* Cameron, Lucy Lyttleton (Butt), no. **148**.

539.1 THE HISTORY OF FISH. [2 lines quot.] New-York: Printed And Sold By S. Wood, At The Juvenile Book-Store. No. 357, Pearl-Street. 1810.
fr.[ii, alphabet], t.[1], [2–3], 4–29 p.; illus.; 10 cm.
MWA-W° (covers wanting).

539.2 ———— New-York: Printed And Sold By Samuel Wood. At The Juvenile Book-store No. 357 Pearl Street. 1812 [cover title].
fr.[ii, alphabet], t.[1], [2–3], 4–29 p.; illus.; 10.5 cm.; pr. & illus. buff paper covers.
CtHi° (t.[1] mut. imprint wanting, fr.[ii], p. [2–3], 27–29 mut.).

539.3 ———— New-York: Printed And Sold By Samuel Wood, At the Juvenile Book-store, No. 357, Pearl-street. 1813.
fr.[ii, alphabet], t.[1], [2–3], 4–29 p.; illus.; 10 cm.; pr. & illus. yellow paper covers; cover dated 1813.
MH°; MWA-T.

539.4 ———— New-York: Printed And Sold By Samuel Wood[,] At The Juvenile Book-Store[,] N. 357, Pearl-Street. 1814.
t.[1], [2–3], 4–28 p.; illus.; 10.5 cm.
MWA-T° (fr.[ii], p. 29 and covers wanting; t.[1], p.[2], 27–28 mut.).

539.5 ———— New-York: Printed And Sold By S. Wood & Sons, At The Juvenile Book-Store, No. 357, Pearl-Street. 1815.
fr.[ii, alphabet], t.[1], [2–3], 4–29 p.; illus.; 10 cm.; pr. & illus. paper covers; front cover undated.
MWA° (fr.[ii], p. 29 & covers wanting); MH; Shaw 34911.

539.6 ———— New-York: Printed And Sold By S. Wood & Sons, At The Juvenile Book-Store, No. 357, Pearl-Street. 1816.
fr.[ii, alphabet], t.[1], [2–3], 4–29 p.; illus.; 10.5 cm.; pr. & illus. paper cover; cover dated 1811.
MWA° (2 copies varied covers); DLC (fr.[ii] & covers wanting); PP (wallpaper covers); Shaw 37840.

539.7 ———— New-York: Published By Samuel Wood & Sons, No. 261, Pearl-Street, And Samuel S. Wood & Co. No. 212, Market-st., Baltimore. 1818.

fr.[ii, alphabet], t.[1], [2–3], 4–29 p.; illus.; 10.5 cm.; blue Dutch paper covers.

NNC-Pl*; MH (pr. & illus. buff paper covers, undated, i. st. p. [2]); Shaw 44328.

539.8 ———— New-York: Published By Samuel Wood & Sons, No. 261, Pearl-street; And Samuel S Wood & Co. No. 212 Market-st. Baltimore. 1820.

fr.[ii, alphabet], t.[1], [2–3], 4–29 p.; illus.; 10.5 cm.; pr. & illus. brown paper covers. Cover title imprint: Printed And Sold By S. [Wood] & Sons, At the Juvenile Book-store, No. 261, Pearl-street, New-York.

NN*; Shoemaker 1602; Weiss 1936.

HISTORY OF FORTUNIO. *See* Aulnoy, Marie Catherine Jumelle de Berneville Comtesse D', no. **50.1.**

540.1 HISTORY OF FOUR-FOOTED ANIMALS. Printed By W. & J. Gilman, Newburyport [Mass.]. Sold at their Book-Store & Printing-Office with a variety of Children's Books, wholesale and retail. 1812.

fr.[2], t.[3], [4–5], 6–27 p.; illus.; 12.5 cm.; pr. & illus. buff paper covers.

CtHi*.

540.2 ———— Animals. Newburyport [Mass.], Printed By W. & J. Gilman. And sold at their Miscellaneous Book-Store, No. 2, Middle-Street. 1814.

fr.[2], t.[3], [4–5], 6–23 p.; illus.; 13 cm.; pr. & illus. buff paper covers.

Cover title: History of Animals.

MSaE*; MNeHi.

541 THE HISTORY OF GEORGE BARNWELL, OF LONDON. Learn to be wise by others harm, and you will do full well. Norwich [Conn.]: Printed by John Trumbull, M,DCC,XCII.

t.[1], [2–3], 4–21 p.; 14.5 cm.

PP*.

HISTORY OF GILES GINGERBREAD. *See* Gingerbread, Giles, no. **451.**

542 THE HISTORY OF GOOD CHILDREN, With An Account Of A Gallery Of Pictures And Museum.

Hartford: Printed by George Goodwin & Sons. 1820.

fr.[2], t.[3], [4–5], 6–23 p.; illus.; 13.5 cm.; pr. & illus. pink paper covers; cover dated 1821. MWA*; Ct (i. st. on fr.[2]); CtHi; MH; NjP (unprinted pale green paper covers); Shoemaker 1604.

THE HISTORY OF GOODY TWO-SHOES. *See* Goody Two-Shoes, no. **463.13.**

HISTORY OF GUY EARL OF WARWICK. *See* Wonderful Exploit Of Guy Earl of Warwick, no. **1450.1.**

543 HISTORY OF HENRY FAIRCHILD AND CHARLES TRUMAN. Philadelphia: Published by the Sunday and Adult School Union. Clark & Raser, Printers. 1819.

t.[1], [2–3], 4–48 p.; title vignette only illus.; 13.5 cm.; pr. & illus. paper covers.

MWA*; Shaw 48230.

THE HISTORY OF HESTER WILMOT. *See* More, Hannah, no. **883.**

544.1 THE HISTORY OF INSECTS. [2 line quot.] New-York: Printed And Sold By S. Wood, At The Juvenile Book-Store, No. 362, Pearl-Street. 1808.

fr.[ii, alphabets], t.[1], [2–3], 4–28, [29] p.; illus.; 10 cm.; Dutch paper covers.

CtHi* (front cover wanting).

544.2 ———— New-York: Printed And Sold By S. Wood, At The Juvenile Book-Store, No. 357, Pearl-Street. 1810.

fr.[ii, alphabets], t.[1], [2–3], 4–28, [29] p.; illus.; 10 cm.; Dutch paper covers.

MWA*.

544.3 ———— New York: Printed And Sold By S. Wood, at the Juvenile Book-store, No. 357, Pearl-Street. 1811.

fr.[ii, alphabets], t.[1], [2–3], 4–28, [29, adv.] p.; illus.; 10 cm.; pr. & illus. yellow paper covers; cover title dated 1811.

Ries*.

544.4 ———— New-York: Printed And Sold By Samuel Wood, At the Juvenile Book-Store, No. 357, Pearl-street. 1812.

fr.[ii, alphabets], t.[1], [2–3], 4–28, [29] p.;

illus.; 10 cm.; pr. & illus. buff paper covers.
DLC.

544.5 ——— New-York: Printed And Sold By
Samuel Wood, At the Juvenile Book-store, No. 357
Pearl-street. 1813.
   fr.[ii, alphabets]; t.[1], [2–3], 4–28, [29, adv.]
p.; illus.; 10 cm.; pr. & illus. buff paper covers.
PP°; DLC (pr. & illus. buff paper covers);
Shaw 28750.

544.6 ——— New-York: Printed And Sold By
Samuel Wood At The Juvenile Book-Store, No.
357, Pearl-Street. 1814.
   t.[1], [2–3], 4–28 p.; illus.; 11 cm.
MWA-T° (fr.[ii] & covers wanting; p. 27–28
mut.).

544.7 ——— Nerv-York [*sic. i.e.* New-York]:
Printed And Sold By S. Wood & Sons, At The
Juvenile Book-Store, No. 357, Pearl-Street. 1816.
   fr.[ii, alphabets], t.[1], [2–3], 4–28 p.; illus.;
9.5 cm.; pr. & illus. paper covers; cover title
undated.
MWA-W°; DLC (fr.[ii] & covers wanting);
MWA; Shaw 37841.

544.8 ——— Nerv-York [*sic. i.e.* New-York]:
Printed And Sold By S. Wood & Sons, At The
Juvenile Book-Store, No. 261, Pearl-Street. 1818.
   fr.[ii, alphabet], t.[1], [2–3], 4–28 p.; illus.;
10 cm.
MWA°; DLC; NNC-PL (orange Dutch paper
covers); PPL; Shaw 44330; Weiss 1942, p. 13.

544.9 ——— New-York: Published By Samuel
Wood & Sons, No. 261, Pearl-Street, And Samuel
S. Wood & Co. No. 212, Market-st. Baltimore.
1818.
   fr.[ii, alphabet], t.[1], [2–3], 4–28 p.; illus.;
10 cm.; green Dutch paper covers.
MWA-W°.

544.10 ——— Nerv-York [*sic. i.e.* New-York]:
Published By Samuel Wood & Sons, No. 261,
Pearl-Street; And Samuel S. Wood & Co. No. 212,
Market-st. Baltimore. 1820.
   fr.[ii, alphabet], t.[1], [2–3], 4–28 p.; illus.;
10.5 cm.; purple & green Dutch paper covers.
Welch°; MH (fr.[ii] & covers wanting); MWA;
NjR (fr.[ii], t.[1], p.[2] wanting); Shoemaker
1605.

545 THE HISTORY OF JACK AND HIS ELEVEN
BROTHERS; Displaying The Various Adventures
They Encountered In Their Travels, &c. Baltimore
[Md.] Published By A. Miltenberger, J. Vance &
Co. and F. Lucas. A. Miltenberger, Print. 1811.
   t.[1], [2–3], 4–108 p.; 14.5 cm.; bound in
leather.
English ed. London 2. ed. E. Langley, 1801.
MWA°.

546 [THE HISTORY OF JACK AND THE GIANTS.
Part. I. To Which is added The Third Voyage Of
Sindbad The Sailor. Newport: Printed by S. Southwick. 1770?] [imaginary title page].
   7–24 p.; 15 cm.; [A]₁–[A]₈ wanting. The book
was once part of a group of five pamphlets
loosely bound together. Three were printed or
believed to have been printed in Newport, and
one in Boston. For this reason the above book
is believed to have been published in Newport.
Alden uses the conjectural title: [The History
Of Jack and the Giant . . . Newport? Printed by
Solomon Southwick? ca. 1770]. The first portion of the imaginary title, given the book in
this bibliography, is patterned after the London
1711 and 1775 editions, because it was probably
copied from an early chapbook form of the book.
The title, Jack The Giant Killer, would be more
suitable since the hero is referred to by this
name on p. 21. This title does not appear to
have been used in English chapbooks until
around 1810. Line 20, p. 21 has the caption:
The Third Voyage of Sindbad the Sailor. The
story ends on p. 24. This is the earliest appearance of *Sindbad the Sailor* in America. There
is a holograph inscription on p. 24: *Jonathan
Shaw Jun. His Book Bought February the 20th:
1771.* The book is printed in 84 or 85 Roman
and italic type similar to S. Southwick's Newport edition of Fox's *Instructions For Right
Spelling, 1769,* and his edition of *The Renowned History Of Giles Gingerbread, 1771,*
no. **452.2.** It is therefore conceivable that the
book was printed in 1770, and by S. Southwick.
English and Scottish chapbook ed., some of
which may be the source books of the above
American ed., Newcastle, entitled: *The Second
Part Of Jack and The Giants.* J. White, 1711.
MWA° (t.[1]–p. 6 & covers wanting); Alden
441; Evans 42108.

THE HISTORY OF JACK IDLE AND DICKY DILIGENT.
See Johnson, Richard, no. **677.**

547.1 THE HISTORY OF JACK JINGLE. Philadelphia: adv. by Francis Bailey, 1793 in **773.1.**

547.2 ——— Hartford: adv. by Peter B. Gleason, 1811 in **1133.2.**

548 THE HISTORY OF JACK THOUGHTLESS. To Which Is Added The Virtue Of A Rod. &c. &c. Adorned with cuts. Norwich [Conn.] Printed by Thomas Hubbard. 1796.
> t.[1], [2–3], 4–28, [29–30, adv. of 12 books sold by T. Hubbard] p.; illus.; 10 cm.; blue marbled paper covers.
> MWA-T°; (not in Evans).

549 THE HISTORY OF JACOB; A Scripture Narrative, In Verse. Nerv-York [*sic. i.e.* New-York]: Published By Samuel Wood & Sons, No. 261, Pearl-Street; And Samuel S. Wood & Co. No. 212, Market-st. Baltimore. 1820.
> fr.[2], t.[3], [4–5], 6–31 p.; 13 cm.; pr. yellowish-buff paper covers; fr.[2] & illus. p. 7, 13, 22, 26, 31 signed A [Alexander Anderson]; cover title undated.
> English ed. London: R. Miller, 2 vols. [1814].
> Welch° (p. 31 wanting); MWA (fr.[2] wanting); RPB; Shoemaker 1607.

550 THE HISTORY OF JESUS. Drawn Up For The Instruction Of Children. To Which Is Added, A Token For Children. Extracted from a late Author, By John Wesley, A. M. [1 line quot.] Prov. xxii. 6. [1 line quot.] First American Edition. New-York: Published By D. Hitt And T. Ware For The Methodist Connection In The United States. J. C. Totten, Printer. 1814.
> t.[i], [ii–iii], iv, [5], 6–95, [96, bl.], [97], 98–160 p.; 11 cm.; bound in leather; caption p. [97]: A Token For Children.
> MWA°; OOxM; Shaw 33644.

551 THE HISTORY OF JOHANNA MARTIN: To Which Is Added, The Interesting Story Of Poor Joseph, With Reflections. Philadelphia: Published by "The Religious Tract Society of Philadelphia," and for sale at their Depository, No. 8, South Front-street. William Bradford—Agent. 1818.
> t.[1], [2], 3–12 p.; title vignette only illus.; 17.5 cm.
> Welch° (covers wanting); MWA; Shaw 44331.

HISTORY OF JOHN GILPIN. *See* Cowper, William, no. **248.**

552 THE HISTORY OF JOHN WISE, A Poor Boy. In Three Parts. Intended For The Instruction Of Young Children, Especially Such as attend Sunday Schools. Hartford: George Goodwin & Sons, Printers. 1820.
> t.[1], [2–3], 4–36 p.; illus.; 14.5 cm.; pink paper covers; illus. p. 9 signed *Barber* [John Warner Barber].
> CtHi°; Ct; MH; PP (pr. & illus. paper covers; front cover dated 1821); Shoemaker 1608.

553 THE HISTORY OF JOSEPH AND HIS BRETHEREN: Wherein we may behold the wonderful Providence of God, in all their Troubles and Advancements. [caption title [p.[1]]. Philadelphia: Printed and sold by Daniel Lawrence, No. 33, North 4th Street. [1792?] [colophon p. 16].
> [1], 2–16 p.; 17 cm.
> PP°; TxU.

THE HISTORY OF JOSEPH, THE SON OF ISRAEL. *See* Macgowan, John, no. **810.1.**

554.1 THE HISTORY OF JOSEPH, THE SON OF ISRAEL. Woodstock [Vt.]: Printed By David Watson. 1819.
> fr.[2], t.[3], [4–5], 6–31 p.; illus.; 9.5 cm.; pr. & illus. paper covers. An abridged ed. of no. **810.1.**
> MWA-W°; VtHi; McCorison 2119; Shaw 48231.

554.2 ——— Woodstock [Vt.]: Printed By David Watson. 1820.
> fr.[2], t.[3], [4–5], 6–31 p.; illus.; 9.5 cm.; pr. & illus. paper covers.
> MWA-T°; (not in Shoemaker).

555.1 THE HISTORY OF LITTLE ANN AND LITTLE JAMES to which is added a Present of Pictures. Boston: adv. by W. Folsom, 1798 in **672.1.**
> English ed. London: John Marshall. [*ca.* 1790]. Evans 33878.

555.2 ——— Exeter [N.H.]: adv. by Henry Ranlet, 1801 in **558.2.**

555.3 ——— Exeter [N.H.]: adv. by Norris & Sawyer, 1808 in **428.3.**

THE HISTORY OF LITTLE CHARLES, And His Friend Frank Wilful. *See* Somerville, Elizabeth, no. **1229.1.**

THE HISTORY OF LITTLE DICK. *See* Little John, no. **773.1**.

THE HISTORY OF LITTLE ELIZA. *See* The History And Adventures Of Little Eliza, no. **516.1**.

556.1 THE HISTORY OF LITTLE FANNY, Exemplified in A Series Of Figures. Boston: Printed By J. Belcher, 1812.
  t.[1], [2–3], 4–17 p.; illus. with 7 moveable figures, head, hats, which lie loose in the book; 10.5 cm.; blue-gray paper covers.
  English ed. London: 1 ed. S. & J. Fuller. 1810. MWA-W° (head, hats, and fig. no. 7 wanting), MHi, MiD (head and 7 figures).

556.2 ———— Figures. First American Edition. Philadelphia: Printed and Sold Wholesale by Wm. Charles, and may be had of all the Booksellers. 1812. Price—18 Cents, Plain,—Coloured, 25 cents. W. M'Culloch, Printer.
  fr.[ii], t.[1], [2–3], 4–14 p.; 6 pl. including front.; 14 cm.; pr. paper covers. Adv. by Wm. Charles, 1815 in **748** as having 7 pl.
  Ball° (wants leaf 8, probably p. 15 and the last pl.).

557 HISTORY OF LITTLE FIDO. Philadelphia: adv. by B. & T. Kite, 1807 in **611.1**.

558.1 THE HISTORY OF LITTLE GOODY GOOSE-CAP, And Her Brother Little Charles. To which is added, The Story of Jonny Badboy. Boston: Printed and sold by John W. Folsom, No. 30, Union Street. 1798.
  fr.[2], t.[3], [4–5], 6–29, [30–31] p.; illus.; 10 cm.; buff paper covers with a striped design in black.
  MSaE° (p. 31 mut.); MH (fr.[2], p. 11–12, 15–18, 21–22 wanting, t.[3] mut.); MWA (fr. [2], p. 13–20, [31] wanting); Evans 48470.

558.2 ———— Exeter [N.H.]: Printed And Sold By H. Ranlet. 1801.
  fr.[2], t.[3], [4–5], 6–28, [29, oval illus.], [30–31, adv. of books] p.; illus.; 10 cm.; illus. buff paper covers; p. 23 wrongly numbered "32".
  MWA°; MSaE (emb. st. on t.[3]); Shaw 658.

558.3 ———— Exeter [N.H.]: adv. by Norris & Sawyer, 1808 in **428.3**.

THE HISTORY OF LITTLE GOODY TWO SHOES. *See* Goody Two-Shoes, no. **463.1**.

559 Price [6½] Cents. Sold At Jansen's [Juv]enile and School Library. THE HISTORY OF LITTLE GOVERNOR PIPPIN. New-York: Printed By L. B. Jansen, [1]16, Broadway, opposite the City Hotel, 1809. [cover title].
  MWA° (pr. & illus. buff paper covers only); Shaw 17756.

560 HISTORY OF LITTLE HENRY. Philadelphia: adv. by William Charles, 1815 in **748**. See no. **517.2** for the actual book.

HISTORY OF LITTLE HENRY AND HIS BEARER. *See* Sherwood, Mrs. Mary Martha (Butt), no. **1196.1**.

THE HISTORY OF LITTLE JACK. *See* Day, Thomas, no. **268.1**.

561 THE HISTORY OF LITTLE JACK, [caption title p. [3]] Hartford Printed by John Babcock. [*ca.* 1800 [imprint below illus. p. [2]].
  illus. [2], [3], 4–30, [31, illus.] p.; illus.; 12 cm.; orange Dutch paper covers. No title page. The text is different from Thomas Day's *The History of Little Jack*, no. **268.1**. *See also* no. **358** which has the same text as no. **561**.
  MWA°; CtY; Evans 49085.

562 THE HISTORY OF LITTLE JOHN. New-York: adv. by William Durell, 1790 in **612.5**.

563.1 HISTORY OF [LITTLE] KING PIPPIN. New-York: adv. by Hugh Gaine, 1786 in John Clarke's *Corderii Colloquiorum Centuria Selecta*.

563.2 THE HISTORY OF LITTLE KING PIPPIN: With An Account of the melancholy Death of four naughty Boys, who were devoured by Wild Beasts. And The Wonderful Delivery of Master Harry Harmless, by a Little White Horse. Philadelphia: Printed and Sold by Young, Stewart, and M'Culloch, the corner of Chesnut and Second-streets. 1786.
  fr.[2], t.[3], [4–5], 6–62, [63, illus.] p.; illus.; 9.5 cm.; buff paper covers speckled with red; p. 43 wrongly numbered "53". On p. 9 there is an illustration of the interior of Young & Co's Bookstore. Adv. by Young & M'Culloch, 1787 in **249.2**; also by William Young, 1794 in **305**.

English, Scottish and Irish ed. London: adv. by
F. Newbery, 1775 in *The Cries Of London*.
MWA*; PP (fr.[2] wanting; t.[3], p. [4] and a
number of other p. mut.); Evans 19711.

563.3 ———— The First Worcester Edition.
Printed at Worcester, Massachusetts. By Isaiah
Thomas, And Sold, Wholesale and Retail, at his
Book-Store. MDCCLXXXVII.

t.[3], [4–5], 6–58 p.; illus.; 9.5 cm.; covers
wanting. Adv. by I. Thomas, 1786 in **395.1**.
MWA-W*; CLU; Evans 20413.

563.4 ———— Hartfor[d:] Printed by Nathaniel
Patten[.] M,DCC,LXXX,IX.

fr.[2], t.[3], [4], 5–59 p.; illus.; 9.5 cm.; Dutch
paper covers.
MWA* (t.[3] mut.).

563.5 ———— Boston: adv. by Samuel Hall, 1791
in **408.3**.

563.6 ———— Boston: Printed and sold by Samuel Hall, No. 53, Cornhill. [1795?].

fr.[2], t.[3], [4–5], 6–60, [61–63, adv. list of 24
books] p.; illus.; 10 cm.; Dutch paper covers.
The advertisement caption p. [61]: *A great
Variety of BOOKS,/designed for the Instruction
and Amusement,/and suited to Children of all
Ages and/Capacities, are constantly kept for
Sale/by S. Hall, No. 53, Cornhill, Boston;/
among which are the following, viz./*[followed
by a list of 24 titles]. No. 5 on the list is *The
Big Puzzling Cap* and 15, *The Royal Alphabet*.
There is a nick in the "d" of the word "and", the
last word in line three, and in the "S" of "S.
HALL" line five. This advertisement caption was
printed by S. Hall from standing type and appears in 10 x 6.5 cm. books of 31 or 61 pages
printed by him in 1794, in **395.3, 408.4, 663.5,
673.8, 1315.8,** and in 1795 in **1384.3**. All these
books printed in 1794 with the exception of no.
673.8 have the letters "d" and "S", mentioned
above printed in perfect type. In Johnson's *The
Hermit Of The Forest*, no. **673.8**, possibly
printed late in 1794 and in *Virtue and Vice*,
1795, no. **1384.3**, the letters show the same
defects described above in *Little King Pippin*,
no. **563.6**. *Little King Pippin* particularly resembles no. **1384.3** in having the list of books,
titles 1–7, and 8–17 on the following page
printed from standing type, with no. 5, *The*

Royal Alphabet and 15, *The Big Puzzling Cap*.
In *The Hermit Of The Forest* and other 1794,
10 cm. books printed by S. Hall, the first two
pages are printed from the same standing type
used in the 1795 ed. of no. **1384.3** but no. 5 is
The Big Puzzling Cap, and 15, *The Royal
Alphabet*, so that these two titles were reset in
1795. From these data *Little King Pippin* is
dated [1795?]. Evans 25605 dates this book
[1793]. This is open to question, because in
1793 the advertisement caption in S. Hall's 10
cm. books of 31 or 63 pages is: *A great Variety
of BOOKS for Children, to be sold by* S. HALL,/
*in Cornhill, Boston; among which are/the fol-
lowing, viz.,* see **1132.2** and **955.3**. Since S. Hall
appears to have usually printed his advertisement captions for a year or two from standing
type he must have changed the type setting in
1794 from the one used in 1793. *King Pippin*
surely was not published in 1793 but later.
Evans 37619 also dates the book [1800]. This
is unquestionably an error because the state of
the illustration of a man on horseback is not
comparable to the print of the cut from the
same block in *Mother Goose's Melody, 1800*,
no. **905.4**.
CtHi*; MWA; NN; PP; Evans 25605 dated
[1793] and 37619 dated [1800].

563.7 ———— The Second Worcester Edition.
Worcester: Printed by Isaiah Thomas, jun. For
Isaiah Thomas And Son, Sold Wholesale And
Retail At Their Respective Bookstores. 1795.

fr.[2], t.[3], [4–5], 6–62, [63, adv. of 6 books]
p.; illus.; 10 cm.; green Dutch paper covers;
copy A, I. Thomas copy rebound in blue mor-
raco. Copy B, same as A but with the last line
of the title page imprint having "Bookstores"
misprinted "okstores", and bound in illus. blue
paper covers.
MWA*; DLC (green Dutch paper covers);
NjP; Evans 28834.

563.8 ———— Philadelphia: Printed By Neal &
Kammerer, Jun. 1796.

fr.[2], t.[3], [4–5], 6–63 p.; illus.; 10.5 cm.;
green Dutch paper covers.
PP*; Evans 47807.

563.9 ———— New-York: Printed by Wm.
Durell, For Cornelius Davis. 1800.

t.[3], [4–5], 6–30 p.; illus.; 11 cm.; the "A" of

"Account", line 6 on the title page, is printed upside down; p. 26 is misprinted "29".
MWA-W* (fr.[2], p. 31–63 and covers wanting); Evans 49086.

563.10 ———— New-York: Printed by Wm. Durell, For Thomas B. Jansen & Co. 1800.
t.[3], [4–5], 6–63 p.; illus.; 10. cm.; text same as no. **563.9** but with the error on the title page corrected.
MWA* (fr.[2], p. 7–8, 25–26 and covers wanting); Evans 37620.

563.11 ———— Third Worcester Edition. Printed at Worcester, Massachusetts, By Isaiah Thomas, Jun. Sold Wholesale and Retail by Him.— MDCCC.
fr.[2], t.[3], [4–5], 6–62, [63, 2 rectangular woodcut illus.] p.; illus.; 10 cm.; illus. blue paper covers.
MWA* (p. 61–62 mut. and lower half of p. wanting); Evans 37621.

563.12 ———— Boston: [Printed and sold by] S. Hall, No. 53, Cornhill, [1]80[1?].
t.[3], [4–5], 6–60 p.; illus.; 10 cm.; the imprint on the title page is worn and the date indistinct but looks as if it might be 1801. The illustration of a man on horseback on p. 33 is printed from the same block used in [1795?], discussed in no. **563.6**. Samuel Hall was at 53, Cornhill alone until 1803. He announced in the *Ind. Chron. April 4, 1803* that the firm of Hall & Hiller at 53, Cornhill had been formed. It was dissolved June 20, 1805. From 1805 to the time of his death Oct. 30, 1807, S. Hall's addresses were "bookseller, house, Half Court Square, 1805", "bookseller, 53 Cornhill, house, Half Court Square, 1806", "bookseller, 53 Cornhill, house, Congress Street, 1807." *The History Of Little King Pippin* could have been printed between 1800 and 1803. Since the state of the illustration of a man on horseback seems a little closer to the state of the cut in 1805 than in 1800, the date [1801?] was probably the correct date of the book.
MH* (i. st. on p. [5]; fr.[2], p. [61–63] & covers wanting; t.[3] & p. [4]–6 mut.; p. 47–48 torn but complete.

563.13 ———— Hartford: Printed by Hale & Hosmer. 1813.

fr.[2], t.[3], [4–5], 6–31 p.; illus.; 10 cm.; pr. & illus. orange paper covers.
MWA*; CtHi (covers wanting); PP; Shaw 28754.

563.14 ———— Hartford: Printed by Hale & Hosmer. 1814.
fr.[2], t.[3], [4–5], 6–31 p.; illus.; 10 cm.; pr. & illus. buff paper covers.
MWA*; CtHi; CtY; Shaw 31720.

563.15 ———— Hartford: Printed by Sheldon & Goodwin. < Stereotyped by J. F. & C. Starr. > [1815]
fr.[2], t.[3], [4–7], 8–31 p.; illus.; 10 cm.; pr. & illus. gray paper covers.
J. F. & C. Starr are known to have been in Hartford in 1815 and 1818. Sheldon and Goodwin were a firm in Hartford from Nov. 1, 1814— Oct. 23, 1815. (MWA cat.).
MWA-W*; CtY; DLC; Shaw 34913.

563.16 ———— Hartford: Printed for J. & W. Russell. < Stereotyped by J. F. & C. Starr. > [1818?].
fr.[2], t.[3], [4–7], 8–31 p.; illus.; 10 cm.; pr. & illus. buff paper covers. John and William Russell began as a firm in Hartford on Nov. 10, 1818 and ran until *ca.* July 28, 1820. J. F. & C. Starr are known to have been in Hartford in 1815 and 1818. (MWA cat.). The book is printed from standing type from no. **563.15** and could have been printed for the Russell brothers in [1818].
MWA-W* (front cover and fr.[2] wanting); CtHi (unprinted pink paper covers).

THE HISTORY OF LITTLE PHOEBE. *See* Somerville, Elizabeth, no. **1230.1**.

564.1 THE HISTORY OF MARGARET, And The Fable Of The Bees. Adorned with Cuts. Sidney's Press. New-Haven. 1813.
fr.[2], t.[3], [4–5], 6–30, [31, adv.] p.; illus.; 10.5 cm.; pr. & illus. green paper covers.
Welch* (covers mut.); MWA; Shaw 28755.

564.2 ———— Windsor, (Vt.) Printed by Jesse Cochran. And Sold [wh]ol[e]sale and retail at his Book-Store 1814.
t.[3], [4–5], 6–30 p.; illus.; 10 cm.
MWA* (fr.[2], p. 31 & covers wanting).

564.3 ——— Windsor, (Vr. [*sic. i.e.* Vt.]) Printed By Jesse Cochran, 1815.

  fr.[2], t.[3], [4–5], 6–31 p.; illus.; 10 cm.; pr. & illus. buff paper covers.
  Cover title: The History of Margaret. Windsor, Vt. Printed and Sold by Jesse Cochran.
  MWA-W°; OClW-LS; McCorison 1743.

565 THE HISTORY OF MARTIN AND JAMES. Boston: adv. by William Spotswood, 1795 in **617.1**. *See also* no. **819.1**.

THE HISTORY OF MARY WOOD. Philadelphia, 1800. *See* Cheap Repository, no. **169.24**.

566 THE HISTORY OF MARY WOOD Published by B Johnson N°. 247 Market Street. Philadelphia. [1807].

  t.[i], [ii], [1], 2–36 p.; title vignette only illus.; 14 cm.
  MWA° (covers wanting); NNC-Sp (bound in vol. I. *Cheap Repository.* 1807); PP (rebound, covers wanting).

567 THE HISTORY OF MASTER FRIENDLY, Together with a number Of Fables: Selected from Æsop. Boston: Printed and sold by N. Coverly. 1792. (Price 4 Coppers).

  t.[1], [2], 3–16 p.; illus.; 10.5 cm.; p. 3–9 copied in part from the English ed.
  English ed. London, entitled: *The History Of Master Billy Friendly, And His Sister Miss Polly Friendly. To which is added, The Fairy Tale of The Three Little Fishes.* John Marshall. n.d. [*ca.* 1783].
  CtHi° (p. 15–16 mut.); MWA-T (p. 1–4 mut.) pink unprinted paper covers; Evans 24397.

568.1 THE HISTORY OF MASTER JACKEY AND MISS HARRIOT. To Which Is Added, A Few Maxims For The Improvement Of The Mind. Dedicated To The Good Children Of The United States Of America. [4 lines of verse]. The First Worcester Edition. Printed at Worcester, Massachusetts. By Isaiah Thomas, And sold, Wholesale and Retail, at his Book-Store. MDCCLXXXVII.

  fr.[2], t.[3], [4–5], 6–31 p.; illus.; 10.5 cm.; illus. buff paper covers. The story entitled "The History Of Master Jackey And Miss Harriot Gracemore" appeared on p. 51–60 in vol. VIII of *The Lilliputian Library; Or Gulliver's Museum. By Lilliputius Gulliver,* with the half title

on p. [v]: The Lilliputian Biographer, Or Lives Of Illustrious Little Heroes, And Others.
English and Irish ed. of *The Lilliputian Library,* 10 vols. London: adv. *London Chronicle, xlvi, May 15–18, 1779.*
English ed. of *The History Of Master Jackey and Miss Harriot* as a separate edition, London: John Marshall [*ca.* 1785].
MWA°; CtHi (fr.[2] & front cover wanting); DLC; Evans 21144 (dated 1788).

568.2 ——— Harriot: Together With A few Maxims For The Improvement of the Mind. Dedicated To The Good Children Of The United States Of America. [4 lines of verse] Boston: Printed and sold by Samuel Hall. [1789?].

  fr.[2], t.[3], [4–5], 6–30, [31 adv. of 7 books] p.; illus.; 10 cm.; illus. brown paper covers. On the recto of fr.[2] and verso of p. [31], both pasted to the inside of the paper covers, 5 lines of letters per page are printed. The illustrations on the covers are printed from the same blocks used to illustrate p. 11, 22, 24 and 28 of Dorothy Kilner's *Little Stories For Little Folks,* no. **729.1**. S. Hall also used cuts from this book to make illustrated paper with which he also bound no. **729.1** and Richard Johnson's *The Hermit Of The Forest,* [1789?], no. **673.1**. The caption p. [5]: THE HISTORY OF *Master* Jackey *& Miss* Harriot. On p. 25 is the earliest located illustration of a man on horseback. It was probably taken from a contemporary edition of *The Royal Alphabet,* because it appears in S. Hall's edition of 1793 of that book. The cut has the letter "H" in the upper left corner and was used for the rhyme "H Was a Horseman." Since no. **568.2** resembles the early format of the book, with paper covers illustrated with cuts taken from *Little Stories,* which has a holograph date 1787 or 1789 on the recto of the frontispiece, it, as well as no. **673.1**, and no. **729.1** are dated [1789].
The illustration, p. 11, supposed to represent "an old woman who used to serve my Lord's house," is a copy of the one printed on p. 29 in *The History Of Little Goody Two-Shoes. London: J. Newbery, 1766.* It shows a front view of Goody Two-Shoes with a basket in her left hand. This illustration is not in the *Charlestown* [*Mass.*]*: J. Lamson, for Samuel Hall, 1797* edition, no. **463.8**, which has entirely different illustrations from those printed by John New-

bery. This illustration on p. 11 appears in all S. Hall editions of the book except no. **568.9**. It is of special interest because it is a clue that Samuel Hall may have published an edition of *The History Of Little Goody Two-Shoes* prior to 1790.

MWA*; NjN (p. 27–31 & covers wanting); Evans 25606.

568.3 [———— Boston: Printed and sold by Samuel Hall, No. 53 Cornhill. 1790?] [imaginary title page].

[5], 6–26 p.; illus.; 10.5 cm. The caption p. [5] is mostly wanting but reads: [The History of Master Jackey and M]iss Harriot. On p. 25 is an illustration of a man on horseback which was reprinted by S. Hall from the same block in all subsequent editions of the book and in different books up to 1805. On the rear cover of Defoe's *Travels Of Robinson Crusoe*. S. Hall, 1790, no. **275.2**, the same illustration is found printed from the same block. Because of the similarity in the breaks in the two books this edition of *Master Jackey . . .* is dated [1790?].

MWA-W*; (fr.[2], t.[3], p. [4], 27–31 & covers wanting); Evans 45887.

568.4 ———— Boston: Printed and sold by Samuel Hall, No. 53, Cornhill. 1791.

The collation is probably the same as in no. **568.5**. The book, according to a letter from the late Mr. Oppenheimer, has the illustration of a man on horseback, which has the same identical breaks as the same illustration has in *Tom Thumb's Folio*. Boston: *S. Hall, 1791*, no. **1315.6**.

Oppenheimer* (not seen); Evans 46191.

568.5 ———— Boston: Printed for and sold by Samuel Hall[,] No. 53, Cornhill. [1792?].

fr.[2], t.[3], [4–5], 6–31 p.; illus.; 10.5 cm.; orange-yellow Dutch paper covers. Adv. by S. Hall, 1792 in **587.34**. Caption p. [5]: The HISTORY of Master Jackey and Miss Harriot. The illustration of a man on horseback is now on p. 24 instead of p. 25. Two breaks in the rule borders are about the same as in the 1791 printing of the illustration. Because of the increase in the extent of a third break, this book is dated [1792?].

RPB*; Evans 46468.

568.6 ———— Boston: Printed and sold by S. Hall, No. 53, Cornhill. 1793.
Greenwood (not available for study).

568.7 ———— Miss Harriot. To Which Is Added, ———— [same as **568.1**] The Second Worcester Edition. Printed at Worcester, Massachusetts. By Isaiah Thomas, And sold Wholesale and Retail, at his Book Store, MDCCXCIV.

fr.[2], t.[3], [4–5], 6–31 p.; illus.; 10 cm.; Dutch paper covers.

MWA* (fr.[2] & p. 29–[30] mut.); Evans 47075.

568.8 ———— Miss Harriot: Together With ———— [same as **568.2**] Boston: Printed and sold by S. Hall, No. 53, Cornhill. [1796?].

fr.[2], t.[3], [4–5], 6–31 p.; illus.; 10 cm.; green paper covers. Adv. by S. Hall 1794 in **673.8**; 1795 in **1384.3**; 1796 in **587.40**; 1796 in **408.6**. Caption p.[5]:[a thick and thin rule] THE HISTORY OF JACKEY AND HARRIOT, [*sic. i.e.* ".] [2 thin rules], [illus.], [2 thin rules]. This differs from the captions in earlier S. Hall editions, **568.2**, **568.3**, **568.5**, but is similar to no. **568.9**, except there is a period after "Harriot." The book resembles the format of no. **568.9** but can be identified by a few characteristic type settings. The caption over the frontispiece: THE PARENTS' ADDRESS TO THEIR CHILDREN. The last line p.[5]: named John, after himself: When Mas-. Decorative bars of printer's ornaments are not present over captions. Two rules are at the head of p. 30, and a thick and thin rule follows the text on p. 31. The book was printed prior to 1800, because the break in the illustration of a man on horseback is close to the state of the break in *The History Of Little King Pippin* [1795?]. The book could have been printed between 1794 and 1799. It was probably not printed in 1794 because it does not contain printer's ornaments of a crown and angel's head commonly used in 1793 and 1794 by S. Hall nor are the letters $\frac{M}{M}$ present on the recto of the frontispiece. No books dated 1797–99 printed by S. Hall with this illustration in it are known. Since the illustration of the man on horseback is so close to that in *Little King Pippin* and yet similar in format to the text of no. **568.9**, the date [1796?] has been selected on present data.

MWA*; NNMM (Dutch paper covers; i. st. on p. [4], 30).

568.9 ———— Boston: Printed by S. Hall, No. 53 Cornhill. [1801?].

fr.[2], t.[3], [4–5], 6–31 p.; illus.; 10.5 cm.; marbled paper covers. Caption p. [5]: [a thick and thin rule] THE HISTORY OF JACKEY and HARRIOT. [2 thin rules] [illus.] [2 thin rules]. The text resembles the format of no. **568.8** but can be identified by a few new type settings. The caption above the frontispiece: THE PARENTS' ADDRESS TO THEIR CHILDREN. The last sentence on p. [5]: John, after himself. When Master. On the bottom of p. 29 the tailpiece consists of a basket of flowers. There is a new illustration representing the "old woman who used to serve my Lord's house," p. 10. It is similar to the one on p. 11, no. **568.2**, but redrawn and shows a side view of the old woman with a basket on her left arm. In this book the break in the illustration of a man on horseback looks slightly more pronounced and closer to the state of the break in *The Sister's Gift, 1805* and identical with the same cut in *The History Of Little King Pippin* [1801?], no. **563.12**. For this reason the book is dated [1801?].

MWA-W*; MHi (caption on p. [5] cut off); NN (dated 1793); Evans 25606, dated 1793; Weiss 136 no. 340, dated [*ca.* 1800].

568.10 ———— Harriot. Being An Essay For The Improvement of the Minds Of All Good Children In The United States. [4 lines of verse] Hudson [N.Y.], Printed by Ashbel Stoddard, And sold Wholesale and Retail, at his Book-Store. 1804.

fr.[2], t.[3], [4–5], 6–30 p.; illus.; 11 cm.; illus.; paper covers.

Ct* (p. 9–10, 31 and rear cover wanting).

569.1 THE HISTORY OF MISS KITTY PRIDE. Together With The Virtue Of A Rod; Or The History of a Naughty Boy. "Vice will always be detected, Virtue ever be protected." First Worcester Edition. Printed at Worcester, Massachusetts, By Isaiah Thomas, jun. Sold Wholesale and Retail by Him. 1799.

fr.[2], t.[3], [4–5], 6–26, [27–28], [29, 2 illus.] [20 adv.], [31, 2 illus.] p.; 11 cm.; orange and green Dutch paper covers; 9 oval illus. on fr.[2], & p. [4], [20], [29], [31] were used by I.

Thomas in *Little Robin Red Breast*, no. **782**. MWA*; Evans 35622.

569.2 ———— Pride. Embellished with Cuts. Shirley [Mass.]: L. Parker, Printer. 1802.

fr.[2], t.[3], [4–5], 6–27, [28, illus., 29, illus.], [30 bl.] [31, illus.] p.; illus.; 9.5 cm.; Dutch paper covers.

PPPrHi*; MWA-W (p. [2–4], 19–20, 27–[31] & covers wanting).

569.3 ———— Harvard [Mass.]: Printed by Sewall Parker. 1803.

t.[3], [4–5], 6–27, [28–29, illus.] p.; illus.; 10 cm.

MWA* (fr.[2]?, & covers wanting); Shaw 4377.

569.4 ———— Pride. Embellished with Facts. [illus. with the word "Windsor" on a stone.] Printed By Nahum Mower. [1805?].

fr.[2], t.[3], [4–5], 6–23, [24–27, 2 cuts on each page]; 10 cm.; brick-red paper covers. Holograph inscription on rear fly leaf: *Relief Crouch her Book She was born September the 12 1803 and died September the 3 1805.*

MWA*; McCorison 2262 (dated 1803–1805).

THE HISTORY OF MR. FANTOM. *See* More, Hannah, no. **884.1**.

570 THE HISTORY OF MR. TOMMY THROUGHGOOD, And Mr. Francis Froward, Both young gentlemen. To which Are Added, A number of Moral Stories; Designed for the Instruction of Youth of both Sexes. Published at the request of several Gentlemen, and Tutors. [one line quot.] Stonington-Port [Conn.], Printed By S. Trumbull. 1800.

t.[1], [2–3], 4–24 p.; 18.5 cm.; printed on blue-gray paper.

English ed. London: the above appeared in *The Lilliputian Magazine. T. Carnan and F. Newbery, 1777.*

CtHi*; Evans 37623.

THE HISTORY OF MOTHER TWADDLE. *See* C., H. A., no. **144**.

571.1 THE HISTORY OF NANCY TRUELOVE. Exhibiting The Advantages Of A Good Education. A Tale. Ornamented with Cuts. Hartford: Printed by Lincoln & Gleason. 1803.

fr.[2], t.[3], [4–5], 6–29, [30–31, adv. list of books] p.; illus.; 10.5 cm.
MWA-W* (covers wanting, t.[3] slightly mut.); NB (Dutch paper covers); Shaw 4378.

571.2 —— Hartford: Printed By Lincoln & Gleason. 1806.
fr.[2], t.[3], [4–5], 6–29, [30, 2 woodcut illus.], [31, adv. list of books] p.; illus.; 10 cm.; blue marbled paper covers.
CtHi*.

571.3 —— Hartford: Printed By Peter B. Gleason & Co. 1811.
fr.[2], t.[3], [4–5], 6–29, [30–31, adv. list of books] p.; illus.; 9.5 cm.
MWA* (covers wanting); Shaw 23013.

572 THE HISTORY OF OLD BRIDGET. A True Story. February—1818. Published by "The Religious Tract Society of Philadelphia," and sold at their Depository, No. 8, South Front-street. Wm. Bradford, Agent.
t.[1], [2], 3–12 p.; title page vignette only illus.; 18.5 cm.
MWA*; Shaw 44337.

THE HISTORY OF POLLY CHERRY. *See* The Entertaining History Of Polly Cherry, no. **359**.

THE HISTORY OF PRINCE ENGLEMONT. New-York: adv. by L. B. Jansen and G. Jansen, 1808 in **766**.

573.1 THE HISTORY OF PRINCE LEE BOO A NATIVE OF THE PELEW ISLANDS brought to England by Capt.ⁿ Wilson a new Edition Printed for B. Johnson & J. Johnson, Philadelphia 1802.
fr.[ii], t.[iii], [iv], [1], 2–143 p.; 7 pl. including engr. (fr.[ii] & t.[iii]; 14.5 cm.; bound in leather. Adv. by Johnson & Warner, 1814 in **1449.2**.
English & Irish ed. London: E. Newbery, 1789. PP*; DeWint; MWA (5 pl. only); PPL; Shaw 2410.

573.2 —— LEE BOO, To Which Is Added, The Life Of Paul Cuffee, Of Westport, In The State Of Massachusetts, A Man Of Colour. Dublin: Printed By M. Goodwin, 29 Denmark-Street. 1818. And Sold By Munroe & Francis, 4 Cornhill, Boston. [cover title].

[3], 4–180 p. illus.; 14 cm.; bound in pr. buff paper over bds. An Irish imprint with Munroe & Francis imprint below that of the Irish publishers.
Adomeit* (t.[1] wanting).

574 HISTORY OF PRICELLA AND LEONARD. Boston: Printed by Lemuel Child. No. 2. West Row. 1812.
fr.[2], t.[3], [4–5], 6–30, [31, illus.] p.; illus.; 10 cm.; pr. & illus. paper covers.
DLC*.

575 THE HISTORY OF RALPH RAYMOND. A new Story for Children. Hartford: Published by S. G. Godwin. Roberts & Burr, Prs. 1819.
fr.[2], t.[3], 4–16 p.; illus.; 10.5 cm.; illus. white paper covers printed in black ink.
MWA*; Shaw 48235.

576 THE HISTORY OF SAMUEL BONNER; Or Cruelty To Animals. By The Author Of "The Returning Prodigal." Boston: Wells And Lilly, Court-Street. 1820.
t.[1], [2–3], 4–24 p.; 15.5 cm.; blue paper covers.
MWA*; Shoemaker 1611.

THE HISTORY OF SINBAD THE SAILOR. *See* Sinbad The Sailor, no. **1212.1**.

577 THE HISTORY OF SOPHIA CARTER. Philadelphia, Published by "The Religious Tract Society of Philadelphia," and sold at the Depository, No. 8, South Front-street. Wm. Bradford, Agent. August, 1820.
t.[1], [2], 3–12 p.; title vignette only illus.; 18.5 cm.
MWA*; Shoemaker 1612.

578.1 THE HISTORY OF SUSAN WARD. Philadelphia, Published by "The Religious Tract Society of Philadelphia" and for sale at their Depository No 8, South Front-street. Wm. Bradford, Agent. April 1817.
t.[1], 2–4 p.; title vignette only illus.; 20.5 cm.; colophon p. 4: Published for the New-York Religious Tract Society, and sold at their Depository, by Whiting & Watson, Theological and Clasical Book-sellers. J. Seymour, Printer. October, 1813.—5000. The page numbers 2–4 are enclosed in parentheses. Page 4 has in the upper

right-hand corner of the page: No. 20. >
NRU°.

578.2 ——— April 1817.
t.[1], [2], 3–12 p.; title vignette only illus.; 18.5
cm. The title page is the same as no. **578.1.** The
text is different being in 12 pages instead of 4
and the page numbers are not enclosed in parentheses. There is no colophon on p. 12 nor "No.
20 >" in the upper right-hand margin of the
page.
MWA°; Shaw 41056.

579 The History of the Apple Pie. Philadelphia: adv. by Wm. Charles, 1810 in **245.5** and
1815 in **748.**
English ed. London: J. Harris June 25–1808.

The History Of The Beggarly Boy. *See* Cheap
Repository, no. **169.21** and The Beggarly Boy, no.
68.

580 History of the Bible. Hudson (N.Y.):
adv. by A. Stoddard, 1804 in **673.21.**

History Of The Bible. *See* Miniature Bible, no.
860.1.

581 A History Of The Bible. Printed In The
Year Of Our Lord, 1819.
t.[1], [2–3], 4–72 p.; 8 cm.; blue paper covers.
MWA°; Shaw 48236.

582 The History of the Bible Abridged.
Philadelphia: adv. by William Young, 1794 in
365. This may be a reprint of *The Holy Bible
Abridged*, no. **612.2.**

The History Of The Birds in the Air. *See*
Whistle, Will, Esq. no. **1426.1.**

The History Of The Birds in the Air. *See*
[Whistle, Will, Esq.], no. **1427.1.**

583 The History Of The Blind Beggar Of
Bethnal Green; Shewing His Birth And Paren-
tage. Printed in New-Haven, M.DCC.XCVII.
t.[3], [4–5], 6–45 p.; illus.; 9.5 cm.; sigs. A_{11},
B_{11} each should be 12, possibly fr.[2], and a
leaf following p. 45 is wanting.
English ed. chapbook version in verse, ———
Of Bednal Green. London: T. Norris [1715].

CtHi° (fr.[2]? and covers wanting); Evans
48144.

The History Of The Children In The Wood.
See Children In The Wood, no. **177.**

The History Of The Davenport Family. *See*
S., H., no. **1136.**

584 History of the Inchanted [*sic. i.e.* En-
chanted] Castle. Worcester: adv. by I Thomas,
1786 in **395.1.**

585 History Of The Famous And Remarkable
Dog, Tobus. Interspersed with interesting Anecdotes and Stories. Second Edition—revised and
improved. vol. I. [II.] Printed For The Proprietors.
[1817].
1st t.[1], [2–3], 4–16, 2nd t.[17], [18–19], 20–
48 p.; 10.5 cm.; buff paper covers. On the front
leaf is a holograph inscription: *Topliff Johnson
from Willm & Henry Webster Albany 1817.*
Topliff Johnson was the son of Jacob Johnson
the Philadelphia publisher of children's books.
Carson°.

586.1 The History of the Holy Bible. Phila-
delphia: Printed and Sold by Young, Stewart and
M'Culloch, the corner of Chesnut and Second
Streets. 1786.
Adv. by Young and M'Culloch, 1787 in **249.2.**
This may be *The Holy Bible Abridged. Phila-
delphia, 1786,* no. **612.2.**
Evans 19508.

586.2 The History Of The Holy Bible, As
contained in the Old and New Testament.
Adorned with Cuts. For the Use of Children. [2
lines quot.] Boston: Printed and sold by J. White
and C. Cambridge, near Charles-river Bridge.
1790.
fr.[ii], t.[iii], [iv–v], vi, [7], 8–96 p.; illus.; 10
cm.; bound in leather. The illus. are printed
from the same woodcut illus. used in *The Holy
Bible Abridged. Boston,* [1782]. *See* no. **612.1.**
MWA-W°; MHi (leather of the cover sewed
across the fr.[ii].

586.3 ——— Boston: Printed and sold by J.
White and C. Cambridge, near Charles-river
Bridge. 1792.
fr.[ii], t.[iii], [iv–v], vi, [7], 8–96 p.; illus.;

10.5 cm.; bound in illus. buff-yellow paper over w. bds.

MWA°; MB (i. st. on t.[iii]; MHi (fr.[ii] & orig. covers wanting; t.[iii] mut. wanting imprint); NjP (front cover broken, t.[iii] slightly worm-eaten); NNC-Pl; Evans 25174; Hamilton 139.

586.4 THE HISTORY OF THE HOLY BIBLE. Illustrated with Notes, And Adorned with Cuts. For the use of Children. [2 lines quot.] Hartford: Printed By John Babcock. 1798.

fr.[2], t.[3], [4–7], 8–120 p.; illus.; 13 cm.; bound in marbled paper over w. bds., leather spine.

CtHi°; CoU; MWA (p. 49–50; 59–62, 71–72, 83–86 and covers wanting; t.[3] mut.); PP; Evans 33411.

586.5 HISTORY OF THE BIBLE. Adorned with Cuts. The Fifth Edition. Philadelphia: Printed for John Wigglesworth, at his Hard-ware, Toy and Brush-Shop, in Second Street. [*ca.* 1798].

t.[1], [2], 3–23, [24, adv.] p.; 4 pl.; 7.5 cm.; text in verse. A different book from any listed under nos. **586** above and from Benjamin Harris' *The Holy Bible In Verse*, no. **492.1**.

MWA°; Evans 48369.

586.6 THE HISTORY OF THE HOLY BIBLE ABRIDGED Embellished with Eight Elegant Copper Plate Prints. Philadelphia, Published By T. T. Stiles. 1807.

fr.[2], t.[3], [4–5], 6–52 p.; 8 pl. some of which can be considered illus. or part of the pagination; 14 cm.; bound in yellow paper over bds., leather spine.

MWA°; CtHi; Shaw 12760.

586.7 ——— Abridged. From Sidney's Press, New-Haven, 1808.

fr.[ii], t.[1], [2–3], 4–62, [63] p.; illus.; 11 cm.; yellow unprinted paper covers.

MWA° (fr.[ii] mut.); CtHi (p. 61–63 wanting; fr.[ii] mut.); Shaw 15244.

586.8 ——— From Sidney's Press, New-Haven, 1809.

fr.[ii], t.[1], [2–3], 4–36 p.; illus.; 13.5 cm.; gray-green pr. & illus. paper covers.

Cover title: History Of The Bible. Published by I. Cooke & Co. Church-Street, New-Haven, opposite Butler's tavern. Where every article may be found usually wanted in Schools and Academies.

MWA°; CtHi; DLC (covers mut.); MH (fr.[ii] wanting); Shaw 17760.

586.9 ——— Abridged Embellished with Eight Elegant Copper Plate Prints. Philadelphia, Published by A. Dickinson 1809.

t.[1], [2–3, bl.], [4, 1st illus.], [5], 6–52 p.; engr. t.[1] with vignette; 6 illus., 1 pl. opp. p. 24; 14 cm.; wallpaper covers; p. no. 26–27 not used, they should be p. 28–29, which would then renumber p. 30–52 to 28–50; 2nd illus. p. [9] numbered 15; 3rd illus. p. [16] numbered 50; pl. opp. p. 24, numbered 22; 4th illus. p. [32] numbered 31; 5th illus. p. [42] numbered 39; 6th illus. p. [47] numbered 46.

PP; CtHi; MWA (t.[1] and several plates wanting); Shaw 17759.

586.10 ——— Abridged. Adorned With Cuts. From Sidney's Press, New-Haven. 1817.

fr.[2], t.[3], [4–5], 6–47 p.; illus.; 13 cm.; illus. pink paper covers.

MWA°.

586.11 ——— New-Haven: Printed For J. Babcock And Son. Sidney's Press. 1819.

fr.[ii], t.[1], [2, adv.–3], 4–36 p.; illus.; 13.5 cm.; pr. brick-red paper covers.

Cover title of PP copy: The Holy Bible. [cut of a man, a hut, a boy and two women]. Published By J. Babcock & Son, Booksellers, Stationers and Printers, adjoining the Post-Office New Haven. Sold by S. & W. R. Babcock, Booksellers and Stationers, Charleston, S. C. PP°.

586.12 ——— New-Haven: Printed For J. Babcock And Son. Sidney's Press. 1820.

fr.[2], t.[3], [4, adv.–5], 6–31 p.; illus.; 15 cm.; pr. & illus. pink paper covers.

Cover title: Bible History. [vignette illus. of Negroes climbing coconut trees.] Published and Sold by John Babcock and Son, New-Haven, and S. & W. R. Babcock. Charleston [S.C.].

MWA° (fr.[2], p. 31 & covers mut.); Ct; CtY; MHi; OOxM; Shoemaker 1615.

587.1 THE HISTORY OF THE HOLY JESUS: Containing, a brief and plain Account of his Birth.

Death, Resurrection and Ascension into Heaven; and his coming again at the great and last Day of Judgement. Being a pleasant and Profitable Companion for Children; compos'd on purpose for their Use. To which is added, two excellent Hymns, one on the presence, the other on the absence of the Lord Jesus Christ; and a Body of Divinity for little Children. By a Lover of their precious Souls. Sold by B. Gray, at the North-side of the Market.

"The above advertisement announcing the book as 'Just Published' appears in the *Boston News Letter* of January 31, 1745. It appears also in the two issues next following with the additional sentence after the word 'little children', 'Adorn'd with sixteen Cuts'. In the absence of further evidence, this is assumed to be the first edition. No copy of this edition is known." Bates (1911).
Bates 5.; Sabin 84553, p. 97.

587.2 THE HISTORY OF THE HOLY JESUS. Containing a brief and plain Account of his Birth, Life, Death, Resurrection and Ascension into Heaven; and his coming again at the great and last Day of Judgement. Being a pleasant and profitable Companion for Children; compos'd on Purpose for their Use. By a lover of their precious Souls. Third Edition. Boston, Printed for B. Gray, on the North Side of the Market. 1746.

fr.[2. portrait], t.[3], [4–47] p.; [A]–[C]$_8$°; 16 illus.; 9.5 cm.; scalloped marble paper covers. Introduction, [A]$_3$ recto & verso; History, [A]$_3$ verso-[C]$_5$ recto; Delight in the Lord Jesus, [C]$_5$ verso-[C]$_6$ recto; Hymn II, [C]$_6$ verso-[C]$_7$ verso; The Child's Body of Divinity, [C]$_7$ verso-[C]$_8$ recto. Six printer's ornaments are used to compose decorative bars at the top of captions or at the end of a section. The large capital "T" of the first word "The" of text is not illuminated. Other characteristic type settings are: [A]$_3$ recto, line 7, "wish" [*sic. i.e.* with]; [A]$_4$ verso, line 12, "Go'd" [*sic. i.e.* Gold]; [A]$_6$ recto, line 3, "First-born" [with a hyphen]; B$_3$ recto, line 1, "astary" [*sic. i.e.* astray]; B$_3$, verso, line 8, "him, - - - - a" [separated by 4 hyphens]; B$_6$ verso, line 1, "o see" [*sic. i.e.* To see]; [C]$_3$ recto, line 8, "Tidings"; [C]$_2$ recto line 1 is 4.8 cm. long [in the MWA copy of the fac.]; the base of the illustration "Darkness over the Land", B$_7$ recto, is along the outside margin of the page. The illustration of

"*Herod slaying* the innocent Children," [A]$_5$ verso, has the signature *J T* in the upper left corner. Bates, when describing the illustrations in the 1747 edition, which are from the same blocks used in the 1746 edition, believed that all of them except perhaps the two smallest, are the work of James Turner who presumably signed this cut.

°In unpaged books, in which reference to certain pages are to be made, signatures will be given in the collation and referred to in the text. MSaE°; MWA (fac. copy of the unique MSaE copy); PP; and other libraries also have copies of this fac. of which 1200 copies were printed; Evans 40398.

587.3 [——— Third Edition. Boston, Printed for B. Gray, on the North Side of the Market. 1746]. [title taken from **587.2**].

A variant of the preceding. A fragmentary copy. The pages are identical with no. **587.2** both in type setting and the breaks in the illustrations. A few corrections have been made: B$_3$ recto, line 1, "astray" is spelled correctly; B$_6$ verso, line 1, has the "T" of "To see" struck. MWA° (fr.[2], t.[3], [4–6], [31–47] wanting; [7–8], [27–30] lower half of the p. and covers wanting); Evans 40398.

587.4 ——— The Fourth Edition. Boston, Printed for D. Gookin in Marlborough-Street. 1747.

fr.[2, portrait], t.[3], [4–47] p.; sigs. [A]–[C]$_8$; illus.; 10 cm.; scalloped marbled paper covers. The text is the same and the type setting is close to the 1746 ed., no. **587.2**. Six printer's ornaments are present. The capital "T" of the first word "The" of the text is 3mm. high. The "e" of the same word lies below the space between the "The" and "Introduction" of the caption. The type setting of **587.5** and **587.7** is the same as in this 1747 edition. The misprintings in the 1746 ed. **587.2**, [A]$_3$ recto line 7, [A]$_4$ verso line 12, B$_3$ recto line 1, are corrected. Other changes are: "First born", [A]$_6$ recto line 3, no longer has a hyphen; only three dashes separate "him, — — —a", B$_3$ verso line 8; and "Tidings", [C]$_3$ recto line 8, is spelled "Tydings"; [C]$_2$ recto line 1, is longer than in no. **587.2**, being 5.5 mm.; the base of the illustration "Darkness over the Land", B$_7$ recto is along the inner margin of the page. On [C]$_6$ recto, line 1, "de^(ar)" is printed with the letters "ar" higher than the "de", and on the line below, "t°" is also misprinted with the "o" higher than the "t"; [C]$_7$ verso line 1 "sp^(re)ad" is printed with the "re" higher than the rest of the word. These misprintings occur only in the 1747 edition. The 16 illustrations are from the same blocks used in the 1746 edition.

CtHi*; Bates p. 5; Evans 5967; Sabin 84553.

587.5 ———— The Fifth Edition. [Bost]on. Printed by J. Green, 1748.

fr.[2, portrait], t.[3], [4–47] p.; [A]–[C]$_8$; 16 illus.; 9.5 cm.; red scalloped marbled paper covers. The text is the same as no. **587.2**. The type setting of most of the pages is from standing type of the 1747 edition. The misprintings on [C]$_6$ recto lines 1 and 2 and [C]$_7$ verso line 1 are corrected. Line 20 [C]$_1$ verso, the "r" of the word "Door" lies between the "e" and "n" of "silent" in the line above, just as in the 1747 edition. In 1749 this line is reset. The word "sound," [C]$_4$ verso line 1, is printed without a space between the "s" and "o" and has a comma after the word, similar to no. **587.4**. See discussion of variations of these points in no. **587.7**. The illustration of "The Prodigal Son", B$_2$ recto, has a break in the double rule border. In 1747 this border is without a break. The picture of "*Abraham* offering up his Son *Isaac*", B$_3$ recto, still has an unbroken border.

MWA-W* (t.[3], p. [4–8] mut.); (not in Evans).

587.6 ———— The Fifth Edition. Boston, Printed by J. Green, 1748.

The printing of line 20 [C]$_1$ verso is the same as in the 1749 edition, no. **587.7**. The word "s ound", [C]$_4$ verso line 1, is printed with a space between the "s" and "o" and without a comma after the word matching MWA copy 1 of the 1749 edition. All illustrations are from the same blocks used in no. **587.5**, but the state of the breaks in the borders of "The Prodigal Son", B$_2$ recto, and the one of "*Abraham* offering up his Son *Isaac*," B$_8$ recto, match the state of the cuts in 1749, with the characteristic breaks. There was apparently a remainder of some leaves or unbound sheets of the 1748 edition which got mixed with those printed in 1749 and both were bound together. This accounts for the presence of 1749 illustrations and

pages in this book with the title page 1748. MWA* (scalloped marbled paper covers); Evans 6157.

587.7 ———— The Sixth Edition. Boston, Printed by J. Bushell and J. Green, 1749.

fr.[2, portrait], t.[3], [4–47] p.; [A]–[C]$_8$; 16 illus.; 10 cm. The text is the same as no. **587.5**. Most of the pages are printed from standing type from the 1747 and 1748 editions, so that they are identical in all three years. Variations occur between copies and certain pages may resemble or differ from no. **587.5**. In the CtHi copy [C]$_4$ verso line 1, "sound," is printed in correctly spaced type with a comma after the word and could have been printed from standing type. In MWA-W copy 2 "s ound" is printed with a space between the "s" and "o" with a comma after the word. In MWA-W copy 2, MWA, and RPJCB copies "s ound" is very close to that in MWA copy 1 but wants a comma after the word. The illustration of "*Abraham* offering up his Son *Isaac*," B$_8$ recto, has a break passing through the double rule left border.

MWA-W* (copy 2, fr.[2], t.[3], p. [4–6], [47] & covers wanting but has illus. of "The Prodigal Son", B$_2$ recto, and "Gabriel", [C]$_4$ recto, centered on the page so that the right rule border is intact); CtHi (scalloped marbled paper covers; fr. [2] wanting, supplied from another copy); CSmH; DLC (fr.[2], t.[3], p. [4–6], [45–47] wanting; on p. 7 there is a holograph date *1749*); MWA (copy 1, fr.[2], [7–8], [15–16], [35–36] mut.); NjP (2 copies: copy 1, complete; copy 2, fr.[2], p. [47] & covers wanting; t.[3] mut. with date wanting; p. [21–28], [43–47] slightly mut.); RPJCB; Bates p. 6; Evans 6631; Hamilton 28; Sabin 94553, p. 98.

587.8 ———— The Sixth Edition. Boston, Printed by J. Bushnell and J. Green, 1749.

A variant of MWA copy 1 of **587.7**. The type setting in both books is identical, but mixed with this typical 1749 edition with the characteristic more extensive break passing through both rules of the border of the illustration of "A careful Mother instructing her Children." [A]$_4$ recto, are typical 1748 illustrations of "The Prodigal Son", B$_2$ recto, and "*Abraham* offering up his son *Isaac*," B$_8$ recto, which lack the

prominent breaks in the borders. The book is a mixture of both editions.
PP°.

587.9 —— The Seventh Edition. [Ne]w-London, Printed [And] Sold by John Green, 1754. t.[3], [4–44] p.;[A]–[C]$_8$ with [A]$_1$; [C]$_7$, [C]$_8$ wanting; 15 illus.; 10 cm. The text is the same no. **587.7**, being 2 mm. high and surrounded by earlier Boston editions. The capital "T" of the first word of the text "The" is smaller than in no. **587.7**, being 2 mm. high and surrounded by an illumination of 8 printer's ornaments. The caption "The Introduction," [A]$_3$ recto, is printed in large Roman type instead of large italics. The missing frontispiece was probably the portrait of The Author from the same block used in no. **587.7**. Fourteen of the illustrations are from the same blocks used in the Boston 1749 edition. Two have new borders. On [A]$_8$ verso the picture of a three-masted square rigger is surrounded by a double rule, and the entire cut is 39 x 53 mm. The florid border of mermaid on either side blowing a horn and much scroll work of the earlier editions is done away with. The small illustration of the fig tree, B$_5$ verso, is crudely redrawn and enclosed in an outer scalloped and inner thin rule border. The illustration of "*Abraham* offering up his Son *Isaac*," with the words "*Genesis 22. 10*" added to the title, B$_8$ recto, has the same break described in no. **587.7**. In no. **587.7** a spot or two confluent spots appear above Isaac's clasped hands. These spots are only a dot in this edition. Other illustrations have additions to the title, a title where none existed before, or the cut is set differently on the page as follows: [A]$_2$ verso, has "*Gen. 3*" following "*Adam and Eve*"; B$_7$ recto, has the title "Darkness over the land, *Luk* [*sic. i.e. Luke*], *23. 44*", below the left double rule margin and along the bottom of the page; [C]$_1$ recto, "An Earthquake"; and [C]$_4$ recto, "GABRIEL."
NN° (fr.[2] & p.[45–47] wanting); Bates p. 6; Evans 7211; Sabin 84553, p. 98.

587.10 —— The Eighth Edition, with some Addition [*sic. i.e.* Additions]. Boston, New-England; Printed and Sold by Fowle & Draper, in Marlboro'-Street. Where may be had a variety of little Books for Children. 1762.
fr.[2], t.[3], [4–32] p.; [A]-B$_8$; 10 illus.; 12.5 cm. Introduction, [A]$_3$ recto and verso; History, [A]$_4$ recto–B$_8$ verso. The text follows that of no. **587.2**. Five printer's ornaments are present as well as an elaborate decorative bar, [A]$_4$ recto, consisting of dolphins, baskets, and scrolls. All the woodcut illustrations are new or redrawn from preceding editions. The frontispiece, [A]$_1$ verso, is the right half of an illustration which came from an unknown edition of *The Prodigal Daughter* and shows the devil dressed up as a fine gentleman. On [A]$_6$ verso the left half of another illustration from *The Prodigal Daughter* portrays the devil in the nude with a tail and horns on his head. This must be meant to illustrate the line on the page opposite "And there the Devil tempts him fore". Two illustrations and a squarish tailpiece 4 x 4.5 cm. with a circular central opening surrounded by a thick ornamental border, [A]$_7$ verso, were used by Daniel Fowle [*ca.* 1756] in *A New Gift for Children*, no. **932**.
MWA° (covers wanting; fr.[2] & p. 15–16] mut.); Evans 41270.

587.11 —— The Eighth Edition. New-London: Printed and Sold by T. Green, 1762.
illus. [1, portrait], fr.[2, portrait], t.[3], [4–48] p.; [A]–[C]$_8$; 18 illus.; 10 cm. The text is the same as no. **587.2**. The type setting is different from the 1754 edition. Two new illustrations have been added. On [A]$_1$ recto is a portrait of a man with a wide ribbon or sash over the right shoulder and extending to the left hip. The other, [C]$_8$ verso, looks as if it might be a supplementary woodcut illustration of the murder of the Innocents. Three soldiers are on the left side of the picture, the middle one seems to be holding up a child possibly siezed from the unhappy mother below him. In the central foreground a body is lying on the ground. To the right among some trees is the outline of a taller figure with arms outstretched towards a smaller one. This illustration is also present in **587.15**, **587.17** and **587.24**. The remaining sixteen illustrations are from the same blocks used in the 1754, New-London edition. The break passing through the left rules of the cut of "*Abraham* offering up his Son *Isaac*, . . ." is similar to that in the same woodcut in 1754, but now a new break appears above the first break, which is merely a hair line and not a definite separation as in the New-London 1766 edition. The

spot above Isaac's clasped hands is as small as in the 1754 New-London edition. The title "GABRIEL" at the bottom of the illustration on [C]₄ recto is printed upside down along the inner margin of the page.

CtHi° (rebound, orig. covers wanting); Bates p. 7; Evans 9138; Sabin 84553, p. 98.

587.12 ——— The Tenth Edition with some Addition [*sic. i.e.* Additions]. Boston, New-England; Printed and Sold by Z. Fowle, at his Printing-Office, in Back Street, 1764. (Price 6 Coppers).

[3–46] p.; would be [A]– C₈ if the copy were complete; 14 illus. and one tailpiece; 10.5 cm. Introduction, [A]₃ recto and verso; History, [A]₄ verso–C₃ verso; Upon the Day of Judgement, C₄ recto and verso; The Child's Body Of Divinity, C₅ recto–C₆ recto; St. Paul's Shipwreck, C₆ verso–C₇ verso, which ends in a tailpiece of 7 lines made up of printer's ornaments, the word "FINIS" and the catchword "Just". The poems "Delight in the Lord Jesus" and "Hymn II. Absence of Christ intolerable" are omitted and three new poems "Upon the Day of Judgement", "The Child's Body of Divinity", "St. Paul's Shipwreck" appear for the first time. The Introduction and History follow that of no. **587.2** and no. **587.10**. The type setting is entirely different from no. **587.10**. Five printer's ornaments are present. The "T" of the first word of the text "The" is 13 mm. high and not illuminated. The portrait of "The AUTHOR," [A]₁ recto in the 1766 edition, no. **587.14**, was probably on the missing leaf [A]₁ in this book. The missing leaf C₈ may have also had at least one illustration. Two illustrations are from the blocks used in no. **587.10**: the Wise Men, [A]₅ recto, and the seated woman holding a baby, [A]₈ recto, now probably representing the woman at the well instead of Eve. There is also a fig tree, B₄ verso, and a kneeling man and woman each before an open book, C₅ recto. This cut was used in 1766, [1767?], 1774, 1779, nos. **587.14**, **587.16** and **587.25–26**. In the Boston [1792?] edition, no. **587.32**, this cut is redrawn and entitled "A little *Boy* and *Girl* at Prayers". Besides these four illustrations there is a squarish tailpiece, C₃ verso with the central space now filled with a square, in which is a design, which might represent a tree. In addition to these there are six illustrations crudely copied in the reverse from the Boston edition of 1746 and each signed *I T*: 1. "*Adam* and *Eve. Gen. 3.6*", [A]₂ verso; 2. "A careful *Mother* Instructing her Children," [A]₄ recto; 3. "*Herod* slaying the innocent Children", [A]₆ recto; 4. "The Prodigal Son", B₂ verso; 5. "Christ teaching the Multitude", B₅ recto; 6. "Abraham offering up his Son Isaac", B₇ recto; 7. "Death with three coffins", B₈ verso. There are three entirely new illustrations: 1. two women, a tree, Christ and a man, in a small rectangular cut, 50.8 x 10.8 mm., [A]₄ verso; 2. a three-masted square rigger meant to depict the ship in which the miracle of the draught of fishes took place, 52.6 x 39 mm., B₁ recto; 3. a picture of another three-masted square rigger, presumably St. Paul's ship, C₆ verso, carrying a flag both forward and aft with a white cross on a black field. Bates discussing the seven cuts signed *I T* in the 1767 edition considers them to be the work of Isaiah Thomas. There is much information to back up Bates' assumption. Isaiah Thomas was bound to Zechariah Fowle as an apprentice, June 4, 1756, when he was 7 years of age. At the age of twelve young Thomas "cut" about a hundred plates for books printed by Z. Fowle. *See* Thomas, vol. I. p. xxv. Hamilton, p. 22, says that in 1762, I. Thomas at the age of 13 cut the plates for Erra Pater's *The New Book of Knowledge*. In the MWA copy of the 1767 edition of Pater's book, Hamilton says "Thomas has written: 'Printed and Cuts engraved wholly by I. Thomas, then 13 years of age, for Z. Fowle when I. T. was his apprentice.' " The seven cuts in no. **587.12** signed *I T*, Hamilton believes were cut by I. Thomas prior to 1765 before Thomas left Fowle.

MWA-W° (fr.[2] & p. [47] or sigs. [A]₁, C₈ and covers wanting); Evans 41450.

587.13 ——— Boston: adv. by Z. Fowle, 1765 in Watts' *A Preservation*.

Evans 10201; Sabin 84553, p. 98.

587.14 ——— The Eleventh Edition. Boston: Printed and Sold by Z. Fowle, at his Printing-Office, in Back-Street. 1766. (Price 4 Pence.).

fr.[2, portrait], t.[3], [4–48] p.; [A]–C₈; 20 illus.; 11 cm.; Dutch paper covers. Introduction, [A]₂ verso–[A]₃ verso; History, [A]₃ verso–C₃ recto; Upon the Day of Judgement, C₃ verso–C₄ recto; The Child's Body of Divinity, C₄ verso–C$_5$ verso; St. Paul's Shipwreck, C$_6$ recto–C$_7$ recto; full page illus. of a standing man and woman facing each other in a two windowed room, furnished with a chair and table, C$_7$ verso; portrait of Queen Charlotte, C$_8$ recto; a man drinking from a bottle, C$_8$ verso. The text follows that of no. **587.12**, but with the various sections and illustrations on different signatures. Four printer's ornaments are present. Nine illustrations are from the same blocks used by Z. Fowle in his 1764 edition, no. **587.12**. Six are full-paged, with five signed *I T*, and three smaller being two-thirds to a quarter of a page in size. The full-paged illustration of "The Wise Men", [A]$_5$ recto, has the same breaks as in no. **587.12**, but now a basal section of the bottom rule border is wanting, leaving a space 12.5 mm. long. "HEROD slaying the innocent Children," is on [A]$_5$ verso instead of [A]$_6$ recto as in the 1764 edition. The smaller illustrations are: Death with three coffins, B$_8$ recto, signed *I T*; the kneeling man and woman each before an open book, C$_4$ verso; and the three-masted square rigger, the ship of the draught of fishes, [A]$_8$ verso. Two new cuts signed *I T* are present: a full page portrait of "The Author," [A]$_1$ verso, which may have been the frontispiece missing in no. **587.12** and a half-page portrait of St. Paul, C$_6$ recto. The remaining unsigned nine illustrations are new. Three full-paged ones are on the last three pages and described above. The other six are small, about a quarter of a page in size and are: "Adam and Eve. *Gen. 3.6.*", [A]$_2$ verso, a crude copy in the reverse of a London, J. Newbery illustration in *The Holy Bible Abridged. 1760;* the woman at the well, [A]$_7$ verso; Christ, a follower and a fig tree, B$_4$ recto; "The Crusifixion", B$_7$ recto; a portly minister, C$_1$ recto; and a small cut 35 x 29 mm. of a man and woman standing on either side of a tree, C$_3$ recto.

MWA* (rear cover wanting); Evans 41626.

587.15 ———— The Eighth Edition. [Ne]w-London: Printed and [sol]d by Timothy Green, 1766. t.[3], [4–48] p.; [A]–[C]$_8$ with [A]$_1$ wanting; 16 illus. with the 17th illus. the portrait of "The Author" wanting; 10.5 cm.; tan paper covers. The text is the same as no. **587.2**. The type setting is different from no. **587.11**. Two printer's ornaments are present. The "T" of the first word of the text "The" is 9 mm. high and

not illuminated. In the succeeding New-London edition of 1769 and New-Haven, 1771, the first portrait on the recto of the frontispiece is not used so it may not have been in this edition. The first illustration of the text, [A]$_2$ verso, has the title "Adam and Eve" in large Roman type. The title is along the left double rule border and at the bottom of the page. The bottom of the illustration is along the outer margin of the page. "The Careful Mother Instructing her Children," [A]$_4$ recto, no longer has a top rule border. The left border of "The Prodigal Son", B$_2$ recto, is no longer present. The top break in the left double rule border of "*Abraham* offering up his son *Isaac, . . .*" is no longer a hair line, as in no. **587.11**, but a marked separation. The spot in the sky above the clasped hands of Isaac, which first appeared in the Boston, 1749 edition as two spots, and was reduced to a dot in the 1754 and 1762, New-London editions, is larger and more prominent. The title "GABRIEL" is printed upside down at the top of the illustration, along the inner margin of the page.

MWA* (fr.[2] wanting, t.[3] mut.); Evans 41627.

587.16 ———— The Fifteenth Edition. Boston: Printed by I. Thomas, for Z. Fowle, in Back-Street, near the Mill-Bridge. (Price 6 Coppers.) [1767?]. fr.[2, portrait], t.[3], [4–47] p.; [A]–C$_8$; 19 illus.; 11 cm. Introduction, [A]$_3$ recto–verso; History, [A]$_4$ recto–C$_3$ verso; Upon the Day of Judgement, C$_4$ recto–verso; The Child's Body of Divinity, C$_5$ recto–C$_6$ recto; St. Paul's Shipwreck, C$_6$ verso–C$_7$ verso; portrait of Queen Charlotte, C$_8$ recto. The text follows that of no. **587.14**, but with various sections and illustrations on different signatures. Four printer's ornaments are present. The letter "T" of the first word of the text "The" is 7 mm. high and not illuminated. The eighteen illustrations are from the same wood blocks used in the Boston, 1766 edition. The third from the last and the last illustration in no. **587.14** are omitted. A new quarter-page picture of "The Annunciation" is on [A]$_4$ recto. "The Wise Men", [A]$_4$ verso, has the same breaks as in no. **587.14**, but now a space 20 mm. long is present. Behind this space 4 mm. have been scooped out from the base of the cut inside of the border.

MWA* (covers wanting); CtHi (fr.[2] wanting); NjN (fr.[2], t.[3], & covers wanting);

Bates p. 7; Evans 41723; Hamilton 68; Sabin 84553, p. 98.

587.17 ——— The Tenth Edition. New-London: Printed and sold by T. Green. 1769.

Portrait [1], [2, bl.], t.[3], 4–48] p.; [A]–[C]$_8$; 17 illus.; 11.5 cm.; bound in leather. The text is the same as no. **587.2**. The type set up and type is different from no. **587.15**. Two printer's ornaments are present. The letter "T" of the first word of text "The" is not illuminated. The identical blocks used in the 1762 edition, no. **587.11**, are present, but the portrait of "THE AUTHOR" is on the recto of [A]$_1$ and is so entitled for the first time. Certain illustrations are placed differently on the page and others have new or more extensive breaks or omissions from the borders. "The careful Mother . . .", [A]$_4$ recto, has the title above the illustration and the base along the outer margin of the page. Comparing it with the impression in no. **587.15**, 15 mm. of the upper half of the left double-rule border is found to be wanting. The illustration of "The Prodigal Son", B$_2$ recto, now has the double rules of both the right and left borders wanting. The twin illustrations of the rich man and Lazarus . . . B$_2$ verso, want the left outer thick rule and the right double rule borders. The title "GABRIEL" to the illustration on [C]$_4$ recto, is printed in larger type than in no. **587.15**, and is printed along the top of the woodcut along the outer margin of the page. CtY*; Evans 41944; Sabin 84553, p. 98.

587.18 ——— The Twenty-Fourth Edition. Boston: Printed for, and Sold by J. Boyles, in Marlborough-Street, 1771.

fr.[2], t.[3], [4–47] p.; [A]–C$_8$; 16 illus., 1 tailpiece; 10.5 cm.; Dutch paper covers. Introduction, p. [5]–7; History, p. 8–38; Upon the Day of Judgment, p. 38–40; The Child's Body of Divinity, p. 41–43; St. Paul's Shipwreck, p. 44–46; a full-page illus. of possibly a portable candle holder with a sconce-like portion attached to a pyramoidal or four-sided triangular metal object with a finial at the top and a looped handle. In front of it is an oval tray with an object on it which could be a snuffer, p.[47]. Printer's ornaments are absent. This is the first paged edition of the book. The last line on p. 16 reads "unto his earnest prayer". The last line on p. 33 is "Even at Jerusalem".

The running title on p. 9, "The Holy Jesus," is 31.2 mm. long, the last "s" of "Jesus" is printed slightly lower than the rest of the word, and the page number 9 is 3 mm. high. Illustrations used in the 1766 edition, no. **587.14**, are: portrait of "The AUTHOR," p. [2]; "HEROD slaying the innocent Children," p. 11; "The careful Mother . . .," p. 13; "The prodigal SON," p. 21; "Abraham . . . ," p. 29; "The Crusifixion", p. 30, with a dent in the upper right-hand corner; "Death . . . ," p. 32. New redrawn illustrations: "ADAM and EVE . . . ," 59.5 x 59.3 mm., p. [5], with the title printed above the cut; "The Annunciation", p. 8; "The Wise Men", p. 9; a large cut of a three-masted square rigger, the ship of the draught of fishes, p. 18, with a break in the thick top rule border. On p. 25 there is an oblong cut of a man looking at a tree with a house in the middle of the illustration. This presumably represents Christ and the fig tree. The sky above the house and tree is clear and does not have any linear blemishes in it. Entirely new illustrations are: a globe, p. 7; "The Ascension", p. 35; a circular tailpiece of a swan surrounded by a thick scroll-like border, p. 40; a cock, p. 46; and a full-page illustration of a triangular object which may be a candle holder of some kind described above.

MWA* (rear cover & p. [47] wanting; p. 45–46 mut.); CtHi (rear cover & p. [47] wanting); NRU (complete); Evans 42245; Sabin 84553, p. 98.

587.19 [——— Boston: Printed For and Sold by J. Boyles, . . . 1771.] [title taken from **587.18**].

A fragmentary variant wanting the title page which is identical with no. **587.18** except that p. 31 is printed p. "33". This was probably the first printing of the book for Boyles, which in the later printing of no. **587.18**, page 31 was correctly numbered.

MWA* (p. [2–12], [47], & covers wanting; p. 13–14 lower half wanting, p. 15–46 mut.).

587.20 ——— The Twenty-Fourth Edition. Boston: N. E. Printed and Sold by N. Coverly, near Liberty-Tree. MDCCLXXI. ☞ Price 6 Coppers. ✒

t.[3], [4], 5–44p.; would be [A]–C$_8$ if the copy were complete; 13 illus., 1 tailpiece; 10 cm. The text is the same as no. **587.18**. The missing illustrations are: The Author, p. [2]; [The

Cock], p. 46; and possibly the illustration on p. [47] in no. **587.18**. The type setting of the title page, except for the imprint, and on most of the pages of the text is identical with no. **587.18**, but variations occur. Printer's ornaments are not present. On p. 10, 12, 14, 15 the catchword is lower than the last line of verse. The last line on p. 16 is the extra line "For the same hour of the day", a duplication of the first line on p. 17. The catchword at the bottom of p. 16 is "The". This may be a misprinting for the word "That", the first word in the second line on p. 17. The last line p. 33 is the same as in no. **587.18**. The catchword p. 36 is "Aud" [*sic. i.e.* And], same as in no. **587.22**. The running title "The Holy Jesus" on p. 9 is printed in larger type than in no. **587.18** and no. **587.22**. The entire line measures 41.2 mm. instead of 31.2 mm. The illustration of the square rigger, the ship of the draught of fishes, p. 18, shows a nail head and an irregular patch in the upper left corner which probably first appeared in no. **587.22**. Unlike no. **587.18** but like no. **587.22**, the thick rule borders are ornamented with a central wavy line.

MWA* (fr.[2], p. 45–47, & covers wanting); Evans 42246; Sabin 84553, p. 98.

587.21 ———— The Twenty-Fourth Edition. Boston: N. E. Printed for, and Sold by J. Perkins, in Union-Street, 1771. Price 6 Coppers.

fr.[2], t.[3], [4–5], 6–44 p.; (45 etc. wanting). MWA*; (not in Evans).

587.22 ———— The Twenty-Fourth Edition. Boston: Printed and Sold by Ez. Russell, in Queen-Street. 1771.

fr.[2, portrait], t.[3], [4–5], 6–38 p.; would be [A]–C_8 if copy were complete. 12 illus.; 10 cm. The text is the same as no. **587.17**. The missing illustrations are those on p. 46, [47] and tailpiece p. 40, if the missing pages of this edition were the same as no. **587.17**. The text and illustrations are identical with no. **587.18** and probably printed from the same type setting except for the imprint on the title page. Printer's ornaments are absent. The running title p. 9, "The Holy Jesus," and the page number 9 are the same as in no. **587.18**. The catchwords on p. 10, 12, 14, 15 are on a level with the last line of verse. The catchword p. 36 is "Aud" [*sic. i.e.* And], same as in no. **587.20**. Both the

last lines on p. 16, "Unto his earnest prayer", and p. 33, "Even at Jerusalem", are the same as in no. **587.18**. This may be the second printing of this edition considering no. **587.18** to be the first. In no. **587.22** the mutilation of the upper left corner of the illustration of the three-masted square rigger, the ship of the draught of fishes, p. 18, probably first appeared, as well as the ornamentation of the thick rule borders with a central wavy line. The mutilation is repaired and shows a nail head and a patch.

MWA* (fr.[2], p. 33–47 & covers wanting); MB (p. 31–47 and rear cover wanting; p. 30 mut.); Evans 12073; Sabin 84553, p. 98.

587.23 ———— The Twenty-Fourth Edition. Boston: Printed for, and Sold by Isaiah Thomas, in Union-Street. 1771.

fr.[2, portrait], t.[3], [4–5], 6–42 p.; would be [A]–C_8 if copy were complete; 13 illus.; 10 cm.; Dutch paper covers. Introduction, p. [5]–7; History, p. 8–38; Upon the Day of Judgement, p. 39–41; The Child's Body of Divinity, p. 42–. The type setting of the text and the illustrations are identical with no. **587.22** up to p. 32, including the illustration of the three-masted square rigger, p. 18, with the nail head and patch and the rule borders ornamented with a wavy central line. Pages 33–42 have a new type setting and are without illustrations. Ten printer's ornaments are present. The last line p. 33 reads "To Olivet with them."

MWA* (p. 43–47 and rear cover wanting; fr. [2], p. 41–42 mut.); RPB (rebound; fr.[2], p. [47] wanting. All of signature C or p. 33–46 match both the N. Coverly, 1771 edition, no. **587.20**, and the Ez. Russell, 1771 edition, no. **587.22**, and appears to be a mixture of no. **587.23** with one of the two other editions); Evans 42247; Sabin 84553, p. 98.

587.24 ———— The Eleventh Edition. New-Haven: Printed by T. and S. Green. 1771.

Portrait [1], [2, bl.], t.[3], [4–48] p.; [A]–[C]$_8$; 17 illus.; 10.5 cm. The text is the same as no. **587.2**. Three printer's ornaments are present. The "T" of the first word of the text "The" is not illuminated. The 17 illustrations are printed from the same blocks used in the 1769 edition, but show characteristic differences. In the twin illustrations of the rich man at table and Lazarus at the gate, B_2 verso, all of the inner left rule border to the left of top of the canopy over the rich man's head is wanting. The top thick rule of this same illustration is mostly broken up and wanting. The title "GABRIEL" at the top of the woodcut, [C]$_4$ recto, is along the outer margin of the page and printed with the same size type as no. **587.14**, but the spaces between the letters are greater.

NjP*; Evans 42244.

587.25 ———— The Twenty-Fifth Edition. Boston: Printed and Sold by John Boyle in Marlborough-Street. 1774.

fr.[2, portrait], t.[3], [4–47] p.; [A]–C$_8$; 19 illus., 1 tailpiece; 9.5 cm.; Dutch paper covers; t.[3] surrounded by an ornamental border. Introduction, [A]$_3$ recto–verso; History, [A]$_4$ recto–C$_3$ verso; Upon the Day of Judgement, C$_4$ recto–verso; The Child's Body of Divinity, C$_5$ recto–C$_6$ recto; St. Paul's Shipwreck, C$_6$ verso–C$_7$ verso; full-page illustration of a skeleton and a man dressed in fine clothes, C$_8$ recto. The text is reset but closely follows the type setting of the [1767?] edition, no. **587.16**. Two figured printer's ornaments and corner ornaments are used for a border around the title page. There are no decorative bars in the text. The "T" of the first word of text "The" is 6 mm. high. Many words are misspelled or abbreviated such as: "Noble Man" [*sic. i.e.* Nobleman], [A]$_8$ verso, line 1; "Barley Loves" [*sic. i.e.* Loaves], B$_3$, verso, line 1; the catchword "Wroship" [*sic. i.e.* Worship], C$_2$ recto; "bro't" [*sic. i.e.* brought], C$_5$ recto, line 2; "Uuto" [*sic. i.e.* Unto], C$_6$ recto, line 6. The catchword "And", B$_6$ recto, is not printed; "But hear ——— the Lord . . .", B$_7$ verso, line 1, has a single dash after "hear" instead of four hyphens "----" as in the [1767?] edition. There is a thick and thin rule above the caption, C$_4$ recto. Fourteen of the nineteen illustrations in no. **587.16** appear in this book. The omitted ones in no. **587.25** are: "The Wise Men", [A]$_4$ verso; "Herod slaying the innocent Children", [A]$_5$ verso; the portly minister, C$_1$ verso; the small cut of the man and woman on either side of a tree, C$_3$ verso; "Queen Charlotte", C$_8$ recto. These are replaced by new or different illustrations: The STAR", [A]$_4$ recto; "HEROD slaying the Innocent", [A]$_5$ verso, is a duplication of "Abraham offering up his son Isaac", B$_7$ recto, with the base and title of the cut, on both pages, along the outer margin of the page, instead of along the inner margin as in no. **587.16**. "The coming of the Holy Ghost", C$_1$ verso, which cut looks more like a representation of the Annunciation; a rectangular cut of two women, a tree, Christ and a man, C$_3$ verso, used in no. **587.12**; a skeleton and a man, C$_8$ recto, mentioned above. On C$_7$ verso is a tailpiece of a double-lined circle enclosing a front view of a nude female figure standing on a wheel, and holding a cloth above her head, which drapes across her loins. The illustration of Death and three coffins, B$_8$ recto, for the first time shows an extensive mutilation. The entire upper left corner is wanting, involving the signature *I T*, a portion of the skeleton's skull, the sky, and the feathered portion of the arrow. This is replaced by an attached corner from another cut.

Welch* (fr.[2] and front cover half wanting, t.[3] mut., p. 47 and rear cover wanting); CtHi (p. [47] wanting); CtY (Pequot); DLC (copy 1, covers wanting; copy 2, fr.[2] half wanting, p.[47] wanting, t.[3] mut.); MB (fr. [2], p. [28–29], [47] wanting); MHi (p. [2]–[32], [47] & covers wanting); MWA; NjP (copy 1, front Dutch paper cover half wanting, p. [21–22] mut.; copy 2, also defective); PP; Bates p. 9; Evans 42625; Hamilton 68; Sabin 84553, p. 98.

587.26 ———— The Twenty-Sixth Edition. Boston: Printed for John Boyle in Marlborough-Street. 1779.

illus.[1], fr.[2], t.[3], [4–48] p.; [A]–C$_8$; 22 illus., 1 tailpiece; 10 cm. The text is the same as no. **587.25**, closely follows the type setting, and has 19 illustrations printed from the same blocks. Two printer's ornaments are present. The letter "T" of the first word of the text "The" is 6.4 mm. high and not illuminated. Many of the misspelled words are now correctly printed such as: "Nobleman", [A]$_8$ verso, line 1; "Loaves", B$_3$ verso, line 1; the catchword "Worship", C$_2$ recto; "brought", C$_5$, recto, line 2; "Unto", C$_6$ recto, line 6. The catchword "And", B$_6$ recto is present. The illustration of "HEROD slaying the Innocent", [A]$_5$ verso, has the base and title along the inner margin of the page. It is the same cut as "Abraham offering . . .", B$_7$ recto, which has the title and base of the cut along the outer margin of the page. Three new full-page illustrations have been added to the blank pages in no. **587.25**; "THE MAN of SIN", [A]$_1$ recto; "The Angel GABRIEL", [A]$_2$ verso; and a boy in baggy trousers standing with legs apart and arms directed to the sides and upward, C$_8$ verso.

MWA* (illus. [1], fr.[2], [47–48] wanting); CtHi (fr.[2], t.[3], p. [5–6], [47] mut.); DLC; MHi (p. 47–48 wanting; illus.[1], fr.[2], [41–46] mut.); NjP; PP (p. [47–48] wanting); RPB (all of [A], B$_1$, C$_4$–C$_8$ wanting); Bates p. 10; Evans 43640; Hamilton 88; Sabin 84553, p. 98.

587.27 ———— The First Worcester Edition. Worcester, (Massachusetts) Printed By Isaiah Thomas, And Sold At His Book Store. MDCCL-XXXVI.

fr.[2], t.[3], [4–5], 6–43, [44–47, adv. list of books] p.; [A]–C$_8$; 19 illus.; 9.5 cm.; illus. buff paper covers, with two rectangular cuts surrounded by a border of ornaments on the front cover. Introduction, p. [5]–6; History, p. [7]–33; The Child's Body of Divinity, p. 34–36; St. Paul's Shipwreck, p. 37–[39]; The Cradle Hymn, p. 40–43; [adv. list of 23 books], p. [44–47]. The last three lines of The History . . . p. 33 are changed from "Amidst devouring Flames,/ While you eternal Praise shall sing/To God and to the Lamb", no. **597.26**, to "And Suffer endless Pain:/But you with Christ, the great, the wise,/ Shall live and ever reign". The Book is smaller than former editions being 9.5 x 6.5 mm. Fifteen printer's ornaments are present. This book and none of the following editions have the letter "T" of the word of the text illuminated, and since different printers used different type, the size of the letter will not be given for the remaining editions. The illustration of Adam and Eve p. [5], and Christ, a follower and the fig tree, p. 21, are from the same blocks used in the Boston [1767?], 1774, and 1779 editions. The remaining cuts are new. With the exception of the frontispiece entitled "The Rev. Mr. *Instructwell*, teaching the Principles of the Christian Religion to Master *Learnwell*", used by I. Thomas in *Little Robin Red Breast, 1786*, and the cut on p. 40, all the illustrations were used by Isaiah Thomas in *The Holy Bible Abridged, 1786*, no. **612.4**, which are copies of woodcuts which appeared in John Newbery's London edition of *The Holy Bible Abridged, 1760*.

MWA-W* (fr.[2]–t.[3] figured in James, p. 24; p. 29–[47] and rear cover wanting) CtHi; MWA; RPB (fr.[2], t.[3], p. [4] wanting); Bates p. 10; Evans 19712; Nichols 1918, 78; Sabin 84553, p. 98.

587.28 ———— Hudson [New-York]: adv. by Ashbel Stoddard in *The Hudson Weekly Gazette*, August 5, 1790, as "Just Published, and sold at this office". Evans 22568; Sabin 84553, p. 99.

587.29 ———— Middletown [Conn.]: adv. by Moses H. Woodward, as "Just printed", *Middlesex Gazette, or Fœderal Adviser*, of Middletown, Conn., April 3, 1970.

Evans 22569; Sabin 84553, p. 99.

587.30 ———— New-York: adv. by William Durell, 1790 in **612.5**.

587.31 ———— Boston: adv. by Samuel Hall, 1791 in **408.3**.

587.32 ———— Sold at the Bible and Heart in Boston. [1792?].

t.[1], [2–40] p.; [A]–B$_8$, C$_4$; 23 illus. and one tailpiece; 10 cm.; marbled paper covers. [An account of Adam and Eve], [A]$_1$ verso; Introduction, [A]$_2$ recto-verso; History, [A]$_3$ verso–C$_2$ recto; Hymn I. Delight in the Lord Jesus, C$_2$ verso–C$_3$ recto; Hymn II., C$_3$ verso–C$_4$ verso. Two printer's ornaments are present. The large capital "T" of the first word of "The Introduction" is 7 mm. high and not illuminated. The account of how Satan brought about Adam and Eve's downfall, [A]$_1$ verso, is added and different from any other edition of the book. The remainder of the text follows no. **587.2** with The Child's Body Of Divinity not present. The book has a holograph inscription *Irene Clark Her Book 1792*. This is probably fairly close to the date of issue. According to MWA cat., the firm of Thomas and John Fleet was at the Bible and Heart from 1776–1797. There are three New England Primer alphabet cuts. Two of them, Adam, [A]$_2$ recto, and Bible, C$_1$ verso, first appeared in Benjamin Harris' *The Holy Bible In Verse. 1717*, no. **492.1**, which was probably printed by John Allen in Boston. The third one, Zaccheus, B$_3$ recto, also undoubtedly belongs to this 1717 series. The set of cuts with the exception of Job appears to have passed into the hands of Thomas Fleet, who was the probable printer of *The Holy Bible In Verse, 1729*. After 1729 various cuts from the set appear in the publications of Thomas and John Fleet such as *Cock Robin's Death And Funeral* [*ca.* 1780], no. **211** and *Tom Thumb's Folio* [*ca.* 1796], no. **1315.1**. The Bible cut was used by Thomas Fleet in 1802 opposite the title page of John Taylor's *Salvador Mundi*, the New Testament portion of his *Verbum Sempiternum*, bound in the same book and dated 1801, no. **1293.10**. Other cuts also found in no. **211** are a coffin ornamented with a skull and crossbones, hourglass and sickle, B_2 verso, and the *New England Primer* cut of the "Pascal Lamb", signed *WG*, B_4 recto. Two other cuts also occur in no. **1315.1**. They are the *New England Primer* illustration, signed *WG*, of a woman and man seated at table in front of a window, $[A]_7$ recto, and one of a woman, a house, and a tree, $[B]_2$ recto, with a rule border in which the rule corners are rounded. The left rule, the upper half of the right rule, and all of the top rule of the border are lacking in *Tom Thumb's Folio*, no. **1315.1**, so that the latter was surely a later printing than no. **587.32** and for this reason has been dated [*ca.* 1796]. Seven small rectangular cuts appear in *The New England Primer Enlarged. . . . Boston: Printed by T. and J. Fleet, at the Bible and Heart in Cornhill.* [n.d]. They are: 1. Adam and Eve, $[A]_1$ verso; 2. a picture without a caption, of a man and woman seated at a round table in front of a window, which in the above *New England Primer* is entitled "A good Boy and Girl at their books", $[A]_7$ recto; 3. the "Pascal Lamb", B_4 recto, the last two are mentioned above under no. **1315.1**; the laying of Christ's body in the Tomb, B_6 verso; 5. a cut of the Annunciation, which presumably represents the coming of the Holy Ghost, B_7 recto; 6. "Christ ascending into Heaven", B_8 recto; 7, "A Little Boy and Girl at Prayers", C_4 verso. A similar small rectangular cut of the temple, $[A]_6$ recto, is a copy of one which appeared in *The Holy Bible Abridged. The Third Edition. London: J. Newbery, 1760*. This Newbery book was first printed in America in Boston by Robert Hodge for Nathaniel Coverly [1782?], no. **612.1**. Another small rectangular illustration supposed to represent the Earthquake, B_6 recto, has a building in it which resembles the Tower of Babel in the Newbery book of 1760 and may have been the source of the artist's inspiration. Redesigned illustrations are: 1. "The Star", with a triangular comet's tail to the right of it, $[A]_3$ verso; 2. a three-masted square rigger, 2.2 x 2.2 cm., $[A]_8$ recto; 3. a feathery fig tree, B_3 verso. Entirely new cuts which are different from any in any other edition of *The History Of The Holy Jesus* are: 1. "The careful and tender Mother", $[A]_3$ recto, showing a crowned woman seated by a fireplace and in front of whom is a couch with a person lying on it; 2. a large cut, $[A]_6$ verso, 5.9 wide by 4.1 cm. high, possibly supposed to represent Nicodemus coming to the Lord by night, which is composed of a half moon, a figure with a crown on his head standing to the left of a central tree, on the opposite side of which are two figures, one a rotund man facing a person, possibly a soldier, with a pointed hat; 3. a blurred cut which looks like a silhouette of a hooded individual, may represent the devil and could have been intended to have something to do with the lines above it: "To tell them of the fatal Doom, they'll have in Hell below", B_1 recto; 4. a small oval cut of a face surrounded by a halo, possibly representing the sun which withdrew its light when Christ died on the cross, B_5 recto; 5. Time, represented by an old man with a scythe and an hourglass, C_2 recto. Besides these is a cut of a battle scene, with infantry and cavalry, supposed to depict Herod's murder of the Innocents, $[A]_4$ recto. This cut and the large ornamental tailpiece on $[A]_5$ recto, composed of a floral design with a bird with outstretched wings perched on a central stand, appeared in Wiggleworth's *A seasonable Caveat against believing every Spirit: . . . Boston: Printed for D. Henchmen, 1735*. MWA-T*; Evans 3975.

587.33 ——— Boston: Printed and sold by Samuel Hall, No. 53, Cornhill. 1792.
fr.[2], t.[3], [4–7], 8–58, [59–62, adv. list of books] p.; [A]–C_8, D_7 one leaf probably p. 63 of adv. wanting; 19 illus.; 10 cm. Introduction, p. [5–6]; History, p. [7]–36; The Child's Body of Divinity, p. 37–39; St. Paul's Shipwreck, p. 40–42; The Cradle Hymn, p. 43–46; Hymns. At Dressing in the Morning, p. 47; At undressing in the Evening, p. 48; The Nativity of Christ, p. 49–50; Sincere Praise, p. 51–53;

Prayers. A Morning Prayer, p. 54–56; An Evening Prayer, p. 56–58; [adv. list of books], p. [59–62 and probably 63]. Adv. by S. Hall, 1793 in **955.3.** Eleven printer's ornaments are present. A large tailpiece on p. 58 is an oval with the word "Finis" in the center and below which are two crossed leafy branches held together with a ribbon. The caption p. [59]: *A great Variety of BOOKS/for Children, to be sold by S. HALL,/in Cornhill, Boston; among which are/the following, viz.* Sixteen illustrations are copies of those in the English edition of *The Holy Bible Abridged. London: J. Newbery, 1760,* but are different from no. **587.27.** The frontispiece and the illustration on p. 43 are redrawn but represent the same subjects as in no. **587.27.** The fig tree p. 23 is entirely different from any previous cuts.

RPJCB* (t.[3], p. [4–6] edge of page frayed, sig. D$_8$ or p. [63] wanting); DLC (fr.[2], t.[3], p. [4], 41–[63] & covers wanting); MWA (fr.[2], t.[3], p.[4]–6, [57–63] and most of 55–56 wanting); Evans 24398; Sabin 84553, p. 99.

587.34 ——— The Second Hudson Edition, Printed at Hudson (New-York) By Ashbel Stoddard, And Sold, Wholesale and Retail, at his Printing-Office. M,DCC,XCIII.

fr.[2, portrait]; t.[3], [4–47] p.; [A]$_8$, B$_4$, C$_8$, D$_4$; 23 illus., 1 tailpiece; 10 cm.; marbled paper covers. Introduction, [A]$_3$ recto-verso; History, [A]$_4$ recto–C$_7$ verso; Upon the Day of Judgement, C$_8$ recto-verso; The Child's Body of Divinity, D$_1$ recto-D$_2$ recto; St. Paul's Shipwreck, D$_2$ verso–D$_3$ verso; illus. of a man and a skeleton, D$_4$ recto. The square shape of the book, size and text follows the Boston 1774 edition, no. **587.25.** Printer's ornaments are not used. Five of the six full-page illustrations are crudely redrawn usually in the reverse with additions from no. **587.25,** as well as 8 small ones on [A]$_3$ recto; [A]$_4$ recto; [A]$_7$ verso; B$_4$ verso; C$_4$ verso; C$_7$ verso; D$_1$ recto; D$_2$ recto and the tailpiece, D$_3$ verso. The remaining small cuts are crudely redrawn and altered in the reverse from those in no. **587.27** or from *The Holy Bible Abridged,* no. **612.4.** "The Annunciation", [A]$_4$ recto, is used also for "The coming of the Holy Ghost", C$_5$ verso. Entirely new ones are: the full-page picture of "ABRAHAM offering up ISAAC", C$_3$ recto, and the small cut of

the three-masted square rigger, [A]$_8$ recto, probably copied from some English children's book.

MWA*; CtHi (several pages bound out of order); NUt (t.[3] bled along the right border affecting the first word of each sentence); Bates p. 11; Evans 25607; Sabin 84553, p. 99.

587.35 ——— New-York: Printed by John Buel, For Wm. Durell. [1793?].

fr.[2], t.[3], [4–5], 6–31 p.; 16 leaves; 11 illus.; 9.5 cm.; Alphabets, p. [4]; Introduction, p. [5]–6; History, p. [7]–28; The Child's Body of Divinity, p. [29]–31. The format and text of this shortened edition is the same as no. **587.27.** This may be the 1790 edition advertised by Durell in *The Holy Bible Abridged,* no. **612.5.** The book is dated [1793] because one copy has a holographic inscription *Rachel Roades Book July 17, 1793.* Eight printer's ornaments are present. The illustrations on p. 8, 10, 15, 16, 19, 23, are redrawn, altered copies of cuts in no. **587.27.** "The Annunciation", p. [7], is similar in the reverse to that in no. **587.16,** [A]$_4$ recto. New ones are: fr. [2], and those on p. [5], 12, 22.

MWA-W* (fr.[2], t.[3], p. [4]–6, [29]–31 and covers wanting); PP; Evans 46784.

587.36 ——— Boston: adv. by S. Hall, 1794 in **1283.4.**

587.37 ——— Hudson (New-York): adv. by Ashbel Stoddard, 1794 in **1220.1.**

587.38 ——— Second Worcester Edition. Printed at Worcester, Massachusetts, By Isaiah Thomas, And Sold Wholesale and Retail at his Book-store. MDCCXCIV.

fr.[2], t.[3], [4–5], 6–63 p.; [A], [B], C–D$_8$; 30 illus.; 10 cm.; Dutch paper covers. Introduction, p. [5]–6; History, p. [7]–33, with the last 4 lines the same as in no. **587.27;** The Child's Body of Divinity, p. 34–36; St. Paul's Shipwreck, p. 37–39; The Cradle Hymn, p. 40–43; Songs for Children, p. 44–63. The format of the book, the text and 18 illustrations up to p. 43 are the same as in I. Thomas' 1786 edition, no. **587.27.** Ten printer's ornaments are present. "Adam and Eve in the Garden of Eden", [A]$_3$ recto, is different from that on the same page in no. **587.27** and is the same as the one used by

I. Thomas, 1786, in *The Holy Bible Abridged*, no. **612.4**. There are two new small tailpiece illustrations which replace groups of printer's ornaments in no. **587.27**: a three-masted square rigger, p. 33; and a tree, p. 43. There are 9 new oval illustrations in the added portion "Songs For Children", p. 44–63. The songs and oval illustrations first appeared in *Little Robin Red Breast. Worcester: I. Thomas, 1786*, no. **782**. MWA* (rebound); CtHi; NRU; PP; Bates p. 11; Evans 27122; Sabin 84553, p. 99.

587.39 ——— The Third Hudson Edition. Printed at Hudson (New-York) by Ashbel Stoddard, and sold at his Book Store, wholesale and retail. M,DCC,XCV.

24 leaves including portrait of the author and 19 other woodcuts; 32 mo. This is probably a ghost. No copy has been located. It may have been taken from an advertisement.

Evans 28836; Sabin 84553.

587.40 ——— Boston: Printed and sold by S. Hall, No. 53, Cornhill. 1796.

fr.[2], t.[3], [4–7], 8–58, [59–63, adv. list of books] p.; [A]–C₈; 19 illus.; 10 cm.; Dutch paper covers. Introduction, p. [5–6]; History, p. [7]–36; The Child's Body of Divinity, p. 37–39; St. Paul's Shipwreck, p. 40–42; The Cradle Hymn, p. 43–46; Hymns. At dressing in the Morning, p. 47; At undressing in the Evening p. 48; The Nativity of Christ, p. 49–50; Sincere Praise, p. 51–53; Prayers. A Morning Prayer, p. 54–56; An Evening Prayer, p. 56–58; [adv. list of books], [59–63]. The format, text and illustrations are the same as no. **587.33**. Comparing **587.33** and **587.40**, the type is reset but closely follows the setting of the earlier edition. Eleven printer's ornaments are present. There is a rule under the running title "Hymns" on p. 47–49, 51, and under "Prayers", p. 54. The caption p. [59] has the same wording as in the 1792 edition but the type setting is different and reads: *A great Variety of BOOKS/for Children, to be sold by S. HALL,/in Cornhill, Boston; among which/are the following, viz.* MWA-W* (fr.[2], p. [63] & covers slightly mut.); CtHi; DLC; MB (per. st. on t.[3]); Bates p. 12; Evans 30564; Sabin 84533, p. 99.

587.41 ——— Boston: adv. by S. Hall, 1798 in **408.6**.

587.42 A History Of The Holy Jesus. Suffield [Conn.]: Printed by Edward Gray. 1803.

t.[1], [2–3], 4–23, [24, portrait] p.; [A]–B₆; 14 illus.; 17 cm.; brownish-buff paper covers. Introduction, p. [3]; History, p. 4–22; Delight in the Lord Jesus, p. 22–23; portrait, p. [24]. The title page has a tapering rule above and below the title vignette of a tree. The printer's ornaments in the text are heavily inked and blurred. Above the caption p. [3] is a decorative bar of printer's ornaments in a rope design. Page 22 has a thin, thick and thin rule. The illustrations are very crudely cut, copied from those in the 1749 edition, no. **587.7**, and are: "The careful Mother . . .", p. 4; "Wise Men come from the East &"c", p. 5; "Herod slaying the innocent Children", in the reverse, p. 6; the three-masted square rigger, in the reverse, p. 9; "The Bible", without the word "Bible" printed across the open pages, p. 10; "The Prodigal Son", p. 11; the fig tree, in the reverse, p. 13; "Darkness over the Land, Luke 23 44", p. 15; "Abraham offering up his Son Isaac. Genesis 22. 10.", p. 16; "An Earthquake", in the reverse, p. 17; "Death . . ." p. 18; "GABRIEL", p. 21. The last full-page illustration is new and consists of a picture of portrait of a man in an oval frame. On the left side of the frame is a trumpeting angel, with very vestigial wings, and on the other side is a standing woman. MWA-W*; CtHi.

587.43 ——— [same as **587.40**] Boston: Printed for Hall & Hiller, No. 53 Cornhill. 1804.

fr.[3], t.[4], [5–7], 8–9, [9], 10–63 p.; [A]–C₈; 19 illus.; 10 cm.; Dutch paper covers. Alphabets p. [5]; Introduction, p. [6–7]; Nativity of Christ, p. 8–9; History, p. [9]–38; The Child's Body of Divinity, p. 39–41; St. Paul's Shipwreck, p. 42–44; The Cradle Hymn, p. 45–48; Hymns. At dressing in the Morning, p. 49; At undressing in the Evening, p. 50; Sincere Praise, p. 51–53; Prayers. A Morning Prayer, p. 54–56; An Evening Prayer, p. 56–58; The Lord's Prayer, p. [59]; Dr. Watts's Catechism, p. [59]–63. The format of the book, text and illustrations are the same as no. **587.33** with "The Nativity of Christ" changed in position and other variations. The type is reset, and pages renumbered. Most of the decorative bars are replaced by rules or a different series of printer's ornaments from the 1796 edition, no. **587.40**. Four figured printer's ornaments and one unfigured ornament are present.

MWA* (copy 1, Dutch paper covers; copy 2. paper covers); CtHi; MB; OCl (fr.[3], t.[4] & p. [4–6] wanting); RPB; Bates p. 12; Sabin 84553, p. 99; Shaw 6478.

587.44 ———— Hudson [N.Y.]: adv. by Ashbel Stoddard, 1804 in **673.21** and 1805 in **663.11**.

587.45 A HISTORY OF THE HOLY JESUS. Suffield [Conn.]: Printed by Edward Gray. 1804.

t.[1], [2–3], 4–23, [24] p.; [A]–B₆; 13 illus.; 17 cm. Introduction, p. [3]; History, p. 4–22; Delight in the Lord Jesus, p. 22–23; portrait, p. [24]. The format, the text and illustrations are the same as no. **587.42**. The type is reset but closely follows the earlier edition. There are two ornamental bars on the title page, mainly made up of oval printer's ornaments with tapering lines at each end. The title vignette could be an open book with a central floral and two crossed trumpet-like designs across the groove in the center. The ornamental bar above the caption p. [3] is composed of two rows of ten braces. The rules on p. 22 in the 1803 edition are replaced by a bar of 17 oval ornaments in a row with tapering lines on each end. *See* no. **587.42** concerning the illustration on p. [24].

MWA*; CtY (t.[1], p. 21–[24] wanting); DLC; MB; Bates p. 12; Sabin 84553, p. 99; Shaw 6479.

587.46 ———— [same as **587.43**] Providence: Printed By Heaton & Williams. [1805?].

t.[i], [ii–iii], iv, [5], 6–24 p.; 12 leaves without sigs.; 2 illus. p. [ii] only illus.; 14 cm. Introduction, p. [iii]–iv; History, p. [5]–24. The text follows that of no. **587.27** without additional poems. There are no printer's ornaments. Two small rectangular woodcuts on p. [ii], are not copies from any blocks used in any former edition or appear to have anything to do with any subject in the book. Heaton & Williams were a firm from 1803–1806.

Welch* (t.[i], p. [ii]–iv, 21–24 & covers wanting); MWA (covers wanting; t,[i], p. [ii] mut.); PP (original paper covers present); Sabin 84553; Shaw 8616.

587.47 ———— Dover, N. H. J. Whitelock, Printer. 1806.

fr.[2], t.[3], [4–6], 7–47 p.; [A]–[C]₈; 15 illus.; 6 tailpiece illus. or ornaments; 10 cm.; gray wallpaper covers. Alphabets, p. [4]; Introduction, p. [5]; History, p. [6]–31; St. Paul's Shipwreck, p. [32]–33; Hymns. The Cradle Hymn, p. [34]–36; At Dressing in the Morning, p. 37; At undressing in the Evening, p. [37]–38; Sincere Praise, p. 38–40; Prayers. Morning Prayer, p. 41–42; Evening Prayer, p. 42–43; Dr. Watts's Catechism, p. 44–47. The format and text follows Hall & Hiller's Boston, 1804 edition, no. **587.43**, with omissions. Decorative tailpieces are: a rose, p. 7; a bird in a tree, p. 31; a house and a tree, p. 33; a vase with flowers, p. 40. The word "FINIS" p. 47 is printed in a rectangular box with a tulip-like ornament at each end. The frontispiece showing a reclining female with a harp is new as well as the small woodcut used for "The Cradle Hymn", p. [34], of a mother teaching a child. The remaining thirteen woodcuts are all copied from no. **587.43**. With the exception of those on p. [6], 21, and 23, all are copied in the reverse.

MWA*; RPB (marbled paper covers; i. st. on fr.[2]); Shaw 10560.

587.48 ———— composed on purpose for their use. Together with a number of Innocent Songs. Second Worcester Edition. Worcester, Massachusetts. Printed By Thomas & Sturtevant, For Isaiah Thomas, Jun. Sold Wholesale and Retail at his Bookstore; by Thomas & Whipple, Newburyport; and by Thomas & Tappan, Portsmouth [N. H.]. 1806.

fr.[2], t.[3], [4–5], 6–69; (70–71, adv. list of books); [A]–F₆; 41 illus.; 14 cm.; bound in brown paper ornamented with black dots, over w. bds., leather spine. Full-page illus. of "The Lamb of God", p. [4]; Introduction, p. [5]–6; History, p. [7]–28; The Child's Body Of Divinity, p. [29]–30; St. Paul's Shipwreck, p. [31]–32; The Cradle Hymn, p. [33]–35; Songs For Children, p. [36]–69; [adv. list of books], p. [70–71]. The text follows I. Thomas' 1794 edition, no. **587.38**, from p. [5]–49. To this has been added "Songs X–XX" with twelve new oval woodcut illustrations, that on p. [36] also being present on p. 62. These songs and all the oval illustrations first appeared in I. Thomas' 1786 edition of *Little Robin Red Breast*, no. **782**. A thick and thin rule is above the caption on p. [5], [7], [29], [31], [33], [36], [70]. Printer's

ornaments are not present. Pages [5]–[31] have seventeen small rectangular illustrations which were in no. **587.38**. The illustration above the caption of *"THE CRADLE HYMN"*, p. [31] is new. Other new cuts are: The frontispiece, a minister seated before a small table in a library, p.[2]; "The Lamb of God", p. [4], both being full-paged ones, and a three-quarter page illustration of a seated Christ[?], with a laurel wreath around his head, surrounded by a halo, and before whom three children and an angel stand, p. 28. The oval cut of a seated minister and a seated boy at a desk, p. 59, was used for the frontispiece in **587.27** and **587.38**.
MWA-W°; CtHi; CtW; ICU; MB; MiD; PP (unprinted pink paper covers); Bates p. 13; Shaw 10561.

587.49 ———— [same as **587.34**] The Fourth Hudson Edition. Hudson [N.Y.]: Printed By Ashbel Stoddard, And Sold Wholesale and Retail at his Book Store, No. 137 Warren Street. 1807.
fr.[2, portrait], t.[3], [4–47] p.; [A]$_8$, B$_4$, C$_8$, D$_4$; 23 illus. and 1 tailpiece; 10 cm.; illus. blue paper covers. Introduction, [A]$_3$ recto–verso; History, [A]$_4$ recto–C$_7$ verso; Upon The Day of Judgement, C$_8$ recto-verso; The Child's Body of Divinity, D$_1$ recto–D$_2$ recto; St. Paul's Shipwreck, D$_2$ verso–D$_3$ verso; illus. of a man and a skeleton, D$_4$ recto. The format and text of the book follows that of the 1793 Hudson edition, no. **587.34**. The type is reset but the illustrations are from the same blocks. Printer's ornaments are absent except on C$_8$ recto which has an ornament composed of a central oval and a tapering ornament on either side. Comparing this edition with no. **587.34**, certain differences can be noted. There are no catchwords. The following illustrations have the title along the outer margin of the page: "The STAR", [A]$_4$ verso; "The careful mother instructing her Children", [A]$_6$ verso, with the "m" of "mother" in the lower case. Other variations: the cut of the three-masted square rigger, [A]$_8$ verso, does not have a double rule along the top border, or along the upper two-thirds of the sides; the title "CHRIST *teaching the multitude*", B$_1$ verso, has the last three words in italics, instead of Roman type, with the *"m"* of *"multitude"* in the lower case; "ABRAHAM *offering up* ISAAC", C$_3$ recto, has the two middle words in italics instead of Roman type. "The *Child's* BODY of

DIVINITY", D$_1$ recto, has *"Child's"* and *"of"* in italics instead of Roman type. The type on D$_1$ recto–D$_2$ verso is smaller in this edition than in no. **587.34**. The first word of the last sentence, D$_2$ recto, is changed to "Zealous" from "Zealously" in no. **587.34**.
Welch°; CtHi; MWA; Bates p. 13; Sabin 84553, p. 99; Shaw 12761.

587.50 ———— Whitehall [Pa.]: [Pri]nted For The Association Of Travelling Booksellers. 1807.
t.[iii], [iv], v–vi, [7], 8–63 p.; would be [A]–D$_8$ if the copy were complete; 18 illus. and probably a missing frontispiece which would make 18 illus. which are the same as no. **587.54**; 10 cm.; marbled paper covers. Introduction, p. [v]–vi; History, p. [7]–36; The Child's Body Of Divinity, p. 37–39; St. Paul's Shipwreck, p. 40–42; The Cradle Hymn, p. 43–46; Hymns. At dressing in the Morning, p. 47; At undressing in the Evening, p. 48; The Nativity of Christ, p. 49–50; Sincere Praise, p. 51–53; Prayers. A Morning Prayer, p. 54–56; An Evening Prayer, p. 56–58; The Ten Commandments, p. 59–62; The Creed, p. 62; The Ten Commandments in Meter, p. 63. Colophon p. 63: Dickinson, Printer. Whitehal[l]. The text up to p. 58 follows the Boston: Hall & Hiller, 1804 edition, no. **587.43**, or Dover, N. H., J. Whitelock, 1806 edition, no. **587.47**. There are no catchwords or ornamental bars of printer's ornaments. A tailpiece of an urn, with a cover, is on p. 36. The page number "v" is on a level with and comes immediately after the caption, instead of being above the caption. The illustrations are completely redrawn, redesigned, and follow the subject of Hall's 1796 edition, no. **587.40**, with many drawn in the reverse. The fig tree, p. 23, is new and shows a tree and Christ standing to the right of it.
N° (fr.[ii] & front cover wanting; t.[iii], & p. [iv]–8, 23–24, 43–44 mut.).

587.51 A History Of The Holy Jesus. Suffield [Conn.] Published By Daniel Smeer E. Gray Printer [1807?].
t.[1], [2–3], 4–23 p.; illus.; 16.5 cm. On p. [2] is a holograph inscription: *Rufus Sikes Book Bought of Chester Allen in The Year 1807.* CtSu°.

587.52 The History Of The Holy Jesus ———— [same as **587.50**] Their Use. Together

With St. Paul's Shipwreck. Exeter [N.H.]: Published by Benjamin P. Sheriff. 1813.

t.[1], [2–4], 5–18 p.; [A]₉; p. [2] only illus.; 13.5 cm.; blue-gray paper covers. Introduction, p. [3]; History, p. [4]–16; The Child's Body of Divinity, p. 16–17; St. Paul's Shipwreck, p. 17–18. The text is the same as no. **587.50** without the additional material. The illustration p. [2] of Jesus leading three children is new. Welch°; CtHi; MH; MWA; NhHi; Bates p. 14; Sabin 84553, p. 99; Shaw 28751.

587.53 ——— [same as **587.2**] Second Edition. Printed at Leominster, Mass. By Salmon Wilder, Jan. 1813.

t.[i], [ii], iii, [iv–vii], viii, [9], 10–32 p.; [A]–B₈; 11 illus.; 13 cm.; paper covers. Alphabets etc. p. [ii]–iii; illus. of "The Man Of Sin," p. [iv]; The Child's body of Divinity, p. [v–vi]; Introduction, p. [vii]–viii; History, p. [9]–28; Essay upon the Day of Judgement, p. [29]–30; St. Paul's Shipwreck, p. [31]–32. The text of The History . . . is the same as no. **587.27**. There are no catchwords. Nine figured printer's ornaments are present. The illustrations are extremely crude, redesigned and copied in the reverse from the Boston, 1779 edition, no. **587.26**. They are: "THE MAN OF SIN", p. [iv]; the woman at the well, p. 13; the three-masted square rigger, p. 14; the "Prodigal Son" p. 16; Christ, a follower, and a tree, p. 20; the "Crusifixion", p. 23; the Angel Gabriel, p. 28; portrait of St. Paul, p.[31]. New small cuts are: a house and a flower, p. 10; a fish and a tree, p. 15; a dog, p. 30. MWA°; PP; RPB (p. [1]–12 mut.); Shaw 28752.

587.54 THE NEW TESTAMENT, IN VERSE; Or The History Of Our Blessed Saviour. Containing A brief account of his Birth, Life, Death, Ressurection, and Ascension, &c. Being a pleasant and profitable companion for Children. Philadelphia: Published by Benjamin Johnson, No. 22, North Second Street. 1813.

fr.[ii], t.[iii], [iv], v, 6–72 p.; A–C₁₂; 18 illus.; 8 cm.; pr. paper covers. Introduction, p. v–7; History, [9]–47; The Child's Body Of Divinity, p. 49–51; St. Paul's Shipwreck, p. 52–55; The Ten Commandments in Metre, p. 55; The Cradle Hymn, p. 56–59; Hymns. At Dressing in the Morning, p. 60; At undressing in the Eve-

ning, p. 61; The Nativity of Christ, p. 62–63; Sincere Praise, p. 64–66; Prayers. A Morning Prayer, p. 67–69; An Evening Prayer, p. 70–72. While the title is different from no. **587.50** the text closely follows it up to p. 72. The Ten Commandments and Creed are omitted. There are no catchwords, ornamental bars of printer's ornaments, or tailpieces in the text. Pages [iv], [8], and [48] are blank. The illustrations are from the same blocks as those used in no. **587.50**. The cut of "The Cradle Hymn", in no. **587.50**, p. 43, is omitted in **587.54**. CtHi°; NWebyC; PP; Bates p. 14; Sabin 84553, p. 99; Shaw 27917 and 28753.

587.55 ——— [same as no. **587.52**] Exeter [N.H.]: Published and sold by Benjamin P. Sherriff. Sold also by W. &. J. Gilman, Newburyport [Mass.]. 1814.

t.[1], [2–3], 4–23 p.; [A]₁₂; illus. p. [2] & [22] only illus.; 12.5 cm.; covers when present are usually unprinted blue-gray paper. The CtHi copy has pr. & illus. paper covers. Illustration [same as in **587.52**], p. [2]; Introduction. p. [3]–4; History, p. [5]–19; The Child's Body of Divinity, p. 19–21; St. Paul's Shipwreck, p. [22]–23. The text follows no. **587.52**. A small rule, 9 mm. long and tapering at the ends, is on p. [3]. On p. 19 there is a bar composed of a small ovoid asterisk-like ornament with a black tapering rule on either side. The illustration, p. [2], is from the same wood block used in the 1813 edition. A new illustration of a three-masted schooner, 5 x 4.7 cm., depicts St. Paul's ship on p. [22]. Cover imprint of the CtHi copy: Newburyport [Mass.], Published by W. & J. Gilman. Sold at their Miscellaneous Book-Store, No. 2, Middle-Street. On the front cover is a holograph inscription *Mary L. Bates's Book Given to her by Betsy Megder as a New Years G. 1818.* MWA-W° (covers wanting); CtHi (pr. & illus. paper covers); DLC; MB (t.[1], p.[2] mut.); NhD; NhHi; PP (original covers wanting); RPB (covers wanting); Shaw 31724.

HISTORY OF THE KING AND THE COBBLER. *See* The King And The Cobbler, no. **738**.

588.1 THE HISTORY OF THE NEW TESTAMENT. New York: adv. by William Durell, 1790 in **612.5**.

Bound with *The Holy Bible Abridged,* no. **612.9**; issued as a separate book, 1800 in **1298**.

588.2 ——— Hudson (New-York): adv. by Ashbel Stoddard, 1794 in **1220.1**, and 1804 in **673.9**. Evans 28288 lists an ed. of 1795.

THE HISTORY OF THE NEW TESTAMENT. *See* Taylor, John, no. **1293.3**.

THE HISTORY OF THE OFFICER's WIDOW. *See* Hofland, Barbara (Wreaks) Hoole, no. **605**.

589.1 No. 1. THE HISTORY OF THE PRODIGAL SON: From The Gospel According To St. Luke, Chapter XV. Illustrated with Six elegant Copperplates. Designed For The Instruction And Amusement Of Youth. New-York: Published by Griffin & Rudd, No. 189 Greenwich-street, and Thomas Gimbrede, No. 101 Read-street. 1813. Price 8 3-4 cents plain, and 25 cents colored. [cover title].
　　[ii, alphabet], [pl. opp. p. [1]], [1], [pl. following p. [1]], 2–6, [7] p. printed on one side of the page only; 6 pl.; 12 cm.; pr. buff paper covers.
　　NHi°.

589.2 ——— SON: Taken From The Gospel ——— [same as **589.1**] New-York: Published by Griffin & Rudd, No. 189 Greenwich-street, and Thomas Gimbrede, No. 101 Read-street. 1813. Price 18 3–4 cents plain, and 25 cents coloured. [cover title].
　　[ii, alphabet], [pl. opp. p. [1]], [1], [pl. following p. [1]], 2–6, [pl. opp. p. 6]; [7] p. printed on one side of the p. only; 6 pl.; 11.5 cm.; pr. paper covers. The date 1813 is indistinct and looks like 1818. The firm of Griffin & Rudd ceased to exist with the death of Charles Rudd on Oct. 2, 1815. (MWA cat.). No. **589.2** has the same text as no. **589.1** except for the addition of the word "Taken" and the spelling of "coloured" in the cover title. Pl. 6 is also opposite p. 6, while in no. **589.1** it is in front of p. 6. MWA°.

589.3 ——— [same as **589.1**] Elegant Engravings. New-York: Printed And Published By Smith & Forman, And for sale at the Franklin Juvenile Bookstores, 190 and 195 Greenwich Street. 1815. [cover title].
　　[2, alphabet], [pl. opp. p. [3]], [3], 4–10, [pl.

opp. p. 10], [11] p.; 6 pl.; 12.5 cm.; pr. paper covers. The rear cover: Of Smith & Forman May Be Had, Recently Published. [followed by a list of 19 children's books, all of which were printed or advertised by Wm. Charles]. MB° (i. st. on each of the 6 pl.).

590 THE HISTORY OF THE PROPHET SAMUEL. Portrayed from the Holy Scriptures. For The Use Of Children. [2 lines quot.] Woodstock [Vt.]: Printed By David Watson. 1820.
　　fr.[2, poem], t.[3], [4–5], 6–31 p.; illus.; 9 cm. MWA-W° (orig. covers wanting); McCorison 2203; Shoemaker 1617.

HISTORY OF THE SEVEN CHAMPIONS OF CHRISTENDOM. *See* Johnson, Richard, no. **668.1**.

591.1 THE HISTORY OF THE SEVEN WISE MASTERS, OF ROME. Containing, Many Excellent and Delightful Examples. With Their Explanations and Modern Significations; which (by way of Allusion) may by [*sic. i.e.* be] termed, An Historical Comparison of sacred and civil Transactions; the better to make an Impression on the Minds of Men. Boston: Printed and Sold by J. White, near Charlestown-Bridge. 1794.
　　fr.[2], t.[3], [4–5], 6–34 p.; front. only illus.; 14 cm.; bound in brown paper over w. bds. Welch° (fr.[2] wanting); BM; DLC; MB; MH (p. 15–22 wanting); MWA; Evans 27669.

591.2 ——— Containing Many Excellent And Useful Examples For Mankind. Together With Their Explanations and Modern Significations; which (by way of Allusion) may be termed; An Historical Comparison Of Sacred And Civil Transactions; the better to make an impression on the Minds of Men. Worcester: 1794.
　　t.[1], [2–3], 4–31 p.; 17.5 cm.
　　See also Roman Histories, no. **1127** and Roman Stories, no. **1128**.
　　MWA° (covers wanting); Evans 27670.

591.3 ——— Boston: Printed and sold by William Spotswood, No. 55, Marlborough-Street. 1795.
　　t.[1], [2–3], 4–100 p.; illus.; t.[1] 12.5 cm. MB° (rebound); Evans 29467.

591.4 ——— Containing Many Ingenious And Entertaining Stories: Wherein The Treachery of

Evil Counsellors is discovered, Innocency cleared, And The Wisdom of the Seven Wise Masters displayed. Philadelphia: Printed And Sold By H. & P. Rice, No. 50 High-Street, Also By J. Rice & Co. Market-Street, Baltimore. 1795.

t.[1], [2–3], 4–100 p.; 14 cm.; bound in gray paper over bds., leather spine.
MWA°; Evans 47597.

591.5 ——— New York. Printed And Sold By John Tiebout, At (Homer's-Head) 358 Pearl-street. 1797.

t.[1], [2–3], 4–95 p.; 12 cm.
MH° (p. 5–6 wanting; p. 84–94 torn); Evans 48249.

591.6 ——— Philadelphia: Printed for the Booksellers. 1798.

t.[1], [2–3], 4–96 p.; 14.5 cm.; bound in black and orange-red wallpaper over bds.
MWA-W°; Evans 48611.

591.7 ——— Hudson, [N.Y.] Ashbel Stoddard, 1801.

123 p.
Shaw 659.

591.8 ——— Wilmington: adv. by P. Brynberg, 1801 in **61.9.**

591.9 ——— Baltimore: adv. by A. Douglas, 1803 in **275.46.**

591.10 ——— Hudson: Printed by Ashbel Stoddard. And sold Wholesale and Retail at his Printing-Office and Book-Store, in the White-House, corner of Warren and Third-Street. 1805.

t.[1], [2–3], 4–106 p.; 15 cm.; bound in illus. blue paper over w. bds., leather spine; text printed on blue-gray paper.
MWA°; MH; N; Shaw 9336.

591.11 ——— Boston: Printed By Nathaniel Coverly, Jun. Corner Of Theatre Alley, Milk-Street. Price one dollar per dozen—12½ cents single. 1811.

t.[1], [2–3], 4–22 p.; 14 cm.
MWA°; Shaw 23016.

591.12 ——— Printed For The Purchasers. 1811.

t.[3], [4–5], 6–34 p.; 14 cm.
MB°.

591.13 ——— Windham [Conn.]: Printed By J. Byrne And Son. 1811.

t.[1], [2–3], 4–84 p.; 13 cm.; bound in marbled paper over w. bds. leather spine.
MWA°; Ct; CtHi (2 copies); MH; PP; PPL; Shaw 23017.

THE HISTORY OF THE TALES OF THE FAIRIES. *See* Aulnoy, Marie, no. **51.**

THE HISTORY OF THE TWO BABES IN THE WOOD. *See* Children In The Wood, no. **178.**

592 THE HISTORY OF THE VOYAGES OF CHRISTOPHER COLUMBUS; And The Discovery Of America, And The West-Indies. New-York: Printed For E. Duyckinck, No. 110, Pearl-Street. By G. Bunce. 1809.

t.[1], [2–3], 4–144 p.; 14 cm.; bound in blue marbled paper over bds., leather spine.
MWA°; Shaw 17761.

THE HISTORY OF THOMAS THUMB. *See* Thomas Thumb, no. **1299.**

593 THE HISTORY OF THREE BROTHERS: A moral and entertaining Tale, founded on Fact. Also The Three Sisters. To Which Is Added, The Little Queen. Embellished with beautiful Cuts. New-York: Printed by Samuel Campbell, No. 124, Pearl Street. 1794.

fr.[2], t.[3], [4–7], 8–106 p.; illus.; 13 cm.; bound in blue marbled paper over w. bds.
English ed. London: adv. by John Stockdale in Camp's *The New Robinson Crusoe.* 1788.
MWA° (rebound); CtHi; DLC; PP; Evans 27124.

THE HISTORY OF TOM JONES. *See* Fielding, Henry, no. **406.1.**

594.1 THE HISTORY OF TOM NODDY AND HIS SISTER SUE. Boston: adv. by John W. Folsom, 1798 in **672.1.**

594.2 ——— Exeter [N.H.]: adv. by Henry Ranlet, 1801 in **558.2.**

594.3 ——— Exeter [N.H.]: adv. by Norris & Sawyer, 1808 in **428.3.**

THE HISTORY OF TOMMY CARELESS. *See* Johnson, Richard, no. **678.1.**

THE HISTORY OF TOMMY GINGERBREAD. *See* Gingerbread, Tommy, no. **453.1**.

THE HISTORY OF TOMMY THROUGHGOOD. *See* The History of Mr. Tommy Throughgood, no. **570**.

THE HISTORY OF TOMMY TITMOUSE. *See* Tommy Titmouse, no. **1322.1**.

HISTORY OF TOMMY TRIP. *See* Tommy Trip, no. **1323.1**.

595.1 [THE HISTORY OF] TOMMY TWO SHOES. Wilmington Del.: adv. "may be had at James Wilson's Book-Store", 1803 in **1081**.

595.2 THE HISTORY OF TOMMY TWO-SHOES, Own Brother To Mrs. Margery Two-Shoes. Adorned With Cuts. Litchfield [Conn.]: Printed By Hosmer & Goodwin. 1808.
　fr.[2], t.[3], [4–5], 6–30, [31, adv.] p.; illus.; 10 cm.; green Dutch paper covers. The book is mainly taken from "Chapter II" and "Appendix" of *The History Of Goody Two-Shoes*. 1775, no. **463.1**, or some English edition. Mary (Belson) Elliot wrote *The Adventures Of Tommy Two-Shoes. Being a Sequel to that of < The Modern Goody Two-Shoes. >* London, W. Darton, jun. 1818. The above Litchfield edition and the following ones are often wrongly ascribed to her as author.
　English ed. York: Wilson, Spence, and Mawman. [*ca.* 1797].
　CtHi°; CtY; Shaw 15245.

595.3 ——— Hartford: Printed by Hale & Hosmer. 1814.
　fr.[2], t.[3], [4–5], 6–30, [31, adv. list of books] p.; illus.; 10 cm.; pr. & illus. green paper covers.
　MWA-W°; CtY (t.[3], wanting); NN-C; RPB; Shaw 31404; Weiss 1935, p. 365.

595.4 ——— Embellished With Cuts. Hartford: by Sheldon & Goodwin. < Stereotyped by J. F. & C. Starr. > [1815].
　fr.[2], t.[3], [4–5], 6–30, [31, adv. list of books] p.; illus.; 10 cm.; pr. & illus. buff paper covers. *See* no. **563.15** concerning the firm of Sheldon & Goodwin. The words "Printed by" are omitted on t.[3].
　Cover title: The Hermit of the Forest, And The

Wandering Infants. Hartford: Printed by Sheldon & Goodwin. Stereotype Edit[ion.] Rear cover an upper illus. of a man and woman and a lower one of a woman milking a cow.
　MWA-W°; CtHi; CtY; MWA; NB; Shaw 43932 (1818?).

595.5 ——— Hartford: Published by J. & W. Russell. [1818?].
　t.[3], [4–5], 6–30, [31] p.; illus.; 10 cm.; illus. buff paper covers. *See* no. **563.16** concerning the firm of J. & W. Russell.
　MWA° (fr.[2] and front cover wanting).

595.6 ——— Two-Shoes. Woodstock [Vt.]: Printed By David Watson. 1819.
　fr.[2], t.[3], [4–5], 6–31 p.; illus.; 9.5 cm.; pr. & illus. paper covers; cover title without imprint or date.
　MWA (fr.[2]. p. 31, & covers wanting); McCorison 2120; Shaw 48239.

THE HISTORY OF TWO GOOD BOYS AND GIRLS. *See* [Richardson, Mr.], no. **1101.2**.

596 THE HISTORY OF TWO HORSES, AND OTHER FABLES, In Verse; With Moral Reflections. Principally Calculated To Inspire The Minds Of Youth With Filial Affection, And A Tenderness towards the Dumb Creation. Philadelphia: Published and sold Wholesale by Wm. Charles, and may be had of all the Booksellers. 1811. W. M'Culloch, Printer.
　fr.[ii], t.[1], [2–3], 4–34 p.; front. only illus.; 13.5 cm.; pr. orange paper covers. Adv. by Wm. Charles, 1814 in **357** and 1815 in **748**.
　MWA°; NNC-Pl; NWebyC; Shaw 23018.

597 HISTORY OF TWO LITTLE GIRLS. Philadelphia: adv. by B. & T. Kite, 1807 in **611.1**.

598 A HISTORY OF WATER BIRDS. Woodstock [Vt.]: Printed By David Watson. 1820.
　fr.[2], t.[3], [4–5], 6–31 p.; illus.; 9.5 cm.; pr. & illus. paper covers.
　MWA°; McCorison 2204; Shoemaker 1620.

599 (No. 23.) THE HISTORY OF WILLIAM BLACK, The Chimney-Sweeper. Published By The Philadelphia Female Tract Society. And for sale at their Depository, No. 20, Walnut Street. [caption title] Printed by Lydia R. Bailey, No. 10, North Alley, Philad. [1817] [colophon p. 8].
　[1], 2–8 p.; 14 cm.

MWA° (bound with other tracts, with which *The Second Annual Report Of The Philadelphia Female Tract Society For The Year 1817* was originally bound); Shaw 41057.

THE HISTORY OF WILLIAM SELWYN. *See* Sandham, Elizabeth, no. 1152.

HOARE, GEORGE RICHARD
600.1 — THE YOUNG TRAVELLER: or, Adventures Of Etienne In Search Of His Father. A Tale For Youth. By G. R. Hoare, Author Of Modern Europe In Miniature. [3 lines quot.] Economy Of Human Life. New-York: Published By William B. Gilley. Van Winkle & Wiley, Printers. 1815.
fr.[ii], t.[i], [ii–iii], iv–viii, [9], 10–93 p.; front. only illus.; 14 cm.; bound in violet-buff paper over bds., green leather spine; front. signed *Scoles sculp.*
English ed. London: J. Harris, 1812.
MWA°; DLC (emb. st. on t.[i]); N; NWebyC; Shaw 34920.

600.2 — ——— [4 lines quot.] Albany: Printed By Websters And Skinners, At their Bookstore, corner of State and Pearl-Streets. 1818.
t.[i], [ii–iii], iv–vi, [7], 8–68, [69–72, adv. of books] p.; 14 cm.; bound in pr. buff paper over bds., green paper spine.
MWA-W°.

THE HOBBY HORSE. *See* Ticklepitcher, Toby, no. **1193.2.**

HOFLAND, BARBARA (WREAKS) HOOLE
1770–1844
601.1 — THE AFFECTIONATE BROTHERS: A Tale By Mrs. Hoffland [*sic. i.e.* Hofland], Author Of The Clergyman's Widow, The Panorama Of Europe, &c.&c. [7 lines of verse] Beattie. New-York: Published By W. B. Gilley, 92 Broadway. Van Winkle & Wiley, Printers. 1816.
fr.[2], t.[3], [4–5], 6–150 p.; front. only illus.; 14.5 cm.; bound in pink paper over bds., green leather spine; front. signed *Scoles sculp.*
English ed. London: A. K. Newman, 1816, 2 vols.
MWA°; DLC; KU; PP; Shaw 37855.

601.2 — ——— Albany: Printed By Websters And Skinners, At their Book-store in the White House, corner of State and Pearl-streets. 1818.

t.[1], [2–3], 4–120 p.; 14 cm.
MWA° (covers wanting); Shaw 44356.

601.3 — ——— [same as **601.1**] New York: Published by W. B. Gilley, 92 Broadway, N. Van Riper, Printer. 1819.
½t.[1], [2, bl.], [i, bl.], fr.[ii], t.[3], [4–5], 6–150 p.; 14 cm.; bound in blue-gray paper over bds., black leather spine; front. signed *Scoles sculp.* Half title p. [1]: The Affectionate Brothers A Tale.
MH°; DLC (½ t.[1] wanting; PP; PPL; Shaw 48253.

602.1 — THE BLIND FARMER, AND HIS CHILDREN. By Mrs. Hopland [*sic. i.e.* Hofland], Author Of The Son Of A Genius; Officer's Widow; Clergyman's Widow; Sisters; Ellen The Teacher; Affectionate Brothers. &c &c. [3 lines of verse] Thomson. Albany: Printed by Websters & Skinners, At their Bookstore, in the White House, corner of State and Pearl Streets—1817.
t.[1], [2–3], 4–120 p.; 14 cm.; bound in pr. violet-buff paper over bds.
English ed. London: J. Harris, 1816.
MWA° (rebound, with rear cover only remaining); Shaw 41065.

602.2 — ——— New-York: Published By William B. Gilley, 92 Broadway. A Paul, Printer 1817.
t.[i], [ii–iii], iv, [5], 6–144 p.; 15 cm.; bound in violet-gray paper over bds., green leather spine.
MWA°; Shaw 41066.

603.1 — ELLEN, THE TEACHER. A Tale For Youth. By Mrs. Hofland, Author Of "The Officer's Widow;" "Son Of A Genius;" And Other Works For Young People. [1 line quot.] Vol. I. [II.] New-York: Published By W. B. Gilley. No. 92, Broadway. 1815.
fr.[ii], 1st t.[1], [2–3], 4–97, [98, bl.], 2nd t.[1] [2–3], 9–93 p.; front. only illus.; 2 vols. in 1; 14.5 cm.; bound in marbled paper over bds., leather spine; front. signed *Scoles sculp.*; illus. p. 32, 82, vol. I., & p. 15, vol. II., signed A., that on p. 64 signed *Anderson* [Alexander Anderson]; p. [2]: Van Winkle & Wiley, Printers.
English ed. London: J. Harris, 1814.
MWA-W°; MH; MNF (imp.); MWA; Shaw 34930.

603.2 — —— [1 line quot.] New-York: Published By W. B. Gilley, 92 Broadway. N. Van Riper, Printer. 1819.

fr.[ii], t.[1], [2–3], 4–189 p.; front. only illus.; 14.5 cm.; bound in blue-gray paper over bds., green leather spine; front. signed *Scoles sculp.;* illus. p. 32, 82, 111 signed *A*, that on p. 159 signed *Anderson* [Alexander Anderson].

MWA°, CtHi; MH; NNG; RPB; Shaw 48254.

604 — THE GOOD GRANDMOTHER AND HER OFFSPRING: A Tale. By Mrs. Hofland, Author of "The Son Of A Genius," &c. &c. [1 line quot.] Proverbs. New-York: Published By James Eastburn & Co. Literary Rooms, Broad-way. E. B. Gould, Printer, 5 Chatham st. 1817.

t.[1], [2–5], 6–170 p.; 15.5 cm.; bound in pr. pink paper over bds.

English ed. London: R. Hunter, 1817.

MWA°; CLU; PP; Shaw 41067.

605 [—] THE HISTORY OF AN OFFICER'S WIDOW And Her Young Family. [2 lines quot.] Congreve. From The Third London Edition. New-York: Published by W. B. Gilley, No. 92 Broadway. Van Winkle And Wiley, Printers. 1815.

fr.[ii], t.[i], [ii–iii], iv, [5], 6–162 p.; front. only illus.; 14.5 cm.; bound in orange-red marbled paper over bds., red leather spine.

English ed. London: 1809.

MWA-W°; MdBP; Shaw 34931 (listed in error as Phil. imprint).

606 [—] MATILDA, Or The Barbadoes Girl. A Tale For Young People. By The Author Of The Clergyman's Widow And Family, Merchant's Widow And Family, Affectionate Brothers, Panorama Of Europe, The Sisters, &c. [2 lines quot.] Bacon. [4 lines quot.] Addison. Philadelphia: Published By M. Carey & Son, No. 121, Chestnut Street. 1817.

t.[1], [2–3], 4–175, [176, bl.], [1], 2 p.; 14.5 cm.; p. [1]–2 at rear adv. list of books; colophon p. 175: Doylestown [Pa.]: Printed By Asher Miner.

English ed. Lond: 1816.

ViU°; MBAt; PPL; Shaw 41068.

607 — THE SISTERS. A Domestic Tale. By Mrs. Hofland, Author Of The Clergyman's Widow And Family; Merchant's Widow And Family; Pano-

rama Of Europe; Young Northern Traveller, &c. &c. [7 lines quot.] Hartford: Printed By Sheldon & Goodwin. 1815.

t.[1], [2–3], 4–212 p.; 15 cm.; bound in leather. Ries°; Shaw 34934.

608.1 [—] THE SON OF A GENIUS; A Tale, For The Use Of Youth. By The Author Of The History of an Officer's Widow and Family, Clergyman's Widow and Family, Daughter-in-Law, &c. &c. [1 line quot.] Proverbs. New-York: Published By Eastman, Kirk & Co. At The Literary Rooms, Corner Of Wall & Nassau Streets. 1814.

t.[i], [ii–iii], iv–vii, [viii, bl.], [9], 10–251 p.; illus.; 14.5 cm.; bound in leather; illus. p. 101 signed *A* [A. Anderson]; colophon p. 251: John Forbes, printer.

English ed. London: 1812.

Welch°; CLU; DLC; MWA (rebound); PP; RPB; Shaw 31737 and 32819.

608.2 [—] —— Second American Edition. New-York. Published By David Bliss, 59 Maiden-Lane. A. Paul, Printer. 1818.

t.[i], [ii–iii], iv–vii, [viii, bl.], [9], 10–251 p.; 14.5 cm.; bound in pink paper over bds., green leather spine.

MWA°; DLC (i. st. on t.[1]); PP; PU; Shaw 44357.

609.1 HOLIDAY ENTERTAINMENT; Or The Good Child's Fairing: Containing the Plays And Sports Of Charles and Billy Welldon, And Other Little Boys and Girls who went with them to the Fair. With The Fancies of the Old Man that lived under the Hill. Ornamented with Cuts. Hartford: Printed By Lincoln & Gleason. 1806.

fr.[2], t.[3], [4–5], 6–31 p.; illus.; 10 cm.; marbled paper covers.

English ed. London: E. Newbery, 1793; adv. by E. Newbery 1786.

NB°; MWA; PP; Shaw 10576.

609.2 —— Hartford: Printed By Peter B. Gleason & Co. 1811.

fr.[2], t.[3], [4–5], 6–31 p.; illus.; 10 cm.; pink paper covers.

MWA-W° (top of t.[3] cropped affecting the upper half of the words "Holiday Entertainment"); OOxM; Shaw 23027.

610 HOLIDAY EXERCISES. Or, The The [*sic*] Christian A. B. C. Consisting Of Seven Alphabets,

With a Text of Scripture affixed to every Letter. [2 lines quot.], [2 line quot.] 2 Tim. 3. 15. Printed By Kline And Reynolds, And Sold by Mr. Bailey, Mr. Aikin, Philadelphia; and Mr. Sam. Loudon, New-York. M,DCCXLXXV [*sic. i.e.* M,DCC-LXXXV].

> t.[1], [2–5], 6–36 p.; 18 cm.; verse.
> NN° (rebound, i. st. on t.[1]); NHi; PU; RPB; Evans 19042.

THE HOLIDAY, OR CHILDREN'S SOCIAL AMUSE-MENT. *See* Dobson, Thomas, no. **293.**

THE HOLIDAY PRESENT: Containing Anecdotes Of Mr. and Mrs. Jennet, And Their Little Family. *See* Kilner, Dorothy, no. **728.**

THE HOLIDAY SPY. *See* Johnson, Richard, no. **679.1.**

HOLLOWAY, WILLIAM
611.1 [—] THE CHIMNEY-SWEEPER'S COM-PLAINT. By The Author Of The Peasant's Fate, Scenes Of Youth, &c. [1 line quot.] Cowper. Philadelphia: Published By B. And T. Kite, No. 20, North Third Street. Fry And Kammerer, Printers. 1807.

> fr.[ii], ½t.[1], [2], t.[3], [4–5], 6–33, [34, bl.] [35–36, adv.] p.; 3 pl. including front.; 14.5 cm.; blue marbled paper covers, pink paper spine. Half title p. [1]: The Chimney-Sweeper's Complaint.
> English ed. London: J. Harris, 1806.
> NNC-Pl°.

611.2 [—] —— Philadelphia: Published By Jacob Johnson, No. 147, Market-Street. 1808.

> ½t.[1], [2,bl.], t.[3], [4–5], 6–32 p.; 14 cm.
> Adv. by Johnson & Warner, 1814 in **1449.3.**
> MWA° (covers and leaves C₅–C₆ wanting); PP; Shaw 14686.

612.1 THE HOLY BIBLE ABRIDGED: Or, The History Of The Old and New Testament Illustrated With Notes, and adorned with Cuts. For the Use of Children. [2 lines quot.] Boston: Printed by Robert Hodge, for Nathaniel Coverly, in New-bury-Street. [1782].

> t.1, [2–7], 8–107 p.; illus.; 13.5 cm.; bound in Dutch paper over w.bds. The OClWHi copy has on p.[4] a holograph inscription: *Patience and Abigail Riders their Book 1783.*

English & Irish ed. London: adv. by John Newbery, 1758.

> MWA° (Dutch paper mostly worn off covers); MB; MNeHi (upper half of t.[1] & p. 103–107 wanting); NjP; OClWHi (p. 15–22, 105–107 & covers wanting); PP; Evans 17474; Hamilton 96; Sabin 5167.

612.2 —— Philadelphia: Printed and Sold by Young, Stewart, and M'Culloch, the Corner of Chesnut and Second-streets. 1786.

> t.[1], [ii–iv], [1], 2–188 p.; illus.; 10 cm.; bound in marbled paper over bds.
> MWA°; Evans 19507.

612.3 —— The First Worcester Edition. Thomas, And Sold At His Book Store. Sold Also By E. Battelle, Boston. MDCCLXXXVI.

> fr.[vi], t.[vii], [viii–x], xi–xiii, [xiv–xx], [21], 22–176 p.; illus.; 10 cm.; illus. buff paper covers.
> MWA° PP (p. 113–114 mut.); Evans 19506.

612.4 —— The First Worcester Edition. Worcester, (Massachusetts) Printed By Isaiah Thomas, And Sold At His Book Store. MDCCL-XXXVI.

> fr.[vi], t.[vii], [viii–x], xi–xiii, [xvi–xx], [21], 22–176 p.; illus.; 10 cm.; bound in illus. buff paper over bds. The described copy is incomplete lacking most of sigs. [A] and C. Same as no. **612.3** but with a different imprint. The above collation is for the complete book, matching this with the preceding.
> MWA-W° (p.[vi], xi–[xvi], 33–48 wanting); NjP (p. 35–36, 45–46, 65–66, 129–130, 143–144 wanting); Evans 44853.

612.5 —— New-York: Printed By William Durell, 198 [*sic. i.e.* 19] Queen-Street. M,DCC,-XC.

> fr.[ii], t.[iii], [iv–v], vi, [7], 8–186 p.; illus.; 10 cm.; bound in Dutch paper over w. bds.; p. [185]–186 adv. list of books.
> MWA°; CtHi; PP; (rebacked, p. 31–34 wanting); Evans 45826.

612.6 —— Children. To which is added, A Complete Abstract Of The Old and New Testament, With the Apocrypha, In Easy Verse. [2 lines quot.] New-York: Printed by Hodge, Allen, and Campbell, And Sold at their respective Book-stores. M,DCC,XC.

fr.[2], t.[3], [4–13], 14–180 p.; illus.; 13 cm.; bound in brown paper speckled with black over bds., leather spine. Frontispiece signed *P. Maverick, Sc. Æ 9 Years.* Peter Maverick, an engraver, was born in 1780 and published his first work at the age of 9. Hamilton considers this engraving to be probably his earliest production. The illustrations in the text are crude copies of those in no. **612.1.** Caption p. [91]: Part II. The New Testament. Caption p. [135]: Complete Abstract Of The Holy Bible in Easy Verse; Containing The Old and New Testaments, With The Apocrypha. This versification of the Bible is not Benjamin Harris' *The Holy Bible In Verse,* no. **492.1.**

MWA-W° (p. 19–22, 81–82 slightly mut.); CCC; CtY (fr.[2] mut.); NjP; NjR (p. [2]–14 wanting); NN (bound in leather); PPL, Evans 22350; Hamilton 127.

612.7 ——— Children. [2 lines quot.] Boston: Printed and sold by Samuel Hall, No. 53, Cornhill. 1791.

fr.[iv], t.[v], [vi], vii–ix, [x–xvi, contents], [17], 18–173 p.; illus.; 10 cm.; bound in marbled paper over w. bds.

MHi°; Evans 46126.

612.8 ——— Children. Sagg-Harbor [New York], Printed by David Frothingham, 1791.

Evans 23182.

612.9 ——— [2 lines quot.] New-York: Printed By William Durell No. 19, Queen-Street. M,DCC,-XCII.

fr.[ii], t.[iii], [iv–v], vi, [7], 8–110, [2 bl. leaves], 2nd t.[3], [4–5], 6–63 p.; illus.; 10.5 cm.; p. 110 printed on the inside of the page. Second title page: The Testament Abridged: Or, The History Of The New Testament. Adorned with Cuts. For the use of Children. [2 lines quot.] Luke xviii. 16. New-York: Printed By William Durell. 1792.

CtHi° (New Testament p. 49–63 and covers wanting); NjP; NNC-LS (complete); Evans 46386.

612.10 [The Holy Bible Abridged ——— [title probably the same as **612.1**]. [Philadelphia: Printed by W. Young, No. 52, Second-street.

M,DCC,XCIII.] [imprint copied from *The History Of Little Goody Two Shoes.* no. **463.5**] [1793].

[1], 2–188 p.; illus.; 10 cm.; bound in leather. The book matches no. **612.2** in having the same cuts, and being in 188 pages. It probably wants the first three leaves sig. A$_1$–A$_3$ of A in 16. t.[1], [ii–iv], 2 leaves similar to the 1786 ed., and a preliminary page which could have been blank as in the 1786 ed. This incomplete copy differs from the 1786 edition by lacking catch words. William Young's 1793 edition of *The History Of Little Goody Two-Shoes,* no. **463.5**, is closer to the type setting of no. **612.10** and catch words are not present. Because of similarities between William Young's printing of *Goody Two-Shoes* and no. **612.10**, the latter is considered to have been printed by William Young in [1793].

MWA-W°.

612.11 ——— New Testament. Being a valuable present for a little Son or Daughter. Illustrated with Notes and adorned with Cuts. [2 lines quot.] Philadelphia: Printed By Francis Bailey, For the Revd Mason L. Weems. M,DCC,XCIV.

fr.[ii], t.[iii] [iv–v], vi, [7], 8–88, Part II. [89], 90–136 p.; illus.; 10.5 cm.; bound in tan paper over bds., leather spine. One illus. signed *I P* according to PP cat. Caption p. [89]: Part II. The New Testament.

MWA°; CLU; CtHi (fr.[ii], t.[iii] & other p. wanting); CtY; MiU; PP (p. [35–46] wanting); PPL; RPJCB; Evans 26650.

612.12 ——— [same as **275.8**] Boston: Printed and sold by Samuel Hall No. 53, Cornhill. 1795.

fr.[ii], t.[iii], [iv–v], vi, [vii–xii], [13], 14–156 p.; illus.; 11 cm.; buff paper covers; tailpiece on p.[xii] composed of three printer's ornaments of crowns set in a triangle.

MWA° (p. 15–16 wanting); CLU (p. 81–82 wanting); CtHi (t.[iii], p. 155–156 mut., bound in Duth paper over w. bds); CtY (yellow Dutch paper over w. bds.); DLC (3 copies); IaB; MB; NjP; PP; Evans 28269; Hamilton 161.

612.13 ——— The Second Worcester Edition. Worcester, (Massachusetts) From The Press Of Thomas Son & Thomas, And Sold At Their Bookstore. MDCCXCVI.

fr.[ii], t.[iii], [iv–vii], viii–ix, [x–xvi], [17], 18–171, [172–175, adv. list of books] p.; illus.;

10.5 cm.; bound in Dutch paper over w. bds. MWA° (2 copies: copy A bound in Dutch paper, copy B rebound in leather with I. Thomas' bookplate); CLU; DLC; MiU; NjP; Evans 30067; Hamilton 170.

612.14 ——— Wilmington [Del.]: Printed and sold by Peter Brynberg. 1797.
t.[1], [2–3], 4–134, [135–136, contents] p.; illus.; 10.5 cm.; bound in tan paper over bds., leather spine.
MWA°; CtY; DeWi (per. st. & i. st. p. [3]); NjP (covers wanting); PP; Evans 31809.

612.15 ——— New-York: Printed by W. Durell, for Evert Duyckinck, Bookseller & Stationer, No. 110 Pearl Street. 1800
fr.[2], t.[3], [4–5], 6–108 p.; illus.; 14 cm.; bound in w. bds., leather spine.
NjP° (paper wanting from w. bds.); Hamilton 189.

612.16 ——— New-York: Printed by W. Durell, for Stephen Stephens and W. Falcouar [*sic. i.e.* Falconer]. 1800.
fr.[2], t.[3], [4–5], 6–108 p.; illus.; 14 cm.
MWA° (covers & p. 107–108 wanting); PP; Evans 36953.

612.17 ——— Testament. For The Use Of Children. Illustrated With Notes, and adorned with Engravings. [2 lines quot.] Boston: Printed For William Norman, Book And Chart Seller. 1802.
fr.[ii], t.[1], [2–7], 8–107 p.; 9 pl. including front.; 14 cm. bound in Dutch paper over w. bds.; copy A, with 9 unnumbered pl. The pl. opp. p. 20, "Rachel watering her flocks", is followed by a duplicate pl. in MWA-W copy which has 10 instead of the usual 9.
Copy B with 8 numbered pl.
Copy C without plates, bound in blue marbled paper, leather spine.
MWA-W° (copy A & C); CtHi (copy A); CtW; DLC (copy C); MBC; MH; MHi (copy C); MSaE; MWA° (copy B, 1 pl. lacking); PP (copy B, 7 pl. only; fr.[ii] & p.[3–4], 21–22 mut.); NNUT; Shaw 1873.

612.18 ——— Testament. Illustrated With Notes And Adorned With Cuts. For The Use Of Children. [2 lines quot.] New-York: Published By

John Tiebout, No. 238 Water-street. W. W. Vermilye, Printer. 1805.
t.[1], [2–3], 4–108 p.; illus.; 13.5 cm.; bound in marbled paper over w. bds.
MH°; IU; Shaw 7994.

612.19 ——— Children. Adorned with Cuts. [2 lines quot.] Boston: Published by Isaiah Thomas, Jun. 1811. S. Avery, printer.
fr.[2], t.[3], [4–5], 6–159, [160, adv.] p.; illus.; 10.5 cm.; bound in gray marbled paper over bds., leather spine.
MWA-W°; CtW; MB; MiU; MWA (I. Thomas copy, rebound in red leather, i. st. on t. [3]); NN (rebound); PP [2 copies]; Shaw 22347.

612.20 ——— The History Of The New Testament. For The Use Of Childrens [*sic. i.e.* Children]. [1 line quot.] Luke xviii. 16. Greenfield [Mass.]: Printed By John Denio. 1811.
t.[1], [2–3], 4–36 p.; 14 cm.
MWA° (covers wanting); DLC; NN; PP; Shaw 22348 and 24818.

612.21 ——— Old And New Testament. Illustrated With notes, for the use of children. [2 lines quot.] Windsor [Vt.]: Printed And Published By Jesse Cochran, 1811.
t.[1], [2–5], 6–180 p.; one tailpiece (illus.) p. 171; 13 cm.; bound in leather.
Welch°; KU; MWA; PP; VtMiS; McCorison 1261; Shaw 22349.

612.22 ——— Old And New Testament. For The Use Of Children. Adorned with Cuts. [2 lines quot.] Barnard, Vt. Published by Joseph Dix. 1813. I. H. Carpenter, printer.
fr.[ii] t.[iii], [iv–v], vi, [7], 8–124 p. illus.; 13 cm.; bound in marbled paper over bds., leather spine.
MWA°; CLU; NN; NjR; PP; VtU; McCorison 1479; Shaw 27899.

612.23 ——— Old And New Testament. Illustrated With Notes and adorned with Cuts, for the use of Children. [2 lines quot.] Hudson [N.Y.]: Printed by Ashbel Stoddard, No. 137, Warren-Street. 1813.
fr.[2], t.[3], [4–6], 7–120 p.; illus.; 13 cm.; bound in paper over w. bds., leather spine.
MWA°; DLC; NHi (fr.[2] wanting); NN; PP; Shaw 27900.

612.24 ———— Old And New Testament. Being a valuable present for a little Son or Daughter. Illustrated with Notes and adorned [wi]th Cuts. [2 lines quot.] Luke xviii. 16. Philadelphia: Published By John Fordyce, No. 368, North Third Street. 1813.

fr.[2], t.[3–4], [v], vi, [7], 8–136 p.; illus.; 10.5 cm.; bound in marbled paper over bds., leather spine.

MWA-T° (title page and pp. 133–136 mut.); (not in Shaw).

612.25 ———— Old And New Testament. For The Use Of Children. Adorned with Cuts. [2 lines quot.] Salem [Mass.]: Published By Thomas Carey. J. D. Cushing, Printer. 1820.

t.[1], [2–3], 4–192 p.; illus.; 11.5 cm.; bound in marbled paper over bds., green leather spine.

Welch°; BM; CtHi; CtY; MSaE; MWA; NNC-T; PP; Shoemaker 410.

THE HOLY BIBLE IN VERSE. *See* Harris, Benjamin, no. **492.1**.

613.1 HONEY JUG. Philadelphia: adv. by B. & J. Johnson, 1801 in **1343**.

613.2 ———— Wilmington, Del.: adv. by J. Wilson, 1803 in no. **1081**.

HORNER, J. *pseud.*
614.1 [—] SILVER PENNY. Wilmington, Del.: adv. ". . . may be had at James Wilson's Bookstore at the sign of Shakespeare, in Market Street", 1803 in **1081**.

614.2 — SILVER PENNY, OR NEW LOTTERY-BOOK, For Children. By J. Horner, Esq. Fellow of the Royal Society of A B C, &c. From Sidney's Press, New-Haven. 1805.

fr.[2], t.[3], [4–5], 6–31 p.; illus.; 10.5 cm.; Dutch paper covers.

English ed. York: J. Kendrew [*ca.* 1820].

MWA°; Shaw 8644.

614.3 ———— From Sidney's Press, New-Haven. 1806.

fr.[2], t.[3], [4–5], 6–31 p.; illus.; 10.5 cm.; violet & green Dutch paper covers.

NB°.

614.4 ———— A, B, C. &c. Embellished with Cuts. Philadelphia: Printed By John Adams. 1806.

fr.[2], t.[3], [4–5], 6–31 p.; illus.; 10 cm.; pr. & illus. blue paper covers; p. 30–31 adv. list of books.

Cover title: Toy-Book, Philadelphia: Sold by James Parke, 1807.

PP°; Shaw 11363 and 13593.

614.5 ———— Philadelphia: adv. by B. & T. Kite, 1807 in **611.1**.

614.6 ———— Horner, Esq. Of The Royal Society Of A.B.C. &c Albany: Printed By E. And E. Hosford. 1809.

fr.[2], t.[3], [4], 5–31 p.; illus.; 10.5 cm.; pr. & illus. buff paper covers.

CtHi°; MWA-T; (not in Shaw).

614.7 ———— Albany: Printed By E. and E. Hosford. 1810.

fr.[2], t.[3], [4], 5–31 p.; illus.; 10 cm.; pr. & illus. buff paper covers.

CtHi°; MWA-W; N; NN-C; NNC-LS; Shaw 20382; Weiss 1936, p. 664.

614.8 ———— Of A. B. C. &c. Ornamented with Engravings. Albany: Printed By E. & E. Hosford. 1813.

fr.[2], t.[3], [4], 5–31 p.; illus.; 11 cm. pr. & illus. buff paper covers.

MWA-W°; (not in Shaw).

614.9 ———— Albany: Printed by E. & E. Hosford. 1814.

fr.[2], t.[3], [4], 5–31 p.; illus.; 10 cm.; pr. & illus. yellow-buff paper covers.

Welch°; ICU; MWA; Shaw 31788.

614.10 ———— Albany: Printed By E. & E. Hosford. 1816.

fr.[2], t.[3], [4], 5–31 p.; illus.; 10 cm.; paper covers.

MWA°; Shaw 37873.

HORWOOD, MISS. *See* Baker, Caroline (Horwood), no. **54**.

615.1 AN HOUR'S AMUSEMENT; Or, Two Entertaining Stories For Young Ladies. Printed at Hudson [N.Y.]: By Ashbel Stoddard, And sold, wholesale and retail, At his Printing-Office, M,DCC,-XCIII.

fr.[2], t.[3], [4], 5–23 p.; illus.; 8 cm.; buff

and red paper covers. Page number 5 printed on the inside margin of the page.
English ed. London: J. Marshall. [*ca.* 1790].
CtHi*; Evans 46786.

615.2 —— Young Ladies. To Which is Added The History Of Augi. Hudson [N.Y.]: Printed by Ashbel Stoddard, And sold Wholesale and Retail, at his Book-Store. 1804.
fr.[2], t.[3], [4–5], 6–30, [31 adv. list of books] p.; illus.; 11 cm.; illus. blue-gray paper covers.
MWA*; Shaw 6505.

615.3 —— Hudson [N.Y.]: Printed By Ashbel Stoddard, And Sold Wholesale and Retail at his Book-Store. 1818.
fr.[2], t.[3], [4–5], 6–31 p.; illus.; 10 cm.; pr. & illus. pink paper covers; cover title dated 1830.
MWA-W*.

616.1 [THE HOUSE THAT JACK BUILT. A Diverting Story for Children of all Ages. To which is added, Some Account of Jacky Jingle; Shewing By what Means he acquired his Learning, and in Consequence thereof got Rich, and Built himself a House. With A Collection of Riddles written by Him. The Whole Adorned with Variety of Cuts By Master Collett. And Set forth at large for the Benefit of those, who being quite destitute, friendless, and poor, Would have a fine House, and a Coach at the Door.] [title taken from the English ed. of John Marshall [*ca.* 1784]]. [Philadelphia: Printed and Sold by William Spotswood. MDCC-LXXXVI.] [Imaginary imprint made up by Charles Evans 1932].
5–28 p.; illus.; 9 cm. The illus. and text are copies of the [*ca.* 1784] ed. of Johns Marshall and for this reason the imaginary title made by Evans 19718 is not used.
English ed. London: John Marshall and Co. [*ca.* 1784].
MWA* (all before p. 5 and all after p. 28 wanting); Evans 19718.

612.2 [—— Built. To Which Are Added. The History Of Miss Kitty Pride. And The Virtue Of A Rod. First Worcester Edition. Printed at Worcester, Massachusetts, By Isaiah Thomas, Jun. Sold Wholesale and Retail by Him. 1786?] [imaginary title made up from the Second Worcester Edition, no. **616.1**.

[3], 4–32 p.; illus.; 10.5 cm.; gold Dutch paper covers.
MWA* (t.[1], p.[2], & front cover wanting);
Evans 19720.

616.3 [—— Built. Also, The History Of Mrs. Williams, and Her Plumb Cake which she mathe- she matically [*sic. i.e.* mathematically] divided among her Pupils, according to their merit. The Story of Little Red Riding Hood. Boston: Printed and Sold by Nath'l Coverly Near the Sign of the White-Horse. [1787?].
t.[1], [2], 3–31, [32 adv. list of books] p.; illus.; 10.5 cm. At the bottom of p. [1] is a holograph inscription: *Elisabeth Bartlett Her Book 1787.* The book contains the earliest printing of *Little Red Riding Hood* in America. Page 18 is numbered "18". The illustrations. p. [2]–18, 11–25 were used by J. White & C. Cambridge, 1790 in **616.5**. "The History of Mrs. Williams and Her Plumb Cake" appeared in England in *The Twelfth Day Gift. London: J. Newbery. 1767.*
MSaE*; Evans 45083.

616.4 [—— Boston: Printed and Sold by Nath'l Coverly Near the Sign of the White Horse. 1788?] [imaginary title made up from **616.3**.]
9–28 p.; illus.; 9.5 cm.; the woodcut illus. are identical with those in no. **616.3**. Except for one, all of them occur on different pages. Page 18 is numbered correctly.
Adomeit* (t.[1], p. [2]–8, 29–31 & covers wanting).

616.5 —— [same as **616.3**] Boston: Printed and sold near Charles-River Bridge. 1790.
t.[1], [2], 3–28 p.; illus.; 8.5 cm.; illus. buff paper covers; thirteen woodcut illus. from the same blocks used in no. **616.3** with the exception of two, those on p. 9 and 10, which are different. The one on p. 9 was used by N. Coverly in *The History Of Little Goody Two-Shoes, 1783,* p. 58. The firm of J. White was printing at the above address in 1790.
NNC-Pl*; MWA (t.[1] torn in half with the last line closely cropped so that the final digits of the date are mostly wanting); Evans 30596 (dated 1796).

616.6 —— Built: to which is added a collection of Riddles. New-York: adv. by William Durell, 1790 in **612.5**.

616.7 [——— Built, A diverting Story for Children Of All Ages. To which is Added some Account of Jack Gingle [*sic. i.e.* Jingle]: Shewing By what means he acquired his learning and in consequence thereof got rich, and built himself a house. With A] [upper half of title page wanting. The above copied from no. **616.24**] [Collect]ion of Riddles, written by him. The whole adorned with a Variety of Cuts by Mr. Collet. And set forth at large for the Benefit of those, Who from being quite destitute, friendless and poor Would have a fine House, and a Coach at the Door. Printed at Hudson [N.Y.]: By Asbel Stoddard, and sold, wholesale and retail, at his Printing-Office, M,DCC, XCIII.

t.[1], [2–3], 4–23, [24, page cropped] p.; illus.; 8.5 cm.; reddish-brown ornamented paper covers.

MWA° (title mut.).

616.8 ——— Built [.] A Diverting Story for Children of all Ages. To which is added Some account of Jack Gingle [*sic. i.e.* Jingle] [.] Shewing By what means he acquired his learning, and in consequence, thereof got rich and built himself a house. With a Collection of Riddles, the [*sic. i.e.* The] whole adorned with a variety of Cuts. And Set forth at large for the benefit of those, [w]ho from being quite destitute, friendless and poor, Would have a fine house, and a coach at the door. Printed By W. Durell. [1793?].

fr.[2], t.[3], [4–7], 8–30 p.; illus.; 10 cm.; brown unprinted paper covers; the word Alphabet on p. [4] is misspelled "ALPHAAET". On p. 20 there is a woodcut illustration of "a coach, driver, and two horses". The same wood block was used by Durell in *Tom Thumb's Folio*, *1793*, no. **1315.7** on p. 27. The cut of "the Maiden all forlorn", p. 8, looks as if it had been badly damaged so that the right border and contiguous portions are lost. The cut must have been unusable by 1800 because a new cut had to be substituted on p. 8, **616.13** and **616.14**. In the cut of "of the man all tattered and torn", p. 9, there is a nick 2 mm. wide in the right rule. This nick by 1800 is about 4 mm. wide in **616.13**, p. 9. No. **616.8** must have been published before 1800 considering the above data. Because of the cut of the "coach, driver and two horses" appearing in **1315.7** and **616.8**, the latter is tentatively being dated [1793?].

Scottish and English ed. Glasgow: J. and M. Robertson, 1793.

MWA-W°; Evans 46787.

616.9 ——— Built. Hudson, N.Y.: adv. by Ashbel Stoddard, 1794 in **1220.1**.

616.10 ——— Built. Philadelphia: adv. by William Young, 1794 in **305,** and 1795 in *Sermons to Children.*

THE HOUSE THAT JACK BUILT. Boston, 1796. Evans 30596. *See no.* **616.5.**

616.11 ——— Built. To Which Are Added. The History Of Miss Kitty Pride. And The Virtue Of A Rod. Second Worcester Edition. Printed at Worcester, Massachusetts, By Isaiah Thomas, Jun. Sold Wholesale and Retail by Him, 1799.

t.[1], [2–3], 4–27, [28 adv. list of books], p.; illus.; 10.5 cm.; orange and silver Dutch paper cover.

MWA°; Evans 48889.

616.12 ——— Built, A Diverting Story for Children Of All Ages. To which is added, Some account of Jack Gingle [*sic. i.e.* Jingle]; Shewing [by] what means he acquired his [le]arning, and in consequence [t]here-of got rich, and built himself a house. With a Collection of Riddles. Adorned With Cuts. New-York: Printed by W. Durell, For Evert Duyckinck. 1800.

fr.[2], t.[3], [4–7], 8–31 p.; illus.; 10 cm.; illus. paper covers.

MWA°; Evans 27656.

616.13 ——— New-York: Printed by W. Durell, For Thomas B. Jansen & Co. 1800.

fr.[2], t.[3], [4–7], 8–31 p.; illus.; 10 cm.; ornamental paper covers.

MWA° (p. 25–31 mut., page numbers wanting); Evans 49090.

616.14 ——— New-York: Printed by W. Durell, For Longworth & Wheeler. 1800.

fr.[2]; t.[3]; [4–7], 8–31 p.; illus.; 10 cm.; illus. buff paper covers.

MWA° (fr.[2], p. 31 & covers mut.); Evans 37055.

616.15 ——— Built, A Story. To which Are Added, The means by which he acquired his learning, and the riches he obtained thereby. Likewise Jack's Riddles, Written for the benefit of all who would be Great and Good. Hudson [N.Y.]. Printed by Ashbel Stoddard, And sold Wholesale and Retail, at his Book-Store. 1804.

    fr.[2], t.[3], [4–6], 7–31 p.; illus.; 11 cm.; illus. blue-gray paper covers.

    MWA-W°; PP (fr. [2] trimmed, p. 29–31 slightly mut.).

616.16 —— Built: To Which Is Added, A Collection Of Entertaining Fables; &c. Embellished with elegant Cuts. Philadelphia: Printed By John Adams. 1805.

    fr.[2], t.[3], [4–5], 6–30 p.; illus.; 10.5 cm.; blue paper covers; p. 28 pr. on the inside of the page; p. 29–30, adv. list of books.

    CtHi°; DLC; Shaw 8647.

616.17 —— Built, A Story. To which is added, Some Account Of Jack Jingle, Shewing how he acquired his learning and thereby his estate. Also, the famous story of the Brazen Head. Portsmouth [N.H.], Printed For C. Peirce By J. Whitelock. 1805.

    fr.[2], t.[3], [4–5], 6–31 p.; illus.; 10 cm.; wallpaper covers.

    NhHi°; Shaw 8648.

616.18 —— Built. To Which Are Added, The History Of Miss Kitty Pride: And The Virtue Of A Rod. Worcester: Printed by Isaiah Thomas, Jun. Sold Wholesale and Retail at his Bookstore. 1805.

    fr.[2], t.[3], [4–5], 6–30, [31, 2 illus.] p.; illus.; 11 cm.; blue paper covers.

    MWA°; Shaw 8649.

616.19 —— Built. To Which Is Prefixed, The History of Jack Jingle, Shewing by what means he acquired his Learning, and in consequence thereof got Rich, and Built himself a House. Set forth for the benefit of those, Who from being quite destitute, friendless and poor; Would have a fine House, and a Coach at the Door. Ornamented with Cuts. Hartford: Printed By Lincoln & Gleason. 1806.

    fr.[2], t.[3], [4–5], 6–30, [31, adv. list of books] p. illus.; 10 cm.; green Dutch paper covers.

    CtHi°; DLC (covers wanting); MWA-T; PP; Shaw 10594.

616.20 —— [same as **616.16**] Entertaining Fables, &c. Embellished With Cuts. Philadelphia: Printed By John Adams. 1806.

    fr.[2], t.[3], [4–5], 6–30, [31, adv.] p.; illus.; 10.5 cm.; wallpaper covers.

    NHi (original covers probably wanting); MWA-W (pr. & illus. blue paper covers).

616.21 —— Built. Philadelphia: adv. by B. & T. Kite, 1807 in **611.1**.

616.22 —— [same as **616.19**] Hartford: Printed By Peter B. Gleason & Co. 1811.

    t.[3], [4–5], 6–30 p.; illus.; 10.5 cm.

    CtHi° fr.[2], p. [31] & covers wanting); Shaw 23053.

616.23 —— Built, A Diverting Story For Children. Ornamented With Cuts. Boston: Printed By N. Coverly, Jun. Milk-Street, 1814.

    t.[1], [2–16] p.; illus.; 9.5 cm.; wallpaper covers.

    MH° (i. st. p. [2]); Shaw 31760.

616.24 —— Built, A diverting Story for Children Of All Ages. To which is added some Account of Jack Gingle [*sic. i.e.* Jingle]: Shewing By what means he acquired his learning and in consequence thereof got rich, and built himself a house. With A Collection of Riddles. The whole adorned with a variety of Cuts And Set-forth at large for the benefit of those Who from being quite destitute, friendless and poor, Would have a fine house and a coach at the door. Hudson [N.Y.]: Printed By Ashbel Stoddard, And Sold Wholesale and Retail, at his Book-Store. 1818.

    fr.[2, alphabet], t.[3], 4–31 p.; illus.; 10.5 cm.; pr. & illus. blue paper covers.

    Cover title: The House That Jack Built. Hudson: Printed By Ashbel Stoddard, And Sold, Wholesale and Retail, at his Book-Store. 1821. N°.

616.25 —— Built. A Diverting Story For Children. Ornamented With Cuts. Boston: Printed by N. Coverly, jun. Milk-Street. 1817.

    t.[1], [2–14], p.; illus.; 10.5 cm.; yellow wallpaper covers.

    MWA°.

616.26 —— Boston: Printed For N. Coverly. Milk Street. 1820.

    t.[1], [2–14] p.; illus.; 10 cm.; paper covers.

The words "THE ALPHABET" on p. [2] are printed entirely in capitals, and the letters of the alphabet are printed in capitals in three rows. The last line p. [8]: built.
ICU°.

616.27 ———— Boston: Printed For N. Coverly. Milk Street. 1820.

Same as no. **616.26** but the type is reset. The words "The Alphabet" are not printed entirely in capitals, and the letters of the alphabet are printed in capitals in four rows. The last line p.[8]: Jack built.
MWA-W° (p. 11–14 wanting).

HOWARD, THOMAS
617.1 [—] THE HISTORY OF THE SEVEN WISE MISTRESSES OF ROME. Containing Many Ingenious And Entertaining Stories; Wherein The Treachery of Evil Councillors is discovered, Innocence cleared, And The Wisdom of the Seven Wise Mistresses displayed. Boston: Printed and sold by William Spotswood, No. 55, Marlborough-Street. 1795.

t.[1], [2–3], 4–114, [115–116, adv. list of books] p.; illus.; 14 cm.; bound in leather.
English and Scottish ed.: By J. C. Blackmore, 1653.
MWA°; CLU; Evans 29492 and 32285 (1797 vol.).

617.2 [—] ———— Philadelphia: Printed And Sold By H. & P. Rice, No. 50 High-Street, Also By J. Rice And Co. Market-Street, Baltimore, 1795.
t.[1], [2–3], 4–114, [115–116, adv. list of books] p.; 14 cm.; bound in leather.
PHi; Evans 47460.

617.3 [—] ———— Philadelphia: Printed for the Booksellers. 1798.
t.[i], [ii–iii], vi [*sic. i.e.* iv], [5], 6–132 p.; 14 cm.; bound in ornamented paper over bds.
MWA°; Evans 48478.

617.4 [—] ———— Wilmington [Del.]: adv. by Peter Brynberg, 1801 in **61.9**.

617.5 [—] ———— Baltimore: adv. by G. Douglas, 1803 in **275.46**.

617.6 [—] ———— Hudson [N.Y.]: Printed by Ashbel Stoddard, And sold Wholesale and Retail,
at his Printing•Office and Book•Store, in the White-House, corner of Warren and Third Streets. 1805.
t.[3], [4–5], 6–99 p.; 15 cm.; bound in illus. blue paper over w. bds.; text pr. on blue paper; p. 76 not struck.
MWA°; N; PP (p. 25–mut.); Shaw 9337.

617.7 [—] ———— Printed For The Purchasers. 1811.
t.[1], [2–3], 4–107 p.; 14 cm.; bound in blue paper over bds., leather spine.
Welch°; DLC; MB; MWA; Shaw 23055.

HOWE, SOLOMON
618 THE YOUNG GENTLEMAN AND LADY'S PLEASANT COMPANION. Containing: A Number of Poems On Natural Moral & Divine Subjects, Entirely New. By Solomon Howe. A.M. [4 lines quot.] Greenwich [Mass.], Printed, By John Howe:—For the Author. Price 12 Cents: 1804.
t.[1], [2], 3–30 p.; 14 cm.
MWA°; CtHi; Shaw 6511.

THE HUBUB. *See* More, Sarah, no. **901**, and The Cheap Repository, no. **169.26**.

HUGHES, MARY (ROBSON)
619 [—] AUNT MARY'S TALES, FOR THE ENTERTAINMENT AND IMPROVEMENT OF LITTLE BOYS. Addressed To Her Nephews. First American From The Third London Edition. New-York: Printed For D. Bliss, No. 59 Maiden Lane. Forbes & Co. Printers. 1817.
fr.[ii], t.[i], [ii–iii], iv, [1], 2–172 p.; front. only illus.; 14.5 cm.; bound in pink paper over bds., leather spine.
English ed. London: 3 ed. Darton, Harvey, and Darton, 1817.
MWA°; PP; Shaw 41093.

620 [—] AUNT MARY'S TALES, FOR THE ENTERTAINMENT AND IMPROVEMENT OF LITTLE GIRLS. Addressed To Her Nieces. First American Edition From The Third London Edition. New-York: Printed For D. Bliss, No. 59 Maiden Lane. Forbes & Co. Printers. 1817.
fr.[ii], t.[i], [ii–iii], iv–vi, [1], 2–168 p.; front. only illus.; 14.5 cm.; front. signed A [Alexander Anderson].
MWA°; CLU; IaU; MB; MH; NB; NN (bound

in pink paper over bds., leather spine; per. st. on t.[i]); Shaw 41094.

621 — The Metamorphoses: Or Effects Of Education. A Tale. By Mrs. Hughes; Author Of Aunt Mary's Tales, The Ornaments Discovered, Stories For Children, Etc. Philadelphia: Printed And Published By Abraham Small, No. 165, Chestnut Street. Nearly opposite to the United States Bank. 1820.
> fr.[ii], t.[i], [ii–iii], iv, [1], 2–286, [287–288, adv. list of books] p.; front. only illus.; 14 cm.; bound in marbled paper over bds., leather spine. English ed. London: William Darton, Jun. 1818. MWA°; CLU; MH; PP; Shoemaker 1695.

622 [—] The Ornaments Discovered: A Story, In Two Parts. By The Author Of Aunt Mary's Tales. New-York: Published By W. B. Gilley, No. 92 Broadway. 1817. D. Fanshaw, Print. 241 Pearl-st.
> t.[1], [2–3], 4–180 p.; 13 cm.
> English ed. London: Wm. Darton jun. 1815.
> MWA° (paper wanting from covers, green leather spine); MH; PP (bound in marbled paper over bds., black leather spine); Shaw 41095.

623 — Stories For Children, Chiefly Confined To Words Of Two Syllables, By Mrs. Hughs [*sic. i.e.* Hughes], Author Of "Aunt Mary's Tales," "Ornaments Discovered," &c. Philadelphia: Printed and Published by Ab'm Small. 1820.
> t.[i], [ii–vi], [1], 2–226, [227–229, adv. list of books written by Mrs. Hughes & published by William Darton Holburn Hill London.], [230, bl.]; [231–233, adv. for Mrs. Hugh's boarding school.] p.; 14 cm.; bound in buff paper over w. bds., red leather spine.
> English ed. London: Wm. Darton, Jun. 1819.
> MWA°; DeWint; MH; PP; PPL; Shoemaker 1696.

624 — The Twin Brothers; Or, Good Luck and Good Conduct. By Mary Hughes. Author of "William's Return; Or, Good News For Cottagers," &c. &c. First Published By The Christian Tract Society. No. XXI. Boston: Wells And Lilly, Court-Street. 1820.
> t.[1], [2–3], 4–180 p.; 14.5 cm.
> MWA°; MHi; Shoemaker 1697.

625.1 The Humorous Alphabet. [illus. of a lion] Newburyport [Mass.], Printed by W. & J. Gilman. Sold at their wholesale and retail Book-Store, No. 2, Middle-Street, and by the Booksellers in Boston. [*ca.* 1814].
> t.[1], [2–3], 4–15, [16, adv. of 17 books] p.; illus.; 10 cm.
> PP° (covers wanting).

625.2 ——— [illus. of a man, woman, house, and trees] Printed by W. & J. Gilman. Sold by the hundred or dozen, at their Book-Store. Middle-Street, Newburyport [Mass.] [*ca.* 1815].
> t.[1], [2–3], 4–16 p.; illus.; 10.5 cm.; pr. & illus. blue-gray paper covers.
> The date is conjectural.
> NNMM° (i. st. p. [2]).

The Humerous Story Of Mrs. Gilpin's Return From Edmonton. *See* [Lemoine, Henry], no. **748**.

The Hunters. *See* Bingham, C., no. **99**.

HURLOTHRUMBO, DR. *pseud.*
626.1 — The Fortune-Teller, By Which Young Gentlemen and Ladies may foretell a variety of future events. By The Renowned Dr. Hurlothrumbo Chief Magician and Astrologer to the King of the Cuckows. Philadelphia: Printed by Francis Bailey, at Yorick's-Head, No. 116, High-Street. 1793.
> t.[3], [4–5], 6–63 p.; illus.; 10.5 cm.
> PP° (p. 31–32, 47–50 wanting); Evans 46752.

626.2 ——— of important Events that will happen both to Themselves and their Acquaintence By the Renowned Doctor, Hurlothrumbo, Chief Magician and Astrologer to the King of the Cuckows. Boston: Printed and sold by John W. Folsom, No. 30, Union-Street. 1798.
> t.[3], [4–5], 6–60, [61–62] p.; illus.; [A]₁₅, B₁₅; 10 cm.
> MWA° (covers, fr.[2]? & p. [63]? wanting, p. [61–62] 99% wanting); Evans 33918.

626.3 ——— Doctor Hurlothrumbo. Chief Magician and Astrologer to the King of the Cuckows. Exeter [N.H.]: Printed And Sold By H. Ranlet. 1801.
> fr.[2], t.[3], [4–5], 6–61, [62–63, adv. list of

books]; illus.; 10.5 cm.; pr. & illus. buff paper covers.
MWA-W°.

626.4 — ——— Exeter [N.H.]: adv. by Norris & Sawyer, 1808 in **428.3**.

627 A HYMN-BOOK FOR THE CHILDREN BELONGING TO THE BRETHEREN'S CONGREGATIONS. Taken Chiefly out of the German Little Book. In Three Books. [1 line quot.] Philadelphia, Printed in the Year MDCCLXIII.
t.[i], [ii], [i], ii–xxvi, 1–64 p.; 13.5 cm.
PP°; Evans 9527.

HYMN FOR THE NURSERY. *See* Hymns For The Nursery, no. **630.2**.

HYMNS AND SONGS OF PRAISE FOR CHILDREN. *See* Gilbert, Ann (Taylor) And Jane Taylor, no. **437**.

628.1 HYMNS AND SONGS OF PRAISE, For The Use Of Children In General, And particularly for those of Sunday and other Schools. New Haven. Printed For J. Babcock & Son. Sidney's Press. 1819.
fr.[ii], t.[1], [2, adv.–3], 4–36 p.; front. only illus.; 13.5 cm.; pr. & illus. yellow-buff paper covers.
Cover title: Sunday School Hymns. Published By J. Babcock & Son, Booksellers, Stationers and Printers.
MWA° (copy 1, fr.[ii] illus. of an Indian; copy 2, fr.[ii] illus. of the fox and the crow); CtHi (fr[ii] illus. of an Indian); MWA-T; NjR; NNC-T (fr.[ii] illus. of a woman on a white horse); PP. (fr. [ii] illus. of two blind men playing a violin and led by a boy); Shaw 48314.

628.2 ——— New-Haven: Printed For John Babcock And Son. Sidney's Press. 1820.
fr.[2], t.[3], [4, adv.], [5], 6–31 p.; front. only illus.; 14.5 cm.; copy A, pr. & illus. yellow-buff paper covers; copy B, pr. & illus. pink paper covers. Rear cover copy A: John Babcock & Son, Booksellers & Stationers, Church St. New-Haven, [18 lines adv.]. Rear cover copy B: Books for Children, For sale by John Babcock & Son. [adv. list of 24 books].
Cover title, copy A: Sunday School Hymns. [illus. of the fox and the crow, signed A [Alexander Anderson]] Sold by John Babcock & Son, New-Haven, and S. & W. R. Babcock, Charleston [S.C.].
Cover title, copy B: ——— [same as copy A] [illus. of two blind musicians led by a boy] Published and Sold by John Babcock and Son, New-Haven, and S. & W. R. Babcock, Charleston.
Adomeit°; CtHi; Shoemaker 1725.

629 HYMNS FOR CHILDREN. [2 lines quot.] Matth. xxi.15. Philadelphia: Printed By Conrad Zentler, In Second, Near Race-Street. 1811.
t.[i], [ii–iii] iv–viii, [1], 2–129 p.; 13 cm.
BM°; Shaw 23078.

HYMNS FOR INFANT MINDS. *See* Gilbert, Ann (Taylor), no. **438.1**.

HYMNS FOR LITTLE CHILDREN. *See* Gilbert, Ann (Taylor) and Jane Taylor, no. **439.1**.

630.1 HYMNS FOR THE NURSERY. Adorned With Cuts. Sidney's Press. New-Haven. 1813.
fr.[2], t.[3], [4–5], 6–31 p.; illus.; 10.5 cm.; pr. & illus. yellow-buff paper covers.
MWA-W°; NjR (t.[3], p. [4] wanting).

630.2 HYMN [*sic. i.e.* Hymns] FOR THE NURSERY. Adorned With Cuts. Sidney's Press. New-Haven. 1813.
fr.[2], t.[3], [4–5], 6–31 p.; illus.; 10.5 cm.; pr. & illus. green paper covers. Same as the preceding but wants the "s" of the word "Hymns" on the title page.
MWA°; CtHi (fr.[2], p. 31 & covers wanting; t.[3] & p. 27–28 mut.); Shaw 28799.

630.3 ——— [same as 630.1] Hartford Printed by Charles Hosmer. 1815.
fr.[2], t.[3], [4–5], 6–30 p.; illus.; 10 cm.; pr. & illus. paper covers; cover title imprint: Hartford: Printed By C. Hosmer. 1815.
MB° (rebound, p. 31 wanting); Shaw 34988.

631 HYMNS FOR THE USE OF CHILDREN. Philadelphia: Printed For The Tract And Book Society Of The Evangelical Lutheran Church of St. John. William Fry, Printer. 1819.
t.[1], [2–3], 4–24 p.; 18 cm.
MWA° (covers wanting); Shaw 48318.

HYMNS IN PROSE FOR CHILDREN. *See* Barbauld, Anna Letitia (Aiken), nos. **60.1–60.41**.

632.1 ICHTHYOLOGY FOR YOUTH; Or, A History Of Nearly All The Known Fishes Of The Ocean. Adorned with upwards of One Hundred Elegant Engravings On Wood. In Six Books. Book I. [II.–IV.] New-York: Published By John Tiebout, No. 238, Water-Street. [Books II.–IV.: Water street.] Southwick & Pelsue, Printers. 1809.

Book I.: t.[i], [ii–iii], iv, [5], 6–32 p.; illus.; 12.5 cm.; pr. & illus. yellow paper covers; cover title dated 1810. Each Book II.–IV.: t.[1], [2–3], 4–32 p.; illus.; 12.5 cm.; pr. & illus. yellow paper covers; each cover title dated 1810. Books I.–IV. and V.–VI. of no. 632.2 in the MWA-W set are in the original green marbled paper case. On the title pages of Books II.–VI. there is a colon after the word "Youth:". Cover title of Books I.–IV. and V.–VI. of no. 632.2: A History Of Nearly All The Known Fishes Of The Ocean.

MWA-W* (Books I.–IV.); MWA (Book III.); MH (Book IV.).

632.2 ——— Book V. [VI.] New York: Published By John Tiebout, No. 238, Water street. Southwick & Pelsue, Printers. 1810.

Book V.: t.[1], [2–3], 4–32 p.; illus.; 12.5 cm.; pr. & illus. pink paper covers. Cover title dated 1820. Book VI.: t.[1], [2–3], 4–31 p.; illus.; 12.5 cm.; pr. & illus. yellow paper covers. Cover title dated 1810. Copy 1: cut of a "Piper" on the front cover and 4 cuts on rear cover; copy 2: cut of a "Turtle" on the front cover and 3 cuts on the rear cover.

MWA-W* (Books V.–VI.; Book VI. copies 1, 2); Ct (Book V. front cover mut.); MH (Book V.); NNC-T (Book V. p. 29–30 wanting).

IDLENESS AND INDUSTRY. See Edgeworth, Maria, no. 318.1.

THE ILLUSTRIOUS AND RENOWNED HISTORY OF THE SEVEN CHAMPIONS OF CHRISTENDOM. See Johnson, Richard, no. 668.1.

633 THE IMPROVED PICTURE ALPHABET; Or, A's Invitation to his Brethren, To Meet For The Amusement And Instruction Of Good Children.

Philadelphia: Published by Wm. Charles No. 32, south Third-street. 1817.

t.[1], [2–16] p.; illus.; 13 cm.; pr. & illus. paper covers.

NNC-Pl* (rear cover wanting); Shaw 41129.

INDUSTRY AND IDLENESS. See Elliott, Mary (Belson), no. 340.

INDUSTRY AND SLOTH. See The Instructive History Of Industry And Sloth, no. 646.1.

634.1 INFANCY. [2 lines quot.] Printed & sold by Samuel Wood, at the Juvenile Book-store, No. 357, Pearl-street, New-York. 1811.

t.[1], [2–16] p.; illus.; 8 cm.; yellow paper covers.

MWA*; Shaw 23092.

634.2 ——— Printed & sold by Samuel Wood, at the Juvenile Book-store, No. 357, Pearl-street, New-York. 1813.

t.[1], [2–16] p.; illus.; 8 cm.

RPB* (covers wanting); Shaw 28811.

634.3 ——— New-York: Printed & sold by Samuel Wood, at the Juvenile Book-store, No. 357, Pearl-street. 1814.

t.[1], [2–16] p.; illus.; 8 cm.; pr. paper covers; cover title undated.

MWA*; CtHi; PP; Shaw 31796.

634.4 ——— Nerv-York [sic. i.e. New-York]: Printed And Sold By S. Wood, at the Juvenile Book-store, No. 357, Pearl-street. 1815.

t.[1], [2–16] p.; illus.; 9 cm.; pr. & illus. buff paper covers; cover title imprint: Sold by Samuel Wood, New-York.

Adomeit*.

634.5 ——— New-York: Printed And Sold By Samuel Wood & Sons, At the Juvenile Bookstore, No. 357, Pearl-street. 1816.

t.[1], [2–16] p.; illus.; 8 cm.; pr. & illus. yellow paper covers; cover title imprint: Sold by Samuel Wood & Sons, New-York.

CLU.

634.6 ——— Nerv-York [*sic i.e.* New-York]: Published by Samuel Wood & Sons, No. 261, Pearl-street, And Samuel S. Wood & Co. No. 212, Market-St. Baltimore. 1818.

t.[1], [2–16] p.; illus.; 8.5 cm.; pr. & illus. yellow paper covers; cover title imprint: Sold by Samuel Wood & Sons, Nerv-York [*sic*.], And Samuel S. Wood & Co. Baltimore. Copy 1: cut of a mole on the front cover, 2 cuts on the rear cover; copy 2: cut of a man plowing on the front cover, 1 cut on the rear cover.

MWA-W* (copy 1, 2).

635 THE INFANT MINSTREL: Or, Poetry, For Young Minds. By Various Female Writers. Philadelphia: Published By Edward Parker, No. 178, Market-street. 1820.

fr.[ii], t.[i], [ii–iii], iv, [5–7], 8–108 p.; front. only illus.; 14 cm.; blue and red marbled paper over bds.; black leather spine.

English ed. London: Darton, Harvey, And Darton, 1816.

FTaSU*; CLU; Shoemaker 1751.

636.1 THE INFANT PREACHER, Or, The Story Of Henrietta Smith. Sabbath Breaking, A Dialogue Between Two Sunday Scholars: Ann Wood: And Other Pieces. Portsmouth, N. H. Printed by T.H. Miller, for Charles Whipple, Newburyport. 1818.

t.[1], [2], 3–36 p.; 14.5 cm.

MNe*; Shaw 44434.

636.2 ——— Smith. Being A Relation Of Facts That Have Taken Place In A Country Town In Connecticut. By A Minister Of The Gospel. New-Haven: Printed At The Office Of The Religious Intelligencer. 1819.

t.[1], [2–3], 4–32 p.; 11 cm.; buff paper covers.

MWA*; Shaw 48340.

636.3 ——— Smith. September, 1819. Published by the Religious Tract Society of Philadelphia, and sold at their Depository, No. 8, South Front-street. Wm. Bradford, Agent.

t.[1], [2], –312 p.; title vignette; 18 cm.

MWA*; PP; Shaw 48341.

636.4 ——— Smith. Boston: Printed For Samuel T. Armstrong, By Crocker And Brewster, No. 50, Cornhill. 1820.

t.[1], [2–3], 4–24 p.; illus.; 13 cm.; pr. & illus. pink paper covers.

MWA*; Shoemaker 1752.

636.5 ——— Smith. [2 lines quot.] New-York: Published By D. H. Wickham, At the Sunday School Depository, No. 59 Fulton-street. 1820.

t. [1], [2–3], 4–24 p.; 12.5 cm.; pr. buff paper covers; cover title dated 1820.

MWA-W*.

636.6 ——— Smith. Sabbath Breaking, A Dialogue Between Two Sunday Scholars. Ann Wood: And Other Pieces. Published By Charles Whipple, Newburyport: Who has for sale a large assortment of Sabbath School Rewards, on the lowest terms. T. H. Miller, Printer, Portsmouth. [1820?].

t.[1], [2], 3–36 p.; 14.5 cm.; blue-gray paper covers.

MH*.

637.1 THE INFANT'S CABINET. New-York: Printed And Sold By S. Wood, No. 357, Pearl-Street 1814.

t.[1], [2–3], [4, bl.] p. followed by 12 books, each [16] p. illus.; 8.5 cm.; bound in marbled paper over bds., leather spine. Each of the books bound under this general title page has a separate title page and dated 1814. The books included in order are: The Book of Letters, The Book of Pictures, The Picture Alphabet, Scripture History, Spring, Summer, Autumn, Winter, Infancy, Childhood, Manhood, Old Age. Adv. by S. Wood, 1816 in **1188.7**.

MWA-W*.

637.2 ——— [cut of a flower] [New-York: Printed And Sold By Samuel Wood & Sons, No. 357, Pearl-Street. 1816] [Imaginary imprint made up from the 1814 ed. with the addition of the words "& Sons".] It is believed that Samuel Wood never printed alone after 1815.

t.[1], [2–3], [4,bl.] p. followed by 11 of 12 books, each [16] p.; illus.; 8.5 cm.; disbound copy. The books are listed on p.[3] and include the same ones found in the 1814 ed., no. **637.1**.

MWA-T* (t.[1], p. [2–4] lower half of page wanting; Scripture History, missing; Infancy, Old Age (imp.)).

638.1 THE INFANT'S DELIGHT. Printed By W. & J. Gilman, Newbury-port. At their Book-Store & Printing Office, with a variety of Children's Books, wholesale and retail. 1812.

fr.[2], t.[3], 4–27 p.; illus.; 15.5 cm.; illus.; paper covers.

English ed. London: J. Marshall [1801?], pl. dated "July 1801."
Adomeit°.

638.2 —— Printed and Sold By W. & J. Gilman, Newburyport. [*ca.* 1814].
t.[1], [2–24] p.; illus.; 11.5 cm. Adv. by W. & J. Gilman. [*ca.* 1814] in **625.1**. The cuts and text are taken from the English edition of [1801?]. MSaE°.

INFANT'S OWN BOOK-CASE. *See* discussion of its contents under Youthful Recreations, no. **1468.**

639 INHABITANTS OF THE WORLD, Alphabetically Arranged. New-York: Published By Samuel Wood & Sons, No. 261, Pearl-Street, And Samuel S. Wood & Co No. 212, Market-st. Baltimore. 1818.
t.[1], [2], 3–28 p.; illus.; 12 cm.; pr. & illus. yellow paper covers; cover title imprint: Nerv-York [*sic. i.e.* New-York]: Published by —— [same as title page] & Sons, And —— & Co. Baltimore.
NhD°.

INNOCENT POETRY. *See* Elliott, Mary (Belson), no. **341.**

640 INSTANCES OF FILIAL INTREPIDITY AND TENDERNESS. Boston: Printed and Sold at No. 53 Cornhill, by Lincoln & Edmands. 1819.
t.[1], [2–3], 4–8 p.; illus.; 11 cm.
MWA°; CLU; Shaw 48345.

641 INSTRUCTION WITH AMUSEMENT, In The Tale Of The Blackbird's Nest. To which is added, The Fruits Of Disobedience, Old Grand-Papa, &c. New-York: Printed And Sold By Mahlon Day, No. 84, Water-Street. 1820.
t.[1], [2–3], 4–36 p.; illus.; 14 cm.; pr. & illus. paper covers.
MWA°; DLC (t.[1] & p. 35–36 mut., covers wanting); Shoemaker 1757.

642 INSTRUCTIONS FOR BABES; Or, Answers In Verse To Scriptual Questions; For the use of Children. [3 lines quot.] New-Haven: For J. Babcock & Son Sidney's Press. 1820.
fr.[2], t.[3], [4–5], 6–30, [31, adv.] p.; front. only illus.; 9.5 cm.; pr. & illus. pink paper covers.
Cover title: —— Babes. Published by J. Bab-

cock & Son, New-Haven, and S. and W. R. Babcock, Charleston.
MWA°.

643.1 THE INSTRUCTIVE ALPHABET. New-York: Printed and Sold by Samuel Wood, No. 362, Pearl-Street. 1808.
t.[1], [2–61], [62, adv. list of books], [63] p.; illus.; 10 cm.; pr. & illus. paper covers.
RPB° (most of rear cover & p. 63 wanting).

643.2 —— New-York: Printed And Sold By S. Wood, At The Juvenile Book-Store, No. 357, Pearl-Street. 1812.
t.[1], [2–45] p.; illus.; 13.5 cm.; pr. & illus. paper covers; cover title dated 1812.
CtHi°; MWA-T (covers dated 1811); NHi; NWebyC; Shaw 25718.

643.3 —— New-York: Printed And Sold By Samuel Wood, At The Juvenile Book-Store, No. 357, Pearl-Street. 1814.
t.[1], [2–45] p.; illus.; 12 cm.; pr. & illus. yellow-buff paper covers; cover title undated.
MWA-W°; CtY (bound with other books); MWA-T; PP (bound with other books); Shaw 31804.

643.4 —— New-York: Printed And Sold By S. Wood & Sons, At The Juvenile Book-Store, No. 357, Pearl-Street. 1816.
t.[1], [2–45] p.; illus.; 12.5 cm.; pr. & illus. yellow-buff paper covers.
NN°; Shaw 37933; Weiss 1942, p. 767.

643.5 —— New-York: Published By Samuel Wood & Sons, No. 261, Pearl-Street, And Samuel S. Wood & Co. No. 212, Market-st. Baltimore. 1818.
t.[1], [2–45] p.; illus.; 13 cm.; pr. & illus. paper covers; cover title undated.
MWA°; Ct; Shaw 44441.

INSTRUCTIVE AND ENTERTAINING DIALOGUES. *See* Guppy, Mrs. (*pseud.*), no. **480.**

INSTRUCTIVE AND ENTERTAINING EMBLEMS. *See* Thoughtful (*pseud.*), no. **1300.1.**

644 AN INSTRUCTIVE AND ENTERTAINING MEDLEY: In Eight Lessons. Being A Pleasant Collection Of Tales, Anecdotes, &c. Chiefly Original.

Philadelphia: Published By Jacob Johnson, No. 147, Market-Street. 1808.
  fr.[ii], t.[1], [2–3], 4–36 p.; engr. front. only illus.; 14 cm.; marbled paper covers; p. [2] & 36: Adams, Printer, Philadelphia.
  PP°; MWA; NjP (bound with other books); Hamilton 269; Shaw 15305.

INSTRUCTIVE HINTS. *See* [C., E.], no. **142.1.**

645 INSTRUCTIVE HINTS, In Easy Lessons, For Children. By E**** C****** Philadelphia: Printed For Jacob Johnson, 147, Market-Street. 1802.
  t.[1], [2–3], 4–59 p.; 12 cm.; green marbled paper covers. *See also* no. **142.1.**
  Adomeit°.

646.1 THE INSTRUCTIVE HISTORY OF INDUSTRY AND SLOTH. Ornamented with Cuts. From Sidney's Press, New-Haven. 1805.
  fr.[2], t.[3], [4–5], 6–30, [31, 2 illus.] p.; illus.; 10 cm. This story is the second tale in *Three Instructive Tales For Little Folks. See* no. **968.**
  MWA° (p. 13–14 wanting); Shaw 8681.

646.2 ——— From Sidney's Press. New-Haven. 1806.
  t.[3], [4–5], 6–30, [31, illus.] p.; illus.; 10.5 cm.; green Dutch paper covers.
  DLC° (fr.[2] and front cover wanting); MWA-T; Shaw 10616.

646.3 ——— [7 lines quot.] Embellished With Cuts. Philadelphia: Printed By John Adams. 1806.
  fr.[2], t.[3], [4–5], 6–31 p.; illus.; 10 cm.; p. 30–31 adv. of 21 books.
  MWA°; Shaw 10617.

646.4 ——— Adorned with Cuts. From Sidney's Press, New-Haven. 1807.
  fr.[2], t.[3], [4–5], 6–29, [30, alphabet–31, adv.] p.; illus.; 10.5 cm.
  CtY° (ornamented paper covers); MWA (p.[2], [31] and covers wanting); Shaw 12815.

646.5 ——— Philadelphia: adv. by B. & T. Kite, 1807 in **611.1.**

646.6 ——— Adorned With Cuts. From Sidney's Press, New-Haven. 1808.

fr.[2], t.[3], [4–5], 6–29, [30, alphabet–31, adv.] p.; illus.; 11 cm.; Dutch paper covers.
  MWA°; Ct (covers wanting); CtHi; MHi; PP; Shaw 50858.

646.7 ——— From Sidney's Press. New-Haven. 1809.
  fr.[2], t.[3], [4–5], 6–29, [30, alphabet–31, adv.] p.; illus.; 10.5 cm.; yellow paper covers.
  MWA° (front cover wanting, rear cover mut.); Shaw 17814.

646.8 ——— Adorned with Cuts. From Sidney's Press. New-Haven. 1810.
  fr.[2], t.[3], [4, alphabet], [5], 6–29, [30, adv.], [31, alphabets] p.; illus.; 10.5 cm.; pr. & illus. buff paper covers; four lines of upper case alphabet with the first line A–F, p. [4]; the last four words p. 28: "that was going for"; 14 blocks of triple rules above the word "Books", line 1, and another 14 blocks below the word "Rags," line 8, p. [30]; [3 lines of the lower case alphabet, with the first line a–l] Capital Letters. [2 lines of upper case alphabet] Double Letters. [1 line of double letters], p.[31]
  Cover title: Industry and Sloth. Published by I. Cooke & Co. Universal Book-Store, Church-Street, New Haven.
  CtHi°; NNC-Pl.

646.9 ——— Adorned with Cuts. From Sidney's Press. New-Haven. 1810.
  fr.[2], t.[3], [4 alphabets], [5], 6–29, [30, adv.], [31, alphabet] p.; illus.; 10.5 cm.; illus. paper covers; a variant of no. **646.8.** There are 7 blocks of triple rules on the title page not present in no. **646.8.** Other differences are: [3 lines of lower case alphabet, with the first line a–k] Capital Letters. ——— [very similar to p. [31], in no. **646.8** except that the rule above the words "Double Letters" is formed of two dashes with a separation between them. In no. **646.8** this rule is formed of three dashes with no separation between them], p.[4]; a printer's ornament, 12. mm. long, below the caption, p.[5], consists of a central cross and tapering lines on either side; last four words, p. 28, "was going for eight"; 4 lines of the upper case alphabet, with the first line A–E, p. [31].
  OOxM°; CtHi (fr.[2], p. [31] & covers wanting); CtY.

647. THE INSTRUCTIVE HISTORY OF MISS PATTY PROUD; Or, The Downfall of Vanity: With The Reward Of Good-Nature. Ornamented with Cuts. For the Amusement and Instruction of Youth. [2 lines of verse] Hudson [N.Y.]: Printed By Ashbel Stoddard, 1820.

fr.[2], t.[3], [4–5], 6–31 p.; illus.; 10.5 cm.; pr. & illus. blue-gray paper covers.
Cover title: The Instructive History Of Miss Patty Proud. Hudson [N.Y.]: Printed By Ashbel Stoddard, And Sold Wholesale and Retail, at his Book-Store. 1821. The book is the same as *The New History Of Miss Patty Proud. Hudson [N.Y.] 1804*, no. **937.3**, up to p. 28. Inserted at the end is a new tale: The Story of A Moor and a Spaniard, p. 29–31 instead of The Boy and the Thief.
NNMM°.

648.1 THE INSTRUCTIVE STORY OF INDUSTRY AND SLOTH. Ornamented with Cuts. Hartford: Printed By J. Babcock. 1796.

fr.[2], t.[3], [4–5], 6–29, [30, adv.–31, 2 illus.] p.; illus.; 10 cm.
MWA° (p. 31 & covers mut.); DLC; PP (violet and green Dutch paper covers); Evans 47815.

648.2 ——— Hartford: Printed By John Babcock. 1798.

fr.[2], t.[3], [4–5], 6–30 [31, 2 illus.] p.; illus.; 11 cm.; Dutch paper covers; p. 30 a tailpiece of "School mistress defending her Scholars from Lucifer." The school mistress has angel's wings and a spear in her hand.
MWA°; CtHi; PP (fr.[2], p.[31] & covers wanting); Evans 33926.

648.3 ——— Hartford: Printed By John Babcock. 1802.

fr.[2], t.[3], [4–5], 6–30 [31, 2 illus.] p.; illus.; 11 cm.; paper covers.
MWA°; Shaw 2451.

648.4 ——— Cuts. To Which Is Added, Learned, Religious, And Moral Lessons for All The Little Gentry In America. Boston: Printed By Hosea Sprague. 1804.

fr.[2], t.[3], [4], 5–31 p.; illus.; 10.5 cm.; Dutch paper covers.
MWA°; Shaw 6542 (The Instructive History [*sic. i.e.* Story]).

648.5 ——— First Windsor Edition. Printed At Windsor [Vt.]: By Farnsworth & Churchill. 1810.

fr.[2], t.[3], [4–5], 6–28, [29, adv.], [30–31, alphabets] p.; illus.; 9.5 cm.; pr. & illus. buff paper covers.
MWA-W°; CLU (rear cover wanting); Vt. (rebound, huge i. st. on t.[3]); McCorison 1181; Shaw 20438.

THE INTELLIGENT MISCELLANY. *See* Velasco, E., no. **1375.1**.

649 AN INTERESTING ACCOUNT OF A CHILD. Hartford: Printed by Peter B. Gleason and Co. 1814.

t.[1], [2–3], 4–11 p.; 14 cm.; blue-gray paper covers.

650 (No. 27.) AN INTERESTING ACCOUNT OF ELIZABETH ALLEN. Published by The Philadelphia Female Tract Society. And for sale at their Depository, No. 20, Walnut Street. [caption title p. [1]] Printed by Lydia R. Bailey No. 20 North Alley, Philad. [1817] [colophon p. 12].

[1], 2–12 p.; 14 cm.
MWA° (bound with other tracts, with which *The second Annual Report Of The Philadelphia Female Tract Society For The Year 1817* was originally bound); Shaw 41146.

THE INTERESTING AND AFFECTING HISTORY OF PRINCE LEE BOO. The commencement of the English title of the London ed., listed under The History Of Prince Lee Boo, no. **573.1**.

651 INTERESTING ANECDOTES OF CHILDREN, Designed Through The Medium Of Example, To Inculcate Principles Of Virtue And Piety. By The Author Of "Lessons for Young Persons in humble Life." Philadelphia: Published By B. & T. Kite, No. 20, North Third-street. 1813.

t.[1], [ii–iii], iv–vi, 7–140 p.; 14.5 cm.; bound in leather.
MWA°; ICU; PP; Shaw 28818.

652 INTERESTING CONVERSATIONS WITH A CRUEL CARMAN, A Beggar, The British Trumper, And A Boy With a Bird's Nest. Hartford, Oliver D. Cooke. 1820.

t.[1], [2–3], 4–16 p.; illus.; 10.5 cm.; pr. & illus. buff paper covers printed in black ink.

MWA-W°; CtY; MWA (t.[1] mut., poor copy); Shoemaker 1761.

THE INTERESTING HISTORY OF LITTLE KING PIP- PIN. Title of English ed. London: J. Imray [*ca.* 1805]. For editions of The History Of Little King Pippin, *see* no. **563.2.**

653 THE INTERESTING HISTORY OF THE PRINCESS DE PONTHIEU. Translated from the French. To Which are added, Henry and Charlotte, A Most Affecting Story: The Happy Deliverance; And The Discontented Villager. Hartford:–Printed By J. Babcock. 1801.
　t.[1], [2–3], 4–108 p.; 13.5 cm.; bound in mar- bled paper over w. bds.
　MWA° (p. 5–8 wanting).

654.1 THE INTERESTING LIFE, TRAVELS, VOY- AGES, AND DARING ENGAGEMENTS, OF THE CELE- BRATED PAUL JONES: Commodore in the American Navy during the late Revolutionary War: Contain- ing Numberous Anecdotes Of Undaunted Courage, In the Prosecution Of His Undertakings. Hudson [N.Y.]: Published By William E. Norman, No. 2, Warren Street. N. Elliott Printer, Catskill. 1809.
　t.[1], [2–3], 4–46 p.; t.[1] 15 cm.
　MWA° (rebound, t.[1] lower half of the page wanting); NN.

654.2 ——— That Celebrated And Justly Re- nowned Commander Paul Jones. Containing Num- berous Anecdotes Of Undaunted Courage, In the Prosecution Of His Various Enterprises. Written By Himself. < The first Philadelphia from the fourth London edition. > Philadelphia: Published By William M'Carty. James Maxwell, printer, No. 50, South Fifth-street. 1812.
　t.[1], [2–3], 4–36 p.; t.[1] 18.9 cm.
　CSmH° (rebound in ¾ black morocco); Shaw 25719.

654.3 ——— That Celebrated And Justly Re- nowned Commander Paul Jones. Containing Num- berous Anecdotes Of Undaunted Courage, In the Prosecution Of His Various Enterprises. Written By Himself. Philadelphia: Published By Robert Desilver, No. 110, Walnut-Street. 1817.

t.[1], [2–3], 4–64 p.; 14.5 cm.; bound in gray paper over bds., leather spine.
MWA°; Shaw 41147.

655 INTERESTING MEMOIR OF H——— G———, Of Philadelphia, A Striking Instance Of The In- fluence Of Divine Grace On The Mind. Philadel- phia: Published by "The Religious Tract Society of Philadelphia," No. 8, South-Front-Street. Wil- liam Bradford—Agent. 1819.
　t.[1], [2], 3–12 p.; title vignette only illus.; 19.5 cm.
　NjR°; Shaw 48347.

656 AN INTERESTING NARRATIVE OF TWO PIOUS TWIN CHILDREN, Who Were Stolen By A Jew And Enslaved To The Turks; Who With Their Father Were Marvellously Delivered From Death. Trans- lated From The German. To Which Is Added, Charles Berry, Or, The Good Son. Hillsborough, (O.) Printed By Moses Carothers. 1820.
　t.[1], [2–3], 4–12 p.; 18 cm.
　MWA°.

657 AN INTRODUCTION TO NATURAL HISTORY, OF BEASTS & BIRDS, In Two Parts; To Which Is Added A Third Part, Consisting Of A Choice Se- lection Of Easy Verse; Taken From The Best Writers, And Well Adapted For The Improve- ment Of Youth. First Edition. Baltimore: Printed By Warner And Hanna, And Sold By Thbm [*sic. i.e.* Them] And John Vance & Co. 1807.
　t.[1], [2–3], 4–180 p.; illus., 16.5 cm.; bound in leather. The woodcuts on p.[3] & 102 are signed *Gobrecht*. Other cuts on p. 6, 20, 33, are signed *G* [Christian Gobrecht]. The cut on p. 29 is signed *Fry*.
　English ed., same as no. **416.1.**
　MWA-W°; DLC (2 copies, copy 1, rebound; copy 2, i. st. on t.[1]); MSaE; MWA; Shaw 12817.

658 ISABEL AND LOUISA. Some Account Of Two Little Girls Who Lived In Boston. By A lady Of Boston. Boston: Printed By Thomas B. Wait And Co. 1813.
　fr.[2], t.[3], [4–5], 6–70 p.; 14.5 cm.; pr. & illus. green paper covers.
　MWA°; NN-C; Shaw 28823.

J

J., S. *See* Jones, Stephen, no. **691.1.**

JACK AND THE BEAN STALK. *See* C., H. A. The History Of Mother Twaddle, no. **144.**

JACK AND THE GIANTS. *See* The History Of Jack And The Giants, no. **546.**

659 THE JACK DAW "AT HOME:" Or, British Nobility Burlesqued. Illustrated With Humerous Engravings. Philadelphia: Published and sold Wholesale by Wm. Charles, and may be had of all the Booksellers. 1815. Price 18¾ cts. plain—25 cts. coloured.
  fr.[ii], t.[1], [2,bl.], [3], 4–16, [pl. opp. p. 16] p.; 6 pl.; 13 cm.; pr. buff paper covers.
  English ed. London: Didier and Tebbett, 1808. NNC-Pl* (rear cover wanting); CLU; DLC (col. pl.); Shaw 35005.

660 JACK HORNER'S HOBBY HORSE. Wilmington, Del.: adv. by J. Wilson, 1803 in **1081.**

JACK THE GIANT KILLER. *See* The History Of Jack and the Giants, no. **546.**

JACK THE GIANT KILLER
661 THE SINGULAR AND VERY SURPRISING LIFE AND ADVENTURES OF JACK THE GIANT KILLER. Illustrated With Elegant Engravings. Philadelphia: Published And Sold Wholesale By Wm. Charles, And May Be Had Of All Booksellers. 1814. Price 18 3–4 Cents. [cover title].
  [1–12] p. engr. on one side only of 12 leaves; illus.; 13 cm.; pr. yellow paper covers. Adv. by Wm. Charles, 1815 in **748.**
  English ed. London: Didier and Tebbett, 1808. MH* (col. illus.).

662 JACK THE PIPER; OR THE PLEASANT PASTIME OF THE FRYAR AND BOY Containing The Witty Adventures betwixt a Fryar and Boy, in relation to his Step-Mother, whom he fairly fitted for her unmerciful cruelty. New-England: Printed for and sold by the Booksellers. Price Nine-pence. 1808.

t.[1], [2–3], 4–23 p.; t.[1], 15 cm.
See also THE FRIAR AND BOY, no. **425** and THE PLEASANT HISTORY OF THE FRIAR AND BOY, no. **1015.**
MWA-W*.

663.1 JACKY DANDY'S DELIGHT. New-York: adv. by Hugh-Gaine, 1786 in *Corderii Colloquiorum.*

663.2 JACKY DANDY'S DELIGHT: Or The History Of Birds And Beasts. In Verse And Prose. Adorned With A Variety Of Cuts. [4 lines of verse.] The First Worcester Edition. Printed at Worcester, Massachusetts, By Isaiah Thomas. Sold at his Bookstore. MDCCLXXXVIII.
  fr.[2], t.[3], [4–5], 6–30 p.; illus.; 10.5 cm.; gold Dutch paper covers.
  English & Scottish ed. London: John Marshall and Co. [1 address] [*ca.* 1783].
  MWA* (emb. st. t.[3]); NjP (3 leaves missing); PP (covers & fr.[2] wanting); Evans 21174.

663.3 ———— Hartford: Printed by Nathaniel Patten. D,DCC,LXXX,IX [*sic. i.e.* M,DCC,-LXXX,IX].
  t.[3], [4–5], 6–29 p.; illus.; 10 cm.
  MWA-W* (fr.[2], last leaf ? & covers wanting).

663.4 ———— Boston: Printed and sold by Samuel Hall, No. 53 Cornhill. 1791.
  fr.[2], t.[3], [4–5], 6–30 p.; illus.; 10.5 cm.
  DLC* (p.[31] & rear cover wanting; fr.[2] mut.) p.; Evans 46199.

663.5 ———— Boston: Printed and sold by Samuel Hall, No. 53, Cornhill. 1794.
  fr.[2], t.[3], [4–5], 6–30, [31, adv. list of books] p.; illus.; 10 cm.; green Dutch paper covers; p.[1] recto of front. pasted to front Dutch paper cover has "M" / M printed on it; advertisement caption p.[31] same as in no. **408.4.** CLU*.

663.6 ———— The Second Worcester Edition. Printed at Worcester, Massachusetts, By Isaiah

Thomas. And Sold Wholesale and Retail at his Bookstore. MDCCXCIV.

> fr.[2], t.[3], [4–5], 6–30 p., illus.; 10.5 cm.; gold Dutch paper covers.
> MWA*; Evans 27160.

663.7 ——— Hudson, N.Y.: adv. by A. Stoddard, 1794 in **1220.1.**

663.8 ——— Newfield [Conn.]: Printed and Sold by Beach and Jones. 1795.

> t.[3], [4–8], 9–28 p.; illus., 9.5 cm.
> CtHi* (fr.[2], p. 29? & covers wanting; t.[3], & p. [5–6] mut.; p. no. torn off p. [6–8], 27–28); Evans 28893.

663.9 ——— Boston: Printed and sold by S. Hall, No. 53, Cornhill. 1798.

> fr.[2], t.[3], [4, alphabet–5], 6–30, [31, adv. list of books] p.; illus.; 10.5 cm.; pr. & illus. buff paper covers.
> Cover title: Parrot and Owl. [cut]. The covers are illustrated with two cuts used by S. Hall, 1797 in no. **997.** Advertisement caption p. [31] same as in no. **673.13.**
> MWA*; Evans 48484.

663.10 ——— Adorned with Cuts. Printed and sold by Nathaniel Coverly. 1799. Great allowance made to those who purchase by the Gross, or Dozen.

> fr.[ii], t.[1], [2–3], 4–16, 15 [*sic. i.e.* 17] p.; illus.; 10 cm.; yellow paper covers. Pages 13–15 [*sic. i.e.* 17] have the same five nursery rhymes discussed in no. **676.**
> MWA*; CtY (fr.[ii] & p. 15 [*sic.* 17] wanting; yellow paper covers); Evans 35659.

663.11 ——— Adorned With Cuts. [4 lines of verse] The Third Hudson Edition. Hudson [N.Y.]: Printed by Ashbel Stoddard, at the White House, corner of Warren and Third Streets. 1805.

> fr.[2], t.[3], [4–5], 6–29, p. [26]–29, Little Red Riding Hood, [30–31 adv. list of books] p.; illus.; 11 cm.; illus, blue paper covers.
> MWA-W* (fr.[2] and front cover wanting); NB (blue-green Dutch paper covers).

663.12 ——— With A Variety Of Cuts. [4 lines of verse] Worcester: Printed by I. Thomas, Jun. Sold Wholesale and Retail at his Bookstore. 1805.

fr.[2], t.[3], [4–5], 6–30, [31, illus.] p.; illus.; 10.5 cm.; redish-orange paper covers.
MWA*; CtHi; Shaw 8689.

JAMES & MARY. A Poem. *See* Watkins, Lucy, no. **1404.**

JAMES MANNERS, LITTLE JOHN, AND THEIR DOG BLUFF. *See* Helme, Elizabeth, no. **499.**

664 JANE LUCY BEN. [caption title p. [1]]. Published For The Hartford Evangelical Tract Society. March, 1818. 5000 [colophon p. 12].

> t.[1], 2–12 p.; 16.5 cm.; grey paper covers.
> CtHi*; MWA; Shaw 44454.

JANEWAY, JAMES 1636?–1674
665.1 —A TOKEN FOR CHILDREN. Being An Exact Account of the Conversion, Holy and Exemplary Lives and Joyful Deaths of several Young Children. By James Janeway, Minister of the Gospel. To which is Added, A Token for the Children of New England. Or, Some Examples of Children, in whom the Fear of God was Remarkably Budding before they Died; In several Parts of New England. Preserved and Published for the Encouragement of Piety in other Children. Boston in N.E. Printed for Nicholas Boone, at his Shop over against the Old-Meeting-House. 1700.

> 1st t.[i], [ii—xii], 1–53, [54, bl.]; 2nd t.[55], [56–60], 61–131, [132, bl.], 3rd t.[1], [2], 3–36 p.; 14 cm.; p. 27 in 3rd vol. is printed "72".
> Second title: A Token For Children. The Second Part. Being A farther Account of the Conversion, Holy and Exemplary Lives, and Joyful Deaths, of several other Young Children, not Published in The First Part. By James Janeway. Minister of the Gospel. Psal. 8. 2.[2 lines quot.] Boston, in N.E. Re-printed by T. Green, for Benjamin Eliot. 1700.
> Third title: A Token, for the Children of New-England. Or, Some Examples of Children, In whom the fear of God was Remarkably Budding, before they Dyed, In Several Parts of New-England. Preserved and Published, for the Encouragement of Piety in other Children. And, Added as Supplement, unto the Excellent Janewayes Token for Children. Upon the Re-printing of it, in this Country. Boston, in N.E. Printed by Timothy Green, for Benjamin Eliot, at his Shop, under the West-End of the Town

House. 1700. P. 27 in his part is printed "72."
English ed. pt. 1, 1671; pt. 2, 1672.
MWA* (rebound); CtHi (p.[v–viii], 35–48, ½
of 61–62, 1–36 at end wanting; p. 29–30 mut.;
bound in original leather); Evans 914.

665.2 —⸺ [same as 1st title, **665.1**] Boston in New-England. Printed for T. Hancock, at
the Bible and Three Crowns near the Town-Dock.
1728.
   t.[i], [ii–iii], iv–xii, 1–117 p.; [A]₄, B–K₆, L₅
with L₆ possibly a blank leaf; 14 cm.
MB*; Evans 3042 with imprint: Boston: 1728.

665.3 —⸺ Boston in New-England Printed
for John Phillips, at the Stationers Arms against
the South side of the Town House. 1728.
   t.[i], [ii–v], vi–xii, 1–117 p.; [A]₄, B–K₆, L₅
with L₆ possibly blank leaf pasted to the inside
of the rear cover; 14 cm.; bound in leather. The
entire book has the identical type setting as no.
665.2 except for the last three lines of the imprint.
MWA* (t.[i] wanting); Evans 39885.

665.4 —⸺ With New Additions. Boston,
Printed: Philadelphia, Reprinted, and sold by B.
Franklin, and D. Hall, MDCCXLIV.
   t.[i], [ii–iii], iv–xii, 1–108 p.; 13 cm.; bound in
leather.
MB* (p. 3–10, 31–34 wanting, t.[i] mut.);
PHi; PP (p. xi–xii mut.); Evans 6339.

665.5 —⸺ Children . . . Boston, Printed
and sold by S. Kneeland. 1752.
   1 p. 1., x, 33 p. 2 leaves, 46, ii, 384 p.; 14 cm.
Evans 40618.

665.6 —⸺ With New Additions. Boston:
Printed and Sold by John Boyles, next Door to the
Three Doves in Marlborough-Street. 1771.
   t.[1], [2], 3–156 p.; 16.5 cm.; bound in leather.
Welch*; MB (per. st. on t.[1]); MWA (re-
bound); Evans 12086.

665.7 —⸺ Boston, in New-England:
Printed and Sold by Thomas and John Fleet, at
the Heart & Crown in Cornhill, 1771.
   1st t.[i], [ii–iv], i–vi, 1–31, [32], 2nd t.[i],
[ii–iv], 1–43, [44, bl.], [1], 2–42 p.; 15.5 cm.;
bound in leather.
Second title: A Token For Children. The Second Part. Being A Farther Account of the Con-

version, Holy and Exemplary Lives, and Joyful
Deaths of several Young Children, not published in the First Part. By James Janeway, Minister of the Gospel. [2 lines quot.] Boston, in
New-England: Printed And Sold by Thomas
and John Fleet, at the Heart & Crown in Cornhill, 1771.
MWA* (2nd part, p. 7–10 mut.); PHi; Evans
12087.

665.8 —⸺ Boston: Printed and Sold by Z.
Fowle, in Back-Street, near the Mill-Bridge. 1771.
   t.[1], [2], 3–156 p.; 17.5 cm. Part of a pub-
lisher's remainder. All copies examined are re-
bound.
MWA* (p. 101–104 wanting); CSmH; CtHi;
DLC (i. st. on t.[1]); ICU; MB; MBAt; MHi;
MiU; MSaE; N; NHi (unbound sheets); NN;
NRU; PHi; PP; OCIW-LS; RPJCB; Evans
12085; Sabin 35754.

665.9 —⸺ several Young Children. In
Two Parts. By James Janeway, Minister Of The
Gospel. [3 lines quot.] Burlington [N.J.], Reprinted by Isaac Collins, MDCCLXXII.
   t.[i], [ii–iv], [1], 2–24, [i–iv], [1], 2–44 p.;
16 cm.; bound in buff paper over bds., leather
spine.
MWA* (p. 3–10, sig. D or p. 25–36 wanting);
PHi; Evans 42350.

665.10 —⸺ Boston: adv. by T. & J. Fleet,
1773 in **1408.3**.

665.11 —⸺ [same as 1st title of **665.1**] Encouragement of Piety in other Children. With New
Additions. Boston, in New-England: Printed and
sold by Thomas and John Fleet, at the Bible and
Heart, in Cornhill. 1781.
   t.[i], [ii–iii], i–v, 1–26, [i–ii], 1–37, [i], 1–38
p.; 16.5 cm.; bound in blue paper over w bds.,
leather spine.
Welch*; CLU; MH; MWA; N; PP; PU; Evans
43985.

665.12 —⸺ [same as **665.9**] [2 lines quot.]
Luke x. 14. Philadelphia: Printed And Sold By
R. Aitken, At Pope's Head, Three Doors Above
The Coffee House, Market Street. M.DCC.LXXXI.
   t.[i], [ii–iii], iv–xiii, [xiv], [15], 16–49, [50]; 2nd
t.[i], [lii–liii], liv–lv, [lvi], [57], 58–102, [103–
105, adv. of books] p.; 12.5 cm.

Second title: p. [li]: ———— Children. Being A farther Account ———— [same as **665.7**] of several other Young Children, ———— First Part. The Second Part. By James Janeway, ————Philadelphia: Printed ———— [same as t.[1]]. DeWint*; NN (1st t.[i] & p. [ii] wanting; bound in leather); PP; Evans 17196; Sabin 35754.

665.13 ———— several young Children. In Two Parts. By James Janeway, Minister Of The Gospel. [2 lines quot.] London, Printed: New-York, Reprinted by W. Ross, No. 33, Broad-street. M.DCC.LXXXVI.
t.[i], [ii–iii], iii [*sic. i.e.* iv], [i], ii–v, [vi, bl.], [i], 2–50 p.; 16.5 cm.; gray paper covers.
MWA*; CtHi (Dutch paper covers); CtY; MWelC; Evans 19734.

665.14 ———— New-York: Reprinted by W. Ross, For Lewis Nicholas, No. 90, Williams-street. 1786.
Evans 19734 (no copy located, probably a ghost; E. A. I. reproduces no. **665.13** for this Evans number).

665.15 ———— By James Janeway, Minister Of The Gospel. To which is added some choice Sayings of Dying Saints. [2 lines quot.] Philadelphia: Printed And Sold By R. Aitken & Son, Market Street, No. 22. M.DCC.XCI.
t.[1], [2–3], 4–127 p.; 13 cm.; bound in leather. Page number "37" and the "6" of page number "64" not struck.
MWA*; PHi.

665.16 ——— Boston: adv. by Samuel Hall, 1793 in **501.2**.

665.17 ——— [same as first title of **665.1**] Printed at Worcester, Massachusetts, By James R. Hutchins, For Nathaniel Ely, Jun. Of Longmeadow. MDCCXCV.
t.[1], [2–3], 4–187 p.; 13.5 cm.; bound in blue paper over bds., leather spine.
Welch* (p. 185–187 mut. but not affecting text); CtHi (p. 142–187 wanting); CtY (p. 187 ½ wanting, p.[1]–10 mut.); DLC; IU; MH; MWA; Evans 33931.

665.18 ———— Printed at Worcester, Massachusetts, For I. Thomas, By James R. Hutchins. 1795.

t.[1], [2–3], 4–187 p.; 13.5 cm.; bound in marbled paper over bds., leather spine.
MWA*; CLU; CtHi (p. 142–187 wanting); MH; NN (bound in yellow paper over w. bds.); PP (bound in leather); Evans 28895; Sabin 35754 and 46555.

665.19 ———— Of Several Young Children. In Two Parts. By The Reverend James Janeway. [3 lines quot.] Elizabeth-Town [N.J.]: Printed by Shepard Kollock, for Cornelius Davis, No. 94, Water-Street, New-York, M,DCC,XCVII.
1st t.[i], [ii, bl.], [i], ii–iii, [iv, bl.], [i], ii–ix, [x, bl.], [1], 2–38; ½ t.[39], [40–45], 46–90 p.; 13.5 cm.; bound in brown paper speckled with black over w. bds. Half title: A Token for Children: Part Second. By The Reverend James Janeway. [3 lines of quot.].
Welch*; MWA; Evans 32315.

665.20 ———— Northampton [Mass.]: Printed For Simeon Butler. 1799.
t.[i], [ii], iii–iv, [i], ii–viii, [1], 2–114 p.; 14 cm.; bound in white paper speckled with brown and green over w. bds., leather spine. Pages 97–144 have Watts' *Divine Songs For Children.*
MWA-W; MH; NB; PPL; Evans 35662.

665.21 ———— [same as **665.15**] Philadelphia: Printed And Sold By R. Aitken, No. 22, Market Street. 1801.
t.[1], [2–3], 4–143, [144, adv. list of books] p.; 14 cm.; bound in leather.
PP* (p. [1]–4 mut. top of page cut off); PHi.

665.22 ———— Several Young Children. In Two Parts. By The Reverend James Janeway. [2 lines quot.] Boston: Printed For Caleb Bingham, No. 44 Cornhill. 1802.
t.[1], [2–3], 4–56; ½ t.[57], [58–59], 60–108 p.; 14.5 cm.; bound in blue paper over w. bds., leather spine. Half title: A Token For Children: Part Second. By The Reverend James Janeway. [2] lines quot.].
MWA*; NN; Shaw 2460.

665.23 ———— James Janeway, Minister Of The Gospel. [2 lines of quot.] Luke X. 14. Stanford (State Of New-York) Printed By Daniel Lawrence, For Henry & John F. Hall. M.DCCC.-III.
fr.[ii], t.[i], [ii], iii–x, 11–101 p.; front. only

illus.; 13 cm.; bound in marbled paper over w. bds.

CtHi; Shaw 4444.

665.24 —⸺— By The Rev. James Janeway. With An Appendix, Containing Additional Lives. [2 lines of quot.] Boston: Published By Caleb Bingham, No. 44, Cornhill. 1804. E. Lincoln, Printer.

    1st t.[1], [2–3], 4–48; ½ t.[49], [50–51], 52–107 p.; 14.5 cm.; bound in paper over w. bds., leather spine. Half title same as no. **665.22**. Welch°; CtHi; MWA; NNC-T (emb. st. on t.[1]); Shaw 6546.

665.25 —⸺— Reverend James Janeway. [2 lines quot.] Charlestown [Mass.]: Printed By Samuel Etheridge, Sold By Him At The Washington Head Bookstore. 1804.

    t.[1], [2–3], 4–108 p.; 14.5 cm.
    MB° (per. st. on t.p.); Shaw 6547.

665.26 —⸺— [same as **665.13**] of the Gospel. To Which Is Added Some Choice Sayings of Dying Saints, [2 line quot.] Philadelphia: From The Press Of The Late R. Aitken, Printed By Jane Aitken, No. 62, North Third Street. 1806.

    t.[1], [2–3], 4–143 p.; 14 cm.; bound in blue marbled paper over bds., leather spine.
    MWA-W°; P; PP; Shaw 10626.

665.27 —⸺— [3 lines quot.] Newark, N. J. Printed By John Austin Crane. 1807.

    t.[1], [2–3], 4–80 p.; 14.5 cm.; bound in marbled paper over bds., leather spine.
    CtHi° (p. 5–6 mut.); MH.

665.28 —⸺— Gospel. [3 lines quot.] Philadelphia: Printed by J. Adams, For Benjamin And Thomas Kite, No. 20, North Third-Street. 1807.

    t.[i], [ii–iii], iv–vi, [7], 8–104 p.; 14.5 cm.; bound in blue marbled paper over bds.
    MWA°; PP (rebacked); Shaw 12826.

665.29 —⸺— [same as **665.24**] Boston: Printed And Published By Lincoln & Edmands, No. 53 Cornhill. 1811. Price $2.25 a doz. 25 cts. single.

    t.[1], [2–3], 4–105, [106–108, adv. list of books] p.; 15 cm..
    MWA°; Shaw 23106.

665.30 —⸺— Children: (The Only Complete Edition Ever Published.) In Two Parts. By James Janeway, Minister Of The Gospel. To Which is added, A Third Part: Containing Some Account Of The Life And God's Gracious Dealings With Hephzibah Mathews. Also, The Child's Monitor, By The Rev. John Cooke, Maidenhead. [2 lines quot.] New-York: Published by Samuel Whiting & Co. at their Theological and Classical Bookstore. No. 96, Broadway. J. Seymour, print. 1811.

    fr.[ii], t.[i], [ii–iii], x [*sic. i.e.* iv], v–vii, [viii bl.], [ix], iv [*sic. i.e.* x], xi–xix, [xx, bl.], [21], 22–67, [68, bl.]; 1st ½ t.[69], [70, bl.], 72–137, [138, bl.]; and 2nd ½ title [139], [140, bl.], [141], 142–236; 2nd t.[237], [238, bl.], [239], [240–250]; 3rd t.[251] p.; 14 cm.; bound in leather; front. signed *Scoles sculp.* First half title: A Token For Children. In Two Parts. By James Janeway. Part The Second. Second half title: A Token For Children. By J. Mathews; Being Intended As A Third Part of The Token For Children Published By the Rev. James Janeway.

Second title: A Child's Monitor; Or The Dying Experience Of Mary Jones, Of North-Town, Near Maidenhead: With Remarks By The Rev. John Cooke. [1 line quot.] New-York: Published By Whiting And Watson.

Third title: —⸺— [same as the 1st title] Cooke. [2 lines quot.] New-York: Published by Whiting & Watson, at their Theological and Classical Book-store, No. 96, Broadway. J. Seymour, print. 1811.

    MWA°; MB; MiU; NN; NNUT; PP; Shaw 23107.

665.31 —⸺— Rev. John Cooke [2 lines quot.] New-York: Published by Whiting & Watson, at their Theological and Classical Book-store, No. 96, Broadway. J. Seymour, print. 1811.

    Same collation, title pages and half titles as preceding. The 1st title page is the same as the 3rd title page. There are only 250 p. in this edition; p. iv and x are correctly printed.
    PP°; KU.

665.32 —⸺— Children; In Two Parts. By James Janeway, Minister Of The Gospel. To which is added, A Third Part; By the Reverend James Mathews. Also, The Child's Monitor; By The Reverend John Cooke. And An Acount Of Mr. John

Rogers. [3 lines quot.] Paris, Kentucky. Printed and Published By J. Lyle. 1814

  1st t.[1], [2–3], 4–139, [140–141]; 2nd or ½ t.[142], [143], 144–261, [262–263]; 3rd t.[264], [265], 266–279, [280–281] p.; 4th t.[282], [283], 284–294 p.; 12.5 cm.

  Second or half title: A Token For Children. By James Mathews; Being Intended As A Third Part Of The Token For Children Published By The Reverend James Janeway.

  Third title: The Child's Monitor, Or The Dying Experience Of Mary Jones, Of North-Town, Near Maidenhead; With Remarks By The Reverend John Cooke. [2 lines quot.] Paris, Kentucky. Printed and Published by J. Lyle.

  Fourth title: An Account Of The Surprising Deliverance Of Mr. John Rodgers, Minister At Crogland, In Cumberland, And The Case Of His Deliverer. Paris, Kentucky. Printed and Published by J. Lyle.

  Shaw 31816.

665.33 —⸻ Children ⸻ [same as **665.1**]; Several Young Children. In Two Parts. By James Janeway, Minister of The Gospel. [5 lines quot.] Paris [Kentucky]: Published By John Lyle. 1814.

  t.[1], [2–3], 4–7, [8, caption 1, pt. I.]; 9–64, 65 [caption 2, pt. II.], 66–139, [140, caption 3], 141–151, [152, caption 4], 153–160 p.; illus.; 13 cm.

  Caption 1: A Token For Children. The First Part.

  Caption 2: Part II.

  Caption 3: An Account Of The Surprising Deliverance Of Mr. John Rodgers, Minister at Croyland, in Cumberland, And The Case Of His Deliverer.

  Caption 4: Examples Of some Eminent Saints, and their exemplary, pious, and holy speeches and sayings, when they were Dying.

  OOxM°.

665.34 —⸻ Children. By James Janeway, Minister Of The Gospel. [3 lines quot.] Bennington, Vt. Published By Joseph Dix. 1815. M. B. Cusack, Printer.

  fr.[ii], [iii], [iv–v], vi–xiv, [23], 24–85 p.; 13.5 cm.; bound in marbled paper over. w. bds., leather spine.

  MWA°; McCorison 1746; Shaw 35008.

665.35 —⸻ James Janeway. [3 lines quot.] Philadelphia: Published And Sold By David Hogan, No. 249, Market Street. 1820. S. Probasco, Printer.

  t.[i], [ii–iii], iv–xv, [xvi, bl.], [17], 18–126, [127–128, contents] p.; 11 cm.; bound in buff paper over bds., leather spine.

  PP.°

A TOKEN FOR CHILDREN. *See* Wesley, John, no. **1423.1**.

JOHN-THE-GIANT-KILLER ESQ, *pseud.*

666 — FOOD FOR THE MIND: Or, A New Riddle-Book, Compiled For The Use Of The Great and the Little Good Boys And Girls, In the United States. By John-The-Giant-Killer, Esq. [2 lines quot.] Homer. [2 lines quot.] Puffendorf. Boston: Printed and sold by S. Hall, No. 53, Cornhill. 1798.

  fr.[ii], t.[iii], [iv], v–vii, 8–63 p.; illus.; 10 cm.; marbled paper covers.

  See also Food For The Mind, no. **415**.

  English ed. London: Listed in *Gentleman's Mag.* Jan. 1757 as by J. Newbery.

  RPB°; Evans 48425.

667 — THE LITTLE RIDDLE-BOOK, Compiled for the Use of the Good Boys and Girls, In England, Scotland, Ireland, & America. By John-The-Giant-Killer, Esq. Boston: Printed and sold by S. Hall, No. 53, Cornhill. 1798.

  fr.[ii], t.[1], 2–29 p.; illus.; 10 cm.

  RPB° (p. 24–29 mut.); Evans 48506.

[JOHNSON, RICHARD] 1573–1659?

668.1 [—] THE MOST ILLUSTRIOUS AND RENOWNED HISTORY OF THE SEVEN CHAMPIONS OF CHRISTENDOM. In Three Parts. Containing the honourable Births, Victories, and notable Atchievements, by Sea and Land, in divers strange Counteries; their Combats with Giants, Monsters, &c. Wonderful! Adventures in Desarts, Wildernesses, inchanted Castles; their Conquests of Empires, Kingdoms; relieving distressed Ladies, with their faithful Loves to them: The Honour they won in Tilts and Tournaments, and Success against the Enemies of Christendom: Also, the Heroic Adventures of St. George's Three Sons. Together, with the manner of their untimely Deaths; and how they came to be stiled Saints, and Champions of Christendom. The Seventeenth Edition. Philadelphia: Printed for Mathew Carey, Bookseller,

Market-street, by Stewart & Cochran, Second-street, M,DCC,XCIV.

fr.[ii], t.[iii], [iv–v], vi, [7], 8–124 p.; front. only illus.; 14 cm.; p. 123–124, adv. list of books.

English unabridged ed. *The most famous history of the seven champions of Christendome.* London: Entered in Stationer's Register in 1596.

English & Scottish abridged ed. or chapbook version, title 1: *The Illustrious and Renowned History Of The Seven Famous Champions Of Christendom.* London: For T. Norris, A. Bettesworth. 1719.

English abr. ed. title 2: *The History and Gallant Achievements of the Seven Champions of Christendom.* London: Didier & Tebbett, 1809. (Clipping from a bookseller's catalogue, copy lacking cover title imprint. Possibly the above 1809 ed.)

English chapbook ed. title 3: *The History Of The Seven Champions Of Christendom.* London.

English chapbook ed. title 4: *The Renowned History of* ———. London: Tho. Norris [1725?].

English abridged ed. title 5: *The Seven Champions of Christendom.* London: Printed for the Booksellers. 1816.

English abridged ed. title 6: *The Surprising Adventures Of the* ———. London: Dean & Munday [1810?].

English abridged ed. title 7: *The Whole History Of The* ———. Manchester: A. Swindells. MWA° (i. st. on p. v.); Evans 27686.

668.2 [—] ——— Containing their honorable Birth, Victories, and notable Atchievements, by Sea and Land, in diverse strange Counteries; their Combats with Giants and Monsters; wonderful Adventures, Fortunes and Misfortunes, in Desarts, Wildernesses, inchanted Castles; their Conquests of Empires, Kingdoms; their relieving distressed Ladies, with their faithful Love to them; Honor they won in Tilts and Tournaments; and Success against the enemies of Christendom. With the Manner of their untimely Deaths; and how they came to be styled Saints and Champions of Christendom. Also, The Heroic Adventures of St. George's three Sons. Amherst, Newhampshire: Printed By Samuel Preston. 1799.

t.[1], [2–5], 6–120 p.; 17 cm.

MWA°; PP (bound in blue paper over w. bds., leather spine); Evans 36291.

668.3 [—] History Of The Seven Champions Of Christendom. New Edition, Carefully Revised And Corrected. Boston: Printed By Hosea Sprague, No. 88, Newbury-Street. 1804.

fr.[2], t.[3], [4–5], 6–128 p.; front. only illus.; 11 cm.; bound in pink and green Dutch paper over w. bds.

MH° (fr.[2] slightly mut.); Shaw 6481.

668.4 [—] ——— [same as **668.1**] St. George's three Sons. Together — with the manner of their untimely Deaths: & how they came to be stiled Saints and Champions of Christendom. The Eighteenth Edition. Wilmington [Del.]: Printed and Sold by Bonsal and Niles — Also Sold at their Bookstore—Market-Street, Baltimore. 1804.

t.[i], [ii–iii], iv, [5], 6–143 p.; 13.5 cm.; bound in gray paper over w. bds.

PP°.

[JOHNSON, RICHARD] 1734–1793

669.1 [—] THE BLOSSOMS OF MORALITY: Intended For The Amusement and Instruction of Young Ladies and Gentlemen. By The Editor Of The Looking-Glass For The Mind. First American Edition. 1795. Philadelphia: Printed by and for William W. Woodward, No. 36, Chesnut Street, on the south side, Franklin's Head, (green sign).

½t.[i], [ii], t.[iii], [iv–viii], [1], 2–212, [213–215 adv.] p.; 16.5 cm.; bound in leather. Half title p. [i]: Blossoms Of Morality.

The editor of this book has been variously ascribed as the Rev. Mr. Cooper, W. D. Cooper, J. Cooper, and the Rev. Charles Cooper. The actual editor appears to have been Richard Johnson, a hack writer who worked for E. Newbery in London.

Entered in Richard Johnson's day book: "*1788 Dec. Mr. Badcock* [E. Newbery's agent]—*to writing The Blossoms of Morality—L 16. 16s.* < *Received 1789 Feb. 4.* >" (Weedon 1949 13).

English and Irish ed. London: E. Newbery, 1789.

MWA°; CtY (½t.[i], p. 213–215 wanting); ICU; NN; PP; Vi; Evans 47468.

669.2 [—] ———— Second American Edition. Wilmington [Del.]: Printed by Joseph Johnson & Co. No. 73, Market-Street. 1796.

t.[1], [2–5], 6–184 p.; 17 cm.; bound in leather. MWA°; CSmH; DeWi (per. st. on t.[1], t.[1] mut.); NN; NNC-LS; PMA; PP; Evans 30277.

669.3 [—] ———— Woodward's Second Edition. Philadelphia: Printed By And For William W. Woodward, No. 17, Chesnut Street. 1798.

t.[1], [2–9], 10–240 p.; 17 cm.; bound in leather. The "2" of p. 238 is not struck; p. [237]–240 a list of subscribers. Welch°; ICU; MWA; PHi; PU; RPJCB (p. 7–10 torn in half, front cover worn); Evans 33568.

669.4 [—] Youth's Library. Vol. II. The Blossoms of Morality ———— With Fifty-One Wood Cuts. New-York [in a vignette] Printed and Published By David Longworth, At the Shakspeare Gallery. MDCCC.

t.[i], [ii], [1–7], 8–258 p.; illus.; 18 cm.; woodcut illus. by A. Anderson; tailpiece p. 258 is signed *A. Anderson Fecit.*
MWA°; MNBedf; NHi; NjP (rebound, upper half of t.[1] wanting); NN; RPJCB; Evans 37248; Hamilton 212.

669.5 [—] ———— same as **669.4** but does not have "Youth's Library Vol. II."] New-York [in a vignette] Printed And Published By David Longworth, At The Shakspeare Gallery. 1802.

t.[i], [ii], [1–7], 8–258 p.; illus.; 18 cm.; bound in leather; woodcut illus. by A. Anderson; tailpiece p. 258 is signed *A. Anderson Fecit.*
MWA-W°; NN; Shaw 1866.

669.6 [—] ———— With Engravings on Wood, By Anderson. New-York: Published By Evert Duyckinck, Bookseller & Stationer. M'Farlane and Long, printers. 1807.

t.[i], [ii, bl.], [iii–iv, adv. or preface], [v, contents], [vi, bl.], [1], 2–196 p.; illus.; 17.5 cm.; bound in leather.
MWA-W°; DLC (i. st. on t.[1]); PP; Shaw 12111 and 12345.

669.7 [—] ———— With Fifty-One Engravings On Wood. Philadelphia: Printed By Thomas And William Bradford, Booksellers And Stationers, No. 8, South Front Street. 1810.

t.[i], [ii, bl.], [iii–iv, adv. or preface], [1, con-

tents], [2–3], 4–199 p.; illus.; 16 cm.; bound in leather.
MWA°; DLC (3 copies); NRU; PP; PPL; PU (p.[iii–iv] [1] are bound after p. 199, having p.[200, bl.], [201–202, adv. or preface], [203, contents]); Shaw 19507 and 19854.

670.1 [—] THE ENTERTAINING TRAVELLER. Philadelphia: adv. by Francis Bailey, 1793 in **773.1.**

670.2 [—] ———— Philadelphia: adv. by John Adams, 1806 in **646.3.**

670.3 [—] THE ENTERTAINING TRAVELLER: Giving A Brief Account Of The Voyages And Travels Of Master Tommy Columbus, In Search of the Island Of Wisdom; With A Description Of That Island: As Also of The Rock of Curiosity, the Court of Ambition, the Field of Luxury, and the Desert of Famine. Philadelphia: Printed For B. & T. Kite. 1807.

t.[3], [4–5], 6–61 p.; illus.; 10.5 cm.; buff paper covers; p. 60–61 adv. list of 28 books pr. & sold by Adams' Printing-Office. Entered in Richard Johnson's day book: "*1780 Oct. 2—Delivered to Do* [Mrs. Newbery] *Journey to the Island of Wisdom. £ 2.2s.*" (Weedon 1949 22).
English ed. London: E. Newbery, n.d.
DLC° (i. st. p. [4]).

671.1 [—] FALSE ALARMS; Or, The Mischievous Doctrine Of Ghosts And Apparitions, Of Spectres And Hobgoblins, Exploded. Philadelphia: Printed for Benjamin Johnson No. 31 High-Street, And Jacob Johnson No. 147 High-Street. 1802.

fr.[ii], t.[1], [2–3], 4–31 p.; front. only illus.; 12.5 cm. pink and gray marbled paper covers. Front. signed *J. Akin del. & Sculp.*
Entered in Richard Johnson's day book: "*1787 June 15, Mr. Badcock* [E. Newbery's Agent]— *To Writing False Alarms—£ 3.3s.*" (Weedon 1949 24).
English ed. London: E. Newbery, 1799.
NjP°; MWA (fr.[ii] wanting); OOxM; PP (fr.[ii] wanting); Hamilton 203; Shaw 2211.

671.2 [—] ———— Keene, N. H. Printed By John Prentiss, And Sold At His Book-Store. 1809.

t.[1], [2–3], 4–64 p.; 10.5 cm.; blue paper covers.
MWA°; CtHi (p. 57–64 mut.); Shaw 17475.

672.1 [—] THE FOUNDLING; OR, THE HISTORY OF LUCIUS STANHOPE. Philadelphia: adv. by Francis Bailey, 1793 in **773.1**.

672.2 [—] THE FOUNDLING; OR THE HISTORY OF LUCIUS STANHOPE. Embellished with Cuts. Boston: Printed and sold by John Folsom, No. 30, Union-Street. 1798.

> fr.[2], t.[3], [4–5], 6–27, [28, alphabet], [29–30, adv. list of books], [31, illus.] p.; illus.; 10 cm.; illus.; paper covers.
> Entered in Johnson's day book: "*1787 July. Mr. Babcock* [E. Newbery's agent.]—*To Writing The Hermit of the Forest— — — — The Foundling* —} £ *2.2s.*" (Weedon 1949 27).
> English ed. London: E. Newbery, 1787.
> MHi° (p. [29–31] mut.); MWA (fr.[2], & covers wanting); Evans 33750.

672.3 [—] ——— Lucius Stanhope. By Edward Ledly, Gent. Printed At Rutland [Vt.]. 1799.

> t.[1], [2–3], 4–30, [31] p.; no illus.; 12.5 cm. The author's name, Edward Ledly, Gent., is fictitious.
> PP° (p. 17–18 and most of [31] wanting, p. 29–30 mut., rebound); McCorison 533; Evans 35732.

672.4 [—] ——— Lucius Stanhope. Embellished With Cuts. Exeter [N.H.]: Printed and Sold by H. Ranlet. 1802.

> fr.[2], t.[3], [4–5], 6–31 p.; illus.; 10 cm.; illus. buff paper covers. Adv. by Henry Ranlet, 1801 in **558.2**.
> MWA°; MSaE (bookplate tipped in at top of t.[3]); Shaw 2243.

672.5 [—] ——— Exeter [N.H.]: adv. by Norris & Sawyer, 1808 in **428.3**.

673.1 [—] THE HERMIT OF THE FOREST, And The Wandering Infants. A Rural Fragment. Embellished with Cuts. Boston: Printed and sold by Samuel Hall, No 53, Cornhill. [1789?].

> fr.[2], t.[3], [4], 5–29, [30–31, adv. list of books] p.; illus.; 10 cm.; illus. buff paper covers printed in red ink. The advertisement caption p. [30]: BOOKS *sold by* S. HALL. Only four 10 cm. books are known printed by S. Hall prior to 1790. *Cock Robin*, no. 213.2, is only a fragment and lacks all before p. 5 and after p. 26. The other 3 are undated. *Little Stories For Little*

Folks, By Dorothy Kilner, no. **729.1**, has a holograph date *1787* or *1789* and is dated [1789?] with the caption on p.[37]: BOOKS *sold by* S. HALL, *in Boston. The History Of Master Jacky And Miss Harriot* can also be dated [1789?]. Its caption p. 31 reads: BOOKS *sold by* S. *Hall, in Cornhill,* BOSTON. From 1790 on, the advertisement caption usually consists of six or more lines instead of one or two, and usually starts *A great Variety . . . See* I. Watts' *Divine And Moral Songs. Boston:* S. *Hall, 1790, no.* **1406.3,** and Henry Fielding's *The Remarkable History Of Tom Jones. Boston:* S. *Hall. 1791, no.* **408.3.** The above edition of *The Hermit Of The Forest* is dated [1789?] because the advertisement caption resembles those found in S. Hall publications printed prior to 1790.
> Entered in Richard Johnson's account book "*1787 July. Mr. Babcock* [E. Newbery's agent] —*To writing The Hermit of the Forest— . . .*" (Weedon 1949 29).
> English and Scottish ed. London: E. Newbery, 1788.
> MWA°; Evans 21884.

673.2 [—] ——— New-York: Printed by William Durell, No. 19, Queen-street. [1791?].

> fr.[2], t.[3], [4–5], 6–28, [29], [30, bl.], [31–32, adv. list of books] p.; illus.; 10 cm.; Dutch paper covers; there is a hole on p. [29] where the page number would be expected to be. Adv. by William Durell, 1790 in **612.5**. The firm of William Durell was at 19 Queen-Street in 1786–1789 and 1791–1793. In 1790 it was at 196 Queen-Street (Evans 22863) and the number 198 on the same street was also used (Evans 22792). Two numbers on Queen-Street appear in Durell's publications in 1791, 198 (Evans 23135, 23213, 23438) and the usual 19. The alphabets p. [4] and all the pages except pages 15, 17, 18, 23, 26 have a similar type setting to the 1792 edition, no. **673.4**. Different decorative bars of printer's ornaments occur in both books. Four printers ornaments are present. The word "the", the last word on page 9, is printed correctly, but the "4" of page number "14" is printed lower than the "1". Because of the similarity of the type setting of most of the pages and especially the alphabets on p. [4] to no. **673.4**, the book is believed to have been printed in [1791?].
> NjR°; MWA-W (p. 29 numbered).

673.3 [—] ——— Embellished With Cuts. Boston: Printed and sold by Samuel Hall, No. 53, Cornhill. 1792.

fr.[2], t.[3], [4], 5–29, [30–31, adv. list of books] p.; illus.; 10.5 cm.; green Dutch paper covers. Advertisement caption p.[30]: *A great Variety of* BOOKS,/*for Children, to be sold by* S. HALL,/*in Cornhill, Boston; among which are/ the following, viz.*

MWA*; PP (p. 31 and rear cover wanting); Evans 46474.

673.4 [—] ——— New-York: Printed By William Durll [*sic. i.e.* Durell] No. 19, Queenstreet [*sic. i.e.* Queen-Street]. M,DCC,XCII.

fr.[2], t.[3], [4–5], 6–29 p.; illus.; 10 cm.; brown Dutch paper covers. At the top and bottom of p.[4] there are a thick and two thin rules. Four printers ornaments are present. The "e" of the last word "th$_e$", p. 9, is lower than the rest of the word. The page number 14 is correctly printed.

CtHi (rear cover wanting); CtY; MWA (fr.[2] wanting); NjP (front Dutch paper cover and fr.[2] mut.); Evans 46475; Hamilton 138.

673.5 [—] ——— Fragment. Adorned with Cut. —New-York:— Printed By William Durell, No. 19, Queen-Street. 1793.

fr.[2], t.[3], [4–5], 6–29, [30] p.; illus.; 10 cm.; green Dutch paper covers.

MiD (fr.[2], & front cover wanting); Evans 46789.

673.6 [—] ——— Philadelphia: adv. by Francis Bailey, 1793 in **773.1.**

673.7 [—] ——— Embellished With Cuts. Philadelphia: Printed by Benjamin Johnson, in Market-Street, the eighth door below Fourth-Street. 1793.

fr.[2], t.[3], [4], 5–31 p.; illus.; 9.5 cm.; paper covers.

Welch*, MWA; Evans 46790.

673.8 [—] ——— Boston: Printed and sold by Samuel Hall, No. 53, Cornhill. 1794.

fr.[2], t.[3], [4], 5–29, [30–31, adv. list of books] p.; illus.; 10 cm.; Dutch paper covers. On p. 5 three printer's ornaments are present composing a decorative bar. On the recto of fr.[2] two large capital letters "$^{\text{M}}_{\text{M}}$" are present.

Advertisement caption p.[30]: *A great Variety of* BOOKS,/*designed for the Instruction and Amusement,/and suited to Children of all Ages and/Capacities, are constantly kept for Sale/by* S. Hall, *No. 53, Cornhill, Boston;/among which are the following, viz.*

MWA-W*; MSaE; PP (p. [31] mut.); Evans 47084.

673.9 [—] ——— Hudson, N.Y.: adv. by Ashbel Stoddard, 1794 in **1220.1.**

673.10 [—] ——— Boston: adv. by Samuel Hall, 1795 in **1384.3.**

673.11 [—] ——— Philadelphia: Printed By Budd & Bartram. 1796.

fr.[2], t.[3], [4], 5–31 p.; illus.; 10 cm.; ornamental paper covers.

PP*; Evans 47818.

673.12 [—] ——— Boston: adv. By John W. Folsom, 1798 in **672.1.**

673.13 [—] ——— Boston: Printed and sold by S. Hall, No. 53, Cornhill. 1798.

fr.[2], t.[3], [4–5], 6–29 [30–31, adv. list of books] p.; illus.; 10 cm.; brown and green Dutch paper covers. Advertisement caption p.[30]: *A great Variety of* BOOKS,/*designed for Instruction and Amusement,/ and suited to Children of all/Ages and Capacities, are constantly/kept for Sale by* S. Hall, *No. 53,/Cornhill, Boston; among which are/the following viz.*

MWA*; PP (blue marbled paper covers); Evans 48487.

673.14 [—] ——— Charleston [Mass.]: Printed and Sold by J. Lamson, at his Office near the Bridge, wholesale and retail. 1798.

fr.[2], t.[3], [4–5], 6–31 p.; illus.; 10 cm.; illus. blue paper covers.

MWA*; MB (fr.[2], mut.); Evans 48488.

673.15 [—] ——— Infants, A Rural Fragment. New-York: Printed by W. Durell, For Evert Duyckinck. 1800.

fr.[2], t.[3], [4–5], 6–30, [31, illus.] p.; illus.; 10 cm.; illus. blue-gray paper covers.

MWA-T*.

673.16 [—] ——— New-York: Printed by W. Durell, For John Harrison. 1800.

fr.[2], t.[3], [4–5], 6–30, [31, illus.] p.; illus.; 10 cm.; pink Dutch paper covers.

MWA° (fr.[2] & p.[31] mut.); Evans 37610.

673.17 [—] ——— New-York: Printed by W. Durell, For Stephen Stephens. 1800.

fr.[2], t.[3], [4–5], 6–30, [31, illus.] p.; illus.; 10 cm.; ornamented paper covers.

OOxM°; MWA; Evans 37611.

673.18 [—] ——— New-York: Printed By William Durell, No. 106 Maiden-Lane. 1801.

fr.[2], t.[3], [4–5], 6–30, [31, illus.] p.; illus.; 10 cm.; orange Dutch paper covers.

MWA-W°.

673.19 [—] ——— Exeter [N.H.]: Printed and sold by Henry Ranlet. 1082 [*sic. i.e.* 1802].

fr.[2], t.[3], [4–5], 6–29, [30, alphabet], [31, illus.] p.; illus.; 10 cm.; illus. paper covers.

Welch° (p. 29–[31] wanting); MWA; PP; Shaw 2398 and 2399.

673.20 [—] ——— Embellished With Cuts. Philadelphia: Published by Jacob Johnson, No. 147, Market Street. 1802.

fr.[2], t.[3], [4], 5–31 p.; illus.; 11 cm.; green paper covers. Part of a large publisher's remainder.

MWA-W°; CLU; CtHi; DLC; NHi; NN; NN-C; OOxM; PHi; PP; Shaw 2399.

673.21 [—] ——— Ornamented with Cuts. A new Edition. Hartford: Printed by Lincoln & Gleason. 1803.

fr.[2], t.[3], [4–5], 6–30, [31, adv. list of books] p.; illus.; 10 cm.; marbled paper covers.

MWA°; Ct (front cover wanting, fr.[2] mut.); CtHi; CtY; MHi (fr.[2], p. 29–[31] wanting, t.[3] and other pages mut.); PP; Shaw 4364.

673.22 [—] ——— Fragment. Hudson [N.Y.], Printed by Ashbel Stoddard, And sold Wholesale and Retail, at his Book-Store. 1804.

fr.[2], t.[3], [4–5], 6–30 [31, adv. list of books] p.; illus.; 10.5 cm.; green Dutch paper covers.

Welch°; MWA; NB; Shaw 6469.

673.23 [—] ——— Ornamented with Cuts. A new Edition. Hartford: Printed by Lincoln & Gleason. 1806.

fr.[2], t.[3], [4–5], 6–30, [31, illus.] p.; illus.; 10 cm.; marbled paper covers.

MWA°; Shaw 10551.

673.24 [—] ——— Embellished With Cuts. Philadelphia: Printed By John Adams. 1806.

fr.[2], t.[3], [4–5], 6–31 p.; illus.; 10 cm.; pr. & illus. blue paper covers; p. 30–31 adv. of 21 books.

Cover title: Toy Book. Philadelphia: Sold by James P. Parke, 1807.

CtHi°.

673.25 [—] ——— Philadelphia: adv. by B. & T. Kite, 1807 in **611.1**.

673.26 [—] ——— Ornamented With Cuts. A new Edition. Litchfield [Conn.]: Printed By Hosmer & Goodwin. 1808.

fr.[2], t.[3], [4–5], 6–30 [31, adv. list of 12 books] p.; illus.; 10 cm.; green Dutch paper covers.

CtHi°; CSmH; Ct. (i. st. on t.[3]; CtY (p. 9–10¾ wanting); fr.[2], p. 29–[31] & covers worm-eaten); Shaw 15219.

673.27 [—] ——— Ornamented with Cuts. A new Edition. Hartford: Printed by Peter B. Gleason & Co. 1811.

fr.[2], t.[3], [4–5], 6–30, [31, adv. list of 7 books] p.; illus.; 10.5 cm.; pr. & illus. buff paper covers.

CtHi°; Shaw 22994.

673.28 [—] ——— Ornamented with Cuts. A New Edition. Hartford: Printed by Hale & Hosmer. 1812.

fr.[2], t.[3], [4–5], 6–30, [31] p.; illus.; 9.5 cm.; pr. & illus. buff paper covers; cover title dated 1813; p. [31]: The Ten Commandments.

MWA-W° (rear cover wanting); CCamarSJ; Ct (i. st. on cover title); CtHi; MB (date torn off imprint, cover title date 1813); MH; Shaw 25637.

673.29 [—] ——— Fragment. Hudson. [N.Y.]: Printed By Ashbel Stoddard, And Sold Wholesale And Retail At His Book-Store. 1812.

fr.[2], t.[3], [4–5], 6–30, [31, adv. list of books] p.; illus.; 11 cm.; illus. blue-gray paper covers.

OClWHi.°.

673.30 [—] ——— Embellished with Cuts. Hartford: Printed by Hale & Hosmer. 1814.

fr.[2], t.[3], [4–5], 6–30, [31] p.; illus.; 10 cm.; pr. & illus. green paper covers; p. [31]: The Ten Commandments; copy 1.

Cover title, copy 1: The Hermit of the Forest ——— Infants. Hartford: Printed by Hale & Hosmer. 1814.

Cover title, copy 2: Fire-Side Amusement, Or A New Collection Of Choice Riddles. Hartford: Printed By Hale & Hosmer. 1814. *See* no. **1082.3** for the book to which this cover title belongs.

MWA-W°; CtHi; MWA; NNC-LS; Shaw 31698.

673.31 [—] ——— Hartford: Printed by Sheldon & Goodwin. < Stereotyped by J. F. & C. Starr. > [1815].

fr.[2], t.[3], [4–5], 6–30, [31, adv. list of books] p.; illus.; 10 cm.; pr. & illus. buff paper covers. Rear cover has two cuts. J. F. & C. Starr are known to have been in Hartford in 1815 and 1818. Sheldon and Goodwin were a firm in Hartford from Nov. 1, 1814–Oct. 23, 1815. (MWA cat.).

MWA-W°; NHi; OOxM; PP (browned copy); Shaw 34893.

673.32 [—] ——— Hartford: Printed by Sheldon & Goodwin. < Stereotyped by J. F. & C. Starr. > [*ca.* 1815] Variant of no. **673.31** differing by having an illus. on. p. [31] instead of adv. list of books. Rear cover has same illus. as fr.[2].

CtHi°; NPV.

673.33 [—] ——— Hartford: Printed for J. & W. Russell. < Stereotyped by J. F. & C. Starr. > [1818?].

fr.[2], t.[3], [4–6], 7–30, [31, illus.] p.; illus.; 10 cm.; pr. & illus. brick-red paper covers. Cover title: The Death And Burial, Of Cock Robin. Hartford, Stereotyped Edition. *See* no. **563.16** for note on printers.

CtHi°; MWA-T (tr.[2], p. 24–[31] wanting).

673.34 [—] ——— Infants. Cooperstown [N.Y.]: Printed and sold by H. and E. Phinney, 1818.

fr.[2], t.[3], [4–5], 6–28, [29–30], [31 adv.] p.; illus.; 10.5 cm.; pr. paper covers.

NUt°; Shaw 44306.

673.35 [—] ——— Cooperstown [N.Y.]: Printed and sold by H. & E. Phinney, 1819.

fr.[2], t.[3], [4–5], 6–28, [29–30], [31, adv.] p.; illus.; 9.5 cm.; pr. & illus. buff paper covers.

MWA°; PP; Shaw 48216.

673.36 [—] ——— Fragment. Hudson: Printed By Ashbel Stoddard. 1820.

fr.[2], t.[3], [4–5], 6–31 p.; illus.; 10.5 cm.; pr. & illus. gray-green paper covers.

Cover title: The Hermit Of The Forest. Hudson: Printed By Ashbel Stoddard, And Sold, Wholesale and Retail, at his Book-Store. 1821.

N°; Shoemaker 1575.

674.1 [—] THE HISTORY OF A DOLL; Containing Its Origin And Progress Through Life. With The Various Calamities That Befel It. By Miss Nancy Meanwell. Boston: Printed and sold by John W. Folsom, No. 30, Union-Street. 1798.

fr.[2], t.[3], [4–5], 6–29, [30–31, adv. list of books] p.; illus.; 10 cm.; illus. buff paper covers. Entered in Richard Johnson's daybook: "*1780 Oct. 30. The History of a Doll. £1. 1s.*" [This line crossed out.]. (Weedon 1949 31).

English ed. London: adv. by E. Newbery, 1800.

CLU°; MWA (p.[31] and rear cover wanting); Evans 34088.

674.2 [—] ——— New-York: Printed by William Durell No. 106 Maiden-Lane. 1800.

t.[3], [4, alphabet–5], 6–30 p.; illus.; 10 cm.; wallpaper covers.

MWA°; (fr.[2] p.[31] & original covers wanting, p. 27–30 slightly mut.); Evans 37945.

674.3 [—] ——— New-York: Printed by W. Durell, For the Book-Sellers. 1800.

fr.[2], t.[3], [4–5], 6–31 p.; illus.; 10.5 cm.; paper covers.

NN°; CtY; Evans 37945.

674.4 [—] ——— Exeter [N.H.]: Printed And Sold By H. Ranlet. 1801.

fr.[ii], t.[3], [4–5], 6–31 p.; illus.; 10.5 cm.; illus. buff paper covers.

MWA° (all p. mut.); Shaw 916.

674.5 [—] ——— Hudson [N.Y.]: Printed By Ashbel Stoddard, And sold Wholesale and Retail at his Book-Store, Corner of Warren and Third-Streets. 1806.

t.[3], [4–5], 6–30 p.; illus.; 11 cm.

CtY° (imp. fr.[2?], p.[31] & covers wanting).

675.1 [—] The History Of A Little Boy Found under a Haycock. Likewise, Little Stories for Little Children. Boston: Printed and sold by J. White. 1790.

t.[3], [4–5], 6–20, [29–30], [31, illus.] p.; illus.; 9 cm. Only a fragment remains of p.[29–30]. The illus. p. [31] is on yellow paper which may have been colored by a child. It might have once been the front cover of the book, but now it is the verso of a leaf pasted to a gray wallpaper cover. Therefore it is considered to be p.[31]. On p. 20 the caption reads: The Adventures Of An Apple Pye. This is followed by the rhyme A Apple Pye/B Bit it.
Entered in Richard Johnson's day book: *"1786 July. Mr. Badcock* [E. Newbery's agent]—*To writing The History of a Little Boy found under a Haycock—Half a Sheet. 32°.—L 1, 1s."* (Weedon 1949 34).
English ed. London: in 2 pts. pt. 1, from which the above American ed. is copied, is entitled: *The Royal Alphabet; Or Child's Best Instructor, To which is added, The History Of A Little Boy, found under a Haycock,* E. Newbery. n.d. *The Royal Alphabet* alone was adv. by E. Newbery in *The Natural History Of Four Footed Beasts. By T. Telltruth.* 1781.; pt. 2 entitled: *The History Of A Little Boy Found under a Haycock, Continued from the First Part, Given in the Royal Alphabet; Or, Child's Best Instructor.* E. Newbery [1787?]. No American edition of pt. 2 has been located, but *see* no. **675.2** for an advertisement. For American ed. of *The Royal Alphabet, see* no. **1132.1**.
MWA° (fr.[2]?, p. 21–28 & front cover wanting); Evans 45896.

675.2 [—] ——— Haycock, concluded from the New Alphabet. Philadelphia: adv. by Francis Bailey, 1793 in **773.1**.

675.3 [—] ——— Haycock. To Which Is Added, The Royal Alphabet. Likewise, Little Stories for Little Children. Boston: Printed by J. White and C. Cambridge, near Charles' River Bridge. [1789].

t.[3], [4–5], 6–30 p.; illus.; 8.5 cm. The Alphabet on p.[20] starts A/For an Angler, that fished/with a hook. On p. 27–30 there are nursery rhymes. J. White and C. Cambridge were together through 1793 only.

CtHi° (fr.[2]?, p. 31? & covers wanting); Evans 21889, dated [1789].

675.4 [—] ——— Boston: adv. by John W. Folsom, 1798 in **672.1**.

675.5 [—] ——— A Haycock. Embellished with Elegant Cuts. Philadelphia: Printed By John Adams. 1805.

fr.[2], t.[3], [4–5], 6–31 p.; illus.; 11 cm.; yellow paper covers. Adv. by John Adams, 1806 in **646.3**.
CtHi° DLC (i. st. on fr.[2] & p.[4]); Shaw 8614.

675.6 [—] ——— Philadelphia: adv. by B. & T. Kite, 1807 in **611.1**.

676 [—] The History Of A Little Child, Found under a Haycock. To Which Is Added, Little Stories For Children. Boston: Printed and sold by N. Coverly. Price Three-Pence. 1794.

t.[1], [2–3], 4–16 p.; illus.; 9.5 cm.; blue-gray paper covers. The cuts on p. 4 & 7 were used by N. Coverly in no. **352**; that on p. 10 appears in his 1783 edition of *Goody Two-Shoes*, no. **463.2**. Five figured type ornaments are present. Under "Little Stories for little Children" are five nursery rhymes.
Welch°; MWA; Evans 47085.

677.1 [—] The History Of Jacky Idle And Dicky Diligent. Philadelphia: adv. by Francis Bailey, 1793 in **773.1**.

677.2 [—] The History Of Jacky Idle And Dicky Diligent, Exhibiting A Striking Contrast Between The Different Consequences Arising From Indolent Inattention And Laudable Perseverance. Embellished With Cuts. Philadelphia: Printed By John Adams. 1806.

fr.[2], t.[3], [4–5], 6–62 p.; illus.; 10.5 cm.; illus. buff paper covers; p. 61–62 adv. list of 23 books.
Entered in Richard Johnson's day book: *"1790 Mr. Badcock* [E. Newbery's agent—*To writing The History of Jacky Idle and Dicky Diligent.—L. 2. 2s."* (Weedon 1949 33).
English ed. London: adv. by E. Newbery in Masson's *Elmina; Or The Flower that never Fades.* 1800.
PP°; MSaE (emb. st. on t.[3]); NWebyC; Shaw 10558.

[—] THE HISTORY OF SANFORD & MERTON. Abridged from The Original. *See* Day, Thomas, no. **271.1**.

678.1 [—] THE HISTORY OF TOMMY CARELESS; Or, The Misfortunes Of A Week. Adorned With Cuts. Wew-York [*sic. i.e.* New-York]: Printed and Sold by William Durell, no. 19, Queen-Street. [1793?].

> fr.[2], t.[3], [4, alphabet], 5–31 p.; illus.; 10 cm.; Dutch paper covers. The frontispiece [2], pages [4], 23 [*sic. i.e.* 29], and 27 [*sic. i.e.* 30] appear to have been printed from standing type used in *The House That Jack Built. Printed By W. Durell.* [1793?], no. **616.8**. Page 31 in no. **678.1** is also printed from standing type used in no. **616.8**, page 26, but with the page number changed to "31" and the first two lines omitted. In both books p. [4], line 1, Alphabet is misspelled "ALPHAAET." A few characteristic type settings are: p. 6, line 14, "misfortunes"; line 15, "summer-house" [with a hyphen]; line 20, "happening"; p. 18, line 6, "a halloo that soon brought the". Durell published an edition of *Tommy Careless* in 1800, no. **678.8**, and used many of the cuts found in no. **678.1**. The illustrations on p. 7, 14, and 27, in no. **678.8**, show nicks in the rule borders which are absent in no. **678.1**, p. 7, 14, 25. The illustrations and text, p. 23 [*sic. i.e.* 29]–31, do not occur in no. **678.8**.
> Entered in Richard Johnson's account book: "*1787 July. Mr. Badcock* [E. Newbery's agent] —*To writing The Misfortunes of a Week—* . . ." (Weedon 1949 38).
> English & Irish ed. London: E. Newbery, 1788. CtHi°; MWA-W (fr.[2], p.[31] & Dutch paper covers wanting; the "1" of page number "18" and the "2" of page number "26" are not struck); Evans 46791.

678.2 [—] ——— Careless. Philadelphia: adv. by Francis Bailey, 1793 in **773.1**.

678.3 [—] "[——— [same as **678.1**] Worcester: From the Press of Isaiah Thomas, Jun. 1795].

> pp. 31, [(1) 32 mo. title from the London edition. Only copy lack the title page." (Evans)
> This unique copy referred to by Evans was probably the A. C. Bates copy in the CtHi. It lacks all before p. [5] and the covers. Bates attributed this book to I. Thomas, 1795, but it

appears to be an edition printed by an unknown publisher. The frontispiece and illustrations are entirely different from any I. Thomas edition. The book does not resemble any American or English edition so far located. The Evans Isaiah Thomas edition can be considered a ghost. Evans 28837.

678.4 [—] ——— Boston: adv. by John W. Folsom, 1798 in **672.1**.

678.5 [—] ——— Adorned With Cuts. Third Worcester Edition. Printed at Worcester: Massachusetts, By Isaiah Thomas, Jun. Sold Wholesale and Retail by Him. 1799.

> fr.[2], t.[3], [4–5], 6–27, [28–31, illus.] p.; illus.; 11 cm.; Dutch paper covers. The three cuts on each page, p. [28–30], appeared in *Mother Goose's Melody. Worcester: I. Thomas, 1799,* no. **905.3**.
> MLuHi (Dutch paper covers); Evans 35623.

678.6 [—] ——— Adorned With Cuts. New-York: Printed by W. Durell, For Evert Duyckinck. 1800.

> fr.[2], t.[3], [4–5], 6–30 p.; illus.; 10 cm.; illus. blue paper covers. This ed. has the identical type setting as **678.7** and **678.8** except for the imprint. Many changes occur in type settings from no. **678.1**. "The Alphabet," p.[4] line 1, is correctly spelled. The first line of text p.[5]: "*I HAVE* heard my papa and" . . . Other chararteristic settings which have been changed are: p. 6, lines 15–16, "misfor-tune"; line 17 "summer house" [without a hyphen]; line 22, "happened"; p. 18, lines 10–11, "a hollow that bro't the". The 1800 ed. lacks the running title "The Misfortunes of a Week" at the top of the page, present in no. **678.1**, p. 6–28. The illustrations on p. 7, 14 and 27 show nicks in the rule borders not present in no. **678.1**. The frontispiece in no. **678.7**, which is probably the missing one in this book, shows a young man seated under a tree instead of Gog and Magog which appears in no. **678.1**.
> MWA-T°; NB (fr.[2], p. 31 and covers wanting); Evans 49095.

678.7 [—] ——— New-York: Printed by W. Durell, For John Harrisson. 1800.

> fr.[2], t.[3], [4–5], 6–31 p.; illus.; 10 cm.; paper covers; same type setting as no. **678.6**.

MWA-W* (p.[2]–14 has the top corner of the page wanting with the page numbers missing from p. 6–14); Evans 49096.

678.8 [—] ——— New-York: Printed by W. Durell, For Thomas B. Jansen & Co. 1800.

t.[3], [4–5], 6–30 p.; illus.; 10 cm.; type setting same as no. **678.6.**

MWA-W* (fr.[2], p. 31 & covers wanting); Evans 49097.

678.9 [—] ——— New-York: Printed By James Oram. [1800?].

fr.[2], t.[3], [4–5], 6–31 p.; illus.; 10 cm. Carson*.

678.10 [—] ——— Misfortunes of a Week. Philadelphia: adv. by John Adams, 1805 in **616.17.**

678.11 [—] ——— Embellished With Cuts. Philadelphia: Printed By John Adams [a row of 4 dots] 1806.

t.[3], [4–5], 6–30 p.; illus.; 10.5 cm.

MWA* (fr.[2], p. 31 and covers wanting).

678.12 [—] ——— Week. Philadelphia: adv. by B. & T. Kite, 1807 in **611.1.**

678.13 [—] ——— Hallowell, (Maine) Published by Ezekiel Goodale. N. Cheever, Printer. [ca. 1809].

fr.[2], t.[3], [4–5], 6–31 p.; illus.; 10.5 cm.; blue marbled paper covers.

MWA*; CLU; PP.

678.14 [—] ——— Easton [Pa.]: Printed by Samuel Longcope. < Price Three Cents. > [n.d.].

fr.[2], t.[3], [4–5], 6–31 p.; illus.; 10 cm.; marbled paper covers.

Carson* (p. 31 mut. with page no. wanting).

679.1 [—] The Holiday Spy. Philadelphia: adv. by Francis Bailey, 1793 in **773.1.**

679.2 [—] The Holiday Spy: Being The Observations Of Little Tommy Thoughtful, On The Different Tempers, Genius & Man[ners] Of The Young Masters & Mi[sses] In The Several Families which [he visited] during his last Break[ing-Up.] First Worcester [Edition.] Worcester, [Massachusetts.] Printed By I[saiah Thomas.] Sold Wholesale [and retail.] [1802?].

t.[3], [4–5], 6–54, [55–58 mut. page no. wanting] p.; illus.; 10 cm.; p.[5], a decorative bar of 8 triangles with stippled interiors. The oval cut, p. 34, is printed with its base along the inner margin of the page. It was used by I. Thomas, 1786 in **782.** The rectangular illustration, p. 53 is also on its side with the base along the outer margin of the page.

Entered in Richard Johnson's day book: "*1780 Sept. 26. Delivered to Mrs. Newbery the Copy of Holiday Anecdotes—L1. 1s.*" (Weedon 1949 39).

English ed. London: adv. by E. Newbery, 1781 in *The Natural History Of Four-Footed Beasts. By T. Teltruth.*

MWA* (covers wanting; t.[3], p.[4]–6, 35–38 mut.); DLC; Shaw 2418.

679.3 [—] ——— Breaking-Up. Adorned With Cuts. Easton [Pa.] Printed by Samuel Longcope. [ca. 1805].

fr.[ii], t.[iii], [iv–v], vi–xviii, [19], 20–57, [58, bl.], [59, alphabets] p.; illus.; 10 cm.; marbled paper covers; p. 52–57 are adv. list of books "Just Published and for sale at the Book-store of Benjamin Johnson, No. 31, High street." Benjamin Johnson used this address 1802 in Kendall's *The Sparrow*, no. **725.** B. Johnson was at 31 Market Street from 1803–06. Market Street is an alternative name for High Street. PP*.

679.4 [—] ——— Hartford: Printed By C. Hosmer. 1815.

fr.[2], t.[3], [4–5], 6–31 p.; illus.; 10 cm.; pr. & illus. green paper covers.

CtHi* (front cover wanting, fr.[2] mut.); DLC; MWA (p.[2], 31 & covers wanting); OClWHi; Shaw 34938.

680.1 [—] The Juvenile Biographer; Containing The Lives Of Little Masters and Misses; Including A Variety Of Good And Bad Characters. By a Little Biographer. The First Worcester Edition. Worcester, (Massachusetts) Printed By Isaiah Thomas, And Sold At His Book Store. Sold Also By E. Battelle, Boston. MDCCLXXXVII.

fr.[ii], t.[iii], [iv], v–viii, [9], 10–119, [120, bl.], [121–24, adv. of books] p.; illus.; 10 cm. MWA copy A, I. Thomas copy bound in leather, probably not part of a remainder. Copy B, bound in gold simulated Dutch paper, part of a large publisher's remainder and represented in all the locations below.

Entered in Richard Johnson's day book: "*1780 Oct. 16. Juvenile Biographer—L1. 1s.*" (Weedon 1949 41).

English ed. London: adv. by E. Newbery in *The Natural History of Four-Footed Beasts. By T. Teltruth. 1781.*

MWA* (A, B); BM; CLU; CtHT; CSmH (rebound in red morocco); CtHi; CtY (Pequot, unbound sheets); DLC (unbound sheets); MB (per. st. on t.[iii]); MH; NjP; NN (2 copies of which are unbound sheets bound in cloth); PP; RPJCB (unbound sheets); Evans 20440; Hamilton 114.

680.2 [—] ——— Biographer. Philadelphia: adv. by Francis Bailey, 1793 in **773.1.**

681.1 [—] Juvenile Trials For Robbing Orchards, Telling Fibs, And Other Heinous Offences. By Master Tommy Littleton, Secretary to the Court; with a Sequel by Dr. Aiken. [2 lines quot.] Boston: Printed For F. Nichols. 1797. < Price twenty cents. >

t.[i], [ii], [i], ii–xvi, [17], 18–118 p.; 13 cm.; bound in marbled paper over bds., red leather spine.

Entered in Richard Johnson's day book: "*1770 Aug. 20. Delivered to Mr Carnan, Juvenile Trials. Value Five Guineas.—*" (Weedon 1949).

English ed. London: T. Carnan, 1772.

MWA-W*; CLU; MB (per. st. on t.[i]); NN; NNC-Pl; PP; RPJCB; Evans 31700.

681.2 [—] ——— And Other Offences. With Alterations And Additions. Recommended by the Author of Evenings At Home. Philadelphia: Printed By B. & J. Johnson, No. 147, High-Street. 1801.

fr.[ii], t.[i], [ii–iii], iv–vi, [7], 8–152 p.; front. only illus.; 11 cm.; bound in leather.

MWA* (fr.[ii] mut.); PP; Shaw 745 and 832.

681.3 [—] ——— Offences. Philadelphia. Published By Benjamin Johnson, No. 22, North Second Street. 1814.

fr.[ii], t.[i], [ii–iii], iv, [5], 6–95 p.; illus.; 13 cm.; bound in pr. & illus gray-green paper over w. bds.

PP*; MWA-T (fr.[ii] & covers wanting); PPL (p. 95 and covers wanting); Shaw 31847.

682.1 [—] The Little Wanderers; Or, The Surprising History And Miraculous Adventures Of Two Pretty Orphans. Embellished with Cuts. Published for all good children. Hartford: Printed by Lincoln & Gleason. 1805.

fr.[ii], t.[iii], [iv–v], vi, [7], 8–63 p.; illus.; 10 cm.; orange and green Dutch paper covers.

Entered in Richard Johnson's day book: "*1786 July. Mr. Badcock* (E. Newbery's agent)—*To writing The Little Wanderers. 3 Half Sheets, 32°. L3. 3s.*" (Weedon 1949 60).

English ed. London: E. Newbery, 1786.

Welch*; CLU; CtHi; CtY; MWA; Shaw 8796.

682.2 [—] ——— New-York: Printed by J. Swaine, No. 49, Pearl-st. 1805.

fr.[ii], t.[1], [2–5], 6–58 p.; illus.; 12 cm.; buff paper covers ornamented with printer's ornaments.

CtY*.

682.3 [—] ——— Embellished with Pictures. Concord N.H. Published By George Hough. Sold wholesale and retail at his Bookstore. 1812.

t.[1], [2, illus.–3], 4–69 p.; illus.; 10 cm.; pr. & illus.; blue-gray paper covers.

MWA*; MiU; Shaw 25871.

682.4 [—] Die Kleinen Wanderer, oder Höchst wunderbare Abentheuer zweyer hübschen Waisen. [4 lines quot.] Philadelphia: Gedruckt bey Conrad Zentler, für Johannes Cline, Buchhändler. 1812.

t.[1], [2–3], 4–74 p.; 10 cm.

MWA*; Shaw 25798.

682.5 [—] ——— Orphans. [2 lines quot.] Philadelphia: Published by J. Pounder, North 4th, opposite St. Georges. Griggs & Dickinsons, Printers. Price 12½ cents. 1814.

fr.[2], t.[3], [4–5], 6–36 p.; illus.; 14.5 cm.; pr. & illus. gray-green paper covers.

NN-C* (i. st. p.[4]; p.[5]–9 cropped at top of the page affecting page numbers); PP.

683.1 [—] Moral Sketches For Young Minds. [6 lines of verse.] Dover, (Delaware) Printed By Wm. Black, 1800. [cover title].

Cover title [i], [ii], [iii, adv.], iv, [1], 2–91 p.; 16.5 cm.; pr. yellowish-buff front paper cover; p.[ii] on the inside of the front cover: Copy-Right Secured according to Law. The advertisement which is really a preface p.[iii]–iv states:

"This work contains a great Variety of short Essays on most of the moral Duties of Life, and were originally written in French by a Pen, which Death has long since silenced. If the Translator of these invaluable Sketches shall be thought to have sent them into the World in an easy and elegant English dress, he aspires to no other Fame."

Entered in Richard Johnson's day book: "*1790 April. Mr Badcock* [E. Newbery's agent]—*To writing Moral Sketches.—L8. 8s.*" (Weedon 1949 65).

English ed. London: E. Newbery, 1790.

DeWi° (per. st. on cover title, & p.[ii]; rear cover wanting); Evans 37994.

683.2 [—] ——— Sketches; Containing Improving And Entertaining Essays On Most Of The Duties Of Life. [6 lines of verse] Dover [Del.]: Printed By William Black. 1802.

fr.[ii], t.[1], [2–5], 6–143 p.; 17.5 cm.; bound in blue marbled paper over bds., leather spine. MWA°; Shaw 2688.

[—] The Mountain Piper. *See* Berquin, Arnaud, no. **90.1.**

[—] The New Robinson Crusoe, . . . Translated from the original German. *See* Campe, J. H. von, no. **158.1.**

684 [—] The Oriental Moralist, Or The Beauties Of The Arabian Nights Entertainments. Translated From The Original, And Accompanied With Suitable Reflections Adapted To Each Story, By the Reverend Mr. Cooper. Author of the History of England, &c, &c, &c. The First American Edition. Dover [N.H.]: Printed By Samuel Bragg, Jr. For Wm. T. Clap, Boston. 1797.

t.[i], [ii–xiv], [1], 2–232, [233, bl.], [234, adv.] p.; 17.5 cm.

Entered in Richard Johnson's account book: "*1791 Mr Badcock* [E. Newbery's agent]—*To abridging The Oriental Moralist—L 16. 16s.*" (Weedon 1949 75).

English ed. London: adv. by E. Newbery in Pinchard's *The Blind Child,* 1791.

MWA°; MB; Bowe mss.; Evans 31743.

685 [—] The Picture Exhibition; Containing The Original Drawings Of Eighteen Disciples. To Which Are Added, Moral And Historical Explana-

tions. Published under the Inspection of Mr. Peter Paul Rubens, Professor of Polite Arts. Printed at Worcester, Massachusetts, By Isaiah Thomas. And Sold Wholesale and Retail, at his Bookstore. MDCCLXXXVIII.

t.[i], [ii–iii], iv–viii, [9], 10–112, [113–119, adv. list of books] p.; illus.; 10.5 cm.; green and gold simulated Dutch paper covers. Part of a publisher's remainder.

Entered in Richard Johnson's day book: "*1772 Jan. 6. Delivered to Mr Carnan The Picture Gallery.—Value Five Guineas.*" (Weedon 1949 76).

English, Irish & Scottish ed. title 1: *The Picture Exhibition.* London: T. Carnan, 1774.

English ed. title 2: *The Picture Room.* York: T. Wilson and R. Spence, 1804.

MWA° (copy 1, rebound in leather with I. Thomas' bookplate; copy 2, simulated Dutch paper covers); BM; CtHi; CtHT; CtY; (Pequot, unbound sheets); DLC (2 copies, one rebound); MB; MH; N; NN (copy 1, simulated Dutch paper covers; copy 2, bound untrimmed sheets); NjP; PP; RPJCB (unbound sheets); Evans 21392.

686 [—] The Poetical Flower Basket, Being A Selection Of Approved And Entertaining Pieces Of Poetry, Calculated For The Improvement Of Young Minds. First American Edition. Printed At Worcester, By Isaiah Thomas, Jun. July. 1799.

fr.[ii], t.[iii], [iv–v], vi, [7], 8–71 p.; illus.; 14 cm.; bound in Dutch paper over w. bds. *The Poetical Flower Basket or the Lilliputian Flight to Parnasus* is vol. VI of *The Lilliputian Library; Or, Gulliver's Museum.*

Entered in Richard Johnson's day book: "*1779 Compiling The Lilliputian Library, 10 vol^s for Mr H. Baldwin in Novr last.—L 21.* May 12 *Received of Mr. Baldwin* 20^1 *deduct thence* 20^s *laid out for Books—L. 19.*" (Weedon 1949 57). These 10 vols were compilations from existing works and probably none of the stories were written by Richard Johnson. *See* no. **568.1.**

English and Irish ed.: *The Lilliputian Library,* 10 vols. *See* **568.1.**

An edition printed in English was published in Berlin: 10 vols. in 2, Sold by Chr. Fridr. Himburg. 1782.

English ed.: *The Poetical Flower Basket.* London: E. Newbery. [n.d.].

MWA-W°; MB; MH; MiD; RPJCB; Evans 36129.

687.1 [—] RURAL FELICITY Or, The History Of Tommy and Sally. Adorned with Cuts. Philadelphia: Printed by Francis Bailey, No. 116, High-Street. 1793.

Entered in Richard Johnson's day book: "*1787 July. Mr Badcock* [E. Newbery's agent]—To writing The Misfortunes of a Week — — — Rural Felicity — 2. 2s." (Weedon 1949 80).
English and Irish ed. London: E. Newbery. [n.d.].
Evans 46792.

687.2 [—] ———— Embellished With Cuts. New-York: Printed by J. Oram, for the Book-binders Society,—1796.— < Price Three Cents. >

fr.[2], t.[3], [4–5], 6–29, [30, bl.], [31, alphabets] p.; illus.; 9.5 cm.; green Dutch paper covers.
MWA-W*; PP; Evans 47819.

687.3 [—] ———— Charlestown [Mass.]: Printed and Sold by J. Lamson, at his Office, near the Bridge. Wholesale and Retail. 1798.

fr.[2], t.[3], [4–5], 6–31 p.; illus.; 10 cm.; green Dutch paper covers.
MWA-W*; Evans 48489.

687.4 [—] ———— Boston: adv. by John W. Folsom, 1798 in **672.1**.

687.5 [—] Tommy and Sally. Wilmington, Del.: adv. "may be had at James Wilson's Book-Store at the sign of Shakespear, in Market-Street . . .", 1800 in **61.8**; 1803 in **1081**. This is probably an edition of *Rural Felicity*.

687.6 [—] Rural Felicity. Philadelphia: adv. by B. & J. Johnson, 1801 in **1046.1**.

688.1 [—] TEA TABLE DIALOGUES; Between Miss Thoughtful, Miss Sterling, Miss Prattle, Master Thoughtful, Master Goodwill, Master Foplin. Embellished With Cuts. [2 lines quot.] Philadelphia: Printed By Joseph James. M.DCC.LXXXIX.

t.[i], [ii–iii], iv–v, [vi], [7], 8–123 p.; illus.; 13.5 cm.
Entered in R. Johnson's day book: "*1770 May 15. Delivered to Mr Carnan, Tea-Table Dialogues.—Value—Five Guineas. 1776 June. Tea-Table Dialogues, for Mr Carnan.—L 5. 5 s. < Paid 1777 Feb. 12 >.*" (Weedon 1949 82).

English ed. London: Entered at Stationer's Hall by T. Carnan, June 21, 1771.
NjP* (rebound, orig. covers wanting); MWA (p. 121–123 and covers wanting); Evans 45501; Hamilton 127.

688.2 [—] ———— Master Foplin, [4 lines quot.] Philadelphia: Printed By Francis Bailey, At Yorick's Head, No. 116, High-Street. 1794.

t.[i], [ii–iii], iv–v, [vi], [7], 8–144 p.; illus.; 10.5 cm.; bound in orange Dutch paper over bds.
CLU* (p. 69–70 mut.); Evans 47086.

689.1 [—] THE YOUTHFUL JESTER, Or Repository of Wit And Ionocent [*sic. i.e.* Innocent] Amusement. Containing: Moral and Humerous Tales—Merry Jests—Laughable Anecdotes—and Smart Repartees. The whole being as innocent as it is entertaining. Baltimore: Printed by Warner & Hanna, corner of Market and South Gay Streets. 1800.

t.[1], [2–3], 4–108 p.; 14 cm.; bound in marbled paper over bds., leather spine.
Entered in Richard Johnson's day book: "*1789 Nov. 25. Mr Badcock* [E. Newbery's agent]— *To the writing of The youthful jester— L 5 5s.* < Paid 1790, Feb. 5 >" (Weedon 1949 91).
English ed. London: E. Newbery. [n.d.].
MWA*; Evans 39160.

689.2 [—] ———— Printed For The Booksellers. 1806.

t.[1], [2–5], 6–108 p.; 13.5 cm.; bound in marbled paper over bds., buff paper spine.
MWA*; Shaw 11912.

[JONES, GILES] [*sic.* author unknown]
690.1 [—] THE LILLIPUTIAN MASQUERADE. Occasioned By the Conclusion of Peace between those Potent Nations, The Lilliputians and the Tommythumbians. [2 lines of verse] The First Worcester Edition. Printed at Worcester Massachusetts. By Isaiah Thomas, And Sold Wholesale and Retail, at his Book-Store. MDCCLXXXVII. Sold also by E. Battelle in Boston.

fr.[2], t.[3], [4–5], 6–61, [62, adv. list of books] p.; illus.; 10 cm.; illus. buff paper covers.
English & Scottish ed. London: adv. by T. Carnan, 1774 in *London Chronicle*.
MWA* (p. 41–42, 59–60, [63] & rear cover wanting; fr.[2]. t.[3], p. [4]–6 mut.; p. 45–46,

57–58, [61] lack the page number); Evans 20434.

690.2 [—] ——— Printed at Worcester, Massachusetts. By Isaiah Thomas, And Sold, Wholesale and Retail, at his Book-Store. MDCCLXXXVII.
fr.[2], t.[3], [4–5], 5–61, [62–63 adv. of 15 books] p.; illus.; 10 cm.; illus. buff paper covers. CLU*.

690.3 [—] ——— The Second Worcester Edition. Worcester: Printed by Isaiah Thomas, Jun. For Isaiah Thomas And Son, Sold Wholesale And Retail At Their Respective Bookstores. 1795.
fr.[2], t.[3], [4–5], 6–61 [62–63, adv. list of books] p.; illus.; 10.5 cm.; green Dutch paper covers.
MWA*; DLC (fr.[2], p. 61–63 & covers wanting), MiU; PP (p. 63 and rear cover wanting); Evans 28908.

690.4 [—] ——— Third Worcester Edition. Worcester: (Massachusetts) Printed by Isaiah Thomas, Jun. Sold Wholesale and Retail at his Printing Office. April–1802.
fr.[2], t.[3], [4–5], 6–61 [62, adv.], [63, 2 oval illus.] p.; illus.; violet and green Dutch paper covers.
MWA*; NN; RPB; Shaw 2538.

690.5 [—] ——— [2 lines of verse] Windsor [Vermont]: Published For J. Stone. Jesse Cochran, Printer. 1816.
fr.[2], t.[3], [4], 5–60 p.; illus.; 10 cm.; blue marbled paper covers. The covers are part of the text of another book which have been marbled.
MWA-W* (p. 61–63 & rear cover wanting, or sigs D$_7$ & D$_8$); McCorison 1849; Shaw 37966.

[JONES, STEPHEN] 1763–1827
691.1 [—] The Life And Adventues Of A Fly. Supposed to have been written by Himself. Illustrated With Cuts. Boston: Printed and sold by John Norman, No. 75 Newbury-street. [*ca.* 1794].
fr.[4], t.[5], [6–17], 18–96 p.; illus.; 10 cm.; bound in marbled paper over bds. The end of the preface p.[16] is signed *S.J.* [Stephen Jones].
English ed. London: adv. by E. Newbery, 1789. MWA-W*; Evans 47087.

691.2 [—] ——— Illustrated with Cuts. Boston: Printed By Samuel Etheridge, Sold By Him, And By The Booksellers. 1797.
fr.[ii], t.[iii], [iv–v], vi–xiv, [15], 16–95 p.; illus.; 11 cm.; bound in paper over w. bds.
MWA*; Evans 48160.

691.3 [—] ——— New-York: adv. by L. B. Jansen and G. Jansen, 1808 in **766.**

691.4 [—] ——— Boston: Published By Bradford & Read, No. 58, Cornhill. 1813.
fr.[ii], t.[i], [ii–iii], iv–xii, [13], 14–94 p.; illus.; 13 cm.; pr. paper covers; cover title dated 1812; page [ii] & colophon p. 94: Watson & Bangs, Printers, 7 State-Street, Boston.
MWA-W*; Shaw 28847.

691.5 [—] ——— Greenfield, Ms. Printed And Published By A. Phelps. 1816.
fr.[ii], t.[iii], [iv–v], vi–x, [11], 12–71 p.; illus.; 12.5 cm.; bound in pr. buff paper over bds.
MWA*; NN-C; Shaw 37968.

691.6 [—] Rudiments Of Reason; Or, The Young Experimental Philosopher: Being A Series Of Family Conferences; In Which the Causes And Effects Of The Various Phenomena That Nature Daily Exhibits, Are Rationally And Familiarly Explained. In Three Volumes. Vol. I. [II.–III.] New-York: Printed for Berry, Rogers, and Berry, No. 35, Hanover Square. 1793.
vol. I.: 1st t.[i], [ii–iii], iv–xvi, [1], 2–160, 2nd t.[i], [ii–iii], iv, 161–163 p.; vol. II.: t.[i], [ii], [1], 2–186 p.; vol. III.: t.[i], [ii], [1], 2–204, [205–224] p.; 3 vols.; 14 cm.; bound in marbled paper over bds., green paper spine. On t.[i], vol. II. the semicolon is omitted after the word "Conferences."
Second title vol. I: ——— [same as 1st title] London: Printed for E. Newbery, at the corner of St. Paul's Church Yard. 1793. < Entered at Stationer's Hall. >
English ed. London: 3 vols. E. Newbery, 1793. MWA* (i. st. on t.[i] of vols. I.–III.); Evans 26109.

692 JOSEPH AND HIS BRETHREN. Baltimore: adv. By G. Douglas in *Robinson Crusoe.* 1803. *See also* The Story Of Joseph and his brethren, no. **1265.1.**

693 A JOURNEY TO LONDON; Or, The World as it Goes: Being A Particular Account Of Master Manley's Tour To That Great City. Ornamented with beautiful Cuts. Printed At Worcester. By Isaiah Thomas, Jun. Sold Wholesale and Retail by him. June 1802.

fr.[ii], t.[1], [2–3], 4–58, [59, adv.], [60–61, illus.] p.; illus.; 11 cm.; over the top of front.: Second Edition.

MWA°; PP (green Dutch paper covers); Shaw 2473.

694.1 JULIA AND THE PET-LAMB; Or, Good Temper And Compassion Rewarded. Philadelphia: Published By Solomon W. Conrad, No. 87, Market Street. 1817. Printed by Lydia R. Bailey.

fr.[ii], t.[1], [2–3], 4–52 p.; front. only illus.; 14 cm.; pr. paper covers.

English ed. London: Darton, Harvey, And Darton, 1813.

PP°.

694.2 —— Philadelphia: Published By Benjamin Warner, No. 147, Market-Street. 1817. Printed by Lydia Bailey.

fr.[ii], t.[1], [2–3], 4–52 p.; 3 pl.; 13 cm.

RPB°.

695 [JULIET; OR, THE REWARD OF FILIAL AFFECTION. A Tale for Youth. Philadelphia: Published By E. And R. Parker, No. 178, Market Street. J. R. A. Skerrett, Printer. 1818.]

[5], 6–71 p.; 13 cm. The above imaginary title made up from the caption on p.[5], the adv. of E & R Parker on the rear cover, and the adv. on the rear cover of *The Juvenile Instructor. E. & R. Parker, 1818,* no. **704.1.**

English ed. London: J. Harris, 1817.

RPB° (t.[1]. p. [2–4] & front cover wanting).

JUSTINEA, OR THE FILIAL DAUGHTER. *See* Sandham, Elizabeth, no. **1155.**

696.1 JUVENAL [*sic. i.e.* JUVENILE] POEMS; Or The Alphabet in Verse. Designed For The Entertainment of all good Boys and Girls, and no others. Adorned with Cuts. Hartford: Printed by John Babcock. 1800.

fr.[2], t.[3], [4], 5–28, [29, alphabets], [30, adv.], [31, illus.] p.; illus.; 11 cm.; Dutch paper covers; text pr. in blue-gray paper.

See also Juvenile Poems, no. **714.1.**

Welch° (p.[3–4] wanting); CtHi (fr.[2], p. [31] and covers wanting); MWA (p.[31] mut.); Evans 49099.

696.2 —— Hartford: Printed by John Babcock. 1802.

fr.[2], t.[3], [4], 5–28, [29, alphabets], [30, adv.], [31, illus.] p.; illus.; 11 cm.; Dutch paper covers.

ICU° (fr.[2], p. 31 & covers mut.).

696.3 —— From Sidney's Press. New-Haven. 1807.

fr.[2], t.[3], [4], 5–28, [29–30, alphabets], [31, adv.] p.; illus.; 10.5 cm.; Dutch paper covers.

DLC°.

696.4 —— entertainment of all Good little Boys and Girls. Ornamented with Engravings. Albany: Printed By E. & E. Hosford. 1808.

fr.[2], t.[3], [4], 5–31 p.; illus.; 10 cm.

MWA° (covers wanting); Shaw 15342.

696.5 —— [same as **696.1**] From Sidney's Press, New-Haven. 1808.

fr.[2], t.[3], [4], 5–28, [29–30, alphabets], [31, adv.] p.; illus.; 10.5 cm.; Dutch paper covers.

PP°.

696.6 —— From Sidney's Press. New-Haven. 1809.

fr.[2], t.[3], [4], 5–28, [29–30, alphabets], [31, adv.] p.; illus.; 10.5 cm.; Dutch paper covers.

CtHi°; DLC (fr.[2] & front cover mut.); Shaw 50947.

696.7 —— Sidney's Press. New-Haven. 1813.

fr.[2], t.[3], [4], 5–28, [29–30, alphabets], [31, adv.] p.; illus.; 10.5 cm.; pr. & illus. buff paper covers.

Cover title: Juvenile Poems.

Welch°; CtY (p. 27–[30] wanting); MWA (t. [3] & p.[4] mut.); NNC-LS; Shaw 28857.

THE JUVENILE BIOGRAPHER. *See* Johnson, Richard, no. **680.1.**

697 THE JUVENILE BUDGET, Being A New Collection Of Entertaining Fables, Intended As a Present for all those Good Girls and Boys who behave according to the following Rules: That Is, Do as they are bid, come when they are called, and shut the door after them. Boston: Printed By N. Coverly. 1803.

t.[1], [2–3], 4–16 p.; illus.; 9.5 cm.; orange paper covers.

MWA-W°; MB.

698 THE JUVENILE BUDGET, Or Entertaining Stories For Little Children. Ornamented With Cuts. Boston: Printed For, And Sold By The Book-sellers. 1810.

fr.[2], t.[3], [4], 5–14, [15] p.; illus.; 10 cm.; wallpaper covers.

DIC° (rebound, per. st. on t.[3], a strip of paper is pasted across the top of p.[15] so that the page number, if any, cannot be seen); Shaw 20474.

699 THE JUVENILE BUDGET, Or Little Stories For Children. Boston: Printed By N. Coverly, Jun. Corner of Theatre-Alley. 1812.

fr.[2], t.[3], [4–15] p.; illus.; 10.5 cm.; yellow wallpaper covers.

MWA°; Shaw 25765.

700 JUVENILE CORRESPONDANCE; Or, Letters, Suited To Children From Four To Above Ten Years Of Age, In Three Sets. New-Haven: Printed By Abel Morse. M.DCC.XCI.

t.[iii], [iv–v], vi, 7, viii, [9–12], 13–106 p.; CtHi°; Evans 23479.

701.1 JUVENILE HISTORY OF BEASTS. Part II. Philadelphia: Published By E. And R. Parker, No. 178, Market street. J. R. A. Skerrett, Printer. 1818.

fr.[ii], t.[1], 2–8, [pl. opp. p. 8] p.; 8 pl. including front.; 12 cm.; pr. buff paper covers; cover title dated 1819. Parts I. & II. adv. by E. & R. Parker, 1818 in **704.1**.

MWA°; RNHi (emb. st. on nearly every p.).

701.2 ——— Beasts. Part I. This useful beast, the Horse, we raise, To draw the waggon, coach, or chaise. Philadelphia: Published By E. And R. Parker, No. 178, Market Street. J. R. A. Skerrett, Printer. 1819.

fr.[ii], t.[1], 2–8 p.; 8 col. pl. including front.; 12 cm.; pr. pink paper covers.

MWA°; PHi; Shaw 48398.

702 JUVENILE HISTORY OF BEASTS AND BIRDS. New-York: adv. by Samuel Wood and Sons, 1819 in **1188.8** and 1820 in **274.2**.

703.1 THE JUVENILE HISTORY OF BIRDS. Part II. Philadelphia: Published by E. And R. Parker, No. 178 Market street. J. R. A. Skerrett, Printer, 1818.

fr.[ii], t.[1], 2–8, [pl. opp. p. 8] p.; 8 pl. in-

cluding front.; 12 cm.; pr. & illus. buff paper covers.

Ross Hopkins°, Eastlake, Ohio.

703.2 ——— Part I. [2 lines of verse] Philadelphia: Published By E. and R. Parker, No. 178 Market Street, J. R. A. Skerrett, Printer. 1819.

fr.[ii], t.[1], 2–8, [pl. opp. p. 8] p.; 8 pl. including front.; 12 cm.; pr. orange paper covers. DLC°.

704.1 THE JUVENILE INSTRUCTOR; Or, A Series Of Moral And Entertaining Tales For the Amusement of Children. With Plates. Philadelphia: Printed By E. And R. Parker, No. 178, Market Street. J. R. A. Skerrett, Printer. 1818.

t.[1], [2], [pl. opp. 3.[3]], [3], 4–23, [24, adv. list of books] p.; 6 col. pl.; 11.5 cm.; pr. buff paper covers.

RPB°; DLC (2 col. pl. wanting); MWA-W (pl. opp. p. [3], [10], [14], [20] wanting); Shaw 44490.

704.2 ——— Philadelphia: Published By E. And R. Parker, No. 178, Market Street. J. R. A. Skerrett, Printer. 1819.

t.[1], [2, bl.], [pl. opp. p.[3]], [3], 4–23, [24, adv.] p.; 6 col. pl.; 12 cm.; pr. buff paper covers. MWA°; Shaw 48399.

JUVENILE LETTERS. *See* Bingham, Caleb, no. **100.1**.

705 THE JUVENILE LIBRARY: Containing The Histories Of Sandford And Merton, Martin And James, And The Young Robber: Designed for the Instruction and Amusement of Youth. New-York: Printed And Sold By J. C. Totten, No. 155 Chatham-street. 1810.

fr.[ii], 1st t.[iii], [iv. bl.]; 2nd t.[1], [2, bl.–3], 4–48; 3rd t.[1], [2, bl.–5], 6–60; 4th t.[i], [ii–iii], iv, [5], 6–48 p.; illus.; 14 cm.; bound in marbled paper over bds., leather spine.

2nd title: The History Of Sandford and Merton. A Work Intended For The Use Of Children. New-York: Published By John C. Totten, No. 155 Chatham-street. 1810. *See also* no. **270.1** for the separate ed. of 1810.

3rd title: Martin And James; Or The Reward Of Integrity: A Moral Tale, For The Amusement And Instruction Of Youth. New-York: Published By John C. Totten, No. 155 Chatham-street. 1810. *See also* no. **817.1** for other separate editions.

4th title: The Young Robber; Or, Dishonesty Punished. New-York: Printed And Sold By John C. Totten, No. 155 Chatham-street. 1810. *See also* no. **1463** for the separate ed. of 1819. NjP°.

706.1 THE JUVENILE MAGAZINE, Or Miscellaneous Repository Of Useful Information. Vol. I. Philadelphia: Printed for Benjamin Johnson, & Jacob Johnson, High-Street. 1802.

vol. 1.: fr.[ii], t.[1], [2–3], 4–214, [215–216, index] p.; 3 pl.; 14.5 cm.; bound in leather; three numbers: No. 1.: [7], 8–72 p.; No. 2.: [pl. opp. p. [73]], [73], 74–144 p.; No. 3.: [pl. opp. p. 145, 145–214, [215–216] p. The three plates are: fr.[ii] signed *Tanner Sc*, pl. opp. p.[73] signed *Stothard del. Tanner Sc.*; pl. opp. p. 145 signed *J. Akin Sc.*

MWA°; PP (p. 5–8, 13–36, 49–60 & binding winting); PPiU (i. st. on t.[1], pl. opp. p. 145 wanting); Shaw 2476.

706.2 ——— Vol. II. [III.–IV.] Philadelphia [printed in a vignette] Printed for Benjamin Johnson, No. 31, High-Street. 1802.

vol. II.: fr.[ii], t.[1], [2–3], 4–214, [215–216, index] p.; 2 pl., 1 full page illus.; 14.5 cm.; bound in leather; three numbers: No. I.: [3], 4–72 p.; No. II. [73 bl.], [74, illus.], [75], 76–144 p.; No. III.: [pl. opp. p.[145]], [145], 146–214 p. The two plates, fr.[ii] signed: *Stothard del. Tanner sc.;* pl. opp. p.[145] signed *J. A.* [James Akin]; illus. p. [74] signed *A* [Alexander Anderson].

vol. III.: fr.[ii], t.[1], [2–3], 4–214, [215–216, index] p.; 3 pl.; 15 cm. bound in leather; three numbers: No. I.: [3], 4–72; No. II. [pl. opp. p.[73]], [73], 74–144 p.; No. III.: [pl. opp. p.[145]], [145], 146–214. The three plates, fr.[ii] & pl. opp. p.[145] signed *Stothard del, Tanner Sc.*; pl. opp. p. [73] signed *J. Akin sc.*

vol. IV.: fr.[ii], t.[1], [2–3], 4–214, [215–216, index] p. Three numbers: No. I. [3]–72 p.; No. II. [pl. opp. p.[73]], [73]–144 p.; No. III. [pl. opp. p.[145]], [145]–214, [215–216] p. Plates: fr.[ii], pl. opp. p.[73], and pl. opp. p.[145] signed *Stothard del Tanner Sc* or *Eng.* Pl. opp. p.[73] also has *Etched by G. Fox. N.Y.*; pl. opp. p.[145] has *Etched by Gilbert Fox.*

MWA° (vols. II.–IV.); DLC (II.–IV.); ICU

(IV.); MH (IV.); MWelC (IV.); NRU (vol. II.); OOxM (vol. IV.); PP (vol. 11. No. II. [pl. opp. p. [73]], p. [73]–74, 149–152 wanting; p.[75]–76 mut.; vol. III. p. 69 incorrectly numbered 67, p. 65–66 bound after p. 68); PPiU (vols. II.–IV. i. st. on each title page).

706.3 ——— Information. Philadelphia [not printed in a vignette]: Printed For Benjamin Johnson, No. 31, High Street. 1803.

vol. II.: t.[1], [2–3], 4–214, [215–216, index] p.; 2 pl., pl. opp. p. 59, 195 p.; 2 full page illus. p. [74], 130, both signed A [Alexander Anderson]; 3 numbers: No. I.: [3]–72 p.; No. II.: [75]–144 p.; No. III.: [145]–214 p.; vol. III.: t.[1], [2–3], 4–214, [215–216, index] p.; 3 pl., pl. opp. p. 61, 106, 196; 3 numbers: No. I.: [3]–72 p.; No. II.: [73]–144; No. III.: [145]–214 p.; vol. IV.: t.[1], [2–3], 4–214, [215–216, index] p.; 3 pl., pl. opp. p. 61, 136, 204; 3 numbers: No. I.: [3]–72 p.; No. II.: [73]–144 p. with pages 76, 81, 84–85, 88–89, 92–93, 96–97, 100, 103, 105, 108, 116 wrongly numbered 40, 45, 48–49, 52–53, 56–57, 60–61, 64, 10, 69, 72, 16 consecutively; No. III.: [145]–214 p.; 3 vols.; 14 cm.; bound in leather. The text of the three volumes is the same as no. **261.2** but with the plates opposite different pages.

CLU° (vols. II.–IV.); MWA (vols. III.–IV.); NB (vol. IV., i. st. on t.[1]; NN (vol. IV.); NRU (vols. II.–IV.); PPL (vol. IV.).

707.1 JUVENILE MISCELLANY, Including Some Natural History, For The Use Of Children. Ornamented with Eighteen Engravings. Philadelphia: Published By Jacob Johnson, No. 147, Market-Street. 1803.

t.[1], [2–72] p.; illus.; 10.5 cm.; bound in leather; colophon p.[72]: J. W. Scott, Printer. MWA-W°; PP.

707.2 ——— Philadelphia: Published By Jacob Johnson, No. 147, Market-Street. 1808.

t.[1], [2–72] p.; illus.; 11 cm.; bound in marbled paper over bds., leather spine; colophon p.[72]: J. Rakestraw Printer. Adv. by Johnson & Warner, 1813 in **1449.2**.

MWA° (p. 61–62 mut.); CtHT; DLC; MSaE (emb. st. on t.[1]); Shaw 15343.

708 THE JUVENILE MISCELLANY, IN PROSE & VERSE. Selected From The Writings Of Eminent

Authors. [1 line quot.] Philadelphia: Printed For The Compiler, By Mordecai Jones, No. 3, Moravian Alley. M,DCC,XCV.

   t.[i], [ii–iii], iv, [5], 6–108 p.; 17 cm.; bound in marbled paper over bds., leather spine.

   NN°; PHi; PP; PSC; Evans 47474.

709 JUVENILE MONITOR; OR THE NEW CHILDREN'S FRIEND. Translated From The German. First American Edition. Boston: Published By Bradford And Read. A. Bowen, Printer. 1814.

   t.[i], [ii–iii], iv–v, [vi], [7], 8–118, [119–120, contents] p.; illus.; 15 cm.; bound in pr. & illus. blue-gray paper over bds.

   MWA°; CLU; PP (t.[i]–v, 115–[120] & rear cover mut.); Shaw 31846.

710.1 THE JUVENILE MONITOR; OR VICE AND PIETY CONTRASTED. Containing Judge Dawes' Address To Three Boys Convicted Of Stealing; And An Account Of Charles Brodhead, A Remarkably Pious Boy, Who Died In New-York. Third Edition. Boston: Printed And Sold By Nathaniel Willis, No. 76, State-Street. 1815.

   fr.[ii], t.[1], [2–3], 4–20, [21, 2 illus.] p.; fr.[ii] & illus. p. [21] only illus.; 14 cm.; pr. & illus. violet paper covers. The book is in two parts: Juvenile Vice consisting of Judge Dawes' address, p.[3]–7 and Juvenile Piety, p.[8]–20. The first part, from a statement on p.[3], was "Extracted from the Palladium [of Dec. 14, 1813]." The second part, according to p.[8] was "Extracted from the Panoplist, of Dec. 1813." *See also* no. **720.1.**

   Cover title: Juvenile Monitor. Judge Dawes' Address To Three Boys convicted of Stealing.

   MWA° (p. 17–[21] and rear cover wanting); PP; Shaw 35038.

710.2 ———— Fourth Edition. Boston: Printed By Nathaniel Willis, Congress-Street. 1818.

   fr.[ii], t.[1], [2–3], 4–20, [21, 2 illus.] p.; fr.[ii] & illus.; p.[21] only illus.; 14 cm.; black paper covers.

   MWA°; MB; PP; Shaw 44491.

711 JUVENILE PASTIMES. New-York: adv. by George Jansen & Lewis Jansen, 1808 in **1232.**

712.1 JUVENILE PIETY; Or, The > [*sic.*] Happiness Of Religion, Exemplified in the Joyful Deaths Of Pious Children. Selected from the Evangelical Magazine. [2 lines quot.] Boston: Printed and sold by Lincoln & Edmands, No. 53 Cornhill. [1819].

   fr.[ii, prose], t.[iii], [iv–v], vi, [7], 8–33, [34–35] p.; illus.; 13.5 cm.; pr. & illus. buff paper covers; fr.[ii]: [a discourse on the] Importance of Sabbath Schools.

   Cover title: Juvenile Piety; Or The Happiness Of Religion. Selected from the Evangelical Magazine. Boston: Printed and sold by Lincoln & Edmands No. 53 Cornhill. 1819.

   MWA°; Shaw 48400.

712.2 ———— Boston: Printed and sold by Lincoln & Edmands, No. 53 Cornhill. [1820].

   fr.[ii, prose], t.[iii], [iv–v], vi, [7], 8–33, [34] p.; illus.; 13.5 cm.; pr. & illus. purple paper covers; fr.[ii]: [a discourse on the] Importance Of Sabbath-Schools; cover imprint: Boston: Printed and [S]old By L[incoln] & Edmands, No. 53 Cornhill 1820.

   MWA° (p.[35]? or sig C₆ and rear cover wanting; front cover mut.); Shoemaker 1822.

713 JUVENILE POEMS Designed Especially For The Improvement And Instruction Of Youth. [3 lines quot.] Deut. vi. 6, 7. Windsor, State Of Vermont. Printed By Alden Spooner. 1792.

   t.[1], [2–3], 4–31 p.; 16 cm.

   MWA° (t.[1], p.[2], 35–36 wanting); MBAt; Evans 25678; McCorison 228.

714.1 JUVENILE POEMS; OR THE ALPHABET IN VERSE. Designed For The Entertainment of all good Boys and Girls, and no others. Philadelphia: Printed by John Adams. 1804.

   fr.[2], t.[3], [4], 5–29 p.; illus.; 10 cm.; p. 29 adv. list of books with numbers "14" and "15" erroneously numbered "4" and "5". Adv. by John Adams, 1806 in **646.3** and 1808 in **1217.** English ed. Taunton: J. Poole for Howard & Evans, London, 1806.

   NNC-Pl°.

714.2 ———— Others. Adorned With Cuts. Philadelphia: Printed By John Adams. 1807.

   fr.[2], t.[3], [4], 5–27, [28–29, adv. list of 28 books] p.; illus.; 10.5 cm.; pr. & illus. blue-gray paper covers; illus. from the same blocks used in no. **714.1**; cover title dated 1808.

   MWA°; Shaw 12852 (probably an error for **714.3** below).

714.3 ——— Philadelphia: Printed For B. And T. Kite. 1807.

fr.[2], t.[3], [4], 5–29, [30–31, adv. list of books] p.; illus.; 10 cm.

DLC* (i. st. p. 5).

714.4 ——— all Good little Boys and Girls. Ornamented with Engravings. Albany: Printed By E. And E. Hosford. 1809.

fr.[2], t.[3], [4], 5–31 p.; illus.; 11 cm.; pr. & illus. buff paper covers; cover title undated.

MWA*; Shaw 17857.

714.5 ——— Albany: Printed By E. And E. Hosford. 1810.

fr.[2], t.[3], [4], 5–31 p.; illus.; 10 cm.; pr. & illus. buff paper covers; cover title undated.

MWA-W*; DLC; N.

714.6 ——— Albany. Printed By E. & E. Hosford. 1811.

t.[3], [4], 5–31 p.; illus.; 10.5 cm.; illus. rear paper cover.

RPB* (front cover, fr.[2] wanting; p. 25–26 mut.); Shaw 23140.

714.7 ——— Albany: Printed By E. & E. Hosford. 1813.

fr.[2], t.[3], [4], 5–31 p.; illus.; 10.5 cm.; pr. & illus. yellow-buff paper covers.

NNC-LS*; OOxM (fr.[2], p. 31 & original covers wanting); Shaw 28856.

714.8 ——— Albany: Printed By E. & E. Hosford. 1814.

fr.[2], t.[3], [4], 5–31 p.; illus.; 10 cm.; pr. & illus. paper covers; cover title imprint: Albany: Printed By E. And E. Hosford.

PP*.

714.9 ——— [same as **714.8**] Girls. Adorned With Cuts. Sidney's Press. New-Haven. 1815.

fr.[2], t.[3], [4], 5–28, [29, upper case alphabet], [30, alphabets], [31, adv.] p.; illus.; 10.5 cm.; illus. yellow covers.

CLU*.

714.10 ——— Sidney's Press. New-Haven. 1817.

fr.[2], t.[3], [4], 5–28, [29, alphabet], [30, 2 illus.], [31, adv.] p.; illus.; 10.5 cm.; illus. green paper covers.

MWA*; CtHi; PP; Shaw 41176.

714.11 ——— [same as **714.4**] Albany: Printed By E. & E. Hosford. 1818.

fr.[2], t.[3], [4], 5–31 p.; illus.; 10 cm.

CtY* (covers wanting); Shaw 44492.

The Juvenile Port-Folio, And Literary Miscellany. *See* Condie, Thomas G., Jun, no. **229.**

715 The Juvenile Repository; Or A Choice Selection Of Interesting And Instructive Pieces In Prose And Verse; For The Use Of Children In Private Families And Schools. By A Friend To Youth. This work was originally designed to go out in separate numbers—but by putting three numbers into a small volume with an index, it is thought, will render it more useful, especially, as a school book. Boston: Printed By Samuel T. Armstrong, Cornhill. 1812.

t.[ii], [1], 2–108, [109, table of contents] p.; 14 cm.; marble paper covers. Caption p.[1]: The Juvenile Repository.

No. 1. July, 1811. Vol. I.; p.[37]: ——— No. 2. August, 1811. Vol. I.; p.[73]: ——— No. 3. September, 1811. Vol. I.

PP*, MWA (No. 1. only).

716 Juvenile Sketches Of Natural History Of Birds. New-York: Printed And Sold By Samuel Wood & Sons, At the Juvenile Book-Store, No. 261, Pearl-Street. 1817.

t.[1], [2–3], 4–68 p.; illus.; 14.5 cm.; pr. & illus. buff paper covers.

CLU*; CtY (t.[1] mut., front cover and most of rear cover wanting); NN (covers wanting); RPB (bound with other books, covers wanting); Shaw 41177; Weiss 1942, p. 767.

717.1 The Juvenile Story Teller, A Collection Of Original Moral Tales. Adorned With Cuts. Sidney's Press. New-Haven. 1815.

fr.[2], t.[3], [4–5], 6–31 p.; illus.; 10.5 cm.; yellow paper covers. An abridged version of the English edition.

English ed. London: James Imray, E. Thomas Printer, 1805.

MWA-W*.

717.2 ——— Sidney's Press. New-Haven. 1817.

fr.[2], t.[3], [4–5], 6–31 p.; illus.; 10 cm.; illus. yellow-buff paper covers.

MWA*; CSmH; Shaw 41178.

717.3 ———— New-Haven. Sidney's Press. For J. Babcock & Son. 1819.

fr.[2], t.[3], [4–5], 6–30, [31, adv.] p.; illus.; 10.5 cm.; illus. buff paper covers printed in pink ink.

MWA°; CLU; CtHi (rear cover wanting); Shaw 48401.

718 THE JUVENILE TRIAL, AND AMUSING STORIES FOR CHILDREN, New-Haven: Printed For John Babcock And Son. Sidney's Press. 1820.

fr.[2], t.[3], [4–5], 6–31 p.; illus.; 15 cm.; pr. & illus. buff paper covers. CtHi copy A has a cut of the fox and the crow on the front cover; copy B has a picture of "The Widow Careful" on the front cover.

Cover title: Juvenile Trial. Published and Sold by John Babcock and Son, New-Haven, and S. & W. R. Babcock, Charleston.

MWA° (B); CtHi (A, B); Shoemaker 1823 and 1824.

719.1 THE JUVENILE TRIAL, AND STORIES FOR CHILDREN. New Haven. Sidney's Press. Printed For J. Babcock & Son. 1819.

fr.[ii], t.[1], [2, adv.–3], 4–35 p.; illus.; 14 cm.; pr. & illus. pink paper covers; copy D.

Copy A: front. an illus. of two men walking, each playing a violin, and a boy holding a bat.

Copy B: front. an illus. of a house with a man standing in the doorway, a man & woman seated in front of a window, and a woman looking out of a second floor window.

Copy C: front. an illus. of a man and boy under a tree looking at wild animals, below which is a cut of a reclining old man and a bear seated in front of him.

Copy D: front. an illus. of an Indian.

Cover title: Published By J. Babcock & Son, Booksellers, Stationers and Printers, adjoining the Post-Office, New-Haven. Sold by S. & W. R. Babcock, Booksellers and Stationers, Charleston, S.C.

MWA° (D); CtHi° (A, B, C); CtY (B, t.[1], & p.[2] wanting); Shaw 48402.

719.2 ———— New Haven. Sidney's Press. Printed For J. Babcock & Son. 1819.

fr.[ii], t.[1], [2–3], 4–36 p.; illus.; pr. & illus. buff paper covers. There is one more page in this edition than in no. **719.1**.

Copy A: front. illus. of two men and an elephant.

Copy B: front. 2 illus. The upper, an eagle chasing a fox; the lower, three peacocks.

Copy C: front. same as copy C, no. **719.1**.

MWA° (A); CtHi° (B, C); Shaw 48403 (35 p. probably a misprint for 36).

JUVENILE TRIALS FOR ROBBING ORCHARDS. *See* Johnson, Richard, no. **681.1**.

720.1 JUVENILE VICE AND PIETY CONTRASTED. Being The Address Of Judge Dawes' To Three Boys Convicted Of Stealing; And An Account Of Charles H. Brodhead, A Remarkably Pious Boy, Who Died In March Last. Boston: Printed And Sold By N. Willis, No. 76, State-Street. (Price 6 cts. single, 50 cts. a doz. $3,50 a hundred.) 1814.

t.[1], [2–3], 4–18 p.; illus. on p.[3] & [8] only illus.; 15 cm.; blue paper covers. The book is in two parts: Juvenile Vice consisting of Judge Dawes' address, p.[3]–6, and Juvenile Piety, p. [7]–20. The first part from a statement on p.[3] was "Extracted from the Palladium of Dec. 14, 1813," while the second part, according to p.[8], was "Extracted from the Panoplist of Dec. 14 1813." *See also* no. **710.1**.

MWA°; PP (p. 17–18 mut.); Shaw 31301 and 31848.

720.2 ———— Who Died In March 1813. The Second Edition. Boston: Printed And Sold By N. Willis, No. 76, State-Street. (Price 6 cts. single, 50 cts. a doz. $3.50 a hundred.) 1814.

t.[1], [2–3], 4–18 p.; 14.5 cm.; brown paper covers.

MWA-T°.

K

KENDALL, EDWARD AUGUSTUS, 1776–1842
721 [—] The Adventures Of Musul Or The Three Gifts: First American Edition. Windsor [Vt.]: Printed for Thomas & Merrifield. Sold Wholesale And Retail At Their Bookstore. 1808. J. Cunningham. Printer.
>t.[1], [2–3], 4–96 p.; 13 cm.; bound in pink paper over w. bds., buff paper spine.
>English ed. London: Vernor and Hood, E. Newbery, 1800.
>MWA* (i. st. on t.[1]); PPL; VtHi; McCorison 964; Shaw 14305.

722.1 [—] The Canary Bird: A Moral Story. Interspersed With Poetry. By The Author Of The Sparrow, Keeper's Travels, The Crested Wren, &c. [1 line quot.]. Philadelphia: Printed For Benjamin Johnson, No. 31 High-Street, And Jacob Johnson No. 147. High-Street. 1801.
>fr.[ii], t.[1], [2–5], 6–80 p.; front. only illus.; 13 cm.; bound in marbled paper over bds. Engraved frontispiece by Tanner.
>English ed. London: E. Newbery, 1799.
>MWA*; CtY (covers wanting); PP; Shaw 747.

722.2 [—] ——— Philadelphia: Printed and Sold By James Stackhouse, No. 177, North Second-street. 1814.
>fr.[ii], t.[1], [2–3], 4–71 p.; front. only illus.; 14.5 cm. buff paper covers.
>MWA*, MSaE (emb. st. on t.[1]); NNC-Pl; Shaw 31081 and 31852.

723.1 [—] Keeper's Travels In Search Of His Master. [2 lines quot.] Langhorne. Philadelphia: Printed By B. & J. Johnson, No. 147, High Street, 1801.
>fr.[ii], t.[i], [ii–iii], iv–vii, [viii, bl.], [9], 10–112 p.; front. only illus.; 13.5 cm.; bound in buff paper over bds., brown paper spine.
>English ed. London: E. Newbery, 1798.
>MWA-W*; ViU; Shaw 748.

723.2 [—] ——— Philadelphia: Published By James Thackara. R. Carr Printer. 1801.
>fr.[vi], t.[vii], viii–ix, [x], [iii], iv–viii, [1], 2–130 p.; front. only illus.; 14 cm.
>OChRHi*.

723.3. [—] ——— [2 lines of verse] Langhorne. Printed For The Booksellers. 1802.
>t.[i], [ii–iii], iv–vi, vi [sic. i.e. vii], [viii, bl.] [9], 10–126 p.; 11 cm.; bound in red scalloped marbled paper over w. bds., leather spine. Probably printed in Philadelphia.
>MWA-W* (paper on covers wanting or faded to brownish-gray, fr.[ii] probably wanting).

723.4 [—] ——— Philadelphia: Published By Johnson & Warner, No. 147, Market Street. 1808.
>fr.[ii], t.[i], [ii, bl.–iii], iv–vi, [7], 8–87, [88, bl.], [89–90, contents] p.; front. only illus.; 14 cm.; bound in olive paper over bds. [Colophon p. 90]: Lydia R. Bailey, Printer, No. 10, North-Alley.
>MWA-W*; CCamarSJ; CaOTP; CLU; CtY; DLC (2 copies); InU; IU; MH; MWA; NN; NNC-Pl; NPU; PHi; PP; PPL; PU; Shaw 15353.

724 [—] Lessons Of Virtue; Or, The Book Of Happiness. Intended For Youth. By The Author Of Keepers Travels, The Crested Wren, The Sparrow, &c. [2 lines quot.] Baltimore [Md.]: Published By Fielding Lucas, Jr. From The Diamond Press. R. W. Pomeroy, Print. 1814.
>t.[1], [2–3], 4–144 p.; 13.5 cm.; bound in green paper over bds., leather spine.
>English ed. 1801.
>CtHi*; MWA.

725 [—] The Sparrow. [2 lines of quot.] Beattie. Philadelphia: Printed For Benjamin Johnson No. 31 High-Street. And Jacob Johnson No. 147 High-Street. 1802.
>fr.[ii], t.[1], [2–3], 4–111 p.; front. only illus.; 13 cm.; bound in marbled paper over bds.; engr. frontispiece signed *Thurston, del, Tanner sc.*
>English ed. London: E. Newbery, 1798.
>Welch*; CtHi; MWA (fr.[ii] wanting); NNC-Pl; PP; Shaw 3105.

A Key To Knowledge. *See* Budden, Maria, no. **130**.

[KILNER, DOROTHY] 1755–1836

726.1 [—] THE GOOD CHILD'S DELIGHT; Or, The Road To Knowledge, In Short, Entertaining Lessons Of One & Two Syllables. Philadelphia, Printed by W. Young, the Corner of Chesnut and Second Streets. M,DCC,XCV.

fr.[2], t.[3], [4–5], 6–64 p.; front. only illus.; 10.5 cm.; gold Dutch paper covers.

Dorothy Kilner often used the pseudonym "M. P."—the initials of Maryland Point where she and her sister lived. At the request of John Marshall she later adopted the pseudonym "Mary Pelham," using the same initials.

English & Irish ed. London: adv. by John Marshall and Co. [1 address] [1783?] in M. A. Kilner's *A Course Of Lectures For Sunday Evenings.*

DLC*; Evans 28760.

726.2 [—] [——— Exeter, N.H.: Printed And Sold by H. Ranlet, 1801.] [imaginary title page].

[5], 6–27, [28, adv. of books sold by H. Ranlet, Exeter] p.; [A]₄–[A]₈, B₁–B₇ only; 10.5 cm. Five printer's ornaments are present.

Whittemore* (all before p.[5] and after p.[28] and covers wanting).

726.3 [—] ——— Exeter [N.H]: adv. by Norris & Sawyer, 1808 in **428.3**.

727.1 [—] THE HISTORY OF A GREAT MANY LITTLE BOYS AND GIRLS, For The Amusement of all Good Children, Of Four and Five Years of Age. Boston: Printed and sold by Samuel Hall, No. 53, Cornhill, 1794.

fr.[iv], t.[v], [vi], vii–viii, 9–66, [67–68, adv. list of books] p.; illus.; 11.5 cm.; Dutch paper covers, no capital letters $\frac{\text{"M"}}{\text{M}}$ on the recto of the frontispiece. On p. vii there is a large decorative bar of 5 printer's ornaments. The ornament of an angel's head is a common one in S. Hall 1794 books, but the crown, also common in S. Hall 1794 10 cm. books, is absent. Adv. by S. Hall, 1796 in **673.8**. The illustrations are mostly copied from John Marshall & Co. [1783?] London edition written in French, which were probably the same illustrations used in the edition printed by him written in English.

English and Irish ed. London: adv. by John Marshall and Co. [1 address] [1783?] in Mary

Ann (Maze) Kilner's *A Course Of Lectures For Sunday Evenings.*

MWA* (p.[69]? and rear cover wanting); CtHi (p.[67]–[69]? and rear cover wanting); Evans 27120.

727.2 [—] ——— Good Children Of Four and Five Years of Age. Hartford: Printed by Charles Hosmer. 1815.

fr.[2], t.[3], [4, alphabet], 5–31 p.; illus.; 10 cm.; pr. & illus. paper covers.

CtHi* (lower half of p. 31 wanting); DLC (1 leaf only, composed of front cover title and illus. on rear cover. Believed to be a printer's proof). NjR (p. 31 wanting); Shaw 34906.

728 [—] THE HOLIDAY PRESENT: Containing Anecdotes Of Mr. and Mrs. Jennet, And Their Little Family,—Viz.—Master George, Master Charles, Master Thomas, Miss Maria, Miss Charlotte, and Miss Harriot. Interspersed with instructive and amusing Stories And Observations. The First Worcester Edition. Printed at Worcester, Massachusetts. By Isaiah Thomas, And Sold, Wholesale and Retail, at his Book Store. MD-CCLXXXVII.

fr.[iv], t.[v], [vi–vii], viii–xi, [xii], 13–106 p.; illus.; 12.5 cm.; bound in Dutch paper over bds. English & Irish ed. London: 2 ed. J. Marshall and Co. [1 address], Dedication p. x signed: *Hamstead Jan. 23, 1781.*

MWA*; Evans 21148.

729.1 [—] LITTLE STORIES FOR LITTLE FOLKS, In Easy Lessons Of One, Two, and Three Syllables. Boston: Printed and sold by Samuel Hall, No. 53, Cornhill. [1789?].

fr.[2], t.[3], [4], 5–32, [33, adv. of 7 books] p.; illus.; 10 cm.; illus. paper covers. The illustrations on the covers are cuts used in the text on p. 28, 22, 8, 18. The author of this book, according to Harvey Darton, is Dorothy Kilner. The recto of the frontispiece has a holograph date *1787* or *1789*. The advertisement caption p.[37]: BOOKS *sold by* S. HALL, *in Boston.* This is an early caption used by S. Hall prior to 1791. *See* discussion no. **568.2**. Adv. by Samuel Hall, 1791 in **408.3**.

English ed. London: John Marshall and Co.; adv. by J. Marshall and Co. [1 address] [1783?] in M. A. Kilner's *A Course Of Lectures, For*

Sunday Evenings, as written by "M.P.", Dorothy Kilner's pseudonym.
MWA°; Evans 21924.

729.2 [—] —— Syllables. Boston: Printed and Sold by Samuel Hall, No. 53, Cornhill. [1793?].

fr.[2], t.[3], [4], 5–70 p.; illus.; 11 cm.; illus. paper covers. Adv. by S. Hall, 1793 in **955.3**; 1794 in **673.8**; 1794 in **1384.3**. There is a printer's ornament of a crown on the title page. This ornament was used in a few books printed by S. Hall in 1793 and many ones printed in 1794. The illustrations are printed from the same blocks used in no. **729.1**. The covers also are illustrated with cuts which appear in the text.
MB° (per st. on t.[3]); Evans 25723.

730.1 [—] The Rational Brutes; Or, Talking Animals. By M. Pelham, Author of the Rochfords, the Village School, and Various other Publications for the Instruction Of Children. [6 lines of verse] Philadelphia: Printed By B. & J. Johnson, No. 147, High-Street. 1801.

fr.[ii], t.[1], [2–3], 4–155 p.; front. only illus.; 13 cm.; bound in blue paper over bds.; front. signed *Satchell del. Tanner sc.*
English ed. London: Vernor and Hood, 1799.
MWA°; MHi (fr.[ii] wanting); NNC-LS; Shaw 761.

730.2 [—] —— Philadelphia: Printed For Benjamin Johnson, No. 22, North Second street, next door to the church. 1813.

t.[1], [2–3], 4–106, [107–108, adv. list of books] p.; 15 cm.; bound in pr. & illus. gray-green paper over bds.
MWA°.

731 [—] The Rotchfords; Or The Friendly Counsellor: Designed For The Instruction And Amusement Of The Youth Of Both Sexes. Two Volumes In One. Vol. I. [II.] [4 lines of verse] From The London Copy. Philadelphia: Printed and Sold by James Humphreys, at the North West Corner of Dock and Walnut-street. 1801.

t.[i], [ii–iii], iv [5], 6–159, [160, bl.]; 2nd t.[161], [162–163], 164–320, [321–324, adv.] p.; 2 vols. in 1, 17.5 cm.; bound in leather.
English ed. London: adv. by John Marshall and

Co. [1 address] [1783?] in M. A. Kilner's *A Course of Lectures For Sunday Evenings.*
MWA°; CLU; DLC; Shaw 762.

732.1 [—] Short Conversations; Or [A]n Easy Road To The Temple of Fame; Which All May Reach Who Endeavor To Be Good. [4 lines of verse.] [Printed A]nd sold by Samuel Hall, No. 53, Cornhill, Boston. 1794.

fr.[2], t.[3], [4], 5–68, [69] p.; illus.; 12 cm. English & Irish ed. London: adv. by John Marshall and Co. [1 address] [1783?] in M. A. Kilner's *A Course Of Lectures For Sunday Evenings*, as written by "M.P.", Dorothy Kilner's pseudonym.
MWA° (t.[3] mut., top of fr.[2] & p.[69] torn away).

732.2 [—] —— Boston: Printed and sold by Samuel Hall, No. 53, Cornhill. 1802.

fr.[2], t.[3], [4–5], 6–70 p.; illus.; 10 cm.
MWA°; Shaw 3067.

732.3 [—] —— Baltimore—Printed by Warner & Hanna, No. 37, Corner of South Gay & Market-streets. 1805.

fr.[2], t.[3], [4–5], 6–72 p.; illus.; 12.5 cm.; wallpaper covers. At the bottom of the frontispiece [2]: First Baltimore Edition.
MdHi°; MWA-T; Shaw 9356.

[KILNER, MARY ANN (MAZE)] b. 1753
733 [—] The Adventures Of A Pincushion. Designed Chiefly For The Use Of Young Ladies. [4 lines of verse] The First Worcester Edition. Printed at Worcester, Massachusetts. By Isaiah Thomas, And Sold, Wholesale and Retail, at his Bookstore. MDCCLXXXVIII.

fr.[ii], t.[iii], [iv], v–viii, 9–104 p.; illus.; 12 cm. English ed. London: adv. by John Marshall and Co. [1 address] [1783] in M. A. Kilner's *A Course Of Lectures For Sunday Evenings.*
MWA°; PMA; PP; RPJCB (p. v–viii, 97–104 wanting); Evans 21187.

734.1 [—] Familiar Dialogues For The Instruction and Amusement Of Children Of Four and Five Years Old. Boston: Printed and sold by S. Hall, No. 53, Cornhill. 1794.

fr.[2], t.[3], [4], 5–68, [69–70, adv. of 12 books] p.; illus.; 12 cm.

English ed. London: adv. by John Marshall

and Co. [1 address] [1783?] in M. A. Kilner's *A Course of Lectures For Sunday Evenings.* Evans 26959.

734.2 [—] ——— Exeter [N.H.]: adv. by Henry Ranlet, 1801 in **558.2.**

734.3 [—] ——— Boston: Printed for Hall & Hiller, No. 53, Cornhill. 1804.
> fr.[2], t.[3], [4], 5–69 p.; illus.; 10 cm.; pr. buff paper covers. Front cover imprint: Boston: Sold at Lincoln & Edmands' Bookstore, No. 53, Cornhill. 1815.
> MWA°; Shaw 6277 and 34671.

734.4 [—] ——— Exeter [N.H.]: adv. by Norris & Sawyer, 1808 in **428.3.**

734.5 [—] ——— Of Little Children From Four To Five Years Old. Embellished With Cuts, Boston: Published By Isaiah Thomas, Jun. 181[3?].
> fr.[2], t.[3], [4–5], 6–48 p.; illus. 13 cm.; wallpaper covers.
> MH°; Shaw 28478.

735 [—] MEMOIRS OF A PEGTOP. By The Author Of Adventures Of A Pincushion. [4 lines of verse.] The First Worcester Edition. Printed at Worcester, Massachusetts, By Isaiah Thomas, And Sold, Wholesale and Retail, at his Bookstore. MDCCLXXXVIII.
> fr.[4], t.[5], [6], 7–208 p.; illus.; 12.5 cm.
> English ed. London: J. Marshall and Co. [1 address] [*ca.* 1783].
> MWA°; MWHi; PP (bound in Dutch paper cover bds.; p. 73–74 wanting; p. 83–84 mut.); Evans 21188.

736 KIMBER & CONRAD's ABC BOOK, With Pictures For Children. Philadelphia: Published By Kimber & Conrad, No. 93, Market Street. Price 6 cents. 12½ cents coloured. [*ca.* 1810?].
> t.[1], [2–24] p.; illus.; 10.5 cm.; buff paper covers. Part of a publisher's remainder. Some of the illustrations are copies of cuts used in I. Thomas' Third Edition of *Mother Goose's Melody.* 1799.
> Welch°; CtHi; DLC; MWA; NN-C; NPV; OOxM; PP; Shaw 10678, 19293, 20497, and 48427 (dated [1819?]).

737 DAS KINDER BÜCHLEIN IN DEN BRÜDER-GEMEINEN. Gedruckt Zu Germanton bey Christoph Sauer. 1775.
> [i], [ii–ix], [x, bl.], [xi], [1, bl.], [2–7], 8–210, [1–61] p.; 8.5 cm.; bound in leather.
> PP° (Catalogued under: Moravian Church. Gesangbuch.); PHi.

KING PIPPIN. *See* The History Of King Pippin, no. **563.1.**

THE KING AND THE COBLER
738.1 THE MOST DELIGHTFUL HISTORY OF THE KING AND THE COBLER. Shewing how the King first came acquainted with the Cobler, and the many pleasant Humours which happened thereupon, &c. [cut.] The Cobler sitting and whistling in his Stall. [cut.] The Cobler's Reception and Behaviour at Court. Printed and Sold by John Boyle, in Marlborough-Street. [*ca.* 1770].
> t.[1], [2], 3–16 p.; title vignettes and tailpiece p. 16 only illus.; 17.5 cm., printed in Boston.
> English ed. title 1: *Cobbler turned Courtier, being a pleasant Humour between K. Henry 8th and a Cobler.* 1680.
> English & Scottish ed. title 2: *The Comical History of the King and the Cobler.* Glasgow.
> English ed. title 3: *The Entertaining History Of* ———. Nottingham: 2 pts. Printed for the Walking Stationers.
> English ed. title 4: *The History Of* ———. London: pt. I. Printed And Sold At The London And Middlesex Printing Office, No. 81, Shoe-lane, Holborn.
> MWA-W° (p. 15–16 wanting); MiU; Evans 42129.

738.2 ——— Sold at the Heart and Crown in Cornhill, Boston. [*ca.* 1770].
> t.[1], [2], 3–16 p.; title vignettes & tailpiece p. 16 only illus.; 16 cm.; printed by Thomas and John Fleet.
> PP° (t.[1], p. 3–4, 15–16 mut.); Evans 42130.

738.3 ——— Printed and sold at the Bible & Heart in Cornhill [Bos]ton. [*ca.* 1785–90].
> t.[1], [2], 3–16 p.; title vignettes & illus. on p. 16 only illus.; 18 cm.

NjP° (t.[1] slightly mut.); Evans 43748; Hamilton 48.

739 KLEINE ERZÄHLUNGEN ÜBER EIN BUCH MIT KUPFERN ODER LEICHTE GESCHICHTE FÜR KINDER. Philadelphia: Gedruckt für Johnson und Warner. 1809.

t.[1], [2–44] p.; illus.; 14 cm.; blue marbled paper covers. A translation into German of *Little Prattle over a Book of Prints*. See no. **777**.

Welch°; CLU; CaOTP; IU; MWA; NHi; PHi; PP; PPL; PU; Shaw 17875.

DIE KLEINEN WANDERER. *See* Johnson, Richard, no. **682.4**.

L

740.1 THE LADDER TO LEARNING, Or, Child's Instructor. Calculated To instruct Little Children, and prepare their minds for Larger Books. It Contains, Lessons for the more easy attaining the true Reading of English.—To which is added,—Entertaining Stories, And The Catechism. First Edition. Stonington-Port [Conn.], Printed By S. Trumbull; Who keeps constantly for sale, very cheap, a large assortment of Books for Children, by the Groce Dozen or Single. [*ca.* 1802].

> fr.[2], t.[3], [4–5], 6–71 p.; illus.; 12 cm.; blue wallpaper covers.
> CtHi°.

740.2 —————— Learning. Baltimore: adv. by G. Douglas, 1803 in **275.46**.

LAMB, CHARLES, 1775–1834 and MARY LAMB, 1764–1847

741 [—] MRS. LEICESTER'S SCHOOL: Or The History Of Several Young Ladies, Related By Themselves. First American Edition. George Town: Published By Joseph Milligan. W. Cooper, Printer, 1811.

> fr.[ii], t.[i], [ii–v], vi–xi, [xii, bl.], [13], 14–165 p.; front. only illus.; 15 cm.; bound in paper over bds.; front. signed *W. Hopwood del. W. R. Jones sc.* The stories "Maria Howe," "Susan Yates," "Arabella Hardy," were written by Charles Lamb, the remainder by his sister Mary Lamb.
> English ed. London: M. J. Godwin, 1809.
> MWA°; CtY; MB; MShM; NcD; NRU; PP; (p. 73–74 wanting); PPL; PSC; Shaw 23173.

742 [—] POETRY FOR CHILDREN, Entirely Original. By The Author Of "Mrs. Leicester's School." Boston: Published By West And Richardson, and Edward Cotton. 1812.

> t.[i.], [ii–iii], iv–vi, [7], 8–144 p.; 15 cm., leather spine; blue marbled paper over bds.; p.[ii]: E. G. House Printer, Court-street. A. E. Newton, 1925, p. 346, quotes Lamb in a letter written in 1827, "One likes to have a copy of everything one does. I neglected to keep one of 'Poetry For Children,' the joint production of Mary and me and it is now not to be had for love or money."

English ed. London: 2 vols., M. J. Godwin, 1809. MWA°; CSmH; CtY; ICU (rebound); FTaSU; MH; MNe (p. 95–96 mut.); N; NRU; PP (copy 1, copy 2 bound in leather wants one leaf); Shaw 25814 and 26489.

743.1 [—] POETRY FOR CHILDREN. Adorned with Cuts. New-Haven. Sidney's Press. For J. Babcock & Son. 1819.

> fr.[2], t.[3], [4–5], 6–30, [31, adv.] p.; illus.; 10.5 cm.; illus. white paper covers pr. in pink ink. An abridged ed.
> MWA°; CtHi; NCooHi; Shaw 49146.

743.2 [—] —————— New-Haven: For J. Babcock & Son. Sidney's Press. 1820.

> fr.[2], t.[3], [4–5], 6–30, [31] p.; illus.; 10.5 cm.; pr. & illus. pink paper covers.
> Cover title: Published by John Babcock & Sons, New Haven, and S. and W. R. Babcock, Charleston.
> MWA°; CtHi; NNC-LS (fr.[2], p.[31], & covers wanting); Shoemaker 1898.

744 — TALES FROM SHAKESPEARE, Designed For The Use Of Young Persons. By Charles Lamb. In Two Volumes. Vol. I. [II.] Philadelphia: Published By Bradford And Inskeep; And Inskeep And Bradford, NEWYORK. J. Maxwell, Printer. 1813.

> vol. I.: ½t.[1], [2, bl.], fr.[ii, portrait], t.[3], [4–5], 6–283 p.; front. only illus. an engr. pl. signed *Zoust pinxit* and *Edwin Sc.*; vol. II.: t.[1]. [2–5], 6–305 p.; no illus.; 2 vols. 17.5 cm.; bound in pr. paper over bds. Half title: Tales From Shakespeare. Written by Charles and Mary Lamb but mostly by Mary. In a letter to Wordsworth, Charles said he was responsible for "Lear," "Macbeth," "Timon," "Romeo," "Hamlet," "Othello," and for occasionally a tailpiece or correction of grammar, for none of the cuts and all of the spelling.
> English ed. London: 2 vols. T. Hodgkins, 1807. PP° (vols. I. II.); MH; MWA (vol. I.); NN (vols. I. II. with ½t.[1] of vol I. wanting); PPL; Shaw 28900.

A Lecture On Heads. *See* Stephens, George Alexander, no. **1257.**

745 Lectures To Young Ladies. To Which Are Added, Short Hymns, Suited To The Subjects. By A Lady. Hartford: Printed By John Babcock. 1801.

t.[1], [2, bl.–3], 4–96 p.; illus.; 13 cm.; bound in brown paper over w. bds.

CtHi°; Ct (rebound; p. 93–96 wanting); MWA; RPB; Shaw 783.

Ledley, Edward. *See* Johnson, Richard, no. **672.2.**

[LEE, RICHARD] 1747–1823
746 [—] The Melancholy End Of Ungrateful Children. Exemplified in the dreadful fate of the Son and Daughter of a wealthy Farmer, who, after receiving and dividing the wealth of their Parents, refused them, in their old age, the shelter of their roof, or a morsel of bread. With an account of the wonderful scenes the Daughter beheld in her trance. Printed for the benefit of the rising Generation, at the particular request of all who were eye-witnesses to the scene. [4 lines of verse]—Rutland [Vt.]:—Printed For Richard Lee. M.DCC.XCV.

t.[1], [2], 3–8 p.; 16.5 cm.

RPB°; DLC; MWA; McCorison 342; Evans 28961.

747 Leisure Hours, Or Evenings At Home, Well Spent In The Improvement of the Mind. New-York: Printed For T. B. Jansen & Co. Booksellers, No. 248, Pearl-Street. 1802.

fr.[ii], t.[1], [2–3], 4–70, [71–72 adv. list of books] p.; 4 pl.; 14.5 cm.; front. signed *A* [A. Anderson], and pl. opp. p. 37, & 60 signed *Anderson.*

NjP°; CLU; Hamilton 216; Shaw 2515.

[LeMOINE, HENRY] 1756–1812
748 [—] The Humourous Story Of Mrs Gilpin's Return From Edmonton. Being the Sequel to Jonny Gilpin. Illustrated With Humourous Engravings, On Copperplate. Philadelphia: Published and sold Wholesale, by Wm. Charles, and may be had of all the Booksellers. 1815. Price, plain, 18 3–4 Cents. Coloured, 25 cents.

fr.[ii], t.[1], [2–3], 4–15 p.; 6 pl. including front.; 12.5 cm.; pr. yellow paper covers.

English ed. London: ——— *Edmonton; being a sequel to the Wedding-Day.* [1784?].

MWA-W° (colored plates), PP (uncolored plates), RPB (colored plates, p. 15 torn in half); Shaw 34462; Weiss 1932b.

LE PRINCE DE BEAUMONT, MARIE 1711–1780
749.1 ——— The Young Misses' Magazine: Containing Dialogues Between A Governess and several Young Ladies of Quality, her Scholars. In Which Each Lady is made to speak according to her particular Genius, Temper, and Inclination; Their several Faults are pointed out, and the easy way to mend them, as well as to think, and speak, and act properly; no less care being taken to form their hearts to goodness, than to enlighten their understandings with useful knowledge. A short and clear Abridgement is also given of sacred and profane History, and some lessons in Geography. The useful blended throughout with the agreeable, the whole being interspersed with proper reflections and moral Tales. Translated from the French of Madam Le Prince De Beaumont. In Four Volumes. Vol. I. [II–IV] Philadelphia, Printed By Mathew Carey. MDCCXCII. Sold by M. Carey, F. Bailey, and T. Lang, in Philadelphia; and by T. Allen, in New-York.

vol. I: t.[1], [2–5], 6–175, [176, bl.]; vol. II: t.[177], [178–179], 180–238 p.; 2 vols. in 1; vol. III: t.[1], [2–3], 4–143, [144, bl.]; vol. IV: t.[145], [146–147], 148–308, [309–312 adv. list of books] p.; 2 vols in 1; 13.5 cm.; bound in leather. The story of "Beauty and the Beast" appears in this work.

English ed. London: 2nd ed. 1757.

MWA° (vols. I–IV); CtY (vols. III–IV); DLC (vol. IV); RPB (vols. III–IV); Bowe mss.; Evans 24472.

749.2 ——— ——— In Four Volumes. Vol. I. [II–IV.] Philadelphia, Printed By Mathew Carey. MDCCXCII.

vol. I: t.[3], [4–5], 6–175, [176, bl.]; vol. II: t.[177], [178–179], 180–328 p.; 2 vols. in one; 14 cm.; bound in leather; Sig [A]₂ is wanting in this volume. If it were present as in the former edition the pagination would be t.[1], [2–5], 6–175 . . . The book except for the imprint is the same as the preceding edition.

MWA° (vols. I–II.); Bowe mss.; Evans 24472.

749.3 ——— ——— Faults are pointed out, and the easy Way to mend them,—The Useful is blended

throughout————moral Tales. Vol. I.[II.] Whitehall [Pa.]: Printed for William Young Bookseller
and Stationer, No. 52 South Second street, Philadelphia. M,DCCC.

vol. I: t.[i], [ii], [1], 2, [5], 6–341, [342, adv.
list of books]; 14 cm.; vol. II: t.[1], [2, bl.],
[3–5], 6–324 p.; 14.5 cm.; 2 vols. bound in
leather.

NN° (vol. II); MWA-T (vol. I); Bowe mss.;
Evans 38324.

749.4 ————— In Four Volumes. Vol. I.[II.]
Brooklyn [N.Y.], Printed By Thomas Kirk. 1806.

vol. I: fr.[ii], t.[1], [2–5], 6–174, [p. 174: End
of Vol. First.], [175], 176–324 [p. 324; End of
Vol. Second] p.; 2 vols. in 1 with the second
vol. without a separate title page; vol. II: fr.
[ii], t.[1], [2–3], 4–143 [p. 143: End of Vol.
Third.]; [144–145], 146–306, [p. 306: End of
the Fourth Volume] p.; 2 vols. in 1 with the
fourth vol. without a separate title page; 14.5
cm.; bound in leather.

MWA° (vols. I–II); PP; Bowe mss.; Shaw
10720.

749.5 ————— De Beaumont. New-York:
Printed For Campbell And Mitchell Booksellers,
124 Pearl-Street. 1807.

vol. I: fr.[2], t.[3], [4–7], 8–174, [p. 174: End
of Vol. First], [175], 176–324, [p. 324: End of
Vol. Second.]; 2 vols. in 1, with the Second Vol.
without a separate title page, 14.5 cm. vol. II:
fr.[ii], t.[1], [2–3], 4–143, [p. 143; End of Vol.
Third.]; [144, bl.]; [145], 146–306, [p. 306:
End of the Fourth and last Volume.] p.; 2 vols.
in 1 with the fourth vol. without a separate
title page; 14 cm.; bound in leather.

MWA° (vol. II); PPL° (vols. I–II); Bowe
mss.; Shaw 12908.

749.6 ————— Two Volumes In One. New-
York: Published By Samuel Campbell And Son,
No. 68 Water-Street, J. & J. Harper, Printers.
1818.

t.[1], [2–5], 6–129, [p. 129: End of Volume
First.], [130, bl.]; [131], 132–240 p.; 2 vols. in
1 with the second vol. without a separate title
page; 16.5 cm.; bound in leather.

MWA°; Bowe mss.; Shaw 44562.

749.7 ————— Two Volumes In One. New-
York: Published By Samuel Campbell And Son,

No. 68 Water-Street, J. & J. Harper, Printers.
1819.

t.[1], [2–5], 6–129, [p. 129: End of Volume
First], [130, bl.]; [131], 132–240 p.; 17.5 cm.;
bound in leather.

MWA°; CtY (i. st. on t.[1]; rebound); MH;
MnU; PP; Bowe mss.; Shaw 48473.

[LE SAGE, ALAIN RENE] 1668–1747

750.1 [—] The Adventures Of Gil Blas, Of San-
tillane, Abridged. Worcester: Printed By Isaiah
Thomas, Jun. Sold Wholesale And Retail At His
Bookstore, At The Sign Of Johnson's Head. 1796.

t.[1], [2–3], 4–196 p.; t.[1] 15 cm.

English ed. London: E. Newbery, 1782.

Welch° (rebound; p. 187–190 wanting); MB;
MHi; MWA; NPV; Evans 30686.

750.2 [—] ————— Leominster [Mass.]: Printed
By Salmon Wilder, For Isaiah Thomas, Jun. September 1810.

t.[1], [2–3], 4–148 p.; 17 cm.; bound in blue
marbled paper over bds., leather spine.

Welch° (p. 107–108 mut.); DLC; MB; MH;
MWA; PP; Shaw 20548.

LESLIE, ELIZA 1787–1858

751 — The Young Ladies' Mentor; Or, Extracts
In Prose And Verse, For The Promotion Of Virtue
And Morality. By Eliza Leslie. [2 lines of verse]
Montaigne. Philadelphia: Printed For Jacob John-
son, No. 187 Market Street. Thomas S. Manning,
Printer. 1803.

t.[i], [ii–iii], iv–vii, [viii, bl.], [9], 10–155 p.;
16 cm.; bound in marbled paper over bds.,
leather spine.

PP°; MWA; Shaw 4518.

752 Lessons For Young Persons In Humble
Life: Calculated to promote their improvement
in the art of reading; in virtue and piety; and, particularly, in the knowledge of the duties peculiar
to their stations. Philadelphia: Printed and Sold by
James Humphreys, Changewalk. 1809.

t.[i], [ii–v], vi–xii, [13], 14–372 p.; t.[i]; 17.5
cm.

English ed. York: 1808.

OOxM°; PP; Shaw 17907.

753 Lessons In Verse. A New Year's Present
For The Children Of The West Church. Boston:
Printed By John Eliot, Jun. 1812.

t.[1], [2–3], 4–54 p.; 14.5 cm.; blue-gray paper covers.
CtHi*; DLC, MB (per. st. on t.[1]); MH; MWA (covers wanting); Shaw 25849.

LESSONS OF VIRTUE. *See* Kendall, Edward A., no. **724.**

L'ESTRANGE, SIR ROGER. *See* Aesop, no. **20.1.**

754.1 LETTERS, WRITTEN FROM LONDON, Descriptive Of Various Scenes And Occurrences Frequently met with in the Metropolis And Its Vicinity. For the Amusement of Children. Illustrated By Plates. Philadelphia: Published By Jacob Johnson, No. 147, Market-Street. 1808.
t.[i], [ii], [1], 2–52 p.; illus.; 16 cm.; yellow paper covers; p.[ii]: Adams, Printer, Philadelphia. On p. 33 is an illus. of the balloon in which Monsieur Garnerin is ascending. Adv. by Johnson & Warner, 1814 in **1449.2.**
English ed. London: Darton & Harvey, 1807.
Welch*; MWA; Shaw 15424.

754.2 ——— Children. With numberous Engravings. Boston: Published By Thomas B. Wait & Co. And Charles Williams. 1813.
t.[3], [4–5], 6–71 p.; illus.; 15 cm. pr. & illus. paper covers; cover title undated. The illus. on p.[5], [8], [15], [53], [54] are signed *N.D.* [Nathaniel Dearborn].
NjP*; Hamilton 688.

THE LIFE AND ADVENTURES OF A FLY. *See* Jones, Stephen, no. **691.1.**

THE LIFE & ADVENTURES OF SINDBAD THE SAILOR. *See* Sindbad The Sailor, no. **1212.4.**

THE LIFE AND DEATH OF TOM THUMB. *See* Tom Thumb, no. **1314.1.**

755 THE LIFE AND MEMORABLE ACTIONS OF GEORGE WASHINGTON, General and Commander Of The Armies Of America. A New Edition Corrected. Frederick-Town [Md.], Printed by M. Bartgis. 1801.
fr.[2], t.[3], [4–5], 6–68 p.; front. only illus.; 15.5 cm.
PHi*; Shaw 1638.

THE LIFE OF JOSEPH. *See* Macgowan, John, no. **810.34.**

THE LIFE OF JOSEPH, A SCRIPTURE NARRATIVE. *See* [Miller, Ebenezer], no. **845.**

756.1 THE LIFE OF JUDAS ISCARIOT. Boston: adv. as "Just Published And to be Sold by Z. Fowle, at his Printing-Office in Back-Street," in *A Chain Of Four Links* [*ca.* 1765].

756.2 THE LIFE OF JUDAS ISCARIOT; Who betrayed his Lord and Master. Embellished with Cuts. Philadelphia: Printed in the Year M,DCC,-XCIV.
fr.[2], t.[3], [4–5], 6–29 p.; illus.; 9 cm.; green Dutch paper covers.
MWA*; Evans 27222.

THE LIFE OF MARY MORDANT. *See* [Marshall, Mrs. L.]. no. **815.**

757.1 THE LIFE OF THAT WONDERFUL AND EXTRAORDINARY HEAVY MAN, DANIEL LAMBERT, From His Birth To The Moment Of His Dissolution; With An Account of Men noted for their Corpulency, and other interesting matter. New-York: Printed And Sold By Samuel Wood, At The Juvenile Book-Store, No. 357, Pearl-Street. 1814.
fr.[ii], t.[1], [2–5], 6–46 p.; front. only illus.; 13 cm.; pr. paper covers; cover title undated.
English ed. Stamford: Drakard's 3 ed. J. Drakard; Crosby and Co., London, 1809.
MWA* (copy 1, with covers; copy 2, bound with other books in no. **191**); MH (p. 45–46 wanting); NRU; Shaw 31934.

757.2 ——— New-York: Printed And Sold By Samuel Wood & Sons, At The Juvenile Book Store, No. 357, Pearl-Street. 1815.
fr.[ii], t.[1], [2–5], 6–46 p.; front. only illus.; 13.5 cm.; pr. buff paper covers; front cover undated; copy A. Rear cover copy A: A General Assortment Of Johnson & Warner's Elegant Juvenile Books, For Sale By Samuel Wood, Agent for them in New-York, On the same terms to the trade given by J. & W. The rear cover of copy B: An Extensive Collection Of Children's Books, School Books, Stationary, &c For Sale Wholesale and Retail, by Samuel Wood No 357 Pea[rl-Street,] New-[York].
MWA-W* (copy A); DLC; MH; MWA* (copy B); NN (copy B); Shaw 35107.

757.3 ——— New-York: Published By Samuel Wood & Sons, No. 261, Pearl-Street; And Samuel

S. Wood & Co. No. 212, Market-street, Baltimore. 1818.

> fr.[2], t.[3], [4–5], 6–46 p.; front. only illus.; 14 cm.; pr. & illus. buff paper covers. The Preface p.[2] is omitted in this ed.
> MWA°; NjN; Shaw 44586; Weiss 1942, p. 767.

758   THE LIFE, TRAVELS, VOYAGES, AND DARING ENGAGEMENTS OF PAUL JONES. Containing Numerous Anecdotes Of Undaunted Courage. To Which Is Added The Life And Adventures Of Peter Williamson, Who was Kidnapped when an Infant, from his Native Place, Aberdeen, And Sold For A Slave In America. Hartford: Printed By John Russell, jr.—State-Street. And for sale, Wholesale and Retail. 1813.

> OOxM.

759   THE LILLIPUTIAN AUCTION. To Which All Little Masters and Misses Are Invited By Charly Chatter, Walk In Young Gentlemen and Ladies, A Going, a Going, a Going! The World's an Auction, where by Young and Old, Both Goods and Characters are bought and sold. Philadelphia: Published by Jacob Johnson, No. 147, Market Street. 1802.

> fr.[2], t.[3], [4], 5–31 p.; illus.; 10.5 cm.; marbled paper covers.
> English ed. London: adv. by T. Carnan and F. Newbery, 1776 in *Nurse Truelove's Christmas Box.*
> MWA°; Shaw 2537.

THE LILLIPUTIAN LIBRARY. *See* Johnson, Richard, The Poetical Flower Basket, Vol. VI., no. **686.**

THE LILLIPUTIAN MASQUERADE. *See* [Jones, Giles] [sic. i.e., author unknown], no. **690.1.**

760   THE LILY: A Book For Children; Containing Twelve Trifles In Verse; Adorned With Cuts. Philadelphia: Published By Johnson & Warner, No. 147, Market-Street. 1809. W. M'Culloch, Printer.

> t.[1], [2–3], 4–35 p.; illus.; 14 cm.; pr. tan paper covers; cover title undated.
> English ed. London: J. Harris, 1808.
> Shaw 17918.

LIMED TWIGS, To Catch Young Birds. *See* Gilbert, Ann (Taylor) and Jane Taylor, no. **440.**

761   A LIST OF NOUNS, Or Things Which May Be Seen. Philadelphia: Published By Jacob Johnson, No. 147, Market-street. 1804.

> t.[1], [2–14] p.; 10.5 cm.; blue marbled paper covers; p. [13–14] adv. list of books.
> MWA°; DLC; MdHi; NNMM; PHi; PP; PPL; RNHi; Shaw 6659.

762   THE LITTLE BEGGAR GIRL. And William And Henry. New-York: Published by L. B. Jansen and G. Jansen. 1808.

> t.[1], [2], 3–24 p.; illus.; 12.5 cm.; pr. & illus. yellow paper covers.
> Cover title: Sold At Jansen's Juvenile & School Library. The Beggar Girl. Ornamented with Cuts. New-York: Published By L. B. Jansen, No. 116 Broadway, opposite the City-hotel. 1802.
> MiD°; MWA; Shaw 15438.

763   A LITTLE BOOK FOR CHILDREN, Containing A few Rules for the Regulation of their Tho'ts, Words and Actions. Portsmouth, New Hampshire: Printed by Daniel Fowle. 1758.

> t.[1], [2–3], 4–16 p.; 9.5 cm. Preface, dated June 22, 1758, p.[2]; Chap. I. For the Regulation of your Thoughts, p.[3]–4; Chap. II. Of Words, p. 4–5; Chap. III. Of Actions, p. 5–9; A Short Catechism, p. 9–11; [Poetry] Children to the eternal God,/Your grateful voices raise, . . . p. 11–13; The Story of Miss Sally Friendly, p. 13–16.
> MB°; Evans 8161.

A LITTLE BOOK FOR LITTLE CHILDREN. *See* White, Thomas, no. **1428.**

764   LITTLE CHARLES. New-York: adv. by T. B. Jansen, [*ca.* 1815] in **47.**

765   LITTLE CHARLES, MARGARET, AND OTHER STORIES. Adorned With Cuts. Sidney's Press. New-Haven. 1817.

> fr.[2], t.[3], [4–5], 6–30, [31, adv.] p.; illus.; 10 cm.; Dutch paper covers. In the MWA-W copy there is a period after "Press." on t.[3].
> CtHi°; DLC (illus. yellow-buff paper front cover; rear cover wanting; p. 29–30 mut.); MWA-W (fr.[2] & front cover wanting); Shaw 41276.

766 LITTLE CHARLES, Or, The Good Son. And Clara And Amelia. New-York: Published by L. B. Jansen and G. Jansen 1808.

t.[1], [2–3], 4–24 p.; illus.; 12.5 cm.; pr. & illus. brownish-buff paper covers; rear cover adv. of 15 books.
Cover title: Sold At Jansen's Juvenile & School Library. Little Charles, And Clara & Amelia. Ornamented with Cuts. New-York: Published By L. B. Jansen 1808.
Adomeit*.

LITTLE CHARLOTTE. *See* Cecil, Sabina, no. **164.**

767.1 THE LITTLE CHRISTIAN: A Novel, Founded On Facts: Designed For The Amusement And Instruction Of Children, Whether Young Or Old. Written By Himself. [4 lines quot.] Published According To Act Of Congress. Boston: Printed By Josiah Ball. Sold by Manning & Loring, No. 2, Cornhill, and Daniel Conant, No. 9, Back-Street, Boston; Barnard B. Macanulty, Salem; Pierce Hill & Pierce, Portsmouth; and other Booksellers. 1805.

t.[1], [2–3], 4–36 p.; 16.5 cm.
NHi* (bound, originally a pamphlet without covers); Shaw 8795.

767.2 ———— [5 lines quot.] Third Edition. Published According To Act Of Congress. Boston: Printed For The Purchaser. 1817.

t.[1], [2–3], 4–58 [i.e. 48] p.; 12.5 cm.; blue paper covers.
MWA-W*.

767.3 ———— A Novel Founded On Fact: ———— [4 lines quot.] Brookfield [Mass.]. Printed For The Author. 1817.

t.[1], [2–3], 4–69 p.; 14 cm.
MWA*; Shaw 41277.

THE LITTLE COUNTRY VISITOR. *See* Pinchard, Mrs., Dramatic Dialogues, no. **1008.**

LITTLE DOG TRUSTY. *See* Edgeworth, Maria, no. **333.**

768 LITTLE EDWARD. Philadelphia: adv. by E. & R. Parker, 1818 in **704.1.**

LITTLE EMMA AND HER FATHER. *See* Baker, Mrs. Caroline (Horwood), no. **56.**

769 THE LITTLE FISHERMAN. Philadelphia: adv. by B. & T. Kite, 1807 in **611.1.**

770.1 LITTLE HISTORIES FOR LITTLE FOLKS. Shewing The Punishment that will befall Naughty Boys And Girls. Adorned with Cuts. New-York: Printed by W. Durell, For Evert Duyckinck. 1800.

t.[3], [4, alphabets], 5–30 p.; illus.; 10.5 cm.
MWA-W*

770.2 ———— Embellished With Cuts. Philadelphia: Printed By John Adams. 1806.

t.[3], [4, alphabets], 5–30 p.; illus.; 10.5 cm.
MWA* (fr.[2]?, p.[31]? & covers wanting, p.[27–30] almost entirely wanting, p. 25–26 mut.).

771 LITTLE HISTORY FOR LITTLE FOLKS. Philadelphia: adv. by B. & T. Kite, 1807 in **611.1.**

772 THE LITTLE ISLANDERS, Or The Blessings Of Industry. Embellished With Copper-Plate Engravings. Philadelphia: Published By Johnson & Warner, No. 147, Market-Street. Brown & Merritt, Printers, 24, Church-ally. 1809.

fr.[ii], t.[1], [2–3], 4–36 p.; 4 pl. including front.; 13 cm.; pr. buff paper covers; four pl. including front. signed *WR sc.* [William Ralph].
Adv. by Johnson & Warner, 1814 in **1449.2.**
English ed. London: J. Harris, 1804.
MWA*; Shaw 17922.

LITTLE JACK OF ALL TRADES. *See* Darton, William, no. **261.1.**

LITTLE JANE. *See* Cecil, Sabina, no. **165.1.**

LITTLE JANE, THE YOUNG COTTAGER. *See* Richmond, Legh, no. **1108.1.**

LITTLE JOHN *pseud.*
773.1 THE HISTORY OF LITTLE DICK. Written By Little John. Philadelphia: Printed by Francis Bailey, at Yorick's-Head, No. 116, High-Street. 1793.

fr.[2], t.[3], [4–7], 8–60, [61–63, adv. list of 35 books]; illus.; 10 cm.; orange wallpaper covers.
English ed. [*ca.* 1790].
MWA-W*; Evans 46783.

773.2 ———— Dick. Wilmington [Del.]: adv. by P. Brynberg, 1801 in **61.9.**

773.3 ——— Dick, Written By Little John. [4 lines of verse] Philadelphia [in a vignette] Published By Jacob Johnson. No. 147, Market-Street. < J. Bioren, Printer. > 1803.

fr.[ii], t.[1], [2–7], 8–112 p.; illus.; 13.5 cm.; bound in blue marbled paper over bds.; p.[97]–112 a "Juvenile Catalogue" of books; 12 full page engr. illus. including front. & 11 tailpiece cuts. The tailpiece cut of a bird on a tree p. 69 is repeated p. 112.

OOxM* (the "3" of the t.[1] date "180[3]" is not struck); MWA (unbound loose sheets, covers and all after p. 44 wanting, the "3" of the date "1803" on t.[1] is struck); Shaw 4374.

773.4 ——— Philadelphia: Published By Jacob Johnson, No. 147, Market Street. 1807.

fr.[ii], t.[1], [2–7], 8–96 p.; illus.; 13.5 cm.; bound in marbled paper over bds., leather spine; p.[87]–96: "A Juvenile Catalogue Of Books For Sale By Jacob Johnson." There are 12 full page engr. plates including the front. and woodcut tailpieces.

MWA* (i. st. on t.[1]; 1 pl. wanting); CtY (p. 13–60, 75–76, 87–94 wanting; t.[1] & p. [3]–8 mut.; p. 61–66 incorrectly bound after p. 82); NNC-T; PHi; PP; Shaw 12759.

774.1 [A Little] Lottery Book. New-York: adv. by Hugh Gaine, 1786 in Clarke's *Corderii Colloquiorum Centuria Selecta.*

774.2 A Little Lottery Book For Children: Containing A new Method of playing them into a Knowledge of the Letters, Figures, &c. Embellished with above Fifty Cuts, And Published with the Approbation of the Court of Common Sense. First Worcester Edition. Printed at Worcester, Massachusetts, By Isaiah Thomas. Sold at his Bookstore in Worcester, and by him and Company in Boston. [1788].

fr.[2], t.[3], [4, bl.], 5–61, [62–63 adv. list of books] p.; illus.; 10.5 cm.; Dutch paper covers. Adv. by I. Thomas, 1787 in **906.2**; 1788 in **685**; 1789 in **954.3**.

English ed. London: adv. by John Newbery, 1759 in *Food for the Mind.*

English ed. entitled: *A New Lottery Book Of Birds and Beasts, For Children.* Newcastle: T. Saint, 1771.

MWA*; NjP (t.[3] wanting); Evans 21205.

775 Little Lucy: Or The Careless Child Reformed. Cambridge [Mass.]: Printed By Hilliard And Metcalf. 1820

t.[1], [2–3], 4–33 p.; 14.5 cm.; pr. buff paper covers.

MWA* (pages dog-eared and mut., p. 13–24, 30–32 wanting); MSaE (2 copies, both complete); PP; Shoemaker 1981.

Little Mary. *See* Cecil, Sabina, no. **166.1**.

The Little Masters And Misses Delight. *See* Slybouts, Young, no. **1216**.

Little Merchants. *See* Edgeworth, Maria, no. **321.1**.

776.1 Little Poems For Children. Windsor, (Vt.) Printed By Jesse Cochran, And Sold Wholesale And Retail, At His Book-Store. 1815.

fr.[2], t.[3], [4–5], 6–31 p.; front. only illus. [a picture of a chair which is not surrounded by a decorative border of printer's ornaments]; 10 cm.; pr. & illus. yellow paper covers. Contains poems by Jane Taylor & Mrs Ann [Taylor] Gilbert and others. The last is a rhymed advertisement.

Cover title: Little Poems. [oval cut of a pigeon on a tree] Windsor, Vt. Printed And Sold By Jesse Cochran.

MWA*; PP; McCorison 1752; Shaw 35119.

776.2 ——— [printer's ornament] Windsor, Vt. Printed and Sold by Jesse Cochran. 1815.

fr.[2], t.[3], [4–5], 6–31 p.; front. only illus., a picture of a chair surrounded with a decorative border of printer's ornaments and a top and bottom inner row of asterisks; 10 cm.; pr. & illus. brownish-buff paper covers. This edition varies from no. **776.1** by having a border around the frontispiece, a varying cover, and the title page imprint differently worded. Five poems have been added to this edition: "The Rose," "Innocent Play," "Good Resolutions," "The Thief" [by I. Watts], "The Drum" by Scott, p. 23–30.

Cover title: Little Poems. [an oval cut of an apple on a table] A copy of an English one used in *The Engraver's Present. London: John Marshall.* [1 address] [178–?] Windsor Vt. ——— Cochran. It is surrounded by a border of printer's ornaments.

Welch*; CLU (a second set of varying covers);

FtaSU; MB; MWA (yellow paper covers); PP;
McCorison 1753.

LITTLE POEMS FOR LITTLE READERS. *See* Gilbert,
Ann (Taylor), no. **441.1.**

777 LITTLE PRATTLE OVER A BOOK OF PRINTS.
With Easy Tales For Children. Philadelphia: Pub-
lished by J. Johnson. 1808.
  t.[1], [2–60] p.; illus.; 13.5 cm. p.[2]: Adams,
  Printer, Philadelphia. Adv. by Johnson and
  Warner, 1809 in **212.2** and 1814 in **1449.3.**
  English ed. London: Wm. Darton and Josh.
  Harvey, Sept. 29, 1804.
  CLU° (orig. covers covered over with yellow
  paper); PP (marbled paper covers); Shaw
  15439.

778.1 A LITTLE PRETTY POCKET-BOOK, Intended
For The Instruction and Amusement Of Little
Master Tommy, And Pretty Miss Polly. With Two
Letters from Jack the Giant-Killer. New-York:
Printed by Hugh Gaine. 1762.
  Evans 9159.

778.2 A LITTLE PRETTY POCKET-BOOK, Intended
For The Instruction and Amusement Of Little
Master Tommy, And Pretty Miss Polly. With Two
Letters from Jack the Giant-Killer; As Also A Ball
and Pincushion; The Use of which will infallibly
make Tommy a good Boy, and Polly a good Girl.
To which is added, A Little Song-Book, Being A
New Attempt to teach Children the Use of the
English Alphabet, by Way of Diversion. The First
Worcester Edition. Printed at Worcester, Massa-
chusetts. By Isaiah Thomas, And Sold Wholesale
and Retail, at his Book-Store. MDCCLXXXVII.
  fr.[2], t.[3], [4–7], 8–122, [123–124 adv. of
  10 juveniles] p.; illus.; 10 cm.; green and gold
  modern simulated Dutch paper covers. This is
  a relatively common book there being a publisher's remainder of it.
  English ed. London: adv. by John Newbery,
  1744 in the *Penny London Morning Advertiser*
  June 18–20, 1744.
  MWA° (2 copies); CLU; CSmH (rebound);
  CtY (rebound); CtY (Pequot, uncut, unbound
  sheets); DLC (rebound); ICU; MH; MWHi
  (not a remainder); NjP; NN (2 copies, 1 copy
  rebound); PP; RPJCB (uncut, unbound sheets);
  Evans 20459; Hamilton 115.

779.1 THE LITTLE PUZZLING CAP. Worcester:
adv. by Isaiah Thomas, 1787 in **906.2;** 1788 in
685; 1789 in **954.3;** 1794 in **1445.2.**

779.2 ———— Philadelphia: adv. by F. Bailey,
1792 in **359.**

780 THE LITTLE RAMBLER; And Other Tales.
Embellished With Three Copper-Plate Engravings. Philadelphia: Published By Jacob Johnson,
No. 147, Market-Street. 1808.
  fr.[ii], t.[1], [2–3], 4–36 p.; A–B₆, C₅ probably
  1 leaf wanting; front. only illus.; 14 cm.; pr. &
  illus. blue paper covers.
  NNC-LS° (p. 35–36, and 2 pl. wanting); ICU
  (3 pl. wanting).

781 THE LITTLE RAMBLER, And Other Tales.
Adorned With Cuts. Sidney's Press. New-Haven.
1815.
  fr.[2], t.[3], [4–5], 6–31 p.; illus.; 10 cm.; green
  paper covers.
  MWA° (p.[2], & 31, and covers mut.); NNC-T;
  Shaw 35121.

THE LITTLE RIDDLE BOOK. *See* John-The-Giant-
Killer, no. **667.**

782 LITTLE ROBIN RED BREAST; A Collection Of
Pretty Songs, For the Instruction and Amusement
of Children: Entirely New. The First Worcester
Edition. Worcester, (Massachusetts) Printed By
Isaiah Thomas, And Sold At His Book-Store
MDCCLXXXVI.
  t.[i], [ii, bl.], [1], 2–120 p.; illus.; 10 cm.,
  bound in Dutch paper over w. bds.; verse. Adv.
  by I. Thomas, 1794 in **1445.2.**
  English ed. London: adv. by E. Newbery, 1784
  in Fielding's *The History And Adventures of
  Joseph Andrews.*
  MWA°; Evans 20461.

783 THE LITTLE SCHOLAR'S PRETTY POCKET
COMPANION, Or Youth's First Step On The Ladder
of Learning, In Rhyme and Prose. [2 lines of
verse] By a friend to the youth of Columbia.
Bennington [Vt.], Printed by Anthony Haswell.
[1795?].
  t.[1], [2–36] p.; illus.; 10.5 cm.; Pages [2–8]
  have an alphabet with each letter, both upper
  and lower case, enclosed in a square of type
  ornaments similar to *Tom Thumb's Play Book.*

CtY* (Pequot, covers wanting); PPL (covers wanting); McCorison 345; Evans 28810.

784 LITTLE STORIES FOR LITTLE CHILDREN, Containing The Story of Mr. Solomon Wiseman, and Jonny Badboy. Adorned with Cuts. Printed at Salem by N. Coverly. 1803.
t.[1], [2–3], 4–16 p.; illus.; 9.5 cm.
MSaE*.

LITTLE STORIES FOR LITTLE FOLKS, *See* Kilner, Dorothy, no. **729.1.**

785 LITTLE STORIES FOR LITTLE FOLKS. Every little moral tale, shall O'er the infant mind prevail. Newburyport, Mass. W. & J. Gilman, 1810.
14 p. This may be an edition of Dorothy Kilner's *Little Stories For Little Folks,* no. **729.1.**
Shaw 20577.

786.1 THE LITTLE TEACHER, For Reading And Spelling Well. By A Parent. Philadelphia: Published By Jacob Johnson, No. 147, Market-Street. 1802. (Price 18 cents).
t.[1], [2–36] p.; 18 full page illus.; 13.5 cm.; marbled paper covers, colophon p.[36]: J. W. Scott, Printer.
English ed. title 1: ——— *Spelling Well.* London: Darton and Harvey, 1798.
English ed. title 2: ——— *Teacher, Or Child's First Spelling Book.* London: Darton, Harvey, And Darton, 1814.
PP*; CtY (Pequot, green paper covers).

786.2 ——— Second Edition. Philadelphia. Published By Jacob Johnson, No. 147, Market Street. 1806. (Price 18 cents).
t.[1], [2–36] p.; 18 full page illus.; 14 cm.; colophon. p. [36]: J. W. Scott, Printer. Adv. by Johnson & Warner, 1814 in **1449.3.**
MWA-T*; NNC-Pl; CtY (Pequot); Shaw 10742.

786.3 ——— Second Edition Improved. Philadelphia: Published By Jacob Johnson, No. 147, Market-Street, 1808. (Price 25 cents).
t.[1], [2–72] p.; 18 full page engr. illus.; 14.5 cm.; blue marbled paper covers; colophon p.[72]: J. Adams, Printer.
OOxM*; Shaw 15440.

THE LITTLE TRIFLER. *See* Pinchard, Mrs., Dramatic Dialogues, nos. **1008** and **1009.1.**

787 THE LITTLE TRINKET. A Collection Of Stories, For Youths Of Both Sexes. [2 lines of verse] Printed And Sold By W. & J. Gilman, Booksellers, Middle-Street, Newburyport [Mass.] [*ca.* 1815].
t.[1], [2–3], 4–22 p.; illus.; 9.5 cm.; pr. & illus. buff paper covers, cover dated 181[5]?; on p. opp. t.[1] a holograph inscription dated *1817.*
MWA* (rear cover wanting); Shaw 35122.

788.1 THE LITTLE VISITOR; Being Observations Of Tommy Thoughtful, On The Different Tempers, Genius, And Manners, Of The Young Masters And Misses In The Several Families which he visited during his last residence in Boston. Boston: Printed and sold by John W. Folsom, No. 30, Union-Street, 1798.
fr.; approx. 11 cm.
Evans 34006.

788.2 ——— [probably the same as **788.1**] [Exeter [N.H.]: Printed And Sold By H. Ranlet. 1801] [imprint copied from no. **626.3**].
5–26 p. only; illus.; 10. cm. The illus. p. 10, 22 were used by H. Ranlet, 1801 in **626.3**, p. 14, 13 respectively. Adv. by Henry Ranlet, 1801 in **558.2.**
MWA-T* (fr.[2], t.[3], p. [4], 27–31 and covers wanting).

788.3 ——— Exeter, [N.H.]: adv. by Norris and Sawyer, 1808 in **428.3.**

THE LITTLE WANDERERS. *See* Johnson, Richard, no. **682.1.**

THE LITTLE WOMAN AND HER DOG. *See* no.**789.1.**

789.1 THE LITTLE WOMAN AND THE PEDLAR, With The Strange Distraction That Seized Her, And The Undutiful Behaviour Of Her Little Dog, On That Occasion. Illustrated With Fifteen Engravings On Copper Plate. New-York: Printed At The Porcupine Office, And may be had of all the Booksellers, twenty-five per cent. less than the London edition. 1810. Price Two Shillings plain and Three Shillings coloured, New-York Currency. [cover title].
[1–16] p. engraved on one side of the page only of 16 leaves; illus.; 11 cm.; pr. brown paper covers; p.[1]: The little Woman & her Dog.

[illus.] A New Edition Published by Wm Charles New York July 1807.

Each leaf has a three-quarter page engraved illustration except p.[2]. The illustrations are from a set of plates which are not heavily lined so that they appear lighter than the following edition. The engraving of "The Little Woman & her dog," p.[1], has white blank spaces in the upper right and left corners of the picture above the fireplace, the little woman's collar is white, weakly shaded with short horizontal lines, and her dress is not covered with crosshatched lines. In illus. p. [14], "Coming home," the moon and clouds stand out in a sky drawn in horizontal lines.

English ed. London: Thos Hodgkins, Dec. 24 1805, cover title dated 1806.

MWA-W°; MWA; Shaw 12934 and 20578.

789.2 ———— New-York: Printed At The Porcupine Office, ———— [same as **789.1**] 1810. Price Two Shillings ———— [same as **789.1**] [cover title].

A variant ed. The text is the same as no. **789.1** but the illustrations are redrawn. The illustrations look as if the engravings in no. **789.1** were darkened by increasing the shading. The illustration on p.[1] has the corners of the picture above the fireplace filled in with the outline of bricks, the little woman's collar is strongly shaded with perpendicular lines, and her dress is darker being covered with strong crosshatched lines. Besides these there are other differences in this cut. In like manner the other cuts have also been darkened by shading. Page [14] "Coming home" has been worked over with crosshatched lines so that the moon and clouds no longer stand out.

MWA-W°; Shaw 12934 and 20578.

790 LIVES OF EMINENT MEN. Embellished with twenty-two Portraits. Philadelphia: Published by Benjamin Johnson, No. 455, Market Street. 1812.

t.[1], [2–3], 4–72 p.; illus.; 14 cm.; brown marbled paper covers.

MWA°; Shaw 25873.

LLOYD, CHARLES 1766–1829

791 [—] TRAVELS AT HOME, And Voyages By The Fire-Side, For The Instruction And Entertainment Of Young Persons. Vol. I. [II]. Europe And

Asia. Philadelphia: Published By Edward Earle. T. & G. Palmer, printers. 1816.

vol. I: t.[i], [ii–iii], iv–xix, [xx], [1], 2–295 p.; vol. II: t.[i], [ii–iii], iv–vi, [1], 2–303 p.; 2 vols.; 14.5 cm. Title of vol. II: ———— Vol. II. Asia, Africa, And America. Philadelphia: Published By Edward Earle. T. & G. Palmer, printers. 1816.

MWA° (vol. I, II); IU, NN (vol. I rebound); PP (vol. I front cover wanting, vol. II rear cover wanting); PPL; Shaw 38085.

792 LONDON; A Descriptive Poem, Nerv-York [*sic. i.e.* New-York]: Published By Samuel Wood & Sons, No. 261, Pearl-Street; And Samuel S. Wood & Co. No. 212, Market-st. Baltimore. 1820.

t.[1], [2–3], 4–32 p. illus.; 13 cm.; pr. & illus. buff paper covers; illus. p.[15] signed A [Alexander Anderson]; cover title undated.

English ed. London: William Darton, Jun. 1811.

MWA-W°; MHa; Shoemaker 2001.

THE LONDON CRIES. *See* The Cries Of London, no. **249.2**.

LONDON IN MINIATURE. *See* Mills, Alfred, no. **848**.

[LONGUEVILLE, PETER] *fl.* 1727

793.1 [—] THE ENGLISH HERMIT; Or, The Adventures Of Philip Quarll. Who was discovered by Mr. Dorrington, a Bristol merchant, upon an uninhabited island;—where he has lived above fifty years, without any human assistance, still continues to reside, and will not come away. Adorned with Cuts. Hartford [printed in a vignette] Printed By John Babcock. 1799.

fr.[2], t.[3], [4–5], 6–95, [96 adv.] p.; illus.; 13.5 cm.; bound in brown paper over w. bds.

English unabr. ed. title 1: *The Hermit, or, the Unparaled Sufferings . . . of Mr. Philip Quarll.* Westminster: J. Cluer and A. Campbell, for T. Warner and B. Creek, 1727.

English unabr. ed. title 2: *The English Hermit,* . . . 1727. This unabridged edition was published in Boston in 1775 and Exeter, N.H., 1795. All unabridged editions are omitted because they are not considered children's books.

English abr. ed. title 1: *The English Hermit.* London: [John Marshall and Co.] [1 address] < Price Six-Pence Bound and Gilt. > [*ca.* 1783].

Scottish abr. ed. title 2: *The Adventures of*

Philip Quarle. Edinburgh: Printed For The Booksellers. 1816.

MWA*; CtHi; CtY (covers wanting); Evans 36187.

793.2 [—] THE HISTORY OF PHILIP QUARLL, Who Lived Thirty Years On An Uninhabited Island. Philadelphia: Published By Bennet & Walton, No. 31, Market-Street. 1814.

t.[1], [2–3], 4–108 p.; 14.5 cm.; bound in pr. blue-gray paper over bds.

MWA-W*.

794 A LOOKING GLASS FOR CHILDREN. Fairhaven [Vt.]: adv. by J. P. Spooner, 1796 in **275.35**.

795 THE LOST CHILD: A Poetic Tale. Founded Upon A Fact. [5 lines of verse] Philadelphia: Published And Sold Wholesale By Wm. Charles, And May Be Had Of All The Booksellers. 1811. W. M'Culloch, Printer.

½t.[i], [ii, bl.], fr.[ii], t.[iii], [iv–v], vi, [7], 8–60 p.; 6 full p. illus. including front.; 17.5 cm.; bound in yellow paper over bds., leather spine. Illus. p. 27 signed *J. Yeager. Sc.* ½t. p. [i]: The Lost Child: A Poetic Tale.

English ed. entitled: ———— *Child. A Christmas Tale*. London: J. Harris, 1810.

MWA-W*; BM; CLU; CSmH; DLC; MB; MH; PP; Shaw 23240.

LOTHROP, JASON

796 — Letters To A Young Gentleman, On A Few Moral And Entertaining Subjects: Written In Prose And Verse, For The Improvement Of The Young. By Jason Lothrop. [2 lines quot.] Published By The Author. 1815. I. & W. R. Hill, Printers.

½t.[i], [ii, bl.], t.[iii], [iv, bl.], [v, label of ownership to be filled in by the owner], [vi, bl.], [vii], [viii, bl.], [ix], x, [11], 12–130, [131–132 bl.], caption t.[1], [2–5], 6–35, [36, contents] p.; 12.5 cm.; bound in red marbled paper over bds., leather spine. I. & W. R. Hill were printers in Concord, N. H. in 1815. Caption title p.[1]: Miscellaneous Poems, Composed For The Amusement And Benefit Of Pious Youth. By Jason Lothrop. [8 lines of verse the beginning of the text].

MWA*; MiD; RPB; Shaw 35134.

797 THE LOTTERY. Published by B Johnson No. 247 Market Street. Philadelphia. [1807].

t.[i], [ii, bl.], [1], 2–36 p.; title page vignette only illus.; 14 cm.; pink paper covers. *See also* The Wonderful Advantages of Adventuring In The Lottery, no. **1449.2** and the Cheap Repository, no. **169.4**.

MWA*; MH; NNC-SP (bound in vol. I. [Cheap Repository, 1807]); PP (rebound, orig. covers wanting, p.[1] torn and repaired); Shaw 12939.

A LOTTERY BOOK FOR CHILDREN. *See* The Little Lottery Book, no. **774**.

798 LOVE PREFERRED TO FORTUNE: Or The History Of Colin & Mira. A Sentimental Tale Founded On Fact. Portsmouth, N. H. Printed At The Oracle-Press, No. 5, Daniel-Street. 1798.

t.[1], [2–3], 4–14 p.; illus.; 11 cm.; illus. paper covers.

MWA* (p. 15–16 wanting).

799 LOVE TRIUMPHANT, Or Constancy Rewarded: In A Series of Familiar Letters, for the Amusement & Instruction Of Youth. In Language suited to their Capacities. To which is Added, a Poetical Appendix. By a Friend to Youth. Troy [N.Y.]: Printed by Luther Pratt & Co. 1797. Copy Right Secured.

fr.[ii], t.[i], [ii, bl.], [iii–iv], [5], 6–122 p.; front. and title vignette only illus.; 13 cm.; bound in leather. Title vignette and frontispiece signed *Abner Reed*.

MWA* (p. 121–122 wanting, t.[1] mut. affecting the imprint); NBuG (p. 13–16, 25–26, 37–38 mut.); Evans 32390.

LOVECHILD, MR. *pseud.*

800 THE GOLDEN PLAYTHING; Or The Way To Be Wise And Happy, By Mr. Lovechild. Boston: Printed And Sold By Hosea Sprague, No 88, Newbury-Street. 1804.

fr.[2], t.[3], [4–5], 6–29, [30, illus.] p.; illus.; 11 cm.; paper covers; p. 29 adv. list of 14 books. CtHi (p. 7–8 ¾ wanting, rear Dutch cover wanting; fr.[2] mut. & p. 9–10 mut. with page numbers wanting); PU (p. 29–[30] & front cover wanting); Shaw 6674.

LOVECHILD, GOODY. *See* Sproat, Nancy, no. **1243.2**.

LOVECHILD, MRS. *See* Fenn, Eleanor (Frere), Lady, no. **397**.

LOVECHILD, MRS. *pseud.*
801 Mrs. Lovechild's Golden Present.
Worcester: adv. by I. Thomas, 1786 in **395.1**

LOVECHILD, NURSE *pseud.*
802.1 [—] T. Thumb's Song Book. New-York:
adv. by Hugh Gaine, 1786 in Clarke's *Corderii
Colloquiorum Centuria Selecta.*

802.2 — Tommy Thumb's Song Book, For All
Little Masters and Misses, To be Sung to them
by their Nurses, until they can sing themselves.
By Nurse Lovechild. To Which Is Added, A Letter
from a Lady on Nursing. The First Worcester
Edition. Printed at Worcester, Massachusetts, By
Isaiah Thomas. Sold at his Bookstore. MDCC-
LXXXVIII.
　　fr.[2], t.[3], [4], 5–59, [60–62, adv. of books]
　　p.; illus. 10 cm.; illus. blue paper covers; con-
　　tains *Mother Goose* rhymes. Evans lists Lady
　　Eleanor Fenn as author. Since she was born in
　　1743, that is not likely.
　　English and Scottish ed. London: vol. II. M.
　　Cooper. [1744?].
　　MWA* (copy 1, blue Dutch paper covers; copy
　　2, illus. paper covers rebound in leather); BM;
　　PPL (p. 2–22, 31–32, 57–62 wanting); Evans
　　21089.

802.3 — The Second Worcester Edition.
Printed at Worcester, Massachusetts. By Isaiah
Thomas, Sold Wholesale and Retail at his Book-
store. MDCCXCIV.
　　fr.[2], t.[3], [4], 5–59, [60–63, adv. of books]
　　p.; illus.; 10 cm., green Dutch paper covers.
　　MWA*.

802.4 — Boston: adv. by Samuel Hall,
1791 in **408.3**; 1792 in **1384.2**; 1793 in **955.3**;
1794 in **1283.4**; 1796 in **587.40**.

LOVECHILD, TIMOTHY *pseud.*
803 The History Of Harry Learnwell. Philadelphia: adv. by William Young, 1794 in **305**.

LOVECHILD, TOMMY *pseud.*
804.1 — Pretty Poems, In Easy Language, For
The Amusement Of Little Boys And Girls. By
Tommy Lovechild. Ornamented with Cuts. Hartford: Printed by Hale & Hosmer. 1813.

　　fr.[2], t.[3], [4–5], 6–30, [31, adv. list of books]
　　p.; illus.; 9.5 cm.; pr. & illus. buff paper covers.
　　MWA*; PP; Shaw 28988.

804.2 — Embellished With Cuts. Hartford: Printed by Sheldon & Goodwin. < Stereotyped by J. F. & C. Starr. > [1815].
　　fr.[2], t.[3], [4–5], 6–31 p.; illus.; 10 cm.; pr. &
　　illus. buff paper covers; p. 31: 6 lines of verse
　　and an illus. of a rose. J. F. & C. Starr are
　　known to have been in Hartford in 1815 and
　　1818. Sheldon and Goodwin were a firm in
　　Hartford from Nov. 1, 1814–Oct. 23, 1815.
　　(MWA cat.).
　　MWA*; FTaSU; PP.

804.3 — [same as **804.2**].
　　fr.[2], t.[3], [4–5], 6–30, [31, adv. list of books]
　　p.; illus.; 10 cm.; pr. & illus. yellow paper cov-
　　ers. A variant issue with a list of 12 books on
　　p. [31] instead of verse and an illus.
　　NNC-Pl (label pasted over fr.[2]).

804.4 — Ornamented with Cuts. Hartford [Conn.]: Printed by Hale & Hosmer. 1818.
　　fr.[2], t.[3], [4–5], 6–30, [31, adv.] p.; illus.;
　　9.5 cm.; pr. & illus. buff paper covers; cover
　　title dated 1813.
　　MWA*.

805.1 The Loving Invitation Of Christ, To
The Aged, Middle-Aged, Youth, And Children.
From The Mouth Of Elizabeth Osborn, Only Three
Years and Nine Months Old. She being dead yet
speaketh. Newburyport [Mass.]; Printed by W. &
J. Gilman, Essex-street. Sold, wholesale and re-
tail, at their Book-Store. 1812.
　　t.[1], [2–3], 4–12 p.; illus.; 15 cm.
　　MWA-W*.

805.2 — Exeter [N.H.]: Printed By C.
Norris & Co. 1811.
　　t.[1], [2–3], 4–8 p.; 12.5 cm.; paper covers.
　　NhD*; MH (blue-gray paper covers); NhHi;
　　Shaw 23609.

806 Lucinda, The Orphan; Or, The Costumes.
A Tale. Exhibited In A Series Of Dresses. Pailadel-
phia [*sic. i.e.* Philadelphia]: Published and sold
by Wm. Charles, No. 32, south Third-street. 1817.

t.[1], [2–3], 4–31 p.; 13 cm.; pr. yellow-buff paper covers.

English ed. London: S. & J. Fuller. 1812. (Illus. with 6 paper doll dresses and head pieces into which a head and torso may be fitted.)

PP* (paper dolls wanting); MWA (paper dolls wanting); NN (paper dolls wanting); Shaw 41300; Weiss 1932b.

807 LUCRETIA, OR THE TRIUMPH OF VIRTUE. New-York: adv. by L. B. Jansen and G. Jansen, 1808 in **766**.

M

[M., A. D.]

808 [—] THE BUTTERFLY'S BIRTH DAY, St. Valentine's Day, And Madam Whale's Ball: Poems, To Instruct And Amuse The Rising Generation. With Elegant Engravings. Burlington, N. J. Printed and published by D. Allinson & Co. 1811.

fr.[ii], t.[1], [2–5], 6–16 p.; 4 pl. including front.; 12 cm.; pr. pink paper covers. A different poem from Roscoe's *The Butterfly's Birthday*, no. **1130.1**. In this book and the London, J. Harris, 1808 edition, p. 8, the end of *The Butterfly's Birth-Day* is signed "A.D.M."
English ed. London: J. Harris, 1808.
MWA° (p. [5]–8 mut., lower ½ of front cover wanting); Shaw 22457.

[M., Y.]

809.1 [—] (No. 26.) MARY THE MILK-MAID. Published By The Philadelphia Female Tract Society. And for sale at their Depository, No. 20, Walnut Street. [caption title]. Printed by Lydia R. Bailey, No. 10, North Alley, Philad. [1817], [colophon p. 12].

t.[1], 2–12 p.; 14 cm.
MWA° (bound with other tracts, with which *The Second Annual Report Of The Philadelphia Female Tract Society For The Year 1816* was originally bound); Shaw 41306.

809.2 [—] MARY, THE MILK-MAID. [n.p., n.d.] [caption p. [2]]. [*ca.* 1820].

illus.[1], [2], 3–14 p.; only one illus.; 11 cm.; pink and gold wallpaper covers.
MWA-W°.

MACGOWAN, JOHN 1726–1780

810.1 — THE LIFE OF JOSEPH, THE SON OF ISRAEL, In Eight Books, Chiefly Designed For The Use Of Youth. Stockbridge (Massachusetts): Printed by Loring Andrews, 1790.

Evans 22629.

810.2 — —— Elizabeth-Town [N.J.]: Printed and sold by Shepard Kollock. 1791.

Evans 23523.

810.3 — —— Youth. Republished, From The First London Edition. Hartford: Published By Elisha Babcock. M,DCC,XCI.

t.[I], [II–III], IV–VIII, [IX–XI], [11], 12–147 p.; 15 cm.; bound in leather. *The Life Of Joseph* may have been a reader used only in schools. The format of the book is not that of a typical reader and is included in this bibliography on the chance that it also may have been used by children for entertainment.
English ed. London: G. Keith, [*ca.* 1771].
MWA°; CtHi; Evans 23524.

810.4 — —— Chiefly designed to allure young Minds to a Love of the Sacred Scriptures. By John Macgowan. A New Edition. Philadelphia: Printed By T. Dobson, At The Stone-House, No. 41, Second-Street. M,DCC,XCI.

t.[1], [2–3], 4, [v], vi–xvii, [xviii, bl.], [xix–xx], [21], 22–295 p.; 15.5 cm.; bound in leather.
MWA°; CLSU; MiD; MiU; NB; PPL; RPJCB (p. 29–32, 97–108, 121–122 wanting); Evans 23525.

810.5 — —— Sagg-Harbour [N.Y.]: Printed and Sold by David Frothingham. [1792].

fr.[ii], t.[i], [ii–iii], iv–xiii, [xiv–xvi], [17], 18–258 p.; front. only illus.; 15.5 cm.; bound in leather; p. 156 is mispaged "165"; front. signed *A. Anderson Sculp.*
NjP°; NEh; NSh; Evans 46493; Hamilton 207a.

810.6 — —— Philadelphia Printed: Carlisle [Pa.] Re-Printed By George Kline M,DCC,XCII.

t.[1], [2–5], 6–144 p.; 14.5 cm.; bound in gray paper over bds., leather spine.
CtY°; Evans 46492.

810.7 — —— [same as **810.3**], [4 lines of verse] Albany: Printed by Barber And Southwick, For Thomas Spencer, and sold at his Book-Store, In Market-Street, A Few Doors North Of The Dutch Church, M,DCC,XCIII.

t.[i], [ii], iii–viii, [ix, bl.], [10], 11–131, [132, adv. of school books and adult books] p.; 16.5 cm.; bound in marbled paper over bds., leather spine.
N° (front cover mut.); CSmH; CtHi; MB; MSaE (ink st. on t.[i]); OCHP; OClWHi; Evans 25742.

810.8 —⸻ Use Of Youth. Hartford: Printed by Elisha Babcock. 1793.
Evans 25743.

810.9 —⸻ Sacred Scriptures. By John Macgowan. The Second Albany Edition. Albany: Reprinted from Dobson's Philadelphia Edition, At the Press of Barber & Southwick, For Thomas Spencer. M,DCC,XCIV.
t.[i], [2–3], 4, [v], vi–xii, [xiii–xiv], [15], 16–187, [188, bl.], [189–192, adv.] p.; 15 cm.; bound in leather.
MWA°; DLC (p. 45–46, 55–58 mut.); N; Nh; NN; PP; Evans 27250.

810.10 —⸻ Use Of Youth. [4 lines of verse] Danbury [Conn.]: Printed And Sold By N. Douglas. MDCCXCIV.
t.[i], [ii–iv], v–viii, [ix, bl.], [x], [11], 12–131 p.; 16 cm.; bound in marbled paper over bds., leather spine.
MWA° (top of p.[iv] cropped so that page number is wanting), CSmH; Evans 47104.

810.11 —⸻ Sacred Scriptures. By John Macgowan. Exeter [N.H.]: Printed by Henry Ranlet for I. Thomas and E. T. Andrews, Boston. MDCCXCIV.
t.[1], [2–3], 4, [v], vi–xiv, [xv–xvi], [17], 18–252 p.; 15 cm.; bound in leather.
MWA° (i. st. on t.[1]); CLU; CtW; MWHi; RPJCB; Evans 27252.

810.12 —⸻ Exeter [N.H.]: Printed and sold by Henry Ranlet. Sold also by most of the Booksellers in Boston. MDCCXCIV.
t.[1], [2–3], 4, [v], vi–xiv, [xv–xvi], [17], 18–252 p.; 15.5 cm.; bound in leather.
PU°; MWA-T; PP (imp.).

810.13 —⸻ Sacred Scriptures. By John Macgowan. A New Edition. Philadelphia: Printed By Thomas Dobson, At The Stone-House, South Second Street. M.DCC.XCV.
t.[1], [2–3], 4, [v], vi–xv, [xvi], [1], 2–259 p.; 18 cm.; bound in leather.
MWA°; PU; ViAl; Evans 29008.

810.14 —⸻ The Use Of Youth. London, Printed: Windsor [Vt.]: Re-printed By Alden Spooner. M,DCC,XCV.

t.[i], [ii–iii], iv–vi, [7], 8–131 p.; 16.5 cm.; p.[130]–131 adv. list of books.
VtHi°; McCorison 349; Evans 29009.

810.15 —⸻ Sacred Scriptures. By John Macgowan. Second Exeter Edition. Printed at Exeter [N.H.], by H. Ranlet, and Sold at his Book-Store, in Main-Street. MDCCXCVI.
t.[1], [2–3], 4, [v], vi–ix, [x], [11], 12–214, [215, adv.] p.; t.[1] 15.5 cm.
MWA° (rebound); DLC; MSaE (emb. st. on t.[1]); PP (15.5 cm., bound in leather); RPJCB; Evans 30718.

810.16 —⸻ Use Of Youth. Hartford: Printed By Elisha Babcock. 1796.
t.[I], [II–III], IV–VIII, [IX–X], [11], 12–142 p.; 16 cm.; bound in blue paper over bds., leather spine.
MWA-W°; CSmH, CtHi; DLC; MB; NN (rebound); PP; Evans 30719.

810.17 —⸻ Use Of Youth. [4 lines of verse] New-York: MDCCXCVI.
t.[i], [ii–iii], iv–viii, [ix, bl.], [x], [11], 12–160 p.; 12.5 cm.; bound in leather.
MWA°; Evans 47829.

810.18 —⸻ Sacred Scriptures. By John Macgowan. The First New-York Edition. New-York: Printed by John Buel, for E. Duyckinck, & Co. No. 110, Pearl-Street. M,DCC,XCVI.
t.[1], [2–3], 4, [v], vi–xii, [xiii–xiv], [15], 16–191 p.; t.[1] 13.5 cm.
DLC° (copy 1, rebound, per st. on t.[1]; copy 2, covers wanting; p. 189–199 mut.); CtY; Evans 30720.

810.19 —⸻ By John Maggowan [*sic. i.e.* Macgowan]. The Fifth Edition. Wilmington [Del.] Printed By Joseph Johnson, Market-Street Opposite The Bank. 1796.
t.[1], [2–3], 4, [v], i [*sic. i.e.* vi], vii–xi, [xii, bl.], [xiii–xiv], [15], 16–173 p.; 16 cm.; bound in gray marbled paper over bds., leather spine.
MWA°; DeWi (bound in leather, p. 173 mut.); DLC (t.[1] mut.); PP (covers wanting); Evans 30721.

810.20 —⸻ Philadelphia: adv. by Thomas Dobson, 1797 in **25.1.**

810.21 —————— Portsmouth, N. H. Printed By Charles Peirce 1797.

t.[1], [2–3], 4, [v], vi–xiv, [xv–xvi], [17], 18–252 p.; 15 cm.; bound in leather.

MWA°; CLU; MH; Evans 32404.

810.22 —————— Windham: (Connecticut) Printed By John Byrne. 1797.

t.[1], [2–3], 4, [v], vi–xi, [xii, bl.], [xiii–xiv], [15], 16–166 p.; 17.5 cm.; bound in leather.

Welch°; CtW; CtY; DLC; MBU; MWA; Evans 32405.

810.23 —————— Dover, N. H. Printed by Samuel Bragg, jun. at the Sun Office. 1800.

t.[1], [2–3], 4, [v], vi–xii, [xiii–xiv], [15], 16–195 p.; 18 cm.; bound in leather.

MWA°; BM; CLU; CtHC; PP; RPJCB; Evans 37870.

810.24 —————— A New Edition. Richmond [Va.]: Published By William Pritchard. 1800.

t.[1], [2–3], 4, [v], vi–xv, [xvi], [1], 2–259 p.; 17 cm.; bound in leather.

MWA°; DLC (rebound); RP; ViU; Evans 37871.

810.25 —————— Sacred Scriptures. By John Macgowan. Windsor, Vermont. Printed And Sold By Nahum Mower. 1801.

t.[i], [ii–iii], iv–xiv, [xv–xvi], [17], 18–252 p.; 15.5 cm.; bound in leather.

MWA°; DLC (per. st. on t.[i]); VtHi; McCorison 608; Shaw 856.

810.26 —————— Use Of Youth. [4 lines of verse] Printed At Worcester, Massachusetts: By Isaiah Thomas, Jun. September. 1801.

t.[i], [ii–iii], iv–viii, [9], 10–129, [130, bl.], [131, adv.] p.; 17 cm.; bound in leather.

MWA° (i. st. on t.[i]); DLC; MiD; MWHi; PP (p.[iii]–vi slightly mut. affecting page no.; bound in blue paper over w. bds.); RPB; Shaw 857.

810.27 —————— Sacred Scriptures. By John Macgowan. New Haven: Printed By William W. Morse. 1802.

t.[i], [ii–iii], iv–x, [xi–xii], [13], 14–208 p.; 13 cm.; bound in leather.

MWA°; DLC; NcD; Shaw 2565.

810.28 —————— Youth. [4 lines of verse] Brookfield Massachusetts, Printed By E. Merriam & Co. July 1803.

t.[i], [ii], iii–ix, [x], 11–153, [154, bl.], [155–156 adv.] p.; 14 cm.; bound in blue marbled paper over w. bds., leather spine.

Welch° (p. v–viii, 65–68, and most of paper from binding wanting); CLU; DLC (2 copies); MWA; MiD; NN; NcD; NjR; PP; Shaw 4568.

810.29 —————— Scriptures. By John Macgowan. New Brunswick [N.J.]: Printed By A. Blauvelt. 1803.

t.[i], [ii–iii], iv, [5], 6–267 p.; 10.5 cm.; bound in leather.

MWA° MiU; NjS; Shaw 4569 and 2564 (dated 1802, is a ghost).

810.30 —————— John Macgowan. Third Exeter Edition. Exeter [N.H.]: Printed For Benjamin P. Sheriff, And Thomas & Whipple, Newburyport. 1805.

t.[1], [ii–iv], v–viii, [9], 10–215, [216, adv.] p.; 14 cm.; bound in leather.

MWA°; OOxM; PP; Shaw 8822.

810.31 —————— John Macgowan. Printed At Greenfield—Massachusetts: By John Denio. 1805.

t.[i], [ii–iv], v–viii, [ix–x], [11], 12–130 p.; 16.5 cm.; bound in leather.

MWA°; DLC; MH; OOxM; Shaw 8821.

810.32 —————— John Macgowan. Minister Of The Gospel. A New Edition. Trenton [N.J.]: Printed By James Oram, And For Sale At His Book Store Near The Presbyterian Church. 1805.

fr.[ii], t.[i], [ii–iii], iv–viii, [ix], [10], 11–171 p.; front. & tailpiece p. 171 only illus.; 17 cm.; bound in marbled paper over bds., leather spine. Engraved front. signed *A. Anderson Sculp.*

MWA°; CLU; DLC; MH; MnU; NjI; NjP (fr. [ii] wanting; i. st. on t.[i]; OCH; PP (rebound); Shaw 8823.

810.33 —————— Israel. Windsor [Vt.]: adv. by O. Farnsworth, in the *Vermont Republican*, Sept. 25, 1809.

810.34 [—] —————— Joseph. Printed By Thomas G. Bradford, Market-street, Nashville, Tennessee. 1811.

t.[i], [ii,bl.] [iii], iv–vi, [7–8], 9–192 p.; 18
cm.
T° (per. st. & i.st. on t.[i]; bound in worn bds.
with an added spine, probably not original);
Shaw 23625.

810.35 ——— Sacred Scriptures. By John
Macgowan. In Eight Books. Walpole, N. H. Pub-
lished By Isaiah Thomas & Co. James G. Watts,
Printer. 1811.
t.[1], [2–3], 4, [v], vi–xi, [xii, bl.], [xiii–xiv],
[15], 16–182 p.; 11.5 cm.; bound in leather.
MWA° (i. st. on t.[1]);CLU; CSmH, NcD;
PP; Shaw 23266.

810.36 ——— By John Macgowan. In Eight
Books. Brattleborough, Vt. Printed By William
Fessenden. 1813.
t.[i], [ii–iii], iv–x, [xi–xii], 13–179 p.; 14 cm.;
bound in marbled paper over w. bds., leather
spine.
MWA°; CLU; DLC; McCorison 1514; Shaw
29017.

810.37 ——— Sacred Scriptures. By John
Macgowan. Williamsburgh [Mass.]: Printed By
Ephraim Whitman. 1818.
t.[1], [2–3], 4–180 p.; 17.5 cm.; bound in
leather.
Welch°; DLC; MWA; Shaw 44654.

THE MAGIC LANTERN. *See* Sandham, Elizabeth,
no. **1153.**

811 MAMMA'S STORIES, Read By Herself To Her
Little Girl. Philadelphia: Published By Benjamin
Warner, No. 147, Market Street. 1816. Printed by
Lydia R. Bailey.
fr.[2], t.[3], [4–5], 6–70 p.; illus.; 14 cm.;
yellow paper covers speckled with gold. Adv.
by Johnson & Warner, on rear cover of no.
1355.3 dated 1817, with title dated 1816.
English ed. London: Darton, 1811.
NNC-Pl.°

812 THE MAN AND THE SNAKE. A New Story
for Children. Hartford: Published by S. G. Goodrich. Roberts & Burr, Prs. 1819.
fr.[2], t.[3], 4–16 p.; illus.; 10.5 cm.; illus.
paper covers pr. in black ink.
CtY°; CtHi (rear cover mostly wanting); Shaw
48572.

813.1 MANHOOD. [3 lines of quot.] Psalm, viii,
1, 4 New-York: Printed & sold by Samuel Wood,
at the Juvenile Book-store, No. 357, Pearl Street.
1810.
t.[1], [2–16] p.; illus.; 8 cm.; ornamental paper
covers. Adv. by S. Wood, 1812 in **439.1.**
N° (covers wanting); MWA-T.

813.2 ——— Printed & sold by Samuel Wood,
at the Juvenile Bookstore, No. 357, Pearl-street,
New-York. 1813.
t.[1], [2–16] p.; illus.; 8 cm.; pr. & illus. pink
paper covers.
Cover title: Manhood. Sold By Samuel Wood,
New-York.
MWA-W°.

813.3 ——— New-York: Printed & sold by
Samuel Wood, at the Juvenile Book-store, No. 357,
Pearl-street. 1814.
t.[1], [2–16] p.; illus.; 8.5 cm.
MWA-W° (bound with other books in no.
637.1).

813.4 ——— Nerv-York [*sic. i.e.* New-York]:
Printed And Sold By S. Wood, at the Juvenile
Book-store, No. 357, Pearl-street. 1815.
t.[1], [2–16] p.; illus.; 8.5 cm.; pr. & illus.
yellow paper covers.
Cover title: Manhood. [cut] Sold by Samuel
Wood, New-York.
CLU°; MWA; Shaw 35179.

813.5 ——— New-York: Printed And Sold By
Samuel Wood & Sons, at the Juvenile Book-store,
No. 357, Pearl-street. 1816.
t.[1], [2–16] p.; illus.; 8 cm.; pr. & illus. buff
paper covers; cover title undated.
MWA°; NNC-LS; Shaw 38137.

813.6 ——— Nerv-York [*sic. i.e.* New-York]:
Published by Samuel Wood & Sons, No. 261 Pearl-
street, And Samuel S. Wood & Co. No. 212,
Market-st. Baltimore. 1818.
t.[1], [2–16] p.; illus.; 8.5 cm.; pr. & illus. buff
paper covers; cover title undated.
MWA-W°; MWA (covers wanting); Shaw
44677 and 45150.

MANT, ALICIA CATHERINE
814 — ELLEN; Or, The Young Godmother. A
Tale For Youth. By Alicia Catherine Mant. First

American, From The Second London Edition. [4 lines of quot.] Philadelphia: Published By M. Carey, Chesnut Street, For Sale Also By Wells And Lilly, Boston. 1816.

[i–ii, adv. of 5 books]; t.[i], [ii–iii], iv, [5], 6–146 p.; 13.5 cm.; bound in brown paper over bds., leather spine. Colophon p. 146: Gillmor & Hamilton, Printers, Harrisburg. English ed. Southampton: T. Skelton; C. Law, London, 1812.
MWA*; CLU; OOxM; PP; Shaw 38139.

MARIA, OR THE EVER-BLOOMING FLOWER. *See* Somerville, Elizabeth, no. **1231.1**.

[MARSHALL, MRS. L.]
815 [—] THE LIFE OF MARY MORDANT. [2 lines of verse] Cowper. By An American Lady. Philadelphia: Published by the Sunday & Adult School Union. Clark & Raser, Printers. 1819.

t.[1], [2–3], 4–48 p.; title page vignette only illus.; 13 cm.; pr. & illus. blue paper covers. MWA*; Shaw 48491.

MARSHALL, LOUISA A.
816.1 — A SKETCH OF MY FRIENDS FAMILY, Intended To Suggest Some Practical Hints On Religion And Domestic Matters. By Mrs. Marshall, Author Of Henwick Tales. Third Edition. [1 line quot.] Boston: Published By Charles Ewer. 1819.

fr.[ii], t.[i], [ii–iii], iv–v, [vi, bl.], [7], 8–164 p. engr. front. only illus.; 14.5 cm.; bound in leather; front. signed *A Bowen Sc.;* p.[ii]: Sylvester T. Goss, Printer.
MWA*; KU; OOxM; PP; Shaw 48587.

816.2 —―――― Fourth Edition. [1 line of quot.] Springfield [Mass.]: Printed By Ira Daniels. 1820.

t.[1], [2–4], 5–108 p.; 15.5 cm.; pr. pink covers. MWA*; Ct; Shoemaker 2112.

[MARTIN, SARAH CATHERINE] 1768–1826
817.1 [—] A CURIOUS ACCOUNT OF THE COMIC ADVENTURES OF OLD MOTHER HUBBARD AND HER DOG. By S. C. M. New York. Published by Wm Charles No 195 Broad way. 1807.

fr.[2], t.[3], [4–17] p. engr. on one side only of 16 leaves; illus.; 12.5 cm.; pr. yellowish-brown covers; front and p.[17] originally may have been glued to the inside of the covers. Cover title: The Comic Adventures Of Old

Mother Hubbard, And Her Dog; Illustrated With Fifteen Elegant Engravings. On Copperplate. By S.C.M. Philadelphia: Published and sold Wholesale by Wm. Charles, and may be had of all the Booksellers. 1810. Price Twenty-Five Cents.
For a scholarly discussion on the history of the name Mother Hubbard, *see* ODNR p. 320–321. While there appears to be a question as to the originality of Miss Martin's work, there is no question that the English 1805 edition was written by her and that possibly due to the format and illustrations the book was enormously popular.
English ed. London: J. Harris, 1805.
NNC-Pl* (rear cover mostly wanting); Shaw 12994.

817.2 [—] THE COMIC ADVENTURES OF OLD MOTHER HUBBARD AND HER DOG; Illustrated With Fifteen Copper-Plate Engravings. New-York: Printed At The Porcupine Office, And may be had of all the Booksellers, Twenty-five percent less than the London Edition. 1808. Price Two Shillings plain, and Three Shillings coloured, New-York Currency. [cover title].

[1–16] p. printed on one side only of 16 leaves; illus.; 11.5 cm.; pr. paper covers. OClWHi*; CtHi; Shaw 14745.

817.3 [—] ―――― New York Printed At The Porcupine Office, And May be had of all the Booksellers, Twenty-five per cent less than the London edition. 1810. Price Two Shillings plain, and Three Shillings coloured. New-York Currency. [cover title].

[1–16] p. pr. on one side only of 16 leaves; 12 cm.; pr. brown paper covers. MWA*; PHi; Shaw 19818.

818.1 [—] A CONTINUATION OF THE COMIC ADVENTURES OF OLD MOTHER HUBBARD AND HER DOG. Philadelphia: adv. by Wm. Charles, 1808 in **1312**.

818.2 [—] A CONTINUATION OF THE COMIC ADVENTURES OF OLD MOTHER HUBBARD, AND HER DOG. Ornamented With Cuts. Boston: N. Coverly, Jr. Printer, Milk-Street. 1813.

fr.[2, alphabet], t.[3], [4–15] p.; illus.; 9.5 cm.; ornamented buff paper covers. CtHi*, DLC; MH (p. 9–10 mut.); Shaw 29057.

819.1 MARTIN AND JAMES; Or, The Reward Of Integrity: A Moral Tale. Designed For The Improvement of Children. Philadelphia: Published For H. & P. Rice, No. 50 High-Street. M,DCC, XCIV.

> t.[i], [ii–iii], iv, [5], 6–64 p.; title vignette only illus.; 10 cm.
> English ed. London: Darton, 1791.
> NNC-Pl° (covers wanting), MWA (t.[i] wanting); Evans 47106.

819.2 ———— Philadelphia: Printed For Mathew Carey, No. 118, Market-Street. 1800.

> t.[i], [ii–iii], iv, [5], 6–64 p.; illus.; 10 cm.; orange and green Dutch paper covers.
> France°; Evans 49112.

819.3 ———— Improvement Of Youth. New-York: Printed And Sold By John C. Totten, No. 155 Chatham-Street, Where may be had a variety of Children's Books. 1807.

> t.[1], [2–3], 4–72 p.; illus.; 13.5 cm,; blue marbled paper covers.
> Welch°; MWA; Shaw 12995.

819.4 ———— New-York.: Published By John C. Totten, No. 155 Chatham-street. 1810.

> t.[1], [2–5], 6–60 p.; illus.; t.[1] 13.5 cm. *See also* no. 705.
> CLU°.

819.5 ———— A Moral Tale, For The Amusement And Instruction Of Youth. New-York: Printed And Sold By J. C. Totten, No. 9 Bowery. 1815.

> t.[i], [ii–iii], iv, [5], 6–48 p.; illus.; 13.5 cm.; pr. & illus. yellow paper covers.
> MWA°, MiU; NNC-T; Shaw 31590.

820 MARTYROLOGY, Or, A brief Account of the Lives, Sufferings and Deaths of those two holy Martyrs, viz. Mr. John Rogers, And Mr John Bradford, Who suffered for the Gospel, by the bloody Tyranny, Rage and Persecution of the Church of Rome, in the Kingdom of England, under the Reign of Queen Mary, and were burnt at Smithfield, the former on the 14th of February 1554, the latter July 1st 1555. [3 lines quot.] Boston: Printed by S. Kneeland and T. Green, in Queen-street, 1736.

> t.[1], [2], 3–19 p.; 13.5 cm.; paper covers.

MWA°; DLC (rear buff paper cover wanting); MB; PP; Evans 4032.

821 MARY AND HER CAT. In Words not exceeding Two Syllables. Philadelphia. Published by Jacob Johnson, No. 147, Market-Street. [*ca.* 1806].

> t.[1], [2–4], 5–35 [36] p.; illus.; 13.5 cm.; paper covers; p.[36] has: Printed by Joseph Rakestraw. Engraved illus. on t.[1] and 11 engraved illus. in text all signed *WSsc* [William Ralph]. Adv. by Jacob Johnson, 1806 in **253.1**; adv. by Johnson & Warner, 1814 in **1449.3**. The author was Mrs. Fenwick.
> English ed. title 1.: *Mary And Her Cat.* London: B. Tabart & Co., 1804.
> Scottish ed. title 2: *The Story Of Mary* ————. Edinburgh: Caw & Elder; G. Ross, 1817.
> MH° (p. 13–14 mut.); CtHi (t.[1], & p. 35–[36] wanting).

MARY THE MILK-MAID. *See* [M.,Y.] no. **809.1**.

MASON, REV. JOHN 1706–1763
822 — SERIOUS ADVICE TO YOUTH. By The Rev. John Mason, A. M. And A Narrative Of The Happy Boatman. Hartford: Published By Oliver D. Cooke. Roberts & Burr, Printers. 1820.

> fr.[2], t.[3], [4–5], 6–32 p.; illus.; 13.5 cm.; pr. & illus. orange paper covers. Front. signed *J. W. B.* [John Warner Barber] All of Mason's works are sermons and not within the scope of this work. This book is included because of "The Narrative of The Happy Boatman."
> Welch°; CtHi; MSaE (covers wanting); MWA; Shoemaker 2135 and 2136.

MASSON, CHARLES FRANCOIS PHILBERT 1762–1807
823.1 [—] ELMINA; or, The flower that never fades. A tale for young people. Ornamented with elegant cuts. Hartford: Advertised "just published Oct. 10, 1790 & for sale by J. Babcock."

> This entry is probably an error for the Hartford, Babcock 1799 edition. (Bowe mss.).

823.2 [—] ELMINA; Or, The Flower that never Fades. A Tale For Young People. Hartford: Printed By John Babcock. 1799.

> fr.[2], t.[3], [4, bl.–5], 6–47 p.; illus.; 13.5 cm.; violet Dutch paper covers.
> English ed. London: E. Newbery, 1791.
> MWA°; CtHi (fr.[2] mut., p. 47 wanting);

CtY (covers wanting); Bowe mss.; Evans 35439.

823.3 [—] —— Embellished with Elegant Cuts. Hartford: Printed By John Babcock. 1800.
fr.[2], t.[3], [4–5], 6–31 p.; illus.; 11 cm.; wallpaper covers; text pr. on light blue paper.
MWA°; CtHi (fair copy); Bowe mss.; Evans 37936.

823.4 [—] —— Hartford; Printed By John Babcock 1802.
fr.[2], t.[3], [4–5], 6–30 p.; illus.; 11 cm.; blue marbled paper covers; text printed on light-bluish paper.
Welch° (front cover wanting); CtHi; MWA (fr.[2] & front Dutch paper cover wanting); Bowe mss.; Shaw 2634.

823.5 [—] —— Philadelphia: adv. by John Adams, 1805 in **1217**; 1806 in **646.3**; and 1807 in **670.3**.

823.6 [—] —— Ornamented with Engravings. Albany: Printed By E. And E. Hosford. 1806.
t.[3], [4–5], 6–30, [31, illus.] p.; illus.; 10 cm.; green Dutch paper covers.
CtHi° (front cover and fr.[2] wanting); N (fr. [2], p.[31] & orig. covers wanting); MWA-T (complete).

823.7 [—] —— [same as **823.3**] From Sidney's Press, New-Haven. 1806.
fr.[2], t.[3], [4–5], 6–30 p.; illus.; 10.5 cm.; Dutch paper covers.
CtY° (covers wanting except for a trace of Dutch paper on part of rear cover); DLC (fr. [2] & covers wanting).

823.8 [—] —— Adorned with Cuts. From Sidney's Press, New-Haven. 1807.
fr.[2], t.[3], [4–5], 6–30 p.; illus.; 10.5 cm.; green Dutch paper covers.
CtY°; PP.

823.9 [—] —— Ornamented with Engravings. Albany: Printed By E. And E. Hosford. 1808.
t.[3], [4–5], 6–30 p.; illus.; 10.5 cm.
NNC-T° (fr.[2], & p.[31] & covers wanting); Bowe mss.; Shaw 15558.

823.10 [—] —— Adorned with Cuts. From Sidney's Press. New-Haven. 1808.
fr.[2], t.[3], [4–5], 6–30, [31, alphabet] p.; illus.; 11 cm.; yellow paper covers.
MWA°; DLC (Dutch paper covers); NNC-T (yellow paper covers); RPB; Bowe mss.; Shaw 15559.

823.11 [—] —— Ornamented with Engravings. Albany: Printed By E. And E. Hosford. 1809.
fr.[2], t.[3], [4–5], 6–30, [31, illus.] p.; illus.; 10 cm.; pr. & illus. buff paper covers.
MWA°; DLC (fr.[2], p.[31] & covers wanting); Bowe mss.; Shaw 18058.

823.12 [—] —— Adorned with Cuts. From Sidney's Press. New-Haven, 1809.
fr.[2], t.[3], [4–5], 6–30, [31, adv.] p.; illus.; 10.5 cm.; buff paper covers.
MWA; Bowe mss.; Shaw 18059.

823.13 [—] —— Ornamented with Engravings. Albany: Printed By E. And E. Hosford. 1810.
fr.[2], t.[3], [4–5], 6–30, [31, illus.] p.; illus.; 10.5 cm.; pr. & illus. buff paper covers.
MWA°; NN (2 copies, one imp.); NNC-Pl; PP; Bowe mss.; Shaw 20706; Weiss 1936, p. 70.

823.14 [—] —— Adorned with Cuts. From Sidney's Press. New-Haven, 1810.
fr.[2], t.[3], [4, alphabet–5], 6–30, [31, adv.] p.; illus.; 11 cm.; pr. & illus. buff paper covers; last three words p.[5]: "loved Lidoriana as"; p. 6 last line: "ing flowers."
Cover title: Elmina. Published by I. Cooke & Co. Universal Book-store, Church-Street, New-Haven.
MWA°; CLU; MBChM (green Dutch paper covers); Bowe mss.; Shaw 20705.

823.15 [—] —— Sidney's Press. New-Haven, 1810.
fr.[2], t.[3], [4, adv.–5], 6–30, [31, alphabet] p.; illus.; 10.5 cm.; pr. & illus. yellow paper covers. A variant of the preceding with an adv. on p.[4], and the alphabet on p.[31]. The last three words p.[5]: "she loved Lidori-"; p. 6 last line: "flowers."
Cover title: —— [same as **823.14**] Book-Store, ——.
CtY°.

823.16 [—] ——— People. First Windsor Edition. Printed At Windsor [Vt.]: By Farnsworth & Churchill. 1810.
  fr.[2], t.[3], [4, bl.–6], 7–31 p.; illus.; 9.5 cm.; pr. & illus. buff paper covers.
  MWA-W*; VtHi (fr.[2] & covers wanting); Bowe mss.; McCorison 1194; Shaw 20707.

823.17 [—] ——— Ornamented with Engravings. Albany: Printed By E. & E. Hosford. 1811.
  fr.[2], t.[3], [4–5], 6–30, [31, illus.] p.; illus.; 10 cm.; pr. & illus. buff paper covers. Page "(6)" enclosed in a parenthesis, other page numbers enclosed in brackets "[ ]". Cover title imprint: Albany: Printed By E. And E. Hosford. [n.d.].
  MWA-W*; Bowe mss.; Shaw 23352.

823.18 [—] ——— Albany: Printed By E. And E. Hosford. 1812.
  fr.[2], t.[3], [4–5], 6–30, [31, illus.] p.; illus.; 10 cm.; pr. & illus. buff paper covers; cover title imprint: Albany: Printed By E. & E. Hosford.
  MWA-W*; CLU; CtHi (fair); Bowe mss.; Shaw 26037.

823.19 [—] ——— Adorned with Cuts. Sidney's Press. New-Haven. 1812.
  fr.[2], t.[3], [4–5], 6–30, [31, alphabet] p.; illus.; 10.5 cm.; yellow paper covers; adv. of I. Cooke & Co. p.[4] of "Books For Children And For Schools."
  Welch*; MWA; NjR (fr.[2], t.[3], p.[4] wanting); Bowe mss; Shaw 26038.

823.20 [—] ——— Ornamented with Engravings. Albany: Printed By E. & E. Hosford. 1813.
  fr.[2], t.[3], [4–5], 6–30, [31, illus.] p.; illus.; 10.5 cm.; pr. & illus. paper covers.
  CtHi*; Bowe mss.; Shaw 29120.

823.21 [—] ——— Adorned with Cuts. Sidney's Press. New-Haven. 1813.
  fr.[2], t.[3], [4–5], 6–30, [31, alphabet] p.; illus.; 10.5 cm.; pr. & illus. paper covers; cover title undated.
  MWA*; CtHi; DLC (fr.[2], p.[31] & covers mut.); PP; RNHi (fr.[2] and front cover wanting; i. st. on t.[3]); Bowe mss.; Shaw 29121.

823.22 [—] ——— Ornamented with Engravings. Albany: Printed By E. & E. Hosford. 1814.

fr.[2], t.[3], [4–5], 6–30, [31, illus.] p.; illus.; 10 cm.; pr. & illus. buff paper covers. Page number 6 enclosed by brackets; other page numbers are enclosed by parentheses. Cover title imprint: Albany: Printed By E. And E. Hosford.
  MWA-W*; Bowe mss.; Shaw 32083.

823.23 [—] ——— Albany: Printed By E. & E. Hosford, 1816.
  fr.[2], t.[3], [4–5], 6–30, [31, illus.] p.; illus.; 10 cm.; pr. & illus. buff paper covers; cover title imprint same as no. **823.22.**
  MWA*; PP; Bowe mss.; Shaw 38195.

823.24 [—] ——— Albany: Printed By E. & E. Hosford. 1818.
  fr.[2], t.[3], [4–5], 6–30, [31, illus.] p.; illus.; 10.5 cm.; gray-green pr. & illus. paper covers; cover title imprint same as no. **823.22.**
  MWA-T*; PP.

MARIA, OR THE EVER-BLOOMING FLOWER. *See* Sommerville, Elizabeth, no. **1231.**

[MATHEWS, ELIZA KIRHAM (STRONG)]
d. 1802
824 — ADELAIDE, Or, Trials Of Fortitude. By Mrs. C. Mathews. [1 line quot.] From Sidney's Press. For I. Cooke & Co. New-Haven. 1813.
  fr.[2], t.[3], [4–5], 6–47 p.; illus.; 11 cm.; illus. paper covers.
  CLU*.

825.1 [—] THE SISTERS, AND THE ROSE; Or, History Of Ellen Selwyn. From Sidney's Press. For I. Cooke & Co. New-Haven. 1812.
  fr.[2], t.[3], [4–5], 6–47 p.; illus.; 11 cm.; pr. & illus. purple paper covers; cover title undated. English ed. entitled: *Lessons Of Truth: Containing The Rose; Or, The History Of Ellen Selwyn; Adelaide, A Tale; And The Sisters.* York: Thomas Wilson and Son, 1811.
  MWA*; CtHi; CtY; Shaw 26741.

825.2 [—] ——— From Sidney's Press. For I. Cooke & Co. New-Haven. 1813.
  fr.[2], t.[3], [4–5], 6–47 p.; illus.; 11 cm.; pr. & illus. pink paper covers.
  MWA*; Shaw 29788.

825.3 [—] ——— Selwyn. Adorned With Cuts. From Sidney's Press. New-Haven. 1817.

fr.[2], t.[3], [4–5], 6–46, [47, adv.] p.; illus.; 12.5 cm.; illus. yellow-buff paper covers. CtY*; Shaw 42121.

825.4 [—] ——— New-Haven: Printed For J. Babcock And Son. Sidney's Press. 1819.
    fr.[ii], t.[1], [2, adv.–3], 4–36 p.; illus.; 13.5 cm.; pr. & illus. buff or green paper covers. CtHi* (2 copies); CtY; DLC (rebound); MWA (fr.[ii] & front cover wanting); Shaw 49423.

MATHEWS, JAMES
826 [—] A Token For Children, part 3 containing some account Of the Life and God's Gracious Dealing with Hephzebah Mathews who departed this Life, June 5, 1790, age 10 years. New-York. 1811.
    MB; NN; PU; Shaw 23107 and 23355.

MAVOR, WILLIAM FORDYCE 1758–1837
827 — A Father's Gift To His Children: Consisting Of Original Essays, Tales, Fables, Reflections, &c. By William Mavor, L.L.D. Rector Of Sonesfield, Oxon, Vicar of Hurley, Berks, Chaplain To The Earl Of Moira, &c. Vol. I. [II.] [1 line quot.] Hor. Philadelphia: Published By M. Carey. 1815.
    vol. I.: t.[i], [ii–v], vi–xiv, [1], 2–215, [216, colopon] p.; vol. II.: t.[i], [ii–v] vi–xii, [1], 2–320 p.; 2 vols.; t.[i] 13.5 cm. Colophon vol. I. p.[216]: George Phillips, Printer. Carlisle, Pa. MWA-W* (rebound, p. [iii], dedication–iv, bl.] wanting); CtW (15 cm. bound in red half calf, blue paper over bds.; vol. I. t.[i] mut.); DLC; PPL (rebound); Shaw 35233.

MAY, ROBERT
828 — The Children's Hymn Book: Being a selection of Hymns from various authors, Including Watts' Divine Songs For Children, And Doddrige's Principles of the Christian Religion. Designed For The Use & Instruction Of The Rising Generation. Selected by Robert May, Missionary. [4 lines of verse] Philadelphia: Published by Thomas & William Bradford, No. 8, South Front Street. 1811.
    t.[1], [2–5], 6–159, [160] p.; 11 cm.; marbled paper covers; colophon p. [160]: T. & W. Bradford, Printers. MWA*; Shaw 24385.

MEANWELL, NANCY (*pseud.*) *See* Johnson, Richard, no. 674.1.

829.1 The Medley. New-York: Printed And Sold By Samuel Wood, At the Juvenile Bookstore, No. 357, Pearl-street. 1813.
    fr.[ii, alphabet], t.[1], [2–3], 4–29 p.; illus.; 10 cm.; pr. & illus. paper covers; cover title dated 1813. MWA*; CtHi; PP (covers wanting); VtHi (covers only); Shaw 29133.

829.2 ——— New-York: Printed And Sold By Samuel Wood, At The Juvenile Book-Store, No. 357, Pearl-Street. 1815.
    fr.[ii, alphabet], t.[1], [2–3], 4–29 p.; illus.; 10 cm.; pr. & illus. paper covers; cover title undated. MWA*; ICU; OClWHi; Shaw 35240.

829.3 ——— [cut] [rule 9 mm. long with a thickened center] Nerv-York [*sic. i.e.* New-York]: Printed And Sold By S. Wood & Sons, At The Juvenile Book-Store, No. 357, Pearl-Street. 1816.
    fr.[ii], alphabet, t.[1], [2–3], 4–28 p.; illus.; 10 cm.; pr. & illus. paper covers; cover title undated. The last line p. 28: "by falling into the deep water." MWA*; Shaw 38217.

829.4 ——— [cut] [a squarish central ornament 2 mm. wide, with a central dot, on either side of which is a dash 5 mm. long] Nerv-York [*sic. i.e.* New York]: ——— [same imprint as 829.3] 1816. A variant of the preceding with a different type ornament on the title page, and variations in type setting. The last line p. 28: "into deep water." MWA-W*.

829.5 ——— Nerv-York [*sic. i.e.* New-York]: Printed And Sold By S. Wood & Sons, At The Juvenile Book-Store, No. 261, Pearl-Street. 1818.
    fr.[ii], alphabet, t.[1], [2–3], 4–28 p.; illus.; 10 cm.; green Dutch paper covers. MWA*; Shaw 44784.

829.6 ——— Nerv-York [*sic. i.e.* New-York]: Published By Samuel Wood & Sons, No. 261, Pearl-Street. And Samuel S. Wood & Co. No. 212, Market-st. Baltimore. 1819.

fr.[ii, alphabet], t.[1], [2–3], 4–28 p.; illus.; 10 cm.; green and violet Dutch paper covers. MWA-W*; PP.

829.7 ——— New-York: Published By Samuel Wood & Sons, No. 261, Pearl-Street, And Samuel S. Wood & Co. No. 212, Market-st. Baltimore. 1820.

fr.[ii, alphabet], t.[1], [2–3], 4–28 p.; illus.; 11 cm.; green Dutch paper covers. Welch*; CLU; CtY; MWA; NjR (fr.[ii] and most of t.[1] wanting); Shoemaker 2207.

THE MELANCHOLY END OF UNGRATEFUL CHILDREN. *See* Lee, Richard, no. **746.**

A MEMORIAL FOR CHILDREN. *See* Hendley, George, no. **504.1.**

A MEMORIAL FOR SUNDAY SCHOOL BOYS. *See* Hendley, George, no. **505.1.**

A MEMORIAL FOR SUNDAY SCHOOL GIRLS. *See* Hendley, George, no. **505.1.**

830 MEMOIRS OF CATHERINE MASON AND JULIA MILLS. Philadelphia: Published by the Sunday and Adult School Union. Clark & Raser, Printers. 1818.

t.[1], [2–3], 4–36 p.; title vignette (illus.) only; 12.5 cm.; pr. & illus. blue paper covers. MWA*; Shaw 44802.

831 No. 3. MEMOIRS OF CHARLES HOWARD BRODHEAD. Published By The Philadelphia Female Tract Society. [caption title p. [1]]. Printed by Lydia Bailey, No. 10, North Alley, Philad. [1816]. [colophon p. 8.].

t.[1], 2–8 p.; 14 cm. MWA* (bound with other tracts, with which *The First Annual Report Of The Philadelphia Female Tract Society For The Year 1816* was originally bound); Shaw 38227.

832.1 MEMOIRS OF DICK, The Little Poney, Supposed to be written by himself; And Published For The Instruction And Amusement Of Good Boys And Girls. Philadelphia: Printed for Benjamin Johnson No. 31 High-Street, And Jacob Johnson No. 147 High-Street. 1802.

fr.[ii], t.[1], [2–5], 6–96 p.; illus.; 12 cm.; bound in Dutch paper over w. bds.; engraved

front. signed *Howitt del. Tanner* [*sc.*]; a different book from no. **773.1.**
English ed. London: Printed for J. Walker; sold by E. Newbery, 1800.
Welch* (rear cover wanting); DLC (fr.[ii], p.[1]–4 and covers wanting, p.[5]–6, p. 95–96 mut.); MWA; PHi; PP; Shaw 2650.

832.2 ——— Philadelphia: Printed For Benjamin Johnson, No. 22, North Second Street. (Next door to the church.) 1813.

fr.[ii], t.[1], [2–5], 6–108 p.; illus.; 15 cm.; bound in pr. & illus. gray-green paper over bds.; front. signed *Howitt del. Tanner sc.* PP*; MB; PHi; Shaw 29148.

833 MEMOIRS OF MARY HALLAM HUNTINGTON, Of Bridgewater, (Mass.) Written By Her Father. Boston: Printed For Samuel T. Armstrong, By Crocker & Brewster, No. 50, Cornhill, 1820.

t.[1], [2–5], 6–36 p.; 14 cm.; pr. & illus. pinkish paper covers; rear cover adv. list of books. Welch*; CLU (imp.); MH; MWA; NNC-T (front cover mut. & half wanting, rear cover & p. 35–36 wanting); Shoemaker 1708 and 2232.

834 MEMOIRS OF MARY W——, Who Died At The Early Age Of Eleven Years and Eight Months. Philadelphia: Published by the Sunday and Adult School Union. Clark & Raser, Printers. 1818.

t.[1], [2–3], 4–32 p.; 10 cm.; pr. blue paper covers. MWA*; Shaw 44803.

835 MEMOIRS OF MISS ELIZA VAN WYCK: To Which Is Added, The Story Of The Happy Waterman. Hartford: Printed By Hudson And Goodwin. 1813.

t.[1], [2–3], 4–34 p.; 13 cm.; blue marbled paper covers. MWA*; Shaw 29149.

836 MEMOIR OF REBECCA M. COIT, Who Died at New York, Dec. 19, 1818, In The Eleventh Year Of Her Age: To which are added, Lines On The Death Of A Young Person. Boston: Printed For Samuel T. Armstrong, By Crocker And Brewster, No. 50, Cornhill. 1820.

t.[1], [2–3], 4–23, [24] p.; illus.; 13 cm.; pr. & illus. pink paper covers. NPV*; Shoemaker 2230.

837 MEMOIR OF MISS SALLY LADD, Daughter Of Lt. Timothy Ladd, Of Dunbarton, New-Hampshire, Who died January 21, 1816, in the 19th year of her age. [caption title] [no place of publication, printer, or date].

    t.[1], 2–12 p.; 17.5 cm.
    MWA*; Shaw 38224.

MEMOIRS OF A PEGTOP. *See* Kilner, Mary Ann, no. **735.**

838.1 MEMOIRS OF THE LITTLE MAN, AND THE LITTLE MAID. So Wonderfully Contrived As To Be Either Sung Or Said. Illustrated With Curious Engravings. Philadelphia: Published and sold Wholesale by Wm Charles, and may be had of all the Booksellers. Price plain 18 1 4 cents. Coloured 31 1 2 cents. 1811. W. M'Culloch, Printer. [cover title].

    [1–12] p. engr. on one side only of 12 leaves; 13.5 cm.; pr. buff paper covers.
    English ed. title 1: *Authentic Memoirs Of The Little Man* . . . London: B. Tabart, 1807.
    English ed. title 2: *Memoirs Of The Little Man* . . . London: Tabart & Co. 1816.
    NHi*.

838.2 ——— Published By Henry Whipple, Salem, Mass. 1814. [cover title].

    1–12 p. engr. on one side only of 12 leaves; 13.5 cm.; pr. paper covers; same plates used in **838.1** and **838.2** but the pages are numbered. CtHi* (rear cover wanting); DLC (rebound; per st. on front blue-gray paper cover; rear cover adv. of 20 books); Shaw 32105.

838.3 ——— Philadelphia: Published and sold Wholesale by Wm Charles, and may [be] had of all the Booksellers. Price plain 18 1 4 Cents. Colo[ured] [31 1 2 Cents.] [*ca.* 1815] [cover title].

    [1–10] p. engr. on one side only of 10 leaves; illus.; 12.5 cm.; pr. tan paper covers; same plates as in no. **838.1**.
    MWA* (3 leaves wanting; covers soiled and mut.); Shaw 32104 (dated 1814).

838.4 ——— Philadelphia: Published and sold Wholesale by Wm. Charles and may be had of all the Booksellers. Price plain, 18 3-4 Cents. Coloured 31 1 4 Cents. 1816. [cover title].

    [1–12] p. engr. on one side only of 12 leaves; illus.; 13 cm.; pr. & illus. brown paper covers.

Rear cover: A New Edition, Of The Little Man And The Little Maid.
    CtHi* (colored illus.); Weiss 1932b.

838.5 ——— Published by Henry Whipple, Salem, Mass. 1818. [cover title].

    1–12 p. engr. on one side only of 12 leaves; illus.; 12.5 cm.; pr. paper covers. Rear cover has adv. of 21 books.
    OChRHi*.

839 MEMOIRS OF THE LIVES OF HANNAH HILL, George Chalkley, And Catharine Burling: With Some Of Their Last Expressions. New-York: Printed By Samuel Wood & Sons, No. 357, Pearl-Street. 1815.

    t.[1], [2–3], 4–11 p.; 12.5 cm.; brown paper covers.
    MWA*; Shaw 35256.

840 THE MENTAL FLOWER GARDEN. New-York: adv. by Thomas B. Jansen, 1805 in **1371.5.**

MERCIER, LOUIS SEBASTIAN 1740–1814
841.1 [—] SERAPHINA: A Novel. From The French of M. Mercier. To which Is Added Auguste & Madelaine. A Real History, By Miss Helen Maria Williams. Charlestown [Mass.]: Printed By John Lamson. 1797.

    t.[i], [ii–iii], iv, [5], 6–102 p.; 10 cm.; green Dutch paper covers.
    MWA*; Bowe mss.; Evans 324672.

841.2 [—] ——— Boston: adv. by John Folsom, 1798 in **558.1.**

842 THE MERMAID AT HOME, Philadelphia: adv. by David Hogan, 1812 in **1392.**

MERRITT, JOHN and SARAH ANN
843 —— A Short Account Of The Life, Sickness, And Death Of Elizabeth Merritt, By Her Father And Mother. John And Sarah Ann Merritt. New-York: Printed By Samuel Wood & Sons, No. 261, Pearl-Street. 1820.

    t.[1], [2–3], 4–13 p.; 14 cm.
    Gardner* (covers wanting; Shoemaker 2244.

THE MERRY CRIES OF LONDON. *See* The Cries Of London, no. **249.14.**

METAMORPHOSIS. *See* Sands, Benjamin, no. **1163.1.**

844 Das Milchmädchen; eine wahrhafte und interessante Erzählung, in fünf Abtheilungen. Philadelphia: Gedruckt und im Verlag bey Conrad Zentler, in der Zweyten Strasse, unterhalb der Rehs-Strasse. 1818.

fr.[2], t.[3], [4–5], 6–88 p.; front. only illus.; 14.5 cm.; bound in glossy marbled paper over bds., leather spine.
P°; PPL; Shaw 44841.

[MILLER, EBENEZER] 1779?–1857
845 [—] The Life Of Joseph, A Scripture Narrative. New-York: Printed And Sold By Mahlon Day, No. 84, Water-street. 1820.

fr.[2], t.[3], [4–5], 6–35 p.; illus.; 14 cm.; pr. & illus. gray paper covers; fr[2] signed A [Alexander Anderson].
PP°.

MILLS, ALFRED
846 — Biography Of Eminent Persons, Alphabetically Arranged. With Portraits, From Drawings By Alfred Mills. New-York: Published by Samuel Wood & Sons, No. 261, Pearl-street; And Samuel S. Wood & Co. No. 212, Market-st. Baltimore. 1819.

t.[1], [2–5], 6–186 p.; illus.; 6.5 cm.; bound in red leather.
English ed. London: Darton, Harvey, & Darton; And J. Harris, 1814.
Welch°; MWA-T; NHi.

847 — Costumes Of Different Nations, In Miniature, From Drawings, By Alfred Mills. With Descriptions. New-York: Printed and Sold by Samuel Wood & Sons, At the Juvenile Book-store, No. 261, Pearl-street. 1817.

t.[1], [2–5], 6–190 p.; illus.; 6.5 cm.; bound in red leather. Adv. by Samuel Wood & Sons, 1819 in **1188.8**.
English ed. London: Darton, Harvey, & Darton, And J. Harris, 1811.
MWA°; Shaw 41438.

848 — London In Miniature: With 47 Engravings Of Its Public Buildings And Antiquities, From Drawings By Alfred Mills. New-York: Printed and Sold by S. Wood & Sons, At the Juvenile Book-store, No. 357, Pearl-street. 1816.

t.[i], [ii–iii], iv, [5, bl.–6, illus.], [7], 8–190 p.; illus.; 7 cm.; bound in leather. Adv. by Samuel

Wood & Sons, 1819 in **1188.8** and 1820 in **274.2**.
English ed. London: Darton, Harvey, & Darton, And J. Harris, 1814.
CtY°.

849.1 — Pictures Of English History, In Miniature, From the reign of Henry VI. to the death of Lord Nelson. Designed By Alfred Mills. With Descriptions. Philadelphia: Printed for Johnson and Warner, No. 147, Market Street. 1815.

t.[i], [ii, bl.], [pl. opp. pl. [1]]; [1], 2–96 p.; 48 pl.; 6.5 cm.; bound in ornamental blue paper over bds., leather spine.
MWA-W°.

849.2 —— Miniature, Designed by Alfred Mills. With Descriptions. Vol. I. New-York: Printed and Sold by Samuel Wood & Sons, At the Juvenile Book-store, No. 261, Pearl-street. 1817.

t.[1], [2–5], 6–192 p.; illus.; 6.5 cm. Adv. by Samuel Wood & Sons, 1819 in **1188.8**.
English ed. London: 2 vols. Darton & Harvey, And J. Harris, 1809.
MWA°; DLC (per. st. on t.[1], bound in leather); Shaw 41439.

850 — Pictures Of Grecian History, In Miniature, Designed by Alfred Mills. With Descriptions. Philadelphia: Published by Johnson and Warner, No. 147, Market Street. 1812.

t.[i], [ii, bl.], [iii, bl.], [iv, illus.], [1], 2–96 p.; illus.; 7 cm.
English ed. London: Darton, Harvey, & Darton, and J. Harris, 1810.
MWA° (p.[1]–2 mut. affecting two words of the last line); CtY; DLC; NHi; NN; PHi; PP (bound in pr. gray-green paper over bds.); Shaw 26083.

851 — Pictures Of Roman History, In Miniature, Designed by Alfred Mills. With Explanatory Anecdotes. Philadelphia: Publishd by Johnson & Warner, No. 147, Market Street. J. Bouvier, Printer. 1811.

t.[i], [ii, bl], [iii, bl.–iv, illus.], [1], 2–96 p.; illus.; 6.5 cm.; bound in green or pink paper over bds.; colophon p. 96: J. Bouvier, printer, Bellavista, Hamilton-ville.
English ed. London: Darton & Harvey; J. Harris, 1809.
MWA° (2 copies with varying covers); CLU

(imp.); CSmH (bound in yellow paper over bds.); MB; NHi (t.[i] wanting); NN; NNMM; PHi (2 copies); PP; PPL; ViU; Shaw 23392.

852.1 — A Short History Of The Bible And Testament, With 48 Neat Engravings, Designed By Alfred Mills. [2nd t. [3]; [a]₂ recto].

Published By Johnson & Warner, No. 147, Market street, Philadelphia. 1809. John Bouvier, Printer. [imprint t. or 1st t.[1]; [a]₁ recto] 1st t.[1], [2, bl.], 2nd t.[3], [4, bl.], [pl. opp. p. [5]]; [5–100] p.; [a]₂; A–M₄; 48 pl.; 7 cm.; bound in marbled paper over bds., leather spine. English ed. London: W. Darton & J. Harvey, And J. Harris, late Newbery, Oct. 10, 1807.

Welch°; MWA; NN; PP (t.[1] bound at the end); PPL; Shaw 18091 and 18607.

852.2 — ———— [2nd t. or t.[3]; [a]₂ recto wanting; probably the same as 852.1].

Published By Johnson & Warner, No. 147, Market street, Philadelphia. 1811. J. Bouvier, Printer. [imprint t. or 1st [1]; [a]₁ recto] 1st [1], [2, bl.], [pl. opp. p.[5]], [5–100] p.; [a]₂, A–M₄; 48 pl.; 6.5 cm.; bound in marbled paper over bds., leather spine.

MWA° ([a]₂ or p.[3–4] wanting); Shaw 23934.

852.3 [—] ———— Engravings. New-York: Printed by Southwick and Pelsue, No. 3, New-Street. 1811.

t.[1], [2–5], 6–192 p.; illus.; 6.5 cm.; bound in leather.

Welch°; DLC; MWA (bound in marbled paper over bds., leather spine); Shaw 23933.

852.4 [—] ———— New-York: Printed by Pelsue and Gould, No. 3 New-Street. 1812.

t.[1], [2–5], 6–192 p.; illus.; 7 cm.; bound in marbled paper over bds., leather spine.

MWA-W°.

852.5 [—] ———— New-York: Pelsue And Gould, Printers, Corner of Wall And Broad-sts. 1812.

t.[1], [2–5], 6–192 p.; illus.; t.[1] 6 cm.

Wightman° (rebound; p. 65–82, 95–[112], [143, bl.–144, illus.] wanting).

852.6 [—] ————New-York: Gould and Van Pelt, Printers, No. 9. Wall-street. 1814.

t.[1], [2–5], 6–192 p.; illus.; 7 cm.; bound in

blue marbled paper over bds., black leather spine.

Welch°; CtY; MWA (bound in leather); PP; Shaw 32768.

852.7 [—] ———— New-York: Published By Wm. B. Gilley, 92 Broad-Way. 1815.

t.[1], [2–5], 6–192 p.; illus.; 6 cm.; bound in pr. & illus. buff paper over bds.

MWA° (front cover wanting); MLuHi; RPB (front cover mut.); Shaw 35932.

852.8 [—] ———— Embellished with neat engravings. Hartford: Published By Cooke & Hale. 1817. B. & J. Russell, Printers.

fr.[2], t.[3], [4–7], 8–190 p.; illus.; 6.5 cm.; bound in tan paper over bds., leather spine.

MWA° (fr.[2] mut.); CtHi; CtY; Shaw 42115.

852.9 [—] ———— Embellished with Engravings, Hartford: Published by Cooke & Hale 1818.

fr.[2], t.[3], [4–7], 8–183 p.; illus.; 7 cm.; bound in blue paper over bds., dark green leather spine; p.[4]: George Goodwin & Sons, Printers, Hartford.

Welch°; CtHi; DLC; MWA (p. 7–8 mut.); Shaw 45716.

MILLS, JULIA

853 — Interesting Memoir Of Miss Julia Mills. Written By Herself. To Which Is Added An Important Discovery. Philadelphia: Published by "The Religious Tract Society of Philadelphia," and for sale at their Depository, No. 8, South Front Street. William Bradford—Agent. October—1818.

t.[1], [2], 3–12 p.; 18.5 cm.

MWA°.

MILTMORE, JAMES *pseud.* acasto 1755–1836

854.1 [—] An Address To A Young Lady. By Acasto. Exeter [N.H.]: Printed By Henry Ranlet, And Sold At His Book-Store. 1805.

t.[1], [2–3], 4–18 p.; title vignette only illus.; 14 cm.; wallpaper covers.

MWA-W°; PP; Shaw 7821.

854.2 [—] ———— Exeter [N.H.]: Printed And Sold By Henry Ranlet. [1805]. Price 3 Cents single, 2 Dolls. 100. [caption title].

[1], 2–8 p.; 18.5 cm.; pr. buff paper covers.

MWA°.

854.3 [—] ——— Newburyport [Mass.], Printed By W. & J. Gilman. Sold at their Miscellaneous Book-Store, No. 2, Middle-Street. 1814.

> fr.[2], t.[3], [4–5], 6–23 p.; illus.; 12 cm.; pr. & illus. paper covers.
>
> MSaE° (copy 1, complete; copy 2, fr.[2], p. 23, & covers wanting). Shaw 30612.

MINIATURE BIBLE often called a Thumb Bible.

All anonymous Bibles under 7 cm. in length have been listed by title under the heading Miniature Bible. Where the author is known the Bible is placed under author as follows:

THE BIBLE. *See* Taylor, John, no. **1293.7–9** and **1293.15**.

THE BIBLE AND APOCRAPHY VERSIFIED. *See* Taylor, John, no. **1293.13**.

AN HISTORY OF THE BIBLE AND APOCRAPHY VERSIFIED. *See* Taylor, John, no. **1293.12**.

THE HISTORY OF THE NEW TESTAMENT. *See* Taylor, John, no. **1293.3**.

THE HOLY BIBLE IN MINIATURE. *See* Taylor, John, no. **1293.11**.

A SHORT HISTORY OF THE BIBLE. *See* Mills, Alfred, no. **852.1**.

VERBUM SEMPITERNUM. *See* Taylor, John, no. **1293.1**, with the New Testament portion entitled: SALVATOR MUNDI.

855 — THE BIBLE. Woodstock [Vt.]: Printed by D. Watson. 1819.

> t.[1], [2–3], 4–251 p. illus.; 5 cm.; bound in leather. American variant of English version 2 with parts of English version 2 re-written. Portions of the first sentence of the first paragraph of selected sections: Preface p.[3]–5: "It is a sorrowful reflection, that in a country . . . have received their completion by the coming of Jesus Christ." [Book I.] Of God and his attributes, p. 8–9: "The Scriptures inform us that God is the Maker, . . . just, faithful, pure and holy." [Book II. Old Testament] Chapter I, p. 12–15: "In the beginning God created the heavens and earth, . . . plenty of fruit hung upon the trees." [New Testament. Book I.] Chap. XIII, p. 151–152: "About 4000 years after the fall of Adam, . . . as had been foretold." English ed. of English version 1, title 1: *Biblia or a Practical Summary of ye Old & New Testaments.* London: R. Wilkin, 1727.
>
> English ed. of English version 1, title 2: *The*

Bible in Miniature or a Concise History of the Old & New Testaments. London: W. Harris, 1771.

Scottish ed. English version 1, title 3: *Bible in Miniature Or, a Concise History of both Testaments.* Edinburgh: 1820.

English ed. English version 1, title 4: *A Concise History Of The Holy Bible. To which Is Added An Appendix containing Several Useful Collections, Never Before Printed.* Liverpool: T. Schofield, 1789.

English ed. of English version 1, title 5: *The History of the Bible, Compiled for the Use of the Emperor of Lilliputia.* [London?] Lilliput: Printed in 1775.

English ed. of English version 2 London: J. Harris, late Newbery, & for Darton & Harvey [*ca.* 1806].

English ed. of English version 3: *The History Of The Holy Bible.* London: R. Snagg, 1802.

English ed. of English version ?, title 3: *The Bible in Miniature Intended as a present for Youth.* [Glasgow]: Lumsden and Son. [n.d]. MWA-W°; McCorison 2093.

856.1 — BIBLE HISTORY. New York: Printed and Sold By S. Wood, No. 357, Pearl-street. 1811.

> fr.[ii], t.[1], [2–3], 4–254 p.; illus.; 5 cm.; bound in leather. American variant 1 of English version 2, no. **855**, with minor differences. The [New Testament] Chap. XIII. has: "About four thousand years" instead of "About 4004 years." Welch°; MH; MWA; NN (fr.[ii] & p. 253–254 wanting); PP; Shaw 22342; Weiss 1942, p. 763.

856.2 — ——— Otsego [Cooperstown, N. Y.]: Printed and Sold by H. & E. Phinney, Jun. 1812.

> fr.[ii], t.[1], [2–3], 4–189 p.; illus.; 5.5. cm.; bound in leather. American variant of English version 2, no. **855**.
>
> MWA°; NCooH; Shaw 24859.

856.3 — ——— New-York: Printed and Sold By S. Wood, No. 357, Pearl-street. 1813.

> fr.[ii], t.[1], [2–3], 4–254 p.; illus.; 4.5 cm.; bound in leather. Same version as no. **856.1**.
>
> Welch°; DLC; MWA (p. 167–171 mut.); NHi; PP (imp.); Shaw 27933.

856.4 — ——— Boston: Published by D. Hale. 1814.

> fr.[2], t.[3], [4–5], 6–256 p.; illus.; 5 cm.;

bound in leather. American variant of English version 2, no. **855**.

MWA° (p.[2], 129–130, 145–146, 153–154 mut.); BM; DLC (p. 113–114 wanting, lower half of p. 5–6, 29–30 wanting); Shaw 30902.

856.5 —— New-York: Printed and Sold By S. Wood, No. 357, Pearl-Street. 1814.

fr.[ii], t.[1], [2–3], 4–254 p.; illus.; 5 cm.; bound in leather. Same version as no. **856.1**.

Welch (p. 253–254 mut.); CLU; MWA; PP; Shaw 30903.

856.6 —— Baltimore. Printed & Published by B. Edes, No. 46, Market-street. 1816.

fr.[ii], t.[1], [2–3], 4–254 p.; illus.; 5 cm.; bound in red leather. American variant of English version 2, no. **855**.

MWA° (shaken copy); Shaw 36992.

856.7 —— Leicester [Mass.]: Printed by Hori Brown. 1816.

fr.[ii], t.[1], [2–3], 4–240 p.; illus.; 5 cm.; bound in leather. American variant of English version 2, no. **855**.

MWA° (2 copies); CLU; PP (rebound); Shaw 36993.

856.8 —— New-York: Printed and Sold By S. Wood & Sons, No. 357, Pearl-street. 1816.

fr.[ii], t.[1], [2–3], 4–254 p.; illus.; 5 cm.; bound in leather. Same as no. **296.1**.

MWA-W°; DLC; ViU; Shaw 36994.

857.1 — THE BIBLE IN MINIATURE or a Concise History of the Old & New Testaments. New York Printed by A. Brower Jun. [1791].

1st t.[i], [ii, bl.], [1], 2–148; 2nd t. [i], [ii, bl], [149–150], [pl. no. "P 151" opp. p. 151], 151–256 p.; 16 pl. including 1st t. & 2nd t.; 5 cm.; bound in red leather; 14 pl. numbered the same as the opp. p.: P 14, P 25, P 52, P 58, P 74, P 93, P 122, P 127, P 143, P 151, P 175, P 248 [*sic. i.e.* 218], P 221, P 247. English version 1, title 2, no. **855**.

2nd title: A Concise History of the New Testament. N York. Printed by A Brower Jun. 1791.

MWA-W°; PP (2nd t.[i] wanting); PPL; Evans 24400.

857.2 — —— Philadᵃ Printed by I. Babcock, Nᵒ 79 N. third Str. [1792].

fr.[ii], engr. 1st t.[1], [ii, bl.], [1], 2–104, engr.; 2nd t.[i], [ii, bl.], 105–181, [182, bl.], [183–190, bl.]; 3rd t.[191, not engr.] p.; A–F₁₆, sig. F includes 4 bl. leaves, and leaf of 3rd t.; 15 engr. pl. including 1st & 2nd t.; 4.5 cm.; bound in leather; 15 pl. including fr.[ii] numbered "I", both title pages and text pl. numbered II–IIII [*sic. i.e.* IV], V, VII–VIII, XI–XV. In the CtY copy the 3rd t. is followed by 2 fly leaves and pl. VI is also wanting. The pl. are copied in the reverse from no. **857.1**. English version 1, title 2, no. **855**.

2nd title: A concise History of the New Testament. Philadᵃ printed by I. Babcock. Nᵒ 79 N. third Str.

3rd title: The Bible In Miniature, or a Concise History of the Old & New Testaments. Hartford, Printed by E. Babcock. M,DCC,XCII.

CtY°; PP (3rd t.[191] pasted to rear cover, fr.[ii] numbered "I", pl. numbered II–XV); Evans 24100.

857.3 — —— New York. Printed by N. Birdsall [1796].

1st t.[i], [ii, bl.], [1], 2–104, 2nd t.[i], [ii, bl.], 105–181 p.; 16 engr. pl. including 1st & 2nd t.; 4.5 cm.; bound in black leather. The 16 pl. are the same as those used in no. **857.1**. The first and second title pages are from the same plates used in no. **857.1** except for the substitution of Birdsall's name and changing the date on the second title page to "1796." The work on the title pages was not carefully done because a trace of the word "Jun" is still present on both and appears to have been erased after printing. In the CtY copy the word "Jun" has not been erased from the second title page. English version 1, title 2, no. **855**.

2nd title: A Concise History of the New Testament. N York. Printed by N. Birdsall 1796.

MWA-W° (p. 81–82, 2nd t.[i], & pl. 52, 58, 93, 122, 145, 221 wanting); CtY (p. 97–112 wanting, p. 113–120 repeated, pl. 58, 127, 248 [*sic.* 218] wanting); NHi (1st t.[i], p. 81–82, & pl. 52, 122, 145 wanting); NN (p. 95–96, pl. 122 wanting); Evans 30083.

857.4 — —— the Old & New Testaments Philadelphia Printed for John Dickins No. 50, Noᵗʰ Second Street [1796].

1st t.[ii], fr.[iii], [iv, bl.], [1], 2–104, [i, bl.];

2nd t.[ii], 105–181 p.; 8 pl. including fr.[iii], and 1st & 2nd t.; 6 cm.; bound in leather. The 8 pl. except 1st t.[ii] are numbered: fr.[iii] numbered 1, 2nd t.[ii] numbered 103 and text pl. 9 is opp. p. 9, 18 opp. p. 17, 37 opp. p. 37, 40 opp. p. 40. English version 1, title 2, no. **855**.
2nd title: A Concise History of the New Testament Philadelphia Printed for John Dickins No 50 North Second Street.
PP°; PPL.

857.5 —––––– Boston: Printed By Hosea Sprague. 1807.
t.[1], 2 [illus.], [3], 4–81, fr.82; 2nd t.[83], 84–144 p.; 2 illus. including fr.82; 7 cm.; bound in green paper over w. bds. English version 1, title 2, no. **855**.
2nd title: A Concise History Of The New Testament. Boston: Printed By Hosea Sprague, 1807.
Welch°; CLU; MB; MWA; PP; Shaw 12116.

857.6 —––––– C. Norris & Co. Printers. 1812.
t.[1], [2–5], 6–80; 2nd t.[81], 82–142 p.; 6.5 cm.; bound in black leather. English version 1, title 2, no. **855**.
2nd title: A Concise History Of The New Testament. Exeter [N.H.]: Printed By C. Norris & Co. 1812.
Welch°; CSmH; MWA; Shaw 24817.

THE BIBLE IN MINIATURE. *See* no. **96** for an edition which is not a miniature Bible in size.

858.1 — A CONCISE HISTORY OF THE HOLY BIBLE. Printed for H. Stead, Philadelphia. 1787.
t.[1], [ii–iii], iv, [5], 6–68; 2nd t.[69], [70, bl.], [pl. opp. p. 71], [71], 72–119; 3rd t.[1], [2–3], 4–10, [11], 12–16 p.; 2 pl. opp. p.[7], [71]; 5 cm.; bound in Dutch paper over bds. English version 1, title 4, no. **855**.
2nd title: A Concise History Of The New Testament. Printed by D. Humphrey's. Philadelphia. 1787.
3rd title: An Appendix Containing the Ten Commandments, And The Old and New Testament Dissected. Printed by D. Humphreys Philadelphia. 1787.
PP°; PHi; PPL; Evans 45053.

858.2 —––––– Philadelphia: Printed in the Year. 1789.

t.[i], [ii–iii], iv, [v–vi, bl.], [1], 2–56, [57–58, bl.]; 2nd t.[59], [60–61], 62–103, [104, bl.]; 3rd t.[1], [2–3], 4–17 p.; 5.5 cm.; bound in black leather. English version 1, title 4, no. **855**.
2nd title: A Concise History Of The New Testament. Philadelphia: Printed in the Year 1789.
3rd title: An Appendix Containing the Ten Commandments, Lord's Prayer & the Creed, And The Old and New Testament Dissected. Printed in the Year 1789.
MWA-W°; Evans 45439.

858.3 —––––– Lansingburgh [N.Y.]: Printed By Luther Pratt, & Co. 1796.
t.[1], [2–3], 4–105, [106, bl.]; 2nd t.[107], [108–109], 110–192 p.; 3 pl.; 5 cm.
2nd title: A Concise History Of The New Testament. Lansingburgh [N.Y.]: Printed By Luther Pratt, & Co. 1796.
Wightman° (rebound); Evans 47724.

858.4 —––––– Philadelphia: Published by J. Peirce. 1814.

858.5 —––––– Philadelphia: Printed and Sold by J. Bioren, 88, Chesnut-street. 1818.
t.[3], [4–5], 6–73, [74]; 2nd t.[75], [76–77], 78–128 p.; illus.; 6.5 cm.; bound in leather. English version 1, title 4, no. **855**.
2nd title: A Concise History Of The New Testament.
MWA°; Shaw 43687.

859 EIN KURZGEFASSTE GESCHICHTE DER BIBEL. Philadelphia: Gedruckt bey C. Zentler. 1811.
fr.[ii], 1st t.[iii], [iv–vi], [1], 2–54, ½t.[55], fr.[56]; 2nd t.[57], [58, bl.], [59], 60–100, capt. t.[101], 102–103, capt. t.[104], 105–106 p.; illus.; 6 cm.; bound in red paper over bds. English version 1, title 4, no. **855**. Half title p. [55]: Kurze Geschichte des Neuen Testaments.
2nd title p.[57]: Kurze Geschichte des Neuen Testaments. Philadelphia: Gedruckt bey C. Zentler. 1811.
Page [101] caption title: Des Alte und Neue Testament zergliedert.
Page [104] caption title: Anhang.
DeWint°; DLC (t.p. coll.).

860.1 HISTORY OF THE BIBLE. Published by Ball & Bedlington. Boston. 1812.

fr.[ii], t.[1], [2–3], 4–254 p.; illus.; 5 cm.; bound in leather; colophon p. 254: Watson & Bangs, Printers. American variant of English version 2, no. **855**.

Adomeit*; MWA (fr.[ii] & p. 13–32, 47–48, 61–62, 113–116, 121–124 wanting; p. 67–68, 95–96 mut.); Shaw 25660.

860.2 —–——— Boston: Published By T. Bedlington & J. Ball. 1814.

fr.[ii], t.[1], [2–3], 4–254 p.; illus.; 5 cm.; bound in leather; p.[2]: Willis, Printer. Same as no. **860.1**.

Welch*; CLU; MB; MH; MWA (fr.[ii] wanting); PP; Shaw 31722.

860.3 —–——— Boston: Printed By Nathaniel Willis 1815.

fr.[ii], t.[1], [2–3], 4–254 p.; illus.; 5.5 cm.; bound in leather. American variant of English version 2, no. **855**.

Welch*; CLU; MB; MHi (rear cover wanting); MWA; NN (2 copies; copy 2, imp.); PP; Shaw 34916.

860.4 —–——— Boston: Published by T. Bedlington. 1819.

fr.[ii], t.[1], [2–3], 4–254 p.; illus.; 5 cm.; bound in leather; p.[2]: Parmenter & Balch Printers. American variant of English version 2, no. **855**.

Welch*; DLC; MB; MWA; MH; PP; Shaw 48237.

860.5 —–——— Lansingburgh [N.Y.]: Published and Sold by Wm. Disturnell. 1820.

fr.[ii], t.[iii], [iv–v], vi–xiii, 14–256 p.; illus.; 5.5 cm.; bound in leather. American variant of English version 2, no. **855**.

Welch*; CLU; MWA; N; NN; Shoemaker 1613.

861.1 — A HISTORY OF THE HOLY BIBLE. Philadelphia: Printed for Pitt Spencer. 1813.

fr.[ii], 1st t.[iii], [iv. bl.-v], vi–viii, [9], 10–120; 2nd t.[121], [122, bl.-123], 124–210; 3rd t.[211], [212, bl.-213], 214–233, [234, bl.]; 4th t.[235], [236, bl.-237), 238–256 p.; illus.; 5.5 cm.; bound in leather, red leather label. English version 1, title 4, no. **855**.

2nd title: A History Of The New Testament. 1813.

3rd title: An Appendix, Containing the Ten Commandments, And The Old and New Testament Dissected. 1813.

4th title: Version Of The Psalms Of David. 1813.

OOxM*; PPL.

861.2 —–——— Cincinnati [O.]: Published by Coleman & Phillips. Morgan, Williams & Co. Printers. 1815.

t.[i], [ii–iii], iv–v, [vi, bl.], [7], 8–76; 2nd t.[77], [78, bl.-79], 80–133, [134, bl.]; 3rd t.[135], [136, bl.-137], 138–150; 4th t.[151], [152, bl.-153], 154–167 p.; 6.5 cm.; bound in leather. English version 1, title 4, no. **855**.

2nd title: A History Of The New Testament. 1815.

3rd title: An Appendix Containing the ten Commandments, And The Old and New Testaments Dissected. 1815.

4th title: Version Of The Psalms Of David. 1815.

PP*; Shaw 34917.

862 MINIATURE BIBLE, Or Abstract Of Sacred History. For the use of Children. [3 lines quot.] Prov. xxii.6. Collated And Abridged By Thomas G. Fessenden. Brattleborough, (Vt.) Published by John Holbrook. 1816. (copy right secured).

fr.[2], t.[3], [4–5], 6–255, [256–257] p.; illus.; 6 cm.; bound in leather. The text is different from any of the preceding miniature Bibles. Portions of the first sentence of the first paragraph of selected sections: Preface, p. [5]: "The object of this little publication . . . truths of the Bible." [The Old Testament] Genesis. Chap. I., p. [9]: "The first book of . . . is named Genesis." Chap. XXXVII. The New Testament, p. [171]: "This book commences . . . the mother of our Saviour."

Welch*; CLU; MWA; N; RNHi (p. 257 wanting); McCorison 1825; Shaw 36958a.

863 THE MINOR CABINET OF USEFUL KNOWLEDGE. Decorated With Engravings On Wood. New-York: Printed For And Sold By T. B. Jansen & Co. No. 248, Pearl-Street. 1802.

t.[1], [2–3], 4–72 p.; illus.; 14.5 cm.; bound with buff paper over bds., leather spine.

MWA-W* (p. 67–68 wanting); Shaw 2664.

864 MIRANDA, OR THE DISCOVERY. A Tale. To Which Are Added, Chariessa, Or A Pattern For

Her Sex. Also, [A]n Original Story, Founded On A Fact. Being a pleasing Companion for young Gentlemen and Ladies. Norwich [Conn.]—Printed by J. Trumbull, 1800.

> t.[1], [2–3], 4–108 p.; 16.5 cm.
> CtHi°; Evans 37970.

MRS. PLEASANT'S STORY BOOK. *See* Pleasant, Mrs. (*pseud.*), no. **1017**.

865 MISCELLANIES, MORAL AND INSTRUCTIVE, In VERSE, Extracted From The Best Authors, For The Improvement Of Young Persons. Baltimore Printed By And For Warner & Hanna, And Sold By Them And John Vance & Co. 1807.

> t.[1], [2–3], 4–60 p.; 16 cm. This is a different book from *Miscellanies, Moral And Instructive, In Prose, and Verse* said to have been compiled by Mrs. Milcah Martha (Hill) Moore.
> CtHi°; DLC; MdBP; MdHi; NN; RPB (rebound; p. [3]–10 wanting); Shaw 13096.

866 THE MODERN STORY TELLER. Contents. The History Of The Three Brothers. The History Of The Three Sisters. The Contrast. Fatal Effects Of Delay. The Nosegay. Courage Inspired By Friendship. And, The Diverting History Of John Gilpin. Embellished With Engravings. Philadelphia: Printed And Sold By H. And P. Rice; Sold Also By J. Rice And Co. Market-Street, Baltimore. 1796.

> fr.[2], t.[3], [4, bl.–5], 6–95, [96, adv.] p.; illus.; 17 cm.; bound in blue-gray paper over bds., leather spine.
> DLC°; Evans 30803.

867 THE MODERN STORY TELLER. Being, A Collection of merry, polite, grave, moral, entertaining, and improving Tales, related with that modesty so as not to offend the most delicate ear, and at the same time calculated to inspire mirth among all degrees of people, of whatever age, sex, or opinion. Philadelphia, Printed and Sold by Peter Stewart, No. 34, South Second-Street. 1802.

> t.[1], [2–3], 4–111, [112, contents] p.; 12.5 cm.; original bds., leather spine.
> PP°.

868.1 THE MODERN STORY-TELLER; Being A Collection Of Merry, Polite, Grave, Moral, Entertaining And Improving Tales. Rutland [Vt.]: Printed At The Herald-Office. 1815.

> t.[1], [2–3], 4–160 p.; 10 cm.; bound in blue marbled paper over w. bds., leather spine. [Fay & Davidson] printers according to McCorison. Context a series of stories about highwayman. A different book from no. **867**.
> MWA-W°; DLC (p. 159–160 mut.); PP; McCorison 1761; Shaw 35296.

868.2 ——— Poughkepsie: Published by Paraclete Potter, P. & S. Potter, Printers. 1816

> t.[1], [2–3], 4–142 p.; 10.5 cm.
> MWA° (all after p. 126 wanting), CtHT; Shaw 38275

868.3 ——— Rutland [Vt.]: Printed at the Herald Office. 1820.

> t.[1], [2–3], 4–158 p.; 10 cm.
> MWA° (covers wanting; 1st pages cropped along the margin so page numbers & first or last letters of words are wanting); DLC (blue marbled paper wanting from w. bds. of covers, leather spine present); PP; McCorison 2217; Shoemaker 2306.

869 A MONITOR FOR PARENTS AND CHILDREN. [11 lines quot.] Charlestown [Mass.]: Printed By Samuel Etheridge, 1803.

> t.[1], [2–3], 4–36 p.; 13 cm.; Dutch paper covers. The History Of Tommy And Harry, p.[3]–20; A Fable. The Boy and his Mother, p. 21–24; A Dialogue, p. 24–35; Select Verses, p. 35–36.
> Welch° (p. 4–5 torn); MB (per. st. & cat. no. on t.[1] rear cover wanting); MWA; Shaw 4670 and 4379.

[MONTOLIEU, MRS.]

870 THE ENCHANTED PLANTS; Fables In Verse. Inscribed To Miss Montolieu, And Miss Julia Montolieu. [4 lines of verse] New-York. Printed And Published By David Longworth, At The Shakspeare-Gallery. 1803.

> ½t.[i], [ii, bl.], [i, bl.], fr.[ii], t.[iii], [iv–vii], viii, [9], 10–117 p.; illus.; 16 cm.; bound in marbled paper over bds.; engr. front. signed W. *Hamilton R.A. Delt. P Maverick Sculp.* Advertisement p.[v]: The few notes she wrote for her children, to whom the poems are inscribed, and which may be of use to young readers, will be found at the end of the book.
> English ed. London: Privately Printed, 1800.
> MWA°, PP (½t.[i] wanting); Shaw 4673.

[MOODY, ELEAZER] *d.* 1720

871.1 [—] THE SCHOOL OF GOOD MANNERS. Containing I. Sundry Mixt Precepts. II. Rules for Children's Behaviour, at the Meeting-house, at Home, at the Table, in Company, in Discourse, at School, Abroad; with an Admonition to Children. III. Good Advices for the ordering of their lives, with a Baptismal Covenant. IV. Some wholesome Cautions. V. A Short Plain & Scriptural Catechism. VI. Eleven short Exortations. VII. The Ten Commandments in verse, with a Compendious Body of Divinity; an Alphabet of Useful Copies & Cyprian's Twelve Absurdities. VIII. Some Prayers for Children; with Graces before and after Meat. New-London: Printed & Sold by T. Green. Also Sold by B. Eliot at Boston, 1715.

t.[i], [ii, bl.], [1], 2–62 p.; 11.5 cm.;
In the preface of *The School of Good Manners. New-London. 1754,* no. **871.3,** p. ii, the printer T. Green says, "The following Institutions were Compiled (chiefly) by Mr. ELEAZER MOODEY Late a Famous School-Master in Boston." R. F. Seybolt in *The Private Schools of Colonial Boston* (Cambridge 1935) p. 5. spells the name "Eleazer Moody" the same as T. Green, so that appears to be the correct spelling of the name. Moody lifted the entire text from *The School Of Manners. By the Author of the English Exercises.* [J. Garretson, School-master] *The Fourth Edition. London. 1701.*
English ed. of Garretson's *School of Manners,* London: 1685.
MHi°; Evans 1778.

871.2 [—] —— Catechism. VI. Principles of the Christian Religion. VII. Eleven short Exhortations. VIII. Good Thoughts for Little Children, A compendious Body of Divinity, an Alphabet of Useful Copies, & Cyprian's Twelve Absurdities, all in Verse. The Third Edition, with Additions. New-London [Conn.], Printed & sold by T. Green. Also Sold by B. Eliot at Boston, 1724.

t.[i], [ii, illus.], [1], [2], 3–78 p.; 1 illus. only; 11.5 cm.
MH° (p.[i], [ii] slightly mut.; p.[1]–2 half wanting).

871.3 [—] —— Manners. Containing I. Twenty mixt Precepts. II. One Hundred and Sixty Three Rules for Children's Behaviour. III. Good Advice for the Ordering of their Lives; With a

Baptismal Covenant. IV. Eight wholesome Cautions. V. A short, plain, & Scriptural Catechism. VI. Principles of the Christian Religion. VII. Eleven short Exortations. VIII. Good Thoughts for Children; a compendious Body of Divinity; An Alphabet of useful Copies; and Cyrpian's Twelve Absurdities. Ec. The Fifth Edition. New-London, Printed & Sold by T. & J. Green. 1754.

t.[i], [ii, alphabets], [i, preface], ii, 1–80 p.; 12 cm.
CtY° (rear cover wanting); PP; Evans 40702.

871.4 [—] —— Manners. Composed for the Help of Parents in Teaching their Children how to carry it in their Places during their Minority. Boston: Re-Printed and Sold by T. & J. Fleet, at the Heart & Crown in Cornhill. 1772.

t.[i], [ii], iii–iv, [5], 6–79, [80] p.; 12 cm.; blue marbled paper covers.
MWA°; MB (per st. on t.[i]; p. iii–iv, 79–[80] mut. blue-gray paper covers); PP; Evans 12553.

871.5 [—] —— Boston: Printed and Sold by John Boyle in Marlborough-Street. 1775.

t.[i], [ii], iii–iv, [5], 6–79, [80] p.; 13 cm.; paper covers.
MB° (per. st. on t.[i]); CtY (p. 79–[80] & covers wanting); MWA (p. 79–[80] & covers wanting); Evans 42886.

871.6 [—] —— Parents—teaching Children how to behave during their minority. Portland [Me.]: Printed, and sold, by Thomas B. Wait. 1786.

t.[1], [2–3], 4–58 p.; 13.5 cm.; blue-gray paper covers.
MWA° (front cover wanting); PP; Evans 19807.

871.7 [—] —— Hartford: Printed, and Sold, by Nathaniel Patten. M,DCC,LXXXVII.

1st t. [1], [2–3], 4–36; 2nd t.[1], [2], 3–12 p.; 15 cm.; bound in Dutch paper over w. bds.
2nd title: Mr. Moody's Discourse To Little Children. The Fourth Edition. Hartford: Printed and Sold, by Nathaniel Patten, M,DDC,LXXXVII.
MWA°; CtHi; PP; Evans 20528.

871.8 [—] —— Parents, in teaching their Children how to behave during their Minority. Boston: Printed and sold by S. Hall, in Cornhill 1790.

t.[iii], [iv–v], vi, [7], 8–55 p.; title vignette only illus.; 10 cm.; blue-gray paper covers.
PP° (covers, & fr.[ii]? wanting); Evans 45914.

871.9 [—] ——— The Seventeenth Edition. Windsor. [Vt.]: Re-Printed By Alden Spooner. M,DCC,XCIII.
t.[i], [ii–iii], iv, [5], 6–40 p.; 13 cm.; bound in brown paper over w. bds., leather spine.
MWA°; McCorison 271; Evans 25834.

871.10 [—] ——— Children how to carry it in their Places during their Minority. Printed by B. Edes & Son, in Kilby-Street, Boston. 1794.
t.[1], [2–3], 4–92 p.; title vignette only illus.; 13 cm.
MB°; ICU; MWA (t.[1] & p.[2], 89–92 mut., covers wanting); NN; PP; Evans 27337; Sabin 77825.

871.11 [—] ——— Printed by B. Edes & Son, in Kilby-Street, Boston. 1794. Sold by them, and also by W. T. Clap, No. 90, Newbury-Street.
t.[1], [2–3], 4–92 p.; title vignette only illus.; 12.5 cm.; bound in orange paper over w. bds., leather spine.
Welch°; CtHi (covers wanting); MWA (p. 57–58 mut.; blue-gray paper covers); PP; Evans 47116.

871.12 [—] ——— Parents, In Teaching Their Children How To Behave In Their Places, During Their Minority. The First Troy Edition. Troy [N.Y.], Printed by Gardner and Billings. MDCCXCV.
fr.[ii], t.[1], [2–5], 6–94 p.; illus.; 11 cm.
RPJCB°; Evans 29094.

871.13 [—] ——— Dover [N.H.]. Printed by Samuel Bragg jun., 1799.
t.[1], [2–4], 5–60 p.; 14 cm.; buff paper covers.
NhHi° (rebound i. st. p.[3]); Evans 35832.

871.14 [—] ——— Children. How To Carry It In Their Places During Their Minority. [3 lines quot.] Printed In The Year 1801.
t.[1], [2–3], 4–48 p.; 11 cm.; paper covers.
See also Green, Samuel. School Of Good Manners. New-London [1801], no. **469.1**.
MWA°; NN (front blue paper cover wanting); Shaw 1301.

871.15 [—] ——— Exeter [N.H.]: adv. by Henry Ranlet, 1801 in **558.2**.

871.16 [—] ——— Haverhill [Mass.]: Printed By Galen H. Fay. 1802.
t.[1], [2–3], 4–40 p.; 15 cm.; bound in brown speckled paper over w. bds., leather spine.
Welch°; MB; MH; MHa (upper half of rear cover wanting); MiD; MWA; Shaw 3054.

871.17 [—] ——— Children how to behave during their Minority. Printed and sold by Manning & Loring, No. 2, Cornhill, Boston. 1804.
fr.[2], t.[3], [4–5], 6–94 p.; front. & title vignette only illus.; 11 cm.; bound in Dutch paper over w. bds., leather spine.
Welch°; MH; MWA (rear cover ½ wanting); Shaw 7249.

871.18 [—] ——— Minority [8 lines of verse] Printed for and sold by Justin Hinds, Walpole, (N.H.) [*ca.* 1804].
t.[1], [2–6] 7–47 p.; 11.5 cm.; green Dutch paper covers.
MWA-W°; MSaE; NhD (p.[1]–4, mut., covers wanting).

871.19 [—] ———Printed and sold by Manning & Loring, No. 2, Cornhill, Boston. 1805.
fr.[2], t.[3], [4–5], 6–95 p.; front. & title vignette only illus.; 11.5 cm.; bound in brown speckled paper over w. bds.; at the top of fr.[2]: Manning & Lorings Second Edition.
MWA° (i. st. on fr.[2]); CtHi; MB; Shaw 8922.

871.20 [—] ——— [same as **871.14**] [2 lines quot.] Printed In 1805.
t.[1], [2–3], 4–48 p.; title vignette only illus.; 11.5 cm.; pink & blue wallpaper covers. [Boston?] usually has been the assigned place for the printing of this book. The title vignette, with its squarish patch missing from the upper right corner, is used for the title vignette of the *Exeter: Norris & Sawyer, 1808* edition, no. **871.23** and the *C. Norris & Co., 1813* edition, no. **821.27**. This edition no. **871.20** is undoubtedly an Exeter publication of Norris & Sawyer and not a Boston one.
MWA-W°; MB; MWA; Sabin 77826; Shaw 8921.

871.21 [—] ——— Newburyport, Published By W. & J. Gilman, Printers & Booksellers, No. 2, Middle-street. [1805?].

fr.[2], t.[4–5], 6–47; illus.; 12.5 cm.; pr. & illus. pink paper covers. Adv. "for sale at this office, wholesale and retail" in W. & J. Gilman's *Merrimac Magazine,* January 4, 1806.
Cover title: The School Of Good Manners. Newburyport: ——— [same as title] Printers, Booksellers, & Librarians, No. 2, Middle-street.
NHi*; MWA (fr.[2], p. 47 & covers wanting).

871.22 [—] ——— Printed and sold by Manning & Loring, No. 2, Cornhill, Boston. 1808.

fr.[2], t.[3], [4–5], 6–95 p.; front. & title vignette only illus.; 11 cm.; bound in marbled paper over w. bds.; at the top of fr.[2]: Manning & Loring's Third Edition.
MWA*; DLC; MSaE; Shaw 16150.

871.23 [—] ——— Children How To Carry It In Their Places During Their Minority. [2 lines of verse] Exeter [N.H.]: Printed by Norris & Sawyer, and Sold at their Book-Store. 1808.

t.[1], [2–3], 4–48 p.; title vignette only illus.; 12 cm.
MWA*; CLU; PP (covers wanting); Shaw 15636 and 16151.

871.24 [—] ——— Children How To Behave During Their Minority. [8 lines of verse] Montpelier, Vt. Printed By Wright And Sibley, For Justin Hinds 1812.

fr.[ii], t.[iii], [iv–v], vi, [7], 8–48 p.; front. only illus.; 12.5 cm.; marbled paper covers.
MWA* (p. 47–48 & rear cover wanting; fr.[ii] and front cover mut.); PP; VtHi (fr.[ii] & covers wanting); McCorison 1408; Shaw 26118.

871.25 [—] ——— Montpelier, Vt. Printed by Wright & Sibley, for P. Merrifield. 1812.

fr.[ii], t.[iii], [iv–v], vi, [7], 8–48 p.; front. only illus.; 12 cm.; pr. & illus. green paper covers.
MWA*; McCorison 1408; Shaw 26119.

871.26 [—] ——— Printed and sold by Manning & Loring, No. 2, Cornhill. Boston,—Sold also by Samuel T. Armstrong, and by Lincoln & Edmands 1813.

fr.[2], t.[3], [4–5], 6–95 p.; front. and title page vignette only illus.; 11 cm.; bound in blue-gray paper over bds.; at the top of fr.[2]: Manning & Loring's Fourth Edition.
MWA*; CtHi (fr.[2] mut., top half wanting); DLC (p. 11–14, 31–42, 75–82, 87–94 wanting); MH; MLuHi; NNC-LS (bound in blue paper over w. bds., leather spine); Shaw 29189 and 29735.

871.27 [—] ——— Children How To Carry It In Their Places During Their Minority. [2 lines of verse] Exeter [N.H.]: Printed by C. Norris & Co. and sold at their Book-Store. 1813.

t.[1], [2–3], 4–48 p.; title page only illus.; 11 cm.; pr. & illus. blue-gray paper covers.
Ries* (front cover ½ wanting); IU (rebound; covers wanting; i. st. on t.[1]; PP.

871.28 [—] ——— Children How To Behave During Their Minority. [8 lines of verse] Published And Sold By Thomas & Whipple, Newburyport [Mass.]. And Henry Whipple, Salem, Mass. W. B. Allen & Co. Printers. 1814.

fr.[ii, 2 cuts], t.[1], [2–3], 4–36, [37, 2 cuts] p.; front. & illus. p. [37] only illus.; 14.5 cm.; p. & illus. paper covers.
Cover title: The School Of Good Manners. Newburyport, Published By W. & J. Gilman, [at] their Miscellaneous Book-Store, No. 2, Middle-Street.
MNe*; MWA (fr.[ii], & p. [37] wanting); Shaw 32724.

871.29 [—] ——— Windsor, Vt. Printed By Jesse Cochran 1815.

fr.[2], t.[3], [4–7], 8–47 p.; front. only illus.; 11.5 cm.; pr. & illus. pink paper covers.
MWA*; DLC; MiU; NNC-Pl; PP; VtHi; McCorison 1762; Sabin 77820; Shaw 35304.

871.30 [—] ——— Montpelier, Vt. Published by E. P. Walton. 1818.

fr.[ii], t.[iii], [iv–v], vi, [7], 8–64 p.; front. only illus.; 10.5 cm.; pr. & illus. buff paper covers.
MWA*; McCorison 2032; Shaw 44879 and 48729 (dated 1819, an error for 1818).

872 MORAL AND ENTERTAINING FABLES, Ornamented With Cuts. For the Amusement of Children. Boston: Published By Charles Williams, No. 8, State-Street. Watson & Bangs, Printers. 1812.

t.[1], [2–3], 4–54 p.; illus.; 13.5 cm.; pr. & illus. buff paper covers.

English ed. London: 2 pts. Darton & Harvey, 1809.

MWA*; CtY; DLC (p. 51–54 wanting); MB; Shaw 26126.

873.1 MORAL AND INSTRUCTIVE TALES For the Amusement of Children of both Sexes. Ornamented With Appropriate Engravings. Philadelphia: Published By E. And R. Parker, No. 178, Market Street. J. R. A. Skerrett, Printer. 1818.

t.[1], [2–3], 4–23, [24, adv. list of books] p.; 6 pl.; 12 cm.; pr. buff paper covers.

MWA-T*; NN.

873.2 ———— Philadelphia: Published By E. And R. Parker, No. 178, Market Street. J. R. A. Skerrett, Printer. 1819.

t.[1], [2–3], 4–23, [24, adv.] p.; 6 pl.; 12.5 cm.; pr. buff paper covers; rear cover adv. list of books.

CLU*.

874 [—] MORAL & INSTRUCTIVE TALES For The Improvement Of Young Ladies; Calculated To Amuse The Mind, And Form The Heart To Virtue. First American Edition. Printed At Leominster, Mass. By Charles Prentiss. 1797.

t.[i], [ii], iii–v, [vi], 7–124 p.; 13 cm.; bound in blue paper over w. bds.

English ed. London: adv. by J. Marshall in M. A. Kilner's *A Course Of Lectures For Sunday Evenings*. [1783].

MWA*; CLU; CtW; MLe; NjP; Evans 32499.

MORAL SKETCHES; Containing Improving And Entertaining Essays On Most Of The Duties Of Life. *See* Johnson, Richard, no. **683.2.**

MORAL SKETCHES FOR YOUNG MINDS. *See* Johnson, Richard, no. **683.1.**

875 MORAL SONGS. Philadelphia: adv. by Johnson & Warner, 1814 in **1449.3.** This book may be by John Oakman, no. **956.**

876 MORAL STORIES. Written for the Instruction of Young Minds. Dedham [Mass.]: First Published by and for H. Mann, who keeps constantly for sale a variety of Childrens' Books. March—1806.

fr.[2], t.[3], [4–5], 6–35 p.; 12 cm.; blue marbled paper covers.
PP* (fr.[2], mut.).

877 THE MORAL STORY TELLER. Uniting Pleasure With Instruction. Nothing is inserted that has not its foundation in Truth. Hartford [Conn.]: Printed By John Babcock. 1797.

t.[1], [2–3], 4–69 [*sic.* 96] p.; t.[1]; 15 cm.

MWA* (rebound; i. st. on t.[1]); CtHi; CtHT (bound with other books); CiY; MH; NN (rebound); Evans 32500.

MORAL TALES FOR YOUNG PEOPLE. *See* Edgeworth, Maria, no. **324.1.**

878 THE MORALIST: Or, Young Gentleman and Lady's Entertaining Companion, &c. Being A Collection Of Moral Tales, And Stories. Selected from the best modern Authors. Boston: Printed and Sold by John W. Folsom, No. 30, Union-Street. MDCCXCI.

t.[1], [2–3], 4–105 p.; 15.5 cm.; bound in leather.

MHi*; Evans 46224.

MORE, HANNAH 1745–1833
[—] BEAR YE ONE ANOTHER'S BURDENS. *See* Cheap Repository, no. **169.27.** For later American editions *see* The Valley Of Tears, no. **899.1.**

[—] BETTY BROWN, THE ST. GILES ORANGE GIRL. *See* Cheap Repository, no. **169.29.**

879.1 [—] BETTY BROWN, THE ST. GILES ORANGE GIRL: With An Account Of Mrs. Sponge, The Money Lender. Philadelphia: Printed By Benjamin Johnson, No. 249, Market Street. 1807.

fr.[ii], t.[1], [2–3], 4–36 p.; engr. front. only illus.; 14 cm.; pink paper covers. Frontispiece: The Orange Girl, Published by B. Johnson No. 247 Market Street. Philadelphia.

English ed. London: John Marshall (pr.); S. Hazard, Bath; J. Elder, Edinburgh. [1797?].

DLC* (fr.[ii], t.[1] and front cover mut.); CLU; MWA (fr.[ii] & covers wanting); NNC-SP (bound with no. **900.1** with spine stamped "Cheap Repository [vol.] 1"); PP (covers wanting, rebound); Shaw 13122.

879.2 [—] ———— Philadelphia: adv. by Benjamin Johnson, 1813 in **899.1.**

879.3　[—] ———— Lender. Ornamented With Cuts. Philadelphia: Published By Benjamin Johnson, 31 Market Street. D. Dickinson, Printer 1817. [cover title].
> [1], 2–24 p.; illus.; 15 cm.; pr. paper covers.
> NjR°; Shaw 40192.

879.4　[—] ———— Philadelphia: adv. by Benjamin Johnson, 1818 in 893.4.

[—] BLACK GILES THE POACHER. *See* Cheap Repository. Philadelphia: 1800, no. **169.11–12**, and The History Of Black Giles, no. **882.1.**

880　[—] THE BLACK PRINCE; Being A Narrative Of The Most Remarkable Occurrences And Strange Vicissitudes, Exhibited In The Life And Experience Of James Albert Ukawsaw Gronniosaw, An African Prince, As Was Related By Himself. Salem [N.Y.]: Printed And Sold By Dodd & Rumsey. 1809.
> t.[1], [2–5], 6–68 p.; 14 cm.
> MWA°.

881　[—] THE FORTUNE TELLER Published by B. Johnson No. 247 Market Street Philadelphia. [1807].
> t.[i], [ii, bl.], [1], 2–36 p.; title vignette only illus.; 14 cm. Caption-title: Tawny Rachel; Or, The Fortune Teller: With Some Account Of Dreams, Omens, And Conjurers.
> MWA° (covers wanting); CLU; CtHi; DLC; NNC-SP (bound with no. **900.1** with spine stamped "Cheap Repository [Vol.] I"); NjR; NPV; PP; Evans 34133 (dated [*ca.* 1798]); Shaw 13125; Weiss 1946, p. 20.

882.1　[—] THE HISTORY OF BLACK GILES Published by' B Johnson, No. 247 Market Street. Philadelphia. [1807].
> t.[i], [ii], [1], 2–72 p.; illus.; 14 cm.; bound in marbled paper over bds., red leather spine; on the spine is stamped "Cheap Repository [vol.] 3."
> Welch° (bound with no. **897** with spine stamped "Cheap Repository [vol.] 3"); CLU (p. 69–72 wanting); CtHi; NNC-SP (bound with no. **897** with spine stamped "Cheap Repository. [vol.] 3"); PP; RPB; Shaw 13127; Weiss 1946, p. 20.

882.2　[—] ———— Black Giles, The Poacher; Or, An Account Of A Family Who Would Rather Live By Their Wits Than Their Work. Philadelphia: Printed For Benjamin Johnson, No. 22, North Second street, next door to the church. 1813.
> fr.[ii], t.[1], [2], 3–48 p.; front. only illus.; 14 cm.; pr. & illus. buff paper covers.
> MWA°; Shaw 28749 and 29208.

882.3　[—] ———— Philadelphia: Published by Benjamin Johnson, No. 31, Market-st. D. Dickinson, Printer. 1818.
> t.[1], [2], 3–48 p.; 14 cm.
> MWA° (covers wanting); Shaw 44900.

883　[—] THE HISTORY OF HESTER WILMOT. Suffer little children to come unto me, and forbid them not. —Mark X.14. Philadelphia: Published by the Sunday and Adult School Union. Clark & Raser, Printers. 1818.
> t.[1], [2–3], 4–48 p.; 13 cm.
> English & Irish ed. London: [pt. 1], II, J. Marshall (pr.), R. White; S. Hazard, Bath; J. Elder, Edinburgh. [1797].
> NN°; MWA; Shaw 44329.

[—] THE HISTORY OF MR. FANTOM. *See* Cheap Repository, no. **169.25.**

884.1　[—] THE HISTORY OF MR. FANTOM, The New Fashioned Philosopher; And His Man William. Printed For The Booksellers. 1802.
> t.[1], [2–3], 4–48 p.; 9.5 cm.; marbled paper covers.
> *See also* The New Fashioned Philosopher, no. **888.**
> NNC-LS° (i. st. on front cover).

884.2　[—] ———— Philadelphia: Published by Benjamin Johnson, No. 22, North Second Street. 1813.
> t.[1], [2] bl, [3], 4–24 p.; 1 illus. only; 14 cm.; pr. & illus. olive paper covers. Holograph inscription opposite t.[1], dated *1815*.
> MWA°; DLC (lacks title page); Shaw 29209; Weiss 1946, p. 21.

884.3　[—] ———— Philadelphia: Published by Benjamin Johnson, No. 31, Market-st. 1817.
> t.[1], [2, illus.], [3], 4–24 p.; illus. p.[2] only illus.; 13.5 cm.; pr. greenish-buff paper covers. Cover title imprint: ———— Johnson, 31 Market street. Dickinson, printer, 100 Race street. 1818.

MWA-W°; NB; PP; Shaw 41480 and 44901; Weiss 1946, p. 21.

[—] THE HISTORY OF TAWNY RACHEL. *See* Cheap Repository, no. **169.13.**

[—] THE HISTORY OF TOM WHITE. *See* Cheap Repository, nos. **169.7** and **169.8.**

885.1 [—] THE HISTORY OF TOM WHITE, THE POSTILLION; Afterwards Called Farmer White. To Which is Added, The History Of Charles Jones, The Footman. Philadelphia: Published By Benjamin And Thomas Kite, No. 20, North Third Street. 1811.

> t.[1], [2–3], 4–72, ½t.[73], [74–75], 76–106 p.; 13.5 cm.; bound in pr. blue paper over bds. Half title: The History Of Charles Jones, The Footman; Written By Himself.
> English & Irish ed. London: J. Marshall (pr.), R. White; S. Hazard. [1795].
> MWA°; MiD; PP; Shaw 23423.

885.2 [—] —— Postilion. Philadelphia: Published by Benjamin Johnson, 31 Market street. Dickinson, printer, 100 Race street. 1818. [cover title].

> t.[1], 2–24+ p.; 13.5 cm.; gray-green paper covers.
> MWA-T° (all after p. 24 wanting, including rear cover).

[—] THE HISTORY OF THE TWO SHOEMAKERS. *See* Cheap Repository, no. **169.14.** *See also* the Two Shoemakers, no. **897.**

886 [—] THE HISTORY OF THE TWO SHOEMAKERS. Part I. Philadelphia. Sold by Johnson & Warner, No. 147, Market-Street. Jacob Meyer, Printer. 1811.

> t.[1], [2–3], 4–107 p.; illus.; 14.5 cm.; bound in blue paper over bds. Caption title p.[27, 53, 79]: The History Of The Two Shoemakers. Parts II, [III–IV].
> English & Irish ed. London: pt. 2 J. Marshall (pr.), R. White; S. Hazard, Bath. [1795].
> MWA°; CLU; CtY; MB; NN (rebound); NNC-Pl; PP; PPL; Shaw 23422; Weiss 1946, p. 20.

887.1 — MOSES IN THE BULRUSHES: A Sacred Drama. In Three Parts By Miss Hannah More . . .

Reprinted at Litchfield, [Conn.] by T. Collier, M,DCCC.

> 23 p.; sq. 16 mo.
> Evans 37995.

887.2 [—] —— Bulrushes: A Sacred Drama. The Subject Is Taken From The Second Chapter Of The Book Of Exodus. First Worcester Edition. Worcester, Massachusetts, Printed by I. Thomas, Jun. Sold Wholesale And Retail By Him. June 1802.

> fr.[2], t.[3], [4–5], 6–31 p.; illus.; t.[3] 10 cm.; violet and green Dutch paper covers.
> MWA° (bound by I. Thomas); Shaw 2702.

887.3 — —— Bulrushes: A Sacred Drama. In Three Parts. The subject is taken from the second chapter of the book of Exodus. By Hannah More. Boston: Published By Isaiah Thomas, Jun. 1813.

> t.[1], [2–3], 4–24 p.; illus.; 12.5 cm.; colored paper covers.
> MWA°; Shaw 29211.

887.4 — —— book of Exodus. [2 lines quot.] Paradise Lost. Printed For The Publisher. 1813.

> t.[1], [2, illus.–3], 4–29, [30] p.; illus. p.[2] only illus.; 10 cm.
> MWA° (p.[31] and covers wanting, t.[1] mut.); Shaw 29210.

887.5 — —— Exodus. By Hannah More. Andover [Mass.]: Printed And Published By Flagg & Gould. 1815.

> t.[1], [2–3], 4–24 p.; illus.; 12.5 cm.; pr. & illus. pink paper covers.
> MWA-W°; NNC-T; Shaw 35318.

888 [—] THE NEW FASHIONED PHILOSOPHER. Published by B. Johnson No 247 Market St. Philadelphia [1807].

> t.[ii], [1], 2–36 p.; title page vignette only illus.; 14.5 cm.; buff paper covers. This is the same as **884.1** and **169.25.** Caption title p.[1]: The History Of Mr. Fantom, The New Fashioned Philosopher, And His Man William.
> NjR°; NNC-SP (bound with no. **902.1** in vol. with spine stamped "Cheap Repository [vol.] 2").

889.1 [—] PARLEY THE PORTER, An Allegory Shewing How Robbers Without Can Never Get

Into An House, Unless There Are Traitors Within. Published By The Cheap Repository Society, London. New-Bedford [Mass.]: Reprinted for, and Sold by A. Sherman, jun. 1810.

½t.[1], [2, bl.], t.[3], [4, bl.–5], 6–23 p.; 19 cm. Half title: Parley The Porter.

MNBedf°; Shaw 20995.

889.2 [—] < No. 17. ―――― Porter. An Allegory. [caption p. [1]] Andover [Mass.]: Printed For The New England Tract Society By Flagg And Gould. 1814. < First edit. 6000.

[1], 2–12 p.; 17.5 cm.; also paged [243], 244–254.

MWA° (bound with other tracts in *Tracts Published By The New England Tract Society. Vol. 1. Andover: Flagg And Gould. 1814*).

889.3 [—] ―――― An Allegory. [1 line quot.] New-York: Printed And Sold By Samuel Wood, No. 357, Pearl-Street. 1814.

t.[1], [2], 3–18 p.; 14 cm.

PP°; MWA-T; Shaw 32159; Weiss 1946, p. 21.

889.4 [—] < No. 17 ―――― An Allegory. [caption title p.[1]] Andover [Mass.]: Printed For The New England Tract Society By Flagg And Gould. 1819. < 4th edit. 6000. [colophon p. 12].

[1], 2–12 p.; 17 cm.; also numbered [197], 198–208 p.

MB° (bound with other tracts of *The Publications Of The New England Tract Society. Vol. 1. Andover: Flagg And Gould. 1820*). Shaw 48750.

890 [—] PATIENT JOE; OR THE NEWCASTLE COLLIER. Philadelphia: Printed And Sold By J. Rakestraw, No. 190, North Third Street. 1808. Price Two Cents.

t.[1], [2], 6 [*sic* 3], 4 p.; title vignette only illus.; 17.5 cm.

PP°; Shaw 15850; Weiss 1946, p. 20.

[—] PATIENT JOE. *See* Sharpless, Joseph, no. **1191.1**.

891.1 [—] Read And Reflect. THE PILGRIMS, AN ALLEGORY. Philadelphia: Printed And Sold By Kimber, Conrad And Co. No. 93, Market Street, And No. 170, South Second Street. 1807. Price Six Cents.

½t. [1], [2], t.[3], [4–5], 6–34 p.; 14 cm. Half title p.[1]: The Pilgrims An Allegory.

English & Irish ed. entitled: *Cheap Repository. Sunday Reading. The Pilgrims. . . .* London: J. Marshall (pr.), S. Hazard, Bath, J. Elder, Edinburgh. [1797]; p. 16 signed Z [Hannah More].

MWA°; DLC (2 copies); MH; NHi; P; PP; PPL; Shaw 13128; Weiss 1946, p. 20.

891.2 [—] THE PILGRIMS, AND PARLEY THE PORTER: Two Allegories. New-York: Printed And Sold By Samuel Wood & Sons, At The Juvenile Booke-Store, No. 357, Pearl-Street. 1815.

t.[1], [2–3], 4–47 p.; illus.; 13.5 cm.; illus. p. 17, 19, 23, 25, 26, signed A [Alexander Anderson].

MWA° (bound with other books in no. **191**).

891.3 [—] ―――― New-York: Printed And Sold By Samuel Wood & Sons, At The Juvenile Book-Store, No. 357, Pearl-Street. 1816.

t.[1], [2–3], 4–47 p.; illus.; 13.5 cm.; pr. yellow paper covers; cover title undated; illus. p. 17, 19, 23, 25, 26, signed A [Alexander Anderson].

MWA°; MH (poor copy, foxed & spotted); Shaw 38286.

891.4 [—] ―――― Nerv-York [*sic. i.e.* New-York]: Published By Samuel Wood & Sons, No. 261, Pearl-street; And Samuel S. Wood & Co. No. 212, Market-St. Baltimore. 1820.

t.[2–3], 4–47 p.; illus.; 14 cm.; pr. paper covers; cover title undated; illus. p. 17, 19, 23, 25, 26, signed A [Alexander Anderson].

MWA°; CCamarSJ; PP; Shoemaker 2336; Weiss 1946, p. 21.

891.5 [—] No. IV. Sunday School Tracts. The Pilgrims, An Allegory [cut] Published by the New-York Sunday School Union Society, and sold at their Depository, by D. H. [Wickham] No. 59 Fulton-street. J. Seymo[ur] [print.] New-York. 1820. [cover title].

[1], 2–24 p.; 13 cm.; pr. & illus. gray paper covers. Colophon p.[24]: Published by the New-York Sunday School Union Society. J. Seymour, Printer. 1820.

MWA°; PP; Shaw 2335.

[—] THE SHEPHERD OF SALISBURY PLAIN. Pr. I. [II.] *See* Cheap Repository, nos. **169.1** and **169.2**,

and The Entertaining, Moral, And Religious Repository, no. **361.1.**

892.1   [—] THE SHEPHERD OF SALISBURY PLAIN.
Philadelphia: Printed By B. & J. Johnson, No 147,
High-Street. 1801.
  fr.[ii], t.[i], [2–3], 4–80 p.; front. only illus.;
  14 cm.; bound in blue marbled paper over bds.,
  dark green paper spine.
  MWA-T°.

892.2   [—] —— PLAIN. In Two Parts. To
Which Is Added, The Sorrows Of Yamba: Or The
Negro Woman's Lamentation. From Sidney's
Press, New-Haven, For Increase Cooke & Co.
1806.
  t.[1], [2–3], 4–108 p.; 13.5 cm. The Shepherd
  Of Salisbury Plain is the most famous of Han-
  nah More's Sunday School Tracts, and was
  originally issued as one of the Cheap Repository
  Tracts.
  Irish ed. Dublin: pt. 2. William Watson. [*ca.*
  1799]. *See also* no. **169.1** for English ed.
  MWA°; CtHi; CtY (rebound, covers wanting);
  Shaw 10904.

892.3   [—] —— Plain. Published by B. Johnson. No. 247 Market Street, Philadelphia. [1807].
  t.[i], [ii, bl.], [1], 2–72 p.; engr. title vignette &
  engr. pl. opp. p. 37 only illus.; 14 cm.; black
  marbled paper covers.
  MWA-T°; NNC-Sp (bound with no. **902.1**
  with spine stamped "Cheap Repository [vol.]
  2"); PP (covers wanting); Shaw 13129; Weiss
  1946, p. 20.

892.4   [—] —— Salisbury-Plain.   Boston:
Printed And Sold By Lincoln & Edmands, No. 53
Cornhill. 1809. Price—6 dolls. a hundred—1 dol.
a doz.—10 cts. single. Who keep for sale a great
variety of Cheap Religious Tracts. The orders of
those, who purchase for distribution, answered
promptly and on the most reasonable terms.
  t.[1], [2–3], 4–36 p.; 17 cm.
  MWA°; Shaw 18120.

892.5   [—] —— Salisbury Plain. In Two Parts.
To Which Is Added, The Sorrows Of Yamba; Or
The Negro Woman's Lamentation. Boston: Printed
By Samuel Avery, No. 10 State-Street. 1810.
  t.[1], [2–3], 4–107 p.; 14 cm.; bound in blue
  paper over bds.
  MWA°; Shaw 20779.

892.6   [—] —— Plain. New-Haven, Published
By Walter, Austin And Co. O. Steele & Co. Printers. 1810.
  t.[1], [2–3], 4–67, [68, bl.], [69–72, adv. list
  of books] p.; 13.5 cm.; purple paper covers;
  colophon p.[72]: Walter, Austin & Co. New-
  Haven, (south corner of the Green,) Feb. 26,
  1810.
  MWA°; CCamarSJ; CSmH; Ct; CtHi; Shaw
  20780.

892.7   [—] Series of Evangelical Tracts, No. 29.
THE SHEPHERD OF SALISBURY-PLAIN. [caption
title p.[1]]. Printed and sold by Lincoln & Edmands, No. 53 Cornhill, Boston. [5 lines adv.]
1812. Price 67 cts. doz. 4,50 cts. a hun. [colophon
p. 24].
  [1], 2–24 p.; 17.5 cm.
  MWA° (bound with other tracts in *Twelve*
  Witnesses. Boston. N. Willis. 1814.); MB;
  Shaw 26130.

892.8   [—] —— Plain. Ornamented With
Cuts. Philadelphia: Published by Benjamin Johnson, No. 22, North Second-Street. 1812. [cover
title].
  [1], 2–48 p.; 4 full page illus.; 14 cm.; pr. &
  illus. buff paper covers. Eight full page illus.
  p.[3], [21], [26], [34].
  MWA°; Shaw 26132.

892.9   [—] —— Plain. In Two Parts. Plattsburgh, N.Y. Published By Heman Cady. 1812.
Azariah C. Flagg, Printer.
  t.[1], [2–3], 4–40 p.; 14.5 cm.; pr. blue-gray
  paper covers; cover title dated 1812.
  N° (rear paper cover wanting); Shaw 26133.

892.10   [—] —— Religious Tracts, No. 4
[caption title p.[1]]. Isaac Collett, Printer, Staun-
ton, Virginia. [*ca.* 1812] [colophon p. 24].
  [1], 2–24 p.; 16 cm.; date obtained from MWA
  cat.
  MWA°; Shaw 26134.

892.11   [—] < No. 10. —— Salisbury Plain.
[caption p. [1]] Andover [Mass.]: Printed For
The New England Tract Society By Flagg And
Gould. 1814. < First edit. 6000. [colophon p. 24].
  [1], 2–24 p.; 17 cm.; also paged [171], 172–
  194; bound with other tracts of Tracts Published By The New England Tract Society. Vol.

1. Andover: Flagg And Gould. 1814. The locations below refer to Vol. 1 of these tracts.
MBAt°; Shaw 32162.

892.12 [—] < No. 10. ——— [same as **892.11**] Gould. 1814. < Second edit. 6000.
Same as no. **892.11** except in the colophon p. 24: < Second edit. 6000.
MH°.

892.13 [—] < No. 10. ——— Salisbury Plain. [caption p.[1]] Published by The Society of the Protestant Episcopal Church for the advancement of Christianity in Pennsylvania. Philadelphia: Printed By J. Maxwell. 1815. [colophon p. 24].
t.[1], 2–24 p.; 19 cm.
PPL°; Shaw 35319.

892.14 [—] < No. 10. ——— Salisbury-Plain. [caption p.[1]] Andover [Mass.]: Printed For The New England Tract Society By Flagg And Gould. 1816. < 3d. edit. 6000.
[1], 2–24 p.; 16 cm.; also paged [125], 126–148.
MB°; Shaw 38287.

892.15 [—] ——— Plain. [caption title p. [1]] Published for gratuitous distribution by The Hartford Evangelical Tract Society. Hudson & Co. Printers. 5000 March 1816. [colophon p. 24].
[1], 2–24 p.; 16.5 cm.; pr. blue paper covers.
Cover title: No. 2. The Shepherd Of Salisbury Plain. List Of Tracts Published By The Hartford Evangelical Tracts Society. March 1816. [a list of 9 tracts].
MWA°; CtHi; Shaw 38288 and 38289.

892.16 — ——— Plain. By Miss Hannah More. With a Short Memoir And an Original Letter, Of The Shepherd. Taken from the London Evangelical Magazine. Boston: Printed and published at No 53 Cornhill, by Lincoln & Edmands, Who have for sale, Bibles, Books, Tracts, and Stationary, in great variety, and on liberal terms. 1817.
fr.[2], t.[3], [4–5], 6–52 p.; front. only illus.; 14 cm.; pr. blue-gray paper covers. Rear cover has an illus. of Lincoln & Edmands Bible Warehouse.
MWA°; CLU; MB; MH; Shaw 41482.

892.17 — < No. 10. The Shepherd Of Salisbury Plain. [caption title p. [1]] Andover [Mass.]: Printed

For The New England Tract Society By Flagg And Gould. 1818. < 5th ed. 6000. [colophon p. 24].
[1], 2–24 p.; 16 cm.
CtHi°.

893 [—] THE SHOEMAKERS. Published by B. Johnson No. 247 Market St. Philadelphia. [1807]. t.[i], [ii], pt. I [1], 2–36, [pl. opp. p. 36] pt. II [1], 2–36, [pl. opp. p.[1]], pt. III [1], 2–36, [pl. opp. p. 36], pt. IV [1], 2–36 p.; 4 engr. pl. including t.[i]; 14 cm.; bound in marbled paper over bds., red leather spine; on the spine is stamped "Cheap Repository [vol.] 3". The caption of each part "The History Of The Two Shoemakers."
English ed., *see* no. **886**, London: J. Marshall (pr.), R. White; S. Hazard. [1795].
MWA-W° (bound with no. **882.1** with spine stamped "Cheap Repository [vol.] 3"); NNC-SP (bound with no. **882.1** with spine stamped "Cheap Repository. [vol.] 3").

[—] THE SHOPKEEPER TURNED SAILOR. *See* Cheap Repository, no. **169.22**.

894.1 [—] THE SHOP-KEEPER TURNED SAILOR: Or, The Folly Of Going Out Of Our Element. Ornamented With Cuts. Philadelphia: Published by Benjamin Johnson, No. 455, Market Street. 1812.
t.[1], [2–3], 4–24 p.; illus.; 13 cm.; blue paper covers; illus. on p. 5, 9, 11, 13, 17, signed *M* [William Morgan], one of Anderson's four pupils.
OClWHi°; PP (p. 5–6, 19–20 wanting); Shaw 26733.

894.2 [—] ——— Philadelphia: adv. by Benjamin Johnson, 1813 in **899.1**.

894.3 [—] ——— Philadelphia: Printed For Benjamin Johnson, No. 22, North Second Street. (Next door to the church.) 1814.
t.[1], [2–3], 4–24 p.; illus.; 14 cm.; pr. & illus. green paper covers.
MH°; MWA-T; PP (t.[1], p. 9–10 torn; p. 13–14 mut.); Shaw 32163.

894.4 [—] ———Philadelphia: Published by Benjamin Johnson, No. 31, Market–st. 1818.
t.[1], [2–3], 4–24 p.; illus.; 14 cm.
MWA°; Shaw 45712.

895.1 [—] Tawny Rachel, or The Fortune Teller. Philadelphia: adv. by Benjamin Johnson, 1813 in 899.1.

895.2 [—] Tawny Rachel; Or, The Fortune Teller: With Some Account Of Dreams, Omens, And Conjurers. Ornamented. With Cuts. Philadelphia: Published by Benjamin Johnson, 31, Market street. Dickinson, printer, 100 Race-street. 1818. [cover title].
 illus. [2], [3], 4–24 p.; illus.; 13.5 cm.; pr. green paper covers.
 MWA*; Shaw 44902.

896.1 [—] 'Tis All For The Best: Exemplified In The Character Of Mrs Simpson. To Which Is Added, The Grand Assizes; Or, General Jail Delivery, &c. &c. &c. Hartford. Printed By Lincoln & Gleason. 1807.
 t.[1], [2–3], 4–71, [72] p.; 13.5 cm.; marbled paper covers.
 English ed. London: J. Evans (pr.), J. Hatchard; S. Hazard, Bath. [*ca.* 1799], holograph date *Dec. 10, 1799.*
 MWA*; CtHi; MB (rebound; p. 5–8 wanting); Shaw 11960 and 13130.

896.2 — —— Best. An Interesting Moral Tract. Illustrating The Happy Effects Resulting From Confidence In The Equity Of Divine Providence. By Miss Hannah More. Boston—Printed. Middlebury, Vt. Re-Printed By J. D. Huntington. 1807.
 t.[1], [2, bl.], [3], 4–23 p.; t.-p. 17 cm.; bound in a book of Religious Tracts.
 Vt* (emb. st. on t.[1]); NcD; McCorison 939; Shaw 13131.

896.3 — Boston Series of Cheap Religious Tracts, No. 7. —— Best. Entertaining, Moral, And Religious. Written by Miss Hannah More. [caption p. [1]] Boston: Printed and sold by Lincoln & Edmands, No. 53, Cornhill. Price 50 cents a doz. 3 dols. 50 cts. a hundred. Who publish a great variety of Cheap Religious Tracts. The charitable, resident in any part of the union, who purchase for distribution, will find their orders liberally and promptly answered. [1810?] [colophon p. [16]].
 [1], 2–15, [16] p.; 16.5 cm.
 MWA*; Shaw 20781.

896.4 — Series of Evangelical Tracts, No. 7. —— Best. Entertaining, Moral, And Religious. Written By Miss Hanna More. [caption p. [1]] Printed By Lincoln & Edmands, And Sold At Their Theological And Miscellaneous Bookstore. No. 53 Cornhill, (Price 50 cts. doz. 3,50 per hun.) [7 lines of adv.] [1810?] [colophon p. [16]].
 [1], 2–15, [16] p.; 16.5 cm.
 MWA* (rebound, bound with other tracts in *Evangelical Tracts Doctrinal, Experimental, And Practical. Vol. I. Boston: Lincoln & Edmands, 1813*); Shaw 26136.

896.5 — —— Best. An Interesting Narrative Of Mrs. Simpson. By Miss Hannah More. [caption p. [1]] Pittsfield [Mass.]: Printed By P. Allen. April, 1810 [colophon p, 24].
 [1], 2–24 p.; 20 cm.
 PPiU*.

896.6 [—] No. I. —— Best. [caption p.[1]] Printed by S. T. Armstrong, and sold by him wholesale and retail, in Charlestown [Mass.], and by Farrand, Mallory & Co. Boston. Price $2.50 Cents per Hundred. [1812?] [colophon p. 24].
 [1], 2–24 p.; 17.5 cm.
 MWA* (bound with other tracts in *Twelve Witnesses. Boston: N. Willis 1814.*), MB; Shaw 26135.

896.7 [—] < No. 11. —— Best. [caption p. [1]] Andover [Mass.]: Printed For The New England Tract Society By Flagg And Gould. 1814. < First ed. 6000. [colophon p. 16].
 [1], 2–16 p.; 17.5 cm.; also paged [195], 196–210.
 MWA* (bound with other tracts in *Tracts Published By The New England Tract Society. Vol. I. Andover: Flagg And Gould. 1814*).

896.8 [—] < No. 11 —— Best. [caption p. [1]] Andover [Mass.]: Printed For The New England Tract Society By Flagg And Gould. 1816. < 3rd Edit. 6000. [colophon p. 16].
 [1], 2–16 p.; 17.5 cm.
 MB* (rebound, per. st. on p. [1]); Shaw 38290 and 39089.

896.9 — (No. 16) —— Best. By Miss Hannah More. Published By The Philadelphia Female Tract Society. [caption p.[1]]. Printed by Lydia R. Bailey, No. 10, North Alley, Philad. [1817] [colophon p. 16].

[1], 2–16 p.; 14 cm.
MWA* (bound with other tracts, with which *The Second Annual Report Of The Philadelphia Female Society For The Year 1817* was originally bound); Shaw 41484 and 41485.

896.10 [—] < No. 11. ——— Best. [caption p. [1]] Andover [Mass.]: Printed For The New England Tract Society By Flagg And Gould. 1818 < 4th ed. 6000. [colophon p. 16].
[1], 2–16 p.; 17 cm.
DLC*; MWA; Shaw 45871.

896.11 [—] ——— Best. Philadelphia: Published by "The Religious Tract Society of Philadelphia," No. 8. South-Front-Street. William Bradford —Agent. February.—1819. [caption title].
[1], 2–12 p.; illus. tailpiece p. 12; 18 cm.
MWA*; Shaw 48752.

896.12 [—] No. 11. ——— Best. [caption p. [1]] Andover [Mass.]: Printed For The New England Tract Society By Flagg And Gould. 1820. < 5th ed. 6000. [colophon p. 16].
[1], 2–16 p.; 17 cm.; also paged [149], 150–164.
MB* (bound with other tracts of *The Publications Of The New England Tract Society, Vol. I. Andover: Flagg & Gould. 1820*).

897 [—] Tom White, The Postilion. Philadelphia: adv. by Benjamin Johnson, 1818 in **893.4**.

[—] The Two Wealthy Farmers; Or The History Of Mr. Bragwell. *See* Cheap Repository, no. **169.5**.

898.1 [—] The Two Wealthy Farmers: Or, The History Of Mr. Bragwell, And His Friend Farmer Worthy. Philadelphia: Published By Benjamin And Thomas Kite, No. 28, North Third-Street. 1807.
t.[1], [2–3],. 4–171 p.; 15.5 cm.; colophon p. 171: R. Bailey, Printer.
English & Irish ed. London: J. Marshall (pr.), R. White; S. Hazard, Bath. [1795].
MWA*; CLU; MH; OClWHi (bound in leather); Shaw 13132.

898.2 —— ——— Farmers; Being An Interesting And Instructive History Of Mr. Worthy And Mr. Bragwell; With A Description Of The Situation and Conduct of their respective Families. From

The Cheap Repository. By Miss Hannah More. To Which Are Added, Several Valuable Religious Pieces. Boston: Published By Lincoln & Edmands, No. 53, Cornhill. 1809.
t.[33], [34, bl.], [35, contents], [36, bl.], [37], 38–156 p.; 17.5 cm.; unbound; portion of a book originally bound in leather.
MWA*; Shaw 18123.

898.3 [—] ——— Philadelphia: Published By Johnson & Warner, No. 147, Market Street. 1811.
t.[1], [2–3], 4–108 p.; 14 cm.; p.[2]: Lydia R. Bailey, Printer, No. 10, North-Alley.
MWA*; DLC (rebound, per. st. on t.[1]), pr. blue paper covers); NjP (rebound); Shaw 23435.

898.4 [—] ——— Farmer Worthy. Philadelphia: Printed For Benjamin Johnson, No. 22, North Second street, next door to the church. 1813.
t.[1], [2–3], 4–95 p.; 14 cm.
MWA*; DLC (per st. on t.[1]); rebound); Shaw 29217.

Bear ye one another's Burdens; Or The Valley Of Tears. *See* Cheap Repository, no. **169.27**.

899.1 [—] The Valley Of Tears, Or, Bear Ye One Another's Burdens. A Vision. Philadelphia: Published by Benjamin Johnson, No. 22, North Second Street. 1813. [cover title].
illus. [2], [3], 4–24 p.; illus. p.[2] only illus.; 13.5 cm.; pr. & illus. green paper covers; illus. p.[2] signed *M* [William Morgan], one of Anderson's four pupils. Colophon p.[24]: Philadelphia: Printed For Benjamin Johnson, No. 22, North Second street, next door to the church. 1813.
English ed. *see* **169.27**.
MWA*; Shaw 29218 and 30395.

899.2 [—] ——— A Vision. With A Frontispiece. Philadelphia: Published by Benjamin Johnson, No. 31, Market-st. 1818.
t.[1], illus. [2], [3], 4–24 p.; illus. p.[2] only illus.; 13.5 cm.
MWA* (covers wanting); Shaw 44903.

[—] The Way To Plenty Or The Second Part Of Tom White. *See* Cheap Repository, 169.8.

MORE, SARAH 1743?–1817

[—] THE CHEAPSIDE APPRENTICE; or, The History Of Mr. Francis H^XXXX. *See* Cheap Repository, no. **169.9.**

900.1 [—] THE CHEAPSIDE APPRENTICE. Published by B. Johnson No. 247 Market St. Philadelphia. [1807].
  t.[i], [ii], [1], 2–36 p.; engr. title page vignette only illus.; 14 cm.; pink paper covers. The Cheapside Apprentice is by Sarah More p. 1–29; Dan And Jane, p. 31–36, by Hannah More. English ed. London: J. Marshall (pr.), R. White; S. Hazard, Bath. [1796]. *See also* no. **169.9.**
  MWA-W°; CLU; CtHi; DLC (covers wanting); MWA (covers wanting); NNC-Sp (bound with no. **879.1** with spine stamped "Cheap Repository [vol.] 1"); PP (rebound); Evans 34135 (dated *ca.* 1798); Shaw 13124; Weiss 1946, p. 20.

900.2 [—] ——— Apprentice, Or The History Of Mr. Francis H^XXXX Philadelphia: Published by Benjamin Johnson, No. 31, Market-st. 1818.
  t.[1], illus. [2], [3], 4–24 p.; illus. p.[2] only illus.; 13.5 cm. MSaE copy cover title imprint: Philadelphia: Published by Benjamin Johnson, 31 Market street. Dickinson, printer, 100 Race street. 1818.
  MWA° (covers wanting); MSaE (pr. olive-green paper covers); Shaw 44906 and 44898.

[—] THE HUBBUB. *See* Cheap Repository, no. **169.26.**

901.1 [—] THE HUBBUB. Published by B. Johnson No. 247 Market St. Philadelphia. [1807].
  t.[ii], [1], 2–35, [36] p.; engraved title with vignette only illus.; 14 cm.
  MWA°; DLC; NNC-Sp (bound with no. **900.1** with spine stamped "Cheap Repository [vol.] 1"); PP (rebound); Evans 34136 (dated [1798]); Weiss 1946, p. 20.

901.2 [—] ——— Philadelphia: adv. by Benjamin Johnson, 1818 in **893.4.**

[—] SORROWFUL SAM; Or, The History of the Two Blacksmiths. *See* Cheap Repository, no. **169.9.**

902.1 [—] SORROWFUL SAM/THE BLACK-SMITH/ Published by B Johnson. N? 247 Market St. Philadelphia. [1807].
  t.[i], [ii], [1], 2–36 p.; engr. title with vignette only illus.; 14 cm. The length of the first line of the title "Sorrowful Sam" measures 63 mm. The title is printed in three lines.
  English ed. Bath: S. Hazard (pr.); J. Marshall (pr.), R. White. [1795] p. 24 signed S [Sarah More]. *See also* no. **169.6.**
  MWA°; NNC-Sp (bound with no. **888** with spine stamped "Cheap Repository [vol.] 2").

902.2 [—] SORROWFUL SAM/THE BLACK-SMITH/ Published by B Johnson. N? 247 Market St. Philadelphia. [*ca.* 1807].
  t.[ii], [1], 2–36 p.; engr. title vignette only illus.; 14.5 cm.; brown marbled paper covers. A variant of no. **902.1** with the title page reprinted in smaller type and the title in two lines instead of three. The length of the first line "Sorrowful Sam" is 33 mm. The engraved title page faces p. [1]. The text is identical in both books.
  MWA°.

902.3 [—] SORROWFUL SAM, Or The Two Blacksmiths. With A Frontispiece. Philadelphia: Published by Benjamin Johnson, No. 31, Market-st. 1818.
  t.[1], illus.[2], [3], 4–24 p.; illus. p.[2] only illus.; 13.5 cm.
  MWA°; Shaw 44907.

MORE TRIFLES! For The Benefit Of The Rising Generation. *See* Sandham, Elizabeth, no. **1160.**

MOSELEY, WILLIAM

903.1 — THE NEW TOKEN FOR CHILDREN; Or A Sequel To Janeway's. Being an authentic account, never before published, of the conversion, exemplary lives, and happy deaths of Twelve Children. By William Moseley, Minister of the Tabernacle, Hanley. First American from the second London edition. [two lines quot.] From Sidney's Press, New-Haven. For Increase Cooke & Co. 1806.
  t.[i], [ii–iii], iv, [5], 6–72 p.; pink wallpaper covers ornamented with a design in blue and red.
  Welch°; MWA.

903.2 —— —— Third Edition, Revised. [2 lines quot.] Philadelphia: Published by Wm. W. Woodward, Corner of Second and Chesnut Streets. 1808.

fr.[ii], t.[iii], [iv–v], vi–viii, [9], 10–142, [143, contents], [144, adv.] p.; front. only illus.; 11 cm.; bound in p.[iv]: Dickinson, Printer, Whitehall.

MWA°; CtY; DLC (p. 129–144, and covers wanting); MiD; Shaw 15663.

903.3 —— —— Fourth Edition, Revised. [2 lines quot.] Jer. iii. 4. Pittsburgh [Pa.]: Published by Patterson & Hopkins. 1812.

t.[i], [ii–iii], iv–vi, [7], 8–128 p.; 11 cm.; bound in blue marbled paper over bds.; p.[ii]: S. Engles & Co. Printers.

MWA-W°.

903.4 [—] —— Children: Being Interesting Memoirs Of Eleven Pious Children. A New Edition. Hartford: Published By W. S. Marsh, And for sale at his Book-Store and Bindery, Main-Street. 1814. B. & J. Russell, Printers.

t.[iii], [iv–v], vi, [vii], [viii, bl.], [9], 10–69 p.; 14.5 cm.; bound in blue paper over w. bds. This is the same as the Pittsburgh 1812 edition, no. 903.3, except that the "Memoir of Ebenezer Kemp," or "Memoir XII" is omitted.

MWA-W°; CtY (p. [v]–vi mut.); PPiU; Shaw 31815.

903.5 [—] —— Fourth Edition Revised [2 lines quot.] Philadelphia: Published By W. W. Woodward, Corner Of Second And Chesnut Streets. A. Griggs & K. Dickinson, Printers. 1815.

fr.[ii]; t.[iii], [iv–v], vi–viii, [9], 10–142, [143, contents–144, adv.] p.; 11 cm.; bound in marbled paper over bds.

MWA-T°; PP° (fr.[ii] wanting); Shaw 35331.

904 A Most Bloody And Cruel Murder, Committed On The Body Of Mrs. Elizabeth Wood, By Her Own Son. Made Public With A View Of Warning The Youth From The Snares And Temptations Of The Wic[ke]d; And To Embrace Virtue And Piety—O[n] T[he] Sure [R]oad To Happiness. To Which Is Added Two Appropriate Hymns. Bennington [Vt.] [:] Printed By Anthony Haswell. [1793?].

t.[1], [2], 3–8 p.; 17 cm.

RPJCB°; McCorison 272.

The Most Delightful History Of The King And The Cobler. *See* The King And The Cobler, no. **738**.

905.1 [Mother Goose's Melody; Or Sonnets for the Cradle. In two Parts. Part 1st. contains the most celebrated Songs and Lullabies of the old British Nurses, calculated to amuse Children and to excite them to Sleep. Part 2d, those of that sweet Songster and Nurse of Wit and Humour, Master William Shakespeare. Embellished with Cuts, and illustrated with Notes and Maxims, Historical, Philosophical, and Critical. The First Worcester Edition. Worcester (Massachusetts) Printed By Isaiah Thomas, And Sold At His Bookstore. [MDCCLXXXVI] [imaginary title compiled from no. **905.2** and I. Thomas' adv. in *The Wisdom Of Crop The Conjurer*, 1787, no. **1445.1**].

13–73, [74, bl.], ½t.[75], 76–82, [83–86] p.; [A]$_7$–[A]$_8$, [B]–E$_8$, with [A]$_1$–[A]$_6$, F$_4$–F$_8$ wanting; illus.; p. 65; 10 mm. Mother Goose's Melody [pt. I.], p. 13–73; Mother Goose's Melody. Part II. Containing The Lullabies of Shakespea[r.] [probably printed without the "e" as in the 2nd & 3rd Worcester editions], p.[75]–80. This fragmentary copy without a title page wants the lower half of most of the pages. On p. 34 there is a characteristic picture of a cock on the right side of the illustration. The cock faces a house on the left, with a pointed roof, a doorway, and a second story window; a tall tree is alongside of the house. This particular cut does not appear in Isaiah Thomas' second or third editions of *Mother Goose's Melody*. Thomas used it in *Nurse Truelove's New Year's Gift*, 1786, no. **955.1**, and in the 1794 edition of the same book, no. **955.5** where it appears on p. 40 in both books. He used it in all his editions of *The House That Jack Built*, [1786?], no. **612.2**, p. 12; 1799, no. **616.11**, p. 12; 1805, no. **616.18**, p. 14. Most of the illustrations closely resemble those in the London edition of Francis Power, 1791. Francis Power undoubtedly printed them from the same blocks used by Thomas Carnan for his edition advertised in 1780, but of which no copy is known. Thomas must have had an early English edition of Carnan's because the format of the book so closely follows that of the Power edition, with the cuts redrawn but very similar. The new illustrations are: a pig, p. 15; the cock, p. 34; a horse, p. 60; a man reading a book, p.

70. On p. 38 the English cut for "Aristotle's Story" is not copied, but the same illustration of two birds standing on a rock appearing on p. 65 for the rhyme "There were two blackbirds Sat upon a hill," copied from the English edition, is repeated. This bird cut is of special interest because in this edition the lower right rule is unbroken. In both the second edition, no. **905.2**, and third edition, no. **905.3**, the rule has two breaks in it near the bottom right corner. This is evidence that this fragment is earlier than no. **905.2** and no. **905.3** and because of the format of the book and the use of the same Isaiah Thomas cuts which appear in the second edition, there is no doubt that the book is the first Worcester edition. Seven printer's ornaments are present. On p. 78, 80, 84 the tailpiece is a small cut of a three-masted square rigger 15 x 15 mm., also used by I. Thomas in his second edition of 1794, no. **905.2** on p. 14 and third edition of 1799, no. **905.3** on p. 80. English ed. London: entered by T. Carnan at Stationer's Hall, Dec. 28, 1780.

MWA* (all before p. 13 and after p. 86 wanting, the lower half of most of the pages 13–86 mut. or wanting); Evans 19105 (dated 1785 and not reproduced in facsimile in Albany, in 1889).

905.2 MOTHER GOOSE'S MELODY: Or Sonnets for the Cradle. In Two Parts. Part I. Contains the most celebrated Songs and Lullabies of the good old Nurses, calculated to amuse Children and to excite them to sleep. Part II. Those of that sweet Songster and Nurse of Wit and Humour, Master William Shakespeare, Embellished With Cuts, And illustrated with Notes and Maxims, Historical, Philosophical, and Critical. The Second Worcester Edition. Worcester, (Massachusetts) Printed By Isaiah Thomas, And Sold At His Bookstore. MDCCXCIV.

fr.[ii], t.[iii], [iv–v], vi–x, [11], 12–73, [74, bl.], ½t.[75], 76–94, [95–96, adv. list of books] p.; [A]–F$_8$; illus.; 10 cm.; illus. buff paper covers. Preface, p.[iv]–x; Mother Goose's Melody [pt. I.], p.[11]–73; Mother Goose's Melody. Part II. Containing The Lullabies of Shakespear [*sic. i.e..* Shakespeare], p.[75]–94; adv. list of books, p.[95–96]. The text is printed from reset type but closely follows that of the first edition, no. **905.1**, with the rhymes on the same pages. On p. 23 line 2, of no. **905.1**, the comma after the world "Hill," lies below and just in front of the base of "W" or "Woman," line 1. In no. **905.2** the comma lies under the middle of the letter "W". Many pages have the same type setting as no. **905.1**. All the cuts are the same in both books except the one on page 34. On this page a new illustration for a cock is used. The cock is 27 mm. high with the body pointed to the right and the bird looking backwards to the left. A portion of a house is drawn on the left side of the cut with a person looking out of a first-story window. The cut of the pot, used for "Pease Porridge Hot," p. 41, is printed upside-down. Eleven printer's type ornaments are present.

MWA*; CSmH (illus. blue paper covers); NjP (t.[iii] ¾ wanting but beautifully repaired with a fac. reproduction of the missing parts); PP illus. blue paper covers); Evans 29122.

905.3 ——— The Third Worcester Edition. Printed at Worcester: Massachusetts, By Isaiah Thomas, Jun. Sold Wholesale and Retail By Him. 1799.

t.[iii], [iv–v], vi–ix, [10], 11–72, ½t.[73], 74–91, [92, illus.] p.; [A]–F$_8$ with [A]$_1$, F$_1$, F$_7$, F$_8$ wanting in both copies; illus.; 10.5 cm. Preface, p.[v]–ix; Mother Goose's Melody. [pt. I.], p.[10]–72; Mother Goose's Melody. Part II. Containing The Lullabies of Shakespear [*sic. i.e.* Shakespeare], p.[73]–91; 3 cuts repeated from p. 48, 41, 58, p.[92]. The text is completely reset and is without catch words. The rhymes are on different pages from no. **905.2**. The illustrations are the same in both books except for the cut on p. 50 illustrating "When I was a little Boy/I liv'd by myself." In this edition a wheelbarrow is substituted for the cut in no. **905.2**, p. 51, of a man wheeling a woman in a wheelbarrow. "Se saw, Margery Daw" is now on p. 26 with "Margery Daw" not printed in italics, and illustrated with the cut of "Se saw, sacaradown" p. 29, no. **905.2**. "Se saw, sacaradown" p. 28, has the cut used in "Se saw, Margery Daw," p. 27 no. **905.2**. Ten printer's ornaments are present.

MWA* (t.[iii], vi–ix, [10], 11–80, 83–91, [92]); Evans 35847.

905.4 ——— Printed by S. Hall, in Cornhill, Boston. 1800.

fr.[ii], t.[iii], [iv, bl.], [v], vi–x, [11], 12–73,

[74, bl.], ½t.[75], 76–95 p.; [A]–F₈; 9.5 cm.; orange Dutch paper covers. Preface, p.[v]–x; Mother Goose's Melody. [pt. I.], p.[11]–73; Mother Goose's Melody, Part II. Containing The Lullabies of Shakespeare, p.[75]–92; Introduction to Spelling, p. 93–95. The type setting follows the format of the Worcester, 1794 edition, no. **905.2** and the Francis Power, London edition of 1791, with the rhymes on the same pages up to p. 80. On p. 80 a portion of the poem "Winter" is added to the bottom of the page and ends p. 81. The remaining poems are on p. 82–92 instead of 83–94. Catch words are not present. Thirty-four of the illustrations are copies of those found in both the London, 1791 and the Worcester, 1794 editions. Two others, that of the pig, p. 15, and the horse, p. 60, are copies of I. Thomas cuts in his editions nos. **905.1–3**, but not in the English one. Six cuts are typically Samuel Hall ones which appear in other books. Those on p. 11, 20, 33, 70 were used by him in *The History Of Master Jackey And Miss Harriot.* [1801?], no. **568.9**, on p. 27, 24, 24, and 12 respectively, and in earlier Samuel Hall editions of the same book. The man on horseback was a favorite one of his used in a number of different books. The illustration on p. 23, appears in *Nurse Truelove's New Year's Gift.* [1796?], no. **955.6**, p. 33. The cut on p.39 was used in *The History Of The Holy Jesus*, no. **587.40**, p. 43. Five more illustrations on p. 24, 26, 32, 34, 41 have not been observed in any other Hall publication. Three figured printer's ornaments are present.
CtHi* (p.[75]–76 wanting with a blank leaf inserted for the missing one); MB* (fr.[ii], t.[iii], p.[iv]–16, 81–95 wanting; p. 17–18 ½ wanting); Evans 49118.

905.5 ———— Cradle, Being the most celebrated Songs and Lullabies of the good old Nurses, Calculated to amuse Children and to excite them to sleep. Embellished with cuts. Printed in the year 1804.
t.[2], 3–15 p.; illus.; 9.5 cm.; illus. yellow paper covers. This edition as well as the following ones are abridged ones which are so completely different from the preceding ones that a description of the cuts will not be made in the same detail. In no. **905.5** the book is illustrated with twelve new very crude cuts. The rectangular

one on p. 4 is a copy, in the reverse, of the cut of the large manor house used by Samuel Hall in *The History Of Master Jackey And Miss Harriot*, no. **568.9**, p. [5]. The cut on p. 12 is the same one used in **675.1** printed in Boston by J. White, 1790. The book of no. **905.5** was probably printed in Boston. The printer could have been either J. White or N. Coverly, because both sometimes used the same cuts.
MWA*.

905.6 ———— Cradle. Boston: Printed By N. Coverl[y] Jun. Corner of Theatr[e] Alley. 1812. fr.[2], t.[3], [4, alphabet], [5–15] p.; illus.; 10.5 cm.; wallpaper covers. This book is illustrated with thirteen crude cuts, eleven of which are pictures of birds. Rhymes about birds are used to match the cuts, and where the verse does not fit the illustration the verse may be altered. For example: "High, diddle, diddle, The bird's in the fiddle, . . .", illustrated with a cut of a pigeon-like bird on a tree, p.[5]; "Ding dong bell, The Lark's in the well, . . .", p.[8], also illustrated with a bird. Other verses are slightly altered and may have an irrelevant cut above them: "Goose goose, gander, Where shall I wander?", p.[7], is depicted as a long pointed-beaked bird; "See saw Margaret Daw, She sold her bed and laid on the straw, . . .", is illustrated with a bird that looks like a duck, p.[11]. Some poems are not taken from *Mother Goose's Melody* and are different from any English Nursery Rhymes recorded in ODNR: "The grateful Lark in air pois'd high, Sings a sweet sonnet to the sky:", p.[6]; "The Ducks by nature do desire, To woddle in the filthy mire, . . .", illustrated with a picture of a long-beaked bird, p.[13]; "The gabbling Goose as white as snow, Seeks the soft winding stream you know; . . .", above which is a bird that looks like a heron. This heron cut was used by N. Coverly for a frontispiece in *The Mother's Gift*, no. **907.1**.
Griffin* (t.[2] cropped along the outer margin of the page affecting a few words of the imprint).

905.7 ———— Cradle. Containing the most celebrated Songs and Lullabies of the good Old Nurses, calculated to amuse Children, and to excite them to sleep. Ornamented with Cuts, And illustrated with Notes and Maxims, historical, philosophical, and critical. Windham [Conn.]:

Printed by Samuel Webb. 1813.

fr.[2], t.[3], [4, alphabet], [5], 6–22 p.; p. 23–31 or last 5 leaves wanting; 10 cm. Alphabet p.[4]; Mother Goose's Melody, p. [5]–21; [beginning of the alphabet] Great A, little a,/ Bouncing B;/The Cat's in the Cupboard,/And she can't see, p. 22. Five printer's ornaments are present. The book has nineteen nursery rhymes which match those on p.[11]–35 in I. Thomas' Second Worcester Edition, 1794, no. **905.2.** Both follow the London edition of 1791. MWA* (p. 23–31 & covers wanting).

905.8 ——— Cradle. Printed At Windsor, (Vt.) By Jesse Cochran, And Sold Wholesale And Retail At His Book-Store. 1814.

fr.[2], t.[3], [4, bl.], 5–31 p.; 22 illus.; 10.5 cm.; pr. & illus. blue paper covers; cover title undated. A particularly interesting abridged edition containing twenty-five rhymes on p.[5]–25, and an alphabet, p. 26–31, which starts: "A a stands for Age, and for Adam, and Awl," and ends "Z z stands for Za-ny, that brings up the rear." Many of the rhymes have changes from no. **905.2** or ODNR: "High Diddle, The Duck's in the Fiddle, . . .", p.[5]; "Baa! Nanny black Sheep, Have you got any wool, No sir—yes sir, I've two bags full, One for my master and one for my dame, and one for the little girl down the lane," p. 11; "There was a man in our town, And he was wondrous wise; He jumped over a hedge, And Scratched out both his eyes; . . .", p. 18; "I had a little hobby horse, His name was hobby gray, His head was made of gingerbread, His tail was made of clay; He could amble—he could trot, He could carry a mustard pot Through the town of Woodstock, Hey, boys, hey!", p. 22. Compare the above with ODNR, p. 203, 88, 402, 210 respectively. Similar to the Coverly edition, no. **905.6**, p.[7], which also changes the rhyme "Goosey, goosey, gander" to "Goose, goose, gander," p. 15. Two rhymes are not located in ODNR, but may be variations of rhymes which start with other words. They are: "Once there was a little boy, He lived in his skin, When he pops out, you may pop in," p. 12; "Father and I went down to Camp Along with captain Goodwin, And there we saw the men and boys As thick as hasty pudding, With fire ribbons in their hats, They look'd so taring fine O, I wish I had just such a one To give

to my Jemimo," p. 13. There are twenty-one illustrations, ten of which are peculiar to this edition. These are the two cuts of the frontispiece, and those on p. 6, 13, 15, 16, 18, 22, 23, 25.

CtHi*; PP (fr.[2], t.[3], p. 4–7 badly browned; pr. & illus. buff paper covers); McCorison 1641; Shaw 32182.

905.9 ——— Windsor, (Vt.) Printed By Jesse Cochran, And sold wholesale and retail, at his Book-Store. 1815.

fr.[2], t.[3], [4–5], 6–31 p.; illus.; 10.5 cm.; pr. & illus. buff paper covers; cover title undated. The book follows the format of the preceding and prints the rhymes on the same pages. The verses "Father and I went down to camp," p. 13, end in "Jemima" instead of "Jemimo." There are only twenty illustrations, the one on p. 25 being omitted. The two cuts making up the frontispiece and those on p. 6, 13 15, 16, 18, 22, 23 are different from those in no. **905.8.** Selected ones are: a man riding upon a bridled goose, p. 15; a stiff-legged horse with a long neck, p. 22; a man on horseback, facing backwards and blowing a horn, p. 23. Ten printer's type ornaments are present. MWA-W*.

905.10 ——— Cradle. Woodstock [Vt.]: Printed By David Watson. 1820.

fr.[2], t.[3], [4–5], 6–30, [31]p.; illus.; 9.5 cm.; printed and illus. paper covers. MWA*.

For other American books containing Nursery Rhymes *see* the following:

906.1 THE MOTHER'S GIFT. The Second Part. New York: adv. by Hugh Gaine, 1776 in *The Young Clerk's Vade Mecum.*

906.2 THE MOTHER'S GIFT: Or, A Present For All Little Children, Who wish to be good. In Two Volumes. I. [II.] The First Worcester Edition. Printed at Worcester, Massachusetts. By Isaiah Thomas, And Sold Wholesale and retail, at his Book Store. MDCCLXXXVII.
　　vol. I: fr.[2], t.[3], [4–6], 7–95 p.; illus.; 10.5 cm.; illus.; buff paper covers; vol. II: fr.[2], t.[3], [4], 5–85, [86–92, adv. list of books] p.; illus.; 10.5 cm.; Dutch paper covers.
　　English & Irish ed. London: 1 ed. Carnan & Newbery, 1769.
　　MWA*; Evans 20536.

906.3 —— Present For All Little Boys, Who wish to be good. Philadelphia: Printed By W. Spotswood. 1791.
　　t.[3], [4–7], 8–63 p.; illus.; 10.5 cm.; green Dutch paper covers. Dedication p. [5] signed *M.S.C.* Adv. by W. Spotswood, 1795 in **1006.2.** DLC* (fr.[2]? and front cover wanting); Evans 23580.

906.4 —— Present for all little Children who wish to be good. Philadelphia: adv. in 2 vols. by F. Bailey, 1792 in **359.**

906.5 —— Present For All Little Boys, Who Wish To Be Good. Hallowell [Me.]: Printed by N. Cheever, for Ezekiel Goodale. 1809.
　　fr.[2], t.[3], [4–5], 6–62 p.; illus.; 10 cm.; pr. & illus. blue-gray paper covers.
　　Welch*; CLU; MWA; MiU; Shaw 18136.

907.1 THE MOTHER'S GIFT, Or Nurse Truelove's Lullaby. Boston: Printed By N. Coverly, Jun. Corner of Theatre Alley. 1812.
　　fr.[2], t.[3], [4, alphabet], [5–15] p.; illus.; 10 cm.; brown paper covers. On the title page the word "Lullaby" is 12 mm. below the words "Nurse Truelove's." A printer's ornament, with tapering ends and lying between the words "Lullaby" and "Boston," has 7 egg-shaped objects in the center. There are ten cuts and two tailpieces which illustrate or ornament ten nursery rhymes. Most of the cuts have little relation to the verses. The frontispiece shows

the heron used in *Mother Goose's Melody,* no. **905.6,** p.[13] for "The gabbling goose." Below is "He who ne'er learn's his A,B,C, Forever will a block head." In holograph some child has added the word "BE" being probably disturbed by the printer's omission. The rhyme is continued on p.[15] under the cut of a long-billed bird printed on the side of the page and ends, "But he who learns bis [*sic. i.e.* his] letters fair, Shall have a coach to take the air." On p.[5] there is a picture of a woman in a room furnished with a chair and a table, also in no. **905.6,** p. 10. Above it is "Rock a-by baby bunt-/ing,/. . ." and "Little Jack Horner," below it. A house p. [6], surrounded by a border of ornaments is above "O my Kitty, my Kitty, And O my Kitty my dreary," but the cut of the horse, p.[7], also in no. **905.6,** p.[12], may refer to this rhyme instead of "Bah! Nanny black Sheep" below it. Jack and Jill, p.[8], is put under the cut of a sailboat. A pigeon-like bird, p.[9], also in no. **905.6,** p.[11], is above a rhyme not found in ODNR, "Little Tommy Thumb/With his little pipe and/drum/Is come to give you a/ dance;/And lovechild so taper,/Will shew you a caper,/Danoyer brought from/France. She is pleas'd that you look,/Into her little book,/And like her songs so well,/That her figures you know/Before that you can go,/And sing them before you/can spell." The cut of the Annunciation p.[13] heads "Two children sliding on the Ice."
　　MWA-W* (t.[3] cropped affecting the word "Theatre" which may have had a dash after it).

907.2 —— Boston: Printed By N. Coverly Jun. Corner of Theatre-Alley. 1812.
　　fr.[2], t.[3], [4, alphabet], [5–15] p.; illus.; 10.5 cm.; wallpaper covers. A variant of no. **907.1.** The word "Lullaby" on the title page is 7 mm. below the words "Nurse Trueloves." The printer's ornament with tapering ends has 9 egg-shaped objects in the center. The text has been reset on many pages and new cuts are substituted. The frontispiece is a cut of a big dog and the word "be." with a period after it is added to the last line underneath it. The illustration on p.[15] has been changed to an arm and hand holding a whip over a cowering dog. This cut used for the frontispiece of *Mother Goose's Melody,* no. **905.6.** The sailboat cut is now above "O my Kitty, my Kitty," p.[6], in-

stead of the house with its frame of printer's ornaments. The illustration of the horse, p.[7] has a new border of a figured flower-like ornament of 6 petals.

MWA-W° (t.[3] slightly cropped along the outer margin affecting the word "Theatre-"; p.[5–6] mut.); CtHi (p.[9–14] wanting).

908 THE MOTHER'S GIFT, OR REMARKS ON A SET OF CUTS FOR CHILDREN. [4 lines of verse] Philadelphia: Published By Johnson & Warner, No. 147, Market-Street. 1809.

t.[1], [2–3], 4–72 p.; 18 engr. pl.; t.[1]; 14.5 cm.; p. "53" numbered "23"; engr. pl. I–XVIII are each divided into six compartments numbered 1–108, a reprint of part I of no. **909** and the first 18 pl.; colophon p. 72: Lydia R. Bailey, Printer, no. 10, North Alley. Adv. by Johnson & Warner, 1814 in **1449.2**.

NN° (rebound); MiD (p. 17–20 wanting; bound in marbled paper over bds.); MWA-T; Shaw 18137.

909 THE MOTHER'S REMARKS ON A SET OF CUTS FOR CHILDREN. Part I. [II.] [4 lines of verse] Philadelphia: Printed for Jacob Johnson, No. 147 Market Street. T. S. Manning, Printer, No. 143 N. Third Street. 1803.

pt. I.: t.[i] [ii–iii], iv–viii, [9], 10–84 p.; pt. II.: t.[1], [2–3], 4–84 p.; 2 vols. 14.5 cm.; bound in blue marbled paper over bds., brown paper spine. These books are part of a set housed in a wooden box, 17.3 x 11.4 x 6.3 cm., with a slide cover. On the cover is a label 10.5 x 7.5 cm. illustrated with a robin perched on a bent tree trunk growing out of a planter or container labled "Douceurs." The colored illustrated label is bordered by two thin, a thick and a thin rule. Outside of the rules is printed: Published by J. Johnson No. 147 Market-Street. [a portion of the label wanting] W.R. [William Ralph] sc. Besides the two volumes there is an advertisement pamphlet of eight pages, three cards and a set of fifty-four engraved sheets or plates referred to as "Douceurs" in the advertisement. Card 1, 14.3 x 9.2 cm.: "For Cutting into Single Letters", has lower case alphabets a–z, a–r, set in ruled compartments. Card 2, 21.1 x 11.8 cm.: consits of lower case consonants with one or two spaces after each, and also ruled into squares. Card 3, 11.5 x 2.9 cm.; "To place after the Consonants", has lower case

vowels and y. The DLC set has two additional cards or 4 and 5. Card 4: "A Frame on which to place the moveable Letters for Spelling Words." Card 5: 13.5 x 8 cm.: "For Concealing the Cuts till the Names have been read." There were probably more cards containing more lower case letters of the alphabet to be cut out as well as sets of upper case alphabets and numerals 1–9, similar to *A New Spelling Alphabet* described below. The fifty-four plates numbered I–LIV are each 14.2 x 8.6 cm., and divided by rules into six compartments each containing a different cut and numbered 1–324. The term "Douceur" is probably an anglicized word for the French word "douze" or twelve. When the plates were printed, they were printed two to a sheet forming twelve cuts per sheet. These double plates were later cut in half. The plates are copied from Darton and Harvey's English edition of 1799 with plates I–XVIII, XLVII–LIV drawn in the reverse. Two English plates, or XLVII–XLVIII are not copied in the American edition and the cuts on plates XLVII–LIV renumbered. In 1824 Harvey and Darton published an English edition of *Mrs Lovechild's Book Of Two Hundred and Sixteen Cuts. Designed By The Late Lady Fenn, to teach Children the Names of Things.* This book of thirty-five plates has the cuts redrawn from the London, 1799 edition. Since the plates were drawn by Lady Eleanor Fenn she must also have written the book on the plates or *Mother's Remarks*. She may also be the author of the other books listed below in Darton's advertisement in *A Present For A Little Boy*. In the MWA-W collection there is a wooden box with a slip cover. The label on the slip cover: "A New Spelling Alphabet for the Instruction of Children." This title is enclosed in an oval green border in which is printed "Kneass sc". Outside of the border are colored illustrations in the corners. At the top of the oval is a scroll-like piece of paper on which is written "J. Johnson No. 147 Market St.". The box contains upper and lower case alphabets which have been cut out of cards and sets of numbers 1–9. This is probably a used supplementary alphabet set issued to be employed with the above set in the box marked "Douceurs".

English ed. adv. title 1: *Lovechild's Douceurs, containing Three Hundred and Thirty six Cuts, with Two Volumes of Mother's Remarks, List* of *Nouns, Dictionary,* and *Book of Nouns, with several sets of Alphabets; a new scheme for the Instruction of Children, in an elegant box, price 9 s.,* London: adv. by Darton and Harvey, 1806 in *A Present For A Little Boy.*

English adv. title 2: *Lovechild's Three Hundred and Thirty-Six copperplate, cuts With Remarks on each, 3 vols. 5 s.,* London: adv. by Darton and Harvey, 1806 in *A Present For A Little Boy.* This must refer to a similarly bound set of the plates and parts I and II of *The Mother's Remarks To A Set Of Cuts.*

English ed. title 3: *Mrs Lovechild's Book of Three Hundred & Thirty six Cuts.* London: Darton, Harvey & Darton, 1813.

English ed. title a: *The Mother's Remarks On A Set Of Cuts For Children. Part I. [II].* London: Darton and Harvey, 1799. The copy described in English title 3 surely consists of the plates or doucers, bound in one volume, which accompanied the two volumes of this book. The plates are numbered I–LVI and have 6 cuts on each plate, which are consecutively numbered 1–336. Signatures A₁, B₁, [C₁], D₁, E₁, F₁ or plates I, XVII, XXV, XXXIII, XLI, XLIX are signed *Willᵐ Darton & Joshʰ Harvey, London Decʳ 31, 1799.*

MWA° (I., II., a set in a wooden box with cards); DLC (I., II., a set with cards 4 & 5, but wooden box wanting); MiD; MWA-W°; NN (I.); NNC-Pl (I., II.); PHi (I., II. complete set in wooden box); PP (I., II. & 54 pl.); PPiU; PPL; Shaw 4688.

MOTT, RICHARD and ABIGAIL
910 — A Short Account Of The Last Sickness And Death Of Maria Mott, Daughter Of Richard and Abigail Mott, Of Mamaroneck, in the State of New-York. New-York: Printed And Sold By Samuel Wood & Sons, No. 357, Pearl-Street. 1817.
t.[1], [2–3], 4–28 p.; 16.5 cm.
PP°.

911 Mounseer Nongtonpaw; A New Version. [4 lines of verse] First American Edition. Philadelphia: Published and sold Wholesale by Wm. Charles, and may be had of all the booksellers. 1814. W. M'Culloch, Printer.
fr.[1], t.[2], [3], 4–16 p.; 12 pl.; 12 cm.; pr. flesh-colored paper covers. Adv. by Wm. Charles, 1815 in 748.

Cover title: Mounseer Nongtongpaw; or The Discoveries of John Bull On A Trip To Paris. Illustrated With Humerous Engravings. Philadelphia: Published and Sold Wholesale by Wm. Charles and may be had of all the Booksellers. Price 25 cents. 1814.
English ed. London: For The Proprietors Of The Juvenile Library, 1808.
Carson° (not seen).

The Mountain Lute. *See* Berquin, Arnaud, no. 89.1.

The Mountain Piper. *See* Berquin, Arnaud, no. 90.1.

The Moving Market. *See* Cries Of London, no. 249.5.

912 Museum Of Beasts, Being A Trifle For A Good Boy. Ornamented With Cuts. Boston: N. Coverly, Printer, Milk-St. 1813.
fr.[2, alphabet], t.[3], [4–15] p.; illus.; 9 cm.; blue wallpaper covers.
CtHi°; MWA-T.

913 The Museum Of Beasts: Being a Trifle For Good Boys And Girls. Ornamented With Cuts. Boston: Printed By N. Coverly, Jun. Milk-Street, 1814.
t.[1], [2–16] p.; illus.; 10 cm.; buff paper covers ornamented with brown lines in a design.
MWA°, NNC-T (imprint torn away; all after the word "Ornament[ed]" wanting); Shaw 32210.

My Brother. *See* Elliott, Mrs. Mary (Belson), no. 342.1.

My Childhood. *See* Upton, Mr., no. 1367.

My Daughter. *See* Gregory, Richard, no. 470.

My Father. *See* Elliott, Mrs. Mary (Belson), no. 343.2.

914 My Father's Present. Containing A lecture on Presence of Mind—Diverting story of Phaeton Junior—Nature and Education, a fable—Aversion subdued—and other instructive pieces, proper to be read by all Young Persons, who wish to be useful and respected in life. Published By

Johnson & Warner, And Sold At Their Bookstores, Philadelphia And Richmond, Virginia. A. Fagan, Printer. 1813.

> fr.[2], t.[3], [4, bl.], [5], 6–71 p.; illus.; 14.5 cm.; yellow paper covers speckled with gold.
> NNC-Pl*; Shaw 29254.

915 My Friend, Or Incidents in Life, Founded On Truth, A Trifle For Children. Philadelphia: Printed For Johnson And Warner, No. 147, Market Street. 1811.

> t.[i], [ii–iii], iv, [5], 6–48 p.; illus.; 15 cm.; pr. pink paper covers. p.[ii]: Lydia R. Bailey, Printer, No. 10, North Alley. Adv. by Johnson & Warner, 1814 in **1449.3**.
> English ed. London: W. And T. Darton, 1810. English ed. entitled: *My Real Friend, or, incidents of life, founded on truth, for the amusement of Children.* London: 2 ed. W. Darton, 1812. This may be the same as the above 1810 ed. but with the title changed.
> CtHi* (poor copy, pages torn; rear cover wanting); CLU; NNC-LS (front pink paper cover wanting, p. 29–32 mut.).

916 My Grandfather. A Poem Illustrated With Engravings. Philadelphia, Published and sold by Wm Charles. Prices Plain 12½ cents Coloured 13¾ Cents 1817. [cover title].

> [1–6] p. engraved on one side of the page only of 6 leaves; 13 cm.; pr. olive-buff paper covers.
> NNC-Pl* (uncolored pl.; rear cover wanting); MWA-W (covers mostly wanting); Shaw 41539.

917.1 My Grand Mother. A Poem Illustrated With Engravings. Philadelphia, Published and sold by Wm. Charles. Price Plain 12½ cents Coloured 18¾ cents. 1817. [cover title].

> [1–6] p. engraved on one side of the page only of 6 leaves; 13.5 cm.; pr. gray-buff paper covers.
> MWA* (rear cover mostly wanting); RPB (col. pl.); Shaw 41540.

917.2 ——— Philadelphia, Published and sold by Wm Charles. Price Plain 12½ cents colourd 18¾ cents. 1818. [cover title].

> [1–6] p. engr. on one side only of 6 leaves; illus.; 13 cm.; pr. yellow-buff paper covers.
> NNC-Pl* (col. pl., p. [1], & [16] torn in half); MWA; Shaw 44958.

918 My Mother's Present. Containing Much Useful Information. Philadelphia: Published by Johnson & Warner, No. 147 Market Street. 1813.

> fr.[2], t.[3], [4–5], 6–71 p.; illus.; 14 cm.; pr. & illus. pink paper covers.
> MWA*; Shaw 29255.

919 My Pony. A Poem Illustrated With Engravings. Philadelphia, Published and sold by Wm Charles. Price Plain 12½ cents Colourd 18 3/4 cents. 1818. [cover title].

> [1–6] p. engr. on one side only of 6 leaves; illus.; 13.5 cm.; pr. buff paper covers.
> English ed. [London]: Published Sept. 9th. 1812. Edition says it is "composed by J. Baker, Esq."
> MWA-T*; PPL (covers wanting).

My Real Friend. *See* My Friend, no. **915**.

My Sister. *See* Elliott, Mrs. Mary (Belson), no. **344**.

My Son. *See* Gregory, Richard, no. **471**.

920.1 My Tippoo. A Poem Illustrated With Engravings. Philadelphia, Published and sold by Wm. Charles. Price Plain 12½ cents Coloured 18¾ cents. 1817. [cover title].

> [1–6] p. engr. on one side only of 6 leaves; illus.; 13 cm.; pr. brown paper covers.
> English ed. entitled: *The Poem of My Tippoo; By J. Baker.* London: William Darton, p.[3] signed *London. Published March 23^d 1813. by Willm Darton Junr.*
> MWA*; PP (col. pl.); Shaw 41541; Weiss, 1932b, p. 10.

920.2 ——— Philadelphia, Published and sold by Wm. Charles. Price Plain 12½ cents Coloured 18¾ cents. 1818.

> [1–6] p. engr. on one side only of 6 leaves; illus.; 13 cm.; pr. brown paper covers.
> Gardner*.

920.3 ——— Illustrated With Elegant Engravings. Philadelphia, Published and sold by Wm Charles. Price Plain 12¼ cents. Coloured 18¾ cents. 1819. [cover title].

> [1–6] p. engr. on one side only of 6 leaves; illus.; 13 cm.; pr. orange paper covers.

NNC-Pl° (rear cover mostly wanting); Shaw 48819.

920.4 [MY TIPPOO, A Poem By J. Baker] [title copied from the English ed. of 1813] [n.p., n.d.]. 2–5 p. engr. on one side only of 5 leaves; illus.; 11.5 cm.; unprinted pink paper covers. The round engraved illustrations are redrawn copies of those in William Darton Junr.'s London, 1813 edition, *see* no. **920.1.** They are different from William Charles' octagonal illustrations in his editions of 1817, 1818, and 1819, nos. **920.1–3,** which are copied in the reverse from the English edition. This fragment was probably published and engraved by J. Scoles, in New York City, who also republished another engraved English Book, *The Doleful Death Of Poor Old Robin. . . By Peter Prim. London: J. Harris, Nov. 1, 1814, see* no. **1063.** He was also the probable publisher of *The History Of An Old Woman Who Had Three Sons,* no. **532,** which was reprinted from the London edition of J. Harris, 1815.

MWA-W° (p. [1], 6 and rear cover wanting).

NARRATIVE PIECES. Baltimore: adv. by G. Douglas, 1803 in **275.46.**

NATURAL HISTORY OF BEASTS. *See* Columbus, Charley (*pseud.*), no. **222.**

921 NATURAL HISTORY OF BIRDS, Containing A Familiar Survey Of The Feathered Creation. To Which Is Added, A Short History Of Beasts. Albany: Printed And Sold By E. And E. Hosford. 1808.
fr.[2], t.[3], [4–5], 6–71 p.; illus.; 13 cm.
MWA° (fr.[2] & paper covers wanting); Shaw 15691.

922 A NATURAL HISTORY OF BRITISH BIRDS. With Plates. G. Love *sc.* Philadelphia Published By B. C. Busby No 2 N-Third St. 1807.
fr.[2], t.[3], [4–5], 6–52 p.; 8 engr. illus. including front. and t.[3]; 14 cm.; pr. & illus. yellow-buff paper covers.
MWA°.

THE NATURAL HISTORY OF FOUR FOOTED BEASTS. *See* Trip, Tommy, no. **1344.1.**

923.1 THE NEW A B C; Being A Complete Alphabet In Verse, To entice Children to learn their Letters. To Which Is Added, A Number Of Tom Thumb's Songs. Worcester: Printed by I. Thomas, Jun. Sold Wholesale and Retail at his Book-Store. 1805.
fr.[2], t.[3], [4–6], 7–31 p.; illus.; 10.5 cm.; red paper covers. Directions To Learners. First begin with A B C,/And rise from low to high degree;/ When A B C you manage well,/ Join syllables, and learn to spell./ . . . p. [6]; [large alphabet letters A–H, J–T, V–Z formed of garlands of flowers] A Stands for Adam, for Acron,/and Awl./ . . . p. 7–17; [12 rhymes taken from *Tommy Thumb's Song Book*, no. **802.2**]. The letter "I" is omitted from the series of alphabet letters. It was printed by I. Thomas in 1798, with the letter "T", in Thomas Thumb's *A Bag Of Nuts, Ready Cracked*, no. **1306.3.**
MWA°; Shaw 8969.

923.2 —— To Which Is Add[ed] [Th]e Famous Histor[y] Of A Little Boy, Found Under A Haycock. Windsor [Vt.]: Printed for Thomas' & Merrifield. Sold wholesale and retail at their Bookstore. 1808.
t.[1], [2–4], 5–28 p.; 9.5 cm.; colophon p.[28]: Rollin Beach, Printer.
MWA° (p. [27–28], top of page dog-eared & page numbers wanting; covers wanting); McCorison 1019; Shaw 15704.

923.3 —— In Verse. To which is added Juvenile Poems. Designed for the Amusement and Instruction of all good little boys and girls. Ornamented with Engravings. Hanover, N.H. Printed by and for Charles Spear. 1811.
fr.[2], t.[3], [4], 5–23 p.; illus.; 10.5 cm.
Oppenheimer° (not available for checking).

924 THE NEW ALPHABET; Or the Child's best instructor, to which is Added The history Of a little Boy found under a Haycock. Philadelphia: adv. by F. Bailey, 1793 in **773.1.**

925 THE NEW CHILDREN'S FRIEND. Or, Pleasing Incitements To Wisdom And Virtue; Conveyed Through The Medium Of Anecdote, Tale, And Adventure. Calculated To Entertain, Fortify, And Improve The Juvenile Mind, Translated Chiefly From The German. Philadelphia: Printed And Sold By Joseph And James Crukshank, No. 87, High-Street. 1801.
t.[i], [ii–iii], iv, [1], 2–103 p.; 14.5 cm.
English ed. London: 2 ed. Vernor And Hood; Darton And Harvey, 1798.
MWA° (rebound); CLU (yellow paper covers); Shaw 993.

926 A NEW COLLECTION OF PICTURES. Printed And Sold By E. Prouty & Co. At The Juvenile Book-Store No. 157 Pearl-Street. 1819.
fr.[ii], t.[1], 2–24, [25] p.; illus.; 7.5 cm.; entire book in holograph mss., written by a child in imitation of the format of a Samuel Wood publication.
NRU°.

927 A NEW COLLECTION OF CHOICE RIDDLES, For the Entertainment of all Good Children. Hartford: Printed by B. & J. Russell. State-Street. 1815.

t.[1], [2–3], 4–16 p.; 7.5 cm.; pink paper covers. MWA-W*.

928 A NEW COLLECTION OF RIDDLES. Ornamented with Engravings. Windsor. (Vt.) Printed By Jesse Cochran, And Sold Wholesale And Retail At His Book-Store. 1815.

fr.[2], t.[3], [4–5], 6–31 p.; illus.; 11 cm.; pr. & illus. paper covers.

VtHi (fr.[2] & covers wanting, p.[3]–6, 29–31 mut.); McCorison 1765; Shaw 32229.

NEW ENGLAND PSALTER. *See* Psalter, no. **1072.1.**

THE NEW ENTERTAINING HISTORY OF POLLY CHERRY. *See* The Entertaining History Of Polly Cherry, no. **359.**

929 NEW FEDERAL SONGSTER. Boston: adv. by John W. Folsom, 1798 in **672.2.**

THE NEW FOUND RELATION, And Dame Burton's Return. *See* Somerville, Elizabeth, no. **1232.**

930 A NEW FRIEND OF YOUTH; or moral and instructive examples for young Ladies and Gentlemen. . . . 1st American edition. [New-Haven], from Sidney's Press for Increase Cooke & Co., 1803.

68 + p.

Shaw 4733.

931.1 A NEW GIFT FOR CHILDREN: Containing Delightful and Entertaining Stories In Two Parts; Viz. 1. The Dutiful Child. 2. The Thief. 3. The Generosity of confessing a Fault. 4. The two good Friends. 5. The Rewards of Virtue. Second Part. 6. The Good Boy. 7. The Good Girl. 8. The Proud Play-mate. 9. The good Girl and the pretty Girl. 10. The meanly proud Girl. 11. The Trifler. 12. The undutiful Child. 13. The lost Child. 14. The Advantages of Truth. 15. Of Tommy Fido. The Fourth Edition. Adorned with Cuts. Boston; New-England: Printed and Sold by Fowle & Draper, in Marlboro's-Street. M,DCCLXII.

t.[i], [ii], [1–2], 3–34 p.; illus.; 16.5 cm. Printer's ornaments are generously used throughout the book.

English ed. London: *A Christmas Box.* Printed and sold by M. Cooper, and M. Boreman, 1746. This book is the English source book for *A New Gift For Children* and *The Careful Parent's Gift.* London: John Marshall & Co. [ca. 1787 or earlier].

PHi*; Evans 9202.

931.2 —— Boston: adv as "Just Published And to be Sold by Z. Fowle at his Printing-Office in Back-Street, Boston" [ca. 1765], in *A Chain Of Four Links.*

932 A NEW GIFT FOR CHILLDREN: Delightful and Entertaining Stories For little Masters and Misses. Boston, Printed by D. Fowle [1756?].

fr.[1, verse], t.[2], [3], 4–30 p.; illus.; 10 cm.; pr. paper covers, extensively decorated with printer's type ornaments. The covers are not separate but the recto and verso of the first and last leaves. To the Tender Parents of my little Benefactors, p. [3]–5, signed "Mary Homebred" (*pseud.*) p. 5; Story I. The Good Boy, p. 5–7; Story II. A good Girl, p. 7–9; Story III. The proud Playfellow, p. 10–11; Story IV. Good Girl & pretty Girl, p. 11–13; Story V. The meanly proud Girl, p. 13–15; Story VI. The Trifler, p. 15–16; Story VII. The undutiful Child, p. 17–18; Story VIII. The lost Child, p. 18–21; Story IX. The Advantages of Truth, p. 22–23; Story X. [Master Tommy Fido], p. 24–25; A Dialogue, p. 26–28; Against Lying [by I. Watts], p. 29–30. The ten stories were printed in no. **931.1** by Fowle and Draper, 1762. Some are abridged versions of the English publication *The Careful Parent's Gift.* London: J. Marshall [ca. 1787 or earlier]. *See* no. **931.1.** The cut of a seated woman holding a child, p. 21 was reprinted in *A New Gift For Children,* 1762, no. **931.1,** on p. 30. The illustration of the seated woman between two trees, p. 26 is also in no. **931.1,** p. 5. The square ornamental cut, p. 29, appears in both books as well as *The History Of The Holy Jesus,* Fowle & Draper, 1762, no. **587.10,** but has different words printed in the center, namely "Tell No Lies, Children." Front cover title: A Little Story-Book For Pretty Boys and [Girls]. Rear cover: Sold at the same Place with this Book Watts's Songs and Catechisms. This Royal Primmer. The Bible In Verse, [cannot make out the title], Fortune Teller. *See also* no **763.**

This paper covered book is the earliest known

non-Biblical child's book, in this format, printed in America. It was preceded by *The Holy Bible in Verse* and *The History Of The Holy Jesus,* both of which were small paperbound books but based on the Bible. The former was usually bound in leather.

CSmH° (fr.[1] & front cover half wanting).

A New Hieroglyphical Bible. *See* Hieroglyphical Bible, no. **513.1.**

933 A New History Of A True Book, In Verse. For Sale at A March's Bookstore; price 6 cents single, and to those who buy to give away 2 dols pr. hundred. [*ca.* 1802].

t.[1], [2], 3–12 p.; 16.5 cm.
From Oct. 31, 1797–Dec. 22, 1797 the firm was publishing as Barrett & March. A March published alone in Newburyport, Mass. from Dec. 23, 1797 to July 12, 1812 the day of his death. The above book was advertised as "Just published" in the *Newburyport Herald,* May 4, 1802. (MWA cat.).
English ed. London: adv. by J. Marshall, R. White; S. Hazard, Bath [1795] in *The Beggarly Boy.*
MWA°; MH; MSaE; NN (rebound, i. st. on p. [2]); RPB; RPJCB; Evans 32543; Shaw 2762.

934 A New History Of Beasts. Embellished with coloured Engravings. Philadelphia: Published By E. and R. Parker, No. 178, Market-Street. J. R. A. Skerrett, Printer. 1818.

fr.[2], t.[3], 4–31, [32, adv. list of books] p.; 8 col. pl.; 12 cm.; pr. & illus. brown paper covers.
MWA° (p. 7–8 & rear cover mut.); PP; Shaw 45000.

New History Of Blue Beard. *See* Perrault, Charles, no. **986.1.**

935 The new History of Polly Cherry and her Golden Apple. To which are added the Adventures of Prince George. Philadelphia: adv. by William Young, 1795 in *Sermons To Children. See also* no. **359.**

936.1 The New Holiday Present; Or, The Child's Plaything Calculated To allure and "teach the young Ideas how to shoot." Boston: Printed

and sold by John W. Folsom, No. 30, Union-Street. 1798.

t.[3], 4–30 p.; illus.; 10 cm. Come hither, pretty little Boy,/Come learn of me your A,B,C,/ . . . p. 4; Alphabets, p. 5; The Alphabet In Verse. "A stands for Apple and Awl, . . ." p. 6–7; Another Alphabet. "A was an Archer, . . ." p. 7–8; Pretty Stories And Songs . . . The History of Master Friendly, p. [9]–16; This is the House that Jack built, p. 17–19; The Old Hound, p. 20–21; Honesty Is The Best Policy, p. 22–23; [Nursery Rhymes] The Jolly Welchman, p. 24; Boys and Girls, p. 25; Little Husband. " I had a little husband,/No bigger than my thumb, . . ." p. 26; A Mouse in a Bag. "There was an old woman/Lived under a hill; . . ." p. 27; Jack and Gill, Jack Horner, The Archer. "Who did kill Cock Robin? . . ." p. 28–29; Three Welch Hunters. p. 29–30.
NPV° (i. st. p. 5; fr.[2] & covers wanting); Evans 34198.

936.2 ——— Exeter [N.H.]: adv. by Henry Ranlet, 1801 in **558.2.**

936.3 ——— Exeter [N.H.]: adv. by Norris & Sawyer, 1808 in **428.3.**

937.1 The New Instructive History Of Miss Patty Proud; Or, The Downfall Of Vanity: With The Reward of Good-Nature. Adorned with Cuts. For the Amusement and Instruction of Youth. [2 lines of verse] Hartford: Printed by John Babcock. 1800.

fr.[2], t.[3], [4–5], 6–31 p.; illus.; 11 cm.; brown speckled paper covers.
English ed. title 1: *The entertaining History of Miss Patty Proud.* London: adv. by J. Hawkins in *The Entertaining and Instructive Tales of Angelo the Hermit of the Wilderness.* Holograph date, "March 16, 1788."
English ed. title 2: *The History Of Miss Patty Proud.* London: S. Carvallo [1820?].
English ed. title 3: *The New Instructive History of* ——— London: adv. by John Marshall [1787] in *The Wisdom Of Crop The Conjurer.*
CtY°; Evans 38061.

937.2 ——— Hartford: Printed by John Babcock. 1802.

fr.[2], t.[3], [4–5], 6–31 p.; illus.; 11 cm.; blue Dutch paper covers.
MWA-W°; CtHi (p.[2]–8 mut.); Shaw 50313.

937.3 ———— Good-Nature. For the Amusement and Instruction of Youth. [2 lines of verse] 1802.
 t.[i], [ii], iii, [4], 5–12 p.; 12 cm.
 Gardner° (t.[i], & p. [ii]–[4], 11–12 mut.).

937.4 ———— Hudson [N.Y.]: Printed By Ashbel Stoddard, And sold Wholesale and Retail, at his Book-Store. 1804.
 fr.[2], t.[3], [4–5], 6–31 p.; illus.; 10.5 cm.; wallpaper covers.
 MWA°; OCl; NRU.

937.5 ———— From Sidney's Press, New-Haven. 1805.
 fr.[2], t.[3], [4–5], 6–31 p.; illus.; 10.5 cm.; orange Dutch paper covers.
 MWA-W°; Shaw 8996.

937.6 ———— From Sidney's Press, New-Haven, 1806.
 t.[3], [4–5], 6–30 p.; illus.; 10.5 cm.
 ICU° (fr.[2], p. 31 & covers wanting); MWA-T (p. 31 & covers wanting).

937.7 ———— Good-Nature. Embellished With Cuts. Philadelphia: Printed By John Adams. 1806.
 fr.[2], t.[3], [4–5], 6–31 p.; illus.; 10 cm.; pr. & illus. blue paper covers; p. 30–31 adv. list of 23 books.
 Cover title: Toy Book. Philadelphia: Sold by James P. Parke. 1807.
 MWA°; Shaw 10973.

937.8 ———— Good Nature. Adorned with Cuts. For the Amusement and Instruction of Youth. [2 lines of verse] From Sidney's Press, New-Haven. 1807.
 fr.[2], t.[3], [4–5], 6–31 p.; illus.; 10.5 cm.; Dutch paper covers.
 CtY°; MWA-T.

937.9 ———— Downfall of Vanity. Adorned with Cuts. Otsego [Cooperstown. N.Y.], Printed by H. & E. Phinney, Jun. 1807.
 t.[3], [4–5], 6–31 p.; illus.; 10 cm.; buff paper covers ornamented with a stippled design.
 MWA; CtY.

937.10 ———— Philadelphia: adv. by B. & T. Kite, 1807 in **611.1.**

937.11 ———— [same as **937.7**] From Sidney's Press, New-Haven. 1808.

t.[3], [4–5], 6–30 p.; illus.; 11 cm.
 CtY° (2 copies; fr.[2], p. 31 & covers wanting); Shaw 4743 (wrongly dated 1803).

937.12 ———— of Youth. [2 lines of verse] Hudson: Printed By Ashbel Stoddard, And sold Wholesale and Retail at his Book-Store. 1809.
 fr.[2], t.[3], [4], 5–31 p.; illus.; 10.5 cm.; illus. blue paper covers.
 MWA°; Shaw 18201.

937.13 ———— Of Goodnature. Adorned with Cuts. [2 lines of verse] From Sidney's Press, New-Haven, 1809.
 fr.[2], t.[3], [4–5], 6–31 p.; illus.; 10.5 cm.; Dutch paper covers.
 CtHi°; CLU; MWA (p.[2], 31 & covers wanting); PHi (wrongly dated 1800 by Evans 38060); Shaw 18202.

937.14 ———— GOODNATURE [*sic. i.e.* GOOD NATURE] [2 lines of verse] From Sidney's Press. New-Haven, 1810.
 fr.[2], t.[3], [4–5], 6–31 p.; illus.; 10.5 cm.; Dutch paper covers; five lines of the upper case alphabet, with the first line A–E, p. [4]; below the caption p. [5] there is a printer's ornament made up of a central cross with tapering lines on either side of it; the last line on p. [5]: "read."; last four words p. 6: "A day is appointed,"; last line p. 31: "them, if he had his due."
 MWA°; Shaw 20869.

937.15 ———— GOOD NATURE. Adorned with Cuts. [2 lines of verse] From Sidney's Press. New-Haven, 1810.
 fr.[2], t.[3], [4–5], 6–31 p.; illus.; 11 cm.; pr. & illus. yellow paper covers. A variant of no. **937.13.** On the title page "GOOD NATURE" has a space between the two words. Other differences are: [3 lines of lower case alphabet] Capital Letters. [2 lines of upper case alphabet] Double Letters. [1 lines of double letters], p. [4]; below the caption p. [5] a line 10 mm. long; last line p. [5]: "you read."; last four words p. 6: "build one. A day"; last line p. 31: "for them, if he had his due."
 Gardner°.

937.16 ———— Reward Of Good Nature. Adorned with Cuts. For the amusement and instruction of youth. First Windsor Edition. Printed At Windsor [Vt.]: By Farnsworth & Churchill. 1810.

 fr.[2], t.[3], [4, bl.], [5–6], 7–31 p.; illus.; 10 cm.; pr. & illus. paper covers.

 MWA*; MB (per st. on t.[3]), MSaE; PP; McCorison 1197; Shaw 208870.

937.17 —— Goodnature. [2 lines of verse] Adorned with Cuts. Sidney's Press. New-Haven. 1812.

 fr.[2], t.[3], [4–5], 6–31 p.; illus.; 10.5 cm.; yellow paper covers.

 MWA*; PP (covers mostly wanting); Shaw 26238.

937.18 —— Sidney's Press. New-Haven. 1813.

 fr.[2], t.[3], [4–5], 6–31 p.; illus.; 10 cm.; pr. & illus. buff paper covers; the "3" of the date "1813" on t.[3] is printed with defective type.

 MWA-W* (front cover has a cut of a man walking in the rain, rear cover a cut of a peacock); CtHi; CtY (yellow paper covers); MWA (has different cuts on the covers from the MWA-W copy); PP.

938 New Political Alphabet: Or, A Little Book For Great Boys. Ornamented with Engravings. Windham [Conn.]: Printed by Samuel Webb. 1813.

 fr.[2], t.[3], [4–5], 6–23 p.; front. only illus.; 10 cm.; pr. yellow paper covers, [alphabets] p.[4]; [alphabet letters] A Stands for Adam's Adminis-/tration,/And B For Betraying the rights of the/nation./ . . . p.[5]–23.

 MWA*; Shaw 29321.

A New Riddle Book. *See* Puzzle, Peter Esq. (*pseud.*), no. **1081.**

The New Robinson Crusoe. *See* Campe, Joachim Heinrich von., nos. **155–158.1.**

939 New Selection of Hymns, for Juvenile Delinquents, Principally Extracted From Watt's Divine Songs. [4 lines of verse] Hymn 8, verse 6. New-York: Printed And Sold By Mahlon Day, No. 84, Water-street. 1820.

 t.[1], [2–3], 4–37, [38, contents] p.; title vignette only illus.; 14 cm.; pr. & illus. brick-red paper covers.

 CtHi*.

940 A New/Story-Book;/ Containing Fables consisting of/Words of one Syllable./Fable I./ The Wolf and the Lamb./ [caption p. [3]].

 [3], 4–30 p.; no illus.; p. [3] 12 cm. On p. 5, 7, 9, 13, 15, 21, 27, there is a decorative bar of a fine small variety of ornament; that on p. 11, 19 is composed of a small 6 pointed asterisk-like ornament. On p. 29 there is a square tailpiece bordered with a row of dagger-like ornaments. The top and left side of the square has short lengths of double thin rules. Inside of the square are 12 index symbols ☞. There are 14 fables taken from *Aesop's Fables.* From the type ornaments and format, this book seems to be an American edition printed sometime during the 18th century.

 MWA* (t.[1], p. [2], 31 and covers wanting).

The New Testament, In Verse. *See* The History of the Holy Jesus, no. **587.54.**

941 The New Testament Of Our Lord And Savior, Jesus Christ: Translated From the Greek. Appointed to be read by Children. Hartford: Printed By John Babcock. 1798.

 fr.[2], t.[3], [4–5], 6–69, [70, adv.], [71, 2 cuts] p.; illus.; 13 cm.; bound in gold Dutch paper over oak bds.

 MWA*; CtHi (fr.[2], p.[7] & covers wanting); DLC; Evans 33417.

942.1 Newtestament [*sic. i.e.* New Testament] Stories and Parables, For Children. From Sidney's Press, New-Haven, 1808.

 fr.[ii], t.[1], [2–3], 4–61, [62, alphabet–63, 2 illus.] p.; illus.; 10.5 cm.; pr. & illus. buff paper covers.

 MWA*; Shaw 14493.

942.2 New Testament Stories. From Sidney's Press, New-Haven. 1809.

 fr.[ii], t.[1], [2–3], 4–35 p.; illus.; 13.5 cm.; pr. and illus. orange-yellow paper covers. Cover title imprint: Published by I. Cooke & Co. New-Haven. [5 lines adv.]. Copy A has a frontispiece of a boy and girl in a wood, a redrawn version of the frontispiece used in *The Tragical History Of The Children In The Wood,* no. **179.6.** The illustration on the front cover has a stump of a tree, a woodchopper with an ax and a little girl carrying a faggot of wood. The rear cover cut contains two dogs in a cart drawn by a dog, along side of which is a man holding a whip in his right hand. Below the picture are 23 lines of advertisement for Increase Cooke & Co. Opposite Butler's Tavern, New-Haven. Copy B has a frontispiece which shows a man seated at a table reading a book. The front cover has a picture of the dog in the manger. The rear cover has at the top of the page an illustration of a woman and a girl seated in a bower, on the left of the cut, and two women walking to the right. Below this are the same 23 lines of advertisement found in Copy A.

MWA-W° (Copy A); MWA° (Copy A, rear cover mut.); MWA-T° (Copy B); Shaw 18223.

942.3 ——— Boston: Printed and sold by Lincoln & Edmands, No. 53, Cornhill. 1810.

t.[2], [3], 4–39 p.; title page vignette only illus.; 10.5 cm.; marbled paper covers. Adv. by Lincoln & Edmands, 1809 in *The Friendly Instructor*.

MWA°; PP (p.[3]–4 mut., top of p. cut off); Shaw 19530.

942.4 ——— From Sidney's Press. For I. Cooke & Co. New-Haven. 1813.

fr.[2], t.[3], [4–5], 6–47 p.; 11 cm.; illus.; paper covers.

OOxM; Shaw 51324.

942.5 ——— Children: Containing A History Of Christ. [3 lines quot.] Middlebury, (Vt.) Printed By T. C. Strong. 1815.

t.[1], [2], 3–32 p.; 10.5 cm.; illus. buff paper covers.

Vt.°; McCorison 1714; Shaw 34086.

THE NEW TOKEN FOR CHILDREN. *See* Mosley, William, no. **903.1**.

THE NEWTONIAN SYSTEM OF PHILOSOPHY. *See* Newbery, John, no. **949.1**.

943 NEW YEAR'S GIFT. Boston: adv. by Lincoln & Edmands, 1819 in *Scripture Questions*.

944.1 A NEW-YEAR'S GIFT [2 lines of quot.] Mat. xxi. 16. Printed and Sold by Samuel Wood, No. 362, Pearl-Street, New-York. 1807.

fr.[2], t.[3], [4–31] p.; illus.; 10 cm.; green

Dutch paper covers. Adv. by Samuel Wood, 1808 in **643.1**.

MWA°; DLC; Shaw 13216.

944.2 ——— Printed and Sold by Samuel Wood, At the Juvenile Book-Store. No. 362, Pearl-Street, New-York. 1809.

fr.[2], t.[3], [4–31] p.; illus.; 10.5 cm.; illus. buff paper covers.

MWA°; CtHi; Shaw 18225; Weiss 1942.

944.3 ——— New-York: Printed And Sold By S. Wood, At The Juvenile Book-Store, No. 357, Pearl Street. 1810.

fr.[2], t.[3], [4–31] p.; illus.; 10 cm.; illus. undated brown paper covers.

MWA°; RPB.

944.4 ——— New-York: Printed And Sold By S. Wood, at the Juvenile Book-store, No. 357, Pearl-street. 1811.

fr.[2], t.[3], [4–31] p.; illus.; 10.5 cm.; pr. & illus. yellow paper covers.

MWA°; Shaw 23539.

944.5 ——— New-York: Printed And Sold By S. Wood, at the Juvenile Book-Store, No. 357, Pearl-street. 1812.

fr.[2], t.[3], [4–31] p.; illus.; 10 cm.; pr. & illus. paper covers.

DLC (fr.[2] & covers wanting).

944.6 ——— New-York: Printed And Sold By Samuel Wood, At the Juvenile Book-store, No. 357, Pearl-street. 1813.

t.[1], [2–30] p.; illus.; 10 cm.

RPB° (fr.[2], p. 31 & covers wanting); PP (covers wanting).

944.7 ——— New-York: Printed And Sold By Samuel Wood, At The Juvenile Book-Store, No. 357, Pearl-Street. 1814.

fr.[2], t.[3], [4–31] p.; illus.; 10 cm.; pr. & illus. paper covers; cover title dated 1813.

MWA° (fr.[2], t.[3], p.[4–6], [31] & covers mut.); PP; Shaw 32270.

944.8 ——— New-York: Printed And Sold By Samuel Wood, At The Juvenile Book-Store, No. 357, Pearl-Street. 1815.

t.[3], [4–30] p.; illus.; 10 cm.

MWA-W° (fr.[2], p.[31] & covers wanting).

944.9 ——— Nerv-York [*sic. i.e.* New-York]: Printed & Sold By S. Wood & Sons, At the Juvenile Book-store, No. 261, Pearl-street. 1817.

fr.[2], t.[3], [4–30] p.; illus.; 9.5 cm.; pr. & illus. brown paper covers; cover title undated. OOxM°.

944.10 ——— New-York: Published by Samuel Wood & Sons, No. 261, Pearl-street, And Samuel S. Wood & Co. No. 212, Market-st. 1818.

fr.[2], t.[3], [4–30] p.; illus.; 10 cm.; paper covers.

CtHi°; MWA; Shaw 51807.

944.11 ——— New-York: Published by Samuel Wood & Sons, No. 261, Pearl-street; And Samuel S. Wood & Co. No. 212, Market-st. Baltimore. 1819.

fr.[2], t.[3], [4–30] p.; illus.; 11 cm.; green Dutch paper covers.

MWA°; CLU; DLC (covers wanting); Shaw 48875 and 48876 (26 p. is incorrect).

945.1 The New Year's Gift. Philadelphia: adv. by Young and M'Culloch, 1787 in **249.2**.

945.2 The New Year's Gift. Containing, diverting and instructive Histories. Philadelphia: adv. by William Young, 1794 in **305**, and 1795 in *Sermons For Children.*

946 A New-Year's Gift, Or Conversations On Several Subjects Of Importance. Published By Johnson & Warner, And Sold At Their Bookstores, Philadelphia, And Richmond, Virginia. A. Fagan, Printer. 1813.

fr.[2], t.[3], [4–5], 6–71 p.; illus.; t.[13] 14 cm.; pr. & illus. pink paper covers.

MWA°; NNC-Pl; Shaw 29324.

The New Year's Gift. *See* Butcher, E. Rev., no. **140**.

947 The New-Year's Gift; Or, The First Book To teach every little Girl and Boy The A B C. Containing The Life and Death of the Apple-Pye, With A was an Archer, Cock Robin's Farewell to all the Birds in the Air, And Naughty Boy Jack. New York: adv. by Hugh Gaine, 1774 in **275.1**.

948.1 A New-Year's Gift, Written A Few Years Ago, By a young Woman in England. And presented to her Nieces and Nephews And Now Re-Published, With desires that it may prove a Blessing to the young and rising generation of both Sexes, unto whom it is at this time affectionately addressed, wherever it may come. To Which Is Annexed, A Few Lines On Procrastination. Concord [N.H.]: Printed By Hough And Russell. M,DCC,XCII.

t.[1], [2–3], 4–8 p.; 18 cm.; verse.

MWA°; DLC; NhD (p.[1]–4, 7–8 torn); Evans 25894.

948.2 ——— Newburyport [Mass.]—Printed For The Purchasers. 1806.

t.[1], [2–3], 4–8 p.; 19 cm.; in verse. MSaE°.

[NEWBERY, JOHN], *ed.* 1713–1767

949.1 [—] The Newtonian System Of Philosophy; Explained By Familiar Objects, In An Entertaining Manner, For The Use Of Young Ladies And Gentlemen, By Tom Telescope, A.M. Illustrated with Copperplates and Cuts. A New Improved Edition, With many alterations and Additions to explain the late New Philosophical Discoveries, &c. &c. By A Teacher Of Philadelphia. Philadelphia: Published By Jacob Johnson, No. 147, High-Street. 1803.

fr.[ii], t.[i], [ii–iv], [1], 2–137, [138], [139–140 adv.] p.; 5 engr. pl. including front.; 17 cm.; bound in leather; pl. opp. p. 5 & 128 signed *W.R. sc.* [William Ralph].

English & Irish ed. title 1: ——— *Philosophy Adapted to the Capacities of young Gentlemen and Ladies, and familiarized and made entertaining by Objects with which they are intimately acquainted: Being The Substance of Six Lectures read to the Lilliputian Society, By Tom Telescope, A.M. And collected and methodized for the Benefit of the Youth of these Kingdoms, By their old Friend Mr. Newbery, in St. Paul's Church Yard; . . .* London: J. Newbery, 1761.

MWA°; CLU; CSmH; CtHi; MH (fr.[ii] & 2 pl. wanting); MiU (p. [iii]–6, 129–130 & pl. 3 wanting); PHi; PPL; ViU; Shaw 5146.

949.2 [—] ——— Illustrated with Copperplates and Cuts. Second Philadelphia Edition: With Notes And Additions, By Robert Patterson. Professor Of Mathematics, In The University Of Pennsylvania. Philadelphia: Published By Johnson &

Warner, No. 147, Market Street. 1808. Lydia R. Railey [*sic. i.e.* Bailey], Printer, No. 10, North Alley.

> fr.[ii], t.[iii], [iv--vi], [1], 2–140 p.; illus.; 17 cm.; bound in leather; 5 engr. pl. including front. Front. signed *W. Ralph sc.* pl. opp. p. 5, 131 signed *W.R. sc.* [William Ralph].
> Welch°; MH; MWA; NN-C (fr.[ii] & pl. wanting); NN (2 copies); NNC-T; NcD; PP; PU; Shaw 16292.

949.3 [—] ——— Lydia R. Bailey, Printer, No. 10, North Alley. Variant of the preceding with "Bailey" spelled correctly on the title page.

> Shaw 15852 and 16291.

NEWTON, JOHN

950.1 — < No. 83. An Account Of Eliza Cunningham. By John Newton. [caption title p. [1]] Andover: Printed For The New England Tract Society By Flagg And Gould. 1817. < 1st edit. 6000. [colophon p. 8].

> [1], 2–8 p.; 19.5 cm.; also numbered [205], 206–212 p.
> MWA°; Shaw 41660.

950.2 — < No. 83. ——— John Newton. [caption title p. [1]] Andover [Mass.]: Printed For The New England Tract Society By Flagg And Gould. 1819. < 4th edit. 6000.

> t.[1], 2–8 p.; 16.5 cm.; also numbered [205], 206–212 p.
> MB° (bound with other tracts of *The Publications Of The New England Tract Society. Vol. IV. Andover: Flagg and Gould. 1820*); Shaw 48928.

951 [—] (No. 6) The Life Of Eliza Cunningham. Published By The Philadelphia Female Tract Society And for sale at their Depository, No. 77, South Second Street. [caption title] Printed by Lydia R. Bailey, No. 10, North Alley, Philad. [1816] [colophon p. 16].

> [1], 2–16 p.; 14 cm.
> MWA° (bound with other tracts with which *The First Annual Report Of The Philadelphia Female Tract Society For The Year 1816* was originally bound); Shaw 38467.

952 [—] Series Of Evangelical Tracts No. 3. Published By Lincoln & Edmands. A Monument To The Praise Of The Lord's Goodness. And

To The Memory Of Eliza Cunningham. [caption p.[1]]. Printed & Published By Lincoln & Edmands, No. 53 Cornhill. Boston, Who publish . . . [4 lines] 1813. Price 33 cts. doz. 2,25 per hun. [colophon p. 12].

> MWA° (bound with other tracts in *Evangelical Tracts. Doctrinal, And Practical. vol. I. Boston: Lincoln & Edmands, 1813*).

953 Nourjahad. Adorned With Cuts. London: Printed For N. Hailes, Juvenile Library, London Museum, Piccadilly. 1817.

> fr.[ii], t.[1], [2–3], 4–92, [93–94, adv. of 4 books] p.; illus.; 6.5 cm.; pr. buff paper covers. Cover title: Nourjahad. Adorned With Cuts. London: N. Hailes, London Museum, Piccadilly. W. Jackson, 71 Maiden-Lane, New-York. Price Sixpence. An English book with an American imprint on the cover title.
> English ed. London: Tabart And Co., 1805. Adomeit.°

NURSE TRUELOVE *pseud.*

954.1 Nurse Truelove's Christmas Box. Worcester: adv. by I. Thomas, 1787 in **906.2**, and 1788 in **685**.

954.2 Nurse Truelove's Christmas Box: Or The Golden Plaything For Little Children. B[y] which they may learn the Le[tters] as soon as they can speak, and [know] how to behave so as to make e[very] Body love them. Hartford [:] Printed by Nathaniel Pat[ten] D,DCC,LXXX,IX [*sic. i.e.* M, DCC, LXXX,IX].

> fr.[2], t.[3], 4–26 p.; illus.; 10 cm.
> English & Irish ed. London: adv. by John Newbery in the *General Advertiser*, Jan. 9, 1750.
> CtHi° (2 leaves wanting, p. 27–30?); Evans 45546.

954.3 ——— The Second Worcester Edition. Printed at Worcester. Massachusetts, By Isaiah Thomas, Sold at his Bookstore, and by Thomas and Andrews in Boston. MDCCLXXXIX.

> fr.[2], t.[3], 4–27, [28–30 adv. list of books], [31, cut] p.; illus. 10 cm.; illus.; buff paper covers.
> MWA°; Evans 22188.

954.4 The Christmas Box [probably stands for Nurse Truelove's Christmas Box] Philadelphia: adv. by Francis Bailey, 1793 in **773.1**.

954.5 [——] [Boston: Printed and sold by S. Hall, No. 53, Cornhill. 1794?].

fr.[2], t.[3], [4], 5–26 p.; illus.; 10 cm.; orange paper covers. Adv. by S. Hall, 1791 in **408.3**; 1792 in **587.33** and **1408.33**; 1793 in **955.3**; 1794 in **1283.4**; and 1796 in **587.40**.
MWA° (t.[3], p. [4] wanting except for a fragment, p. 27–31 wanting; p. 5–6 mut.); Evans 47143.

954.6 —— The Third Worcester Edition. Printed at Worcester, Massachusetts, By Thomas, Son & Thomas, Sold at their Bookstore. MDCC-XCVI.

fr.[2], t.[3], 4–29, [30] p.; illus.; 10 cm.; illus. blue paper covers.
MWA°; Evans 31317.

954.7 —— Charleston [Mass.]: Printed and Sold by S. Etheridge. 1802.

fr.[2], t.[3], 4–29, [30–31] p.; illus.; 9 cm.; Dutch paper covers.
MWA° (fr.[2], p.[31] mut.).

954.8 —— Worcester: Printed by I Thomas, Jun. Sold Wholesale and Retail at his Book Store. 1805.

fr.[2], t.[3], [4], 5–30, [31, 2 cuts] p.; illus.; 10.5 cm.; dark blue paper covers. The date on the MWA copy is not clear and could be mistaken for 1806.
MWA (fr.[2], p. 31 and covers wanting); Shaw 11051 (wrongly dated 1806).

955.1 Nurse Truelove's New-Year's Gift: Or, The Book of Books for Children. Adorned With Cuts. And designed for a present to every little Boy who would become a great Man, and ride upon a fine Horse; and to every little Girl, who would become a fine Woman, and ride in a Govenour's Coach. But let us turn over the leaf and see more of the Matter. The First Worcester Edition. Worcester, (Massachusetts) Printed By Isaiah Thomas And Sold At His Bookstore. MDCC-LXXXVI.

fr.[2], t.[3], [4–5], 6–58, [59–62 adv. list of books], [63, illus.] p.; illus.; 10 cm.; illus. paper covers; p. 31–40: The House That Jack Built. English & Irish ed. London: adv. by [J. Newbery] in the *Public Advertiser*, Dec. 18, 1753.
MWA°; MH (p. 45–48, 57–58 wanting); PP (fr.[2], p. 63 & covers wanting); Evans 20033.

955.2 —— Girl, who would become great Men and Women. Plymouth [Mass.]: Printed And Sold By Nathaniel Coverly. M,DCCLXXX-VII.

t.[1], [2–3], 4–32 p.; illus.; 9.5 cm.; yellow paper covers. "The House That Jack Built" is not in this edition. Many woodcuts in the text were used by N. Coverly in his edition of *The History . . . Of Little Goody Two-Shoes*, 1783 in **463.2**.
MWA°; Evans 45117.

955.3 —— [same as **955.1**] Boston: Printed and sold by Samuel Hall, in Cornhill. 1793.

t.[3], [4–5], 6–58, [59–62, adv. list of books], [63, illus. & prose] p.; illus.; 10 cm.; Dutch paper covers. The advertisement caption p. [59]: *A great Variety of* BOOKS,/*for Children, to be sold by* S. Hall,/*in Cornhill, Boston; among which are/the following, viz.* On p.[62] no. 28 reads: Tommy Trip's Pictures of Beasts & Birds, with a familiar Description of each, in Verse and Prose. Published for the Benefit of little Masters and Misses of the United States of America. < This Book contains Pictures of 70 different Birds and Beasts of the most curious kinds. >
MLuHi°; MWA; Evans 26284.

955.4 The New-Year's Gift [probably Nurse Truelove's New-Year's Gift] Philadelphia: adv. by Francis Bailey, 1793 in **773.1**.

955.5 —— [same as **955.1**] The Second Worcester Edition. Printed at Worcester, Massachusetts, By Isaiah Thomas, And Sold Wholesale and Retail, at his Book-Store. MDCCXCIV.

fr.[2], t.[3], [4–5], 6–54 p.; illus.; 10.5 cm.; Dutch paper covers; p. 31–40: The House That Jack Built.
MWA° (rear cover and all after p. 54 wanting); Evans 27820.

955.6 —— Children [remainder of the title wanting] [Boston: Printed and sold by S. Hall, No. 53, Cornhill. 1796?] [imaginary title copied from 1793 ed.].

fr.[2], t.[3], [4–5], 6–58, [59–62, adv. list of books] p.; illus.; 10 cm.; Dutch paper covers; p. 31–40: The House That Jack Built. Advertisement caption p. [59]: *A great Variety of* BOOKS/*for Children, to be sold by* S. Hall,/

in *Cornhill, Boston; among which are/the fol-lowing,* viz. The first two lines of the caption match the advertisement caption in S. Hall's 1796 edition of *The History Of The Holy Jesus,* no. **587.40,** also without a comma after the word "Books". The last two lines match the advertisement caption in the 1793 edition, **955.3** and S. Hall's 1793 edition of *The Royal Alphabet,* no. **1132.2,** in everything except the word *"viz"* which in both these books is printed in italics but not in no. **955.3.** On p. [62] no. 23: [*Pictures*] *of seventy-two Beasts and* [*Birds*] *with a familiar description of each,* [*in verse*] *and prose.* . . . An edition with the title *Pictures Of Seventy-Two Beasts & Birds,* no. **997,** was published in 1796. In S. Hall's 1796 ed. of *The History Of The Holy Jesus,* no. **587.40,** both *Nurse Truelove's New Year's Gift* and *Pictures*

of Seventy-Two Beasts & Birds are advertised. Because of these advertisements and the simi-larity of the first two lines of the advertisement caption in **587.40,** this edition of *Nurse True-love's New-Year's Gift* is dated [1796].

MWA-W° (t.[3] mut. with lower two-thirds of the page cut away; fr.[2], p. 61–62 and front cover mut., rear cover & p.[63] wanting); NN-C (fr.[2], t.[3] & p. 61–62 wanting, p.[5]–6½ wanting, p. 7–10, [31]–32 mut.); Evans 47872.

955.7 ———— Third Worcester Edition. Printed at Worcester, Massachusetts, By Isaiah Thomas, Jun. Sold Wholesale and Retail by Him. 1800.
fr.[2], t.[3], [4–5], 6–60 p.; illus.; 10 cm.
MWA-W° (original covers wanting); Evans 49126.

O

OAKMAN, JOHN

956 MORAL SONGS, For The Instruction And Amusement Of Children; Intended As A Companion To Dr. Watts' Divine Songs. By John Oakman, And Others. Philadelphia: Published By Benjamin Johnson, No. 249, Market Street. 1806.

t.[1], [2–3], 4–48 p.; illus.; 18 cm.; bound in brown paper over bds., leather spine; bound with *Divine Songs For Children. By Isaac Watts DD. Philadelphia. Benjamin Johnson.* Cuts on p.[1], 26, 28, 47 signed A [Alexander Anderson]. *See* no. **1409.1**.

English ed. London: Darton And Harvey, 1802. Welch°; MWA (bound in blue marbled paper over bds.); OOxM; PP; Shaw 11052.

[O'KEEFFE, ADELAIDE] 1776–1855

957.1 [—] ORIGINAL POEMS; Calculated To Improve The Mind Of Youth, And Allure It To Virtue. By Adelade. Part II. Ornamented With Elegant Engravings. Philadelphia. Published By Johnson & Warner, No. 147 Market-Street. Brown & Merritt Printers, No. 24, Church-alley. 1809.

fr.[ii], t.[1], [2–3], 4–16, [pl. opp. p. 16] p.; 8 pl. including front.; 12.5 cm.; wallpaper covers. A Philadelphia ed. published by Benjamin Warner in 1821 has the cover title dated 1809 and is identical with the title page of no. **957.1**. It was probably the original cover used for the above 1809 ed.

MWA° (rear cover wanting); NNC-Pl (covers wanting); PP° (1821 ed. with cover title dated 1809); Shaw 18284.

957.2 [—] —— Part I. Ornamented With Elegant Engravings. Philadelphia. Published By Johnson & Warner, No. 147, Market-Street, Brown & Merritt, Printers, No. 24, Church-alley, 1810.

fr.[ii], t.[1], [2–3], 4–14, [15–16], [pl. 8] opp. p.[16]] p.; 8 pl. including front.; 13 cm.; yellow paper covers; front. signed N. Charles Sculp.

English ed. London: Harris, 1808. CLU (7 pl.); DLC (pl.[7], [8] wanting); MWA (pl.[7] & covers wanting); PP; PPL; Shaw 20949.

958.1. OLD AGE [2 lines of quot.] Printed & Sold by Samuel Wood, at the Juvenile Book-store, No. 357, Pearl-Street, New-York. 1810.

t.[1], [2–16] p.; illus.; 8 cm.; buff paper covers ornamented with a design in black. MWA°; Shaw 20951.

958.2 —— Printed & sold by Samuel Wood, at the Juvenile Bookstore, No. 357, Pearl-street, New-York. 1811.

t.[1], [2–16], p.; illus.; 8 cm.; pink covers. Welch°; MWA (black paper covers); Shaw 23595.

958.3 —— New-York: Printed & sold by Samuel Wood, at the Juvenile Book-store, No. 357, Pearl-street. 1813.

t.[1], [2–16] p.; illus.; 8.5 cm.; pr. & illus. buff paper covers. Cover title: Old Age. Sold By Samuel Wood. New-York. MWA°; PP.

958.4 —— New-York: Printed & sold by Samuel Wood, at the Juvenile Book-store, No. 357, Pearl street. 1814.

t.[1], [2–16] p.; illus.; 8.5 cm. MWA-W° (bound with other books in no. **637.1**); PP.

958.5 —— Nerv-York [*sic. i.e.* New-York]: Printed And Sold By S. Wood, at the Juvenile Book-store, No. 357, Pearl-street. 1815.

t.[1], [2–16] p.; illus.; 8.5 cm.; pr. & illus. buff paper covers. Cover title: Sold by Samuel Wood, New-York. MWA°.

958.6 —— New-York: Printed And Sold By Samuel Wood & Sons, at the Juvenile Book-store, No. 357, Pearl-street. 1816.

t.[1], [2–16] p.; illus.; 8.5 cm.; pr. & illus. buff-yellow paper covers; Cover title: Old Age. Sold by Samuel Wood & Sons, New-York. MWA-W°; MWA; NNC-T; Shaw 38516.

958.7 —— Nerv-York [*sic. i.e.* New York]: Published by Samuel Wood & Sons, No. 261, Pearl-street. And Samuel S. Wood & Co., No. 212, Market-st. Baltimore. 1818.

t.[1], [2–16] p.; illus.; 8 cm.; pr. & illus. buff paper covers.

Cover title: Old Age. Sold by Samuel Wood & Sons, New-York, And Samuel S. Wood & Co. Baltimore.

MWA-W°; CtHi; MH; PP; Shaw 45150.

959.1 OLD DAME MARGERY's HUSH-A-BYE: Embellished With Fifteen Elegant Engravings On Copper-Plates. Philadelphia: Published By Jacob Johnson, No 147 Market Street. Whitehall [Pa.]. Printed by A. Dickinson. 1807.

t.[2], fr.[i], [ii–iii, bl.], [iv, pl. opp. p.[3]]. [3–16] p.; 8 pl. including front.; 10 cm.; pr. paper covers. Contents a collection of nursery rhymes.

MSaE°.

959.2 —— Philadelphia: Published By Johnson & Warner, No. 147 Market-Street. Ann Coles, Printer. 1814.

t.[1], [2, bl.], [pl. opp. p. [2]], [pl. opp. p. [3]], [3–16] p.; 1 full page pl., 7 pl. in two compartments; 12 cm.; pink paper covers. Eighteen of the twenty nursery rhymes in the book are the same or show slight variations from ODNR. The one on p. [5] not in ODNR, is "Tom Tinker's Dog." *Bow, wow, wow./Whose dog are thou?/Little Tom Tinker's dog,/Bow, wow, wow.* An interesting variation of "A was an Archer, and shot at a Frog," ODNR p. 48, is "The Alphabet In Verse." *A—was an Archer, you saw on the heath;/B—was a Beauty that shew'd her white teeth,* p. [8–9]. Part of a publisher's remainder.

MWA°; CLU; DLC; NHi; PP; PPL; Shaw 32399.

959.3 —— Bye, And Hymns For Infant Minds. Adorned With Cuts. Sidney's Press. New Haven, 1817.

fr.[2], t.[3], [4–5], 6–30, [31, adv.] p.; illus.; 10.5 cm.; illus. buff paper covers.

NNC-T° (front cover wanting, rear cover worn).

959.4 —— Bye, And Little Hymns. Adorned With Cuts. From Sidney's Press, For John Babcock And Son. 1818.

fr.[2], t.[3], [4], 5–30, [31, adv.] p.; illus.; 10 cm.; illus. paper covers printed in pink ink. Adv. by J. Babcock & Son, 1819 in **481.6**.

CtY°; PP.

OLD FRIENDS IN A NEW DRESS Or Familiar Fables In Verse. *See* Sharpe, Richard Scrafton, no. **1190**.

960.1 OLD GRAND-PAPA, And Other Poems For The Amusement Of Children. By A Young Lady. Embellished With Wood Engravings, Philadelphia: Printed For Benjamin Warner, No. 147, Market Street. Lydia Bailey Printer. 1817.

t.[1], [2–3], 4–48 p.; illus.; 16 cm.

English ed. London: Darton, Harvey And Darton, 1812.

MH° (covers wanting, p. 3–4 mut.); RPB (t. [1], & p.[2] wanting); Shaw 41692.

960.2 —— Of Children. New-York: Published By Samuel Wood & Sons, No. 261, Pearl-Street; And Samuel S. Wood & Co. No. 212, Market-street, Baltimore. 1818.

t.[1], [2–3], 4–66 p.; illus.; 14 cm.; pr. & illus. yellow paper covers; cover title undated.

MWA° (rear cover wanting); MH; Shaw 45155.

OLD MOTHER HUBBARD. *See* Martin, Sarah Catherine, no. **817.1**.

961.1 THE OLIO. [cut] Lambert's Leap. New-York: Printed And Sold By Samuel Wood, No. 357, Pearl-Street. 1813.

t.[1], [2–3], 4–48 p.; illus.; 13.5 cm.; pr. & illus. buff paper covers.

MWA°; Shaw 29411.

961.2 —— New-York: Printed And Sold By Samuel Wood, At The Juvenile Book-Store, No. 357, Pearl-Street. 1815.

t.[1], [2–3], 4–48 p.; illus.; 13.5 cm.

NHi° (bound with other books in no. **191**, vol. 1); PP (bound with other books in no. **191**, vol. 1)

961.3 —— New-York: Printed And Sold By Samuel Wood & Sons, At The Juvenile Book-Store, No. 357, Pearl-Street. 1816.

t.[1], [2–3], 4–48 p.; illus.; 14 cm.; pr. & illus. buff paper covers.

MWA°; CtY (p.27–30 mut.); MSaE; N; NNC-LS; Shaw 38518.

961.4 ——— New-York: Published By Samuel Wood & Sons, No. 261 Pearl-street; And Samuel S. Wood & Co. No. 212, Market-[Street] Baltimore. 1820.

t.[1], [2–3], 4–48 p.; illus.; 13.5 cm.; pr. & illus. paper covers; cover title undated.

RPB° (t.[1] mut.).

OPIE, AMELIA (ALDERSON) 1769–1853
962.1 — THE BLACK VELVET PELISSE, And The Mother And Son. From The Tales Of Mrs. Opie. New-York: Printed and Published by Elliot & Crissy, 114 Water-street; sold also by T. Powers, 116 Broadway; A. Devillers, Charleston [S.C.]; Bonsall, Conrad & Co., Norfolk [Va.]; Somerville & Co. Petersburgh; and Warner & Hanna, Baltimore. 1810.

t.[1], [2–3], 4–87 p.; title vignette only illus.; 14.5 cm.; bound in blue paper over bds., orange paper spine.

Mrs. Opie's novels are not considered children's books. The above appears to have been issued as a child's book in printed paper covers. In the New-York edition printed by John Low it is advertised among a list of "Books For Children."

MWA°; RPB; Shaw 20957.

962.2 —— ——— Pelisse. From The Tales Of Mrs. Opie. Boston: Published By Thomas Wells, No. 3, Hanover Street. J. Eliot, Printer. 1815.

fr.[ii], t.[1], [2–3], 4–32, [33] p.; front. & title vignette only illus.; 14.5 cm.; pink paper covers.

MWA°; CCamarSJ; KU; MiD (rear cover wanting); PP; Shaw 35538.

962.3 [—] ——— Pelisse, Or The Reward of Generosity, Exemplified In The Character Of Miss Julia Beresford. Ornamented With Cuts. New-York: Printed And Sold By John Low, No. 17 Chatham-Street. 1815.

t.[3], [4–5], 6–36 p.; illus.; 14 cm.; pr. gray-green paper covers; cover title dated 1815; rear cover adv. list of books for children.

MWA-W°; MB; MnU; MSaE; Shaw 34137.

963 THE ORATOR. New York: adv. by T. B. Jansen, [ca. 1815] in **47**.

964 ORIGINAL AND SELECT JUVENILE HYMNS. Adapted To the Use of Free Schools; more particularly to those called Sunday or Sabbath Schools. New-York: Printed And Sold By Samuel Wood & Sons, At The Juvenile Book-Store, No. 261, Pearl-Street. 1817.

fr.[ii], t.[1], [2–3], 4–68 p.; 14.5 cm.; pr. & illus. paper covers. Adv. by Samuel Wood, 1819 in **1188.8**, and 1820 in **274.2**.

NB°; NHi.

ORIGINAL HYMNS FOR SABBATH SCHOOLS. *See* Gilbert, Ann (Taylor), no. **443.1**.

ORIGINAL POEMS; Calculated To Improve The Minds Of Youth. *See* O'Keeffe, Adelaide, no. **957.1**.

ORIGINAL POEMS FOR INFANT MINDS. *See* Gilbert, Ann (Taylor), no. **444.1**.

ORIGINAL TALES NEVER BEFORE PUBLISHED. *See* Fitz, Daniel, no. **413.1**.

ORIGINAL TALES; WRITTEN FOR THE IMPROVEMENT OF YOUTH. *See* Fitz, Daniel, no. **413.2**.

THE ORNAMENTS DISCOVERED. *See* Hughes, Mary (Robson), no. **622**.

THE ORPHAN. *See* Richmond, Legh, no. **1110**.

THE ORPHAN BOY. *See* Elliot, Mary (Belson), no. **345.1**.

965 THE ORPHAN BOY. New-York: Published By D. Wickham, At the Sunday School Depository, No. 59 Fulton-street. 1820. [cover title].

t.[1], 2–24 p.; front cover title vignette only illus.; 13 cm.; pr. & illus. buff paper covers.

MWA-T°.

THE ORPHAN SISTERS. *See* P., M. A., no. **969**.

966.1 THE ORPHANS, Or, Honesty Rewarded. Ornamented with Copper-plate Engravings. Philadelphia: Published By Bennett And Walton, No. 31, Market Street. 1808.

fr.[ii], t.[1], [2–3], 4–34, [35, adv.] p.; 3 pl. including front.; 14 cm.; blue marbled paper covers.

English ed. London: J. Harris, 1804.

MWA° (col. pl.); PP; NjP (bound with other books); Hamilton 269; Shaw 15822.

966.2 ——— Embellished With Three Copper-Plate Engravings. Philadelphia: Published By Jacob Johnson, No. 147, Market-Street. 1808.

fr.[ii], t.[1], [2–3], 4–36 p.; 3 pl. including front.; 13.5 cm.; pr. & illus. blue marbled paper covers; p.[2]: Adams, Printer, Philadelphia. Adv. by Johnson & Warner, 1814 in **1449.3**.
MWA*; MWA-W (p. 23–36 & 1 pl. wanting); OOxM; ScU; Shaw 15823.

966.3 ——— Together With Select Hymns. Adorned With Cuts. From Sidney's Press New-Haven. 1817.

fr.[2], t.[3], [4–5], 6–46, [47] p.; illus.; 13 cm.; illus. buff paper covers.
CtHi*; Shaw 41710.

967 OUR SAVIOR. A Poem By a Christian. Illustrated With Engravings Philadelphia Published and sold by Wm. Charles Price Plain 12½ cents Coloured 18¾ cents. 1816. [cover title].

[1–6] p. engr. on one side only of 6 leaves; 13 cm.; pr. yellow-buff paper covers.
CtHi*; DLC (rear cover wanting); NjR; NNC-Pl; RPB (colored illus., p. 6 mut.); Shaw 38538; Weiss 1932, p. 10.

P

P—, C. [PALMER, CHARLOTTE]
968 — THREE INSTRUCTIVE TALES FOR CHIL-
DREN: Simple And Careful, Industry And Sloth,
And The Cousins. By C.P—, Boston: Printed By
Hosea Sprague. No. 44, Marlboro' Street. 1802.
    t.[1], [2–3], 4–61 p.; 10.5 cm.; blue paper
covers.
    See also no. **646.1.**
    English ed. London: adv. by E. Newbery in
The Triumph Of Good-nature. [1800].
    PP*.

P., M. A.
969 [—] THE ORPHAN SISTERS. Boston: Wells
And Lilly, Court-Street. 1820.
    t.[1], [2–3], 4–88 p.; 14 cm.; end of text p. 88
signed: M.A.P.
    MWA* (covers wanting); Shoemaker 2630.

THE PANORAMA OF YOUTH. *See* Sterndale, Mary,
no. **1255.**

970 PAPA'S PRESENT; Or, Pictures Of Animals,
With Descriptions In Verse. New-York; Published
by Samuel Wood and Sons, No. 261, Pearl-Street;
And Samuel S. Wood & Co. No. 212, Market-st.
Baltimore. [1821? or later].
    t.[1], [2–3], 4–31 p.; illus.; 12.5 cm.; pr. paper
covers. Cover title imprint, same as the title
page, but "New-York" spelled "Nerv-York."
Adv. by Samuel Wood, 1820 in *The Decoy*,
New York. The [1821?] edition is the only edition located and is included to represent what
the 1820 edition may have been.
    English ed. London: Darton, Harvey And Dar-
ton, 1819.
    NB (p. 9–24 wanting).

971 THE PARENT'S PRESENT TO THEIR HAPPY
FAMILY; Containing the Poems of My Father,
Mother, Sister, & Brother, In Imitation of Cowper's
Mary. Embellished With Fifty Fine Engravings.
Published By Johnson & Warner, And Sold At
Their Bookstores, Philadelphia And Richmond,
Virginia. A. Fagan, Printer. 1813.
    fr.[2], t.[3], [4–6], 7–101 p. paged continu-
ously, but printed on one side only of 50 leaves,

with the even-numbered pages [4]–100 blank;
illus.; 14 cm.; pr. pink paper covers.
    English ed. London: J. Arliss. [1809], paper
watermarked 1808, holograph date *1810*.
    MWA*; NcD; NHi; NN (rear cover wanting);
Shaw 29436.

972 THE PARLOUR TEACHER. Philada. Printed by
Jacob Johnson 147, Market Street. 1804.
    t.[1], [2–32] p.; illus.; 16 cm. Adv. by Johnson
& Warner, 1814 in **1449.2.**
    English ed. London: W. Darton & J. Harvey,
1802.
    NNC-LS* (covers wanting); DLC (gray mar-
bled paper covers); PP (p.[1–6], [23–28]
wanting); Shaw 6989.

PARNELL, THOMAS 1679–1718 and OLIVER
GOLDSMITH 1728–1774
973.1 [—] THE HERMIT AND THE TRAVELLER
New-York: Printed And Sold By Samuel Wood.
At the Juvenile Book-Store, No. 357, Pearl-Street.
1813.
    t.[1], [2–3], 4–48 p.; illus.; 14 cm.
    English ed. *The Hermit* first appeared in
Thomas Parnell's *Poems on several occasions.*
London: B. Lintot, 1722.
    English ed. *The Traveller* by Oliver Goldsmith.
London: J. Newbery, 1765.
    MWA* (covers wanting); DLC; NHi (pr. &
illus. green paper covers); Shaw 28651 and
29445.

973.2 [—] ——— New-York: Printed And Sold
By Samuel Wood, At The Juvenile Book-Store,
No. 357, Pearl-Street. 1814.
    t.[1], [2–3], 4–48 p.; illus.; 13.5 cm.; pr. &
illus. buff-yellow paper covers.
    MWA-W*; MHa; MWA (2 copies; copy 2,
bound with other books in vol. II of no. **191**);
Shaw 31597; 31697 and 32440.

973.3 [—] ——— New-York: Printed And Sold
By Samuel Wood & Sons, At The Juvenile Book-
Store, No. 357, Pearl-Street. 1816.
    t.[1], [2–3], 4–48 p.; illus.; 14 cm.; pr. & illus.
buff paper covers. Cover imprint: Printed ———

[same as title] Pearl-Street, Nerv-York [*sic. i.e.* New-York].

MWA*; CSmH; NN; PHi; PP; PPL; RPB (covers wanting); Shaw 38560; Weiss 1936, p. 274.

973.4 [—] ——— New York: Published By Samuel Wood & Sons, No. 261, Pearl-Street; And Samuel S. Wood & Co. No. 212, Market-street, Baltimore. 1818.

t.[1], [2–3], 4–48 p.; illus.; 14 cm.; pr. & illus. buff paper covers.

Cover title imprint copy 1: Nerv-York [*sic. i.e.* New-York]: Published By ——— [same wording and type as t.[1] in 4 lines] Baltimore.

Cover title imprint copy 2: Nerv-York [*sic. i.e.* New-York]: Published By Samuel Wood & Sons, No. 261, Pearl-Street, And By Samuel S. Wood & Co. No. 212, Market-street. Baltimore.

MWA* (copy 1, 2); CtHi; ICU; RPB (covers wanting); Shaw 45209.

974 THE PARROT'S ALPHABET. Philadelphia: adv. by E. & R. Parker, 1818 in **704.1**.

975.1 PASTORAL LESSONS, AND PARENTAL CONVERSATIONS, Intended As A Companion, To E. [*sic. i.e.* A. L.] Barbauld's Hymns In Prose. Philadelphia: Printed By B. Johnson, No. 31, High-Street. 1803.

t.[1], [2–3], 4–96 p.; 12.5 cm.; bound in green paper over bds., blue paper spine. The advertisement p. 4 is dated London, 1797.

English ed. London: 2 ed. Darton and Harvey, 1797.

CLU*.

975.2 ——— E. [*sic. i.e.* A. L.] Barbauld's Hymns In Prose. New-York: Printed And Sold By Samuel Wood, At The Juvenile Book-Store, No. 357, Pearl-Street. 1813.

t.[1], [2–5], 6–68 p.; 14 cm.; bound in gray-green paper over bds., leather spine.

MWA*; DLC; Shaw 29451.

975.3 ——— New-York: Printed And Sold By Samuel Wood & Sons, At The Juvenile Book-Store, No. 357, Pearl-Street. 1816.

t.[1], [2–5], 6–68 p.; 14 cm.; bound in blue-gray paper over bds., leather spine.

MWA*; Shaw 38562.

976 PATERNAL ADVICE TO CHILDREN. To Which Is Prefixed, A Short Narrative Of The Awful Event

By Which It Was Occasioned. Philadelphia: Published by the Sunday and Adult School Union. Clark & Raser, Printers. 1818.

[1], [2–3], 4–32 p.; 10 cm.; pr. blue paper covers; cover title dated 1818.

MWA*; Shaw 45212.

THE PATERNAL PRESENT. *See* Pratt, Samuel Jackson, no. **1045.1**.

PATHS OF VIRTUE DELINEATED. *See* Richardson, Samuel, no. **1102.1**.

977 PATHS OF VIRTUE, EXEMPLIFIED IN THE LIVES OF EMINENT MEN AND WOMEN. Interspersed With Moral Reflections. The First American Edition. Philadelphia: Printed and sold by Daniel Lawrence, No. 33, North 4th Street, near Race. MDCC.XCII.

t.[i], [ii, bl.], iii–v, [vi, bl.], [7], 8–167 p.; 13.5 cm.; bound in brown paper speckled with black over bds., leather spine.

English ed. London: F. Newbery, 1777.

MWA*; Evans 46537.

PATIENT JOE. *See* More, Hannah, no. **890**.

PATTY PRIMROSE; Or The Parsonage House. *See* Peacock, Lucy, no. **968**.

PATTY PROUD. *See* The New Instructive History Of Miss Patty Proud, no. **937.1**.

PEACOCK, LUCY 1786–1815

[—] AMBROSE AND ELEANOR. *See* Ducray Duminil, Francois Guillaume, no. **300.1**.

978 [—] PATTY PRIMROSE; Or, The Parsonage House. By The Author Of "A Visit for a Week," &c. &c. Philadelphia: Published By Benjamin Warner, No. 147, Market-Street. 1817.

fr.[ii], t.[1], [2–3], 4–72 p.; front. only illus.; 14 cm.; pr. green paper covers.

English ed. London: Darton, Harvey, And Darton, 1810.

PP*; CLU; DLC; MSaE (t.[1] wanting); NNC-Pl (fr.[ii] wanting).

979.1 [—] VISIT FOR A WEEK, Or, Hints on the Improvement of Time. Containing, Original Tales, Entertaining Stories, Interesting Anecdotes, And Sketches From Natural and Moral History. To

Which Is Added, A Poetical Appendix, Designed
For The Amusement Of Youth. [4 lines quot.]
Voltaire. Embellished With An Elegant Frontispiece. Philadelphia Printed By Ormrod And Conrad, No. 41, Chesnut-Street. 1796.

> fr.[ii], t.[i], [ii–iii, bl.], [iv], [1], 2–275, [276,
> adv. of books] p.; front. only illus.; 17 cm.;
> bound in leather; front. signed *Thackara sc.*
> English ed. London: Hookham and Carpenter,
> 1794.
> MWA°; MiU; NN; PP (fr.[ii] & p. 265–266;
> 275–[276] wanting & p. [1]–2 mut.); Evans
> 30966.

979.2 [—] ——— [4 lines of verse] A New
Edition. Philadelphia: Printed For J. Ormrod, J.
Sparhawk, J. & J. Crukshank, M. Carey, J. Conrad
& Co. and H. & P. Rice. 1801.

> fr.[ii], t.[1], [2–5], 6–301, [302–304, adv. list
> of books] p.; front. only illus.; 16.5 cm.; bound
> in leather. Front. signed *Thackera sc.*
> MWA°; MB; OOxM; PHi; PPL; Shaw 1108.

979.3 [—] ——— Moral History. [4 lines quot.]
A New Edition. Philadelphia: Printed by J.
Adams, For Benjamin And Thomas Kite, No. 28,
North Third Street, And No. 21, South Fourth
Street. 1807.

> t.[1], [2–3], 4–234 p.; 15.5 cm.
> MH°.

979.4 [—] ——— Philadelphia: Published By
Johnson And Warner, Thomas And William Brad-
ford, Kimber And Conrad, Bennett And Walton,
B. B. Hopkins And Co., Mathew Carey, Stephen
Pike, And Benjamin And Thomas Kite. 1811.

> t.[1], [2–3], 4–235 p.; t.[1] 17.5 cm.
> MWA° (rebound); CSmH; DLC (bound in
> leather); MBAt; MH; PP; PPL; Shaw 23043.

THE PEASANT'S REPAST. *See* Berquin, Arnaud, no.
91.1.

PEDDER, JAMES 1775–1859
980 [—] THE YELLOW SHOE-STRINGS; Or, The
Good Effects. Of Obedience to Parents. Philadel-
phia: Published By Benjamin Warner, And Sold
At His Book-Stores, Philadelphia, And Richmond
Virginia, 1816.

> fr.[ii], t.[1], [2–5], 6–48 p.; 3 pl. including
> folded front.; 16.5 cm.; pr. paper covers; colo-
> phon p. 48: A Bowman, Printer. Cover title
> dated 1816; the PP copy dated 1817.

English ed. London: W. Darton [n.d.] plates
dated Dec. 17, 1814.
MWA°; CtY (fr.[ii] & front cover wanting);
MBSPNEA; MiD (covers wanting); PP; RPB;
Shaw 38572, 39890 and 41747 (dated 1817).

981 A PEEP INTO THE SPORTS OF YOUTH, And
The Occupations And Amusements Of Age. To
which is added, The Ship-Wrecked Sailor Boy.
Embellished with Fifty-Five Copper-plates. Phila-
delphia: Published By Johnson & Warner, No. 147,
Market-Street. 1809. Wm. M'Culloch, Printer.

> fr.[2], t.[3], [4–35] p.; engr. illus.; 13.5 cm.;
> pr. pink paper covers; cover title dated 1809.
> DLC°; PP; Shaw 18327.

982.1 PEOPLE OF ALL NATIONS; An Useful Toy
For Girl Or Boy. Philadelphia Published by Jacob
Johnson, No. 147, Market-street. 1802.

> English ed. London: 2 vols. Darton and Harvey
> [pt. I.] 1800; pt. II. 1801. Two of 8 six mm.
> books that come in a box with a label on the back
> of the box: Infants own Book Case Sold By Dar-
> ton, Harvey [and] Darton, Price 4 s.; each book
> has a front cover label: The Infant's own Book.
> *See* discussion under no. **1468.**
> Shaw 2880.

982.2 ——— Philadelphia [a row of 7 dots] Published by Jacob Johnson, No. 147, Market-street,
1807.

> t.[1], [2–128] p.; illus.; 6.5 cm.; bound in mar-
> ble paper over bds., leather spine; colophon p.
> [128]: Whitehall [Pa.]: Printed by A. Dickin-
> son. Adv. by Johnson & Warner, 1814 in **1449.2.**
> MWA°; CLU; DLC (2 copies, copy 2 wants
> p.[1–16]); MH; NHi; NN; NNC-PL; PHi; PP;
> Shaw 13354.

982.3 ——— Albany [N.Y.]: Printed and Published by H. C. Southwick, No. 73, State-Street.
[1812].

> t.[1], [2–128] p.; illus.; 6.5 cm. In 1812 the firm
> of H. C. Southwick was at 73 State-Street.
> According to the Albany directories, Southwick
> was printing at 94 State Street from 1813–1815
> and at 5 Union Street in 1816. (MWA cat.).
> MWA-T°.

983.1 THE PEOPLE OF ALL NATIONS, Being a
miniature description of the manner and customs
of the inhabitants of the different nations of the

world. Designed For The Improvement Of Youth. Ornamented With Sixty-Two Elegant Engravings. Auburn [N.Y.]: Printed by J. Beardslee & Co. 1818.

> t.[1], [2–3], 4–64 p.; illus.; 10.5 cm.; pr. & illus. paper covers. The same as no. **982.1** in larger format with a new title page.
> MWA° (rear cover mut.); Shaw 45265.

983.2 ———— Auburn [N.Y.]: Printed by D. Rumsey. 1819.

> t.[2], [2–3], 4–64 p.; illus.; 10 cm.; pr. & illus. blue paper covers; cover title undated.
> MWA-W°; NB (i. st. on t.[2], covers mut., p. 41–42 torn).

PERCIVAL, THOMAS 1740–1804
984.1 — A Father's Instructions: Consisting Of Moral Tales, Fables, And Reflections; Designed To Promote The Love Of Virtue, A Taste For Knowledge, And An Early Acquaintance With The Works of Nature: By Thomas Percival, M.D. F.R.S. & S.A. Member Of The Medical Societies Of London And Edinburgh, And Of The Royal Society Of Physicians At Paris. Philadelphia: Printed For Thomas Dobson, At The Stone House, In Second Street. M DCC LXXXVIII.

> t.[1], [2–5], 6, [vii], viii–xi, [xii], [13–15], 16–238, [239–243], [244, bl.], [245–248, adv.] p.; 14 cm.; bound in leather.
> English and Irish ed. entitled: *A Father's Instructions To His Children*. London: 2 ed. J. Johnson, 1776.
> MWA° (i. st. on t.[1]); CtY; PHi; PP; PPL; Evans 21382.

984.2 ————— By Thomas Percival, M.D. F.R.S. And A. S. Lond. F.R.S. And R.M.S. Edinb. President Of The Literary And Philosophical Society Of Manchester, And Member Of Various Foreign Societies. The Ninth Edition. Philadelphia: Printed by T. Dobson, No. 41 S. Second-Street. 1797.

> t.[i], [ii–iii], iv–xii, [1], 2–219 p.; 17 cm.; bound in leather.
> MWA°; MiD; Evans 32666.

984.3 ———— The Ninth Edition. Richmond [Va.]: Published By William Pritchard. 1800.

> t.[i], [ii–iii], iv–xii, [1], 2–219 p.; 17.5 cm.; bound in leather.
> MWA°; KyHi; MSaE; N; NcD; NN; PU; Evans 38232.

[PERRAULT, CHARLES] 1628–1703
985.1 [—] Fairy Tales, Or Histories Of Past Times. With Morals: Containing, I. The Little Red Riding-Hood. II. The Fairy. III. Blue Beard. IV. The Sleeping Beauty in the Wood. V. The Master-Cat: or, Puss in Boots. VI. Cinderilla: or, The little Glass-Slipper. VII. Riquet with the Tuft. VIII. Little Thumb. IX. The Discreet Princess. Haverhill [Mass.], Printed By Peter Edes. MDCCXCIV.

> t.[1], [2–3], 4–83 p.; 15.5 cm.; bound in white paper ornamented with zigzag lines in orange over w. bds. The tales are usually ascribed to Charles Perrault, who is assumed to have written under his son's name, Pierre Perrault-Darmancour (1678–1700), because at that time it was beneath the dignity of an adult author to write children's stories. Another theory holds that Pierre Perrault-Darmancour actually wrote the tales with assistance from his father. It has been noted that the tales were written with outstanding logic, with every detail worked out to completion with legal precision. Since Charles Perrault was a lawyer, this is the kind of work one would expect from a legal mind rather than a 17-year-old youth.
> English and Scottish ed. title 1: *Histories, Or Tales of past Times*. London: J. Pote; R. Montague, 1729.
> English ed. title 2: *Histories Or Tales of Passed Times, Told By Mother Goose*. Salisbury: 3 ed. B. Collins; W. Bristow, London. 1763.
> English ed. title 3: *Histories of Passed Times, or The Tales Of Mother Goose*. London: Fr & Eng. 2 vols. Sold at Brussels by B. Le Francq, Bookseller, 1785.
> English ed. title 4: *The Celebrated Tales Of Mother Goose*. London: J. Harris, 1817.
> Scottish ed. title 5: *The Entertaining Tales Of Mother Goose*. Glasgow: Jas. Lumsden & Son. [*ca.* 1815].
> English ed. title 6: *Fairy Tales by Mother Goose*. York: adv. under Twelvepenny Books by Wilson Spence & Mawman, 1797 in S. Bunyano's *The Prettiest Book For Children*.
> Scottish ed. title 7: *Fairy Tales of Mother Goose: Containing The Stories of Cinderella*: Glasgow: J. Lumsden & Son. [n.d.].
> Scottish ed. title 8: *Fairy Tales Of Times From Mother Goose*. Edinburgh: G. Ross, 1805.
> English ed. title 9: *Mother Goose's Histories or Tales Of Passed Times. Containing, I. The Little*

Red Riding-Hood. II. The Fairy. III. Blue Beard. London: C. Sympson, chapbook ed.

English ed. title 10: *Mother Goose's Tales.* Short title adv. used by members of the Newbery family. The actual title may have been the same as title 2. London: adv. by F. Newbery, 1769, "9d," in Samuel Richardson's *The History of Pamela.*

English ed. title 11: *History and Tales of Mother Goose.* London: adv. by H. Turpin [*ca.* 1784] in The History Of Harloquin & Columbine.

Scottish ed. title 12: *Mother Goose's Fairy Tales.* Edinburgh: J. Morren [1800?].

Irish ed. title 13: *New Fairy Tales. Taken from the Most Polite Authors.* Dublin: Richard Cross, 1790. (a chapbook form).

English ed. title 14: *Tabart's Collection Of Popular Stories For The Nursery. Part II.* London: Tabart & Co. 1804. On p.[2]: < Entered at Stationer's Hall. > The Stationer's Hall entry for parts 1 and 2 was made by R. Phillips September 14, 1804. Phillips appears to have done a considerable amount of publishing under Tabart & Co.'s imprint.

English ed. title 15: *Tales of Passed Times, By Mother Goose.* London: Eng. & Fr. 6 ed. Printed for S. Van den Berg, Bookseller, 1764.

English ed. title 16: —— *Times. By Old Mother Goose: With Morals.* London: 22 ed. W. Osborne and J. Griffin; and J. Mozley, Gainsbrough, 1786.

MHa°; MSaE (rear cover half wanting); MWA-W (t.[1], p.[2]–4, 75–83 wanting); Bowe mss.; Evans 29299 (dated 1795, probably from an adv. for the 1794 ed.).

985.2 — TALES OF PASSED TIMES BY MOTHER GOOSE. With Morals. Written In French by M. Perrault, and Englished by R. S. Gent. To which is added a New one, viz. The Discreet Princess. The Seventh Edition, Corrected, and Adorned with fine Cuts. New-York: Printed for J. Rivington, Bookseller and Stationer, No. 56, Pearl-Street. 1795.

fr.[ii], [1, bl.] 1st English t.[2], 1st French t.[3], [4, bl.], [5–6], 7–149, [150, bl.] 2nd French t.[151], [152, bl.], 2nd English t.[153], [154, bl.], [155], 156–227 p.; 9 pl. including front.; 18 cm.; bound in leather. The plates are signed *Anderson S.* or *Anderson Sculp.* [Alexander Anderson].

2nd English title: The Discreet Princess; Or The, Adventures Of Finetta. A Novel. Printed in the Year M.DCC.LXIV. [*sic. i.e.* M.DCC.XCV]. English ed. title 7, no. **985.1.**

MWA-T° (9 pl.); CLU (pl. wanting); DLC (8 pl. pl. opp. p. 82 wanting); MB (pl. wanting); MH (bound in leather, 9 pl.; p. 101–102 mut.); PP (9 pl.); MWA-W (bound in green paper over bds., buff paper spine; pl. wanting); Bowe mss.; Evans 29300.

985.3 [—] FAIRY TALES, OR HISTORIES OF PAST TIMES. Containing The Little Red Riding Hood. The Fairy. Blue Beard. The Sleeping Beauty in the Wood. The Master Cat, or Puss in Boots. Cinderilla, or the Little Glass Slipper. Riquet with the Tuft. Little Thumb. New-York. Printed By John Harrisson, And Sold at his Book Store, Peck Slip. 1798. < Price Twelve Cents >

fr.[2], t.[3], [4–5], 6–107 p.; illus.; 11.5 cm.; bound in buff paper ruled with red lines and spotted with black dots.

MWA-W° (p. 19–30 wanting; p. 99–107 mut.); Bowe mss.

[PERRAULT, CHARLES] Selections from *Fairy Tales*

BLUE BEARD (arranged chronologically)

986.1 [—] A NEW HISTORY OF BLUE BEARD, Written By Gaffer Black Beard, For the Amusement Of Little Lack Beard, and his Pretty Sisters. Adorned with Cuts. Hartford: Printed by John Babcock. 1800.

fr.[2], t.[3], [4–5], 6–31 p.; illus.; 11 cm.; violet and green Dutch paper covers.

English ed. title 1: *Blue Beard,* London: [included in] Tabart's Collection Of Popular Stories For The Nursery. Part II. Tabart & Co. 1804.

English ed. title 2: *Blue Beard; Or, The Fatal Effects of Curiosity And Disobedience.* In verse. London: J. Harris, 1808.

English ed. title 2a: —— *Female Curiosity, And Little Red Riding Hood; Tales For The Nursery.* London: 5 ed. Tabart And Co., 1804.

English ed. title 3: *Blue Beard; Or, Female Curiosity, A Juvenile Poem.* London: J. and E. Wallis. [n.d.].

English ed. title 4: *The History of Blue Beard.* [London]: Whittington and Arliss. 1815.

MWA-W° (p. 29–30 mut.); CtHi; Bowe mss.; Evans 38059.

986.2 [—] ——— Stonington [Conn.]: Printed by Samuel Trumbull. 1801.
> fr.[2], t.[3], [4, alphabets–5], 6–23 p.; illus.; 12.5 cm.; wallpaper covers.
> MWA*; Bowe mss.; Shaw 1010.

986.3 [—] ——— Adorned with Cuts. Hartford: Printed by John Babcock. 1802.
> fr.[2], t.[3], [4, alphabets–5], 6–29 p.; illus.; 10.5 cm.; green Dutch paper covers.
> DLC*; CtHi (fr.[2] bound out of place, 7 pages at the rear mut., p. [27–29] cropped so that the page numbers are wanting); Bowe mss.; Shaw 2882.

986.4 [—] ——— Philadelphia: Printed By John Adams. 1804.
> fr.[2], t.[3], [4, alphabets–5], 6–31 p.; illus.; 10.5 cm.; buff-brown paper covers.
> MWA*; CCamarSJ; CLU; CSmH; DLC; IU; MiU (2 copies); NB (i. st. on t. [31]); NHi; NN (2 copies); OCLW-LS; OOxM; PHi; PP (2 copies); PPL; PU; Bowe mss.; Shaw 6869 and 7025.

986.5 [—] ——— Sisters. Stonington [Conn.]: Printed by Samuel Trumbull, 1804.
> fr.[2], t.[3], [4–5], 6–28, [29–31] p.; illus.; 9.5 cm.; illus. buff paper covers; entire book printed on blue paper.
> MWA-W*; Bowe mss.

986.6 [—] ——— Adorned with Cuts. From Sidney's Press, New-Haven. 1805.
> fr.[2], t.[3], [4, alphabets–5], 6–30 p.; illus.; 10.5 cm.; Dutch paper covers.
> MWA* (top of t.[3], [4] & front cover wanting); Bowe mss.; Shaw 56709.

986.7 [—] ——— Blackbeard. For the Amusement of all good Boys and Girls. Albany: Printed And Sold By The Gross Or Dozen. By E. And E. Hosford. 1806.
> fr.[2], t.[3], [4–5], 6–31 p.; illus.; 10.5 cm.
> PP; Bowe mss.

986.8 [—] ——— [same as **986.1**] Adorned with Cuts. From Sidney's Press, New-Haven. 1806.
> fr.[2], t.[3], [4, alphabets–5], 6–30 p.; illus.; 10.5 cm.; pink and green Dutch paper covers.
> MWA* (fr.[2] wanting); CtHi (rear cover wanting); CtY (fr.[2] & covers wanting); NjN;

PP (fr.[2] wanting, rebound); Bowe mss.; Shaw 50709.

986.9 [—] ——— From Sidney's Press, New-Haven. 1807.
> fr.[2], t.[3], [4, alphabets–5], 6–29, [30, alphabets], [31, adv.] p.; illus.; 10.5 cm.; Dutch paper covers; p. 6, line 1, the last word "nobleman," has a comma after it.
> CtY*; Bowe mss.

986.10 [—] [——— From Sidney's Press, New-Haven. 1807.]
> A variant ed. of no. **986.9**; p. 6, line 1, the last word "nobleman'" has an apostrophe after the "n" instead of a comma.
> Adomeit* (fr.[2], t.[3], p.[4], 29–[31] wanting; p.[5]–6½ wanting); Bowe mss.

986.11 [—] ——— For the amusement of all good Boys and Girls. Ornamented with Engravings. Albany: Printed By E. And E. Hosford. 1808.
> fr.[2], t.[3], [4, alphabets–5], 6–30, [31, illus.] p.; illus.; 10.5 cm.; pr. & illus. buff paper covers.
> MWA*; CLU (fr.[2], p. 29–30 wanting); Bowe mss.; Shaw 15900.

986.12 [—] ——— [same as **986.1**] Sisters. From Parks Press; Montpelier, Vt. 1808.
> t.[1], [2–3], 4–25, [26–27, alphabet], [28, numerals punctuation, etc.], [29, adv.] p.; 9.5 cm.; blue paper covers.
> MWA-W* (pr. buff paper covers printed in red ink); VtHi (p. 27–28 mut.); Bowe mss.; Mc Corison 1021; Shaw 15901.

986.13 [—] ——— Adorned With Cuts. From Sidney's Press, New-Haven. 1808.
> fr.[2], t.[3], [4, upper case alphabet], [5], 6–29, [30, alphabets], [31, adv.] p.; illus.; 10.5 cm.; green and gold Dutch paper covers
> MWA-W*; Bowe mss.

986.14 [—] THE HISTORY OF BLUE-BEARD, To Which Is Added The Entertaining History Of Little Red Riding Hood. Northampton [Mass.]: Printed And Published By P. Mackenzie. Price One Penny. 1808.
> fr.[2], t.[3], [4–5], 6–31 p.; illus.; 9.5 cm.
> DLC*; Bowe mss.

986.15 [—] ——— [same as **986.11**] and Girls. Printed By E. And E. Hosford. 1809.

t.[3], [4, alphabets–5], 6–30, [31, illus.] p.; illus.; 10 cm.; illus. buff rear paper cover.
MWA° (fr.[2] and front cover wanting); Bowe mss.; Shaw 18200.

986.16 [—] ———— [same as **986.1**] Sisters. From Sidney's Press. New Haven. 1809.
fr.[2], t.[3], [4, alphabets–5], 6–29, [30, alphabet–31, adv.] p.; illus.; 10 cm.; Dutch paper covers.
MWA°; CtY; Bowe mss.

986.17 [—] ———— [same as **986.11**] Girls. Albany: Printed By E. & E. Hosford. 1810.
fr.[2], t.[3], [4, alphabets–5], 6–30, [31, illus.] p.; illus.; 10 cm.; pr. & illus. buff paper covers; cover title undated.
MWA°; MB; MSaE; N; Bowe mss.; Shaw 20867.

986.18 [—] ———— [same as **986.8**] pretty Sisters. Adorned with Cuts. From Sidney's Press. New-Haven, 1810.
fr.[2], t.[3], [4, adv.–5], 6–29, [30, alphabet] p.; illus.; 10.5 cm.; adv. p. [4] last line: "for Rags."; 5 lines of upper case alphabet with the first line "A–E", and last line "V–Z", p. [30].
MWA° (p. [31] & covers wanting, fr.[2] mut., lower half wanting); Bowe mss.; Shaw 51030.

986.19 [—] ———— sisters. Adorned with Cuts. From Sidney's Press. New-Haven, 1810.
fr.[2], t.[3], [4, adv.–5], 6–29, [30–31, alphabets] p.; illus.; 10.5 cm.; pr. & illus. buff paper covers. A variant of the above with last line p. [4]: "Rags."; a rule 10 cm. long under the caption, p. [5]; [3 lines of lower case alphabet] Capital Letters [2 rows of upper case alphabet] Double Letters [1 line of double letters], p. [30]; 4 lines of upper case alphabet with the first line "A–G", and the last line "XYZ", p. [31].
Cover title: Blue Beard. Published by I. Cooke & Co. Universal Book-Store, Church-Street, New-Haven.
MWA°; NjR (fr.[2] & covers wanting); Bowe mss.

986.20 [—] BLUE BEARD; Or, The Fatal Effects Of Curiosity And Disobedience. Illustrated With Elegant And Appropriate Engravings. Philadelphia: Published and sold Wholesale by Wm.

Charles, and may be had of all the Booksellers. 1810. W. M'Culloch, Printer.
fr.[ii], t.[1], [2–3], 4–16 p.; 8 pl. including front.; 12.5 cm.; pr. buff paper covers.
CtY° (Pequot, rear cover mostly wanting); Bowe mss.; Shaw 19582.

986.21 [—] ———— [same as **986.11**] and Girls. Ornamented With Cuts. First Windsor Edition. Printed At Windsor [Vt.]. By Farnsworth & Churchill. 1810.
fr.[2], t.[3], [4–5], 6–27, [28, alphabets], [29, adv.], [30–31, 2 cuts per page] p.; illus.; 10 cm.; blue paper covers.
MWA°; CtHi; VtHi (blue marbled paper covers); Bowe mss.; McCorison 1199; Shaw 20868.

986.22 [—] ———— Ornamented with Engravings. Albany: Printed By E. & E. Hosford. 1811.
fr.[2], t.[3], [4, alphabets–5], 6–30, [31, illus.] p.; pr. & illus. buff paper covers; cover title undated.
MWA° (fr.[2], p.[31] & covers wanting); CtHi (top half of t.[3] torn away); Bowe mss.; Shaw 23524.

986.23 [—] ———— [same as **986.1**] Sisters. Sidney's Press, New-Haven. 1812.
t.[3], [4, alphabets–5], 6–29, [30, adv.] p.; illus.; 10.5 cm.; pinkish-brown wallpaper covers.
CtHi° (fr.[2], p.[31] and rear cover wanting); Bowe mss.; Shaw 26433.

986.24 [—] ———— [same as **986.11**] Engravings. Albany: Printed By E. & E. Hosford. 1813.
fr.[2], t.[3], [4, alphabets–5], 6–30, [31, illus.] p.; illus.; 10.5 cm.; pr. & illus. buff paper covers. Cover title: Blue Beard. Albany: Printed By E. and E. Hosford.
MWA° (p.[31] and rear cover wanting); PP (p. 27–30 wanting); Bowe mss.; Shaw 29309.

986.25 [—] ———— Albany: Printed By E. & E. Hosford. 1814.
fr.[2], t.[3], [4, alphabets–5], 6–30, [31, illus.] p.; illus.; 10.5 cm.; pr. & illus. paper covers; cover title undated.
CCamarSJ; DLC (p.[31] & rear cover wanting); Bowe mss.; Shaw 32472.

986.26 [—] ———— (Ornamented with Cuts.) Windsor, (Vt.) Printed by Jesse Cochran. And

Sold whole-sale and retail at his Book-Store. 1814.
fr.[2], t.[3], [4–5] 6–31 p.; illus.; 10 cm.; pr. &
illus. blue-gray paper covers, or buff paper
covers.

MWA* (2 copies; copy 2, has the top of t.[3]
wanting); VtHi (rear cover wanting); Bowe
mss.; McCorison 1649; Shaw 32473.

986.27 [—] Blue Beard; Or The Fatal Effects
Of Curiosity And Disobedience. Illustrated with
Elegant And Appropriate [*sic. i.e.* Appropriate]
Engravings, On Copperplate. Philadelphia: Published and sold Wholesale, by Wm. Charles, and
may be had of all the Booksellers. 1815.
fr.[ii], t.[1], [2–3], 4–16 p.; 8 pl. including
front.; 12.5 cm.

RPB* (covers wanting); Bowe mss.; Shaw
51526.

986.28 [—] ——— [same as **986.26**] Windsor,
(Vt.) Printed By Jesse Cochran, 1815.
fr.[2], t.[3], [4–5], 6–31 p.; illus.; 10.5 cm.; pr.
& illus. blue-gray paper covers.

MWA*; VtHi; Bowe mss.; McCorison 1770;
Shaw 35616.

986.29 [—] ——— Ornamented with Engravings. Albany: Printed By E. & E. Hosford. 1816.
fr.[2], t.[3], [4, alphabets–5], 6–30, [31, illus.]
p.; illus.; 10 cm.; pr. & illus. buff paper covers.
Cover title imprint: Albany: Printed By E. And
E. Hosford.

MWA-W*; MH (fr.[2], p. 27–[31] wanting);
N (i. st. on front cover); NNC-LS; NUt; PP;
Bowe mss.; Shaw 38402.

986.30 [—] ——— Albany: Printed By E. & E.
Hosford. 1818.
fr.[2], t.[3], [4–5], 6–30, [31, illus.] p.; illus.;
10.5 cm.; pr. & illus. blue-gray paper covers.
Cover title imprint: Albany: Printed by E. And
E. Hosford.

MWA*; DLC; N (i. st. on front covers); Bowe
mss.; Shaw 45001.

986.31 [—] Blue Beard, And Little Red Riding-
Hood; Tales For The Nursery. With Three Copper-Plates. A New Edition. New-York: Published
By L. & F. Lockwood, No. 110 Chatham-Street.
1818.
fr.[ii], t.[1], [2–3], 4–18 p.; 3 pl. including

front.; 13.5 cm.; pr. purple paper covers. The
cover title imprint: ——— Birch & Kelley Printers. 1818.

MWA-W*; Bowe mss.; Shaw 43400.

CINDERILLA OR CINDERELLA (arranged
chronologically)

"Cinderilla" is spelled with an "i" in the first English ed. of *Histories, Or Tales of Past Times,* 1729
and in the three first American editions of the
Tales, nos. **985.1–3**. The conventional spelling of
the name "Cinderella" with an "e" appears in the
earliest publication of the story in Solomon Winlove's *An Approved Collection of Entertaining
Stories.* Worcester, Massachusetts. *Isaiah Thomas,
1789,* no. **1437.1**, which was reprinted from the
English, F. Newbery ed. of 1770. In the following
listing of editions both spellings will be used.

987.1 [—] Cinderilla; Or The Little Glass
Slipper. [13 lines of quot.] Litchfield [Conn.]:
Printed by T. Collier. [*ca.* 1800].
fr.[2], t.[3], [4–5], 6–29, [30, bl.], [31, illus.]
p.; illus.; 9 cm. "Cinderella's slipper was originally not of glass but of *vair*, which as Balzac
explains in *Catherine de Medici* was the rarest
of costly furs, in early times restricted by law
to the use of the highest royalty. Through a
printer's error *vair* was spelt *verre*, which means
glass; but the magic that made little Cinderella
a princess was fur, not glass." Sidney Grumbie.
Frontiers and the Fur Trade. The Johns Clay
Co. New York. 1929, p. 33.
English ed. title 1: *Adventures of the Beautiful
Little Maid Cinderilla.* York: J. Kendrew. [*ca*
1820].
English ed. title 2: *The Adventures Of Cinder-
ella.* London: J. Mckenzie.
English ed. title 3: *Cinderella.* Short title adv.
York: adv. by R. Spence [*ca.* 1788] "Price One
Penny" in *Fairy Tales.*
English & Scottish ed. title 4: *Cinderella; or,
The Little Glass Slipper.* London: G. Thompson,
43, Long Lane, West Smithfield. [*ca.* 1800], in
verse.
English ed. title 5: *Cinderella* ——— *Slipper:
A Tale For The Nursery.* London: Sixteenth
[*sic. i.e.* six] ed. Tabart & Co. 1804.
English ed. title 5a: *Cinderella* ——— *Slipper.*
[in verse]. London: J. Harris, 1808.
Scottish ed. title 6: *The Entertaining Story of
Little Cinderella and the Glass Slipper.* Glas-

gow: Lumsden and Son. This is the closest to the American ed. no. **987.1.**

English ed. title 7: *The Interesting Story of Cinderella and her glass slipper.* Banbury: J.G. Rusher [*ca.* 1820].

Irish ed. title 8: *History of a Glass Slipper.* Dublin: adv. by Wm. Jones [*ca.* 1800] under "Penny Books" in R. Johnson's *The Flights Of A Lady Bird.*

English ed. title 9: *Marshall's Edition Of The Popular Story of Cinderella.* London: John Marshall, 1817.

MiU*; Bowe mss.; Evans 49134.

987.2 [—] CINDERELLA: Or, The History Of The Little Glass Slipper. Philadelphia: Printed For Mathew Carey, No. 118, Market-Street. 1800.
 fr.[2], t.[3], [4–5], 6–32 p.; illus.; 10 cm.; green Dutch paper covers.
 CSmH*; Bowe mss.

987.3 [—] CINDERILLA: OR, THE LITTLE GLASS SLIPPER. Desinged [*sic. i.e.* Designed] For The Entertainment Of All Little Misses. Ornamented with Cuts. Albany: Printed And Sold By The Gross Or Dozen, By E. And E. Hosford. 1806.
 fr.[2], t.[3], [4, alphabets–5], 6–31 p.; illus.; 11 cm.; pink and gold Dutch paper covers. In all Hosford editions *Cinderella* is spelled *Cinderilla.*
 Welch*; MWA (fr.[2], t.[3] slightly mut.); Bowe mss.

987.4 [—] —— Designed For the Entertainment of all good Little Misses. Ornamented with Engravings. Albany: Printed By E. and E. Hosford. 1806.
 fr.[2], t.[3], [4, alphabets–5], 6–30, 27 [*sic i.e.* 31] p.; illus.; 10 cm.; green Dutch paper covers.
 NN* (i. st. p.[4]; the upper edge of p. 15, 18, 27 [*sic.* 31] cropped); Bowe mss.; Shaw 10145.

987.5 [—] —— Albany: Printed By E. And E. Hosford. 1808.
 fr.[2], t.[3], [4, alphabets–5], 6–31 p.; illus.; 10.5 cm.; pr. & illus. buff paper covers; cover title undated.
 MWA*; CLU; KU; Bowe mss.; Shaw 14696.

987.6 [—] —— Albany: Printed By E. and E. Hosford. 1809.
 fr.[2], t.[3], [4, alphabets–5], 6–31 p.; illus.;

10.5 cm.; pr. & illus. buff paper covers; cover title undated.
 MWA-W*; OClW-LS; Bowe mss.

987.7 [—] —— Albany: Printed By E. And E. Hosford. 1810.
 fr.[2], t.[3], [4, alphabets–5], 6–31 p.; illus. 10 cm.; pr. & illus. buff paper covers; cover title undated.
 MWA-W* (p. 29–30 lower ¼ wanting); MB (a front., similar to the one used in no. **177**, but with a different border and words below it, is tipped in between p. 30–31); MWA; NNC-Pl; PP; Bowe mss.; Shaw 19780.

987.8 [—] —— Albany: Printed By E. And E. Hosford. 1811.
 fr.[2], t.[3], [4–5], 6–31 p.; illus.; 10 cm.; pr. & illus. buff paper covers.
 N* (front cover mut.); NN-C (fr.[2] & covers mut.); Bowe mss.

987.9 [—] —— Albany: > Printed By E. & E. Hosford. 1813.
 fr.[2], t.[3], [4–5], 6–31 p.; illus.; 10.5 cm.; pr. & illus. buff paper covers. cover title imprint: Albany: Printed by E. And E. Hosford. In the Ct copy the bracket after "Albany: >" on the title page is sharp, while in the MWA copy it is indistinct. The date 1813 is very clear in the MWA copy, but in the Ct one the loop of the "3" is filled with ink and can easily be confused with the number "5". But on studying the date of the Ct copy under a low-powered microscope, the top of the last figure is rounded similar to the number "3" at the bottom of p.[4] of this book and does not have the convex upward curve of the "5" also on p.[4]. The type setting of both copies is identical.
 MWA*; Ct* (p. 29–31 & covers wanting); Bowe mss.

987.10 [—] —— Albany: Printed By E. & E. Hosford. 1814.
 fr.[2], t.[3], [4–5], 6–30, [31, illus.] p.; illus.; 10 cm.; pr. & illus. buff paper covers.
 MWA*; CtHi (front. mut.); PP; Bowe mss.; Shaw 31156 and 32471.

987.11 [—] CINDERELLA; OR THE LITTLE GLASS SLIPPER: BEAUTIFULLY VERSIFIED; Illustrated With Elegant Figures, To Dress And Undress.

Philadelphia: Published and sold wholesale by Wm. Charles, and may be had of all the Booksellers. 1815.

t.[1], [2–3], 4–24 p.; 13.5 cm.; pr. yellow-buff paper covers; text in verse. The covers were added after 1820. Cover imprint: Philadelphia: Published By Morgan & Sons. Price 18 3/4 cents plain—coloured 25 cents.

English ed. London: S. And J. Fuller, 1814, with seven paper dolls inserted loose in the text. MWA° (figures wanting); NN (figures wanting); Bowe mss. Shaw 51527 (Cinerella [*sic. i.e.* Cinderella] on t.[1] an error in Shaw).

987.12 [—] Cinderilla ——— [same as **987.4**] Albany: Printed By E. & E. Hosford. 1816.

fr.[2], t.[3], [4, alphabets–5], 6–30, [31] p.; illus.; 10 cm.; pr. & illus. buff paper covers. Cover title imprint: Albany: Printed By E. and E. Hosford.

MWA-W°; NB; NNC-LS; PP (pr. & illus. buff paper covers); Bowe mss.; Shaw 37246.

987.13 [—] Cinderella; ——— Slipper, Designed For The Entertainment Of All Good Little Misses. Boston: Printed By Munroe, Francis and Parker, At Their Juvenile Library, Cornhill, And At Francis' Bookstore, Newbury Street, Near Boylston Market. [*ca.* 1816].

fr.[2], t.[3], [4, adv.–5], 6–34, [35, illus.] p.; illus.; 15 cm.; pr. & illus. paper covers.

CtHi°; Bowe mss.

987.14 [—] Cinderilla ——— [same as **987.4**] Albany: Printed By E. & E. Hosford. 1818.

fr.[2], t.[3], [4, alphabets–5], 6–30, [31] p.; illus.; 10 cm.; pr. & illus. blue-gray paper covers; cover title imprint same as t.[3] but undated.

MWA°; MH; N (cover title: *The Puzzling Cap.* Albany: Printed By E. & E. Hosford. n.d.; pr. green paper covers.); NB (i. st. on t.[3]; front cover wanting); Bowe mss.; Shaw 43622.

Note. Shoemaker 2724 lists a Cooperstown [N.Y.]: H. & E. Phinney, 1820, edition. At first glance the date on the NB copy looks like 1820, but, under a low-powered dissecting microscope, it can readily be seen that the date is definitely 1829 with the last figures a short curved tailed "9" filled with ink. The paper and cuts are definitely later than 1820.

LITTLE RED RIDING HOOD (arranged chronologically)

988.1 [—] Little Red Riding-Hood, The Fairy, And Blue Beard; With Morals. Philadelphia: Printed and sold by John M'Culloch, No. 1. North Third-Street. MDCCXCVII.

t.[3], [4–5], 6–31 p.; 10 cm.; orange Dutch paper covers. The story of *Little Red Riding-Hood* first appeared in Solomon Winlove's *An Approved Collection of Entertaining Stories.* Worcester, Massachusetts. I. Thomas, 1789, no. **1437.1**.

English ed. title 1: *The Affecting Story Of Little Red Riding Hood.* London: G. Martin. [*ca.* 1815].

English ed. title 2: *The Diverting Story Of Little Red Riding Hood.* [London] G. Thompson And J. Evans. [*ca.* 1800].

English ed. title 3: *The Entertaining Story of Little Red Riding Hood, And Tom Thumb's Toy.* York: J. Kendrew [*ca.* 1820].

English and Irish ed. title 4; *History Of Little Red Riding Hood.* York: adv. by R. Spence [*ca.* 1788] "Price One Penny" in *Fairy Tales.*

English ed. title 5: *Little Red Riding Hood.* Mostly short title adv. London: adv. by J. Evans [*ca.* 1800] under "Penny Books" in *A Concise History Of All The Kings And Queens Of England.*

MWA-W° (bottom of t.[3] cropped with only the top third of the date remaining, p. 13–14 slightly mut.); Bowe mss.; Evans 48226.

988.2 [—] The Entertaining Stories of Little Red Riding-Hood, and the Master Cat, or Puss in Boots. Adorned with Cuts. For the Amusement and instruction of Youth. New-York: Printed & sold by Smith & Formen, No. 70 Vesey-street, and 13 Corner of Greenwich and Barclay-sts. Where children's books of every description may be had. 1808.

fr.[2, alphabet], t.[3], [4–5], 6–31 p.; illus.; 10 cm.

Oppenheimer°; Bowe mss.; Shaw 15899.

Peter Prim (*pseud.*). *See* Prim, Peter no. **1063**.

989 Peter Prim's Present. Philadelphia: adv. by Wm. Charles, 1815. No edition before 1820 is known. A later edition is given below. It is a reprint of a William Charles one printed prior to

1820: Peter Prim's Profitable Present to the little Misses and Masters of the United States. [2 lines of verse] Illustrated with neat engravings. Philadelphia: Published by Morgan & Sons [*ca.* 1821] [cover title].

   [1–8] p. engr. on one side only of 8 leaves; illus.; 13 cm.; pr. paper covers. At the foot of p.[1]: Philadela. Pub. and sold by W. Charles. English ed. London: J. Harris, Dec. 17, 1809. PP°; CLU; NNC-Pl; PHi.

990 PETER PRIM'S PRIDE, Or Proverb's, That Will Suit The Young Or The Old. Philadelphia: Published By Johnson & Warner, No. 147, Market Street. 1812.

   fr.[ii], t.[i], [ii, bl.], [1], 2–16, [pl. opp. p. 16] p.; 17 pl.; 13.5 cm.; pr. buff paper covers. Engiish ed. London: J. Harris, 1810. NN° (i. st. p. [17]); CtHi (3 pl. wanting).

PETER PUZZLE ESQ. *See* Puzzle, Peter, Esq. (*pseud.*), no. **1081.**

PETER PUZZLEWIT ESQ. *See* Puzzlewit, Peter, Esq. (*pseud.*), no. **1084.**

991 PETER PRY'S PUPPET SHOW. Part the First. [Second.] Philadelphia: Published and Sold Wholesale by Wm. Charles, and may be had of all the Booksellers. Price, plain, 12 1–2 cents.—Colored, 18 3–4 cents. 1814. [cover titles].

   Pt. I: t.[1], [2–8] p. engr. on one side only of 8 leaves; illus.; 13 cm.; pr. buff paper covers. Title: Peter Pry's Puppet Show Part the First. There is a Time for all things A Time to work and a Time to play.

   Pt. II: [2–8] p. engr. on one side only of 8 leaves; 13 cm.; pr. paper covers. MWA° (pt. I.); ICU° (pt. II, p.[1] wanting); Shaw 32477.

PHILIP AND AGNES. *See* Sandham, Elizabeth, no. **1153.**

992.1 THE PICTURE ALPHABET, For Little Children. New-York: Printed & sold by Samuel Wood, at the Juvenile Book-store, No. 357, Pearl-street. 1813.

   t.[1], [2–16] p.; illus.; 8 cm.
   MWA-T° (covers wanting).

992.2 ——— New York: Printed and sold by Samuel Wood, at the Juvenile Book store, No. 357, Pearl-street. 1814.

   t.[1], [2–16] p.; illus.; 8.5 cm.; paper covers. Adv. by S. Wood, 1808 in **643.1** and 1812 in **439.1.**
   MWA°; (not in Shaw).

992.3 ——— Nerv-York [*sic. i.e.* New-York]: Printed And Sold By Samuel Wood & Sons, at the Juvenile Book-store, No. 357, Pearl-street. 1815.

   t.[1], [2–16] p.; illus.; 8 cm.; pr. & illus. tan paper covers; cover title; imprint: Sold by Samuel Wood, New-York.
   MWA°; Shaw 35640.

992.4 ——— Nerv-York [*sic. i.e.* New York]: Printed And Sold By Samuel Wood & Sons, at the Juvenile Book-store, No. 357, Pearl-street. 1816.

   t.[1], [2–16] p.; illus.; 7.5 cm.
   MH°; MWA-T (bound with other books in **637.1**); Shaw 38637.

992.5 ——— Nerv-York [*sic. i.e.* New-York]: Published by Samuel Wood & Sons, No. 261, Pearl-street, And Samuel S. Wood & Co. No. 212, Market-st. Baltimore. 1818.

   t.[1], [2–16] p.; illus.; 8 cm.
   Cover title: Sold by Samuel Wood & Sons, New-York, And ——— & Co. Baltimore.
   MWA°; OClW-LS (pr. & illus. buff paper covers); Shaw 45334.

993 A PICTURE BOOK, FOR LITTLE CHILDREN. Philadelphia: Published By Kimber And Conrad, No. 93, Market Street. Merritt, Printer. [*ca.* 1812].

   t.[1], [2–24], p.; illus.; 14 cm.; yellow paper covers. The cuts on t.[1], p.[12], [14], [23] are redrawn cuts with a similar design to those in *The Wonderful Life And Adventures Of Robinson Crusoe.* Albany: E. And E. Hosford, *1810,* no. **275.73.** Those on p.[6], [16], [17], [20] were also probably used with the above for an unknown edition of *Robinson Crusoe.* The two cuts on p.[18] and the bottom one on p.[20] are copies of those on p.[11], 19 and 21 respectively in *Mother Goose's Melody.* Worcester, *I. Thomas, 1794,* no. **936.2.** The book is part of a large publisher's remainder. Welch°; CaOTP; CLU; CSmH; CtHi; DeWint; DLC; IU; MWA; NB (i. st. on t.[1]); NHi; NN;

NN-C; NNMM; NRU; OOxM; PHi; PP; PPL; PU; ViU; Shaw 11163, 15947 and 26465.

THE PICTURE EXHIBITION. *See* Johnson, Richard, no. **685.**

994.1 PICTURE EXHIBITION, Or, The Ladder To Learning. Step The First. Adorned With Cuts. First Worcester Edition. Worcester; Printed by Isaiah Thomas, Jun. Sold Wholesale and Retail at his Book-Store.— September, 1798.
fr.[2], t.[3], [4–13], 14–30, [31, adv.] p.; illus.; 10.5 cm.; paper covers.
Evans 48578.

994.2 —— Second Worcester Edition. Worcester: Printed by I. Thomas, Jun. Sold Wholesale and Retail at his Book Store. 1805.
fr.[2], [3], [4–13], 14–29, [30, adv.], [31, 2 oval cuts] p.; illus.; 10.5 cm.; brick-red paper covers.
MWA° fr.[2], p. 29–31 & covers mut.); DLC; Shaw 9147.

THE PICTURE ROOM. *See* Johnson, R., no. **685.**

995 PICTURES OF LONDON With Plates. Philadelphia: adv. by Johnson & Warner, 1817 in **1355.3.**

996 PICTURES OF BIBLE HISTORY With Suitable Descriptions. Hartford: Oliver D. Cooke. 1820.
t.[1], 2–24 p.; illus.; 14 cm.; pr. & illus. green paper covers; cover title dated 1820.
MWA°; CtHi; OClWHi; RPB; Shoemaker 2778.

997 PICTURES OF SEVENTY-TWO BEASTS & BIRDS, With A Familiar Description Of Each, In Verse And Prose. Published for the Benefit of the Lovers of Natural History, and for the Instruction of the Youth of America. Boston: Printed and sold by Samuel Hall, in Cornhill, 1796.
fr.[2], t.[3], [4], 5–118 p.; illus.; 10 cm.; blue marbled paper covers. The earliest known American edition of *A Pretty Book of Pictures or Tommy Trip's History of Beasts and Birds,* first adv. by J. Newbery in *Food For The Mind.* 1759., but having a new title and omitting the *History of Tommy Trip, and his Dog Jawler, and Wolog the great giant. See* discussion of

this book under *Tommy Trip's History of Beasts and Birds,* no. **1326.**
Welch° (p. 115–118 wanting); MWA (complete); Evans 47884.

THE PILGRIMS. *See* More, Hannah, no. **891.1.**

PILKINGTON, MARY (HOPKINS) 1766–1839
998 — BIOGRAPHY FOR BOYS; Or Characteristic Histories, Calculated To impress the Youthful Mind With An Admiration Of Virtuous Principles, And A Detestation Of Vicious Ones. By Mrs. Pilkington. Philadelphia. Published By Johnson & Warner, No. 147, Market Street. 1809.
fr.[ii], t.[1], [2–3], 4–137, [138 bl.–139] p.; front. only illus.; 14.5 cm.; bound in marbled paper over bds., leather spine; colophon p. 137: Lydia R. Bailey Printer. No. 10, North Alley.
English ed. London: 1799.
MWA°; CLU; MNF; NN (bound with other pamphlets, covers wanting); PP (bound in marbled paper over bds.); Shaw 18392.

999 — BIOGRAPHY FOR GIRLS; Or, Moral And Instructive Examples For The Female Sex. The Fourth Edition. By Mrs. Pilkington. Philadelphia: Published By Johnson And Warner, No. 147, Market-Street. 1809. Printed by J. Adams.
fr.[ii], t.[i], [ii–iv], [1], 2–129 p.; front. only illus. signed *W R sc* [William Ralph]; 14 cm.; 14 cm.; marbled paper over bds.
English ed. London: Vernor and Hood and E. Newbery, 1799.
MWA° (i. st. on t.[i]); DLC (fr.[ii] wanting); MB; MSaE; NN (rebound, per st. on t.[i]); PHC; PHi (fr.[ii] omitted); PP (fr.[ii] omitted); Shaw 18393.

1000 — CONFIDENCE IN PARENTS, The Only Security For Happiness; Or, the misery that is certain to attend Deceit. By Mrs. Pilkington. From Sidney's Press. New-Haven. 1817.
t.[1], [2–3], 4–46, [47, adv. of books], [48, adv. of school books and stationary] p.; 14 cm.; pr. & illus. red paper covers; cover title dated 1818.
MWA°; CtHi; Shaw 41826.

1001 — HENRY; OR, THE FOUNDLING: To Which Are Added, The Prejudiced Parent; Or, The Virtuous Daughter. Tales, Calculated To Improve The Mind And Morals Of Youth. By Mrs. Pilkington. Philadelphia: Published By James Thackara, No. 43, South Second-Street, R. Carr, Printer. 1801.

> t.[1], [2–3], 4–162 p.; 14 cm.; paper covers; bound in blue paper over bds., red leather spine.
> English ed. London: Vernorn & Hood, 1799.
> DLC*; Shaw 1156.

1002.1 — MARVELOUS ADVENTURES; OR, THE VICISSITUDES OF A CAT. By Mrs. Pilkington Baltimore: Published by F. Lucas, Jun. 138, Market-street. J. Robinson, printer. 1814.

> fr.[ii], t.[1], [2–3], 4–161 p.; 13.5 cm.; bound in brown paper over bds., leather spine.
> English ed. London: Vernor and Hood and J. Harris, 1802.
> MWA* (fr.[ii] wanting); ICU; MdBE (fr.[ii] wanting, per st. on t.[1] & p.[3]); PP; Shaw 32512.

1002.2 — ———— Baltimore: Published by F. Lucas, Jun. and J. & T. Vance. J. Robinson, printer. 1814.

> fr.[ii], t.[1], [2–3], 4–161 p.; front. only illus.; 14 cm.; bound in marbled paper, black leather spine.
> NN*.

1003.1 — MENTORIAL TALES, FOR THE INSTRUCTION OF YOUNG LADIES Just Leaving School And Entering The Theatre Of Life. By Mrs. Pilkington. Vol. I. [II.–III.] Philadelphia: Published By Jacob Johnson, Market-Street. 1803. < T. L. Plowman, Printer. >

> vol. I.: t.[i], [ii–iii], iv, [3–5], 6–131, [132, bl.] p. 2 bl. leaves; vol. II.: t.[i], [ii, bl.]; [1], 2–136 p., 2 bl. leaves; vol. III.: t.[1], [2–5], 6–107 p.; bound in 1 vol.; 14 cm.; bound in leather.
> Title page vol. II.: ———— [same as vol. I.] Philadelphia: Published By J. Johnson, Market-Street. 1803. < Eaken & Mecum, Printers.>
> Title page vol. III.: ———— [same as vol. I.] Philadelphia: Published By Jacob Johnson, No. 147, Market-Street. A. And G. Way, Printers. 1803.
> English ed. London: 1802.
> MWA*; MH; MSaE (vol. I. wants t.[1] & p. [2]–[4]; NHi (vol. II. only. p. 81–84 ½ wanting); NjR (vol. I.); PHi; Shaw 4870.

1003.2 — ———— Ladies. New-York: adv. by Thomas B. Jansen, 1805 in **1371.5.**

1003.3 — ———— Philadelphia: adv. by Jacob Johnson, 1806 in **1047.**

1003.4 — ———— Philadelphia: Published By Johnson And Warner, No. 147, High-Street. 1811.

> t.[i], [ii–iii], iv, [v], [vi, bl.], [5], 6–292 p.; 14 cm.; bound in leather.
> MWA*; CLU; MB; MSaE; NjR; NcD; NjP; Shaw 23694.

1004 — MRS. PILKINGTON'S NATURAL HISTORY. Philadelphia: adv. by Johnson & Warner, 1812 in **497.**

1005 [—] TALES OF THE HERMITAGE; Written For The Instruction And Amusement Of The Rising Generation. Philadelphia: Published By James Thackara. H. Maxwell, Printer. 1800.

> fr.[ii], t.[1], [2–5], 6–158 p.; front. only illus.; 14 cm.; bound in marble paper over bds., leather spine; front. signed *Engraved by James Akin Philad. Pub. by J. Thackara Octr. 23rd 1800.*
> English ed. London: Vernor & Hood, 1798.
> Carson*; Evans 38269.

PINCHARD, MRS. ELIZABETH (of Taunton)
1006.1 [—] THE BLIND CHILD, OR ANECDOTES OF THE WYNDHAM FAMILY. Written For the Use Of Young People, By A Lady. Philadelphia: Printed For W. Spotswood, & H. And P. Rice, Market-Street. 1793.

> fr.[ii], t.[i], [ii–iii], iv–vii, [viii], [9], 10–192 p.; front. only illus.; 10 cm.
> English ed. London: E. Newbery, 1791, front. dated Octbr. 29 1791.
> MWA* (p. 97–98, 101–102, 123–124, 127–128 wanting); DLC (fr.[ii] & p. 99–126 wanting, bound in green Dutch paper over bds.); Evans 26004.

1006.2. [—] ———— Boston: Printed And Sold By W. Spotswood, No. 55 Marlborough-Street. 1795.

> fr.[ii], t.[i], [ii–iii], iv–vii, [viii, bl.], [9], 10–191, [192, adv. list of books] p.; front only illus.; 10.5 cm.; bound in leather; front. signed *Smither sc.* [James Smither].
> MWA-W* (fr.[ii] signature *"Smither"* rubbed off, p. 133–134 mut.); MH; MWA; NRU (fr.[ii] wanting); PP (fr.[ii] signature *"Smither"* wanting); Evans 29325.

1006.3 [—] ———— Philadelphia: Printed And Sold By H. & P. Rice, No. 50 High-Street, And J. Rice & Co. Market-Street, Baltimore. 1795.

fr.[ii], t.[i], [ii–iii], iv–vii, [viii, bl.], [9], 10–191, [192, adv. list of books] p.; 10.5 cm.; bound in Dutch paper over bds. This is the same as the preceding with a different title page.

MWA-W° (fr.[ii] wanting); PHC; Evans 47559.

1006.4 [—] ———— Worcester: Printed By Isaiah Thomas, jun. Sold Wholesale And Retail At His Bookstore, At The Sign Of Johnson's Head. 1796.

fr.[ii], t.[i], [ii–iii], iv–vii, [viii], [9], 10–190 p.; front. only illus.; 10 cm.; silver paper covers. Welch°; CtHi; MB; MWA; PP (fr.[ii] wanting; p. 189–190 mut.; rebound); Evans 31013.

1006.5 [—] ———— Boston: Published By Isaiah Thomas, Jun. No. 6, Marlborough Street. 1813.

fr.[ii], t.[iii], [iv–v], vi–vii, [viii], [9], 10–176 p.; front & illus. p.[viii] only illus.; 10.5 cm.; bound in leather (copy 1); copy 2 bound in yellow paper over bds., leather spine.

MWA-W° (copy 1 & 2); MB (per. st. on t.[ii]); MH; MSaE; PP; Shaw 29520.

1006.6 [—] ———— Hartford: Printed by Hale & Hosmer. 1814.

fr.[ii], t.[iii], [iv–v], vi, [7], 8–90 p.; front. only illus.; 14 cm., bound in buff marbled paper over bds., red leather spine.

Welch°; CLU; Ct (fr.[ii], p.[7]–8 mut.); CtHi; MWA; PP; Shaw 32513.

1007 [—] THE BLIND CHILD OR, ANECDOTES OF THE WINTHROP FAMILY. New-York: Published By L. B. Jansen, & G. Jansen. 1808.

t.[1], [2–3], [4–9 mut., page numbers wanting], 10–22, [23–24 page numbers wanting] p.; illus.; 12.5 cm.; marbled paper covers. The story is the same as no. **1006.1** with some of the names changed, and some parts rewritten. The place is New York instead of London.

CtHi°.

1008 [—] DRAMATIC DIALOGUES, For The Use of Young Persons. By The Author Of The Blind Child, &c. [4 lines of quot.] Essay On Solitude, By Zimmerman. Boston: Printed For W. Spotswood. 1798.

fr.[ii], general t.[i], [ii, adv. list of 8 books–iv],

1st book, fr.[ii] 1st t.[1], [2–3], 4–42 p., bl. leaf; 2nd book, fr.[ii], t.[1], [2–3], 4–50 p.; 3rd book, t.[1], [2–3], 4–95 p.; 4th book fr.[ii], t.[1], [2–3], 4–38 p.; 5th book, fr.[ii], t.[1], [2–3], 4–45 p.; 6th book, [fr.[ii], t.[1], [2–3], 4–22 p.; 7th book, [1], 2–28 p.; 5 pl. or front. only illus.; 11 cm.; bound in leather.

Title page of the 1st book: The Misfortunes Of Anger. A Drama In Two Parts. [2 lines of verse] Waller. Boston: Printed For William Spotswood. 1798.

Title page of the 2nd book: Sensibility. A Drama. In Two Parts. [6 lines of verse] Sensibility.—Miss More: ———— W. Spotswood. 1798.

Title page of the 3rd book: The Little Trifler. A Drama. In Three Parts. [6 lines quot.] Johnson. ———— 1798.

Title page of the 4th book: The Little Country Visitor. A Drama. In Two Parts. [2 lines of quot.] Miss More's Pastoral. Boston: Printed For W. Spotswood.

Title page of the 5th book: The Distrest Family. A Drama. In Two Parts. [6 lines of quot.] Poems by R. Burns. ———— W. Spotswood.

Title page of the 6th book: The Village Wedding. A Drama, In One Part. [4 lines of quot.] Shenstone. ———— W. Spotswood.

Caption title of the 7th book: The Mocking Bird's Nest. A Dialogue. [caption title].

English ed. London: E. Newbery, 1792.

Welch° (2nd book, fr.[ii] wanting); DFo; MH; MWA; OOxM (1st t.[i] wanting); PP (1st book, t.[i], p.[2]–8; 2nd book, p. 39–40 mut.); Evans 34381.

1009.1 [—] THE LITTLE TRIFLER. ———— [same as **1008**, 3rd book].

fr.[ii], t.[1], [2–3], 4–95 p.; front. only illus.; 10.5 cm.; gold Dutch paper covers.

MWA°; Evans 34005.

1009.2 [—] THE MISFORTUNES OF ANGER. ———— [same as **1008**, 1st book.].

fr.[ii], t.[1], [2–3], 4–42 p.; front. only illus.; 10.5 cm.

MWA°; OOxM; Evans 48579.

1009.3 [—] THE VILLAGE WEDDING. ———— [same as **1008**, 6th book] bound with The Mocking Bird's Nest. A Dialogue. [caption title].

fr.[ii], t.[1], [2–3], 4–28 p.; front. only illus.; 10.5 cm.
MWA°; Evans 3011.

1010.1 [—] THE TWO COUSINS, A Moral Story, For The Use Of Young Persons. In Which Is Exemplified The Necessity Of Moderation And Justice To The Attainment Of Happiness. By The Author of the "Blind Child," and "Dramatic Dialogues." [10 lines of quot.] Beaumont And Fletcher. From the Press Of Samuel Etheridge, Sold By Him, And By The Booksellers. Boston, 1796.
  fr.[ii], t.[i], [ii–iii], iv, [5], 6–142 p.; engraved front. only illus.; 14 cm.; bound in leather.
  English ed. London: entered at Stationer's Hall by E. Newbery, July 25, 1794.
  MWA° (i. st. on t.[i]); CLU; MB (emb. st. on t.[i]); MHi; NN; PP; PPiU (i. st. on t.[i]); Evans 31014.

1010.2 [—] —— New-York: Printed And Sold By John Tiebout, No. 358, Pearl-Street. 1799.
  t.[i], [ii–iii], iv, [5], 6–130 p.; 13 cm.
  MWA° (covers and all after p. 130 wanting); Evans 36120.

THE PIOUS AND INDUSTRIOUS SAILOR BOY. *See* Ventum, Harriet, no. **1377.**

1011 THE PIOUS GIFT; Consisting Of A Dialogue Between Two Seamen, After A Storm; The Wonderful Cure Of General Naaman; The Blind Irishman Restored To Sight; An Account Of Some Seaman In The Battle Of The Nile; Hymns, &c. Suitable For Sabbath-School Premiums. New-York: Printed And Sold By Mahlon Day, No. 84, Water-street. 1820.
  fr.[ii], t.[1], [2–3], 4–43 p.; illus.; 13.5 cm.; pr. & illus. blue paper covers.
  MWA-W°; NjR.

THE PIOUS INDIAN. *See* Boudinot, Elias, no. **119.1.**

THE PIRATE BLACKBEARD. *See* Blackbeard, Or The Captive Princess, no. **103.1.**

1012 THE PIRATE. A Tale For the Amusement and Instruction of Youth. Embellished with cuts. To which is added: Several Selected Pieces in Prose and Verse. Philadelphia: Published by Johnson & Warner. William Green, Printer, 1813.
  fr.[2], t.[3], 4–108 p.; illus.; 14 cm.
  PHi°; PP; Shaw 29522 and 30505.

PITY's GIFT. *See* Pratt, Samuel Jackson, no. **1046.1.**

1013 PLAIN TALES, FOR THE IMPROVEMENT OF YOUTH. Philadelphia. Printed by John Bioren, No. 88, Chesnut Street. 1802.
  fr.[ii], t.[1], [2–3], 4–30 p.; front. only illus.; 13.5 cm.; marbled paper covers; front. signed *Tanner* sc.
  MWA°.

THE PLEASANT AND DELIGHTFUL HISTORY OF JACK AND THE GIANTS. *See* The History Of Jack and The Giants, no. **546.**

1014 THE PLEASANT AND PROFITABLE COMPANION Being A Collection Of Ingenious and Diverting Historys; With Suitable Applications or Morals for instructing the Mind, and encouraging Virtue. [2 lines of verse] Boston: Printed for J. Edwards, & H. Foster, in Cornhill. 1733.
  fr.[ii], t.[iii], [iv, bl.], 1–176 p.; 13.5 cm.; bound in leather. The book contains 60 stories most of which are reprinted from B.P.'s version of *Gesta Romanorum*, English edition title 2. The *Gesta Romanorum* came to England about 1300. There it was copied in monasteries in Latin for the use of monks when compiling sermons. It is rich in stories which later were adopted for children. The book contains an early form of "Guy of Warwick: the Story of the Three Caskets and the Jew's Bond," which later appeared in *The Merchant Of Venice*. There is also a version somewhat similar to *King Lear*, also the story of "The Hermit" which Parnell later retold. The book was printed by Wyken de Worde in the early part of the 16th century. The British Museum has an edition of 1539. Over the years many editions were printed of this popular book, but only those English editions used to compare the text with the American one will be listed.
  English ed. title 1: *A Record Of Ancient Histories, Entitled in Latin Gesta Romanorum*. London, T. Basset, R. Chiswell, A. Mill, G. Conyers, and M. Wotton. 1689.
  English ed. title 2: *Gesta Romanorum: Or, Fifty-*

Eight Histories. London: G. Conyers at the Ring on Little Britain.
MWA°; Evans 40027.

1015 THE PLEASANT HISTORY OF THE FRYAR AND BOY; Or The Young Piper's Pleasant Pastime. Containing The witty Adventures between the Fryar and the Boy; in relation to his Step Mother, whom he fairly fitted for her unmerciful cruelty. [8 lines of verse] Keene, New-Hampshire: Printed By Henry Blake, & Co. MDCCXCIII.

t.[1], [2–3], 4–14 p.; [A]₄, B₃ sig. B₄ wanting, or p. 15–16?; 16.5 cm.
See also The Friar And Boy, no. **425.**
MH°; MLuHi; Evans 26007.

1016 PLEASANT STORIES, AND LESSONS FOR CHILDREN. Fairhaven [Vt.]: Printed By J. P. Spooner. 1797.

t.[3], [4–5], 6–30 p.; 10 cm.
VtHi° (fr.[2]?, p. [31]? & covers wanting); McCorison 448; Evans 48233.

PLEASANT, MRS. *pseud.*
1017.1 MRS. PLEASANT'S STORY BOOK. Philadelphia: adv. by David Hogan, 1798 in [Nathaniel Bacon's] *A Relation Of the Fearful State Of Francis Spira.*

1017.2 MRS. PLEASANT'S STORY BOOK, Composed For The Amusement Of Her Little Family: To Which are Added, Instructions For The Proper Application Of Them. Philadelphia: Printed By Robert Johnson For B. and J. Johnson, No. 147 High-Snreet [*sic. i.e.* Street]. [*ca.* 1802].

fr.[2], t.[3], [4–5], 6–93 p.; illus.; 11 cm.; bound in silver paper over bds.
English ed. title 1: *Mrs. Norton's Story Book.* London: J. Marshall. [*ca.* 1795].
English ed. title 2: *Mrs. Pleasant's Story Book.* York: T. Wilson And R. Spence. 1804.
MWA-W° (p. 91–92 slightly mut. affecting the last word of 4 lines on p. 91, and the first word of the first 6 lines on p. 92); CtHi (orange Dutch paper covers, dated [*ca.* 1790]); PP (p. 65–66 mut.); Shaw 2678 (dated 1802).

1018 A PLEASING ACCOUNT OF GEORGE CROSBY; Aged Twelve Years. Philadelphia: Published by the Sunday & Adult School Union. Clark & Raser, Printers. 1820.

fr.[2], t.[3], [4–5], 6–30, [31, illus.] p.; illus.;

10 cm.; pr. & illus. blue paper covers; cover title dated 1820.
MWA°; Shoemaker 2799.

1019 PLEASING AMUSEMENT. Philadelphia: adv. by William Young, 1794 in **305.**

1020 PLEASING AMUSEMENTS, pt. 1. [2.] Philadelphia: adv. by Francis Bailey, 1793 in **773.1.**

1021.1 A PLEASING HISTORY. [*sic. i.e.* HISTORY] OF BEASTS AND BIRDS. Windsor, Vt. Printed and Sold by Jesse Cochran. 1815.

fr.[2], t.[3], [4–5], 6–31 p.; illus.; 10 cm.; pr. & illus. paper covers; fr.[2] a cut of a giraffe. Caption p.[5]: [a double rule]/*PLEASING HISTORY.*/The last line p. 6: "years they inhabit Asia, Africa &c." On p. 8 there is a rectangular cut of man on horseback with a sword in his hand. The tailpiece, p. 24, shows the sun and moon above a pair of dividers, a miter square and a log.
Cover title: [circular cut of a bird] Windsor, Vt. Printed and Sold by Jesse Cochran. *See also* no. **1204.**
OClW-LS°; DLC (p. 31 & rear cover wanting); McCorison 1774; Shaw 35654.

1021.2 [———— Windsor, Vt. Printed and Sold by Jesse Cochran. [*ca.* 1816]] [the title and imprint are taken from **1021.1.** The date is conjectural].

fr.[2], [5], 6–31 p.; illus.; 10 cm.; pr. & illus. paper covers; fr.[2] has two cuts with the upper illus. a lighted candle. Caption p. [5]: [a double rule]/*PLEASING HISTORY.*/The last line p. 6: "a dark brown, approaching to a black." On p. 8 there is a cut of a horse. The tailpiece p. 24 shows a portion of a broken fence with various objects in front of it.
Cover title: Pleasing History Of Beasts and Birds. [cut of a squirrel seated on a limb of a tree eating a nut]/Windsor, Vt. Printed and Sold by Jesse Cochran.
VtHi° (t.[3], p. [4] wanting).

1022 PLEASING INCITEMENTS TO WISDOM AND VIRTUE, Conveyed Through The Medium Of Anecdote, Tale, And Adventure: Calculated To Entertain, Fortify, And Improve The Juvenile Mind. Translated chiefly from the German. Philadelphia: Re-printed by James Humphreys, From the London Edition. 1800.

> t.[i], [ii–iii], iv, [v, contents], [vi, bl.], [1], 2–120 p.; 14 cm.
> MWA° (rebound); ICU; Evans 38282.

THE PLEASING, INTERESTING, AND AFFECTING HISTORY OF PRINCE LEE BOO. (Title of English ed.). For other editions and titles of Prince Lee Boo, *see* **573.1** and the entry below **650.**

1023 THE PLEASING MORALIST; Containing Essays On Various Subjects, Including Dr. Watts' Advice To A Young Man, On His Entrance Into The World. New-York: Published By Samuel Wood & Sons, No. 261, Pearl-Street; And Samuel S. Wood & Co. No. 212, Market-street, Baltimore. 1818.

> t.[i], [ii–iii], iv, [5], 6–80 p.; illus.; 14 cm.; bound in blue-gray paper over bds.
> English ed. —— *Or, Young Gentleman And Ladies Preceptor; Containing* —— *Subjects: Pride, Envy, . . . To which is added Advice To A Young Man,* —— *World. By Solomon Winlove, Esq. With Cuts By Bewick.* York: A. Miller, W. Law, And S. Carter; And For Wilson, Spence, And Mawman, 1798.
> OClWHi°; CLU; MWA; Shaw 45348.

1024.1 A PLEASING TOY. New-York: Printed And Sold By S. Wood, At the Juvenile Book-store, No. 357, Pearl-street. 1811.

> fr.[ii, alphabet], t.[1], [2–3], 4–27 p.; illus.; 10 cm.; pr. & illus. buff paper covers.
> MWA°; CLU; Shaw 23703.

1024.2 —— New-York: Printed And Sold By Samuel Wood, At the Juvenile Book-Store, No. 357, Pearl-street. 1812.

> fr.[ii, alphabet], t.[1], [2–3], 4–27, [28–29, adv. list of books] p.; illus.; 10 cm.; pr. & illus. buff paper covers.
> OOxM°.

1024.3 —— New-York: Printed And Sold By Samuel Wood, At the Juvenile Book-store No. 357, Pearl street. 1813.

> fr.[ii, alphabet], t.[1], [2–3], 4–27, [28–29, adv. list of books] p.; illus.; 10 cm.; pr. & illus. paper covers; cover title imprint: —— Sold By S. Wood, —— 1813.
> PP°.

1024.4 —— New-York: Printed And Sold By Samuel Wood, At The Juvenile Book-Store, No. 357 Pearl-Street. 1814.

> fr.[ii, alphabet], t.[1], [2–3], 4–27, [28–29, adv. list of books] p.; illus.; 10.5 cm.; pr. & illus. buff paper covers; cover title imprint: New-York: —— S. Wood, At the Juvenile Book-store, No. 357, Pearl-street. 1813.
> MWA° (fr.[ii], & front cover mut.); DLC (p. [1]–4, 25–28 wanting, p. 9–10 mut.; front cover dated 1814).

1024.5 —— *Nerv-York* [sic. i.e. New-York]: Printed And Sold By Samuel Wood, At The Juvenile Book-Store, No. 357, Pearl-street. 1815.

> fr.[ii, alphabet], t.[1], [2–3], 4–27, [28–29, adv. list of books] p.; illus.; 10 cm.; pr. & illus. buff paper covers; cover title undated.
> MWA°; NN; Shaw 35655.

1024.6 —— *Nerv-York* [sic. i.e. New-York]: Printed And Sold By S. Wood & Sons, At The Juvenile Book-Store, No. 261, Pearl-Street. 1817.

> fr.[ii, alphabet], t.[1], [2–3], 4–27 p.; illus.; 10 cm.; pr. & illus. buff paper covers; cover title imprint: Printed And Sold By S. Wood & Sons, —— Pearl Street. New-York.
> MWA°; PP (Dutch paper covers); Shaw 41842.

1024.7 —— New-York: Published By Samuel Wood & Sons, No. 261, Pearl-Street, And Samuel S. Wood & Co., No. 212, Market-st. Baltimore. 1818.

> fr.[ii, alphabet], t.[1], [2–3], 4–27 p.; illus.; 10.5 cm.; violet and green Dutch paper covers.
> OClW-LS°; NPV (emb. st. on t.[1], p. 11–12 wanting, violet & green Dutch paper covers); Shaw 45349.

1024.8 —— *Nerv-York* [sic. i.e. New-York]: Published By Samuel Wood & Sons, No. 261, Pearl-Street, And Samuel S. Wood & Co. No. 212, Market-st. Baltimore. 1819.

> fr.[ii], t.[1], [2–3], 4–27 p.; illus.; 10.5 cm.; no front. in this ed.
> MWA° (fr.[ii] & covers wanting); CLU; ICU (covers wanting); PP; PPL; RP; RPB (bpl. over t.[1]); Shaw 49130.

1025 A PLEASING TOY. Hudson [N.Y.]: Published by W. E. Norman. n.d. [*ca.* 1820].

> t.[1], 2–8 p.; illus.; 5.5 cm.; pr. & illus. yellow

paper covers. A different book from no. **1024.8.**
MWA-W°.

1026 PLEASING TRACTS SELECTED FOR THE
BENEFIT OF YOUTH. The Boy Of Dundee. *"A
Youth to Fortune and to Fame unknown."* [cap-
tion p. 1] Boston: Printed By Timothy Fletcher,
In Cambridge-Street, 1808. [colophon p. 12].
t.[1], 2–12 p.; 16 cm.
MWA-T°.

1027 PLEASING TRAITS IN THE CHARACTERS OF
CHILDREN: Suitable For A Sabbath School Reward. [2 lines of quot.] David. Boston: Printed and
sold by Lincoln & Edmands, No. 53 Cornhill. 1819.
t.[1], [2–3], 4–16 p.; title vignette only illus.;
12.5 cm.; pr. & illus. violet-gray paper covers;
cover title undated. Copy 1 has a cut of a tree
on the front cover title. Copy 2 has a cut of
flowers on the cover title.
MWA° (copies 1, 2); PP; Shaw 49131 and
49132.

1028.1 THE PLEASURES OF PIETY IN YOUTH
EXEMPLIFIED, In The Life And Death Of Several
Children. Extracted from Brown's Young Chris-
tian. Precious Testimony. Janeway's Token For
Children. Rowland Hills Token Of Love. Will's
Spiritual Register. &c. From The Second English
Edition. Boston: Printed By E. Lincoln, Water-
Street. 1805.
t.[1], [2–3], 4, [5], 6–90 p.; 13.5 cm.; gray
paper covers.
MWA°; Shaw 9158.

1028.2 ———— of several Children. Extracted
from unquestionable authorities. Boston: Printed
& published by Lincoln & Edmands. Sold at their
Bible Ware House, and Theological & Miscellaneous Bookstore, No. 53 Cornhill. 1815.
fr.[2], t.[3], [4–5], 6–70, [71] p.; front. and
illus. p. [71] only illus.; 14.5 cm.; pr. & illus.
buff paper covers.
MWA-W°; Shaw 35656.

1028.3 ———— Boston: Printed and sold at No.
53 Cornhill, by Lincoln & Edmands, Who publish
a great variety of books, suitable for instruction
and rewards in sabbath schools. 1819.
fr.[2], t.[3], [4–5], 6–70, [71] p.; front. and
title vignette only illus.; 14 cm.; pr. & illus.
paper covers.

MWA° (p. 71 wanting, fr.[2], t.[3], & p. 4–10
mut. with page numbers wanting); MSaE; NN;
PP; RPB; Shaw 49133, 49134, 49135, and
49136.

1029 THE POACHER'S DAUGHTER. Philadelphia:
Published by the Sunday and Adult School Union.
Clark & Raser, Printer's. 1818.
t.[1], [2–3], 4–36 p.; title vignette only illus.;
12 cm.; pr. & illus. blue-gray paper covers.
CLU°; MWA.

POEMS FOR CHILDREN. *See* Gilbert, Ann (Taylor),
no. **445.1.**

1030 POEMS FOR CHILDREN, Or The School
Teacher's Present. Hartford: Sold By Cooke And
Hale. Copy Right Secured. [*ca.* 1818].
t.[1], [2], 3–16 p.; illus.; 6 cm.; pr. & illus.
violet-buff paper covers.
MWA-W°; CtHi (pr. paper covers); Shaw
38665 (dated [1816]).

1031 POEMS FOR LITTLE CHILDREN. 1820 [no
place or printer].
t.[1], [2], 3–12 p.; illus.; 8 cm.
PP° (covers wanting).

POEMS FOR LITTLE CHILDREN. *See* Gilbert, Ann
(Taylor), no. **446.**

POEMS ON DIFFERENT SUBJECTS, By A Lady. *See*
Sprout, Nancy, no. **1247.**

1032 POEMS, ON DIFFERENT SUBJECTS: Calculated To Improve And Edify Young Christians.
Albany, Printed by Charles R. and George Webster, No. 36 State-street, near the English Church
[1790?].
t.[1], [2], 3–12 p.; 12.5 cm.
RPB° (covers wanting); Evans 45973.

1033.1 POEMS, OR, THE ALHPABET [*sic. i.e.*
ALPHABET] IN VERSE. Designed for the Entertainment of all good Boys and Girl. Adorned With
Cuts. Sidney's Press. New-Haven. 1817.
fr.[2], t.[3], [4], 5–26, [27–28], [29, upper case
alphabet], [30, 2 cuts], [31, adv.] p.; illus.; 11
cm.; Dutch paper covers; p. [27–28] are cropped
at the top of the page taking the page numbers
off these pages when they were cut.
TxU° (p. 5–6, 26, [27–30] cropped at the top
of the page affecting page number).

1033.2 —— [same as **1033.1**] Sidney's Press. New-Haven, 1818.

fr.[2], t.[3], [4], 5–28, [29, 2 cuts], [30, upper case alphabet], [31, adv.] p.; illus.; 10.5 cm.; illus. white paper covers printed in black ink. MWA-T°.

1033.3 —— Alphabet in Verse. For The Entertainment of all good Children. Adorned with Cuts. New-Haven. Sidney's Press. For J. Babcock & Son. 1819.

fr.[2], t.[3], [4, alphabet–5] 6–30, [31, adv.] p.; illus.; 10 cm.

NN° (covers wanting; fr. [2] mut.); CtY.

1034 POEMS, SELECTED FROM THE WORKS OF APPROVED AUTHORS. Dublin: Printed by William Espy, Little Strand-street. 1818. Price bound in Sheep—Eightpence—in Grain–Sixpence.

fr.[1], t.[2], [3, bl.], [4], 5–179 p.; illus.; 14 cm.; bound in pr. orange-buff paper over bds. The imprint on the front cover: Dublin: Printed By William Epsy [*sic. i.e.* Espy], Little Strand-Street. 1818. And Sold By Munroe & Francis, 4, Cornhill. Boston. Rear cover: Uniform Editions of the following popular Works for Children, selected by the Society of Friends in Dublin for distribution among all classes, may be had at the low price of 25 ct. each, of Munroe & Francis, No. 4, Cornhill, Boston. [followed by a list of 21 titles].

MWA° (i. st. on cover title); Shaw 45364.

1035 A POETIC SELECTION FOR SABBATH SCHOOLS. Boston: Printed and sold at No. 53 Cornhill, by Lincoln & Edmands, Who publish a great variety of books suitable for Instruction and Rewards in Sabbath Schools. 1819.

t.[1], [2–3], 4–16 p.; illus.; 12.5 cm.; pr. & illus. paper covers; cover title undated.

MWA°; CCamarSJ; MHi; MSaE (cover p. 15–16 wanting); RPB; Shaw 49144.

POETIC TALES FOR CHILDREN. *See* Sproat, Nancy, no. **1248.1**.

1036 THE POETICAL BALANCE; or the Fates of Britain and America compared: A Tale. Philadelphia: adv. by Francis Bailey, 1792 in **1459**, and 1793 in **773.1**.

1037 A POETICAL DESCRIPTION OF SONG BIRDS: Interspersed with Entertaining Songs, Fables, And Tales, Adapted to each Subject: For The Amusement Of Children. [2 lines of verse] The First Worcester Edition. Printed at Worcester, Massachusetts, By Isaiah Thomas, Sold at his Bookstore in Worcester, and by him and Company in Boston. MDCCLXXXVIII.

fr.[2], t.[3], [4], 5–88 p.; front. only illus.; 12 cm.; bound in Dutch paper over bds. Adv. by I. Thomas, 1787 in **906.1**.

English ed. title 1: *The Poetical History Of Song Birds*. Adv. by T. Carnan in the London Chronicle May 15–18, 1773.

English title 2: *Poetical Description of Birds*. London: adv. by F. Power & Co., 1790 in *The Adventures Of A Bee*.

CtHi°; MB; MWA (p. 15–16, 21–22 wanting; lower half of p. 19–20 wanting; p. 29–30 mut.); NN (rebound); RPJCB (covers detached, poor copy); Evans 21399.

THE POETICAL FLOWER BASKET. *See* Johnson, Richard, no. **686**.

1038.1 POETICAL PRECEPTS. Comprising A Number Of Short Moral Poems, For The Use Of Children. By a Friend To Youth. [3 lines of quot.] Watts. [2 lines of quot.] Solomon. Concord [N.H.]: Printed by I. & W. R. Hill. 1814.

½t.[i], fr.[ii], t.[iii], [iv–v], vi, [7], 8–24 p.; front. only illus.; 12 cm.; marbled paper covers. ½ title: Poetical Precepts.

MWA°; MH; MSaE; PP; Shaw 32528.

1038.2 —— Exeter [N.H.]: Printed For The Author. 1815 .

fr.[2], t.[3], [4–6], 7–24 p.; illus.; 12.5 cm.; pr. pink paper covers. The leaf of fr.[2] is conjugate with the blank leaf following p. 24; the leaf of t.[3], p.[4], is conjugate with that of p. 23–24.

CtY°; DLC; Shaw 35660.

1038.3 —— Exeter [N.H.]: Printed for the Author. 1815.

fr.[2], t.[3], [4–6], 7–24, [25, bl.], [26, illus. used for front. of the above edition, **1038.2**], [27, adv.] p.; illus.; 12.5 cm.; illus. paper covers; fr.[2] conjugate with p.[27], the leaf of p. 23–24 conjugate with the leaf of p. [25–26].

CtY°.

1039   POETRY AND PROSE FOR CHILDREN. [4 lines of verse] Greenfield [Mass.]: Published By Clarke & Tyler. H. Graves, Printer. 1820
    fr.[2], t.[3], [4–5], 6–14 p.; illus.; 10.5 cm.
    MWA-T* (covers wanting); PP.

POETRY FOR CHILDREN. *See* Lamb, Charles, no. **742.**

THE POLITE LITTLE CHILDREN. *See* Cameron, Lucy Lyttelton (Butt), no. **150.**

POLLY CHERRY. *See* The Entertaining History Of Polly Cherry, or The New History Of Polly Cherry, no. **359.**

1040.1   POMPEY THE LITTLE WHO WAS TIED TO THE KETTLE. New York Published Jan.ʸ 1808 by Wᵐ Charles ———— Nº 195 Broad Way.
    t.[1], [2–13] p. engr. on one side only of 13 leaves; illus.; 11 cm.; pr. & illus. paper covers. Cover title imprint: Philadelphia: Published By Benjamin Johnson, No. 219 Market Street. 1809.
    MWA*; NRU; Shaw 15970.

1040.2 ———— A New Edition With Additional Plates. Philadelphia Published & sold wholesale by Wᵐ Charles Price 18¾ Cents 1812 [cover title].
    [2–15] p. engr. on one side only of 14 leaves; illus.; 13 cm.; pr. & illus. paper covers. The plates are redrawn in the reverse. The new plates are engr. p. [9–10].
    MWA*; Shaw 26492.

POOR SARAH. *See* Boudinot, Elias, no. **120.1.**

1041   THE PORT FOLIO; Or, A School Girl's Selection. By a Lady. [11 lines of verse] New-York: Published By A. T. Goodrich & Co. No. 124 Broadway, Corner of Cedar-Street. J. Seymour, Printer. 1818.
    t.[1], [2–3], 4–132 p.; 14 cm.
    MWA*; RPB; Shaw 45379.

1042   PORTRAITS OF CURIOUS CHARACTERS IN LONDON, &c. &c. With Descriptive and Entertaining Anecdotes. [2 lines of verse] Philadelphia: Published By Jacob Johnson, Nº 147, Market-Street. 1808.
    t.[1], 2–70, [71] p.; illus.; 14 cm.; colophon p.[71] Lydia R. Bailey, Printer, No. 84, Crown Street. Adv. by Johnson and Warner, 1814 in **1449.3.**
    English ed. London: W. & T. Darton, 1806.
    MWA* (i. st. on t.[1]; has I. Thomas' bookplate); PP (bound in marbled paper over bds., red leather spine); Shaw 13987.

1043   THE POST BOY. Clear the road! Clear the road! make room for me That ev'ry little child may learn, its A.B.C. Philadelphia. Published by Jacob Johnson, Nº 147 Market-Street. [1807].
    t.[1], [2–40] p.; illus.; 15 cm.; marbled paper covers. Adv. by Johnson & Warner, 1814 in **1449.2.**
    English ed. London: W. Darton and J. Harvey, 1802.
    PP* (copy 1, p.[19–20] wanting, p.[3–4] mut.; copy 2, p.[13–16], [25–28] wanting, p.[27–28], [29–30] in duplicate in place of missing pages); FTaSU (Sig C₂ wanting); MLuHi; MWA.

[POUPARD, JAMES] METAMORPHOSIS. *See* Sands, Benjamin, no. **1163.**

1044   No. 14. THE POWER OF TRUTH. An Authentic history of a poor villager. [caption title]. Andover [Mass.]: Printed For The New England Tract Society. By Flagg And Gould. 1820. 5th ed. 6,000. [colophon p. 12].
    [1], 2–12 p.; 17 cm.; also numbered [173], 174–184.
    MB* (bound in vol. 1 of publications of the N. Eng. Tract Soc. Andover 1820).

PRATT, SAMUEL JACKSON 1749–1814
1045.1 — THE PATERNAL PRESENT. Being A Sequel To Pity's Gift. Selected from the Writings of Mr. Pratt. New-York. Printed For Robert Moore, No. 38, Pearl-street. 1804.
    t.[1], [2–3], 4–107 p.; illus.; 13.5 cm.; ornamented blue-gray paper covers.
    English ed. London: C. Whittingham for T. N. Longman and O. Rees, and J. Harris, 1802.
    MWA* (rebound); DLC; ICN; PP; Shaw 7105 with Parental [*sic. i.e.* Paternal]).

1045.2 ———— Chiefly Selected From The Writings Of Mr. Pratt. Ornamented With Vignettes. Philadelphia: Published By Jacob Johnson. No. 147, Market–Street. 1807.
    t.[i], [ii–iii], iv, [5], 6–144 p.; illus.; 14 cm.; bound in marbled paper over bds., red leather

spine; colophon p. 144: Joseph Rakestraw, Printer. Adv. by Johnson & Warner, 1814 in **1449.2.**

MWA-W° (p. 99–106 wanting); CLU; DLC; MdHi; Shaw 13427.

1046.1 — PITY'S GIFT: A Collection Of Interesting Tales, To Excite The Compassion Of Youth For The Animal Creation. Selected By A Lady, From The Writings Of Mr. Pratt. The First Philadelphia Edition. Philadelphia: Printed By B. & J. Johnson, N° 147, High Street. 1801.

fr.[ii], t.[i], [ii–v], vi–vii, [viii, bl.], [9], 10–85, [86 adv.] p.; front. only illus.; bound in marbled paper over bds., yellow paper spine.

English ed. London: T. N. Longman, and E. Newbery, 1798.

MWA-W°; CLU; PP; Shaw 1178.

1046.2 — ——— The Animal Creation. From The Writings Of Mr. Pratt. Ornamented With Vignettes. Selected By A Lady. Philadelphia: Published By J. Johnson, No. 147, Market-Street. 1808. J. Adams, Printer.

t.[i], [ii–v], vi–vii, [viii, bl.], [1], 2–135 p.; illus.; 14.5 cm.; bound in marbled paper over bds., red leather spine; illus. p. 67, 72, 81, 84, 110, 129 signed A [Alexander Anderson]. Adv. by Johnson & Warner, 1814 in **1449.2.**

MWA-W°; DLC; MB; MH; NHi; NNC-Pl; OOxM; Shaw 15991.

1047 A PREMIUM. Philadelphia: Published by Jacob Johnson, 147 Market-Street 1806.

t.[1], [2–72] p.; [A]–B$_4$, C–D$_2$, E$_4$, F$_2$, G$_4$, H$_2$, I–K$_4$, L–M$_2$; illus.; t.[1] 14 cm.; illus. on [A$_2$] verso show the front of Jacob Johnson's Book Store. The title page vignette [A$_1$] recto and illustration on [A$_4$] verso, that on C$_2$ verso, E$_1$ recto, E$_4$ verso, G$_4$ verso, I$_1$ recto, I$_4$ verso, L$_2$ verso, are signed *W.R.* [William Ralph] sc. The colophon p. [72]: Joseph Rakestraw, Printer. Adv. by Johnson & Warner, 1812 in **497**, and 1814 in **1449.3.**

MWA-T° (p. [27–30] or E$_2$–E$_3$ wanting); CLU° (p. 3–4, 33–34, 37–38 or sigs. [A$_2$], F$_1$, G$_1$ wanting).

A PREMIUM FOR SABBATH SCHOOLS. *See* Children's Hymn Book, no. **184.**

1048 A PRESENT FOR A GOOD CHILD Illustrated with Engravings Philadelphia Published & sold

Wholesale by Wm Charles Price 6¼ Cents Coloured 12½ cents [1820] [cover title].

[1–8] p. engr. on one side only of 8 leaves; illus.; 11 cm.; pr. buff paper covers; on the blank recto of p. [1] is a mss. inscription *Martin Bael his Book 1820.*

MWA°; Shoemaker 2860.

A PRESENT FOR A LITTLE BOY. *See* Darton, William, no. **264.1.**

A PRESENT FOR A LITTLE GIRL. *See* Darton William, no. **265.1.**

1049 A PRESENT FOR CHILDREN. New-York: adv. by S. Wood, 1820 in **274.2.**

1050 A PRESENT FOR GOOD BOYS. In Which They Will Find Much Amusement And Instruction. Published By Johnson & Warner, And Sold At Their Bookstores, Philadelphia, And Richmond, Virginia. A. Fagan, Printer. 1813.

fr.[2], t.[3], [4–5], 6–71 p.; illus.; 14 cm.; pr. & illus. pink paper covers.

MWA°; NHi; NNC-Pl; Shaw 29576.

1051 A PRESEN[T] FOR A LITTLE B[OY.] [2 lines of verse] Adorned With Cuts. Portsmouth [N.H.]. Printed For The Purchasers. 1805.

fr.[2], t.[3], [4–5], 6–21 p.; illus.; 10 cm.; wallpaper covers. The Illustrations of the "Drum" and "Eagle" p. [5], the "Heron" p. 16, the "Quale" p. 17 appeared in *The Mother's Gift. Boston: N. Coverly. 1812*, no. **907.2**, on p. 14, fr.[2], and p. 9 respectively. This is a different book from no. **264.1.**

MWA° (t.[3], p. 13–14 mut.).

1052.1 A PRESENT FOR SABBATH SCHOOL CHILDREN. [1 line of quot.] Newburyport [Mass.], Printed By W. & J. Gilman. Sold at their Book-Store and Library, No. 2, Middle-Street. 1818.

t.[1], [2–3], 4–15 p.; illus.; 12 cm.; pr. & illus. paper covers; cover title undated.

MSaE°.

1052.2 ——— Boston: Printed and sold by Lincoln & Edmands, No. 53 Cornhill. 1819.

t.[1], [2–3], 4–16 p.; title vignette & illus.; 12.5 cm.; pr. & illus. buff paper covers; cover title undated.

MWA°; CCamarSJ; CLU; MWHi; OOxM; PP; Shaw 49188.

1053 No. I. Sunday School Rewards. A PRESENT FOR SUNDAY-SCHOOL CHILDREN. Boston: Printed By Ezra Lincoln. 1817.

t.[1], [2], 3–11, [12] p.; title vignette only illus.; 16.5 cm.; the title page is both title and cover title; p. [12] is not part of the text but printed as a rear cover. Caption p.[12]: Rules And Regulations, For the Sunday Schools established by the Society for the Moral and Religious Instruction of the Poor in Boston.
Welch°; MWA; Shaw 41883 and 42235.

1054 [A] PRESENT FROM PHILADELPHIA. Ornamented With Fourteen Handsome Engravings. Printed And Sold By Benjamin Johnson, No. 31, High Street, Philadelphia. 1803.

fr.[2], t.[3], [4–47] p.; sigs. [A]$_{12}$, B–C$_6$; illus.; 13.5 cm.; buff paper covers. Cover label: Pres[ent From] Phil[adelphia.]
MWA-T° (½ of the front cover and fr.[2] wanting; sig.[A]$_7$, [A]$_{12}$ or p. 13–14, 23–24 wanting, one of these pages probably have the two missing pl. illus., because only 12 are present).

A PRESENT TO CHILDREN. By The Author of Ditties For Children. *See* Sproat, Nancy, no. **1249**.

1055.1 A PRESENT TO CHILDREN. Consisting of several new Divine Hymns and Moral Songs. New-London: Printed by T. Green. [1782?].

t.[1], [2], 3–15, [16] p.; 12 cm.; verse. Title page not surrounded by a border. Since the 1783 edition, no. **1055.2**, is known this is probably earlier [1782?].
PP° (mss. inscription on t.[1] below the imprint: "*Eber Chapman His Book 1783*"); CtY (mss. inscription on t.[1] below the imprint: "*Eber Chapman His Book 1783*"); Evans 44248.

1055.2 ——— New London: Printed by T. Green. 1783.

t.[1], [2], 3–16 p.; 12 cm.; verse.
CtY°.

1055.3 ——— Norwich [Conn.], Printed By Ebenezer Bushnell. 1792.

t.[1], [2–3], 4–14, [15, lower case alphabet] p.; 11 cm.; verse.
CtY° (top half of p.[15] torn away); Evans 46551.

1056 A PRESENT TO CHILDREN CONSISTING OF SEVERAL NEW DIVINE HYMNS, MORAL SONGS & ENTERTAINING STORIES. Printed For Chapman Whitcomb [Leominster Mass. *ca.* 1800].

t.[1], [2], 3–12 p.; 16 cm.; blue-gray paper covers. This is a different book from nos. **1055.1–3**.
MWA° (bound as a book).

1057 PRESENTS FOR GOOD BOYS. In words of One and two Syllables. London: Printed for Tabart & Co. at the Juvenile & School Library, 157 New Bond Street March 1st 1805. and sold by all Booksellers & Toy Shops in the Empire. Price One Shilling.

t.[1], [2–3], 4–36 p.; illus.; 14 cm.; pr. paper covers. Cover title imprint: Philadelphia: Published And Sold By H. Conrad & E. Parsons, N. E. Corner of Fourth and Chesnut Streets, 1805. Colophon p. 36: W. Marchant, Printer, 3 Greville-street, Holborn.
PP°.

1058.1 PRESENTS FOR GOOD GIRLS. Philadelphia. Published by Jacob Johnson, No. 147, Market Street. 1806.

t.[1], [2–48] p.; illus.; 13 cm.; blue marbled paper covers; colophon p.[48]: Robert Bailey, Printer, No. 48, Crown-Street. Engravings signed *W R sc* [*i.e.* William Ralph].
English ed. London: Entered at Stationer's Hall by R. Phillips July 24, 1804.
MWA-W°.

1058.2 ——— New-York. Published By Wm B. Gilley, 92 Broadway. Sold Wholesale And Retail By The Principle Booksellers. Gould and Van Pelt, Printers, 9 Wall-street. 1814.

t.[1], [2–3], 4–36 p.; illus.; 14 cm.; pr. paper covers. Cover title imprint: New-York. Published By William B. Gilley, No. 92 Broadway. 1814.
MWA°.

1058.3 ——— New-York: Published by Gould and Van Pelt, No. 9 Wall St. Sold Wholesale And Retail By The Principle Booksellers. Gould and Van Pelt, Printers, 9 Wall street. 1814.

t.[1], [2–3], 4–36 p.; illus.; 14 cm.; paper covers.
CtY°; MWA (p.[3]–4, 21–36 & covers wanting); Shaw 32566.

A PRETTY BOOK OF PICTURES. *See* Tommy Trip's Pictures Of Beasts And Birds, no. **1326.**

1059 PRETTY HYMNS, FOR YOUNG CHILDREN. Newburyport [Mass.], Published By W. & J. Gilman. Sold at their Bookstore and Printing-Office, No. 2, Middle-Street. 1819. [cover title].

    [1], 2–16 p.; illus.; 12.5 cm.; pr. & illus. paper covers; colophon p. 16: Newburyport [Mass.]: Printed By W. & J. Gilman, No. 2, Middle-Street. 1819.

    MSaE*.

A PRETTY NEW YEAR'S GIFT. *See* Sobersides, Soloman, no. **1221.1.**

1060 THE PRETTY ORPHANS: A Tale. Shewing [*sic. i.e.* Showing] how Farmer Townsend took home three Orphan Children, who had neither Father nor Mother, and brought them up as his own. Cambridge [New-York]: Printed By Tennery & Stockwell, And sold Wholesale and Retail, at their Printing Office & Bookstore. n.d. [1805?].

    fr.[2], t.[3], 4–31 p.; illus.; 10 cm.; marbled paper covers. Joseph Tennery published the *Cambridge Gazette* at Cambridge N.Y. Dec. 7, 1803–4. William Stockwell was at Cambridge, N.Y. 1805–1808. (MWA cat.).

    MWA-W*; (not in Shaw).

1061.1 A PRETTY PLAY-THING FOR CHILDREN of all Denominations. New-York: adv. by Hugh Gaine, 1774 in **275.1**, and 1776 in *The Young Clerk's Vade Mecum.*

1061.2 A PRETTY PTAYTHING [*sic. i.e.* PLAY-THING] FOR CHILDREN of all Denominations. Containing, I. Tom Noddy and his Sister Sue, a Lilliputian Story. II. An Alphabet in Prose, interspersed with proper Lessons in Life, for the use of Great Children. III. A few Maxims for the Improvement of the mind. IV. The sound of the Letters explained by visible Objects. V. The Puzzling-Cap: a choice collection of Riddles, in Familiar Verse. The whole embellished with a variety of Cuts. Philadelphia: Printed by Benjamin Johnson No. 147 Market street. 1794.

    t[iii], iv, 5–62+ p.; illus.; 10 cm.

    English ed. *A Pretty Play-Thing For Children of all Denominations: Containing I. The Alphabet in Verse, for the Use of little Children. II. An Alphabet in Prose, interspersed with proper Les-sons in Life, for the Use of Great Children. III. The Sound of the Letters explained by visible Objects, delineated on Copper Plates. IV. The Cuz's Chorus, set to Music, To be sung by Children, in order to teach them to join their Letters into Syllables, and pronounce them properly. V. An exact Representation of a good Fat Cuz arrayed in the Robes of his Order. The Whole embellished with Variety of Cuts, after the Manner of Ptolomy. Alexandria: Printed for the Booksellers of Egypt and Palmyra, and sold at the Bible and Sun in St. Paul's Church-Yard. Price bound half a Shass or 3d. English.* [*ca.* 1759] London: adv. by J. Newbery, 1759 in John-The-Giant Killer's (*pseud.*) *Food For The Mind.*

    MWA* (p.[ii?], 63? and covers wanting); Evans 47187.

1062 PRETTY POEMS FOR CHILDREN. Newburyport [Mass.], Printed By W. & J. Gilman. And sold at their Miscellaneous Book-Store, No. 2, Middle-street. 1814.

    fr.[2], t.[3], [4], 5–23 p.; illus.; 13.5 cm.; pr. & illus. buff paper covers; cover title undated.

    MWA*; PP (rebound; fr.[2], p. 23 & covers wanting); Shaw 32567.

PRETTY POEMS. *See* Lovechild, Tommy (*pseud.*), no. **804.1.**

A PRETTY RIDDLE BOOK FOR CHILDREN. *See* Conundrum Christopher (*pseud.*), no. **232.**

PRIM, PETER *pseud.*
1063 — THE DOLEFUL DEATH OF POOR OLD ROBIN with the Distribution of his Valuable Property as related And Exhibited in beautiful Engravings By Peter Prim. Engraved & Published by J. Scoles, New York. [*ca.* 1815].

    t.[2], [1–15] p. engraved on one side of 16 leaves; 13.5 cm. The date is conjectural. J. Scoles was an engraver & bookseller in New York, 1794–1820. The collation is taken from the English edition which has 16 leaves, and pages 1–15 numbered.

    See also Peter Prim's Pride, no. **990.**

    English ed. London: Harris Nov. 1–1814.

    Not in Shaw.

PRINCE LEE BOO. *See* The History Of Prince Lee Boo, no. **573.1;** The Interesting And Affecting History Of Prince Lee Boo, entry below no. **650**; The Pleasing, Interesting, and Affecting History of Prince Lee Boo, entry below no. **1022**.

1064 PRISCILLA THE ORPHAN. New-York: adv. by L. B. Jansen and G. Jansen, 1808 in **766**.

1065 THE PRIZE. Being A Selection Of Stories, Calculated To Attract The Attention Of Children. Warren [R.I.]: Printed At The Office Of The Columbian Post-Boy, Next Room To The Post-Office. 1812.
> t.[3], [4], 5–30 p.; 10.5 cm.; blue paper covers. Printed by [Mason & Bird]. Joseph Mason Jr. & James Bird were printers & publishers in Warren, R.I. 1812–1813. (MWA cat.).
> MWA* (p. 27–30 worm-eaten); Shaw 26530.

1066 THE PRIZE; OR, THE LACE MAKERS OF MISSENDEN. A Tale. Philadelphia: Published By M. Carey & Son, No. 126, Chestnut-street. October–1817.
> [i–ii, adv.], t.[i], [ii], [1], 2–139 p.; 14.5 cm.; colophon p. 139; Doylestown, Bucks County [Pa.], printed By Asher Miner.
> MH*; Shaw 41890.

1067.1 THE PRIZE FOR YOUTHFUL OBEDIENCE. From Sidney's Press. For Increase Cooke & Co. 1803.
> t.[3], [4–5], 6–72 p.; illus.; 13.5 cm.; buff paper cover. New-Haven.
> English ed. London: [pt. I.] Darton And Harvey, 1800.
> DLC*; Shaw 4921.

1067.2 ———— Part I. [II.] Philadelphia: Published By Jacob Johnson, No. 147, Market Street. T. L. Plowman, Printer. 1803.
> Two vols. 16 cm.
> Pt. I: t.[1], [2–60] p.; illus.; bound in brick-red marbled paper over bds.; Pt.[II]: t.[1], [2–60] p.; illus.; bound in green marbled paper over bds.; 2 vols. 16 cm.; some cuts in both vols. signed A [Alexander Anderson].
> Welch* (pts. I, D_2–D_3 wanting; II); DLC; MWA (pt. II, p. 49–51 wanting); NN (pt. II); NNC-Pl (pt. II); NNC-T; NNMM (pt. II); PHi (pt. II); PP (pt. II); PPL (pt. II); Shaw 4922.

1067.3 ———— From Sidney's Press. For Increase Cooke & Co. 1806.
> t.[3], [4–5], 6–72 p.; 13.5 cm.; bound in marbled paper over w. bds.; printed in New-Haven.
> MWA*; Shaw 11217.

1067.4 ———— Obedience. Part I. [II.]. Philadelphia: Published By Jacob Johnson, No. 147 Market Street, John Bioren, Printer, 1807.
> pt. I: t.[1], [2–54] p.; illus.; pt. II: t.[1], [2–51] p.; illus.; 2 vols. 16 cm.; pink paper covers; some cuts in both vols. signed A [Alexander Anderson].
> MWA* (pts. I, II), CaOTP (pt. II); CSmH (pt. II); CtY (pt. I, II); DLC (pts. I, II); NHi (pts. I, II); NNC-Pl (pt. II); PHi (pt. II); PP (pts. I, II); PPL; Shaw 13440.

1067.5 ———— Obedience. From Sidney's Press, New-Haven. 1808.
> t.[1], [2–3], 4–64 p.; [A]–B_{16}; 10.5 cm.; pr. yellow paper covers.
> Cover title: The Prize. Contents include pt. I of no. **1067.2**.
> CtHi* (rear cover wanting); Shaw 50883.

1067.6 ———— Obedience. From Sidney's Press, New-Haven. 1809.
> fr.[ii], t.[1], [2–3], 4–35 p.; illus.; 13.5 cm.; pr. & illus. brown paper covers. Cover imprint: Published by I. Cooke & Co. New-Haven, Who have a universal assortment of Books and Stationery, for wholesale and retail.
> MWA*; CtY (rebound); PP; Shaw 18446.

1067.7 ———— Sidney's Press. Published by John Babcock & Son, New-Haven. S. & W. R. Babcock, No. 163 King-Street, Charlestown, And M'Carty & Davis; Philadelphia. 1820.
> fr.[2], t.[3], [4–5], 6–31 p.; illus.; 14.5 cm.; pr. & illus. yellow paper covers, cover title undated.
> CtHi*; CtW; MHa; NB (i. st. on t.[3]); Shoemaker 2873.

1067.8 ———— Obedience. New·Haven: Printed For John Babcock And Son. Sidney's Press. 1820.
> fr.[2], t.[3], [4–5], 6–31 p.; illus.; 15 cm.; pr. & illus. blue-gray paper covers.
> Copy A: The frontispiece shows an owl in a tree with seven birds around him. Cover title: The

Prize. [illus. of two men walking while each is playing a violin. In front of them a child is walking.] Published and Sold by John Babcock and Son, New-Haven, and S. & W. R. Babcock, Charleston.

Copy B: Cover title: The Trize [*sic. i.e.* Prize]. [illus. of the trunk of a tree with a sow and her litter of page at the foot of the tree.] Published and Sold ——— [same as in copy A] Charleston.

MWA-T* (copy A); Adomeit* (copy B; pr. & illus. blue paper covers; fr. [2], p. 31 wanting).

THE PRODIGAL DAUGHTER (arranged chronologically)

Many of the editions of *The Prodigal Daughter* are undated and difficult to describe. For this reason all possible means to distinguish each issue will be employed. Of prime importance is the kind of type used in printing the first three words or more of the title and the punctuation after the word "Daughter". For this reason the first words of the title will not be put in small capitals as in all other books in this bibliography. Instead an attempt will be made to give some idea of the type used. Besides this, the ending of each line on the title page through the first line of explanation of text, usually printed in smaller type, the last line of the explanation, and the imprint will be shown by a cross line. Some characteristic variations on the title page, the first page of text, the last page on which the end of the poem appears, and the page containing Rev. Mr. Williams' sermon will be mentioned.

1068.1 THE PRODIGAL DAUGHTER:/Or a strange and wonderful Relation/Shewing how a gentlemean of a vast Estate in *Bristol* had a/proud and disobedient Daughter, who because her Parents would not support her in all her Extravagance, bargaind [*sic. i.e.* bargain'd] with the Devil to poison them. How an Angel informed her Parents of their Daughter's Design. How she lay in a Trance four Days, and when she was put into the Grave, she came to Life again, and related the wonderful Things she saw in the other World. Likewise the Substance of a Sermon preached on this Occasion by the Reverend Mr./Williams, from Luke 15.24./Printed and sold at the Heart and Crown in Boston. [*ca.* 1737–1741].

t.[1], [2], 3–8+ p.; 3 illus.; 17 cm. The title page is the usual one found in most editions. Some peculiarities are: a colon after "Daughter:", line 1; "*Bristol*", line 3, in italics; "bargaind [*sic. i.e.* bargain'd]", line 5; "their Daughter's Design,", line 7; "into the Grave", line 8. The caption, p. 3, is in four lines. There is a

comma after "Daughter," and "Or,", lines 2 and 3; "LADY", line 4, is printed entirely in capitals; "Reclaim'd, &c", line 4, is printed with a capital "R", " 'd" followed by "&c." in italics. Below the caption and seven blocks of a single rule there are 12 lines of verse, lines 5–16, the same as no. **1068.5,** but differs in having "pen'd", line 6, spelled with one "n"; "*Bristol*", line 9, in italics. Page 5, like the remainder of the book, is printed in 88 (20 line measure) type. *See* note under no. **492.1.** All after p. 8 is wanting.

The illustration and text except for page [6] and 7, are the same as no. **1068.5,** and occur on the same pages. Page [6] has 9 lines of text, with the last line ending "something surpriz'd." Page 7 is in 31 lines with the first line: "But want of Grace so blinded had her Eyes." Only the first three of the usual four large different illustrations, 9–9.5 cm. high by 7.3–7.9 cm. wide, are in this fragmentary copy. Cut 1 shows the Prodigal Daughter in her coffin, on the right, above her head a burning candle in a holder on the right side of an oval mirror, the minister in the center and the mother standing on the left. It is signed *P. F.* Isaiah Thomas, 1874, vol. 1, p. 99 says that Thomas Fleet has a negro slave who "was an ingenious man, and cut on wooden blocks, all the pictures which decorated the ballads and small books of his master." Isaiah Thomas also notes that Fleet had two negro boys named Pompey and Caesar who were young men when their master died, but worked after his death in his printing house, and believed them to be the sons of the "ingenious" negro slave. Hamilton 51.(1) thinks the signature *P. F.* on cut 1 "may be the work of Pompey Fleet or perhaps that of the ingenious negro himself, Pompey's father, who may have borne the same name." Cut 2, the devil, on the left, dressed as a gentleman and facing the Prodigal Daughter, on the right, p. 6, has no breaks in the thick and thin rules of the left border. Behind the devil's legs and the tip of his cane there are shadows, represented by cross lines. These were removed from the cut in the Heart and Crown edition of [1769?], no. **1068.5,** and are absent in all later printings of the illustration. Cut 3, the parents in bed, on the left, above whom and to the right is a huge robed angel, p. 8, has the left ruled border damaged. In this region of the left border, an upper and lower piece, each 2 mm. long, are missing, leaving a central fragment 2 mm. long.

Small printer's ornaments are not present in this edition. On page 3 there is a large ornamental cut of a battle scene which has nothing to do with the poem. Going through Evans and checking D. Henchman and Thomas Fleet imprints, on the microcards of Early American Imprints, it was found that this figure first appeared in Edward Wigglesworth's *A seasonable Caveat against believing every spirit. Boston: Printed For D. Henchman, 1735*, Evans 3975, Hamilton 16.

The Heart and Crown was the name of Thomas Fleet Sr.'s firm 1731–1758. His sons Thomas and John Fleet continued the firm under the same name 1758–1779. In 1780 the name was changed by them to The Bible and Heart, when, according to Isaiah Thomas, crowns became unpopular. From the above data this fragmentary copy was surely printed prior to 1780, because the firm's name is the Heart and Crown. Cut 2, p. 6, has no breaks in the thick and thin rules of the left border and shadows are present behind the devil's legs and cane. In *The History Of The Holy Jesus. Boston: Fowle & Draper*, 1762, the left half of cut 2, drawn in the reverse, is present and is the only other representation of cut 2 showing the devil with leg and cane shadows. It was probably an illustration used in no. **1068.2**. Since all later editions of *The Prodigal Daughter*, with this cut, lack these shadows, we can assume that the Fleet fragmentary copy was printed prior to 1762, when possibly shadowed versions of the picture were considered so old-fashioned that Fowle & Draper cut up the cut or discarded it as an illustration to be used in *The Prodigal Daughter*. This cut could have been discarded because, like his having a cloven foot, the devil may not have been supposed to cast a shadow. If it is assumed that Evans has some basis for his entry no. 4069, the 1736 printing of the book could have been the first edition. It is then possible that the borders of all the cuts were intact at that time and showed no breaks. The battle-scene cut, which shows no nick in the shield in 1735, could have acquired the nick in 1736 since it is present from 1737 on. In NjP copy of Evans 4145 the nick is smaller than in Evans 4210. The cut was used frequently in Thomas Fleet Sr.'s publications from 1737 to 1741. Printers, on acquiring a new cut or type ornament, used it often in the first years after obtaining it. Because of the repeated use of the battle-scene cut, just after 1735, no. **1068.1** has been given the date [*ca.* 1737–1741] until another copy is located, which hopefully may have an inscribed date in it.

Irish broadside ed. title 1: *The Prodigal Daughter; Or, The Disobedient Child Reclaimed, being a full and true Relation of one Jane Nicholson, the only daughter of a Rich Merchant living in Merchant-Street*, St. James's, London. Newry: Robert Moffet, 18;. [*sic. i.e.* 1804?]. Many of the verses of this Irish edition and the broadside editions below, show variations from those in American editions. The location of the story is always London and not Bristol, as in the American editions.

English broadside ed. title 2: *The Prodigal Daughter: Or, The disobedient Lady Reclaim'd.* [n.p.], [n.d.].

English chapbook ed. title 1: *The Prodigal Daughter: Or, The Disobedient Child Reclaimed.* Newcastle: M. Angus & Son. [n.d.].

NjP* (all after p. 8 wanting); Evans 41867; Hamilton 51.

1068.2 [The Prodigal Daughter . . .] [part of the probable title on missing p. [1]].

Sold at The New Printing-Office, [*ov*]*er-against the Old Brick Meetin, near the* Cour[t] House, *in Cornhill*, BOSTON. [1758?] [p. [15]]. [11–16] p.; 2 illus.; 15 cm. This fragmentary copy is mostly wanting. Line 25 p. [12]: "He said, *But you have been a Sinner wild*", printed in italics, except for "He said", has the same wording found in most editions. *See* no. **1068.16** for exceptions. The poem ends in 8 lines on p. [15] with the last four lines: "I hope this will a good Example be./Children, your Parents honour and obey, /And then the Lord will bless you here on Earth,/And give you a Crown of Glory after Death." Comparing the last 24 lines of the poem, p.[13–15], with those on p. 15, **1068.3**, the following differences in **1068.2** are: "*Return*", p. [13], line 25, in italics with a capital "R"; a period after "*paid.*", line 27; "Misery,", line 29, "me,", p. [14], line 1, "free,", line 2, are all followed by a comma; "me", p. [13], line 30, without punctuation; "desire;", p. [15], line 2, with a semicolon; "be.", line 5, followed by a period. The caption p. [16]: "THE SERMON/Luke XV. *and the first Part of the 24th*

Verse,/For this my Son was dead, and is alive, he was [lost]/*and is found.",* is mostly printed in italics. The Rev. Mr. Williams' sermon is broken up into three paragraphs with spaces between them. "Finis" at the bottom of the page is printed in large capital italics and measures 42. mm. in length. Two printer's ornaments are present. Between the two decorative bars there is a large ornament of a hand holding a bunch of flowers and surrounded, at the wrist, by a frilled cuff.

The two illustrations are redrawn in the reverse from no. **1068.1** and measure 10 cm. high by 8 cm. wide. In complete copies of the book in later editions these two cuts are numbered 1 and 4. Cut 1 portrays the Prodigal Daughter in her coffin, on the left, a central minister, and her mother on the right, p. [11]. This picture is usually a duplicate of the one used on the title page. Cut 4, the devil in his true form, naked, with horns, tail, and a cloven hoof, on the left, is opposite the Prodigal Daughter, on the right, p. [14]. It is also drawn in the reverse of the one in **1068.5**, and probably occurred in **1068.1**, from which the drawing in the Mecom edition could have been copied. One side of the girl's face is shaded in both illustrations. The block used in the Mecom edition was cut in half and the left half, showing only the naked devil, was used in *The History Of The Holy Jesus. Boston: Fowle & Draper, 1762*, no. **593**. Another half cut, serving for the frontispiece in no. **593**, has the devil, on the right, dressed as a gentleman, but having a cloven hoof, shadows behind his legs and tip of his cane. It is surely the right half of cut 2 which probably appeared in Mecom's edition. This half cut and the one in no. **1068.1** are the only illustrations showing leg and cane shadows.

Benjamin Mecom's firm was "At the New Printing-Office, opposite the Old Brick Meeting, in Cornhill" in 1758, *see* no. **1068.8**. Evans lists the address: "At the New-Printing-Office, near, the Town House [Court-House, on Cornhill] 1757–1762." Janeway's *Heaven Upon Earth. Boston: Reprinted by Z. Fowle & Draper, for B. Mecom. 1760*, Evans 8625, is evidence that Fowle & Draper printed for B. Mecom. Because of the cut in both **593** and **1068.2**, it is probable that the latter book was printed by Z. Fowle & S. Draper for B. Mecom. The date [1758?], given by the MWA, is reasonable, be-

cause it allows a sufficient number of years for the cut on p. [11] to have been used, before being cut up vertically to be printed in no. **593**. MWA° (p. [1–10] or sigs [A]$_1$–[A]$_4$, B$_1$ wanting); Evans 41867.

1068.3 THE PRODIGAL DAUGHTER: BEING/A strange and wonder [*sic. i.e.* wonderful] Relation of a young Lady in *Bristol,/*who, because her Parents would not support her in her Extravagance, bargained with the Devil to poison them. – – – – How an Angel informed her Parents of her Design. – – – – How she lay in a Trance four Days. – – – – How she came to Life again, &c, &c. – – – – Likewise the Sub-/stance of a Sermon on this Occasion, from *Luke xv.* 24./Printed and Sold in *Back-street*, BOSTON. [1767?].

t.[1], [2–3], 4–15, [16] p.; 7 illus. including a duplicate on p. 12 of the one on t.[1]; 18 cm. The firm of Zachariah Fowle was in Back-street, Boston, 1763–1770. The title page in this book has "BEING", line 3, instead of the usual "Or", as in no. **1068.1** and later editions; "wonderful" is misspelled "wonder", line 4. The entire explanation is a contracted version with many of the usual words omitted. "them. – – – –", "Design, – – – –", "four Days. – – – –", lines 7, 8, are each followed by a period and four dashes. The four-lined caption p.[3], has a semicolon after "Daughter;", line 2, and "reclaim'd, &c.", line 4, has a lower case "r" and "&c." in italics. Below the caption, p.[3], and the decorative bar, line 5, there are 8 lines of verse, or lines 6–13. Line 6: "Let every wicked graceless Child attend". In line 7 "penn'd" is spelled with two "ns"; "Bristol", line 10, printed in regular type; line 13 reads: "Whom he most tenderly did love so dear." The text on p. 11 is printed entirely in 74 (20 line measure) type. *See* note under no. **492.1**. The last 24 lines of the poem are on p. 15, with the substance of Rev. Mr. Williams' sermon on p. [16], in three paragraphs.

Six figured printer's ornaments are present.

Four different cuts are used. Two of these, or cuts 1 and 4, are redrawn versions of those on p. [11], [14] in no. **1068.5**. Cut 1 shows the Prodigal Daughter in her coffin, on the left, a central minister, and the mother on the right, signed *I T*, t.[1], p. 12. Hamilton thinks that the initials *I T* are those of Isaiah Thomas. Cut 2, also printed in 1787 depicts the devil dressed as a gentleman, on the left, facing the Prodigal Daughter on the right, p. 6. Cut 3 of the mother and father in bed, on the left, above whom, on the right, is a flying, nude, warning angel, is printed from the same block used in 1787. Cut 4 is the I. Thomas version of the devil in his true form, on the left, facing the Prodigal Daughter on the right, p. 10. It is the same one used in the [1772?] ed. Besides these there are two new, small, rectangular cuts numbered 5 and 6. Cut 5 portrays the Prodigal Daughter arguing with her mother, with a round table between them. Cut 6 is the Crucifixion used by Z. Fowle in *The History Of The Holy Jesus, 1766,* B₇ recto, no. **587.14.** Hamilton lists no. **1068.3** under the date 1767, because it was the last year in which I. Thomas worked for Fowle as an apprentice. He says that the cuts may have been made earlier and the book could have been printed any time between 1763 and 1771. The date 1767 seems most plausible, since the cut of the Crucifixion was used in no. **587.14** in 1766.

NjP* (p. [3]–4 slightly mut.); MWA* (t.[1], p.[2] & ¼ of [3]–4 wanting, p. 15–[16] mut.); Evans 41754; Hamilton 45.

1068.4 ——— Daughter./Or a strange ——— [same as **1068.1**] Relation, shewing how a/——— in Bristol, had a proud ——— bargained with the Devil ——— of her Design. ——— four Days; ——— put in the Grave, she came to life again, ——— Preach'd on the Occassion/by the Rev. Mr. Williams, from Luke XV. 24./Providence: Printed and Sold at the New-Printing/Office, at the Paper-Mill./[1768?].

t.[1], [2], 3–16 p.; 6 illus. including the duplicate on p. 12 of the one on t.[1]; 18 cm. Printed by John Waterman. The title and text are the same as in no. **1068.1,** but title has a period after "Daughter.", line 1; "shewing", line 2, has a lower case "s"; "Bristol", line 3, in small capitals; "bargained", lines 5, 6, spelled with an "ed"; "her Design.", line 7, instead of "Daughter's Design,"; a semicolon after "Days;", line 8; "in the Grave,", lines 8, 9; "life", line 9, with the "l" in lower case; "preach'd", line 11; "Williams", "Luke XV", line 12, not in italics. The caption, p. 3, is the same as in **1068.1,** but the "r" in "reclaim'd, &c." in the lower case and "&c," not in italics. Below the caption and decorative bar, line 5, the 12 lines of verse are

the same as in no. **1068.1,** with "pen'd,", line 7, spelled with one "n"; "Bristol", line 10, printed in regular type. The type, measured on p. 5, is 80 (20 line measure). *See* note under **492.1.** The last 16 lines of the poem are on p. 15 with "s" of "saviour's", line 2, in the lower case; no comma after "free", line 2; a period after "require.", line 9. Page 16 has the caption: "THE/ SERMON." The word "SERMON." and period measure 52.5 mm. in length.

Four printer's ornaments are present.

The four different large cuts are redrawn or influenced by those in earlier editions. Cut 1, the Prodigal Daughter in her coffin, on the right, having above her head a burning candle in a holder, to the left of an oval mirrow, is signed *I.W.* possibly John Waterman, t.[1], p. 12. Cut 2 is a crude representation of the devil, dressed as a French gentleman, on the left, facing the Prodigal Daughter on the right, p. 6. A print from the same block appears in the Newport, 1770 edition. Cut 3, the parents in bed on the right, a huge robed angel to the left, p. 8, is the reverse of the one in no. **1068.1.** Cut 4, the devil in his true form, on the left, p. 10, closely resembles the one in no. **1068.2,** p. [14]. On p. 15, an additional cut is used for a tailpiece, consisting of 5 figures, three of which are in ministers' robes.

MWA* t.[1], p. 3–7 mut. affecting text); RHi; Evans 41868.

1068.5 ——— Daughter:/Or a strange and wonderful Relation, Shewing how a/——— [same as **1068.1**] *Bristol,* had a proud and disobedient Daughter, who, because ——— bargained with the Devil to poison them.—How an Angel ——— her Design. — How she lay in a Trance four Days; ——— in the Grave, ——— Sermon Preach'd on this Occa-/sion by the Rev. Mr. *Williams,* from *Luke* XV, 24./Sold at the Heart and Crown, in Cornhill, *Boston./*[1769?].

t.[1], [2], 3–16 p.; illus. including the duplicate on p. 12 of the one on t.[1]; 18 cm.; colophon p. 16 same as the imprint on t.[1]; above the imprint on t.[1] there is a single thin rule. The firm of Thomas and John Fleet was at the above address 1757–1776. The title page is reset, closely follows **1068.1,** but has a colon after "Daughter:", line 1; "bargained", line 5; "them. — ", "Design. — ", lines 6, 7, followed by a

period and a dash; a semicolon after "Days;",
line 7; "in the Grave", line 8; "preach'd", line
10; "Luke XV", line 11. The caption in four
lines, p.[3], similar to **1068.1,** has a colon after
"Daughter:", line 2, and "reclaimed, *&c.*", line
4, with a lower case "r", ending in "ed", and
"*&c.*" printed in italics with the "*&*" capitalized.
Below the decorative bar, line 5, there are the
same 12 lines of verse with "penn'd,", line 7,
spelled with two "ns"; the "C" of "Child", line 6,
capitalized, also the "L" of "Lines", line 7, the
"W" of "Warning", line 8, and many other
words. The type setting of the remainder of
the text is very close to no. **1068.1** with the
same verses on the identical pages except pages
6 and 7. Page 6 is in 8 lines instead of 9, and
p. 7 has 32 lines instead of 31. The type in
which the book is printed, measured on p. 5, is
83 (20 line measure). *See* note under no. **492.1.**
The poems ends, p. 15 in 16 lines. "The Substance of a SERMON" is on p. 16.

Three figured printer's ornaments are present.
Cuts 1, 2, 3, are printed from the same blocks
used in no. **1068.1.** The left border of cut 2, the
devil dressed as a gentleman, on the left, facing
the Prodigal Daughter on the right, p. 6, for the
first time shows a wedge-shaped break 7 mm.
from the lower left corner. The shadows behind
the devil's legs and cane have been removed.
Cut 3, the parents in bed, is in the same state as
printed in no. **1068.1.** Cut 4, the devil in his
true form, with horns, tail, cloven foot, on the
right, talking to the Prodigal Daughter on the
left, p. 10, has the right side of the girl's face
shaded, and the nose intact. The top double
ruled border is broken. There is a break between
the left end of the lower rule and the left double
ruled border. This may be due to inking, because, when the same illustration was printed
from the same block in no. **1068.1** [*ca.* 1790],
more of the double top rule border is present.
Because of the wedge-shaped break in the lower
left border of cut 2, p. 6, which appears in all
later editions printed by the Fleets and Nathaniel Coverly, this book is without doubt a
later printing of no. **1068.1.** Hamilton also
thought **1068.5** was printed after **1068.1.** The
date [1769?] is chosen because of the manuscript inscription in the Emerson Greenaway
copy "Moses Sargent Morell his book. 1769".
NjP° (p. 15–16 wanting; t.[1], p. 13–14 mut.);
Evans 41996; Hamilton 51. (1).

1068.6 THE/Prodigal Daughter:/Or, a ——
[same as **1068.4**] Relation,/shewing —— BRIS-
TOL, had/—— Daughter, who, because ——
Trance Four Days; —— Grave she ——
SERMON —— Mr. WILLIAMS,/from LUKE
XV.24./ NEWPORT: Printed 1770 [imprint
printed in the space in the cut below the coffin].
t.[1], [2], 3–16 p.; 5 illus. including the duplicate on p. 12 of the one on t.[1]; 18 cm. The
title page is very close to no. **1068.4,** with a
few differences. It is the earliest edition with
a comma after "Or,", line 3. "Four", line 9, has
the "F" capitalized; there is no comma after
"Grave", line 9; "SERMON", is printed in large
capitals. The four-lined caption, p. 3, has a
colon after "DAUGHTER:", line 2; no comma
after "OR", line 3; "reclaimed, *&c.*", line 4, ends
in "ed". The first 12 lines of the poem are
printed in 15. They are the same as in no.
1068.4 including "pen'd," line 9, spelled with
one "n". Line 16 is different and reads: "Whom
he most tenderly lov'd so dear.", instead of
". . . . did love so dear." The last 16 lines of the
poem, p. 15, are very similar to nô. **1068.4,**
except for "Saviour's", line 2, with a capital
"S"; a comma after "require,", line 9. "THE/
SERMON." is on p. 16 with the word "Sermon." and period 71 mm. long. The text is
printed in 84.5 (20 line measure) type, taking
the measurement on p. 5. *See* note under no.
492.1.
Ten printer's ornaments are present. The five
illustrations are printed from the same blocks
used by John Waterman in no. **1068.4,** and are
the same pages. The cuts are in good condition
and show no breaks in the ruled borders.
RHi°.

1068.7 THE/PRODIGAL DAUGHTER;/Or a
—— [same as **1068.5**] relation, shewing, how
a/—— because her parents —— her extravagance, —— informed her parents of her design. —— trance four days; —— grave, she/
came to life again, &c. &c./Boston, printed and
sold at I. Thomas's Printing-Of-/fice near the Mill
Bridge./[1772?]
t.[1], [2], 3–15, [16] p.; illus.; including a
duplicate on p. 12 of the one on t.[1]; 18 cm.
The shortened title page has the same wording
as no. **1068.6** with the first three words printed
in two lines; a semicolon after "DAUGHTER;",

line 2; no comma after "Or", line 3; the words "relation", "parents," "extravagance", "parents", "design", "trance", "grave", lines 3, 5, 6, 8, 9 respectively, have the first letter in the lower case; "shewing," line 4, is followed by a comma. The caption p. 3 is the same as in no. **1068.6** except for a comma after "OR,", line 3. No illumination is present around the letter "L" of "Let", line 6, below the decorative bar, line 5. Below the bar, the 12 lines of verse, line 6–17, are closer to the type setting of **1068.4** than to **1068.6**. All three editions have "pen'd", line 7, spelled with one "n". There is a comma after "attend,", line 6. Line 9: "To love their friends . . ." is peculiar to this edition. Line 13 reads: "Whom he most tenderly did love so dear." This is similar to no. **1068.4**. Page 15 is in 24 lines instead of 16 in no. **1068.4**. A semicolon follows "free;", line 10; a comma after "require," line 17. Page [16] has the caption: "THE/SUBSTANCE of a SERMON,/Preached on the occasion." It is printed in much smaller type than no. **1068.4** with the word "SERMON" measuring 35 mm. long. Large cuts 1, 2, 3, 4, on t.[1], p. 12 and p. 6, 8, 10 and small cut 5, p. 4, are printed from the same blocks used in the Z. Fowle [1767] edition, no. **1068.3** and placed on the same pages. Small cut 6 of the Crucifixion is omitted. Two figured printer's ornaments are present. The large dolphin ornament above the caption, p. 3, appears in John Lathrop's *The Importance of Early Piety. Boston: Printed by Isaiah Thomas at the New-Printing-Office in Union-Street, near the Market.* MDCCXXI, Evans 12093 It was also employed in Ezra Weld's *A Sermon Preached At The Ordination Of The Reverend Samuel Niles. Boston: Printed by Isaiah Thomas, at the South Corner of Marshall's—Lane, near the Mill-Bridge.* MDCCLXXII, Evans 12610. On page [2] there is a mss. date "October 9, 1773". Since the address in *The Prodigal Daughter,* **1068.7**, is similar to Ezra Weld's book of 1772 and the manuscript date in **1068.7** is 1773, the American Antiquarian Society's date of [1772?] is being used.

MWA* (p. 5–6, 7–8, 11–12, 15–16 mut., entire book torn in half but repaired); PP*; Evans 12352 with the imprint "Boston, 1772" may be this edition.

1068.8 THE PRODIGAL/DAUGHTER:/Or, a strange ———— [same as **1068.6**] Relation,/shewing how ———— Estate in/BRISTOL, had ———— disobedient Daughter, who, because her Parents ———— her Extravagance, ———— in a Trance Four Days; ———— in the Grave ———— SERMON preach-/ed on the Occasion, by the Rev. Mr. WIL-/LIAMS, from *Luke* xv. 24./DANVERS: Printed and Sold by E. RUSSELL, next Bell-Tavern./[*ca.* 1776].

t.[1], [2–3], 4–16 p.; 5 illus. including a duplicate, p. 12, of the one on t.[1]; 18.5 cm. The wording, punctuation and capitalization of the first letter of various words on the title page are the same as in no. **1068.6**, except for a different type setting; the words "The Prodigal" are printed on line 1; "preached", lines 14, 15, spelled "ed" instead of "'d". The caption p. [2]: "The following Resolution passed in the House of Representatives,/for this State [Mass.], February, 16, 1776." This resolution concerned the saving of rags for the paper-mills, because of the shortage of paper. Page [3] has an entirely different type setting from previous editions. There are no type ornaments present and it is printed in 25 lines. The caption, in 4 lines, is the same as in no. **1068.6** with a colon after "DAUGHTER:", line 2. It differs in having a comma after "OR,", line 3; "reclaimed, &c.", line 4, with "&c." not in italics. Below the caption, lines 5–25, there are 5 sets of 4 lines of verse with a space between them. The text throughout the book is printed in this manner. The word "pen'd", line 6, has one "n". Comparing the book with no. **1068.6** differences are found. The "P" of "Parents", line 8, and "G" of "Gentleman", line 10, are capitalized; "fair,", line 11, is followed by a comma instead of a colon; "loved", line 12, instead of "lov'd"; "array"; is followed by a semicolon. The text is printed with similar type to no. **1068.11** or 93.5 (20 line measure). *See* note under no. **492.1**. This is the earliest of the E. Russell editions which all have a new set of cuts redrawn from the usual four illustrations described in no. **1068.4**. They are smaller being 6.8–7 cm. high by 7.3–7.5 cm. wide. Cut 1, the Prodigal Daughter in her coffin, t.[1], p. 12, has no candle or mirror above the girl's head. Cuts 1 and 4, printed from the same blocks, were used in Russell's 1794 edition. Cuts 2, 3, 4, are on p. 6, 8, 10, respectively. Type ornaments are not used, but a thick and thin rule are above the caption p. [3].

NjP°; Evans 43144.

1068.9 ———— Daughter,/Or a ———— [same as **1068.7**] Relation, shewing how a Gentle-/man ———— because her Parents ———— Extravagance, ———— informed her Parents ———— Trance Four Days; ———— the Grave, she came to Life again, and related the wonderful Things she saw in the other World. Likewise the Substance of a Sermon preached on the occa-/sion, by the Rev. Mr. WILLAMS, from *Luke* xv.24./PRINTED AT WORCESTER, (*Massachusetts*) MDCCLXXXVII.

t.[1], [2], 3–12 p.; 3 large illus., 3 small oval illus.; 19 cm. Printed by Isaiah Thomas. The title page differs from Isaiah Thomas' earlier edition, no. **1968.7**, in having the first three words on one line, with a comma after "Daughter,", and the first letter of "Relation", "Parents", "Extravagance", "Parents", "Trance Four Days", "Grave", "Life", lines 2, 4, 5, 6, 7, 8 capitalized. After the word "again", line 8, three and a quarter lines are added instead of "&c. &c.". The caption p. [3] has the same wording and punctuation as no. **1068.7**. The verses, lines 5–32, are printed in sets of 4 lines with a space between the sets. The word "penn'd", line 6, is printed "nn" as in no. **1068.3**. "Gentleman", line 10, has a Capital "G". On page 12, lines 1–10, end the poem; line 11 is a decorative bar; the caption: The/Sermon/Luke XV, . . . , lines 12–15; followed by lines 16–32.

Four printer's ornaments are present. Three illustrations are the usual large ones printed from the same blocks and described in no. **1068.3** under cuts 1, 2, 3. They appear in this book on t.[1], p. 4, and 6 respectively. Besides the large illustrations three small oval cuts are found on p. 3, 8, 9. They were first used in *Little Robin Red Breast. Worcester: I. Thomas, 1786*, no. **782**, and have nothing to do with the story in this book.

MWA° (entire book silked; p. 11–12 mut.); Evans 45146.

1068.10 ———— Daughter:/Or, a strange and wonderful Relation: Shewing how a /———— [same as **1068.5**] in *Bristol* had — Daughter; who, because ———— Devil to poison them ———— How an Angel ———— Design. — How she lay in a Trance four Days, and, when ———— saw/in the other World./Printed and sold at the *Bible* and *Heart* in Cornhill, *Boston.*/[*ca.* 1790] [date conjectural].

t.[1], [2], 3–16 p.; 5 illus. including the duplicate on p. 12 of the one on t.[1]; 19.5 cm.; no colophon p. [16]; 12 blocks of a thick and thin rule above the imprint on t.[1]. The firm of Thomas and John Fleet was named the Bible and Heart in 1780, when crowns became unpopular, according to Isaiah Thomas. While the title page closely follows no. **1068.5**, the last two lines: Likewise the ———— Luke XV. 24", are omitted. The same words in both books have the first letter capitalized. The editions mainly differ in punctuation. This book is the earliest Fleet edition having "Or,", line 2, followed by a comma; "Relation:", on the same line, followed by a colon. Because of these particular variations occurring in later Fleet editions, **1068.16** and **1068.17** and not in earlier ones, no. **1068.3** and **1068.5**, this book is dated [*ca.* 1790]. Other differences on the title page are: no comma after "*Bristol*", line 3; a semicolon after "Daughter;", line 4; no period after "them", line 6; a comma after "Days,", line 8. The caption on p. 3 is the same as in no. **1068.5**. Below the decorative bar, line 6, there are 14 lines of verse or lines 7–20. These are two more than in no. **1068.5** because the illumination around the letter "L" has pushed the first 4 lines to the right. This caused the last word in line 7 to be dropped below in line 8, where it is printed "< penn'd;" with a bracket in front of the word and followed by a semicolon. In like manner "< Company." has been dropped a line and placed in line 11. "*Bristol*,", line 12, is in italics. The type, measured on p. 5, is 84.5 (20 line measure). *See* note under no. **492.1**. Like no. **1068.5** many lines are in italics. The 16 lines, the end of the poem, on page 15, are the same as in no. **1068.5**, except there is a semicolon after "me;", line 1, and the lines are in sets of four with spaces between them. This is different from the rest of the book and no. **1068.5** which are without spaces. "The Substance of a Sermon,/. . . is on page 16.

Three printer's ornaments are present. The illumination around the letter "L", p. 3, consists of a standing angel on either side of a central square. The "L" in the MWA copy is added in ink and may be superimposed over the printed "L" below it. This angel ornament was used by

[Thomas Fleet Sr.] for D. Henchman, 1735 in Wigglesworth's *A Seasonable Caveat against Believing Every Spirit*, Evans 3975, and by Thomas Fleet, 1802 in J. Taylor's *Salvator Mundi*, p.[iv], no. **1293.10**.

The illustrations are printed from the same blocks used in no. **1068.5**. Cut 1, the Prodigal Daughter in her coffin, t.[1], p. 12, for the first time is wanting any trace of a top line border above the illustration itself. The basal thick rule is intact. Cut 2, the devil dressed as a gentleman, talking to the Prodigal Daughter on the right, as in no. **1068.5**, has no shadows behind the devil's legs and cane. The wedge shaped break in the lower left ruled border has not increased in size over that shown in no. **1068.5**. Cut 4, the devil in his true form talking to the Prodigal Daughter on the left, still has the right half of the girl's face shaded and the nose intact. The top border is more complete than in any previous Fleet edition.

MWA°; Evans 43751.

1068.11 THE PRODIGAL / DAUGHTER: / Or, —— [same as **1068.8**] Relation,/shewing —— Trance four Days: —— preach'd on the Occa-/sion, by the Rev. Mr. WILLIAMS, from *Luke* xv.24./BOSTON: Printed and Sold by E. RUSSELL,/next Liberty-Pole, 1790.—Where Town/ and Country Shop-keepers, Travelling tra-/ders, Town-flys, &c. may be supplied with a Number of other curious Books, Verses, &c.

t.[1], [2–3], 4–16 p.; 10 illus. including the duplicate on p. 11, of the one on t.[1]; 16.5 cm. The title page is printed in smaller type than no. **1068.8**, but has the same wording, punctuation and capitalization of the first letter of words which occur in the earlier E. Russell edition. *See* note under no. **492.1** for the type measurement. Variations are: "four Days:", line 7, with the "f" in the lower case and a space between "Day" and the colon where the "s" is almost entirely worn away; "preach'd", line 11. The type setting on p. [3] follows no. **1068.8**, but has a three-lined caption instead of four. Below the thin rule, under the caption, are 24 lines of verse, or lines 4–27, in which textual variations are: "ev'ry", line 4; the "C" of "Child", line 4, the "D" of "Daughter", line 10, capitalized; no comma after "pen'd", line 5, with one "n"; a comma after "company,", line 7; "*Bristol*", line 8, is in italics; "lov'd", line

11; line 12, "costly" not followed by a comma; "array;" followed by a semicolon; the "C" of "Child", line 13, in upper case. The type measurement on p. [3] is 93.5 (20 line measure). *See* note no. **492.1**. This is the same size type throughout the book and in no. **1068.8**. The poem ends on page 14 lines 1–22 and does not have spaces between sets of verses, but otherwise has the same type setting as no. **1068.8**. The caption below the cut at the bottom of p. [15]: THE FUNERAL/SERMON/LUKE . . . The Sermon is completed on p. 16. Type ornaments are absent in this edition.

Four of the illustrations are the usual ones printed from the same blocks described in no. **1068.8** under cuts 1, 2, 3, 4, which appear in this book on t.[1], p. 11 and pages 5, 7, 9 respectively. Cuts 1 and 4 in Russell's 1794 edition, no. **1068.12**, were also printed from these blocks as well as cuts 2 and 3. On p. [2], above the advertisement, a man's portrait makes its first appearance in this Russell edition. It is one of John Dickinson, the work of Paul Revere, who according to Hamilton, p. 19, and Brigham, p. 135, charged Russell two pounds for this and another cut. On p. [15] a large cut supposedly represents the Rev. Mr. Williams delivering "The Funeral Sermon."

MB°; Evans 45978.

1068.12 —— PRODIGAL / DAUGHTER: / Or, —— [same as **1068.11**] RELATION,/shewing —— in BRIS-/TOL had —— Trance four Days; —— World. Also, the —— Sermon preached on the/Occassion, by the Rev. Mr. WILLIAMS./[3 lines quot. on outer margin of page parallel to the right border of the cut, with the last line next to the cut.]/Boston: Printed and Sold by E. RUSSELL, near/Liberty-Pole, 1794; (Price Six Pence.)— Where/Town and Country Shop-keepers, Travelling-tra-/ders, &c. may be supplied with sundry Books, &c.

t.[1], [2], 3–16 p.; 10 illus. including the duplicate, p. 11, of the one on t.[1]; 19 cm. The reset title page has the wording, punctuation and capitalization of the first letter of various words found in no. **1068.8** from the first three words, printed in two lines, to "Mr. WILLIAMS", line 14. The quotation, for the first time, is given in full on the title page and placed on the right side of the cut. It reads: "LUKE XV.24. *For this my/Son was dead, and is alive,/he was* *lost and is found."* The four-lined caption p.[3] is the same as no. **1068.8** except for *"&c.",* which is printed in italics. Below the decorative bar, line 5, and above the catch word "Come", line 28, there are 22 lines of verse, or lines 6–27. These more closely follow no. **1068.11** in every respect, but show variations. There is a comma after "pen'd," line 7; no comma after "Parents", line 9; lines 12–13 read: "A Pious Man, and eke of mighty fame;/But view the Picture, there you'll see his name;"; a comma after "costly," and "array,", line 16. The type measured on p. [3] is 94.7 (20 line measure). *See* note under no. **492.1**. Page 14, lines 1–20, are printed in five sets of four lines, which are exactly the same as the last 5 sets in no. **1068.8**, except, "bed", line 10, is not followed by a comma; "sacrament", line 13, has a lower case "s"; "They gave her then, . . .", line 14, instead of "They gave it her then, . . ." The caption p. [15]: "The FUNERAL SERMON./ . . . , is followed with the sermon itself on p. 16.

Two printer's type ornaments are present.

Cuts 1, 2, 3, 4 and other illustrations are from the same blocks used in no. **1068.11**. The portrait of John Dickinson, p. [3], discussed in no. **1068.11**, has the right portion of the base omitted and the words "John Bricket Esq." printed below the rolled paper in the man's hand. A new small cut is on the upper left corner of page 16. Within a central oval, above the letter "T", is an angel's head with outspread wings. Below the letter "T" is a skeleton, on the left, and a burning candle in a large candlestick on the right.

Welch* (t.[1], p. [2], 7–8 mut.) MHi (p. 15–16 wanting); MWA (t.[1], p. [2], [15]–16 mut.); RPJCB; Evans 27563.

1068.13   THE / PRODIGAL / DAUGHTER: / OR, THE / DISOBEDIENT LADY / *RE-CLAIMED,* &c./[3 lines quot. parallel to the right border of the cut with the first line of the quot. next to the cut]/*BOSTON:* Printed and Sold at Russell's Of-/fice, Essex-Street, near Liberty-Pole; (Price/Six Pence.)—Where Persons may/be supplied with sundry/Books, &c./1797.

t.[1] [2–3], 4–16 p.; 10 illus.; including the duplicate, p. 11, of the one on t.[1]; 21 cm. The title, in six lines, with the three-lined quotation to the right of the cut, is entirely different from all preceding editions. The portrait of John

Dickinson labeled "John Bricket, Esq." is omitted, on page 2. In its place is a half title: "The Prodigal Daughter: Or, a/strange and wonderful Relation, *shewing/*——— [same as **1068.12**, but mostly printed in italics.]/*the* Rev. Mr. Williams." Above and below the half title are double rules. Page [3] has a similar type setting to no. **1068.12**, with the four-lined caption, and lines 12–13, "A Pious Man, . . . /But view the picture, there you'll see his name." Only in this case the picture of John Bricket, Esq. is omitted on p.[2]. The words, "Disobedient Lady", in the caption, are printed in capitals and larger type than no. **1068.12**. The two words measure 61.2 mm. in length, instead of 40.4 mm. The "S" and "T" of "Dis-obedient" and the "A" and "Y" of "Lady" are printed in italics. "Reclaimed, &c." are also in italics. The word "pen'd", line 7, is the same as in no. **1068.12** and the last edition in which this word is spelled with one "n". The type has been reset on p. 14–16 but is very close to no. **1068.12**. The type measurement on p. [3] is 95 (20 line measure). *See* note under no. **492.1**. The illustrations are printed from the identical blocks used in no. **1068.12** and appear on the same pages. Three printer's ornaments are present.

MWA*; Evans 48236.

1068.14   THE / PRODIGAL DAUGHTER, / or / *A strange and wonderful Relation,/*SHEWING,/ *How a Gentleman of great estate in Bristol,/had a proud and disobedient daughter, who,/because her parents would not support her in/all her extravagance, bargained with the devil/to poison them.—How an angel informed them/of her de-sign.—How she lay in a trance four/days; and when she was put into the grave,/she came to life again, and related the wond-/derful things she saw in the other world.—/*Hartford: Printed for the *Travelling Booksellers.* 1799.

t.[1], [2–3], 4–12 p.; 16 cm. This unillustrated edition has most of the title pages printed in italics. The type setting of the text ending page 12 differs from preceding editions although the old form of the letter "s" is still used. Comparing this book with no. **1068.10** differences are noted. The main part of the title, on the title page, through "SHEWING", is in 5 lines in-stead of 2; the "H" of "How", line 6 is capital-ized; "great estate", line 6, is used instead of "vast estate"; "*Bristol*", line 6, is in large italics; with the exception of "*Gentleman*", line 6, "*How*", lines 10 and 11, the first letter of every word in the subtitle is printed in the lower case; there is a dash after "world.—", line 14. The caption p.[3] is in 4 lines, followed by 25 lines of verse. There is a comma after "attend,", line 5; "penn'd;" is spelled with two of the letter "n", which spelling is used in all following editions; "warning", line 7, "parents", line 8, "estate", line 10, and other words usually capitalized, have the first letter in the lower case. "Bristol", line 9, is in regular type; "clothed" line 13, is used instead of "cloathed"; "LORD", line 28, entirely in capitals. The book is printed in 83.6 (20 line measure) type. *See* note under no. **492.1**. Line 6, page 11 ends "sinner wild." The last 30 lines of the poem are on p. 12, and show variations. One of these is "crowns", line 30, instead of "crown".

MWA*; Ct; DLC; Evans 36166.

1068.15 THE / PRODIGAL / DAUGHTER, / OR A / STRANGE AND WONDERFUL/RELA-TION./*Shewing how a* ——— [same as **1068.14**] *in Bris-/tol, had* ——— *daughter,/who,* ——— *support/her* ——— *with/the Devil to poison them.—How an Angel in-/formed them of her design.—How she lay in a/trance four days: And when* ——— *and related/the wonderful things she saw in the other/world.*/NEW-YORK:/ *Printed for the Traveling Booksellers./*1799.

t.[1], [2–3], 4–8+ p.; 16 cm. The type setting resembles that of no. **1068.14** in largely being printed in italics. The main title is in 6 lines instead of 5 and ends with "*Relation.*" The subtitle, in italics, follows the wording of no. **1068.14** and differs in not having a dash after "*word.*", line 16. The caption, p. [3], in 4 lines, has "*Prodigal Daughter,*", line 2, in large italics and followed by a comma. The verses below the caption and the text of the book closely resemble the type setting of no. **1068.14** and printed in the same size type. Only one type ornament is present. The modern form of the letter "s" is used.

RPJCB* (all after p. 8 wanting, probably p. 9–12).

1068.16 THE/PRODIGAL DAUGHTER:/Or, [same as **1068.10**] Relation: Shewing how a/ ——— in BRISTOL, in *England,* had ——— bar-gained with the *Devil* to poison them.—How an Angel informed her Parents of her Design.—How ——— Trance four days, ——— life again ——— Things/she saw in the other World./ Printed and sold at the *Bible & Heart,* Cornhill, BOSTON./[*ca.* 1802].

t.[1], [2], 3–12+ p.; 4 illus.; 17 cm. The type setting and wording of the title page, which ends with the word "World" resembles no. **1068.10,** but the first three words are printed in two lines instead of one. This is the second Fleet edition with a comma after "Or," and a colon after "Relation:", line 3. "BRISTOL,", line 4, is printed in small capitals, followed by a comma. This edition is the first Fleet edition to add "in *England*", after "BRISTOL", line 4. The word "them.—", line 9 is followed by a period and a dash; "days", line 9, has a lower case "d"; the "l" of "life", line 10, is in the lower case. Page 3 has an entirely different type setting from **1068.10** and is closer to **1068.5.** The caption reads: The/*Prodigal Daughter:*/Or/ The Disobedient Lady Reclaimed, &c./[16 lines of verse, or lines 6–21]. The following words have the first letter in the lower case, where in no. **1068.5** it is capitalized: "child," line 6, "line", line 7, "parents-" followed by a dash, line 9; "estate", lines 11, "array", line 14; "child" and "truth", line 15; "heart" and "pride", line 16; "delight", "vanity", line 16. Line 7 has "penn'd" with two of the letter "n"; "Bristol", line 10, is printed in regular type. The type measured on p. 5 is 83.5 (20 line measure). *See* note under no. **492.1.** Line 29, p. 12, ends "a sinner vile". This is first edition in which "vile" is substituted for "wild", and appears only in later editions printed by Thomas Fleet, the son of John Fleet, **1068.17,** and by Nathaniel Coverly, **1068.21–25.** Pages 13–16 are missing from this edition. The type setting of the text is quite different from **1068.10**, because in the earlier book many portions are in italics, while in **1068.16** none of the text is in italics.

Three printer's ornaments are present. The illustrations are printed from the same blocks used in no. **1068.10,** but now characteristic breaks and differences appear. Cut 1, the Prodigal Daughter in her coffin, t.[1], no longer has the signature *P.F.* Cut 2, the devil dressed as a gentleman talking to the Prodigal Daughter, p. 6, has a very thin broken line for a basal rule. The wedge-shaped break in the lower left double-ruled border, first noted in no. **1068.5**, is still 3.8–5 mm. wide. Cut 3, the parents in bed, being warned by a huge angel, p. 8, shows little actual variation from its state in no. **1068.1**. Cut 4, the devil in his true form, talking to the Prodigal Daughter, p. 10, has been damaged. There is now no shading on the right side of the girl's face, both eyes are altered and the outline of the nose is wanting. This damaged illustration is the characteristic one in the 1807 edition, no. **1068.17**, and all later ones printed by Nathaniel Coverly. The use of the old form of the letter "s" and the word "vile", p. 12; cut 1 without the signature *P.F.*, but having a new depression on the left portion of the illustration; the new break in cut 2; the altered face of the girl in cut 4, with an enlargement of the break along the left top rule border, indicate that this book is an intermediate edition between **1068.10** [*ca.* 1790] and **1068.17**, 1807, but closest to the later edition. Thomas Fleet Sr., a bachelor, died March 2, 1797, at the age of 65, according to Isaiah Thomas. John Fleet and his son Thomas Jr. continued the business. Even before his uncle's death, Thomas Jr. was printing at the Heart and Crown under his own name. After Thomas Fleet Sr.'s death the firm was continued under the same name through 1802, by John and his son Thomas with Thomas sometimes printing under his own name. The book was advertised on p. [45] in Watts' *Divine Songs Attempted In Easy Language For The Use Of Children. Boston: Printed by J. and T. Fleet, at the Bible and Heart*, 1802, no. **1408.57**. Based on this evidence it is believed that no. **1068.16** was printed by John and Thomas Fleet, [*ca.* 1802].

MWA-W*; Evans 45804.

1068.17   THE / PRODIGAL DAUGHTER: / Or, ⸺ [same as **1068.16**] Relations: Shewing how a / ⸺ in BRISTOL, in England, had / ⸺ the DEVIL ⸺ ANGEL informed ⸺ in a trance four days, ⸺ grave, ⸺ wonderful / things she saw in the OTHER WORLD. / Sold at the Printing Office, No. 5, Cornhill, BOSTON. 1807.

t.[1], [2], 3–15, [16, illus.] p.; 5 illus.; 18.5 cm. Printed by Thomas Fleet Jr. whose firm was at the above address in 1807. The book is reset using the modern form of the letter "s". Many of the lines on the title page and in the text show variations from no. **1068.16**. The word "BRISTOL;", line 4, is followed by a semicolon; "DEVIL", line 7, is in small capitals; the first six lines end with the same word, but in line 7 the last two words are "—How an" instead of "—How an Angel"; "ANGEL", line 8, is in small capitals; the "d" of "design", line 8, is not capitalized; as well as the "t" of "trance", line 9, and the "g" of "grave", line 10; the words "OTHER WORLD", line 11, are printed in small caps. On p. 3 most of the caption is in italics and the text below it and the decorative bar is in 16 lines. The caption is in three lines. "*Bristol*", line 9, is in italics, the rest of the poem is printed exactly like p. 3 in no. **1068.16**. The type measured on p. 5, is 84 (20 line measure). *See* note under no. **492.1**. Page 14, in 20 lines, has lines 17–20 in italics except "GLORY" and "DEATH", which are printed in small capitals. Cuts 1, 2, 3, 4, are printed from the same blocks used in no. **1068.16**. Cut 1, the Prodigal daughter in her coffin, t.[1], is similar to the state of the cut in no. **1068.16** in not having the signature *P.F.*, but having a shallow depression at the left end of the top of the illustration. Cut 2, the devil dressed as a gentleman, talking to the Prodigal Daughter, p. 6, has the usual wedge-shaped break through the rules of the lower left border and the new 2 mm. break in the outer left rule of the left border, 41.5 mm. from the top of the cut, first seen in no. **1068.16**. Cut 3, the parents in bed, p. 8, shows little change. Cut 4, the devil in his true form, talking to the Prodigal Daughter, p. 10, has only a single top rule, the former lower top rule. All trace of the upper broken top ruled border in no. **1068.16** is gone. On p. [16] a new cut appears for the first time. It shows a church with the words "Laus Deo" above it. Welch* (t.[1] slightly mut.); CCamarSJ; MH; MHi; MWA; RPB; Shaw 13441.

1068.18   THE / PRODIGAL DAUGHTER, / OR, A / STRANGE AND WONDERFUL RELATION. / SHEWING / How a Gentleman ⸺ [same as **1068.14**] Bristol, had a / proud ⸺ in all her pride, agreed with the Devil to poison them. How an Angel informed her parents of her horrid design. How she lay in a Trance four days; and while she was about to be laid in the grave, she came to life again, and related the wonderful things she saw in the other World. Likewise, the sub- / stance of

a Sermon preached on this occasion./Second Edition / PROVIDENCE / PRINTED, / BY / DAVID HEATON./AND SOLD AT HIS BOOK STORE MAIN STREET./1808.

t.[1], [2–3], 4–12 p.; oval illus. p. 12 only illus.; 17 cm. The caption p. [3]: "The Prodigal Daughter", is in one line. Below it are 31 lines of verse. Page [3] has similar wording and punctuation to that in no. **1068.14**. In both editions "penn'd", line 3, has two of the letter "n", but variations occur. There is no comma after "late", line 6, "cloath'd", line 10, instead of "clothed"; no comma after "say", line 11, and "high", line 12; "Lord", line 23, printed in regular type. Line 30, page 9 ends "sinner wild". This is the first of the editions not printed in Boston which returns to the use of "wild" instead of "vile". Other editions using "wild" are **1068.19–20** and **1068.26–29**. Three figured printer's ornaments are present. The oval cut on p. 12 shows a gentleman with his hand on a man's shoulder and a third man standing in front of them. MWA*; Shaw 16002.

1068.19   The/Prodigal Daughter,/*OR*/A strange ——— [same as **1068.14**] Relation,/SHEWING/ How ——— in BRISTOL, had/a ——— them— How an angel informed her parents of her design —How she ——— in the grave, ——— world.— Likewise, the substance of a/sermon preached on the occasion./[initials "J.B." [John Byrne]] So[ld] the Printing Office, Windham [Conn.]. [prior to 1811].

t.[1], [2–3], 4–12 p.; 14 cm.; text printed on blue-gray paper. The book is mostly printed in very small type or in 67 (20 line measure). *See* note under no. **492.1**. The wording of the title page and text matches that of no. **1068.14** with textual differences. The "P" of "Prodigal Daughter" on the title page is much larger than in no. **1068.14**. The words "A strange and wonderful", line 4, are not printed in italics. There is no comma after "Shewing", line 5; lines 6–15 are printed in 67 (20 line measurement) except for "BRISTOL", line 6 printed in small capitals; no period following "them/—", line 9; "her parents", line 10, replace "them" in no. **1068.14**; "design—", line 11, has a dash after it but no period; "in the grave", line 16, instead of "into the grave"; "world.—", line 14 is followed by "Likewise . . . occasion." In the four-lined caption, p. [3], there is a colon after "Daughter:",

line 2; "reclaimed, &c.", line 4, has a lower case "r" and "&c." after it. In the 22 lines of verse below the caption, "liv'd", line 10, and "cloath'd", line 13, are spelled "'d"; "Lord", line 26, is printed in regular type. Line 3, p. 10, ends "a sinner wild". The end of the poem, on page 11, is in 24 lines. They have the same wording as no. **1068.14**. In line 19 "christian", is entirely in the lower case. The caption p. 12: "The Substance of a/SERMON,/ . . . The word "FINIS.", line 26, is 22 mm. long including the period. Four figured printer's ornaments are present. Above the title page imprint on either side of the scroll-like initials *J. B.* are large fronds with many leaflets. John Byrne was printing in Windham, Conn., 1791–1827. After 1810 he stopped using the old form "s" in the *Windham Herald*. (MWA cat.).

MWA-W* (t.[1] slightly mut.).

1068.20   THE / PRODIGAL DAUGHTER: / OR A / STRANGE AND WONDERFUL RELATION,/SHEWING/How a ——— [same as **1068.19**] Bristol, had a proud/and disobedient Daughter, ——— preach-/ed on this occasion./ SOLD AT THE PRINTING OFFICE./GREENFIELD [Mass.]. [prior to 1811].

t.[1], [2–3], 4–12 p.; 16 cm. The old style "s" is used throughout most of the title page and text. Lines 6–14 on the title page are printed in smaller type than the text, p. [3]–11. The larger text type measures 81 (20 line measure). *See* note under no. **492.1**. It follows the type setting on p. [3] of no. **1068.19**. Two printer's type ornaments are present. The caption, in four lines, has a colon after "Daughter:", line 2, and "RECLAIMED, &c." line 4, with the "R" capitalized. Line 3, page 10 ends "a sinner wild", instead of "vile". The last 24 lines of the poem are on p. 11, with p. 12 having the caption: "THE/SUBSTANCE OF A/SERMON,/ . . . " The word "FINIS.", at the bottom of the page, including the period, is 28 mm. long. These pages use the same wording and type setting as no. **1068.19**. Because of the similarity of the two books they were probably printed about the same time so no. **1068.20** is also being dated [prior to 1811]. DLC*.

1068.21   THE/PRODIGAL/DAUGHTER:/Or, a strange and wonderful Relation; Shewing how a

Gentle-/man ——— [same as **1068.17**] Bristol; in England, had proud/and ——— wonder-/ful things she saw in the other world [on the right side of the cut] Printed By Nathaniel Coverly, jun'r. [on the left side of the cut] corner of theatre alley, boston. [1812].

t.[1], [2–3], 4–14 p.; 4 illus.; 18 cm. Nathaniel Coverly used the above address in *The Mother's Gift*. 1812, nos. **907.1–2**. The title page has some distinctive features. The main title is in three lines instead of two as in no. **1068.17**. The size of the type in successive lines is larger. "Relation;", line 4, is followed by a semicolon; "England", line 5, is in small capitals. This is the first edition with the imprint on both sides of the illustration. The text, p. [3], in 21 lines, has the last line: "Come, come, my child, this course in time refrain." "Let", the first word of the poem, is 14.5 mm. long; *Bristol*, line 9, is in italics. The type, measured on p. 5, is 95 (20 line measure). *See* note under no. **492.1**. The last four lines of the poem, p. 14, are printed in italics except for "glory" and "death", which are in small capitals. The substance of a sermon was probably on missing pages 15–16. Two printer's ornaments are present.

The illustrations are printed from the same blocks used by Thomas Fleet Jr. in no. **1068.17**. Coverly undoubtedly acquired them from Thomas Fleet Jr., because they appear in all subsequent Coverly editions. Cuts 1, 2, 3, 4 are on t.[1], p. 6, 8, 10. Cut 1, the Prodigal Daughter in her coffin, t.[1], shows a faint trace of the top rule border above the illustration, not seen in **1068.16**, or **1068.17**. Cut 2, the devil dressed as a gentleman, talking to the Prodigal Daughter, p. 6, now has a break in the devil's cane. Cut 4, the devil in his true form, talking to the Prodigal Daughter, p. 10, has a larger break in the top rule which is 15 cm. long, and extends to the edge of the left rule border.

MH° (t.[1] & p. [3]–4, 13 mut. affecting the text).

1068.22 THE PRODIGAL/DAUGHTER:Or, a strange and wonderful Relation: Shewing how a/ ——— [same as **1068.21**] in Bristol, in England, had/ ——— Daughter; who, ——— poison them. — How an ——— Parents of her design. — How ——— wonderful/things she saw in the

other world./☞ N. Coverly, Jr. Printer, *Milk-St. Boston./[ca.* 1813].

t.[1], [2–3], 4–12 p.; 4 illus.; 18 cm. This edition is characterized by having the first three words of the title in two lines. There is a colon after "Daughter:", line 2; a semicolon after "disobedient Daughter;", line 5; a period after "them.—", line 7; the "P" of "Parents", capitalized, line 8; "*Boston|*", line 12 followed by a line with a thin place in the middle of it, possibly a defective bracket. The text is printed in much smaller type, 69.1 (20 line measure), than no. **1068.21**. *See* note under no. **492.1**. Page [3] has 36 lines instead of 24. The first word of text, on p.[3], "Let" is 6 mm. long; "Parents—", line 8, is followed by a single dash; "bristol", line 9, is printed in small capitals; the "n" of "ru^n", line 27, is higher than the rest of the word; there is a comma after "mother,", line 29. Line 36 reads: "Therefore I'll take my comfort while I'm here." The last four lines of the poem, or lines 17–20 are printed on p. 12 in regular type except "crown" and "glory after death", line 20, which words are in small capitals. Lines 21–39 are the substance of Rev. Mr. Williams' sermon. There is a dash after "observe—", line 25, four dots after "Secondly . . . .", line 30, and many other distinctive variations.

The illustrations are printed from the same blocks used in no. **1068.21**. Cuts 1 and 3 show the same defects as the earlier book, although cut 1 does not have a hairline rule above it. Cut 2, the devil dressed as a gentleman talking to the Prodigal Daughter, p. 5, no longer has thick double basal rules. The lower one is a thin hairline, while the thin upper one has a break 15 mm. wide, just below the tip of the broken devil's cane. This could be due to poor inking, because the break is only 4 mm. wide in no. **1068.23**. Cut 4, the devil in his true form talking to the Prodigal Daughter, p. 9, for the first time is missing a squarish piece from the side of the dressing table, along the left side of the cut. N. Coverly's firm used the Milk Street address in 1810, 1813–16, without a number. From 1818–1821 it was 16 Milk Street. Since cuts 2 and 3 have new characteristic defects this edition is surely later than no. **1068.21** and the tentative date [*ca.* 1813] has been assigned to it.

MWA°; NjP°.

1068.23 THE PRODIGAL/DAUGHTER,/Or, a ———— [same as **1068.22**] Relation: Shewing how a/Gentleman ———— Bristol in England, had/a ———— Daughter: who, ———— poison them — How ———— wonderful/things she saw in the OTHER WORLD./☞ N. COVERLY, JR. Printer. Milk-St. Boston. [*ca.* 1814].

t.[1], [2–3], 4–12 p.; 4 illus.; 20.5 cm. The title page differs from no. **1068.22** in having the words "The Prodigal" printed in smaller type, and a comma after "Daughter". There is no comma after "Bristol", line 4; there is no period after "them—" line 7. The text is printed in the same size type, with 36 lines on p. [3], and ending with the identical line, but shows variations. On line 8 "parents," is followed by a comma; "Bristol," line 9, printed in regular type followed by a comma; "run", line 27, is correctly printed; "mother", line 29, is not followed by any punctuation. Pages [6–7] are not numbered. The last four lines of the poem, p. 12, lines 17–20, are entirely printed in regular type, including the last three words "glory after Death." Lines 21–39 contain the substance of the Rev. Mr. Williams' sermon, which is followed by the word "FINIS.", which is shorter than in no. **1068.22**. A few other characteristics are: a semicolon after "alive;", line 22; a comma after "observe," line 25; three dots after "Secondly . . .", line 30; three dots after "lastly . . .", line 34. Line 33 reads: "for the sake of a sinner's repentance,", with the apostrophe of sinner's printed in the reverse.

Cuts 1, 2, 3, 4 on t.[1], and p. 5, [7], 9 respectively, are printed from the same blocks used in no. **1068.22**. Cut 1 is the same in both editions. Cut 2, the devil dressed as a gentleman talking to the Prodigal Daughter, p. 5, has only the upper thin much broken basal rule remaining, in which there is a space 4 mm. long, below the tip of the devil's cane. The small end piece of the right border extending down towards the basal rule is broken, has a forked end and is 1.5 mm. long. In no. **1068.22** this piece is unbroken, the end is squared off and it is 3 mm. long. Cut 3, the angel warning the sleeping parents, p. [7], has an oval piece wanting from the right side near the angel's wing. Since this oval piece is not wanting in no. **1068.25**, this is probably due to some error in printing. Cut 4, the devil in his true form, p. 9, closely resembles the state of the cut in no. **1068.22**, only more

of the left end of the top rule is present. This is probably the result of heavier inking when it was printed. *See* no. **1068.22** for a discussion of the dates at which N. Coverly was at addresses in Boston. This book is a later edition than no. **1068.22**, because of the lack of the basal rule in cut 2. The date is conjectural, but in order to show the possible sequence of editions, this book is dated one year later or [*ca.* 1814].
Griffin*.

1068.24 THE/PRODIGAL DAUGHTER,/OR THE / DISOBEDIENT LADY, / IN FIVE PARTS,/BEING A TRUE RELATION OF ONE/JEAN NICHOLSON,/The only Daughter of a wealthy Merchant, living in/Merchant-Street, St. James's London./SHEWING,/I. How she being much indulged by her parents, fell into all manner of disobedience. Wickedness and debauchery. II. How the devil appeared to her, and advised her to poison her parents, which she consented to. III. How her parents were forewarned by an Angel of her wicked design, and gave the poisoned meat she had prepared for them to dogs. IV. How at the sight thereof she fell down dead, and was thereupon buried. V. How they heard her as they were closing the grave, give several groans, at which they broke open the coffin. How she sat up in her coffin, telling the minister and several more persons, what strange and dreadful things she had seen in her trance, concerning the torments of hell: With an account of the comforts and inconceiva-/ble glories of heaven./Printed for the Itinerant Booksellers./[*ca.* 1816].

t.[1], [2], 3–8 p.; 17.5 cm. Inserted in this book is a slip of paper with a holograph inscription: *Sally Green's property Whiringham October 2nd 1816.* The late Clarence Brigham believed this book was printed in Hudson [N.Y.] [*ca.* 1816]. This is the only American version of the book which lays the scene in London instead of Bristol. In this respect it is similar to the English broadside editions, *see* no. **1068.1**, title 2. No type ornaments or illustrations are in this edition. The caption p. [3] is in two lines ending with "DAUGHTER." Below the caption are 36 lines printed in small 69 (20 line measure) type. *See* note under no. **492.1**. Line 27, p. 7, ends "sinner vile," as in all the Boston editions from no. **1068.16** on. This is the only edition broken up into five parts.
MWA*.

1068.25 *THE*/Prodigal Daughter:/Or, a ———— [same as **1068.23**] Relation: shewing/how ———— in Bristol in England, had a/ proud ———— devil to poison them. How an ANGEL informed/her parents of her design How she lay in a trance four/days — and when ———— OTH-/ER WORLD./ *N. Coverly, Printer, Milk-street, Boston.* [*ca.* 1816].

t.[1], [2–3], 4–12 p.; 4 illus.; 18 cm. This is the first edition of this book printed by N. Coverly that does not have the first three words on the title page printed in large capital letters. "The", line 1, is printed in large italics, and "Prodigal Daughter:", line 2, is in large type with only the first letter of each word capitalized. The "s" of "shewing", line 3, is in the lower case; "Bristol", line 4, is not followed by a comma; the "d" of "devil", line 7, is not capitalized; "them.", line 7, is followed by a period; "ANGEL", line 7, is in large capitals; "design", line 8, has no punctuation after the word; "days —", line 9, is followed by a dash; an index symbol is lacking before the imprint, printed in large and smaller italics. Page [3] is in 36 lines, with the caption in 4 lines, similar to no. **1068.23**. There is no punctuation after "DAUGHTER", line 2. Line 12 reads: "whom he so tenderly did love so dear", instead of "whom he most tenderly did love so dear" in no. **1068.23**. The "s" and "h" of "s he", line 29, has a space between the letters; a colon is after "destroy:", line 32; the last two words in line 35 are "would care". Line 5, page 11, ends "sinner vile,". The poem ends on line 19, p. 12, with the last four lines of verse printed as in no. **1068.23**. Lines 20–39 are the substance of Rev. Mr. Williams' sermon, ending: "to repent-/ance. Finis." The type setting of the entire page closely follows no. **1068.23**. The illustrations are printed from the same blocks. Cut 1, the Prodigal Daughter in her coffin, t.[1], has a new break between the end of the right rule border and the thick basal rule. Cut 2, the devil dressed as a gentleman talking to the Prodigal Daughter, p. 5, has a single broken thin basal line, which also appears in no. **1068.23**, as well as the break in the devil's cane. The end of the downward projecting right border now ends in a point instead of a fork. In this book there is a trace of the basal thin ruled line below the tip of the devil's cane instead of a space as in no. **1068.23**. Cut 4, the devil in his true form, talking to the

Prodigal Daughter, p. 9, now has a longer break in the top left rule border. The shortened left rule border and the squarish piece wanting from the side of the dressing table are the same size as in no. **1068.23**. This book is certainly a later edition than no. **1068.23** and is tentatively dated [*ca.* 1816].
RPB°.

1068.26 THE/PRODIGAL/DAUGHTER;/OR, A/*STRANGE AND WONDERFUL*/RELA-TION./Shewing ———— [same as **1068.14**] who, when her parents ———— poison them, — How ———— four days: And when ———— into the grave, ———— she saw in/the other world./Philadelphia: Printed and sold by D. Dickinson, No. 100, Race street. [1819?].

t.[1], [2], 3–8 p.; title vignette only illus.; 21.5 cm. The modern form of the letter "s" is used. The title page has the first portion to "Relation" separated into 6 lines instead of 3 as in no. **1068.1**; line 8 has "when her parents" instead of "because her parents"; a comma after "them,", line 10; a colon after "days:", line 12. Page [2], in 39 lines, has the caption in 4 lines, instead of 3, and a comma after "DAUGHTER," line 2; line 12, "Whom he most tenderly did love so dear," is the same as in no. **1068.24**; "(for truth they say,)", enclosed in parentheses, line 14; "Holy Scriptures", line 18, has the first letter of each word in capitals; "break", line 22 is not followed by a comma. The type measured on p. 3, is 84 (20 line measure). *See* note under no. **492.1**. Line 27, page 7, ends "sinner wild". Lines 1–39, page 8, printed in regular type, complete the poem. The words "The End.", line 40, are used instead of the usual "Finis". No text illustrations or type ornaments are present. The title vignette is a square cut with an inner circle. Within the circle is a seated woman drinking out of a bottle and holding a cane in her right hand. The firm of David Dickinson was at 100 Race street in 1819.
MWA°; Shaw 49193.

1068.27 THE/PRODIGAL/DAUGHTER,/OR A/*STRANGE AND WONDERFUL*/RELA-TION./Shewing how a Gentleman of great estate in/Bristol, ———— [same as **1068.2**] she saw in/ the other world./*Philadelphia:*/Printed and sold, Wholesale and Retail, no. 100, Race street./ [1819?].

t.[1], [2], 3–8 p.; 22 cm. The type has been reset but closely follows no. **1068.26** using the modern form of the letter "s". The book was probably printed by D. Dickinson, who was at 100 Race street in 1819. The title is the same as no. **1068.26** except for a comma after "DAUGHTER," instead of a semicolon. The four-lined caption, p. 2, is similar to that in no. **1068.26** except for not having a comma after "DAUGHTER", line 2. Below the caption there are 33 lines of verse instead of 39, but the type setting and punctuation is the same in both books except for a comma after "break,", line 22. Page 2 to page 5, line 32, are printed in 84 (20 line measure) type, measured on p. 5. Page 5, lines 33 to 40, page 8, are in 68.5 (20 line measure) type, measured on p. 8. *See* note under no. **492.1**. The end of the poem, in 42 lines, is on p. 8, which page is remarkably close to that of no. **1068.26**. The only differences are: "sin", line 4, instead of "sins"; "End.", line 43, in place of "The End." There are no illustrations. DLC°; Shaw 9200 (dated 1805).

1068.28　THE/PRODIGAL/DAUGHTER,/OR, A/STRANGE AND WONDERFUL/RELATION. Shewing ——— [same as **1068.26**] estate in/Bristol, had ——— poison them. — How an ——— saw in/the other world./[vignette of a coffin with initials "J. B" on the lid]/PHILADELPHIA:/Printed and sold, No. 212 Market Street, corner of Decatur Street. [*ca.* 1820].

　t.[1], [2], 3–8 p.; title vignette only illus.; 20 cm. The date is conjectural. The type setting, with the modern form of the letter "s", closely resembles no. **1068.26**, up to "Relation", line 6, being printed in six lines, but "Daughter,", line 3, is followed by a comma; "Or", line 4, has no punctuation after it. The remainder of the title is very close, only "them.—", line 11, is followed by a period. Page [2], in 37 lines and a caption in 4 lines, has a semicolon after "DAUGHTER;", line 2, instead of a comma; "holy scriptures", line 18, entirely in the lower case. The type setting of the rest of the page is that of no. **1068.26**. The same is true for page 8, which is in 42 lines of verse, below which, is "END". Line 35, page 7, ends "sinner wild". No type ornaments or text illustrations are present. Because of the similarity in the type setting to **1068.26**, even to using the word "END" instead of "Finis" on p. 8, it is believed that the book

was printed sometime close to **1068.26** and is therefore dated [*ca.* 1820]. MWA°.

1068.29　THE/PRODIGAL/DAUGHTER./ [*ca.* 1820] [half title p. [1]].

　½t.[1], [2, bl] [3], 4–12 p.; 18 cm. There is no imprint or date. All three words on the half title are printed in large capitals. Page [3] is as follows: THE/PRODIGAL DAUGHTER:/OR THE/DISOBEDIENT LADY RECLAIMED./SHEWING,/*How* ——— [same as **1068.27**, but printed in 8 lines instead of 10 and entirely in italics except for "BRISTOL", line 6, which is in small capitals] *estate in* BRISTOL, *had a*/proud———wonderful/things she saw in the other world./[8 lines of verse printed in regular type]. Line 11, page 11 ends "sinner wild". The last 27 lines of the poem, on p. 12, are in 84 (20 line measure) type which is used throughout the book. *See* note under no. **492.1** for this measurement. Some lines have been omitted. Lines 15–16: "But first behold the wretched place of doom,/ [2 lines in no. **1068.27** omitted]/I saw the burning lake of misery,/I saw the man there that first tempted me,/[2 lines omitted]/He told me he at last was sure of me./I said my Saviour's blood has set me free./[2 lines omitted]/When thus ——— [same 8 lines at **1068.27**] doth pursue./Finis." There are no illustrations. MWA°.

PROFITABLE AMUSEMENT. *See* Tales Uniting Instruction With Amusement, no. **1288.1**.

1069　THE PROGRESS OF THE DAIRY; Descriptive Of The Method Of Making Butter And Cheese For The Information Of Youth. *Nerv-York* [*sic. i.e. New-York*]: Published By Samuel Wood & Sons, No. 261, Pearl-Street; And Samuel S. Wood & Co. No. 212, Market-st. Baltimore. 1819.

　fr.[ii], t.[1], [2–3], 4–25 p.; illus.; 13.5 cm.; pr. & illus. paper covers; cover title undated; seven full-paged illus., including front., signed *A* [Alexander Anderson]. Adv. by Samuel Wood & Sons, 1820 in **274.2**. English ed. London: J. Wallis, 1800. MWA°; Shaw 49194.

PROUDFIT, ALEXANDER MONCREIF **1070.1**　— SCRIPTURE INVITATIONS AND PROMISES FOR LITTLE CHILDREN: With Practical Addresses And Select Hymns. By Alexander Proudfit. [1 line quot.] The Second Edition. Salem [N.Y.]: Printed And Sold By Dodd And Stevenson, At The Salem Book-Store. 1815.

t.[1], [2–3], 4–56 p.; 12.5 cm.; pr. blue-gray paper covers; cover title dated 1815. MWA-T*.

1070.2 —— The Fourth Edition. Salem, N.Y. Printed And Sold By Dodd And Stevenson, At The Salem Book-Store. 1820.

t.[1], [2–3], 4–72 p.; 12.5 cm.; paper covers. This is a preachment type of book and would not be included in this bibliography, but on p. 38 the author makes the following observation for the benefit of children which is too nice to omit: "Need I inform you my dear young readers, that you are naturally polluted in every part; that your hearts are deceitful above all things and desperately wicked; that every imagination of your thoughts is only evil continually."

MWA*; Shoemaker 2906.

1071 THE PROVERBS OF SOLOMON; AND ECCLESIASTICS: Newly translated out of the Original Tongues. Very necessary for the Instruction Of Youth. Philadelphia: Printed And Sold By Peter Stewart, West Side Of Second-Street, Ninth Door Above Chesnut-Street. M,DCC,LXXXVIII.

t.[1], [2–3], 4–60 p.; 17.5 cm. PP* (rebound); Evans 20965.

PSALTER (arranged chronologically)

1072.1 THE NEW ENGLAND PSALTER: Or, Psalms of David. With The Provers of Solomon. And Christ's Sermon on the Mount. Being a proper Introduction for the Training up Children to the Reading of the Holy Scriptures. Boston, N. E. Printed for Thomas Hancock at the Bible and Three Crowns, 1730.

t.[1], [2–191] p.; [A]–M$_8$; 16.5 cm. Two printer's ornaments are present. RPJCB*; Evans 39942.

Note: The letter "J" is not used for a signature designation in this edition or in the following ones.

1072.2 —— Boston: Printed by S. Kneeland and T. Green, for T. Hancock at the Bible and Three Crowns in Ann-Street near the Town-Dock. 1732.

t.[1], [2–128+] p.; sigs should be [A]–L$_8$, or p.[1]–[176] similar to no. **1072.3**; 15 cm.; bound in leather. The type setting is different but very close to no. **1072.3**. The Psalms in both books end on H$_8$ verso, p. [128]; The Proverbs of Solomon, I$_1$ recto–L$_5$ recto, p. [129–169], Christ's Sermon on the Mount, L$_5$ recto–L$_8$ verso, p. [169–176]; The Nicean Creed, L$_8$ verso, p. [176], in no. **1072.3**, are wanting in this copy but were probably on the same pages. Three printer's ornaments are present. MWA* (p. [7–10], [23–26] and all after p. [128] or H$_8$, I–L$_8$ wanting; C$_1$, torn; C$_2$, ½ wanting; t.[A]$_1$ recto, mut.); Evans 39984.

1072.3 —— Boston: Printed by S. Kneeland & T. Green for N. Proctor in Fish Street. 1738.

t.[1], [2–176] p.; [A]–L$_8$; 15.5 cm.; bound in leather. Eight printer's ornaments are present. MHi*; Evans 40133.

1072.4 —— Scripture [*sic. i.e.* Scriptures]. Boston: Printed by J. Draper for T. Hancock in Ann-Street 1740.

t.[1], [2–176] p.; A–L$_8$; 15 cm. bound in leather. The book is reset but closely follows no. **1072.3**, having the same text on the same pages. There is a large decorative bar above the caption, A$_2$ recto, of the Phoenix rising from its ashes with scrolls and two cupids. On L$_8$ verso there are two decorative bars. MWA*; Evans 40187.

1072.5 —— Philadelphia: Printed and Sold by B. Franklin. 1744.

t.[1], [2–176] p.; [A]–L$_8$; t.[1] 15.5 cm. Seven printer's ornaments are present. Above the caption, p. A$_2$ recto, there is a wide bar composed of five rows of ornaments. PHi (rebound); Evans 5336.

1072.6 —— Boston: Printed and Sold by Green And Russell, in Queen-street. M,DCC,LVII.

t.[1], [2–3], 4–191, [192] p.; 15 cm.; bound in leather. MB* (emb. st. on t.[1]; t.[1] & p. [3]–12, 191–[192] mut.); Evans 40876.

1072.7 —— Boston: Printed and Sold by Edes & Gill at their Printing-Office in Queen-Street, M,DCC,LVIII.

t.[1], [2–167+] p.; [A]–K$_8$, L$_4$; 15.5 cm.;

bound in buff paper over w. bds.

MB° (G$_7$, L$_2$, L$_3$, wanting); MH; Evans 40949.

1072.8 ——— Boston: Printed and Sold by Benjamin Mecom, at the New Printing-Office, opposite the Old Brick Meeting, in Cornhill; where Printing Work is done cheap. 1758.

t.[1], [2–132+] p.; A–B$_6$, C$_4$, D$_6$, D$_2$; E$_4$, F$_2$, G$_4$,H$_2$, I$_4$, K$_2$, L$_4$, M$_2$, N$_4$, O$_2$, P$_4$, Q$_2$, R$_4$, S$_2$; 16 cm.; bound in leather.

MWA° (60 leaves only, ending with Proverbs of Solomon, Chapter XI, Psalm II, verse 5, p. [132]); Evans 40950.

1072.9 ——— Boston: Printed and Sold by S. Kneeland, opposite the Probate-Office in Queen-Street, M,DCC,LX.

t.[1], [2–150] p.; [A]$_6$, B$_7$, C$_2$, D–N$_6$, sig. F$_1$ printed "E"; 16.5 cm.; bound in leather; sig. B$_7$ is an inserted leaf printed in larger type.

MWA° (p. [9–14], [37–38] mut.); Evans 41110.

1072.10 ——— Psalter Improved, By the Addition of a Variety of Lessons in Spelling, accented and divided according to Rule. Likewise, Rules for Reading, and particularly of the Emphasis belonging to some special Word or Words in a Sentence. Instruction for Reading Verse; as also of the different Letters used in printed Books, and particularly of the Use of Capitals, Notes and Points, made Use of in Writing and Printing. Likewise, some Account of the Books of the Old-Testament: Of the Books of the Prophets: Of the Apocryphal Books, and of the Books of the New-Testament. The Whole being a proper Introduction, not only to Learning, but to the training up Children in the Reading of the Holy Scriptures in Particular. Philadelphia: Printed and Sold by W. Dunlap at the Newest-Printing Office, in Market-Street, M, DCC,LX.

t.[1], [2–3], 4–116 p.; 16 cm.; bound in green Dutch paper over bds., leather spine.

PHi°; DLC; MB; MWA (t.[1] mut., imprint wanting, p. 11–12 mut., lower half of page torn away); NN; Evans 8543.

1072.11 ——— [same as **1072.1**] Scriptures. Boston: Printed (by B. Mecom) for Green and Russell, in Queen-Street. 1761.

t.[1], [2–3], 4–158, [159], p.; t.[1] 15 cm. Three printer's ornaments are present. On the title page there is a large crown. The tailpiece, p. 158, is a hand, surrounded at the wrist by a cuff and holding a bunch of flowers.

NN° (copy 1, rebound, p. 159 wanting; copy 2, t.[1] wanting, either **1072.11** or **1072.12**, p. [3], 31–32, 153–159 mut.); MWA (t.[1] wanting, either **1072.11** or **1072.12**); Evans 8795.

1072.12 ——— Boston: Printed (by B. Mecom) for D. Henchman, J. Edwards, T. Leveret in Cornhill, M. Dennis near Scarlett's Warf, J. Winter in Union-Street, S. Webb in Ann-Street, and J. Perkins near the Mill-Bridge. 1761.

t.[1], [2–3], 4–159, [160] p.; 15 cm.; bound in leather. The type setting is the same as no. **1072.11**, only the title page imprint is different. MWA-T°; MB (emb. st. on t.[1]); N (closely trimmed copy, some captions and page numbers blurred, all after p. 142 wanting); Evans 8796.

1072.13 ——— Boston: Printed by D. and J. Kneeland, opposite The Probate-Office, in Queen-Street, for John Perkins, in Union-Street. 1764.

t.[1], [2–3], 4–158, [159] p.; [A]–K$_8$; 15.5 cm.; bound in leather.

CLU°.

1072.14 ——— Boston, Printed by D. and J. Kneeland, opposite the Probate-Office, in Queen-Street, for S. Webb, in Cornhill. 1764.

t.[1], [2], 3–158+ p.; 1 cm.; bound in leather. MB° (per. st. on t.[1]; p. [159] wanting); Evans 41430.

1072.15 ——— Boston: Printed by D. and J. Kneeland, for Wharton and Bowes. 1764.

Evans 9603. The DLC copy has been considered to be this edition. It is figured in EAI, which shows that most of the title page is wanting including the imprint. The remaining upper third of the title page and the remainder of the book matches the text of **1072.32**, and could be either that edition or **1072.30** or **1072.31**. Evans gives "PHi" for a location, but no copy is in that library. He may have obtained the above imprint from an advertisement.

1072.16 ——— New-York, Printed and sold by H. Gaine, 1766.

132 p.; 16 cm.

Evans 41604.

1072.17 —— Boston: Printed by Edes and Gill, in Queen-Street, MDCCLXVIII.

t.[1], [2–168] p.; [A]–K₈, L₄; 16 cm.; bound in leather; Nicene Creed on the lower half of p. [168].

DLC° (i. st. on t.[1]); CSmH; Evans 10835.

1072.18 —— Boston: Printed by Edes and Gill, in Queen-Street, For John Perkins in Union-Street, M,DCC,LXVIII.

t.[1], [2–168] p.; [A]–K₈, L₄; 16 cm.; bound in leather.

MB° (per. st. on. t.[1]); Evans 41797.

1072.19 —— Boston: Printed and Sold by William McAlpine in Marlborough-Street, M,DCC,LX,VIII.

t.[1], [2–4], [5–6, a portion of leaf wanting including p. no.], 7–159, [160]; t.[1] 15.5 cm.; bound in leather; Nicene Creed on the lower two thirds of p. 159, and the upper fourth of p. [160] below which is an adv. of W. M'Alpine. Five figured type ornaments are present as well as two unfigured ones.

RPJCB°; NN (p. 3–8, 11–14, 17–26, 41–48, 91–94, 115–118, 127–132, all after p. 144 wanting); Evans 10834.

1072.20 [—— Boston: Printed and Sold by William McAlpine in Marlborough-Street,] [*ca.* 1768] [conjectural title mostly copied from **1072.19**].

33–194, [195–196] p.; 15 cm.; bound in leather; Nicene Creed on p. [195] and the upper fourth of p. [196], below which is an adv. of William M'Alpine. Among the items offered were *The Death of Abel*, published by Z. Fowle & N. Coverly in 1765, and Jonathan Edward's *Treatise*, published in New York in 1768 from which the Boston Edition was reprinted. The above advertised books may help date this book [*ca.* 1768]. Five printer's ornaments are present. MWA° t.[1], p.[2]–32, 75–82, 99–106 wanting; p. 33–36 ¾ wanting, p. 37–38, 140–141, 167–168, 185–186 mut.).

1072.21 —— Boston: Printed by D. Kneeland, in Queen-Street, for Nicholas Bowes, opposite the old Brick Meeting-House in Cornhill. 1770.

t.[1], [2–176] p.; [A]–K₈; 16 cm.; bound in leather.

PMA° (interleaved with notes in James Win-throp's handwriting; sig. H₄ wanting, but text appears to be complete); Evans 42061.

1072.22 —— Boston: Printed by D. Kneeland, in Queen-Street, For Thomas Leverett in Cornhill. 1770.

t.[1], [2–176] p.; [A]–L₈; 16 cm.; bound in leather.

NN° (A₆, B₁, F₂ mut.); Evans 11567.

1072.23 —— Boston: Printed by D. Kneeland, in Queen-Street, for John Perkins in Union-Street. 1770.

t.[1], [2–175], [176, Nicene Creed] p.; [A]–L₈; 16 cm.

DLC°; Evans 11568.

1072.24 —— Boston: Printed and Sold by William M'Alpine, about Mid-way between the Governor's and Dr. Gardner's, Marlborough-Street. 1770.

t.[1], [2–3], 4–194 p.; [A]–Q₆ [R. wanting]; 15.5 cm.; bound in leather, the last page with the Nicene Creed is wanting.

DLC° (mut.); Evans 42062.

1072.25 —— Boston: Printed and Sold by D. Kneeland, next to the Writing-School in Queen-Street. 1771.

t.[1], [2–176] p.; [A]–L₈; 16 cm.; bound in leather.

NhD°; Evans 42214.

1072.26 —— Boston: Printed and Sold by William McAlpine in Marlborough-Street. MDCCLXXI.

t.[1], [2–3], 4–159, [160] p.; 16 cm.; bound in leather. Five printer's ornaments are present.

MWA° (p. 3–4, 159–[160] mut.; i. st. on t.[1]); MB (per st. on. t.[1]; p. 113–114, 147–150 mut.); Evans 11986.

1072.27 —— Boston: Printed and Sold by John Perkins, in Union-Street, near the Market. 1771.

t.[1], [2–3], 4–159, [160] p.; 16 cm.; bound in leather; p. 40 not numbered.

MWA° (p. 3–6 wanting); NN (rebound; p. 27 cropped; p. 41–48 wanting); Evans 11987; Sabin 52737.

1072.28 ———— Boston: Printed and Sold by John Boyles, in Marlborough-Street. 1773.

t.[1], [2–3], 4–158, [159] p.; 16 cm.; bound in leather. Title page bordered with ornament; no decorative bars of ornaments in text.

MWA* (p. 113–[159] wanting); NBuG (p. 65–80 wanting); Evans 12672.

1072.29 ———— Boston: Printed by John Boyles, for John Perkins in Union-Street. 1773.

t.[1], [2–3], 4–158, [159] p.; 15.5 cm.; bound in leather. Same as no. **1072.26** except for the imprint.

MWA-W* (upper ¼ of t.[1] wanting, p. 11–14, 19–22, 25–32, 43–46, 113–122, 127–128 wanting); Evans 42407.

1072.30 ———— Boston, N. E. Printed for, and sold by John Boyle, in Marlborough-Street. M,DCC,LXXIV.

t.[1], [2–3], 4–159, [160] p.; 16.5 cm.; bound in blue paper over bds., leather spine. Six printer's ornaments are present.

MWA-W*; Evans 42558.

1072.31 ———— Boston, N. E. Printed and Sold at Greenleaf's Printing-Office, in Hanover-Street, M,DCC,LXXIV.

t.[1], [2–3], 4–159, [160] p.; 16.5 cm.; bound in leather. Same as no. **1072.30** except for imprint.

MWA*; CtW (p. [160] wanting); CtY; PP (p. 81–96 duplicated); PPL; Evans 13148.

1072.32 ———— Boston, N. E. Printed for and sold by John Perkins, at his shop in Union-Street. M,DCC,LXXIV.

t.[1], [2–3], 4–159, [160] p.; 16.5 cm.; bound in leather. Same as no. **1072.25** except for the imprint. The imprints of **1072.31** and **1072.32** are closest to Evans 13148 which reads: "Boston: Printed at Greenleaf's Printing Office for John Perkins. 1774."

MWA-W* (p. [3]–6 slightly mut., p. 6–9, 19–24 cropped); DLC; MB (per. st. on t.[1]); N (t.[1], p. 19–22, 47–48, 85–86 mut.); NN (p. 27–28 cropped; p. 41–48 wanting); Evans 42559; Sabin 52737.

1072.33 ———— Boston: Printed and sold by Benjamin Edes & Sons, in Cornhill. M,DCC,-LXXXIV.

t.[1], [2–3[, 4–171, [172] p.; 16 cm.; bound in leather.

PP* (Q₂, Q₃ wanting); DLC; MWA; NN; Evans 18358.

1073.1 THE PSALTER: Or, Psalms of David: With The Proverbs of Solomon, And Christ's Sermon on the Mount. Being An Introduction for training up Children in the Reading of the Holy Scriptures. Boston: Printed by T. And J. Fleet, at the Bible and Heart in Cornhill. M,DCC,LXXXI.

t.[1], [2], 3–157, [158] p.; 16.5 cm.; bound in leather.

MWA*.

1073.2 ———— Boston: Printed by T. and J. Fleet, at the Bible and Heart in Cornhill. 1783.

t.[1], [2], 3–156, 175 [*sic. i.e.* 157], [158] p.; 16.5 cm.; bound in paper over w. bds.

MWA*; MB (rebound); MHi (bound in blue-gray paper over w. bds.; p. 157 printed correctly); RPJCB.

1073.3 ———— Being an Introduction for Children to the Reading of the Holy Scriptures. Carefully copied from the Holy Bible. Worcester, Massachusetts, Printed by Isaiah Thomas, at his Office near the Court-House. MDCCLXXXIV.

t.[1], [2–3], 4–160 p.; 17 cm.; bound in leather.

MWA* (i. st. on t.[1]); MHi (p. 3–6 wanting).

1073.4 ———— Worcester, Massachusetts, Printed by Isaiah Thomas, for Ebenezer Battelle, in Boston. MDCCLXXXIV.

t.[1], [2–3], 4–160 p.; 16 cm.; bound in paper over w. bds.

MWA*; DLC.

1073.5 ———— Boston: Printed and sold by John Norman in Marshal's Lane, near the Boston-Stone [*sic. i.e.* Store]. MDCCLXXXVII.

fr.[ii], t.[1] [2–158] p.; [A]–I₈, K₇ with K₈ bl. plus fr.[ii]; 16.5 cm.; bound in blue-gray paper over w. bds., leather spine; front. by W. Norman according to Hamilton.

NjP*; DLC (p. 156–158 wanting); MWA (fr.[ii], p. 129–158 wanting; rebound); Hamilton 117.

1073.6 ———— Boston: Printed by Benjamin Edes, for James White, at Franklin's Head, Court-Street. MDCCXCVI.

t.[1], [2–3], 4–158 p.; 17.5 cm.; bound in gray paper over w. bds., leather spine.

MWA*, NN (t.[1] mut., p. 3–10, 17–20, 53–56, 137–140, 149–152 wanting).

1073.7 ———Being An Introduction For The Training Up Of Children To The Reading Of The Holy Scriptures. Boston: Published by Hastings, Etheridge & Bliss, No. 8, State Street. And By Said Etheridge, Charlestown. 1808. S. Etheridge, Printer, Charlestown, Mass.

t.[1], [2–3], 4–157, [158] p.; 17.5 cm.; bound in gray paper over w. bds.

MWA*; DLC; KU; Shaw 14504.

1073.8 ——— Being An Introduction For Children To The Reading Of The Holy Scriptures. Carefully Copied from the Holy Bible. Baltimore: Printed By Warner & Hanna. 1808.

t.[1], [2–3], 4–170, [171], [172, adv. of school books] p.; 17 cm.; bound in gray paper over bds., blue cloth spine.

MWA*; DLC; Shaw 14503.

1073.9 ——— Baltimore: Printed By Warner & Hanna. For John Vance & Co. No. 178, Market Street. 1808.

t.[1], [2–3], 4–170, [171], [172, adv. of school books] p.; t.[1] 16 cm.

MdBE* (rebound, extensive per. st. on t.[1], per st. on p. [3]).

[PUCKLE, JAMES]
1074 [—] The Club: Or, A Grey Cap For A Green Head; In A Dialogue Between Father And Son. [1 line quot.] Philadelphia: Printed By Francis Bailey, At Yorick's Head, No. 116, High-Street. M,DCC,XCV.

t.[i], [ii–iii], iv–v, [vi], [7–9], 10–198 p.; 15.5 cm.

MWA*.

1075 [—] A Gray-Cap For A Green-Head, In A Dialogue Between Father And Son. The first American Edition, from the fourth British Edition. Philadelphia: Printed By And For Samuel Longcope, No. 147, Spruce Street. M.DCC.XCVIII.

t.[5], [6, bl.–13], 14–159 p.; 17.5 cm.; bound in leather.

MWA*; DLC (3 copies); PHi; PP; PPL; Evans 34426.

1076 Pug's Visit; Or, The Disasters Of Mr. Punch. A Poetic Tale. Illustrated With Sixteen Elegant Engravings On Copper-Plate. Philadelphia: Published and sold Wholesale by Wm. Charles, and may be had of all Booksellers. 1809. Price 25 Cents. [cover title].

[1–16] p. engr. on one side only of 16 leaves; 12.5 cm.; pr. paper covers.

English ed. London: J. Harris, April 10th, 1806.

MWA* (front cover mut.); Shaw 18468.

1077.1 Pug's Visit To Mr. Punch. Illustrated With Eight Whimsical Engravings. Philadelphia: Published and sold by Wm. Charles, and may be had of all the Booksellers. 1810. Price 12 1–2 Cents.

[1–8] p. engr. on one side only of 8 leaves; illus.; 13.5 cm.; pr. buff paper covers.

PP*; NNC-Pl (rear cover ⅞ths wanting); PHi; Shaw 21162.

1077.2 ——— Illustrated With Eight Whimsical Engravings. Philadelphia: Published and sold Wholesale by Wm. Charles, and may be had of all the Booksellers. 1815. Price, 12 1–2 Cents. [cover title].

[1–8] p. engr. on one side only of 8 leaves; illus.; 13.5 cm.; pr. buff paper covers.

MWA*; PP; Shaw 35733.

1078 The Pullet; Or A Good Foundation For Riches And Honour. Philadelphia. Printed For Johnson And Warner, No. 147, Market Street. 1810. Lydia R. Bailey, Printer, No. 10. North-Alley.

fr.[ii], t.[1], [2–3], 4–36 p.; 3 pl. including front.; 13.5 cm.; pr. buff paper covers; 3 pl. signed *WR Sc* [William Ralph].

English ed. London: J. Harris, 1808.

MWA* (rear cover wanting); OOxM; PP; Shaw 21163.

1079.1 Punch's Visit To Mr. Pug. Illustrated With Eight Whimsical Engravings. Philadelphia: Published And Sold Wholesale By Wm. Charles, And May Be Had Of All Booksellers. 1810. Price 12 1–2 Cents. [cover title].

[1–8] p. engr. on one side only of 8 leaves; illus.; 12.5 cm.; pr. buff paper front cover.

DLC* (rear cover wanting); Shaw 21164.

1079.2 ——— Philadelphia: Published and sold Wholesale, by Wm. Charles, and may be had of all the Booksellers. 1815. Price, 12 1–2 Cents.

[1–8] p. engr. on one side only of 8 leaves; illus.; 13.5 cm.; pr. paper covers.
MWA°; Shaw 35734.

1080 Punishment, though late, overtakes the sinner at last. Boston: adv. by Thomas B. Wait And Co. And Charles Williams, 1812 in *The Columbian Centinel.*

PUZZLE, PETER, ESQ. *pseud.*
1081 — A New Riddle-Book, Published for the use of all good little Boys and Girls. By Peter Puzzle, Esq. [2 lines of verse] Homer. Wilmington [Del.], Printed & Sold Wholesale and Retail by J. Wilson, at the Mirror Printing-Office & Book-Store. 1803.

t.[1], [2, adv.], [3], 4–32 p.; 10 cm. Adv. by J. Wilson, 1800 in **61.8.**
CtY°.

PUZZLEBRAIN, JEFFREY *pseud.*
1082.1 — Fire-Side Amusement: A New Collection Of Choice Riddles, Printed for the Entertainment of all the good and merry little Boys and Girls, who are so lucky as to obtain it. By Jeffrey Puzzlebrain. Ornamented With Cuts. Litchfield [Conn.]: Published By Hosmer & Goodwin. 1808.

fr.[2], t.[3], [4–5], 6–31 p.; illus.; 10 cm.
CtY° (fr.[2] ½ torn away).

1082.2 — ——— Hartford: Printed by Hale & Hosmer. 1812.

fr.[2], t.[3], [4–5], 6–31 p.; illus.; 9.5 cm.; pr. & illus. buff paper covers.
MWA-W° (covers mut.); CtHi (front cover mut., rear cover wanting; poor copy); CtY (covers, fr.[2], & p. 31 wanting); RPB; Shaw 25427.

1082.3 — ——— Adorned with Cuts. Hartford: Printed by Hale & Hosmer. 1814.

fr.[2], t.[3], [4–5], 6–31 p.; illus.; 9.5 cm.
MWA-W copy 2 of no. **673.30** has printed & illus. buff paper covers which are probably duplicates of the missing ones in this book.
Cover title: Fire-Side Amusement, Or A New Collection Of Riddles. Hartford: Printed by Hale & Hosmer. 1814.
MWA-W° (covers wanting).

1083 Puzzles for Little Folks, Philadelphia: adv. by Wm. Charles, 1809 in **254.1.**

PUZZLEWIT, PETER, ESQ. *pseud.*
1084 — A Bag Of Nuts Ready Crack'd: Being A Choice Collection Of Riddles, Paradoxes, &c. By Peter Puzzlewit, Esq. Dover, N. H. J. Whitlock, Printer. 1807.

fr.[2], t.[3], [4–5], 6–30, [31, illus.] p.; illus.; 10 cm.; wallpaper covers. *See also* no. **1191.1.**
NhHi°; Shaw 12021.

The Puzzling-Cap. *See* The Big Puzzling Cap, no. **98.1** or The Little Puzzling Cap, no. **779.1.**

The Puzzling-Cap. *See* Wiseman, Billy (*pseud.*), no. **1446.1.**

1085.1 [The Puzzling Cap, ——— [probably the same as **1085.2**] Boston: Printed and Sold by N. Coverly. 1790?] [imaginary title mainly composed from **1085.2**].

5–24 p.; illus.; 9.5 cm. This fragmentary copy has twenty illustrations, two cuts on each even-numbered page, with two riddles on the opposite odd-numbered page. Most of the cuts are printed from the same blocks as in N. Coverly's 1792 edition, no. **1085.2**. The one for "A Husband", p. 18, and "A Gooseberry Bush", p. 20, are peculiar to this edition, as well as "A Pair Of Stays", p. 12, which with its riddle is omitted from no. **1085.2**. In **1085.2** there is only one cut per page and each riddle, matching a cut, is printed below the illustration and has a different Roman number from no. **1085.1**. In no. **1085.1** the picture of "A Barrel Of Beer", p. 10, has an unbroken curved line along the top side of the barrel. The title "Wheel-Barr$_{\text{ow}}$", p. 16, has the letters "ow" lower than the rest of the word. On the same page the cut entitled "A Water No Pot" [*sic. i.e.* Watering Pot] has the handle of the pot without a nick and the spout is intact. In 1792 the cut is damaged but correctly labeled "Watering Pot". "Gooseberry Bush", p. 20, is correctly spelled. Because so many of the illustrations are the same in both **1085.1** and **1085.2**, this fragment is believed to have been printed by N. Coverly. It must be pointed out however that this fragment could have been printed by C. White and C. Cambridge in Boston, since this firm often printed editions of the same books and illustrated them with pictures from blocks used by N. Coverly. However until a copy with a title page is found, no. **1085.1** will be considered to be from N. Coverly's press. The book was undoubtedly printed prior to 1792 because the cuts are without breaks and the spelling error on p. 16 is corrected in 1792. The date [1790?] is selected as a possible date when the book was published. English and Scottish ed. London: adv. by F. Newbery, 1771 in *The Sugar Plumb*.

MWA-W° (all before p. 5 and all after p. 24 wanting).

1085.2 THE PUZZLING CAP, A Choice Collection Of Riddles, In familiar Verse: With a curious Cut to each Riddle, Boston: Printed and Sold By N. Coverly. 1792. Price, 5 Coppers.

t.[1], [2–3], 4–32 p.; illus.; 11 cm. The illustrations are mostly from the same blocks used in no. **1085.1**. Except for the first cut entitled "The Puzzling Cap", p. [2], which has the riddle or "Riddle I", on the opposite page, there is only one illustration on a page with the accompanying riddle below it. The title "A Pin", p. 8, has the "A" lower than the rest of the line. The cut of "A Barrel Of Beer" has a break in the curved line along the top side of the barrel. The page number above this cut is blurred, but looks like "17" [*sic. i.e.* 10]. The picture entitled, "Pair Of Spectacles", with "Riddle XV" [*sic. i.e.* XIV] below it, precedes "A Watering Pot", "Riddle XIV" [*sic. i.e.* XV] on the opposite page, p. 17. The page number of the former is "16" printed on the inside of the page. The cut of the watering pot has a nick in the handle and the spout above the crosspiece is missing. The illustrations on p. 18, 19, 26 are not in no. **1085.1**. Those on pages 18 and 26 were used by N. Coverly, 1783 in *The History Of Little Goody Two-Shoes*, p. 52 and 58 respectively. In the title for "Riddle XVII", p. 19, the word gooseberry is misspelled "Goosbury". Page 32 has verses entitled "The wonder, or The Riddle of Riddles." They are a rewritten version of those which appeared in *A Little Book For Little Children: . . . By T. W. London, Printed for G. C. and sold at the Ring in Little-Britain* [*ca.* 1705].

MWA°; Evans 25195.

1085.3 ———— Boston: Printed and Sold By N. Coverly. 1792. Price, 5 Coppers.

A variant of no. **1085.2**. The differences are: the page number on p.[10] is wanting; page number "16" is printed on the outside of the page; the riddles on page 16 and 17 are correctly numbered "XIV" and "XV" respectively. The text of the remainder of the book is identical with no. **1085.2**.

MB° (per st. on t.[1] which is also mut.; the book has 4 leaves bound with it of an edition of *The House That Jack Built*).

1085.4 ———— Cap; being a pretty collection of Riddles. Philadelphia: adv. by Francis Bailey, 1793 in **773.1**.

1085.5 ———— [same as **1085.2**] Verse. With a curious Cut to each. Philadelphia: Printed By John Adams. 1805.

fr.[2], t.[3], [4–5], 6–31 p.; illus.; 10.5 cm.; olive-gray paper covers.

MWA°; CtY (p.[5]–8, 25–28 wanting); DLC; NHi; NN; NNC-Pl; PP; Shaw 9225; Weiss 1936, p. 610.

1085.6 ———— To Each. To which is added, Description Of The Swan And Good Boy. Hartford: Printed By Lincoln & Gleason. 1806.

fr.[2], t.[3], [4–5], 6–30, [31, adv. list of books] p.; illus.; 10 cm.; Dutch paper covers.

RPB° (bound with other books); CtHi; DLC (fr.[2], p.[31] & covers mut.); PP (marbled paper covers); Shaw 11232.

1085.7 ———— Philadelphia: adv. by, B. & T. Kite, 1807 in **611.1**.

1085.8 ———— Being A Choice Collection Of Riddles. Ornamented with Engravings. Albany: Printed By E. & E. Hosford. 1808.

fr.[2], t.[3], [4–5], 6–31 p.; illus.; 10.5 cm.

MWA° (fr.[2], p. 31, & covers wanting); Shaw 16028.

1085.9 ———— Albany: Printed By E. And E. Hosford. 1810.

fr.[2], t.[3], [4–5], 6–31 p.; illus.; 10.5 cm.; pr. & illus. buff paper covers; cover title undated.

MWA° (2 copies; copy 1, cover title: "Wisdom In Miniature"; copy 2, cover title: "The Puzzling Cap," i. st. on p.[5]); Shaw 21165.

1085.10 ———— Ornamented With Cuts. Boston: Printed For, And Sold By The Booksellers. 1810.
  fr.[2], t.[3], [4–5], 6–15 p.; illus.; 10 cm.; brown or gray marbled paper covers.
  MWA-W°.

1085.11 ———— Ornamented with Engravings. Albany: Printed By E. & E. Hosford. 1813.
  fr.[2], t.[3], [4–5], 6–31 p.; illus.; 10.5 cm.; pr. & illus. paper covers. Cover title imprint: Albany: Printed By E. And E. Hosford.
  OClWHi°; CLU; MWA-T; Shaw 29607.

1085.12 ———— Ornamented With Cuts. Boston: N. Coverly, Printer, Milk-St. 1813.

fr.[2, alphabet], t.[3], [4–15] p.; illus.; 9.5 cm.; wallpaper covers.
  MH° (i. st. p.[4]; p. 7–10 mut. lower half of the page torn away).

1085.13 ———— Riddles. Ornamented with Engravings. Albany: Printed by E. & E. Hosford. 1816.
  fr.[2], t.[3], [4–5], 6–31 p.; illus.; 10 cm.; pr. & illus. buff paper covers, cover title undated.
  MWA-T°; NNC-LS (i. st. on front cover).

1085.14 ———— Ornamented With Cuts. Boston: Printed For N. Coverly, Milk-Street. 1820.
  t.[1], [2–16] p.; illus.; 10 cm.; yellow wallpaper covers.
  MWA°; Shoemaker 2919.

R

[R., J.]
1086 [—] YOUTH'S MONITOR: Or, Histories Of The Lives Of Young Persons [4 lines of verse] Cowper. The First American Edition. Philadelphia: Printed For Geo. W. Mentz, 71, Race Street. Griggs and Dickinsons [*sic. i.e.* Dickinson] Printers. 1815.

fr.[ii], t.[iii], [iv–v], vi–viii, [9], 10–127 p.; front. only illus.; 10.5 cm.
MWA°; PP; Shaw 35739.

R., R. [RANSOM, R.] *See* THE GOOD BOY'S SOLILOQUY, no. **460.**

THE RATIONAL BRUTES. *See* Kilner, Dorothy, no. **730.1.**

RATIONAL SPORTS. *See* Fenn, Eleanor (Frere) Lady, no. **401.1.**

RAWES, WILLIAM
1087.1 — EXAMPLES FOR YOUTH, In Remarkable Instances Of Early Piety. Selected By William Rawes, Jun. [2 lines quot.] New-York: Printed By Isaac Collins & Son. 1802.

t.[i], [ii–iii], iv–vi, [7], 8–263, [264, adv. list of books] p.; 14 cm.; bound in leather. According to the British Museum Catalogue the selections were made from John Tompkins' *Piety Promoted,* the 2 ed. of which was printed in London, 1703.
English and Irish ed. London: 1797.
MWA°; CtY (p. 105–108, 143–146 wanting); MiD; PSC; Shaw 2964.

1087.2 — —— New-York: Printed By Samuel Wood, No. 362, Pearl-Street. 1809.

t.[i], [ii–iii], iv–v, [vi], [7], 8–191, [192, adv.] p.; 17 cm.; bound in leather.
MWA°; MH; NcD; PHC; PSC; Shaw 18477.

RAYMOND, JANE (OSBORN)
1088 [—] EARLY PIETY EXEMPLIFIED IN ELIZABETH OSBORN, Only Three Years And Nine Months Old. She being dead yet speaketh. Boston: Printed and Sold at No. 53 Cornhill, by Lincoln & Edmands, 1819.

[*366*]

t.[1], [2–3], 4–8 p.; illus.; 11 cm.; p.[3]: The substance of this Narrative was related to Ebenezer L. Boyd, at Dorchester, Massachusetts, in 1809, by widow Raymond, the surviving sister of Elizabeth Osborn . . . An Account Of . . . < Taken by her sister, Mrs Jane Osborn > MWA°; Shaw 49241.

1089 THE RECONCILED SISTERS: Or, The Prudent Explanation. Philadelphia: Published By Benjamin & Thomas Kite, No. 20, North Third-Street. Brown & Merritt Printers, No. 24, Church-alley. 1810.

t.[1], [2–3], 4–36 p.; 12 cm.
MWA° (covers wanting); Shaw 21178.

[REDE, SARAH]
1090.1 [—] A TOKEN FOR YOUTH, Or Comfort to Children Being the Life & Christian Experience of the wonderful workings of the Spirit of God on Cartaret Rede. From her Infancy to her last Moments, as it was faithfully taken from her own Mouth, by her Mother. The Twenty-fifth Edition. [5 lines of quot.] Boston: Reprinted & Sold at the Printing-house in Newbury-Street. 1729.

t.[i], i–iii, 1–30+ p.; 15 cm.; p. 27–30+ I. Watts' *Divine Songs.*
MWA° (last leaf sig. C6 wanting, t.[i] mut.).

1090.2 [—] —— Mother. The Twenty-Seventh Edition. [4 line quot.] Boston, Printed and Sold by S. Kneeland, In Queen-Street. 1766.

t.[1], [2–4], 5–24 p.; 17.5 cm.
MWA°; RPJCB (p.[24] not numbered).

1091 RELIGION WITHOUT LEARNING; OR, THE HISTORY OF SUSAN WARD. [caption p. 1]. Published For The Hartford Evangelical Tract Society. March, 1818. 5000. [colophon p. 16].

[1], 2–16 p.; 16.5 cm.; pr. blue paper covers. Cover title: Little Henry And His Bearer. Rear cover unprinted. *See* no. **578.1.**
MWA-T°; MWA.

1092.1 THE REMARKABLE HISTORY OF AUGI: Or A Picture Of True Happiness. Together with The Story Of The Dreamer. First American Edition.

Worcester: Printed By Isaiah Thomas jun Sold Wholesale And Retail At His Bookstore, At The Sign Of Johnston's Head. 1796.

> fr.[2], t.[3], [4–5], 6–31 p.; front only illus.; 9.5 cm.; Dutch paper covers.
> MWA° (bound in leather, I. Thomas copy); NjP; PP; Bowe mss.; Evans 31080.

1092.2 ———— Second Worcester Edition. Printed at Worcester, Massachusetts: By Isaiah Thomas, Jun. Sold Wholesale and Retail by Him. 1799.

> fr.[2], t.[3], [4–5], 6–31 p.; 11 cm.
> MWA° (the "1" of p. "31" is not struck in this copy); CLU (fr.[2] wanting); RPJCB°.

1092.3 ———— Massachusetts, Printed For The Booksellers [*ca.* 1802].

> fr.[2], t.[3], [4–5], 6–31 p.; 10.5 cm. The frontispiece is the same as the one used in *The New England Primer . . . New England Printed For The Booksellers* [*ca.* 1802–1810].
> MWA°.

THE REMARKABLE HISTORY OF TOM JONES. *See* Fielding, Henry, no. **408.1**.

1093.1 REMARKS ON CHILDREN'S PLAY. [4 lines of quot.] Watts. New-York: Printed And Sold By S. Wood, At The Juvenile Book-Store. No. 357, Pearl-Street. 1811.

> t.[1], [2–3], 4–44, [45, adv.] p.; illus.; 12.5 cm.; pr. & illus. yellow paper covers.
> NHi°.

1093.2 ———— New-York: Printed And Sold By Samuel Wood, At the Juvenile Book-Store, No. 357, Pearl-street. 1814.

> t.[1], [2–3], 4–44, [45, adv.] p.; illus.; 12.5 cm.; unprinted yellow paper covers.
> PP°; CtY (bound with other books); NWebyC (incomplete); Shaw 26588.

1093.3 ———— New-York: Printed And Sold By S. Wood & Sons, At The Juvenile Book-Store, No. 357, Pearl-Street. 1816.

> t.[1], [2–3], 4–44, [45, adv.] p.; illus.; 12 cm.; pr. & illus. paper covers; cover title imprint: Printed And Sold ——— Pearl-Street, *Nerv-York* [*sic. i.e.* New-York].
> MWA°.

1093.4 ———— New-York: Printed And Sold By S. Wood & Sons, At The Juvenile Book-Store, No. 261, Pearl-Street. 1817.

> t.[1], [2–3], 4–44, [45, adv.] p.; illus.; 13 cm.; pr. & illus. paper covers; cover title worn, undated.
> MWA° (rear cover mut.); Shaw 41947.

1093.5 ———— New-York: Published By Samuel Wood & Sons, No. 261, Pearl-Street; And Samuel S. Wood & Co. No. 212, Market-st Baltimore. 1819.

> t.[1], [2–3], 4–44, [45, adv.] p.; illus.; 13 cm.; pr. & illus. buff paper covers; cover title undated.
> CtHi°.

THE RENOWNED HISTORY OF GILES GINGERBREAD. *See* Gingerbread, Giles (*pseud.*), no. **452.1** and addenda.

1094.1 THE REPROBATE'S REWARD, Or, A Looking-Glass For Disobedient Children, Being A full and true account of the barbarous and bloody murder of one Elizabeth Wood, living in the city of Cork, by her own Son, as she was riding, upon the 28th day of July, to Kingsale market. How he cut her throat from ear to ear; as also how the murderer was found out by her apparition or ghost; the manner of his being taken; his dying words at the place of execution: with a true copy of verses written by his own hand in Cork jail, being a warning to all disobedient children to repent, and obey their parents. Philadelphia: Printed In The Year M, DCC, XCIII.

> t.[1], 2–8 p.; 18 cm.; in verse.
> English ed. London: J. Evans, and Co. [n.d.].
> NN° (rebound); Evans 46863.

1094.2 ————verses written by his own hand in Cork jail, being a warning to all disobedient Children to repent, and obey their Parents. Philadelphia: Printed In The Year M,DCC,XCVIII.

> t.[1], 2–8 p.; 12.5 cm.; gray paper covers.
> PP°; Evans 48590.

1094.3 ———— riding upon the road one day with articles for sale to market. ——— [same as **1094.1**] Rhode-Island: Reprinted at the request of a number of Country Inhabitants, 1802.

> t.[1], [2, bl.–3], 4–11 p.; 19 cm.
> MWA°; RPB; Shaw 2974.

1095 THE RETURNING PRODIGAL. In Two Parts. First Published By The Christian Tract Society. No. XX. Boston: Wells and Lilly, Court-Street. 1820.
t.[1], [2–3], 4–51 p.; t.[1] 15.5 cm.
MWA° (bound with other tracts); Shoemaker 2989.

1096.1 THE REWARD OF AVARICE: Or, Abdalla And The Iron Candlestick. A Turkish Tale. To Which Is Added, The Story Of Whang The Miller. Hartford: Printed By John Babcock. 1798.
fr.[2], t.[3], [4–5], 6–29, [30, adv.], [31, 2 cuts] p.; 11.5 cm.; yellow Dutch paper covers.
English ed. London: Printed by F. Newbery, 1777 in *The Amusing Instructor,* p. 93 with the caption: Ingratitude punished.
PP°; Evans 48591.

1096.2 ——— First Windsor Edition. Printed At Windsor [Vt.]: By Farnsworth & Churchill. 1810.
fr.[2], t.[3], [4, bl.], [5–6 alphabets], [7], 8–29, [30–31, 2 cuts per page] p.; illus.; 9.5 cm.; pr. & illus. white paper covers; p. 19 printed "91".
Cover title: Abdalla. Printed At Windsor: By Farnsworth & Churchill 1810.
MWA°; PP (fr.[2], p.[31] & covers wanting); Vt; McCorison 1204; Shaw 21203, also 21204 (under wrong title: *The Reward of Virtue*).

1097 THE REWARD OF INGRATITUDE. An Eastern Tale. Adorned with Cuts. New-Haven: For J. Babcock And Son. Sidney's Press. 1820.
fr.[2], t.[3], [4–5], 6–31 p.; illus.; 11 cm.; pr. & illus. brown paper covers.
MWA-W°; CtY; Shoemaker 2993.

1098 THE REWARD OF INTEGRITY, Or, The History Of Martin And James, A Moral Tale. Designed For The Improvement Of Youth. To which is added, A Short Account Of Jack Easy. New-York: Printed and Sold by John C. Totten, No. 9 Bowery. 1819.
fr.[ii], t.[iii], [iv–v], vi, [7], 8–46 p.; illus.; 14 cm.; pr. & illus. paper covers.
CtHi°; MWA (covers wanting, t.[iii] frayed; a dog-eared copy); PP; Shaw 49272.

1099 RHYMES FOR CHILDREN. New-York: Published By Thomas B. Jansen, Bookseller, No. 11 Chatham-street, opposite the City Hall. 1817.
t.[1], [2–5], 6–36 p.; illus.; 14 cm.; pr. & illus. pink paper covers. Contents consist of Nursery Rhymes.
Cover title: Jansen's Edition. Rhymes For Children. New-York: Sold by T. B. Jansen, Bookseller And Stationer, No. 11 Chatham-st. opposite the City-Hall. Price 12 1–2 Cents.
MWA-T°; DLC.

RHYMES FOR THE NURSERY. *See* Gilbert, Mrs. Ann (Taylor), no. **447**.

RHYMING ALPHABET; OR, TOM THUMB'S DELIGHT. *See* Thumb, Thomas, no. **1307**.

1100 RICHARD AND JAMES, Or, The Duty Of Obedience: A Tale, Designated For The Instruction Of Young Persons: To which are added, A Short Account Of Samuel And James, Two Pious Brothers; And Some Intresting Anecdotes. Boston: Printed For Samuel T. Armstrong, By Crocker & Brewster, No. 50, Cornhill. 1820.
fr.[2], t.[3], [4–5], 6–34, 24 [*sic. i.e.* 35] p.; front., title vignette & illus. p. 24 [*sic.* 35] only illus.; 14 cm.; pr. & illus. blue-gray paper covers; rear cover adv. list of books.
Cover title: Richard And James; Or, The Duty Of Obedience. ———[imprint same as t.[3]] 1820. Vignette on front cover signed *Akin.*
MWA-W°; DLC; MB; Shoemaker 3007.

[RICHARDSON, MR.]
1101.1 [—] THE HISTORY OF TWO GOOD BOYS AND GIRLS, To which is added, The Story of Three Naughty Girls and Boys: Together with the Father's Advice. Boston: Printed and sold by N. Coverly 1793, Price 4 Coppers.
½ t.[1], fr.[2], t.[3], 4–16 p.; illus.; 10 cm.; p. 6 wrongly numbered "9". Half title: The History Of two good Boys & Girls, &c. Caption p. 4: The Story of the Good Boys and Girls; from the works of Mr. Richardson.
MWA°; Evans 46868.

1101.2 [—] ——— The Story o[f] Three Naughty Girls and Boys, Together with a Dialogue Between a little Boy and Girl. Boston. Printed and sold by N. Coverly 1793. Price 5 Coppers.
t.[3], 4–30 p.; illus.; 8 cm.
MWA-T° (covers wanting); MWA.

RICHARDSON, SAMUEL 1689–1761

CLARISSA HARLOWE (arranged chronologically)

1102.1 [—] THE PATHS OF VIRTUE DELINEATED; OR, THE HISTORY IN MINIATURE OF THE CELEBRATED CLARISSA HARLOWE, Familiarised and Adapted To the Capacities of Youth. [2 lines of quot.] Congreve. Philadelphia: Printed and Sold by W. Woodhouse, at the Bible, N⁰ 6, South Front-street. M.DCC.XCI.

fr.[ii], t.[1], [2–3], 4–135 p.; front. only illus.; 16.5 cm.
English 1st unabridged ed.: *Clarissa; Or The History Of A Young Lady.* London: 7 vols. Printed for S. Richardson, And Sold by A. Millar, J. and Ja. Rivington; John Osborn and J. Leake at Bath, 1748.
English abr. ed. version 1: *The Paths Of Virtue deliniated; Or, The History In Miniature Of The Celebrated Pamela, Clarissa Harlowe, And Sir Charles Grandison.* London: 1 vol. R. Baldwin, MDCCLVI.
English abr. ed. adv. title 1, probably the same as version 2, title 2. *The History of Clarissa,* &c. London: adv. by Newbery and Carnan, 1768 in *The History of Little Goody Two-Shoes.*
English abr. ed. version 2, title 2: *Clarissa; Or The History Of A Young Lady.* London: New Ed. E. Newbery [n.d.].
PP°; Evans 23740.

1102.2 — CLARISSA; OR THE HISTORY OF A YOUNG LADY. Comprehending The Most Important Concerns Of Private Life. Abridged from the Works of Samuel Richardson, Esq. Author of Pamela, and Sir Charles Grandison. The First Boston Edition, adorned with Cuts. Boston: Printed and sold by Samuel Hall, No. 53, Cornhill. 1795.

fr.[2], t.[3], [4–5], 6–142, [143–146, adv. list of books] p.; illus.; 14 cm.; bound in violet and green Dutch paper over bds.
English abr. ed. version 2, title 2, no. **1102.1.**
MWA-W°; CtHi (fr.[2], t.[3], & rear cover wanting); CtY; MB (per. st. on t.[3], fr.[2], & p. 143–144 wanting); MH; NjP (rebound); PPL; RPJCB.

1102.3 [—] —— [same as **1102.1**] Youth. [2 lines quot.] Congreve. With Copper Plate Engravings. Cooperstown [N.Y.]:—Printed And Sold By E. Phinney—First Door East Of The Court-

House; Wholesale And Retail. MDCCXCV.

t.[3], [4–5], 6–154, [155, adv.] p.; 16.5 cm.; bound in gray paper over w. bds.
English abr. ed. version 1, no. **1102.1.**
MWA°; CLU; PP (the words "With Copper Plate Engravings." have been erased from t.[3]); Evans 29414.

1102.4 — THE HISTORY OF MISS CLARISSA HARLOWE, Comprehending The Most Important Concerns Of Private Life, And Shewing Wherein The Arts Of A Designing Villain, And The Rigour of Parental Authority, conspired to complete the Ruin of a Virtuous Daughter. Abridged From The Works of Samuel Richardson, Esq. Author of Pamela, and Sir Charles Grandison. Philadelphia: Printed For The Booksellers. 1798.

t.[1], [2–3], 4–117 p.; t.[1] 15.5 cm.
English abr. ed. version 2, title 2, no. **1102.1.**
On the title page the letter "m" in "com-plete" is higher than the "co".
Welch° (covers wanting); CtY; MiU; MWA (bound in marbled paper over w. bds.; 16 cm.; p. 117 mut.); MB; Evans 34464.

1102.5 — CLARISSA; —— [same as **1102.2**] Grandison. Printed At Suffield [Conn.], By H. & O. Farnsworth, For Oliver D. & I. Cooke. Booksellers, Hartford. MDCCXCVIII.

t.[1], [2–3], 4–138, [139, adv. list of books] p.; 16 cm.; bound in marbled paper over w. bds., leather spine.
English abr. ed. version 2, title 2, no. **1102.1.**
MWA°; CLU; CtSu; CtY; DLC; NN (rebound, p. [139] wanting); Evans 34463.

1102.6 — —— Author of Pamela, *Ec.* From The Press Of William W. Morse. Corner of Elm and High Street. New Haven. M,DCCC.

t.[3], [4, adv.], [5], 6–138 p.; 14.5 cm.; bound in wallpaper over w. bds., leather spine.
English abr. ed. version 2, no. **1102.1.**
MWA°; Evans 38403.

THE HISTORY OF PAMELA (arranged chronologically)

1103.1 [—] THE PLEASING HISTORY OF PAMELA; Or Virtue Rewarded. Being An Entertaining History of a beautiful young Damsel, who rose from almost the lowest to the highest Situation of Life, with many important and entertaining Subjects, intended to cultivate the Principles of Virtue and Religion in the Minds of both Sexes. Boston: Printed and sold by Samuel Hall, No. 53, Cornhill. [*ca.* 1793].

    fr.[2], t.[3], [4–5], 6–96 p.; 3 pl. including front.; 11.5 cm.

    English 1st unabr. ed.: *Pamela; Or Virtue Rewarded.* London: 4 vols. Printed for S. Richardson And Sold by C. Rivington and J. Osborn, 1741.

    English abr. ed. version 1, *see* no. **1102.1.**

    English and Scottish abr. ed. version 2: *The History Of Pamela.* London: adv. by Newbery and Carnan, 1768 in *The History of Little Goody Two-Shoes.*

    MWA° (rebound); Evans 26088.

1103.2 — ——— Samuel Richardson Esq. Philadelphia: Printed and Sold by William Gibbons, Cherry-Street, between Third and Fourth Streets. M.DCC.XCIV.

    t.[1], [2–4], 5–107 p.; 16.5 cm.; bound in black paper ornamented with zigzag and scalloped lines and bands of buff over bds.

    English abr. ed. version 2, no. **1103.1.**

    P°; MWA (p. 39–48, 75–82 wanting; p. [1]–4, 33–34, 37–38 mut.); Evans 47203.

1103.3 — THE HISTORY OF PAMELA; Or, Virtue Rewarded. Abridged from the Works of Samuel Richardson, Esq. Adorned with Copperplates. The First Worcester Edition. Printed at Worcester, Massachusetts, by Isaiah Thomas. Sold at his Bookstore in Worcester; by said Thomas and Andrews in Boston, and by said Thomas and Carlisle, in Walpole [Vt.]. MDCCXCIV.

    fr.[ii], t.[i], [ii–vi], [1], 2–168 p.; 6 pl. including front.; 13.5 cm.; bound in leather.

    English abr. ed. version 2, no. **1103.1.**

    MWA° (i. st. on t.[1]); CtY (6 pl. bound before t.[i]); MB (fr.[ii] wanting; per. st. on t.[i]); MiU (fr.[ii] wanting); MWHi (fr.[ii], p. [iii]–4 wanting); NN; NNC; PP (6 pl. bound before t.[i]); Evans 27622.

1103.4 — ——— Lansingburgh [N.Y.]: Printed by Luther Pratt, & Co. Sold Wholesale and Retail, at their Printing-Office, King street. MDCCXCVI.

    fr.[ii], t.[1], [2–3], 4–146 p.; 12.5 cm.; bound in marbled paper over bds.

    English abr. ed. version 2, no. **1103.1.**

    MWA°; N; Evans 47901.

1103.5 — ——— New-York: Printed By Mott & Lyon, For Evert Duyckinck, & Co. No. 110, Pearl-Street. 1796.

    t.[1], [2–5], 6–144 p.; 14 cm.; bound in gray paper over w. bds.

    English abr. ed. version 2, no. **1103.1.**

    MWA-W°; CtY; PU; Evans 31101.

1103.6 — ——— New-York: Printed and sold, by Tiebout & O'Brien, No. 358, Pearl-street, and all Booksellers in Town and Country. 1796.

    fr.[2], t.[3], [4–5], 6–141, [142–144, contents] p.; front. only illus.; 14 cm.; bound in brown paper speckled with black over w. bds.

    MWA-T°; Evans 47902.

1103.7 — ——— Boston: Printed and sold by S. Hall, in Cornhill. 1797.

    fr.[2], t.[3], [4–7], 8–142 p.; 14 cm.; bound in Dutch paper over w. bds.

    English abr. ed. version 2, no. **1103.1.**

    MWA°; DLC; MB (fr.[2] wanting, per. st. on t.[3]); Evans 22763.

1103.8 — ——— New-York, Printed by T. Kirk, No. 112, Chatham-street, for Cornelius Davis, No. 94, Water-street. 1798.

    fr.[2], t.[3], [4–5], 6–90, [91–92] p.; 16.5 cm.; bound in gray paper over w. bds.

    English abr. ed. version 2, no. **1103.1.**

    MWA°; Evans 48595.

1103.9 — ——— New-York, Printed by T. Kirk, No. 112, Chatham-street, for John Tiebout No. 358, Pearl-street. 1798.

    fr.[2], t.[3], [4–5], 6–90, [91–92] p.; 16 cm.

    English abr. ed. version 2, no. **1103.1.**

    MWA° (fr.[2], almost entirely wanting); Evans 48598.

1103.10 — ——— S. Richardson, Esq. New-York, Printed By T. Kirk, No. 112, Chatham-street, for Naphtali Judah, No. 47, Water-street. 1798.

    fr.[2], t.[3], [4–5], 6–90, [91–92, contents] p.; front only illus.; 16 cm.; bound in buff paper over bds., leather spine; p. 49 printed "94".

    English abr. ed. version 2, no. **1103.1.**

    CtY° (small hole in p. 51–52); Evans 48596.

1103.11 — ——— New-York, Printed by T. Kirk, No. 112, Chatham-street, for Stephen Stephens, No. 165, Pearl-street. 1798.

fr.[2], t.[3], [4–5], 6–90, [91–92] p.; front only illus.; t.[3]; 16.5 cm.
English abr. ed. version 2, no. **1103.1**.
MWA-W° (covers wanting).

1103.12 —————— Norristown [Pa.]: Printed and sold by David Sower. 1799.
t.[1], [2–7], 8–156 p.; 14 cm.; bound in marbled paper over bds., leather spine.
English abr. ed. version 2, no. **1103.1**.
MWA°; PHi; PP; Evans 36230.

1103.13 —————— Fairhaven [Vermont], Printed By Jeddah P. Spooner, and sold wholesale and retail. M,DCC,XCIX.
t.[3], [4–5], 6–106 p.; 14.5 cm.
English abr. ed. version 2, no. **1103.1**.
VtHi°; Evans 26231.

1103.14 — —————— Philadelphia: Published By Mathew Carey, 122, Market-Street. 1808. Printed By T. & G. Palmer.
t.[i], [ii–iii], iv, [5], 6–107 p.; 14.5 cm.; bound in blue marbled paper over bds., leather spine.
English abr. ed. version 2, no. **1103.1**.
Welch°; CLU; MWA; NN; Shaw 16077.

1103.15 — —————— Philadelphia: Printed In The Year, 1812.
t.[1], [2–3], 4–108 p.; 13.5 cm.; bound in green Dutch paper over bds.
English abr. ed. version 2, no. **1103.1**.
Welch°; Shaw 26623.

1103.16 — —————— Wilmington [Del.]: Printed By R. Porter. 1817.
t.[1], [2–3], 4–106 p.; 13.5 cm.; bound in pr. blue-gray paper over bds.
English abr. ed. version 2, no. **1103.1**.
DeWi° (per. st. on p.[1], pr. paper on rear cover mostly wanting); Shaw 41980.

SIR CHARLES GRANDISON (arranged chronologically)

1104.1 — THE HISTORY OF SIR CHARLES GRANDISON, Abridged From The Works Of Samuel Richardson, Esq. Author of Pamela, and Clarissa. The Tenth Edition. Philadelphia: Printed by Carey, Stewart, and Co. North Front-street, No. 22. [*ca.* 1790].
t.[1], [2–3], 4–160 p.; 10.5 cm.; bound in Dutch paper over bds.

English abr. ed. version 2 below with the last sentence omitted and the book ending on the next to the last sentence: "Their piety and virtue are the sources of the noblest pleasures that can fill the human mind." Mathew Carey and Peter Stewart were publishing together 1790–1791.
English 1st unabr. ed.: *The History of Sir Charles Grandison*. London: 7 vols. Printed for S. Richardson, and Sold by C. Hitch and L. Hawes, J. and J. Rivington, Andrew Millar, R. and J. Dodlsey, and J. Leake at Bath, 1754. [Vol. 7 has the additional imprint] and by R. Main, In Dublin, 1754.
English abr. ed. version 1, *see* no. **1102.1**.
English abr. ed. version 2: —————[same as title of 1st ed.] *Grandison, Abridged*. London: adv. by F. Newbery, 1769 in *The History Of Pamela*. Welch° (p. 3–4 slightly mut.); MWA (rebound); PP (bound in orange Dutch paper over bds.); Evans 22852.

1104.2 — —————— First Boston Edition, adorned with Cuts. Boston: Printed and sold by Samuel Hall, No. 53, Cornhill. 1794.
fr.[ii], t.[1], [2–3], 4–113, [114–116] p.; 14 cm.; bound in green Dutch paper covers.
English abr. ed. version 2, no. **1104.1**.
MWA-W°; CLU; CtY; MB; MH; RPJCB; Evans 527623.

1104.3 — —————— Eleventh Edition. Philadelphia: Printed For Mathew Carey, By R. Folwell. M.DCC.XCIV.
t.[1], [2–3], 4–160 p.; t.[1]; 10.5 cm.
English abr. ed. version 2, no. **1104.1**.
MWA° (rebound); CtY; MH; MHi (Dutch paper covers); Evans 29415.

1104.4 — —————— Printed For John West, Bookseller, In Boston. M, DCC, XCVI.
t.[1], [2–3], 4–176 p.; 13.5 cm.; bound in buff paper over w. bds.
English abr. ed. version 2, no. **1104.1**.
MWA°; MHi; Evans 47903.

1104.5 — —————— From The Tenth London Edition. Suffield [Conn.]: Printed By Havila & Oliver Farnsworth, For Oliver D. & I. Cooke, Booksellers—Hartford. MDCCXCVIII.
1st t.[1], [2–3], 4–143, [144, bl.]; 2nd t.[1], [2–3], 4–138, [139, adv. list of books]; 16.5 cm.; bound in leather.

English abr. ed. version 2, no. **1104.1**.
2nd title: *Clarissa: Or The History Of A Young Lady.*——— [same as **1104.5**] Suffield [Conn.], By H. & O. Farnsworth ——— [same as **1104.5**] MDCCXCVIII.
MWA°; CtHi; CtY; DLC (p. 139–143 wanting); PPL; RPJCB; Evans 34465.

1104.6 ——— and Clarissa. Avery's Edition. Boston: Printed by Samuel Avery, No. 79, State-street. 1810.
t.[1], [2–3], 4–156 p.; 10 cm.; bound in gray-green paper over bds.
English abr. ed. version 2, no. **1104.1**.
MWA°; CtY (front cover pr. green paper over bds. with imprint: Boston: Printed By Samuel Avery, No. 91, Newbury Street. 1814; rear cover wanting); Shaw 21222.

1104.7 ——— and Clarisa [*sic. i.e.* Clarissa] Tenth Edition. From Sidney's Press, For Increase Cooke & Co. Book-Sellers, New-Haven. 1810.
t.[1], [2–3], 4–132 p.; 14 cm.; bound in gray-green paper over bds., leather spine.
English abr. ed. version 2, no. **1104.1**.
MWA°; Shaw 21223.

1104.8 ——— Eleventh Edition. Wilmington [Del.]: Printed By R. Porter. 1812.
t.[1], [2–3], 4–107 p.; 14.5 cm.
English abr. ed. version 2, no. **1104.1**.
DLC°; MWA-T (bound in pink & green marbled paper over bds.); Shaw 26624.

RICHMOND, LEGH 1772–1827
1105.1 — < No. 53. THE AFRICAN SERVANT. By Rev. Legh Richmond, Rector Of Turvey, Bedfordshire, Eng. An authentic narrative. [caption p.[1]]. Andover [Mass.]: Printed For The New England Tract Society By Flagg And Gould. 1816. < 3rd Edit. 6000. [colophon p. 16].
[1], 2–16 p.; 18.5 cm.; also paged [25], 26–40.
MB° (rebound; per. st. on p. [1]); Shaw 38804.

1105.2 ——— narrative. [caption p. [1]]. Andover [Mass.]: Printed For The New England Tract Society By Flagg And Gould. 1820. < 5th ed. 6000. [colophon p. 16].
[1], 2–16 p.; 17 cm.; also paged [25], 26–40.
MB° (bound with other publications of the

N. Eng. Tract Soc. vol. III. Andover: Printed by Flagg & Gould, 1820); Shoemaker 3009.

1106.1 — ANNALS OF THE POOR. Containing The Dairyman's Daughter, (With considerable additions.) The Negro Servant, And The Young Cottager. By The Rev Legh Richmond, A.M. Rector of Turvey, Bedfordshire; and Chaplin to His Royal Highness the Duke of Kent and Strathern. [1 line quot.] Baltimore: Published By Neal, Wills And Cole. Benjamen Edes, printer. 1815.
t.[1], [2–5], 6–288 p.; 14 cm.; bound in leather.
Page 6: ". . . It has been thought that such a volume [Annals Of The Poor] may prove an acceptable present to families in general, and to young people in particular."
While on the Isle of Wight Richmond collected local experiences which he afterwards used as a basis for his famous stories "The Dairyman's Daughter," "The Negro Servant," and "The Young Cottager." In 1809 he wrote the stories after moving away from the Isle of Wight. He contributed them, under the pseudonym of "Simplex," the *The Christian Guardian,* vols. 1–6, 1809–1814. They were reprinted together later under the general title *Annals Of The Poor.* English ed. London: Religious Tract Society, 1814.
CtSoP° (p. 287–288 wanting); Shaw 35781.

1106.2 ——— Hartford: Printed By Sheldon & Goodwin. 1815.
t.[i], [ii–iii], iv–vi, [7], 8–216 p.; 15.5 cm.; bound in pr. buff paper over bds.
MWA°; CtY; Shaw 35782.

1106.3 ——— Strathern. [1 line quot.] New-Haven: Published By Whiting and Tiffany, Sign Of Franklin's Head, Corner of College Green. 1815.
t.[1], [2–5], 6–288 p.; 14 cm.
MWA°; CtY; NcD; OO; PPL; Shaw 35783.

1106.4 ——— New-York: Published By Whiting And Watson, Sold by D. Whiting, Troy, and Camp, Merrill, and Camp. Utica. 1815.
t.[1], [2–5], 6–288 p.; 14 cm.
MWA°; NB (i. st. on t.[1]); PPL; Shaw 35784 (placed under title of *The Negro Servant,* but is probably **1106.4** which contains this tract and *The Young Cottager*).

1106.5 —— —— Baltimore: Published By Neal, Wills, & Cole. 1816. Pomroy & Toy, Printers.

  t.[1], [2–5], 6–288 p.; 14 cm.

  ViU°; MWA-T; Shaw 38806.

1107.1 [—] Series of Evangelical Tracts, No. 34. THE DAIRYMAN'S DAUGHTER: Extracted from an authentic and interesting Narrative, Communicated by a Clergyman of the Church of England. [caption p. [1]]. Boston: Printed and sold by Lincoln & Edmands, 53 Cornhill, (Price 67 cts. a doz. 4.50 a hundred.) Who are constantly adding new Numbers to their Series of Tracts. In addition to their great variety of books, suitable for social, village, and private libraries, they have bound their Series of Tracts in two vols. which they recommend for their appropriate, seasonable, and various subjects. Price 2 dollars. [1813] [colopohn p. 24].

  [1], 2–24 p.; illus. p. [1] only illus.; 17 cm.; p. 24 above the colophon: "Note. The mother died about six months after her daughter; . . . The father continued after her, . . . Whether he yet lives, I know not; but probably before this time, (1812) the daughter and both her parents are met together in 'the land of pure delights, where saints immortal reign.' " This note signifies that the book this edition was copied from was not printed in England before 1812. *See* no. 1106.1 on the history of this book. *The Dairyman's Daughter* was greatly enlarged after its first publication and was very popular. In 1816 it was reprinted twice in editions of twenty thousand each. *See* no. 1107.4 for a wrongly dated edition of [1812], Shaw 27567. Shaw 50604 lists a Philadelphia edition "Published by the Philadelphia Tract Society. William Bradford, Agent. [1805?] (PPL)." Based on examination of selected pages of the PPL copy, the book surely is printed after 1820. Since the book was not printed in England as early as [1805] the date is an error. A Philadelphia Tract Society, according to Edwin Wolf 2nd, was founded in 1827. It may be the one who published this pamphlet.

English serial ed. in *The Christian Guardian.* London:

Title a: *The Dairyman's Daughter.* vol. II, nos. 14, 15, 17, 20, February–August 1810.

Title b.: *The Funeral Of The Dairyman's Daughter.* vol. III, no. 3, March 1811. In this number the note, on p. 24, in no. **1107.1**, first appears without the date 1812.

Title c: *Recollections Concerning The Dairyman's Daughter.* vol. VII, no. 3, March 1, 1815.

Title d: *Recollections Relative To The Dairyman's Daughter.* No. II. vol. VII, no. 9, September, 1815.

Title e: *Recollections Of The Dairyman's Daughter. No. III.* vol. VIII, no. 3–4, March 1,–April 1, 1816.

MWA°; PPL; Shaw 25210 (dated [1812?]) and 29664 (dated [1813?]).

1107.2 [—] —— Daughter. An Authentic And Interesting Narrative. Harrisonburg [Va.]: Published by Davison & Bourne. 1813.

  t.[1], [2–3], 4–108 p.; 12.5 cm.

  MWA°; MH (emb. st. on t.[1]); Shaw 29665.

1107.3 [—] < No. 9. —— Daughter. Extracted from an authentic and interesting Narrative, Communicated by a Clergyman of the Church of England. [caption p.[1]]. Andover, [Mass.]: Printed For The New England Tract Society By Flagg And Gould. 1814. First ed. 600. [colophon p. 24].

  [1], 2–24 p.; 17.5 cm.; also paged [147], 148–170 p.; paper covers.

  MWA° (bound with other tracts in *Tracts Published By The New England Tract Society.* Vol. I. Andover: Flagg And Gould. 1814); DLC; Shaw 32649.

1107.4 [—] The Dairyman's Daughter —— [caption p.[1]]. Printed by N. Willis, 76, State-Street, Boston: (Price 67 cts. a doz. $4.50 a hundred.) Who have for sale a variety of interesting Religious Tracts. Usual discounts made. [colophon p. 24] [1814?].

  [1], 2–24 p.; 16.5 cm.

  MWA° (bound with other tracts in *Twelve Witnesses. Boston: N. Willis. 1814*); MB (bound with other tracts in *Twelve Witnesses. 1814*); MHi (separate pamphlet); Shaw 27567 dated [1812] and 32650.

1107.5 [—] —— [same as **1107.1**] Narrative. Sold for the benefit of the Virginia Religious Tract Society. Harrisonburg, [Va.] Published by Davison & Bourne. 1814.

  t.[1], [2–3], 4–108 p.; 12 cm.; paper covers.

  ViU°; Shaw 32651.

1107.6 [—] —— Daughter. To which is added, An Interesting Account Of A Child. Hartford: Printed by Peter B. Gleason & Co. 1814.

t.[i], [ii], [1], 2–36 p.; 14 cm.; blue-marbled paper covers.

MWA°; CtHi°; MB; PP; Shaw 32652.

1107.7 [—] —— [same as **1107.1**] Narrative, In Five Parts. Communicated By A Clergyman Of The Church Of England. Third American, from the fifth English Edition. Hudson [N.Y.]: Published By William E. Norman. 1814.

t.[1], [2–5], 6–70 p.; 16 cm.; pr. paper covers; cover title dated 1818.

MWA°; MH; N (rebound; red back cover wanting; front cover dated 1818); Shaw 32653.

1107.8 [—] —— England. Second American, From The Fifth British Edition. New-Haven: Printed by Oliver Steele. 1814.

t.[1], [2–3], 4–47 p.; 20 cm.

MWA°; CtHi; Shaw 32654.

1107.9 [—] —— England. From The Fifth British Edition. New-York: Printed and sold by T. & J. Swords, No. 160 Pearl-Street. 1814.

t.[1], [2–5], 6–70, [71–72, adv. list of books] p.; 14 cm.; pr. yellowish-olive paper covers.

NN°; Shaw 32655.

1107.10 [—] —— England. Second American Edition. Poughkeepsie [N.Y.]: Published by Paraclete Potter. P. & S. Potter, Printers. 1814.

t.[1], [2–5], 6–63, [64–70, adv. and recommendations] p.; 14.5 cm.; bound in blue marbled paper over bds., leather spine.

CLU°; Shaw 31286.

1107.11 [—] < No. 9. —— [same as no. **1107.6**] England. [caption p.[1]]. Andover [Mass.]: Printed For The New England Tract Society By Flagg And Gould. 1815. <Second edit. 6000.

[1], 2–24 p.; 18.5 cm.; p. also numbered [101], 102–124.

MB° (rebound); Shaw 35785.

1107.12 — —— In Five Parts. By The Reverend Legh Richmond, A.M. Rector Of Turvey, Bedfordshire, (Eng.) [4 lines of verse] Gray. Newark [N.J.]: Published And Sold By William

Tuttle, At His Book And Stationary Store. John Tuttle & Co. Printers. 1815.

t.[1], [2–3], 4–72 p.; 14 cm.

NN° (covers wanting); CtY (rebound; pr. olive paper covers); DLC; NjR (p. 65–72 & covers wanting); PP.

1107.13 [—] < No. 31. —— [same as **1107.6**] England. [caption p.[1]]. Published By The New-York Religious Tract Society. J. Seymour, Printer. < Nov. 1815—5000. >

t.[1], 2–24 p.; 18 cm.

NjR°; Shaw 34510.

1107.14 — Religious Tracts, No. 9. —— [same as **1107.3**] Narrative. By The Reverend Legh Richmond, A.M. A Minister of the Church of England. [caption p. [1]]. Published by the Society of the Protestant Episcopal Church for the Advancement of Christianity in Pennsylvania. Philadelphia: Printed By J. Maxwell. 1815. [p. [34]].

[1], 2–33, [34] p.; p. [1]; 18 cm.

PPL°.

1107.15 [—] < No. 9 —— An Authentic Narrative. Andover, Mass., Printed For The New England Tract Society by Flagg and Gould. 1816. < 3rd. edit. 6000.

[1], 2–24 p.; 18 cm.; p. also numbered [101], 102–124.

MnU; Shaw 51623.

1107.16 [—] —— Daughter. A Narrative From Real Life: < First Part. > Published by "The Religious Tract Society of Philadelphia," and for sale at their Depository, No. 8, South Front-street. William Bradford—Agent. April [5 dots] 1816.

t.[1], [2–3], 4–42 p.; 18 cm.

MWA°; Shaw 38807.

1107.17 [—] —— Daughter. < Second Part. > Published by "The Religious Tract Society of Philadelphia." and for sale at their Depository, No. 8, South Front-street. May [6 dots] 1816. [caption p. [1]].

[1], 2–12 p.; 18 cm.

MWA°; NjR; Shaw 37381 and 38808.

1107.18 — The Dairyman's Daughter ——— [same as **1107.6**] England. [caption p. [1]]. Published For The Hartford Evangelical Tract Society. March, 1818. 5000. [colophon p. 24].

[1], 2–24 p.; 16.5 cm.

CtHi*; Shaw 45542.

1107.19 — No. 9. ——— Daughter. An Authentic Narrative. By Rev. Legh Richmond, Rector of Turvey, Bedfordshire, England. [caption p.[1]]. Andover [Mass.]: Printed For The New England Tract Society By Flagg And Gould. 1819. < 5th edit. 6,000. [colophon p. 24].

[1], 2–24 p.; 17 cm.; also numbered [101], 102–124 p.

MB* (bound with other publications of the N. Eng. Tract Soc. Vol. I Andover: Printed by Flagg & Gould. 1820.); Shaw 49290.

1107.20 [—] ——— Daughter, An Authentic And Interesting Narrative In Two Parts—Part II. Philadelphia: Published by the Sunday and Adult School Union. Clark & Raser, Printers. 1819.

t.[1], [2–3], 4–48 p.; title vignette only illus.; 13 cm.; pr. & illus. blue paper covers. Cover title imprint: Philadelphia: Published by the Sunday and Adult School Union, And For Sale At Bradford's Book-store, No. 8, south Front Street. 1818. Clark & Raser, Printers.

MWA-T*.

1107.21 [—] ——— Daughter. Extracted From An Authentic And Interesting Narrative, Communicated By A Clergyman Of The Church Of England. [caption p. [1]]. Printed By Ephram Whitman, Goshen [Mass.]: (Price 8 cts. singel, 67 a doz. $4.50 a hundred.) Who has for sale a variety of interesting Religious Tracts. [1819] [colophon p. 23].

t.[1], 2–23 p.; 18 cm. Ephraim Whitman printed in Goshen, Mass. only in 1819. He died in Goshen, September 14, 1819. (MWA cat.). Above the colophon p. 23 is the same note which appears above the colophon in no. **1107.1**.

NN* (dated [1812] probably an error in mistaking the date in the note for the date of the publication).

1107.22 [—] ——— [same as **1107.2**] New York: Printed and sold by T. and J. Swords, 1820.

t.[1], [2] 3–24 p.; 18.5 cm.

MWA*.

1108.1 [—] LITTLE JANE, THE YOUNG COTTAGER. A True Narrative, By the Author of the Dairyman's Daughter. Published by "The Religious Tract Society of Philadelphia," and for sale at their Depository, No. 8, South Front-street. Wm. Bradford—Agent. [caption p. [1]]. January —1816. [bottom of p. [1]].

[pt. I]: [1], 2–12 p.; pt. II.: [1], 2–12 p.; 2 vols.; 18.5 cm.; pt. II. undated.

NjR*; Shaw 38080.

1108.2 [—] ——— Daughter. Published by "The Religious Tract Society of Philadelphia," and sold at their Depository, No. 8, South Front-street Wm. Bradford. Agent. [1818?] [caption p. [1]].

pt. I.: [1], 2–12 p.; pt. II.: [1], 2–12 p.; 2 vols. 21 cm.

NjR*; Shaw 44595.

1109.1 [—] THE NEGRO SERVANT, An Authentic And Interesting Narrative, Communicated by a Clergyman of the Church of England. [caption p. [1]]. Printed By N. Willis, No. 76, State Street, Boston. [1814] [colophon p. 16].

[1], 2–16 p.; 17.5 cm. *See* no. **1105.1** on the history of the book.

English serial ed. in The Christian Guardian. London: title: *The Negro Servant.* vol. I, no. 5, 8, May & August 1809, vol. II., no. 13, January 1810.

English pamphlet ed. London: F. Collins, 1810. MWA* (bound with other publications in *Twelve Witnesses. Boston: N. Willis. 1814.*); MB (bound with other publications in *Twelve Witnesses, 1814*); Shaw 32220 and 32656.

1109.2 [—] No. 53. THE NEGRO SERVANT, ——— [caption p. [1]]. Andover [Mass.]: Printed For The New England Tract Society By Flagg And Gould. 1815. First ed. 6000. [colophon p. 16].

[1], 2–16 p.; 18.5 cm.; also paged [25], 26–40.

DLC*; Shaw 35786.

1109.3 ——— An Authentic Narrative. By The Reverend Legh Richmond, A.M. Rector of Turvey, Bedfordshire; and Chaplain to his Royal Highness the Duke of Kent and Strathern. New-York: Published By Whiting And Watson. Sold by D. Whiting, Troy [N.Y.], and Camp, Merrill, and Camp, Utica [N.Y.]. 1815.

t.[1], [2–3], 4–51 p.; 14 cm.; blue-gray paper covers; p.[2]: Fanshaw and Clayton, Letterpress and Copper-plate Printers 241 Pearl and 10 Cliff streets. The "2" of "241" is written in ink.

MWA°; CtY (rebound); Shaw 35788; and 35784 (refers to **1109.4** which contains **1109.3**).

1109.4 [—] —— Servant. By The Author Of The Dairyman's Daughter. Philadelphia. Published by "The Religious Tract Society of Philadelphia," at their Depository, No. 8, South Front Street. 1817. Wm. Bradford, Agent.

t.[1], [2], 3–12 p.; 19 cm.
MWA°; PPPrHi; Shaw 41982.

1110 [—] (No. 29.) THE ORPHAN. By The Author Of The Young Cottager. Published By The Philadelphia Female Tract Society. And For Sale at their Depository, No. 20, Walnut Street. [caption p. [1]]. Printed by Lydia R. Bailey No. 10, North Alley Phila. [1817] [colophon p. 12].

[1], 2–12; p. 14 cm.
MWA° (bound with other tracts, with which *The Second Annual Report Of The Philadelphia Female Tract Society For The Year 1817* was originally bound); Shaw 41983.

1111.1 — THE YOUNG COTTAGER. An Authentic Narrative. By The Reverend Legh Richmond, A.M. Rector of Turvey, Bedfordshire; and Chaplain to His Royal Highness the Duke of Kent and Strathern. Hartford: Printed By Sheldon & Goodwin. 1815.

t.[1], [2–3], 4–76 p.; 14 cm.; buff paper covers. *See* no. **1105.1** on the history of this book. English ed. London: Printed For The Author, And sold by J. Hatchard; Longman, Hurst, and Co.; L. B. Seeley; Nisbet; Kent; Williams and Son; T. Inkersley, Bradford; Robinson and Co., Leeds; J. Hurst, Wakefield; M. Richardson, Manchester; Holden, Halifax; R. Wilson, Knaresbrough; Earnshaw, Colne, 1815.
PP°.

1111.2 —— —— New-Haven: Published By Whiting And Tiffany, Sign Of Franklin's Head, Corner of College Green. 1815.

t.[1], [2–3], 4–100 p.; t.[1] 14 cm.
CtY° (covers wanting).

1111.3 —— —— An Authentic Narrative. By The Reverend Legh Richmond, A.M. Rector of Turvey, Bedfordshire; and Chaplain to His Royal Highness the Duke of Kent and Strathern. New-York: Published By Whiting And Watson. Sold by D. Whiting Troy [N.Y.], and Camp, Merrill, and Camp, Utica. [N.Y.] 1815.

t.[1], [2–3], 4–100 p.; 14 cm.
N° (per st. on t.[1]); Shaw 35789.

1111.4 — < No. 79. The Young Cottager, By Rev. Legh Richmond, Rector Of Turvey, Bedfordshire, Eng. An authentic narrative. [caption p.[1]]. Andover [Mass.]: Printed For The New England Tract Society By Flagg And Gould. 1816. < First edit. 10,000. [colophon p. 36].

[1], 2–36 p.; 17.5 cm.; also paged [129], 130–164.
DLC°; Shaw 38809.

1111.5 [—] No. 9. —— List Of Tracts Published By The Hartford Evangelical Tract Society. March, 1816. [list of 9 tracts] [cover title].

[1], 2–28 p.; 16.5 cm.; pr. paper covers, pr. on both sides of the leaf. Caption on inside of front cover: An Address To Christians. Recommending The Distribution Of Cheap Religious Tracts. [29 lines of text]. The text ends on the inside of the rear cover. Caption on back of rear cover: Meditations: [2 lines quot.] [32 lines of text].
MWA°; CtHi; Shaw 38810.

1111.6 —— —— [same as **1111.3**] Paris, (Ky.) Printed And Published By John Lyle, Bookseller. 1816.

t.[1], [2–3], 4–120 p.; 13 cm.
ICU° (t.[1] mut., i. st. p.[3]); Shaw 38811.

1111.7 — < No. 79. —— Bedfordshire, Eng. An Authentic Narrative. [caption p. [1]]. Andover [Mass.]: Printed For The New England Tract Society By Flagg And Gould. 1817. 2d ed. 6,000. [colophon p. 36].

[1], 2–36 p.; 17.5 cm.; p. also numbered [129], 130–164.
MB° (rebound, per. st. on p.[1]); Shaw 41984.

1111.8 —— —— An Authentic Narrative. Abridged, From The "Annals Of The Poor," By The Rev. Legh Richmond, Rector Of Turvey, Bedfordshire, England. [1 line of quot.] New-York:

Printed By S. Seymour, No. 49 John Street. 1817. [cover title].

[1], 2–36 p.; cover title vignette only illus.; 13.5 cm.

MWA*; Shaw 41985 and 42990.

1111.9 — No. 79. ——— Bedfordshire, Eng. [caption p. [1]]. Andover [Mass.]: Printed For The New England Tract Society, By Flagg And Gould. 1820. 4th edit. 6,000 [colophon p. 36].

[1], 2–36 p.; 14 cm.; p. also numbered [129], 130–164.

MB* (bound with other tracts in *Tracts Published By The New England Tract Society. Vol. IV. Andover: Printed By Flagg And Gould. 1820*); Shoemaker 3016.

1111.10 — ——— Published For The Hartford Evangelical Tract Society. And To Be Had Of Their Agent, Mr. James R. Woodbridge, In Hartford, And At Their Depository In The Principal Towns In This State. Price, 3 cents; or $3 per 1000. Hartford, Conn. 1820. [cover title].

[1], 2–28 p.; 19 cm.; pr. paper covers. Front cover paged [1], 2, rear cover 3–4. Caption on inside of front cover: Extract. Trust In God. [followed by 38 lines of text] [the text ends on p. 4 of rear cover].

CtHi*; Shoemaker 3017.

1112.1 THE RIDDLE BOOK. For The Entertainment Of All Young Masters and Misses. Adorned With Cuts. Sidney's Press. New-Haven, 1817.

fr.[2], t.[3], [4], 5–30, [31, adv.] p.; illus.; 10.5 cm.; illus. yellow-buff paper covers.

MWA-W*; CtY.

1112.2 ——— Sidney's Press. New-Haven, 1818.

fr.[2], t.[3], [4], 5–30, [31, adv.] p.; illus.; 10 cm.; illus. paper covers; rear cover a picture of the building containing the "Books & Stationary" shop of "J. Babcock & Son," and the "Post-Office" which has "W.H. & A.S. Jones" below it, "Church Street New-Haven."

MWA*; CtY; NHi; Shaw 45545.

1112.3 ——— New-Haven. Sidney's Press. For J. Babcock & Son. 1819.

t.[3], [4–5], 6–30 p.; illus.; 10.5 cm.

MWA* (fr.[2], & p.[31], and covers wanting); Shaw 49293.

[RIDLEY, JAMES] 1736–1765

1113 [—] THE ADVENTURES OF URAD; Or The Fair Wanderer. Boston: Printed by Mein and Fleeming, and to be sold by John Mein at the London Book-Store, North-side of King-street, Boston. MDCCLXVII. At which Place may be had, A great variety of Entertaining and Instructive Books for Children.

[ii], [iii, bl.], fr.[iv], t.[v], [vi, bl.], [1], 2–58 p.; front & illus. p. 50 only illus.; 10.5 cm.; bound in green Dutch paper over bds. The story is tale 5 in James Ridley's *Tales Of The Genii.*

English ed. *Tales Of The Genii.* London: 1764. MWA* (p.[ii] mut.); MB (per st. on t.[v]; p.[ii] pasted to rear cover); MH (p.[ii]–10 or all of sig.[A]); PP (t.[v] mut. affecting imprint); Evans 41762.

[RILEY, GEORGE]

1114.1 [—] THE BEAUTIES OF THE CREATION; Or, A New Moral System Of Natural History; Displayed In The Most Singular, Curious, And Beautiful, Quadrupeds, Birds, Insects, Trees, And Flowers: Designed to inspire Youth with Humanity towards the Brute Creation, and bring them early acquainted with the wonderful Works of the Divine Creator. [3 lines quot.] Blackmore on the Creation. Philadelphia: Printed By William Young, Bookseller, Nº. 52, Second-Street, The Corner Of Chesnut-Street. M,DCC,XCII.

t.[i], [ii–iii], iv–ix, [x–xii], [13], 14–348 p.; 17 cm.; bound in leather. Publisher's adv. of books p.[344]–348.

English ed. London: Vol. I. [II.], Printed For G. Riley; And sold by Mess. Champante And Whitrow; S. Hazard, Bath, 1790.

MWA-W*; CtY; KyLx; MiU; NN (rebound); OOxM; RPJCB; Evans 24745; Sabin 71393.

1114.2 [—] ——— Second American Edition. [3 lines quot.] Blackmore on the Creation. Philadelphia: Printed by William Young. Bookseller, No. 52, Second, corner of Chesnut-street. 1796.

t.[i], [ii–iii], iv–ix, [x–xii], [13], 14–346, [347–348] p.; 17 cm.; publisher's adv. of books p.[344]–[348].

MWA*; CSt; DLC; IaDmD; MnU; PHi; PP; PU; RPJCB; Evans 31105.

1114.3 [—] ———Third American Edition. Worcester: Printed By Isaiah Thomas, Jun. Sold

By Him At His Bookstore, Opposite The Gaol. September—1798.

fr.[ii], t.[iii], [iv–vii], viii–xii, [i] ii–ix, [x–xii], [13], 14–274, [275–276] p.; no illus. in text except tailpiece cuts: a tree, p. xii; a dog, p. ix; an angel holding a scroll with the words "The End" on it, p. 274; 15.5 cm.; bound in leather; on p. [275] there is a decorative adv. of an oval ornamented with books and floral designs. MWA* (I. Thomas copy); DLC; ICU; MH; NN; OClWHi; PMA; PPL; PU; RPJCB; Evans 34470.

1115 RILEY'S EMBLEMS. Philadelphia: adv. by Francis Bailey, 1793 in **773.1.** *See* Wynne, J.H., no. **1457.1.**

1116.1 THE ROAD TO LEARNING MADE PLEASANT, With Lessons And Pictures. Philadelphia: Published By Jacob Johnson, No. 147, Market-Street. 1803.

t.[1], [2–48] p.; illus.; 16 cm.; paper covers. Adv. by Johnson & Warner, 1814 in **1449.2.** English ed. London: adv. by Darton And Harvey, 1806 in *Instructive Hints.* MWA*; CtHi; NNC-LS (incomplete); Shaw 4987.

1116.2 ——— Philadelphia, J. Johnson, 1807. [46] p. Shaw 13504.

1117 THE ROBBER. Montpelier: adv. by E. P. Walton, 1819 in **134.10.**

1118 THE ROBBER OR SONS OF NIGHT: A True Story. Weathersfield [Vt.]: Published by L. Roberson. A. D. Pier, Printer. 1816.

t.[3], [4–5], 6–31 p.; illus.; 10 cm.; pr. & illus. gray-green paper covers. The illustrations are copies of cuts in S. Hall's editions of *The History Of Master Jackey And Miss Harriot,* no. **568.2.** Roberson was a pseud. of Lewis Robinson of Reading (McCorison). MWA*; CtY; McCorison 1864; Shaw 38818.

1119.1 (No. 30.) THE ROBBER'S DAUGHTER. Founded On Fact. Published By The Philadelphia Female Tract Society. And for sale at their Depository, No. 20, Walnut Street. [caption title]. Printed by Lydia R. Bailey, No. 10, North Alley, Philad. [1817] [colophon p. 16].

[1], 2–16 p.; 14 cm. MWA* (bound with other tracts, with which *The Second Annual Report Of The Philadelphia Female Tract Society For The Year 1817* was originally bound); Shaw 41991.

1119.2 THE ROBBER'S DAUGHTER. A Tale, Founded On Fact. Middlebury, Vt. Printed at the Messenger Office. 1818.

t.[1], [2], 3–24 p.; 14 cm. MWA* (bound, pamphlet); McCorison 2049; Shaw 45550.

1119.3 THE ROBBER'S DAUGHTER. The Sunday-School Convert. A Narrative founded on Fact. Boston: Printed and sold at No. 53 Cornhill, By Lincoln & Edmands. 1819.

t.[1], [2–3], 4–24 p.; title vignette & illus. p.[2] only illus.; 13 cm.; pr. & illus. blue paper covers. MWA-W*.

1119.4 ——— Daughter. Boston: adv. by S. T. Armstrong, and by Crocker & Brewster, 1820 in *Original Hymns For Sabbath Schools.*

ROBERTS, MARGARET (WADE) d. 1812?

1120 [—] Cottage, a Tale for Youth. New-York: adv. by W. B. Gilley, 1816 in **1152.**

1121 — DUTY, OR THE WHITE COTTAGE. A Novel. By The Late Mrs. Roberts, Author Of "Rose And Emily:" Interspersed With Poetry; And Preceded By A Character Of The Author, By Mrs. Opie. In Two Volumes. Vol. I. [II.] London, Printed. New-York: Re-printed And Published By I. Riley. 1815.

vol. I.: t.[i], [ii–iii], iv–xxii, [1], 2–220 p.; vol. II.: t.[1], [2–3], 4–234 p.; 2 vols. in one 14.5 cm.; bound in leather. English ed. London: 1814. MWA*; PPL; Shaw 35797.

1122.1 — ROSE AND EMILY; Or, Sketches Of Youth. By Mrs. Roberts, Author Of "Moral Views; Or, The Telescope For Children." [2 lines quot.] Psalm xxxvii. New-York: Published By Eastburn, Kirk & Co. No. 86, Broadway. 1813.

fr.[ii], t.[1], [2–3], 4–240 p.; front. only illus. signed *Rollinson,* [William Rollinson]; 14.5 cm.; bound in leather, red label on spine; colophon p. 240: Pray & Bowen, Printers, Brooklyn.

English ed. London: Longman, Hurst, Rees, Orme, & Brown, J. Harris, 1812.
MWA*; PP (p. 209–210 slightly mut.); Shaw 29671 and 29672.

1122.2 —— —— New-York: Published By Eastburn, Kirk & Co. No. 86, Broadway; And Cummings & Hilliard, Boston. 1813.
fr.[ii], t.[1], [2–3], 4–240 p.; front. only illus. signed *Rollinson* [William Rollinson]; 14.5 cm. bound in leather; colophon p. 240; Pray & Bowen, Printers, Brooklyn.
MWA*.

1122.3 —— —— New-York: adv. by W. B. Gilley, 1816 in **1152.**

1123.1 Robin Goodfellow, A Fairy Tale. Written By A Fairy For The Amusement Of All The Pretty Little Faies & Fairies, In the United States of America. Philadelphia: Printed by Francis Bailey, No. 116, High-Street. [1790?].
fr.[2], t.[3], [4–5], 6–62, [63, adv. of 8 books] p.; illus.; 9.5 cm.; blue paper covers. Adv. by Francis Bailey, 1792 in **359**, and 1793 in **773.1.**
English ed. London: adv. by F. Newbery, 1769 in Solomon Winlove's *Moral Lectures, On The Following Subjects. Pride . . .*
NN*.

1123.2 —— —— Worcester Massachusetts: adv. by I. Thomas, 1786 in **395.1.**

Robin Hood. *See* The Adventures of Robert Earl Of Huntington, no. **10.** The large number of English editions of *Robin Hood* are omitted because they are versions never printed in America. *See* no. **1124** below.

1124 —— The Life and Death of Robin Hood, Complete In Twenty-Four Songs. New-York: Printed in the year 1800. < Price Twelve Cents. >
t.[1], [2–3], 4–80 p.; illus.; 16 cm.
MWA*; PP; Evans 37838.

1125.1 The Robin's Nest. Also The Decayed Merchant's Dutiful Daughter. Adorned With Cuts. From Sidney's Press New Haven. 1817.
fr.[2], t.[3], [4–5], 6–47 p.; illus.; 13 cm.; illus. buff paper covers.
Ct* (i. st. on front cover & fr.[2]).

1125.2 —— —— Nest, And The Decayed Merchant's Dutiful Daughter. Adorned With Cuts. New Haven: Printed For J. Babcock & Son. Sidney's Press. 1819.
fr.[ii], t.[1], [2–3], 3–35.; illus.; 14 cm.; pr. & illus. green paper covers.
Cover title: Robin's Nest. Published By J. Babcock & Son, Booksellers, Stationers and Printers, adjoining the Post-Office, New-Haven. Sold by S. & W. R. Babcock, Booksellers and Stationers Charleston, S.C.
MWA*; CtHi (pr. & illus. green paper covers); CtY (p. 31–32 mut.); Shaw 49306.

ROCHE, REGINA MARIA (DALTON) 1764?–1845
1126 —— Melinda, Or The Victim Of Seduction. A Moral Tale [4 lines of verse] By Mrs. Roche. Danbury [Conn.]: Printed For The Booksellers. 1804.
t.[1], [2–3], 4–23 p.; 14 cm.; blue-gray paper covers.
CtHi*; Shaw 50474.

1127 Roman Histories: Or, The History Of The Seven Wise Masters Of Rome. Containing Seven Days Entertainment, In Many Pleasant & Witty Tales & Stories. The Fiftieth Edition. Printed For, And Sold By James Wilson, Book Binder, &c. No. 5. High-street, opposite the upper Market, Wilmington. 1796.
t.[1], [2–3], 4–103 p.; 13 cm.; bound in buff paper over bds.
DeHi*; Evans 47913.

1128.1 Roman Stories: Or The History Of The Seven Wise Masters Of Rome Containing Seven Days Entertainment, In many Pleasant and Witty Tales, or Stories, Wherein The Treachery of evil Councillors is discovered Innocency cleared, and the Wisdom of Seven Wise Philosophers displayed. Newly Corrected, and better Explain'd, and Enlarg'd. Adorned with many pretty Pictures, lively expressing each History. The Thirty-fourth Edition. New-York: Printed for Benjamin Gomez, No. 97 Maiden-Line, 1795.
fr.[2], t.[3], [4, adv.], [5], 6–144 p.; illus.; 13 cm.
English ed. London: 5 ed. T. Sabine & Son. [1820?].
MWA*; NjP (bound in ornamental buff paper over bds., leather spine); Evans 29466; Hamilton 164.

1128.2 ——— Wilmington [Del.]: Printed and Sold by Peter Brynberg. 1796.

 t.[1], [2–3], 4–103 p.; 13.5 cm.; bound in brown paper over bds.

 Ries*.

ROMAN STORIES OF THE HISTORY OF THE SEVEN WISE MISTRESSES OF ROME. Title of English ed. London: J. Hodges, 1754. *See* Howard, Thomas for English and American Editions of The History Of The Seven Wise Mistresses Of Rome.

ROSCOE, WILLIAM 1753–1831
1129 — THE BUTTERFLY'S BALL, And The Grasshopper's Feast. By Mr. Roscoe. To Which Is Added, An Original Poem, Entitled, A Winter's Day. By Mr. Smith Of Stand. Philadelphia: Published By B. C. Buzby, At His Juvenile Book Store, No. 2, North Third Street. 1809.

 fr.[ii], t.[1], [2–3], 4–16 p.; 8 pl. including front.; 12.5 cm.; pr. & illus. paper covers; p.[2]: Joseph Rakestraw, printer.

 English ed. London: original holograph mss.; J. Harris Jany 1st. 1807.

 CtY* (front cover ¾ wanting).

1130.1 [—] THE BUTTERFLY'S BIRTH-DAY. By The Author Of The Butterfly's Ball. Philadelphia: Published by B. & T. Kite, No. 20, N. Third Street. 1810.

 ½t.[1], [2], [i, bl.], fr.[ii], t.[3], [4–5], 6–15 p.; 6 pl. including front.; 11.5 cm.; pr. yellow paper covers; page [2]: Printed by Jane Aitken. Half title p.[1]: The Butterfly's Birth-Day.

 English ed. London: J. Harris, [n.d.], front. dated 1806.

 CSmH*; MWA; NNPM; Shaw 19991 and 21240.

1130.2 [—] ——— Illustrated with Elegant Engravings. New-York: Published And Sold By D. Longworth. No. 11 Park, For D. W. Smith, No. 90 Anthony-St. And May Be had Of All The Principle Booksellers. 1816.

 ½t.[1], [2, bl.], [i, bl.], fr.[ii], t.[3], [4–5], 6–14, [15] p.; 2 pl. including front.; 13 cm.

 CtHi* (covers and all but a fragment of p.[15] wanting); NPV (2 pl. wanting); Shaw 37130.

1131 THE ROSE'S BREAKFAST. Illustrated With Elegant And Appropriate Engravings. Philadelphia: Published By B. C. Buzby, At His Juvenile Book Store, No. 2, North Third Street. 1809.

fr.[ii], t.[1], [2–3], 4–32 p.; 8 pl. including front.; 13 cm.; pr. & illus. paper covers; colophon p. 32; Joseph Rakestraw, printer.

 English ed. London: J. Harris, 1808.

 DLC* (covers mut.); CtHi (fr.[ii] & covers wanting, t.[1] mut. imprint wanting); MWA (t.[1] & p.[2]–6, 27–32 wanting); PP (pl. opp. p. 17 torn); Shaw 18535.

1132.1 THE ROYAL ALPHABET; Or, Child's Best Instructor. To Which Is Added, The History Of A Little Boy Found Under A Haycock. The First Worcester Edition. Printed at Worcester, Massachusetts. By Isaiah Thomas, And Sold, Wholesale and Retail, at his Book-Store. MDCCLXXXVII.

 fr.[2], t.[3], [4, alphabet], 5–31 p.; illus.; 9.5 cm.; Dutch paper covers.

 English ed. London: adv. by F. Newbery in the *London Chronicle* Dec. 31, 1778–Jan. 2 1779.

 MWA*; Evans 20688.

1132.2 ——— Boston: Printed for and sold by Samuel Hall, No. 53, Cornhill. 1793.

 fr.[2], t.[3], [4], 5–30, [31, adv. list of books] p.; illus.; 10 cm.; Dutch paper covers. Adv. by S. Hall [1789?] in **568.2**; 1790 in **1406.3**; 1791 in **408.3**; 1794 in **408.4**; 1796 in **587.0**.

 NNC-Pl*; Evans 46870.

1132.3 ——— Hudson (New-York): adv. by Ashbel Stoddard, 1794 in **1220.1**. Evans 29442 lists an ed. of 1795 probably from a similar adv.

1132.4 ——— Boston: Printed and sold by Samuel Hall in Cornhill. [*ca.* 1795?].

 fr.[2], t.[3], [4], 5–30 p.; illus.; 9.5 cm.

 MB* (p.[31] and rear cover wanting); Evans 29441.

1132.5 ——— Boston: S. Hall, 1798.

 Evans 48602.

1132.6 ——— Boston: Printed and sold by Samuel Hall, No. 53, Cornhill. 1802.

 t.[3], [4], 5–30 p.; illus.; 11.5 cm.

 CLU* (fr.[2], p. 31 and covers wanting).

1132.7 ——— Hudson [N.Y.], printed by Ashbel Stoddard And sold Wholesale and Retail at his Book-Store. 1804.

fr.[2], t.[3], [4–5], 6–28, [29], [30–31, adv. list of books] p.; illus.; 11 cm.; illus. blue-gray paper covers.

MWA-W*; Shaw 7211.

1133.1 THE ROYAL FABULIST; Being A Choice Collection Of Entertaining Fables. Intended As a Present for all those Good Girls and Boys who behave according to the following Rules: That Is, Do As They Are Bid, Come When They Are Called, And Shut The Door After Them. Ornamented with Cuts. Hartford: Printed By Lincoln & Gleason. 1806.

fr.[2], t.[3], [4 alphabets–5], 6–30, [31, adv. list of 12 books] p.; illus.; 10 cm.

Scottish ed. Edinburgh: G. Ross, 1815.

MWA* (covers wanting); CtHi; CtY; Shaw 11301.

1133.2 ——— Hartford: Printed By Peter B. Gleason & Co. 1811.

fr.[2], t.[3], [4–5], 6–30, [31, adv. list of 12 books] p.; illus.; 10 cm.; pr. & illus. buff paper covers.

Cover title: The Royal Fabulist. Hartford: Printed By Peter B. Gleason & Co. 1824.

MWA*; CtHi; NRU; Shaw 23841.

RUDIMENTS OF REASON. *See* Jones, Stephen, no. **691.6.**

1134 Sunday School Tract. No. 111. Anniversary Reward. RULES FOR GOOD LIVING. New-York: Published by P. W. Gallaudet, at his Theological Bookstore, No. 59 Fulton-street. J. Seymour, printer. 1819.

t.[1], [2], 3–16 p.; title page vignette only illus.; 13.5 cm.; pr. & illus. buff-brown paper covers; cover title dated 1819.

CtHi* (rear cover mut.).

RURAL FELICITY Or The History Of Tommy and Sally. *See* Johnson, Richard, no. **687.1.**

1135 RURAL SPORTS ILLUSTRATED WITH EMBLEMATICAL PRINTS. Philadelphia: Published and sold Wholesale by Wm Charles. Price 6¼ Cents. [Prior to 1814] [cover title].

[1–8] p. printed on one side only of 8 leaves; engr. col. illus.; 10 cm.; printed buff paper covers. This 10 cm. book is the same size as no. **242**, *Country Scenes. Philadelphia: W^m. Charles.* This later book is known only by the covers which were found pasted, face down, to the inside covers of the MWA-T copy of *The Entertaining History Of Jobson & Nell. Philadelphia: Wm. Charles, 1814,* no. **357.** Therefore this book was printed prior to 1814, and since *Rural Sports* is the same size it is a possibility that it also was published around the same time.

MWA*.

S

S., H.

1136.1 THE HISTORY OF THE DAVENPORT FAMILY: In which is displayed A Striking Contrast Between Haughty Indolence and Healthful Activity, In the Characters of the Young Davenports, and their Cousins, Sophia and Amelia Easy. Interspersed with Moral Reflections. By H. S. Two Volumes In One. Embellished with Engravings. Boston: Printed And Sold By Spotswood And Etheridge. 1798.

    fr.[ii], t.[1], [2–3], 4–144 p.; illus.; 14 cm.; bound in marbled paper over bds.

    English ed. London: [vol. I.] E. Newbery. [n.d.] [ca. 1793].

    Welch* (p. 13–14, 49–50 wanting; p. [3]–4, 23–24 mut.); DLC (rebound; i. st. on t.[1]); MSaE; MWA; OOxM; Evans 34504.

1136.2 [—] ——— Family. Adorned With Cuts. Montpelier [Vt.]: Published by Wright & Sibley. 1812.

    t.[1], [2–3], 4–180 p.; 10 full page illus.; 13.5 cm.; bound in buff paper over w. bds.

    MWA-T*.

1137 SACRED BIOGRAPHY, Exhibiting The History Of The Old Testament. From a Plan Suggested by Dr. Watts. Published by Johnson & Warner, Philadelphia. 1809. Lydia R. Bailey, Printer.

    t.[1], [2], 3–64 p.; illus.; 11 cm.; paper covers.

    PP*; Shaw 18557.

1138 THE SAILOR'S DAUGHTER: Or, Filial Affection. Embellished With Three Copper-Plate Engravings. Philadelphia: Published By Jacob Johnson, No. 147, Market-Street. 1808.

    fr.[ii], t.[1], [2–3], 4–36 p.; 3 pl. including front.; 13.5 cm.; pr. & illus. blue paper covers; p.[2]: Adams, Printer, Philadelphia. Adv. by Johnson & Warner, 1814 in **1449.2**.

    English ed. London: J. Harris, 1804.

    MWA-W*; Shaw 16121.

SAINT-PIERRE, JACQUES HENRY BERNADIN DE, 1737–1814 [KENDALL, EDWARD AUGUSTUS] tr. 1776–1824

1139.1 — THE INDIAN COTTAGE. Translated From The French Of Monsieur De St. Pierre. Author of Paul and Mary, &c. &c. To which Is Added, Palaemon, A Pastoral Tale. From The French Of M. Marmontel. Philadelphia: Printed And Sold By William Spotswood. 1794.

    t.[1], [2–3], 4–79, [80, bl.] [81–84 adv. list of books for sale by William Spotswood, Boston, Henry and Patrick Rice, and Benjamin Johnson, Philadelphia] p.; 16.5 cm.; bound in leather.

    English ed. London: 1791.

    MWA* (bound with **1140.1**); Bowe mss.

1139.2 ——— Cottage Or A Search After Truth. By M. Saint-Pierre, Author of The Voyage to The Isle Of France, The Studies Of Nature, Shipwreck, Or Paul And Mary, &c. [1 line quot.] New-York: Printed By M. M'Farlane. 1800.

    t.[i], [ii, bl.], [i], ii–v, [6, bl.], [7], 8–114 p.; 12 cm.; bound in blue marbled paper over bds., leather spine.

    MWA*; Bowe mss.

1139.3 ——— Cottage. Translated From The French Of St. Pierre, Author of Paul and Mary, &c. &c. Boston: Printed And Sold At Hosea Sprague's Printing-Chamber, No. 44, Marlboro, Street. 1803.

    t.[1], [2–3], 4–110 p.; 11.5 cm.; bound in leather.

    MWA*; MSaE; Bowe mss.; Shaw 5012.

SAINT-PIERRE, J. H. B. DE, 1737–1814 [MALTHUS, DANIEL] tr.

1140.1 — PAUL AND MARY, An Indian Story. To Which Is Added, The Indian Cottage. Translated From The French Of Monsieur De St. Pierre. [3 lines quot.] Georg. Virg. [4 lines quot.] Pitt. Philadelphia: Printed And Sold By William Spotswood. 1794.

    fr. [ii], 1st t.[iii], [iv], [1], 2–166, 2nd t.[1], [2–3], 4–79, [80, bl.], [81–84], adv. list of books for sale by William Spotswood, ——— [same as **1139.1**] p.; front. only illus.; 14.5 cm.; bound in leather.

    2nd title page: The Indian Cottage ——— [same as **1139.1**.] Philadelphia: Printed And Sold By William Spotswood. 1794.

    MWA*; PPL; Evans 27667.

1140.2 —————— Story. Translated from the French of Monsier De St. Pierre. [7 lines of verse] Salem: — Massachusetts: — Printed by William Carlton and sold by Cushing and Carlton, at the Bible and Heart, Essex-street. < October 27, 1795. >

t.[1], [2–3], 4–105 p.; 17 cm.; bound in red scalloped marbled paper, leather spine.

MWA°; Bowe mss.; MSaE; Evans 29460.

SAINT-PIERRE, J. H. B. DE, 1737–1814 ALEA, JOSE MIGUEL, tr. d. 1800?

1141.1 PABLO Y VIRGINIA. Por Jacob Bernardino Henrique De Saint-Pierre. Traducido En Español Por Don Jose Miguel Aléa. [1 line quot.] Enei. lib. 1. Philadelphia: En La Imprenta De M. Carey. 1808.

t.[i], [ii–iii], iv–v, [vi, bl.], [7], 8–180 p.; 17.5 cm.; bound in leather.

MWA°; PP; PPL; Bowe mss.; Shaw 16127.

1141.2 —————— Philadelphia: En La Imprenta De. M. Carey. 1810.

t.[i], [ii–iii], iv, [7], 8–146 p.; 14.5 cm.; green, yellow and red marbled paper covers, red leather spine.

MWA°; PPL; Bowe mss.; Shaw 21260.

SAINT-PIERRE, J. H. B. DE, 1737–1814 HUNTER, HENRY, tr. 1741–1802

1142 — THE BEAUTIFUL HISTORY OF PAUL AND VIRGINIA, An Indian Story. Translated from the French of J. H. B. de Saint Pierre, Author of The Studies of Nature, By H. Hunter, D.D. [1 line quot.] Exeter [N.H.]: Printed And Sold By Henry Ranlet. 1798.

t.[1], [2–3], 4–163, [164–166, adv. list of books], 14 cm.; bound in blue paper over w. bds., leather spine.

Welch°; MWA (bound in leather); Bowe mss.

1143.1 — PAUL AND VIRGINIA, An Indian Story. Translated from the French of J. H. B. De Saint Pierre, Author of the Studies of Nature, By H. Hunter, D.D. Embellished With Engravings. [1 line quot.] Aeneid. Lib. I. [1 line quot.] Boston: Printed For W. Spotswood & J. Nancrede. 1796.

fr.[ii], t.[1], [2–3], 4–264 p.; 3 engr. pl. signed S. *Hill Sculp.*, front., & pl. opp. p. 219, 220; 11 cm.

MWA° (rebound; fr.[ii] mut.); Bowe mss.; Evans 31150.

1143.2 —————— [Vol. I.], Vol. II. Boston: Printed For W. Spotswood & J. Nancrede. 1796. [vol. I.]: French t.[2], [i, bl.], fr.[ii], English t.[3], [4–5], 6–291 p.; front. only illus.; vol. II: French t.[2], [i, bl.], fr.[ii], English t.[3], [4–5], 6–241, [242, bl.], [243–252, adv. list of French books] p.; 2 pl., front., pl. opp. p. 149; signed S. *Hill Sculp.*; 11 cm.; 2 vols. bound in yellow paper over bds., black leather spine; front. Vol. II a duplicate of the one in Vol. I.

French title: Paul Et Virginie. Histoire Indienne. Par Jacques-Henri-Bernadin De Saint Pierre. Avec Figures. [1 line quot.] Aeneid Lib. 1. [Tome I.], Tome II. A Boston: Imprimé Pour Guillame Spotswood, Et Joseph Nancrede. 1796.

MB° (vol. [I] French t.[1] mut., II emb., st. on French titles of vols. [I], II.); MWA (vol.[I]); Bowe mss.; Evans 31148.

1143.3. —————— Printed At Wrentham, (*Mass.*) By Nathl. and Benj. Heaton, For E. Goodale, Mendon [Mass.]; And S. Warriner, Jun. Wilbraham [Mass.]. M,DCC,XCIX.

t.[1], [2–3], 4–180 p.; 14.5 cm.; bound in leather.

Welch°; CtY; DLC; MWA (in. st. t.[1]); NN; PP; RPJCB, Evans 36267.

1143.4 —————— Baltimore, Printed and sold by Bonsol & Niles, No. 173, Market-street. 1800.

t.[1], [2–3], 4–201 p.; 13.5 cm.; bound in leather.

MWA°; MdHi; PP; Bowe mss.; Evans 38450.

1143.5 —————— Virginia. By James-Henry-Bernadin De Saint-Pierre. Translated By Henry Hunter, D.D. Minister Of The Scots Church, London-Wall. Philadelphia: Printed By Abraham Small, For Birch And Small. 1808.

fr.[ii], t.[iii], [iv, bl.], [1], 2–160, [161–162, adv. list of books] p.; front. only illus.; 17.5 cm.; bound in leather; front. signed *Lawson* [Alexander Lawson].

MWA°; CLU; MB; Bowe mss.; Shaw 16128.

1143.6 —————— Virginia. By J. H. B. De. Saint-Pierre. Translated —————— [same as **1143.5**] Alexandria [Va.]: Printed by John A. Stewart. 1813.

t.[i], [ii–iii], iv–vi, [7], 8–216 p.; 9.5 cm.; bound in leather.

MWA°; Bowe mss.; Shaw 29711.

SAINT-PIERRE, J. H. B. DE, 1737–1814 WIL-
LIAMS, HELEN MARIA, tr. 1762–1827
1144.1 — PAUL AND VIRGINIA. Translated From
The French Of Bernadin Saint-Pierre. By Helen
Maria Williams, Author of Letters on the French
Revolution, Julia, a Novel, Poems, &c. Philadel-
phia: Printed By Wm. Duane, And Published At
The Aurora Bookstores, No. 106, Market street,
Philadelphia, and Square 450, Pennsylvania Ave-
nue, Washington City. 1802.
　　t.[i], [ii–iii], iv–xii, 1–212 p.; 16.5 cm.; bound
　　in leather; preface p. xii, signed *Helen Maria*
　　Williams, Paris, June, 1795.
　　French 1st ed. Paris; de l'impr. de Monsieur,
　　1789.
　　English ed. London: [n.p.] 1795.
　　Bowe°; Bowe mss.; Shaw 3037.

1144.2 — Paul & Virginia ———— [same as
1144.1] Williams. With Engravings On Wood,
By Anderson. New-York: Published By Evert
Duyckinck, No. 110 Pearl-Street. L. Nichols,
Printer. 1805.
　　fr.[ii], t.[iii], [iv, bl.], [i], ii–v, [vi, bl.], [7],
　　8–154 p.; front., pl. opp. p. 37, 94, 137, title
　　vignette & tailpieces only illus.; 17.5 cm.; bound
　　in leather.
　　MWA°; Bowe mss.; Shaw 9298.

1144.3 ————— New-York: Published By
Evert Duyckinck, No 110 Pearl-Street. George
Long, printer. 1811.
　　fr. [ii], t.[iii], [iv, bl.], [i], ii–v.[vi, bl.], [7],
　　8–154 p.; front., pl. opp. p. 37, 94, 137, title
　　vignette & tailpieces same as no. **1144.2**; 18
　　cm.; bound in leather.
　　MWA° (fr.[ii] wanting); Bowe mss.; Shaw
　　23862.

SAINT-PIERRE, J. H. B. DE [anon. version]
1145.1 — Paul and Virginia: With The Indian
Cottage. Newly translated from the French of
Jas. Henry Bernadin De Saint Pierre. Published
By Fielding Lucas, Jr. 138, Market-Street, Baltimore. 1814. J. Robinson, Printer.
　　fr.[ii], engr. 1st t.[iii], [iv, bl.], 2nd t.[1],
　　[2–3], 4–146, ½ t. [147], [148–149], 150–205
　　p.; engr. front. & engr. title vignette only illus.;
　　11 cm.; bound in leather.
　　MWA°; Bowe mss.; Shaw 32700.

1145.2 — ———— Virginia. Translated From The
French Of St. Pierre. Cabinet Edition. Philadel-

phia: Published And Sold By D. Hogan, No. 249,
Market Street. 1820.
　　t.[1], [2–3], 4–168 p.; 10 cm.; bound in leather.
　　MWA°; PHi; Bowe mss.

SALVADOR MUNDI. *See* Taylor, John, no. **1293.1.**

SALZMANN, CHRISTIAN GOTTHILF
1744–1811
1146.1 — ELEMENTS OF MORALITY, For The
Use Of Children; With An Introductory Address
To Parents. Translated From The German Of The
Rev. C. G. Salzmann. The First American Edition.
Printed At Providence (R. Island) By Carter And
Wilkinson, And Sold At Their Book And Stationary Store, Opposite The Market. M,DCC,XCV.
　　fr.[ii], t.[i], [ii–iii], iv–xix, [xx, bl.], [21], 22–
　　306, [307–308, adv. list of books] p.; 2 pl. &
　　ornamental tailpieces; 17 cm.; bound in leather;
　　fr.[ii] signed *S. Hill, Boston.*
　　English ed. London: entered Stationer's Hall,
　　July 12, 1790; 2 vols. 1790. 3 vols. Printed by
　　J. Crowder for J. Johnson, 1791.
　　MWA°; NN (2 copies: copy 1, fr.[ii] badly
　　foxed, other pl. wanting; copy 2, fr.[ii] wanting;
　　rebound); CtY; DCU; ICU; MBC; MH; NNS;
　　PP; PPL; RPB; Evans 29464.

1146.2 — ———— Rev. C. G. Salzmann. Illustrated With Twenty Copper-Plates. In Two Volumes. Vol. I. [II.] Philadelphia: Printed By J.
Hoff & H. Kammerer, Jun. M,DCC,XCVI.
　　vol. I: ½t.[i], [ii], fr.[pl. 1], t.[iii], [iv–v], vi–
　　xxxiv, [35], 36–248 p.; 10 plates including
　　frontispiece, signed *Weston fc.;* vol. II: ½t.[1],
　　[2], fr.[pl. 1], t.[3], [4–5], 6–259, [260–262]
　　p.; 10 plates including frontispiece signed *Wes-
　　ton* or *H. W. &c.;* 2 vols; 16.5 cm.; bound in
　　leather.
　　MWA° (vols. I, II, i. st. on t.[iii]); CLU; CtHt
　　(vol. 1 only); DLC; MH; NB; PHi; PP (bound
　　in 1 vol.); PPL; Evans 31156.

1146.3 — ———— Salzmann. The Third American Edition. Wilmington [Del.]: Printed by Joseph
Johnson Market-Street Opposite The Bank. 1796.
　　t.[i], [ii, bl.–iii], iv–xiv, [15], 16–232 p.; 17 cm.;
　　bound in leather.
　　MWA°; DeHi (p.[15]–24, 231–232 mut.);
　　DeWi (per st. on t.[i]); DLC (rebound; i. st.
　　on t.[i]); PP; PU; Evans 31157.

1146.4 ——— First Baltimore Edition, Revised and Corrected. Printed And Published By Joseph Robinson, Baltimore 1811.

t.[1], [ii–iii], iv–xvi, [17], 18–267, [268, adv. list of school books] p.; 16.5 cm.; bound in leather; colophon p. 267: Printed by J. Robinson. This book is listed, p.[268], as a school book.

MWA° (i. st. on t.[i]); BM; CSmH; CtY; MB; MH; OClWHi; PPi; PPL; RPB; Shaw 23865.

SANDERS, CHARLOTTE

1147.1 — HOLIDAYS AT HOME. Written For The Amusement Of Young Persons. By Charlotte Sanders. [2 lines of verse] New-York: Printed By J. Swaine, For T. H. Burnton, No. 116, Broad-Way, Opposite the City Hotel. 1804.

t.[1], [2–5], 6–268 p.; 18 cm.; bound in leather; dedication p. [3] signed *C. Saunders* [*sic. i.e. Sanders*]. January, 1803.

English ed. London: J. Mawman; T. Wilson and R. Spence, York, 1803.

MWA°; DLC; PP; Shaw 7231.

1147.2 ——— By Charlotte Saunders. [*sic. i.e.* Sanders] [2 lines of verse] New-York: Printed and sold by T. & J. Swords, No. 160 Pearl-Street. 1814.

t.[1], [2–5], 6–226 p.; t.[1] 12.5 cm.; dedication p.[3] signed: *C. Saunders* [*sic. i.e. Sanders*]. January, 1803.

KU° (rebound, p. 221–224 wanting); MWA; Shaw 32718.

1148 — THE LITTLE FAMILY. Containing A Variety Of Moral And Philosophical Matter. Written For the Amusement And Instruction Of Young Persons. By Charlotte Sanders. Vol. I. [II.] [5 lines of verse] Thomson. Printed at Haverhill, Massachusetts: By Moore & Stebbins, For David West, No. 59, Cornhill, Boston. 1799.

1st t.[i], [ii, bl–iii], iv–v, [vi, bl.], [7], 8–143, [144, bl.]; 2nd t.[1], [2, bl.–3], 4–140 p.; bound in 1 vol.; 17.5 cm.; bound in leather. vol. I. p. 133 incorrectly numbered 123.

English ed. Bath: 2 vols. R. Cruttwell, 1797. MWA° (i. st. on t.[1]); MHa; NN; Evans 36274; Sabin 76349.

SANDHAM, ELIZABETH

[—] CARELESS ISABELLA. *See* separate issues from The Magic Lantern Exhibition, no. **1154.2**.

1149 — DEAF AND DUMB! By Miss Sandham, Author of "The Twin Sister," &c &c. [2 lines quot.] Cowper. Philadelphia, Published By Isaac Peirce, No. 5, North Front Street. 1818.

fr.[ii], t.[1], [2–3], 4–103, [104, bl.], [105–108, adv. list of books] p.; front. only illus.; 15.5 cm. English ed. London: Darton, Harvey, And Darton, 1810.

MWA°; RPB; Shaw 45633.

1150 [—] THE FISHERMAN; A Tale, For Young Persons, By The Author Of A Cup Of Sweets, Godmother's Tales, &c. &c. New-York: Published By W. B. Gilley, No. 92 Broadway. T. & W. Mercein, print. 1816.

fr.[ii], t.[1], [2–3], 4–116 p.; front only illus.; 15 cm.; bound in orange marbled paper over bds., red leather spine; fr.[ii] signed *Scoles sculp.*

English ed. London: J. Harris, 1815.

Welch°; CLU; MWA; OOxM; PP; Shaw 37608.

1151 [—] THE GODMOTHER'S TALES. By The Author Of Short Stories, Summer Rambles, Cup Of Sweets, &c. &c. New-York: Published By A. T. Goodrich & Co. No. 124 Broadway, Corner Of Cedar-Street. J. Seymour, Printer. 1818.

t.[i], [ii, bl.–iii], iv, [v], [vi, bl.], [1 leaf], [7], 8–135 p.; 15.5 cm.; bound in gray paper over bds.; pink front cover label.

English ed. London: J. Harris, 1808.

CLU°.

1152 — THE HISTORY OF WILLIAM SELWYN. By Miss Sandham. Author Of The Twin Sisters, And Other Works For Young People. [1 line quot.] Cowper. New-York: Published By W. B. Gilley, No. 92 Broadway, T. & W. Mercein, Print. January 1816.

fr.[ii], t.[i], [ii–iii], iv–vi, [1], 2–220, [221–226, adv. list of books] p.; front. only illus.; 15.5 cm.; bound in pr. gray-green paper over bds.; front. signed *Morgan del Scoles Sculp.*; cover title dated February, 1816.

English ed. London: J. Harris, 1815.

MWA°; CSmH; MB; PP; RPB; Shaw 38870.

1153 [—] THE MAGIC LANTERN; Or, Amusing And Instructive Exhibitions For Young People. With Ten Coloured Engravings. Philadelphia: Published By Benjamin Johnson, No. 249 Market Street. 1807.

Following the title page there are 10 separate stories with a colored plate facing the caption title of each booklet, which are all 12 pages long; 17 cm.; bound in marbled paper over bds., leather spine. The caption titles in order are:

1. The Story Of Charles Maitland; Or, The Dangers Of A Meddling Disposition.
2. Justina; Or, the Filial Daughter.
3. Emma Clifford; Or, Impertinent Curiosity Punished.
4. Anna, The Tale Bearer.
5. Harrington; Or, The Artful Boy Discovered.
6. Wandering William; Or, The Disadvantages Of An Unsettled Disposition.
7. The Story Of Constance, The Proud Girl.
8. The Story Of Peevish William.
9. Philip And Agnes; Or, The Benevolent Children.
10. Careless Isabella; Or, The Dangers of Delay.

On p. 12 of each book the colophon reads: John Bouvier printer.

The English ed. —— [same as above] *With Eleven Coloured Engravings. By The Authoress Of Short Stories, Summer Rambles, The Red And Black Book, &c. &c.* London: Printed For Tabart And Co. 157, New Bond-Street; And To Be Had Of W. Gibbons, Bath; M. Keene, Dublin; And Of All Other Booksellers. Price 6 S. half-bound. < Printed by J. Adlard, Duke-street. [*ca.* 1806] Front has: "London Pub. Mar. 4–1806, by Tabart & Co. 157 New Bond St."

MWA°; DLC (p. and pl. wanting or mut.); PP (bound in green paper over bds., leather spine); Shaw 12975.

1154.1 [—] CARELESS ISABELLA; Or, The Dangers Of Delay. Embellished with a Magic Lantern Exhibition. Published By Benjamin Johnson, No. 249, Market Street, Philadelphia. 1806. [cover label].

pl. [ii], [1], 2–12 p.; one col. pl. only illus.; 16.5 cm.; orange paper covers.

NN° (bound with *The Story Of Constance* [caption p.[1]]; [1], 2–10 p. [p. 11–12 wanting]); Shaw 10085.

1154.2 [—] —— Published by Johnson and Warner, No. 147, Market Street, Philadelphia. 1812. [front cover label].

pl. [ii], [1], 2–12 p.; one col. pl. only illus.; 17

cm.; gray paper covers; colophon p. 12: John Bouvier, Printer.
PP°.

1155 [—] JUSTINEA; Or, The Filial Daughter. Embellished with a Magic Lantern Exhibition. Published by Benjamin Johnson, No. 249, Market Street, Philadelphia. 1806. [front cover label].

pl. [ii], [1], 2–12 p.; one col. pl. only illus.; 17 cm.; bound in gray marbled stiff paper covers. MSaE° (pl. [ii] wanting).

1156 [—] THE STORY OF CHARLES MAITLAND; Or, The Dangers Of A Meddling Disposition. [caption title] [Embellished with . . . Published By Benjamin Johnson, . . . Philadelphia. 1806.] [remainder of title and imprint taken from the cover label of **1155**].

pl. [ii], [1], 2–12 p.; one col pl. only illus.; 17 cm.; orange paper covers.
MWA-W° (cover label wanting).

1157 [—] THE STORY OF CONSTANCE, The Proud Girl. [caption title p.[1]] [Embellished with a Magic Lantern Exhibition. Published by Benjamin Johnson, No. 249, Market Street, Philadelphia.–1806.] [remainder of title and imprint taken from the cover label of no. **1155**].

pl. [ii], [1], 2–12 p.; one col. pl. only illus.; 16.5 cm.; orange paper covers.
OClWHi° (cover label wanting).

1158 [—] THE STORY OF PEEVISH WILLIAM. Embellished with a Magic Lantern Exhibition. Published By Benjamin Johnson, No. 249 Market Street, Philadelphia. 1806. [front cover label].

[1], 2–12 p.; 17 cm.; gray marbled paper covers.
CtHi° (pl. wanting); MWA (pl. wanting, p. [1]–2 mut.); Shaw 11418.

1159 [—] WANDERING WILLIAM, Or, The Disadvantage Of An Unsettled Disposition. Embellished with a Magic Lantern Exhibition. Published By Benjamin Johnson, No. 249, Market Street, Philadelphia. — 1806. [front cover label].

pl.[ii], [1], 2–12 p.; one col. pl. only illus.; 17 cm.; brown paper covers.
PHi°.

1160 [—] MORE TRIFLES! For The Benefit Of The Rising Generation: By The Author Of "Juliana."—"Trifles, Or, Friendly Mites." "Easton

House."—Addresses Of An Affectionate Mother," &c. &c. Poughkeepsie [N.Y.]: Published By Paraclete Potter. P. & S. Potter, Printers. 1814.

t.[1], [2–3], 4–106 p.; 14 cm.; bound in blue paper over bds., leather spine. *Trifles, Or, Friendly Mites* is by Elizabeth Sandham.
English ed. London: J. Harris, 1804.
MWA°; DLC; MH; NPV; Shaw 32166 and 32709.

1161.1 [—] THE TWIN SISTERS, Or The Advantages Of Religion. By Miss Sandham, Author Of Many Approved Works For Young Persons. First American Edition. [4 lines of verse] Boston: Published By Bradford & Read, No. 58, Cornhill. Watson & Bangs, Printers. 1813.

t.[i], [ii–iii], iv, [5], 6–213 p.; 14.5 cm.; bound in marbled paper over bds., red leather spine.
English ed. London: 4 ed. J. Harris, 1810.
MH°; CtY (rebound); Shaw 29719.

1161.2 [—] —— Persons. Second American Edition. [4 lines of verse] Poughkeepsie [N.Y.]: Published By Paraclete Potter, Main-Street. P. & S. Potter, Printers. 1813.

t.[i], [ii–iii], iv, [5], 6–168 p.; 14.5 cm.; bound in paper over bds., leather spine.
MWA°; NN; Shaw 29720.

1161.3 [—] —— Second American Edition. [4 lines of verse] Middlebury [Vt.]: Printed And Published By William Slade, Jun. 1815.

t.[i], [ii–iii], iv, [5], 6–215 p.; 13.5 cm.; bound in marbled paper over bds., leather spine.
MWA°; CSt; DLC (i. st. on t.[1]); ICU; NN; PP (bound in marbled paper over bds., red leather spine); Vt; VtHi; VtMiS; McCorison 1780; Shaw 35848.

1162 [—] URSULA; Or The Insufficiency Of Human Attainments: By The Author Of The "Twin Sisters," "Orphan," &c. [5 lines of verse] Beattie. Philadelphia: Published By Johnson & Warner, No. 147, Market Street. 1811.

t.[1], [2–3], 4–130 p.; t.[1] 13 cm.; colophon p. 130: J. Bouvier, Printer, Bellavista, Hamilton-[ville] [Pa.].
MWA° (rebound; p. 129–130 mut.); MHi (pr. & illus. paper covers, dated 1811; 14 cm.); Shaw 23868.

[SANDS, BENJAMIN]
1163.1 [—] [Metamorphosis. Philadelphia, *ca.* 1787].

[2–6] p.; illus.; 14.5 cm.; verses [1–21] unnumbered.

All American editions of *Metamorphosis*, nos. **1163.1–1163.39**, are an oblong sheet of paper usually 33 cm. by 28 cm., printed on the recto and verso and folded perpendicularly three times into 4 leaves 8 cm. wide. The top 8 cm. and bottom 6 cm. of the sheet are now horizontally folded inward over the central 14 cm. and four .5 mm. pieces are cut out of these folded portions between the leaves to a depth of 8 cm. along the top fold and 6 mm. along the bottom fold, so that each page has a top flap, or extension 8 cm. long and a bottom flap 6 cm. long. Pages [2–5] on the verso of the sheet each show an illustration. Contiguous pages [1], [8], [7], on the recto of the sheet are blank in no. **1163.1** but in later editions may be printed or illustrated. These are followed by p. [6] on the recto, with 12 lines of verse enclosed in a border of type ornaments, and is the back of p. [5]. In these booklets the recto and verso of the original sheet will be considered rather than the sides of the individual leaves after folding. Pages [2] and [3], [4] and [5] when folded have facing full-page illustrations. The recto of each top and bottom flap on being folded inwardly come together at the middle and form a picture with 4 lines of verse, enclosed in a border of printer's ornaments above it. These pages formed by the union of two flaps, "a" and "b", designating upper and lower flaps respectively, have the same page numbers with "a" or "b" added as the underlying illustrations. On the verso of each top and bottom flap, or the underneath portion when folded, there are 12 lines of verse. By lifting or folding down the flaps, combinations of illustrations on the flaps with portions of the underlying page form new pictures. Thus when flaps [2a] and [2b] are folded over p. [2], a full-page illustration of Adam is seen. If flap [2a] is lifted, the upper portion of p. [2] comes to view and the illustration changes to Eve. When flap [2b] is turned downward, so that all of p. [2] comes to view, Eve turns into a mermaid. In like manner the cut of the lion, flaps [3a] and [3b], on lifting flap [3a] changes into a griffin, with the combination of upper p. [3] and flap [3b]. When flap [3b] is turned down, bringing all of p. [3] to view, the picture changes into an eagle with an infant in his claws. Flap [4a] shows a festooned drapery, held in three places, hanging over the upper fourth of a heart. Flap [4b] depicts a gentleman with a cane looking at a fox seated on a column. When flap [4b] is turned down, the lower three-fourths of a heart comes to view, lying between the legs of a table. On raising flap [4a], all of p. [4] is shown which is a cut of a man counting out money on a table with the three-quarter heart below it. Combined flaps [5a] and [5b] depict a front and larger view of the gentleman with a cane already seen on opposite flap [4b]. When flap [5b] is turned down, the lower portion of the underlying illustration, p. [5], is a man dying in bed. On turning up flap [5a] the complete illustration, p. [5], shows an erect skeleton, in front of a coffin, holding a downward pointed arrow in the right hand, and standing over the bed of a dying man. At the top and bottom of the illustration on p. [2–5] there is a border 10 mm. wide composed of an upper-case alphabet, numbered 1–9 and 0, which according to the statement on the title page of no. **1163.12** were printed "To Aid Females In Marking Linen, &c." The bottom border on p. [5] has the author's name "B. Sands" followed by an ornamental grouping of squares which does not resemble any letter of the alphabet. This border is present in all editions except no. **1163.12**. From 1807 on, a title page is always on p. [1]. The 1810 edition has illustrations on p. [7] and [8]. From 1810–1820 pages [1], [8], [7], [6] are on the recto of the sheet and are either printed, illustrated, or both. The text of no. **1163.1** is curious and rewritten from the English edition of 1654. For comparison's sake, the first 12 sets of verses from **1163.1** will be given with the verse number taken from **1163.3**.

[1] Adam comes first upon the Stage.
     And Eve from out his Side,
     Who was given to him in Marriage:
     Turn up, and see his Bride. [flap [2a]
     recto]

[2] Here Eve in shape you may behold,
     One body sheweth Twain:
     Once more do but the Leaf downfold,
     And it's as strange again. [flap [2a] verso]
     [below 6 lines:
     [13] Adam and Eve in Innocence,/ . . .]

[3] Eyes look not on the Mermaid's Face,
     Let Ears forebear her Song;
     Her Features have an alluring Grace
     More Charming than her Tongue. [flap
     [2b] verso] [above 8 lines:
     [17] Eve did the fatal Apple take,/ . . .]

[4] A Lion rousing from his Den,
     On Purpose for to range
     Is soon turn'd into another Shape:
     Lift up, and see how strange. [flap [3a]
     recto]

[5] A Griffin here you may behold,
     Half Beast half Fowl to be
     Once more do but the leaf downfold,
     And a frightful Sight you'll see. [flap [3a]
     recto] [below 8 lines:
     [14] In happy Eden see them
     plac'd,/ . . .]

[6] Behold within the Eagle's Claws
     An Infant there doth lye!
     Which he hath taken as a Prey
     With Wings prepar'd to fly. [flap [3b]
     verso] [above 8 lines:
     [18] The Tree of Life now in that
     Land/ . . .]

[7] Now I've escaped the Eagle's Claws,
     And am from Dangers free,
     I've set my Heart to gather Gold:
     Turn down the Leaf, and see. [flap [4a]
     recto]

[8] A Heart here is oppress'd with Care,
     What Salve can cure the same?
     Under the Leaf you'll find a Cure:
     Lift up, and see how plain. [flap [4b]
     verso] [about 8 lines:
     [19] Or who before his awful
     Bar/ . . .]

[9] A Purse with Gold and Silver-Store
     Has cur'd my Heart, I'm sick no more;
     But am from Cares and Dangers free;
     What wordly Cares can trouble me. [flap
     [4a] verso] [below 8 lines:
     [15] This Land they freely might
     possess,/ . . .]

[10] Now I've got Gold & Silver Store,
     Brides from the Rich, Pawns from the
     Poor,
     What wordly Cares can trouble me?
     Turn down the Leaf, and then you'll see.
     [flap [5a] recto]

[11] Sickness is come, and Death draws nigh,
     Help Gold and Silver, ere I die;

It will not do, for it's but Dross;
Turn up and see Man's End at last. [flap
[5b] verso] [above 8 lines:
[20]   Now Christ is come to set us
free/ . . .]

[12]   O! Man; now see, thou art but Dust,
Thy Gold and Silver is but Rust;
Time now is come, thy Glass is spent;
What Wordly Cares can Death prevent?
[flap [5a] verso] [below 8 lines:
[16]   Had they obey'd their Maker's
Voice,/ . . .]

Textural differences between this edition and no. 1163.3: The verses are unnumbered; each 4 lines of verses [1–20] are separated by a space; flap [2a] recto, verse [1], "Stage,", line 1, followed by a comma; both editions have a colon after "Marriage:", line 3; flap [2a] verso, verse [2], "Twain:", line 2, followed by a colon; flap [3b] verso, verse [18], "Face.", line 8, with a period; flap [4a] recto, verse [7], "Gold:", line 3, with a colon; flap [4a] verso, verse [9], "me.", line 4, followed by a period; flap [4b] verso, verse 6, "lye!", line 2, spelled with a "y"; flap [5b] verso, verse [11], "Dross:", line 3, with a colon; flap [5a] recto, verse [16], "eat,", line 7, with a comma; verse 12, "Man;", line 1, with a semicolon.

Fourteen printer's ornaments are present.

The illustrations, on either the flaps, or pages, are enclosed by an outer thick and an inner thin rule border. The cuts were printed again and again. With the passage of time the rules became more and more nicked or broken. These particular illustrations are probably type metal cuts because some of the rules are bent, or have a curve in them. The presence or absence of certain rules or nicks in borders are of little value in dating these booklets, because they appear to a greater or lesser extent in all editions using the Poupard cuts and may be entirely due to how well the cut was inked at the time of printing. It is believed that 1163.1 is an earlier printing than 1163.3 because of the old spelling "lye" of the word "lie," the unnumbered verses, and the fact that the ruled borders are less defective.

Solomon Wieatt in his edition printed in 1807, no. 1163.9, employed the author's name "Benjamin Sands" on the title page. The name "B. Sands" occurs on the bottom border of p. [5] in all editions using Poupard blocks. S. Wieatt

printed two more editions of the booklet; another in 1807, no. 1163.10, and one in 1810, no. 1163.11. In each of these the author's name is left off the title page and does not appear in any other edition of the book. Since the name "B. Sands" appears on p. [5] in all Poupard illustrated editions, it is safe to assume he is the author. The book was rewritten from the English edition of *The Beginning and Progress of Man.* London: E. Alsop, 1654, whose author is unknown.

These "Metamorphoses" were extremely popular and children made colored manuscript copies of them. There is a manuscript one with the inscription: *Designed by Katherine Fisher 18 years of age 1789.* (MDeHi). Other manuscript copies appeared in America during the latter part of the eighteenth and early nineteenth centuries.

The signature, *J. Poupard,* appears at the base of all the illustrations except the one on p. [4]. James Poupard, according to Groce and Wallace, was in Philadelphia from 1769–1807. Hamilton quotes Stauffer as saying that Poupard's earliest engraving was mentioned in the *Pennsylvania Gazette* of *June 29, 1774.* The *Pennsylvania Magazine, February 1775,* Hamilton 76, contains a cut signed *J. P.,* probably James Poupard. There are eleven illustrations signed *J. Poupard* in Croxall's *Fables Of Aesop And Others. Philadelphia: R. Aitken, 1777,* no. 18.1. The date Rosenbach 82 gives 1163.3 is [1775]. This date seems too early, for if 1163.3 were the first edition, it would have all the rule borders in perfect condition, which is not the case. It is believed to be later than no. 1163.1 for reasons mentioned above. Even no. 1163.1 has breaks in the borders. The earliest known dated edition is the MDeHi manuscript copy dated 1789. If that date is correct, then the printed edition possibly could have been printed several years before that date. On this assumption the conjectural date [*ca.* 1787] is assigned no. 1163.1. This at least allows sufficient time for the Poupard blocks to acquire the breaks which appear in 1807, no. 1163.9. If the cuts had been used over a period of 32 years, more and larger breaks would be expected.

English ed. & version entitled: *The Beginning, Progress and End of Man.* London: E. Alsop for T. Dunster, 1654.

NjP°; MWA-T° (flap [5b] wanting); Evans 46569; Hamilton 1168.(1), (dated [*ca.* 1775]).

1163.2 [—] [———— Philadelphia, *ca.* 1788] [German ed.].

[2–6] p.; illus.; 14.5 cm.; verses [1–21] unnumbered, similar to no. **1163.1**. *See* no. **1163.1** for a description of the format of this booklet. Typographical characteristics, comparing **1163.2** with **1163.4**, are: flap [2a] recto, verse [1], a period after "Seit.", line 2; a comma after "wars,", line 3; flap [2a] verso, verse [13], "gewand.t", line 4, with ".t" instead of " 't".; flap [2b] verso, verse [3], "reizende,", line 3, spelled without a "t"; flap [3b] verso, verse [18], "Erkänntnitz", line 2, has two "ns"; flap [4b] verso, verse [8], no comma after "gedrückt", line 1; flap [5a] recto, verse [10], "Welch weltlich", line 3, in 2 words; flap [5a] verso, verse [12], no comma after "Zeit", line 3; p. [6], verse [21], an exclamation mark after "verhüten!", line 4, spelled with one "t".

Sixteen printer's ornaments are present.

The illustrations are printed from the same blocks used in no. **1163.1** and show the same breaks and imperfections in the rule borders. From the above data, including the fact that the verses are unnumbered, evidently the book was printed close to no. **1163.1**. For this reason the conjectural date [*ca.* 1788] is being given to no. **1163.2**.

Ries° (flap [3a] wanting).

1163.3 [—] [———— Philadelphia, *ca.* 1792].

[2–6] p.; illus.; 14 cm.; verse I numbered in small Roman type; verses 2–21 numbered in Arabic numerals. *See* no. **1163.1** for a description of the format of this booklet. The type setting is similar to no. **1163.1** but shows variations: flap [2a] recto, verse 1, a period after "Stage.", line 1; flap [3a] recto, verse 4, no period after "Den," line 1, "range", line 2; flap [3b] verso, verse 6, "lie!", line 2, spelled with an "i"; verse 18, "Face?", line 8, followed by a question mark; flap [4a] recto, verse 7, "Gold.", line 3, followed by a period; flap [4a] verso, verse 15, "Lord", line 5, not followed by a comma, flap [5a] recto, verse 10, "Gold and Silver", line 1, with "and" spelled out; flap [5a] verso, verse 16, "eat;", line 7, followed by a semicolon; "God", line 8, instead of "Gods".

Eighteen printer's ornaments are present.

The illustrations are printed from the Poupard blocks used in no. **1163.1**. From data on the imperfections in the ruled borders, in conjunction with the newer spelling of the word "lie", flap [3b] verso, instead of "lye", and the fact that the verses are numbered for the first time, it is believed that **1163.3** was printed later than **1163.1** and **1163.2**. The conjectural date [*ca.* 1792] is being given the book.

PP; Evans 45354 (dated [1788]).

1163.4 [—] [———— Philadelphia *ca.* 1793] [German ed.].

[2–6] p.; illus.; 14.5 cm.; verses printed in German; verse I, numbered with a small Roman numeral; verses 2–21 numbered in Arabic similar to no. **1163.3**. *See* no. **1163.1** for a description of the format of this booklet. The text differs from no. **1163.2** by having on flap [2a] recto, verse I, no period after "Seit", line 2; no comma after "wars", line 3; flap [2b] verso, verse [3], "reitzende", line 3, spelled "tz"; flap [3b] verso, verse 18, "Erkäntnitz", line 2, with one "n"; flap [4b], verse 8, a comma after "gedruckt,", line 1; flap [5a] recto, verse 10, "Welch-weltlich", line 3, in one word; flap [5a] verso, verse 12, a comma after "Zeit,", line 3; p. [6], verse 21, "verhutten", line 4, not followed by an exclamation point, and spelled with two "ts".

Twelve printer's type ornaments are present.

The illustrations are printed from the Poupard blocks used in no. **1163.3** and show all the imperfections in the rule borders of that edition. In addition a new nicked area appears for the first time in the cut of Adam, flap [2a] recto. This edition is believed to have been printed later than no. **1163.3** because of presence of this new nicked area. The characteristic that links it to no. **1163.3** is the use of Roman numeral "I" for verse "1". All later editions have the "1" printed with an Arabic numeral. The booklet is dated [*ca.* 1795].

Welch°; MWA-T; PP; PPL; Evans 46570.

1163.5 [—] [———— Philadelphia, *ca.* 1796–1801].

[2–6] p.; illus.; 14.5 cm.; verse 1, 2–21 numbered with Arabic numerals. *See* no. **1163.1** for a description of the format of the booklet. The text shows variations in type setting when compared with no. **1163.3** Flap [2a] recto, verse 1,

"Marriage?", line 3, is followed by a question mark instead of a colon and is similar to no. 1163.4; flap [2a] verso, verse 2, "Body," line 2, has a capital "B", instead of "b"; flap [4a] recto, verse 7, "Gold;", line 3, is followed by a semicolon instead of a period; flap [4a] verso, verse 9, "me!", line 4, has an exclamation mark instead of a question mark; flap [4b] verso, verse 8, "oppress'd", line 1, has the first "s" printed in the old form "s" and the second one in the modern form of the letter; verse 19, "Head,", line 6, followed by a comma instead of a period; "bride", line 7, has a lower case "b" instead of "B"; flap [5b] verso, verse 20, "love.", line 4, with a lower case "l" instead of "L"; "Propos'd", line 7, and "purchas'd", line 8, both have the modern form of the letter "s" instead of the old form.

Six printer's type ornaments are present.

The illustrations are printed from the Poupard blocks. This edition is probably later than 1163.3 and 1163.4 because the modern form of the letter "s" is used in three words, where the old form of the letter was present in 1163.3. Arabic numeral "1" numbers the first verse and does so in all later editions. The conjectural date [*ca.* 1796–1801] has been assigned to this book. NjP°; Hamilton 1168.(2).

1163.6   [—] [——— Philadelphia, *ca.* 1802].
p.[2] including flaps [2a–2b] only; illus.; 14.5 cm.; verse "1" numbered with an Arabic number. *See* no. 1163.1 for a description of the format of this booklet. The text has the same type-setting, punctuation, capitalization and spelling as no. 1163.5.

Seven printer's type ornaments are present.

The Poupard cuts have the same imperfections noted in no. 1163.5. Since the type setting of the text is the same as 1163.5; with the old form of the letter "s" at the beginning of words still in use; the border ornaments similar, but having variations, and the borders around the cuts having no new imperfections, 1163.6 was probably printed sometime near 1163.5 and is dated [*ca.* 1802].

MWA-T° (p. [2] and flaps [2a–2b] only are present in this fragmentary copy).

1163.7   [—] ——— Philadelphia, *ca.* 1803–1804].
[2–6], p.; illus.; 14.5 cm.; verses 1–21 numbered in Arabic numerals as in all the following edi-tions. *See* no. 1163.1 for a description of the format of this booklet. The text shows variations from no. 1163.5. Flap [2a] recto, verse 1, "Marriage:"; line 3, followed by a colon; "see", line 4, spelled with the modern form of the letter "s" and so are all words throughout the text starting with a lower case "s", or having the letter somewhere in the word; flap [2b] verso, verse 17, "Righteousness,", line 4, followed by a comma; flap [3b] verso, verse 6, "prepared", line 4, instead of "prepar'd"; flap [4b] verso, verse 19, "Bride,", line 7, with a capital "B"; flap [5b] verso, verse 20, "God,", line 7, followed by a comma.

Seven printer's type ornaments are present.

The illustrations printed from the Poupard blocks show no new breaks or bends not found in no. 1163.5. Since the modern form of the latter "s" is used throughout, the booklet was possibly printed [*ca.* 1803–1804]. NjP°; Hamilton 1168.(3), fig. 26.

1163.8   [—] [——— Philadelphia, *ca.* 1805–1806].
[2–6] p.; illus.; 14.5 cm.; verses 1–21 numbered in Arabic numerals. *See* no. 1163.1 for a description of the format of this booklet. The modern form of the letter "s" is used throughout and in all later editions. The text shows variations from no. 1163.7. Flap [2a] recto, verse 1, "side," line 2, has a lower case "s"; flap [3a] recto, verse 4, "shape:", line 3, with a lower case "s"; flap [3b] verso, verse 6, "prepar'd", line 4, spelled " 'd"; flap [4a] verso, verse 9, "Silver-store", line 1, with the "s" of "store" in the lower case; the following words all have the first letter in the lower case: flap [5a] recto, verse 10, "store", line 1; flap [5a] verso, verse 16, "voice,", line 1, "choice,", line 2, verse 12, "dust;", line 1, "death," line 4; flap [5b] verso, verse 11, "end", line 4, verse 20, "view", line 5, "eternal", line 7, "blood", line 8; p. [6], verse 21, "space", line 5, "length", line 6, "span", line 6, "space", line 9, "eternity", line 10, "time", line 12, all have the first letter of each word in the lower case.

Nine printers' ornaments are present.

The Poupard blocks show two new breaks. The first passes through both rules of the left border of picture of the upper half of Adam, flap [2a] recto. The second bisects both rules of the right border of the cut of the upper half of the lion, flap [3a] recto. Both breaks occur in no. 1163.9

and later editions. By means of them this book is dated prior to 1807 or [*ca.* 1805–1806]. MWA-T°.

1163.9 [—] METAMORPHOSIS, OR A TRANSFORMATION OF PICTURES, With Poetical Explanations: For The Amusement Of Young Persons. By Benjamin Sands. Philadelphia: Printed For And Sold By Solomon Wieatt, No. 368, North Second Street. 1807.

t.[1], [2–6] p.; illus.; 14.5 cm. *See* no. **1163.1** for a description of the format of this booklet. This is the first edition with a title page, which occurs in all succeeding editions. The name of the author, Benjamin Sands, appears on the title page of only this edition. *See* no. **1163.1** for a discussion of the author. The type setting is close to no. **1163.8** with relatively few differences. Flap [2a] recto, verse 1, "Marriage;", line 3, is followed by a semicolon; flap [2b] verso, "grace," line 3, has a lower case "g"; flap [5a] verso, verse 16, "fruit," line 7, a lower case "f", "Good", line 8, a capital "G"; p. [6], verse 21, "life", line 7, a lower case "l".
Eight printer's type ornaments are present.
The illustrations printed from the Poupard blocks show the same imperfections shown in **1163.8,** plus a new break the same as in **1163.12.**
MWA-W°; CLU; RPB; Shaw 13547.

1163.10 [—] ———— Children. Philadelphia: Printed For And Sold By Solomon Wieatt, No. 368, North Second Street. 1807.

t.[1], [2–6] p.; illus.; 15 cm. This is a new printing of no. **1163.9** without the author's name, Benjamin Sands, and a border of type ornaments around the title page. *See* no. **1163.1** for a description of the format of this booklet and a discussion of the author. In this and all following editions textual variations will not be given since all the complete copies are dated and such data are not essential to describe and date a particular edition. Ten printer's type ornaments are present. The ruled borders around the Poupard blocks are the same as in no. **1163.9** and show no new breaks.
OClWHi°; PP; Shaw 13547.

1163.11 [—] ———— Philadelphia, Published By Solomon Wiatt, No. 104, North Second street. 1810.

t.[1], [2–8] p.; illus.; 14.5 cm.; p. [7], [8] illustrated for the first time. *See* **1163.1** for a description of the format of the booklet. Seven printer's type ornaments are present. Three new illustrations are used. The title vignette signed *MICAH, C^h, IV. 4.* shows a man reading a book under a tree. That on p. [7] depicts a man seated in a chair and handing a boy a book. The picture on p. [8] portrays a woman in chains in a prison. It was used for a frontispiece to portray Maria Martin in *The History Of The Captivity and Sufferings Of Maria Martin. Philadelphia: Printed and sold by Joseph Rakestraw, 1809.*
MWA°; NN (i. st. on p.[2, 3, 4, 5, 6]); Shaw 21282.

1163.12 [—] ———— Philadelphia, Published By Jonathan Pounder, No. 104, North Second Street. 1811.

t.[1], [2–8] p.; illus.; 14.5 cm.; p. [7–8] illus. signed *A* [Alexander Anderson]. *See* no. **1163.1** for a description of the format of this booklet. Seven printer's type ornaments are present. The Anderson illustration on p. [7] shows a girl standing beneath the branches of a tree and a seated or crouching Negro to the left of her. The Anderson cut on p. [8] has a central group of a man and a woman and dark shaded figures.
Welch°; CLU; MSaE; MWA; NN-C (t.[1], flaps [2a–2b], p. [2] only); PP; Shaw 23869.

1163.13 [—] ———— Philadelphia: Printed And Sold By Joseph Rakestraw, No. 248, North Third Street. 1811.

t.[1], [2–8] p.; illus.; 14.5 cm. *See* no. **1163.1** for a description of the format of the booklet. Four printer's ornaments are present. The illustrations are printed from the identical blocks employed in no. **1163.12,** without any new defects in the rule borders.
MSaE° (flaps [5a–5b] and p. [6] wanting).

1163.14 [—] ———— Frederick Town, Md. Printed by Matthias Bartgis, 1813.

t.[1], [2–8] p.; illus.; 16 cm.; p. [7–8] illus. *See* no. **1163.1** for a description of the format of this booklet. Nine printer's type ornaments are present. The title vignette and all the illustrations are copied, in the reverse, from no. **1163.16.** The artist did such a careful job of copying that he even reproduced the signature

MICAH. C IV. *4* on the title page vignette. MdHi° (i. st. on p. [7]); MdBE (i. st. on t.[1]); Shaw 29152.

1163.15 [—] —— New-York: Printed by Pelsue and Gould, No. 9 Wall-street. 1813.
t.[1], [2–3], [8] p. only. illus.; 15 cm. *See* no. **1163.1** for a description of the format of this booklet. Nine printer's type ornaments are present. The text and illustrations are probably copies of the Poupard ones in no. **1163.16** or some earlier Philadelphia edition. The title vignette, of an angel or cherub seated on clouds and holding a table, is new. The cut of the three-masted schooner, flying the American flag, appears in this edition, p. [8], and resembles the one later used by Joseph Rakestraw in his Philadelphia edition printed for New York publisher Samuel Wood in 1814, no. **1163.19**. The blocks were used with new border ornaments around the title page and flaps in an edition "Published by Wm. Hazen & Co., Pottersville, Hunterdon Co., N.J. 1875." The cuts present on the missing pages and flaps in no. **1163.15** are present in this edition and were probably the ones used by Pelsue and Gould in 1813.
MWA° (complete); Shaw 29153.

1163.16 [—] —— Philadelphia, Printed By Joseph Rakestraw, No. 256, North Third Street. 1813.
t.[1], [2–8] p.; illus.; 14.5 cm.; p. [7], [8] illus. *See* no. **1163.1** for a description of the format of this booklet. Seven printer's type ornaments are present. The title vignette and the Poupard text illustrations are printed from the same blocks used in no. **1163.12**. Two new oval illustrations appear for the first time in a Philadelphia edition. They were copied in no. **1163.14**. The one on p. [7] shows a man seated with his back to a small hill and facing a horse. On top of the hill is a tree with a long overhanging branch. The illustration on p. [8] includes a man and woman standing in front of a haystack with trees in the background.
MWA° (flaps [4a–5a], [4b–5b], p. [4–7] wanting); Shaw 29721.

1163.17 [—] —— Cheshire, Conn.: Published And Sold By Shelton & Kensett. 1814. Hale & Hosmer, Printers, Hartford.

t.[1], [2–8] p.; illus.; 14.5 cm.; p. [7–8] illus. *See* no. **1163.1** for description of the format of this booklet. Two printer's type ornaments are present. The text illustration are copies of the Poupard ones in no. **1163.16**. There are new illustrations: the title vignette of a vase filled with flowers; a seated woman reading a book, p. [6]; a branch with two roses, two buds, and leaves, p. [7]; a three-masted schooner, p. [8]. CtHi°; MWA; Shaw 32710; Weiss 1932, p. 104.

1163.18 [—] Metamorphosis; oder eine Verwandlung von Bildern, mit einer Auslegung in Versen, zum Vergnügen jungen Leute. Hannover, in Pennsylvanien; Gedruckt bey Stark und Lang. 1814.
t.[1], [2–8] p.; illus.; 15 cm.; p. [7], [8]. *See* no. **1163.1** for a description of the format of this booklet. Nine printer's type ornaments are present. The title vignette signed *MICAH, C. IV. 4* and cuts in the text are copied in the reverse from those in **1163.11**. On p. [7] there is a picture of a wingless cherub seated on a cloud with a lyre. That on p. [8] shows a crossed horn and lyre entwined with flowers. Both cuts are new.
MWA-W°.

1163.19 [—] —— [same as **1163.9**] New-York: Published By Samuel Wood, No 357, Pearl Street. [11 dots] Printed by Joseph Rakestraw, Philadelphia. [9 dots] 1814.
t.[1], [2–8] p. illus.; 14 cm.; p. [7] 9 lines of explanation, p. [8] illus. of a three-masted schooner flying an American flag; "New-York:" on the title page, is 19 mm. long including the colon. *See* no. **1163.1** for a description of the format of this booklet. Eight printer's type ornaments are present. The title vignette shows a column of stone with an urn on top of it. On the side of the column is a carved face with a stream of water coming out of the mouth, and falling into a round bowl in front of the column. Behind the column are shrubs. The cut of the three-masted schooner, p. [8], appears for the first time in a Philadelphia, J. Rakestraw edition.
MWA-W°; CLU (t. [1], p. [2], flaps [2a], [2b] wanting); CtHi; NNMM.

1163.20 [—] —— New-York: Published By Samuel Wood, No. 357, Pearl Street. [11 dots]

Printed by Joseph Rakestraw, Philadelphia. [9 dots] 1814.

t.[1], [2–3], [8] p. only; illus.; 14.5 cm.; p. [7], [8] same as no. **1163.19**; "New-York:" on the title page, 19 mm. long, including the colon. A variant of **1163.19**. The leaf of the title page and p. [2] with its flaps are the same as **1163.19**. The leaf following this, having p. [3] and [8] and flaps [3a], [3b], shows differences in corner ornaments.

CLU* (p. [4–7] wanting).

1163.21 [—] ——— New-York: Published by Samuel Wood, *No. 357, Pearl street.* [no dots] J. Rakestraw, printer, Philadelphia. [9 dots] 1814.

t.[1], [2–8] p.; illus.; 14.5 cm.; p. [7], [8] same as no. **1163.19**; "New-York:" on. t.[1], 19 mm. including the colon. A variant of no. **1163.19** with Samuel Wood's address in italics, not followed by a row of 11 dots, and "J. Rakestraw, printer," is used instead of "Printed by Joseph Rakestraw." The printer's type ornaments and their distribution in borders around the title page, and verses on the flaps and p.[6], [7] are the same as no. **1163.19** with variations in the corner ornaments.

PPL*; NB (b. pl. on t.[1], flap [2b] wanting); NHi.

1163.22 [—] ——— [same as **1163.21**] New-York: Published By Samuel Wood, [no dots] *No. 357, Pearl street.* J. Rakestraw, printer, Philadelphia. 1814.

t.[1], [2–8] p.; illus.; 14.5 cm.; A variant of no. **1163.21**. The book closely matches no. **1163.21**, but has some different corner ornaments.

MWA-W*.

1163.23 [—] ——— New York: Published By Samuel Wood, No. 357, Pearl Street. [no dots] Printed by Joseph Rakestraw, Philadelphia [9 dots] 1814.

t.[1], [2–8] p.; illus.; 14.5 cm.; p. [7], [8] same as in **1163.19**; "New York:", on t.[1], 14 mm. long including the colon. *See* no. **1163.1** for a description of the format of this booklet. The booklet is a variant of no. **1163.19** with "New York:" printed in smaller type and not separated by a dash, no row of 11 dots after "Pearl Street", and "Pearl Street" printed in regular type. The eight printer's type ornaments are the same as in no. **1163.19**, but the corner orna-

ments show variations.

MWA*; Shaw 32711.

1163.24 [—] ——— [same as **1163.23**] New-York: Published by Samuel Wood, No. 357, Pearl Street. Printed by Joseph Rakestraw, Philadelphia. [9 dots]. 1814.

t.[1], [2–8] p.; illus.; 14.5 cm. A variant of no. **1163.23**, with which it is identical, except for certain corner ornaments.

DLC*.

1163.25 [—] ——— Philadelphia: Printed And Sold By Joseph Rakestraw, No. 256, North Third Street. [9 dots] 1814.

t.[1], [2–3], [8] p.; illus.; 14.5 cm.; p. [7], [8] same as no. **1163.19**; "Philadelphia:", on t.[1], 19 mm. long, including the colon; the line "No. 256, North Third Street." is 26.8 mm. long. The book has a similar type setting to no. **1163.19**, with the same illustrations and printer's type ornaments, but with different corner ornaments.

MWA*; PP; Shaw 32712.

1163.26 [—] ——— Philadelphia: Printed And Sold By Joseph Rakestraw, No. 256, North Third Street. 1814.

t.[1], [2–3] p.; only; illus.; 14.5 cm.; p. [8] same as no. **1163.19**; "Philadelphia:", on t.[1], is 24 mm. long including the colon, and the line "No. 256, North Third Street." is 40 mm. long including the period. This variant of no. **1163.21** has the imprint printed in larger type, "Joseph Rakestraw", instead of "J. Rakestraw", and shows differences in the corner ornaments of the decorative borders. The eight printer's type ornaments are those of no. **1163.19**, with the triple-bordered title page identical in both.

KU* (p. [4–7] and flaps wanting).

1163.27 [—] ——— Philadelphia: Printed And Sold By J. Rakestraw, No. 256, North Third Street. [9 dots] 1814.

t.[1], [2–8] p.; illus.; 14 cm.; p. [7], [8] same as no. **1163.19**; "Philadelphia:" on t.[1] 19 mm. long including the colon, the line "No. 256, North Third Street.", measured with the period, is 26.8 mm. long. A variant of no. **1163.25** having the same title page but a different distribution of corner ornaments.

DeWint*.

1163.28 [—] ———— Philadelphia: Printed And Sold By J. Rakestraw, No. 256, North Third street. [9 dots] 1814.

t.[1], [2–8] p.; illus.; 14.5 cm. A variant of no. **1163.27**. The title page is the same as in **1163.27** including the borders of printer's type ornaments. The corner ornaments on the flaps are different.

MWM°; Weiss 1933b.

1163.29 [—] ———— Young Persons. Also, An Alphabet Of Large And Small Letters To Aid Females in Marking Linen, &c. Wilmington [Del.]: Printed And Sold By Robert Porter, No. 97, Market-Street. 1814.

t.[1], [2–8] p.; illus.; 14.5 cm.; p. [7] 6 lines of explanation, p. [8] U. S. seal. *See* no. **1163.1** for a description of the format of this booklet. Six printer's ornaments are present. There is no title vignette. The text illustrations are copies of the Poupard ones in no. **1163.25**, or some earlier Philadelphia edition. All of them are signed *Bowen* [Abel Bowen] except the one on p. [4]. RPB° (p. [4], and flaps [4b], [5b] mut.); MWA; OOxM (flap [2a], [5b] wanting); Shaw 51437.

1163.30 [—] ———— [same as **1163.25**] New-York: Sold By Samuel Wood And Sons, No. 357 Pearl street. Joseph Rakestraw, Printer, Philadelphia. [16 dots] 1815.

t.[1], [2–8] p.; illus.; 14.5 cm.; p. [7], [8] same as no. **1163.19**. *See* no. **1163.1** for a description of the format of this booklet. Eight printer's ornaments are present. The ornaments have the same distribution on the different pages and flaps as in no. **1163.19**, but the corner ornaments are new. The illustrations are the same as in no. **1163.19**.

MWA-W°; NNC-T; PP (1 flap wanting).

1163.31 ———— Philadelphia: Printed And Sold By Joseph Rakestraw, No. 256, North Third Street. [9 dots] 1815.

t.[1], [2–8] p.; illus.; 14.5 cm.; p. [7], [8] same as no. **1163.19**. *See* no. **1163.1** for a description of this booklet. The eight printer's ornaments in no. **1163.19** are use in the borders in the book. Only the corner ornaments show variations. The illustrations are the same as in no. **1163.19** with no new defects.

MWA°; Shaw 35849.

1163.32 [—] [Philadelphia: J. Rakestraw, 1815?].

[2–7] p.; illus.; 14.5 cm. A variant of no. **1163.31** lacking the title page, printed by Joseph Rakestraw for either a Philadelphia or New-York edition. The border of ornaments is the same in both booklets except for two corner ornaments on two flaps.

MWA° (t.[1], p.[2] and flaps wanting).

1163.33 [—] ———— New-York: Sold By Samuel Wood And Sons, *No. 357, Pearl Street*. Printed by J. Rakestraw, Philadelphia. [16 dots] 1816.

t.[1], [2–8] p.; illus.; 14.5 cm.; p. [7], [8] same as no. **1163.19**. *See* no. **1163.1** for a description of the format of this booklet. Eight printer's ornaments are present. The type setting resembles no. **1163.19** with the same illustrations, borders and separating bars of type ornaments. Only the corner ornament formulas differ. The identical blocks used in no. **1163.19** are in this edition without any new marked defects in the ruled borders of the illustrations.

MWA°; MH (t.[1] slightly mut.); PP; Shaw 8871; Weiss 1933b.

1163.34 [—] ———— New-York: Sold By Samuel Wood And Sons, *No. 357, Pearl Street*. Printed by J. Rakestraw, Philadelphia. [16 dots] 1816.

A variant of no. **1163.33**. The book is identical with no. **1163.25** in every way and differs only in the corner ornament formula in the double border on p. [7].

MWA-T°; CLU°; MSaE.

1163.35 [—] ———— New-York: Sold by Samuel Wood And Sons, *No. 357, Pearl Street*. Printed by J. Rakestraw, Philadelphia. [16 dots] 1817.

t.[1], [2–8] p. illus.; 14.5 cm.; p. [7], [8] same as no. **1163.19**. *See* no. **1163.1** for a description of the format of this booklet. The illustrations and the borders of type ornaments, and separating bars are the same as no. **1163.33**, with some corner ornaments showing differences.

MWA°; Shaw 42048.

1163.36 [—] ———— Philadelphia: Printed And Sold By J. Rakestraw, *No. 256, North Third Street*. [16 dots] 1818.

t.[1], [2–8] p.; illus.; 14.5 cm.; p. [7], [8] same as no. **1163.19**. *See* no. **1163.1** for a description of the format of this booklet. The illustrations are the same as in no. **1163.35**. The printer's ornaments on the borders and separating bars are the same as no. **1163.35**, except one ornament on the title page is not used and the corner ornaments show variations.

NjR°; Shaw 44824.

1163.37 [—] [———— Philadelphia: J. Rakestraw, 1818?].

[4–7] p. flaps [4a–5b] only. A variant of no. **1163.36**, lacking the title page, printed by Joseph Rakestraw for either a Philadelphia or New-York edition. It has the same border ornaments and corner ornament formulas as no. **1163.36**, except flap [5a] recto and p. [7].

MWA° (t.[1], p. [2–3], [8] and flaps [2a–3a], [2b–3b] wanting, flap [4b] found with another edition, was attached to this edition, because it is the same as no. **1163.36** and probably belonged to it).

1163.38 [—] ——— New-York: Sold By Samuel Wood And Sons, *No. 261, Pearl Street.* Printed by J. Rakestraw, Philadelphia. [11 dots] 1819.

t.[1], [2–8] p.; illus.; 14.5 cm.; [7], [8] same as no. **1163.19**. *See* no. **1163.1** for a description of the format of this booklet. The illustrations and printer's type ornaments in the borders are the same as in no. **1163.36**. The corner ornaments are changed.

MWA-W° (2 copies); MH; NhD; Shaw 44824.

1163.39 [—] ——— New-York: Sold By Samuel Wood And Sons, No. 261, Pearl Street. Printed by J. Rakestraw, Philadelphia. [11 dots] 1820.

t.[1], [2–8] p.; illus.; 14.5 cm.; p. [7], [8] same as no. **1163.19**. *See* no. **1163.1** for a description of the format of this booklet. The illustrations are printed from the same blocks used in no. **1163.38**. The eight printer's ornaments and their distribution in borders are those of no. **1163.19**. MWA-T° (flaps [2b], [4b] wanting); MB° (per. st. on t.[1]); Shoemaker 2247.

SAVAGE, SARAH 1784–1837
1164 [—] THE FACTORY GIRL. By A Lady. [2 lines quot.] Boston: Published By Munroe, Francis & Parker, No. 4, Cornhill. 1814.

t.[1], [2–3], 4–112 p.; 14 cm.; bound in pr. yellow paper over bds.; cover title dated 1815. MWA°; CtY; MNF; Shaw 32719.

1165 [—] FILIAL AFFECTION. Or The Clergyman's Granddaughter. A Moral Tale. By The Author Of The Factory Girl. [4 lines of quot.] Boston: Published By Cummings And Hilliard. 1820.

t.[1], [2–5], 6–162 p.; 15 cm.; bound in brown paper over bds., leather spine. MWA°; Shoemaker 3113.

THE SCHOOL OF GOOD MANNERS. *See* Green, William, no. **468**.

THE SCHOOL OF GOOD MANNERS. *See* Moodey, Eleazer, no. **871.1**.

1166 THE SCHOOL: Or, A Present From A Preceptress To Her Pupils, On The First Of January 1813. By A Lady Of Boston. Boston: Published By Thomas B. Wait And Co. 1813.

fr.[2], t.[3], [4–5], 6–34 p.; illus.; 13.5 cm.; orange marbled paper covers. MWA° (fr.[2] wanting); PP; Shaw 29733.

SCOLFIELD, WILLIAM
1167.1 — BIBLE STORIES. Memorable Acts Of The Ancient Patriarchs, Judges And Kings: Extracted From Their Original Historians. For The Use Of Children. By William Scolfield. In Two Volumes. Vol. I. [II.] London, Printed: Albany, Re-Printed By Charles R. And George Webster, At Their Bookstore. 1803.

vol. I.: t.[i], [ii–iii], iv–xiii, [xiv, bl.], [15], 16–173, [174, bl.] p.; vol. II.: t.[1], [2–3], 4–162, [163–164, contents] p.; 2 vols. in 1; 15 cm.; bound in leather.

English ed. London: 2 vols. R. Phillips; Benj. Tabart, 1802. MWA°; N; Shaw 5025.

1167.2 — ——— William Scolfield. Philadelphia: Printed By Thomas And Wm. Bradford, No. 8, South Front Street. 1803.

fr.[ii], t.[iii], [iv, bl.], [i], ii–ix, [x, bl.], [xi–xiv, contents], [1], 2–200 p.; 2 pl. including front.; t.[i] 13.5 cm.; colophon p. 200: Thomas & William Bradford, Printers. RNHi° (rebound, emb. st. on t.[i]); MB (per. st. on t.[i], rebound pl. opp. p. 198 wanting); Shaw 5026.

1167.3 — ——— By William Scolfield. Philadelphia: Printed For Jacob Johnson, Book-Seller, No. 147, Market Street. 1803.

fr.[ii], t.[iii], [iv, bl.], [i], ii–ix, [x, bl.], [xi–xiv, contents]. [1], 2–200 p.; 2 pl. including front.; 14.5 cm.; blue marbled paper over bds., leather spine; colophon p. 200: Thomas & William Bradford, Printers.
MWA-W*.

1167.4 —— —— For The Use Of Children. By William Scolfield. New-York: Printed And Sold By Isaac Collins And Son, No. 189, Pearl-Street. 1804.
t.[i], [ii], [1], 2–12, [1], 2–257, [258–261, contents] p.; t.[1] 13 cm.
NN* (rebound, per st. on t.[i]); Shaw 5846.

1167.5 —— —— For The Use Of Schools. By William Scolfield. Wilmington [Del.]: Printed For Mathew R. Lockerman, Robert Porter, Printer. 1812.
t.[i], [ii–iii], iv–xi, [xii–xvi], [17], 18–216 p.; 15 cm.; bound in leather.
DLC*; DeHi (2 copies); DeU; DeWi (per. st. on t.[i] & p.[17]); Shaw 26701.

1168 Scriptural Stories, For Very Young Children. By the Author of "The Decoy, Natural History of Quadrupeds," &c. With Elegant Wood-Cuts. London Printed. Philadelphia Re-Printed: For Kimber And Conrad, No. 93, Market-Street. 1814.
fr.[2], t.[3], [4–5], 6–68 p.; illus.; 14 cm.; yellow paper covers. Part of a large publisher's remainder.
Welch*; CtHi; CtY; MiD; MWA; NhD (covers wanting); NHi; NN; PP; PPL; Shaw 32733.

1169.1 Scripture History. [2 lines quot.] Printed & sold by Samuel Wood, at the Juvenile Book-store No. 357, [Pear]l-Street. New-York. 1810.
t.[1], [2–16] p.; illus.; 8 cm.
MSaE* (covers wanting).

1169.2 —— New-York: Printed & sold by Samuel Wood, at the Juvenile Book-store, No. 357, Pearl Street. 1811.
t.[1], [2–16], p.; illus.; 8 cm.; Dutch paper covers. Adv. by S. Wood, 1812 in **1188.3.**
MWA*; CLU; Shaw 23903.

1169.3 —— New-York: Printed & sold by Samuel Wood, at the Juvenile Book store, No. 357, Pearl-street. 1814.

t.[1], [2–16] p.; illus.; 8 cm.; yellow wallpaper covers.
MWA*; NB.

1169.4 —— Nerv-York [*sic. i.e.* New-York]: Printed And Sold By Samuel Wood & Sons, at the Juvenile Book-store, No. 357, Pearl-street. 1815.
t.[1], [2–16] p.; illus.; 8 cm.; pr. & illus. yellow-buff paper covers.
Cover title: Scripture History. Sold by Samuel Wood & Sons, New-York.
OOxM*; FTaSU; Shaw 3856.

1169.5 —— New-York: Printed And Sold By Samuel Wood & Sons, At the Juvenile Book-store, No. 357, Pearl-street. 1816.
t.[1], [2–16] p.; illus.; 7.5 cm.; pr. & illus. paper covers. Cover title imprint: Sold by Samuel Wood & Sons, New-York.
MWA*; PP; Shaw 38902.

1169.6 —— Nerv-York [*sic. i.e.* New-York]: Published by Samuel Wood & Sons, No. 261, Pearl-street, And Samuel S. Wood & Co., No. 212, Market-st. Baltimore. 1818.
t.[1], [2–16] p.; illus.; 8 cm.; pr. & illus. paper covers. Cover title imprint of copy 1: Sold by Samuel Wood & Sons. Nerv-York [*sic. i.e.* New York], And Samuel S. Wood & Co. Baltimore. Cover title imprint copy 2: Sold by Samuel Wood & Sons, New York.
MWA* (copy 1, 2); CtHi; MSaE; Shaw 45674 and 45675.

1170 Scripture History, Abridged. In which it is designed to give Children Such a taste of the writings of the inspired penmen, as may engage them diligently to Study The Sacred Scriptures. Ornamented with cuts. [woodcut] "Search the Scriptures." Boston: Printed and sold by Lincoln & Edmands, No. 53, Cornhill. 1819.
fr.[2], t.[3], [4–5], 6–70, [71] p.; illus.; 14.5 cm.; pr. & illus. green paper covers; cover title dated 1819.
MWA-W*; CCamarSJ; CtHi; DLC; NB; PP; PPL; Shaw 49386 and 49387.

1171.1 The Seasons. [4 lines of verse] New York: Printed And Sold By S. Wood, At The Juvenile Book-Store, No. 357, Pearl-Street. 1810.

t.[1], [2–3], 4–44, [45, adv.] p.; illus.; 12.5 cm.; pr. & illus. paper covers; cover title dated 1809. This book includes the text and cuts of Samuel Wood's *Spring*, no. **1125**; *Summer*, no. **1277.1**; *Autumn*, no. **52.1**; and *Winter*, no. **1439.1**.
MWA°; MSaE; PP; Shaw 21315.

1171.2 ———— New York: Printed And Sold By S. Wood, At The Juvenile Book-Store, No. 357, Pearl-Street. 1811.
t.[1], [2–3], 4–44, [45, adv.] p.; illus.; 12 cm.; pr. & illus. buff paper covers; cover date 1811.
MWA°; CLU; CtY (cover title dated 1811; t.[1] & p.[2] wanting); Shaw 23907.

1171.3 ———— New-York: Printed And Sold By S. Wood, At the Juvenile Book-Store, No. 357, Pearl-street. 1812.
t.[1], [2–3], 4–44, [45, adv.] p.; illus.; 12 cm.; pr. & illus. buff paper covers.
CtHi° (p.[45] mut.); NHi.

1171.4 ———— New-York: Printed And Sold By Samuel Wood, At The Juvenile Book-Store, No. 357, Pearl-Street. 1814.
t.[1], [2–3], 4–44 p.; illus.; 13 cm.
MWA° (original covers wanting); CLU; CtY (bound with other books, p. 7–38 wanting); PP (bound with other books); Shaw 32736.

1171.5 ———— New York: Printed And Sold By S. Wood & Sons, At The Juvenile Book-Store, No. 357, Pearl-Street. 1815.
t.[1], [2–3], 4–43 [44, adv.] p.; illus.; 12 cm.; illus. buff paper covers; cover title undated.
MWA°; MB; MH; RPB; Shaw 35886.

1171.6 ———— New-York: Printed And Sold By S. Wood & Sons, At The Juvenile Book-Store, No. 357, Pearl-Street. 1816.
t.[1], [2–5], 6–44, [45, adv.] p.; illus.; 12 cm.; pr. & illus. yellow-buff paper covers.
DLC°; MH; Shaw 38908.

THE SECOND CHAPTER OF ACCIDENTS. *See* Darton, William, no. **258.1**.

1172 THE SECOND SPIRA: Or The Blaspaemers Justly Reproved. To which is added, A Sermon, Which was preached on that occasion. From Parks' Press. Montpelier, Vt. 1808.

t.[3], [4–5], 6–13 p.; 9 cm.; pr. paper covers.
MWA°.

1173.1 SELECT FABLES, IN PROSE AND VERSE. [8 lines quot.] Moore. New-York: Printed And Sold By Samuel Wood, At The Juvenile Book Store, No. 357, Pearl-Street. 1811.
t.[3], [4–5], 6–50 p.; illus.; 13 cm.; pr. & illus. buff paper covers; p. 45 numbered "54".
MWA°; RPB; Shaw 23909.

1173.2 ———— New-York: Printed And Sold By S. Wood, At The Juvenile Book-Store, No. 357, Pearl-Street. 1812.
t.[3], [4–5], 6–50 p.; illus.; 13.5 cm.; pr. & illus. buff-brown paper covers.
MWA-W° (rear paper cover wanting).

1173.3 ———— New-York: Printed And Sold By Samuel Wood, At The Juvenile Book-Store, No. 357, Pearl-Street. 1814.
t.[1], [2–3], 4–48 p.; illus.; 13.5 cm.; pr. & illus. yellow paper covers; cover title dated 1814.
MWA°; CaOTP; CtHi; ICU, NHi; NN (2 copies varying covers); NNC—T (emb. st. on t.[1]); PP; PPL; Shaw 32738; Weiss 1936, p. 644.

1173.4 ———— New-York: Printed And Sold By Samuel Wood; At The Juvenile Book-Store, No. 357, Pearl-Street. 1815.
t.[1], [2–3], 4–48 p.; illus.; 14 cm.
NHi° (bound with other books); PP.

1173.5 ———— New-York: Printed And Sold By Samuel Wood & Sons, At The Juvenile Book-Store, No. 357, Pearl-Street. 1817.
t.[1], [2–3], 4–48 p.; illus.; 13.5 cm.; pr. & illus. paper covers. Cover title imprint: Printed And Sold By Samuel Wood, At The Juvenile Book-Store, No. 357, Pearl-Street, New-York.
MWA°; MSaE; Shaw 42086.

1173.6 ———— [3 lines quot.] Cooperstown [N.Y.]: Printed and sold by H. & E. Phinney. 1819.
fr.[2], t.[3], [4–5], 6–29, [30, adv.] p.; illus.; 10 cm.; pr. & illus. brown paper covers.
MWA-W°.

1174 SELECT PIECES FROM SCRIPTURE. Philadelphia: adv. by Wm Charles, 1808 in **231.1**.

1175 SELECT RHYMES, AND AMUSING POEMS, FOR CHILDREN. Newburyport [Mass.]: Printed By W. & J. Gilman. Sold at their Book and Stationery Store, Middle-Street [5 dots] 1810.

t.[1], [2–3], 4–36 p.; illus.; 13 cm.; paper covers.
MSaE°.

SELECT RHYMES FOR THE NURSERY. *See* Gilbert, Mrs. Ann (Taylor), & Jane Taylor, no. **448.1.**

1176 SELECT VERSES FOR LITTLE MASTERS AND MISSES; Ornamented With Alphabetical Cuts; New-York: Printed by William Durell, No. 198, Queen Street. M,DCCXC.

fr.[2], t.[3], [4–27] p.; illus.; 10 cm.; illus. white paper covers.
CtHi°; MWA (fr.[2], & p.[21–22], [27], and covers wanting); Evans 22883.

1177 SELECT VERSES FOR LITTLE MASTERS AND MISSES. Ornamented With Cuts. Hartford: Printed by Charles Hosmer. 1815.

fr.[ii], t.[3], [4, alphabet], 6 [*sic. i.e.* 5], [6], 7–26, 28 [*sic. i.e.* 27], 29 [*sic. i.e.* 28], 30 [*sic. i.e.* 29], 29 [*sic. i.e.* 30], 31 p.; illus.; 10 cm.; pr. & illus. buff paper covers; cover title undated. Except for the verses below the frontispiece this is a different book from no. **1176.**
MWA°; CSmH; Shaw 35894.

1178.1 A SELECTION OF BIBLE LESSONS, With Reflections On Each Subject, Adapted To The Capacity Of Children. [2 lines of quot.] By A Friend To Sabbath Schools. Hartford: Printed By G. Goodwin & Sons, And for sale by them: also, by Howe & Spaulding, and J. Babcock & Son, New-Haven: Simeon Butler, Northampton: and Oliver Goodwin, Litchfield. Price 12 1–2 cents single, $1 12 1–2 per doz. and $7 50 per hund. 1820.

fr.[2], t.[3], [4–6], 7–72 p.; illus.; 14.5 cm.; unprinted paper covers.
MWA°; CtHi; CCamarSJ; DLC; RPB; Shoemaker 3165.

1178.2 ——— Schools. Second Edition. Hartford: Printed By G. Goodwin & Sons, And for sale by them: also, by Howe & Spalding, and J. Babcock & Son, New-Haven: Simeon Butler, Northampton: and Oliver Goodwin, Litchfield. < Price 12 1–2 cents single, $12 1–2 per dozen and $7 50 per hun. > 1820.

fr.[2], t.[3], [4–6], 7–72 p.; illus. 14.5 cm.
CtHi° (fr.[2] mut.); MWA; PP; Shoemaker 3166.

1179 A SELECTION OF HYMNS, FOR INFANT MINDS. Boston: Printed By Sylvester T. Goss. 1820.

t.[1], [2], 3–40 p.; title vignette only illus.; 8.5 cm.; paper covers.
MWA°; PP (covers wanting); Shoemaker 3167.

1180.1 A SELECTION OF HYMNS; INCLUDING DR. WATT'S DIVINE SONGS, Suited To The Capacities Of Children. [1 line quot.] Philadelphia: Printed by Thomas and William Bradford, No. 8, South Front Street. 1812.

t.[1], [2–3], 4–64 p.; 10.5 cm.; marbled paper covers.
ICU°.

1180.2 ——— New-York: Published by Dodge & Sayre, No. 242 Pearl Street. 1814.

t.[1], [2–3], 4–64 p.; 10.5 cm.; buff paper covers; p.[2]: Printed by D. & G. Bruce, Slote-lane.
OOxM°; Shaw 32742.

1181 A SELECTION OF MISCELLANEOUS PIECES, In Verse And Prose. Respectfully Dedicated To The Youth Of Both Sexes. Part I. Philadelphia: Printed And Sold By Daniel Lawrence, No. 78, North 4th Street, Near Race. M.DCC.XCIII.

t.[i], [ii], [1], 2–80, [81–82] p.; 16 cm.; bound in red scalloped marbled paper over bds.; p. 55 caption title: Miscellaneous Pieces In Prose Part II.
NN°; DLC; MiU; PHi; PP; Evans 24777.

1182 A SELECTION OF NEW TESTAMENT STORIES AND PARABLES. For The Use Of Children. Windsor [Vt.]: Published by Merrifield & Cochran. Sold, wholesale and retail at their Bookstore, sign of the Bible. 1811.

t.[1], [2–3], 4–58 p.; 12.5 cm.; blue marbled paper covers.
MWA-W°; McCorison 1262; Shaw 22381.

1183 A SELECTION OF POEMS, FOR YOUNG CHILDREN. Philadelphia, Printed By Meyer & Jones. 1810.

t.[1], [2–3], 4–40 p.; illus.; 17 cm.; paper covers.
MWA° (front cover wanting); Shaw 21321.

SELLON, WILLIAM

1184 — An Abridgement Of The Holy Scrip-
tures. By The Rev. Mr. Sellon, Late Minister Of
St. James's, Clerkenwell. [3 lines quot.] Hartford:
Printed and sold by Hale & Hosmer. 1813.

t.[i], [ii–iii], iv–ix, [x, bl.], [1], 2–215, [216,
bl.], [217–218, adv. list of books] p.; 14 cm.;
bound in leather.
English ed. London: 1781.
MWA°; CtW; CtY; DLC; MB; NN (per st.
on t.[i]); Shaw 29770.

1185 — A Concise History Of The Holy
Scriptures. By William Sellon. First American
Edition; Corrected And Enlarged. Philadelphia:
Published By Joseph Sharpless, No. 4, Franklin-
Court, (Market-Street, Between Third And Fourth
Streets, South Side.) J. Rakestraw, printer. 1813.

t.[i], [ii–iii], iv–xii, [13], 14–223 p.; 18 cm.;
bound in leather.
MWA°; Shaw 29771.

Seraphina, *See* Mercier, Louis Sebastian, no.
841.1.

1186 Serious Soliloquies, Interspersed With
Hymns; To Which Are Added, Anecdotes For The
Instruction And Entertainment Of Children. Bos-
ton: Printed By Sewell Phelps, No. 5, Court
Street. 1819.

t.[1], [2–3], 4–24 p.; 17 cm.
MWA° (covers wanting); Shaw 49398.

1187 Set of Flowers, Alphabetically Ar-
ranged, For Little Children. [cut] Yellow-Lupin.
New-York: Published By Samuel Wood & Sons,
No. 261, Pearl-Street, And Samuel S. Wood &
Co. No. 212, Market-st. Baltimore. 1819.

t.[1], 2–24 p.; illus.; 12.5 cm.; pr. & illus. paper
covers; cover title imprint: *Nerv-York* [*sic. i.e.
New-York*]:——— & Sons, And Samuel S.
Wood & Co. Baltimore.
MWA°; CtY; OOxM; PP; Shaw 49401.

The Seven Champions Of Christendom. *See*
Johnson, Richard, no. **668.1.**

The Seven Wise Master's Of Rome. *See* The
History Of The Seven Wise Master's Of Rome,
no. **591.1.**

The Seven Wise Mistresses Of Rome. *See* Howard, Thomas, no. **617.1.**

1188.1 The Seven Wonders Of The World.
and other magnificent buildings, &c. [1 line quot.]
Eccl. 1, 2. New-York: Printed And Sold By S.
Wood, At The Juvenile Book-Store, No. 357
Pearl-Street. [2 rows of 10 dots] 1810.

t.[1], [2–3], 4–42, [43, adv. list of books] p.;
illus.; 12.5 cm.; pr. & illus. buff paper covers;
cover title dated 1809.
Welch°; MWA; PP.

1188.2 ——— *NEW-YORK:* Printed And Sold
By S. Wood, At The Juvenile Book-Store, No. 357,
Pearl-Street. [2 rows of 10 dots.] 1810.

t.[1], [2–3], 4–42 [43, adv. of 30 books] p.;
illus.; 13 cm.; pr. & illus.; yellow paper covers.
On t.[1] there is a semicolon after "World;".
Cover title: The Seven Wonders Of The World.
NEW-YORK: Printed ——— [same as t.[1]],
[1 row of 9 dots] 1811.
MWA-T° (the lower ¼ of p. 21–24 wanting);
Weiss 1942, p. 770.

1188.3 ——— New-York: Printed And Sold By
S. Wood, At the Juvenile Book-Store, No. 357,
Pearl-street. [a row of 10 dots] 1812.

t.[1], [2–3], 4–42, [43, adv. list of books] p.;
illus.; 12 cm.; pr. & illus. buff-brown paper
covers; cover title imprint below a cut of a
ship: ——— [same as t.[1]] Pearl-street. [a
row of 11 dots] 1812.
Welch°; MWA; NHi; PP (p. [43] & covers
wanting); Shaw 26721.

1188.4 ——— Otsego [N.Y.] Printed by H. &
E. Phinney, Jun. 1812.

t.[1], [2–3], 4–41, [42, bl.], [43, adv.] p.; illus.;
12.5 cm.; illus. blue-gray paper covers.
PP° (covers wanting except for ½ of rear cover).

1188.5 ——— New-York: Printed And Sold By
Samuel Wood, At The Juvenile Book-Store, No.
357, Pearl-Street. 1814.

t.[1], [2–3], 4–42, [43–44, adv. list of books]
p.; illus.; 12.5 cm.; pr. & illus. yellow paper
covers; cover title imprint below cut of a branch
of a pea plant: New-York: ——— [same as
1188.3] Pearl-street. [a row of 10 dots] 1812.
MWA°; MH (i. st. on t.[1], cover title dated
1814); NjR; PP (covers wanting, bound with
other books); Shaw 32751.

1188.6 ———— *Nerv-York* [*sic. i.e.* New-York]: Printed And Sold By Samuel Wood, At The Juvenile Book-Store, No. 357, Pearl-street. 1815.

t.[1], [2–3], 4–42, [43–44, adv. list of books] p.; illus.; 12.5 cm.; pr. & illus. paper covers; cover title imprint: Printed ———— Pearl-Street. New-York.

MWA°; CtY (cover title dated 1814); Shaw 35905.

1188.7 ———— New-York: Printed And Sold By S. Wood & Sons, At The Juvenile Book-Store, No. 357, Pearl-Street. 1816.

t.[1], [2–3], 4–42, [43–45, adv. list of books] p.; illus.; 13 cm.; pr. & illus. buff paper covers. Cover title imprint of MWA-W copy: ———— Book-Store, No. 261, Pearl-Street, *Nerv-York* [*sic. i.e.* New York]. Cover title imprint of MWA copy: ———— [same as title but dated 1814].

MWA-W°; DLC (front cover mut.); MWA; PP (covers wanting); Shaw 38915 and 38916.

1188.8 ———— New-York: Published By Samuel Wood & Sons, No. 261, Pearl-Street; And Samuel S. Wood & Co. No. 212, Market-st. Baltimore. 1819.

t.[1], [2–3], 4–42, [43–45, adv. list of books] p.; illus.; 12.5 cm.; pr. & illus. brownish-buff paper covers. Cover title imprint: *Nerv-York* [*sic. i.e.* New-York]: ———— Sons, And Samuel S. Wood & Co. Baltimore.

MWA-W°; DLC; NjN; OOxM; Shaw 49402.

[SEWALL, SAMUEL] 1652–1730

1189.1 [—] EARLY PIETY, EXEMPLIFIED IN ELIZABETH BUTCHER OF BOSTON: Who was born *June* 14th. 1709. And Died *July* 13th. 1718. Being Just Eight Years & Eleven Months Old. The Third Edition. [3 lines quot.] Boston Printed by S. *Knee-land,* for *Samuel Gerrish,* and Sold at his Shop near the Old Meeting House. 1725.

t.[i], [ii, bl.], i–iv, 1–18 p.; 14.5 cm. The end of the preface, p. iv, is signed *Joseph Sewall. Boston, August 20th 1719.* Evans 1973, an unlocated edition of 1718, is open to question since the above preface is dated 1719. The second edition of 1719, Evans 2038, also unlocated, is a more probable edition. The first edition could have been printed in 1719. According to EAI this 1719 edition "is assumed from an entry in Judge Sewall's diary. See Holmes. Cot-

ton Mather, 1, 285." The authorship is also based on Holmes. On p. 18 a mss. inscription: *Elizabeth Allyn her Book given to her by Mary Mather.*

MWA-T° (no covers).

1189.2 [—] Early Piety: Exemplified ———— [same as **1189.1**] The Fourth Edition. ———— Boston: Printed by J. Draper, for C. Harrison over against the Brazen-Head in Cornhill. M,DCC,XLI.

t.[i], [ii, bl.], i–iv, 1–17, [18, adv.] p.; 13 cm. MWA°; PPL; Evans 5008.

[SHARPE, RICHARD SCRAFTON] d. 1752

1190 [—] OLD FRIENDS IN A NEW DRESS; Or, Familiar Fables In Verse. [cut] See page 15. Philadelphia: Published By Jacob Johnson, No. 147, Market-Street. 1808.

fr.[2], t.[3], [4–5], 6–46, [47, 2 cuts] p.; illus.; 14 cm.; pr. & illus. paper covers; front cover undated. Adv. by Johnson & Warner, 1809 in **212.2**, and 1814 in **1449.3**.

English ed. London: W. And T. Darton, 1807. MnU; NNC-Pl; PPL; RPB (bound with other books); Shaw 15798.

SHAKESPEARE, WILLIAM. *See* ENTERTAINING STORIES OF KING LEAR AND HIS DAUGHTERS, no. **365**, and Lamb, Charles, no. **744**.

SHARPLESS, JOSEPH

1191.1 — THE STORY OF JOSEPH AND HIS BRETHREN, Set Forth In A Pleasing And Instructive Manner; And Adapted To the capacities of Children. By Joseph Sharpless. Frankford, Penn. Published By The Author. 1812. Joseph Rakestraw, Printer.

1st t.[i], [ii–iii], iv, [5], 6–113, [114]; 2nd t.[115], [116–117], 118–119 p.; 3 pl.; 5 cm.

2nd title: Patient Joe; Or The Newcastle collier. Frankfort, Penn. Published By Joseph Sharpless. 1812. *Patient Joe* is by Hannah More. MWA°; CLU; CSmH; DLC; PP; PSt; Shaw 26238 and 26724.

1191.2 ———— Sharpless. Second Edition. Corrected. Philadelphia: Published By The Author. Merritt, Printer. 1814.

1st t.[i], [ii–iii], iv, [5], 6–113, [114]; 2nd t.[115], [116–117], 118–119 p.; 14.5 cm.; bound in leather.

2nd title: Patient Joe, Or, The Newcastle Collier. Philadelphia: Published By Joseph Sharpless. 1814. *Patient Joe* is by Hannah More.

MWA°; PHi; RNHi; Shaw 32160 and 32754.

1191.3 — —— Philadelphia: Published By The Author. Merritt, Printer. 1814.

1st t[i], [ii-iii], iv, [5], 6–113, [114]; 2nd t.[115], [116–117], 118–119; 3rd t.[i], [ii–iii], iv, [5], 6–107 p.; 15 cm.

3rd title: Bunyan's Pilgrim's Progress, Versified; For The Entertainment And Instruction Of Youth. By George Burder, Author Of Village Sermons, &c. With Other Poems Subjoined. Philadelphia: Published By Joseph Sharpless. Merritt, Printer. 1814. A variant of the preceding edition having Burder's *Bunyan's Pilgrims Progress Versified*, no. **136.4**, bound at the rear of the book.

MWA°; Shaw 32755.

1192 THE SHEPHERD AND HIS FLOCK. [3 lines quot.] Portland [Me.]: Published By William Hyde. A. Shirley, Printer. 1820. [cover title].

illus. [2], [3], 4, [5], 6–35 p.; front. only illus.; 14.5 cm.; pr. brownish-buff paper covers; p. "5" is not struck in the Welch copy, but is present in MWA copy.

English ed. London: 2 ed. 1813.

Welch°; MWA; Shoemaker 3200.

SHERWOOD, MRS. MARY MARTHA (BUTT)
1775–1851

1193.1 — THE HEDGE OF THORNS. By Mrs. Sherwood, Author of "The History of the Fairchild Family, Little Henry, and his Bearer," &c. Nerv-York [*sic. i.e.* New-York]: Published By Samuel Wood & Sons, No. 261, Pearl-Street; And Samuel S. Wood & Co., No. 212, Market-st. Baltimore. 1820.

fr.[ii], t.[1], [2–5], 6–87, [88, adv. list of books] p.; 15 cm.; bound in gray-green paper over bds., red leather spine. The type ornament above the words Nerv–York: [*sic.*] is 2.5 cm. long. The word "Thorns" in the title is printed with white letters outlined by their lines. Front. signed: *Scoles sculp.* [John Scoles].

English ed. London: J. Hatchard, 1819.

Welch°; CLU; MWA; PPL.

1193.2 — —— Nerv-York: [*sic. i.e.* New-York]: Published By Samuel Wood & Sons, No.

261, Pearl-Street; And Samuel S. Wood & Co., No. 212, Market-street, Baltimore. 1820.

Varied issue with a different type setting from the preceding. The ornament above Nerv-York: [*sic.*] is 10 mm. long, instead of 20 mm. long. The word "Thorns" is printed in solid black letters instead of white. In the imprint the word "street" is spelled out in "Market-street."

MWA°; MB (per. st. on t.[1]); Shoemaker 3204.

1193.3 — —— Philadelphia: Published By The Sunday & Adult School Union. Clark & Raser, Printers. 1820.

90 p.

Shoemaker 3205.

1194.1 — THE HISTORY OF EMILY AND HER BROTHERS. By Mrs. Sherwood, Author of "Little Henry and his Bearer," First American Edition. Philadelphia: Published By The Sunday & Adult School Union. Clark & Raser, Printers. 1819.

t.[1], [2–3], 4–32 p.; 9.5 cm.; pr. blue-gray paper covers.

MWA°; Shaw 49411.

1194.2 — —— Bearer," etc. Second American Edition. Philadelphia: Published By The Sunday & Adult School Union. Clark & Raser, Printers. 1820.

t.[1], [2–3], 4–32 p.; 10 cm.; pr. blue-gray paper covers.

DLC°; Shoemaker 3206.

1195 — THE HISTORY OF LITTLE GEORGE AND HIS PENNY. By Mrs Sherwood, Author of "Little Henry and His Bearer." Portland [Me.]: Published By William Hyde, And for sale at his Bookstore, No. 3, Mussey's Row, Middle-street. 1820.

fr.[2], t.[3], [4–5], 6–31 p.; illus.; 10.5 cm.; pr. & illus. brown paper covers; cover title undated; colophon p. 31: A. Shirley, Printer. *See Little George And His Penny*, no. **1198**.

MWA° (p. 31 mut.); CtY; Shoemaker 3207.

1196.1 [—] THE HISTORY OF LITTLE HENRY AND HIS BEARER. From the second London Edition. Andover [Mass.]: Published By Mark Newman. Flagg & Gould printers. 1817.

fr. [ii], t.[1], [2–3], 4–86 p.; front. only illus.; 14.5 cm.; bound in pr. buff paper over w. bds.; front. signed *Bowen S.* [John Bowen].

English ed. Wellington: F. Houlston and Sons. 1814.

MWA-W°; MSaE; NNC-Pl; Shaw 41051 and 42109.

1196.2 [—] ——— Bearer. Second American, From the Second London Edition. Hartford: Hudson And Co. Printers. 1817.

t.[1], [2–3], 4–32 p.; 16.5 cm.; blue paper covers.

MWA-W°; CtHi; CtY; DLC; Shaw 41052 and 42110.

1196.3 [—] ——— Second American Edition. Middlebury, Vt. Published By F. Burnap. 1817.

t.[1], [2–3], 4–64 p.; 11.5 cm.; marbled paper covers.

MWA°; CLU; MiU; Vt (per st. on t.[1]); VtHi (rebound); McCorison 1953; Shaw 42111.

1196.4 [—] ——— The second Andover Edition. Andover [Mass.]: Published By Mark Newman. Flagg & Gould [3 dots] printers. 1818.

fr.[2], t.[3], [4–5], 6–72 p.; front. only illus.; 14 cm.; pr. gray-green paper covers.

MWA°; KU; MLuHi; MSaE; Shaw 44332 and 45702.

1196.5 [—] ——— His Bearer. This little book, now re-published, was sent by Mrs. Bardwell to her mother, and contains an interesting history of facts, which occurred in the Eastern World, and furnishes ample proof of the usefulness of Female Missionaries. Boston: Printed & sold by Lincoln & Edmands, No. 53 Cornhill. 1818.

t.[1], [2], 3–36 p.; title vignette only illus.; 14.5 cm.; pr. & illus. blue-gray paper covers. Copy A, cut of a manor house on the front cover, the same one used by Samuel Hall [1801?] in *The History Of Master Jackey And Miss Harriot*, no. **568.9.** Copy B has a cut of a ship on the front cover.

Welch° (A); DLC; MH; MWA (A, B); NN (covers wanting; p. 35–36 mut.); OClW-LS; RP; Shaw 44333 and 45703.

1196.6 [—] ——— Bearer. Third American Edition. Catskill [N.Y.]: Published By Nathan Elliott. Croswell & Son, Printers. 1818.

t.[1], [2–3], 4–54 p.; 14 cm.; pr. green paper covers; p. 49 printed correctly. In CtY copy p. 49 is incorrectly printed "48".

MWA°; CaOTP; CCamarSJ; CLU; CSmH; CtHi; CtY; DLC; MiD; N; NHi; NN (2 copies, 1 copy bound with other books); PHi; PP; PPL; Shaw 44334 and 45704; Weiss 1936, p. 335.

1196.7 [—] ——— Third American Edition. New-Haven: Printed At Sidney's Press, For John Babcock & Son. 1818.

t.[1], [2–3], 4–48 p.; 14 cm.; pr. buff paper covers.

Cover title: The India Orphan, Or The History Of Little Henry And His Bearer. New-Haven: Printed At Sidney's Press. 1818.

MWA°; CtY (2 copies: copy 1, rebound; copy 2, rear cover wanting); OOxM; Shaw 45706.

1196.8 [—] ——— Second American Edition. New-Haven: Published By Nathan Whiting. 1818.

[i, adv.], [ii, bl.], t.[1], [2–3], 4–48 p.; 14 cm.; pr. pink paper covers; cover title dated 1818.

CtHi°; CtY (p.[i–ii] absent); DLC (p.[i–ii] absent); Shaw 45705.

1196.9 [—] ——— Bearer. Portland [Me.]: Published by Wm. & H. Hyde, And For Sale At Their Book-Stores In Portland And Bath. Printed By A. & J. Shirley. 1818.

t.[1], [2–3], 4–48 p.; 13 cm.; pr. & illus. gray-green paper covers.

MWA°; NhD (cover mut.); PP; Shaw 44335.

1196.10 [—] ——— Bearer. From the second London Edition. Utica [New York]: Published By Merrell And Hastings. William Williams [4 dots] Printer. 1818.

t.[1], [2–3], 4–45 p.; 13.5 cm.; pr. paper covers.

MWA° (p. 45 & rear cover wanting); NUt; PP; Shaw 45707.

1196.11 [—] ——— Bearer. Woodstock [Vt.]: Printed By David Watson. 1818.

fr.[2], t.[3], [4–5], 6–66 p.; illus.; 13 cm.; pr. & illus. buff paper covers.

VtHi°; MiD; NNC-T; Vt.; McCorison 2041; Shaw 45708.

1196.12 [—] ——— Bearer. Albany [N.Y.]: Published by Websters & Skinners, and D. Steele. Packard & Van Benthuysen, Printers. 1819.

fr.[2], t.[3], [4–5], 6–69 p.; front. only illus.; 13.5 cm.; pr. green paper covers.

NN-C°; MWA-T.

1196.13 [—] ——— Bearer. Newburyport [Mass.], Printed By W. & J. Gilman. Sold at their Book Store and Printing-Office. NO [*sic. i.e.* No.] 2, Middle-Street. 1819. [cover title].

> [3], 4–50 p.; illus.; 13.5 cm.; pr. & illus. brick-red paper covers.
> MWA°; Shaw 48233 and 49413.

1196.14 [—] ——— Bearer. From the eighth London edition. New-York: Printed And Sold By J. C. Totten, No. 9 Bowery. 1819.

> fr.[2], t.[3], [4–5], 6–58 p.; front. only illus.; 14 cm.; pr. paper covers.
> MWA°; NjN; Shaw 48232 and 49412.

1196.15 [—] ——— Bearer. Philadelphia: Published by the Sunday and Adult School Union. Clarke & Raser, Printers. 1819.

> t.[1], [2–3], 4–87 p.; title page vignette only illus.; 14 cm.; marbled paper covers.
> MWA-T° (p. 63–66 mut.); CoU (p. 75–87 wanting); PHi.

1196.16 [—] < No. 107. Little Henry And His Bearer. [caption p. [1]] Andover [Mass.]; Printed For The New England Tract Society By Flagg And Gould. 1820. < 1st edit. 6000. [colophon p. 32].

> [1], 2–32 p.; 16.5 cm.; also numbered [277], 278–308.
> MB° (bound with other tracts of the *Publications Of The New England Tract Society, Vol. 5. Andover [Mass.]: Printed By Flagg And Gould. 1820*); Shoemaker 3208.

1196.17 [—] The History Of ——— Bearer. Boston: adv. by Samuel T. Armstrong, 1820 in **443.1**.

1196.18 [—] ——— Hartford; George Goodwin & Sons. Printers. 1820.

> t.[1], [2–3], 4–32 p.; illus.; 10.5 cm.; blue marbled paper covers.
> MWA-T°; MB (rebound); Shoemaker 3209.

1196.19 [—] ——— Bearer. Newburyport: Printed By W. & J. Gilman. Sold at their Book-Store and Library, No. 2, Middle-Street. [*ca.* 1820].

> fr.[ii], t.[1], [2–3], 4–50 p.; illus.; 13.5 cm.; pr. & illus. paper covers.
> MNe°.

1197 — The History Of Theophilus And Sophia. By Mrs. Sherwood, Author of "Little Henry and his Bearer," &c. &c. First American Edition. Andover [Mass.]: Published By Mark Newman. 1820.

> t.[1], [2–3], 4–51 p.; 14.5 cm.; pr. buff paper covers; cover title dated 1820.
> English ed. Wellington, Salop: 2nd ed. F. Houlston and Son, sold by Scratcherd and Letterman, London, 1818.
> MWA-W°; ICU; MSaE; Shoemaker 3210.

1198 [—] Little George And His Penny. Newburyport, Printed By W. & J. Gilman. Sold at their Book-Store and Printing-Office No. 2, Middle-Street. 1820. [cover title].

> [1], 2–12 p.; illus.; 13.5 cm.; pr. & illus. olive-green paper covers. Caption p.[1]: The History Of Little George And His Penny. By Mrs. Sherwood, Author of 'Little Henry and his Bearer.'
> MWA°; Shoemaker 3212.

1199 — The Two Sisters. By Mrs. Sherwood, Author of "The History of the Fairchild Family," "Little Henry and his Bearer." &c. &c. First American Edition. Philadelphia: Published by the Sunday and Adult School Union, And for sale at their Depository, 29 N. Fourth Street. Clarke & Raser, Printers. 1820.

> fr.[2], t.[3], [4–5], 6–34, [35, cut] p.; illus.; 12.5 cm.; pr. & illus. blue paper covers.
> English ed. Wellington, Salop: 3 ed F. Houlston And Son. Sold by Scratcherd And Letterman, 1820.
> MWA°; MSaE; Shoemaker 3213.

1200.1 [—] The Wishing-Cap. Newburyport [Mass.], Printed By W. & J. Gilman. Sold at their Book-Store and Printing-Office, No. 2, Middle-Street. 1820. [cover title].

> [1], 2–12 p.; illus.; 13.5 cm.; pr. & illus. blue-gray paper covers. Caption p.[1]: The Wishing Cap. By Mrs. Sherwood, Author of 'Little Henry and his Bearer.' Colophon p. 12: Newburyport, Printed and sold by W. & J. Gilman, No. 2, Middle-Street. 1820.
> MWA°; MSaE; Shoemaker 3214.

1200.2 —— ——— By Mrs. Sherwood, Author of "Little Henry and his Bearer." Portland [Me.]: Published By William Hyde, And for sale at his Bookstore, No. 3, Mussey's-Row, Middle-street. 1820.

fr.[2], t.[3], [4–5], 6–29 p.; illus.; 10.5 cm.; pr. & illus. buff paper covers; cover title undated; colophon p. 29: A. Shirley, Printer. MWA°; Shoemaker 3215.

1201 THE SHIPMATES. An Evening Conversation; Being A Supplement To The Tract, Entitled Conversation In A Boat, By The Same Author. [caption p.[1]]. Published For The Hartford Evangelical Tract Society March, 1818. 5000 [colophon p.24].

t.[1], 2–24 p.; 16 cm.; pr. blue-gray paper covers.
Cover title: The Shipmates, Or A Sequel To A Conversation In A Boat.
NN°; Shaw 45710; Weiss 1936, p. 658.

1202.1 THE SHIPWRECK AND BENEVOLENCE REWARDED. New-York: adv. by L. B. Jansen and G. Jansen, 1808 in **766.**

1202.2 THE SHIPWRECK, OR HUMANITY REWARDED. New-York: Published By Thomas Powers, Book-Seller, 116 Broadway, opposite the City-Hotel. G. Long, Printer. 1810.
t.[1], [2–3], 4–24 p.; illus.; 12.5 cm.
MWA° (covers wanting); Shaw 21339.

1202.3 ——— New-Haven: For J. Babcock & Son. Sidney's Press. 1820.
fr.[2], t.[3], [4–5], 6–30, [31, adv.] p.; front. and title vignette only illus.; green and violet Dutch paper covers.
Welch°; CSmH (covers, fr.[2], p.[31], wanting. Book placed in covers with frontispiece & p.[31] glued to inside belonging to another book); Ct; CtHi; MWA; NPV; Shoemaker 3218.

SHOP-KEEPER TURNED SAILOR. *See* More, Hannah, no. **893.1.**

1203.1 A SHORT ACCOUNT OF THE DEATH OF A PROFLIGATE YOUTH, That, By Bad Company, Learned To Deny, In Heart And Life, The Savior Of The World. [1 line quot.] Springfield [Mass.]; Printed By T. Ashley. 1800.
t.[1], [2–3], 4–12 p.; 16.5 cm.
MWA°; Evans 38500.

1203.2 ——— Deny, In Heart And Life, The Savior Of The World. [1 line quot.] [n.d.] [n.p.]
t.[1], [2–3], 4–15 p.; 16 cm.
MB° (per. st. on t.[1]).

1204 A SHORT AND PLEASING HISTORY OF THE MOST REMARKABLE BEASTS & BIRDS. Woodstock, Vt. Printed By O. Farnsworth. 1818.
fr.[2], t.[3], [4–5], 6–31 p.; front. only illus.; 10.5 cm.; illus. paper covers. Cut of "Elephant" p.[5] printed upsidedown.
Cover title: Beasts & Birds.
VtHi°; McCorison 2042; Shaw 45714.

1205 A SHORT AND TRUE ACCOUNT OF A YOUNG YOUTH; Born in Philadelphia of honest and true Christian Parents; who was taken away by an Angel the 31st of January 1768, up to the Coelestial Parts, where the Lord of Host show'd her great Wonders and supernatural Things. Ezek. el, Chap. 33, vers. ix. [4 lines quot.] Translated from the German. Philadelphia printed by Anthony Armbruster in Third-street, 1768.
t.[1], [2], 3–8 p.; 18.5 cm.
PPL°; Evans 11069.

SHORT CONVERSATIONS; OR, AN EASY ROAD TO THE TEMPLE OF FAME. *See* Kilner, Dorothy, no. **732.1.**

SHORT HISTORY OF THE BIBLE AND TESTAMENT. *See* Mills, Alfred, no. **852.1.**

1206 SHORT STORIES FOR YOUNG PEOPLE. Contents. 1. The Little Hopper. 2. The White Chicken. 3. Charlotte. 4. The Sly Child. 5. The Untidy Girls. 6. The Good Child. The Second Windsor Edition. Printed at Windsor, Vermont. By Nahum Mower. And sold Wholesale and Retail, at his Printing-Office. 1806.
fr.[2], t.[3], 4–27 p.; illus.; 10.5 cm.; gray paper covers; 16 leaves; leaf 15 has been mostly cut away, and may have been blank; leaf 16 blank and originally pasted to the rear cover. The date 1806 on the title page at a quick glance can be mistaken for 1800. Mower was not printing in Windsor in 1800, but in Worcester, Mass. (McCorison).
VtHi°; Evans 38502 (dated 1800); McCorison 873; Shaw 11362.

SILVER PENNY. *See* Horner, J., Esq. (*pseud.*), no. **614.2.**

THE SILVER THIMBLE, *See* Trimmer, Sarah (Kirby), no. **1341.**

1207 Simon the Miller. Wilmington, Del.: adv. by James Wilson, 1803 in **1081.**

1208 Simons the Miller, Philadelphia: adv. by B. & J. Johnson, 1801 in **1046.1.**

1209 Simple Ballads For Children. Adorned With Cuts. Sidney's Press, New-Haven, 1818.
fr.[2], t.[3], [4, alphabet–5], 6–30, [31, adv.] p.; illus.; 10 cm.; illus. buff paper covers. NN°; Shaw 45719.

1210 Simple Ballads; Intended For The Amusement And Instruction Of Children. Philadelphia: Published By Johnson And Warner, No. 147 Market Street, J. Bouvier, Printer. 1811.
fr.[ii], t.[1], [2, bl.–5], 6–108 p.; engraved front. only illus.; 15 cm.; bound in pr. pink paper over bds.; colophon p. 108: Printed by John Bouvier. Written by E. L. Avelin.
English ed. London: W. & T. Darton, 1810.
PP°; NN; NNC–PL; PHi; Shaw 23939.

1211.1 Simple Stories For Children. Philadelphia. Published By Jacob Johnson. 1808.
fr.[2], t.[3], [4–47] p.; illus.; 14 cm.; p.[4]: Dickinson, Printer, Whitehall. Adv. by Johnson & Warner, 1814 in **1449.3.**
English ed. London: W. & T. Darton, 1807, front. dated Feb. 25, 1807.
RPB°; MWA (incomplete; p. 5–6 torn; 7–8 mut.); Shaw 16194.

1211.2 ———— Adorned With Cuts. Sidney's Press. New-Haven. 1813.
fr.[2], t.[3], [4–5], 6–31 p.; illus.; 10.5 cm.; pr. & illus. yellow paper covers.
MWA°.

1211.3 ———— Sidney's Press. New-Haven. 1817.
fr.[2], t.[3], [4–5], 6–31 p.; illus.; 10.5 cm.; illus. yellow paper covers.
MWA°.

Simple Truths In Verse. *See* Elliott, Mary (Belson), no. **346.**

SINBAD THE SAILOR (arranged chronologically)

1212.1 The History Of Sinbad The Sailor: Containing An Account Of His Several Surprising Voyages And Miraculous Escapes. Printed and sold by S. Hall, No. 53, Cornhill, Boston. 1794.
fr.[ii], t.[1], [2–3], 4–121, [122, adv. list of books] p.; 7 full p. illus. including front.; 11 cm.; p. 70 & 104 have tailpiece ornaments of a crown and angel's head.
English ed. title 1: ———— [same as above] London: E. Newbery, 1794.
English ed. title 2: *The Seven Voyages Of Sinbad The Sailor.* London: Ann Lemoine; J. Roe, [n.d.], front. dated Aug. 1803.
English ed. title 3: *The Voyages Of Sinbad The Sailor. A Tale For The Nursery.* London: Tabart And Co. 1805.
MWA°.

1212.2 The Seven Voyages Of Sindbad The Sailor. And The Story Of Aladdin; Or, The Wonderful Lamp. Philadelphia: Printed And Sold By H. And P. Rice, N° 50, High-Street. 1794.
t.[1], [2–3], 4–96 p.; 16.5 cm.; bound in gray paper over bds., leather spine.
PP° (copy 1, p. 51–52 lower 1/8th wanting; p. 53–54 mostly wanting; copy 2, rebound, p. 11–14 mut.); MWA-T; Bowe mss.

1212.3 Sindbad the Sailor. New-York: adv. by L. B. Jansen and G. Jansen, 1808 in **765.**

1212.4 The Life & Adventures Of Sindbad the Sailor With Plates. G. Love Sc. Philadelphia. Published By T. T. Stiles. N° 12 Walnut St. 1808.
t.[1], [2–3, bl.], illus. [4], [5], 6–52 p.; engr. title page and 7 full page illus.; 13.5 cm.; pr. & illus. purple paper covers; p. 51 printed "52". The full page illus. between p. 26 and 27, 30 and 31 are probably bound out of order and are the missing pages 23–24, 33–34.
MWA°; Shaw 16196.

1212.5 The History Of Sindbad The Sailor. Containing, An Account Of His Several Surprising Voyages, And Miraculous Escapes. Newburyport: [Mass.]: Printed By W. And J. Gilman. Sold At Their Book And Stationery Store, Middle-Street. 1809.
t.[3], [4–5], 6–71, [72, adv.] p.; illus.; 14.5 cm.; blue marbled paper over bds.
MWA°; KU (p. 65–68 & covers wanting); Bowe mss.; Shaw 50944.

1212.6 ———— Sailor. In Seven Voyages. Philadelphia. Printed and Sold by J. & A. Y. Humphreys. 1812.
fr.[ii], t.[1], [2–3], 4–58 p.; engraved front. only illus.; 13.5 cm.
MWA°; CLU; Shaw 25659.

1212.7 ———— Sailor. Also, The Celebrated Travels And Adventures, By Sea And Land, Of The Renowned Baron Munchausen. Chillicothe [O.]: Printed For The Publishers. 1817.
t.[1], [2–3], 4–36 p.; 13.5 cm.; pr. blue paper covers.
MWA° (p. 33–34 mut.); Shaw 41055 and 42119.

THE SINGULAR AND VERY SURPRISING LIFE AND ADVENTURES OF JACK THE GIANT KILLER. See Jack The Giant Killer, no. **661.**

SIR FRANCIS AND HENRY. *See* C., C. no. **141.**

SIR JOHN DENHAM AND HIS WORTHY TENANT. *See* Berquin, Arnaud, no. **92.**

THE SISTERS. A DOMESTIC TALE. *See* Hofland, Mrs. Barbara (Wrecks) Hoole, no. **607.**

THE SISTERS, AND THE ROSE, OR The History Of Ellen Selwyn. *See* Mathews, Eliza Kirkham (Strong), no. **825.1.**

1213.1 THE SISTER'S GIFT; Or, The Naughty Boy Reformed. Published For The Advantage Of The Rising Generation. O now, while Health and Vigour still remain, Toil, toil, my Lads to purchase honest Gain! Shun Idleness! shun Pleasure's tempting Snare, A Youth of Folly, breeds an Age of Care. Worcester (Massachusetts) Printed by Isaiah Thomas; And Sold At His Book-Store, MDCCLXXXVI: Where may be had a Variety of Little Books for Children.
fr.[2], t.[3], [4–5], 6–31 p.; illus.; 10 cm.; Dutch paper covers.
English & Irish ed. London: adv. by F. Newbery, 1769 in Solomon Winlove's *Moral Lectures.*
MWA°; Evans 19989.

1213.2 ———— The Second Worcester Edition. Printed at Worcester, Massachusetts, By Isaiah Thomas, Sold at his Bookstore, and by Thomas and Andrews in Boston. MDCCLXXXIX.

fr.[2], t.[3], [4–5], 6–31 p.; illus.; 10 cm.; Dutch paper covers.
MWA°; Evans 22145.

1213.3 ———— [4 lines of verse] New York. 1790. illus. [2], [3, bl.], fr.[4], t.[5], [6–7], 8–29 p.; illus.; 10 cm.; illus. buff paper covers. Pages 8–19, 24–29 have the page numbers printed on the outside of the page. On p. 20–23 the page numbers are on the inside of the page. The illustration on p.[2] shows Abraham about to sacrifice his son.
MWA°; CtY; Evans 45992.

1213.4 ———— Boston: adv. by Samuel Hall, 1791 in **408.3**, and 1792 in **1408.33.**

1213.5 ———— Philadelphia: adv. by Francis Bailey, 1792 in **359**, and 1793 in **773.1.**

1213.6 ———— Boston: adv. by S. Hall, 1793 in **955.3.**

1213.7 ———— The Third Worcester Edition. Printed at Worcester, Massachusetts, By Isaiah Thomas, Jun. For Isaiah Thomas, Sold at their respective Book-stores, and by Thomas and Andrews in Boston.—MDCCXCV.
fr.[2], t.[3], [4–5], 6–31 p.; illus.; 10 cm.; Dutch paper covers.
MWA°; Evans 47602.

1213.8 ———— Boston: adv. by S. Hall, 1796 in **587.40.**

1213.9 ———— Generation. Ornamented with Cuts. Hartford: Printed by Lincoln & Gleason. 1803.
fr.[2], t.[3], [4–5], 6–31 p.; illus.; 10 cm.; blue marbled paper covers.
MWA°; CLU; CtHi; PP; Shaw 5053.

1213.10 ———— Generation [4 lines of verse] Boston: Printed for Hall & Hiller, and sold by them at No. 53, Cornhill. 1805.
fr.[2], t.[3], [4], 5–31 p.; illus.; 10 cm.; buff and green Dutch paper covers. On p. 13 is the cut of a man on horseback used so much in S. Hall editions of *The History Of Master Jackey And Miss Harriot,* no. **568.3.**
DLC° (p. 13–14 mut.); Shaw 9363.

1213.11 ——— Hartford: Printed by Lincoln & Gleason. 1806.

fr.[2], t.[3], [4–5], 6–31 p.; illus.; 10 cm.; green Dutch paper covers.

MWA-W*; NB.

1213.12 ——— Reformed. Boston: Printed By Lemuel Child, No. 2, West Row, No. 33, Court-Street. [1809?].

t.[3], [4–5], 6–28 p. Lemuel Child Jun. [or Lemuel Child] was in 1808–1809 Boston, Mass. Printer and Bookseller. 1810 New Bedford, Mass. Printer. 1819 Southbury, Conn. (MWA cat.).

MWA* (fr.[2?], p. 29–31 and covers wanting); Shaw 18619.

1213.13 ——— Generation. [5 lines of verse] Hallowell [Me.]: Printed by N. Cheever, for E. Goodale. 1809.

fr.[2], t.[3], [4–5], 6–31 p.; illus.; 10.5 cm.; green Dutch paper covers.

MWA*; CLU; DLC (fr.[2], p. 31 & covers wanting); Shaw 18620.

1213.14 ——— Generation. Ornamented with Cuts. Hartford: Printed By Peter B. Gleason & Co. 1811.

fr.[2], t.[3], [4–5], 6–31 p.; illus.; 9.5 cm.; pr. paper covers.

MWA-W* (covers wanting, p. 27–31 bled at the top of the page); CtHi (p.[2–4]. wanting; NRU p. 31 and rear pr. cover wanting, front cover title dated 1824).

1214.1 Sister's Gift. Newburyport [Mass.], Printed by W. & J. Gilman, No. 2, Middle-Street. 1815. [cover title].

t.[1], [2–3], 4–16 p.; illus.; 8.5 cm..; pr. & illus. buff paper covers. Title page [1]: The Sister's Gift. New[buryport,] Printe[d by W. & J. Gilman Book-] s[ellers, No. 2, Middle-Street, 1815]. A different book from no. **1213.1**. [alphabets], p. [2]; The Watch, [verse], p. [3]; The Beggar Boy, p. 4–5; illus. p. 6; Pity the sorrows of a poor / old man/ ... [verse], p. 7–8; An Hour Glass, p. 9; illus. p. 10; The Gardeners, p. 11–12; A Flower Pot, p. 13; The Nightingale, [verse], p. 14; The Fox, [verse], p. 15; illus. "Ah here is the picture of a little Boy..." p. 16.

MWA-W* (t.[1] & p.[2] mut. imprint mostly wanting).

1214.2 The Sister's Gift. Newburyport [Mass.], Published and Sold by W. & J. Gilman, No. 2 Middle-street. [ca. 1820].

t.[1], [2–3], 4–15, [16] p.; illus.; 7 cm.; pr. & illus. brick-red paper covers. [alphabets] p.[2]; [illus.] What a sad thing it is to be a Beggar! ...p. [3]–4; Little Cow brindle, let / down thy milk,/ ... [verse] p. 5; [illus.] p. 6; Pity the sorrows of a poor / old man, / ...[verse] p. 7–8; An Hour Glass, p. 9; [illus.] p. 10; The Gardeners, p. 11–12; [illus.] Oh, here is a very pretty Flower Pot,... p. 13; [1st 8 lines of Dr. Watts' Cradle Hymn] p. 14; [illus.] p. 15; If parent, aunt, or liberal/friend,/ With pretty *cents* should/ line your purse, / ...[verse] p. [16]. After 1820 the firm of W. & J. Gilman was located at No. 9, State-Street.

Cover title: Sister's Gift. Printed and Sold By W. & J. Gilman, Booksellers, No. 2 Middle-street, Newburyport.

MWA-W*.

Six Penny Worth Of Wit. *See* Twelve Cents Worth Of Wit, no. **1224**.

[SLACK, MRS. ANN (Fisher)] *comp.* 1719–1778

1215 [—] The Pleasing Instructor, Or Entertaining Moralist; Consisting of Select Essays, Relations, Visions and Allegories, Collected from the most eminent English Authors. To Which Are Prefixed, New Thoughts on Education. A New Edition. Boston, Printed By J. Bumstead, Sold By Him, No. 20, Union-Street; By B. Larkin, And E. Larkin. Cornhill; And By D. West, Marlboro-Street. 1795.

t.[i], [ii–iv], v–x, [11], 12–312, [313–315, contents] p.; 18 cm.; bound in leather.

English ed. Newcastle upon Tyne: 3 ed. enlarged, 1760.

MWA*; CtY (rebound, p.[313–15] wanting); DLC; NjP; PP; Evans 29518.

SLYBOOTS, YOUNG *pseud.*

1216 — The Little Masters And Misses Delight: Containing Polite Histories, Stories, Tales, Lives, & Adventures, For the early Improvement of Youth, In Virtue and good Manners. A New Edition, Improved By Young Slyboots. Published by Authority. Wilmington: (Del.) Printed and Sold by P. Brynberg. 1801.

t.[1], [2, alphabets], 3–85, [86, cut of a bell]

p.; illus.; 10 cm.; buff paper covers ornamented with a design printed in blue ink, blue-gray paper spine. The History of St. George and the Dragon, p. 20–24; The Character Of Prudinaa [*sic. i.e.* Prudiana], p. 28–31; The Story of Cinderilla; . . . p.59–74; The Master Cat; Or, Puss in Boots, p. 75–85.

English ed. London: H. Turpin. [*ca.* 1784?]. PP°; NNC-Pl; Shaw 831.

SMART, CHRISTOPHER 1722–1770
1217 [—] CHOICE EMBLEMS, FOR CHILDREN. Embellished With Cuts. Philadelphia: Printed By John Adams [4 dots] 1806.

t.[3], [4, alphabets], [5], 6–28, [29, adv.], [30, list of books], [31, alphabet] p.; illus.; 10 cm.; illus. gray paper covers.

MWA° (fr.[2], and front cover wanting).

1218 — HYMNS FOR THE AMUSEMENT OF CHILDREN. By the Rev. Christopher Smart, M.A. To Which Are Added. Watt's Divine Songs For Children. Philadelphia: Printed By William Spotswood. 1791.

t.[i], [ii], iii–iv, 1–92 p.; illus.; 13 cm.; bound in brown and green Dutch paper over bds.; p. 65–92 are *Divine Songs For Children*, By Isaac Watts, D.D.

English & Irish ed. London: entered by T. Carnan at Stationer's Hall, Dec. 24, 1770.

MWA-W° (bound with **60.4**, dated 1797); Evans 23765.

SMITH, CHARLOTTE (TURNER) 1749–1806
1219 — RURAL WALKS: In Dialogues. Intended For The Use Of Young Persons. By Charlotte Smith. Two Volumes In One. Volume I. [II.] Philadelphia: From The Store Of Thomas Stephens, Nº 60, South Second Street. 1795.

fr.[ii], 1st t.[i], [ii–iii], iv–xi, [xii], [13], 14–97, [98, bl.], 2nd t.[99], [100–101], 102–199, [200–204] p.; front. only illus.; 2 vols. in 1; 17.5 cm.; colophon vol. I. on p.[97], & 199: "Wrigley and Berriman Printers No. 149: Chesnut Street."; vol. II. same colophon p. 199 but has "149," followed by a comma. Frontispiece signed *Thackara sc.* Preface p. vi signed *Charlotte Smith. Nov. 19, 1794.*

English ed. London: T. Cardell jun and W. Davies, 1795.

MWA°; CLU; NNC-T; PP; Evans 29525.

SMYTHIES, MISS. *See* THE HISTORY OF A PIN, no. **525.1.**

SOBERSIDES, SOLOMON *pseud.*
1220.1 — CHRISTMAS TALES, For The Amusement and Instruction of Young Ladies & Gentlemen In Winter Evenings. By Solomon Sobersides. [4 lines of verse] Printed in Hudson (New-York) by Ashbel Stoddard, and sold, at his Book Store, Wholesale and Retail. M,DCC,XCIV.

fr.[2], t.[3], [4], 5–159, [160, adv. list of books] p.; illus.; 10 cm.; bound in brown paper over bds.

English ed. London: R. [*sic. i.e.* J.] Marshall [*ca.* 1780].

MWA° (fr.[2], t.[3] mut); N; Evans 29540.

1220.2 —————— Sobersides. [2 lines of verse] Philadelphia: Printed By Robert Johnson, For B. And J. Johnson, No. 147, High-Street. 1799.

t.[3], [4], 5–156 p.; illus.; 11 cm.; bound in Dutch paper over bds.; p. 145–156 follow p. 112, p. 113–114 follow p. 156.

PHi°; Evans 36329.

1221.1 — A PRETTY NEW-YEAR'S GIFT; Or, Entertaining Histories, For The Amusement and Instruction Of Young Ladies and Gentlemen, In Winter Evenings. By Solomon Sobersides. [2 lines of verse] The First Worcester Edition. Worcester, (Massachusetts) Printed By Isaiah Thomas, And Sold At His Book Store. MDCCLXXXVI.

fr.[2], t.[3], [4], 5–152, [153–156, adv. list of books] p.; illus.; t.[3] 10 cm.; the same text as *Christmas Tales*, no. **1220.1.**

MWA° (rebound in leather, with Isaiah Thomas' bookplate); BM; CtHT; NjP (bound in illus. blue paper over bds.); PP (bound in illus. buff paper over bds.); RPJCB; Evans 19995; Hamilton 109.

1221.2 —————— Worcester, (Massachusetts) Printed By Isaiah Thomas, And Sold At His Book Store. Sold Also By E. Battelle, Boston. MDCCLXXXVI.

fr.[2,], t.[3], [4], 5–152, [153–156, adv. list of books] p.; illus.; 10 cm.; bound in illus. buff paper over bds.

MWA° (i. st. on t.[3]); Evans 44967.

1221.3 —————— The Second Worcester Edition. Worcester (Massachusetts) Printed by Thomas, Son & Thomas, And Sold At Their Bookstore. 1796.

fr.[2], t.[3], [4, bl.], 5–135, [136, adv. list of books] p.; illus.; 10.5 cm.; bound in Dutch paper over w. bds.

MWA* (copy 1, Dutch paper covers; copy 2, illus. blue paper covers); DLC (rear illus. blue-gray paper cover wanting); NN (rebound, p. 135–[136] mut.); PP; Evans 31218; Weiss 1936, p. 603.

1222 SOME ACCOUNT OF MARIA HUGHES, A Poor But Pious Child, Who died January 31, 1816, Aged Thirteen. By A Clergyman. Published by "The Religious Tract Society of Philadelphia," and for sale at their Depository, No. 8, South Front-street. William Bradford—Agent. July—1817.

t.[1], [2–3], 4–12 p.; title page vignette only illus.; 18.5 cm.

MWA*.

1223 (No. 15.) SOME ACCOUNT OF THE HAPPY DEATH OF EDWIN TAPPER, Aged 15 years. Published By The Philadelphia Female Tract Society [caption title]. Printed by Lydia R. Bailey, No. 10, North Alley, Philad. [1816] [colophon p. 12].

[1], 2–12 p.; 14 cm.

MWA* (bound with other tracts with which *The First Annual Report Of The Philadelphia Female Tract Society For the Year 1816* was originally bound); Shaw 38975.

1224 (No. 21.) SOME ACCOUNT OF THE HAPPY DEATH OF PETER V - - - Of Somerville, New Jersey. Published By The Philadelphia Female Tract Society [caption title.] Printed by Lydia R. Bailey, No. 10, North Alley, Philad. [1817] [colophon p. 8].

[1], 2–8 p.; 14 cm.

MWA* (bound with other tracts with which *The Second Annual Report of The Philadelphia Female Tract Society For The Year 1817* was originally bound); Shaw 42160.

1225 SOME VERY GENTLE TOUCHES TO SOME VERY GENTLE—MEN By a humble country Cousin of Peter Pindar Esq. Dedicated to all the little Girls & Boys of the City of New-York [*ca.* 1806].

t.[1], 2–16 p. engr. on one side only of 16 leaves; illus.; 13 cm.; orange marbled paper covers.

MWA-W* (col. pl.); NN (copy 1, t.[1] and covers wanting; copy 2, complete but looks like a reprint of the book or facsimile); Shoemaker 3269.

SOMERVILLE, ELIZABETH

1226.1 — THE AMBITIOUS SHEPHERD, A Moral Story, For Youth. By Elizabeth Sumerville [*sic. i.e.* Somerville] To which is added, Goodnatured Credulity—The Noble Basket-Maker—and Tenderness to Mothers. From Sidney's Press, New-Haven. 1809.

fr.[ii], t.[1], [2–3], 4–35 p.; front. only illus.; 13.5 cm.; pr. & illus. paper covers.

Cover title: Ambitious Shepherd. Published by I. Cooke & Co. New-Haven, Who have a universal assortment of Books and Stationery, for wholesale and retail.

MWA*; CtY; Shaw 18655.

1226.2 — —— By Elizabeth Somerville. To which are added, Good natured Credulity.—Tenderness to Mothers.—Sloth contrasted with Industry.—The Linnets' Nest.—The Oak. Wilmington, Del. Printed And Sold By James Wilson. No. 105, Market Street. 1813.

t.[1], [2, alphabets], [3], 4–36 p.; illus.; 13.5 cm.

Cover title: New Year's Gift: Containing The Ambitious Shepherd, &c. Printed And Sold By J. Wilson At The Watchman Printing Office And Bookstore, No. 105, Market Street, Wilmington, Delaware. (DeWI copy).

MWA* (covers wanting, p. 35–36 mut.); DeWi (pr. & illus. blue-gray paper covers); Shaw 29827.

1226.3 — —— By Eliza Sumerville [*sic. i.e.* Somerville]. To which is Added, Several Entertaining Stories, For the Instruction & Amusement of all Good Children. Hartford: B. & J. Russell, Jr. —Printers. State-Street. 1813.

fr.[2, alphabet], t.[3], [4–5], 6–62, [63, adv.] p.; 10 cm.

CtHi*; Shaw 29901.

1227.1 [—] CHARLOTTE, OR, THE PLEASING COMPANION, For Young Misses. Written by a Lady. With Beautiful Engravings. [Printer's ornament with letters "T.B.J." in the center] New-York: Printed For T. B. Jansen. & Co. Booksellers And Stationers, No. 248, Pearl-Street. 1803.

fr.[ii], t.[1], [2–5], 6–68, [69–71, adv. list of books], [72, adv.] p.; 4 pl. including front. also tailpieces illus.; 15 cm.; bound in marble paper over bds., leather spine; p. 67 wrongly paged "46". Plates signed *Anderson* [Alexander Anderson]. The text is the same as p.[3]–68 of *The Village Maid*, no. **1233.2**.

Welch* (pl. opp. p. 24 wanting); MWA; Shaw 5079.

1227.2 [—] ———— New-York: Printed For T. B. Jansen & Co. Booksellers And Stationers, No. 248, Pearl-Street. 1803.

   fr.[ii], t.[1], [2–5], 6–37 p.; front. only pl., also tailpiece illus.; 14 cm.; blue-gray marbled paper covers. A variant of the preceding with less pages, and paper covers.
   MWA-W*.

1228 [—] Choice Tales, For The Improve-ment Of Youth Of Both Sexes. New-York: Printed And Sold By G. & R. Waite, No. 64, Maiden-Lane. [*ca.* 1803].

   t.[1], [2–3], 4–72 p.; illus.; 9.5 cm.; The stories are taken from Elizabeth Somerville's *Village Maid*, no. **1133.2**.
   MWA-W*; (covers wanting); CLU; Shaw 50476.

1229.1 [—] The History Of Little Charles, And His Friend Frank Wilful. Embellished With Cuts. Litchfield [Conn.]: Printed By Hosmer & Goodwin. 1808.

   fr.[2], t.[3], [4–5], 6–29, [30], [31 adv.] p.; illus.; 10 cm.; Dutch paper covers. The story is taken from Elizabeth Somerville's *The Village Maid*, no. **1133.2**.
   CtHi*; CLU; Shaw 15242.

1229.2 [—] ———— Hartford: Printed By Hale & Hosmer. 1812.

   fr.[2], t.[3], [4–5], 6–29, [30], [31 adv. list of 12 books] p.; illus.; 9.5 cm.; pr. & illus. yellow paper covers; cover title dated 1813; p.[31] adv. of 12 juveniles.
   MWA*; Shaw 25657.

1229.3 [—] ———— Hartford: Printed by Hale & Hosmer. 1814.

   fr.[2], t.[3], [4–5], 6–29, [30], [31, adv. list of 12 books] p.; illus.; 10 cm.; pr. & illus. paper covers.
   MWA* (rear cover wanting); Ct; NB; Shaw 31719.

1229.4 [—] ———— Hartford: Printed by Shel-don & Goodwin. < Stereotyped by J. F. & C. Starr > [1815].

fr.[2], t.[3], [4–5], 6–30, [31, adv. list of 12 books] p.; illus.; 10 cm.; pr. & illus. paper covers.
Cover imprint: ———— [same as title page] Goodwin. Stereotype Edition. *See* no. **563.15** for note on printers.
MWA*; CtHi (fr.[2], p.[31] & covers wanting); NN; PP; Shaw 34912; Weiss 1936, p. 334.

1230.1 [—] The History Of Little Phoebe, And The Reclaimed Child. Embellished With Cuts. Litchfield [Conn.]: Printed By Hosmer & Goodwin. 1808.

   fr.[2], t.[3], [4–5], 6–31 p.; illus.; 10 cm.; green Dutch paper covers. Taken from Elizabeth Somerville's *Village Maid*, no. **1133.2**.
   CtHi* (p. 25–26 mut.); Shaw 50854.

1230.2 [—] ———— Phoebe, The Reclaimed Child. And The Old Woman's Story. New-York: Published by George Jansen, 116 Broadway, And Lewis B. Jansen, opposite the New City-Hall, 253 Broadway. 1808.

   fr.[36], t.[37], 39–74 p.; illus.; 14 cm.; blue marbled paper covers; fr.[36] & p. 39–74 are part of T. B. Jansen's New-York 1803 edition of Elizabeth Somerville's *Village Maid*, no. **1133.2**, to which a new leaf p. [37–38] has been added. The frontispiece is signed *Anderson* [Alexander Anderson] and is the same illus. used opposite p. 73 in no. **1133.2**. Page 65 is printed "56".
   DLC*; PP.

1230.3 [—] ———— Child. Embellished with Cuts. Hartford: Printed by Hale & Hosmer. 1812.
   fr.[2], t.[3], [4–5], 6–31 p.; illus.; 9.5 cm.
   MWA* (p. 31 slightly mut., covers wanting); CtHi (fr.[2], p. 31 & covers wanting); Shaw 25658.

1230.4 [—] ———— Hartford: Printed by Hale & Hosmer. 1814.
   fr.[2], t.[3], [4–5], 6–31 p.; illus.; 10 cm.; pr. & illus. buff paper covers.
   Welch*; CtHi; MWA; NjP; Shaw 31721.

1230.5 [—] ———— Hartford: Printed by Shel-don & Goodwin. < Stereotyped by J. F. & C. Starr. > [1815].
   fr.[2], t.[3], [4–5], 6–31 p.; illus.; 9.5 cm.; pr. & illus. buff paper covers; p. 31 has 6 lines of verse and an illus. of two roses on a forked stem. *See* no. **563.15** on printers.

CtHi°; DLC (copy 1, fr.[2] & covers wanting; copy 2, complete copy); Shaw 34914.

1230.6 [—] ——— [same as above].
fr.[2], t.[3], [4–6], 7–30, [31, adv. list of books] p.; illus.; 10 cm.; pr. & illus. buff paper covers. Variant of preceding with pages [6], [16], [18], [31] unnumbered; p.[31], adv. of books. Welch°; CtHi (Bates p. [6], [18], & [20] not numbered; fr.[2], p. [31] & covers wanting); MWA (p.[31] bled at top of page); NB.

1230.7 [—] ——— Adorned With Cuts. Hartford: Printed for J. & W. Russell. < Stereotyped by J. F. & C. Starr. > [1818?].
fr.[2], t.[3], [4–6], 7–31 p.; illus.; 10 cm.; pr. & illus. whitish-buff paper covers; pages [6], [16], [18], [20], [27] unnumbered. *See* no. **563.15** on printers.
MWA° (the top of p.[5–6], 28–30 cropped affecting p. numbers).

1231.1 [—] MARIA, OR THE EVER-BLOOMING FLOWER. (A Tale for Young Ladies.) Adorned with Cuts. Sidney's Press. New-Haven, 1818.
fr.[2], t.[3], [4–5], 6–30 p.; illus.; 10.5 cm.; illus. white paper covers pr. in green ink. Taken from Elizabeth Somerville's *Village Maid,* no. **1133.2.** The story of Maria closely follows that of *Elmina,* written by Charles Masson, with a few textual changes or omissions.
CtHi°; (p. [31] & rear cover wanting); Shaw 44692.

1231.2 [—] ——— New-Haven. Sidney's Press. For J. Babcock & Son. 1819.
fr.[2], t.[3], [4–5], 6–30, [31, adv.] p.; illus.; 11 cm.; illus. buff paper covers pr. in blue ink. Welch° (rear cover mut.); CSmH; CtHi (fr.[2], p. [31] & covers wanting); CtY (covers wanting); MSaE (pr. in pink ink); MWA; Bowe mss.; Shaw 48583.

1232 [—] THE NEW FOUND RELATION, And Dame Burton's Return. Ornamented with Cuts. New-York; Published by George Jansen, No. 116 Broadway. And Lewis B. Jansen, 253 Broadway, Opposite the New City-Hall. 1808.
fr.[ii], t.[iii], [iv, adv.], 75–108 p.; illus.; 14 cm.; marbled paper covers; p. 75–108 are identical with the same p. in Elizabeth Somerville's *The Village Maid,* no. **1133.2.**
DLC°.

1233.1 [—] THE VILLAGE MAID; Or, Dame Burton's Moral Stories For The Instruction And Amusement Of Youth. By Elizabeth Somerville. To Which Are Added, Plain Tales. Philadelphia: Printed And Sold By John Bioren, No. 88, Chesnut Street. 1802.
fr.[ii], t.[iii], [i, bl.–ii, contents], iii [contents], [1], 2–143 p.; front. only pl., 6 tailpiece illus.; 13.5 cm.; bound in marble paper over bds., leather spine; front. signed *Tanner Sc.*
English ed. London: J. Bonsor for Vernor and Hood; E. Newbery, 1801.
CLU°; DeWint.

1233.2 [—] ——— Youth. By Elizabeth Somerville. [printer's ornament with letters T. B. J.] New-York: Printed For T. B. Jansen & Co. Booksellers And Stationers, No. 248, Pearl-Street. 1803.
fr.[ii], t.[1], [2–5], 6–144 p.; 8 pl. including front.; 14.5 cm.; bound in blue marbled paper over bds., leather spine; 8 pl. signed *Anderson.* Adv. by Thomas B. Jansen, 1805 in **1371.5.**
Welch° (fr.[ii] wanting); MWA; NjP; NjR; Hamilton 223; Shaw 5080.

1234 [—] THE VILLAGE TALES, Or Juvenile Amusements. With Cuts. New-York: Printed For T. B. Jansen, Bookseller, No. 248, Pear-Street. 1803.
fr.[ii], t.[i], [2, bl.], 3–72 p.; 4 pl. including front.; t.[1] 15 cm.; 4 pl. including front. signed *Anderson* [Alexander Anderson]. The book is identical with the first 72 p. of *The Village Maid,* no. **1133.2.**
MWA° (rebound); PP (pl. opp. p. 24 mut.; bound in marbled paper over bds., leather spine); Shaw 5508.

SON OF A GENIUS. *See* Hofland, Barbara (Wreaks) Hole, no. **608.1.**

1235 A SONG-BOOK FOR LITTLE CHILDREN. Newburyport [Mass.]: Printed by W. & J. Gilman, No. 2, Middle-Street. 1818.
t.[1], [2–3], 4–16 p.; illus.; 7.5 cm.; pr. paper covers.
MB°; MH (fine copy with two sets of printed red paper covers; front cover undated); MWA-T (p. 15–16 & covers wanting; t.[1], p. [2] mut.); Shaw 45759.

1236 SONGS AND LULLABIES OF THE GOOD OLD NURSES. Calculated to Amuse Children. Embellished With Cuts: And illustrated with Notes and Maxims, Historical, Philosophical, and Critical. First Worcester Edition. Printed at Worcester: Massachusetts, By Isaiah Thomas, Jun. Sold Wholesale and Retail by Him. 1799.

fr.[2], t.[3], [4–5], 6–29, [30–31, illus.] p.; illus.; 10.5 cm. The text is a reprint from standing type of pages [10]–13, 19, 30, 26–27, 31, 14–17, 25, 28, 23, 22, 21, 18, 29, 44, 43, 24, 32, 20, on pages [5]–29 respectively, with only the page numbers and the running caption changed from "Mother Goose's Melody" to "Songs and Lullabies" from I. Thomas' Worcester edition of *Mother Goose's Melody*, 1799, no. **905.3**.
MWA*; PP (fr. [2] & covers wanting); Evans 36335.

1237 — SONGS FOR THE AMUSEMENT OF CHILDREN. Middletown [Conn.]. Printed By M. H. Woodward. M,DCC,XC.

t.[1], [2], 3–31 p.; 9 cm.; The verses in this book are entirely different from Christopher Smart's *Hymns For The Amusement Of Children*.
MB* (per. st. on t.[1]); Evans 22894.

1238.1 SONGS FOR THE NURSERY, Collected From The Works Of The Most Renowned Poets And Adapted To Favorite Melodies. Carlisle [Pa.]: Printed by Archibald Loudon. 1812.

t.[1], [2–3], 4–72 p.; 13 cm.; contains Nursery Rhymes.
English ed. London: entered at Stationer's Hall by R. Phillips and a certificate was given Jan. 12, 1805.
MWA* (covers wanting).

1238.2 — Nursery. New-York: Published By Thomas B. Jansen, Bookseller, No. 11 Chatham-street; opposite the City-Hall. 1817.

t.[1], [2–5], 6–36 p.; illus.; 14 cm.; pr. & illus. pink paper covers.
N*.

1238.3 — Nursery, Collected From The Works Of The Most Renowned Poets, And Adapted To Favorite Melodies. Hudson: Printed By Ashbel Stoddard. 1819.

t.[1], [2–3], 4–33 p.; 14 cm.; paper covers.
MB*; Shaw 49457.

1239.1 THE SONGSTER'S OF THE GROVE, or a Description of Singing Birds. Boston: adv. by John W. Folsom, 1798 in **672.1**.

1239.2 THE SONGSTER'S OF THE GROVE or a Description of Singing Birds with Practical Instructions For Chusing, Feeding, and Teaching them to sing; ornamented with the Figures of Each species exactly copied from Nature. Harvard [Mass.]: Printed by Sewall Parker, 1803.

fr.[2], t.[3], [4–5], 6–31 p.; illus.; 9.5 cm.
Oppenheimer* (not available for checking).

THE SORROWS OF YAMBA, A Poem. *See* Cheap Repository, no. **169.2**.

1240.1 THE SORROWS OF YAMBA: Illustrating the cruelty of the Slave-trade. Together with Reflections of a Minister in a day of Declension. [2 lines of verse] Greenwich [Mass.]: Printed By John Howe—For Ezekiel Terry, of Palmer. 1805.

t.[1], [2], 3–12 p.; 16.5 cm.; no covers. This tract may not be a child's book. The book was published by tract societies and appeared with other tracts intended for children. It is included in this bibliography for completeness.
English ed. London: entered at Stationer's Hall, October 29, 1795, as owned by Hannah More, who was the editor of The Cheap Repository. English broadside ed. title 1: The Sorrows of Yamba; Or, The Negro Woman's Lamentation. To the tune of Hosier's Ghost. London: J. Marshall, pr. R. White, S. Hazard, Bath. pr. [n.d.] paper watermarked "1795", 40 stanzas.
NHi*; Shaw 9400.

1240.2 — Yamba; Or The Negro Woman's Lamentations. A Poetic Fact, Describing The Cruelties Inflicted On The Africans By Men Who Are Destitute Of Humanity; In which is shewn The Power Of God In Bringing Good Out Of Evil, By Sometimes Converting These Captives To A Better Hope Than That Of Being Released From The Bonds Of Those Masters Into Whose Hands They Have Fallen. New-Haven: Printed by Joseph Barber. 1811.

t.[1], [2], 3–12 p.; 18 cm.
MWA*.

1240.3 (No. 24.) — Lamentation. Published By The Philadelphia Female Tract Society. And for sale at their Depository, No. 20, Walnut

Street. [caption title]. Printed by Lydia R. Bailey, No. 10, North Alley, Philad. [1817] [colophon p. 8].

  [1], 2–8 p.; 14 cm.
MWA° (bound with other tracts, with which *The Second Annual Report Of The Philadelphia Female Tract Society For The Year 1816* was originally bound); Shaw 42168.

1240.4 ——— Lamentation. < Taken from the Cheap Repository. > Boston: Printed and Sold at No. 53 Cornhill, by Lincoln & Edmands. 1819.
  t.[1], [2], 3–8 p.; illus.; 11.5 cm.; paper covers. RPB°; Shaw 49460.

1240.5 ———— Lamentation. Mountpleasant [?]: Printed By B. Bates & H. Howard. 1820.
  t.[1], [2–3], 4–12 p.; 11 cm.; paper covers. DLC°; Shoemaker 3275.

1241 THE SPANISH GUITAR, a Tale For young Persons. New-York: adv. by William B. Gilley, 1816 in **1152**.

THE SPARROW. *See* Kendall, Edward Augustus, no. **725**.

1242.1 SPRING. [cut] Infancy,—The Spring of Life. New-York: Printed & Sold by Samuel Wood, at the Juvenile Book-store, No. 357, Pearl-street. 1811.
  t.[1], [2–16] p.; illus.; 8 cm. Adv. S. Wood, 1808 in **643.1**; 1810 in **1188.1**; 1812 in **1188.3**. MWA° (covers wanting); RPB (covers wanting); Shaw 23971.

1242.2 ——— New-York: Printed & sold by Samuel Wood, at the Juvenile Book-store, No. 357, Pearl street. 1814.
  t.[1], [2–16] p.; illus.; 8 cm.; pr. & illus. paper covers.
Cover title: Spring. Sold by Samuel Wood, New-York.
MWA°; MWA-W (bound with other books in no. **637.1**); Shaw 32837.

1242.3 ——— *Nerv-York* [*sic. i.e. New-York*]: Printed and sold By S. Wood, at the Juvenile Book-store, No. 357, Pearl-street. 1815.
  t.[1], [2–16] p.; illus.; 8 cm.; illus. rear paper cover.
MWA° (front cover wanting); Shaw 35995.

1242.4 ——— *Nerv-York* [*sic. i.e. New-York*]: Printed And Sold By Samuel Wood & Sons, at the Juvenile Book-store, No. 357, Pearl-street. 1816.
  t.[1], [2–16] p.; illus.; 7.5 cm.; pr. & illus. paper covers; cover title undated.
MWA°; PP; RPB; Shaw 38997.

1242.5 ———*Nerv-York* [*sic. i.e. New-York*]: Published by Samuel Wood & Sons, No. 261, Pearl-street, And Samuel S. Wood & Co., No. 212, Market-st. Baltimore. 1818.
  t.[1], [2–16] p.; illus.; 8 cm.; blue wallpaper covers.
NhD (covers wanting).

SPROAT, NANCY 1766–1826
1243.1 [—] DITTIES FOR CHILDREN. By A Lady Of Boston. Philadelphia: Published By Johnson & Warner, No. 147, Market-St. 1813. W. Brown, Printer.
  fr.[ii], t.[1], [2–5], 6–45 p.; illus.; 14 cm.; pr. & illus. pink stiff paper covers.
MWA° (p. 41–44 & covers wanting); DLC (title page coll.); MSaE (emb. st. on t.[1]; p.[5]–6 and rear cover mut.); NjR; Shaw 28337.

1243.2 [—] ——— Philadelphia: Published By Benjamin Warner, No. 147, Market Street. Lydia R. Bailey, Printer. 1818.
  t.[1], [2], 3–36 p.; illus.; 14 cm.; pr. & illus. paper covers.
MWA° (p. 15–16, 21–22 wanting); RPB; Shaw 43865.

1244 — FAMILY LECTURES. By Mrs. N. Sproat. Boston: Printed By Samuel T. Armstrong, No. 50, Cornhill. 1819.
  t.[i], [ii–iii], iv. [9], 10–202 p.; 16.5 cm.; bound in gray-green paper over bds.
MWA° (i. st. on p.[9]); MH; NN (has signature "N. Sproat" inscription on t.[i], per. st. on t.[i], i. st. on p.[ii]); RPB (front cover wanting); Shaw 49488.

1245.1 [—] THE GOOD GIRL'S SOLILOQUY; Containing Her Parents' Instructions, Relative To Her Disposition And Manners. *Nerv-York* [*sic. i.e. New-York*]: Published By Samuel Wood & Sons, No. 261, Pearl-Street, And Samuel S. Wood & Co., No. 212, Market-street, Baltimore. 1819.
  fr.[ii], t.[1], [2–3], 4–30 p.; illus.; 13 cm.; pr. &

illus. green paper covers; cover title undated; fr.[ii] signed *A* [Alexander Anderson].
RPB°; CtHi; PP (fr.[ii] & p. 29–30 bound in the middle of the book).

1245.2 [—] —— *Nerv-York* [*sic. i.e. New-York*]: Published By Samuel Wood & Sons, No. 261, Pearl-Street; And Samuel S. Wood & Co., No. 212, Market-st. Baltimore. 1820.
  fr.[ii], t.[1], [2, bl.], [3], 4–24+ p.; illus.; 13 cm.; pr. & illus. paper covers.
  NN° (p. 13–16, 25–30, rear cover & most of front cover wanting); NCooHi; Shoemaker 1411.

1246 — LULLABIES FOR CHILDREN. By Mrs. N. Sproat, Authoress Of "Ditties For Children." "Poetic Tales," &c. &c. Taunton, Mass.: Printed By A. Danforth. 1818.
  t.[1], [2–3], 4–12 p.; 14 cm.; paper covers.
  RPB°; MH; NN (p.[3]–4 wanting); OClWHi.

1247 [—] POEMS, ON DIFFERENT SUBJECTS. By A Lady. [2 lines of verse] Boston: Published By West & Richardson, No. 75, Cornhill. E. G. House, printer: 1813.
  t.[1], [2–3], 4–117 p.; 13.5 cm.; bound in gray-green paper over bds.
  MWA°; RPB; Shaw 29535.

1248.1 [—] POETIC TALES, For Children. By the Authoress of "Stories for Children, by Goody Love-child," and "Ditties for Children, by a Lady of Boston," New-York: Printed And Sold By Samuel Wood, At The Juvenile Book-Store, No. 357, Pearl-Street. 1814.
  t.[1], [2–3], 4–48 p.; illus.; 14 cm.; pr. & illus. buff paper covers.
  MWA°; NN (top of t.[1] cut off); Shaw 32527; Weiss 1942.

1248.2 [—] —— New-York: Printed And Sold By Samuel Wood; At The Juvenile Book-Store, No. 357, Pearl-Street. 1815.
  t.[1], [2–3], 4–48 p.; illus.; 14 cm.
  PP° (bound with other S. Wood publications in vol. 1. of *The Children's Magazine*, no. **191**); NB; NHi (bound with other S. Wood publications in no. **191**); Shaw 51537.

1248.3 [—] —— New-York: Printed And Sold By Samuel Wood & Sons, At The Juvenile Book-Store, No. 357, Pearl-Street. 1815.

t.[1], [2–3], 4–48 p.; illus.; 14 cm.; pr. & illus. yellow-buff paper covers.
Cover title: Poetic Tales. Printed And Sold By Samuel Wood & Sons At The Juvenile Book-Store, No. 357, Pearl Street. *Nerv-York* [*sic. i.e. New-York*].
NWebyC°; CtHi; NjR.

1248.4 [—] —— New-York: Published By Samuel Wood & Sons, No. 261, Pearl-Street; And Samuel S. Wood & Co. No. 212, Market-street. Baltimore. 1819.
  t.[1], [2–3], 4–48 p.; illus.; 13.5 cm.; pr. & illus. paper covers; cover title undated.
  MWA°; MH; RPB (covers worn); Shaw 49489.

1249 [—] A PRESENT TO CHILDREN. By The Author of "Ditties for Children, Poetic Tales, Good Girl's Soliloquy." &c. &c. *Nerv-York* [*sic. i.e. New-York*]: Published By Samuel Wood & Sons, No. 261, Pearl-street; And Samuel S. Wood & Co., No. 212, Market-Street, Baltimore. 1820.
  t.[1], [2–3], 4–29 p.; illus.; 13 cm.; pr. & illus. paper covers; cover title undated; 8 illus. signed *A* [Alexander Anderson].
  MWA-W°; NjR; Shoemaker 3296.

1250 [—] THE SECOND PART OF DITTIES FOR CHILDREN. By The Authoress Of "Ditties For Children," &c. &c. Boston: Published By West And Richardson. T. W. White, Printer. 1816.
  fr.[2], t.[3], [4–5], 6–36 p.; illus.; 14 cm.; pr. paper covers.
  MSaE°.

1251.1 [—] STORIES FOR CHILDREN; In Familiar Verse. By Goody Lovechild. Boston: Published By West And Richardson, No. 75, Cornhill. 1813.
  t.[1], [2–3], 4–35 p.; 14.5 cm.; pr. & illus. paper covers.
  MWA°; Shaw 28986.

1251.2 [—] —— Boston: Published By West And Richardson, No. 75, Cornhill. E. G. House, Printer, Court-Street. 1813.
  fr.[ii], t.[1], [2–3], 4–36 p.; illus.; 14.5 cm.; pr. & illus. paper covers.
  MWA° (p. 35–36 & rear cover worm-eaten); Shaw 28987.

1251.3 [—] —— Colchester [Conn.]: Published By Thomas M. Skinner & Co. 1814.

t.[1], [2 adv.–3], 4–35 p.; 13.5 cm.; pr. paper covers.

MWA*; CtHi; RPB; Shaw 31961.

1251.4 [—] —— Familiar Verse. By The Author Of "Poetic Tales," &c. Illustrated with engravings. Boston: Published By Munroe & Francis, No. 4, Cornhill, (Corner of Water-street;) And David Francis, No. 90, Newbury-Street, (Five doors north of Boylston Market.) 1819.

t.[3], [4], 5–35 p.; illus.; 14 cm.; pr. & illus. yellow paper covers.

RPB*; NN (p. 15–22 wanting); Shaw 49490.

1251.5 [—] —— Verse. By Goody Lovechild, Authoress of "Poetic Tales," and "Ditties for Children, by a Lady of Boston." Philadelphia: Printed By Joseph Rakestraw, No. 256, North Third Street. 1819.

t.[1], [2–3], 4–36 p.; illus.; 14 cm.; pr. & illus. gray paper covers; illus. p.[3] signed *Anderson*. The illus. on the rear cover of a girl beneath the limb of a tree with a seated negro behind her is signed *A* [Alexander Anderson]. It was used by J. Rakestraw, 1811 in **1163.13**. Cover title undated.

MWA-W*.

1252 The Squirrel. Entered according to Act of Congress, Sept 26 1814. New-York: Sold By T. B. Jansen, No. 11 Chatham-street. 1814.

t.[1], [2–3], 4–16 p.; illus.; 6.5 cm.; caption p. [2]: The Discontented Squirrel. The story first appeared in England in *Choice Tales; . . . London: S. Rousseau, For Vernor And Hood, 1799*. This book was printed in America in Philadelphia by Joseph Charless, 1800 in **202**.

MWA-T*.

STANFORD, JOHN

1253 The Death Of Euphemia Mitchell, Improved In A Letter To A Young Friend. By John Stanford, M.A. [3 lines quot.] New-York: Printed By Thomas And James Swords, No. 27, William-Street. 1792.

½ t.[1], [2, bl.], t.[3], [4, bl.], [5], [6, bl.], [7], 8–22, [23] p.; 16.5 cm.; Half title: The Death Of Euphemia Mitchell; p.[23]: To Be Sold By Robert Hodge, No. 11, Water-Street, The Death of Euphemia Mitchell, An Essay on the Law of God, And Hymns for Youth By John Stanford, M.A.; p.[5] Advertisement: "The following Let-

ter was written, and printed, on the earnest request of the Friends of Euphemia, and was introduced into several periodical Publications in England.—On the solicitation of American Friends, and a wish to promote the Virtue And Happines Of Youth, it is again presented to the Public. J. S. New York Sept. 24, 1792."

English ed. Hammersmith, 1784.

MWA*; BM; Evans 24811.

[STERNDALE, MARY]

1254 — Delia's Birth Day. New-York: adv. by W. B. Gilley, 1816 in **1374**.

1255 [—] The Panorama Of Youth. In Two Volumes. [4 lines of verse] First American Edition. Volume II. Philadelphia: Printed By Mathew Carey, No. 121, Chesnut Street. 1816.

t.[1], [2–3], 4–151, [152, bl.], [1]–21, [22] p.; 17.5 cm.; bound in gray-green paper over bds., red leather spine; p. [1]–[22] at rear adv. of books.

NjR*; MSaE.

1256 — The Sisters. New-York: adv. by W. B. Gilley, 1816 in **1374**.

[STEVENS, GEORGE ALEXANDER] 1710–1784

1257 [—] A Lecture On Heads. Philadelphia: Published and Sold by Wm. Charles, No. 32 south Third-street. 1817.

t.[1], [2–3], 4–12 p.; text illus.; 13 cm.; red paper covers. This book, or the English edition from which it was reprinted, probably contained 6 paper dolls. It slides into a printed buff paper slipcase whose rear cover has a list of books published by Wm. Charles. Cover title of slipcase: —— Heads. For the Amusement of all Ages. First American, from the Third London edition. [4 lines of verse] Philadelphia: Published by Wm. Charles, No. 32, South Third-street. 1817.

English unabridged ed. London: J. Pridden [1770?]. This and others listed in BM cat. are not children's books, but the original edition from which the abridged edition may have been compiled. No copy of the English abridged edition has been located.

MWA*; NN; Shaw 42217; Weiss 1932a, p. 9.

Stories For Children; In Familiar Verse, By Goody Lovechild. *See* Sproat, Nancy, no. **1251.2.**

1258 Stories For Good Children, Or, A Birth-Day Present. Hartford: Sold by Cooke & Hale. [*ca.* 1818].

t.[1], [2], 3–16 p.; illus.; 6.5 cm.; buff paper covers.
PP*.

1259 Stories From Scripture. For Small Children. Adorned with Cuts. New-Haven: For J. Babcock And Son. Sidney's Press. 1820.

fr.[2], t.[3], [4–5], 6–30, [31, adv.] p.; illus.; 11 cm.; pr. & illus. pink paper covers.
CtHi*; CSmH; MSaE; MWA-T; Shoemaker 3344.

1260 Stories, Original And Selected, In Prose And Poetry. Adorned With Cuts. From Sidney's Press. For I. Cooke & Co. New-Haven. 1813.

fr.[2], t.[3], [4–5], 6–47 p.; illus.; 11 cm.; pr. & illus. green paper covers.
Cover title: Biography For Girls.
MWA-W*; CtY; MWA (fr.[2], p. 47 & covers wanting, p. 45–46 mut.); Shaw 29883.

The Story Of Ali Baba. *See* Ali Baba, no. **27.9.**

1261 The Story Of Careless Mary; Who Lost A Charming Ride In A Fine Coach, By Not Being Careful Of Her Bonnet. Boston: Printed by Nathaniel Willis. 1816.

fr.[2], t.[3], [4], 5–14, [15, illus.] p.; illus.; 11 cm.; illus. paper covers.
MWA*; Shaw 39021.

The Story Of Constance, The Proud Girl. *See* Sandham, Elizabeth, no. **1153.**

The Story Of Charles Maitland. *See* Sandham, Elizabeth, no. **1156.**

1262 The Story Of Idris. Together With The Story Of Arachne And Melissa. To Which Is Added, The Little Moralist. Second Newburyport Edition. Printed And Sold By W. & J. Gilman, No. 2, Middle-Street. n.d. [*ca.* 1820].

fr.[2], t.[3], [4–5], 6–23 p.; illus.; 13 cm.
NB* (i. st. on t.[3], b. pl. over front.); MH; NNC-T (p. 23 wanting).

1263 The Story Of James And Fanny, Ann And Mary, And Margaret, The Little Wanderer. Cooperstown [N.Y.]: Printed and sold by H. & E. Phinney. 1817.

10.5 cm.; illus.; pr. & illus. paper covers.
Cover title: James & Fanny. Cooperstown: Printed and sold by H. & E. Phinney. 1817.
Oppenheimer*.

1264.1 The Story Of Joseph. Philadelphia: Printed for Joseph Crukshank, No. 87, High-street. 1797.

t.[1], [2–3], 4–48 p.; 10.5 cm.; Dutch paper covers.
MWA*; Evans 48261.

1264.2 ———— Printed For John G. Ustick, No. 79, North Third-street, Philadelphia. 1799.

t.[1], [2–3], 4–39 p.; 11 cm.; marbled paper covers.
MWA*; Evans 37377.

The Story Of Joseph And His Brethren. *See* Cheap Repository, no. **169.17.**

1265.1 The Story Of Joseph And His Brethren. In Three Parts. Written For The Benefit Of Youth. To Which Is Added, The Awful Death Of An Impious Youth: A Fragment. Philadelphia: Published by D. Hogan, No. 249, Market Street. 1811.

t.[1], [2–3], 4–106 p.; 14 cm.; bound in buff wallpaper with a three-pronged design in black. Joseph And His Brethren, p.[3]–29; Part II, p. [30]–58; Part III, p. [59]–68; The Awful Death Of An Impious Youth, p. [69]–84; The Harvest Home, p.[85]–103; The True Heroes; Or The Nobel Army Of Martyrs, p. [104]–106.
MWA-T* (front cover wanting).

1265.2 ———— In Three Parts. Philadelphia: Sold by Johnson & Warner, No. 147, Market-Street. Jacob Meyer, Printer. 1811.

fr.[2], t.[3], [4–5], 6–105 p.; illus.; 14.5 cm.; bound in blue-gray paper over bds. The Story, &c. [pt. I.], p. [5]–33; Joseph And His Brethren. Part II, p. 35–66; Joseph And His Brethren. Part III, p. 67–78; The History Of Diligent Dick, p. [79]–98; The Prodigal Son, p. 100–101; Extract From a late Author, on Detraction. p. 102–105.
Cover title: ———— Brethren. By Hannah More

[*sic.*] Philadelphia: Published By Johnson & Warner, No. 147, Market-[Street.] 1811.
MWA°; PHi; Shaw 23992.

1265.3 ———— Pittsburgh: Printed and sold by Cramer & Spear, Franklin Head Bookstore, Market Street. 1817.
84 p.; 12 cm.
PPi°.

1265.4 ———— In Three Parts. Written For The Benefit Of Youth. To Which Is Added, The History Of Charles Jones. Wilmington [Del.]: Printed By R. Porter. 1819.
t.[1], [2–3], 4–106 p.; 13.5 cm.; bound in pr. blue paper over bds.; cover title undated.
MWA°; DeHi; DeWi (per. st. on t.[1], & p. [3]); PP (covers wanting); Shaw 48462 and 49515.

1266 THE STORY OF LITTLE JUDITH. New-York: adv. by George Jansen & Lewis B. Jansen, 1808 in **1232.**

1267 A STORY OF LITTLE THOMAS AND BETSEY. A new Tale for Children. Hartford: Published by S. G. Goodrich. Roberts & Burr, Pr's. 1819.
fr.[2], t.[3], 4–16 p.; 10.5 cm.; illus. white paper covers pr. in red ink.
MWA-T°.

THE STORY OF MARY AND HER CAT. *See* Mary And Her Cat, no. **821.**

THE STORY OF PEEVISH WILLIAM. *See* Sandham, Elizabeth, nos. **1153** and **1158.**

1268 THE STORY OF QUASHI; Or, The Desperate Negro. To Which Is Added, The Story Of Sinbad the Sailor And The Elephants. Together With The Story of Mendaculus. Newburyport Edition. Printed And Sold By W. & J. Gilman, Booksellers, No. 2, Middle-Street. [1820].
fr.[2], t.[3], [4, illus.–5], 6–23 p.; illus.; 13.5 cm.; pr. & illus. paper covers; front cover dated "1820."
MWA°; PP (p. 9–10, 13–23 mut.); Shoemaker 3349.

THE STORY OF THE CRUEL GIANT BARBARICO. *See* Fielding, Sarah, no. **410.**

1269 A STORY OF THE ENVIOUS MAN. Together With The Dead Man's Resurrection; And The Waterman And Drowned Dog. A.L.T.D.H. Printer's. 1813.
t.[1], [2–3], 4–24 p.; 13 cm.; green, red and brown marbled paper covers.
Carson° (not seen).

1270 THE STORY OF THE FOX THAT LOST HIS TAIL. Concord [N.H.]: Published and sold by Daniel Cooledge at his Book-Store.—1812. Geo. Hough, Printer.
fr.[2], t.[3], [4–5], 6–23 p.; illus.; 10 cm.; pr. & illus. paper covers.
Cover title: Concord Toy. No. 2.
NRU°; Shaw 26814.

1271 THE STORY OF THE HAPPY WATERMAN. Designed For The Amusement Of All Good Little Masters And Misses. Hartford, Printed By Hudson And Goodwin. 1813.
t.[1], [2], 3–12 p.; tailpiece p. 12 only illus.; 13 cm.; gray paper covers.
CtY°.

1272.1 THE STORY OF THE INNOCENT AMELIA; Or, The Treacherous Brother. In A Series Of Letters. Being A Fact. Putney, Ver. Printed For, And Sold By J. Hinds, Walpole, New Hampshire. 1799.
t.[3], [4–5], 6–59 p.; 10.5 cm.; wallpaper covers. Cornelius Sturtevant Jr. & Co. printer was the only one in Putney Vt. between 1798–1799 according to McCorison. The book is juvenile in size & format, but there is a question whether it should be considered a child's book.
MWA°; McCorison 541; Evans 36378.

1272.2 ———— Printed At Leominster, (Massachusetts.) By Salmon Wilder. 1811.
t.[1], [2–3], 4–32 p.; 12.5 cm.; no covers.
MWA°; VtHi; Shaw 23993.

1273 THE STORY OF WILLIAM AND ELLEN. Hartford: Sold By Cooke & Hale. < Copy right secured. > [*ca.* 1816].
t.[1], [2], 3–16 p.; illus.; 6 cm. Oliver D. Cooke and Horatio G. Hale were known as a booksellers firm in Hartford only from 1816–1819. (MWA cat.).
NRU° (covers wanting).

STOWELL, HUGH, REV.
1274 — A NARRATIVE OF THE LIFE OF MISS

Sophia Leece. By The Rev. Hugh Stowell, Rector Of Ballaugh, Isle Of Man. Philadelphia: Published By The Sunday And Adult School Union, And For sale at their Depository, 29 North Fourth St. Clarke & Raser, Printers. 1820.

fr.[2], t.[3], [4–5], 6–108 p.; front. only illus.; 14.5 cm.; bound in marbled paper over bds., leather spine.

PP*; Shoemaker 3350.

STRETCH, L. M.

1275 — The Beauties Of History; Or, Pictures Of Virtue And Vice, Drawn From Real Life; Designed For the Instruction and Entertainment of Youth. By L. M. Stretch, M.A. The Seventh Edition. Vol. I. [II.] Springfield [Mass.]: Printed By Edward Gray. M,DCC,XCIV.

vol. I: t.[iii], [iv, bl.–v], vi–xxiv, [1], 2–360 p.; vol. II: t.[iii], [iv, bl.–v], vi–xi, [xii, bl.], [1], 2–348 p.; 2 vols.; 17.5 cm.; bound in leather. Title to vol. II: —— Stretch, M.A. Vicar of Twyford and Ouselbury, Hampshire, The Seventh Edition. Vol. II. Springfield [Mass.]: Printed By Edward Gray. M,DCC,XCIV. English ed. London: Printed for the Author, 1770.

MWA* (vols. I., II., i. st. on t.[iii] of both vols.); BM; CtY (vol. II.); ViU; Evans 27749.

1276 The Sugar Plumb; Or, Sweet Amusement For Leisure Hours: Being An Entertaining and Instructive Collection of Stories. Embellished With Curious Cuts. The First Worcester Edition. Printed at Worcester, Massachusetts, By Isaiah Thomas, And Sold, Wholesale and Retail, at this Book-Store. MDCCLXXXVII.

fr.[2], t.[3], [4–5], 6–123, [124, adv.] p.; illus.; 10.5 cm.; bound in Dutch paper over bds. *See* no. 1282.1. English ed. London: F. Newbery, 1771.

MWA* (2 copies: copy 1, bound in Dutch paper; copy 2, rebound, I. Thomas' copy); CLU; CtHi; Evans 20735.

1277.1 SUMMER. [cut] Youth — The Summer of Life. New-York: Printed & sold by Samuel Wood, at the Juvenile Book-store, No. 357, Pearl Street. 1809.

t.[1], [2–16] p.; illus.; 8 cm. Adv. by Samuel Wood, 1808 in 643.1 and 1810 in 1188.1.

MWA* (covers wanting); Shaw 18706.

1277.2 —— New-York: Printed & sold by Samuel Wood, at the Juvenile Book-store, No. 357, Pearl Street. 1811.

t.[1], [2–16] p.; illus.; 8 cm.; Dutch paper covers. Adv. by S. Wood, 1812 in 1188.3.

MWA*; Shaw 23999.

1277.3 —— New-York: Printed & sold by Samuel Wood at the Juvenile Book-store, No. 357, Pearl-street. 1813.

t.[1], [2–16] p.; illus.; 8 cm.; pr. & illus. pink paper covers. Cover title undated: Summer. Sold by Samuel Wood. New-York.

MWA-W*; MWA-T; N (i. st. on t.[1]).

1277.4 —— New-York: Printed & sold by Samuel Wood, at the Juvenile Book-store, No. 357, Pearl-street. 1814.

t.[1], [2–16] p.; illus.; 8 cm.; pr. & illus. yellow-buff paper covers. Cover title MWA copy: Summer. Sold by Samuel Wood, New-York.

Welch* (copy 1, covers wanting; copy 2, bound with other books in no. 637.1); MWA*; Shaw 32891.

1277.5 —— Nerv-York [*sic. i.e. New-York*]: Printed And Sold By S. Wood, at the Juvenile Book-store, No. 357, Pearl-street. 1815.

t.[1], [2–16] p.; illus.; 8 cm.; pr. & illus. buff paper covers. Cover title: Summer. Sold by Samuel Wood, New-York.

MiD*; CLU.

1277.6 —— Nerv-York [*sic. i.e. New-York*]: Printed And Sold By Samuel Wood & Sons, at the Juvenile Book-Store, No. 357, Pearl-street. 1816.

t.[1], [2–16] p.; illus.; 8 cm.; pr. & illus. yellowish-buff paper covers. Cover title: Summer. Sold by Samuel Wood & Sons, New-York.

MWA-W*; KU; MWA (p. 11–14 mut., leaves torn); NN; PP; Shaw 39035.

1277.7 —— Nerv-York [*sic. i.e. New-York*]: Published by Samuel Wood & Sons, No. 261, Pearl-street, And Samuel S. Wood & Co. No. 212, Market-st. Baltimore. 1818.

t.[1], [2–16] p.; illus.; 8 cm.; pr. & illus. paper covers.

Cover title: Summer. Sold by Samuel Wood & Sons, New-York, And Samuel S. Wood & Co. Baltimore.
MWA*; PP; Shaw 45819.

A SUMMER'S WALK. *See* Barbauld, Anna Letitia (Aikin), nos. **62.1** and **62.2**.

1278 THE SUNDAY SCHOLARS, Joseph And James. Middlebury, Vt. Printed at the Messenger Office. 1818.
t.[1], [2], 3–12 p.; 14.5 cm.
MWA*; McCorison 2049; Shaw 45825.

1279.1 THE SUNDAY SCHOOL CHILDREN. Philadelphia: Published By The Sunday and Adult School Union. Clark & Raser, Printers. 1819.
t.[1], [2–3], 4–36 p.; title page vignette only illus.; 12.5 cm.
MiD*.

1279.2 ——— Philadelphia: Published by the Sunday and Adult School Union, And for sale at their Depository, 29 N. Fourth Street. Clark & Raser, Printers. 1820.
t.[1] [2–3], 4–36 p.; title page vignette only illus.; 12.5 cm.; pr. & illus. paper covers; rear cover adv. list of books.
MWA*; RPB; Shoemaker 3367.

1280 THE SUNDAY SCHOOL OR VILLAGE SKETCHES. [2 lines of verse] Cowper. Andover [Mass.] Printed By Flagg And Gould. 1820.
t.[i], [ii, bl.], [i, Contents], [ii, Errata], [iii, Preface], iv–vi [end of Preface], [7], 8–251 p.; 14.5 cm.
NN*; Shoemaker 3368.

1281 (No. 13.) A SUNDAY'S EXCURSION. Published By The Philadelphia Female Tract Society. [caption title]. Printed by Lydia R. Bailey, No. 10, North Alley, Philad. [1816] [colophon p. 12].
[1], 2–12 p.; 14 cm.
MWA* (bound with other tracts, with which *The First Report Of The Philadelphia Female Tract Society for 1816* was originally bound); Shaw 39036.

1282.1 SWEET AMUSEMENT, For Leisure Hours: Being An Entertaining And Instructive Collection Of Stories. [2 lines of verse] First Exeter Edition.

Printed and Sold by H. Ranlet, Exeter [N.H.], Where a number of pretty books for children are constantly for sale. 1797.
t.[1], [2], 3–62 p.; illus.; 13 cm. With exception of the first story, "The History Of The Children in The Wood.", all the stories are taken from *The Sugar Plumb*, no. **1276**. Adv. by H. Ranlet, 1801 in **558.2**.
MWA* (lower half of p. 60–62 & covers wanting); Evans 34623.

1282.2 ——— Exeter: adv. by Norris & Sawyer, 1808 in **428.3**.

SWIFT, JONATHAN 1667–1745

GULLIVER'S TRAVELS abr. (arranged chronologically)

1283.1 [—] THE ADVENTURES OF CAPT. GULLIVER, Worcester: adv. by I. Thomas, 1786 in **395.1**.

1283.2 — THE ADVENTURES OF CAPTAIN GULLIVER, In A Voyage To the Islands of Lilliput and Brobdingnag. Abridged from the Works of The Celebrated Dean Swift. Adorned With Cuts. Philadelphia: Printed by Young and M'Culloch, the corner of Chesnut and Second-streets. 1787.
fr.[2], t.[3], [4], 5–128 p.; illus.; 10.5 cm.; Dutch paper over bds., leather spine.
English 1st unabridged ed.: *Travels into several Remote Nations Of The World, by Lemuel Gulliver.* London: 2 vols. for Benj. Motte, 1726.
English abr. ed. title 1; *Travels into* ——— *World. By Captain L. G.* London: For J. Stone, and R. King, 1727.
English & Scottish abr. ed. title 2: *The Travels and adventures of Capt. L. G.* London: [1750?] a chapbook.
English abr. ed. title 3: *The Adventures Of Captain Gulliver.* London: adv. by F. Newbery, 1777 in *Lives Of The British Admirals.*
English & Scottish abr. ed. title 4: *Gulliver's Travels.* York: adv. by Wilson Spence & Mawman [ca. 1797] in *The New Puzzling-Cap.*
Scottish abr. ed. title 5: *Gulliver's Voyage To Lilliput.* Glasgow: adv. by J. & M. Robertson, 1802 in Tommy Trip's *The Natural History Of Four Footed Beasts.*
Scottish abr. ed. title 6: *The Surprising Adven-*

tures Of Captain Gulliver In A Voyage To The Kingdom Of Lilliput. Glasgow: Lumsden & Son. [1800?].

Scottish abr. ed. title 6a: ———— *In A Voyage To Lilliput*. Glasgow: J. Lumsden & Son. 1815. English abr. ed. title 7: *The Wonderful Adventures And Discoveries Of Captain Lemuel Gulliver*. London: A. K. Newman, 1811.

PP* (p. 63–64 9/10 wanting; sig. D is misprinted being printed on both sides of the sheet with pages of the outer form, instead of the pages of the outer and inner forms, so that p. 98, 99, 102, 103, 106, 107, 110, 111, 114, 115, 118, 119, 122, 123, 126, 127 were never printed); Evans 45170.

1283.3 ———— Philadelphia: Printed by W. Young, Bookseller, No. 52. Second-street, Corner of Chesnut-street. M,DCC,XCI.

fr.[2], t.[3], [4], 5–120 p.; illus.; 11 cm.; paper covers.

DeWint* (p. 25–32, 49–68 wanting); Evans 46294.

1283.4 ———— New-York: Printed and Sold by W. Durell, No. 19, Queen-Street. [*ca.* 1793].

fr.[2], t.[3], [4], 5–16 p.; illus.; 10 cm.; Dutch paper front cover.

MWA* (all pages after p. 16 wanting); Evans 26239.

1283.5 ———— Lilliput & Brobdingnag. Abridged from the Works of The celebrated Dean Swift. Adorned With Cuts. Boston: Printed and sold by S. Hall, No. 53, Cornhill. 1794.

fr.[4], t.[5], [6, bl.], 7–119, [120, bl.], [121–126, adv. of books] p.; illus.; 11 cm.; bound in Dutch paper over bds.

MWA-W* (fr.[4], t.[5] mut., p. 125–126 wanting); CtY; DLC; MH; NjP; Evans 29599; Hamilton 148.

1283.6 ———— Abridged fron [*sic. i.e.* from] the Works of the Celebrated Dean Swift. Adorned With Cuts. Philadelphia: Printed By W. Young, No. 52, Second-Street, the Corner of Chesnut-Streets. M,DCC,XCIV.

fr.[2], t.[3], [4], 5–159, [160, adv.] p.; illus.; 10.5 cm.; bound in Dutch paper over bds.

NjP; Evans 47224.

1283.7 ———— To the Islands of Lilliput. Abridged from the Works of The Celebrated Dean Swift. Printed at Fairhaven [Vt.], and Sold cheap by the gross, dozen, or single. Prince single, 12 Cents. [1796].

t.[3], 4–47 p.; illus.; 12 cm. Adv. by J. P. Spooner, Fairhaven [Vt.], [1796] in Defoe's *The Wonderful Life . . . Robinson Crusoe*, no. **275.35.**

PP* (t.[3], p. 4 mut.); McCorison 401; Evans 47927.

1283.8 ———— Lilliput and Brobdingnag. Abridged from the Works of The celebrated Dean Swift. Adorned With Cuts. Philadelphia: Printed by H. Sweitzer, No. 85, Race-street. M,DCC,-XCIX.

fr.[2], t.[3], [4–5], 6–257 [*sic. i.e.* 157] p.; illus.; 11 cm.; bound in marbled paper over bds. PP*.

1283.9 ———— Lilliput. Abridged from the Works of the Celebrated Dean Swift. First Worcester Edition. Worcester, (Massachusetts) Printed by I. Thomas, Jun. Sold Wholesale and Retail by him.—November, 1802.

t.[3], [4–5], 6–59, [60–61], [62–63, 2 illus. per page] p.; illus. p.[62–63] only illus.; 10 cm.; green Dutch paper covers.

MWA*; CtHi; Shaw 3129.

1283.10 ———— Lilliput and Brobdingnag. Abridged from the Works of The celebrated Dean Swift. Adorned With Cuts. Wilmington [Del.]: Printed and sold by Bonsal and Niles. Also at their Book-Store, Market-Street, Baltimore. 1804.

t.[1], [2], 3–143, [144, adv.] p.; illus.; 13.5 cm.; bound in buff paper speckled with red and gray over bds.; p.[103]–133, The Misfortunes Of An Inchanted [*sic. i.e.* Enchanted] Prince; p. [135]–143, Drusilla: Or The Fate Of Harold.

MWA-W*; OOxM.

1283.11 [—] CAPTAIN GULLIVER. New-York: adv. by L.B. Jansen and G. Jansen, 1808 in **766.**

1283.12 [—] THE SURPRISING ADVENTURES OF CAPTAIN GULLIVER in a Voyage to the Kingdom of Lilliput. Philadelphia Published By B. C. Buzby, N<u>o</u>. 2, N<u>H</u> 3. S<u>T</u> 1808.

fr. [2], t.[3], [4–5], 6–52 p.; 7 engr. illus. including front. and t.[3]; 13 cm.; paper covers. MiU*.

1283.13   [—] Voyages And Travels, Of Captain Gulliver. New-York: adv. by Thomas B. Jansen, 1805 in **1371.5.**

1283.14   [—] Gulliver's Travels. Philadelphia: adv. by William Charles, 1811 in **838.1;** 1814 in **357;** 1815 in **748.**

Note—There are small 14.5–16 cm. editions of *Gulliver's Travels* which are not abridged and therefore not included, because they are not considered children's books.

T

T., B. A.

1284.1 [—] THE DISASTROUS EVENTS WHICH ATTENDED JOE DOBSON, Illustrated With Sixteen Elegant Engravings. Philadelphia: Published and sold wholesale by Wm. Charles, and may be had of all the Book-sellers. 1809. Price 25 Cents. [cover title].

    [1–16] p.; engr. on one side only of 16 leaves; illus.; 13.5 cm.; pr. brownish-buff paper covers. English ed. London: entitled: *Cobler! stick to your last; Or, The Adventures Of Joe Dobson. . . . By B.A.T.* London: J. Harris, 1807.
    DLC* (rear cover mostly wanting); Shaw 17391.

1284.2 [—] ——— Philadelphia Published and Sold Wholesale by Wm. Charles, and may be had of all the Booksellers. 1813. Price 25 cents. [cover title].

    [1–16] p. engr. on one side only of 16 leaves; illus.; 13 cm.; pr. buff paper covers.
    PP*.

1284.3 [—] ——— Philadelphia: Published and sold by Wm. Charles, No. 32, S. Third-st. Price 25 cents. 1817. [cover title].

    [1–16] p. engr. on one side only of 16 leaves; col. illus.; 12.5 cm.; pr. buff paper covers.
    NCooHi*.

1285.1 TAKE YOUR CHOICE: Or The Difference Between Virtue And Vice, Shown In Opposite Characters. Philadelphia: Printed By Jacob Johnson, No. 147, Market-Street. 1804.

    ½t. [1], fr.[2], t.[3], [4–56], [57–58, adv. list of books] p. illus.; 16 cm. Half title: Take Your Choice.
    English ed. London: Harris, 1802.
    PP*; Shaw 7330.

1285.2 ——— Philadelphia: Printed By Jacob Johnson, No. 147, Market-Street. 1808. Adams, Printer.

    ½t.[1], fr[2], t.[3], [4–56] p.; illus.; 14 cm.; gray marbled paper covers.
    MWA*; NNC-Pl; Shaw 16279.

TALES FOR YOUTH. *See* Wynne, John Huddlestone, no. **1460.1**.

TALES OF THE HERMITAGE. *See* Pilkington, Mary (Hopkins), no. **1005**.

1286.1 TALES OF THE HERMITAGE. Written by a Lady, for the improvement of Youth. New-York: T. B. Jansen & Co. Bookseller. No. 248, Pearl-Street. 1802.

    CLU*.

1286.2 ——— New-York: adv. by Thomas B. Jansen, 1805 in **1371.5**.

1286.3 ——— New Haven: Printed For John Babcock And Son. Sidney's Press. 1820.

    fr.[2], t.[3], [4–5], 6–31 p.; front. and title vignette only illus.; 14.5 cm.; pr. & illus. buff paper covers. A different book from Pilkington's *Tales Of The Hermitage.*
    Cover title: The Hermitage. Sold by John Babcock & Son, New-Haven, and S. & W. R. Babcock, Charleston. The front cover illus. and fr.[2] are signed A [Alexander Anderson].
    English ed. London: J. Harris, 1815.
    MWA-W*; CtHi; CtY; MWA; PP; Shoemaker 2786.

1287 TALES OF THE POOR; Or, Infant Sufferings; Containing, The Chimneysweeper's [*sic. i.e.* Chimney Sweeper's] Boy; Sally Brown, The Cotton Spinner; The Orphans; And Mary Davis. [1 line quot.] *Nerv-York* [*sic. i.e. New-York*]: Printed And Sold By Samuel Wood & Sons, At The Juvenile Book-Store, No. 357, Pearl-Street. 1816.

    t.[1], [2, bl.], ½t.[3], [4, illus.], [5], 6–70 p.; illus.; 14 cm.; pr. & illus. yellow-buff paper covers; illus. p. [50], [58] signed A [Alexander Anderson]. Half title p. [3]: TALE I THE *Chimneysweeper's* [*sic. i.e. Chimney Sweeper's*] BOY. Adv. by S. Wood & Sons, 1819 in **1188.8**.
    PP* (rear cover wanting); Shaw 39048.

1288.1 TALES UNITING INSTRUCTION WITH AMUSEMENT: CONSISTING OF THE BOY WITH A BUNDLE; The Boy who told Lies; Willy and his

Dog Diver; and The Girl Who Was Fond Of Flowers. Ornamented With Copper-Plate Engravings. Philadelphia: Published By Johnson & Warner, No. 147, Market Street. 1809.

fr.[ii], t.[1], [2–3], 4–36 p.; 3 pl. including front.; 12.5 cm.; pr. paper covers.; colophon p. 36: Lydia R. Bailey, Printer, No. 10, North Alley.

Cover title: Johnson & Warner's Juvenile Library, The Boy With A Bundle; And Other Tales. No. 417, Market-Street. 1809. These stories appeared in England in *Profitable Amusement For Children. London: Vernor And Hood; J. Harris, 1802.*

PP°; RP; Shaw 18718.

1288.2 ——— Amusement: Consisting Of The Children who were fond of Climbing; Matty in the Flower-Garden; The Boys who tore their Clothes; And The Girl Who Was Kind To The Poor. Ornamented With Copper-Plate Engravings. Philadelphia: Published By Johnson & Warner, No. 147, Market Street. 1809.

fr.[ii], t.[1], [2–3], 4–36 p.; 3 pl. including front.; 12.5 cm.; pr. blue-gray paper covers; colophon p. 36: R. Bailey, Printer, No. 10, North Alley.

Cover title: Johnson & Warner's Juvenile Library, The Children Who Were Fond Of Climbing; And Other Tales. No. 147, Market-Street. Philadelphia. For English source book *see* no. **1173.1.**

PP°.

1289.1 ——— Amusement: Consisting of The Little Rambler; Playing With Fire; The Child And The Chimney Sweeper, And How To Guard Against A Fall. Ornamented with Copper-plate Engravings. Philadelphia: Published By Bennett And Walton, No. 31, Market Street. 1808.

fr.[ii], t.[1],[2–3], 4–24 p.; 3 pl. including front.; 14 cm.; gray marbled paper covers. For English source book *see* no. **1288.1.**

NNC-Pl°.

1289.2 ——— Amusement: Consisting of Throwing Squibs; And The Boy With A Bundle. Ornamented with Copper-plate Engravings. Philadelphia: Published For Bennet And Walton, No. 31, Market Street. 1808.

fr.[ii], t.[1], [2], 3–22, [23, adv.] p.; 2 pl. including front.; 13.5 cm.; pr. paper covers;

cover title dated 1813. For English source book *see* no. **1288.1.**

MiD° (p. 23 wanting; marbled paper covers); Shaw 16280.

The Talking Bird. *See* The Adventures Of Old Dame Trudge, no. **9.1.**

1290 The Tame Goldfinch: Or, The Unfortunate Neglect. Embellished With Three Copper-Plate Engravings: Philadelphia: Published By Jacob Johnson, No. 147, Market-Street. 1808.

fr.[ii], t.[1], [2–3], 4–36 p.; 3 pl. including front.; 13.5 cm.; blue marbled paper covers; p.[2]: Adams, Printer, Philadelphia. Adv. by Johnson & Warner, 1814 in **1449.2.** Part of a large publisher's remainder.

English ed. London: J. Harris, 1804.

MWA° (rebound); CLU; CSmH; CtHi; CtY; DLC; NB; NHi; NNC-Pl; PP; Shaw 16281.

TAYLOR, ANN. *See* Gilbert, Ann (Taylor) no. **436.**

TAYLOR, ANN & JANE. *See* Gilbert, Ann (Taylor), no. **436.**

TAYLOR, JANE 1783–1824

1291 — Display. A Tale For Young People. By Jane Taylor, One of the authors of "Original Poems for Infant Minds," "Hymns for Infant Minds," &c. [1 line quot.] Jurieu. Boston: Published By John Eliot. 1815.

t.[1], [2–3], 4–106 [*sic. i.e.* 206] p.; 15.5 cm.; p. 204–206 wrongly printed 104–106. The NNC-Pl copy has p. 204–206 correctly printed.

English ed. London: Taylor and Hessey and J. Conder, 1815.

MWA° (emb. st. on t.[1]); CLU; MH; MSaE; NNC-Pl; NPV; PP; PPL; Shaw 36052 and 36053.

1292 — Essays In Rhyme, On Morals And Manners. By Jane Taylor. Author of 'Display: a Tale.' And one of the Authors of 'Original Poems for Infant Minds.' 'Hymns for Infant Minds,' &c. [7 lines of verse]. Boston: Published By Wells And Lilly. Sold by Van Winkle and Wiley, New-York; and by M. Carey, Philadelphia. 1816.

t.[i], [ii–iv], [1], 2–117, [118, bl.], [1], 2–4 p.;

15 cm.; bound in leather; p.[1]–4 at rear adv. of books.

English ed. London: 1816.

MWA°; CSmH; DLC; MH; NcD; NjR; NN (bound in green paper over bds.); PHi; PP; PPL; Shaw 39060.

[TAYLOR, JOHN] 1580–1654

THUMB BIBLES (arranged chronologically)

1293.1 [—] Verbum Sempiternum. The Seventh Edition with Amendments. New-York: Printed for S. P. [1760?].

1st ½ t.[i], [ii, bl.], 1st t.[iii], [iv–xii], [1], 2–148, 2nd ½ t.[149], [150, bl.], 2nd t.[151], [152–155], 156–275 p.; 5 cm.; bound in leather. *S.P.* probably stands for Samuel Parker who issued what he called a Seventh Edition in New-York.

1st half title: The Bible.
2nd half title: The New Testament.
2nd title: The History Of The New-Testament. New-York: Printed for S.P.
English & Scottish ed. title 1: *Verbum Sempiternum*. London: Verbum Sempiternae [*sic. i.e.* Sempiternum]. Jo Beale for John Hamman. 1614.
English ed. title 2: *The Epitome of the Bible, Briefly Explaining the Contents of the several Books of the Old and New Testament. Penned in Metre for the great Delight and better Remembrance of the Reader.* London. Jonathan Robinson, 1768.
English ed. title 3: *A New History of the Old and New Testament, In a Short, easy and Instructive Manner.* London: Printed for the Author. M,DCC,LXXI.
PP° (1st ½ t.[i], p. xi–xii wanting); MH (1st ½ t.[1] wanting, p. 275 mut.); NN (p. 263–275 wanting); Evans 41171.

1293.2 [—] ——— The Third Edition with Amendments. Boston: Printed for, and Sold by N. Procter near Scarlet's-Wharffe. [*ca.* 1765].

1st ½ t.[i], [ii, bl.], 1st t.[iii], [iv–vii], [viii, bl.], [i–iv], [1–148], 2nd ½ t.[i], [ii, bl.], 2nd t.[iii], [iv, bl.], [v–vi], [1–107], [108, bl.], [i–iv], [i–iv] p.; A–I$_8$, K$_8$, L–R$_8$, S$_5$, plus 2 fly leaves and a leaf pasted to the inside of the back cover which makes a total of 8 leaves for S; 5 cm.; bound in leather.

1st half title: The Bible.

2nd half title: The New Testament.

2nd title: Salvator Mundi. The Third Edition with Amendment [*sic. i.e.* Amendments], Boston: Printed for N. Procter near Scarlet's Wharffe. 1765. There is no "s" on "Amendment" or a period "." after the word in the 2nd title in the MWA copy, but both are present in the DLC, NN, and PP copies. Sig. D$_2$ is misprinted "E$_2$" in MWA, DLC and PP copies, but is correctly printed in the NN copy.

MWA°; DLC (rebound; 2nd t.[iii] mut., last half line wanting); DeWint (last 2 leaves wanting); MH; NN (rebound; 1st ½ t.[i] wanting); PP; RPJCB (sig. A$_1$ & A$_8$ wanting); Evans 10179.

1293.3 [—] ——— The Seventh Edition With Amendments. Boston: Printed by Mein & Fleeming. [*ca.* 1768].

1st ½ t.[i], [ii, bl.], 1st t.[iii], [iv–xii], [1], 2–148, 2nd ½ t.[149], [150, bl.], 2nd t.[151], [152, bl.], [153–155], 156–275 p.; 4.5 cm.; bound in dark red leather.

1st half title: The Bible.

2nd half title: The New/Testa/ment.

2nd title: The History Of The New-Testament. Boston: Printed by Mein & Fleeming.

MH°; MB (emb. st. on 1st t.[iii]; p. 179–180, [247–250]; 255–258, 265–272, 275 wanting); MWA (New Testament only issued as a separate book, p. 263–275 wanting); Evans 41889.

1293.4 [—] ——— Philadelphia: Printed by A. Steuart. [1769?].

1st ½ t.[i], [ii, bl.], t.[iii], [iv, bl.], [v–vi],[i–vi], [7–154], 2nd ½ t.[155], [156, bl.], 2nd t.[157], [158, bl.], [159–268], 269–272, [273–280] p.; [a]$_2$, a$_{14}$, B–H$_{16}$, I$_{15}$+1 leaf; 5 cm.; bound in Dutch paper over bds. Holograph signature p. [ii]: *Elizabeth Wiggins Ju^r the 20th. of the 5 Month A.D. 1769.*

1st half title: The Bible.

2nd half title: The New TESTA-/MENT.

2nd title: The History Of The New Testament. Philadelphia: Printed by A. Steuart.

MWA-W°; CLU; DLC (sigs. loose in binding); PP; Evans 42009.

1293.5 [—] ——— The Third Edition with Amendments. Providence: Printed and Sold by John Waterman at the Paper Mills. [*ca.* 1768].

1st ½ t.[i], [ii, bl.], 1st t.[iii], [iv–vii], [viii, bl.],

[i–iv], [1–148], 2nd ½ t.[i], [ii, bl.], 2nd t.[iii], [iv, bl.], [v–vi], [1–107], [108, bl.], [i–iv], [i–iv], p; A–R$_8$, S$_5$, no J; 5.5 cm.; The pagination of the Boston 1786 edition was followed in supplying the page numbering. Text same as no. **1293.2** and appears to have been printed from standing type.

1st half title: The Bible.

2nd half title: The New Testament.

2nd title: Salvator Mundi. The Fifth Edition with Amendments. Providence, Printed and Sold by John Waterman.

MH° (D$_7$, S$_5$ mut.); MWA (sig.[A]–[A]$_8$, H$_2$–H$_3$ [L]$_1$, [L]$_2$, S$_5$ wanting, D$_6$ mut.); RHi (wants 1st title, and 2nd ½ title); MWA-W (sig. [A]$_1$, B$_8$, C$_1$, D$_8$, E–H$_8$, I$_2$–I$_8$, K–M$_8$, wanting; S$_4$–S$_5$ mut.); PP; Evans 11086.

1293.6 [—] ———— The Twelvth [*sic. i.e.* Twelfth] Edition, with Amendments. Boston: Printed in 1786.

1st ½ t.[i], [ii], 1st t.[iii], [iv–v], vi–vii, [viii, bl.], [i], ii–iii, v [*sic. i.e.* iv], I, 2–148, 2nd ½ t.[i], [ii, bl.], 2nd t.[iii], [iv, bl.], [v], vi, [1], 2–107, [108, bl.], [i], ii–iv, [i], ii–iv p.; [A]–H$_{16}$, I$_{13}$; 5 cm.; bound in leather over w. bds.; p. I, [A]$_7$ is a Roman numeral; p. 9, [A]$_{11}$ is printed in larger type than the other page numbers.

1st half title: The Bible.

2nd half title: The New Testament.

2nd title: Salvator Mundi. The Twelvth [*sic. i.e.* Twelfth] Edition, with Amendments. Boston: Printed in 1786.

MWA-W°; MB (emb. st. on t.[iii], ½ t.[i], p.[ii], [v]–vi, 17–18, 21–22, 55–56); MH (p. [i–viii], 1–16, 93–94 wanting, p. 83–84 mut.); MiD; Evans 44974.

1293.7 [—] THE BIBLE. The Eighth Editio$_n$ [with the "n" lower than the rest of the word]. Philadelphia: Printed for Sower & Jones, 6$_6$, with the second "6" lower than the first] No. Third-street. by Jacob Johnson & Co. [1796?].

fr.[2], 1st t.[3], [4–8], 9–162, ½ t.[163], fr.[164], 2nd t.[165], [166–169], 170–286 p.; illus.; 5.5 cm.; bound in leather; illus. p. [177] signed *F. Reiche Sc;* that on p. [202] signed *FR.* The dedication p.[6]: "Most hopeful George,° into thy hands we give. The Sum of that which makes us ever live." The asterisk after the name refers to the footnote "°G. Wash-

ington," so that there can be no doubt that King George is not referred to. The footnote is followed by the catchword "And." On p. 285 the page number is printed "2". Sower & Jones printed at 66 N. Third-street in 1793–1794 according to Evans but H. Glenn and Maud O. Brown state that they were there in 1795–1796 with the first member of the firm being spelled Sauer. If Evans' dates are too early, then his date [1794] for this book is open to question and the date [1796] would be preferable being closer to the 1798 ed., no. **1293.8**, which closely resembles this book except for a few differences.

Half title: The New Testament.

2nd title: The History Of The New Testament. F$_3$.

MWA° (rebound); Ahlstrom; MH; NN (copy 1, bound in leather; copy 2, bound in marbled paper over bds.); PP; Evans 26649.

1293.8 [—] ——— The Ninth Edition. Philadelphia: Printed for W. Jones, No. 30, N. Fourth st. 1798.

fr.[ii], 1st t.[1], [2, bl.], 2nd t.[3], [4, bl.], [5–8], 9–162, ½ t.[163], fr.[164], 2nd t.[165], [166, bl.], [167–169], 170–286 p.; illus.; 5.5 cm.; bound in leather. The text is the same as no. **1293.7** but some pages have been changed and reset. The dedication p.[8]: "Most worthy George,° into thy hands we give, The sum of that which makes us ever live, °G. Washington [no catch word]." Page number 285 is printed "2 8". In the PP copy 1st t.[1] is pasted over 2nd t.[3] so that the title page of the earlier edition is cancelled. The MWA-W copy has the 2nd t.[3] unpasted from the preceding leaf or 1st t.[1].

2nd title: The Bible. The Eighth Editio$_n$ [with the "n" lower than the rest of the word]. Philadelphia: ——— [same as 1st t.[3] of **1293.7**]. The ½ t.[163] and 2nd t.[165] are the same as those on the same pages in no. **1293.7**.

MWA-W°; PP; Evans 33510.

1293.9 [—] ——— The ninth Edition. New-England, Printed For The Purchaser. [*ca.* 1800].

fr.[2], t.[3], [4–8], 9–154, 156 [*sic. i.e.* 155], 155 [*sic. i.e.* 156], ½ t.[157], [158–159], 160–274 p.; front. only illus.; 5 cm.; bound in leather over w. bds.

Half title: The New Testament.

MWA-T° (p. 49–72, 225–240, 265–274 wanting); PP (p. 274 slightly mut. affecting page no.); Evans 35190.

1293.10 [—] Verbum Sempiternum. A New Edition. Boston: Printed by Thomas Fleet, 1801.
1st ½ t.[1], [2], 1st t.[3], [4–12], 13–160, 2nd ½ t.[i], [ii], 2nd t.[iii], [iv–v], vi, [1], 2–107, [108], [i], ii–iv, [i], ii–iv p.; 5.5 cm.; bound in leather over w. bds. On p. [162] the cut of an open book with the word "Bible" on it is a *New England Primer* alphabet cut used in *The Holy Bible In Verse* in 1717 in **492.1**; 1724 in **492.3**; 1729 in **492.4**. The cuts on p.[4] and [108] of the Salvator Mundi are the same ones used by T. & J. Fleet for a capital, p. 3, in *The Prodigal Daughter*, Boston, [*ca.* 1790], no. **1068.10**.
1st half title: The Bible.
2nd half title: The New Testament.
2nd title: Salvator Mundi. Thirteenth Edition, with Amendments. Boston: Printed by T. Fleet. 1802.
MWA-W° (1st ½ t.[1], p.[2] 25–26, 49–50, 71–72 of Verbum Sempiternum wanting); MB; Shaw 1383.

1293.11 [—] The Holy Bible In Miniature: Printed by Samuel Sower. 1802.
fr.[2], 1st t.[3], [4, bl.], [5–8], 9–160, 1st ½ t.[161], [162, bl.], 2nd ½ t.[163], [164, bl.], [165–167], 168–283, [284], [285–288] p.; illus.; 5.5 cm.; bound in black leather.
1st half title: The New Testament. 1803.
2nd half title: The History of the New Testament.
p.[5]: Dedication to his Excellency G. Washington, President of the United States of America; p. 284: The Bible is the property of; p.[285]: Family Record. Marriages.; p.[286–287] Family Record. Births.; p.[288]: Family Record. Deaths.
MdHi°; DLC (marbled paper covers); MdBE (fr.[2], p. 285–288 wanting); Shaw 1880 and 3792 (dated 1803).

1293.12 [—] An History Of The Bible And Apocraphy Versified, And Adorned With Cuts. 1805.
t.[3], [4–9], 10–69, [70, bl.], ½ t.[71], [72–74], 75–127, [128] p.; illus.; 6.5 cm.; bound in yellow wallpaper ornamented with a black and white chain design.
Half title: The New Testament Versified.
Walcott°.

1293.13 [—] The Bible And Apocraphy Versified, And Adorned With Cuts. 1805.
t.[3], [4–9], 10–69, [70, bl.], ½ t.[71], [72–74], 75–127, [128] p.; illus.; 6 cm.; marbled paper covers. The text is identical with no. **1293.12** only t.[3] has been changed.
MWA-W°.

1293.14 [—] Verbum Sempiternum. A New Edition. Wm. Powers. [1810].
1st ½ t.[1], [2], 1st t.[3], [4–12], 13–160, 2nd t.[i], [ii, bl.], 2nd t.[iii], [iv, bl.], [v–vi], [1], 2–107, [108, bl.], [i], ii–iv, [i], ii–iv p.; 5.5 cm.; bound in leather.
1st half title: The Bible. 1810.
2nd half title: The New Testament.
2nd title: Salvator Mundi. A New Edition. Wm. Powers, Printer. 1810.
Welch°; CLU; MH (1st t.[1] wanting); MWA (bound in lilac paper over bds.); NN (p. 71–72, 97–98 of Verbum Sempiternum, [iii]–2 of Salvator Mundi, & covers wanting); Shaw 19540.

1293.15 [—] The Bible. Ninth Edition. Rutland [Vt.]: Printed by Fay & Davison. [*ca.* 1813].
fr.[2], t.[3], [4–8], 9–161, [162, bl.], 1st ½ t.[163], fr.[164]; 2nd ½ t.[165] [166–169], 170–286 p.; illus.; 5.5 cm.; bound in buff paper, ornamented with blue dots, over bds. The front fly leaf has a holograph inscription: *Amelia Vernon, March 8, 1813.* The firm of Fay & Davison was in existence from June 28, 1813— Dec. 31, 1816. (MWA cat.).
1st half title: The New Testament.
2nd half title: The History Of The New Testament.
Welch°; DLC; MWA; VtHi; McCorison 1537; Shaw 27930.

TAYLOR, JOSEPH 1761 or 1762–1844
1294 — Tales Of The Robin, And Other Small Birds; Selected From The British Poets, For The Instruction and Amusement of Young People. By Joseph Taylor, Compiler of the General Character of the Dog, Wonders of the Horse, &c. &c. [2 lines of verse] Philadelphia: Published And Sold By Wm. Charles, No. 32, South Third Street. M'Carty & Davis, Printers. 1817.
fr.[ii], t.[i], [2–3], 4–140, [141–144, contents] p.; 6 pl. including front.; 14.5 cm.; bound in buff paper over bds., green leather spine.

English ed. London: W. & T. Darton. 1808.
MWA° copy 1, uncolored pl.; copy 2, colored
pl.); PP (col. pl.); Shaw 42252.

1295 The Teaching Parrot For Children.
Philadelphia: Published By Johnson & Warner,
No. 147, High Street. J. Bouvier, Printer. 1809.
t.[1], [2–36] p.; illus.; 13 cm.; pink paper covers.
Adv. by Johnson & Warner, 1814 in no. **1449.2.**
English ed. London: Darton And Harvey, 1802.
NNC-Pl°; Shaw 18733.

Tea-Table Dialogues. *See* Johnson, Richard, no.
688.1.

Telescope, Tom (*pseud.*) *See* [Newbery, John]
ed., no. **949.1.**

1296 Mr. Telltruth's Natural History Of
Birds. Worcester: adv. by I. Thomas, 1786 in
395.1.

TELLTRUTH, T. *pseud.*
The Natural History Of Four-Footed Beasts.
See Columbus, Charley (*pseud.*), The Natural
History Of Beasts, no. **222.**

THACKWRAY, WILLIAM
1297.1 — Ten Commandments, Philadelphia:
adv. by E. & R. Parker, 1818 in **704.1.**

1297.2 — The Ten Commandments, In Verse.
By William Thackwray, Walworth. Embellished
with Engravings. Philadelphia: Published by E.
and R. Parker, No. 178, Market Street. J. R. A.
Skerrett, Printer. Price coloured, 12 cents—Plain,
6 cts. 1819.
fr.[2], t.[3], [4–5], 6–30, [31, illus.] p.; 8 full
page illus.; 9.5 cm.; pr. & illus. paper covers.;
no illus. for 1st, 3rd, 7th commandments; pages
16–17, 24–25, 28–29 blank.
MWA-T°.

1298 The Testament Abridged: Or The His-
tory Of The New Testament. Adorned with Cuts.
For The Use Of Children. [2 lines quot.] Luke
xvii, 16. New-York: Printed by William Durell,
No. 106, Maiden-Lane. 1800.
fr.[2], t.[3], [4–5], 6–63 p.; illus.; 10.5 cm.
Adv. by W. Durell, 1790 in **612.5**; bound with
The Holy Bible Abridged, 1792 in **612.9.**
MWA° (p. 15–16 mut.).

Think Before You Speak. *See* Dorset, Catherine
Ann. no. **297.1.**

THOMAS THUMB

1299 The History Of Thomas Thumb, With
His wonderful Adventures; And Some Anecdotes
respecting Grumbo The Great Giant. Wilmington
[Del.]: Printed by James Adams, North-Side of
the upper Market-House, M,DXX,XCVII.
fr.[2], t.[3], 4–27, [28, illus.], [29], 30, [31,
adv.] p.; front. & illus. p. [28] only illus.; 8 cm.;
illus. white paper covers; p. [29]–30 adv. list of
20 books.
PP°; PHi (i. st. on t.[3]); Evans 32931.

THOUGHTFUL, MISS *pseud.*
1300.1 — Instructive And Entertaining Emblems, On Various Subjects, In Prose And Verse.
By Miss Thoughtful. Hartford: Printed By J. Babcock. 1795.
fr.[2], t.[3], [4, adv.], 5–31 p.; illus.; 10 cm.;
paper covers.
CLU°; CtHi° MWA; Evans 47466.

1300.2 — ——— Hartford: Printed By J. Babcock. 1796.
fr.[2], t.[3], [4–5], 6–30, [31, adv.] p.; illus.;
10 cm.; orange paper covers.
MWA-W°; MiU; Evans 47814.

1300.3 — ——— Hartford: Printed by John
Babcock. 1798.
fr.[2], t.[3], [4–5], 6–30, [31, adv.] p.; illus.;
11.5 cm.; violet and silver Dutch paper covers.
CtHi°; NN (i. st. p. [4], & 29, p. 9–10, 15–18,
23–24 wanting, p. 13–14, 19–20 mut.); Evans
48482; Weiss 1936, p. 395.

1301.1 Thoughtlessness Corrected; or, The
History of Emily Willis. Boston, Pr. by Munroe &
Francis, 1813.
15 p.
Shaw 29948.

1301.2 Thoughtlessness Corrected: Or The
History of Emily Willis. First Published By The
Christian Tract Society. No. XXII. Boston: Wells
And Lilly, Court-Street. 1820.
t.[1], [2–3], 4–20 p.; 16 cm.
MSaE°.

1302 THE THREE BROTHERS, a moral tale; the Three Sisters, a moral tale; and Courage inspired by Friendship, a moral tale; the whole embellished with a number of engravings. Boston: adv. by W. Spotswood, 1795 in **1006.2.**

1303 THREE EVENINGS AMUSEMENT FOR CHILDREN Of Ten To Twelve Years Of Age. Philadelphia: adv. by Johnson & Warner, 1813 in **1050,** and 1814 in **1449.2.** This is the cover title of *The Budget; Or Three Evenings Amusement,* no. **133.**

THREE INSTRUCTIVE TALES. *See* P—, C. [Palmer, Charlotte], no. **968.**

THREE STORIES FOR YOUNG CHILDREN. *See* Edgeworth, Maria, no. **333.**

1304 THROWING SQUIBS, Or The Unlucky Boy. Ornamented with Cuts. Windham [Conn.]: Printed by Samuel Webb. 1813.

> t.[3], [4–5], 6–21, [22, alphabet] p.; illus.; 10 cm. The story appeared in England in *Profitable Amusement For Children. London: Vernor And Hood; J. Harris, 1802.*
> MWA° (two leaves or fr.[2]? & p. [23]? & covers wanting); Shaw 29951.

THUMB, THOMAS *pseud.*
1305 [—] A BAG OF NUTS. New-York: adv. by Hugh Gaine, 1786 in John Clarke's Tr. *Corderii Colloquiorum.*

1306.1 — A BAG OF NUTS, READY CRACKED: Or, Instructive Fables, Ingenious Riddles, And Merry Conundrums. By the Celebrated and Facetious Thomas Thumb, Esq. Published for the Benefit of all little Masters and Misses who love Reading as well as Playing. The First Worcester Edition. Worcester, (Massachusetts) Printed By Isaiah Thomas, And Sold At His Book-Store, MDCCLXXXVI.

> fr.[ii], t.[iii], [iv–v], vi–xiii, [14], 15–95 p.; illus.; 10 cm.; Dutch paper covers. *See also* no. **1084.**
> English & Scottish ed. London: adv. by F. Newbery, 1775 in *The Cries Of London.*
> MWA°; Evans 20748.

1306.2 ——— Philadelphia: Printed by W. Young, No. 52, Second-street, the corner of Chesnut-street. M,DCC,XCIII.

> fr.[ii], t.[iii], [iv–v], vi–viii, 9–52+ p.; illus.;

10 cm.; Dutch paper covers. Adv. by W. Young, 1794 in **305.**
MWA-W° (all after p. 52, 6 leaves, probably p. 53–63 and rear cover wanting).

1306.3 ——— Second Worcester Edition. Worcester, Massachusetts: Printed By I. Thomas, Jun. Sold Wholesale and Retail at his Book-Store. September 1798.

> fr.[2], t.[3], [4–5], 6–95 p.; illus.; 10.5 cm.; green Dutch paper covers; illus. p. 78, 82, [89], 92 were used by I. Thomas in no. **782;** the caption p. 22: The Greddy [*sic. i.e.* Greedy] Mouse. Large letters "IT", formed of flowers, are on p. 21, which are absent in no. **1306.1.**
> Welch° (p.[3–4], 95 mut.); MWA; PP (fr.[2], 93–95 & covers wanting; p. 91–92½ wanting, p.[3]–11, 83–90 slightly mut. affecting page numbers.

THUMBE, THOMAS *pseud.*
1307 — RHYMING ALPHABET; Or, Tom Thumb's Delight. By Thomas Thumbe. Hartford: Printed by B. & J. Russell, State-Street. 1815.

> t.[1], [2–3], 4–14, [15–16] p.; 7.5 cm.; paper covers.
> CtHi°; Shaw 35779.

1308 THE THUNDERSTORM; Or, The History Of Tom Watson, The Unnatural Son; Being a Warning to all Parents. Philadelphia: Published by the Philadelphia Tract Society, and for sale at their Repository, No. 8, South Front street. Wm. Bradford, Agent. November, 1817.

> t.[1], [2], 3–12 p.; title page vignette only illus.; 18 cm.
> English ed. London: *Cheap Repository.* J. Evans And Co Pr., J. Hatchard; S. Hazard, Bath.
> MWA-T°; NjR; Shaw 41483.

TICKLEPITCHER, TOBY *pseud.*
1309.1 — THE HOBBY HORSE. Worcester: adv. by I. Thomas, 1786 in **395.1.**

1309.2 — THE HOBBY HORSE; Or, Christmas Companion: Containing, Among other interesting Particulars, The Song of a Cock and Bull, A Canterbury Story, And A Tale Of A Tub. Faithfully copied from the original Manuscript, in the Vatican Library. By Toby Ticklepitcher. Embellished with elegant Cuts. Boston: Printed By Hosea Sprague. 1804.

t.[1], [2], 3–55 p.; 10 cm.; pages 52–54 have
English nursery rhymes.
English ed. London: adv. by F. Newbery in
London Chronicle Jan. 8–10, 1771.
MWA°; Shaw 6484a and 7350.

'TIS ALL FOR THE BEST. *See* More, Hannah, no.
895.1.

TITMOUSE, TOMMY. *See* Tommy Titmouse. The
History Of Tommy Titmouse, no. **1322.1.**

1310 (No. 14.) TO A YOUTH AT SCHOOL. Published By The Philadelphia Female Tract Society.
[caption title]. Printed by Lydia R. Bailey, No. 10,
North Alley, Philad. [1816] [colophon p. 12].
  [1], 2–12 p.; 14 cm.
  MWA° (bound with other tracts, with which
*The First Annual Report Of The Philadelphia
Female Tract Society For The Year 1816* was
originally bound); Shaw 39091.

1311 A TOKEN FOR YOUTH; Containing Several
Advices And Directions To Children And Youth.
Also The Lives And Glorious Martyrdoms Of Sev-
eral Young Persons. . . . To Which Is Added An
Account of God's Gracious Dealings With Some
Young Persons And Children. By J.J. Twenty-Fifth
Edition. Boston 1727.
  Evans 2886.

A TOKEN FOR YOUTH, Or Comfort to Children.
See Rede, Sarah, no. **1090.1.**

1312 TOM THE PIPER'S SON, In Two Parts, Illustrated With Whimsical Engravings. Part The First.
Philadelphia Published and sold wholesale, by Wm.
Charles, And may be had of all the Book-sellers.
1808. price 12½ cents. [cover title].
  [1–8] p. engr. on one side only of 8 leaves; illus.;
12.5 cm.; pr. yellow paper covers.
  English ed. London: J. E. Evans [1803?].
  DLC° (rear cover ¾ wanting); MWA (front
cover worn & mut.); Shaw 16334.

TOM THE PIPER'S SON. PT. II. *See* A Continuation
Of Tom The Piper's Son, no. **231.1.**

TOM THUMB (arranged chronologically)

1313.1 THE EXHIBITION OF TOM THUMB; Being
An Account Of many valuable and surprising

Curiosities Which he has collected In the Course
of his Travels, For The Instruction and Amuse-
ment Of the American Youth. The First Worcester
Edition. Printed at Worcester, Massachusetts, By
Isaiah Thomas And sold, Wholesale and Retail, at
his Book-Store. MDCCLXXXVII. Sold also by E.
Battelle, in Boston.
  fr.[2], t.[3], [4–5], 6–60, [61–63, adv. list of
books] p.; illus.; 10 cm.; Dutch paper covers.
  Adv. by I. Thomas 1786 in **395.1** under the title:
Tom Thumb's Exhibition.
  English ed.; *Tom Thumb's Exhibition.* London:
adv. by F. Newbery, 1775 in *The Cries Of
London.*
  MWA°; PP; Evans 20749.

1313.2 ———— The Second Worcester Edition.
Printed At Worcester, Massachusetts, By James R.
Hutchins, For Isaiah Thomas, And Sold Wholesale
and Retail, at His Book-Store.—MDCCXCV.
  fr.[2], t.[3], [4–5], 6–60, [61–63, adv.] p.; illus.;
10.5 cm.; illus. blue paper covers.
  MWA°; Evans 29632.

1314.1 THE LIFE AND DEATH OF TOM THUMB,
The Little Giant. Together with some Curious
Anecdotes Respecting Grumbo, The Great Giant,
King of the country of Eagles. Embellished with
Cuts. Hartford: Printed By John Babcock. 1800.
  fr.[2], t.[3], [4–5], 6–31; illus.; 11 cm.; orange
Dutch paper covers.
  English & Scottish ed.: *The Life And Death Of
Tom Thumb.* Gainsbrough: Mozley's Lilliputian
Book Manufactory. [*ca.* 1796].
  NjP°; Ct (fr.[2], p. 31 & covers wanting); Evans
49107; Hamilton 190.

1314.3 ———— From Sidney's Press, Hew-Haven
cock. 1802.
  fr.[2], t.[3], [4–5], 6–31 p.; illus.; 11.5 cm.;
marbled paper covers; p. no."）9)" the front
bracket printed backwards.
  MWA°; CtY (p. 29–30 misbound after p.[4];
marbled paper covers); Shaw 2534.

1314.2 ———— Hartford: Printed By John Bab-
[*sic. i.e.* New-Haven]. 1805.
  fr.[2], t.[3], [4–5], 6–31 p.; illus.; 10.5 cm.;
orange Dutch paper covers.
  MWA° (date torn off of t.[3]); Shaw 8785.

1314.4 ——— Ornamented with Cuts. From Sidney's Press. New-Haven. 1806.

　　fr.[2], t.[3], [4–5], 6–31 p.; illus.; 10.5 cm.; buff Dutch paper covers.

　　MWA°; CtHi; Shaw 10728.

1314.5 ——— Philadelphia: adv. by John Adams, 1806 in **646.3**.

1314.6 [———] From Sidney's Press, New Haven. 1807?] [imaginary title and imprint mostly taken from **1314.4**].

　　7–28 p.; illus.; 10.5 cm. This fragment of the [1807?] edition has a similar format and the same cuts as editions of 1805 in **1314.3**; 1806 in **1314.4**; 1809 in **1314.7**. Because of the closeness of this book to the 1806 edition with the breaks in the cut on p. 24 closest to the 1809 edition this book has been dated [1807?].

　　MWA°.

1314.7 ——— Embellished with Cuts. Philadelphia: Printed For B. & T. Kite. 1807.

　　fr.[2], t.[3], [4–5], 6–30 p.; illus.; 10.5 cm.; pr. & illus. blue paper covers.

　　CtHi°.

1314.8 ——— Litchfield [Conn.]: Printed By Hosmer & Goodwin. 1808.

　　fr.[2], t.[3], [4–5], 6–31 p.; illus.; 10 cm.; orange paper covers.

　　MWA-W°; CtHi (Dutch paper covers); Shaw 50891.

1314.9 ——— Adorned With Cuts. Sidney's Press, New Haven. 1808.

　　fr. [2], t. [3], [4–5], 6–31p.; illus.; 10.6 cm.; Dutch paper covers

　　MWA°.

1314.10 ——— From Sidney's Press, New-Haven. 1809.

　　fr.[2], t.[3], [4–5], 6–31 p.; illus.; 10.5 cm.; yellow paper covers.

　　Welch° (fr.[2] & front cover wanting, t.[3] mut.); MWA.

1314.11 ——— New-Haven, 1810.

　　fr.[2], t.[3], [4–5], 6–31 p.; illus.; 10.5 cm.; buff paper covers.

　　MWA°; CtHi; Shaw 51019.

1314.12 ——— From Sidney's Press. New-Haven, 1812.

　　fr.[2], t.[3], [4–5], 6–31 p.; 10 cm.

　　CtHi°; DLC (p. 29–30 upper half wanting, p. 26, 31 mut.); MWA-T; Shaw 25866.

1314.13 ——— Thumb, The Little Giant. Ornamented With Cuts. Boston: Printed By N. Coverly, jun. Milk-Street. 1813.

　　t.[1], [2–15] p.; illus.; 10 cm.; wallpaper covers.

　　DLC° (buff paper covers ornamented with red, rear cover wanting); Shaw 29957.

1314.14 ——— Boston: Printed By N. Coverly, Jun. Milk-Street, 1814.

　　t.[1], [2–16] p.; illus.; 10 cm.; wallpaper covers.

　　PP°; MB (p.[15–16] wanting); Shaw 31928.

1314.15 ——— Tom Thumb, The Little Giant. ——— [same as no. **1314.1**] Hartford: Printed by Sheldon & Goodwin. Stereotyped by J. F. & C. Starr. [1815].

　　fr.[2], t.[3], [4–5], 6–31 p.; illus.; 10 cm.; pr. & illus. paper covers. *See* **563.15** for note on printers.

　　MWA°; CLU; Ct (i. st. on front cover); CtHi.

Tom Thumb's Exhibition. *See* Exhibition of Tom Thumb, no. **1313.1**.

1315.1 Tom Thumb's Folio, For Little Giants. To which is prefixed, An Abstract Of The Life of Mr. Thumb. And an Historical Account of The wonderful Deeds he performed. Together with Some Anecdotes respecting Grumbo, the great Giant. Sold at the Bible and Heart, in Cornhill, Boston. [*ca.* 1780].

　　t.[1], 2–32 p.; illus.; 10 cm.; blue marbled paper covers. Some of the illustrations are *New England Primer* alphabet cuts used in *The Holy Bible In Verse, 1717*. *See* discussion under Benjamin Harris, no. **492.1**. Thomas and John Fleet printed at The Bible and Heart, 1780–1795. The original name of the firm was The Crown and Heart, but according to I. Thomas when crowns became unpopular the Bible was substituted for a crown.

English, Scottish & Irish ed. London: adv. by J. Newbery, 1767 in *The History Of Little Goody Two-Shoes*.

　　CtHi°; MWA; PP; Evans 43755.

1315.2 ——— Folio, Or a new Play-Thing for little Boy's And Girls. To which is prefixed An Abstract of The Life of Mr. Thumb, And An Historical Account of the Wonderful Deeds he performed. Together With some Anecdotes respecting Grumbo the Great Giant. Boston: Printed and Sold by Nathaniel Coverly, near the White-Horse. 1783.

t.[1], 2–32 p.; illus.; 10.5 cm.; black paper covers.

MWA°; Evans 44470.

1315.3 ——— Folio: Or, A New Threepenny Play Thing For Little Giants. To which is prefixed, An Abstract of The Life of Mr. Thumb, And An Historical Account of the Wonderful Deeds he performed. Together with Some Anecdotes respecting Grumbo the Great Giant. The First Worcester Edition. Printed at Worcester, Massachusetts. By Isaiah Thomas, And Sold, Wholesale and Retail, at his Book Store. MDCCLXXXVII.

fr.[2], t.[3], [4–6], 7–28, [29–30 adv. of books], 31 p.; illus.; 10 cm.; illus. blue paper covers.

MWA° (p. [5]–13 closely trimmed; p. 19–24 mut.); Evans 20750.

1315.4 ——— Hartford: Printed by Nathaniel Pat[ten]. M,DCC,LXXX,IX.

fr.[2], t.[3], [4–5], 6–29 p.; illus.; 9.5 cm.; Dutch paper covers.

CtHi° (fr.[2], t.[3] mut.); Evans 45620.

1315.5 ——— New-York: adv. by William Durell, 1790 in **612.5**.

1315.6 ——— Boston: Printed and sold by Samuel Hall, No. 55, Cornhill. 1791.

fr.[2], t.[3], [4–5], 6–31 p.; illus.; 9 cm.; Dutch paper covers; p. [29–30] adv. of 15 titles; p. 31 the cut of a man on horseback used in S. Hall editions of *The History Of Master Jackey And Miss Harriot*. Adv. by S. Hall, 1792 in **1408.33**. Advertisement caption same as in no. **408.3**.

CtHi°, MB (p. 31 wanting); MWA-W (fr.[2], t.[3], p. [4], 25–31 & covers wanting); Evans 46305.

1315.7 ——— Folio; Or, A New Play-Thing For Little Giants ——— [same as Worcester 1787 edition] —New York:—Printed By William Durell. No. 19, Queen-Street. 1793.

fr.[2], t.[3], [4], 5–30 p.; illus.; 9.5 cm.; reddish-brown paper covers. Adv. by William Durell, 1790 in *The Holy Bible Abridged*.

MWA-W°; Evans 46890.

1315.8 ——— [same as **1315.3**] Boston: Printed and sold by Samuel Hall, No. 53, Cornhill. 1794.

fr.[2], t.[3], [4, alphabet], [5], 6–28, [29–31, adv.] p.; illus.; 10 cm.; Dutch paper covers. On the recto of fr.[2] there are two large capital "M"s one above the other $_{\text{"M"}}^{\text{M}}$.

PP° (front cover wanting; fr.[2], mut.); MH; NjP (Dutch paper covers); Evans 47239; Hamilton 155.

1315.9 ——— An Abstrbct [*sic. i.e.* Abstract] Of The Life ——— [same as **1315.3**] Giant. Printed By John Norman, No. 75, Newbury-Street, Boston. [1794?].

t.[3], [4–5], 6–29 p.; illus.; 9 cm. On p. 15 the page number is misprinted "51". John Norman appears to have written his address No. 75 Newbury St. from 1790–1794. Also in 1794 and from 1796–1798 the address is printed No. 75 Newbury-Street with the word "Street" spelled out. Earlier than this, 1790–1792 his address was: At his Office, No. 75 Newbury-Street, Opposite the sign of The Lamb. From these data on addresses obtained from Evans the book is dated [1794?]. Also, no. **1315.10** has the manuscript date 1795 written in it.

PP° (rebound; fr.[2] & covers wanting); Evans 47238.

1315.10 ——— An Abstract Of The Life ——— [same as **1315.9**] Giant. Printed By John Norman, No. 75, Newbury-Street, Boston. [1795?].

fr.[2], t.[3], [4–5], 6–29 p. illus.; 9 cm.; gray paper covers; a variant of no. **1315.9**. The word "Abstract" on the title page is correctly spelled, and the page number on p. 15 is correctly printed. On p. 26 there is a manuscript inscriptions *Saley Smith Her Book 1795*. This helps date this book. It could have been a corrected edition printed in [1794?] or printed a year later in [1795].

MWA-W°; Evans 47238.

1315.11 ——— Philadelphia: adv. by William Young, 1794 in **305**.

1315.12 ———— The Second Worcester Edition. Printed at Worcester, Massachusetts, By Isaiah Thomas. And Sold Wholesale and Retail at His Bookstore. MDCCXCIV.
fr.[2], t.[3], [4–5], 6–31 p.; illus.; 10.5 cm.; green Dutch paper covers.
MWA°; NjN; Evans 27800.

1315.13 ———— Boston: adv. by S. Hall, 1796 in **587.40**.

1315.14 ———— Folio: Or, A New Penny Play-Thing For Little Giants. ———— [same as no. 1315.3] Giant. New-York: Printed by J. Oram, for the Society of Bookbinder's 1796. Price Three Cents.
fr. 2, t.[3], 4–30 p.; illus.; 10 cm.; paper covers.
NB° (bpl. pasted over fr.[2]); NNMM (i. st. on t.[3], p. 5, 18, 28; covers wanting; p. 29–30 upper third of page wanting; fr. 2, t.[3], p. 19–20 mut.); Evans 47940.

1315.15 ———— Hudson [N.Y.]: Printed by Ashbel Stoddard, And sold Wholesale and Retail, at his Book-Store, corner of Warren and Third Streets. 1806.
fr.[2], t.[3], [4–5], 6–31 p.; illus.; 11 cm.
OChRHi° (page number torn away from p. 6; p. 31 mut.); Shaw 11458.

1316.1 Tom Thumb's Little Book. Boston: adv. by Samuel Hall, 1790 in **1406.3**; 1791 in **408.3**; 1792 in **1408.33**; 1793 in **955.3**; 1794 in **673.8**; 1795 in **1384.3**. Evans 29635 lists an edition dated [1795] but gives no location.
Since no copy of no. **1316.1** has been located it is a matter of conjecture what the text was. It may have been the same as no. **1316.2** below, although Nathaniel Coverly had a way of changing the usual format of the book by omitting or adding certain portions. Another possibility is that the text was the same as *Tom Thumb's Play Book* with the title page changed. No. **1318.8** is fragmentary copy of a book listed as *Tom Thumb's Play Book* which is lacking the title page. It may actually be a Samuel Hall edition of *Tom Thumb's Little Book*.

1316.2 Tom Thumb's Little Book, To Teach Children their Letters As soon as they can speak. Being a new and pleasant Method to allure Little Children In the first Principles Of Learning.

Boston: Printed and sold by N. Coverly, 1794. (Price Three Pence).
½t.[1], fr.[2], t.[3], 4–16 p.; front. only illus.; 9.5 cm.; marbled paper covers. The text is the same as *Tom Thumb's Play-Book*, no. **1318.1**, through "Grace after meat," with the final five prayers at the end omitted. Half title: Tom Thumb's Little Book.
MWA-W°; DLC (covers wanting); Evans 27801.

1317.1 Tom Thumb's New Riddle Book; Containing A variety of Entertaining Riddles for the Amusement of Young Masters and Misses. To which is added The new A,B,C; Being A Complete Alphabet in Verse, to entice Children to learn their Letters. Boston: Printed and sold by John W. Folsom, No. 30, Union-Street. 1798.
fr.[2], t.[3], [4–5], 6–31 p.; front. & illus. p. 8, 10, 18 only illus.; 10 cm.; illus. paper covers.
MSaE°.

1317.2 ———— Exeter [N.H.]: adv. by Henry Ranlet, 1801 in **558.2**.

1317.3 ———— Exeter [N.H.]: adv. by Norris & Sawyer, 1808 in **428.3**.

1318.1 Tom Thumb's Play-Book; To teach Children their Letters as soon as they can speak. Being A New and pleasant Method to allure Little Ones in the first Principles of Learning. Boston: Printed for and sold by A. Barclay in Cornhill. [1764].
t.[1], [2–3], 4–31, [32, alphabet] p.; 6.5 cm.; illus. paper covers. [blank] p.[2]; Alphabet. Double Letters, p.[3]; [alphabet rhyme] A a Apple pye, p. 4–5; [alphabet rhyme]A was an Archer, p. 6–17; [double letters] Ab eb ib ob, ub ac ec ic oc/ab [*sic. i.e.* ad] ed id ob [*sic. i.e.* od] ud af if of/ . . . , p. 18; [triple letters] Bla ble bli . . . , p. 19; A Scripture Catechism, p. 20–23; Grage [*sic. i.e.* Grace] before Meat, p. 23–24; Grace after Meat, p. 24; A Prayer at your uprising, p. 25–26; A Prayer before you sleep, p. 26–27; The young Child's Morning Prayer, p. 28–29; The young Child's Evening Prayer, p. 29–30; The Lord's Prayer, p. 30–31; [upper case alphabet] A–Z, p. [32]. Eleven printer's ornaments are present. On the blank page opposite the title page there is a holograph inscription written in Isaiah Thomas' handwrit-

ing: *Printed by I. Thomas when A'prentice in 1764. for A. Barclay.* The date at first glance could be taken for 1761 or 1762 but it appears to be 1764. Comparison of **1318.1** and **1318.4** shows that p. 5–30 are identical in both books. The 1771 edition has these pages printed from standing type. Page 4 in the 1771 edition has an extra line "L l Long'd for it," and in the following line "Mourn'd" is spelled with an "'d" instead of "Mourned" in the earlier edition. The omission of a line on this page and also on p. 31 in the Barclay edition, could easily have been done by an apprentice. It must be noted, however, that in the case of the omission on p. 4, it is possible that the original book from which Thomas copied the book may have lacked it also, because the Edinburgh [*ca.* 1786] ed. also wants this line. The words wanting in the Barclay edition p. 31 are: "forgive us our trespasses as we". These have been added to p. 31 in the 1771 edition and appear on the first three lines. The remaining four lines on p. 31 are printed from standing type. Page 3 and [32] of no. **1318.1** are not present in the 1771 edition. Instead there is a frontispiece, p.[2], which seems to be made up of portions of p.[32] and p.[3] of no. **1318.1**. The decorative bar at the top of the frontispiece matches the lower bar on p.[32] of no. **1318.1**. The next six lines match the same six lines in no. **1318.1**, on p.[3]. This is followed by 4 new lines: Great Letters./[3 lines of the upper case of the alphabet], below which is the same decorative bar used on p.[3] of no. **1318.1** in the middle of the page. The similarity of the Barclay edition to the Kneeland and Adams 1771 edition does not change belief in Isaiah Thomas' written statement.

Tom Thumb's Play Book contains the famous alphabet rhyme "A. was an Archer and shot a frog." This verse and "D. was a drunkard, and had a red face," first appeared in England in *A Little Book For Children: Wherein are set down, in a plain and pleasant way, Directions for Spelling, and other remarkable matters. Adorned with cuts. By T. W. London, Printed for G. C. and sold at the Ring in Little-Britain.* [*ca.* 1712].

The next appearance of "A" was an Archer" is in *The Child's new Play-thing,* 2 ed. 1743, no. **194.1**. The rhyming alphabet except for the letters A and D is entirely rewritten and is the version used in all editions of *Tom Thumb's*

Play-Book. The Child's new Play-thing also contains another equally famous rhyme "A Apple Pye, B bit it, . . ." which is in all editions of Tom Thumb's Play-Book.

English, Scottish and Irish ed. title 1: *Tom Thumb's Play-Book*. London: entered at Stationer's Hall by Mathew Unwin, August 6, 1747. English & Irish ed. title 2: *Tom Thumb's Play-Thing*. Newry: adv. by D. Carpenter, 1782 in *The History Of Little King Pippin*.

MWA°; Evans 10189 with imprint: [Boston: Printed by Isaiah Thomas For Andrew Barclay. 1765].

See also no. **198**, and no. **1316.1**.

1318.2 ———— Providence, Printed and sold by John Waterman, at the new Printing Office at the Paper-Mill. M.DCC.LXVIII.

[1, capital letter "S", ornamented with a ship], fr.[2, lover case alphabet], t.[3], 4–30, [31, upper case alphabet], [32, illus. of an Indian] p.; illus. p. [1], 19, [32] only illus.; 8 cm.; marbled paper covers. The text p. 4–19 follows no. **1318.1** on the same pages: A Scripture Catechism, p. 20–22; Graces. Grace before Meat, p. 23; Grace after Meat, p. 23–24; Prayers. A Prayer at your uprising, p. 24–25; A Prayer before you go to bed, p. 26–27; The young child's morning prayer, p. 27–28; The young child's evening prayer, p. 28–29; The Lord's prayer, p. 29–30; [upper case alphabet in large letters] A–Z, &, p.[31]; illus. p.[32]. The alphabet sets used with "A was an Archer" are differently set. Those on p. 6 are "A a/B a". "B b/b e". Nine printer's ornaments are present. MWA°; NjP; Evans 41891; Hamilton 50.

1318.3 ———— Boston, Printed for, and Sold by J. Boyles, in Marlboro'-Street. 1771.

t.[1], [2, bl.], 3–32 p.; 18 cm.; paper covers. The text is the same as no. **1318.1**, but with the word "Grace" spelled correctly on p. 23, and the book reset. Eight printer's type ornaments are present.

PP°; CtY (Pequot, rear Dutch paper cover mut.).

1318.4 ———— Boston: Printed and sold by Kneeland and Adams, in Milk-Street. 1771 .

fr.[2, alphabets], t.[3], 4–31 p.; 7 cm. Many pages printed from standing type from no.

1318.1. *See* discussion concerning this book under no. **1318.1.**
MWA° (p. 31 slightly mut.); DLC (lower half of p. 31 and rear cover wanting); NRU (gray-green paper covers); PP (fr.[2] & p. 31 mut. but not affecting text); Evans 12250.

1318.5 ——— Worcester, (Massachusetts) Printed by Isaiah Thomas, And sold at his Book-Store, MDCCLXXXVI.
fr.[2], t.[3], 4–30, [31, lower case alphabet] p.; front. only illus.; 6.5 cm.; Dutch paper covers. This is the first American edition with a frontispiece showing Tom Thumb's standing in the palm of his father's right hand. *The A B C.* [alphabet rhyme] A a Apple Pye, p. 4–5; [alphabet rhyme] A was an Archer, p. 6–17; a e i o u [double letters] Ab eb ib ob ub ac ec/ic oc uc ad ed id od ud/ . . . , p. 18–19; A Scripture Catechism, p. 20–23; Graces. Grace before Meat, p. 24; Grace after Meat, p. 24–25; Prayers. A Prayer at your up-rising, p. 25–26; A prayer before you go to Bed, p. 26–27; The young Child's Morning Prayer, p. 27–28; The young Child's Evening Prayer, p. 28–29; The Lord's Prayer, p. 29–30; [lower case alphabet in large type], p.[31]. Seven printer's ornaments are present.
MWA°; MiD (rebound in red morocco); Evans 20021.

1318.6 ———Printed at Worcester, Massachusetts, By Isaiah Thomas, And Sold at his Book-store. MDCCXCIV.
fr.[2], t.[3], 4–30, [31, lower case alphabet] p.; front. only illus.; 6.5 cm.; black paper covers. The frontispiece and text are the same as no. **1318.5,** but different type ornaments are used. Seven printer's ornaments are present.
MWA°; Evans 47240.

1318.7 ——— Norwich [Conn.]: Printed by T. Hubbard. 1795.
t.[1], [2], 3–32 p.; 7 cm.; Dutch paper covers. [lower case alphabet], p.[2]; The A B C. [alphabet rhyme] A a Apple Pye, p. 3–4; [alphabet rhyme] A was an Archer, p. 5–16; a e i o u [double letters] Ab eb ib ob ub ac ec/ic oc uc ad ed id od/ . . . , p. 17–18; A Scripture Catechism, p. 19–22; Graces. Grace before Meat, p. 23; Grace after Meat, p. 24; Prayers. A Prayer at your Up-rising, p. 24–26;

A prayer before you go to Bed, p. 26–28; The Young Child's morning Prayer, p. 28–29; The young Child's Evening Prayer, p. 30–31; The LORD's PRAYER, p. 31–32. Four printer's ornaments are present.
CtHi°.

1318.8 [——— n.p. 179–?]
fr.[2], 7–28, [31, lower case alphabet] p.; front only illus.; 7.5 cm.; ornamented paper covers. [alphabet rhyme, A was an Archer] C was a Captain, all cover'd with Lace. . . . , p. 7–17; a e i o u [double letters] Ab eb ib ob ub ac ec/ic oc uc ad ed id od/ . . . p. 18– ; p. [19–22 wanting]; Graces. Grace before Meat, p. 23; Grace after Meat, p. 23–24; PRAYERS. A Prayer at your Up-rising, p. 24–25; A Prayer before you go to Bed, p. 26–27; The young Child's Morning Prayer, p. 27–28; The young Child's Evening Prayer, p. 28– ; p. [29–30 wanting] [lower case alphabet in large type] a–z &c./f[l]–ff./[portion wanting], 3–9 [o?, number indistinct], p. [31]. The frontispiece, showing Tom Thumb standing in the palm of his father's hand, is redrawn. It is possibly a copy of the one used in no. **1318.5** or some English edition. Seven printer's ornaments are present.
MWA° (t.[3], p. 4–6, 29–30 wanting); Evans 48645.

1318.9 [——— [n.p.]179–?]
7–26 p. only; 7.5 cm. [alphabet rhyme, A was an Archer] C. was a Captain all covered with lace. . . . , p. 7–17; [double letters] Ab eb ib, ob ub ac ec ic oc/uc ad ed id od ud af ef if of/ . . . , p. 18–19; [4 lines of triple letters] Bla, ble, bli blo blu cla/ . . . , p. 19; A Scripture Catechism, p. 20–23; Grace before Meat, p. 23; Grade after Meat, p. 23–24; PRAYERS. A prayer at your uprising, p. 24–25; A Prayer before you go to bed. Eight printer's ornaments are present. Page 7 is stained and worn and the type ornaments difficult to identify.
MWA-W° (fr.[2], t.[3], p. 4–6, 27–30, [31], [32?] & covers wanting).

1319 TOMMY AND SALLY. Wilmington, Del.: adv. by J. Wilson, 1803 in **1081.**

1320.1 THE FAMOUS TOMMY THUMB'S LITTLE STORY-BOOK: Containing His Life and surprising Adventures; To which are added, Tommy Thumb's

Fables, with morals and, at the end, pretty Stories, that may be Sung or Told. (Adorned with many curious Pictures.) Boston: Printed and Sold by W. M'Alpine in Marlborough-street, 1768.

fr.[2], t.[3], 4–30 p.; [A]–B$_8$, if the book were complete; illus.; 9.5 cm.; scalloped marbled paper covers. [Tom Thumb's life] p. 4–15; Tommy Thumb's Fables. The APE and her young ones, p. 15–17; The KID and the WOLF, p. 17–18; the COUNTRYMAN and the STORK, p. 19–20; The old DOG and his MASTER, p. 21–22; The THIEF and the DOG, p. 27–28; Tomy [*sic. i.e.* Tommy] Thumb's Stories &c. There was a man of Thessary, p. 28–29; Sliding on the Ice, p. 29. Cock Robbin [*sic. i.e.* Robin] [1st 16 verses], p. 29–30; When I was a Little Boy, p. 30. This is the earliest known American child's book containing the first four verses of *Cock Robin* and nursery Rhymes which later appeared in *Mother Goose's Melody*. It is also the fourth earliest known book containing such rhymes, since no copy is known of the one advertised by Mein and Fleeming in 1768, no. **1320.2**. All but "Sliding on the Ice" appeared first in *Tommy Thumb's Pretty Song Book*. See below a list of English books printed prior to 1768 containing nursery rhymes. Three printer's ornaments are present. The illustrations on p. 15, 17, 19, 21, 27 are enlarged, and redrawn with variations, in the reverse from the English edition [*ca.* 1760].

English ed. of children's books containing nursery rhymes printed prior to 1768:

1. *Tommy Thumb's Pretty Song Book. Voll,* [*sic. i.e.* Vol.] *II. Sold by M. Cooper, According to Act of Parlia[ment.]* [*ca.* 1744], contains thirty-eight nursery rhymes, including the above rhymes except "Sliding on the Ice," and an additional rhyme of recommendation signed *N. Lovechild.*

2. *The Top Book of All, For Little Master's and Misses. . . . sold only at R. Baldwin's, and S. Crowder's Booksellers in Pater-noster-Row, London; and at Benj. Collins's, in Salisbury.* [*ca.* 1760], contains 9 nursery rhymes, but only "The wise man of Thistleworth" with variations occurs in no. **1320.1**. On p. [63] two sides of an English coin dated 1760 are printed.

3. *The Famous Tommy Thumb's Little Story-Book. London: Printed for S. Crowder, and sold by B. Collins, Salisbury.* [*ca.* 1760] containing nine nursery rhymes. This book is always found in fine condition and is probably part of a publisher's remainder.

NjP° (p. 23–26, 31–32 and rear cover wanting); Evans 41890.

1320.2 —— Boston: adv. by Mein & Fleeming, 1768 in **452.1**.

1320.3 —— Printed and sold at the Printing-Office [in Marlborough Street, 1771].

fr.[2], t.[3], 4–32 p.; illus.; 11 cm.; the last line of the title page is bled so that only the top of the last three words and date remain. The book was printed by John Boyle. [Tom Thumb's life] p. 4–17; Tommy Thumb's Fables. The APE and her young ones, p. 15–16; The KID and the WOLF, p. 17–18; The COUNTRYMAN and the STORK, p. 18–19; The old DOG and his MASTER, p. 20–21; The APE and FOX, p. 22–23; The TORTOISE and the EAGLE, p. 24–25; The THIEF and the DOG, p. 26–27; Tommy Thumb's Stories, &c. There was a man of Thessary, p. 28; Sliding on the Ice, p. 28; Cock Robbin [*sic. i.e.* Robin] p. 29; When I was a little boy, p. 29–30; O my Kitten, p. 30; This Pig went to Market, p. 31; The Sow came in, p. 31; Boys and girls, p. 32; Little Boy Blue, p. 32. This copy of the 1771 edition is complete and has the 5 rhymes missing in no. **1320.1**. "O my Kitten and Boys and girls" first appeared in *Tommy Thumb's Pretty Song Book* [*ca.* 1744]. "The Sow came in" occurs both in *The Top Book Of All* [*ca.* 1760] and with "Sliding on the Ice" and "Little Boy Blue" in the English ed. of *The Famous Tommy Thumb's Little Story Book* [*ca.* 1760]. No type ornaments are present in this edition. On p. 28–32 the rhymes are set apart by a single rule. The frontispiece, title vignette and illustrations in the text are from the same blocks used in no. **1320.1**. The cuts in **1320.3** for the stories on missing pages 23–26, in **1320.1**, are like the other text cuts enlarged and redrawn, with variations, in the reverse from the English edition of [*ca.* 1760].

MB° (covers wanting); Evans 12040.

TOMMY THUMB'S SONG BOOK. *See* Lovechild, Nurse, no. **802.1**.

TOMMY TITMOUSE (arranged chronologically)

1321 ADVENTURE [*sic. i.e.* Adventures] OF TOMMY TITMOUSE. Exeter [N.H.]: adv. by Norris & Sawyer, 1808 in **428.3**.

1322.1 THE HISTORY OF TOMMY TITMOUSE. A Little Boy, Who became a Great Man by minding his Learning doing as he was bid, and being good-natured and obliging to every Body. Together With The Adventures of the Old Man of the Woods, and other Stories equally pleasing and instructive. Embellished with Cuts. Boston: Printed and sold by John W. Folsom, No. 30, Union-Street. 1798.

t.[3], [4–7], 8–58 p.; [A]$_{15}$, B$_8$, C$_5$, probably [A]$_1$, C$_6$–C$_8$ wanting; illus.; 10 cm.

English & Irish ed. London: adv. by E. Newbery in the *London Chronicle*, Dec. 27–29, 1787.

Griffin* (fr.[2], all after p. 58 and covers wanting); Evans 48471.

1322.2 —— Exeter [N.H.]: Printed And Sold By H. Ranlet. 1801.

fr.[2], t.[3], [4–7], 8–61, [62] p.; illus.; 10.5 cm.; illus. buff paper covers; front cover illus. same as the front. used by H. Ranlet, 1802 in **673.18**.

MWA-W* (rear cover wanting, including sig. D$_8$ or p.[63] which may have been blank).

TOMMY TRIP (arranged chronologically)

1323.1 THE HISTORY OF TOMMY TRIP, AND HIS DOG JOWLER. And Of Birds and Beasts. Adorned With Cuts. Sidney's Press. New-Haven. 1815.

fr.[2], t.[3], [4–5], 6–30, [31, adv.] p.; illus.; 10.5 cm.

MWA; Shaw 34918.

1323.2 —— Sidney's Press. New-Haven. 1817.

fr.[2], t.[3], [4–5], 6–30, [31, adv.] p.; illus.; 10.5 cm.; illus. blue paper covers.

CtY*; DLC (fr.[2] mut.); Shaw 41658.

1323.3 —— Sidney's Press. New-Haven. 1818.

fr.[2], t.[3], [4–5], 6–30, [31, adv.] p.; illus.; 10 cm.; illus. buff paper covers printed in red ink.

MWA-W*.

1323.4 —— New-Haven: For J. Babcock And Son. Sidney's Press. 1820.

fr.[2], t.[3], [4–5], 6–30, [31, adv.] p.; illus.;

10.5 cm.; pr. & illus. yellow-buff paper covers. NN* (i. st. p.[31]); Shoemaker 1618.

1324 TOMMY TRIP'S HISTORY OF BEASTS IN VERSE AND PROSE, Ornamented with Elegant Engravings. To Which Is Added, The Story of little Pheebe [*sic. i.e.* Phoebe] and her Lamb. Now published for the benefit of the little Masters and Misses of The United States of America. New-York: Printed and Sold by Wm. Durell No. 106, Maiden-Lane, 1800.

fr.[2], t.[3], [4], 5–31 p.; illus.; 10.5 cm.; Dutch paper covers.

PP* (t.[3] cropped at the bottom affecting the lower portion of the date); Evans 49154.

1325 —— Beasts. With a Cut to each Page. Published for the instruction and Amusement of all little Masters and Misses. Philadelphia. Printed by John Adams. 1805.

fr.[2], t.[3], [4–5], 6–31 p.; illus.; 11 cm.; Dutch paper covers.

MWA*.

1326 TOMMY TRIP'S PICTURES OF BEASTS AND BIRDS with a familiar Description of each, in Verse and Prose.—Published for the Benefit of the little Masters and Misses of the United States of America. < This Book contains Pictures of 70 different Birds and Beasts, of the most curious kinds. > Boston: adv. by S. Hall, 1791 in **408.3**; 1793 in **955.3**; 1794 in **673.8**; 1798 in **673.13**. The title was changed in 1796 to *Pictures of Seventy-Two Beasts & Birds* —— Benefit of the *Lovers of Natural History, and for the Instruction of the Youth of America*, no. **997**. This book was advertised by S. Hall, 1796 in **587.40** as *Descriptions of seventy-two Beasts and Birds*.

TOMMY TWO SHOES. *See* The History Of Tommy Two Shoes, no. **595**.

1327 A TOY-SHOP FOR CHILDREN. In Which Good Little Girls And Boys Will Find Amusement And Instruction. Philadelphia: Published By Jacob Johnson, No. 147 Market-street. 1804.

t.[1], [2–58] p.; 28 full page engr. illus.; 7.5 cm.; bound in green paper over bds. The illustrations are drawn in the reverse from engraved colored plates issued in 1801 by John Marshall in London, England and housed in a wooden box with a sliding cover. On the cover is pasted a colored illustrated piece of paper entitled "The

Infant's Cabinet Of Various Objects." Accompanying the cards are two 5 cm. books: *A Description of Various Objects. Volume I. [II.] London: Printed and sold by John Marshall 140 Fleet Street From Aldermary Church Yard.* [n.d.]. The two volumes were reprinted by J. Johnson, 1803 in **283.1** and **283.2**, without the plates. The text of *The Toy-Shop* is different from *A Description Of Various Objects* and probably came from an unknown edition by John Marshall.

MWA°; Shaw 7380.

1328.1 THE TRAGICAL DEATH OF AN APPLE-PYE, Who was Cut in Pieces, And Eat By Twenty-Five Gentlemen. For all Pretty Masters and Misses. New-York: Printed for T. B. Jansen & Co. No. 248 Pearl-Street. 1803.

t.[1], [2–3], 4–15, [16, adv. list of books] p.; illus.; 8 cm.

English ed. [London]: R. Marshall [1780?].

MWA° (covers wanting).

1328.2 ———— Apple-Pie. Newburyport [Mass.], Printed by W. & J. Gilman. Sold at their Miscellaneous Book-Store, No. 2, Middle-Street. 1814.

t.[1], [2–3], 4–16 p.; illus.; 8.5 cm.; pr. & illus. yellow-buff paper covers; cover title undated. The nursery rhyme "Jack and Jill" is on p. 16. Two rhymes have the first two lines altered: "Little Miss Leech,/Sat upon a bench, ———" [remainder same as "Little Miss Muffet." ODNR, p. 323], p. 10; "I'll tell you a story,/Of Jack in his glory, ———" [remainder same as "———/ About Jack a Nory," ODNR, p. 233], p. 11.

MWA°; Shaw 32951.

1328.3 ———— Newburyport [Mass.], Printed and Sold by W. & J. Gilman, No. 2, Middle-street. [1820?].

t.[1], [2–3], 4–16 p.; illus.; 7.5 cm.; pr. & illus. paper covers. A reprint of the text and cuts of the 1814 edition, no. **1328.2**. On p. 16 below the rhyme of "Jack and Jill" another is added: To Boston, to Boston,/To buy a fine book;/ Home again, home again,/only look.

MH° (i. st. p.[3]).

TRAGICAL HISTORY OF THE CHILDREN IN THE WOOD. *See* Children In The Wood, no. **179.1**.

1329 THE TRAGICAL WANDERINGS OF GRIMAL-KIN. [caption title p.[1]]. [Philadelphia: Published

and sold wholesale by Wm. Charles and may be had of all Booksellers 1815?] [imprint from Cowper's *The Diverting History Of John Gilpin*, which this book resembles in format].

[1–8] p. engr. on one side only of 8 leaves; illus.; 13 cm.; pr. paper covers; rear cover, adv. list of books.

English ed.: London, Tabart, 1808.

MWA° (front cover wanting); Shaw 36106; Weiss 1932b.

TRAGI-COMIC HISTORY OF THE BURIAL OF COCK ROBIN. *See* Cock Robin, no. **215**.

1330.1 THE TRANSMIGRATIONS OF INDUR. Also, The Travellers' Wonders. Ornamented With Plates. New-York, Published By T. B. Jansen, Book-Seller, 116 Broadway, opposite the City-Hotel. L. Nichols, Print. 1805. Price 1 shilling.

fr.[ii], t.[1], [2–3], 4–36 p.; illus.; 14 cm.; paper covers; front. signed *Anderson* [Alexander Anderson]. The story is taken from *Evenings At Home*. Vol. II., no. **25.1**, written by John Aikin and Mrs. A. L. Barbauld.

MWA°; CtHi; PP; Shaw 9495. Weiss, 1923b.

1330.2 ———— New-York: Published By Thomas Powers, Book-Seller, 116 Broadway, opposite the City-Hotel. 1810.

fr.[ii], t.[1], [2–3], 4–36 p.; illus.; 14 cm.; pr. & illus. paper covers; front. signed *Anderson* [Alexander Anderson]; cover title undated.

MWA°; CLU; Shaw 21510.

TRAPWIT, TOMMY *pseud.*

1331.1 ——— BE MERRY AND WISE; Or, The Cream of the Jests, And The Marrow of Maxims, For the Conduct of Life. Published for the Use of all good Little Boys and Girls. By Tommy Trapwit, Esq. Adorned with Cuts. [3 lines quot.] Grotius. The First Worcester Edition. Worcester, (Massachusetts) Printed By Isaiah Thomas, And Sold At His Book Store. MDCCLXXXVI.

fr.[ii], t.[iii], [iv], v–vi, 7–128 p.; illus.; 10 cm.; bound in Dutch paper over bds.

English & Irish ed. London: adv. by J. Newbery, in *Gentleman's Magazine* Feb. 1753 and *London Magazine* Feb. 1753 as *Collections of Jests & Maxims*.

MWA° (i. st. on t.[iii], fr.[ii] wanting); CLU; DeWint; Evans 44851.

1331.2 — —— The First Worcester Edition. Worcester, (Massachusetts) Printed By Isaiah Thomas, And Sold At His Book Store. Sold Also By E. Battelle, Boston. MDCCLXXXVI.

Same collation as preceding, the book differing only in the imprint.

MWA° (rebound in leather, with I. Thomas' bookplate); PP (rebound); Evans 20028.

1332.1 THE TRAVELLERS; Exhibiting A Variety of Characters Mounted upon Curious and Wonderful Animals. New-York: Printed by J. Oram, for the Book-sellers in Town and Country. 1795.

fr.[2, alphabet], t.[3], [4], 5–30, [31, alphabet] p.; illus.; 10 cm.; Dutch paper covers. English ed. Coventry: N. Merridew [*ca.* 1804]. OOxM°; Evans 29655.

1332.2 —— New-York: Printed by W. Durell, For Thomas Kirk. 1800.

fr.[2], t.[3], [4], 5–31 p.; illus.; 10.5 cm.; violet and green Dutch paper covers. MWA°; Evans 38664.

1333 A TRIFLE FOR A GOOD BOY. Ornamented With Fourteen Handsome Engravings. Philadelphia: Printed For And Sold By Benjamin Johnson, No. 249, High-Street. 1807. Dickinson, Printer. Whitehall.

fr.[2], t.[3], [4–47] p.; illus.; 13.5 cm.; marbled paper covers; front. and illus. p.[46–47] signed A [Alexander Anderson]; those on p.[13], [16], [18–19], [24] signed *J. Aikin*. MWA°; PP; Shaw 13744.

1334.1 A TRIFLE FOR A GOOD GIRL. Ornamented With Fourteen Handsome Engravings. Printed And Sold By B. Johnson, No. 31, High Street. Philadelphia. 1803.

fr.[2], t.[3], [4–47] p.; [A]₆, C₆, B₆, C₆; illus.; 13.5 cm.; paper covers. Label on front cover: Trifle for a good Girl. MWA°; RPB.

1334.2 —— Philadelphia: Printed For And Sold By Benjamin Johnson, No. 249, High-Street. 1807. Dickinson, Printer. Whitehall.

t.[3], [4–46] p.; illus.; 13.5 cm. CtY° (covers, fr.[2], & p.[47] wanting).

1335.1 THE TRIFLE-HUNTER: Or, The Adventures Of Prince Bonbennin. A Chinese Tale. Hartford: Printed By John Babcock. 1798.

fr.[2], t.[3], [4–5], 6–28, [29, adv.], [30–31, 2 cuts per page] p.; illus.; 11 cm.; Dutch paper covers. The story appeared in London, England in 1788 in *The Palace Of Enchantment* under the title: *The Curious Story Of The White Mouse*. MWA°; Evans 48646.

1335.2 —— First Newport Edition. Newport [R.I.]: Printed by O. Farnsworth. 1799.

fr.[2], t.[3], [4–5], 6–29, [30, 2 cuts], [31, adv.] p.; illus.; 11.5 cm.; Dutch paper covers. MWA° (fr.[2], t.[3], and front cover mut.); RNHi; Evans 36450.

1335.3 —— Tale. Ornamented with Cuts. Printed At Providence. [*ca.* 1800].

illus.[1], [2, bl.], t.[3], [4, alphabet], [5], 6–32 p. illus.; 10.5 cm.; no covers. The illustrations are redrawn versions of the Hartford, John Babcock, 1798 edition, no. **1335.1**. They are printed from the same blocks used by O. Farnsworth in the Newport, 1799 edition, **1335.2**, and the Windsor [Vt.], 1810 edition, **1335.4**. The illustration, p.[1], **1335.3**, and fr.[2], **1335.4**, of a seated man showing the palms of his hands on either side of his face, has a break 5 mm. long in the basal outer thick rule border near the right corner. This break is not present in the same cut in the frontispiece of the 1799 edition. The cut of the old woman and Prince Bonbennin, p. 18, no. **1335.2**, and p. 20, no. **1335.3**, has a jagged piece scooped out of the lower left corner. By 1810 the left corner is rounded. The picture of Prince Bonbennin, the cat and the white mouse, p. 29, no. **1335.3**, has a break 1 mm. long in the outer top rule border near the left corner. In no. **1335.2**, p. 26, the border is not broken. By 1810, no. **1335.4**, p. 26, the same 1 mm. break is present and the cut is printed upside down. Because of the breaks in the rule borders of the above cuts, the Providence edition surely was printed between 1799 and 1810. Since the cut on p. 19 has a scooped out left lower corner identical with that in the 1799 edition, it is believed that these breaks occurred close together and that the new breaks occurred soon after 1799. For these reasons no. **1335.3** is being dated [*ca.* 1800].

Adomeit°.

1335.4 ———— First Winsor Edition. Printed At Windsor [Vt.]: By Farnsworth & Churchill. 1810.
fr.[2], t.[3], [4–7], 8–28, [29, adv.], [30–31, 2 cuts per page] p.; illus.; 9.5 cm.; pr. & illus. buff paper covers.
MWA-W*; MH (fr.[2], t.[3], & p. [4] mut. NHi; VtHi; McCorison 1216; Shaw 21520.

1336 Trifles For Children; Part I [II–III] Think nought a Trifle Though it small appear. Philadelphia Published by J. Johnson, no. 147, Market-Street. 1804.
pt. I–III, each pt.: t.[1], [2–48] p.; illus.; 14 cm.; pt. I, pr. & illus. brown paper covers; cover title dated 1809; pt. II, green paper covers; pt. III, marbled paper covers. The 1804 covers for the three parts were probably marbled paper. The illus. B$_{11}$ recto, pt. II, is signed A [Alexander Anderson]. The title pages of pt. II and III do not have "Think nought a Trifle Though it small appear."
English ed. London: pts. I, II, Darton and Harvey, Dec. 30, 1796.
MWA* (pt. I–II); MWA-W (pt. III); CtHi (pt. III); NNC-Pl (pt. I, blue marbled paper covers; pt. III, pr. & illus. paper covers; cover title dated 1809); PP (pt. II, unprinted green paper covers); RPB (pt. II); Shaw 7387 (pt. I); 7388 (pt. II); (pt. III) not in Shaw.

1337 Trifles For Good Boys. Philadelphia: adv. by Johnson and Warner, 1814 in **1449.3**.

1338 Trifles For Good Girls. Philadelphia: adv. by Johnson and Warner, 1814 in **1449.3**.

TRIMMER, SARAH (KIRBY) 1741–1810
1339.1 — A Concise History Of England, Comprised In A Set Of Easy Lessons: Being A Continuation Of A Series Of Historical Books For Children. Brought Down To The Peace Of Paris. In two volumes. By Mrs. Trimmer. To Which Are Added, Tables Of Chronology, Events, &c. Boston: Published By Munroe & Francis, No. 4, Cornhill, And David Francis, No. 90, Newbury-Street. 1818.
vol. I., t.[3], [4–5], 6–189 p.; illus.; 15 cm.; bound in leather.
MWA*; Shaw 45897.

1339.2 — ———— Chronology, Events, &c. Vol. II, Boston: Published By Munroe & Francis, No.

4, Cornhill, And David Francis, No. 90, Newbury-Street. 1819.
vol. II., t.[3], [4–5], 6–180 p.; illus.; 15 cm.; bound in leather.
MWA*; Shaw 49635.

1340.1 — An Easy Introduction To The Knowledge Of Nature. Adapted To The Capacities Of Children. By Mrs. Trimmer Revised, Corrected, and greatly augmented; and adapted to the United States of America. Boston: Printed by Manning and Loring, For David West. 1796.
t.[i], [ii–iii], iv–ix; [xi, bl.], [12], 13–147, [148, bl.], [1], 2–8 p.; 13.5 cm.
English ed. London: Printed for the Author, And Sold by J. Dodsley; J. Robson; T. Longman; G. Robinson; J. Johnson; Wells and Grosvenor, and J. Shave, 1780.
CLU*; MWA; Evans 31316.

1340.2 — ———— 1st American Edition. Alexandria, DC. Printed by Cotton and Stewart. 1804.
MWA*; PPL; Shaw 7390.

1341 — Easy Lessons Of Scripture History, From The Old Testament. Ornamented with Cuts. By Mrs. Trimmer. New-York: Printed and sold by T. & J. Swords, No. 160 Pearl-street. 1813. Price twenty Cents. [cover title].
t.[1], [2–3], 4–82 p.; 11 cm.; pr. buff paper covers. The cover title was probably a remainder used with the 1821 reprint of the book. Title page: ———— By Mrs. Trimmer. Second American Edition. New-York: Printed and sold by T. & J. Swords, No. 160 Pearl-street. 1821.
English ed. title 1: *A Description Of A Set Of Prints Of Scripture History: Contained In A Set Of Easy Lessons* [vol. I.]; *A Series Of Prints Of Scripture History* [vol. II.]. London: [vol. I.] entered Stationer's Hall, by John Marshall & Co., May 8, 1786.
English ed. title 2: *Scripture Lessons designed to accompany a Series of Prints from the Old Testament. By Mrs Trimmer.* [vol. I.] London: entered Stationer's Hall by J. Marshall, April 1, 1797; *A Series Of Prints Taken From The Old Testament.* [vol. II.]. London: J. Marshall, [1797], plate dated 1797.
English ed. title 3: *A New Series Of Prints, Accompanied By Easy Lessons: Being an improved Edition of the First Set Of Scripture Prints. From The Old Testament.* London: 2

vols. J. Harris; J. Hatchard; B. Tabart, 1803, printed dated June 1st, 1803.
NCooHi°.

1342 — FABULOUS HISTORIES, Designed For The Amusement & Instruction Of Young Persons. By Mrs. Trimmer. Philadelphia: Printed And Sold By William Gibbons. 1794.
t.[i], [ii–iii], iv–viii, [9], 10–214 p.; 16 cm.; bound in marbled paper over bds., leather spine.
English ed. title 1: *Fabulous Histories, Designed for the Instruction of Children, Respecting Their Treatment Of Animals*. London: T. Longman, and G. G. and J. Robertson; and J. Johnson, 1786. Dedicatory letter signed Nov. 3, 1785.
English ed. title 2: *Fabulous Histories, By Mrs Trimmer: Or, The History Of The Robbins*. London: 12 ed. N. Hailes, 1818.
English ed. title 3: *History Of The Robbins*. London: John Offor, 1819.
MWA°; PPL; PPPrHi; VtNN.

1343 [—] THE SILVER THIMBLE. By The Author Of Instructive Tales, &c. Philadelphia: Printed By B. & J. Johnson, No. 147, Market Street. 1801.
fr.[ii], t.[1], [2–3], 4–123, [124–125, bl.], [126–127, adv.] p.; engr. front only illus.; 13.5 cm.; bound in marbled paper over bds., green paper spine.
English ed. London: E. Newbery, 1799.
Welch°; CLU; MWA; Shaw 1324 and 1435.

TRIP, TOMMY *pseud.*
1344.1 — THE NATURAL HISTORY OF FOUR FOOTED BEASTS. By Tommy Trip. Adorned With Cuts. Printed in Hudson (New-York) by Ashbel Stoddard, & sold at his Book Store, Wholesale and Retail. M,DCC,XCV.
t.[1], [2–3], 4–158, [159], [160, adv. list of books] p.; illus.; 11 cm.; bound in leather, over w. bds.
English ed. title 1: *The Natural History Of Four Footed Beasts by T. Teltruth*. London: E. Newbery, 1781.
Scottish ed. title 2: ——— *By Tommy Trip*. Glasgow: J. & M. Robertson And J. Duncan, 1784. Scottish ed. are the immediate source books of the American one. They were derived from E. Newbery's publication.
PP°; Evans 29565.

1344.2 ——— Hudson: (N.Y.) Printed By Ashbel Stoddard, And Sold at his Book-Store, Wholesale & Retail. 1802.
t.[1], [2], 3–128 p.; illus.; 10.5 cm.; bound in yellow wallpaper over w. bds.
Welch°; MWA; NNC-LS (i. st. on t.[1], covers and p. 33–128 wanting); Shaw 2725.

1345.1 [TRIP'S HISTORY OF BEASTS; Being A Trifle For A Good Boy. Ornamented with Engravings. Albany: Printed And Sold By The Groce Or Dozen By E. and E. Hosford. 1806?] [Title copied from the Albany 1808 edition.] [imprint taken from **987.3**].
[5], 6–28 p.; illus.; 10 cm. The illustrations are the same as those used in the Albany editions of E. & E. Hosford 1808–1818. The type setting of some pages is identical with the Hosford 1809 and 1813 editions. The woodcut of "The Bear", p. 8, has a surrounding double rule border, with 8 mm. of the lower left border wanting. All Hosford editions from 1808–1818 do not have a double rule border on the top and sides of the cut of "The Bear", but retain the double rule at the bottom of the cut. Because of this border the book is believed to have been printed before 1808 and probably in 1806. In the 1806? and 1809 editions, p. 16, the word "color" is spelled "colour", in 1813 it is spelled "color."
MWA-W° (fr.[2], t.[3], p.[4], 29–31 & covers wanting).

1345.2 TRIP'S HISTORY OF BEASTS; Being A Trifle For A Good Boy. Ornamented with Engravings. Albany: Printed By E. And E. Hosford. 1808.
fr.[2], t.[3], [4–5], 6–31 p.; illus.; 10 cm.; pr. & illus. buff paper covers.
Cover title: History of Beasts: Albany: Printed By E. & E. Hosford.
MWA° (covers worn); Shaw 16347.

1345.3 ——— Embellished With Cuts. Litchfield [Conn.]: Printed By Hosmer & Goodwin. 1808.
fr.[2], t.[3], [4–5], 6–31 p.; illus.; 10 cm.; Dutch paper covers.
Griffin°.

1345.4 ——— Ornamented with Engravings. Albany: Printed By E. And E. Hosford. 1809.
fr.[2], t.[3], [4–5], 6–31 p.; 10.5 cm.; pr. & illus.

buff paper covers; cover title undated, same as
no. **1345.2**.
Welch°; CtHi; MWA.

1345.5 ——— Albany: Printed By E. And E.
Hosford. 1810.
fr.[2], t.[3], [4–5], 6–31 p.; illus.; 10.5 cm.;
pr. & illus. yellow paper covers.
MB°; DLC; PP (p. 29–31 & rear cover wanting); Shaw 21521.

1345.6 ——— Albany: Printed By E. & E. Hosford. 1811.
fr.[2], t.[3], [4–5], 6–31 p.; illus.; 10 cm.;
pr. & illus. buff paper covers; cover title imprint
same as no. **1345.2**.
MWA°; CLU; Shaw 24062.

1345.7 ——— Albany: Printed By E. & E. Hosford. 1812.
fr.[2], t.[3], [4–5], 6–31 p.; illus.; 10.5 cm.;
pr. & illus. paper covers; cover title undated
same as no. **1345.2**.
MWA°.

1345.8 ——— Hartford: Printed by Hale &
Hosmer. 1812.
fr.[2], t.[3], [4–5], 6–31 p.; illus.; 9.5 cm.;
pr. & illus. buff paper covers.
Cover title: Trip's History of Beasts. Hartford:
——— Hosmer. 1813.
MWA-W°.

1345.9 ——— Albany: Printed By E. & E. Hosford. 1813.
fr.[2], t.[3], [4–5], 6–31 p.; illus.; 10.5 cm.;
pr. & illus. paper covers; cover title undated,
same as no. **1345.2**. The right parenthesis enclosing p. "(9)" is lower than the left one. The
"3" in the date 1813, on t.[3], is printed in
defective type.
Welch°; MWA; PP; Shaw 29973.

1345.10 ——— Good Boy. Ornamented with
Engravings. Jaffrey [N.H.]: Printed By Salmon
Wilder. 1813.
fr.[2], t.[3], [4–5], 6–31 p.; illus.; 10 cm.
MWA°; NhHi (fr.[2], p. 31 & covers wanting);
Shaw 29974.

1345.11 ——— Good Boy. Ornamented with
Engravings. Jaffrey, < N.H. > Printed By Salmon
Wilder. —1813—

fr.[2], t.[3], [4–5], 6–31 p.; illus.; 10 cm.;
pr. & illus. yellow paper covers.
Cover title: History of Beasts. Printed by S.
Wilder. A variant of the preceding edition, with
a new title page, in which there is a comma
after the words "Beasts," instead of a colon
":"; thickened rules above and below the line
"Ornamented with Engravings"; < N.H. > in
brackets instead of being omitted; no ornament
above the date, and "—1813—" set off with
dashes.
MWA-W° (p. 31 mut.); NhD (white unprinted
paper covers).

1345.12 ——— Adorned with Cuts. Hartford:
Printed by Hale & Hosmer. 1814.
fr.[2], t.[3], [4–5], 6–31 p.; illus.; 10.5 cm.
MWA°; Shaw 32967.

1345.13 ——— Adorned With Cuts. Hartford:
Printed by Sheldon & Goodwin. < Stereotyped
by J. F. & C. Starr. > [ca. 1815].
fr.[2], t.[3], [4–5], 6–31 p.; illus.; 10.5 cm.;
pr. & illus. paper covers;
Cover title: Trip's History of Beasts. ———
[same as t.[3]] Stereotype Edition. *See* no.
563.15 on printers.
MWA°; CtHi (fr.[2], t.[3] mut.); DLC.

1345.14 ——— Ornament with Engravings.
Albany: Printed By E. & E. Hosford. 1816.
fr.[2], t.[3], [4–5], 6–31 p.; illus.; 10 cm.;
pr. & illus. paper covers; cover title undated,
same as no. **1345.2**. It is strange that no 10 cm.
children's books printed by E. & E. Hosford in
1815 are known.
MWA°; Shaw 39118.

1345.15 ——— Albany: Printed By E. & E.
Hosford. 1818.
fr.[2], t.[3], [4–5], 6–31 p.; illus.; 10 cm.;
pr. & illus. paper covers; cover title undated,
same as no. **1345.2**.
MWA°; Shaw 45898.

1345.16 ——— A Good Boy. Ornamented with
Cuts. Hudson [N.Y.]: Printed By Ashbel Stoddard.
1820.
fr.[2], t.[3], [4–5], 6–31 p.; illus.; 10.5 cm.;
pr. & illus. blue-gray paper covers.
Cover title: HISTORY/OF/BEASTS./ Hudson
[N.Y.]:/ Printed by Ashbel Stoddard,/And

Sold, Wholesale and Retail at his/Book-Store./ 1821./The woodcuts are the same as those used in no. **1344.2**. The cut of "The Leopard", p. 10, has the entire left-hand corner wanting in both 1802 and 1820 editions. In the 1820 edition a new break appears at the middle of the upper part of the cut. The cut of "The Squirrel,", p. 25, in 1820 edition, wants the lower right hand corner. In the 1802 printing, p. 108, the cut is intact.

MWA-T°; CtHi (front cover, fr.[2], t.[3] mut.).

1346 THE TRIUMPH OF GOODNATURE, Exhibited In The History Of Master Harry Fairborn And Master Trueworth. Interspersed With Tales and Fables. Boston—Printed By Hosea Sprague. 1804.

t.[1], [2–3], 4–48 p.; 12 cm.; Dutch paper covers.

English ed. London: E. Newbery [1801] manuscript inscription and dated "1801".

MWA°; DLC (per. st. on t.[1]); MB; OOxM; Shaw 7391.

TRUE, ELEZA S.

1347 THE AMARANTH: Being A Collection Of Original Pieces, In Prose And Verse, Calculated To Amuse The Minds Of Youth Without Corrupting Their Morals. By Eleza S. True. [4 lines of verse] Portland [Me.]: J. M'Kown, Printer. 1811.

t.[i], [ii–iii], iv, [5] 6–108 p.; 17.5 cm.

MWA° (covers wanting, p. 107–108 mut.); DLC (bound in green marbled paper, leather spine; emb. st. on t.[i]); Shaw 24063.

1348 THE TRUE AND PLEASANT HISTORY OF ELIZABETH LOVELESS, Very Interesting To All Young Persons: The History Of William Black, The Chimney-Sweeper: And The Prodigal Son, In Verse. New-York: Published By The Female Union Society For The Promotion Of Sabbath Schools. J. Seymour, printer. 1816.

t.[1], [2–3] 4–36 p.; 14 cm.; pr. yellow paper covers.

CSmH°; Shaw 38122.

1349 THE TRUE HISTORY OF A LITTLE BOY, WHO CHEATED HIMSELF; Founded On Fact: And Adorned With Engravings. Philadelphia, Published by W. Charles, No. 32 South third St. Price plain 18¾ Cents, colour'd 31¼ [*ca.* 1817] [cover title].

[1–12] p. engr. on one side only of 12 leaves;

illus.; 13.5 cm.; pr. paper covers. William Charles was at 32 South Third St. 1817–1818. English ed. London: Tabart & Co. 1809. NNC-Pl° (rear cover wanting).

1350 TRUE STORIES, OR, INTERESTING ANECDOTES OF CHILDREN: Designed Through The Medium Of Example, To Inculcate Principles Of Virtue And Piety. By The Author Of "Lessons For Young Persons In Humble Life." Poughkeepsie [N.Y.]: Published by Paraclete Potter. P. & S. Potter, Printer. 1815.

t.[1], [2–3], 4–108 p.; 14 cm.; bound in marbled paper over bds., leather spine.

English ed. York: T. Wilson and Son; For Longman, Hurst, Rees, Orme, And Brown, London; Wilson And Son, York. Sold Also By Hatchard, London. 1810.

MWA°; ICU; MSaE; NP; Shaw 36128.

1351 TRUE STORIES; OR INTERESTING ANECDOTES OF YOUNG PERSONS: Designed Through The Medium Of Example. To Inculcate Principles of Virtue And Piety. By The Author of "Lessons For Young Persons Of Humble Life." Philadelphia; Published By Benjamin & Thomas Kite, No. 20, North Third-Street. J. Bouvier, printer. 1811.

t.[1], [2–3], 4–365; 17.5 cm.; bound in leather. A different book from no. **1350**.

English ed. York: 2 ed. Thomas Wilson and Son; For Longman, Hurst, Rees, Orme, And Brown, London: And For Wilson And Son, York. Sold Also By J. Hatchard, London. 1812.

Ries°; DLC; MnU; Shaw 24065.

1352.1 TRUE STORIES RELATED. By A Friend To Little Children. New-York: Printed And Sold By S. Wood, At the Juvenile Book-Store, No. 357, Pearl-street. 1812.

t.[1], [2–3], 4–45 p.; illus.; 12.5 cm.; pr. & illus. paper covers.

NHi°; CLU.

1352.2 —— New-York: Printed And Sold By Samuel Wood, At The Juvenile Book-Store, No. 357, Pearl-Street. 1814.

t.[i], [ii–iii], iv, [5], 6–45 p.; illus.; 12.5 cm.

MWA° (covers wanting; p. 45 mut.); CtY (bound with other books); PP (bound with other books); Shaw 32970.

1352.3 ——— New-York: Printed And Sold By S. Wood & Sons, At The Juvenile Book-Store, No. 357, Pearl-Street. 1815.

t.[i], [ii–iii], iv, [5], 6–45 p.; illus.; 12 cm.; pr. & illus. paper covers; cover title imprint: Printed ——— Pearl-Street. *Nerv-York* [*sic. i.e. New York*].

MWA°; PP; Shaw 36129.

1352.4 TRUE STORIES/RELATED/BY/A FRIEND TO /LITTLE CHILDREN./WINDSOR, (Vt.)/PRINTED BY/ JESSE COCHRAN,/*And sold, wholesale and retail, at his*/BOOK-STORE. 1815.

fr.[2], t.[3], [4–5], 6–31 p.; front. only illus.; 10.5 cm.; pr. & illus. buff paper covers. Front. illus. has two cuts. The upper one shows a butterfly; the lower, two flying ducks.

MWA°; NN-C (covers wanting); PP (front cover wanting); VtHi (pr. & illus. blue-gray paper covers); McCorison 1786; Shaw 36130.

1352.5 ——— BY [this word and the next two lines printed in smaller type than **1352.4**]/A FRIEND TO/LITTLE CHILDREN./Windsor, (Vt.)/ PRINTED BY/JESSE COCHRAN,/*And sold, wholesale and retail, at his*/Book-Store./[10 dots] 1815.

fr.[2], t.[3], [4–5], 6–31 p.; front. only illus.; 10 cm.; pr. & illus. blue-gray paper covers. Front. illus. consists of two cuts. The upper one shows a man in a chair on the left, and a seated woman on the right in a room with one window. The lower one, also a rectangular cut, has an inner oval, inside of which two standing boys are shown.

MWA-T°; CLU.

1352.6 ——— New-York: Printed And Sold By S. Wood & Sons, At The Juvenile Book-Store, No. 357, Pearl-Street. 1817.

t.[i], [ii–iii], iv, [5], 6–43 p.; illus.; 12 cm.; pr. & illus. paper covers; cover title imprint: Printed ——— Pearl-Street, New-York.

MWA°; PP; Shaw 42333.

1352.7 ——— *Nerv-York* [*sic. i.e. New-York*]: Published By Samuel Wood & Sons, No. 261, Pearl-Street, And Samuel S. Wood & Co., No. 212, Market-st. Baltimore. 1819.

t.[1], [2–5], 6–43 p.; illus.; 12 cm.; pr. & illus. paper covers; cover title imprint: *Nerv-York* [*sic. i.e. New-York*]: ——— & Sons; And Samuel S. Wood & Co. Baltimore.

MWA°; CLU; ICU; Shaw 49639.

1353 THE TULIP: Containing Twelve Trifles For Children. Philadelphia: Published By Johnson & Warner, No. 147, Market-Street. 1809. W. M'Culloch, Printer.

t.[1], [2, bl.], 3–36 p.; illus.; 14 cm.; pr. buff-brown paper covers. Adv. by Johnson & Warner, 1814 in **1449.3.**

Cover title: The Tulip, Containing Twelve Trifles In Verse For Children.

MWA°; NNC-Pl; Shaw 18794.

[TURNER, MRS. ELIZABETH] 1774?–1846

1354 [—] THE COWSLIP, Or More Cautionary Stories, In Verse. By The Author Of That Much Admired Little Work, Entitled The Daisy. Illustrated With Thirty Engravings. Published By Johnson & Warner, And Sold At Their Bookstores, Philadelphia, And Richmond, Virginia. Griggs and Dickinson, Printers. 1813.

½t. [3], fr.[4], t.[5], [6, bl.], [7], 8–70, [71, adv.] p.; illus.; 14 cm.; pr. & illus. pink paper covers. Many of the cuts are signed A [Alexander Anderson]: Half title: The Cowslip, Or More Cautionary Stories. In Verse.

Cover title: ——— [same as title page] In Verse. Adapted To The Capacities Of Children At An Early Age. By The Author Of The Daisy. Illustrated With Thirty Engravings. Philadelphia: Published by Johnson & Warner, No. 147, Market Street. 1813.

English ed. London: J. Harris, and B. Crosby, 1811.

MWA°; NB (i. st. on t.[3]); NjR (all before p. 15, p. 17–20, & covers wanting; p. 29–23 half wanting); NNC-Pl; PP (covers wanting); Shaw 28237 and 29993.

1355.1 [—] THE DAISY; Or, Cautionary Stories In Verse, Adapted To The Capacities Of Children From Four To Eight Years Old. Illustrated With Engravings On Copper-Plate. Part II. Philadelphia: Published by Jacob Johnson, No. 147, Market street. 1808. W. M'Culloch, Printer.

1st t.[1], [2–36] p.; 13.5 cm.; bound in blue marbled paper over bds., red leather spine.

MWA-T°; OOxM; PHi.

1355.2 [—] ——— Old. Illustrated With Sixteen Engravings On Copperplate. Part I. Philadelphia: Published By Jacob Johnson, No. 147, Market-Street. (J. Adams, Printer). 1808.

½t.[1], [2, bl.], t.[3], [4–35], [36, adv.] p. [as

they should have been printed]; illus.; 14 cm.; orange paper covers. Part of a large publisher's remainder. The pages are all out of order with the plates printed on the wrong leaves. The pages are bound or printed in the following order: [1], [18], t.[3], [2̲1̲], [17], [2], [15], [33], [13], [6], [11], [8], [9], [2̲7̲], [7], [12], [5], [14], [23], [32], [25], [30], [1̲0̲], [28], [29], [30], [31], [24], [4̲], [22], [35], [20], [1̲6̲], [34], [19], [36]. The pages underlined are illus. printed upside down; p. 18 engr. The correct paging is taken from volume 2 of **1355.1** and **1355.3**. This publisher's remainder is such a printer's botch it is doubtful that Jacob Johnson ever allowed these books to be put on sale.

Welch°; CaOTP; CCamarSJ; CLU; CSmH; CtHi (covers wanting); CtY; DeWint; DLC (2 copies); IU; MH; MWA; MiD; NHi; NN; NN-Pl; NRU; OOxM; PHi; PP; PU; ViU; Shaw 14821 and 16353.

1355.3 [—] ——— Philadelphia: Published By Benjamin Warner, No. 147, Market [Str]eet. 1816. Printed by Lydia R. Bailey.
½t.[1], [2, bl.]. t.[3], [4–35] p.; p. 18 engr.; illus.; 14 cm.; pr. brown paper covers; half title: The Daisy; Or, Cautionary Stories in Verse. Cover title: The Daisy, Or Stories in Verse. Part First. Philadelphia: Published by Benjamin Warner, No. 147, Market Street. 1817.
MWA-W° p. 7–8 mostly wanting); PP.

[—] THE LILLY. *See* no. **760.**

1356 TWELVE CENTS WORTH OF WIT, Or, Little Stories For Little Folks Of All Denominations. Adorned With Cuts. Unhappy Wit, like most mistaken Things, Atones not for the Envey which it brings. So singeth that excellent Poet Master Pope; and therefore, when you have read this *Twelve cents worth of Wit* you would do well to buy *Twelve cents worth of Wisdom*, which is much better, and may be had at the Place where this is sold. With and Wisdom should always be blended together; for, as Mrs. Margery Two-Shoes, observes, Wit is Folly, unless a wise Man hath the keeping of it. Philadelphia: Printed for John Curtis, Bookbinder and Stationer, North 4th street No. 43. [*ca.* 1795].
[1], fr.[2], t.[3], [4], 5, vi–xx, 21–128 p.; illus.; 10 cm.; gray marbled paper covers. Colophon

p. 128: Printed By Ormrod & Conrad, ☞ No. 41, Chesnut-street. p.[1]: To The Young Gentlemen, And Ladies Of America, This Book Is Inscribed By Their Good Friend. J. C. [John Curtis].
English ed. London: entitled: *Six Pennyworth of Wit; Or, Little Stories for Little Folks of all Denominations.* ——— [same as above American ed.] J. Newbery. [n.d.].
MWA°; Evans 28521.

1357 Hercules in his Cradle Strangles two Serpents. [illus.] THE TWELVE LABOURS OF HERCULES. Son of Jupiter and Alcmena. Philaᵈᵃ Pubᵈ & sold by Wᵐ Charles Price 18 Cents [1815?] [cover title].
[1–12] p. engr. on one side only of 12 leaves; illus.; 13.5 cm.; pr. front paper cover, rear cover unpr. Adv. by Wm. Charles, 1815 in **748.**
English ed. London: Didier & Tebbett, 1808.
Ball° (rebound).

THE TWIN BROTHERS. *See* Hughes, Mary, no. **624.**

THE TWIN SISTERS. *See* Sandham, Elizabeth, no. **1161.1.**

THE TWO APPLE TREES. *See* Berquin, Arnaud, no. **93.**

1358 (No. 10) THE TWO APPRENTICES: A Narrative And Conversation, Written To Shew The Excellency And Use Of Scripture. Published By The Philadelphia Female Tract Society. [caption title p. [1]]. Printed by Lydia R. Bailey, No. 10, North Alley. 1816. [colophon p.8].
[1], 2–8 p.; 14 cm.
MWA° (bound with other tracts with which *The First Annual Report Of The Philadelphia Female Tract Society For The Year 1816* was originally bound); Shaw 39134.

THE TWO BABES IN THE WOOD. *See* Children In The Wood, no. **180.**

1359 THE TWO BOYS: Or, The Reward Of Truth. Philadelphia: Printed For Johnson And Warner, No. 147, Market Street. 1810. Lydia R. Bailey, Printer, No. 10, North-Alley.
fr.[ii], t.[1], [2–3], 4–36 p.; 4 pl. including front.; 13 cm.; pr. buff paper covers; front.

signed *WR sc* [William Ralph]. Adv. by John-
son & Warner, 1814 in **1449.3.**
English ed. London: J. Harris, 1808.
MWA°; Shaw 21542.

1360.1 THE TWO BROTHERS: Or, The History
Of Charles And John Spencer. An American Tale.
Ornamented with Cuts. Hartford: Printed by
Lincoln & Gleason. 1803.
    fr.[2], t.[3], [4–5], 6–29, [30–31, adv. list of
    books] p.; illus.; 10 cm.; blue marbled paper
    covers.
    MWA°; Ct (covers wanting); CtHi; PP; Shaw
    5186.

1360.2 ———— Adorned With Cuts. Hudson
[N.Y.]: Printed by Ashbel Stoddard, at the White
Horse, corner of Warren and Third Street. 1805.
    fr.[2], t.[3], [4–5], 6–30, [31, adv.] p.; illus.;
    10.5 cm.; marbled paper covers.
    NNC-LS (i. st. on front cover).

1360.3 ———— Ornamented with Cuts. Hartford: Printed By Lincoln & Gleason. 1806.
    fr.[2], t.[3], [4–5], 6–29, [30, bl.], [31, adv.
    of 12 books] p.; illus.; violet and green Dutch
    paper covers.
    MWA-W°; WaPS; Shaw 11488.

1360.4 ———— Hartford: Printed By Peter B.
Gleason & Co. 1811.
    fr.[2], t.[3], [4–5], 6–29, [30, illus.], [31, adv.
    list of books] p.; 9.5 cm.; pr. purple paper
    covers.
    Cover title: History Of Charles And John
    Spencer. Hartford: Printed By Peter B. Gleason
    & Co. 1813.
    MWA° (top of book cropped); CtHi; Shaw
    24072.

THE TWO COUSINS, A Moral Story. *See* Pinchard,
Mrs., no. **1010.1.**

1361 THE TWO DOVES, AND THE OWL. A new
story for Children. Hartford: Published by S. G.
Goodrich. Roberts & Burr, Pr's. 1819.
    fr.[2], t.[3] 4–16 p.; illus.; 10.5 cm.; illus. white
    paper covers printed in pink ink.
    MWA-W°; CtHi; MWA (top of fr.[2] mut. but
    not affecting illus.); PP; Shaw 49655.

1362 TWO ENTERTAINING STORIES FOR YOUNG
LADIES. Hudson (New-York): adv. by Ashbel
Stoddard, 1794 in **1220.1.**

THE TWO LAMBS. *See* Cameron, Lucy Lyttleton
(Butt), no. **151.1.**

THE TWO SISTERS, Or The Cavern. *See* Herbester,
Mrs., no. **508.1.**

U

1363 The Uncle's Present, A New Battledoor. Published by Jacob Johnson. 147 Market Street, Philadelphia. [*ca.* 1810].
>[1–4] p.; illus.; 17 cm.; pr. & illus. paper covers. The title is on a flap of p.[1]. Each letter of the alphabet is illustrated with one of the Cries of London.
>Cover title: Read And Be Wise. [3 lines upper case alphabet] [illus.] [numbers 1–9 and 0] Philadelphia: Sold By Benjamin Warner, 147, Market Street.
>MWA°; CLU; CSmH; CtHi; DeWint; DLC; ICU; IU; MiD; NHi; OClW-LS; OOxM; PP; PU; Shaw 14251 and 21546.

1364 Unterhaltungen für Deutsche Kinder. Philadelphia: Gedruckt bey Conrad Zentler, in der Zweyten Strasse, nah am Eck der Rehs-Strasse. 1808.
>t.[1], [2–3], 4–36 p.; illus.; 14 cm.; brown paper covers speckled with black.
>MWA°; Shaw 16611.

1365 Die Unterredung: Ueber die Feyer-tage, Eines Schul-Lehrers und seiner Kin-dern. In Frag und-Antwort. Das 2te deutsche Virginische Kinderbuch. Neumarket Virginien: Gedruckt bey Ambrozius Henkel. 1807.
>t.[1], [2–5], 6–32 p.; illus.; 12 cm.; illus. buff paper covers printed in red ink.
>MWA° (p. [5]–6 mut.); Shaw 14105.

1366 Eine Unterredung Zwichen Knaben und Magdchen auf das Oster-Fest samt einer schönen Geschechte Taglöhners Abend-Essen genannt. Neu-Market [Va.]: Gedruckt und zu haben bey Ambrozius Henkel und Co. 1813.
>t.[1], [2–3], 4–31, [32, adv. list of books] p.; illus.; 14 cm.; paper covers.
>ViU°; Shaw 30390.

UPTON, MR.
1367 — My Childhood A Poem By Mr. Upton. Illustrated With Engravings. Philadelphia Published and sold by Wm. Charles. Price Plain 12½ cents, Coloured 18¾ cents. 1816. [cover title].
>[1–6] engr. on one side only of 6 leaves; 13 cm.; pr. paper covers.
>MWA° (rear cover wanting); Shaw 39652.

Urad, Or The Fair Wanderer. *See* Ridley, James, no. **1113**.

Ursula, Or The Insufficiency Of Human Attainments. *See* Sandham, Elizabeth, no. **1162**.

1368 Useful Essays, And Instructive Stories, Selected For The Improvement of the Minds, And The Forming of the Manners, Of The Youth of the United States. By a Friend to Science. [4 lines of verse] From the Press of Anthony Haswell, Bennington, Vermont, 1807.
>t.[1], [2, bl.–3], 4–111, [112] p.; 13 cm.
>MWA°; VtHi (bound in blue paper over w. bds.; blue paper mostly wanting from covers); McCorison 951; Shaw 14108.

V

1369 THE VAGABOND. A new Story for Children. Hartford: Published by S. G. Goodrich. Roberts & Burr, Pr's. 1819.

fr.[2], t.[3], 4–16 p.; front. only illus.; 10.5 cm.; illus. white paper covers printed in pink ink, copy 1; black ink, copy 2. The illustrations on the covers of copy 1 are oval, horizontal and printed on the side. In copy 2 the illustration on the front cover is diamond-shaped and perpendicular, while that on the rear cover is oval and perpendicular.
MWA-W° (copy 1, copy 2, front cover and fr. [2] wanting); CSmH; CtHi (copy 2); Shaw 49968.

1370 THE VAIN COTTAGER: Or, The History Of Lucy Franklin. To Which Are Prefixed A Few Hints To Young Women In Humble Life, Respecting Decency And Propriety Of Dress. From Sidney's Press. New-Haven; For Increase Cooke And Co. 1807.

t.[1], [2–3], 4–72 p.; 15 cm.
MWA°; Shaw 14109.

VALENTINE AND ORSON (arranged chronologically)

1371.1 THE RENOWNED HISTORY OF VALENTINE AND ORSON, The Two Sons Of The Emperor Of Greece. Haverhill [Mass.], Printed By Peter Edes. MDCCXCIV.

t.[1], [2–3], 4–100 p.; 15 cm. English abr. ed. title 8, London, 1724.
English unabr. ed.: [*Valentine And Orson.* Wynkyn de Worde].
English unabr. ed. title 1: *The History of the two Valyaunt Brethern Valentyne and Orson.* [Translated From The French by H. Watson] London: William Coplande, [1565?]. [B.L.].
English unabr. ed. title 2: *Valentine And Orson.* London: T. Pnrfoot [*sic. i.e.* Purfoot] 1637.
English abr. ed. title 1. *The Adventures Of Valentine and Orson.* London: Tabart And Co. 1804.
English abr. ed. title 2. *The Famous History Of Valentine And Orson. . . . Written by Laurence Price.* London: W. Whitwood, 1673.

English abr. title 2a. ——— *Orson.* [author unknown] London: 16 ed. For A. Bettsworth, C. Hitch, J. Osborn and J. Hodges, 1736.
English abr. ed. title 3: *The Famous and Renowned History Of Valentine and Orson.* [London]: C. Bates, [1680?].
English, Scottish & Irish abr. ed. title 4: *The History Of Valentine and Orson.* Dublin: Luke Dillon, 1734.
English abr. ed. title 5: *The History & Adventures Of Valentine and Orson.* London: Didier & Tebbett, 1808.
Scottish ed. title 6: *The History Of The Famous Valentine and Orson.* Edinburgh: Printed for the Company of Flying Stationers. [1800?].
English abr. ed. title 7: *The New History Of Valentine and Orson.* London: For E. Midwinter. [1750?].
English & Scottish abr. ed. title 8: *The Renowned History Of Valentine And Orson.* London: D. Pratt, 1724.
English abr. ed. title 9: *Valentine And Orson.* [London: A. M. for E. Tracy, [1700]].
MWA°; CLU; MHa; MSaE; RPJCB; Evans 27605.

1371.2 ——— New-York—Printed By G. Forman, For B. Gomez, No. 32, Maiden-Lane. 1794.
fr.[2], t.[3], [4, adv.], [5], 6–138, [139–142] p.; front. only illus.; 13.5 cm.; bound in leather. English abr. ed. title 7, no. **1371.1.**
Bowe mss.; Evans 47309.

1371.3 ——— Newly Corrected And Amended. Hartford: Printed By J. Babcock. 1800.
t.[1], [2–3], 4–141, [142–143, adv.] p.; 13 cm.; bound in marbled paper over w. bds.
English abr. ed. title 7, no. **1371.1.**
MWA°; CiHi; Bowe mss.; Evans 38368.

1371.4 ——— Greece. Elizabeth-Town [N.J.]: Printed By John Woods, For Evert Duyckinck, New-York. 1802.
t.[1], [2–3], 4–108 p.; 14 cm.; bound in illus. paper over bds., leather spine.
English abr. ed. title 7, no. **1371.1.**
PP°; Bowe mss.

1371.5 THE ADVENTURES OF VALENTINE AND ORSON. A Tale For Youth. Ornamented With Plates. New-York: Published By T. B. Jansen, Book-Seller, 116 Broadway, opposite the City-Hotel. L. Nichols, Print. 1805.

fr.[ii], t.[1], [2–3], 4–35, [36, adv. list of books] p.; front. & title vignette only illus.; 13.5 cm.; marbled paper covers; front. signed *Anderson.*
PP°; NRU (p. 1–8, 13–14, 35–36 mut.); MB; Bowe mss.; Shaw 7840 and 50491.

1371.6 ——— New-York: Published By Thomas Powers, Book-Seller, 116 Broadway, opposite the City-Hotel. 1810.

fr.[ii], t.[1], [2–3], 4–36 p.; illus.; 13.5 cm.; pr. & illus. paper covers.
Cover title: History Of Valentine And Orson. New-York: ——— Bookseller and Stationer, No. 116 Broadway, ——— Hotel. Price 12½ cents.
MWA°; DLC; CCamarSJ; MiD; OOxM; Bowe mss.; Shaw 19314.

1371.7 ——— Ornamented With Nine Engravings. Boston: Printed and published by Samuel Avery, at the Juvenile Bookstore, No. 91 Newbury Street. 1811.

fr.[ii], t.[1], [2–3], 4–36 p.; illus.; 14 cm.; pr. & illus. paper covers.
Cover title: The History Of Valentine And Orson. Boston: ——— 1811. Price 12½ Cents.
MWA° (fr.[ii], p. 9–10, 27–28 wanting; first word "The" on t.[1] is cut off; p. 29–32, 35–36 ½ wanting); DLC (fr.[ii], t.[1], p. [2], 35–36 wanting; MiU; MSaE (t.[1] wanting); Shaw 24329.

1371.8 ——— Youth. Otsego [N.Y.]: Printed By H. & E. Phinney, Jun. And Sold By Them Wholesale And Retail, 1811.

t.[1], [2–3], 4–44 p.; 12.5 cm. April 16, 1807 was the first date the *Otsego Herald* changed the name of the town from Cooperstown to Otsego. N. Y. The imprint of the paper changed back to Cooperstown N. Y., July 17, 1813. (MWA cat.).
NCooHi° (covers wanting); MWA-T.

1371.9 ——— Youth. Ornamented With Eight Engravings. Boston: Published by Thomas Wells, No. 3, Hanover-Street. 1812.

fr.[ii], t.[1], [2–3], 4–32 p.; illus.; 14.5 cm.; pr. & illus. blue paper covers; cover title dated 1813.
MWA° (rear cover wanting); Shaw 27372.

1371.10 ——— Boston: Published By Watson & Bangs, No. 7, State-Street. 1813.

fr.[ii], t.[1], [2–3], 4–32 p.; illus.; 14 cm.; pr. & illus. violet paper covers.
Cover title imprint of MH copy: Boston: Published by Thomas Wells, No. 3, Hanover-Street. 1813.
MWA° (covers worn, rear cover mut.); MB; MH (copy 1, pr. & illus. gray paper covers; copy 2, fr.[ii] mut. and defaced; pr. & illus. violet paper covers); Shaw 30393.

1371.11 THE HISTORY AND ADVENTURES OF THE RENOWNED PRINCES VALENTINE AND ORSON. Philadelphia: Published and Sold Wholesale by Wm. Charles, and may be had of all the Booksellers. Price 18 3-4 Cents. 1813. W. M'Culloch, Printer. [cover title].

[1–12] p. engr. on one side only of 12 leaves; illus.; 13.5 cm.; both pr. paper covers bordered with ornaments in each corner. Page [1]: Frontispiece. [illus.] Prince Orson suckled by a Bear. The History & Adventures of the Renowned Princes. Valentine & Orson.
English abr. ed. title 5, no. **1371.1.**
MWA-W°; DLC (i. st. p. [1]); RPB; Shaw 30394.

1371.12 ——— [same as **1371.10**] Boston: Published By R. P. & C. Williams, No. 8, State-Street. 1814.

fr.[ii], t.[1], [2–3], 4–32 p.; illus.; 14.5 cm.; pr. & illus. paper covers; colophon p. 32; Thomas G. Bangs, Printer.
MWA°; MHi (fr.[ii], p. 31–32 & covers wanting); RPB; Shaw 33521.

1371.13 ——— [same as **1371.11**] Philadelphia: Published and sold Wholesale by Wm. Charles, No. 32, South Third-street, and may be had of all the Booksellers. Price 18 3-4 cents. 1817.

[1–12] p. engr. on one side only of 12 leaves; col. illus.; 13 cm.; pr. paper covers.
English abr. ed. title 5, no. **1371.1.**
MWA-W°.

THE VALLEY OF TEARS. *See* More, Hannah, no. **899.1.**

1372 VARIETY, IN PROSE AND VERSE, FOR LITTLE CHILDREN. New-York: Published By Samuel Wood & Sons, No. 261, Pearl-street; And Samuel S. Wood & Co., No. 212, Market-Street, Baltimore. 1820.

t.[1], [2–3], 4–32 p.; illus.; 12.5 cm.; pr. paper covers. Adv. by S. Wood, 1819 in **1188.8**.
MWA*; Shoemaker 4081.

1373 VARIOUS MODES OF CATCHING. Philadelphia, Published by J. Johnson N⁰ 147 Market-Street. [1802].

t.[1], [2–32] p.; 16 engr. illus. p. including t.[1] and exclusive of duplicate p. [4] and [29]; 9.5 cm.; yellow paper covers speckled with gold. This book and its companion volume, *Youthful Recreations*, no. **1468** and a smaller book, *People of All Nations*, no. **982.1** were published in London, England in 1801 by Darton and Harvey and probably were all part of a set of books printed for *The Infant's Own Bookcase. See* discussion no. **1468**. Since all three were issued by Jacob Johnson it is logical to suppose he reprinted them in the same year as no. **982.1** or 1802. Adv. by Johnson & Warner, 1814 in **1449.3**. Part of a publisher's remainder.
English ed. London Wᵐ Darton and Jʰ Harvey, 1801.
MWA*; CtY; NHi; PHi; PP; Shaw 21887 dated [1810?]).

VAUX, FRANCES BOWYER
1374 — HENRY. A Story, Intended For Little Boys And Girls. From Five To Ten Years Old. By Frances Bowyer Vaux. First American Edition. Philadelphia: Published and Sold by Wm. Charles, No. 32, South Third street. 1817.

½t.[1], fr.[ii], t.[iii], [iv–v], vi–vii, [viii, bl.], [9], 10–60 p.; engraved folded copper plate front only illus.; 18 cm.; bound in green paper over bds.
English ed. London: W. Darton, Jun. 1815.
PP*; ICU; Shaw 42768.

VELASCO, E.
1375.1 — THE INTELLIGENT MISCELLANY. For the Amusement and Instruction of Youth. By E. Velasco. [2 lines quot.] Vol. I. From Wilder's Press. [Jaffrey, N.H.] 1814.

fr.[2], t.[3], [4–5], 6–30, [31, illus.] p.; illus.; 10 cm.
MWA*; Shaw 33529.

1375.2 ———— By E. Velasco. [4 lines of verse] Weems Life of Washington. Vol. II. From Wilder's Press. [Jaffrey, N.H.] 1815.

t.[3], [4–5], 6–81 [*sic. i.e.* 31] p.; illus.; 10.5 cm.; brown paper covers.
Welch°; MWA; NhHi; PP; Shaw 36430.

VENTUM, HARRIET
1376 — THE HOLIDAY REWARD; Or Tales To Instruct And Amuse Good Children, During The Holiday and Midsummer Vacations. By Mrs. Ventum. New-York: Published By W. B. Gilley, 92 Broadway. N. Van Riper, Printer. 1819.

t.[1], [2–5], 6–129, p.; 14.5 cm.; bound in green paper over bds., black leather spine.
English ed. London: J. Harris, 1806.
MWA-W° (original rear cover & leather spine wanting); DLC; PP; PPL; NN (rebound); RPB; Shaw 49979.

1377 [—] THE PIOUS AND INDUSTRIOUS SAILOR BOY, And The Sick Soldier. Sidney's Press. Published by John Babcock & Son, New-Haven, S. & W. R. Babcock, No. 163 King-Street, Charleston, and M'Carty & Davis, Philadelphia. 1820.

fr.[2], t.[3], [4–5], 6–31 p.; illus.; 14.5 cm.; pr. & illus. paper covers; fr.[2] signed A [Alexander Anderson].
The above two stories are taken from Harriet Ventum's *Holiday Reward,* no. **1376**.
MWA° (p. 31 mut.); CtHi; MB (per. st. on t.[3]); MH; PP; Shoemaker 2788.

VERBUM SEMPITERNUM. *See* Taylor, John, no. **1293.1**.

1378 VERSES FOR LITTLE CHILDREN. *Nerv-York* [*sic. i.e. New-York*]: Published By Samuel Wood & Sons, No. 261, Pearl-street; And Samuel S. Wood & Co., No. 212, Market-Street, Baltimore. 1820.

fr.[ii], t.[1], [2–3], 4–30 p.; illus.; 12.5 cm.; pr. buff paper covers; cover title undated.
English ed. London: Darton, Harvey And Darton. 1810.
MWA°; CtHi (fr.[ii] mut.); NjP; Shoemaker 4100.

1379 VICE IN ITS PROPER SHAPE; Or, The Wonderful and Melancholy Transformation Of Several Naughty Masters and Misses Into Those Contemptible Animals which they must resemble in

Disposition. Printed for the Benefit of all Good Boys and Girls. First Worcester Edition. Printed at Worcester, Massachusetts, By Isaiah Thomas, Sold at his Bookstore, and by Thomas and Andrews in Boston. MDCCLXXXIX.

> fr.[ii], t.[iii], [iv–v], vi–xi, 12–128 p.; illus.; 10 cm.; bound in Dutch paper over w. bds.
> English ed. London: adv. by F. Newbery, 1775 in *The Cries Of London*.
> MWA° (copy 1, Dutch paper covers, i. st. on t.[iii]; copy 2, rebound in leather, I. Thomas copy); CLU; NjP; PP; Evans 22221; Hamilton 128.

1380 THE VICTIMS OF PLEASURE; Being Scenes In Humble Life: Exemplifying the Evil of Sabbath-Breaking. Boston: Printed By Crocker And Brewster, No. 50, Cornhill, Sold by them, wholesale and retail, and by the Booksellers generally throughout the United States. 1820.

> fr.[2], t.[3], [4–5], 6–124 p.; 14 cm.; bound in paper over w. bds., leather spine.
> English ed. London, Oxford [printed], 1816.
> MB° (emb. st. on t.[3]); Shoemaker 4103 and 4388.

1381 VILLAGE ANNALS, Containing Austerus And Humanus. A Sympathetic Tale. Embellished With Fine Engravings. Philadelphia: Published By Johnson & Warner, No. 147, Market Street. Griggs & Dickinson, Printers. 1814.

> fr.[2], t.[3], [4–5], 6–35 p.; illus.; 14 cm.; green paper covers. Part of a large publisher's remainder.
> English ed. London: J. Arliss, 1808.
> Welch° CaOTP; CCamarSJ; CLU; CSmH; CtHi; CtY; DeWint; DLC; MiD; MWA; NN (2 copies); NNC-Pl; NRU; PHi; PP; PPL; PU; ViU; Shaw 33546.

THE VILLAGE MAID. *See* Somerville, Elizabeth, no. **1233.**

1382.1 THE VILLAGE ORPHAN: A Tale For Youth. To Which Is Added, The Basket-Maker, An Original Fragment. Philadelphia: Printed By John Thompson, For James Thackara, No. 177, South Second-Street. 1800.

> t.[i], [ii], [1], 2–152 p.; 13.5 cm.; bound in leather.
> English ed. London: Longman & Rees. [*ca.* 1800].
> MWA°; Evans 38940.

1382.2 ——— Fragment. Ornamented With Vignettes On Wood. Philadelphia: Published By Johnson And Warner, No. 147, Market-Street. J. Bouvier, Printer. 1810.

> t.[1], [2–5], 6–136 p.; illus.; 15 cm.; bound in pink paper over bds. Adv. by Johnson & Warner, 1812 in **104.1**; 1814 in **1449.3**; 1817 in **1355.3**.
> MWA°; NNC-Pl (bound in pr. & illus. pink paper over bds.; cover title dated 1811); Shaw 21912.

VILLAGE TALES, OR JUVENILE AMUSEMENTS. *See* Somerville, Elizabeth, no. **1234.**

1383 VIRTUE AND INNOCENCE; A Poem For Children. Philadelphia: Published by Johnson and Warner, No. 147, Market Street. 1812. [cover title].

> fr.[ii], t.[iii], [iv, bl.], [1], 2–16, ½t.[17], [18–19], 20–23, [24, illus.] p.; illus.; 15 cm.; pr. & illus. olive paper covers. Adv. by Johnson & Warner, 1813 in **971**.
> Engr. t.[iii]: Virtue And Innocence—A Poem. [cut] [2 lines of quot.]. ½t. p.[17]: The Ten Commandments; To Which Is Profixed The Collect Of The Communion Service; In Verse. Adapted To Youth.
> English ed. London: W. and T. Darton, 1808.
> MWA°; CLU; NN; TxU; Shaw 27413.

1384.1 VIRTUE AND VICE: Or The History Of Charles Careful, And Harry Heedless, Shewing the Good Effects of Caution and Prudence, And the many Inconveniences that Harry Heedless experienced from his Rashness and Disobedience, while Master Careful became a great Man, only by his Merit. The First Worcester Edition. Printed at Worcester, Massachusetts, By Isaiah Thomas, And sold, Wholesale and Retail, at his Book-Store. MDCCLXXXVII.

> fr.[2], t.[3], [4–5], 6–61, [62–63, adv.] p.; illus.; 10.5 cm.; illus. buff paper covers.
> English ed. London: adv. by E. Newbery in *London Chronicle* 19–21 Dec: 1780.
> MWA (copy 1, rebound, scalloped marble paper covers; copy 2, illus. buff paper covers, t.[3] wanting); Evans 20851.

1384.2 ——— Merit. Boston: Printed and sold by Samuel Hall, No. 53, Cornhill. 1792.

> fr.[2], t.[3], [4–5], 6–61, [62–63, adv. list of

books] p.; illus.; 10 cm.; Dutch paper covers.
MWA°; Evans 46665.

1384.3 ———— Boston: Printed and sold by
Samuel Hall, No. 53, Cornhill. 1795.
fr.[2], t.[3], [4–5], 6–61, [62–63, adv. list of
17 books] p.; illus.; 10 cm.; violet and green
Dutch paper covers. Two printer's ornaments
are present. The advertisement caption p.[62]:
*A great Variety of BOOKS,/designed for In-
struction and Amusement,/and suited to Children of All Ages and/Capacities, are constantly
kept for Sale/by S. HALL, No. 53, Cornhill,
Boston;/among which are the following, viz.*
DLC; NN-C (fr.[2], t.[3], p.[4], [63] mut.);
Evans 29818.

1384.4 ———— The Second Worcester Edition.
Printed at Worcester, Massachusetts. By Thomas,
Son & Thomas. And Sold, Wholesale and Retail,
at their Book-store. MDCCXCVI.
fr.[2], t.[3], [4–5], 6–61, [62–63, adv. list of
books] p.; illus.; 10.5 cm.; illus. blue-gray paper
covers.
MWA°; Evans 31514.

1384.5 ———— Third Worcester Edition. Printed
at Worcester, Massachusetts, By Isaiah Thomas,
Jun. Sold Wholesale and Retail by Him. MDCCC.
fr.[2], t.[3], [4–5], 6–61, [62–63, 2 cuts per
page] p.; illus.; 10.5 cm.; pink Dutch paper
covers.
MWA°; Evans 38968.

1385.1 VIRTUE IN A COTTAGE, Or, A Mirror
For Children, Displayed In The History Of Sally
Bark And Her Family. [2 lines of verse] Hartford:
Printed By J. Babcock. 1795.
fr.[2], t.[3], [4–5], 6–31 p.; illus.; 10.5 cm.;
green Dutch paper covers. Mrs. Trimmer in
The Guardian Of Education. Vol. I, May to
December, 1802 lists this book under "M.P."
[Dorothy Kilner].
English ed.; *Virtue In A Cottage; Or, A Mirror
For Children In Humble Life.* London: J. Mar-
shall, [2 addresses] [1797?] mss. date "1797"
on the recto of the front fly leaf which was
pasted originally to the front cover.
MWA°.

1385.2 ———— Hartford: Printed By J. Babcock. 1802.
fr.[2], t.[3], [4–5] 6–46 p.; illus.; 12.5 cm.;
pink and blue scalloped marbled paper covers;
text printed on blue-gray paper.
MWA-W°.

VISIONS, FOR THE ENTERTAINMENT AND INSTRUC-
TION OF YOUNG MINDS. *See* Cotton, Nathaniel,
no. **240.1.**

VISIONS IN VERSE, For The Entertainment and
Instruction Of Younger Minds. Title of English
ed. *See* Cotton, Nathaniel, no. **240.1.**

1386 THE VISION OF MIRZA, Exhibiting A Picture Of Human Life, A Tale. Ornamented with
Cuts. Windham [Conn.]: Printed by Samuel
Webb. 1813.
fr.[2], t.[3], [4–5], 6–21, [22, alphabet], [23,
2 cuts] p.; front. & illus. p. [23] only illus.;
9.5 cm.; pr. & illus. yellow paper covers. The
story is taken from *The Amusing Companion,*
no. **39.**
MWA-W°; Shaw 30430.

VISIT FOR A WEEK. *See* Peacock, Lucy, no. **979.1.**

1387 A VISIT TO A SABBATH EVENING SCHOOL,
A Narrative For Children. By A Sabbath School
Teacher. [4 lines of verse] New-York: Published
by P. W. Gallaudet, at his Theological Bookstore,
No. 49, Fulton-street. 1818.
t.[1], [2–3], 4–36 p.; 14.5 cm.; pr. brown paper
covers; colophon p. 36: Birch And Kelley,
Printers.
DLC°; MH.

1388 A VISIT TO A SABBATH SCHOOL, A Narrative For Children. By a Sabbath School Teacher.
Boston: Printed For Samuel T. Armstrong, By
Crocker & Brewster, No. 50, Cornhill. 1820.
t.[1], [2], 3–36 p.; title vignette only illus.; 14
cm.; pr. & illus. green paper covers; rear cover
adv. of books.
MWA-W° (copy 1, pr. & illus. paper covers;
copy 2, green unprinted covers with a label:
Sunday School Premium Attendance); MB; NN
(i. st. on t.[1], covers wanting); OClW-LS;
Shoemaker 4126 and 4389.

1389 Visit To My Friend's Family. Philadelphia: adv. by The Sunday and Adult School Union, 1819 in **1279.1,** and 1820 in **1279.2.**

1390 A Visit To The Bazaar. New-Haven: Published By A. B. Goldsmith And N. & S. S. Jocelyn. 1819.
    fr.[ii], t.[1], [2–3], 4–29 p.; 8 col. pl. including front.; 13 cm.; pr. buff paper covers. Colophon p. 29: A. H. Maltby & Co. Printers, New-Haven. English ed. London: J. Harris, 1818.
    MWA° (pl. opp. p. 25 wanting; t.[1] torn); CtHi (all after p. 23 wanting); Shaw 50001.

1391 Voyages And Travels Of A Bible. By J. Campbell, Author of Worlds Displayed, Picture of Human Life, Alfred and Galba; &c. [3 lines quot.] Second American, From The Fourth London, Edition. Windsor [Vt.]: Printed And Published By Pomroy & Hedge. 1816.
    t.[1], [ii–iii], iv, [5], 6–77, [78 contents] p.; 13.5 cm.; bound in pr. & illus. buff paper over w. bds. In the advertisement, p.[iii], the author says "The first two chapters of this history of a Bible, were formerly published at the end of *World's Displayed* [*see* no. **154**]. Several highly respected friends have recommended an enlargement of that history: in compliance with their recommendation I have attempted it; . . . shall entertain, but also edify young readers." The end of the advertisement, p. iv, is signed *John Campbell. Kingsland, June 1, 1807.* The cover title is undated.
    MWA-T°.

W., S.

1392 — SCENES AT HOME; Or Sketch Of A Plain Family. By S. W. Author Of A Puzzle For A Curious Girl, A Visit To A Farm House, &c. Philadelphia: Published By David Hogan, No. 249, Market-Street. Griggs & Dickinson, Printers. 1812.

t.[1], [2–3], 4–108 p.; 13.5 cm.; bound in blue paper over bds., leather spine; p. 104–108 adv. "Juvenile Publications For Sale By David Hogan," many of which are undoubtedly publications of Jacob Johnson, Johnson & Warner and William Charles.

English ed. London: B. Tabart And Co., 1810.

MWA-W°; CtHi; Shaw 26698.

1393 — A VISIT TO LONDON, Containing A Description Of The Curiosities In The British Metropolis. By S. W. Author Of The Visit To A Farm-House, And The Puzzle For A Curious Girl. With Six Copper Plates. A New Edition, with Additions and Improvements. Philadelphia: Published By Benjamin Warner, No. 147, Market-st. Sold Also At His Store In Richmond, Virginia. Wm. Greer, Printer. 1817.

fr.[ii], t.[1], [2–5], 6–111 p.; 6 pl. including front.; 14 cm.; bound in marbled paper over bds., leather spine.

MWA°; Shaw 42802.

WAKEFIELD, PRISCILLA (BELL) 1751–1832
1394.1 — A BRIEF MEMOIR OF THE LIFE OF WILLIAM PENN. Compiled For the use Of Young Persons. By Priscilla Wakefield. Philadelphia, Published By Isaac Peirce, No. 5, North Front Street. 1818. Shinn, Printer, Fetter Lane.

fr.[ii], t.[1], [2–3], 4–47 p.; front. only illus.; 14 cm.; pr. olive paper covers; front. signed *J. Henry sc.*

PSC° (p. 1–6 mut.).

1394.2 — —— New-York: Printed And Sold By Mahlon Day, No. 84, Water-Street. 1820.

fr.[ii], t.[1], [2–3], 4–31, [32–33, adv.] p.; front. only illus.; 14 cm.; pr. & illus. paper covers.

PP°; ICU; PHi; Sabin 100979; Shoemaker 4140.

1395 — DOMESTIC RECREATION; Or Dialogues Illustrative Of Natural And Scientific Subjects. By Priscilla Wakefield, Author Of Mental Improvement. &c. Philadelphia: Published By Jacob Johnson. No. 147, Market Street. Printed By Robert Carr. 1805.

fr.[ii], ½t.[i], [ii, bl.], t.[iii], [iv–v], vi, [7], 8–192 p.; 6 pl. including front.; 15 cm.; bound in gray & pink marbled paper over bds., red leather spine. Six plates: fr.[ii], and 5 pl. in text signed *Ralph sc* [William Ralph].

English ed. London: Darton And Harvey, 1805.

MWA-W°; DLC (copy 1, fr.[ii] precedes ½t.[i]; copy 2, fr.[ii] follows ½t.[i]); MH; NcD; NN; NNC-T; NRU; PP; Shaw 9679.

1396 — A FAMILY TOUR THROUGH THE BRITISH EMPIRE; Containing some Account of its Natural And Artificial Curiosities, History and Antiquities; Interspersed With Biographical Anecdotes. Particularly adapted to the Amusement And Instruction Of Youth. By Priscilla Wakefield. Philadelphia: Published And Sold By Jacob Johnson & Co. Sold Also By C. Peirce, And W. & D. Treadwell, Portsmouth; W. P. & L. Blake, Boston; Beers & How, New-Haven; Whiting, Backus & W. Albany; O. Penniman & Co. Troy; Thomas & Whipple, Newbury-Port; George Hill, And Warner & Hanna, Baltimore; R. & J. Grey, Alexandria, And S. Pleasants, And W. Prichard, Richmond. 1804. < A. Bartram, Printer. >

fr.[ii, folded col. map], t.[i], [ii, bl.–iii], iv, [1], 2–354, [355–368] p.; front map only illus.; 17 cm.; bound in blue marbled paper over bds., leather spine.

English ed. London: Darton and Harvey, 1804.

MWA-W°; BM; PP; PPi; Shaw 7683.

1397 — INSTINCT DISPLAYED, In A Collection Of Well-Authenticated Facts, Exemplifying The Extraordinary Sagacity Of Various Species Of The Animal Creation. [6 lines of verse]. By Priscilla Wakefield. First American from the second London edition. Boston: Published By Cummings And Hilliard, And Timothy Swan, At The Boston Bookstore, No. 1, Cornhill. Flagg & Gould, Printers. 1816.

t.[i], [ii–iii], iv–xvi, [13], 14–335 p.; 14.5 cm.; bound in pr. brown paper over bds., red leather spine.

English ed. London: 1811.

MWA*; DLC; OClWHi; PHC; PP; PPL; Shaw 39675.

1398 — JUVENILE ANECDOTES, Founded On Facts. Collected For The Amusement Of Children. By Priscilla Wakefield, Author Of Mental Improvement, Leisure Hours, &c. Philadelphia: Published By Johnson & Warner. 1809.

t.[i], [ii–iii], iv–vi, [1], 2–171 p.; 14.5 cm. bound in blue marbled paper over bds., red leather spine. In the NNC-Pl & PP copies the "Preface" p. [iii]–iv follows the "Contents" p. [v]–vi.

English ed. London: vol. [I.], 1795.

MWA-W*; DLC (rebound, i. st. on t.[i]); KU; NNC-Pl; PP (rebacked); Shaw 19127.

1399.1 — MENTAL IMPROVEMENT: Or The Beauties And Wonders Of Nature And Art. In A Series Of Instructive Conversations. By Priscilla Wakefield, Author Of Leisure Hours. First American, From The Third London Edition. New-Bedford: Printed By Abraham Shearman, Jun. For Caleb Green & Son. 1799.

t.[i], [ii–iii], iv, [v–vi], [7], 8–264 p.; 17.5 cm.; bound in leather.

English ed. London: entered at Stationer's Hall by Darton & Harvey, 1794.

MWA*; CLU; CtY; DLC; MB; MH; MiU; MWiW; PHi; PPL; PU; RPJCB; Evans 36664.

1399.2 — ——— Second American From The Fifth London Edition. New-Bedford [Mass.]: Printed And Sold By A. Shearman, Jun. 1809.

t.[i], [ii–iii], iv–ix, [x], ½t.[xi], [xii], [13], 14–278, [279–280] p.; 18 cm.; bound in leather.

MWA*; BM; MB; MH; PHC; PPF; PU; Shaw 19128.

1399.3 — ——— Third American, From The Fifth London Edition. Philadelphia: Published By Johnson And Warner, No. 147, Market Street, And Benjamin Johnson, No. 22, North Second Street, 1814.

t.[i], [ii–iii], iv–ix, [x], [11], 12–240 p.; 18.5 cm.; bound in leather.

MWA*; DLC (i. st. on t.[i]); MH; PPL; PU; Shaw 33560.

1399.4 — ——— Fourth American, From The Fifth London Edition. Philadelphia: Published By Benjamin Johnson, No. 31, Market Street. 1819. Greggs & Co., Printers.

t.[i], [ii–iii], iv–ix, [x], [11], 12–240 p.; t.[i] 18.5 cm.; bound in blue paper over bds., cloth spine.

MWA*; DLC (rebound); MB; MH; PP; Shaw 50010.

1400 — SKETCHES OF HUMAN MANNERS, Delineated In Stories Intended To Illustrate The Characters, Religion, And Singular Customs, Of The Inhabitants Of Different Parts Of The World. By Priscilla Wakefield. First American Edition. Philadelphia: Published By Johnson & Warner, And Sold At Their Stores, In Philadelphia, In Richmond, (Vir.) And Lexington, (K.). 1811.

fr.[ii], t.[1], [2–7], 8–252 p.; front. only illus.; 14 cm. Colophon p. 252: William Greer, Printer. The frontispiece is signed *H. Anderson fs.* [Alexander Anderson].

English ed. 1807.

MWA*; DLC; MH (p. 157–160 wanting); NcU; NN (rebound); OClWHi; PHC; PPL; PP (bound in marbled paper over bds., leather spine); Sabin 100984; Shaw 24353.

1401 — VARIETY; Or, Selections And Essays, Consisting Of Anecdotes, Curious Facts, Interesting Narratives, With Occasional Reflections. By Priscilla Wakefield. London Printed. Philadelphia: Published By James P. Parke, No. 119, High Street. Brown & Merritt, Printers, 24, Church-alley. 1809.

t.[i], [ii–iii], iv–viii, [1], 2–207 p.; 18 cm.

English ed. London: Darton and Harvey, 1809.

MWA* (rebound); DLC; MB; NcD; NN; PHC; PPG; PSC; PU; ViU; Shaw 19129.

1402 A WALK AND CONVERSATION, Between A Fond Father And His Little Son, As They Took A Walk Through The Fields And Meadows, &c. For The Use Of Children. Norwich: Printed, By Charles E. Trumbull. MDCCCIV.

t.[1], [2], 3–31 p.; 11 cm.; paper covers.

CtHi; Shaw 50480.

WALKS OF USEFULNESS IN LONDON And Its Environs. *See* Campbell, John, no. **153.1**.

WALTON, ELIAKIM PERSONS 1812–1890

1403 [—] CHILD'S SPELLING BOOK. Montpelier, Vt. Published at the Book-Store. 1818. [cover title].

t.[1], [2–3], 4–6, [7], 8–12 p.; 14 cm.; pr. & illus. buff paper covers.

Cover title: The Child's Spelling Book; Or, The Poetical A, B, C. With Lessons In Spelling And Reading. [2 lines quot.].

VtHi*; Shaw 43606.

WANDERING WILLIAM. *See* Sandham, Elizabeth, no. **1153.**

A WARNING TO LITTLE CHILDREN. *See* Dow, Hendrick, no. **298.1.**

WATERS. *See* [Johnson, Richard], THE POETICAL FLOWER BASKET, no. **686.** The BM catalogue gives "Waters" for the name of the author.

WATKINS, LUCY

1404 — THE HISTORY AND ADVENTURES OF LITTLE JAMES AND MARY. An Instructive and Entertaining Tale for Youth. Written By Lucy Watkins. Philadelphia: Published And Sold By W. Charles, No. 32, South Third-street. [1819].

fr.[ii], t.[1], [2–3], 4–15 p.; 4 pl. including front.; 13 cm.; pr. buff paper covers; the tail of the "9" of the date "1819" on the cover title is prolonged into a curved line. At first glance the date looks as if it were 1810. Colophon p. 15: H. C. Lewis, Printer, No. 272 Market-St.

Cover title: James & Mary. A Poem. Illustrated With Engravings. Philadelphia, Published and sold by Wm. Charles, Price Plain 12¼ cents— Coloured 18¾ cents. 1819. The word "Poem" on the cover title is an error because the text is in prose.

NNC-Pl* (col. pl.); PP; Shaw 21963 (dated [1810]).

1405 — SOPHY: Or, The Punishment Of Idleness And Disobedience. A Moral Tale. Written By Lucy Watkins. Philadelphia: Published & Sold By Wm. Charles, No. 32, South Third street. 1819.

fr.[ii], t.[1], [2–3], 4–16 p.; probably 6 pl., front. & pl. opp. p. 5, 7, 9, 11, 13; 13 cm.; pr. brown paper covers; colophon p. 16: M'Carty & Davis, printers.

English ed. London: Dean And Munday, 1812.

MWA-W* (col. pl. opp. p. 5, 7, 9, 11 wanting);

DLC (col. pl. opp. p. 7, 9, wanting); Shaw 50053.

WATTS, ISAAC

1406.1 [— DIVINE AND MORAL SONGS FOR CHILDREN. Newport: Printed and sold by Solomon Southwick. 1773.]

See no. **1408.5.**

Evans 13066.

1406.2 — DIVINE AND MORAL SONGS FOR CHILDREN; Revised And Altered So As To Render Them Of General Use. To Which Are Added, A Short Catechism And Prayers. By Isaac Watts, D.D. Printed at Worcester, Massachusetts, By Isaiah Thomas. And Sold, Wholesale and Retail, at his Bookstore. MDCCLXXXVIII.

fr.[ii], t.[iii], [iv], v–ix, [x–xiv], [15], 16–118 p.; illus.; 11 cm.; bound in Dutch paper over bds.

English ed. title 12.

Welsh ed. title 1: *Caniadau Durviole* [Divine Songs]. Crefyddole: 1771.

English ed. title 2: *Divine and Moral Songs.* Derby: R. Miller. 1816.

English ed. title 3: *Divine and Moral Songs Attempted in Easy Language For The Use Of Children.* Beverly: M. Turner, For Messers. Crosby and Co. London; G. Turner, Hull; and M. Turner, Beverly, 1815.

English ed. title 4: *Divine and Moral Songs for Children.* London: Printed for the Booksellers, By J. Moore, Ilminster, [1814].

English ed. title 5: *Divine and Moral Songs For The Use Of Children.* London: W. Darton, 1812.

English ed. title 6: *Divine and Moral Songs In Easy & Pleasing Language. For The Instruction Of Children.* London: Edward Lacey, [1810?] [ca. 1830 or later].

English, Scottish & Irish ed. title 7: *Divine Songs Attempted In Easy Language for the Use Of Children.* London: M. Lawrence, 1715.

English ed. title 7a: *Divine Songs Attempted in Easy Language For The Instruction of Young Children in The First Principles of Morality.* London: *Printed for the* Booksellers, 1794.

English & Scottish ed. title 8: *Divine Songs for Children.* London: Darton and Harvey, 1802.

English ed. title 9: *Divine Songs For The Use Of Children.* Coventry: [1787?].

English & Scottish ed. title 10: *Divine Songs in*

Easy Language, For The Use Of Children. Glasgow: J. Lumsden & Son, 1814, part of a publisher's remainder.

English ed. title 11: *Dr. Watts's Divine And Moral Songs For Children: Revised And Altered So As To Render Them Of General Use. To which are added, A short Catechism And Prayers.* London: Printed by Permission of the Proprietors, For J. Johnson, 1787.

English ed. title 12: *Dr. Watts's Divine Songs For Children.* London: adv. by J. Mackenzie, [*ca.* 1790] in *The Entertaining History of Palidor and Fidele.*

English ed. title 13.: *Dr. Watts's Divine Songs In Easy Language For The Instruction Of Christian Children.* London: W. Mason [*ca.* 1810].

English ed. title 14: *Dr. Watts' Hymns, and Moral Songs for the Use of Children, Revised and Altered. To Which are, Added Prayers For The Use Of Children. By A Lady.* London: entered at Stationer's Hall Dec. 28, 1785 by Marshall & Co.

English ed. title 15: *Dr. Watts's Hymns For Children.* Exeter: T. Besley, Sold also by J. Johnson and Co., London; P. Hegland, Exeter; Rees and Curtis, Plymouth; and J. Belcher, Birmingham, 1812.

English ed. title 16: *Dr. Watts's Moral Songs.* Banbury: J. G. Rusher. [*ca.* 1815] part of a publisher's remainder.

English ed. title 17: *Hymns and Moral Songs.* York: adv. by Wilson, Spence and Mawman, 1797, in Bunyano's *The Prettiest Book For Children.*

English ed. title 18: *Select Songs for Children . . . By Isaac Watts, the Rev. Mr. Foxton and other eminent divines.* Newcastle: S. Hodgson, 1793.

English ed. title 19: *Songs Divine And Moral . . . A New Edition Revised by J. Owen.* London: J. Sharpe, And N. Hailes, And J. Hatcherd, 1809.

English ed. title 20: *Songs, Divine and Moral, For The Use Of Children.* Knaresbrough: J. Hargrove, 1819. Cover title: Watts's Divine and Moral Songs.

English ed. title 21: *Specimen of Moral Songs.* Chelmsford: I. Marsden. [1820?] part of a publisher's remainder.

English ed. title 22: *Spiritual Lessons for Children to read . . . Chiefly selected from the Divine Songs of Dr. Watts.* [1780?].

English & Scottish ed. title 24: *Watts' Divine Songs For Children.* London: adv. by H. Turpin, [*ca.* 1776] in *The History of Harloquin & Columbine.*

English & Scottish ed. title 25: *Watts Divine Songs For The Use Of Children.* Glasgow: Lumsden & Son [*ca.* 1804] bound with other books dated 1804, the American ed. copied from this one, no. **1420.1,** was printed in 1807.

English ed. title 26: *Watts's Hymns For Children, complete with Prayers.* London: adv. by J. Marshall pr.; R. White; S. Hazard at Bath; J. Elder, at Edinburgh, [1796?] in *Cheap Repository.*

MWA*; MWiW; PP (rebound); Evans 21576.

1406.3 — DIVINE AND MORAL SONGS, ATTEMPTED IN EASY LANGUAGE, For The Use Of Children. Revised And Corrected. By Isaac Watts, D.D. [2 lines quot.] Boston: Printed and sold by Samuel Hall, in Cornhill.— MDCCXC.

t.[i], [ii–iii], iv–vi, [7], 8–71, [72–74, adv.] p.; illus.; 10 cm. Caption p. [72]: *A great Variety of instructing,* entertain-/*ing, and very useful BOOKS for*/CHILDREN, most of them adorened with suitable Pictures, are printed by *Samuel Hall,* near the *State-/House, in Cornhill,* BOSTON, and are/sold very cheap; among which are/the following, viz. The cuts on p. 39, 41, 45, and 59 were used by Samuel Hall [*ca.* 1789] in D. Kilner's *Little Stories For Little Folks,* Boston, no. **729.1;** those on p. 43, 47, and 57 in *The Royal Alphabet,* 1793, no. **1132.2.**
CtY* (sigs. [A$_1$] [E$_8$] & covers wanting); Evans 46090.

1406.4 ———— Children. Bennington [Vt.]: adv. by Haswell and Russel, April 5, 1790 in the *Vermont Gazette.*

1406.5 ———— Songs, Attempted [same as **1406.3**] Boston: Printed and sold by Samuel Hall, in Cornhill. 1796.
fr.[ii], t.[i], [ii–iii], iv–vi, [7], 8–70 p.; illus.; 10.5 cm.; Dutch paper covers. Ornamental tailpiece on p. 70 consists of two crowns and two angel heads below them.
MWA*; DLC (p. 69–70 wanting); MB (per st. on t.[i], fr.[ii], & covers wanting); Evans 31577.

1406.6 —————— Revised And Altered So As To Render Them Of General Use. By Isaac Watts, D.D. Leominster [Mass.]: Printed By Charles Prentiss. Sold Wholesale & Retail at his Bookstore. 1796.

> t.[i], [ii], iii–x, [11], 12–72 p.; 11.5 cm.; blue-gray paper covers.
> Welch° (p. 71–72 mut. rear cover wanting); MWA (p. 71–72 mut., rear cover wanting).

1406.7 —————— Isaac Watts, D.D. Second Leominster Edition. Printed By Charles Prentiss. 1797.

> t.[i], [ii], iii–x, [11], 12–48 p.; 12.5 cm.
> MWA°; Evans 48313.

1406.8 —————— [same as **1406.3**] Printed and sold by Samuel Hall, No. 53, Cornhill, Boston. 1799.

> fr.[ii], t.[i], [ii–iii], iv–vi, [7], 8–70 p.; illus.; 10.5 cm.; marbled paper covers. Two printer's ornaments of an angel's head and a crown extensively used by S. Hall in his 1794 publications and other ornaments are present.
> MWA° (p. 69–70 & rear cover wanting); MB (i. st. on both fr.[ii] & t.[i]); NjP (Dutch paper covers); NNC-Pl; Evans 36075.

1406.9 —————— Songs In Easy Language For The Use Of Children. By I. Watts. D.D. [2 lines quot.] Matth. xxi. 16. Printed In Catskill [N.Y.], [B]y M. & H. Crosswell, For Geo. Chittenden, Sign Of The Bible, Hudson. Where they may be had by the gross, dozen, or single—also, a variety of Books & Stationery. [1800].

> t.[1], [2], 3–36 p.; 13.5 cm.; wallpaper covers. Mackay and Harry Croswell printed as a firm in Catskill, New York 1800–1801. (MWA cat.).
> MWA-W°; Evans 49185.

1406.10 —————— [same as **1406.3**] Boston: Printed And Sold By E. Lincoln, Water-Street. 1802.

> t.[i], [ii–iii], iv, [5], 5–36 p.; 14 cm.
> MWA-W° (covers wanting); PP; RPB; Shaw 3501.

1406.11 —————— Charlestown [Mass.]: Printed And Sold By Samuel Etheridge. 1802.

> fr.[ii], t.[i], [ii–iii], iv–vi, [7], 8–70 p.; illus.; 10 cm.; Dutch paper covers.
> MWA°.

1406.12 —————— Printed and sold by Manning & Loring, No. 2, Cornhill, Boston. 1803.

> fr.[ii], t.[iii], [iv–v], vi–viii, [9], 10–72 p.; illus.; 10.5 cm.; ornamented brown paper covers.
> MWA°; DLC (scalloped red paper covers); Shaw 5548.

1406.13 —————— Songs For Children; Revised And Altered So As To Render Them Of General Use. By Isaac Watts, D. D. Brookfield, (Massachusetts) Printed By E. MERRIAM & CO. 1803.

> t.[i], [ii, bl.], iii–x, [11], 12–50, [51–52 top of leaf torn off] p.; 15.5 cm.; blue paper covers.
> CtHi° (rear cover wanting).

1406.14 —————— Songs For Children. By Isaac Watts, D.D. Cambridge [Mass.] Printed At The University Press By W. Hilliard. MDCCCIII.

> t.[i], [ii–iii], iv, [5], 6–36 p.; 15.5 cm.
> NN° (rebound); ICU; PP.

1406.15 —————— Watts, D.D. [cut of a coat of arms] Phillips. Cambridge Printed At The University Press By W. Hilliard. MDCCCIII. Num. Edit. 4000.

> t.[i], [ii–iii], iv, [5], 6–36 p.; 15.5 cm.; buff wallpaper covers ornamented with blue and brown squares.
> Welch° (front cover wanting); CtY (Pequot); MB (rebound); MSaE; MWA; PP; RP; Shaw 5547.

1406.16 —————— Revised and Corrected. By Isaac Watts, D.D. [2 lines quot.] Kennebunk, (Maine) Printed By S. Sewall, For William & Daniel Treadwell, Printers and Stationers, Portsmouth, (N.H.) 1803.

> t.[i], [ii–iv], v, [vi, bl.], [7], viii [*sic. i.e.* 8], 9–48 p.; 12 cm.
> MWA° (p.[iii–iv] mut. with page no. wanting from p. iv; covers wanting); MH.

1406.17 —————— Revised And Altered, So As To Render Them Of General Use. To Which Are Added, A Short Catechism, And Prayers. By Isaac Watts, D.D. Printed At Worcester, Massachusetts, By Isaiah Thomas, Jun. Sold Wholesale and Retail by him. 1803.

> fr.[ii], t.[iii], [iv–v], vi–xii, [13], 14–62, [63, 2 illus.] p.; illus.; 10 cm.; Dutch paper covers.
> MWA° (front cover wanting).

1406.18 ——— Moral Songs, Attempted In Easy Language, For The Use Of Children. Revised And Corrected. By Issac Watts, D.D. [3 lines quot.] Boston—Printed By Hosea Sprague, 1804. < Price Six Cents. >

fr.[2], t.[3], [4], 5–63 p.; illus.; 11 cm.; marbled paper covers. Front. shows a man sitting at a table under a tree.

CtHi°; NNC-Pl; Shaw 7705.

1406.19 ——— Boston—Printed By Hosea Sprague, No. 88, Newbury-Street. 1804.

fr.[2], t.[3], [4], 5–60 p.; illus.; 11 cm. A variant of no. **1406.7** with a different imprint on the title page. The frontispiece shows another variation being an illustration of a seated man at table in a library.

CtHi° (p. 61–63 wanting).

1406.20 ——— Moral Songs For Children. By Isaac Watts, D.D. The Second Cambridge Edition. Printed By W. Hilliard. 1804.

t.[i], [ii–iii], iv, [5], 6–36 p.; 16 cm.; buff wallpaper covers ornamented with crosses of black, squares of brown, and circles of light green.

Welch°; CtHi; FTaSU; MB; MSaE; MWA; PP; Shaw 7707.

1406.21 ——— Songs, Attempted In Easy Language, For The Use Of Children. By Isaac Watts, D.D. [2 lines quot.] Charlestown [Mass.]: Printed By Samuel Etheridge. Sold By Him At The Washington Head Bookstore. 1804.

t.[i], [ii–iii], v [*sic. i.e.* iv], [5], 6–36 p.; 14.5 cm.; blue paper covers.

MWA°; N.

1406.22 ——— Children, To Which are added, Catechisms for Children and for Youth, Prayers, &c. Revised and Corrected. Isaac Watts, D.D. [1 line quot.] Mat. xxi. 16. From Sidney's Press, New Haven, 1804.

t.[i], [ii–iii], iv–vi, [7], 8–72 p.; 13.5 cm.; marbled paper covers.

MH°; Shaw 7706.

1406.23 ——— Songs, In Easy Language, For The Use Of Children. By I. Watts, D.D. [2 lines quot.] Matth. xxi. 16. Hudson [N.Y.], Printed and sold by Ashbel Stoddard, At his Book-Store and Printing-Office, Corner of Warren and Third Streets. 1805.

fr.[2, poem], t.[3], [4], 5–35 p.; tailpiece p. 35 only illus.; 13.5 cm. blue paper covers.

MWA°.

1406.24 ——— Children; Revised And Altered So As To Render Them Of General Use. By Isaac Watts, D.D. To Which Is Added, The Doctor's Wonderful Dream. Keene, < N.H. > Printed By And For John Prentiss. 1805. Sold at his Bookstore, Wholesale and Retail.

t.[i], [ii–iii], iv–v, [vi], [7], 8–72 p.; 11.5 cm.; green marbled paper covers.

MWA°; Shaw 9694.

1406.25 ——— Northampton, Mass. 1805. Shaw 9695.

1406.26 ——— [same as **1406.18**] Children. Corrected And Revised By Isaac Watts, D.D. [2 lines quot.] Printed By Hosea Sprague, No. 88, Newbury-Street, Boston, 1806.

t.[1], 2–36 p.; 14 cm.; paper covers.

MWA°; Shaw 11812.

1406.27 ——— Revised and Corrected.— Printed & sold by Lincoln & Edmands, No 53, Cornhill, Boston. 1808.

fr.[ii], t.[iii], [iv, bl.–v], vi–viii, [9], 10–71 p.; illus.; 11 cm.; marbled paper covers. The illus. p. 45, 49, and 59 are cuts used by S. Hall in *The Royal Alphabet*, no. **1132.4**.

MWA°; DLC; MB; NN (fr. [ii] & front cover wanting; rebound); Shaw 16674.

1406.28 ——— Children. By Isaac Watts, D.D. To which are added Catechism And Prayers. Boston: Printed and sold wholesale and retail, By Samuel T. Armstrong, Cornhill. 1811.

fr.[ii], t.[iii], [iv–v], vi, [7], 8–72 p.; illus.; 14.5 cm.; marbled paper covers.

PP°.

1406.29 ——— Prayers. Boston: Printed by Samuel T. Armstrong, For Isaiah Thomas, Jun. 1811.

t.[iii], [iv–v], vi, [7], 8–72 p.; illus.; t.[iii] 14 cm. The book is identical with no. **1406.28** except for the imprint on the title page.

MWA-T° (fr. [ii] wanting); CtHC (fr. [ii] wanting; bound with other books); Shaw 24387.

1406.30 — < No. 32. DIVINE AND MORAL SONGS FOR CHILDREN. By Isaac Watts, D.D. [caption title p. [1]]. Andover [Mass.]: Printed For The New England Tract Society By Flagg And Gould. 1814. < First edit. 6000. [colophon p. 20].

[1], 2–20 p.; 18 cm.; also paged [37] 38–56.
MWA° (bound with other tracts in *Tracts Published By The New England Tract Society. Vol. II. Andover: Flagg And Gould. 1814*); Shaw 33603.

1406.31 — < No. 32. ——— [same as **1406.30**] [caption title p. [1]]. Andover [Mass.]: Printed For The New England Tract Society By Flagg And Gould. 1816. < 3d Edit. 3000. [colophon p. 20].

[1], 2–20 p.; 17.5 cm.; also paged [37], 38–56.
MWA° (bound with other tracts in *Tracts Published By The New England Tract Society. Vol. II. Andover: Flagg And Gould. 1815*).

1406.32 — < No. 32. ——— [caption title p. [1]]. Andover ([Mass.]: Printed For The New England Tract Society By Flagg And Gould. 1816. < 4th edit. 6000. [colophon p. 20].

[1], 2–20 p.; 17 cm.
DLC°.

1406.33 — ——— Children; Revised And Altered, So As To Render Them Of General Use. By Isaac Watts, D.D. New-Ipswich [N.H.]: Printed By S. Wilder. 1818.

t.[1], [2–46] p.; [A]₆; B₄, B₂, C₄, C₇ and a fly leaf C₈; 8.5 cm.; ornamental paper covers.
MWA° (upper half of t.[1] wanting); PP°; Shaw 46712.

1406.34 — < No. 32. DIVINE AND MORAL SONGS FOR CHILDREN. By Isaac Watts, D.D. [caption title p. [1]]. Andover [Mass.]: Printed For The New England Tract Society By Flagg And Gould. 1819. < 5th edit. 6000. [colophon p. 20].

[1], 2–20 p.; 18 cm.; paper covers; also numbered p.[37], 38–56.
CtHi°; MB; Shaw 50056.

1407 — DIVINE HYMNS, IN VERSE, FOR CHILDREN. By The Rev. Dr. Watts. The Thirteenth Edition With Moral Songs, Sacred Hymns, &c, &c, &c. By other Eminent Divines. Baltimore: Printed By W. Corbet, At R. Wild's, No. 130. Market-Street. 1799.

t.[i], [ii, bl.], [1], 2–70 p.; 16.5 cm.; marbled paper covers.
MWA°; Evans 36676.

1408.1 — DIVINE SONGS ATTEMPTED IN EASY LANGUAGE FOR THE USE OF CHILDREN. By I. Watts, D.D. [2 lines quot.] The Seventh Edition. Boston, N.E. Printed by S. Kneeland and T. Green, for D. Henchman, in Cornhill, 1730.

t.[i], [ii, bl.], [i], ii–iv, [1–2], 3–42 p.; 13.5 cm. PREFACE, p. [i]–iv; DIVINE SONGS FOR CHILDREN, p.[1]–28; *The* TEN COMMANDMENTS *out of the Old Testament put into short Rhime for Children*, p. 28; *The sum of the Commandments out of the New Testament*, p. 29; *Our Saviour's Golden Rule*, p. 29; *Duty to God and our Neighbour*, p. 29; *The Hosanna; or Salvation ascribed to Christ. Long Metre*, p. 30; *Common Metre*, p. 30; *Short Metre*, p. 30 *Glory to the Father, and the Son, &c Long Metre*, p. 31; *Common Metre*, p. 31; *Short Metre*, p. 31; *A Slight Specimen of Moral Songs*, p. 32; *The Sluggard*, p. 32–33; *Innocent Play*, p. 34; *To fill up a few Vacant* PAGES, Here are added, . . . p. 35; *A Prayer to be Us'd by Children*, p. 35–37; *A Paraphrase on the* LORD'S PRAYER, p. 37–38; *A Prayer proper to be put up by Parents for their Children*, p. 38–42. Nine printer's ornaments are present.
MWA° (p. [1]–16, 31–32, 39–42 mut.); Evans 39960.

1408.2 — ——— Philadelphia: adv. by B. Franklin, 1736 in the *Pennsylvania Gazette*.

1408.3 — ——— The Eighth Edition. Boston: N.E. Re-printed by J. Draper For T. Hancock in Ann-Street. 1738.

[1], 2–48, 5[0] [*sic. i.e.* 49], [50] p.; [A]–E₆; 11.5 cm.; the last leaf is slightly mut. affecting the page numbers. Printed in 67 (20 line measure) Roman type, measured on p. [49]. *See* note on type measurement under no. **492.1**. The text is the same as the Draper edition of 1744, no. **1408.5** and appears on the same pages. Eight printer's ornaments are present. This book differs from no. **1408.5** in not only having different decorative bars on the same pages, but also having a large number of illuminations around the first letter of each song p. [1]–34. On p. 43, a large diamond-shaped ornament signed *I B*, is used as a tailpiece and appears in books

printed by both Kneeland and Green, Evans 4301 and J. Draper, Evans 4488. Most of the capital letters of the first word of each song are not illuminated in **1408.1** and **1408.5** in which respect these editions differ from **1408.3**. Both **1408.3** and **1408.5** have the same characteristic type. On p. 43, in each of these books, the words *"THE END"* are printed in the same large italic type. The signature "E" is printed from the same type font in both books, being a large upper case letter instead of the usual small signature letter such as "D", p. 31. The catch number "II¹", in both books, has the last Roman number "I" higher than the rest of the number. MWA° (sig. [A]₁–[A]₃, E₅–E₆ wanting or t.[i], p. [ii], [i–iv], 51–54 wanting); CtHi (rear cover wanting); Evans 40222 with the imprint [The Ninth Edition? Boston, 1740?].

1408.4 ——— Ninth Edition Boston: N.E. Reprinted by J. Draper, for J. Blanchard, at the Bible and Crown in Dock-Square. 1744.
 t.[i], [ii], iii–v, [1], 2–53 p.; 12.5 cm.; bound in Dutch paper over bds.
 MWA°.

1408.5 ——— By I. Watts. [2 lines quot.] Matth. xxi. 16. The Ninth Edition. Boston: N. E. Re-printed by J. Draper, for D. Henchman, in Cornhill. 1744.
 t.[i], [ii, bl.], i–[iv], [1], 2–53 p.; A–E₆; 13.5 cm.; marbled paper covers. Printed in 65 (20 line measure) Roman type, measured on p. 49. *See* note on types under no. **492.1**. In both **1408.1** and **1408.6**, Song V, verse II, lines 1 and 2, p. 7 read: "Tis to Thy Sov'reign Grace I owe,/That I was born on *British* Ground." In the Hartford 1783 edition, no. **1408.24**, "British Ground" is changed to "Christian ground", which is usual in most American editions printed after 1783. The Newburyport edition of 1784, no. **1408.26**, is an exception and has "gospel ground". Fourteen figured printer's ornaments are present. The RP imperfect copy of this book has been considered to be [*Divine And Moral Songs For Children. Newport* [*R.I.*]: *Printed and sold by Solomon Southwick. 1773*], Evans 13066.
 CLU°; RP (t.[i], p. [ii], 53 wanting).

1408.6 ——— The Twelfth Edition. London, Printed: Philadelphia, Re-printed, and Sold by B. Franklin, and D. Hall, at the Post-Office. MDCCL.
 t.[i], [ii], iii–iv, 1–41 p.; t.[i]; 12.5 cm.; the text follows no. **1408.1** up to p. 38; The Cradle Hymn is on p. 39–41. Three printer's ornaments are present.
 PHI° (rebound); Evans 40574.

1408.7 ——— By I. Watts. [2 lines quot.] Matth. xxi. 16. The Eleventh Edition. Boston: N. E. Reprinted and Sold by Z. Fowle and S. Draper, opposite to the Lion & Bell, in Marlboro'-Street, 1759.
 t.[i], [ii], [i], ii–iv, [1], 2–42+ p.; 14 cm. This edition is heavily ornamented with printer's ornaments. Each song has one or more bars of them above it. Twenty ornaments are present.
 MWA° (all after p. 42 wanting); Evans 41090.

1408.8 ——— The Fifteenth Edition. Portsmouth, in New-Hampshire: Printed and Sold by Daniel & Robert Fowle. 1764.
 t.[1], [2–5], 6–32 p.; 16.5 cm.
 MWA°; Evans 41509.

1408.9 ——— [2 lines quot.] The Fifteenth Edition. Boston: N.E. Re-printed by D. & J. Kneeland for Thomas Leverett, in Corn-hill. 1765.
 t.[1], [2–3], 4–36 p.; 14.5 cm.
 MWA° (p. 29–36 mut., 7–26 mut. but **not** affecting text); Evans 41598.

1408.10 ——— The Fourteenth Edition corrected. Boston: Printed for and sold by John Perkins in Union street. MDCCLXXI.
 t.[1], [ii, illus.], iii–v, 6–47 p.; 4 illus.; 13 cm.; scalloped marbled paper covers. Illus. p.[ii] shows a minister in a pulpit. It was used in E. Russell's Boston 1797 edition, no. **1068.12**, of *The Prodigal Daughter*. That on p. 39 is a lamb. The one on p. 17 of a skeleton holding a scythe signed *I T*, and the illus. p. 42 of a kneeling man and woman, each before an open book, were used in *The History Of The Holy Jesus*, no. **587.14**.
 NjP° (front cover wanting); MWA (t.[i], p.[ii], 43–47, & covers wanting, pp. slightly mut., page numbers wanting); Evans 12272; Hamilton 58.

1408.11 ——— New-London, printed and sold by T. Green. 1772.

t.[i], [ii], iii–iv, [5], 6–35 p.; 14.5 cm.
CtY* (rebound); Evans 42386.

1408.12 —— —— Fifteenth Edition corrected.
Boston: N.E. Printed for and Sold by Nicholas
Bowes, in Corn-hill. MDCCLXXIII.

t.[i], [ii], iii–v, [1], 2–42 p.; 14.5 cm.; p. 2–7
printed on the inside of the page. There is no
p. [8]. The "9" of p. no. "19" is not struck.
MWA*; MHi (t.[i] wanting, p. iii–v, [1]–16
mut.); Evans 42533.

1408.13 —— —— The Fifteenth Edition. Boston; N.E. Printed and Sold by T. and J. Fleet, at
the Heart and Crown, in Cornhill. 1773.

t.[i], ii–iv, 5–44 p.; 16 cm.; illus. front paper
cover. Front cover has a cut of a church and
the date 1773. The inside of the front cover the
fr.[ii] has a list of books: "Just Re-printed. And
to be Sold at the Heart and Crown, in Cornhill,
Boston, The Holy Bible epitomiz'd in Verse. Very
pleasant and profitable, and greatly tending to
encourage Children, and others to read, and also
to understand what they read in that Sacred
Book. < Price 6 Cop. > Also A Token For
Children: . . . < Price 8d. > ˙Likewise, The
School of Good Manners. . . . < Price 7 Coppers. > " The inside of the rear cover has a list
of three books.
MWA*; Evans 42534.

1408.14 —— —— The Fifteenth Edition corrected. Boston: N.E. Printed for and Sold by
Thomas Leverett in Corn-hill. MDCCLXXIII.

t.[i], [ii], iii–v, [1], 2–42 p.; 15 cm.; p.[3]–7
pr. on the inside of the leaf. There is no p.[8].
The "9" of p. no. "19" is not struck.
MWA* (t.[i], pp. [ii]–7 mut., remaining p.
mut. but not affecting text); Evans 42535.

1408.15 —— —— The Sixteenth Edition. Phila-
delphia: Printed by Joseph Crukshank, for R.
Aitken, Bookseller, opposite the London Coffee-
House, in Front-street. [1773?].

fr.[ii], t.[1], [2, bl.], [3], 4–29, [30, adv. of
books] p.; 10 cm.; marbled paper covers.
MWA*; NjP; Evans 13065.

1408.16 —— —— The Fourteenth Edition.
Boston, New-England: Printed and Sold at Greenleaf's Printing-Office, Hanover-Street. 1774.

t.[i], ii–iv, 5–44 p.; 14.5 cm. Seven printer's
type ornaments are present.
MWA-W* (p. 41–44 mut.); PP.

1408.17 —— —— [3 lines quot.] The Fourteenth Edition. Boston: Printed for, and sold by
A. Barclay at the sign of the Gilt Bible, in Cornhill. M,DCC,LXXV.

t.[i], [ii, illus.], iii–v, 6–47, [48, portrait] p.;
2 illus.; 13.5 cm. The illustration p. [ii] shows
a minister in a pulpit. The lower part of the cut
is ragged and a section of the base present in
1408.18 and **1408.19** is missing, as well as the
words "Dr. Watts." This book is probably the
last 1775 printing of the book by Nathaniel
Coverly since the other editions do not have this
cut damaged. The portrait, p. [48], looks like
Oliver Cromwell. Below it the sentence reads:
"☞ The Price of this Book is/Eight Coppers. ☜ "
MB*; Evans 42980.

1408.18 —— —— The Fourteenth Edition.
Boston: Printed and Sold, by N. Coverly, near
Christ-Church, North-End. M,DCC LXXV.

t.[i], [ii, illus.], iii–v, 6–47, [48, portrait] p.;
2 illus.; 14.5 cm. The illustration, p. [ii], of the
minister in the pulpit is entitled "Dr. Watts".
It is signed *N C* in the lower left corner of
the cut. It is possible that the signature *N C*
stands for Nathaniel Coverly. On p. [48] the
portrait of Oliver Cromwell, used in no. **1408.17**,
is present as well as the words below it. The
three 1775 editions, **1408.17**, **1408.18**, and
1408.19, are printed from standing type.
MWA*; Evans 42981.

1408.19 —— —— Edition. Printed for, and
Sold by Mascoll Williams, at the sign of the Bible,
in King-Street. Salem. M.DCC LXXV.

t.[i], [ii, illus.], iii–v, 6–47, [48, adv. of Mascoll
[W]illiams] p.; 1 illus.; 13.5 cm. The illus. of
the preacher, p. [ii], entitled "Dr. Watts", is
intact as in **1408.18**, with the signature *N C*
in the lower left-hand corner. The portrait of
Oliver Cromwell is replaced by a page of advertisements of Mascoll Williams. Nathaniel Coverly undoubtedly printed this book for Williams
from standing type.
NjP*.

1408.20 —— —— The Seventeenth Edition.
Norwich: Printed by Green & Spooner. 177[7]
(Price Nine-pence).

t.[i], [ii–iii], iv, [5], 6–36 p.; 16.5 cm.
Griffin* (covers wanting); Evans 43405.

1408.21 —————— By I. Watts, D.D. To which is added the Delightful and Entertaining Stories viz. Of Tommy Fido/The undutiful Child./The Proud Girl/Of Gog/Of Magog. Boston [Printed] & sold by Nathaniel Cover[ly] in Marlboro-Street. M,DCCLXXVIII. < Price Two Shillings. >

t.[i], [ii], iii–v, 6–48 p.; illus. p. 29, and title vignette of a central bird with a bee on either side, only illus.; 15.5 cm.; page numbers 13–36 pr. on the inside of the page. The three stories at the end: Of Master Tommy Fido, p. 45–46; The undutiful Child, p. 46; The meanly proud Girl, p. 47, first appeared in America in *A New Gift for Children*, 1762, no. **931.1**. The book ends with: The Description of Gog and Magog, p. 47–48, which has the same text as the English edition of *The Gigantic History Of the two famous Giants, And other Curiosities In Guildhall, London. Third Edition, corrected. Printed for Thomas Boreman, London, 1741.*
MWA* (t.[i], p. [ii], 27–28, 33–35, 38, 46, 48 mut. affecting text or page number); MWA-T (t.[i] wanting); Evans 43593.

1408.22 —————— viz. Of Tommy Fido. The undutiful Child. The Proud Girl/Of Gog/Of Magog. Boston: Printed & sold by Nathaniel Coverly, in Marlboro'-Street. M,DCCLXXVIII. < Price Two Shillings. >

t.[i], [ii], iii–v, 6–48 p.; illus. p. 29, 37 and title vignette of a central eagle with a bee on either side, only illus.; 14 cm.; bluish-gray paper covers. A variant of no. **1408.21** with p. 37 having a new type setting which includes an illustration of a horse and a ship not found in the preceding book. Page numbers 13–32 are printed on the inside of the page as in no. **1408.21**.
NjP*; MWA (t.[i], [ii]–10, 43–48 wanting, p. 11–12 ½ wanting); Evans 43592; Hamilton 85.

1408.23 —————— By I. Watts, D.D. [2 lines quot.] The Twentieth Edition, Corrected. [imprint torn off] [*ca.* 1780].

t.[1], [2–3], 4–46+ p.; [A]–C₆, D₅, D₆ wanting; 14 cm.; p. no. < 4 > – < 7 > enclosed in brackets, p. numbers (8)–(46) enclosed in parentheses. Preface, p. [3]–6; [Divine Songs], p. 7–34; *Our Saviour's Golden Rule*, p. 34; *The* Ten Commandments *out of the Old Testament, put into short Rhime for Children*, p. 34; *The Sum of the* Commandments *out of the New Testament.* Matthew 22.37, p. 35; *Duty to*

GOD *and our Neighbours*, p. 35; *Out of my Book of* Hymns, *I have here added The* Hosanna, *and* Glory to the Father, *&c*, . . . *The* Hosanna; *or Salvation ascrib'd to* CHRIST. *Long Metre.* . . . *Common Metre*, p. 36; *Short Metre*, p. 37; Glory *to the* FATHER *and the Son, &c. Long Metre*, . . . *Common Metre.* . . . *Short Metre.* p. 37; A Slight SPECIMEN of *Moral* SONGS, p. 38; The Sluggard, p. 39–40; Innocent Play, p. 40; PRAYERS. A Prayer to be used by Children, p. 41–43; A Paraphrase on the LORD'S Prayer, in the Words of the *Assembly's shorter Catechism*, p. 43–44; A PRAYER *proper to be put up by* PARENTS *for their* CHILDREN, p. 45–46 and probably ended on p. 48 which is missing. No printer's type ornaments are present. A single rule separates each song. Song V, verse 2, line 2: That I was born on *British* ground.
MWA* (D₆ or p. 47–48 wanting, the lower half of p. [1]–4 wanting; p. 8, 13–16, 19–23, 27, 39–40, 45–46 mut. affecting text); Evans 43914.

1408.24 —————— Children. By I. Watts, D.D. Hartford: Ptinted [*sic. i.e.* Printed] By Hudson & Goodwin: M,DCC,LXXXIII.

t.[i], [ii–iii], iv–v, [vi]; 7–60 p.; 13 cm.; bluegray paper covers. Song V, verse 2, line 2 has "British' ground" changed to "Christian ground." Three printer's ornaments are used in the border around the title page, the only place ornaments occur.
MWA* (front cover wanting); Evans 44494.

1408.25 —————— By Isaac Watts D.D. To Which Is Added, The Wonderful Dream, by the Author. Also Four Delightful and Entertaining Stories, viz. I. Of Master Tommy Fido. II. The undutiful Child. III. The meanly proud Girl. IV. Description of Gog and Magog. Norwich [Conn.] Printed by J. Trumbull. M,DCC,LXXXIII.

t.[i], [ii, bl.], iii–v, 6–48 p.; 17.5 cm.; p. 10, Song V, verse 2, line 2: "My birth on fair Columbia's ground". *See* no. **1408.21** on the three stories at the end and the "Description of Gog and Magog."
CtHi*; CtY (t.[i] & p. 17–18, 45–48 mut.); Evans 18294.

1408.26 —————— The Twenty-Fifth Edition. With some additional composures. Hartford:

Printed and sold by Z. Webster a few rods South-East of the Court-House. [1784].

½t.[i], [2, bl.], t.[3], [4–5], 6–47 p.; portrait p. [1] only illus.; 14.5 cm. Zephaniah Webster printed in Hartford in 1784. Half title p. [1]: Divine Songs Attempted In Easy Language For The Use Of Children. [portrait] By I. Watts, D.D.

CtHi°; CtHT (p. 47–48 wanting); Evans 44627.

1408.27 —— Use Of Children. By I. Watts, D.D. [two lines quot.] Newbury-Port [Mass.]: Printed and Sold by John Mycall, M,DCC,LXXXIV.

t.[i], [ii–iii], iv–vi, [7], 8–54 p.; 11.5 cm.; Song V, verse 2, line 2 has "British ground" changed to "gospel ground." Five printer's ornaments are present.

MWA°; CtHi; DLC (green-speckled paper covers); MNe (p. 53–54 wanting; p. 51–52 mut.); MSaE (covers, and all after p. 36 wanting); Evans 44627.

1408.28 —— The Seventeenth Edition. Philadelphia: Printed And Sold By Joseph Crukshank, In Market-Street, Between Second And Third Streets, MDCCLXXXIV.

t.[1], [2–3], 4–24 p.; 13.5 cm. Song V, verse 2, line 2, has *British* ground." Six printer's ornaments are present, as well as one unfigured one.

MWA°; P (yellow and green, Dutch paper covers); Evans 44628.

1408.29 —— [2 lines quot.] Matt. xxi. 16. The Seventy Eighth Edition. Printed in Bennington, In the State of Vermont, by Haswell & Russell. In the Year of our Lord. M,DCC,LXXXV.

t.[i], [ii–iv], [5], 6–24+ p.; 16.5 cm.

MWA° (all after p. 24 wanting); Evans 44828.

1408.30 —— Children. By I. Watts, D.D. New-Haven, Printed By J. Meigs. M,DCC,-LXXXIX.

t.[i], [ii–iii], iv–v, [6], 7–8+ p.; 16 cm.

CtHi° (all after p. 8 wanting); Evans 45739.

1408.31 —— By Isaac Watts, D.D. Author of the Lyric Poems. [2 lines quot.] Matt. xxi. 16. Middletown [Conn.]: Printed by Moses H. Woodward. M,DCC,XC.

t.[1], [2–3], 4–32 p.; illus.; p.[2] only illus.;

9.5 cm.; the words, on. t[1], "[Printed b]y" are not struck in the MWA copy.

MWA° (covers wanting); CtHi (p. 31–32 mut. with the page numbers torn off; covers wanting); Evans 46091.

1408.32 —— By I. Watts, D.D. New-Haven: Printed By A. Morse; M. DCC. XC.

t.[iii], [iv–v], vi–vii, [viii, bl.], [9], 10–66 p.; 13.5 cm.; illus. blue-gray paper covers.

MWA°; Evans 46092.

1408.33 —— Watts, D.D. [2 lines quot.] Boston: Printed and sold by Samuel Hall, in Cornhill. MDCCXCII.

fr.[ii], t.[i], [ii, bl.–iii], iv–vi, [7], 8–71, [72–74, adv.] p.; illus.; 10.5 cm.

MB° (per st. on t.[i]); MWA-W (fr.[ii]–p. 14, p. 65–[74] & covers wanting); Evans 46669.

1408.34 —— [2 lines quot.] Matthew xxi. 16. The Fifty First Edition. Boston: Printed by T. Fleet, jun. MDCCXCIII.

t.[i], [ii], iii–v, 6–46 p.; 15.5 cm.; blue-gray paper covers.

MWA-W°; MBC; MH; Evans 26436.

1408.35 —— I. Watts, D.D. And The Principles Of The Christian Religion; Expressed In Plain And Easy Verse. By P. Doddridge, D.D. [2 lines quot.] To Which Are Added Supplementary Hymns, By Various Authors. Exeter [N.H.]: Printed And Sold By Henry Ranlet. MDCCXCIII.

t.[i], [ii–iii], iv–viii, [9], 10–96 p.; 15 cm.; bound in marbled paper over bds.

MWA°; NN (scalloped marbled paper covers, rebound); Evans 26437.

1408.36 —— I. Watts, D.D. [2 lines quot.] Enlarged And Improved. Printed At Newburyport, By George Jerry Osborne, Guitemberg's (*sic. i.e.* Gutemberg's) Head. MDCCXCIII.

t.[i], ii–iv, 5–48 p.; 15 cm.

MWA°; Evans 26438.

1408.37 —— Printed At Newburyport, By George Jerry Osborne, Gutemberg's Head. MDCCXCIII.

t.[i], ii–iv, 5–48 p.; 14.5 cm. Same as preceding edition but with "Gutemberg's Head" spelled correctly.

MWA°; Evans 26438.

1408.38 —————— [2 lines quot.] Matthew XXI. 16. (The Sixty fourth Edition.) Boston: Printed and sold by N. Coverly, Over the sign of the Indian Chief, North side the Market. 1794. (Price Six Pence).

t.[i], [ii, bl.–iii], iv–vi, 7–48 p.; 16 cm.

Griffin° (p. 33–34 mut.); MWA (t.[i], p. [ii]–vi, 41–48 wanting); Evans 47320.

1408.39 —————— [3 lines quot.] Matthew xxi. 16. (The Sixty fifth Edition.) Canaan [Cooperstown]: Printed and sold by E. Phinney,—By the gross, dozen or single,—MDCCXCIV.

t.[1], [2–3], 4–36 p.; 13 cm.; paper covers.

CSmH°.

1408.40 —————— [2 lines quot.] Hartford: Printed By Elisha Babcock 1794.

fr.[2], t.[3], [4–5], 6–31 p.; front. only illus.; 10.5 cm.; blue-gray paper covers.

MWA°; CtHi; Evans 28034.

1408.41 —————— [2 lines quot.] Matth. xxi. 16. Bennington [Vt.]: Printed By Anthony Haswell. 1795.

t.[3], [4–6], 7–35 p.; 13.5 cm.

MiU°; CSmH (p. 35 mostly wanting); McCorison 366.

1408.42 —————— Printed At Dover [N.H.], By Samuel Bragg, Jun. And For Sale At His Office. 1795.

t.[1], [2–3], 4–34 p.; 13.5 cm.; gray paper covers.

MWA°; Evans 29841.

1408.43 —————— I. Watts, D.D. Hartford: Printed By J. Babcock. 1795.

fr.[2], t.[3], [4–5], 6–31 p.; illus.; 10 cm.; speckled-brown paper covers.

MWA°; CtHi (t.[3] mut.); PP (fr.[2] mut.; covers wanting).

1408.44 —————— [2 lines quot.] Third Dover [N.H.] Edition. Printed By Samuel Bragg, Jr. 1796.

t.[1], [2–3], 4–32+ p.; 12.5 cm.

See also *Divine Songs in Easy Language*, no. **1410.2.**

MH° (t.[1], p.[2]–4, 29–32 mut., all after p. 32 wanting); Evans 48021.

1408.45 —————— (The Sixty-fourth Edition.) Haverhill [Mass.]: Printed and sold by N. Coverly, 1797. (Price Nine Pence).

t.[1], [2–3], 4–36 p.; illus.; 18 cm.

MSaE° (t.[1], & p.[2], 35–36 mut.); MB (p. 31–32 mut., p. 35–36, and the lower half of p. 33–34 wanting); MHa (p. 15–22, 25–26, 29–32, 35–36, wanting); NN (rebound); Evans 33162.

1408.46 —————— [2 lines quot.] To Which Are Added The Principles Of The Christian Religion, Expressed in Plain and Easy Verse. By P. Doddridge, D.D. London Printed, Re-Printed By George Bunce, New-Haven. 1797.

t.[i], [ii–iii], iv–vi, [7], 8–72 p.; 13.5 cm.; ornamental paper covers.

CtY; Evans 48312.

1408.47 —————— Newark [N.J.]: Printed by Pennington & Dodge, For Cornelius Davis, New-York. 1797.

t.[i], [ii–iii], iv–vi, [7], 8–72 p.; 12.5 cm.; blue paper over w. bds., leather spine.

MWA°; CtY (marbled paper covers); Evans 33163.

1408.48 —————— [2 lines quot.] Boston: Printed By B. Edes. Jun. 1798.

t.[i], [ii–iii], iv–vi, [7], 8–47 p.; 12.5 cm.; blue-gray paper covers.

MWA°; Evans 34965.

1408.49 —————— By I. Watts, D.D. To Which Are Added, Dr. Watt's Wonderful Dream; His Catechisms, for Children three or four years old, and for youth eight or ten years of age. Morning and Evening Prayers, &c. Hartford: Printed By John Babcock. 1798.

t.[1], [ii–iii], iv–v, 6–60 p.; 16.5 cm.

CtHi°; Evans 48754.

1408.50 —————— [2 lines of quot.] Matthew xxi. 16. < The Ninety fourth Edition. > Medford (Massachusetts.) Printed and sold by Nathaniel Coverly. 1799. < Price Twelve Cents. >

t.[1], [2–3], 4–5, 4 [*sic. i.e.* 6], 7–32 p.; 18 cm.

MWA° (p. 31–32 wanting; p. 27–30 mut.); DLC (rebound, i. st. on t. [1]); MHi; Evans 36677.

1408.51 ———— By Isaac Watts, D.D. [3 lines quot.] < The Ninety fifth Edition. > Boston: Printed and sold by N. Coverly. < Price 12 Cents. > ☞ Great allowance made by the Gross or Dozen. [1800?].

t.[1], [2–3], 4–36 p.; 15.5 cm. MWA copy has a mss. note on inside back cover, "Nancy Norris April 13ᵗʰ 1801." Coverly was printing in Medford, Mass. in January and February of 1800 according to mss. notes in his pamphlets and from his imprints. He probably went from Medford to Boston in 1800 and from Boston to Salem in 1801.

MWA-W*; CtHi; CtHT; MSaE; MWA (blue paper covers); RPJCB; Evans 49184.

1408.52 ———— [2 lines quot.] New-Haven: Printed By Read & Morse. 1800.

fr.[ii], t.[iii], [iv–v], vi–viii, [9], 10–64 p.; 12 cm.

MB* (per st. on t. [iii]); Evans 39026.

1408.53 ———— Children. By Isaac Watts, D.D. Author of the Lyric Poems. [2 lines of quot.] Matt. xxi. 16. Philadelphia: Printed and sold by John M'Culloch, No. 1, North Third-street. 1800.

t.[3], [4, alphabet], [5], 6–31 p.; 10.5 cm.; blue-gray front cover.

Carson* (rebound, rear cover wanting; p. 31 mut.; 15 leaves only, fr.[2]? could be on the missing leaf); Evans 49186.

1408.54 ———— Salem: Printed by Joshua Cushing, for T. C. Cushing. 1800.

t.[i], [ii–iii], iv–vi, [7], 8–48 p.; 15 cm.; blue paper covers.

MWA* (p. 47–48 mut.); MB; MSaE; Evans 39025.

1408.55 ———— By I. Watts, D.D. Matthew, xxi. 16. [2 lines quot.] Baltimore: Printed By Warner & Hanna, No. 37, Market-Street, Corner Of South Gay-Street. 1801.

t.[I], [II–III], IV–VI, [VII–VIII], [1], 2–62 p.; 13.5 cm.; yellow wallpaper covers.

PP*; Shaw 1616.

1408.56 ———— [2 lines quot.] To Which are added. The Principles Of The Christian Religion, Expressed in plain and easy Verse. By P. Doddridge, D.D. —New York:— Printed And Sold By J. Tiebout, No. 216, Water-Street. 1801.

t.[i], [ii, adv.–iii], iv, [5], 6–72 p.; illus.; 13 cm.; bound in ornamental paper over bds., leather spine.

MWA*; Shaw 50263.

1408.57 ———— By Isaac Watts, D.D. [2 lines quot.] Matthew xxi. 16. Boston: Printed By J. & T. Fleet, at the Bible and Heart, Cornhill, 1802.

t.[i], ii–iv, 5–44, [45, adv.] p.; 15.5 cm.; light-blue paper covers.

MWA* (front cover wanting); NNC-Pl; Shaw 3502.

1408.58 ———— By I. Watts. [2 lines quot.] Lewiston: (Penn.) Printed By Edward Cole. 1802.

t.[i], [ii–iii], iv, [5], 6–48 p.; t.[i], 17.5 cm. PPL*.

1408.59 ———— By I. Watts, D.D. [2 lines quot.] To Which Are Added, The Principles Of The Christian Religion, In Plain And Easy Verse. By P. Doddridge, D.D. New-York: Printed For John Tiebout, No. 246, Water-Street, By L. Nichols. 1802.

t.[i], [ii–iii], iv, [5], 6–72 p.; 11 oval illus. and 1 tailpiece, p. 37; 13 cm.; bound in buff paper over bds., leather spine.

MWA-W*; ICU.

1408.60 ———— Hartford: adv. by Lincoln & Gleason, 1803 in **571.1**.

1408.61 ———— I. Watts, D.D. [2 lines quot.] Providence [R.I.]: Printed By Heaton & Williams. 1804.

t.[i], [ii–iii], iv, [5], 6–36 p.; 13.5 cm.

MWA* (p. 31–32 mut.); RPB (p. 36 mut.); Shaw 7708.

1408.62 ———— New-York: Printed For J. & T. Ronalds, 188 Pearl-Street. 1806.

t.[3], [4–5], 6–46 p.; 10 cm.; marbled paper covers.

MWA*; Shaw 11813.

1408.63 ———— I. Watts, D.D. Matt. xxi. 16. [2 lines quot.] London: Printed. Hartford, Re-printed By Hudson & Goodwin. 1807.

fr.[ii], t.[iii], [iv–v], vi–x, [11], 12–120 p.; illus.; 11 cm.; bound in greenish-gray paper over bds., leather spine.

Welch*; BM; CtHi; DLC (2 copies); MiDW; MWA; NHi; NNC-Pl; PP; Shaw 14167.

1408.64 —————— I. Watts, D.D. [2 lines quot.] Northampton [Mass.]: Published By S. & E. Butler. 1807. T. M. Pomroy. Printer.

t.[i], [ii–iii], iv–vi, [vii–ix], [x, bl.], [1], 2–62 p.; 14.5 cm.

MWA* (covers wanting); Shaw 14168.

1408.65 —————— [2 lines quot.] [cut showing two beehives] Utica [N.Y.]: Printed and Sold by Seward and Williams. 1810.

t.[i], [ii–iii], iv, [5], 6–36 p.; title page vignette only illus. except for ornamental headpieces and tailpieces; 13 cm.; Copy 1: bound in blue paper over bds., leather spine. Copy 2: unprinted pink paper covers. Copy 3: pr. & illus. yellow paper covers with the cover title: Watt's & Doddridge's Songs. [2 lines quot.] [cut of a dragonfly] Utica: William Williams. Mdcccxxxi. Bound with and before no. **1415.1**.

OOxM* (copy 1); MWA (copy 2, 3); N; NUt; PP; Shaw 21873 and 21979.

1408.66 —————— [2 lines quot.] To Which Are Added, The Principles Of The Christian Religion, Expressed in plain and easy Verse. By P. Doddridge, D.D. Utica [N.Y.]: Printed and Sold by Seward and Williams. 1810.

t.[i], [ii–iii], iv, [5], 6–72 p.; illus. p. [38] only illus. except for ornamental headpieces and tailpieces; 13.5 cm.; bound in blue paper over w. bds., brown paper spine. The book is a variant of no. **1408.65**. The title page has no title vignette. The text has the identical type setting of **1408.65** with the same headpieces and tailpieces except for the tailpiece on p. 36, which is a rose, instead of the one in **1408.65** of a full quiver of arrows crossed with a flaming torch. Page [37] is blank, the title page for "Moral Songs" being omitted. The page numbers are continuous with "Moral Songs" on pages [1]–36, and "Principles of the Christian Religion," on pages [37]–72. The illustrations of the seated helmeted woman surrounded by books, a shutter, a globe and furniture, p.[38], is the same as in no. **1408.65**, p. [2], of "Moral Songs."

NUt*; PP (rebound); Shaw 21971 (under the title *Divine and Moral Songs*).

1408.67 —————— By Isaac Watts, D.D. [2 lines quot.] Printed by W. & J. Gilman, For Wil-

liam Sawyer & Co. Booksellers, No. 3, Market-square, Newburyport. [*ca*. 1811].

t.[1], 2–36 p.; 14 cm.

NNC-T*.

1408.68 —————— Children. To Which Is Added Several Useful And Instructive Passages From Scripture. By Isaac Watts, D.D. [2 lines quot.] Walpole, N.H. Published By Isaiah Thomas, & Co. And Sold At Their Bookstore. James G. Watts, Printer. 1811.

t.[1], [2–5], 6–47, [48, adv.] p.; 12 cm.; bound in leather.

MWA* (i. st. p.[3]); PP (blue marbled paper covers); Shaw 24388.

1408.69 —————— By Isaac Watts, D.D. [2 lines quot.] Mathew xxi. 16. Boston: Printed By Nathaniel Coverly, Jun'r. Corner Of Theatre Alley. Price 50 Cents per Dozen, 8 single. [*ca*. 1812].

fr.[ii], t.[iii], iv–v, 6–23 p.; front. only illus.; blue-gray paper covers. The page numbers on pages 7–12 are printed on the inner margin of the page, those on p. 13–23 on the outer margin. The frontispiece illustration of a church was used in *The Prodigal Daughter* by John & Thomas Fleet in 1807, no. **1068.17**.

MWA*; MB (per st. on t.[iii]); Shaw 27470.

1408.70 —————— By I. Watts, D.D. [2 lines quot.] Hartford: Printed by Sheldon & Goodwin. 1815.

fr.[ii], t.[iii], [iv–v], vi–x, [11], 12–125, [126] p.; illus.; 11 cm.; bound in marbled paper over bds.

MWA*; Ct; CtHi; Shaw 36498.

1408.71 —————— By Isaac Watts. [2 lines quot.] Boston: Published By Samuel T. Armstrong, And sold wholesale and retail by him, No. 50, Cornhill, U. Crocker, Printer. 1819.

fr.[ii], t.[iii], [iv–v], vi, [7], 8–36 p.; illus.; 14.5 cm.; blue marbled paper covers. The illus. p. 9, 10, 17, 19 are signed J. F., that on p. 13, *Fisher 1812* [Jonathan Fisher].

MWA*; MH; OOxM; PP; Shaw 50057.

1409.1 — Divine Songs For Children. By Isaac Watts, D.D. [2 lines quot.] [cut] The Good Samaritan. Philadelphia: Published By Benjamin Johnson, No. 249, Market Street. 1807.

t.[1], [2–3], 4–48 p.; illus.; 16 cm.; bound in

brown paper over bds., leather spine. Bound with no. **956**, dated 1806. The cut on p. 24 is signed *Anderson*. The remainder, with the exception of the unsigned one on p. 18, are signed A [Alexander Anderson].

Welch°; MB; MWA; NNC-Pl; PHi; Shaw 14169.

1409.2 — Divine Songs; For Children, Attempted In Easy Language. By I. Watts, D.D. Ornamented with Cuts. Matt. xxi. 16. [2 lines quot.] From Sidney's Press, New-Haven. 1808.

fr.[ii], t.[i], [ii–iii], iv–vi, [7], 8–63 p.; illus.; 10.5 cm.; pr. & illus. buff paper covers.

Ct° (i. st. on fr.[ii]).

1409.3 — ——— Children. Attempted In Easy Language. By I. Watts, D.D. Ornamented with Cuts. Matt. xxi. 16. [1 line quot.] From Sidney's Press, New-Haven. 1809.

fr.[ii], t.[1], [2–3], 4–36 p.; illus.; 14 cm.; pr. & illus. blue paper covers.

Cover title imprint: Published by I. Cooke & Co. New-Haven. Book-Sellers, Stationers, and Printers.

MWA°; Shaw 19157.

1409.4 — ——— By I. Watts, D.D. [2 lines of quot.] From Sidney's Press, For I. Cooke & Co. New-Haven. 1812.

fr.[2], t.[3], [4, bl.–5], 6–47 p.; illus.; 11 cm.; pr. & illus. yellow-buff paper covers.

Cover title: Watts's Divine Songs. Published by I. Cooke & Co. New-Haven, at whose new brick store, opposite Butler's tavern, every article necessary in the education of young Ladies and Gentlemen, may at all times be had.

MWA°; Shaw 27471 (with wrong title).

1409.5 — ——— Children. By Isaac Watts, D.D. [2 lines quot.] To Which Is Added Dr. Watts' Plain And Easy Catechisms: Together With A Collection Of Prayers, &c. Designed And Arranged For Sunday Schools. Printed and Published by A. H. Maltby & Co. No. 4, Glebe Building, Chapel-street, New-Haven. 1819.

t.[1], [2–3], 4–36 p.; 13.5 cm.; brown and blue marbled paper covers.

Welch°; CaOTP; CLU; CtHi; CtW; DLC; FTaSU; MSaE; MWA; NB (i. st. on t.[1]); NHi; NN; NNC-Pl; PHi; PP; PPL; Shaw 50058.

1409.6 — ——— I. Watts. An unfilled command. Ed. 2. Andover Mass., Pr. by Flagg & Gould for the Baptist General Tract Soc. and for the New England Tract Society, 1820.

24 p.

Shoemaker 4193.

1410.1 — Divine Songs: In Easy Language, for the use of Children. By the late Reverend and Pious Doctor Watts. Ornamented with Cuts from Original Designs. [2 lines of quot.] Printed at Springfield [Mass.]: MDCCLXXXVIII.

fr.[2, portrait], t.[3], [4–5], 6–31 p.; illus.; 10 cm.; illus. paper covers.

MWA°; Evans 45408.

1410.2 — ——— Pious Doctor Watts. [2 lines quot.] Matt. xxi. 16. New-London [Conn.]: Printed And Sold Wholesale And Retail, By James Springer. 1796.

fr.[ii], t.[1], [2–3], 4–28 p.; illus.; 9.5 cm.

CtHi°; PP (green Dutch paper covers).

1411.1 — Dr. Watts' Divine And Moral Songs, For The Use Of Children. Boston: Published By Benjamin Crocker. 1819.

t.[3], [4–5], 6–35 p.; title vignette only illus.; 14 cm.; pr. buff paper front cover, rear cover unprinted.

MWA-W°; MWA-T.

1411.2 — ——— Moral Songs; With Prayers For Children. Philadelphia: Published And Sold By D. Hogan, No. 249, Market-Street. 1820.

t.[1], [2–3], 4–32 p.; 12.5 cm.

PP°; Shoemaker 4192.

1412.1 — Dr. Watts' Divine Songs, Attempted In Easy Language, For The Use Of Children. [2 lines quot.] Newburyport [Mass.]: Printed By W. & J. Gilman. Sold at their Book and Stationary Store, Middle-Street [5 dots] 1810.

t.[1], [2, illus.], [3], 4–36 p.; illus.; 14 cm.; pr. & illus. paper covers.

Cover title: Watts' Divine Songs. [a cut of a man and woman looking at two kneeling children] [a bar of oval ornaments] NEWBURY-P[ORT] PRINTED BY W. AN[D J. GIL-MAN.] MIDDLE-ST[REET.]. The rear cover has three illustrations and a top and bottom bar of ornaments. On p. [2] the cut, printed on the side, shows Christ seated and surrounded with children and people. This illustration, the title vignette, and that on p. 24 are signed *Gilman*. MSaE* (front cover mut.); MWA (p. 29–36 wanting); Shaw 21972.

1412.2 — —— Newburyport [Mass.]: PRINTED BY W. & J. GILMAN. Sold at their Book and Stationary Store, Middle-Street [5 dots] 1810.

fr.[2], t.[3], [4–7, 2 cuts on each p.], [8 full p. illus.], [9], 10–48 p.; illus.; 12.5 cm.; gray-green paper covers.

Cover title: Dr. Watts' Divine Son[gs.] [a cut of a boy and girl on the right and two beehives on the left.] [a bar of oval ornaments] Pr[remainder of cover torn away]. The rear cover has two cuts and an upper and lower bar of ornaments. The frontispiece of Christ seated among the children and people is the same as in no. **1412.1**, p. [2]. One cut on p. [4], [7], [8] is signed *Gilman*. Pages [9]–47 are not illustrated. MWA* (front cover half wanting, rear cover mut.); Shaw 21974 (28 p. probably an error for 48 p.).

1412.3 — —— Newburyport: Printed By W. & J. Gilman. Sold at their Book and Stationery Store, Middle-Street, and by E. Stedman, Sign of the Bible and Quadrant, Merrimack-street. 1810.

fr.[2], t.[3], [4–9], 10–48 p.; illus.; 13 cm.; marbled paper covers. MNeHi*.

1413 — DR. WATTS' DIVINE SONGS FOR CHILDREN. Sold by Lincoln & Edmands, No. 53 Cornhill. [ca. 1819] [caption p.[1]].

[1], 2–24 p.; illus.; 13 cm.; pr. & illus. brick-red paper covers. The cut on p. 18 was used earlier by Lincoln & Edmands in Watts' *Divine & Moral Songs*, 1808 in **1406.27**. Possibly because of this cut, in the past this book has been dated [ca. 1808]. The cuts on p. 2 and 22 are in Lincoln & Edmands 1819 edition of *Scripture History Abridged*, no. **1170**. The top and basal decorative bars on the front and back covers have two printer's ornaments identical with those on the front and back covers of E. Lincoln's *Scripture Questions. Second Edition, enlarged. Boston: Lincoln & Edmands, 1819*. This last book has the same format in size, type of paper used for the cover and the identical wording of the advertisement caption on the back

cover as no. **1413**. The advertisement caption of no. **1413** differs only in having certain words capitalized. In *Scripture Questions* "Watt's Divine Songs" is advertised for sale at "$2,50 per hun." but is omitted in no. **1413**. In Clowes' *The Gooseberry Bush And Caterpillars*, no. **209**, Lincoln and Edmands used the same shade of brick-red colored paper for the covers in 1818. This book was also advertised in no. **1413** and in *Scripture Questions*. Only one edition of no. **209** is known. Because of these data the book is dated [ca. 1819]. It could not have been printed earlier than 1818, but its type ornaments and the advertisements seem to favor the later date 1819.

MWA*; Shaw 16675 (under the title *Mr.* [*sic. i.e. Dr.*] *Watt's Divine Songs For Children . . .* [1808?]).

1414.1 — DR. WATT'S DIVINE SONGS, FOR THE USE OF CHILDREN. [2 lines quot.] Hartford: Published By Oliver D. Cooke. Roberts & Burr, Printers. 1820.

t.[1], [2], 3–24 p.; title vignette only illus.; 13.5 cm.; pr. & illus. orange paper covers.

MWA*; NNC-Pl; Shoemaker 4194 and 4195.

1414.2 — —— Children. Newburyport [Mass.]: Published By W. & J. Gilman. Sold at their Miscellaneous Book-Store, NO. 2, Middle-Street. [a row of 12 dots] Price 12½ cents. [ca. 1820].

fr.[ii], t.[1], [2–3], 4–36, [37] p.; illus.; 14.5 cm.; pr. & illus. yellow paper covers; the abbreviation "NO." on the title page is printed with both letters in capital letters. The title vignette is a large bird perched on a branch and facing to the left. The figure on p.[3], signed *Gilman*, showing two kneeling children holding a sheet of paper entitled "Hymns," was used for the title vignette by W. & J. Gilman, 1810 in **1412.1**. The one on p. 28 of a boy, a girl and two beehives is also signed *Gilman*. With the text, p. 5–36, different frontispieces, pages 37, and covers were added. These are described below under copies 1 to 5. The text was probably printed [ca. 1820] because the firm of W. & J. Gilman was at No. 2, Middle Street in 1820. *See* no. **1198**. After that date it moved to No. 9, State-Street. Earlier publications of the Gilmans are usually, but not invariably, dated. Copy 1 backs up this conclusion, because it has a mss. inscription *Rebecca Wrights Book 1821*. The book could have been published a year earlier and is dated [*ca. 1820*].

Copy 1: The frontispiece, 5.2 cm. high by 7 cm. wide, is printed on the side and shows a woman reading to a girl in an arbor with two standing ladies to the left. Page [37] has a cut of a seated man and woman facing two kneeling children. Below the figure is "The Lord's Prayer". Six printer's ornaments are present on the covers and p. [37]. The front cover has a cut of a seated man on a porch, with a boy in front of him, below which is the imprint: Newburyport: PRINTED BY W. *&* J. GILMAN, NO. 2, Middle-Street. [a row of 10 dots] Price 12½ cents. The rear cover has an advertisement of 22 books.

Copy 2: The frontispiece depicts a man reading a book with three beehives on the left of the cut. Page [37] has eight lines of verse below a cut of a boy in a graveyard.

Copy 3: The frontispiece shows Christ seated and surrounded by children and people and is signed *Gilman*. Below the illustration: "< See the Hymn at the end—Page 37. >" There is no cut on p. 37, which has the page number printed on the page. Below the caption there are twenty-eight lines of verse. The front cover cut shows two kneeling children reading a sheet of paper labled "Hymn". In the background is a spouting whale in the sea on the right, and to the left an elephant, and a tree trunk with birds on a few remaining branches. The imprint reads: Newburyport: PUBLISHED BY W. & J. GILMAN, NO. 2, Middle-Street. [a row of 6 dots] Price 12½ cents. The rear cover has 13 lines of advertisement by W. & J. Gilman.

Copy 4: The frontispiece is the same as in copy 3, but does not have anything printed below it. Page [37] is not numbered and has a cut of a woman looking at a child in a cradle, below which are 8 lines of Watt's "Cradle Song." The illustration on the front cover is the same as in copy 3, with a different imprint below it: BOSTON: PUBLISHED BY THOMAS WELLS, *No.* 3, *Hanover-Street*. [row of 6 dots] Price 12½ cents. The rear cover has 13 lines of advertisement for Thomas Wells.

Copy 5: Pages [5]–36 are the same as the above copies, but the title page vignette has a new cut. It portrays a church, a building, two trees, a winding road, and people in the foreground.

The remainder of the title page is the same as in copies 1 to 4. The frontispiece and p. [37] are the same as copy 2.

MWA* (copy 1; copy 2, covers wanting); NjP* (copy 3); MWA-W* (copy 4); MSaE* (copy 5); Shaw 19158 (dated [1809?]) and 19159 (dated 1809).

1415.1 — DR. WATTS' DIVINE SONGS, SUITED TO THE CAPACITIES OF CHILDREN. New-York: Printed by J. Seymour, for P. W. Gallaudet, 1818. Shaw 46713.

1415.2 ——— [1 line quot.] Pittsburgh [Pa.]: Published For The Sabbath Schools of The Western Country, and for sale by R. Patterson & Lambdin. Butler & Lambdin, Printers. 1819.

t.[1], [2–3], 4–32 p.; 11 cm.; pr. buff front cover, rear cover unprinted.
MWA*; Shaw 50059.

1415.3 ——— New-York: Published By R. & W. A. Bartow, 347 Pearl-Street, Franklin-Square, And W. B. Bartow, Richmond, (Vir.) J. Grey & Co., Printers. 1820.

t.[1], 2–24 p.; 13.5 cm.; pink paper covers.
MWA*; Shoemaker 4198.

1416 — MORAL SONGS, ATTEMPTED IN EASY LANGUAGE, For The Use Of Children. By I. Watts, D.D. [2 line quot.] To Which Are Added, The Principles Of The Christian Religion, Expressed in plain and easy Verse. By P. Doddridge, D.D. Utica [N.Y.]: Printed and Sold by Seward and Williams. 1810.

t.[1], [2, illus.], [3], 4–36 p.; illus. p. [3] only illus. except for ornamental headpieces and tailpieces; 13 cm.; bound in blue paper over bds., leather spine. Bound with and following no. **1408.65**. A Slight Specimen Of Moral Songs, p. [3]–14; The Principles Of The Christian Religion, p. [15]–36.
OOxM*; MWA; N; NUt; PP; Shaw 21980.

1417 — SELECT SONGS FOR CHILDREN. In Three Parts. I. Divine Songs, attempted in Easy Language. II. Moral Songs, in the most familiar manner. III. Psalms in Verse, Spiritual Hymns, and Serious little Poems. By I. Watts, D.D. The Rev. Mr. Foxton, M. A. and other eminent Divines. [2 lines of quot.]. New-York: Printed by J. Harrison, Yorick's Head No. 3 Peck-Slip. 1794.

t.[1], [2, bl.–3], 4–68, [69–71, contents] p.; 13 cm.; paper covers.

English ed. title 18.

DLC°; Evans 47323.

1418.1 — SONGS, DIVINE AND MORAL, FOR THE USE OF CHILDREN. By Isaac Watts. [2 lines quot.] Mat. xxi. 16. New-York: Printed And Sold By S. Wood, At The Juvenile Book-Store, No. 357, Pearl-Street. 1809.

t.[1], [2–3], 4–44 p.; illus.; 13 cm.

N° (covers wanting).

1418.2 ——— New-York: Printed And Sold By S. Wood, At The Juvenile Book-Store, No. 357, Pearl-Street. 1811.

t.[1], [2–3], 4–45 p.; illus.; 12.5 cm.; pr. & illus. paper covers.

Cover title: Watts' Divine And Moral Songs. New-York: Printed And Sold By S. Wood, At the Juvenile Book-Store, No. 357, Pearl street. 1811.

MWA°; MiD; Shaw 24397.

1418.3 ——— New-York: Printed And Sold By S. Wood At The Juvenile Book-Store, No. 357, Pearl-Street. [2 rows of 9 dots] 1812.

t.[i], [2–3], 4–45 p.; illus.; 12.5 cm.; pr. and illus. yellow-buff paper covers.

Cover title: Watts' Divine And Moral Songs. New-York: ——— At the Juvenile Book-store, No. 357, Pearl street. 1812.

Adomeit°.

1418.4 ——— New-York: Printed And Sold By S. Wood, At the Juvenile Book-Store, No. 357, Pearl-street. 1813.

t.[1], [2–3], 4–45 p.; illus.; 12.5 cm.; pr. & illus. paper covers.

Cover title: Watt's Divine Songs. New-York: ——— [same as title] 1813.

NHi°.

1418.5 ——— By Isaac Watts. [3 lines quot.] Windham [Conn.]: Printed by Samuel Webb. 1813.

fr.[2], t.[3], [4–5], 6–22, [23, alphabet] p.; illus.; 9 cm.; pr. & illus. yellowish-buff paper covers. Alphabets p.[4]; A CRADLE HYMN, p.[5]–8; illus., p. 9; THE BEGGAR'S PETITION, p. 10–13; *A Summer Evening*, p. 14–15; [illus. of] THE THIEF, p. 16, *The Thief*, p.

17–18; *Mother Goose's Melody*. Robin and Richard/Were two pretty Men; . . . Boys and Girls, come out to play; . . . p. 20; *A Local Song; or the Conjuror's/Reason for not getting Money./I Would, if I could;/If I couldn't, how cou'd I?/I cou'dnt without I cou'd, cou'd I?/ Cou'd you, without you cou'd, cou'd/ye?/Cou'd ye, cou'd ye?/Cou'd you, without you cou'd, cou'd/ye?/Note. . . . Dickery, Dickery Dock, p. 21; There were two Blackbirds/Sat upon a Hill;/ . . A SEASONABLE SONG. Piping hot, smoking hot;/What I've got,/You have not;/ Hot Grey Pease, hot, hot, hot,/Hot Grey Pease hot,/p. 22; Upper case alphabet and numbers, p.[23].

Cover title: Divine And Moral Songs. Printed by S. Webb, Windham. 1813.

MWA-W°.

1418.6 ——— New-York: Printed And Sold By Samuel Wood At The Juvenile Book-Store, No. 357, Pearl-Street. 1814.

t.[1], [2–3], 4–45 p.; illus.; 12.5 cm.; pr. & illus. paper covers.

Cover title: Watts' Divine And Moral Songs. New York: Printed And Sold By S. Wood, At the Juvenile Book-store, No. 357, Pearl-street. 1812.

NHi°; CtY (front cover mut. & worn, dated 1814); ICU; PP (bound with other books); Shaw 33604.

1418.7 ——— Watts. [2 lines quot.] New-York: Printed And Sold By Samuel Wood, At The Juvenile Book-Store, No. 357, Pearl-Street. 1815.

t.[1], [2–3], 4–46 [*sic., i.e.* 45] p.; illus.; 12.5 cm.; pr. & illus. paper covers.

Cover title: Watts' Divine Songs. Printed And Sold By S. Wood & Sons At The Juvenile Book-Store, No. 357, Pearl-Street. New-York. [n.d.].

MSaE°; Ct (front cover wanting).

1418.8 ——— New-York: Printed And Sold By S. Wood & Sons, At The Juvenile Book-Store, No. 357, Pearl-Street. 1816.

t.[1], [2–3], 4–44 p.; illus.; 12.5 cm.

RPB° (p. 45 and covers wanting, p. 19–44 mut.); Shaw 39739.

1418.9 ——— [2 lines quot.] To Which Are Added, The Principles Of The Christian Religion, In Plain And Easy Verse. By P. Doddridge, D.D.

New-York: Printed And Sold By T. And J. Swords, No. 160 Pearl-street. 1817.

t.[1], [2–3], 4–64 p.; 10.5 cm.; blue-gray paper covers.

MWA-W*.

1418.10 — ——— [same as **1418.7**] Watts. [2 lines quot.] New-York: Printed And Sold By S. Wood & Sons, At The Juvenile Book-Store, No. 261, Pearl-Street. 1817.

t.[1], [2–3], 4–45 p.; illus.; 12.5 cm.; pr. & illus. buff paper covers.

Cover title: Watts' Divine Songs. Printed ——— [same as t.[1]] Pearl-Street. New-York.

MWA*.

1418.11 — ——— Watts, D.D. [3 lines quot.] Albany: Printed By Websters And Skinners, at their Book store, corner [of] State and Pearl-Streets. 1818.

t.[1], [2–3], 4–36+ p.; illus.; 13 cm.

Adomeit* (p. 35–36 mostly wanting).

1418.12 — ——— New-York: Published By Samuel Wood & Sons, No. 261, Pearl-Street; And Samuel S. Wood & Co., No. 212, Market-st. Baltimore. 1818.

t.[1], [2–3], 4–45 p.; illus.; 13 cm.; pr. & illus. buff paper covers.

Cover title: Watts' Divine Songs. *Nerv-York* [*sic. i.e. New-York*]: Published by Samuel Wood & Sons, And Samuel S. Wood & Co. Baltimore. [n.d.].

CtY*; DLC.

1418.13 — ——— And Moral, For Children: By Isaac Watts, D.D. From The London Edition —Complete. Albany: Printed and sold by G. J. Loomis & Co. State street. 1819.

t.[1], [2–3], 4–48 p.; 12.5 cm.; blue-gray paper covers.

MWA*; MB (per st. on t.[1]); Shaw 50060.

1418.14 — ——— and Moral, For The Use Of Children. By Isaac Watts. [2 lines quot.] New-York: Published By Samuel Wood & Sons, No. 261, Pearl Street; And Samuel S. Wood & Co No. 212, Market-st. Baltimore. 1819.

t.[1], [2–3], 4–45 p.; illus.; 13 cm.; pr. & illus. buff paper covers.

Cover title: Watt's Divine Songs. New-York:

Published by Samuel Wood & Sons; And Samuel S. Wood & Co. Baltimore. [n.d.].

MWA*; PCC; Shaw 50061.

1418.15 — ——— New-York: Published By Samuel Wood & Sons, No. 261, Pearl Street; And Samuel S. Wood & Co. No. 212, Market-st. Baltimore. 1820.

t.[1], [2–3], 4–45 p.; illus.; 13 cm.; pr. & illus. buff paper covers. Cover title same as cover title of no. **1418.14**.

MWA*; NNMM (front cover wanting; p. 27–28, 43–44 mut.); Shoemaker 4206.

1419 — Watts Divine Songs for children. New-York: adv. by William Durell, 1790 in **612.5**. This may be an edition of *Divine Songs Attempted In Easy Language for the Use of Children.*

1420.1 — Watts Divine Songs For the use of Children With Plates. G. Love sc. Ph[il]adelphia Published By J. Johnson. 1807.

fr.[2], t.[3], [4, bl.–5], 6–52 p.; 8 engr. pl. or illus. including fr.[2] & t.[3]; 13.5 cm.; green paper covers. The "il" of "Philadelphia" is hidden by a wing of the middle angel in the illustration above the word. Colophon p. 52: A. Dickinson, Printer. Whitehall. The plates are crudely copied in the reverse from Scottish ed. title 24, Glasgow: Lumsden & Son. [*ca.* 1804].

MWA-W*; CLU; CtHi; MSaE; NHi; NN; NNC-Pl; PP; Shaw 14170.

1420.2 — Watt's Divine Songs For The Use Of Children. Published by John Lyle, Paris, Kentucky. 1814.

t.[1], [2], 3–32 p.; 13.5 cm.; pr. blue-gray paper covers.

Cover title: D[i]vine Songs For Children. [2 lines quot.] By Isaac Watts, D.D. Paris, KY. Printed And Published By John Lyle[.] 1814. Rear cover: Just Published By John Lyle, And Sold At His Book-Store, Main-Street, Paris, Ky. "Janeway's Token for Children." Also "Watt's Catechisms for Children." He Has For Sale A Great Variety Of Books for-Children, And Many Other Useful Books; Together With An Assortment Of Blank-Books."

PPPrHi* (i. st. on t.[1], front cover worm-eaten, affecting the word "Divine," and period after "Lyle."; p. 30 had a fold in the leaf, when printed, so that the last verse of Song XXV and

first verse of Song XXVI are mostly unprinted);
Shaw 33605.

1420.3 — WATTS' DIVINE SONGS FOR THE USE
OF CHILDREN. Adorned With Cuts. New-Haven:
Sidney's Press. 1817.
> fr.[2], t.[3], [4–5], 6–47 p.; illus.; 13 cm.; illus.
> buff paper covers.
> MWA* (p.[2–4] mut.); Shaw 42844.

1420.4 — ——— New-Haven: From Sidney's
Press. 1818.
> t.[1], [2–3], 4–36 p.; illus.; 14 cm.; paper
> covers.
> MWA* (covers wanting); PP (p. 35–36 & rear
> cover wanting); Shaw 46711.

1420.5 — ——— Children. Sidney's Press. For
John Babcock And Son, New-Haven, S. And W. R.
Babcock, 163 King-St. Charleston, And M'Carty
And Davis, Philadelphia. 1820.
> fr.[2], t.[3], [4, adv.–5], 6–31 p.; illus.; 14.5
> cm.; pr. & illus. paper covers; cover title un-
> dated.
> CtHi*; CtY (copy 1, covers wanting; copy 2,
> fr.[2], p. 31 & covers wanting); NB (i. st. on
> t.[3], bpl. over t.[3], fr.[2], p. 31 and covers
> wanting); Shoemaker 4196.

1420.6 — ——— New-Haven: Printed For
John Babcock And Son. Sidney's Press. 1820.
> fr.[2], t.[3], [4–5], 6–31 p.; illus.; 15 cm.; pr. &
> illus. gray-green paper covers; fr.[2] and cover
> title vignette signed A [Alexander Anderson].
> Cover title: Watts' Divine Songs. Published and
> Sold by John Babcock and Son, New-Haven,
> and S. & W. R. Babcock, Charleston [S.C.].
> MWA*; Ct (p. 29–30 mut. & ½ wanting); PP;
> Shoemaker 4197.

1421 — A WONDERFUL DREAM, By I. Watts,
D.D. Eighth Edition: Greenwich [Mass.]: Printed
and sold Price 50 Cents per Dozen 6 Cents single,
March,—1804.
> t.[1], [2], 3–16 p.; title vignette only illus.; 14.5
> cm.; printed by John Howe. While this book is
> not considered a child's book, this edition is
> included because the advertisement on p. [2]
> states: ". . . the Editor is encouraged to publish
> this Piece, tho' a Dream for the benefit of youth,
> as it is likely to have a good tendancy to pro-
> mote Piety and Deter from Profanity."
> Welch*; MWA; OOxM; Shaw 7716.

WESLEY, JOHN 1703–1791
1422 — THE HISTORY OF JESUS. Drawn Up For
The Instruction Of Children. To Which Is Added,
A Token For Children. Extracted from a late Au-
thor, By John Wesley, A.M. [2 lines quot.] First
American Edition. New-York: Published By D.
Hitt and T. Ware, For The Methodist Connection
In The United States. John C. Totten Printer.
1814.
> t.[i], [ii–iii], iv, [5], 6–160 p.; 11 cm.; bound in
> leather.
> MWA*; Shaw 33644.

1423.1 — A TOKEN FOR CHILDREN; Extracted
From A Late Author, By John Wesley, A.M. First
American edition [3 lines of quot.] Philadelphia:
Sold by Wiatt & Delaplaine, No. 104, North
Second-street. Stiles, printer. 1810.
> t.[1], [2–3], 4–79 p.; 10 cm.; bound in mar-
> bled paper over bds., leather spine.
> DLC*.

1423.2 — ——— Trenton [N.J.]: Published by
D. Fenton, Nearly opposite the Bank. 1812.
> t.[1], [2–3], 4–79 p.; 12 cm.; bound in pr. &
> blue paper over bds.
> MWA-W*.

1423.3 — ——— Second American Edition [3
lines quot.] Philadelphia: Printed For, And Sold
By J. Pounder, No. 352, North Third Street. A.
Dickenson, Printer [4 dots] 1813.
> t.[1], [2, bl.], [3], 4–96 p.; 11 cm.; bound in
> pr. buff paper over bds.
> MWA*; Shaw 28829 (listed under Janeway,
> James).

1423.4 — ——— Third American Edition. [2
lines quot.] Mark x. 14. Philadelphia: Published
By Solomon Wiatt, Bookseller. 1814.
> t.[1], [2–3], 4–96 p.; A_{16}, $C–D_{16}$, no sig. B;
> 10.5 cm.; bound in marbled paper over bds.
> NNC-LS* (i. st. p.[3]); PSC.

1423.5 — ——— Fourth Amrican [*sic. i.e.*
American] Edition. [3 lines quot.] New-York:
Printed And Sold By John C. Totten, No. 9
Bowery. 1815.
> t.[1], [2–3], 4–60 p.; 13.5 cm.; pr. reddish
> paper covers.
> CtHi*; NN; Shaw 35009 and 36540.

1423.6 —— —— Fifth American Edition. New-York: Printed And Sold By John C. Totten, No. 9 Bowery. 1819.

t.[1], [2–3], 4–48 p.; 14.5 cm.; pr. & illus. yellow-buff paper covers; cover title dated 1819. MWA-W°.

1424.1 The Whim-Wham: Or, Evening Amusement, For All Ages And Sizes. Being an Entire New Set Of Riddles, Charades, Questions, and Transportations. By A Friend To Innocent Mirth. Philadelphia: Published By Johnson & Warner, No. 147, High-Street. Sweeny & M'Kenzie, Printers. 1811.

fr.[ii], t.[1], [2–5], 6–33 p.; front. only illus.; 14 cm.; buff paper covers; front. signed *Charles sc.* [William Charles]. Adv. by Johnson & Warner, 1814 in **1449.3**.

English ed. London: W. & T. Darton, 1810.

MWA°; MH; P; PP; RPB; Sabin 103294; Shaw 24428.

1424.2 —— Hartford: Printed By Charles Hosmer. 1815.

fr.[2], t.[3], [4–5], 6–31 p.; illus.; 10 cm.; pr. & illus. buff paper covers.

MWA-W° (rear cover wanting); MWA° (covers, fr.[2] & p. 31 wanting).

1425.1 Whimsical Incidents or The Power Of Music. Wm. Charles. Philadelphia 1811 [cover title].

t.[1], [2–16] p. engr. on one side only of 16 leaves; illus.; probably 13 cm.; pr. & illus. paper covers.

Cover title: Whimsical Incidents or The Power of Music, a Poetic Tale: By a near Relation Of Old Mother Hubbard.

English ed. London: J. Harris, 1805.

Oppenheimer° (not available for checking, 2 p. are wanting).

1425.2 —— Music. A Poetic Tale. Present For The New-Year. 1816. [cover title].

t.[1], [2–16] p. engr. on one side only of 16 leaves; illus.; 13 cm.; pr. & illus. buff paper covers. The title page is the same as no. **1425.1**. MWA°; CLU; PP (t.[1], p.[2–3], 7, 16 mut.); Weiss 1936, p. 11.

1425.3 —— A Poetic Tale. Published by Henry Whipple. Salem Mass. [*ca.* 1820] [cover title].

t.[1], [2–16] p. engr. on one side only of 16 leaves; illus.; 12.5 cm.; pr. & illus. brownish-buff paper covers. Title page same as 1811 ed. Harriet S. Tapley in *Salem Imprints*, p. 462, dates this [*ca.* 1820]. (MWA cat.).

MWA°; CLU; MSaE; Sabin 103295; Shoemaker 4264.

WHISTLE, WILL ESQ. *pseud.*

1426.1 — The History Of The Birds In The Air. By Will Whistle, Esq. Albany: Printed And Sold By The Gross Or Dozen, By E. And E. Hosford. 1806.

t.[3], [4, alphabets], 5–30 p.; illus.; 10.5 cm. *See Will Whistle's History Of The Birds In The Air*, no. **1431.1**.

NHi° (fr.[2], p. 31, & covers wanting; p. 29–30 mut. page numbers torn away).

1426.2 —— —— Albany: Printed By E. And E. Hosford. 1806.

fr.[2], t.[3], [4, alphabets], 5–31 p.; illus.; 10 cm.; Dutch paper covers.

MWA° (p. 31 mut. affecting the last 2 lines of text); Shaw 11863.

1426.3 —— —— Albany: Printed By E. And E. Hosford. 1809.

fr.[2], t.[3], [4, alphabets], 5–31 p.; illus.; 10 cm.; pr. & illus. buff paper covers; cover title undated.

NB°; NN (i. st. on t.[3]); PP; Shaw 19216.

1427.1 [—] The History Of The Birds in the Air: Designed For the Amusement of all good little Boys and Girls. Ornamented with Engravings. Albany: Printed By E. And E. Hosford. 1810.

fr.[2], t.[3], [4, alphabets], 5–30, [31, 2 cuts] p.; illus.; 10 cm.; pr. & illus. buff paper covers; cover title undated.

Welch° (p. 31 mut., rear cover wanting); DLC (p. 29–31 & rear cover wanting); MSaE (fr.[2], p. 31, & covers wanting); MWA; NNC-LS (covers, fr.[2], & p. 31 wanting, i. st. on front paper cover which is not the original cover); PP (fr.[2], p.[31] & covers wanting); Shaw 20340.

1427.2 [—] —— Albany: Printed By E. & E. Hosford. 1814.

fr.[2], t.[3], [4, alphabets], 5–31 p.; illus.; 10 cm.; pr. & illus. buff paper covers.

Cover title: History Of Birds. Albany: Printed By E. And E. Hosford.
MWA-W°; MH; Shaw 31718.

1427.3 [—] ———— Albany: Printed By E. & E. Hosford. 1816.

fr.[2], t.[3], [4, alphabets], 5–31 p.; illus.; 10 cm.; pr. & illus. buff paper covers; cover title undated.
MB°; DLC; Shaw 37844.

1427.4 [—] ———— Albany: Printed By E. & E. Hosford. 1818.

fr.[2], t.[3], [4, alphabets], 5–30, [31, 2 illus.] p.; illus.; 10.5 cm.; pr. & illus. blue-gray paper covers; cover title undated.
N° (a very browned copy); MWA (fr.[2], p. 31 & covers wanting).

THE WHITSUNTIDE PRESENT. *See* Allgood, Nurse (*pseud.*), no. **30.1.**

WHITE, THOMAS [d. 1672?]
1428.1 [—] A LITTLE BOOK FOR LITTLE CHILDREN. Wherein are set down several Directions for Little Children: And several Remarkable Stories both Ancient and Modern, of little Children. Divers whereof are of those Lately Deceased, Boston, in N.E. Reprinted by T. Green, for Nicholas Buttolph, at the corner of Gutteridges Coffee-House. 1702.

t.[1], [2], 3–94 p.; 14.5 cm. This is the second earliest American children's book containing religious narratives. The first is Janeway's *A Token For Children*, 1700, no. **665.1.** The only extant English edition is the twelfth of 1702, which has on pages [91–93]: "Youth's Alphabet: Or, Herbert's Morals." Selected verses are given below:

A.
Awful Revere is unto Kings most due,
For they're our Father's, and our country's too.
C.
Children that make their Parent's heart's Bleed,
May live t'have children to revenge that deed.
D.
Dare to be true, nothing can need a lie;
A fault which needs it most, grows two thereby.

The last leaf H_6 is blank in the Boston edition and Youth's Alphabet is not included. The American book has an added paragraph at the end, p. 94, in which the author asks children to remember him in their prayers. The book is a gruesome compilation containing some of the most harrowing stories taken from Foxe's *Book Of Martyrs*. The account of the mother and the seven martyred sons is a grisly one. Books such as this one and Janeway's *A Token For Children* were considered suitable literature intended to bring joy to the youth of their day.
English ed. London: adv. by Thomas Parkhurst, 1674 in Thomas Lye's *The assemblies shorter catechism drawn out into distinct propositions.* MWA° (p. 61–62, 93–94 mut.); Evans 1056.

1428.2 [—] ———— Boston, in N. E. Reprinted by T. Green, for Benjamin Eliot, at his shop, under the West-End of the Exchange. 1702.

t.[1], [2–3], 4–94 p.; 14.5 cm.
MWA°.

1428.3 [—] ———— Boston: adv. by N. Buttolph, 1705 in Secker's *A Wedding Ring.*

WHITTINGTON, RICHARD (arranged chronologically)

1429.1 THE FAMOUS AND REMARKABLE HISTORY OF SIR RICHARD WHITTINGTON, Three Times Lord-Mayor Of London. Who lived in the time of King Henry the Fifth. Boston: Printed and sold at the Heart & Crown in Cornhill. [*ca.* 1770].

t.[1], [2], 3–16 p.; title page vignette & illus. p. 16 only illus.; 21.5 cm. At the top of p. 3 the word Fleet is printed in the center of the decorative bar of printer's ornaments. Thomas and John Fleet printed at the Heart and Crown from 1731 to 1776. The above chapbook could have been printed at the same time as *The Most Delightful History Of The King and the Cobler*, [*ca.* 1770], no. **738.2.** According to Ashton the common story of Sir Richard Whittington is quite incorrect. He actually was the third son of Sir William Whittington, lord of the manor of Pauntley, in Gloucestershire, who died in 1360. The son became enormously rich after having been sent to London to learn to be a merchant and became mayor of London in 1397, 1406, and 1419. How the cat got into the story nobody seems to know. Some say that Whittington made his money by carrying coals in vessels called cats or "cattes". Another theory is that he made his money by "achats" the French word for trading.

Early English ed. title 1: *The famous and re-markable history of Sir Richard Whittington, thrice lord mayor of London, . . . Written by T. H.* [probably Thomas Heywood] London: F. Coles, 1656.

English ed. title 2: *An Old Ballad of Whittington and his Cat.* London: [1710?] [broadside fol.].

English ed. title 3: *The History Of Sir R.W.* [*or*] *Richard Whittington.* Durham: I. Lane [1730?].

English ed. title 4: *The Adventures of Sir Whittington.* Brentford: P. Norbury. London: Printed and Sold by all Book-sellers in Town and Country. [n.d.].

English ed. title 5: *The Ancient And Renowned History Of Whittington And His Cat.* London: Darton, Harvey, And Darton, 1812.

English ed. title 5a: *The Ancient History Of Whittington And His Cat.* London: W. Darton, 1817.

English ed. title 6: *The Entertaining History Of Dick Whittington.* [cover title] Title: *The Pleasing and Renowned History . . .* Banbury: J. G. Rusher. [1814?].

English & Scottish ed. title 7: *The Famous History Of Whittington And His Cat.* London: Printed for and sold by all the Stationery and Toy Shops in Town and Country. [1803?] manuscript date on p.[4] "1803."

English & Scottish ed. title 8: *The History Of Whittington . . . and his Cat.* London: 3 ed. Tabart & Co. 1804.

English & Irish ed. title 9: *Whittington and His Cat.* York: adv. by Wilson, Spence & Mawman, 1797 in Bunyano's *The Prettiest Book For Children.*
MB° (per st. on t.[1]); Evans 42049.

1429.2 ———— Sold at the Bible and Heart in Cornhill, Boston. [*ca.* 1780].
t.[1], [2, bl.], 3–16 p.; title page vignette and illus. p. 16 only illus.; 16 cm. Thomas and John Fleet changed the name of their firm to Bible and Heart when crowns became unpopular in 1780. The two illustrations are the same as in no. **1429.1**. The one on p. 16 was used in their edition of *The Wonderful Life. . . . of Robinson Crusoe* [*ca.* 1792], no. **275.18**.
Fitzhugh°.

1429.3 THE FAMOUS HISTORY OF WHITTING-TON AND HIS CAT. Shewing, How from a poor Country Boy, destitute of Parents or Relations, he obtained great Riches, and was promoted to the high and honorable dignity of Lord Mayor of London. Adorned with Cuts. Hartford: Printed by Nathaniel Patten. M,DCC,LXXX,VIII.
fr.[ii], t.[1], [2], 3–27, 8 [*sic. i.e.* 28], [29, illus.] p.; illus.; 9.5 cm.; Dutch paper covers.
CtHi°; MWA (p. 29 and rear cover wanting; page number of p. "28" printed correctly); Evans 21602; Weiss 1938b.

1429.4 ———— London. Adorned with Cuts. Middletown [Conn.]: Moses H. Woodward, M,DCC,XC.
t.[1], [2–3], 4–27 p.; illus.; 8.5 cm.
MWA-W°; CtHi; CtW (p. 23–24 wanting); Evans 23083; Weiss 1938b.

1429.5 ———— New-York: Printed & Sold by William Durrell, No. 19, Queen street. [*ca.* 1791].
fr.[2, alphabet], t.[3], [4–30] p.; 10 cm. William Durell was at 19 Queen street from 1786–1789, and 1791–1793. Adv. by Wm. Durell, 1790 in **612.5**.
CLU; Evans 46357.

1429.6 ———— of Parents obtained great Riches, and was promoted to the high dignity of Lord Mayor of London. Embellished With Cuts. Printed for and Sold by John Fisher, Stationer, in Market-street, Baltimore. 1794.
fr.[2], t.[3], [4], 5–31 p.; illus.; 10 cm.; red scalloped marbled paper covers.
MWA°; Evans 47328.

1429.7 ———— [same as **1429.3**] London. Adorned With Cuts. Newfield [Conn.]: Printed by Beach and Jones. [*ca.* 1795].
t.[1], [2], 3–27, [28, full page cut] p.; illus.; 10 cm.; Dutch paper covers.
MWA°; Evans 47684.

1429.8 ———— Exeter [N.H.]: adv. by H. Ranlet, 1798 in **1142**.

1429.9 ———— New-York: Printed by W. Durell, For Evert Duyckinck. 1800.
fr.[2], t.[3], [4–5], 6–31 p.; illus.; 10 cm.; illus. blue paper covers.
NB°; Evans 49193.

1429.10 ——— New-York: Printed by W. Durell. For John Harrison. 1800.

fr.[2], t.[3], [4–5], 6–31 p.; illus.; 10 cm.; Dutch paper covers.

MWA* (p. 31 & rear cover mut.); OClWHi; Evans 37395; Weiss 1938b.

1429.11 ——— New-York: Printed By W. Durrell [*sic. i.e.* Durell], for Stephen Stephens. 1800. Evans 37395.

1429.12 ——— New-Haven: Printed By William W. Morse. 1802.

t.[3], [4–5], 6–30 p.; illus.; 10 cm. The illustration on p. 15 depicts Christ and his disciples in a ship during a tempest; that on p. 19 shows Christ at the last supper. These cuts are redrawn from *The Holy Bible Abridged*, no. **612.4**. The printer possibly thought the first cut could do for the ship Whittington's cat boarded and the second would represent the king at table before the rats descended upon him. Did the children reading this book think that kings usually had a halo?

MWA-W* (covers wanting); CtHi; DLC (green Dutch paper covers); Shaw 3555; Weiss 1938b.

1429.13 THE HISTORY OF WHITTINGTON AND HIS CAT. Shewing ——— [same as **1429.3**] Relations; he attained great Riches, and was promoted to the high and honorable dignity of Lord Mayor of London. Embellished with Cuts. Philadelphia: Published by Jacob Johnson, Nº 147, Market-Street. 1802.

fr.[2], t.[3], [4], 5–31 p.; illus.; 11.5 cm.; olive-buff paper covers. Part of a large publisher's remainder.

MWA*; CtHi; DLC; NB; NHi; NN; NNC-Pl; NNMM; PHi; PP; Shaw 3556; Weiss 1938b.

1429.14 THE FAMOUS HISTORY ——— [same as **1429.3**] Ornamented with Cuts. Hartford: Printed By Lincoln & Gleason. 1806.

fr.[2], t.[3], [4–5], 6–29, [30], [31, adv.] p.; illus.; 10.5 cm.

Ct (i. st. on t.[3], Dutch paper covers); NRU (p. 29–[31] wanting, 25–26 mut.); Shaw 10384.

1429.15 ——— Hartford: Printed By Peter B. Gleason & Co. 1811.

fr.[2], t.[3], [4–5], 6–30, [31] p.; illus.; 10.5 cm.; pr. & illus. buff paper covers. Cover title dated 1824.

MWA-W*; CtHi (covers & p. [31] wanting); CtY (cover title dated 1817); MWA (cover title dated 1811;) Shaw 24440.

1429.16 ——— Printed And Sold By Nathaniel Coverly, Jun'r. Corner of Theatre-Alley. Boston. ☞ Price 75 Cents Per Dozen, 12 Single. n.d. [*ca.* 1812].

t.[1], [2], 3–16 p.; illus.; 14 cm.

MWA-W* (blue wallpaper covers probably added by a former owner); MSaE (p. 15–16, mut.); Shaw 27544.

1429.17 THE RENOWNED HISTORY OF SIR RICHARD WHITTINGTON, AND HIS CAT. Adorned With Cuts. Sidney's Press, New-Haven. 1817.

fr.[2], t.[3], [4, alphabet–5], 6–31 p.; illus.; 10.5 cm.; illus. paper covers.

OOxM*.

1429.18 ——— Sidney's Press, New-Haven, 1818.

fr.[2], t.[3], [4, alphabet–5], 6–30, [31, adv.] p.; illus.; 10.5 cm.; illus. paper covers. Adv. by J. Babcock & Son, 1819 in **481.6**.

CtY* (2 copies varied covers); MWA (front cover & p.[2–4] mut.); Shaw 46801.

1429.19 THE ANCIENT AND RENOWNED HISTORY OF WHITTINGTON AND HIS CAT. New-York: Printed and Published by J. Robertson, 121 Water-street, 1818.

5⅝ x 3½ inches; 36 p.; stiff paper covers; title on front cover; cut on title page.

Weiss 1938b, p. 485.

1430 THE WIDOW'S SON, AND TRUTH REWARDED. New-York: adv. by L. B. Jansen and G. Jansen, 1808 in **766**.

1431.1 WILL WHISTLE'S HISTORY OF THE BIRDS IN THE AIR. Here's Will Whistle's History of the Birds in the air, It may serve for a present from market or fair, Yet if it should not it will learn you to read, And that you must own in a good thing indeed. Hartford: Printed by John Babcock, 1802.

fr.[2], t.[3], [4, alphabets], 5–28, [29, adv.] p.; illus.; 11 cm.

See Whistle, Will Esq. *The History Of The Birds in the Air*, no. **1427.1**.

MWA*.

1431.2 ——— or fair. Philadelphia: Printed by
John Adams. 1805.
  fr.[2], t.[3], [4, alphabets], 5–31 p.; illus.; 10.5
  cm.; illus. buff paper covers pr. in red ink;
  p. 30–31, adv. of books.
  MWA°; Shaw 9722.

1431.3 ——— [same as **1431.1**] indeed. Hartford: Printed by Lincoln & Gleason. 1806.
  fr.[2], t.[3], [4], 5–31 p.; illus.; 10.5 cm.
  MSaE°.

1431.4 ——— indeed. From Sidney's Press,
New-Haven. 1806.
  fr.[2], t.[3], [4, alphabets], 5–29, [30, adv.] p.;
  illus.; 11 cm. The first word of verse on p. 5–9,
  11–22, is printed entirely in capital letters. The
  cut of "The Woodcock and Snipe", p. 9, is
  printed right side up. The illustration of "The
  Swan", p. 13, shows an erect swan.
  RPB (Dutch paper covers, i. st. on t.[3]).

1431.5 ——— Birds. Part First. [4 lines of verse
same as **1431.2**] Philadelphia: Printed By John
Adams. 1806.
  fr.[2], t.[3], [4, alphabets], 5–31 p.; illus.; 10.5
  cm.; pr. & illus. blue paper covers; p. 30–31
  adv. of 31 books.
  Cover title: Toy-Book. Philadelphia: Sold by
  James P. Parke, 1807 .
  MWA-W°.

1431.6 ——— From Sidney's Press, New-Haven.
1807.
  fr.[2], t.[3], [4, alphabet], 5–29, [30, alphabets],
  [31, adv.] p.; illus.; 10.5 cm.; Dutch paper
  covers. The first word of verse on p. 5–15,
  17–22, is printed entirely in capital letters. The
  picture of "The Woodcock and Snipe" is printed
  on the side. The cut of "The Swan", p. 13, looks
  like a heron whose head and neck are curved
  down to the left towards a long-necked bottle
  and is printed on the side.
  MWA-W° (fr.[2], t.[3], p. 29–31 & covers
  worm-eaten).

1431.7 ——— From Sidney's Press, New-Haven.
1808.
  fr.[2], t.[3], [4, alphabet], 5–29, [30, alphabets],
  [31, adv.] p.; illus.; 10.5 cm.; red & green Dutch
  paper covers. The first word of verse p. 5–8,

10–11, 14–15, 17–22 is printed entirely in
capital letters. The illustration, p. 9, of "The
Woodcock and Snipe", is printed on the side.
The cut of "The Swan", p. 13, is the same as
in no. **1431.6** and printed on the side.
  MWA-W°; CLU; DLC (2 copies); MSaE;
  RPB; Shaw 16738.

1431.8 ——— From Sidney's Press, New-
Haven, 1810.
  fr.[2], t.[3], [4, alphabet], 5–29, [30, alphabets],
  [31, adv.] p.; illus.; 10.5 cm.; pr. & illus. yellow
  paper covers.
  Cover title: Will Whistle. Published by I. Cooke
  & Co. Universal Book-Store, Church-Street,
  New-Haven. The first word of verse, p. 5–8,
  11–13, 17–22, is printed entirely in capital letters. The cut of "The Woodcock and Snipe", p.
  9, is printed right side up. The illustration of
  "The Swan", p. 13, is the same as no. **1431.6**
  and printed on the side. Page "19" has the page
  number printed with the "9" lower than the "1".
  MWA°; DLC; MWA-W; NCooHi; Shaw 22033.

1431.9 ——— Hartford: Printed By Peter B.
Gleason & Co. 1811.
  fr.[2], t.[3], [4, alphabets], 5–31 p.; illus.; 10
  cm.; pr. buff paper covers; cover title dated
  1811; p. no. 29 printed on the inside of the
  page.
  MWA° (fr.[2], p. 31 & covers mut.); CtHi
  (2 copies; copy 1, cover title dated 1824);
  Shaw 23015 and 24430.

1431.10 [——— From Sidney's Press, New-
Haven. *ca.* 1811 or later] [conjectural title mainly
composed from **1431.8**].
  [5], 6–28+ p.; illus.; 10 cm. Page number "5"
  is slightly lower than the caption, "The Eagle",
  on p. 5, instead of being on a line with the caption. The first word of verse on p. 5–8, 13–15,
  17–22, is printed entirely in capital letters. The
  illustration of "The Woodcock and Snipe", p. 9,
  is printed right side up. The illustration of "The
  Swan", p. 13, is the same as no. **1431.6** and
  printed on the side of the page with page number "19" printed correctly. The fragment is
  closest to no. **1431.8** and is dated [*ca.* 1811 or
  later]. Until a copy is found of this book, the
  precise date cannot be ascertained.
  OOxM° (fr.[ii], t.[3], p. [4], 29–[31] wanting).

1431.11 —— From Sidney's Press, New-Haven. 1812.

fr.[2], t.[3], [4, adv.], 5–29, [30, upper case alphabet] p.; illus.; 10.5 cm.

MSaE°.

1432 WILLIAM AND ELIZA. New-York: adv. T. B. Jansen, [*ca.* 1815] in **47.**

1433 WILLIAM AND JACOB; Or, The Advice Of A True Friend. Boston: Wells And Lilly, Court-Street. 1820.

t.[1], [2–3], 4–7 p.; 14 cm.; verse; signed *A. H.* on p. 7.

MWA°; Shoemaker 4289.

1434 (No. 25.) WILLIAM BRYANT, Or The Folly Of Superstitious Fears. Published By The Philadelphia Female Tract Society. And for sale at their Depository, No. 20, Walnut Street. [caption title p. [1]]. Printed by Lydia R. Bailey, No. 10, North Alley, Philad. [1817] [colophon p. 12].

[1], 2–12 p.; 14 cm.

MWA° (bound with other tracts, with which *The Second Annual Report Of The Philadelphia Female Tract Society For The Year 1817* was originally bound); Shaw 42915.

1435.1 WILLIAM AND THE YOUNG EAST INDIAN. New-York: adv. by L. B. Jansen and G. Jansen, 1808 in **766.**

1435.2 WILLIAM AND THE YOUNG EAST-INDIAN. New-York: Published By T. Powers, 116 Broadway. 1809.

t.[1], [2], 3–24 p.; illus.; 13 cm.

Adomeit°.

[WILLIAMS, HELEN MARIA]

1436 [—] THE HISTORY OF PEROUROU, The Bellows-Mender. With Other Amusing And Instructive Histories. Baltimore: Printed For G. Douglas, Bookseller. 1801.

t.[1], [2–3], 4–179, [180, adv. list of books] p.; 14 cm.; bound in leather. The History Of Perourou, p. [3]–41; The Story Of La Roche, p. [42]–63; The Use And Excellence Of Religion [verse], p. 64; The History Of Auguste and Madelaine, p. [65]–81; A Provincal Tale, p. [82]–91; Alonzo The Brave And Fair Imogene [verse], p. [92]–95; Sir Bertrand, A Fragment,

p. [96]–102; Bishop Bruno, An Ancient Fragment [verse], p. [103]–105; Cornelius Agrippa's Bloody Book [verse], p. [106]–108; Narrative Of The Sufferings Of James Bristow. . . , p. [109]–179; adv. list of 7 books only one of which, *The Surprising Adventures of Robinson Crusoe,* is a child's book. *The History Of Perourou* and *The History Of Auguste and Madelaine* can be considered children's books. The others in this volume are open to question. The book is included because of these two tales. Scottish ed. title: *The History Of Perourou; Or, The Bellows Mender; . . .* By Miss Williams. Edinburgh: J. Morren, 1817.

Bowe°; Shaw 3559.

WINLOVE, SOLOMON, Esq. *pseud.*

1437.1 — AN APPROVED COLLECTION OF ENTERTAINING STORIES. Calculated Instruction and Amusement Of All Little Masters and Misses. By Solomon Winlove, Esq. The First Worcester Edition. Printed at Worcester, Massachusetts, By Isaiah Thomas. Sold at his Bookstore in Worcester, and by him and Company in Boston. MDCCLXXXIX.

fr.[2], t.[3], [4–7], 8–128 p.; illus.; 10.5 cm.; bound in red scalloped marbled paper over bds. This book contains the first American printing of Perrault's *Cinderella* and an early printing of *Little Red Riding Hood* which appeared earlier in *The House That Jack Built.* [1787?], no. **616.3.**

English ed. London: adv. by F. Newbery in *London Chronical,* 27–9 Dec. 1768.

Welch° (p. 17–18, 49–50, 63–64; 119–122; 127–128 wanting); MWA; Evans 22283.

1437.2 —— —— Boston: Printed and sold by Samuel Hall, No. 53 Cornhill. 1796.

fr.[2], t.[3], [4–7], 8–128 p.; illus.; 10 cm. Printer's type ornaments are present. Adv. by Samuel Hall, 1792 in **1408.33;** 1794 in **673.3;** 1795 in **1384.2;** 1798 in **408.6.**

MWA° (rebound, fr.[2], wanting); MB (bpl. pasted over fr.[2]); NjP (bound in violet and green Dutch paper over bds.); Evans 48029; Hamilton 166.

1438 — MR WINLOVE'S LECTURES ON MORAL SUBJECTS < Price six-pence > Philadelphia: adv. by Francis Bailey, 1793 in **773.1.**

1439.1 WINTER [cut] Old Age—the Winter of Life. Printed & sold by Samuel Wood, No. 362, Pearl-Street. New-York. 1807.

t.[1], [2–16] p.; illus.; 8 cm.; green Dutch paper covers. Adv. by S. Wood, 1808 in **643.1.**
MWA°; Shaw 14231.

1439.2 ——— Printed & sold by Samuel Wood, at the Juvenile Book-store, No. 357, Pearl-Street. New-York. 1809.

t.[1], [2–16] p.; illus.; 8 cm.; buff paper covers speckled with black. Adv. by S. Wood, 1810 in **1188.1,** and 1812 in **1188.3.**
NHi°.

1439.3 ——— New-York: Printed & sold by Samuel Wood, at the Juvenile Book-store, No. 357, Pearl-street. 1814.

t.[1], [2–16] p.; illus.; 8.5 cm.; pr. & illus. buff paper covers.
MWA°; MWA-W (bound with other books in no. **637.1**); Shaw 33706.

1439.4 ——— *Nerv-York* [*sic. i.e.* New-York]: Printed And Sold By S. Wood, at the Juvenile Book-store, No. 357, Pearl-street. 1815.

t.[1], [2–16] p.; illus.; 8.5 cm.; pr. & illus. paper covers.
Cover title: Winter. Sold by Samuel Wood, New-York.
MWA°; CtHi (covers wanting).

1439.5 ——— *Nerv-York* [*sic. i.e.* New-York]: Printed And Sold By Samuel Wood & Sons, at the Juvenile Book-store, No. 357, Pearl-street. 1816.

t.[1], [2–16] p.; illus.; 8 cm.
MWA-T° (bound with other books in *The Infant's Cabinet. See no.* **637.2.**

1439.6 ——— *Nerv-York* [*sic. i.e.* New-York]: Published by Samuel Wood & Sons, No. 261, Pearl-street, And Samuel S. Wood & Co. No. 212, Market-st. Baltimore. 1818.

t.[1], [2–16] p.; illus.; 8 cm.
MWA° (covers wanting); Shaw 46835.

1440 THE WINTER EVENING, Or Stories Instructive and Amusing. For Young Persons. With Cuts. New-York: Printed For T. B. Jansen & Co., Booksellers, No. 248, Pearl-Street. 1802.

t.[1], [2–3], 4–31 p.; illus.; 14 cm.; marbled paper covers. Adv. by Thomas B. Jansen, 1805

in **1371.5.** Adv. by George Jansen & Lewis B. Jansen, 1808 in **1232.**
NNC-T°.

1441 WISDOM IN MINIATURE: An Excellent Toy For Good Little Children. By A Friend Of Youth. S. Ide's print [4 dots] N. Ipswich [N.H.] 1815.

t.[1], [2–3], 4–28 p.; 9.5 cm.; ornamental buff paper covers; 14 leaves, one leaf at both front and rear probably missing.
MWA°; Shaw 36601.

1442.1 WISDOM IN MINIATURE; Or Instruction for Infant Minds. Adorned with Cuts. Rutland [Vt.]: Printed by Fay & Davison. 1813.

t.[3], [4–5], 6–14 p.; illus.; 10 cm.
VtHi°; McCorison 1558; Shaw 30559.

1442.2 ——— Windsor (Vt.), Printed by Jesse Cochran. And sold whole-sale and retail at his Book-Store. 1814.

fr.[2], t.[3], [4–5], 6–31 p.; illus.; 10 cm.; pr. & illus. brownish-buff paper covers.
MWA° (fr.[2], p. 31 & covers mut.); McCorison 1687; Shaw 33710.

1442.3 ——— Windsor (Vt.), Printed By Jesse Cochran. And sold whole-sale and retail at his Book-Store. 1815.

fr.[2], t.[3], [4–5], 6–31 p.; illus.; 10 cm.; pr. & illus. buff paper covers.
MWA°; CLU; CtHi; VtHi; McCorison 1801; Shaw 36602.

1443.1 WISDOM IN MINIATURE: Or The Young Gentleman's and Lady's Magazine.— < No. 1. > Being a collection of Sentences Divine and Moral. [3 lines quot.] Hartford: Printed By J. Babcock. 1796.

fr.[2], t.[3], [4–5], 6–30, [31] p.; illus.; 10 cm.; orange paper covers.
MWA°; CLU; CtHi (p.[31] & rear cover wanting); MB; NN (fr.[2], p.[31] & covers wanting; rebound); PP (fr.[2], p.[31] & covers wanting); Evans 37650.

1443.2 ——— Magazine. Being a collection of Sentences, Divine and Moral. [3 lines quot.] Hartford: Printed By John Babcock. 1798.

fr.[2], t.[3], [4–5], 6–30, [31, cut] p.; illus.; 11 cm.; buff paper covers, speckled with green and brown.
MWA°; CtHi; DLC; MH; Evans 35045.

1443.3 —— Hartford: Printed by John Babcock. 1800.

fr.[2], t.[3], [4–5] 6–30, [31, illus.] p.; illus.; 11 cm.

CtHi*; DLC; Evans 29125.

1443.4 —— Stonington [Conn.]—Printed by S. Trumbull. 1801.

t.[3], [4–5], 6–30 p.; illus.; 10 cm.

CtHi* (fr.[2], p. 31 & covers wanting); Shaw 50268.

1443.5 —— Hartford Printed by John Babcock. 1802.

fr.[2], t.[3], [4–5], 6–30, [31, illus.] p.; illus.; 11 cm.; Dutch paper covers.

MWA-W*; CtHi (p. [2–4] & cover wanting); MH (i. st. p. [17]); MWA-T; Shaw 3571.

1443.6 —— Philadelphia: Printed By John Adams For Jacob Johnson. 1802.

[1], t.[2], [3, alphabet], [4], 5–23, [24] p.; illus.; 9 cm.; p.[1] and [24] each have an illustration surrounded by a wide border and serve for the covers, since there are no separate paper covers.

CtHi*.

1443.7 —— Newport [R. I.]: Printed by Oliver Farnsworth. 1803.

fr.[2], t.[3], [4–5], 6–30, [31, alphabet] p.; illus.; 11 cm.; gray wallpaper covers.

MWA*.

1443.8 —— [2 lines of quot.] From Sidney's Press, Hew-Haven [*sic. i.e.* New-Haven] 1805.

fr.[2], t.[3], [4–5], 6–30, [31, illus.] p.; illus.; 10.5 cm.; orange Dutch paper covers.

MWA*; NRU; Shaw 9753.

1443.9 —— Embellished with cuts. Philadelphia: Printed By John Adams. 1805.

fr.[2], t.[3], [4, alphabets–5], 6–30, [31, adv.] p.; illus.; 10 cm.; olive paper covers. Part of a large publisher's remainder, all of which have olive paper covers. RWe copy with pink paper covers is not part of the remainder.

MWA-W*; CCamarSJ; CLU; CSmH; CtHi; DLC; MiU; NHi; NN; NNC-Pl; PHi; PP; RP; RWe; Shaw 9752.

1443.10 —— Moral. Albany: Printed And Sold By The Gross Or Dozen, By E. And E. Hosford. 1806.

fr.[2], t.[3], [4, alphabets–5], 6–30, [31, illus.] p.; illus.; 10 cm.; green Dutch paper covers.

MWA-W*.

1443.11 —— Moral. Ornamented with Engravings. Albany: Printed By E. And E. Hosford. 1806.

fr.[2], t.[3], [4–5], 6–30, [31, illus.] p.; illus.; 10 cm.; paper covers.

Greenaway*.

1443.12 —— Moral. [2 lines quot.] From Sidney's Press, New-Haven. 1806.

fr.[2], t.[3], [4, alphabets–5], 6–30, [31, illus.] p.; illus.; 10.5 cm.; wallpaper covers.

MWA-W*; CtY (Dutch paper covers); NN-C covers wanting, i. st. on t.[3]); Shaw 11888.

1443.13 —— From Sidney's Press, New-Haven. 1807.

fr.[2], t.[3], [4, alphabet–5], 6–30, [31, illus.]; illus.; 10.5 cm.; violet and green Dutch paper covers.

Welch*; CLU; CtHi; MWA; Shaw 14232.

1443.14 —— Moral. Ornamented with Cuts. Albany: Printed By E. & E. Hosford. 1808.

fr.[2], t.[3], [4–5], 6–30, [31, illus.] p.; illus.; 10 cm.

MWA*; (p.[5]–6 & covers wanting); NNC-PL; Shaw 16754.

1443.15 —— [2 lines quot.] From Sidney's Press, New-Haven. 1808.

fr.[2], t.[3], [4, alphabet–5], 6–30, [31, illus.] p.; 10.5 cm.; paper covers. The first parenthesis around p. "8)" is wanting.

CtHi*; MSaE; MWA (fr.[2], p.[31] & covers wanting); Shaw 16756.

1443.16 —— Moral. Ornamented with Engravings. Albany: Printed By E. And E. Hosford. 1809.

fr.[2], t.[3], [4–5], 6–30, [31, illus.] p.; illus.; 10.5 cm.

MWA* (original covers wanting); OCHP; Shaw 19251.

1443.17 ——— [3 lines quot.] Montreal [Canada]: Printed By Nahum Mower. 1809.
t.[3], [4–5], 6–31 p.; 10.5 cm.
MSaE°.

1443.18 ——— [2 lines quot.] Adorned with Cuts. From Sidney's Press, New-Haven, 1809.
fr.[2], t.[3], [4, alphabet–5], 6–30, [31, adv.] p.; illus.; 11 cm.; green Dutch paper covers. Page [5] the woodcut shows a side view of a woman facing three children, p. 24, last line, first word "For" spelt "Fur."
MWA-W°.

1443.19 ——— Adorned with Cuts. From Sidney's Press New-Haven. 1809.
fr.[2], t.[3], [4–5], 6–30, [31, adv.] p.; illus.; 10.5 cm.; Dutch paper covers. A variant of the preceding Sidney's Press 1809 edition. The woodcut on p. [5] shows a back view of a seated woman facing four children. The type setting and other cuts are identical with no. **1443.18.**
DLC°; MWA; (p.[2–4], 29–[31], & covers wanting); Shaw 19252.

1443.20 ——— Ornamented with Engravings. Albany: Printed By E. And E. Hosford. 1810.
fr.[2], t.[3], [4–5], 6–30, [31, illus.] p.; illus.; 10.5 cm.; pr. & illus. buff paper covers; cover title undated.
MWA°; CtY; MNF; NPV; PP (fr.[2], p.[31] & covers wanting); Shaw 22072.

1443.21 ——— [2 lines quot.] Adorned with Cuts. From Sidney's Press. New Haven, 1810.
fr.[2], t.[3], [4, alphabet–5], 6–30, [31] p.; illus.; 11 cm.; pr. & illus. yellow paper covers.
Cover title: Wisdom In Miniature. Published by I. Cooke & Co. Universal Book-Store, Church-Street, New-Haven. In the word "collection" on t.[3] the "c" is lower case & "Press" is spelled with 2 "ss"; the date 1810 is 8 mm. long; p. [4] has the alphabet, with line 1, A–F; p. 20, line 8, "Virtne" [*sic. i.e.* Virtue]; p. 27, line 2, "control," spelled correctly; last line p. 30, "ven".
MWA-W; MHi.

1443.22 ——— From Sidney's Press. New-Haven, 1810.
fr.[2], t.[3], [4–5], 6–30, [31] p.; illus.; 10.5 cm.; red paper covers. This variant can be identified as follows:

Cover title: Wisdom In Miniature./[a cut of a Grecian temple]/Published by I. Cooke & Co./ Universal Book-Store, Ch[urch-]/Street, New-Hav[en.] In the word "Collection" on t.[3] the "C" is in caps., the word "Press" is spelled "fs" & the 1810 is smaller; p.[4], line 1, includes letters A–E; p. 20, line 8, "virtue" is spelled correctly; p. 27, line 2, "control" is spelled "controul," The type setting on p. 27 and 30 is different from the above. The last line p. 30: "into Heaven."
MWA°; Shaw 22073.

1443.23 ——— Windsor, (Vt.) Printed by Farnsworth & Churchill. 1810.
fr.[2], t.[3], [4–5], 6–30, [31, alphabets] p.; illus.; 9.5 cm.; pr. & illus. buff paper covers.
MWA°; CLU; NPV; PP; VtHi (p.[31] wanting); McCorison 1240; Shaw 22074.

1443.24 ——— And Moral. Ornamented with Engravings. Windham [Conn.]: Printed by Samuel Webb. 1813.
fr.[2], t.[3], [4–5], 6–23 p.; illus.; 9.5 cm.; blue-gray marbled paper covers.
MWA°; Shaw 30560.

1443.25 ——— Ornamented with Engravings. Albany: Printed By E. & E. Hosford. 1814.
fr.[2], t.[3], [4–5], 6–30, [31, illus.] p.; illus.; 10 cm.; pr. & illus. buff paper covers; cover title imprint: Albany: Printed By E. And E. Hosford.
MWA°; CtHi; PP (covers wanting); Shaw 33709.

1443.26 ——— Albany: Printed By E. & E. Hosford. 1816.
fr.[2], t.[3], [4–5], 6–30, [31] p.; illus.; 10 cm.; pr. & illus. buff paper covers; text pr. on blue-gray paper; cover title imprint: ——— E. And E. Hosford.
MWA°; NNC-Pl; NNG; Shaw 39845.

1443.27 ——— Albany: Printed By E. & E. Hosford. 1818.
fr.[2], t.[3], [4–5], 6–30, [31] p.; illus.; 10.5 cm.; pr. & illus. blue paper covers; cover title undated.
MWA°; DLC; Shaw 46841.

1444.1 WISDOM IN MINIATURE; Or The Young Gentleman's And Lady's Pleasing Instructor, Being A Collection Of Sentences, Divine, Moral And Historical, Selected from the writings of many ingenious and learned Authors, both ancient and modern. Intended not only for the use of Schools, but as a Pocket Companion for the Youth of both Sexes. First Worcester Edition. Worcester, From The Press Of Isaiah Thomas, jun. 1795.

fr.[ii], t.[i], [ii–iii], iv–viii, [9], 10–222 p.; front. only illus.; 11 cm.; bound in leather.

English ed. title 1: *Wisdom In Miniature; Or The Young Gentleman and Lady's Pleasing Instructor.* Coventry: 2 ed. Luckman. [n.d.].

English ed. title 2: *Wisdom In Miniature Or The Pleasing Instructor.* London: Lane And Newman, 1804.

MWA*; CLU; CtHi (t.[1] mut.); NNC-Pl; PP (p. 215–216 mut.); Evans 29914.

1444.2 ——— Second Worcester Edition. Printed at Worcester (Massachusetts), By Thomas, Son & Thomas: Sold Wholesale And Retail By Them, At Their Bookstore.—October, 1796.

fr.[ii], t.[i], [ii–iii], iv–viii, [9], 10–192 p.; engr. front only illus. signed *Doolittle Sc* [Amos Doolittle]; 11 cm.; bound in leather.

Welch*; BM; CLU; CtHi; CtHT; CtY; DLC (p. 177–178 mut.); MB (per st. on t.[i]); MH; MWA (copy 1 rebound, I. Thomas copy; copy 2, rebound in blue leather); MWHi; N; NN (rebound); NNC-Pl (p. 13–14 mut.); PP (fr.[ii] wanting); RPJCB; Evans 31651; Weiss 1936.

1444.3 ——— Pocket Companion for the Youth of Both Sexes in America. Third Edition. Brooklyn [N.Y.]: Printed by T. Kirk. 1800.

t.[i], [ii–iii], iv–v, [vi, bl.], [7], 8–208 p.; 10.5 cm.; bound in leather.

CtY*; NNC-Pl (t.[i] mut.); PP; Evans 39126.

1444.4 ——— Youth of both Sexes. [2 lines quot.] Philadelphia: Printed By S. W. Conrad, For Ezekiel Cooper, No. 118, North Fourth-Street. 1801.

t.[1], [ii–iii], iv–vi, [7], 8–235, [236–237, contents], [238–240, adv. list of books] p.; 10.5 cm.; bound in leather.

MWA*; Shaw 50267.

1444.5 ——— and modern. Designed not only for the use of Schools, but as a Pocket Companion

for the Youth of both Sexes. [1 line quot.] Psalm cxi. 10. Bennington [Vt.]: Printed By Anthony Haswell. 1808.

t.[i], [ii–iii], iv–v, [vi, bl.], [7], 8–144 p.; 14 cm.; bound in blue paper over w. bds., leather spine.

MWA*; ICU; Vt. (per st. on t.[i]); VtHi (covers wanting); McCorison 1050; Shaw 16755.

1445.1 THE WISDOM OF CROP THE CONJUROR. Exemplified In several Characters of Good and Bad Boys with an impartial Account of the celebrated Tom Trot, Who Rode before all the Boys in the Kingdom till he arrived at the Top of the Hill, called Learning. Written For the Imitation of those who love themselves. The First Worcester Edition. Worcester, (Massachusetts) Printed By Isaiah Thomas, And Sold At His Book Store. MDCCLXXXVI.

fr.[ii], t.[iii], [iv], v–viii, 9–43, [44–47, adv. list of books]; illus.; 9.5 cm.; Dutch paper covers.

English ed. London: John Marshall and Co. at No. 4, *Aldermary Church-Yard,* in *Bow-Lane.* < Price Two PENCE Bound and Gilt. > [1787?], mss. inscription, p. [iv]: "William Wilde his Book 1788 87".

MWA* (rebound); PP; Evans 20153.

1445.2 ——— themselves. To Which Are Added, The Farmer, And His Two Daughters, And The Old Mouse. The Second Worcester Edition. Printed at Worcester, Massachusetts, By Isaiah Thomas, Sold Wholesale and Retail at his Bookstore. MDCCXCIV.

fr.[ii], t.[iii], [iv], v–viii, 9–59, [60–63, adv. list of books] p.; illus.; 10 cm.; silver paper covers; p. 42 [*sic. i.e.* 43]. The oval cut, p. 44, shows "The Farmer" standing between his two daughters. Another oval cut, p. 53, depicts "The Old Mouse" talking to her family. Neither of these cuts was used in I. Thomas' 1786 edition of *Little Robin Red Breast,* no. **782.**

MWA-W* (p. [63] mut.); MB; MWA (rebound); PP; Evans 28117.

1445.3 [——— The Third Worcester Edition. Printed at Worcester Massachusetts, by Isaiah Thomas Jun. 1804?] [imaginary title].

fr.[ii], [v], vi–vii, [viii bl.], [9], 10–63 p.; illus.; 10 cm.; the "3" of p. 38 is not struck, p. [51] is not struck. The above edition and imprint

are conjectural. The cuts on most of the pages are the same as those found in the first and second Worcester editions of Isaiah Thomas, **1445.1** and **1445.2**. The book was undoubtedly printed by him. The cut on p. 11 has the same breaks in the right top border as in no. **1445.2**, p. 11. On p. 33 the tailpiece of the three-masted square rigger does not appear in no. **1445.2**.
MH° (t. [iii] & p. [iv] wanting; p. 23–26 bound after p. 30).

WISEMAN, MASTER BILLY *pseud.*
1446.1 — THE PUZZLING CAP: A Choice Collection of Riddles, In Familiar Verse. By Master Billy Wiseman [4 lines of verse] Adorned With Cuts.— New-York e— [*sic. i.e.* "—"] Printed By William Durell For Thomas B. Jansen & Co. 1800.
  fr.[2], t.[3], [4, alphabets], 5–31 p.; illus.; 10 cm.; front, brown paper cover speckled with black; rear, brown wallpaper cover; p. 29[*sic. i.e.* 21].
  English & Scottish ed. London: adv. by F. Newbery, 1775 in *The Cries Of London.*
  MWA-W° (p. 23–24, 27–31 wanting); Evans 49141.

1446.2 — ——— New-York e— [*sic. i.e.* "—"] Printed by William Dur[ell] For John Low. 1800.
  fr.[2], t.[3], [4, alphabets], 5–31 p.; illus.; 10.5 cm.; buff paper covers speckled & circled with red; p. 29 [*sic. i.e.* 21]. The book is identical with no. **1446.1** except for the third line of the imprint on the title page: "For John Low." Both books were probably printed at the same time and the name of the bookseller left vacant until each individual placed an order.
  MWA-W° (fr.[2], t.[3], p.[4] have the outer eighth of the page wanting affecting some of the letters along the margin of the page); Evans 39127.

1446.3 — ——— Of Riddles, By Master Billy Wiseman. [3 lines of verse] Ornamented with Engravings. Hudson [N. Y.]: Printed by A. Stoddard, 1812.
  fr.[2], t.[3], [4, alphabets–5], 6–31 p.; illus.; 10.5 cm.; illus. blue-gray paper covers.
  MWA-W°.

1446.4 [— ——— Albany: Printed By E. & E. Hosford. *ca.* 1813] [imaginary title, imprint and date].

[5], 6–28 p.; illus.; 10.5 cm. The text is the same as no. **1446.3** except that p. 20 in this edition has "A Fish." [cut of a fish] [8 lines of verse], while in the Hudson edition there is "A Man In The Stocks" [cut] [7 lines of verse]. All illustrations are E. and E. Hosford cuts. The cut of the bear, p. 28, does not have a double rule border at the top and sides. This is the state of the cut from 1808–1818. The rest of the cuts give no clue as to the possible date. The illustration of the "Grass-Hopper," p. 16, has a nick in the left end of the top border which seems to be as wide as in the impressions of the cut from 1808–1810. The date [*ca.* 1813] is conjectural being the midpoint between 1808 and 1818.
NB° (fr.[2], t.[3], p.[4], 29–31 and covers wanting).

1447.1 A WONDERFUL ACCOUNT OF A LITTLE GIRL of nine years old, Who lives in the Town of Jerico, in the State of Vermont; by the name of Hannah Coy. Who was Converted to the knowledge of the Gospel of Jesus Christ in a marvelous manner, as she has often related, and is still ready to relate to all that ask her. Also, An Account Of A Girl of twelve years of age, Who lived on Lord Collier's Manor, in the Province of Lower Canada; who was converted to the love of God in a wonderful manner, and it proved to be the hopeful conversion of the whole family, and a great many of the neighbors in the town. Likewise An Account Of The Vision or Trance of a Young Woman, Who lives on the West side of Lake Champlain, in the State of New-York, in the town called Pleasant Valley. Her wonderful discoveries and conversion, and a wonderful reformation which followed it. The whole being taken from the mouths of these three Girls before a great number of witnesses. Together With An Account Of The Sickness And Death, As Was Supposed, Of The Wife of Mr. Stone, of Stockbridge, State Of Vermont. Who from a state of Death, to appearance, opened her eyes, called for her clothes, got up and dressed herself, and said, God hath healed me. Printed For The Purchaser. 1800.
  t.[1], [2–3], 4–12 p.; 19 cm. According to McCorison the pamphlet was printed in Windsor, Vermont by A. Spooner and advertised in the *Vermont Journal,* May 25, 1801.
  VtHi°; McCorison 590; Evans 39129.

1447.2 ———— [same as **1447.1**] Hannah Coy. — Who ———— she has often related. Also, An Account Of A Girl of twelve years of age, ———— proved to be a hopful conversion of the whole family, ———— Vision and Trance of a young woman, who lived on ———— Printed at Wrentham [Mass.], 1813.

　　t.[1], [2–3], 4–12 p.; 16 cm.
　　MH*.

1448 A WONDERFUL ACCOUNT OF THE CONVERSION OF TWO YOUNG GIRLS. Windsor, (Vermont) Printed By A. Spooner. 1795.

　　t.[1], [2–3], 4–12 p.; title page vignette only illus.; 17 cm.
　　Nh*; McCorison 379.

THE WONDERFUL ADVANTAGES OF ADVENTURING IN THE LOTTERY!!! *See* Cheap Repository, no. **169.4.**

1449.1 THE WONDERFUL ADVANTAGES OF ADVENTURING IN THE LOTTERY! The Gamester; And Black Giles, &c. Philadelphia: Published By Benjamin & Thomas Kite, No. 20, North Third Street. William Brown Printer, 24 Church-alley. 1811.

　　t.[1], [2–3], 4–108 p.; 13.5 cm.; bound in pr. blue paper over bds.; cover title imprint: Philadelphia: Published By Johnson & Warner, No. 147, Market Street. 1811.
　　English ed. London: Entered at Stationer's Hall, January 26th 1797, by Hannah More [for the *Cheap Repository*]. See no. **169.4** for English editions.
　　MWA*; NNC-Pl (bound in unprinted blue paper over bds.); Shaw 24480.

1449.2 ———— Lottery. Philadelphia: Printed For Benjamin Johnson, No. 22, North Second street, next door to the church. 1813.

　　fr. [ii], t.[1], [2–3], 4–23 p.; illus.; 13 cm.; pr. & illus. paper covers.
　　PPeSchw*; Shaw 27669.

1449.3 ———— New-York: Printed And Sold By Samuel Wood, At The Juvenile Book-Store, No. 357, Pearl-Street. 1814.

　　t.[i], [ii–iii], iv–viii, [9], 10–42, [43–46, adv. list of books] p.; illus.; 14 cm.; pr. & illus. yellow paper covers.
　　Cover title: The Lottery. New-York: ————

1814; p. [44–46] adv. of books printed by Johnson & Warner, Philadelphia.
　　MWA-W* (rebound); CtY (covers wanting); Shaw 33712.

1449.4 ———— New York: Printed And Sold By Samuel Wood, At The Juvenile Book-Store, No. 357, Pearl-Street. 1815.

　　t.[i], [ii–iii], iv–viii, [9], 10–45, [46–49, adv. list of books] p.; illus.; 13.5 cm.; pr. & illus. buff paper covers.
　　Cover title: The Lottery. Printed ———— Pearl-Street. New-York.
　　MWA* (copy 1, a separate copy; copy 2, bound with other books in vol. II of no. **191**; Shaw 36606.

1449.5 ———— *Nerv-York* [*sic. i.e.* New-York]: Published By Samuel Wood & Sons, No. 261, Pearl-Street; And Samuel S. Wood & Co. 212, Market-street, Baltimore. 1820.

　　t.[i], [ii–iii], iv–viii, [9], 10–45 p.; illus.; 14.5 cm.; pr. & illus. buff paper covers.
　　Cover title: The Lottery. New-York: Published by ———— Baltimore.
　　NWebyC*; Shoemaker 2010.

1450.1 THE WONDERFUL EXPLOIT OF GUY, EARL OF WARWICK. With Original Plates. Philadelphia: Published and Sold Wholesale by Wm. Charles, and may be had of all the Booksellers. Price, plain, 12 1-2 Cents—Colored, 18 3-4 Cents. 1814. [cover title].

　　[1–8] p. engr. on one side only of 8 leaves; illus.; 13.5 cm.; pr. paper covers. Adv. by Wm. Charles, 1815 in **748**.
　　Ball.*

1450.2 ———— Philadelphia: Published and sold by Wm. Charles, No. 32, S. Third-st. Price, plain, 12 1–2 cents—coloured, 18 3–4 cents. 1817. [cover title].

　　[1–8] p. engr. on one side only of 8 leaves; illus.; 12.5 cm.; pr. buff paper covers.
　　DLC* (rear paper cover mostly wanting); Shaw 40971.

1451.1 THE WONDERFUL HISTORY OF AN ENCHANTED CASTLE, Kept By Giant Grumbo, The Most Humaine And Tender-Hearted Giant In The Known World. Embellished with Cuts. Albany:

Printed And Sold By The Gross Or Dozen, By E. And E. Hosford. 1806.

> fr.[2], t.[3], [4–5], 6–31 p.; illus.; 10.5 cm.; ornamented yellow-brown paper covers.
> English ed. York: adv. by R. Spence, [*ca.* 1789] for 1d. under the title *The History of an Enchanted Castle kept by the Giant Grumbo, in Fairy Tales, Pleasing and Profitable For All Little Gentlemen and Ladies.*
> MWA°; Shaw 11893.

1451.2 ―――― Ornamented with Engravings. Albany: Printed By E. And E. Hosford. 1806.

> fr.[2], t.[3], [4–5], 6–31 p.; illus.; 10 cm.; blue and pink marbled paper covers; the cut on p. 7 is printed upside down.
> MWA-W°.

1451.3 ―――― Albany: Printed By E. And E. Hosford. 1808.

> t.[3], [4–5], 6–30 p.; illus.; 10.5 cm.
> MWA° (fr.[2], p.[31] and covers wanting); Shaw 16760.

1451.4 ―――― Albany: Printed By E. And E. Hosford. 1809.

> fr.[2], t.[3], [4–5], 6–31 p.; illus.; 10.5 cm.; pr. & illus. buff paper covers;
> Cover title: The Enchanted Castle. Albany: Printed By E. And E. Hosford.
> MWA°; N. (three-fourths of p. 31 and rear cover wanting, fr.[2], and front cover mut.); NNC-LS (covers wanting, i. st. on p.[1]); Shaw 19257.

1451.5 ―――― Albany: Printed By E. And E. Hosford. 1810.

> fr.[2], t.[3], [4–5], 6–31 p.; illus.; 10.5 cm.; pr. & illus. paper covers; cover title undated.
> RPB°; MWA-W (mut.); NNC-LS (i. st. on front cover); Shaw 22079.

1451.6 ―――― Albany: Printed By E. & E. Hosford. 1811.

> fr.[2], t.[3], [4–5], 6–31 p.; illus.; 10 cm.; pr. & illus. buff paper covers; cover title same as no. **1451.4**.
> MWA-W°.

1451.7 ―――― Albany: Printed By E. & E. Hosford. 1813.

> fr.[2], t.[3], [4–5], 6–31 p.; illus.; 10 cm.;

pr. & illus. buff paper covers; cover title same as no. **1451.4**.
MWA°; CSt; CtY; PP (front cover mut.); Shaw 30563.

1451.8 ―――― Giant In The World. Hartford: Printed By C. Hosmer. 1815.

> fr.[2], t.[3], [4, alphabets–5], 6–31 p.; illus.; 10 cm.; pr. & illus. paper covers; cover title imprint: Hartford: Printed by Charles Hosmer. 1815.
> IU°.

1451.9 ―――― Ornamented with Engravings. Albany: Printed By E. & E. Hosford. 1816.

> fr.[2], t.[3], [4, alphabets–5], 6–31 p.; illus.; 10 cm.; pr. & illus. buff paper covers; cover title imprint: Albany: Printed By E. And E. Hosford.
> NCooHi°; MWA-T.

WOODD, BASIL 1760–1831

1452.1 ― MEMOIR OF MOWHEE, A Youth From New Zealand, Who died at Paddington, December 28, 1816. By The Rev. Basil Woodd. Philadelphia: Published by the Sunday and Adult School Union. Clark & Raser, Printers. 1818.

> t.[1], [2–3], 4–48 p.; title vignette only illus.; 13.5 cm.
> NN° (rebound, with other books, covers wanting, i. st. on t.[1]).

1452.2 ― MEMOIR OF MOWHEE, A Young New Zealander, Who Died At Paddington, On Saturday, December 28, 1816. In a Letter Addressed To The Rev. Josiah Pratt B.D. Secretary of the Church Missionary Society. By The Rev. Basil Wood, [*sic. i.e.* Woodd] M.A. From the Second London Edition. Published By S. G. Goodrich, At The Hartford Sunday School Repository. 1820.

> t.[1], [2], 3–24 p.; 13.5 cm.; blue paper covers.
> CtHi°; DLC (buff paper covers); Shoemaker 4321.

WOODLAND, MISS M. *fl.* 1804

1453 ―TALES FOR MOTHERS AND DAUGHTERS. By Miss Woodland. Volume I. [II.] New-York: Published By W. B. Gilley, No. 92 Broadway. 1818.

> vol. I: ½t.[1], [2, bl.], [i, bl.], fr.[ii]; 1st t.[3], [4–5], 6–8, 2nd t.[7], [8–9], 10–96, [i, bl.], fr.[ii]; 3rd t.[3], [4–5], 6–144 p.; 2 front. only illus.; vol. II: ½t.[1], [2, bl.], [i, bl.], fr.[ii],

1st t.[3], [4], 2nd t.[3], [4–5], 6–106, [1–2, bl.], [i, bl.], fr.[ii], 3rd t.[3], [4–5]; 6–112 p.; 2 front. only illus.; 2 vols.; 14.5 cm.; bound in blue paper over bds., red leather spine. The imprints of the 2nd and 3rd title pages in vols. I. [II] are: New-York: Published By W. B. Gilley, No. 92 Broadway. 1818. The printer's name "N. Van Riper . . . printer . . . Greenwich." appears on the verso of the 2nd & 3rd title pages of vol. I. [II] and the verso of ½t.[1] of Vol. II.

Vol. I. 2nd title: A Tale Of Warning; Or, The Victims Of Indolence. By Miss Woodland.

———

Vol. I. 3rd title: Bear And Forebear; Or, The History Of Julia Marchmont. By Miss Woodland.———

Vol. II. 2nd title: Rose And Agnes; Or, The Dangers of Partiality. By Miss Woodland.

———

Vol. II. 3rd title: Matilda Mortimer; Or, False Pride. By Miss Woodland.———

English ed. of *Matilda Mortimer*. London: Tabart & Co. 1809, with frontispiece dated May 1807.

MWA-W* CLU (vol. I.); DLC; MnU; NjR (vol. I. all before 2nd t.[7], fr.[ii], 3rd t. [3] & covers wanting); PP (imp.); RWe; Shaw 46856.

1454.1 THE WORLD TURNED UPSIDE DOWN or the Comical Metamorphoses A Work entirely calculated to excite Laughter in Grown Persons and promote Morality in the Young Ones of both Sexes: Decorated with 34 Copper Plates curiously Drawn and elegantly Engraved [4 lines of verse] Boston Printed and Sold by John D. M'Dougall [an]d Company two doors South of the Treasurer's Office. [1780?].

t.[iii], [iv, bl.], [1], 2–64 p.; 29 engr. pl. including t.[iii]; 12 cm.; marbled paper covers. Comparing this edition with the English Ryland edition, from which it was probably reprinted and the plates copied, there should be 34 plates, fr.[ii], t.[iii], pl. opp. p.2, followed by 31 pl. each, opposite uneven-numbered pages or pages 3–63. The plates are copied in the reverse from the London Ryland edition. The pl. opp. p. 2 "A Man struggling through the Globe" faces the "Introduction," p.[1], in the English ed. John M'Dougall & Co printed only in 1780–81. (MWA cat.).

English ed. title 1: *The World Turned Upside Down; or the Comical Metamorphoses.* London: Edward Ryland. [*ca.* 1765].

English ed. title 2: *The World Turned Upside-Down Illustrated by Wonderful Prints.* [London?]: [1805?].

English ed. title 3: ——— *Upside Down, or the folly of man exemplyfy'd in twelve comical relations.* London: C. Dicey. [n.d.].

English ed. title 3a: ——— *exemplefied* [*sic. i.e.* exemplified] ——— [London] [1750?] [a chap-book].

English ed. title 3b: ——— *exemplified* ——— London: [n.d.].

English ed. title 4: ——— *Upside Down; Or no News, and Strange News.* York: J. Kendrew. [*ca.* 1820].

OO* (fr.[ii]), p. 59–60, pl. opp. p. 9, 11, 13, 59 wanting); Evans 43918.

1454.2 ——— Boston Printed and Sold by I. Norman N⁰ 75 Newbury Street. [1795?].

fr.[ii], t.[i], [ii–iii, bl.], [iv, pl. opp. p. [2]], 2–64, [pl. opp. p. [64] p.; 34 engr. pl. including fr.[ii], t.[i], pl. opp. p. [2], pl. [I–XXX] or a pl. for each of 30 tales, plus pl. [XXXI] opp. p. 64, or the pl. for the conclusion; 10.5 cm.; buff paper covers; plates redrawn from the London Edward Ryland, English ed. title 1, probably by John Norman. The front fly leaf of the MWA-W copy has a mss. inscription, "Aaron Toppen Townsends' fine Picture Book 1795". The MWA copy also has a mss. fly leaf inscription: "Henry Mathewson's Book Stolen from a thief in the year 1797".

MWA-W* (rear cover wanting); MWA (bound in Dutch paper over w.bds.; p. [49]–62, pl. [XXIV–XXXI] or pl. opp. p. [49], [51], [53], [55], [58], [60] wanting); CtHi* (p.[53]–60, pl. [XXV–XXX] or pl. opp. p. [51], [53], [55], [58], [60], [62] wanting, rear cover half wanting); Evans 45805.

WORLD'S DISPLAYED. *See* Campbell, John, no. **154.1**.

WRIGHT, JOHN *fl. ca.* 1720–1730
1455.1 — SPIRITUAL SONGS FOR CHILDREN: Or Poems On several Subjects and Occasions. By J. Wright. The Fourth Edition. Boston: Printed and Sold by Z. Fowle, at his Printing-Office, in Back-Street. 1764.

t.[1], [2], 3–64 p.; 11 cm.

English ed. London: Joseph Marshall, 1727.

MWA° (rear cover wanting); Evans 41512.

1455.2 ——— The Seventh Edition. London: Printed. Boston Reprinted, By Nathaniel Coverly. MDCCLXXXIV.

t.[1], [2–4], 5–47 p.; 17 cm.; p. 27 numbered "2".

MSaE° (p. 47, mostly wanting p. [1]–12, 43–46 mut.); MWA (p.[1]–6 wanting); Evans 44635.

WYNNE, JOHN HUDDLESTONE 1743–1788

1456.1 [—] CHOICE EMBLEMS, For The Improvement And Pastime Of Youth. Woodstock [Vt.]: Printed By David Watson. 1819.

fr.[2], t.[3], [4, alphabets–5], 6–31 p.; illus.; 9.5 cm.; pr. & illus. paper covers.

Cover title: Choice Emblems. A selection of emblems taken from Wynne's larger work *Choice Emblems Natural, Historical, Fabulous, Moral And Divine* . . . , no. **1457.1**.

Griffin°.

1456.2 [—] ——— Youth. No. II. Woodstock [Vt.]: Printed by David Watson, 1820.

fr.[2], t.[3], [4–5], 6–31 p.; illus.; 9.5 cm.; pr. paper covers.

Cover title: No. II. Choice Emblems.

MPlyA (not seen); McCorison 2194; Shoemaker 737.

1457.1 [—] CHOICE EMBLEMS, NATURAL, HISTORICAL, FABULOUS, MORAL, AND DIVINE, For The Improvement And Pastime Of Youth: Ornamented With Near Fifty handsome Allegorical Engravings, designed on purpose for this Work. With pleasing and familiar Descriptions to each, in Prose and Verse, Serving to display the Beauties and Morals of the Ancient Fabulists. The whole calculated to convey the golden Lessons of Instruction under a new and more delightful Dress. [4 lines of verse] Goldsmith. Philadelphia: Printed And Sold By Joseph Crukshank, In Market Near Third-Street. MDCCXC.

t.[i], [ii, bl.], iii–xii, [1], 2–166 p.; illus.; 13 cm.; bound in scalloped marbled paper over bds.

English & Irish ed. title 1: *Choice Emblems, Natural, Historical, Fabulous, Moral And Divine.* London: G. Riley, 1772.

English ed. title 2: *Riley's Emblems, Natural,*

Historical, ——— [same as title 1]. London: 3 ed. F. Newbery & G. Riley, 1779.

MWA°; CtY; DLC; NcD; NjP; PPL; Evans 22854; Hamilton 131.

1457.2 [—] ——— Youth; Calculated to convey the Golden Lessons of Instruction, under a new and more delightful dress. Written For The Amusement Of A Young Nobleman. [5 lines of verse] Hartford: Printed by Hale & Hosmer. 1814.

fr.[2], t.[3], [4–5], 6–30, [31, adv. list of 12 books] p.; illus.; 10.5 cm.; pr. & illus. buff paper covers.

MWA°; Shaw 33742.

1457.3 [—] ——— dress. First American from the tenth London Edition. New-York: Published By James Oram. C. Wiley, Printer. 1814.

t.[i], [ii–iii], iv–vi, [vii–viii, contents], [1], 2–189 p.; illus.; t.[i] 14 cm. Cuts on p.[2], [71], [116], [124] signed L [Garret Lansing]. NN° (rebound); ICU; PPL; Shaw 31146.

1457.4 [—] ——— Youth; Displaying The Beauties And Morals Of The Ancient Fabulists: The whole calculated to convey the Golden Lessons of Instruction under a new and more delightful dress. Hartford: Published By Oliver D. Cooke, 1815. Seth Richards, Printer [8 dots] Middletown [Conn.].

fr.[ii], t.[1], [2–3], 4–72 p.; front only illus.; 14 cm.; pr. & illus. green paper covers. Cover title imprint: Hartford: Published By O. D. Cooke. 1814. The MWA copy has a pl. opp. p. 12.

MWA-W°; CLU; CtHi; CtY (copy 1, cover title dated 1814; copy 2, cover title dated 1914 [*sic. i.e.* 1814]; MWA (copy 1, covers wanting); copy 2, bound with the *Christian Occonomy . . . Hartford: O. D. Cooke 1814.*); NN; PP; Shaw 33743 and 36655; Weiss 1936, p. 93.

1457.5 [—] ——— Youth; Calculated to convey the Golden Lessons of Instruction, under a new and more delightful dress. Written For The Amusement Of A Young Nobleman. [6 lines of verse] Hartford: Printed by Charles Hosmer. 1815.

fr.[2], t.[3], [4–5], 6–31 p.; illus.; 10 cm.; pr. & illus. green paper covers; cover title dated 1815.

CtHi°; MWA-T (covers wanting); Shaw 36656.

1457.6 [—] ——— Youth; Displaying The Beauties And Morals Of The Ancient Fabulists. New-York: Printed And Sold By Samuel Wood, At The Juvenile Book-Store, No. 357, Pearl-Street. 1815.

t.[i], [ii–v], vi–x, [11], 12–184 p.; illus.; 14 cm.; bound in pr. buff paper over bds. Cuts on p. 40, 46, 60, 81, 97, 118 signed *L,* that on p. 126 *G.L.* [Garret Lansing]. Hamilton ascribes all the cuts in this book to Garret Lansing. MWA°; CLU; NjP; Hamilton 967; Shaw 36607 and 36657.

1457.7 [—] ——— [same as **1457.5**] dress [5 lines of verse] New-York: Published by P. W. Gallaudet, at his Theological Bookstore, No. 49 Fulton-street. 1818.

t.[1], [2–3], 4–23, [24, adv.] p.; 12 cm.; pr. & illus. gray paper covers; colophon p. 23: "Birch And Kelley, Printers." MWA°; CtHi; DLC (t.[1], p. [2], 23–[24] wanting); Shaw 46888.

1457.8 [—] ——— Of Youth; Displaying The Beauties And Morals Of The Ancient Fabulists. New-York: Printed And Sold By Samuel Wood & Sons, At The Juvenile Book-Store, No. 261, Pearl-Street. 1818.

t.[i], [ii–iii], iv–viii, [9], 10–180 p.; illus.; 14.5 cm.; bound in buff paper over bds., leather spine. The cuts on p. 40, 43, 46, 57, 60, 81, 85, 97, and 118 are signed *L,* and that on p. 126, *G.L.* [Garret Lansing]. Hamilton ascribes all the cuts in this book to Garret Lansing. MWA-W°; NjP; Hamilton 968; Shaw 46889; Weiss 1942.

1457.9 [—] ——— Youth: Calculated To Convey The Golden Lessons of Instruction, Under a new and more Delightful Dress. [4 dots quot.] Boston: Printed by Lincoln & Edmands, No. 53, Cornhill, 1819.

t.[1], [2–3], 4–23, [24] p.; illus.; 12.5 cm.; pr. & illus. blue paper covers; front cover undated and illustrated with a cut of a tree not surrounded by a border. MWA copy 1, rear cover adv. of Tracts and Bibles; MWA copy 2, purple paper covers, front cover undated and has a cut of a tree in a pot enclosed by a ruled border. MWA° (copy 1, 2); CtHi; Shaw 50179 and 50180.

1458 [—] EMBLEMS AND FABLES, NATURAL, HISTORICAL, MORAL, AND DIVINE Conveying The Golden Lessons Of Instruction Under A Delightful Dress. Hartford: Oliver D. Cooke. 1820.

t.[1], [2–24] p.; illus.; 13.5 cm. MWA°; Shoemaker 4351.

1459 [—] EMBLEMS NATURAL, HISTORICAL, FABULOUS, MORAL, AND DIVINE. For The Improvement And Pastime Of Youth. The Whole calculated to convey the Golden Lessons of Instruction under a new and more delightful Dress. Part II. [4 lines of verse] Philadelphia: Printed by Francis Bailey, No. 116, High Street. — < —1792.— >

t.[1], [2], 3–30, [31–32, adv. list of books] p.; illus.; 8 cm.; pr. & illus. paper covers. Part I and II were adv. by Francis Bailey, 1793 in **773.1**. PHi°.

1460.1 [—] TALES FOR YOUTH. Part I [II–IV] [no title page to Part V is known] Philadelphia: Printed Sold By W. Spotswood. MDCCCII.

pt. I. 1st t.[i], [ii, bl.], [1], 2–30 p. [tales I–VIII]; pt. II: 2nd t.[i], [ii], [1], 2–29 p. [Tales IX–XV]; pt. III: 3rd t.[1], [2, bl.], [3], 4–31 p. [Tales XVI–XXII]; pt. IV: 4th t.[1], [2, bl.], [3], 4–32 p. [Tales XXIII–XXX]; pt. V: 5th t.[1], [2] [both pages torn out of MWA-W copy but a fragment of the leaf remains], [3], 4–32 p. [Tales not numbered. They are additional tales not by J. H. Wynne]; 30 text illus., a title vignette to pt. I, III, IV, and tailpieces; 5 pts. bound in 1 vol.; 12 cm.; bound in red and blue marbled paper over bds., black leather spine; the text illustrations are copies of the London, 1794 edition. English ed. title 1: *Tales For Youth; In Thirty Poems: To Which are Annexed, Historical Remarks And Moral Applications In Prose. By The Author Of "Choice Emblems For The Improvement Of Youth,"* &c. London: J. Crowder, For E. Newbery, 1794. English ed. title 2: *Amusing And Instructive Tales For Youth In Thirty Poems.* London: J. Crowder, for E. Newbery, 1800. MWA-W° (t.[I], to pts. II & V wanting; 5 pts. bound in one vol.); NNC-Pl (pt. IV, p. 31–32 mut., Dutch paper covers); OOxM (pt. II, 11 cm. cream-buff paper covers); Shaw 3134 (pt. I); 3135 (pt. II); 3136 (pt. III); 3137 (pt. IV); 3138 (pt. V).

1460.2 [—] ———— Youth, In Thirty Poems. To Which Are Annexed, Historical Remarks And Moral Applications In Prose. Boston: Printed and Sold by the Booksellers. 1814.

title page 11.5 cm.

MWA-W* (all the book wanting except the title page).

Y

YELLOW SHOE-STRINGS. *See* Pedder, James, no. **980**.

1461.1 THE YOUNG CHILD'S A B C, Or, First Book. New-York: Published By Samuel Wood, No. 362 Pearl-Street. 1806.

t.[1], [2], 3–16 p.; illus.; 10 cm.; illus. blue paper covers; colophon p. 16: J. C. Totten, print. No. 155 Chatham-street.

MWA*; CLU; CSmH; CtHi; CtY; DLC; NHi; NNC-Pl; PP; PPL; Shaw 11909.

1461.2 ——— From Sidney's Press, New-Haven. 1807.

fr.[2], t.[3], [4–5], 6–31 p.; illus.; 10.5 cm.

MWA*; PPL.

1461.3 ——— Adorned With Cuts. Hallowell, Maine, Printed and published by N. Cheever, and sold at his Printing-Office. 1809.

fr.[2], t.[3], [4], 5–30, [31, adv.] p.; illus.; 10 cm.

MWA*; Shaw 19287.

1461.4 ——— First Book. From Sidney's Press. New-Haven. 1810.

fr.[2], t.[3], [4], 5–31 p.; illus.; 10.5 cm.; yellow paper covers.

MWA* (covers mostly wanting).

1461.5 ——— From Sidney's Press, New-Haven. 1812.

fr.[2], t.[3], [4], 5–31 p.; illus.; 10.5 cm.; yellow paper covers.

MWA*; Shaw 27637.

1461.6 ——— From Sidney's Press, New-Haven. 1813.

fr.[2], t.[3], [4], 5–31 p.; illus.; 10.5 cm.; pr. & illus. yellow paper covers.

Welch*; MWA; MWHi; OCl; PP; Shaw 30597.

1461.7 ——— New-York: Printed And Sold By Samuel Wood, No. 357, Pearl-Street. 1813.

t.[1], [2–16] p.; illus.; 9.5 cm.; pr. & illus. blue-gray paper covers.

MWA*; MH; NN; NNC-Pl (t.[1] torn in half); Shaw 30598.

1461.8 ——— New-York: Printed And Sold By Samuel Wood & Sons, At The Juvenile Book-Store, No. 357, Pearl-Street. 1816.

t.[1], 2–16 p.; illus.; 10 cm.; pr. & illus. green paper covers.

Copy 1, cover title: ——— A, B, C: Or, First Book. [cut of 3 boys playing] Printed And ——— [same as t.[1]] Pearl-Street, New-York.

Copy 2, cover title: ——— Book. [cut of 2 children playing with racquets] ——— New-York.

Copy 3, cover title: ——— Book. [cut of a person between two bushes] ——— New-York: Published by Samuel Wood & Sons, No. 261, Pearl-Street; And Samuel S. Wood & Co. No. 212, Market-street, Baltimore.

Copy 4, cover title: ——— Book. [cut of a man with a cloth over his shoulder facing a youth to the left] New-York: ——— [same as copy 3] Baltimore.

Copy 5, cover title: ——— Book. [cut of birds] *Nerv-York* [*sic. i.e.* New-York]: ——— [same as copy 3] Baltimore.

MWA* (copies 1–5); CLU; MSaE; ICU; Shaw 39899 and 39900.

1461.9 ——— Georgetown, D.C. Printed By W. Duffy, Book-Seller And Stationer. 1817.

t.[1], 2–16 p.; illus.; 9.5 cm.

PP* (covers wanting; p. 15–16 mut.).

THE YOUNG COTTAGER. *See* Richmond, Legh, no. **1112.1**.

1462 THE YOUNG FLORIST'S COMPANION, Being Concise Explanations Of Botanical Terms Used In Describing Flowers; Together with illustrations of the Classes and Orders, by familiar Examples. Hartford: Published By S. G. Goodrich. Roberts & Burr, Printers. 1819.

t.[1], [2], 3–31 p.; 14 cm.

CSmH*; Shaw 50188.

THE YOUNG MISSES MAGAZINE. *See* Le Prince De Beaumont, no. **749.1**.

1463 THE YOUNG ROBBER; Or Dishonesty Punished. To Which Is Added, Mr. Goodman and his

Children, The Way To Be Good And Happy, And The Ditch. New-York: Printed And Sold By J. C. Totten, No. 9 Bowery. 1819.

> fr.[ii], t.[iii], [iv–v], vi, [7], 8–46 p.; illus.; 14 cm.; pr. & illus. buff paper covers.
> English ed. London: J. Harris, 1804.
> NHi°; NNC-Pl; PHi; PP; Shaw 50189.

1464 YOUTHFUL AMUSEMENTS, A New Edition. Philadelphia: Published by Johnson & Warner N⁰. 147 Market Street 1810

> t.[1], [2, bl.–3], 4–47, [48] p.; illus.; 13.5 cm.; blue marbled paper covers; engr. t.[1] vignette & text illus. signed *WR sc* [William Ralph].
> MWA°; NHi; Shaw 22129.

1465 THE YOUTHFUL ENQUIRER: Or, The Story Of Joseph Careful. Newburyport [Mass.], Printed And Sold by W. & J. Gilman, No. 2, Middle-Street. [1819] [cover title].

> [1], 2–8 p.; illus., 13 cm.; pr. & illus. blue-gray paper covers. On p.[1] is a holograph inscription "Elizabeth Fowle 1819 Sabbath School."
> MWA-W°.

1466 YOUTHFUL FOLLY DETECTED. Written For The Benefit Of Youth, Particularly The Female Sex, [8 lines of verse] Walpole, N. H., Printed At The Observatory Press, By David Newhall. 1804.

> t.[1], [2–5], 6–32 p.; 13 cm.; marbled paper covers.
> CLU°.

THE YOUTHFUL JESTER. *See* [Johnson, Richard], no. **689**.

1467 YOUTHFUL PIETY: A Memoir Of Miriam Warner, Who Died at Northampton, Feb. 21, 1819, in the 11th year of her age; And Of Eliza M'Carty, Who Died at Aurora, N.Y. Dec. 4, 1818, in the 14th year of her age. Boston: Printed For Samuel T. Armstrong, By Crocker And Brewster, No. 50, Cornhill. 1820.

> t.[1], [2–3], 4–23, [24] p.; illus.; 13 cm.; pr. & illus. brick-red paper covers.
> MWA-W°; MWA; NN (p. 23–[24] & covers wanting); Shoemaker 4368.

1468 YOUTHFUL RECREATIONS. Philadelphia Published by J. Johnson No. 147 Market Street. [1802].

> t.[1], [2–32] p.; illus.; 9.5 cm.; yellow paper

covers speckled with gold. Jacob Johnson was of the firm of Johnson & Warner 1808–1816. He was alone from 1802–1808, 1816–1819. (MWA cat.). The English edition appeared in 1801, therefore it is logical to suppose this book was printed in [1802].

> English ed. London: W᷾ᵐ Darton & J᷾ᵇ Harvey, 1801., 9 cm., cover label: "The Infant's own Book, by Darton & Harvey, London."
> MWA°; CaOTP; CLU; CSmH; CtHi; DLC; FTaSU; NHi; NNC-Pl; NNMM; NRU; PHi; PP; PPL; Shaw 22130 dated ([ca. 1810]).

1469 YOUTHFUL SPORTS Philadᵃ Published by Jacob Johnson N⁰ 147 Market-St 1802.

> t.[1], [2, bl.], [3–24], [25], 26–59, [60, adv.] p.; illus.; 13.5 cm.; marbled paper covers. Engraved title page and 11 engraved illus. printed on one side only of 12 leaves, include p.[2–24]. The blank pages are part of the pagination. Colophon p. [60]: John Bioren, printer. Adv. by Johnson & Warner, 1809 in **212.2**, and 1814 in **1449.3**.
> English ed. London: Darton & Harvey, 1801.
> MWA° (p. 59–[60] mut.); ICU (p.[23–24] or pl. [11] wanting); PP (blue marbled paper covers, 11 plates bound in the front of the book); Shaw 3605.

1470 THE YOUTH'S AMUSEMENT; Containing A Variety Of Moral And Interesting Matter, For The Improvement Of Young Persons. Charlestown [Mass.]: Printed By S. Etheridge, And Sold By Him And E. Cotton. 1806.

> t.[1], [2–3], 4–72 p.; 13 cm.; bound in blue paper over bds., leather spine.
> MWA°; Shaw 11913.

1471 YOUTH'S CABINET. Vol. I > Utica [N.Y.] [4 dots] Friday, March 31, 1815 < No. 1. [caption p. [1]].

> [1–4] p.; 16.5 cm.
> ——— Vol. I. > Utica [4 dots] Friday, April 7, 1815. < No. 2. [caption p. [1]].
> [1–4] p.; 16.5 cm.
> ——— Vol. I. > Utica [4 dots] Friday, April 14, 1815. < No. 3. [caption p. [1]].
> [1–4] p.; 16.5 cm.
> ——— Vol. I. > Utica [4 dots] Friday, April 21, 1815. < No. 4. [caption p. [1]].
> [1–4] p.; 16.5 cm.
> MB°.

1472.1 THE YOUTH'S CABINET OF NATURE, For The Year; Containing Curious Particulars Characteristic Of Each Month. Intended To Direct Young People To The Innocent And Agreeable Employment Of Observing Nature. [6 lines quot.] New-York: Printed And Sold By S. Wood, At The Juvenile Book-Store, No. 357, Pearl-Street. 1811.

t.[1], [2–3], 4–52 p.; illus.; 13 cm.; pr. & illus. pinkish-buff paper covers; cover title dated 1811. The book is a rewritten version of John Aikin's *The Calendar Of Nature*, no. **24.** The title of **1472.1** was changed to *The Cabinet Of Nature*, 1815–1817, *see* **147.1–2.**
English ed. London: R. Harrild, 1812.
CtHi°; MWA-T; NHi; NjP.

1472.2 ——— New-York: Printed And Sold By Samuel Wood, At The Juvenile Book-Store, No. 357, Pearl-Street. 1812.

t.[1], [2–3], 4–52 p.; illus.; 13.5 cm.; pink paper covers.
Welch°; MWA; PP; PPL; Shaw 27639.

1472.3 ———New-York: Printed And Sold By Samuel Wood, At The Juvenile Book-Store, No. 357, Pearl-Street. 1814.

t.[1], [2–3], 4–52 p.; illus.; 13.5 cm.; pr. & illus. buff paper covers. Part of a large publisher's remainder.
Welch°; CaOTP; CCamarSJ; CLU; CSmH; CtHi; CtY; DLC; ICU; IU; MiD; MWA (copy 1, covers present; copy 2, bound with other books in no. **191;** NHi; NN; PHi; PP; PPL; PU; Shaw 33755.

1473.1 YOUTH'S GUIDE TO HAPPINESS, Consisting Of Poems, Essays, & Sermons, Particularly calculated for the Pious Instruction Of The Rising Generation. [2 lines quot.] Published By S. Dodge. Manning, Printer. 1810.

t.[1], [2–3], 4–107 p.; 14 cm.; bound in leather. Contents: A few poems, sermons, & Doddridge's Principles of the Christian Religion. On p. 62–75 is, "some account of the Happy Death Of Edwin Tapper aged 15 years."
MWA°; CtHi; RPB (front cover wanting); Shaw 22131.

1473.2 ——— Newark: Printed By John Tuttle & Co. 1814.

t.[1], [2–3], 4–105 p.; 14 cm.; bound in green paper over bds., leather spine.
MWA°; Shaw 33756.

1473.3 ——— Norwich [Conn.]: Printed And Sold By R. Hubbard. 1814.

t.[1], [2–3], 4–95, [96] p.; 14 cm.; marbled paper covers.
RPB°; Shaw 33757.

1474 THE YOUTH'S GUIDE TO WISDOM, Containing A Choice Selection Of Maxims And Morals For The Rising Generation. Embellished With Many Engravings. Boston: Published By T. B. Wait And Co. And Charles Williams. 1812.

fr.[2], t.[3], [4–5], 6–31 p.; illus.; 14 cm.; pr. violet-gray paper covers.
English ed. London: R. Harrild, 1807.
MWA°; RPB (p. 31 wanting); Shaw 27640.

1475 THE YOUTH'S MANUEL. Containing Prayers And Hymns, And The Catechism, Of The Protestant Episcopal Church In America. [4 lines quot.] Boston: Published By Charles Williams. T. B. Wait & Co. Printers. 1813.

t.[i], [ii–iii], iv, [5], 6–54 p.; 14.5 cm.
CSmH°.

1476 THE YOUTH'S MONITOR: Or A Collection Of Thoughts On Civil, Moral, And Religious Subjects: Selected From Different Authors. [1 line quot.] Leominster [Mass.]: Printed For The Purchaser. 1799.

t.[1], [2, bl.–3], 4–48 p.; 17.5 cm.; bound in yellow paper over bds., leather spine.
MWA°; NjR; NN (rebound); RPJCB; Evans 36748.

YOUTH'S MONITOR: OR, HISTORIES OF THE LIVES OF YOUNG PERSONS. *See* [R., J.], no. **1086.**

1477 THE YOUTH'S NEWS PAPER. < 3 Dols. P. Ann. > < No. 1 > New-York, Saturday, September 30, 1797. Printed by J. S. Mott, for the Editor, and C. Smith, No. 51 Maiden-Lane. [caption title p. [1]].

[1], 2–8 p.; 20 cm.
——— < 2 Dols. P. Ann. > < No. 2. > New-York, Saturday, October 7, 1797. Printed by ——— [caption title p.[9]].

[9], 10–16 p.; 20 cm.
——— < 2 Dols. P. Ann. > < No. 3. > New-York, Saturday, October 14, 1797. Printed by ——— [caption title p.[17]].

[17], 18–24 p.; 20 cm.
——— < 2 Dols. P. Ann. > < No. 4. > New-

York, Saturday, October 21, 1797. ——— [caption title p.[25]].

   [25], 26–32 p.; 20 cm.

——— < 2 Dols. P. Ann. > < No. 5. > New-York, Saturday, October 28, 1797. ——— [caption title p.[33]].

[33], 34–40 p.; 20 cm.

——— < 2 Dols. P. Ann. > < No. 6. > New-York, Saturday, November 4, 1797. ——— [caption title p.[41]].

   [41], 42–48 p.; 20 cm.

NN°; Evans 33258.

Z

1478 ZWEEN BETTELKNABEN. eine Lehrreiche Geschichte für Umsere Deutschen Kinder. nebst Zwo Todesgeschichten. Philadelphia, Gedruckt bey Henrich Schweitzer, an eck der Rees und viertn Strasse, und zu haben einz. In und beym Dutzend bey O. Gassner in Schulhause, in der Cherrystrasse bey J. Johnson in der Marktstrasse, und beym Drucker, 1806.

t.[1], [2], 3–28 p.; illus.; 13.5 cm.; blue marbled paper covers.

MWA*; Shaw 11918.

Index of Printers, Publishers, and Imprints

(CHRONOLOGICALLY ARRANGED UNDER NAME)

A

Adams, James (1797 Wilmington, Del.) 1299.

Adams, John (1802–1809 Philadelphia) 1443.6, 714.1, 986.4, 214, 275.55, 616.16, 675.5, 678.10, 1085.5, 1325, 1413.2, 1443.9, 533.1, 614.4, 612.20, 646.3, 670.2, 673.24, 677.2, 678.11, 770.1, 937.7, 1217, 1314.5, 1413.5, 249.9, 295.2, 665.28, 714.2, 979.3, 1046.2, 1138, 1285.2, 999.

Aitken, Mr. (1785 Philadelphia) 610.

Aitken, Jane (1806–1810 Philadelphia) 665.26, 1130.1.

Aitken, Robert (1773–1802 Philadelphia) 1408.15, 226, 665.12, 18.2, 665.21, 18.5.

Aitken, R., & Son (1791–1792 Philadelphia) 665.15, 18.3.

Aitken, The Press of The Late R. (1806 Philadelphia) 665.26.

Akerman, Samuel (1804 Philadelphia) 265.1.

Alexandria [D.C.] (1802) 16.2.

Allen, Horatio G. (1814 Newburyport, Mass.) 438.13, 438.14.

Allen, P. (1810 Pittsfield, Mass.) 895.5.

Allen, T. (1792 New York) 749.1.

Allen, William B. [Brown] (1809–1812 Haverhill, Mass.) 278, 33.

Allen, William B., & Co. (1813–1816 Newburyport, Mass.) 153.3, 438.13, 871.28, 438.19.

Alleyne, Abel D. (1816 Dedham, Mass.) 65.1, 65.2, 65.4.

Allinson, David (1816 Burlington, N.J.) 151.1.

Allinson, David, & Co. (1811 Burlington, N.J.) 808.

A. L. T. D. H. (1813 n.p.) 1269.

Andrews, Loring (1790 Stockbridge, Mass.) 810.1.

Armbruster, Anthony (1786 Philadelphia) 1205.

Armstrong, Samuel T.[urrell] (1811–1820 Boston) 473.1, 475.1, 475.2, 438.1, 1406.29, 895.6, 438.7, 871.26, 99, 438.12, 438.25, 506.1, 507.1, 1244, 1408.71, 118, 438.25, 443.1, 505.2, 507.2, 636.4, 833, 836, 1100, 1119.4 [adv.], 1196.17 [adv.], 1388, 1467.

Ashley, T.[imothy] (1800 Springfield, Mass.) 1203.1.

The Association of Travelling Booksellers (1807 Whitehall, Pa.) 587.50.

The Aurora Bookstores (1802 Philadelphia and Washington City) 1144.1.

Author, Printed For The (1769 n.p.) 273.2; (1817 Brookfield, Mass.) 767.3; (1815 [Concord, N.H.] [Jason Lathrop]) 796; (1815 Exeter [N.H.]) 1038.2, 1038.3; (1804 Greenwich, [Mass.] [Solomon Howe]) 618; (1769 Newport [R.I.]) 273.1, 273.2.

Avery, Joseph (1820 Plymouth, Mass.) 512.2.

Avery, Samuel (1810–1811 Boston) 134.5, 892.5, 1104.6, 612.19, 1371.7.

B

B., H. (1814 Philadelphia) 275.81.

B., J. [Byrne, John] (prior to 1811 Windham, Conn.) 1068.19.

Babcock, Elisha (1791–1796 Hartford) 810.3, 810.8, 1408.40, 810.16.

Babcock, I. ([1792] Philadelphia) 857.2.

Babcock, John (1799–1802 Hartford) 823.1, 1300.1, 1385.2, 1408.43, 90.2, 173.1, 648.1, 1300.2, 267, 1443.1, 877, 90.3, 173.2, 282, 586.4, 648.2, 941, 1096.1, 1300.3, 1335.1, 1408.49, 1443.2, 390, 793.1, 823.2, 158.1, 275.41, 696.1, 823.3, 937.1, 986.1, 1314.1, 1371.3, 1443.3, 561, 200, 347.1, 392, 426, 653, 745, 134.2, 213.10, 275.44, 648.3, 696.2, 823.4, 937.2, 986.3, 1314.2, 1385.2, 1431.1, 1443.5.

Babcock, John And Son (1811–1820 New Haven) 959.4, 1196.7, 26.5, 49.2, 60.36, 308, 82, 158.5*, 160.3*, 168, 308, 455.1, 455.2, 481.6, 538, 586.10, 628.1, 717.3, 719.1, 719.2, 743.1, 825.4, 1033.3, 1112.3, 1125.2, 1231.2, 1429.18 [adv.], 27.9, 58.2, 60.40, 64, 85, 104.4, 111, 158.6, 159, 311, 401.2, 438.35, 455.3, 455.4, 464, 481.9, 481.10, 502, 503, 527.3, 586.12, 628.2, 642, 718, 743.2, 1067.7, 1067.8, 1097, 1178.1, 1178.2, 1202.3, 1259, 1286.3, 1323.4, 1377, 1420.5, 1420.6.

Babcock, S. & W. R. (1819–1820 Charleston, S.C.) 308*, 158.5*, 160.3*, 481.6*, 719.1*, 1125.2*, 586.11, 111*, 159, 311, 401.2, 438.35,

E

Eichbaum and Johnson (1818 Pittsburgh, Pa.) 236.13.

Eliot, Benjamin (spelled "Elliot", 1700 Boston) 665.1; (1702 Boston) 1428.2; (1715 New London) 871.1; (1724 Boston) 871.2.

Eliot, John (1815 Boston) 1291; (spelled "Elliot") 962.2.

Eliot, Jun., John (1812 Boston) 753.

Elliot, Benjamin (*see* Eliot, Benjamin).

Elliot & Crissy (1810 New York) 962.1.

Elliot, J., (*see* Eliot, John).

Elliot, Nathan (1807–1809 Catskill, N.Y.). 179.5, 154.7, 654.1, 1196.6.

Ely, Jun., Nathaniel (1795 Longmeadow, Mass.) 665.17.

Engles, S. (1815 Pittsburgh) 236.12.

Etheridge, Samuel (1796–1797 Boston) 271.3, 1010.1, 691.2; (1802–1808 Charleston, Mass., sometimes spelled "Charlestown") 501.3, 954.7, 1406.11, 501.4, 869, 1406.21, 1470, 1073.7.

Ewes, Charles (1819 Boston) 750.1, 816.1.

F

Fagan, A. (1811–1815 Philadelphia) 109, 25.3, 131, 133, 375, 420, 914, 946, 971, 1050, 264.3.

Fairhaven, Vt. ([1796] no printer's name) 1283.7.

Falconer, W. (1800 New York) 612.16.

Falcouer [*sic.*] (*see* Falconer, W.).

Fanshaw, D. (1817 New York) 476.5, 622.

Farnsworth & Churchill (1809–1810 Windsor, Vt.) 275.72, 81, 90.6, 648.5, 823.16, 937.16, 986.21, 1096.2, 1335.4, 1443.23.

Farnsworth, Havila & Oliver (1798–1799 Suffield, Conn.) 1102.5, 1104.5, 90.4, 173.3, 275.39.

Farnsworth, Oliver (1799–1803 Newport, R.I.) 1335.2, 281.1, 173.5, 275.48, 281.2, 1443.7 (1809–1818 Windsor, Vt.) 173.7, 281.3, 810.33 [adv.], 1204.

Farrand, Mallory, & C ([1812?] Boston) 895.6.

Fay & Davison (1813–[*ca.* 1813] Rutland, Vt.) 37, 1442.1, 1293.15.

Fay, Galen H. (1802 Haverhill, Mass.) 871.16.

Fay, William, & Co. (1813 Rutland, Vt.) 461.

The Female Union Society For The Promotion Of Sabbath Schools (1816 New York) 1348.

Fenton, D. (1812 Trenton, N.J.) 1423.2.

Fessenden, William (1813 Brattleborough, Vt.) 810.36.

Fisher, John (1794 Baltimore) 1429.6.

Flagg, Azariah C. (1812 Plattsburgh, N.Y.) 892.9.

Flagg and Gould (1814–1820 Andover, Mass.) 154.11, 401.1, 438.11, 476.1, 889.2, 892.11, 892.12, 895.7, 1107.3, 1406.30, 153.5, 476.2, 887.5, 1107.11, 1109.2, 476.3, 892.14, 895.8, 1105.1, 1107.15, 1111.4, 1397, 1406.31, 1406.32, 476.4, 950.1, 1111.7, 1196.1, 521.4, 892.17, 895.10, 1196.4, 239.2, 889.4, 950.2, 1107.19, 1406.34, 233.3, 481.8, 505.1, 521.5, 895.12, 1044, 1105.2, 1111.9, 1196.16, 1280, 1409.6.

Fleet, J. & T. (1802 Boston) 1408.57.

Fleet, Thomas (1751 Boston) 492.5 [adv.].

Fleet, Jun., T. (1793 Boston) 1408.34.

Fleet, Thomas and John (1771–1783 Boston) 665.7, 871.4, 493, 665.10, 1408.13, 665.11, 1073.1, 1073.2.

Fletcher, Timothy (1808 Boston) 1026.

Folsom, John W. ([1790?]–1798 Boston) 71.1, 878, 39, 395.6 [adv.], 428.1, 453.2, 555.1 [adv.], 558.1, 594.1 [adv.], 626.2, 672.2, 673.12 [adv.], 674.1, 675.4 [adv.], 678.4 [adv.] 687.4 [adv.], 788.1, 841.2 [adv.], 929 [adv.], 936.1, 1239.1 [adv.], 1371.1, 1322.1, 213.6 [adv.].

Folwell, R. (1794 Philadelphia) 1104.3.

Forbes & Co. (1817 New York) 619, 620.

Forbes, John (1814 New York) 608.1.

Fordyce, John (1813 Philadelphia) 145, 612.24.

Forman, George (1794–1809 New York) 1371.2, 361.5, 275.69.

Foster, H. (1733 Boston) 1014.

Fowle, Daniel ([1756?] Boston) 932; ([*ca.* 1756] Boston) 492.7 [adv.]; (1758 Portsmouth, New Hampshire) 763.

Fowle, Daniel & Robert (1764 Portsmouth, N.H.) 1408.8.

Fowle and Draper (1762 Boston) 3.1, 587.10, 931.1.

Fowle, Z. (1764–1771 Boston) 587.12, 1455.1, 587.13, 484.1, 756.1, 931.2, 587.14, 587.16, 665.8.

Fowle, Z. and S. Draper (1759 Boston) 1408.7.

Francis' Bookstore, Printed at ([*ca.* 1816] Boston) 987.13.

Francis, David (1810–1819 Boston) 207.1, 337, 404, 1339.1, 1251.4, 1339.2.

Francis, Munroe And Parker (1808 Boston) 444.3.

Franklin, B. (1737–1744 Philadelphia) 1408.2 [adv.], 1072.5.

Franklin, B., and D. Hall (1744–1750 Philadelphia) 665.4, 1408.6.

Frary, Erastus (1808 Johnstown) 501.5.

Frothingham, David (1791–[1792] Sagg Harbor, N.Y.) 612.8, 810.5.

Fry And Krammerer (1807 Philadelphia) 523, 611.1.

Fry, William (1818 Philadelphia) 60.33, 631.

G

M

O

Office Of The Phoenix (1815 Binghamton, N.Y.) 40.

Office Of The Religious Intelligencer (1819 New Haven) 636.2.

Olds, Benjamin (1820 Newark, N.J.) 104.5.

Oliver, Daniel (The Rev.) (1809 Charlestown, Mass.) 473.1.

Oram, James (1796–1811 New York) 453.1, 687.2, 1315.14, 678.9, 154.1, 154.3, 500, 810.32, 236.6, 1457.3.

Ormrod & Conrad (1796–1798 Philadelphia) 979.1, 77.1.

Ormrod, John (1798–1801 Philadelphia) 77.1, 979.2.

Osborne, George Jerry (1793 Newburyport, Mass.) 1408.36, 1408.37.

Orborne's Office (1793 Newburyport, Mass.) 245.2, 275.22.

Osborne's Press (1793 Newburyport, Mass.) 245.1.

P

Packard & Van Benthuysen (1819 Albany, N.Y.) 1196.12.

Palmer, T. & G. (1808–1816 Philadelphia) 1103.14, 791.

Park, James (also spelled "Parke") (1807 Philadelphia) 614.4.

Parke, James P. (also spelled "Park" (1809 Philadelphia) 436, 1401.

Parker, E. & R. (1818–1819 Philadelphia) 106, 165.1, 166.1, 167.1, 255, 405, 429, 701.1, 703.1, 704.1, 768, 873.1, 934, 974, 1297.1, 164, 165.2, 166.2, 167.2, 387, 701.2, 703.2, 704.2, 873.2, 1297.2.

Parker, Edward ([1814]–1820 Philadelphia) 328.2, 635.

Parker, L. (1802 Shirley, Mass.) 457, 569.2.

Parker, Samuel H. (1803 Boston) 23.

Parker, Sewall (1803 Harvard, Mass.) 569.3, 1239.3.

Parks, Josiah (1810 Montpelier, Vt.) 424.2.

Park's Press (1807–1808 Montpelier, Vt.) 275.60, 245.3, 986.12, 1172.

Parmenter And Balch (1819 Boston) 60.33.

Pat [*sic*.], Nathaniel (*see* Patten, Nathaniel).

Paterson, R. (1815 Pittsburgh) 236.11.

Patten, Nathaniel (1787–1789 Hartford) 871.7, 1429.3, 128.2, 563.4, 663.3, 954.2, 1315.4.

Patterson & Hopkins (1812 Pittsburgh, Pa.) 903.3.

Patterson, R., & Lambdin (1819 Pittsburgh, Pa.) 1415.2.

Paul, Abraham (1817–1818 New York) 602.2, 324.4, 608.2.

Peirce, C. (1797–1805 Portsmouth, N.H.) 810.21, 1396, 616.17.

Peirce, Isaac (1818 Philadelphia) 1149, 1394.1.

Peirce, J. (1814 Philadelphia) 858.4.

Pelsue and Gould (1812–1814 New York) 852.5, 430.2, 1163.15, 438.16.

Penniman, O., & Co. (1804 Troy) 1396.

Pennington & Dodge (1797 Newark, N.J.) 1408.47.

Perkins, John (1761–1774 Boston) 1072.12, 1072.13, 1072.18, 1072.23, 1072.27, 1408.10, 1072.29, 1072.32.

Phelps, A. (1816 Greenfield, Mass.) 691.5.

Phelps, Sewell (1819 Boston) 1186.

Philadelphia ([1819?]–[*ca.* 1820]) (no printer's name) 1068.27, 1068.28.

Philadelphia Female Tract Society ([1816]–1819 Philadelphia) 22, 203.1, 285, 376, 482, 831, 951, 1223, 1281, 1310, 1358, 388, 476.6, 476.7, 485, 520.2, 599, 650, 809.1, 895.9, 1110, 1119.1, 1224, 1240.3, 1434, 154.14.

Philadelphia, Printed in the Year (1763–1812) (no printer's name) 627, 858.2, 1094.2, 174.1, 1094.1, 756.2, 1103.15.

Philadelphia Tract Society (perhaps Philadelphia Female Tract Society) (1817 Philadelphia) 1308.

Phillips, John (1728 Boston) 665.3.

Phinney, E. (1794–1795 Cooperstown, N.Y.) 1408.39, 1102.3.

Phinney, H. & E. (1814–1820 Cooperstown, N.Y.) 275.80, 249.22, 1263, 673.34, 26.4, 249.23, 673.35, 1173.6, 351.4.

Phinney, Jun., H. & E. (1807–1812 Otsego, [N.Y.]) 937.9, 1371.8, 856.2, 1188.5.

Pier, A. D. (1816 Weathersfield, Vt.) 1118.

Pierce, Hill & Pierce (1805 Portsmouth, N.H.) 767.1.

Pike, Stephen (1811 Philadelphia) 979.4.

Pleasants, S. (1804 Richmond) 1396.

Plowman, T. L. (1803 Philadelphia) 1003.1, 1067.2.

Pomeroy, R. W. (1814 Baltimore, Md.) 724.

Pomroy & Hedge (1816 Windsor, Vt.) 151.2, 1391.

Pomroy, T. M. (1807 Northampton, Mass.) 1408.64; (1811 Windsor, Vt.) 134.6.

Pomroy & Toy (1816 Baltimore) 1106.5.

Porcupine Office (1808–1810 New York) 817.1, 789.1, 789.2, 817.3.

Porter, Robert (1812–1819 Wilmington, Del.) 1104.8, 1167.5, 1163.29, 1103.16, 1265.4.

Potter, P. & S. (1813–1816 Poughkeepsie, N.Y.) (sometimes spelled "Poughkepsie") 1161.2, 1107.10, 1160, 317.4, 1350, 868.2.

Potter, Paraclete (1812–[1818?]) Poughkeepsie, N.Y.) (sometimes spelled "Poughkepsie") 237.1, 1161.2, 1107.10, 1160, 317.4, 1350, 868.2, 146.

Pounder, Jonathan (1811–1814 Philadelphia) 1163.12, 266.3, 1423.3, 682.5.

Powers, Thomas (1809–1810 New York) 1435.2, 26.2, 50.2, 58.1, 158.4, 962.1, 1202.2, 1330.2, 1371.6.

Powers, Wm. ([1810] no location) 1293.14.

Pratt, Luther & Co. (1796 Lansingburgh, N.Y.) 467, 858.3, 1103.4; (1797 Troy, N. Y.) 799.

Pray & Bowen (1813 Brooklyn) 1122.1, 1122.2.

Prentiss, Charles (1796–1797 Leominster, Mass.) 1406.6, 874, 1406.7.

Prentiss, John (1805–1809 Keene, N.H.) 1406.24, 373.1, 671.2.

The Press of Charles & Hale, Printed At (1807 Walpole, N.H.) 424.1.

The Press of Walton & Goss, From (1810 Montpelier, Vt.) 424.2.

The Press of William W. Morse (1800 New Haven) 1102.6.

Preston, Samuel (1799 Amherst, N.H.) 668.2.

Prichard, W. (*see* Pritchard) (1804 Richmond) 1396.

Printed For Messrs. Everybody (1813 Philadelphia) 117.

Printed in (1716) 1425.2; (1717) 492.1; (1718) 492.2; (1724) 492.3; (1729) 492.4; (1793) 197.5; (1800) 1124; (1801) 871.14; (1804) 905.5; (1805) 871.20; (1820) 1031.

Printed in The Year of Our Lord (1819) 581.

Printing-house (1729 Boston) 1090.1.

Printing Office (1771 Boston) 1320.3.

Printing Office ([*ca.* 1799] Albany) 174.2.

Printing Office (1807 Boston) 1068.17.

Printing Office (prior to 1811 Greenfield, Mass.) 1068.20.

Pritchard, William (1800 Richmond, Va.) 810.24, 984.3.

Probasco, S. (1820 Philadelphia) 655.35.

Procter, N. (*see* Proctor, N.) [*ca.* 1765] Boston) 1293.2.

Proctor, N. (*see* Procter, N.) (1738 Boston) 1072.3.

The Proprieter [-tor] Of The Boston Book-Store ([1793?]–[1793] Boston) 71.2, 74.

Proprietors (1817 [Albany]) 585.

Providence, Printed At ([*ca.* 1800]) 1335.3.

Pryor, George (1806 Philadelphia) 450.2.

The Publisher (1813 no location) 887.4.

Publishers (1817 Chillicothe, O.) 1212.7.

Purchaser (1800–1815 no location) 1447.1, 937.3, 2.

The Purchaser (1799 Leominster, Mass.) 1476.

The Purchaser ([*ca.* 1800] New England) 1293.9.

Purchasers (1811 no location) 591.12, 617.7.

The Purchasers (1805–1806 Newburyport, Mass.) 232, 1051, 948.2.

Putney, Ver. (1799) 1272.1.

R

Railey [*sic.*] (*see* Bailey, Lydia R.).

Rakestraw, Joseph (1804–1820 Philadelphia) 193.1, 289, 394, 821, 350.4, 1045.2, 414.1, 707.2, 890, 1131, 1163.13, 1191.1, 1163.16, 1185, 1163.19, 1163.20, 1163.21, 1163.22, 1163.23, 1163.24, 1163.25, 1163.26, 1163.27, 1163.28, 1163.30, 1163.31, 1163.33, 1163.34, 1163.35, 346, 1163.36, 1163.38, 1163.39.

Ranlet, Henry (1792–1805 Exeter, N.H.) 393, 1408.35, 240.1, 810.11, 810.12, 810.15, 1282.1, 1142, 1429.8 [adv.], 218.8 [adv.], 428.2, 453.3 [adv.], 555.2 [adv.], 558.2 [adv.], 594.2 [adv.], 626.3, 674.4, 675.2 [adv.], 788.2 [adv.], 871.15 [adv.], 936.2 [adv.], 1317.2 [adv.], 1322.2, 672.3, 673.19, 854.1.

Read, Ezra (1817 Boston) 316.3, 330.3.

Read & Morse (1800 New Haven) 1408.52.

Reed, A. (1807 Hartford) 249.8.

The Religious Tract Society of Philadelphia (1816–1820 Philadelphia) 1107.16, 1107.17, 1108.1, 578.1, 578.2, 1109.4, 1222, 551, 572, 853, 1108.2, 48, 488.3, 636.3, 655, 895.11, 120.2, 151.7, 577.

Rice, Henry & Patrick (1794–1801 Philadelphia) 1006.1, 819.1, 1139.1 [adv.], 1140.1 [adv.], 1212.2, 268.2, 591.4, 617.2, 1006.3, 866, 979.2.

Rice, James, and Co. (1795–1796 Baltimore) 268.2, 591.4, 617.2, 1006.3, 866.

Riley, I. (1811–1815 New York) 155, 244, 1121.

Richards, Seth (1815 Middletown, Conn.) 1457.4.

Rivington, J. (1795 New York) 985.2.

Roberson, L. (*pseud.*) (1816 Weathersfield, Vt.) 1118.

Roberts & Burr (1819–1820 Hartford) 524, 575, 812, 1267, 1361, 1369, 1462, 243, 438.31, 438.32, 443.2, 822, 1414.1.

Robertson, J. (1818 New York) 1429.19.

Robinson, Joseph (1811–1818 Baltimore) 1146.4, 1002.1, 1002.2, 1145.1, 104.2.

Robinson, Lewis, of Reading (1816 Weathersfield, Vt.) 1118.

Ronalds, J. (1804 New York) 76.6.

U

Union Tract Association Of Friends in the Western Countries of the State of New York (1818–1819 Auburn, N.Y.) 190.1, 190.2.

United Company Of Flying Stationers ([1795?] New York) 180.

Ustick, John G. (1799 Philadelphia) 1264.2.

Ustick, S. C. (1799 Philadelphia) 486.

Ustick, Stephen C. (1807 Burlington, N.J.) 136.1, 136.2.

Ustick, T. (1796 Philadelphia) 38.1.

Utica (1815 Utica, [N.Y.], no printer's name) 1471.

V

Vance, J. & T. (1814 Baltimore) 1002.2.

Vance, John, & Co. (1806–1811 Baltimore) 143.1, 265.2, 350.3, 416.2, 417.2, 657, 865, 1073.9, 269.10, 321.2, 545.

Van Riper, J., & Co. (1819 New York) 130.2.

Van Riper, N. (1818–1819 New York) 508.2, 345.2, 601.3, 603.2, 1376.

Van Winkle & Wiley (1815–1816 New York) 489, 600.1, 603.1, 605, 129, 601.1.

Vermilye, W. W. (1805 New York) 612.18.

The Virginia Religious Tract Society (1814 Harrisonburg, Va.) 1107.5.

W

Wait, Thomas B. (1786–1793 Portland, Me.) 871.6, 275.10, 501.1, 61.4, 61.5, 61.6.

Wait, Thomas B., And Co. (1812–[1814] Boston, Mass.) 396, 430.1, 1080 [adv.], 1474, 69.1, 249.14, 368, 227, 261.2, 658, 754.2, 1166, 1475, 261.1, 328.2.

Waite, G. & R. (1801–1804 New York, N.Y.) 361.9, 1228, 76.6.

Walker (1809 New Brunswick, N.J.) 271.5.

Walter, Austin And Co. (1810 New Haven, Conn.) 892.6.

Walton, E. P. (1818–1819 Montpelier, Vt.) 86.2, 871.30, 69.2, 134.10, 192, 1117.

Warner, Benjamin (1816–1818 Philadelphia, Pa.) 340, 389.3, 811, 980, 1355.3, 694.2, 960.1, 978, 980, 1393, 61.15, 456.4, 1243.2; (1816–1818 Richmond, Va.) 980, 1393, 456.4.

Warner & Hanna [William Warner & Andrew Hanna] (1798–1810 Baltimore, Md.) 300.1, 300.2, 689.1, 213.7, 269.7, 1408.55, 1396, 275.52, 732.3, 143.1, 265.2, 350.3, 416.2, 417.2, 657, 875, 143.2, 1073.8, 1073.9, 269.9, 269.10, 962.1.

Warner, William (1812–1816 Baltimore, Md.) 10, 236.7, 115.5, 350.7, 275.83, 276.2, 269.11.

Warren, R. I. (1812 [Mason & Bird]) 1065.

Warriner, John S. (1799 Wilbraham, Mass.) 1143.3.

Wartman, Lawrence (1813 Harrisonburg, Va.) 42.

Waterman, John (1768–[1768] Providence, R.I.) 1318.2, 1293.5.

Watson & Bangs (1812–1814 Boston) 872, 1161.1, 27.1, 1371.10, 27.3, 27.4, 413.2.

Watson, David (1818–1820 Woodstock, Vt.) 90.10, 1196.11, 275.93, 554.1, 595.6, 855, 1456.1, 90.11, 275.94, 554.2, 590, 598, 905.10, 1456.2.

Watts, James G. (1811 Walpole, N.H.) 810.35, 1408.68.

Way, A. and G. (1803 Philadelphia, Pa.) 1003.1.

Webb, Phinehas (1811 Ballston Spa, N.Y.) 520.1.

Webb, S. (1761–1764 Boston, Mass.) 1072.12, 1072.14.

Webb, S. (1812 Norwich, Conn.) 438.6.

Webb, Samuel (1813 Windham, Conn.) 123.1, 905.7, 938, 1304, 1386, 1418.5, 1443.24.

Webster, C. R. & G. [Charles R. & George Webster] (1790–1803 Albany, N.Y.) 275.12, 1167.1.

Webster, J. ([1814] Philadelphia, Pa.) 224.1.

Webster, Z. ([1784] Hartford, Conn.) 1408.26.

Websters And Skinners (1806–1819 Albany, N.Y.) 60.11, 602.1, 153.8, 600.2, 601.2, 1418.11, 1196.12.

Weems, Revᵈ Mason L. (1794 Philadelphia, Pa.) 612.11.

Wells & Lilly (1815–1819 Boston, Mass.) 308 [adv.], 310.2 [adv.], 313.1, 314.1, 320.3 [adv.], 322, 323 [adv.], 326.1, 327 [adv.], 331.1 [adv.], 334 [adv.], 335.1 [adv.], 307.3, 308 [adv.], 309.1, 310.2 [adv.], 313.2, 315, 320.3 [adv.], 323 [adv.], 326.2, 327 [adv.], 331.1 [adv.], 332, 334, 335.1 [adv.], 335.2, 814, 1292, 61.4, 308 [adv.], 328.3, 60.35, 309.2, 309.3 [adv.], 313.3, 314.2, 320.3 [adv.], 321.3, 323 [adv.], 326.2 [adv.], 327 [adv.], 331.2, 334 [adv.], 335, 141, 424.3, 462, 576, 624, 969, 1095, 1301.2, 1430.

Wells, Thomas (1812–1816 Boston, Mass.) 1371.9, 27.1, 249.18, 962.2, 27.6.

Wells, W. ([1814] Boston, Mass.) 328.2.

West, D. (1790–1796 Boston, Mass.) 157.1, 1215, 295.1.

West, David (1796–1808 Boston, Mass.) 1340.1, 1148, 444.3.

Y

Z

* cover title.